READER'S DIGEST

COMPLETE GUIDE TO Gardening SEASON BY SEASON

READER'S DIGEST

COMPLETE GUIDE TO Gardening

SEASON BY SEASON

PUBLISHED BY THE READER'S DIGEST ASSOCIATION LIMITED
LONDON • NEW YORK • SYDNEY • MONTREAL

about this book 8
useful terms 8

year-round garden 10

- early spring surprises *12*
- late spring bulbs *14*
- summer climbers *16*
- late summer colour *18*
- autumn grasses *20*
- winter highlights *22*

early spring *practical diary* 24

- perennials *26*
- annuals & biennials *28*
  feature bedding schemes *32*
- bulbs & tubers *34*
- roses *36*
- climbers *40*
- shrubs & trees *42*
  feature designing a border *50*
- alpine gardens *52*
- water gardens *54*
- patios & containers *56*
- lawns *58*
- fruit *60*
- vegetables *64*
- herbs *70*
- the greenhouse *72*

early spring *plant selector* 78

- perennials *80*
  feature hellebores *84*
- annuals & biennials *85*
- bulbs *86*
  feature daffodils *92*
  feature spring-flowering crocuses *94*
- climbers *95*
- shrubs & trees *96*
  feature camellias *108*
- alpines *109*
- waterside & water plants *113*
- herbs & vegetables *114*
- choosing the best plants *118*

contents

late spring
practical diary 120

- perennials *122*
- annuals & biennials *126*
- bulbs & tubers *128*
- roses *130*
- climbers *132*
- shrubs & trees *136*
- alpine gardens *140*
- water gardens *142*
- patios & containers *146*
  feature permanent containers *150*
- lawns *152*
  feature new lawns *154*
- fruit *158*
- vegetables *160*
- herbs *164*
- the greenhouse *166*

late spring
plant selector 170

- perennials *172*
- annuals & biennials *182*
- bulbs *184*
  feature tulips *186*
- climbers *188*
- shrubs & trees *190*
  feature rhododendrons *199*
- alpines *200*
- waterside & water plants *203*
- herbs, vegetables & fruit *204*
- choosing the best plants *206*

summer
practical diary 208

- perennials *210*
- annuals & biennials *214*
- bulbs & tubers *216*
- roses *218*
- climbers *220*
- shrubs & trees *222*
- alpine gardens *228*
- water gardens *230*
  feature creating a healthy pond *232*
- patios & containers *234*
  feature easy patio watering *236*
- lawns *238*
- fruit *240*
- vegetables *244*
- herbs *250*
- the greenhouse *254*

summer
plant selector 260

- perennials *262*
  feature pelargoniums *273*
- annuals & biennials *274*
- bulbs *278*
- climbers *280*
  feature clematis *282*
  feature climbing roses *284*
- shrubs & trees *285*
  feature shrub roses *290*
- alpines *292*
- waterside & water plants *294*
- herbs, vegetables & fruit *296*
- choosing the best plants *300*

late summer
practical diary 302

- perennials *304*
- annuals & biennials *308*
- bulbs & tubers *310*
- roses *314*
- climbers *316*
- shrubs & trees *318*
- alpine gardens *322*
- water gardens *324*
- patios & containers *326*
- lawns *328*
- fruit *330*
- vegetables *336*
- herbs *342*
  feature creating a herb garden *344*
- the greenhouse *348*

late summer
plant selector 352

- perennials *354*
- annuals & biennials *366*
- bulbs *370*
  feature lilies *372*
- climbers *373*
  feature honeysuckles *375*
- shrubs & trees *376*
  feature fuchsias *382*
  feature hydrangeas *383*
- alpines *384*
- waterside & water plants *386*
- herbs, vegetables & fruit *388*
- choosing the best plants *392*

autumn
practical diary 394

- perennials *396*
- annuals & biennials *400*
- bulbs & tubers *402*
- roses *404*
- climbers *408*
- shrubs & trees *412*
  feature planting a hedge *416*
- alpine gardens *420*
- water gardens *422*
- patios & containers *424*
- lawns *426*
- fruit *430*
  feature creating a fruit garden *434*
- vegetables *438*
- herbs *442*
- the greenhouse *444*

autumn
plant selector 448

- perennials *450*
  feature asters *457*
- annuals & biennials *458*
- bulbs *463*
  feature dahlias *465*
- climbers *466*
  feature late flowering clematis *467*
- shrubs & trees *468*
  feature acers *476*
- alpines *477*
- waterside & water plants *480*
- herbs, vegetables & fruit *482*
- choosing the best plants *486*

contents

winter *practical diary* 488

- perennials *490*
- annuals & biennials *492*
- bulbs & tubers *494*
- roses *496*
- climbers *498*
- shrubs & trees *502*
- alpine gardens *514*
- water gardens *516*
- patios & containers *518*
- lawns *520*
- fruit *522*
- vegetables *524*
  feature making a vegetable plot *528*
- herbs *536*
- the greenhouse *538*

winter *plant selector* 542

- perennials *544*
- annuals & biennials *546*
- bulbs *547*
  feature dwarf irises *550*
- climbers *551*
  feature common or english ivy *552*
- shrubs & trees *554*
  feature holly *570*
  feature heaths *571*
- alpines *572*
- herbs, vegetables & fruit *574*
- choosing the best plants *578*

gardening basics 580

- tools & equipment *582*
- understanding your soil *592*
- compost & leaf mould *596*
- mulches *600*
- summer watering *602*
- summer feeding *604*
- cloches & coldframes *606*
- types of cloche *608*

index 610

acknowledgements 638

about this book

The *Complete Guide to Gardening - Season by Season* provides a comprehensive practical and inspirational guide to making the most of your garden right through the year, with detailed information to help you plan, plant and maintain the garden of your dreams. To reflect the pattern of garden activity, the bulk of the book is divided into six seasons: early spring, late spring, summer, late summer, autumn and winter.

year-round garden This opening chapter offers an inspiring source of design and planting ideas taken from contemporary and traditional gardens photographed through the year. Many of the plants have been identified to enable you to adapt the ideas to your own garden scheme.

practical diary Presented season by season, these chapters detail the most important tasks to be done in the garden at different times of the year. The information is divided into subject areas – such as Perennials, Climbers, or Lawns – that reflect particular gardening interests. Within each season, the headings appear in the same order, making it easy to find the section you need. Under each heading is a list of the main tasks for the time of year, and the most important jobs are then explained in more detail. Since many jobs may require follow-up attention in a later season,

useful terms

alpine Although this strictly refers to a mountain plant that grows naturally in free-draining soil at high altitude, the term is used by gardeners to mean any plant suitable for growing in a rock garden.
annual A plant that grows, flowers, sets seed and dies in one growing season.
anther The part of the flower that produces pollen.
aquatic plant In its widest sense, this can mean any water plant, but usually refers to plants such as water lilies that grow in deeper water, rooted in the bottom of the pond or in special baskets.
bareroot This refers to plants, usually trees and shrubs, that have been dug up and supplied to the customer without any soil on their roots. Roses are often supplied in this way.
bedding (plant) A plant used outdoors for temporary or seasonal display, often as part of a planned 'bedding scheme'.
biennial A plant that completes its life cycle in two growing seasons.
biological control The treatment or prevention of pests, diseases or weeds by natural, rather than chemical, methods, usually involving a naturally occurring parasite or predator.
cloche A glass or plastic cover used to shelter plants from cold or windy weather. Cloches are available as separate units or in tunnel form, often called 'continuous cloches'.
coldframe A low, unheated structure with a transparent top, in which plants can be grown in protected conditions.
cordon A plant restricted by pruning and training to a single, unbranching stem. Examples include apples, tomatoes and sweet peas grown on canes.
corm The swollen stem base of plants like crocuses and gladioli, where food is stored during winter. A new corm forms each year on top of the shrivelled remains of last year's.
cultivar A distinct, named plant variety that has originated in cultivation, rather than in the wild. Cultivars are often simply (but incorrectly) called 'varieties'.
deadhead To cut off the spent flowers.
die-back The result of attack by a fungal disease, which causes shoots or branches to die back from their tips.
direct sow To sow seeds in the ground where the plants are to grow, rather than starting them indoors or in a temporary seedbed for later transplanting.
drill A furrow or channel made in the soil at the correct depth for sowing seeds.
ericaceous Any plant belonging to the erica or heather family, for example pieris and rhododendrons. Also refers to the acid conditions these plants like and the special lime-free compost in which they are potted.
espalier A tree such as an apple or cotoneaster that is pruned and trained as a single upright trunk, with side branches extending horizontally to form symmetrical layers or 'tiers'.
foliar feed Liquid fertiliser sprayed or watered on the leaves of plants, usually applied for rapid results or when plants are not actively absorbing nutrients through their roots (after injury or in cold weather, for example).
glyphosate A chemical weedkiller that is absorbed through leaves and moves through the plant so that all parts, including roots, are killed (see systemic).
habitat The natural home of a plant growing in the wild. Not to be confused with habit, which is the typical form or shape of a plant.
harden off To gradually acclimatise a plant previously grown indoors to unprotected conditions outside in the garden.
hardwood cutting A piece of this year's shoot taken for propagation from a shrub, tree or climber during the autumn, when their stems are hard and ripe.
heel A small strip of bark torn from the main stem when a sideshoot is pulled off to make a (heel) cutting.
heel in To bury the roots of a plant in a temporary hole or trench when it is not to be planted immediately.
humus The dark, water-retentive component of soil that results from the decay of organic material.
in situ Literally, in position, or where plants are to grow permanently.
internodal cutting A cutting that is trimmed midway between two leaf-joints, rather than immediately below the leaves.
layering A method of propagation in which a shoot is rooted while still attached to the

a 'Looking ahead' feature indicates where you will find details of what you will need to do later in the year.

plant selector These six directories describe the best plants for each season, as selected by our gardening experts. Within each subject grouping, the plants are arranged by colour, and within each colour sequence they are generally listed alphabetically by botanical name. Each plant is shown in a photograph, with information supplied including the plant's common name, size, site and soil preferences, best uses, general care and suggestions for good companions. Each plant is also given a 'hardiness' rating:

- 'Hardy' plants can be grown outdoors in all parts of the British Isles.
- Plants rated 'not fully hardy' can be grown outdoors in milder parts of the British Isles but elsewhere will need some protection in winter.
- 'Half-hardy' plants can withstand temperatures down to 0°C (32°F). They are often grown outdoors in summer displays, but propagated and kept under glass between autumn and late spring.
- 'Tender' plants require protection under glass for all or part of the year.

At the end of each of the seasonal plant selectors, there are lists of the plants best suited to different garden conditions and soil types.

gardening basics The concluding chapter of the book offers essential information for every gardener. It includes a guide to tools and equipment, describes the different types of soil and how to identify what you have in your garden and improve it, and takes a look at composts and mulches. It also provides information on watering and feeding, and how best to make use of cloches and coldframes.

parent plant. Rooting a branch where it touches the ground is called simple layering, while serpentine layering involves rooting a long flexible stem in several places; long stems can be tip layered by burying their growing tips.

loam A type of soil that contains a balanced mixture of sand, clay and organic material.

marginal plant A waterside plant that is grown at the edge of the pond, either in shallow water or on the bank.

mulch Any material used to cover and protect the soil surface. Organic mulches include straw, manure and lawn mowings, while polythene sheet and stones are examples of inorganic mulches.

naturalise To deliberately plant, or allow plants to grow and spread, as in the wild.

node The place on a plant's stem where a leaf forms.

nursery bed A piece of ground specially reserved for raising young plants.

organic This literally refers to any material derived from decomposed animal or plant remains. It is also used to describe a gardening approach that uses little or no obviously chemical substances such as fertilisers and pesticides.

perlite A granular, absorbent soil or compost additive made from expanded volcanic rock.

perennial **(correctly herbaceous perennial)** A durable non-woody plant whose soft, leafy growth dies down in winter, but grows again the following year.

pinch out To remove a growing tip, using finger and thumb.

pot on To move a potted plant into a larger container.

pot (up) To transfer a plant from a seed tray or open ground into a pot.

prick out To transplant seedlings from where they have been sown to a container or piece of ground where they will have more space to grow.

rhizome An underground root (strictly, a stem) that behaves like a bulb by storing food from one season to the next. Also used to describe the buried creeping shoots by which some plants, especially grasses, spread underground.

rootballed This describes plants packaged for delivery by wrapping their mass of roots and soil or compost in a net bag.

rootstock (or stock) The rooted portion of a grafted tree. This usually influences the habit and ultimate size of the selected variety joined onto it (the scion).

seedbed A piece of ground for raising seeds, specially prepared by removing all weeds, stones and large lumps of soil.

semi-ripe cutting A section of this year's stem cut off for propagation, usually during summer while the tip is still soft but the base has become firm and woody.

softwood cutting A cutting prepared from a portion of a young new shoot that has not started to harden.

spit A measurement of depth equal to the length of a spade-blade (about 25cm/10in).

standard A trained form of woody plant with a single upright stem that is clear of all leaves and shoots. Full standard trees have trunks about 2m (6ft) high, half-standards 1.2m (4ft). Standard roses are about 1m (3ft) high, while half-standards have 75cm (2ft 6in) stems.

subsoil The lower layer of ground below the topsoil (see below). Often paler and relatively infertile, this is usually coarser in texture and hard to cultivate.

sucker A shoot growing from below ground and away from the main stem of a plant, sometimes from its rootstock.

systemic A type of pesticide, fungicide or weedkiller sprayed onto leaves and absorbed into all plant parts in its sap.

tender perennial A plant that can live for several years but cannot tolerate frost or very cold conditions.

thin out To reduce the number of plants, buds or fruit so that those remaining have enough room to develop fully.

tip cuttings Softwood cuttings (see above) formed from the outer ends of young shoots.

top-dressing An application of fertiliser, organic material or potting compost spread on the surface. Also refers to replacing the top layer of compost in a large container with a fresh supply.

topgrowth The upper, visible part of a plant above ground level.

topsoil The upper layer of soil, usually darker and more fertile than the layers below (see subsoil), and where plants develop most of their feeding roots.

tuber A fat, underground root (in dahlias, for example) or stem (begonias), constructed differently from a bulb or corm but used in the same way for storing food from one season to the next.

variety Botanically, a distinctly different variation of a plant that has developed in the wild, but commonly used to mean the same as cultivar (see left).

year-round garden

A garden can inspire all year round. Early spring offers a taste of things to come, with hellebores and early crocus pushing up beneath the bare deciduous trees. Late spring boasts the freshest of greens and the prettiest of flowers. Summer delights with new blooms every day, while the golden glow of late summer enhances the vibrancy of dahlias and heleniums. In autumn, grasses and plants billow and riot in the borders as their final flowers turn to seed heads and fruit, while multicoloured leaves rustle overhead. The crystal clear mornings of winter reveal fascinating patterns and shapes, enhanced by fragrant winter honeysuckle and cheered by the appearance of snowdrops and yellow aconites. Spring is just around the corner.

early spring surprises

As the gradual increase in daylight hours and spells of warm weather wake plants from their winter rest, buds burst into new life. The thrusting growth and sudden explosion of colour can take even the seasoned gardener by surprise.

A far cry from its cousin the weeping willow, *Salix hastata* 'Wehrhahnii' makes a small, slow-growing shrub whose bare twigs come alive with a fine display of soft silvery catkins in spring (above). These mature to show yellow pollen as bright green leaves burst from their buds.

Lenten roses (*Helleborus hybridus*) are a promiscuous bunch, capable of seeding around and producing some beautiful hybrids. This ruby-flowered plant pierces a ground covering of hardy *Cyclamen coum* (right). Both enjoy well-drained, humus-rich soil in partial shade.

Early spring is when drifts of purple *Crocus tommasinianus* and clumps of naturalised snowdrops coincide with the flowering of hellebores (above). For the best show, remove shabby hellebore leaves as flower buds form, and divide large clumps after flowering.

A young shuttlecock fern (*Matteuccia struthiopteris*) unfurls perfect new fronds, breaking through the leaf litter in a woodland situation (below).

The early, fragrant blooms of *Hyacinthus* 'Amethyst' make an ideal accompaniment to emerging peony stems (right). As spring progresses, a ground cover of forget-me-nots will rise up to mask the dying hyacinths and continue the display through into summer.

Thrusting their way through bare earth after a long winter, these daffodil shoots are full of promise (below). The bulbs are well adapted to withstand even wet winters and, from their early autumn planting, should emerge to flower in spring year after year.

late spring bulbs

Bulbs are the mainstay of spring in all their glorious colours and extraordinary flower forms. When they have finished flowering, they gradually disappear below ground, to build up their resources for the following year.

Crown imperials (*Fritillaria imperialis*) are the largest of the fritillaries. They require a rich, well-drained soil in sun or semi-shade.

An American dog's-tooth violet (*Erythronium oregonum*) thrives with the European native *Cyclamen repandum* in dappled shade (right).

Lily-flowered *Tulipa* 'West Point' is a mid to late flowering hybrid that is an excellent choice for containers.

A meadow-land plant, snakeshead fritillary (*Fritillaria meleagris*) in its white and purple forms naturalises well in moist grassland (below).

Summer snowflake (*Leucojum aestivum*) is a superb bulb for dry shade and best left alone once planted (left).

A naturalistic planting (below left) combines *Anemone blanda* and wild daffodils (*Narcissus pseudonarcissus*) with wild violets and primroses.

Tulips look best massed in groups according to colour (below right). These are Darwin hybrids 'Apeldoorn' (red) and 'Apeldoorn's Elite' (yellow).

Hyacinthus orientalis 'Carnegie'

summer climbers

Rosa and *Clematis*

Vertical planting provides an extra dimension, especially useful in a small garden. Doorways and arches as well as walls and fences can be framed and draped with foliage and flowers.

A brick wall pierced by an arch is embellished by a collection of wall shrubs and climbers (above). The clematis blooms will have been preceded by the fragrant blossoms of the wisteria, whose foliage still makes a contribution. The pale blue ceanothus will have been blooming since spring.

The rambler rose 'Félicité Perpétue' flowers in perfect harmony with *Clematis* 'Comtesse de Bouchaud' (right). This rose does not repeat, but the clematis will bloom sporadically until autumn.

Climbing rose 'Bantry Bay' has been teamed with the maroon clematis 'Royal Velours' (above). Select clematis that can be pruned hard in winter, when the rose is taken down for an overhaul.

The potato vine (*Solanum crispum* 'Glasnevin') will grow vigorously through summer, constantly in flower (above). To keep it within bounds, prune back to its main framework each year in spring, when frost is unlikely to damage the tender young growths.

Clematis 'Comtesse de Bouchaud' and *Rosa* 'Minnehaha' scramble together (below) without constraint, but each winter they must be unravelled and separately pruned.

Unlike the annual sweet pea, the everlasting pea (*Lathyrus latifolius*) is a long-lasting perennial that produces many stems from its rootstock every year (below).

late summer colour

Colour in the garden is never more glorious than in late summer. While random mixtures of colour work well in a cottage-style garden, careful blending of harmonious hues will have a more dramatic impact elsewhere.

Single colour borders can be effective but call for judicious planting. This superb all-red border uses a range of different flowers: penstemons, petunias, tobacco plants and dahlias provide the brightest reds, with dark-leaved *Amaranthus* to tone things down.

Dahlias are dependable perennials for late summer colour, but their flowers can be large and their hues strident, so careful siting is essential. Lift and divide dahlia tubers each autumn, and store.

Cannas are tropical plants (left), but grow so vigorously that they will develop and flower within a single summer, if planted out in May. They need moist, fertile soil and full sun. This is 'Rosemond Coles'.

An unusual mix of tropical and temperate-climate plants has been used here to develop a luxuriant display (left). The large banana leaves make a striking foil for *Lobelia* x *gerardii* and *Acanthus spinosus*.

Hot colours work well in full sunshine, and this double border at Great Dixter in Sussex is a shining example of bold planting (below). The large dahlia flowers harmonise with the soft, misty purple *Verbena bonariensis*, which seeds itself freely.

The bold curve enhances this mixed border and increases its length, providing more planting opportunities. The cool blue hydrangea at one end contrasts beautifully with the brilliant red and orange crocosmias at the other.

autumn grasses

The movement and texture of grasses brings a welcome softness to the autumn garden. Most flower in late summer and early autumn, and pass the rest of the season with pale, glistening seed heads. Grasses associate effortlessly with other plants.

Ornamental grasses require little more upkeep than a gentle shearing over before new growth appears in spring. They are ideal choices for a small, low-maintenance garden where the traditional lawn has been replaced by a wide path (above). Here a shingle mulch suppresses weeds and conserves moisture.

Different heights are used to great effect here, with a stand of tall reed grass (*Calamagrostis brachytricha*) behind *Imperata cylindrica* 'Rubra' (right). This red-leaved beauty may need a protective winter mulch in cold regions.

The criss-crossing stems of purple moor grass (*Molinia caerulea* subsp. *caerulea* 'Heidebraut') make fine lattice-work behind *Berberis* x *media* 'Red Jewel' (above). This elegant grass appreciates moist, neutral to acid soil.

The soft, feathery flower sprays of *Stipa tenuissima* (above) make it one of the most beautiful ornamental grasses, forming billowing, wispy mounds. It suits most soils and makes a fine complement to other plants, including the mauve-flowered heather *Calluna vulgaris* 'Spring Torch'.

Grasses lend themselves brilliantly to low-maintenance, prairie-style perennial plantings and have a unifying effect (above). Planted randomly among yellow coreopsis, sedums and soft-leaved *Stachys byzantina* is the grass *Stipa tenuissima*, turning parchment coloured with age.

The tall, straw-coloured plumes of *Miscanthus* and teasel heads (below) are caught by the slanting rays of late autumn sunshine. If you leave such elegant dead stems in place during winter, not only do they benefit wildlife, but they will create enchanting scenes like this.

One of the best tufted-hair grasses is *Deschampsia cespitosa* 'Tautrager' (right). Most grasses perform well in a sunny position and in well-drained soil. This one can cope with dry or damp soil and sun or partial shade, but it dislikes chalky or alkaline soils.

winter highlights

Plants whose chief display is timed for the colder months provide the gilding of the winter garden. Shrubs with colourful stems, bark and twiggy outlines lend a permanent beauty, while those with berries and flowers give a succession of surprises.

Massed plantings of burgundy-leaved *Cotoneaster horizontalis* and the grass *Stipa arundinacea* look most effective during winter (left). Snowy birch stems complete the scene.

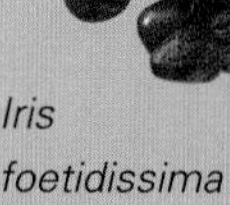

Iris foetidissima

Plants chosen for their dramatic stem colours work well in bold groups (below). The ghostly wands of *Rubus thibetanus* rise from winter-flowering heathers behind the rounded leaves of *Bergenia* 'Sunningdale'. Prune this rubus by cutting all stems back hard, almost to the base, in spring.

The Himalayan birch (*Betula utilis* var. *jacquemontii*) has brilliant white bark (below).

Of all the dogwoods grown for their winter stems, *Cornus sanguinea* 'Winter Beauty' (left) is probably the best for smaller gardens as it grows slowly and to less stature than some of its cousins. The frost-covered, shrimp-pink stems associate well with the *Juniperus virginiana* behind.

If considering a small tree for the garden, bear in mind the witch hazels (*Hamamelis*). These slow-growing plants (below) have abundant spidery, scented flowers of yellow, orange or red that open against bare branches in late winter. They enjoy sheltered woodland conditions.

Some evergreen shrubs present lively and often scented winter flowers as well as colourful foliage. *Mahonia* x *wagneri* 'Moseri' (left) will reach 1.5m (5ft). It will grow in shade, but its leaves colour best in sun.

Plants whose fruit persists well into winter breathe colour and life into gardens sleeping under winter's mantle. *Cotoneaster frigidus* 'Cornubia' makes a large shrub liberally strung with shiny red fruit (right).

early spring

practical diary

The first stirrings of spring rekindle our enthusiasm for gardening. An early start puts the gardener ahead for the whole season, making tasks more leisurely and enjoyable. When soil conditions allow, digging and forking the kitchen garden beds prepares the ground for later sowings and plantings. Owners of a greenhouse can start sowing seeds indoors, while several garden shrubs, including roses, can be pruned early in the year. And a few minutes spent tidying containers planted in autumn, or cutting away dead and damaged leaves of hellebores, will make you feel that the new season has begun.

perennials

The earliest perennials are already gracing the garden with colourful blooms, while clumps of fresh green foliage herald the show to come. Early spring is an excellent time to plant and propagate many more plants by seed, cuttings or division, to fill your garden with flowers for very little outlay.

now is the season to . . .

■ **weed, feed and mulch** established plants. Cut off any remaining dead growth, and tidy up evergreens (see opposite).

■ **lift, divide and replant** established clumps of ornamental grasses and those perennials that flower from mid to late summer onwards (see page 399 and below).

■ **plan new planting schemes,** then buy and plant new perennials and grasses while weather conditions are cool and moist. Well-established plants in large pots are a good buy as you can divide them immediately into several smaller clumps.

■ **divide and repot container-grown** perennials and grasses that have become congested, and top-dress those remaining in their pots with fertiliser and fresh compost (see page 40).

■ **harden off plants** you have raised or overwintered under cover before planting them out.

■ **pot up young plants** that have developed from root cuttings taken in autumn or winter.

■ **protect new shoots** from slugs and snails, particularly on delphiniums, lupins, peonies, hostas and other susceptible plants (see page 123).

Emergent peony shoots are a cheering sight, but must be protected from slugs and snails.

■ **remove winter protection** once weather conditions improve, although in cold areas vulnerable plants may need protecting throughout early spring.

■ **take basal cuttings** of suitable perennials (see opposite).

■ **sow seeds** of many perennial species, either bought or those you collected the previous year (see opposite).

■ **pot on tender perennials** overwintering under cover into fresh compost and water well to encourage new growth. Soft-tip cuttings can be taken from the young shoots (see page 139).

and if you have time . . .

■ **take root cuttings** while plants are dormant (see page 491).

maintaining established perennial borders

You need to prepare established perennials and grasses for the coming year, before they start to grow rapidly and form new shoots that could be damaged by the work.

- **first lift,** divide and replant young, vigorous portions of older perennials that have formed congested clumps.
- **then lightly fork** over the bare soil between plants, mixing in a dressing of slow-release fertiliser at the same time.

Pulmonarias enjoy shady conditions and are one of the earliest perennials to flower. *Pulmonaria officinalis*, with spotted leaves and long-lasting funnel-shaped pink-and-blue flowers, makes good ground cover.

tidying a perennial border

Dig out all perennial weeds, such as tap-rooted dandelions and thistles.

Cut dead and untidy stems from grasses and perennials to make way for fresh new growth.

- **remove all weeds,** particularly the roots of perennial ones, and closely inspect each clump of plants for weeds that may have taken root within the plant itself.
- **cut out to ground level any dead stems** that were not removed previously.
- **remove dead foliage** from evergreen grasses by combing carefully through the clump with your fingers, and cut off tatty leaves from evergreen perennials such as bergenias.
- **finally, mulch the bare soil** with a 5cm (2in) thick layer of organic matter, such as well-rotted manure, garden compost or chipped bark.

propagation

As new growth appears, it is time to take basal cuttings of a number of perennials including achillea, anthemis, chrysanthemums, delphiniums, gypsophila and lupins. Sever the new shoots when they are 8–10cm (3–4in) high and insert them in a pot of cuttings compost; keep covered until they root (see page 125).

DIVIDING TIP Newly purchased grasses provide more value for money if you divide them into several smaller clumps which can then be planted separately. Once established, they will spread out in the bed.

The young foliage of *Alchemilla mollis* pushes through dead leaves.

sowing seed

This is the time to sow many perennials and grasses, which is an economical way of stocking a new garden or border. Certain varieties will even bloom this year if you sow them early and under cover (see below). A few perennials need a period of cold in order to germinate, which you can achieve by putting the seed in a polythene bag with a little damp sand, and placing it in the refrigerator for several weeks before sowing in the following way:

- Sow seed in pots or trays of moist seed compost, or direct into the soil in a coldframe or protected by a cloche.
- If sowing direct, draw out shallow drills with a hoe and mix a little potting compost into the drill bottom to help retain moisture. Water the drill before sowing.
- Sow sparingly, then cover seeds with a thin layer of compost. Keep moist at all times.
- Once the seedlings are big enough to handle, prick out into modular trays, so each plant develops a compact root system.

looking ahead . . .

- ☑ LATE SPRING Put in supports for tall-growing perennials such as delphiniums and phlox.
- ☑ Continue taking basal cuttings and pot up when rooted.
- ☑ Continue to prick out seedlings and pot on young plants.

some perennials that flower in their first year

• *Achillea* Summer Pastels Group • *Agastache cana* • *Anaphalis margaritacea* • *Chrysanthemum* varieties • *Coreopsis grandiflora* 'Early Sunrise' • *Helenium* 'Autumn Lollipop' • *Malva moschata* • *Papaver orientale* 'Checkers' • *Rudbeckia* Satellite Mixed • *Tanacetum coccineum* Robinson's Mixed Single • *Verbascum* Sunset Shades

annuals & biennials

Most summer annuals and bedding plants are sown now, indoors in the warmth of the greenhouse, or outside in a prepared nursery bed. Meanwhile, spring bedding transplanted in autumn will be coming into flower as the days lengthen.

now is the season to . . .

- **sow tender bedding plants** and other half-hardy annuals under glass in early March (see pages 30 and 74). Include plants such as nemesias, impatiens, petunias, nicotianas, gazanias and mesembryanthemums.
- **sow annual climbers** to make a good size by planting time. Cobaea, rhodochiton, thunbergia, morning glory, canary creeper and nasturtiums can all be started in small pots indoors in warmth (see page 41).
- **buy seedlings and plug plants** from garden centres, and pot up to grow indoors until planting time (see page 30).
- **prick out seedlings sown** earlier, to give them more space to develop (see page 31).
- **protect all indoor sowings** and seedlings against damping-off disease (see page 76).
- **repot overwintered** tender perennials, such as pelargoniums and fuchsias, and water more freely to start into growth (see page 73). Take cuttings when new growth is long enough.
- **plant out autumn-sown** sweet peas with suitable supports (see right). Move spring-sown plants to a coldframe, and sow a final batch in warmed soil where they are to flower.
- **remove cloches** and other frost protection from autumn-sown annuals, and thin seedlings if necessary. Lift thinnings carefully, without damaging the roots, using an old kitchen fork or seed label, and transplant elsewhere. Protect seedlings from slugs and snails.
- **dig or fork sites** for new flower beds. Ground dug in autumn can now be raked and levelled, ready to prepare seedbeds for outdoor sowing (see right).
- **late in the season, begin transplanting** hardy annuals from their winter quarters to flowering positions; check seed packets for the correct spacing.
- **at the end of March, start sowing** hardy annuals outdoors (see right) or under glass if conditions are unsuitable for direct sowing.
- **protect newly planted** seedlings from wind.

and if you have time . . .

- **weed among spring bedding** when the ground is dry, and hoe lightly to loosen the surface.

planting out sweet peas

1 Space 2.5m (8ft) long canes 30–45cm (12–18in) apart in rows or as wigwams, and make sure they are firm.

2 Using a trowel or dibber, plant one potful or paper tube of sweet peas next to each cane; water in well.

3 Secure young shoots to the cane with a loop of string or special sweet pea rings. Once plants start growing, tie in new growth every two or three days.

planting out sweet peas

Before planting out autumn-sown sweet peas still in pots or paper tubes, you need to harden them off gradually by leaving them outside during the day to accustom them to outdoor conditions. After a week of this they should be ready to plant.

sowing annuals direct

Many half-hardy annuals make the strongest bushy plants if sown under glass. But for large displays this is laborious, and it is often better to sow direct in late March or April.

Prepare the ground as soon as it is workable by forking the soil one spade blade deep where it has not been cultivated since last autumn. Sites that have already been dug over should need only light forking to break up the surface and any

Protect a seedbed from heavy rain or prolonged dry weather with a portable coldframe.

Double daisies (*Bellis perennis*) make colourful and long-lasting spring bedding if sown the previous spring or early summer.

large clods. Then rake to level and to leave a fine tilth, ready for sowing. You can protect this seedbed from heavy rain or prolonged dry weather by covering it with a plastic sheet, weighted down with bricks, or a portable coldframe. This will also warm the soil, and after two to three weeks you can sow seeds you have bought or saved last year with a good chance of rapid germination.

Lavatera trimestris 'Mont Blanc'

annuals to grow for cut flowers

• annual chrysanthemums • annual grasses • calendula • candytuft • china asters • clarkia • clary • cornflowers • eschscholzia • flax (*Linum*) • godetia • gypsophila • honeywort (*Cerinthe*) • larkspur • lavatera • malope • nigella • poppies • red orache (*Atriplex*) • scabious • sunflowers • woodruff (*Asperula*) • zinnia

hardy annuals for cutting

Many annuals make long-lasting cut flowers. Surplus plants at bedding time can be lined out in the vegetable garden or beside paths, or you can sow direct in rows solely for this purpose. Water plants regularly, and mulch and support them to ensure long, straight stems.

thinning outdoor seedlings

Thin autumn-sown outdoor seedlings in stages to 8cm (3in) apart while they are still small and the soil is damp.

thinning outdoor seedlings

1 **Pull up and discard** surplus seedlings while pressing firmly with your fingers around seedlings to be retained, so they are not disturbed. Alternatively, chop out spare seedlings with a narrow onion hoe.

2 **Always clear and destroy** thinnings as they can attract pests and diseases.

3 **Thin outdoor annuals** again when they touch each other, this time spacing them at their recommended distance apart. Intermediate seedlings will be large enough to lift carefully with a kitchen fork or a seed label for transplanting elsewhere. Water well after thinning.

annuals & biennials/2

raising annuals under glass

Half-hardy annuals cannot stand frost. They are always sown under glass because if you wait until conditions are warm enough to sow outdoors, the plants will flower very late. Most can be sown now, but some need a long growing season, and antirrhinums, pelargoniums and *Begonia semperflorens* are best sown in late winter if they are to make substantial plants in time for bedding out (see page 493).

For successful germination you need to provide an ambient temperature of about 18°C (64°F) in a greenhouse or propagator. If this is not possible, wait until March, when artificial heating to 10°C (50°F), combined with increased sunlight, should still ensure success.

Where an unheated greenhouse or coldframe is the only aid available, buy temperature-sensitive plants like begonias, lobelia and petunias as seedlings or plugs, and concentrate on sowing more robust, faster-growing tender annuals like china asters, dahlias, nemesia, tagetes and zinnias in April.

These ready-made sowing disks come in a plastic tray. The seeds start to germinate when water is added.

Lack of heat is no handicap with hardy annuals. These are normally sown direct outdoors, but may also be started indoors without artificial heat in early March to provide strong, branching plants for transplanting outdoors in late April or May. Use this method to raise superior plants of calendulas, clary, dimorphotheca, lavatera, nasturtiums and larkspur for containers and greenhouse pot plants, and for filling gaps in borders.

potting on plug plants

Small plug plants need to be potted on into 8cm (3in) containers as soon as possible after buying, so that their roots can develop and the plants grow on to a suitable size for planting out.

Early spring is a busy time for sowing. Seeds of half-hardy annuals should be sown under glass; those of hardy annuals can also be sown direct outdoors.

pricking out seedlings

1 **Make sure seedlings** are moist before you ease a cluster out, using the forked end of a dibber or the point of a seed label. Gently separate the seedlings and spread them on a board.

2 **Fill a seed tray** with compost and make holes about 5cm (2in) apart; four rows of six is a useful plan. Handle seedlings by their leaves (the fragile stems are easily crushed) and insert each into a hole, then gently firm.

3 **Once the tray is full,** water with a fine rose and label the tray. Keep in a well-lit place, but shade the seedlings from hot, bright sunlight for a few days, and plant out when the leaves are touching each other.

the importance of thinning

Most annuals germinate very quickly if sown in the right conditions, and tagetes, annual chrysanthemums and zinnias emerge less than a week after sowing. They soon develop into dense clusters of seedlings, all struggling for light and becoming spindly, conditions that often encourage the spread of damping-off disease.

To avoid early overcrowding, sow seeds as sparingly as possible. Prick out or thin seedlings as soon as they are ready, to ensure that they have space to grow strongly and avoid the soft, leggy growth and matted roots that result from overcrowding.

pricking out

By the end of February, some of the earliest seedlings should have one or two true leaves above the initial pair of seed leaves, and will be large enough to handle comfortably. Prick them out into trays, preferably modular ones of 6, 9 or 12 compartments, which gives them room to develop individually, or space them out in plain seed trays (see above). Pot up larger seedlings individually in 6–8cm (2½–3in) pots.

annual grasses

Most annual grasses are very easy to grow and produce graceful, airy plants for garden display and also for drying. They tend to mature quickly, rather than last the whole season, but you can avoid an untidy appearance in late summer by cutting off the dry seed heads for indoor use, clearing plants and replacing them with late flowering annuals or more grasses from a later sowing made in June.

- Sow and keep indoors in 8cm (3in) pots during March, because seedling grasses are hard to distinguish from weed grasses.
- Grow a few seeds in each pot, and thin if necessary to leave several evenly spaced seedlings.
- Harden off and plant out in late May, or early June for tender species such as sorghum.
- Plant in bold groups, or thread the grasses between other bedding for maximum effect.
- Cut for drying just before seeds are ripe, as they shed easily, and hang up in a warm, airy place.

looking ahead . . .

- ☑ LATE SPRING Buy and harden off summer bedding plants.
- ☑ Sow biennials.
- ☑ SUMMER Clear spring displays.
- ☑ Plant out summer bedding.
- ☑ Transplant biennials.
- ☑ LATE SUMMER: Take cuttings of tender perennials, which are treated as annuals.

there is still time to . . .

- **order seeds, seedlings and plug** plants from catalogues, but make haste before order books close.
- **transplant biennials** for spring bedding to their flowering positions from early March, and fill gaps in autumn-planted displays.
- **sow slow-maturing** tender bedding such as pelargoniums and begonias in a warm greenhouse.
- **direct sow** sweet peas in soil warmed by cloches.

hardy annual grasses

• foxtail millet (*Setaria italica*) 60cm (2ft) • greater quaking grass (*Briza maxima*) 45cm (18in) • hare's tail (*Lagurus ovatus*) 45cm (18in) • purple millet (*Panicum miliaceum* 'Violaceum') 60cm (2ft) • squirrel tail grass (*Hordeum jubatum*) 45cm (18in)

bedding schemes

Annual bedding is a traditional celebration of a season, in which a bed or border is planted up with a variety of easy-care flowers that bloom simultaneously over a long period to create a choreographed riot of colour.

seasonal schemes

Plants for bedding may be hardy or half-hardy annuals, biennials, bulbs or tender perennials, according to the season in which they flower. Spring bedding is normally composed of bulbs such as daffodils, tulips and hyacinths, planted in autumn together with biennials like wallflowers, pansies and forget-me-nots, and dug up when flowering ceases. Summer bedding uses hardy and half-hardy annuals, often blended with tender perennials such as pelargoniums and fuchsias, and carries the display from the end of the spring bedding season through to the autumn, when the cleared plants are replaced once more with spring bedding plants.

bedding styles

Formal bedding depends on symmetry: the plants are set out in a geometrical pattern, with taller varieties ('dot' plants) at the back, or in the centre of island beds, and the smallest plants along the edges. The space in between is filled with intermediate-height plants, grouped in a mosaic of repeated shapes (see opposite).

Informal bedding dispenses with the geometry of straight lines and patterns, instead setting out the plants in relaxed groups that may overlap and even flower at different times to produce a more natural effect. A version of the herbaceous border (see Winter), this often uses hardy and native annuals rather than tender bedding plants.

long-flowering annuals and tender perennials

FOR SUMMER BEDDING SCHEMES • *Ageratum houstonianum* • *Begonia semperflorens* • gazania • heliotrope • busy lizzie (*Impatiens*) • *Lobelia erinus* • alyssum (*Lobularia maritima*) • *Nemesia strumosa* • pelargonium • petunia • *Phlox drummondii* • *Solenostemon* • *Tagetes*

FOR HARDY ANNUAL BEDS • *Antirrhinum* • *Calendula* • cornflower (*Centaurea cyanus*) • *Convolvulus minor* • cosmos • love-in-a-mist (*Gypsophila*) • *Salvia viridis*

sowing a hardy annual bed

Short-lived but inexpensive hardy annuals are great summer bed or border fillers. Of all seasonal flowers, they are the easiest to grow, as seed is sown directly in the soil where they are to flower. In a new garden or cleared patch, they can be sown in spring to cover an entire area by summer, creating a colourful blaze. In an established border, you can use annuals as gap-fillers for extra bursts of colour. In the right conditions many will self-seed freely, which means virtually no work apart from thinning out congested clumps of seedlings.

1 **Weed and rake** the soil to a fine tilth, then mark out an informal shape for each variety by trickling sand onto the ground.

2 **Within each outlined shape,** draw out shallow lines or drills with a trowel, using a stick as a guide.

3 **Sow seed thinly** in each drill. Cover with a little soil, and firm down using the back of a rake. After a few weeks, remove weed seedlings by hand and thin annual seedlings as needed (see page 27).

Hardy annuals look best in informal groups. Here, purple, pink and white *Salvia viridis* and pink lavatera form colourful drifts in a border (above).

formal bedding scheme

This example of a symmetrical summer bed is filled with half-hardy annuals and tender perennials. It will provide three months of vibrant colour, starting around midsummer.

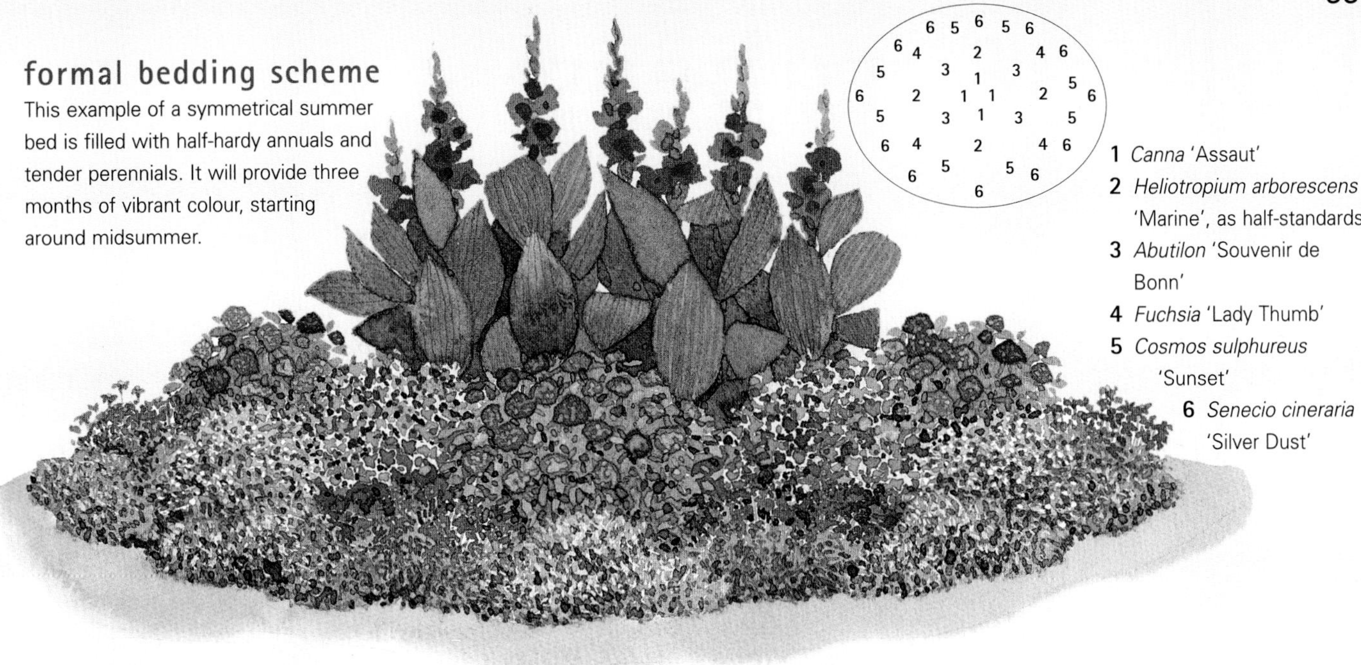

1 *Canna* 'Assaut'
2 *Heliotropium arborescens* 'Marine', as half-standards
3 *Abutilon* 'Souvenir de Bonn'
4 *Fuchsia* 'Lady Thumb'
5 *Cosmos sulphureus* 'Sunset'
6 *Senecio cineraria* 'Silver Dust'

formal bedding guidelines

- **choose an open sunny site,** sheltered from strong winds, especially if you include tall central 'dot' plants over 60cm (2ft) high, such as cordylines, cannas or standard plants.
- **keep the design bold and simple.** In large beds, use large blocks of plants – smaller ones can look too fussy.
- **make sure plants** are acclimatised, and water before planting.
- **begin in the centre** with the dot plants, spacing them 1m (3ft) apart; support with canes if needed.
- **frame the bed with edging plants,** 15cm (6in) from the sides and 10–15cm (4–6in) apart, according to size and vigour.
- **finally, fill in the spaces** with flowers of medium height, spaced 23–30cm (9–12in) apart.

colour schemes

For the best results, plan out the scheme before planting. There are no firm rules about colour combinations; you could blend a few complementary shades in a gentle or subtle design, or mix a whole rainbow of contrasting colours. Reds and oranges have a hot impact, while blue, mauve and white are tranquil. Remember that leaves can be as colourful as flowers, and many foliage plants such as coleus, silver senecio and golden helichrysum make a real contribution to a scheme.

raising the plants

Even a small flower bed can absorb a surprisingly large number of plants. You need to decide whether to buy them as young plants, which can be expensive but is less demanding on time and care, or to grow them from seed, a much cheaper option but dependent on having a greenhouse and lots of attention while the seedlings grow to flowering size.

Popular annuals and tender perennials are usually offered by garden centres as seedlings or plug plants early in the season, or as larger plants in bud or flower a few weeks later. A much wider range is available if you grow them from seed, starting 12–16 weeks before you need to plant out – spring bedding in mid-autumn and summer bedding after the last spring frosts. Remember that half-hardy annuals like begonias and impatiens need heat for germination and early growth. The most successful are F_1 hybrids, which produce uniform plants with large, bright flowers.

maintaining a scheme

Thoroughly water the bed immediately after planting, and repeat every seven days if there is no substantial rainfall. Keep the ground bare of weeds, at first by hoeing and later, when the bedding plants have filled out, by hand weeding. A mulch of lawn garden compost will help suppress weeds as well as keep the soil moist. Give plants a high-potash feed at midsummer and repeat monthly to keep them in peak condition; prolong flowering by deadheading.

At the end of the season, clear the exhausted plants en masse and prepare the ground for the next display. After the spring bedding, dig up and dry bulbs, and discard herbaceous flowers; remove weeds, tidy the edges, spread a dressing of general fertiliser and rake the surface level or into a gentle mound ready for the summer plants. When these have finished in mid-autumn, clear the bed; compost the annuals after saving any seed, and transfer tender perennials to a greenhouse. Fork in a 5cm (2in) layer of garden compost all over the bed and level, ready for the next season.

bulbs & tubers

Early spring is the time when you really appreciate bulbs and the colour they bring to the garden. With a minimum of effort now you can ensure this colour year after year – and with a little more you can enjoy bulb displays into the summer months.

now is the season to . . .

- **check bulbs in winter store,** to ensure they are still in good condition, and make plans for planting them in batches for extended summer flowering.
- **bring indoors the last potted spring bulbs** and keep in a cool, well-lit place until buds show colour.
- **move or divide clumps** of snowdrops and winter aconites while they are still in leaf (see opposite).
- **plant lilies outdoors in borders** or pots. You can transplant lilies by digging them up with large, undisturbed rootballs while the stems are still short.
- **feed bulbs naturalised in grass** in March, and those in pots and borders after flowering (see right).
- **sprout gladioli corms under glass.** Press them into a tray of compost and keep them moist and warm, then plant them out in March, together with some dormant corms that will bloom two to three weeks later.
- **take dahlia cuttings from tubers** sprouted in winter, and start more tubers into growth (see opposite).
- **mark the position of outdoor bulbs** that might need moving.
- **plant summer-flowering bulbs** in mild gardens (see opposite).
- **pot up begonias, ranunculus and other bulbs** in coldframes and unheated greenhouses for flowering indoors.

and if you have time . . .

- **pot or repot tender bulbs,** such as vallotas and clivias, together with a last batch of amaryllis (see page 495).

The cheerful yellow trumpets of daffodils are one of the most welcome sights of spring.

after flowering

- **deadhead outdoor bulbs** by pinching off large heads such as daffodils and stripping off the faded flowers of hyacinths, but leave the stalks and leaves intact to die down naturally.
- **when indoor bulbs finish flowering,** cut off the dead heads and stand them, in their pots or bowls, in an unheated room or a coldframe. Continue to water and feed them with a high-potash liquid fertiliser. In March, harden them off for a few days, then plant the contents intact in the ground, where the foliage can die down naturally. Let the bulbs flower normally next year, but lift them again for forcing the year after.

Deadhead daffodils singly, as their flowers fade and die.

For hyacinths, strip off the small blooms individually because the stem continues to manufacture food in the same way as the leaves.

the importance of leaving bulb foliage

Leaves are a plant's food factory, so their early removal can weaken a bulb and prevent it from flowering the following year. Over several years, bulbs can die out altogether if the foliage is tidied excessively. Never knot or cut off bulb foliage until it starts to yellow naturally – usually six weeks after flowering. If dying foliage spoils the appearance of a border, sprinkle seeds of a fast-growing annual such as nigella around the leaves to disguise them.

bulbs in lawns

Naturalised bulbs such as narcissi, crocuses and fritillaries can compete comfortably with the grass in a lawn, provided you do not feed that area with a lawn fertiliser, as the high nitrogen content will boost the growth of the grass more than that of the bulbs. Instead, feed the bulbs as they appear in early spring with a light watering of high-potash liquid fertiliser or a sprinkling of bone meal, which will benefit the bulbs without stimulating grass growth.

starting dahlias for soft-tip cuttings

One of the easiest ways to propagate dahlias is to take soft-tip cuttings in spring and root them in gentle heat. Start in early spring by checking the tubers and cleanly cutting off any withered sections, before burying them in trays of moist compost.

Bury dahlia tubers to half their depth in a tray of moist compost to encourage them to shoot.

- Space the tubers so that they sit on a shallow layer of compost in the trays and heap more compost around them until the lower half is buried; water once thoroughly.
- Keep in a warm, well-lit position as the buds break and develop into new shoots.
- Sever the shoots just below the lowest leaf when about 5–8cm (2–3in) long, and root in a propagator.
- Let the parent plant continue to grow until late spring, when it can be planted outdoors, or potted up in a deep, 10–13cm (4–5in) container.

looking ahead . . .

- ☑ LATE SPRING Continue to feed bulbs outdoors.
- ☑ Plant out well-rooted dahlias and begonias.
- ☑ SUMMER Lift and dry spring bulbs.

summer bulbs

Most summer bulbs are planted from late April onwards (see page 128), but it is worth starting a few earlier in mild gardens and warm, sheltered positions. Suitable bulbs include brodiaea, eucomis, galtonia, sparaxis, tigridia and tritonia. Make sure the site gets full sun and drains freely; in heavy soils, bed the bulbs on a 5cm (2in) layer of grit and plant 8–10cm (3–4in) deep.

dividing aconites

Like snowdrops, winter aconites are best divided and transplanted 'in the green', before their leaves die down.

dividing winter aconites

1 Transplant established aconites by forking up a dense clump shortly after flowering.

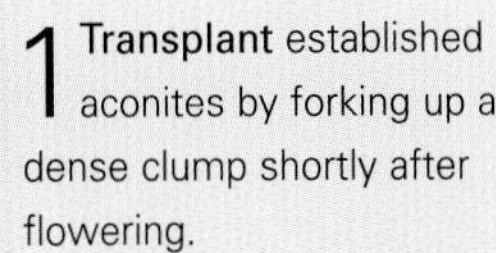

2 Tease the clump apart to separate individual tubers or small clusters, according to the number of plants you require.

3 Use a narrow trowel to open up small holes in fresh ground or part of the lawn, spaced 15cm (6in) apart. Replant a tuber in each hole, making sure it is deep enough to bury the white portion of stem; gently tread firm all round.

roses

This is the main pruning season for all except rambler roses. A little care now will ensure shapely bushes, strong, youthful growth and masses of blooms later in the year. As you prune, watch for early signs of pests and diseases, and clear up the debris afterwards.

now is the season to . . .

- **refirm roses** if frost has lifted their roots.
- **finish planting bare-rooted roses** and tidying rose beds, clearing away fallen leaves and other winter debris.
- **trim and tidy ground cover** and edging plants growing in rose beds and borders.

On climbing roses growing up supports, loosen or replace any ties that are too tight and tie in new growth as it appears.

- **check climbers and ramblers,** making sure the supports are in good repair, and that ties are secure and not too tight.
- **mist roses in pots under glass** with water occasionally to stimulate new growth and deter red spider mite. Keep the plants at about 10–15°C (50–60°F) for early flowers; watch out for pests and diseases, and feed at every other watering once new growth appears.
- **cut out dead and damaged** wood from all roses early on, in preparation for pruning.
- **sow rose seeds** that have been exposed to cold over winter (see opposite and page 497).
- **remove winter protection** from young and newly planted roses.
- **start pruning roses,** beginning with climbers, if not done in late winter. Then move on to shrub roses (see page 38), before pruning hedges and other kinds.
- **protect bushes** with wire guards where rabbits are a problem; keep in place until buds have opened into strong new shoots.
- **in a mild season, feed pruned roses** in late March with a balanced dry fertiliser or special rose feed (see page 130), and hoe or rake into the soil surface.
- **watch out for the first signs** of pests and diseases; these can appear as early as February in warm weather (see opposite).

and if you have time . . .

- **start weeding between roses** during mild spells.

The red-tinged early shoots on rose bushes and climbers are a sign of healthy new growth but also a magnet for greenfly, so keep an eye open.

good companions for roses

SMALL BULBS • chionodoxa • crocus • dwarf narcissi • snowdrops • *Tulipa turkestanica*

SPRING FLOWERS • aubrieta • primroses • violas

SHORT ANNUALS • ageratum • candytuft • nasturtiums

PERENNIALS • *Alchemilla mollis* • hardy geraniums • stachys

EVERGREEN SHRUBS • cotton lavender • dwarf lavender • rosemary • sage • thyme

Tulipa turkestanica

underplanting roses

Opinions are divided about the merits of growing other kinds of plants between roses. They can impede access for pruning and other maintenance work, you need to take more care when mulching the roses, and cultivation can take longer because you may have to hand weed rather than hoe. On the other hand, suitable companion plants can complement and enhance the display, shroud bare stems and supply colour when the roses are not in leaf or bloom. As a compromise, you might prefer to limit planting to a perennial or annual edging.

Choose plants with short, compact growth and shallow roots to avoid competing with the roses, and be prepared to feed and water a little more often in a dry season so there are adequate resources for all plants. Make sure that none of the companion plants obscure or clash with the roses; if you wish, select softer, more pastel coloured flowers or confine your choice to plants with variegated foliage.

sowing roses

Seeds extracted from rose hips and exposed to cold (see page 497) can now be sown in pots or trays of soil-based compost. Space them 2–3cm (1in) apart, cover with a thin layer of compost and keep in gentle heat, no higher than 15°C (60°F). Seedlings emerge erratically over several months. Prick them out individually into 8cm (3in) pots and stand in a coldframe or a cool, well-lit place. Pot on as they grow and plant out next spring.

pests and diseases

Some roses are prone to more than their fair share of ailments, especially where they are growing in less than ideal situations. A few simple precautions can stop a minor outbreak developing into a serious problem.

- **choose disease-resistant varieties,** some of which have remarkably good health under normal garden conditions.
- **buy healthy plants** and plant them in well-prepared sites.
- **inspect plants regularly,** in particular shrub roses, which often begin growing first and offer an early bridgehead for aphids and diseases.
- **feed plants at the right time;** avoid over-feeding or the excessive use of high-nitrogen fertilisers, which can cause roses to develop soft, vulnerable growth.
- **clear up all leaves,** dead material and prunings promptly, especially where diseases like black spot have occurred before.
- **treat problems straight away,** choosing the right product and measuring out and applying it exactly according to the instructions.
- **if you grow a lot of roses,** consider starting a regular spraying plan early in the season to prevent outbreaks (see page 131).
- **disperse roses** in a mixed border to reduce the incidence of diseases.

common rose pests and diseases

1 black spot
2 mildew
3 greenfly

Many roses are prone to particular ailments. It is important to recognise the symptoms so that you can deal with them promptly, but, better still, try to prevent them taking hold (see below).

Take preventative measures by spraying new growth against common rose problems.

disease-resistant varieties

• 'Albéric Barbier' • Bonica • 'Buff Beauty' • 'Cécile Brünner' • 'Charles de Mills' • 'Félicité Perpétue' • 'Fritz Nobis' • Gertrude Jekyll • Just Joey • 'Maigold' • 'Paul's Himalayan Musk' • 'Penelope' • Remembrance • 'Roseraie de l'Haÿ' • Winchester Cathedral

roses/2

pruning

To prevent your roses turning into shapeless, tangled shrubs with few flowers, it is necessary to prune them annually. In an average year this should be done in mid-March in the south and west of the British Isles, and in late March in central areas, but in northern gardens and those on high or exposed ground, delay the job until April. The danger of pruning too early is that buds are stimulated into life and may then be injured by hard frosts. Pruning too late, when the sap is rising, means you cut off growing shoots, wasting the plant's energy and exposing open wounds to disease.

identifying rose types

It is important to know a rose's type, so you can prune it to achieve the best results.

- **hybrid teas** have long, sturdy stems with flushes of large shapely blooms borne singly or in small groups at the ends of a few sideshoots.

PRUNING Limit the main stems to about five per bush, and shorten these to four or five buds from the base, or just two buds for extra vigour and fewer, superior flowers.

You may need to use a pruning saw or long-handled pruners to cut through old, woody stems on roses that are too thick for secateurs.

differences between climbers and ramblers

CLIMBERS Stiff, thick stems with large flowers, held singly or in small trusses on thin, twiggy sideshoots

prune in late winter to retain a framework of mature branches.

examples • Compassion • Golden Showers • 'Pink Perpétue' • 'Zéphirine Drouhin'

RAMBLERS Vigorous, pliable stems with small flowers in huge trusses borne on new shoots, often in a single summer display

prune after blooming by cutting out much of the flowered growth for replacement by young stems.

examples • 'Albertine' • 'Dorothy Perkins' • 'New Dawn' • 'The Garland' • 'Wedding Day'

Rambler *Rosa* 'The Garland'

- **floribundas** bear smaller flowers in clusters or sprays almost continuously throughout the season on freely branching bushes. Patio roses are compact, bushy floribundas that seldom exceed 60cm (2ft) in height, with trusses of proportionately smaller flowers.

PRUNING Keep five or six stems on each plant, and prune older stems to five or seven buds long; lightly trim young new shoots or leave them unpruned.

- **climbers** have stiff stems pruned in winter to retain a framework of mature branches (see page 497). The large flowers often come in flushes or are borne continuously throughout summer.
- **ramblers** have long, flexible stems with smaller flowers in large trusses, usually borne in a single spectacular display.

PRUNING In late August or September, prune to replace flowered stems with young shoots (see page 315).

- **shrub roses** are a varied group. Some old roses, like rugosas and centifolias, may only bloom once a year, whereas others, sometimes classed as modern shrub roses, are repeat flowering and vary from dainty bushes to virtual climbers.

PRUNING Lightly prune to shape, thin any overcrowded shoots, and cut one or two of the oldest branches to ground level or a low sideshoot to stimulate new growth.

- **ground-cover roses** are a kind of shrub rose with low, dense, spreading growth that can cover large areas.

PRUNING Treat like shrub roses, but also cut out any vigorous upright stems that disturb the low profile of the plant.

- **miniature roses** are no more than about 45cm (18in) high, usually bushy, sometimes with a slightly tender constitution.

PRUNING Prune lightly to maintain size, or fairly hard for improved flower quality, cutting all stems back to four or five buds.

- **standard roses** These are hybrid tea or floribunda roses grafted on a tall stem. PRUNING They should be pruned according to their type. Weeping standards are mostly grafted forms of rambler roses, and are pruned in the same way as ramblers.

looking ahead . . .

☑ LATE SPRING Finish pruning roses.
☑ Feed outdoor roses.
☑ LATE SUMMER Collect rose hips for seed.
☑ Start pruning ramblers.

the three degrees of pruning

The basic pruning routine (see below) can be adapted for all kinds of rose. The severity of your pruning will affect the size, vigour and flowering of a rose, and needs to be adjusted according to the type and variety, and also the amount of growth it makes in your soil.

- **light pruning** Shorten older stems by no more than a third and remove the tips from young shoots. This restrains very vigorous varieties, which would produce even stronger stems if they were hard pruned, and maintains size, especially on poor or dry soils.
- **moderate pruning** Cut the main stems to half their length, and shorten weaker shoots to two or three buds. This suits general garden purposes, ensuring a healthy balance between flowers and new growth.
- **hard pruning** Reduce main stems to two or three buds from the base. This is used for most shrub roses immediately after planting, but is otherwise reserved for hybrid teas intended for exhibition and for rejuvenating overgrown shrub roses.

shearing roses

Trials have shown that simply shearing off excess growth is just as effective as the traditional rose pruning methods; plants are equally healthy and vigorous afterwards, provided they are fed and well-tended. Some gardeners prefer this less time-consuming approach to rose pruning. Prune at the normal time, using garden shears, secateurs or a hedge trimmer to cut bushes down to about half their height, leaving the weaker, twiggy growth unthinned but removing all dead stems at their base.

there is still time to . . .

- **plant bare-rooted roses,** provided you complete this by early April.
- **prepare planting sites** for container-grown roses.

basic moderate pruning of shrub roses

1 **Cut out all dead stems** and trim parts that are damaged or diseased back to healthy wood, which will show a white cut surface.

2 **Remove thin, spindly** shoots, and any that cross one another or that are growing into the centre of the plant. Also cut out or pull off any suckers.

3 **Shorten the remaining** strong, healthy branches by half to an outward-facing bud or shoot. Compost or dispose of the prunings.

4 **Prune out** one or two of the oldest branches to ground level using long-handled pruners, to stimulate strong new growth.

climbers

This is an excellent time to prune, put in new plants, particularly evergreens, and sow some annual climbers to enjoy their colourful, if short-lived, contribution to summer. After pruning, make a habit of tying in new growth regularly to prevent it from becoming tangled.

now is the season to . . .

- **plant new climbers early,** before the weather becomes warm and dry. Spring is the best time to plant evergreen climbers and wall shrubs, and any plants on the borderline of hardiness (see page 134).
- **prune winter jasmine** (*Jasminum nudiflorum*) if you have not already done so (see page 499), as well as overgrown deciduous climbers like common jasmine (*Jasminum officinale*) and honeysuckle.
- **prune clematis** that flower in summer and autumn (see opposite).
- **repair or replace supports** before climbers grow strongly.
- **remove winter frost protection** as soon as weather conditions permit.
- **protect blooms of early flowering climbers** such as *Akebia quinata* and *Clematis* 'Early Sensation' from late hard frosts. Cover whole plants with fleece overnight, but remove it during the day.
- **mulch all climbers** and apply a slow-release fertiliser.
- **sow annual climbers** under cover (see opposite).
- **trim back self-clinging climbers,** such as ivy, climbing hydrangea and parthenocissus, to keep them well away from woodwork, roofs and guttering.
- **tie new shoots** into wires on walls and fences.
- **pot up semi-ripe cuttings** taken in late summer, if rooted.
- **check layers** prepared the previous year.
- **top-dress, feed and water** container-grown climbers (see right).
- **prune out frost-damaged shoots** in April, cutting them back to healthy growth.

and if you have time . . .

- **propagate climbers** by layering (see pages 133 and 500).

Carefully check to see whether layers started last year are well rooted, disturbing them as little as possible.

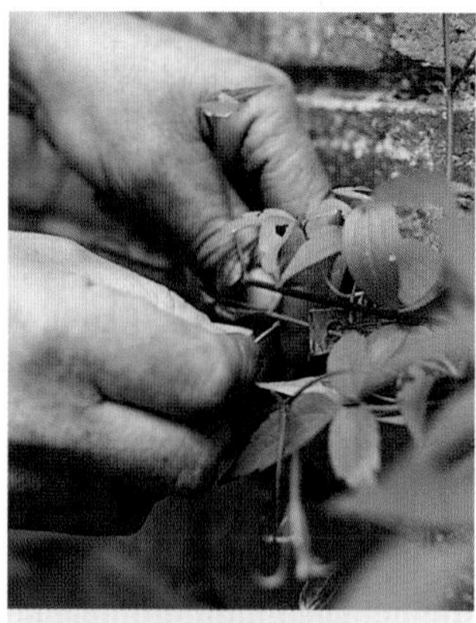

Tie in the new growth of herbaceous climbers to their wires, using soft string or sweet pea rings.

upkeep of climbers in containers

Climbers that have been in the same pot for more than two years should be replanted into a larger container. If the plant is already in a large pot, or if repotting is difficult because climbers are entwined with trellis or wires, top-dressing will keep the plant growing strongly. This involves gently scraping off the top few centimetres of old compost and replacing it with fresh soil-based potting compost mixed with controlled-release fertiliser. Water regularly and do not allow the compost to dry out.

The chocolate vine (*Akebia quinata*) flowers early, but may need to be protected if spring frosts threaten.

Brightening a fence in spring, *Clematis* 'Early Sensation' is one of the first clematis to flower. Protect its blooms in the event of late frosts.

pruning and training

After pruning, get into the habit of tying in new growth regularly to prevent it from becoming tangled and messy.

pruning clematis

The severity of pruning will vary according to the flowering time of the variety.

- **large-flowered clematis** that bloom in early to midsummer, such as 'Lasurstern', 'Nelly Moser' and 'The President': first remove all dead, damaged or weak shoots, then cut back healthy stems to a strong pair of buds. Hard prune some shoots and lightly prune others for a plant that flowers from top to bottom.
- **species and large-flowered hybrids** that bloom in late summer, such as 'Ernest Markham', 'Gipsy Queen', 'Jackmanii', *Clematis tangutica* and *C. viticella* and its hybrids: cut back all stems to 30–60cm (1–2ft), just above a strong pair of buds.
- **if you are not sure** of the variety, then treat as for the first group mentioned above to be sure of a good crop of flowers and to encourage strong, healthy shoots.

annual climbers to sow now

HARDY ANNUALS • canary creeper (*Tropaeolum peregrinum*) • climbing nasturtiums • rhodochiton • sweet peas (sow a few now for late blooms)

HALF-HARDY ANNUALS • *Cobaea scandens* • morning glory (*Ipomoea*) • thunbergia

overgrown climbers

Take the opportunity now to prune overgrown specimens of campsis, common jasmine (*Jasminum officinale*) and honeysuckle (*Lonicera periclymenum*) so that they have time to produce new flowering stems for the coming year.

Take out any crossing stems that may rub together, and shorten long, straggly stems.

sowing annual climbers

Annual climbers are splendid for summer colour. They grow rapidly from seed and may reach 2.5m (8ft) by the end of summer, smothered in colourful blooms. You can direct sow hardy annuals outside, but the best results come from seeds sown in pots or modular trays of moist potting compost (see below). Half-hardy annuals must be raised under cover and planted out once frosts are past.

Sweet peas do best in paper tubes or root trainers to develop their deep root system (see page 445). Transfer hardy annuals to a cool, frost-free coldframe or greenhouse; half-hardy annuals need a warmer environment.

looking ahead . . .

☑ LATE SPRING Plant out annual climbers.
☑ Propagate late flowering clematis.

sowing seeds of morning glory

1 Sow two or three seeds to a cell in a six-cell tray. Stand the tray in a warm place or propagator.

2 Move to a well-lit spot as soon as the seedlings appear, a week or so later. Transplant to one plant per 8cm (3in) pot and stake them as growth develops.

shrubs & trees

Spring is the season for trimming evergreens into shape and there is plenty of pruning and propagation to do, but take time to enjoy the froth of blossom on early flowering shrubs and trees.

now is the season to . . .

■ **continue planting deciduous species,** but try to get all bare-rooted plants in the ground by the end of March.

■ **refirm recent plantings** if their roots have been lifted by wind or frost. In a dry season, water and mulch to keep the roots moist.

■ **inspect all supports** and tree ties, and repair or adjust where necessary.

■ **cover vulnerable plants** such as cistus and hydrangeas if frost threatens.

Where a shrub has succumbed to frost damage, or 'scorch', prune out the affected shoots before new growth gets started.

■ **shelter recently planted** evergreens from wind and frost by erecting a temporary windbreak of hurdles or netting.

■ **watch out for** early signs of pests and diseases, and take prompt action to prevent them spreading; some evergreen diseases, such as mahonia rust, are present or visible all the year round (see page 44).

■ **prune late flowering shrubs** such as buddleia, perovskia and caryopteris, together with frost-shy shrubs like hardy fuchsias and hydrangeas (see pages 45 and 137).

■ **trim winter-flowering heaths** to remove dead blooms and keep plants compact (see page 44).

■ **start pruning early flowering shrubs** such as forsythia and winter jasmine (see page 498) as their display finishes.

■ **prune mahonias** to prevent leggy growth (see page 44).

■ **hard prune shrubs with coloured stems**, such as cornus and salix, to encourage vivid young growth, and cut back canes of white-stemmed brambles (*Rubus*) to the ground (see page 512).

■ **renovate overgrown evergreens** and evergreen hedges by pruning them hard in late March (see opposite).

■ **move misplaced evergreen shrubs** growing on heavy soil (see page 504).

■ **pull up or cut off suckers** from shrubs such as lilac and sumach, or mow them off if they are growing in a lawn.

■ **layer shrubs and trees** that are difficult to propagate from cuttings. Plants with low pliable branches can be layered in the ground (see page 139), while those with stiffer upright stems are better air layered (see page 47).

■ **sow tree and shrub seeds** that have been stored over winter.

■ **pot up seedlings and cuttings** started last autumn, and grow on ready for planting in a nursery bed in early summer.

■ **take root cuttings** of shrubs such as sumach, aralia and ceanothus, and root them in a coldframe or indoors in warmth (see page 46).

■ **trim or start training topiary** plants towards the end of March (see page 48).

■ **trim rose hedges** in late March; use shears or a hedge trimmer to clip them to size, then prune out any dead and diseased wood. Feed after pruning.

■ **water plants in containers** if prolonged drought or winds have dried out the compost.

and if you have time . . .

■ **paint tree trunks** and branches of deciduous plants with an antiseptic winter wash if pests and diseases have been a problem. Do this as early as possible and before buds start to open. Cover all plants beneath to prevent injury from splashes.

avoiding the dangers of late frost

Spring frosts are unpredictable and potentially lethal to flower buds, young growth and plants that originated in warm climates. Injury can be serious after a sequence of warm weather, followed by a sharp frost and then another mild spell. Use fleece or a similar temporary cover to protect vulnerable plants when frost threatens. The young shoots of hydrangeas and fuchsias are also vulnerable, together with plants of borderline hardiness, such as forms of rosemary and lavender (see below).

plants vulnerable to spring frost

• camellia • grey and silver-leaved shrubs (especially cistus and halimium) • hydrangeas • lavenders (*Lavandula lanata* and *L. latifolia*) • *Magnolia stellata* • romneya • rosemary (*R.* 'Prostratus')

Camellia japonica 'Akashigata'

hard pruning overgrown evergreens

Laurel, holly and rhododendrons are typical of evergreen shrubs that require little annual pruning, but eventually become too straggly or outgrow their allotted space. You can cut them back radically between late March and early June, to stumps about 45–60cm (18–24in) high. Remove damaged or diseased wood and weak growth, leaving only the strongest stumps to regrow.

Renovating an overgrown laurel hedge by pruning in late March will ensure plenty of healthy new growth.

Overgrown evergreen hedges, such as box, holly and yew, are treated similarly (see below), but the work is better spread over a few years to ensure regrowth all over the hedge.

- **start by cutting** the top to the required height, then trim all the branches on one side almost back to the main stems. Feed and mulch the hedge; water well in dry weather.
- **when new shoots are growing well** on the cut face, which may be two or three years later, the second side may be hard pruned in the same way.

HEDGE SHAPING TIP Where a hedge acts as a windbreak, you can sculpt the top in free-form undulations or castellate it like battlements. This helps to filter the wind, whereas a level top makes a barrier rather like a solid wall or fence, causing wind turbulence.

hard pruning a box hedge

1 **Set up a string line** at the desired height and cut the top of the hedge to this height using hedging shears.

2 **Clear away** clippings before tackling one face of the hedge. Trim branches almost back to the main stems (see above).

Hazel catkins (*Corylus avellana*) are one of the distinguishing sights of a new year in the garden. Developed during winter, the male catkins expand to shed their pollen in early spring.

regenerating overgrown shrubs

If neglected or only lightly pruned over a number of years, shrubs such as cornus, *Buddleja davidii* and many hydrangeas become tall and leggy, with a bare base and fewer, small flowers. You can often rejuvenate them by cutting them hard back in early spring, leaving a series of healthy stumps to regrow. Small shrubs can be cut back in one go, but larger specimens, such as mature hydrangeas, are better tackled in stages, spreading the work over two or three years by cutting back a third or half of the stems each year. Feed after pruning and leave the new growth unpruned for a year to become established. Always check when you buy a shrub that it withstands hard pruning, because some kinds, such as brooms (*Cytisus*), do not regenerate well from old stems.

shrubs & trees/2

early spring pruning

This is pruning time for shrubs that bloomed late last year and those that have just finished flowering. By doing this annually you will keep the plants shapely and encourage plenty of flowers for next year. Some early blossom and new growth is particularly vulnerable to frost, but a combination of late pruning and protection will keep damage to a minimum.

trimming heathers

If left unpruned, heathers and heaths often become tall, leggy and straggly, with a lot of dead growth that can shorten their lives. Do not prune so hard that you cut into the old, tough wood, which often cannot regenerate.

One-handed shears or large scissors are the best tools for clipping off all the dead flowerheads and some of the young growth of heathers, to leave a neat, compact finish.

- **prune winter-flowering heaths** (mainly *Erica* x *darleyensis* and cultivars), now, as flowers fade and new growth appears.
- **you can prune summer and** autumn-flowering heathers such as *Calluna vulgaris*, *Daboecia cantabrica*, *Erica cinerea*, *E. ciliaris* and *E. tetralix* and their varieties after flowering, but as the dead flowerheads of many varieties remain attractive over winter, you may prefer to leave pruning until March.
- **check variegated heathers** for all-green reversions, and cut these out at their base.

pruning mahonia

1 **As soon as** flowering finishes, trim off the end rosettes of foliage, cutting just above the next set of leaves down the stem.

2 **If you want** a more compact bush, use long-handled loppers to prune the stems harder, down to a low sideshoot.

mahonias

Tall mahonias such as *M. japonica* develop long bare stems unless pruned annually (see above). You can prune shorter-growing *Mahonia aquifolium* in the same way, unless it is grown as a hedge or ground cover, in which case shear off all the stems, almost to ground level, to keep growth young and leafy. You can use the prunings to propagate (see page 47).

- **mahonia rust** is present all the year round and causes deep reddish purple patches on older leaves, with powdery brown pustules on the undersides. Prune and burn diseased foliage, and spray young growth with copper-based fungicide at monthly intervals during the growing season.

winter and early flowering shrubs

Shrubs such as winter-flowering *Viburnum* x *bodnantense* and *V.* x *burkwoodii*, which flower early on stems produced the previous year, are pruned as soon as their blooms fade. New stems grow freely from the base of these shrubs, so cut out about a third of the oldest branches, and trim the rest to shape; in this way the plants are constantly rejuvenated, with enhanced flowering.

On ornamental quince (*Chaenomeles* x *superba* 'Nicoline'), clusters of waxy cups open on bare stems. Prune after flowering, cutting back flowered shoots on wall-trained specimens to within three or four buds of the permanent framework.

late flowering shrubs

Most late flowering shrubs, including *Buddleja davidii*, caryopteris, lavatera, leycesteria, perovskia and santolina, produce their blooms on growth made in the current year, and these stems need pruning now, just before or as their new leaves begin to open.

- Shorten all the shoots that flowered last year to within one or two buds from their base.
- Thin congested growth by removing or shortening some of the older stems.

Shear off the dead and untidy stems of potentillas to neaten their growth before summer flowering.

pruning hydrangeas

This is the best time to prune hydrangeas such as *H. paniculata*, *H. arborescens* and *H. macrophylla* hybrids, both lacecap and mophead (Hortensia) types. The dead flowers are usually left untouched over winter, because they are considered to provide a degree of frost protection.

- Cut old flowering stems to two or three buds from the base.
- Remove any weak or old exhausted shoots.
- Mulch plants with a deep layer of rotted manure.

pruning hardy fuchsias

Fuchsias are also often left until spring before pruning, especially in colder gardens, for the sake of the frost protection given by the old growth. Now all this must be cut back hard, almost to ground level.

In milder areas you can prune more lightly, allowing a framework of permanent older branches to develop. You then simply remove any framework branches that are exhausted, shorten the sideshoots to their base, and lightly trim the remaining stems to shape.

pruning cotinus

Prune smokebush (*Cotinus*) now, according to the effect you require (see below). Cutting back large bushes hard will restore their shape and vigour, stimulating more handsome and colourful foliage, whereas light pruning maintains size and allows the bush to flower more lavishly.

pruning cotinus

1 **An overgrown cotinus** can be hard pruned in early spring to a more manageable shape, resulting in vigorous new growth with improved leaf size and colour.

2 **Use loppers or a saw** to remove complete branches, cutting back to a main stump or the junction with another, better placed branch.

3 **Thinner growth** can be left unpruned to maintain a leafy, although reduced canopy, or it can be trimmed off to leave a clean cut.

4 **Alternatively,** shorten the younger shoots by half for a compromise between total renewal and retaining some of the flowering wood.

shrubs & trees/3

With its attractive rounded leaves and pink, bell-shaped blooms, *Rhododendron* Temple Belle Group brings long-lasting colour to the early spring garden.

propagation

Shrubs and trees can be propagated in several ways at this time of year. Air layering is a traditional method that is particularly satisfying, as you get a sizable plant that needs less cosseting than one raised from cuttings. Also, being above ground it is less likely to suffer accidental damage than layers in the soil.

The advantages of taking root cuttings are simplicity and reliability. No elaborate equipment is necessary unless you choose to take the cuttings under glass, and you will often have 100 per cent success.

Besides the more conventional cuttings taken from shoots or leaf buds, some evergreen shrubs can be propagated from stem cuttings taken when pruning the plant (see opposite).

taking root cuttings

Root cuttings from shrubs and trees are treated like those taken from fleshy rooted perennials (see page 490).

- In late winter and early spring, while the plants are still dormant, scrape away some of the soil until part of the root system is exposed.
- Cut off a few roots at least 5mm (¼in) thick and close to the stem. Keep them moist until preparation.
- Trim the cuttings to about 15cm (6in) long and remove any fine side roots. Make a flat cut at the top (the end that was nearer the stem) and a sloping cut at the base.
- Plant the cuttings in a coldframe, outdoors in a well-drained spot and covered with a cloche, or in deep pots of cuttings compost in the greenhouse. Insert them upright with the flat cut at the top, spacing them 5–8cm (2–3in) apart. Cover the tops with a thin layer of soil or compost.
- Rooting takes about six weeks under glass or two to three months outdoors. Pot up growing cuttings individually or transplant 15cm (6in) apart in a nursery bed.

shrubs to grow from root cuttings

• ailanthus • aralia • ceanothus • clerodendron • embothrium • gymnocladus • koelreuteria • myrica • paulownia • rhus • robinia • sassafras • sorbaria • zanthoxylum

Rhus typhina

propagating mahonia from stem cuttings

1 **Use mahonia prunings** as propagating material by selecting a firm green (not brown) stem and cutting this just above a leaf joint and about 4cm (1½in) below it.

2 **To save space** under glass and reduce water loss, trim the stem back to just beyond two or three pairs of leaflets.

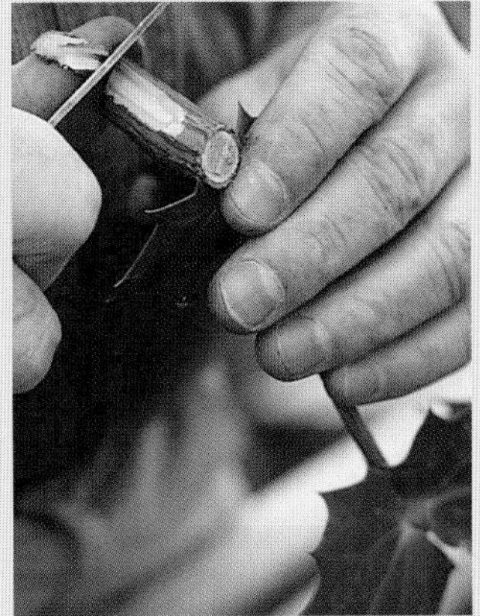

3 **With a sharp knife,** trim off the rough edges round the bottom of the cutting and peel a strip of bark from one side to increase the rooting area.

4 **Insert an upright cutting** to the base of its first leaf in a 10–13cm (4–5in) potful of cuttings compost. Firm and water in well, then keep warm in a propagator.

air layering

Some shrubs and trees are reluctant to root as cuttings, while simple layering in the ground is impossible because of the lack of suitable low, flexible branches. Air layering is the solution. You can air layer stems any time from early spring to late summer; it takes about a year to ensure a good supply of roots (see right). When you can see roots appearing at the surface of the moss, remove the plastic carefully and cut off the stem just below the rooted area. Plant the layer outside in a nursery bed and leave for a year or pot up the cutting in a 10–13cm (4–5in) pot of soil-based compost.

shrubs and trees to air layer

- citrus • hawthorn (*Crataegus*) • quince (*Cydonia*) • davidia • ginkgo • witch hazel (*Hamamelis*) • kalmia • liquidambar • magnolia • medlar • rhododendron • styrax

Ginkgo biloba

air layering a rhododendron

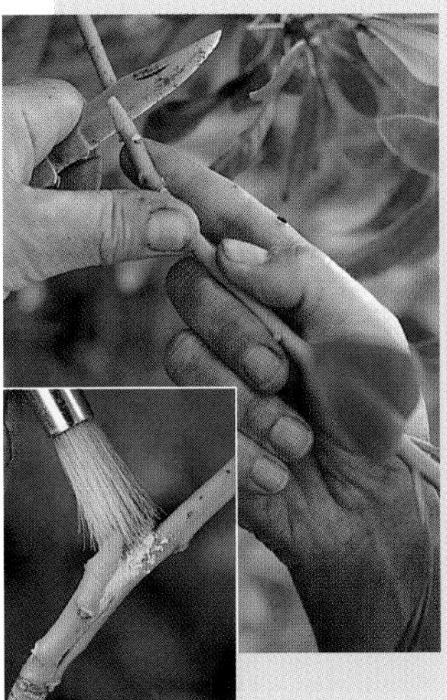

1 **Choose a young,** straight branch. About 30cm (12in) from its tip, make an angled cut half way through the branch to form a tongue about 5cm (2in) long. Dust the cut surfaces with hormone rooting powder (inset).

2 **Wedge the tongue** open with a fragment of moist sphagnum moss, then wrap more moss round the cut like a fat bandage.

3 **Hold the moss** in place with a square of clear plastic sheeting, tightly sealed with waterproof tape at top and bottom, and along the overlapping edge.

shrubs & trees/4

training and topiary

When creating a large shape from an established shrub, such as this yew teddy bear, you may have to shorten some thicker branches with a saw or loppers. New growth will soon appear to cover the bare patch.

It takes about five to ten years to train and clip evergreen shrubs into simple geometric shapes such as balls, cubes and pyramids, and a little longer to sculpt more complex representational figures like birds and small animals. Box and yew are the classic plants for this traditional art form, although some larger-leaved species such as holly, bay and portugal laurel (*Prunus lusitanica*) can also be used. Deciduous plants like hawthorn (*Crataegus*) and golden privet (*Ligustrum*) also clip well into simple shapes.

topiary training techniques

Start with an existing bushy specimen, larger than the finished shape, and carve it freehand with secateurs or one-handed shears. Alternatively, plant a smaller container-grown bush inside a wire former and use this as a template to guide your cutting (see opposite). The bush will eventually cover the former completely.

A standard bay (*Laurus nobilis*) makes an immaculate and traditional centrepiece for a herb garden, or two can be planted in a pair of matching large containers to flank a doorway. You can buy fully formed specimens, but it is not difficult to train your own from a single-stemmed plant, a rooted offshoot or a strong cutting (see below).

Most topiary figures need clipping at least twice a year, in April and late summer. More frequent trimming maintains a precise outline and bushy growth; fast-growing species like privet may need four or five trims a year. Feed topiary in early spring with a general fertiliser to sustain replacement growth.

FROST-PROTECTION TIP Standard plants such as bay, yew or box kept in containers are vulnerable to temperatures below -4°C (25°F), so insulate both tree and container, or move them under cover when hard frost is forecast.

training a standard bay

1 **Pot up** a straight-stemmed rooted cutting or offshoot in a 10cm (4in) container of potting compost mixed with extra grit. This may take a year or more to start growing well, during which time keep it in a warm greenhouse and occasionally mist to keep humidity high.

2 **As the plant** grows, pot it on into a larger container and trim off the lower leaves and sideshoots to start developing the clear trunk. Support the stem with a cane and tie it in several places to keep it straight. Continue potting on and tying in as necessary.

3 **When the young tree** is a little taller than the required height, prune off the growing tip. Remove shoots forming on the trunk, and cut or pinch out the tips of sideshoots in the head when about 15cm (6in) long. Shorten sideshoots growing from these in the same way.

4 **Keep pinching out** the tips of sideshoots to encourage a dense, shapely ball of leafy growth. Repot or topdress annually in spring, and trim the head with secateurs twice a year.

using a ready-made frame

2 As the plant grows, trim its foliage with scissors or small shears at least once a year wherever it protrudes beyond the wire former.

1 For small topiary items, plant the shrub centrally in the pot, then anchor the frame's 'legs' firmly in the compost. Choose a bushy, small-leaved species like box.

Well-established ivy against a wall has been trimmed with shears into an ornamental 'house', while the impact of a dominating conifer has been cleverly reduced by exposing part of the stem to admit light and cutting the base to create the effect of a standard growing in a pot.

using a self-assembly frame

1 Topiary frame kits are easy to construct. Stand the base in the bottom of a pot and half-fill with soil-based compost. Assemble the components, securing them with wire twists; here, they form a sphere.

2 Plant the young shrub in the centre, then fill with more compost. Trim off any foliage extending beyond the frame, or tie the flexible shoots of a plant like this *Cotoneaster horizontalis* to the wires for faster coverage.

making decorative stems

While trees are young you can sculpt their flexible stems by training them round formers, such as spirals of wire, or plait them for a 'barleysugar' twist that is retained even when the trunk has firmed up. Start while stems are young and pliable and can be bent without cracking. Twist or ply multiple stems evenly (see below), holding them in place with ties. When the tree reaches the desired height, allow the sideshoots to develop into a head. Shorten these top branches by half to encourage dense busy growth.

Pot up the young plant and, if it has several stems, gently plait these together, then secure them to a strong cane with string or wire twists. Trim all shoots, buds and leaves from the lower part of the stems to reveal their decorative arrangement.

there is still time to . . .

- **move shrubs and trees** to new positions, but complete this work by early March (see page 504).

designing a border

Border plants are a wonderful investment, increasing in size and beauty over time. Because there is a vast range to choose from, advance thought and careful selection will produce the best results.

the right conditions

A few plants thrive almost anywhere, but most have preferences as to where they grow. Matching a plant to its preferred site will ensure that it flourishes and remains healthy without undue attention. Plants that enjoy the same conditions often make good-looking combinations. Find out what grows well in your area by doing a bit of local research. Walk around your neighbourhood to see which plants thrive there, visit open gardens and talk to knowledgeable neighbours or staff at nearby nurseries and garden centres.

year-round interest

Borders need to earn their keep, and there can be something of colour and interest in every month of the year. The planning guidelines described here can help you to create a border with year-round structure and form. Take care when choosing the flowering plants: it is all too easy to end up with lots of summer blooms and very little at other times. Start by listing suitable plants for the winter months, when blooms are at their most scarce, then work through autumn, spring and finally summer.

One of the most attractive trees for small gardens, *Prunus serrula* has beautiful peeling red-brown bark that is handsome all year round (above).

Beneath deciduous trees are opportunities to plant drifts of shade-lovers such as tiarellas, aquilegias, phlox, ferns and trilliums (right).

climate and location

As well as assessing conditions such as soil and aspect, the climate and location of your garden are important factors in choosing plants. Many plants that happily thrive outdoors in warmer parts of the country would be killed by the winter cold in more northerly areas or on exposed hilltop sites. In coastal places, the sea has a tempering influence on climate and keeps the winter temperatures higher than they are just a few miles inland, but it is vital to select plants that are tolerant of salt-laden winds. There is a big difference between town and country, too, as the warmth and shelter created by tall buildings makes for a warmer, more protected environment than in open, rural areas.

how many, how far apart?

Trees and shrubs must be spaced sufficiently far apart to allow room for their eventual height and spread. Correctly spaced plants will look 'gappy' at first, but will fill out surprisingly quickly; in between you can plant annuals or perennials and grasses that are quite happy to be moved later on.

In small to medium-sized gardens, the largest plants should be planted singly, while small shrubs, perennials and grasses look most effective in groups of three or five. Bulbs look wonderful planted in large quantities, particularly if you limit the number of varieties to create a real impact.

planning guidelines

Whether you are planning planting schemes for a whole new garden or just one or two beds or borders, the best

Upright juniper gives height to the border.

Deciduous and evergreen climbers clad the fence backing the border.

Fragrant *Choisya ternata* gives two seasons of flower.

Spiky phormium brings a strong year-round outline.

Plant spring bulbs between perennials for additional early colour.

Low ground-covering plants go at the front.

mixed border in early summer

Backed by deciduous and evergreen climbers, this border shows a good proportion of shapely evergreen shrubs infilled by flowering shrubs and herbaceous perennials for all seasons.

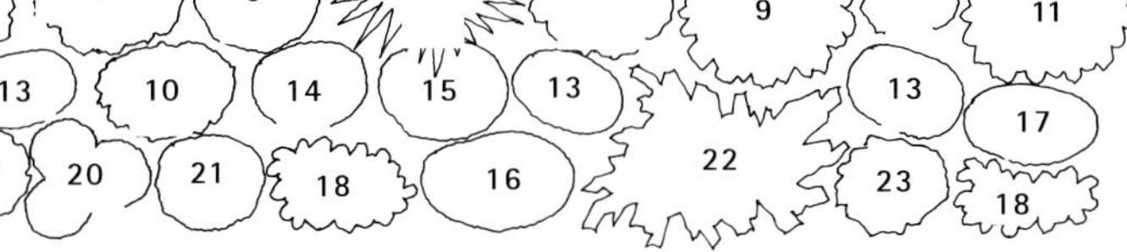

1 *Vitis coignetiae*
2 *Trachelospermum jasminoides*
3 *Lonicera* x *americana*
4 *Arbutus unedo*
5 *Berberis* x *stenophylla*
6 *Juniperus communis* 'Hibernica'
7 *Phormium* 'Sundowner'
8 *Viburnum tinus*
9 *Rhododendron* 'Bow Bells'
10 *Pittosporum tobira*
11 *Garrya elliptica*
12 *Choisya ternata*
13 *Miscanthus sinensis* 'Silberfeder'
14 *Hemerocallis* 'Catherine Woodbery'
15 *Osmanthus delavayi*
16 *Geranium* x *magnificum*
17 *Lilium regale*
18 *Bergenia* 'Ballawley'
19 *Iris* 'Jane Phillips'
20 *Hebe* 'Boughton Dome'
21 *Arabis alpina* subsp. *caucasica* 'Variegata'
22 *Juniperus virginiana*
23 *Skimmia japonica* 'Rubella'

starting point is to sketch out a planting plan on paper, then draw it to scale on graph paper. In a large garden you may find it easier to make a separate plan for each border rather than tackling the whole plot at one go.

If you select your plants in the following sequence, you can build up a framework of permanent planting, which you can then fill in with a succession of seasonal colour.

- **trees** are the most dominant occupants of the garden. Consider how different shapes of tree will fit into your garden, and how many seasons of interest they will provide. Those with green or softly coloured leaves are a safer choice than golds or purples, which can look overpowering when large.
- **evergreen shrubs and conifers** should make up about a third of all the medium to large plants, to give year-round structure and colour, which is particularly important in winter. Choose some that are architectural in form, with large or spiky leaves or a striking shape, as well as some of a gentler habit to provide a backdrop to flowers.
- **deciduous shrubs** offer attractive shapes or colourful or variegated foliage, and often a dramatic flowering season. Those with small, plain green leaves make an effective backdrop to flowers.
- **flowering shrubs** can be selected to bloom at different times of year, to create a succession of interest.
- **herbaceous perennials,** grasses and smaller shrubs can be used as infill, once all the key plants are in place.
- **bulbs** can be planted in the spaces between groups of plants to grow up through carpets of ground cover.
- **seasonal bedding** like annuals, biennials and frost-tender perennials can provide spectacular, long-lasting summer colour. Use them to fill gaps while the permanent planting matures, or to make a display in their own right.

alpine gardens

Many alpines will be coming into flower at this time, and those with silvery leaves, especially, still need their roots and foliage kept dry if they are to survive a wet spring. As the growing season gets under way, prepare troughs, sinks or raised beds for planting.

now is the season to . . .

- **prepare beds** and other areas for planting alpines.
- **protect vulnerable plants** from slugs and snails (see opposite) before they can eat new shoots.
- **protect plants** against wet spring weather to prevent basal rot from developing, especially on plants with silver or hairy leaves, by covering them with a pane of glass balanced on pots or bricks (see page 514).

Trim the growth of untidy alpines by cutting back long straggly shoots.

- **trim any straggly plants,** and those that have encroached on their neighbours, by cutting back the long growth to 8–10cm (3–4in) above the ground.
- **control weeds** by carefully hoeing between plants to take out annual weeds before they can produce seed. Treat perennial weeds as they emerge by spot treating them with a weed pen or paint-on gel to avoid disturbing the soil.
- **replenish gravel mulches** over alpine beds and borders to a depth of at least 2–3cm (1in). This will improve drainage, prevent weed seeds from germinating and deter slugs and snails.
- **divide oversized plants** in the same way as border perennials, but leave those coming into flower until early summer or autumn.
- **check root cuttings** taken in autumn; if they have rooted, plant them out in April or pot up individually.
- **propagate new alpines** from seeds and cuttings (see opposite).
- **visit shows** and Internet sites, and scrutinise catalogues in search of new plants to add to the alpine garden.

Tidy individual alpines by removing any dead or dying leaves before replenishing the gravel mulch.

Cushion-forming *Draba rigida* (below) is a hardy evergreen perennial, bringing spring colour to rock gardens, troughs and raised beds. It is vulnerable to excessive damp; protect with a pane of glass if needed.

preparing an alpine bed

Good drainage is essential to the success of alpines, together with an open, sunny site clear of trees. Whether you plan to grow alpines in a raised bed, or in the open garden, you need to prepare the site thoroughly by breaking up the lower levels and incorporating plenty of drainage material to keep the growing medium open and free draining. Fill the bottom third of a raised bed with pea shingle, top up with a mix of soil-based compost or good quality garden soil and grit, then leave it to settle for two to three weeks before you plant. It is worth making up a fresh compost mix when you are replenishing a tired alpine sink or trough (see below).

replenishing an alpine sink

1 In a bucket, mix a quantity of sterilised loam-based compost, such as John Innes No. 2, with equal parts of horticultural sand or grit. Use washed sand or grit to ensure that it is free of clay particles.

2 Take the plants carefully out of the sink and trim any straggly ones, then remove the upper third of compost and replace with the fresh mix.

3 After replacing the old plants, and adding any new ones, mulch with a layer of gravel or coarse grit to a depth of 2–3cm (1in).

slug control

Young plants and new shoots need protection from foraging slugs and snails. Biological control in the form of parasitic nematodes is of no use at this time of year as the soil will be too cold for them to survive, but there are other measures you can take.

- **use citrus peel** as a bait and dispose of the slugs and snails while they are feeding.
- **lay extra grit** around the base of plants to act as a barrier.
- **apply slug bait** as granules or pellets at about 10 per m^2 (9 per sq yd).

propagating

Keep a close watch on seed trays in the coldframe, as many alpine seeds sown in winter will start to germinate (see page 515). Carefully prick out individually those that have germinated and replace trays in the coldframe in case more seeds germinate later.

You can also sow seeds outdoors now, including any you have collected and stored over winter in a refrigerator (see page 420). Sow seeds thinly in a clay pot or pan filled with equal parts of John Innes seed compost and grit, cover with a layer of grit and label; the grit helps the stems to elongate, making the tiny seedlings easier to prick out. Place the pots in a cool, exposed position before watering thoroughly.

taking cuttings

Many alpines can be increased from cuttings at this time, but the method will vary according to the growth habit of the particular plant.

- **take advantage of new shoots** to take basal cuttings, and trim them to about 2–3cm (1in).
- **detach individual rosettes** from saxifrages and pot up (see page 514).
- **root branching succulents** from sideshoots, and sedums from individual leaves.
- **insert all these cuttings** into pots or pans of cuttings compost, mixed with an equal amount of extra grit or perlite. Water them from below by standing the container in a dish of water until the compost surface is moist, then cover the surface with 5mm (¼in) of grit; label the cuttings.

water gardens

As temperatures rise it is time to remove ice protection and reintroduce the pump as the pond starts into life. Any cleaning that is necessary should be done early, before plants develop and pond creatures begin to breed. In milder areas you can start planting and can divide overgrown plants.

now is the season to . . .

■ **order new aquatic plants** from mail-order or Internet suppliers. Start planting new pond plants in mild areas, or leave it until late spring in colder ones (see page 144).

■ **remove, clean and store** pond heaters or other ice-guard devices.

■ **replace a submersible pump** that has been stored over winter after checking that it works properly. Stand it on a brick or a block of wood to avoid drawing in sediment from the base of the pond.

■ **test external pumps** after removing winter insulation.

■ **refill barrel and other container ponds** towards the end of the season and reintroduce plants or fish that have been kept under cover for the winter (see page 233).

■ **start to feed fish** as the weather warms up. Feed daily but take care to give only as much food as the fish will eat in about half an hour, as uneaten food is a major cause of green algae in ponds. Net the pond to protect fish from herons if not already done (see page 423).

■ **divide established clumps** of early flowering marginals such as kingcup (*Caltha palustris*) as soon as possible (see page 143). There is less urgency for marginal grasses and plants that flower later, although they should also be divided during spring – except irises, which are divided in summer after flowering.

■ **divide bog garden plants** in the same way as perennials once they have formed established clumps (see page 399). If you plan a new, large bog garden, growing from seed is an economical way of raising new plants, including cuckoo flower (*Cardamine pratensis*), many moisture-loving primulas and purple loosestrife (*Lythrum salicaria*).

■ **protect frog and toad spawn** from birds by netting that area of the pond. Do not transfer spawn from other ponds as this can spread disease.

■ **clean out ponds** if necessary (see opposite).

■ **set up a water butt** to collect rainwater for topping up the pond, which will be much better for pond life than nutrient-rich tap water.

The unfurling leathery leaves and spiny stems of a dramatic *Gunnera manicata* erupt into growth in early spring, emerging from a protective winter covering of straw.

cleaning out the pond

All ponds tend to turn green in spring. This is caused by algae that feed on the nutrients that proliferate in the water at this time of year. The water usually clears once the pond plants begin growing strongly, taking up the nutrients and starving out the algae (see page 143).

A total clean out is a major job that is only necessary every five years or so for small ponds and double that for larger ones. The exception is if the water is black, smelly and obviously polluted, such as occurs when leaves and debris have been left to rot in the pond.

Choose a time in early spring, before fish and other creatures start breeding, to empty your pond if it needs a total clean out, so that it has time to settle down before winter. Take the opportunity to check the liner and make any necessary repairs, and to divide and replant any plants that are overgrown. Inspect pond snails and dispose of those with spiral shells (great pond snails), as they eat plants.

spring cleaning a pond

1 **Remove all pond plants** and place them on a plastic sheet if they will be out of the water for a few hours only; if longer, stand them in buckets part-filled with water. Get ready three large bowls of clean water. Scoop out fish and other wildlife, and keep fish, spawn and snails in separate bowls (fish need wide containers for plenty of oxygen). Put some plants in with the fish for shelter and food.

2 **To siphon out the water,** take a 1.5m (5ft) length of hose and place in the pond so it fills with water. Holding one end under water with your thumb sealing it, quickly bring the other end out of the pond to a lower point than the one in the pond, releasing your thumb at the same time. The pull of gravity should start the flow of water, which can be caught in a bucket. If there is a lot of debris in the pond, place an old sieve on the pond end of the hose to stop it from getting blocked. If you cannot find a lower point, you will have to bale or pump out all the water.

3 **After baling out** the last few centimetres of water with a container, scoop out the mud from the bottom using a net or sieve – don't worry about removing every last bit. Pile the mud on a plastic sheet next to the pond and leave it there for a couple of days so that any creatures can crawl back into the water.

4 **Scrub inside the pond** with a stiff brush and clean water; do not use detergents. Bale out the resulting dirty water. Refill the pond, using rainwater first and topping up with tap water, then replace the plants. Allow temperatures to stabilise for a day or so before replacing fish, spawn and snails.

patios & containers

It is a good idea to get a head start on the year and take care of as many jobs as possible on fine early spring days. Start planning and planting now so you can enjoy colourful containers right through the summer.

now is the season to . . .

- **clean patios and decking** before the space is filled with container displays.
- **remove winter protection** and return pots to their original positions as soon as the weather permits. However, keep some fleece handy to protect susceptible young growth and flowers if late frosts threaten.
- **brighten up your containers** and patio borders with spring bedding plants that are tough, colourful and long flowering. There is plenty of choice in garden centres or nurseries, including double daisies (*Bellis perennis*), forget-me-nots, primulas and wallflowers, plus ready-grown bulbs.
- **water regularly** as the weather warms up, particularly on breezy days when containers dry out rapidly.
- **order young tender perennials** and bedding plants from mail order or Internet suppliers.
- **protect the blooms of spring-flowering shrubs** like camellias, rhododendrons and azaleas by placing containers in a sheltered spot away from the early morning sun.
- **mulch rhododendrons** with chipped bark to protect their shallow roots from extremes of temperature.
- **feed spring bulbs in containers** while they are in flower and until the leaves start to yellow and die, so they will make a superb display next spring. Label each container so that you can identify the bulbs when dormant.

Deadheading winter pansies will prolong their flowering display into early summer.

- **deadhead winter pansies** to encourage new flowers.
- **plant lily bulbs** to twice their depth in soil-based potting compost. Put three bulbs in a 25–30cm (10–12in) deep pot and stand in an unheated greenhouse or coldframe or a sheltered spot outside.
- **plant up containers** of tender plants in a heated greenhouse or conservatory; small plug plants are very useful for hanging baskets and flower pouches (see below). By growing the displays under cover through spring, you will have well-established containers to put out after the frosts.
- **plant perennials,** ornamental grasses and ferns. Many of them make low-maintenance container plants; they will establish quickly if planted now. Good-looking foliage and early flowering perennials are particularly useful during spring when there is little else around. Some tolerate shade and so are perfect for brightening gloomy corners (see opposite).
- **prune patio roses,** removing all dead, weak and damaged shoots and shortening sideshoots.
- **pot up roses and shrubs** (see page 149).
- **top-dress permanent plants** by replacing the top few centimetres of compost with an appropriate compost mixed with controlled-release fertiliser (see page 40).
- **in April, start to harden off** shrubs of borderline hardiness that overwintered under cover (see page 167), so that they acclimatise to outside conditions before being returned to the patio in late spring.
- **control weeds in paving cracks** at an early stage, by hand or with a weedkiller or garden flame gun. Once the cracks are clear, and if you like an informal garden, sow seed of plants that thrive in crevices such as mexican daisy (*Erigeron karvinskianus*) and yellow fumitory (*Corydalis lutea*).
- **bring garden furniture out of store** and clean or treat if necessary. Resin furniture only requires washing with hot water and a mild detergent. Wooden furniture usually needs treating with stain or preservative every other year; choose the right product for hardwood or softwood furniture.

Plug plants can be ordered by mail. They should be potted on into 8cm (3in) pots as soon as they arrive, to grow on to a larger size.

looking ahead . . .

☑ LATE SPRING Harden off containers of tender plants.
☑ Move container shrubs of borderline hardiness outside.

In a large galvanised planter, spring bulbs (*Narcissus*) and *Helleborus foetidus* make colourful companions for permanent pieris and ivy.

cleaning patios and decking

Patios, decks and paths look much better for a thorough cleaning at the end of winter, and are much safer to walk on, as algae can make surfaces dangerously slippery. Shady areas are the worst affected by moss and algae, as the surface tends to stay damp for long periods. The best method of cleaning is to use a pressure washer, but first make sure that the water can drain away freely.

When using a pressure hose on brick paving, take care not to wash the sand out of the joints.

You can use the washer alone or in conjunction with a proprietary cleaner, in which case choose an environmentally friendly product to avoid harming living things. Apply cleaner before using the washer and carefully follow the manufacturer's instructions. Bear in mind the following points:

- **paviors and some types of slab** may be damaged if water is applied at high pressure. On these surfaces, use moderate pressure of around 1000 psi, or hold the applicator high above the surface of the paving to lessen the force of the water.
- **when cleaning concrete,** do not concentrate pressure on a single area for more than a few seconds, or it could begin to damage the surface.
- **patios should slope gently** to allow water to drain readily, so start at the highest point and work downhill.
- **for decking,** use low pressure of around 750 psi, as water applied at high pressure can drive dirt into the wood. After cleaning, allow decking to dry, then apply a sealer to the surface, according to the manufacturer's instructions.

perennial plants for containers

FOLIAGE PLANTS • grasses, such as *Hakonechloa macra* 'Aureola' (sun or part shade) and *Festuca glauca* (sun) • hardy ferns, such as *Athyrium filix-femina* and *Asplenium scolopendrium* (shade) • heucheras (sun or part shade) • hostas (part or full shade) • dead-nettles, *Lamium maculatum* varieties (part or full shade)

SPRING FLOWERS • lily-of-the-valley, *Convallaria majalis* (shade) • *Dicentra formosa* 'Alba', *D.* 'Langtrees', *D.* 'Luxuriant' (sun or part shade) • *Erysimum* 'John Codrington' (sun) • *Primula* 'Wanda' (sun or shade) • *Viola sororia* 'Freckles' (sun or part shade)

lawns

Often early spring is catch-up time for doing any maintenance and repair jobs that were missed in autumn, especially if the grass was wet under foot. Now that the lawn is coming to life and starting to grow again, this is also the time to get it into good condition to cope with the stresses of the year ahead.

now is the season to . . .

- **keep off the lawn** if it is frosted or very wet.
- **brush off worm casts** regularly (see right).
- **trim the edge** of your lawn (see opposite) and repair any broken edges if necessary (see page 429).
- **level any humps or hollows** that have developed in the lawn over the winter months (see page 428).
- **aerate the lawn** with a hollow-tiner, spiked roller or garden fork to improve drainage and ease surface compaction. Then apply a top-dressing of equal parts loam, sand and peat substitute at a rate of 1.5kg m^2 (3lb per sq yd). For heavier soils with high clay content, use a mix of four parts horticultural sand to one part loam or garden compost.
- **start mowing the grass** if it begins to grow (see opposite).
- **re-seed** any bare patches (see opposite).
- **start feeding lawns** with a spring fertiliser.
- **control weeds** and moss (see right).

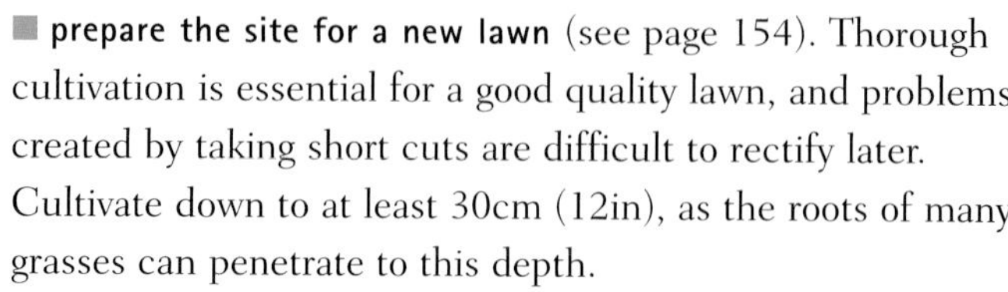

- **prepare the site for a new lawn** (see page 154). Thorough cultivation is essential for a good quality lawn, and problems created by taking short cuts are difficult to rectify later. Cultivate down to at least 30cm (12in), as the roots of many grasses can penetrate to this depth.

and if you have time . . .

- **brush the lawn** to knock off any heavy dew. If it is left, the humid conditions can encourage the spread of fungal disease.

controlling weeds and moss

The most effective way of controlling lawn weeds is through a combination of chemical and cultivation practices, which involves weedkiller use in conjunction with frequent mowing.

- **use a fan-shaped rake** to lift low-spreading weeds, such as speedwell and yarrow, before mowing, so that the blades slice off their topgrowth.
- **kill tap-rooted weeds** like dandelion and dock by digging down and cutting them off about 8cm (3in) below soil level.
- **control larger areas** of spreading weeds by applying a spray or granular lawn weedkiller, which will kill broad-leaved weeds without harming the grass.
- **brush off worm casts** as these contain weed seeds brought up from below ground, which will germinate when exposed to daylight. Always brush the lawn before mowing, using a stiff brush or besom to scatter the casts. Brushing in this way helps to reduce wear and tear on mower blades caused by the gritty nature of the casts and prevents them being smeared over the lawn by the mower, smothering the grass beneath and causing a patchy appearance.

moss control

If there is too much moss to control by raking, apply a mosskiller, such as lawn sand or a liquid formulation containing sulphate of iron. The moss will turn black, but wait until it then turns brown before raking out dead remains. Re-treat any patches where moss reappears about three weeks after the first application.

WEED AND FEED TIP To save time, use a combined weed and feed formulation, which will kill off the weeds with a selective chemical herbicide while it feeds the grass.

Early spring is the ideal time to aerate your lawn. This will help to get it back into condition and looking its best for the months of use ahead.

trimming a lawn edge

1 **Use a half-moon** edging tool to cut a clean edge to the lawn. On straight edges, stand on a plank and use it as a cutting line.

2 **Neaten lawn edges,** if necessary, using long-handled edging shears.

trimming lawn edges

The edge of a lawn often sags and crumbles as a result of frost action on the bare soil. Remove the narrowest strip possible to reinstate a clean edge; collect the trimmings and add them to the compost heap.

looking ahead . . .

☑ LATE SPRING Sow grass seed or lay turf for a new lawn.

dealing with bare patches

Bare patches may be due to weeds smothering the grass, or part of the lawn being covered with an object; whatever the cause, the grass will eventually die due to lack of light. Spills of concentrated fertiliser or other chemicals may 'burn' the grass and kill it off in patches. Fortunately, these areas can be re-seeded to restore the lawn to its original condition (see below).

spring feeding

Start feeding lawns now, especially in milder areas where growth starts early. Use a spring or summer fertiliser which is high in nitrogen and phosphates to promote growth and root development of the grass. If you use a powdered or granular formulation, rather than liquid feed, wait for a day when the grass is dry and the soil is moist, so that the fertiliser settles on the soil. If there is no rain within 48 hours, water the lawn lightly to wash in the fertiliser.

mowing the lawn

Once the soil temperature rises above 5–7°C (40–45°F), the grass starts growing and you need to mow. The exact timing will vary from year to year, depending on the weather. Make the first cuts with the mower blades set high. As the rate of growth increases, the lawn will need more frequent mowing, and the height of cut can gradually be lowered. Aim to reduce the grass by a third of its height at each cutting; do not cut it too short, as this weakens the grass and exposes bare soil where moss and weeds can easily establish.

re-seeding bare patches

1 **First go over the area** with a spring-tined rake. Rake vigorously to drag out all the old dead grass, including pieces of dead root, and to score the soil surface. Use a garden fork to break up the surface and ease soil compaction. Jab the tines into the soil to a depth of 2–3cm (1in).

2 **Rake the soil** to a depth of 1–2cm (½–¾in) to level it and to create a fine seedbed.

3 **Sow grass seed** evenly over the area, at a rate of about 30g per m^2 (1oz per sq yd), and lightly rake it in.

4 **Cover the area** with sacking until the seeds germinate; water in dry weather.

fruit

This is the turn of the year in the fruit garden, when stored crops come to an end and blossom heralds the harvest to come. Check and feed all your fruit ready for the new season, and remember to protect early flowers on wall-trained fruit whenever frost is forecast.

now is the season to . . .

- **check fruits** in store frequently as the end of the keeping season approaches, and use up the good samples quickly.
- **inspect supports** for trained fruit, and replace or repair them if necessary. Check and loosen ties before new growth starts. Tie in new stems while they are flexible.
- **thin spurs on trained** apples and pears (see opposite); complete this and all winter pruning, except for stone fruits, as soon as possible (see page 522).
- **prune new bush** and cane fruit before growth starts (see opposite).
- **plant autumn-fruiting raspberries,** and cut old canes in existing rows down to the ground.
- **tie in new blackberry canes** if not done in autumn (see below).
- **plant perpetual strawberries** for fruit later this year. Remove the first flush of flower buds from summer-fruiting varieties planted in autumn and all buds from those put in now, to allow plants to build up strength.
- **divide alpine strawberries,** and sow new plants under glass (see page 63).
- **weed and lightly cultivate** round all fruits, before feeding and mulching (see below).
- **protect blossom from frost,** especially early flowering apricots and peaches (see opposite).
- **watch for signs of pests and disease,** including scale insects (see page 63).
- **start early vines** under glass into growth (see page 62).
- **pollinate early blossom** on greenhouse fruits (see page 62).
- **remove grease bands** from fruit trees in April.
- **water new fruits in a dry spell,** especially those near walls and fences where the soil is sheltered from rain.
- **pick forced rhubarb** under pots.

tying in blackberries and hybrid berries

In mild gardens, new stems are usually trained in autumn, after the old fruited canes are removed, but in colder gardens the young canes are loosely bundled along a wire for protection (see page 432). You can untie these now and fan the canes out evenly on the wires, securing them with string or plastic twists. Very long canes can be cut off at the top wire, or you can tie them along the wire as a thick rope, or arch them above the supports, tying the tips to the top wire to form gentle loops.

feeding and mulching

All fruit plants, except very large trees, respond to feeding in March or early April. Apply a general-purpose fertiliser at the rate of 100–140g per m^2 (3–4oz per sq yd), using the higher rate on poor or light soils. After pruning and weeding, sprinkle the fertiliser evenly over a slightly larger area than is shaded by the branches, and lightly rake in. After two weeks, mulch with a 5–8cm (2–3in) layer of garden compost or well-rotted manure.

Forced rhubarb is one of very few crops to be harvested in the fruit garden in early spring, but there is much to do now to ensure good fruit crops later in the year.

pruning new bush and cane fruits

Most new cane and bush fruits need formative pruning so that they grow into the desired shape. You can do this straight after planting, or wait until early in their first spring.

- **raspberries, blackberries and hybrid berries** Cut each cane to a bud 15–23cm (6–9in) above ground.
- **blackcurrants** Cut all stems to about 5cm (2in) high. Retain the best four or five shoots that appear later; if these are less than 45–60cm (18–24in) long at the end of the season, cut growth back again next spring.
- **gooseberries, red currants and white currants** Cut back all shoots by half to an upward-pointing bud. Prune cordons and other trained forms by cutting back main branches by half, and all sideshoots to 2–3cm (1in). Remove all growth on the lower 10–15cm (4–6in) of the main stem to establish a clear 'leg'.

protecting blossom

Wall-trained fruits that flower early are more at risk from spring frosts than those in the open garden, because of the still conditions that prevail near boundaries and garden structures. Protect the blossom by draping plants with fleece or net curtaining at night.

Strawberries need similar protection, or you can cover plants with cloches. If the open flowers do get frosted, it is possible to wash off the frost early, before sunshine can damage the frozen blooms and turn the centres black. Fit a fine spray attachment to a hosepipe or hand sprayer and mist the flowers until all signs of frost have gone.

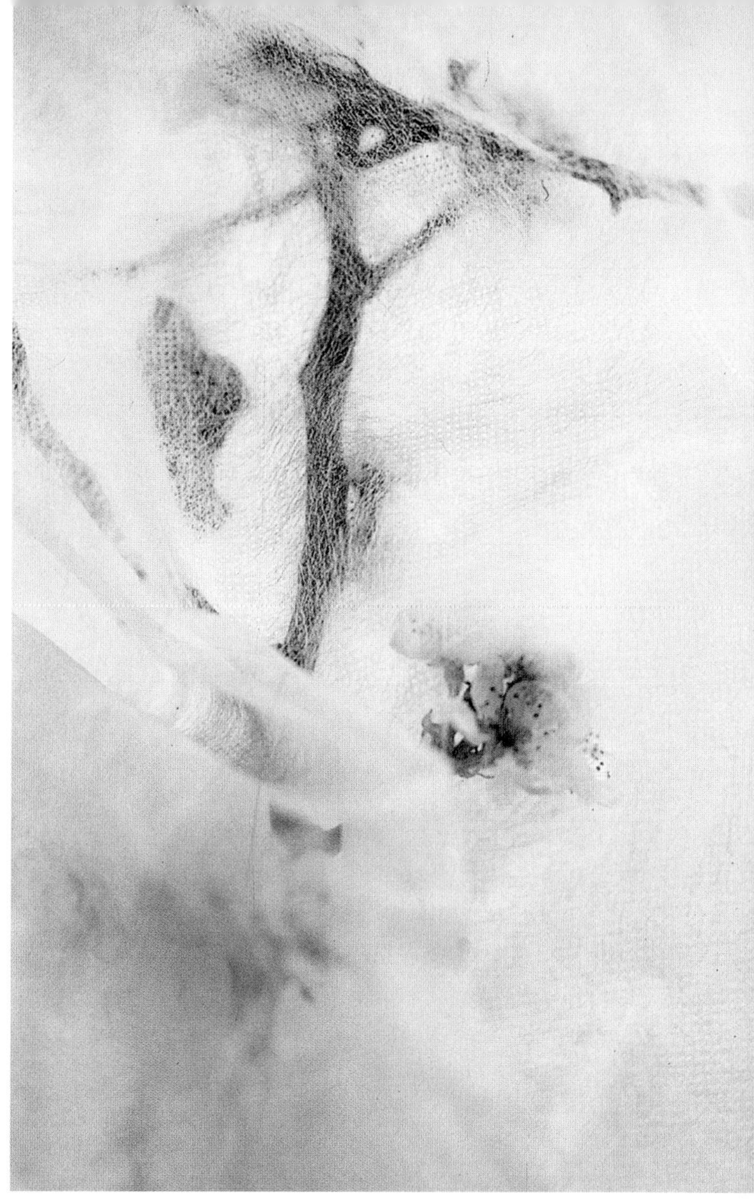

Protect wall fruit against spring frost by draping it with horticultural fleece at night. Remove it by day to allow access for pollinating bees.

thinning spurs on trained apples and pears

1 **Thin fruiting spurs** that have become crowded or cross each other by cutting some out at their base, or where they branch.

2 **Remove any young shoots and** buds that are going to become inaccessible, emerge close to main branches or point in the wrong direction.

3 **Aim to leave an** open, balanced arrangement of sideshoots to admit plenty of air and light; clear away all prunings when you have finished.

fruit/2

fruit under glass

Apricots, peaches and vines will be coming into flower in the greenhouse, while forced rhubarb and strawberries should be ready for picking. Discard rhubarb crowns after forcing, but plant strawberries in the garden after hardening off; they may crop again in late summer. Alpine strawberries make attractive plants, and sowing seeds under glass now is a good way to build up stocks of unusual varieties.

pollinating and thinning

Apricots, peaches and strawberries grown in the greenhouse often flower before many pollinating insects are about, especially if the weather is cold. On a warm day, open wide the ventilators and doors, but otherwise you will need to fertilise the open flowers yourself, around midday if possible. Early outdoor apricots and peaches on warm walls may also flower too early for insects, and they will benefit from hand pollination too.

In a mild season, the earliest varieties can set a heavy crop of fruitlets by the end of March, and these should be thinned as soon as possible to ensure good-sized fruits. Reduce clusters to leave one or, at the most, two fruitlets in each. Thin crowded stems to leave a fruitlet every 5–8cm (2–3in). If all these develop, you should thin them further in late spring.

greenhouse grapes

In unheated greenhouses, grape vines will be coming into leaf and flower, especially if the stems are sprayed every day or two with warm water to stimulate the buds to open. If you lowered the main stems in winter to encourage the buds to break evenly (see page 540), you can retie them on their wires when the majority of buds show early leaf. In heated greenhouses and conservatories, the vines will be flowering now, so tap the stems every day with a cane to fertilise the flowers.

thinning grapes

- **as trusses often set too many fruits,** thin a heavy set when grapes are the size of small peas, to prevent the developing fruits from crowding each other. You may need to do this in April in a warm greenhouse, but wait until early summer in an unheated one. Using a pair of pointed, long-bladed scissors, remove most of the grapes in the centre of the bunch, and the smallest grapes around the point of the bunch, but leave plenty in the widest part or 'shoulders'; aim to leave at least a pencil thickness between grapes.
- **pinch out the shoots** at the second leaf beyond a truss of setting fruit.

If insects have not done the job of pollination (above), use a soft, small paintbrush to stroke the centre of each bloom lightly (left) and transfer the pollen from one flower to another.

alpine strawberries

Many alpine strawberries do not make runners in the same way as large-fruited kinds, but instead grow into large clumps like a border perennial. Although these will fruit if left alone, yield and quality are greatly improved if you split large clumps into smaller segments every few years (see below).

raising from seed

Use a soil-based compost, and sow the seeds sparingly in trays or pots. Cover them thinly with compost and keep them in a propagator or greenhouse at about 18°C (64°F) until seedlings appear. Prick these out individually into small pots when they have two true leaves, and plant out in May or June.

dividing alpine strawberries

1 **Shear off the old foliage** during early March and dig up the clump with a fork.

2 **Either cut a plant** into several portions or simply tear it apart with your hands; discard the old woody centre.

3 **Replant the young outer** portions about 30cm (12in) apart in fresh ground that has been dug and manured. They make an attractive edging to a bed in the kitchen garden.

dealing with scale insects

1 **Check plants** in early spring for the brownish scales, particularly on the woody stems of vines, apricots and peaches.

2 **Wipe them off** using a cotton bud or a soft cloth, dipped in alcohol.

scale insects

These minute sap-feeding insects can attack fruit trees and vines, especially those growing under glass. They shelter under waxy oval scales on shoots and branches where they lay their eggs safe from most insecticides, so you will have to remove them by hand (see above). Spraying with insecticide is effective only against the migrating juveniles, which usually emerge in early summer outdoors, but much earlier under heated glass. Inspect stems closely in warm spells during spring and summer, and spray if the minute crawling insects are seen. Spray again a fortnight later to catch survivors and late hatchings, if possible before they can develop their protective scales.

there is still time to . . .

- **check blackcurrants for big bud mites;** infected buds are conspicuous and are easily removed for destruction (see page 523).
- **cover rhubarb** outdoors with forcing pots, boxes or buckets to produce early tender stalks.
- **cover strawberries** with cloches or polythene tunnels to advance their harvest by a few weeks.
- **protect peaches** and nectarines from peach leaf curl by covering the trees with screens, and by applying a copper-based fungicide spray.

looking ahead . . .

☑ LATE SPRING Prune stone fruits such as plums and cherries.
☑ Plant out alpine strawberries.
☑ SUMMER Thin grapes in unheated greenhouses.
☑ LATE SUMMER Summer-prune trained fruit.
☑ Cut down summer-fruiting raspberries.
☑ AUTUMN Cut down blackberries and hybrid berries after fruiting.

vegetables

Although there is no real end to the cropping year in a well-planned kitchen garden, early spring feels like the year's beginning as the weather improves. This is the best time to sow seed under cover and plant out a wide range of hardy vegetables.

now is the season to . . .

■ **order seeds** and young vegetable plants for delivery later. Although young plants and seedlings are becoming available now, do not be tempted to buy too early in cold areas unless you can provide them with the protection they may need.

■ **inspect stored vegetables** at regular intervals and remove any showing signs of mould or rot before they infect their neighbours. Use up quickly those that show signs of growth or withering. Stored crops could include beetroot, carrots, garlic, onions, potatoes, shallots, swedes and turnips.

■ **begin to harden off** and plant out hardy crops, such as peas, started off in pots under glass in winter.

■ **continue preparing seedbeds** (see page 525). Break the soil down to a roughly level surface, so that it can dry out during sunny or windy weather. This will help you to create a fine surface, or tilth, when the seedbed is raked level (see page 161).

■ **monitor the soil temperature** to see how quickly it is warming up. Many seeds need temperatures of 5–7°C (40–45°F) in the upper layer of soil before they will germinate.

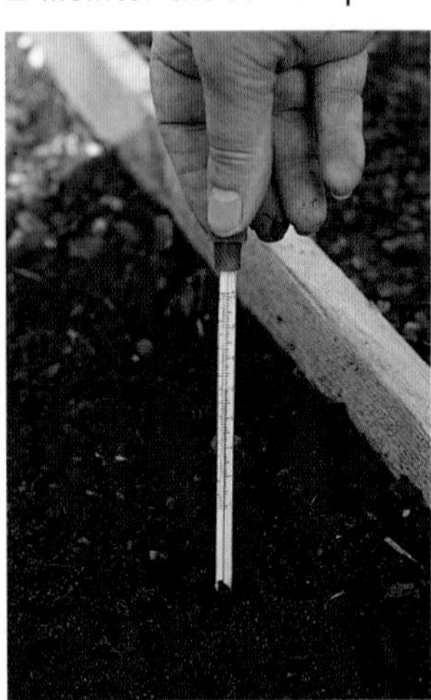

To test the soil temperature, insert an outdoor thermometer into the upper 8–10cm (3–4in) layer of earth and leave it for about an hour.

■ **warm the soil** before sowing or planting by covering areas with cloches, low polythene tunnels or black plastic sheeting. If the weather is dry and windy, remove the covers to allow the soil to dry before sowing (see page 525).

■ **make early sowings** of crops such as beetroot, broad beans, carrot, lettuce, peas, radish, spinach and turnips when soil conditions become suitable. Choose early varieties of these crops where possible.

■ **plant onions sets,** early potatoes, asparagus and globe artichokes (see page 69).

■ **prepare trenches** for planting runner beans, peas, marrows or pumpkins in late spring or early summer (see below).

■ **dig areas as they become** clear of crops and compost the plant waste. Dig in any overwintering green manures.

■ **if the soil is wet,** dig trenches 15–20cm (6–8in) deep and wide at 1.2m (4ft) intervals. This creates mini raised beds in between, with improved drainage.

Digging shallow trenches creates raised beds, allowing you to plant or sow even on heavy soil or a high water table.

■ **protect seedbeds and seedlings from birds** by covering them with fleece or netting, or using bird scarers. Brassicas are particularly vulnerable, and wood pigeons will feed on any cauliflowers they can reach.

■ **watch for slugs** and early signs of other pests (see opposite).

■ **during dry periods, take the opportunity** to hoe off weed seedlings, but remember that disturbing the soil encourages more weed seeds to germinate as the weather turns milder.

Cover the kitchen waste with soil dug from the next section.

trench composting

You can compost a small supply of waste in a trench as a source of nourishment and consistent moisture for tall peas, runner beans, marrows, squash and pumpkins. Mark out a trench 30cm (12in) wide where they are to grow. Dig out a short section at one end, the depth of a spade blade. Fill the trench to half its depth with kitchen and vegetable waste, and cover with soil. Continue until the trench has been filled along its length; cover the last section with the soil from the first. Leave to settle for a month or two. For beans on 'wigwams', or pumpkins, dig a pit 1m (3ft) across for each plant and fill in the same way.

avoiding later pest problems

Pests and diseases become more prevalent as the weather turns milder. Slugs start to feed soon after hatching, but if this first generation can be controlled it will be months before the population builds up to epidemic proportions.

protecting seedlings from slugs

The juicy young leaves of seedlings will always attract slugs but there are various ways to deter them.

1 Scatter grit around young plants, using a pot as a guide

2 Buy a proprietary slug pot filled with a toxic mixture

3 Cut a serrated collar from a plastic bottle using pinking shears

4 Place the base of a clear plastic bottle filled with old beer near young plants, to act as a trap – or use upturned grapefruit skins

harvesting now

• asparagus • brussels sprouts • calabrese • celeriac • jerusalem artichokes • kale • leeks • parsnips • salad onions • spring greens • sprouting broccoli • winter cabbage and cauliflower • winter lettuce • winter radish • winter spinach

Sprouting broccoli

• **look out for aphids** by inspecting the outer leaves of cabbages, cauliflowers and other vegetables.

• **control blackfly** on broad beans by pinching out the growing tips when they begin to flower.

• **clear away all plant debris** to the compost heap rather than bury it, as it provides food for hatching slugs at this time.

You can buy lettuce and brassicas as young plants. If weather conditions or soil are unsuitable for immediate planting, transplant into pots or modular trays and grow on under glass or on a windowsill until you can plant out.

vegetables/2

sowing and planting

Early spring is the time for putting into practice the plans you made during the winter months, and for sowing and planting the crops you enjoy eating. The weather and your garden conditions play a part in the precise timing of your sowing and planting, as do the varieties you choose.

varieties

If you look through seed catalogues or along a stand of seed packets, you will see that some crops, such as peas, carrots and potatoes, have early and maincrop varieties. Maincrops are sown later in the season than earlies, and usually take longer to mature. You can sow some early varieties of carrot in late summer, as they are quick to mature, but with lettuce it is vital to sow the right variety for the season.

'Purple Cape' is a winter cauliflower variety, with purple-red curds, harvested in March.

One way to mark a straight drill is to press the handle of a rake or hoe into the soil to make a groove.

Seed tape with pre-spaced seed saves thinning crops such as lettuce, radish and carrots, which are easily sown too thickly.

Vegetable seeds come in a wide and colourful array of shapes and sizes; the bigger they are, the easier to space correctly.

sowing into a coldframe

1 **Using the corner of a hoe,** make straight, shallow drills in a seedbed you have prepared and raked to a fine tilth.

2 **If the soil is dry,** trickle water into the drills before sowing the seeds.

3 **Sow the seeds thinly** and cover them lightly with soil. Water gently through a fine rose before closing the lid of the coldframe. The seeds should have germinated in 14–21 days.

timing

Many crops can be sown or planted over several months. Bear in mind that most seeds and young plants can only grow when the soil temperature reaches a minimum requirement; the danger of sowing too early is not frost, but that seeds will sit in cold, damp soil and rot before they germinate. Many of the earlier sowings will be more successful under glass – a greenhouse or coldframe – or with cloche protection than in open ground. Sowings made under glass in modular trays incur less root disturbance than those made in trays or pots and then pricked out. This is a useful way of getting a head start and avoiding the unpredictability of the weather at the start of the year. Using modular trays is also a way to minimise root disturbance when transplanting vegetables, as they are planted with an intact rootball, avoiding the risk of tearing young roots as you tease seedlings apart.

Space young leeks or other crops closer than recommended if you wish to harvest and eat them as baby, or mini, vegetables.

spacing crops

Plants grow better without too much competition, which is why regular weeding and correct spacing are important. It is worth thinning seedlings in stages rather than all in one go, to avoid gaps, conserve moisture and suppress weeds. Later thinnings can often be used in salads, or as immature or baby vegetables, leaving the rest wider-spaced to mature fully. You may in any case prefer smaller roots and cabbages, in which case grow them closer together; the seed packet usually states whether a variety is suitable for growing this way.

extended harvesting

For the harvesting period to last as long as possible, make a number of small successional sowings every few weeks and include early, maincrop and seasonal varieties. Protecting early and late crops with cloches is another way to extend the harvest. With peas and beans, regular picking in itself prolongs the season.

Use cloches to protect early and late salad crops and extend the harvest.

The yield you can expect from a crop is greatly influenced by growing conditions. If your soil is well prepared, regularly enriched with organic matter and kept weed free, your yield will be much higher than where the soil is dry, weedy and exhausted. Other influencing factors are the weather and your choice of variety; some varieties simply yield more heavily than others.

vegetables/3

sowing and planting by crop

Spring is the best sowing and planting time for many crops, including perennial asparagus and both globe and jerusalem artichokes.

peas and beans

- **sow early varieties of peas** in 8–10cm (3–4in) pots, two or three seeds per pot, then place in a cool greenhouse or coldframe, if not already done in late winter. The plants will be large enough for planting out by mid-spring, with those sown in a length of guttering (see page 160) a little later. Plant them 8–10cm (3–4in) apart, preferably in pre-warmed soil to avoid any check to growth.
- **as the weather warms, remove cloches** from autumn-sown peas, but harden them off first by removing alternate cloches during the day and ventilating them increasingly at night for a couple of weeks.
- **thin peas sown in autumn or late winter** by removing alternate plants.
- **sow early peas and broad beans outdoors** as a follow-on crop to those raised in pots, or sown outdoors under cloches or polythene tunnels.
- **harden off and plant out** broad beans sown in pots under cover in winter, 25–30cm (10–12in) apart.

Traditional forcing pots are used to cover kale plants, forcing a crop of tender young shoots.

cabbage family

- **finish harvesting last year's brussels sprouts** as the last 'buttons' swell; snap off the leafy tops and use as greens.
- **sow brussels sprouts, sprouting broccoli** and varieties of summer cabbage and cauliflower in pots or in a seedbed for transplanting in May or June.
- **harvest kale** by picking the young shoots, leaving the large outer leaves intact to fuel the plants' growth.
- **continue to harvest winter cabbages,** cutting the whole head, and start picking the secondary crop of leafy greens produced by the stumps of previously harvested cabbages (see page 526).
- **transplant autumn-sown** spring cabbages early, spacing plants about 30cm (12in) apart (see page 439).
- **spring greens** planted in autumn will be ready for harvest. Pick some of the young leaves, as more will develop, or remove alternate plants so that those left will form a head.

onion family

- **finish planting shallots, and plant onion sets** early on a well-drained site. Check them regularly until they have started to root, as birds foraging for food often move them about. Replant them if necessary.
- **inspect stored onions and garlic;** dispose of any showing signs of rot or mould, and quickly use up any that are shooting.
- **lift mature leeks** as required. If you need the ground for planting other crops in April, lift any that remain and heel them in spare ground out of the sun.
- **continue to sow leeks and onions** in modular trays or pots in the greenhouse. Sow four or five seeds per pot to transplant in late spring.
- **sow salad onions** from late March in short rows.

Plant onion sets 1cm (½in) deep and 10–15cm (4–6in) apart in rows 25cm (10in) apart.

Where mice are a problem, start onion sets in pots to plant out once they are bigger.

root crops

- **make first sowings** of early varieties of beetroot, carrot and turnip unless the soil is cold and wet, in which case wait for it to warm up. For the earliest sowings, use cloches, or cover the soil for a week or two with plastic sheeting to provide warmer conditions and encourage rapid seed germination.

SOWING CARROTS TIP Cover carrots with fleece tucked into the soil to give an earlier crop and to protect against carrot fly.

- **sow kohl rabi and parsnips** outdoors in late March or April. As parsnips are slow to germinate, sow radish or beetroot in between as markers; these fast-maturing crops will be ready for pulling before the parsnip roots start to develop.
- **sow celeriac** under cover in modular trays.

planting early potatoes

METHOD 1 **When each chitted** potato has formed four or five shoots 2–3cm (1in) long, dig a trench 10cm (4in) deep and place them in it, rose end up, and 25–30cm (10–12in) apart; fill in with soil.

METHOD 2 **Plant the chitted** tubers in individual holes, using a trowel, at the same depth and distance, in rows 40–50cm (15–20in) apart. Fill in each hole with soil.

potatoes

It is advisable to buy seed potatoes that are certified disease-free stock, rather than be tempted to plant tubers you have bought from the greengrocer or supermarket. The size of seed potatoes depends on the variety, but they should be about the size of a hen's egg. Before planting, you need to sprout, or chit, potatoes indoors (see page 527). Do this first with earlies, for planting out in March or early April, and two to three weeks later for maincrop varieties, planted in late spring. Soil temperature at the planting depth should be at least 6°C (43°F) for four or five days before planting, so that the shoots will grow unchecked.

salad crops

- **continue to protect early sowings** with cloches or low polythene tunnels, giving ventilation on sunny days. Thin when necessary; there may be pickings in a mild season.
- **make successional sowings of lettuce,** radish and spinach in the open ground, preferably warmed by plastic sheeting.

perennial crops

Globe artichokes and asparagus, in particular, need a lot of space and should be planted in a sheltered, sunny position. The soil should be well drained, deeply dug, enriched with plenty of rotted manure or garden compost and cleared of all traces of perennial weeds. These long-term crops need two years to establish before you can enjoy a harvest.

- **take globe artichoke offsets** or buy small plants. Cut offsets from the edge of an established plant and set them just deep enough to stand upright, about 5cm (2in); each plant will need about 1m^2 (10sq ft). Cover with fleece if frost threatens.
- **asparagus crowns** must not be allowed to dry out, so plant as soon as possible (see below). Young plants are also sold in pots ready for transplanting, or you can raise plants from seed sown in modular trays under glass. Start to harvest established plants when spears are 15cm (6in) tall.
- **jerusalem artichokes** will tolerate light shade. Plant tubers 30cm (12in) apart and 10cm (4in) deep in well-prepared soil. The plants grow tall, reaching 3m (10ft), and will crop this year.

planting asparagus crowns

1 **Dig a trench** 45cm (18in) deep and incorporate plenty of well-rotted organic matter. Make a shallow ridge down the centre.

2 **Plant the crowns** 10–15cm (4–6in) deep, spreading out the roots, crab-wise, either side of the ridge. Space them 30cm (12in) apart in rows 45cm (18in) apart. Earth over the trench and fork in more compost. On heavy soils, plant the crowns more shallowly, but earth up the stems as they grow.

herbs

With spring in the air there is a rapid revival of growth, so finish tidying up and dividing large clumps of perennial herbs, and start feeding the young plants. Begin sowing, at first under glass and later outdoors, and planting hardy herbs outside and in containers.

now is the season to . . .

- **tidy herb beds and borders** before new growth gets under way. Clear the dead foliage of herbaceous herbs such as salad burnet and fennel, then weed and prick over the soil with a fork.
- **feed perennial herbs** such as marjoram and tarragon with bone meal or a high-potash granular fertiliser.
- **warm the ground** before sowing by covering prepared soil with cloches, plastic sheeting or a light coldframe to encourage rapid germination. Start sowing two to three weeks later.
- **thin autumn-sown** seedlings.
- **pot up rooted cuttings** under glass into 8cm (3in) pots of soil-based compost.
- **check any layers of thyme,** rosemary, sage and other herbs started the previous year. Pot them up if they have rooted.
- **propagate perennial herbs** by division (see opposite).
- **finish laying out** new herb gardens (see page 443).
- **prune lavender, sage and rosemary** in a mild season; avoid cutting back into old wood, which may not regenerate.

and if you have time . . .

- **plant out potted** hardy herbs used indoors over winter after feeding with general fertiliser and hardening them off for 10–14 days. Keep tender herbs frost free in a coldframe or greenhouse until late spring.

dividing basil

1 **First acclimatise** the plant by standing the pot in its plastic sleeve in a cool, well-lit place. Gradually turn down the sleeve a little more each day. Water gently if dry.

2 **When you can remove** the plastic sleeve without the plants drooping, gently tap out the contents of the pot.

3 **Slice the rootball** into several segments with a sharp knife. Pot up each piece in a 10cm (4in) pot of soil-based compost, water gently and stand in a lightly shaded place.

4 **Once the plants recover** and stand upright, you can grow and pot them on in the usual way.

repotting tender herbs

French lavender (*Lavandula stoechas*), rosemaries such as *R. officinalis* 'Prostratus', and lemon verbena can be trimmed to shape now, before potting on or repotting. Cut out dead wood, shorten very long shoots and remove one or two older branches on lemon verbena; lightly clip evergreens to a balanced shape.

- **pot on young plants** into the next size pot, using a soil-based compost and putting plenty of drainage material in the bottom.
- **repot larger specimens** by carefully knocking them from their pots. Tease the outer 2–3cm (1in) of compost from the roots, shortening any that spiral all round the pot, and replace in the same container, working fresh soil-based compost between the roots with your fingers.

dividing bought herbs

You can divide up pots of culinary herbs, such as parsley, coriander and basil, bought from a supermarket (see above).

herbs to sow now

IN A WARM GREENHOUSE IN LATE MARCH • basil • coriander • dill • marjoram • parsley • rue

IN A COOL GREENHOUSE OR COLDFRAME • lemon balm • lovage • sage • sorrel • summer savory

OUTDOORS • borage • caraway • chervil • chives • fennel

planting a herb tower

A terracotta 'tower' with several planting pockets around the sides is ideal for growing a basic selection of culinary herbs or a collection of the same herb, such as thymes or basils, in different varieties.

dividing perennial herbs

By dividing perennial herbs you can produce smaller and younger plants that will grow more vigorously.

- **early in the season** you can divide chives, lemon balm, marjoram, mint, sorrel and tarragon.
- **late in the season** you can divide any of the above, plus lovage, pennyroyal, rue, salad burnet, thyme, winter savory and any herbs growing in cold gardens.
- **dig up clumps,** split them with a spade or sharp knife, or tear them apart with your fingers, and replant the outer portions in fresh soil, discarding the woody centre.

looking ahead . . .

☑ SUMMER Plant out tender herbs and those raised from seed, cuttings, layers and divisions.

☑ LATE SUMMER Pot up herbs for winter use.

there is still time to . . .

- **order annual herb seeds** before the main sowing season, or get ahead by buying seedlings or dividing pots of herbs sold for kitchen use (see opposite).
- **take root cuttings** of bergamot, chamomile, mint, hyssop, sweet cicely, sweet woodruff and tarragon (see page 490).

planting a thyme tower

1 Spread a layer of gravel, 5cm (2in) deep, in the base of the pot and in the centre of it stand a length of perforated watering pipe, or plastic drainpipe with holes drilled every 10cm (4in). Pour in a handful or two of gravel to keep the pipe in place, and fill around it with soil-based compost up to the level of the first planting pocket.

2 Set a thyme plant in position, then add compost up to the level of the next planting hole.

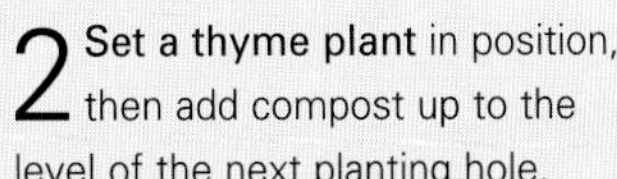

3 Continue adding compost and planting thymes in the pockets. Fill to just below the rim of the pot and finish by planting two or three thymes on top.

4 Use a watering can to fill the pipe with water, which will percolate through to all layers.

The finished tower (right) can become a focal point, especially when the thymes are in flower.

the greenhouse

The greenhouse is at the centre of early spring activities. Its protected surroundings allow early sowings, but you do need to be organised, as seedlings of all kinds jostle for space with cuttings and overwintering plants. As the weather warms up, and on sunny days, ventilate and water more often.

now is the season to . . .

- **gradually increase watering** as temperatures rise. Pots and trays can dry out rapidly on warm sunny days, so keep newspapers handy to shade seedlings in particularly bright weather.
- **ventilate more freely,** especially on still sunny days, but remember to close the vents at night.
- **harvest strawberries and rhubarb** forced in winter. Discard forced rhubarb crowns at the end of the season.
- **check heaters** are working efficiently before seeds of all kinds start to germinate.
- **keep insulation in place** for a few more weeks. If the season is very warm, remove fixed insulation cautiously, but keep newspapers and fleece handy for sudden cold spells.
- **monitor pests** (see opposite) and guard against diseases such as damping-off (see page 76).
- **sow your home-saved seeds** at the appropriate time, after checking that they are still in good condition (see page 77).
- **sow greenhouse crops** such as tomatoes and cucumbers, and if outdoor conditions are unsuitable sow vegetables like peas, broad beans, lettuce and summer cabbages.
- **continue sowing annual bedding** plants and hardy annuals (see page 30).
- **prick out seedlings** as soon as they can be handled easily (see page 31).
- **pot up rooted cuttings** that have overwintered under glass.
- **pot on rootbound plants** when they show signs of new growth (see opposite).
- **let bees fertilise indoor fruits** such as apricots, peaches and strawberries by opening vents wide on mild days, or pollinate the open flowers by hand (see page 62).
- **tie up grape vines** as soon as their buds break and train new shoots (see page 62).
- **revive tender perennials** (see opposite).
- **take cuttings** from the new shoots of tender perennials.

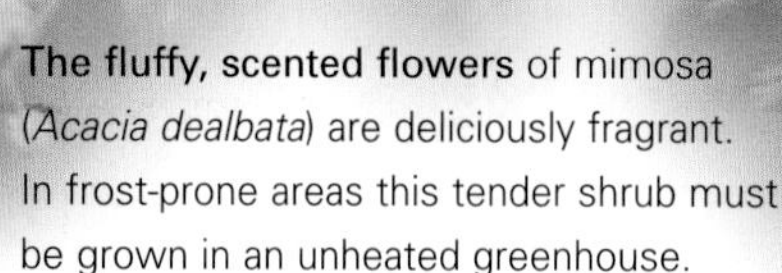

The fluffy, scented flowers of mimosa (*Acacia dealbata*) are deliciously fragrant. In frost-prone areas this tender shrub must be grown in an unheated greenhouse.

- **propagate tender succulents** (see page 75).
- **take cuttings of begonias,** chrysanthemums, dahlias and gloxinias forced in winter, when their shoots are about 8cm (3in) long (see page 540).
- **cut forced** *Anemone coronaria* for the house; continue to water and feed plants when flowering finishes.
- **liquid-feed greenhouse pot plants** such as calceolarias and cinerarias as they come into flower.
- **pot up lily bulbs** for early flowers. Plant out those that have flowered, after feeding and hardening off.

and if you have time . . .

- **pot up lily-of-the-valley** for fragrant indoor blooms.

reviving tender perennials

1 Tidy the plant by cutting back leggy stems, which will promote healthy new growth.

2 Remove the plant from its pot and tease out the roots using a pencil or plant label.

3 Re-pot into a larger container and fill the space round the sides with new compost.

4 Pack the compost down firmly with a cane and water carefully.

awakening overwintered perennials

From early March you can revive tender perennials such as pelargoniums, fuchsias, marguerites (*Argyranthemum*), heliotrope and coleus that have been kept barely moist and dormant over winter. Move plants to a well-lit position. Prune hard by shortening thin stems and sideshoots to about 2–3cm (1in), and remove all dead material. Give a little water; if this runs straight through, stand pots in a tray of water for a while until the compost is uniformly moist. Once young shoots appear, increase watering, take soft-tip cuttings if required and repot or pot on into larger containers if you want to plant them out in late spring.

potting up lily-of-the-valley

It is not too late to dig up some roots of lily-of-the-valley to enjoy the heavily fragrant white bells indoors. Make sure the roots have plenty of pinkish white, pointed tips and plant several roots in a 10–13cm (4–5in) pot, with the tips just below the surface. Water and keep cool in a well-lit place.

potting on

As soon as roots poke through the bottom of a pot, start checking whether the plant needs a larger container by gently tapping it from the pot. If only a few roots are visible at the edges it is not ready, so slide the plant back in the pot and settle it by firmly knocking the base of the pot on the staging. The right moment for potting on is when there are plenty of roots round the sides, but before they encircle the rootball. Choose a pot 2–3cm (1in) larger for plants in pots up to 13cm (5in), or 5cm (2in) wider for those in larger pots (see right).

monitoring pests

Many pests can survive winter cosseted in the warmth of a greenhouse and start multiplying very early in the year. To check for their presence, hang sticky yellow traps just above plants and inspect regularly, brushing the plant leaves first to disturb any flying pests. Raise the traps as plants grow, and move them round the greenhouse every week or so.

potting on a tender shrub

1 Spread a drainage layer of gravel or crocks in the bottom of the new pot and cover with a little compost. Stand the potted plant in the centre, still in its pot, and add or remove compost until the rims are level. Twist the smaller pot to free it, then lift it out, leaving behind a neatly moulded hole.

2 Tap the plant from its pot, fit it in the hole and settle it in place by patting or knocking the pot on the staging. Water from above to consolidate the compost.

the greenhouse/2

propagation

This is the prime time for sowing seeds. The basic technique is the same for vegetables and flowers, although the amount of heat and light individual crops require may differ. For this reason, make a point of always reading the instructions on the seed packet before you start to sow. As new growth gets under way, it is also time to take cuttings of soft shoots and succulents. If you have a cool or unheated greenhouse, you can give seeds and cuttings the higher temperatures they require by using a heated propagator.

sowing techniques

You can sow seeds indoors in a variety of containers including trays, modular trays, pans or, if there are just a few of them, in small pots. The standard method is the same for all these containers (see right), but make sure they are scrupulously clean and use fresh seed compost to avoid possible problems. After sowing, place the container in a propagator or cover it with a sheet of glass to prevent the compost from drying out, but remove this as soon as germination takes place.

seeds large and small

Space large seeds, such as nasturtiums and sweet peas, individually at regular intervals in a tray, or sow two or three seeds in small pots and press them down into the compost.

Tiny seeds produced by plants such as petunias and begonias are difficult to sow. Mix them thoroughly with some dry silver sand and sprinkle this over the surface to distribute evenly.

Nasturtium (*Tropaeolum* 'Alaska')

sowing seeds

1 **Overfill the container** with moist seed compost and level off with a piece of board.

2 **Press lightly** with a tamping board to firm and level the surface of the compost.

3 **Tip some of the seeds** into one hand, and sprinkle a pinch at a time evenly and sparingly across the surface.

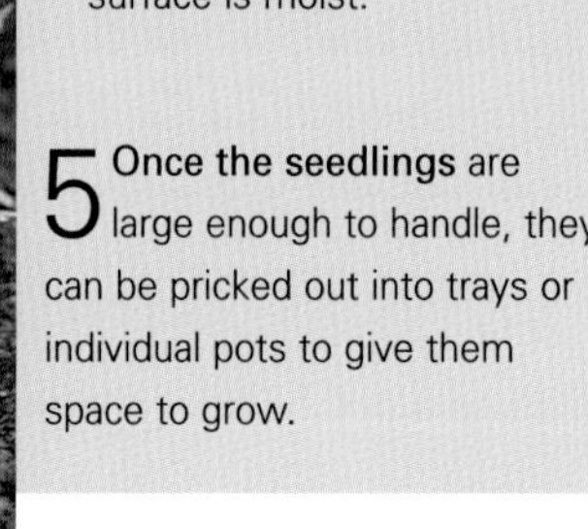

4 **For seeds** needing darkness, sieve a thin layer of compost over the surface. Mist with water or stand the tray in shallow water until the surface is moist.

5 **Once the seedlings** are large enough to handle, they can be pricked out into trays or individual pots to give them space to grow.

taking aeonium cuttings

1 **Cut sideshoots** off at their base with a sharp knife or snap them off cleanly by hand.

2 **Pull off the lower leaves** and insert the bare stem upright in a small pot of sandy cuttings compost or a soil-based compost blended with extra grit.

A collection of succulents, including aloe and agave, sit on metal trays filled with gravel, which ensures the free drainage these plants need.

taking cuttings of succulents

Tender succulents such as aeoniums, echeverias and kalanchoes kept dry through winter can be watered now to plump up their leaves and start them growing. Branching kinds like *Aeonium arboreum* often produce sideshoots that root easily to make vigorous new plants (see above). Water and keep in a warm place out of full sun until rooted. If you want lots of plants, insert individual leaves (those you removed from the stems) in a tray of gritty compost and place in a propagator.

propagators

The easiest and best way to provide the right amount of warmth for germinating seeds or rooting cuttings – and to confine this heat to the plants that need it – is to use a covered propagator. Some models are shaped like small coldframes, or simply trays with clear lids, often fitted with ventilators but without additional heating. Other models are more sophisticated, with a thermostatically controlled heating element and perhaps a misting unit.

You can make your own propagator by constructing a box on the greenhouse staging, topped with a clear, hinged lid. For additional heat, buy a soil-heating cable of adequate wattage for the temperature range you require, and lay this in a bed of horticultural sand at the bottom of the case. Fit a thermostat, with the control box on the outside, together with a maximum-minimum thermometer to monitor temperatures. A simpler method is to buy a propagating tray with a self-contained heating element and capillary mat for watering. Stand containers of seeds or cuttings on the tray and cover them individually with plastic domes or all together with the clear top supplied. Narrow windowsill models are available for holding two to five seed trays, allowing you to raise seed indoors.

The hinged lid of this home-made propagator is covered with clear plastic sheeting for insulation and to cut out bright light.

looking ahead . . .

- ☑ LATE SPRING Start hardening off young bedding and overwintering tender plants to acclimatise them to outside conditions.
- ☑ Continue to take soft-tip cuttings.
- ☑ SUMMER Move out summer bedding and tender plants for the patio.
- ☑ Introduce biological pest controls.

there is still time to . . .

- **sow varieties of** half-hardy bedding annuals that germinate and grow fast (see page 30).
- **buy plug plants** and seedlings of vegetables and annual flowers to pot up or prick out in a cool greenhouse.

the greenhouse/3

avoiding propagation problems

Fluctuating temperatures mean that early spring is a fickle season under glass, and ventilation becomes increasingly important as plants start growing from seed or cuttings. The soft growth is very susceptible to pests and diseases, and you need to be sensitive to the needs of these young plants to avoid common problems.

damping-off disease

This very troublesome disease can result in the death of many kinds of seedlings, both indoors and out. It is caused by a range of virulent soil-borne fungi, which are particularly liable to affect fast-growing annual bedding flowers, and also some vegetables, while they are very young.

Seedlings develop dark leaves and then collapse in patches, their white stems becoming as thin as hairs, turning brown and shrivelling at soil level. The condition can quickly affect a whole tray or bed of seedlings. Treatment is difficult and control depends on precautionary good hygiene.

- **use fresh seed compost** (low in nutrients), and sterilise garden soil used for compost mixes (see right).
- **wash and disinfect old pots,** containers and seed labels.
- **mix extra horticultural sand into compost** to improve drainage for susceptible plants such as nemesia and antirrhinums, and cover seeds with a thin layer of sand.
- **sow sparsely,** and prick out or thin before the seedlings are overcrowded.
- **use modular trays,** sowing a few seeds in each cell, to confine infection, which spreads easily throughout ordinary seed trays.

When sowing seeds of plants vulnerable to damping-off disease, mix sharp sand into the seed and cuttings compost to improve drainage.

Sowing seeds in individual disposable pots or modular trays will help to reduce the risk of disease spreading.

- **water containers from below** using mains water, as rainwater from butts is often a source of the fungi. Avoid overwatering.
- **water with a copper-based fungicide** after sowing and pricking out.
- **keep seedlings at the right temperature,** ideally in a heated propagator: cold draughts and cool, wet soils or composts are lethal.

sterilising soil for compost

If you make your own composts, it is important to sterilise garden soil before adding it to the mix in order to kill most of the disease pathogens and weed seeds. You can do this by using a chemical disinfectant, available for this purpose, or by pasteurising the soil in a conventional or microwave oven.

- **in a conventional oven** Spread moist soil 8–10cm (3–4in) deep in a tray, cover with kitchen foil and heat at 80°C (175°F) for 40 minutes. Uncover and leave to cool.
- **in a microwave oven** First sieve out the stones and organic material. Weigh 2kg (4lb 8oz) of soil into a bowl, cover and cook on maximum for five minutes. Spread on a tray to cool.
- **do not sterilise** garden compost or leaf-mould, as heat can reduce their food value.

Half-hardy annuals such as antirrhinums grown under glass are readily affected by damping-off disease, which can decimate sowings. Reduce the risk of infection by using clean equipment and fresh compost and watering with a copper-based fungicide.

testing old seed

1 **Spread and moisten** two or three thicknesses of absorbent paper in a saucer or shallow pan, and sprinkle a few seeds on the surface.

2 **Cover with plastic** film and keep in a warm place, in light or darkness according to the type of seed. Do not allow the paper to dry out.

3 **Leave for** up to three weeks and watch for signs of germination. If half or more start to grow, the seed will be worth sowing.

why seeds fail to germinate

There are many reasons why seeds fail to germinate. The most common causes are:

- **using old seed** that has lost its viability, or its ability to germinate
- **using stale compost** left over from a previous season, or a potting mixture rather than a special seed compost
- **using compost** that is too wet, or that has been allowed to dry out before seedlings emerge
- **surroundings** too cold or too hot
- **compost pressed too firmly** after sowing, or compacted by heavy watering from above
- **seeds covered with compost** when they need light, or buried too deeply

testing seeds

All seeds eventually lose their ability to germinate. If yours are more than two or three years old, or might have been exposed to damp or heat, test a sample before sowing to see how well they germinate (see left).

USING OLD SEED TIP Mix together all the old seed varieties that showed poor germination, and scatter them fairly thickly on a bare patch of soil. Before the plants flower, dig them in as green manure.

making liquid feed

You can make your own liquid fertiliser by growing comfrey or nettles and harvesting the plants, then soaking the leaves in a net in a bucket of water for about two weeks.

making liquid fertiliser

1 **Shear off the fresh young** growth of comfrey or nettles in spring, using a pair of garden shears.

2 **Pack the leaves** into a net bag and tie it at the top.

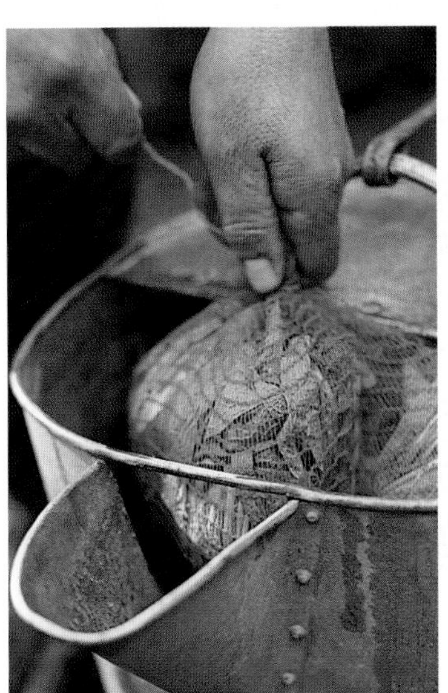

3 **Suspend this** in a tank or bucket of water for 10–14 days, occasionally squeezing the bag. Dilute the resulting liquor to look like weak tea before applying.

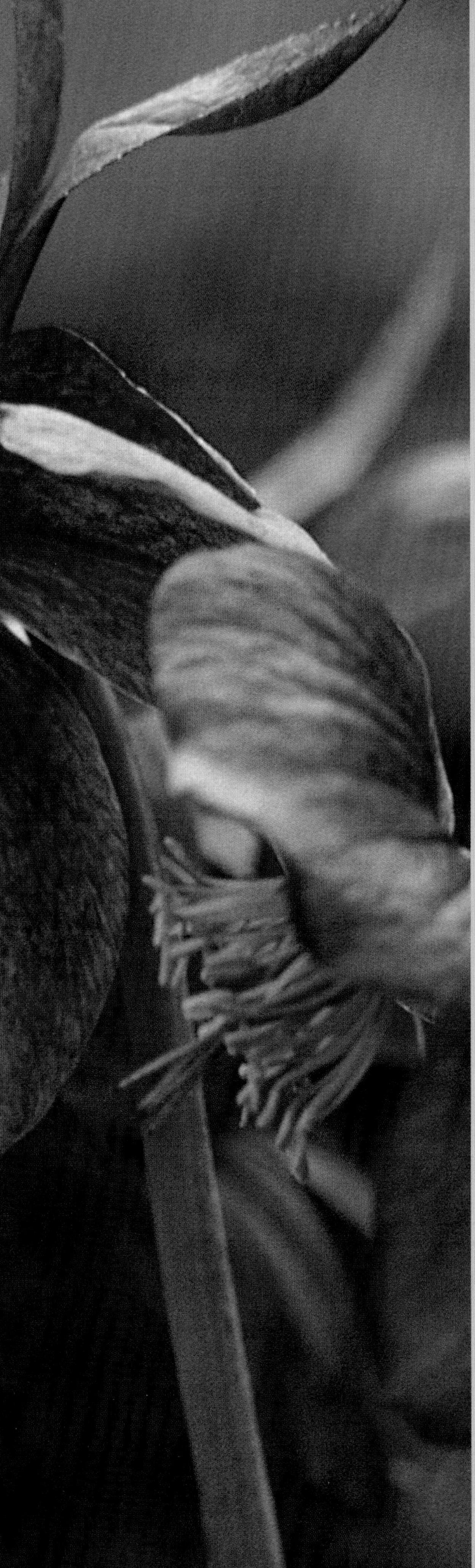

early spring

plant selector

A well-planted garden in early spring is wreathed with blossom, studded with early bulbs and alight with flowering shrubs and clumps of narcissus and Lenten roses. Breathtaking carpets of bulbs will take the eye away from leafless branches and bare canopies. Most early spring bulbs naturalise and spread unaided, but if you note star performers which suit the garden now, you can lift and divide them later. Early flowering cherries, camellias and early rhododendrons will make fine specimen trees, while even the tiniest of gardens can enjoy great variety through alpines, many of which bloom in early spring.

Helleborus hybridus 'Pluto'

perennials

Most non-woody durable plants are herbaceous (that is, they die down in winter), but some of the most important that flower in early spring are evergreen. Plant in the dormant season, preferably in autumn.

purple, blue and violet

1 Corydalis flexuosa

The long season of this compact perennial begins in early spring, when ferny leaves are topped by sprays of tubular flowers in various shades of blue. The foliage can be light green, blue-green or purplish green with red marks. In dry summers the leaves die down, but re-emerge in the autumn, sometimes with a scattering of flowers. Cultivars include the aptly named 'China Blue', 'Père David', with sky-blue flowers, and 'Purple Leaf', the most purplish in flower and leaf. Hardy.

Height: 30cm (12in) **Spread:** 25cm (10in)
Site: Partial shade. Humus-rich and moist but well-drained soil
Compost: Soil-based (John Innes No. 2)
Use: Container, shady border, underplanting for shrubs, woodland garden
Good companions: *Erythronium dens-canis, Galanthus* 'S. Arnott', *Tiarella wherryi*

2 Omphalodes verna

Blue-eyed mary, Creeping forget-me-not

Spreading mats of green tapered leaves provide good ground cover between shrubs. In spring sprays of small blue flowers with a white eye are a bonus. Hardy.

Height: 20cm (8in) **Spread:** 30cm (12in)
Site: Partial shade, shade. Humus-rich and moist but well-drained soil
Use: Ground cover, shady border, wild garden, woodland garden
Good companions: *Galanthus nivalis, Primula vulgaris, Pulmonaria angustifolia* 'Munstead Blue'

3 Primula auricula 'Blue Velvet'

Border auricula

The border auriculas are a group of evergreen primulas that thrive in the open garden. They have leathery, sometimes white-mealy leaves and produce erect stems that carry terminal clusters of usually fragrant, flat-faced flowers. 'Blue Velvet' has plush, rich blue-purple flowers with a white centre. Hardy.

Height: 15cm (6in) **Spread:** 20cm (8in)
Site: Sun, partial shade. Humus-rich and moist but well-drained soil
Use: Sunny or lightly shaded border

3

4

1

2

5

6

Good companions: *Narcissus* 'Cedric Morris', *Polygonatum* x *hybridum*, *Primula auricula* 'Old Yellow Dusty Miller'

4 Primula 'Miss Indigo'
Primrose

This primrose forms a characteristic rosette of bright green, deeply veined leaves. Nestling among these are rich purple, double flowers, the petals finely edged in creamy white. Hardy.
Height: 15cm (6in) **Spread:** 30cm (12in)
Site: Partial shade, sun. Humus-rich and moist but well-drained soil
Compost: Soil-based (John Innes No. 2) or soil-less
Use: Container, front of border, woodland garden
Good companions: *Galanthus elwesii*, *Primula vulgaris* 'Alba Plena', *Scilla siberica* 'Spring Beauty'

5 Pulmonaria saccharata 'Frühlingshimmel'
Jerusalem sage, Lungwort

Like many pulmonarias, this has grey-spotted leaves. From late winter to late spring it produces sprays of pale pink buds, red-brown at the base, that open to clear mauve-blue flowers. Hardy.
Height: 25cm (10in) **Spread:** 60cm (2ft)
Site: Partial shade. Humus-rich and moist but well-drained soil
Use: Ground cover, shady border, wild garden, woodland garden
Good companions: *Corydalis ochroleuca*, *Narcissus* 'February Gold', *Waldsteinia ternata*

6 Symphytum 'Hidcote Blue'
Comfrey

This leafy plant has green rough-textured foliage and makes a good filler between shrubs, but is potentially invasive. Red buds are gathered on a coiled stem and as this unrolls the tubular flowers change to blue and white. Hardy.
Height and spread: 45cm (18in)
Site: Partial shade, sun. Moist but well-drained soil
Use: Underplanting for shrubs, wild garden, woodland garden
Good companions: *Digitalis purpurea*, *Euphorbia amygdaloides* 'Purpurea', *Lunaria annua*

pink and mauve

7 Bergenia 'Schneekönigen'
Elephant's ears

Clump-forming perennial with large leaves partially curled at the edges. The large, very pale pink flowers are borne throughout spring. Hardy.
Height: 40cm (16in) **Spread:** 60cm (2ft)
Site: Sun, partial shade. Well-drained, preferably moist soil
Use: Front of border, gravel garden, ground cover
Good companions: *Allium hollandicum* 'Purple Sensation', *Deutzia* x *rosea*, *Stachys byzantina* 'Silver Carpet'

8 Bergenia stracheyi
Elephant's ears

One of the smallest of the bergenias, this forms a clump of upright oval leaves, which in early spring cradle short-stemmed sprays of fragrant pink flowers. The Alba Group is white flowered. Hardy.
Height: 20cm (8in) **Spread:** 25cm (10in)
Site: Sun, partial shade. Moist but well-drained soil
Use: Front of border, woodland garden
Good companions: *Epimedium* x *rubrum*, *Galanthus nivalis*, *Geranium sanguineum*

9 Bergenia 'Sunningdale'
Elephant's ears

Clump-forming evergreen with spoon-shaped red-backed leaves that develop rich bronze tints in autumn and winter. During spring bright red stems carry sprays of vivid purplish pink flowers. Hardy.
Height and spread: 40cm (16in)
Site: Sun, partial shade. Well-drained, moist soil
Use: Front of border, gravel garden, ground cover
Good companions: *Artemisia arborescens*, *Bergenia* 'Ballawley', *Cistus ladanifer*

10 Epimedium grandiflorum 'Rose Queen'
Barrenwort, Bishop's mitre

The deep pink flowers have white-tipped spurs and are held clear of the foliage, which is of great beauty. The young leaves emerge bronzed in spring and later turn green. Hardy.
Height: 25cm (10in) **Spread:** 30cm (12in)
Site: Partial shade. Moist but well-drained soil
Use: Ground cover, shady border, woodland garden
Good companions: *Geranium macrorrhizum* 'Ingwersen's Variety', *Tellima grandiflora* 'Purpurteppich', *Viburnum* x *bodnantense* 'Dawn'

11 Primula 'Guinevere'
Primula

Evergreen perennial with heavily corrugated bronze-purple leaves and erect stems that carry heads of yellow-centred, mauve-pink flowers. Hardy.
Height: 15cm (6in) **Spread:** 25cm (10in)
Site: Partial shade, sun. Humus-rich and moist but well-drained soil
Compost: Soil-based (John Innes No. 2) or soil-less
Use: Container, front of border, woodland garden
Good companions: *Galanthus* 'S. Arnott', *Narcissus* 'Dove Wings', *Polemonium* 'Lambrook Mauve'

7

8

9

10

11

red and russet

1 Pulmonaria rubra 'David Ward'
Lungwort

The coral red flowers are a vivid feature in spring, but at least of equal value is the evergreen foliage. The pale green leaves are edged with creamy white and form large rosettes. Hardy.

Height: 30cm (12in) **Spread:** 1m (3ft)

Site: Partial shade, shade. Humus-rich and moist but well-drained soil

Use: Ground cover, shady border, woodland garden

Good companions: *Brunnera macrophylla, Cornus controversa* 'Variegata', *Pulmonaria saccharata* 'Frühlingshimmel'

yellow

2 Epimedium perralderianum
Barrenwort, Bishop's mitre

Evergreen foliage plant with glossy, deep green toothed leaves, bronze-tinted when young. The bright yellow flowers have short spurs. Hardy.

Height: 30cm (12in) **Spread:** 60cm (2ft)

Site: Partial shade. Moist but well-drained soil

Use: Ground cover, shady border, woodland garden

Good companions: *Corydalis ochroleuca, Epimedium* x *warleyense* 'Orangekönigin', *Mahonia japonica*

3 Euphorbia amygdaloides var. robbiae
Mrs Robb's bonnet

Spreading evergreen with red-tinted upright stems densely set with dark green leaves that have reddish backs. Greenish yellow flowerheads are borne in spring and early summer. Potentially invasive, but useful in shade where soil is poor. Harmful if ingested and contact with the milky sap may cause skin reactions. Hardy.

General care: Cut flower stems to the base in summer when flowering is over.

Height and spread: 60cm (2ft)

Site: Partial shade. Well-drained, preferably moist soil

Use: Shady border, wild garden, woodland garden

Good companions: *Helleborus foetidus, Pachysandra terminalis, Vinca minor* 'La Grave'

4 Euphorbia characias subsp. wulfenii

Milkweed, Spurge

Evergreen shrubby perennial that makes a large clump of stiff stems crowded with blue-grey leaves. From early spring until early summer large yellow-green flowerheads top the clump. Harmful if ingested and contact with the milky sap may cause skin reactions. Hardy.

General care: Cut flower stems to the base in summer when flowering is over.

Height and spread: 1.2m (4ft)

Site: Sun. Well-drained soil

Use: Gravel garden, sunny border

Good companions: *Eryngium* x *tripartitum*, *Sedum* 'Herbstfreude', *Stipa gigantea*

5 Euphorbia rigida

Milkweed, Spurge

Evergreen with initially upright stems covered with blue-green narrow leaves. Plants tend to sprawl in spring when the stems produce heads of long-lasting yellow-green flowers. Harmful if ingested and contact with the milky sap may cause skin reactions. Hardy.

Height: 45cm (18in) **Spread:** 60cm (2ft)

Site: Sun. Well-drained soil

Use: Gravel garden, raised bed, rock garden, sunny border

Good companions: *Cytisus* x *praecox* 'Allgold', *Lavandula* x *intermedia* Dutch Group, *Ruta graveolens* 'Jackman's Blue'

6 Primula auricula 'Old Yellow Dusty Miller'

Border auricula

This evergreen primula (see 3, *Primula auricula* 'Blue Velvet', page 80) has spoon-shaped leaves dusted with white meal and rich yellow flowers with white-mealy eyes. Hardy.

Height: 15cm (6in) **Spread:** 25cm (10in)

Site: Sun or partial shade. Humus-rich and moist but well-drained soil

Use: Sunny or lightly shaded border

Good companions: *Myosotis sylvatica* 'Royal Blue', *Narcissus* 'Jack Snipe', *Tulipa* 'Orange Emperor'

7 Primula vulgaris

Primrose

The bright green, deeply veined leaves form a more or less evergreen clump. The odd flower may be found in late winter, but the main season is spring, when plants produce clusters of pale yellow, often fragrant flowers. Hardy.

Height: 20cm (8in) **Spread:** 35cm (14in)

Site: Partial shade. Moist but well-drained soil

Compost: Soil-based (John Innes No. 2) or soil-less

Use: Container, front of border, wild garden, woodland garden

Good companions: *Anemone blanda*, *Chionodoxa luciliae* Gigantea Group, *Muscari aucheri*

cream and white

8 Bergenia ciliata

Elephant's ears

Unlike the majority of bergenias, the large rounded leaves of this species are hairy, and it is only reliably evergreen in frost-free areas. The white flowers are carried in sprays on red-tinted stems. The petals emerge from brown-pink bases. Hardy.

Height: 30cm (12in) **Spread:** 45cm (18in)

Site: Sun. Well-drained, preferably moist soil

Use: Front of border, gravel garden

Good companions: *Eryngium alpinum*, *Osteospermum jucundum*, *Verbena bonariensis*

9 Pachyphragma macrophyllum

The smell of the small four-petalled flowers is rank, but the billowing mass creates snowy brightness under deciduous trees and shrubs. Mounds of overlapping rounded leaves make good cover throughout summer and persist until the new leaves emerge the following spring. Hardy.

Height: 30cm (12in) **Spread:** 75cm (2ft 6in)

Site: Partial shade. Moist but well-drained soil

Use: Ground cover, wild garden, woodland garden

Good companions: *Euphorbia amygdaloides* 'Purpurea', *Geranium phaeum* 'Album', *Helleborus foetidus* Wester Flisk Group

10 Primula vulgaris 'Alba Plena'

Primrose

White double forms of the primrose (see 7, above) have been cultivated for centuries. 'Alba Plena' often begins flowering in winter and picks up momentum in early spring. The flowers have several layers of pure white, deeply notched petals around a muddled centre. Hardy.

Height: 15cm (6in) **Spread:** 30cm (12in)

Site: Partial shade. Moist but well-drained soil

Compost: Soil-based (John Innes No. 2) or soil-less

Use: Container, front of border, wild garden, woodland garden

Good companions: *Aquilegia* 'Hensol Harebell', *Galanthus* 'Atkinsii', *Helleborus hybridus*

11 Pulmonaria 'Sissinghurst White'

Jerusalem cowslip, Lungwort, Spotted dog

The bristly evergreen foliage is covered with grey-white spots. In the shade that it prefers the white funnel-shaped flowers, which open from pale pink buds, strike a cool note. Hardy.

Height: 30cm (12in) **Spread:** 45cm (18in)

Site: Partial shade. Humus-rich and moist but well-drained soil

Use: Ground cover, shady border, wild garden, woodland garden

Good companions: *Anemone sylvestris*, *Magnolia denudata*, *Omphalodes cappadocica*

hellebores

The long-lasting muted magnificence of hellebores in flower often begins in late winter and their fingered, sometimes evergreen leaves are pleasing over many months. Most hellebores do well in a wide range of conditions, but are generally at their best in dappled shade under a canopy of deciduous trees or shrubs, in moist but well-drained soil that is preferably neutral to alkaline. All parts are harmful if eaten.

1 Helleborus torquatus Party Dress Group

Cultivars of *H. torquatus* are usually deciduous; the leaves are composed of numerous tapered leaflets and appear after flowers begin to open in late winter or early spring. The nodding or outward-facing double flowers of the Party Dress Group are greenish brown to pink and are borne profusely. Hardy.

Height and spread: 30cm (12in)

Good companions: *Asplenium scolopendrium, Cyclamen hederifolium, Lonicera* x *purpusii* 'Winter Beauty'

2 Helleborus orientalis subsp. guttatus

Lenten rose

The leathery fingered leaves overwinter, but are usually blemished and therefore best removed by the time the nodding or outward-facing single flowers open in late winter or early spring. These are creamy white, sometimes tinted pink, with green centres surrounded by red-purple speckling. Hardy.

Height and spread: 45cm (18in)

Good companions: *Eranthis hyemalis, Primula* 'Miss Indigo', *Primula vulgaris*

3 Helleborus x sternii 'Boughton Beauty'

This hybrid combines subtly coloured flowers with handsome, dark green, usually toothed foliage, over which plays a flicker of silver. The stems and veins of the three-lobed leaves are maroon or purplish pink and the single flowers, dark pink in bud opening to greenish pink, are filled with cream stamens. Not fully hardy.

Height and spread: 50cm (20in)

Good companions: *Erythronium dens-canis, Galanthus nivalis, Sarcococca hookeriana* var. *digyna*

4, 5, 6, 7, 8 Helleborus hybridus

Lenten rose

The dark green leaves of this clump-forming evergreen perennial have often become shabby by late winter, but the nodding saucer-shaped flowers are subtly tinted with intriguing deep shades. A vast number of un-named seedlings come in a wide colour range that extends from off-white and greenish cream or yellow through pink and red to dark plum. Buy Lenten roses when in flower to be sure of selecting colours you like. Many seedlings have single flowers (5, 7), but some are double or anemone-centred (8). The Ashwood Garden hybrids (4) offer a selection of good quality un-named plants. Named forms, such as 'Pluto' (6), tend to be expensive. Hardy.

Height and spread: 45cm (18in)

Good companions: *Galanthus elwesii, Lilium martagon* 'Album', *Philadelphus* 'Manteau d'Ermine'

1

2

3

4

8

7

6

5

annuals & biennials

At this time of year short-lived plants raised as biennials give good value over many weeks. Those that flower in early spring combine well with bulbs to add colour to formal beds and containers.

purple, blue and violet

1 Viola x wittrockiana Princess Series

Pansy

The pansies are short-lived evergreen perennials usually grown as annuals or biennials. The season of winter-flowering kinds extends into spring and even into early summer. In the small-flowered Princess Series the colour range includes white, cream, yellow, blue and purple. Hardy.

General care: Sow seed outdoors in summer for winter and early spring flowers or under glass in late winter for spring and summer flowers.

Height: 15cm (6in) **Spread:** 30cm (12in)

Site: Sun, partial shade. Moist but well-drained soil

Compost: Soil-based (John Innes No. 2) or soil-less

Use: Container, formal bedding, front of border

Good companions: *Hyacinthus orientalis* 'Carnegie', *Narcissus* 'Little Gem', *Scilla siberica*

red, russet and maroon

2 Bellis perennis 'Kito'

Double daisy

For lawn purists the common daisy is a tiresome perennial weed, but doubles have been cultivated, usually as biennials, since the sixteenth century. 'Kito' is readily raised from seed, and has very double red-pink flowerheads. The spoon-shaped leaves are bright green. Hardy.

General care: Sow seed outdoors in early summer and plant out in early autumn.

Height: 15cm (6in) **Spread:** 15cm (6in)

Site: Sun, partial shade. Moist but well-drained soil

Compost: Soil-based (John Innes No. 2) or soil-less

Use: Bedding, sunny or shady border, container, edging

Good companions: *Crocus vernus* 'Pickwick', *Iris* 'Natascha', *Tulipa* 'Heart's Delight'

1

4

2

3

5

3 Erysimum cheiri 'Blood Red'

Wallflower

The wallflower is a short-lived perennial and plants naturalised in old brickwork often survive for several years. As a garden plant it is almost invariably treated as a biennial and valued for its upright stems crowded with fragrant velvety flowers in spring. 'Blood Red' has relatively early scented flowers of an intense deep red. Hardy.

General care: Sow seed outdoors in late spring or early summer and plant out in mid-autumn.

Height: 45cm (18in) **Spread:** 30cm (12in)

Site: Sun. Well-drained soil, preferably limy

Compost: Soil-based (John Innes No. 2)

Use: Container, formal bedding, sunny border

Good companions: *Fritillaria imperialis*, *Tulipa* 'Estella Rijnveld', *Tulipa* 'Purissima'

4 Primula Prominent Series

Polyanthus

The polyanthus primulas are short-lived evergreen perennials usually grown as biennials. Sturdy stems carry a truss of scented flowers above a rosette of deeply veined leaves. In this dwarf selection the brightly coloured or white flowers, usually with a conspicuous yellow eye, appear in late winter or early spring. Hardy.

General care: Sow seed in summer and plant out in autumn.

Height and spread: 15–20cm (6–8in)

Site: Sun, partial shade. Moist but well-drained soil

Compost: Soil-based (John Innes No. 2) or soil-less

Use: Container, formal bedding, front of border

Good companions: *Bellis perennis* 'Kito', *Hyacinthus orientalis* 'Anna Marie', *Tulipa* 'Cape Cod'

5 Primula Silver-laced Group

Polyanthus

Like Gold-laced Group primulas (see Late Spring), these short-lived semi-evergreen perennials are often grown as biennials, but are less widely available. Upright stems carry four to eight flowers, which have a yellow eye and mahogany lobes outlined in white. Hardy.

General care: Sow seed outdoors in early summer and plant out in autumn. Divide plants after flowering or in autumn.

Height: 25cm (10in) **Spread:** 30cm (12in)

Site: Partial shade. Fertile and moist but well-drained soil

Compost: Soil-based (John Innes No. 2) or soil-less

Use: Container, formal bedding, greenhouse or conservatory, shady border

Good companions: *Fritillaria meleagris*, *Narcissus* 'Rip van Winkle', *Primula* Cowichan Garnet Group

bulbs

Much of the colour that brings the garden to life in early spring comes from bulbs. The term is used loosely to cover all those perennials that develop underground storage organs.

purple, blue and violet

1 Anemone coronaria Saint Bridgid Group

Windflower

The wild plant, a native of the Mediterranean with knobbly tubers and prettily divided leaves, bears single flowers that are white or various shades of blue and red. Saint Bridgid anemones have double or semi-double flowers in a richer colour range, much valued for cutting. Hardy.

General care: For flowers in late winter or early spring plant in early to mid-autumn with the top of the corm about 8cm (3in) deep. Plant in mid-spring for flowers in summer.

Height: 30cm (12in) **Spread:** 15cm (6in)

Site: Sun. Well-drained soil

Compost: Soil-based (John Innes No. 2) with added grit

Use: Container, sunny border, raised bed

Good companions: *Chaenomeles speciosa* 'Nivalis', *Paeonia lactiflora* 'Festiva Maxima', *Tulipa* 'Purissima'

2 Chionodoxa luciliae Gigantea Group

Glory of the snow

This fleshy bulb produces narrowly strap-shaped leaves and sprays of usually three mid-blue flowers with a white eye. Hardy.

General care: Plant in early to mid-autumn with the top of the bulb about 8cm (3in) deep.

Height: 20cm (8in) **Spread:** 5cm (2in)

Site: Sun. Well-drained soil

Compost: Soil-based (John Innes No. 2)

Use: Container, front of border, raised bed, rock garden

Good companions: *Crocus chrysanthus* 'Cream Beauty', *Iris* 'Joyce', *Tulipa* 'Heart's Delight'

3 Chionodoxa sardensis

Glory of the snow

Small slender bulb with sprays of up to 12 eye-catching starry flowers that are vivid blue with a very small white eye. Hardy.

General care: Plant in early to mid-autumn with the top of the bulb about 8cm (3in) deep.

Height: 15cm (6in) **Spread:** 5cm (2in)

Site: Sun. Well-drained soil

Compost: Soil-based (John Innes No. 2)

Use: Container, front of border, raised bed, rock garden

Good companions: *Bellis perennis*, *Galanthus* 'S. Arnott', *Primula* 'Guinevere'

4 Ipheion uniflorum

The bulb smells slightly of garlic, as do the linear pale green leaves if bruised. In early to mid-spring, each bulb produces pale to purplish blue, upward-facing starry flowers, the segments usually with a darker centre line. 'Wisley Blue' has violet-blue flowers. Leave bulbs undisturbed to develop into dense clumps. Not fully hardy.

General care: Plant in autumn or straight after flowering with the top of bulb 8cm (3in) deep.
Height: 15cm (6in) **Spread:** 5cm (2in)
Site: Sun. Moist but well-drained soil
Compost: Soil based (John Innes No. 2) with added leaf-mould and grit
Use: Front of border, rock garden
Good companions: *Campanula persicifolia, Lilium regale, Paeonia lactiflora* 'Karl Rosenfield'

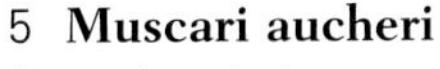

5 Muscari aucheri

Grape hyacinth

In early to mid-spring this bulbous species produces rather narrow leaves and upright stems topped by a tight stack of small bell-shaped blue flowers that narrow at the mouth. Hardy.

General care: Plant in autumn with the top of the bulb about 10cm (4in) deep.
Height: 20cm (8in) **Spread:** 5cm (2in)
Site: Sun. Moist but well-drained soil
Compost: Soil-based (John Innes No. 2)
Use: Sunny border, raised bed, rock garden
Good companions: *Chionodoxa forbesii* 'Pink Giant', *Magnolia stellata, Tulipa clusiana*

6 Puschkinia scilloides

Starry flowers, about six to a loose spray, are pale blue with a darker centre line to each segment. Variety *libanotica* is usually all white. Hardy.

General care: Plant in early autumn with the top of the bulb about 8cm (3in) deep.
Height: 20cm (8in) **Spread:** 5cm (2in)
Site: Sun, partial shade. Well-drained soil
Compost: Soil-based (John Innes No. 2)
Use: Container, front of border, raised bed, rock garden, underplanting for perennials and shrubs
Good companions: *Muscari botryoides* 'Album', *Tulipa clusiana, Tulipa humilis* Violacea Group

7 Scilla bifolia

Squill

In late winter or early spring this small bulb produces a loose spray of about 10 starry flowers. Usually purplish to turquoise-blue, there are also white and pink-flowered forms. Hardy.

General care: Plant in late summer or early autumn with the top of the bulb about 8cm (3in) deep.
Height: 15cm (6in) **Spread:** 5cm (2in)
Site: Sun, partial shade. Humus-rich, well-drained soil
Compost: Soil-based (John Innes No. 2) with added leaf-mould and grit
Use: Container, front of border, raised bed, rock garden, underplanting for perennials and shrubs
Good companions: *Lonicera* 'Winter Beauty', *Narcissus* 'Jack Snipe', *Puschkinia scilloides* var. *libanotica*

8 Scilla mischtschenkoana

Squill

This dwarf bulb flowers in late winter or early spring, when leaves are still short. The flowers, usually four to a stem, are pale blue, darker on the backs of the segments and with a dark line down the centre of each. Hardy.

General care: Plant in late summer or early autumn with the top of the bulb 8cm (3in) deep.
Height: 10cm (4in) **Spread:** 5cm (2in)
Site: Sun, partial shade. Humus-rich, well-drained soil
Compost: Soil-based (John Innes No. 2) with added leaf-mould and grit
Use: Container, front of border, raised bed, rock garden, underplanting for perennials and shrubs
Good companions: *Chaenomeles* x *superba* 'Pink Lady', *Chionodoxa forbesii* 'Pink Giant', *Narcissus* 'Dove Wings'

9 Scilla siberica 'Spring Beauty'

Siberian squill

Brilliant blue flowers, usually several to a bulb, hang on loose stems over strap-like leaves. Hardy.

General care: Plant in early autumn with the top of the bulb about 8cm (3in) deep.
Height: 15cm (6in) **Spread:** 5cm (2in)
Site: Sun, partial shade. Humus-rich, well-drained soil
Compost: Soil-based (John Innes No. 2) with added leaf-mould and grit
Use: Container, front of border, raised bed, rock garden, underplanting for perennials and shrubs
Good companions: *Galanthus elwesii, Narcissus obvallaris, Primula vulgaris*

pink and mauve

10 Chionodoxa forbesii 'Pink Giant'

Glory of the snow

The delicate pink, white-centred stars of this vigorous bulb are useful for contrasting with the more usual blue flowers of the species. Hardy.

General care: Plant in early to mid-autumn with the top of the bulb about 8cm (3in) deep.
Height: 20cm (8in) **Spread:** 5cm (2in)
Site: Sun. Well-drained soil
Compost: Soil-based (John Innes No. 2)
Use: Container, front of border, raised bed, rock garden
Good companions: *Chionodoxa luciliae* Gigantea Group, *Scilla siberica* 'Spring Beauty', *Tulipa* 'Heart's Delight'

11 Corydalis solida 'George Baker'

Tuberous plant with ferny grey-green leaves, fleshy stems and small pink-red snapdragon-like flowers. Needs a sheltered position. Hardy.

General care: Plant in autumn with the top of the tuber about 10cm (4in) deep.
Height: 25cm (10in) **Spread:** 15cm (6in)
Site: Sun, partial shade. Sharply drained soil
Compost: Soil-based (John Innes No. 2) with added grit
Use: Container, raised bed, rock garden
Good companions: *Crocus angustifolius, Crocus minimus, Geranium cinereum* 'Ballerina'

pink and mauve (continued)

1 Hyacinthus orientalis 'Anna Marie'

Hyacinth

The powerfully scented spikes of the numerous hyacinth cultivars are densely set with waxy bell-shaped flowers. 'Anna Marie' is pale pink, but other colours are available. Prepared bulbs can be forced for winter flowering. Hardy.

General care: Plant in autumn with the top of the bulb about 10cm (4in) deep.

Height: 25cm (10in) **Spread:** 8cm (3in)

Site: Sun, partial shade. Well-drained soil

Compost: Soil-based (John Innes No. 2) or bulb fibre if planting in containers without drainage holes

Use: Container, formal bedding, front of border

Good companions: *Bellis perennis*, *Hyacinthus orientalis* 'Jan Bos', *Primula* 'Guinevere'

2 Tulipa 'Apricot Beauty'

Single early flowering tulip

The soft salmon-pink cups are edged with orange. Single Early Group tulips can be forced for winter flowering. Hardy.

General care: Plant in late autumn or early winter with the top of the bulb 10–15cm (4–6in) deep.

Height: 40cm (16in) **Spread:** 15cm (6in)

Site: Sun. Well-drained soil

Compost: Soil-based (John Innes No. 2)

Use: Border, container, formal bedding

Good companions: *Erysimum cheiri* 'Ivory White', *Primula* Gold-laced Group, *Viola* x *wittrockiana* Universal Series

3 Tulipa 'Couleur Cardinal'

Triumph Group tulip

Most Triumph tulips flower in mid-spring, so are useful for beds that need to be cleared early for summer bedding. 'Couleur Cardinal' is compact. The single cups have plum outer petals, but are glowing crimson inside. Hardy.

General care: Plant in late autumn or early winter with the top of the bulb 10–15cm (4–6in) deep.

Height: 35cm (14in) **Spread:** 15cm (6in)

Site: Sun. Well-drained soil

Compost: Soil-based (John Innes No. 2)

Use: Border, container, formal bedding

Good companions: *Anemone coronaria* De Caen Group, *Muscari aucheri*, *Myosotis sylvatica* 'Royal Blue'

4 Tulipa 'Peach Blossom'

Double early flowering tulip

Peak flowering time for these tulips is mid-spring, but they can be forced for winter blooms. 'Peach Blossom' has deep pink flowers, the base often green-tinged cream. Hardy.

General care: Plant in late autumn or early winter with the top of the bulb 10–15cm (4–6in) deep.

Height: 30cm (12in) **Spread:** 15cm (6in)

Site: Sun. Well-drained soil

Compost: Soil-based (John Innes No. 2)

Use: Border, container, formal bedding

Good companions: *Bellis perennis*, *Hyacinthus orientalis* 'Ostara', *Tulipa* 'Heart's Delight'

red and russet

5 Anemone coronaria De Caen Group

Windflower

The single flowers of these vigorous anemones are in various shades of red, pink and white. Hardy.

General care: For flowers in late winter or early spring, plant in early to mid-autumn with the top of the corm about 8cm (3in) deep. Plant in mid-spring for flowers in summer.

Height: 25cm (10in) **Spread:** 15cm (6in)

Site: Sun. Well-drained soil

Compost: Soil-based (John Innes No. 2) with added grit

Use: Container, sunny border, raised bed

Good companions: *Centaurea cyanus*, *Consolida ajacis* Giant Imperial Series, *Gladiolus* 'The Bride'

6 Hyacinthus orientalis 'Jan Bos'

Hyacinth

Although this early cultivar produces a slimmer spike than many hyacinths, the stem is still densely set with fragrant, bright crimson-red bells. Prepared bulbs are suitable for forcing. Hardy.

General care: Plant in autumn with the top of the bulb about 10cm (4in) deep.
Height: 25cm (10in) **Spread:** 8cm (3in)
Site: Sun, partial shade. Well-drained soil
Compost: Soil-based (John Innes No. 2) or bulb fibre if planting in containers without drainage holes
Use: Container, formal bedding, front of border
Good companions: *Muscari aucheri*, *Primula* Cowichan Garnet Group, *Viola* Sorbet Series

7 Tulipa clusiana var. chrysantha
Lady tulip

In early to mid-spring this graceful plant bears a large yellow flower, stained red or brown-purple on the outside. *T. clusiana* itself is white with crimson-pink markings. Hardy.
General care: Plant in late autumn or early winter with the top of the bulb about 10cm (4in) deep.
Height: 30cm (12in) **Spread:** 8cm (3in)
Site: Sun. Well-drained soil
Compost: Soil-based (John Innes No. 2)
Use: Border, container, formal bedding
Good companions: *Aubrieta* 'Greencourt Purple', *Campanula carpatica*, *Daphne cneorum* 'Eximia'

8 Tulipa hageri 'Splendens'

In early to mid-spring this tulip bears up to four large star-shaped flowers to a stem. Each one is up to 9cm (3½in) across, crimson-scarlet, tinged green on the outside with a black base and brown-red inside. Hardy.
General care: Plant in late autumn or early winter with the top of the bulb about 10cm (4in) deep.
Height: 30cm (12in) **Spread:** 15cm (6in)
Site: Sun. Well-drained soil
Compost: Soil-based (John Innes No. 2)
Use: Border, container, formal bedding, raised bed, rock garden
Good companions: *Aurinia saxatilis* 'Citrina', *Tulipa orphanidea* Whittallii Group, *Tulipa urumiensis*

9 Tulipa 'Heart's Delight'
Kaufmanniana tulip

The flowers of this low-growing mottle-leaved tulip are carmine-red on the outside, paler at the margins, and off-white inside, giving an overall impression of pinkish red. The base is yellow with red marks. Hardy.
General care: Plant in late autumn or early winter with the top of the bulb 10–15cm (4–6in) deep.
Height: 20cm (8in) **Spread:** 15cm (6in)
Site: Sun. Well-drained soil
Compost: Soil-based (John Innes No. 2)
Use: Border, container, formal bedding, raised bed, rock garden
Good companions: *Iris* 'George', *Primula* 'Guinevere', *Tulipa humilis* Violacea Group

10 Tulipa 'Madame Lefeber'
Fosteriana tulip

One parent of the Fosteriana Group of tulips is red-flowered *T. fosteriana*, a species that produces single bowl-shaped flowers in mid-spring. The sheeny, searing red flowers of this hybrid are borne slightly earlier. Hardy.
General care: Plant in late autumn or early winter with the top of the bulb 10–15cm (4–6in) deep.
Height: 35cm (14in) **Spread:** 15cm (6in)
Site: Sun. Well-drained soil
Compost: Soil-based (John Innes No. 2)
Use: Border, container, formal bedding
Good companions: *Bellis perennis* 'Kito', *Erysimum cheiri* 'Blood Red', *Hyacinthus orientalis* 'Jan Bos'

11 Tulipa praestans 'Fusilier'

The relatively small red flowers are carried in bouquets of up to five per stem over slightly downy grey-green leaves. Hardy.
General care: Plant in late autumn or early winter with the top of the bulb 10–15cm (4–6in) deep.
Height: 30cm (12in) **Spread:** 15cm (6in)
Site: Sun. Well-drained soil
Compost: Soil-based (John Innes No. 2)
Use: Border, container, formal bedding, raised bed, rock garden
Good companions: *Muscari aucheri*, *Myosotis sylvatica* 'Royal Blue', *Primula* Prominent

12 Tulipa 'Red Riding Hood'
Greigii tulip

Greigii tulips have handsome leaves with dark markings. This is one of the best, with bright scarlet single flowers and attractively maroon-mottled foliage. Hardy.
General care: Plant in late autumn or early winter with the top of the bulb 10–15cm (4–6in) deep.
Height: 20cm (8in) **Spread:** 15cm (6in)
Site: Sun. Well-drained soil
Compost: Soil-based (John Innes No. 2)
Use: Border, container, formal bedding, raised bed, rock garden
Good companions: *Armeria maritima* 'Düsseldorfer Stolz', *Festuca glauca* 'Seeigel', *Muscari botryoides* 'Album'

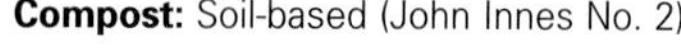

red and russet (continued)

1 Tulipa 'Shakespeare'

Kaufmanniana tulip

The blooms of this sturdy tulip, which flowers in the first half of spring, are an unusual blend of salmon and scarlet with yellow at their base. Hardy.

General care: Plant in late autumn or early winter with the top of the bulb 10–15cm (4–6in) deep.

Height: 25cm (10in) **Spread:** 15cm (6in)

Site: Sun. Well-drained soil

Compost: Soil-based (John Innes No. 2)

Use: Border, container, formal bedding, raised bed, rock garden

Good companions: *Chionodoxa forbesii* 'Pink Giant', *Hyacinthus orientalis* 'Jan Bos', *Muscari aucheri*

yellow and orange

2 Fritillaria imperialis

Crown imperial

Sturdy stems carry tiers of glossy green leaves for up to two-thirds of their height and then are topped by more leaves, below which hangs a ring of bell-shaped flowers up to 5cm (2in) across. The most common colour is reddish orange, but there is considerable variation: 'Rubra' and 'Rubra Maxima' are deep orange-red; 'Lutea' and 'Lutea Maxima' are bright yellow. Hardy.

General care: Plant the large hollow-crowned bulb on its side on a bed of coarse sand about 20cm (8in) deep.

Height: 75cm (2ft 6in) **Spread:** 30cm (12in)

Site: Sun, partial shade. Well-drained soil. Good on lime

Use: Border

Good companions: *Muscari aucheri, Stipa gigantea, Tulipa orphanidea* Whittallii Group

3 Tulipa 'Cape Cod'

Greigii tulip

This hybrid has handsomely mottled foliage. The yellow flowers are shaded apricot on the outside and tinted bronze around the black base inside. The segments have a central red stripe. Hardy.

General care: Plant in late autumn or early winter with the top of the bulb 10–15cm (4–6in) deep.

Height: 20cm (8in) **Spread:** 15cm (6in)

Site: Sun. Well-drained soil

Compost: Soil-based (John Innes No. 2)

Use: Border, container, formal bedding, raised bed, rock garden

Good companions: *Achillea* x *lewisii* 'King Edward', *Haplopappus glutinosus, Helianthemum* 'Wisley Primrose'

4 Tulipa 'Orange Emperor'

Fosteriana tulip

The large flowers of this vigorous hybrid are usually borne in mid-spring over broad grey-green leaves. They are glowing orange, less intense inside, with a yellow base. Hardy.

General care: Plant in late autumn or early winter with the top of the bulb 10–15cm (4–6in) deep.

Height: 40cm (16in) **Spread:** 15cm (6in)

Site: Sun. Well-drained soil

Compost: Soil-based (John Innes No. 2)

Use: Border, container, formal bedding

Good companions: *Crocus vernus* 'Remembrance', *Erysimum cheiri* 'Orange Bedder', *Tulipa* 'Prinses Irene'

5 Tulipa orphanidea Whittallii Group

The impression of this subtly coloured tulip is of bronzed orange, but the outer segments are tinged green and the base inside is black. The almost spherical flowers open to a star. Hardy.

General care: Plant in late autumn or early winter with the top of the bulb about 10cm (4in) deep. Clumps are best left undisturbed.

Height: 35cm (14in) **Spread:** 10cm (4in)

Site: Sun. Well-drained soil

Compost: Soil-based (John Innes No. 2)

Use: Border, container, raised bed, rock garden

Good companions: *Crocus angustifolius, Crocus chrysanthus* 'Zwanenburg Bronze', *Iris danfordiae*

6 Tulipa 'Prinses Irene'

Triumph Group tulip

In mid-spring this hybrid bears cup-shaped orange flowers with a purple 'flame' on the outer segments. Hardy.

General care: Plant in late autumn or early winter with the top of the bulb 10–15cm (4–6in) deep.

Height: 35cm (14in) **Spread:** 15cm (6in)

1

2

3

Site: Sun. Well-drained soil
Compost: Soil-based (John Innes No. 2)
Use: Border, container, formal bedding
Good companions: *Primula* Gold-laced Group, *Tulipa* 'Couleur Cardinal', *Viola* x *wittrockiana* Ultima Series

7 **Tulipa urumiensis**

Linear, grey-green leaves form a flat rosette from which rises a short stem carrying one or two starry flowers. These are bright yellow inside and bronze-yellow on the exterior. Hardy.
General care: Plant in late autumn or early winter with the top of the bulb about 10cm (4in) deep.
Height: 35cm (14in) **Spread:** 10cm (4in)
Site: Sun. Well-drained soil
Compost: Soil-based (John Innes No. 2)
Use: Border, container, raised bed, rock garden
Good companions: *Rhodanthemum hosmariense*, *Sedum* 'Bertram Anderson', *Tulipa orphanidea* Whittallii Group

cream and white

8 **Anemone nemorosa**
Wood anemone

This creeping rhizomatous plant can spread rampantly. The white nodding flowers are often flushed pink or mauve; 'Allenii' is mauve-blue, 'Alba Plena' is white and double. Hardy.
General care: Best planted after flowering, while plants are still in leaf. Alternatively, plant fresh rhizomes horizontally about 5cm (2in) deep in early autumn.
Height: 10cm (4in) **Spread:** 25cm (10in)
Site: Partial shade. Moist, humus-rich but well-drained soil
Use: Underplanting for shrubs, woodland garden
Good companions: *Galanthus nivalis*, *Narcissus* 'Dove Wings', *Viola riviniana* Purpurea Group

9 **Leucojum vernum**
Spring snowflake

In late winter or early spring strap-shaped deep green leaves emerge with a leafless stem that carries one or two white drooping flowers. The segments are tipped with green. Hardy.
General care: Plant in late summer or early autumn with the top of the bulb about 10cm (4in) deep.
Height: 25cm (10in) **Spread:** 10cm (4in)
Site: Sun, partial shade. Moist, humus-rich soil
Use: Border, in grass, waterside
Good companions: *Astilbe* x *arendsii* 'Irrlicht', *Cornus alba* 'Kesselringii', *Leucojum aestivum* 'Gravetye Giant'

10 **Ornithogalum oligophyllum**
Star-of-bethlehem

The bright green linear leaves lie almost flat with above them a cluster of up to five unscented flowers that are almost wholly green on the outside and glistening white inside. Hardy.
General care: Plant in autumn with the top of the bulb about 10cm (4in) deep.
Height: 10cm (4in) **Spread:** 15cm (6in)
Site: Sun. Well-drained soil
Use: Naturalised in short grass, raised bed, rock garden
Good companions: *Aurinia saxatilis* 'Citrina', *Euphorbia myrsinites*, *Tulipa orphanidea* Whittallii Group

11 **Tulipa 'Purissima'**
Fosteriana tulip

Stems rise from bright green leaves carrying large, long-lasting flowers that open milky white then turn pure white with a soft yellow centre. Hardy.
General care: Plant in late autumn or early winter with the top of the bulb 10–15cm (4–6in) deep.
Height: 35cm (14in) **Spread:** 12cm (5in)
Site: Sun. Well-drained soil
Compost: Soil-based (John Innes No. 2)
Use: Border, container, formal bedding
Good companions: *Buxus sempervirens*, *Hyacinthus orientalis* 'Anna Marie', *Viola* x *wittrockiana* Universal Series

12 **Tulipa turkestanica**

A few grey narrow leaves accompany up to seven flowers on a slender stem. The star-like flowers are ivory with a yellow centre. Hardy.
General care: Plant in late autumn or early winter with the top of the bulb about 10cm (4in) deep.
Height: 30cm (12in) **Spread:** 8cm (3in)
Site: Sun. Well-drained soil
Compost: Soil-based (John Innes No. 2)
Use: Border, container, formal bedding, raised bed, rock garden
Good companions: *Crocus chrysanthus* 'Cream Beauty', *Euphorbia myrsinites*, *Tulipa urumiensis*

daffodils

In spring, yellow or white daffodils make an enormous impact in the garden – in borders or naturalised in grass – and as cut flowers. They vary in vigour, size, number of flowers and colour, but the structure of the flower is essentially always the same – six petals around a short cup or long trumpet – apart from double forms. Plant in late summer or early autumn in a well-drained sunny or partially shaded site, with the top of the bulb at a depth twice its height. In containers, use soil-based (John Innes No. 2) compost with added grit. Daffodils described here are hardy and can be forced for winter flowering.

1

2

1 Narcissus 'Dutch Master'
Trumpet daffodil

This all-yellow hybrid conforms to the classic daffodil pattern – a ring of six petals backing a trumpet at least as long as the petals.
Height: 40cm (16in) **Spread:** 10cm (4in)
Good companions: *Forsythia giraldiana, Lonicera x purpusii* 'Winter Beauty', *Narcissus* 'Saint Keverne'

2 Narcissus 'Jack Snipe'
Cyclamineus daffodil

The flowers of this vigorous Cyclamineus daffodil (see 4) are long-lasting, from early to mid-spring. The white petals are swept back from a short lemon-yellow trumpet.
Height: 20cm (8in) **Spread:** 8cm (3in)
Good companions: *Primula vulgaris, Pulmonaria officinalis* 'Sissinghurst White', *Viburnum farreri*

3 Narcissus 'Tête-à-Tête'

This dwarf daffodil is very compact, early and bears one to three bright yellow flowers on each stem, the long cups slightly darker than the swept-back petals. It is excellent for growing in containers indoors or outside, alone or with other small bulbs or shrubby plants.
Height: 15cm (6in) **Spread:** 5cm (2in)
Good companions: *Narcissus* 'Little Gem', *Salix reticulata, Scilla siberica* 'Spring Beauty'

4 Narcissus 'February Gold'
Cyclamineus daffodil

Hybrids derived from the bright yellow *N. cyclamineus* are generally considerably larger than this dwarf moisture-loving daffodil, but share the sharply angled single flowers of their common parentage, with segments swept back from a relatively long trumpet. They flower in late winter and early spring. This vigorous hybrid has yellow petals and a long, slightly richer-coloured frilled trumpet.
Height: 30cm (12in) **Spread:** 8cm (3in)
Good companions: *Chimonanthus praecox, Chionodoxa luciliae* Gigantea Group, *Clematis macropetala* 'Maidwell Hall'

5 Narcissus 'Dove Wings'
Cyclamineus daffodil

One of the first Cyclamineus daffodils to flower (see 4, above). 'Dove Wings' has a pale yellow trumpet and white petals.
Height: 30cm (12in) **Spread:** 8cm (3in)
Good companions: *Anemone blanda, Narcissus* 'Jack Snipe', *Primula vulgaris* 'Alba Plena'

6 Narcissus 'Little Gem'
Dwarf trumpet daffodil

Several dwarf daffodils that flower in early spring make an attractive alternative to large

3

4

5

trumpet daffodils. 'Little Gem' is sturdy and compact with bright yellow petals and trumpet.
Height: 15cm (6in) **Spread:** 10cm (4in)
Good companions: *Crocus chrysanthus* 'Zwanenburg Bronze', *Iris histrioides* 'Major', *Veronica peduncularis* 'Georgia Blue'

7 Narcissus 'Barrett Browning'
Small-cupped daffodil

The small-cupped daffodils flower in early to mid-spring and produce a single bloom to a stem, with a cup up to a third the length of the flower segments. 'Barrett Browning' has a bright orange cup surrounded by white segments.
Height: 40cm (16in) **Spread:** 15cm (6in)
Good companions: *Myosotis sylvatica* 'Royal Blue', *Primula* Gold-laced Group, *Tulipa* 'Prinses Irene'

8 Narcissus obvallaris
Tenby daffodil

In early spring, stiff stems bear single flowers with petals pointing forward around a slightly frilled trumpet. Petals and trumpet are an almost uniform rich yellow. This sturdy daffodil is excellent for naturalising in the wild garden.
Height: 30cm (12in) **Spread:** 8cm (3in)
Good companions: *Crocus speciosus, Eranthis hyemalis, Galanthus nivalis*

9 Narcissus 'Rip van Winkle'
Double daffodil

Double daffodils tend to be knocked around by rough weather, but this dwarf is a good garden plant, each flower a bright yellow mophead of numerous pointed segments.
Height: 15cm (6in) **Spread:** 5cm (2in)
Good companions: *Hyacinthoides non-scripta, Narcissus obvallaris, Tulipa sprengeri*

10 Narcissus 'Sun Disc'
Jonquil

Most of the jonquils have very narrow leaves and round stems that bear two or three sweetly scented small-cupped flowers. 'Sun Disc' bears a single small rounded flower per stem. It is yellow at first but pales to cream.
Height: 20cm (8in) **Spread:** 5cm (2in)
Good companions: *Crocus chrysanthus* 'Cream Beauty', *Hypericum olympicum, Tulipa urumiensis*

11 Narcissus 'Liberty Bells'
Triandrus daffodil

Narcissus triandrus is a dainty species, having several small-cupped flowers to a stem. The charming hybrids that share these characteristics usually flower around the middle of spring. In mid-spring, 'Liberty Bells' bears two lemon-yellow flowers to a stem.
Height: 30cm (12in) **Spread:** 8cm (3in)

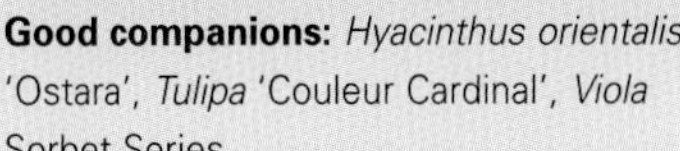

Good companions: *Hyacinthus orientalis* 'Ostara', *Tulipa* 'Couleur Cardinal', *Viola* Sorbet Series

12 Narcissus 'Saint Keverne'
Large-cupped daffodil

In general, large-cupped daffodils are a showy group with trumpets that are more than a third the length of the petals. 'Saint Keverne' is almost uniformly yellow, with broad petals. It is excellent for naturalising in grass or borders.
Height: 45cm (18in) **Spread:** 15cm (6in)
Good companions: *Berberis darwinii, Kerria japonica* 'Pleniflora', *Muscari armeniacum*

spring-flowering crocuses

The strong colours of crocuses make a considerable impact from winter to early spring, particularly when they are grown densely in containers or as large colonies in grass, where drifts of one colour are more effective than random mixtures. Many are also good for raised beds and rock gardens. Plant crocuses in autumn, the smaller species as early as possible, with the top of the corm 5–8cm (2–3in) deep in well-drained gritty soil, or in soil-based compost (John Innes No. 2) with added grit. All crocuses described here are hardy.

1 Crocus vernus 'Pickwick'

Dutch crocus

The large goblet-shaped flowers of the vigorous Dutch crocuses open out in sunshine to reveal bright orange stigmas. This cultivar is pale mauve striped purple and has a purple base.

Height: 12cm (5in) **Spread:** 5cm (2in)

Good companions: *Corylus avellana* 'Contorta', *Crocus* x *luteus* 'Golden Yellow', *Narcissus* 'Rijnveld's Early Sensation'

2 Crocus flavus

Scented bright yellow to orange flowers, up to four to a corm, are produced with the leaves.

Height: 8cm (3in) **Spread:** 5cm (2in)

Good companions: *Crocus chrysanthus* 'Ladykiller', *Scilla bifolia, Tulipa* 'Cape Cod'

3 Crocus angustifolius

Cloth of gold crocus

Small, intense orange-yellow flowers with mahogany-stained outer segments that recurve when fully open. Flowers are produced in late winter or early spring at the same time as leaves.

Height and spread: 5cm (2in)

Good companions: *Crocus minimus, Tulipa orphanidea* Whittallii Group, *Tulipa urumiensis*

4 Crocus x luteus 'Golden Yellow'

Dutch yellow crocus

Each corm produces up to five vivid orange-yellow flowers at the same time as the leaves, in late winter or early spring. This crocus does not set seed, but cormlets are produced freely so that colonies steadily expand.

Height: 10cm (4in) **Spread:** 5cm (2in)

Good companions: *Colchicum speciosum* 'Album', *Crocus speciosus, Crocus vernus* 'Purpureus Grandiflorus'

5 Crocus minimus

In early to mid-spring each corm produces one or two flowers with the leaves. The outer segments are buff with deep purple markings, the inner segments mauve-purple around the orange-yellow stigmas.

Height: 8cm (3in) **Spread:** 5cm (2in)

Good companions: *Crocus korokolwii, Pulsatilla vulgaris, Tulipa hageri* 'Splendens'

6 Crocus vernus 'Jeanne d'Arc'

Dutch crocus

This Dutch crocus (see 1, above) is pure white with a hint of violet at the base.

Height: 12cm (5in) **Spread:** 5cm (2in)

Good companions: *Betula utilis* var. *jacquemontii* 'Silver Shadow', *Crocus vernus* 'Remembrance', *Narcissus* 'Dove Wings'

1

7 Crocus vernus 'Remembrance'

Dutch crocus

One of the first of the Dutch crocuses (see 1, above) to flower, this cultivar bears violet-purple goblets with a bright green sheen over leaves with a white midrib.

Height: 12cm (5in) **Spread:** 5cm (2in)

Good companions: *Anemone blanda, Eranthis hyemalis, Narcissus* 'February Gold'

8 Crocus vernus 'Purpureus Grandiflorus'

Dutch crocus

The fine satin sheen of this Dutch crocus (see 1, above) shows off its rich purple colouring.

Height: 12cm (5in) **Spread:** 5cm (2in)

Good companions: *Colchicum* 'Rosy Dawn', *Crocus vernus* 'Jeanne d'Arc', *Crocus vernus* 'Pickwick'

climbers

Climbers twine, cling with small stem roots or clasp with tendrils. Those that flower in early spring bring welcome colour to walls, fences and architectural supports. Plant in the dormant season.

purple, blue and violet

1 Akebia quinata

Chocolate vine

The brown-purple flowers of this semi-evergreen climber are somewhat hidden in spring by the five-lobed leaves, but their pervasive spicy scent betrays their presence. After a hot summer purple, sausage-shaped fruits may follow and are produced most freely if two plants are grown close together. Hardy.

General care: Prune lightly immediately after flowering.

Height: 8m (25ft) **Spread:** 4m (12ft)

Site: Sun, partial shade. Moist but well-drained soil

Use: Pergola, tree climber, wall

Good companions: *Clematis montana* var. *rubens* 'Elizabeth', *Rosa* 'Aimée Vibert', *Wisteria sinensis*

pink and mauve

2 Clematis alpina 'Ruby'

The colour range of the alpine clematis, all spring-flowering, slender deciduous climbers, is centred on blue and white. Most are in flower by mid-spring, but 'Ruby' often produces occasional blooms in summer. It is a useful alternative in red-pink with greenish white petal-like stamens. Hardy.

General care: Plant with the base in shade. Prune lightly immediately after flowering.

Height: 3m (10ft) **Spread:** 1.5m (5ft)

Site: Sun, partial shade. Fertile, humus-rich and well-drained soil. Good on lime

Compost: Soil-based (John Innes No. 3)

Use: Container, shrub climber, training on tripod, wall

Good companions: *Clematis macropetala*, *Tulipa* 'Couleur Cardinal', *Tulipa* 'Purissima'

3 Clematis macropetala 'Maidwell Hall'

This slender deciduous clematis is usually in bloom by mid-spring and often continues into early summer. The freely produced deep mauve flowers appear double because petal-like stamens fill the centre. Fluffy seed heads follow. Hardy.

General care: Plant with the base in shade. Prune lightly immediately after flowering.

Height: 3m (10ft) **Spread:** 1.5m (5ft)

Site: Sun, partial shade. Fertile, humus-rich and well-drained soil. Good on lime

Compost: Soil-based (John Innes No. 3)

Use: Container, shrub climber, training on tripod, wall

Good companions: *Clematis* 'Abundance', *Rosa* 'Parade', *Solanum laxum* 'Album'

cream and white

4 Clematis armandii

This vigorous evergreen species is a very fine plant, with glossy dark green leaves and in early spring numerous clusters of scented white flowers. Hardy.

General care: Plant with the base in shade. Prune lightly immediately after flowering.

Height: 5m (15ft) **Spread:** 4m (12ft)

Site: Sun, partial shade. Fertile, humus-rich and well-drained soil. Does well on lime

Use: Arch, pergola, wall

Good companions: *Lonicera periclymenum* 'Serotina', *Rosa* 'Madame Alfred Carrière', *Rosa* 'Veilchenblau'

5 Hedera colchica 'Dentata Variegata'

Bullock's heart ivy, Persian ivy

Evergreen self-clinging plant that is equally at home on a large wall or making effective ground cover. The large unlobed leaves have curled-under edges and are grey-shaded bright green with irregular creamy yellow margins that become milky white as the leaves mature. Hardy.

General care: Prune at any time to restrict growth.

Height: 5m (15ft) **Spread:** 4m (12ft)

Site: Sun, partial shade. Well-drained soil

Use: Ground cover, wall

Good companions: *Buxus sempervirens*, *Hedera colchica* 'Dentata', *Prunus laurocerasus*

green

6 Holboellia coriacea

Fragrant evergreen twining climber with clusters of purplish male blooms carried at stem ends, greenish female ones lower down. Inedible purple fruits appear after a hot summer. Not fully hardy.

General care: Prune lightly after flowering.

Height: 6m (20ft) **Spread:** 2.5m (8ft)

Site: Sun, partial shade. Humus-rich and well-drained soil

Use: Arch, pergola, tree climber, wall

Good companions: *Buddleja crispa*, *Solanum crispum* 'Glasnevin', *Trachelospermum jasminoides*

1

2

3

4

5

6

shrubs & trees

Massed blossom often precedes or eclipses the beautiful foliage tints of early spring when deciduous trees and shrubs start to break into leaf. Plant in the dormant season, preferably in autumn or early spring.

2

purple, blue and violet

1

1 Erica x darleyensis 'Kramer's Rote'

Darley dale heath

Like other darley dale heaths, this bushy evergreen is lime-tolerant and flowers over a long season in winter and spring. The foliage is bronze tinted and the flowers are magenta. Hardy.

General care: Trim plants in spring, after flowering.

Height: 30cm (12in) **Spread:** 60cm (2ft)

Site: Sun. Well-drained soil

Compost: Soil-based, preferably lime-free (ericaceous)

Use: Container, ground cover, heather garden, raised bed, rock garden

Good companions: *Erica carnea* 'King George', *Erica* x *darleyensis* 'Furzey', *Juniperus* x *pfitzeriana* 'Wilhelm Pfitzer'

2 Rhododendron Blue Tit Group

This dense evergreen dwarf bush has foliage that is yellow-green when young, but later turns mid-green. The small funnel-shaped flowers are borne in clusters of two or three at the tips of the stems and are soft mauve-blue. Excellent for a sunny rock or heather garden. Hardy.

Height and spread: 1m (3ft)

Site: Partial shade. Lime-free, humus-rich but well-drained soil

Compost: Soil-based (ericaceous)

Use: Container, heather garden, rock garden

Good companions: *Disanthus cercidifolius*, *Gaultheria mucronata* 'Bell's Seedling', *Ledum groenlandicum*

3 Rhododendron 'Penheale Blue'

Free-flowering, compact evergreen shrub with small glossy leaves, this can be grown in full sun. In early and mid-spring it bears dense clusters of funnel-shaped flowers that are violet-blue with red undertones. Hardy.

Height and spread: 1.2m (4ft)

Site: Partial shade, sun. Lime-free, humus-rich but well-drained soil.

Compost: Soil-based (ericaceous)

Use: Container, heather garden bed, rock garden

Good companions: *Acer japonicum* 'Vitifolium', *Hamamelis* x *intermedia* 'Pallida', *Rhododendron* 'Golden Torch'

4 Salix gracilistyla 'Melanostachys'

This deciduous shrub is startling in spring before the leaves develop. The blackish catkins have brick-red anthers, the combination creating a purplish effect on the naked branches. The leaves are silky grey before they turn glossy green and are retained well into autumn. Hardy.

Height: 3m (10ft) **Spread:** 4m (12ft)

Site: Sun. Moist but well-drained soil

Use: Border, waterside

Good companions: *Cornus alba* 'Kesselringii', *Miscanthus sinensis* 'Silberfeder', *Salix irrorata*

5 Vinca minor 'La Grave'

Lesser periwinkle

Vinca minor itself is a low evergreen shrub with trailing branches and glossy pointed leaves. It is a vigorous coloniser and stems root readily. This large-flowered selection bears purplish blue flowers in spring and early summer. Of similar vigour, f. *alba* is a white-flowered form, but variegated forms, such as blue-flowered 'Argenteo-Variegata' with creamy leaf margins, spread less aggressively. All forms flower best if grown in full sun. Hardy.

Height: 15cm (6in) **Spread:** Indefinite

Site: Sun, partial shade. Well-drained soil

Use: Ground cover

Good companions: *Euphorbia amygdaloides* 'Purpurea', *Hedera helix* 'Ivalace', *Iris foetidissima*

pink and mauve

6 Chaenomeles x superba 'Pink Lady'

Flowering quince, Japanese quince

This deciduous shrub is one of several hybrids that make spiny spreading bushes. It often starts flowering on bare stems in winter and continues into late spring. Bright pink cup-shaped flowers open from strongly coloured buds. Hardy.

General care: Prune immediately after flowering, on wall-trained specimens cutting back flowered shoots to within three or four buds of a permanent framework of branches.

Height: 1.5m (5ft) **Spread:** 2m (6ft)

Site: Sun, partial shade. Well-drained soil

Use: Border, wall

Good companions: *Chionodoxa forbesii* 'Pink Giant', *Galanthus elwesii*, *Muscari armeniacum*

7 Daphne bholua var. glacialis 'Gurkha'

Rather upright deciduous shrub that begins flowering in winter and extends into early spring. The purplish pink flowers are borne in clusters on stem tips and have a strong sweet scent. Hardy.

Height: 2.5m (8ft) **Spread:** 1.5m (5ft)

Site: Sun, partial shade. Humus-rich and moist but well-drained soil

Use: Border, woodland garden

Good companions: *Geranium phaeum*, *Magnolia* x *loebneri* 'Leonard Messel', *Omphalodes cappodocica*

8 Erica erigena 'Irish Dusk'

Irish heath, Mediterranean heath

This compact dark-leaved form of a low-growing lime-tolerant species often starts to flower in winter and bears spikes of honey-scented pink flowers throughout spring. Hardy.

General care: Trim plants in late spring or early summer, after flowering.

Height: 60cm (2ft) **Spread:** 45cm (18in)

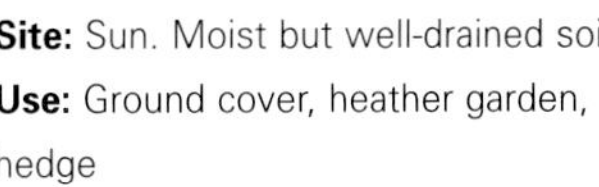

Site: Sun. Moist but well-drained soil
Use: Ground cover, heather garden, hedge
Good companions: *Erica carnea* 'Springwood White', *Erica erigena* 'Brightness', *Picea abies* 'Little Gem'

9 Magnolia campbellii subsp. mollicomata

Once it is mature, after 10 years, this deciduous tree is magnificent in spring when it bears large, upright pink or purplish pink blooms. Hardy.
Height: 15m (50ft) **Spread:** 10m (33ft)
Site: Sun. Moist but well-drained soil, preferably lime-free
Use: Canopy in border, woodland garden
Good companions: *Davidia involucrata, Disanthus cercidifolius, Viburnum plicatum* 'Mariesii'

10 Magnolia x loebneri 'Leonard Messel'

This densely branched, deciduous tall shrub or small tree flowers before the foliage develops. Purplish pink globular buds open to form a paler star of 10–12 narrow, somewhat limp petals. Hardy.
Height: 8m (25ft) **Spread:** 6m (20ft)
Site: Sun. Moist but well-drained soil
Use: Canopy in border, specimen shrub, woodland garden
Good companions: *Epimedium* x *youngianum* 'Niveum', *Omphalodes verna, Tiarella wherryi*

11 Pieris japonica 'Blush'

The glossy leaves of this evergreen compact shrub are coppery when young. In late winter and early spring it is covered with drooping sprays of deep pink buds. These open to pale pink waxy flowers that age to white. Hardy.
Height: 4m (12ft) **Spread:** 3m (10ft)
Site: Sun, partial shade. Lime-free, moist but well-drained soil
Use: Border, woodland garden
Good companions: *Gaultheria mucronata* 'Wintertime', *Kalmia latifolia* 'Ostbo Red', *Rhododendron* Temple Belle Group

12 Prunus x blireana

Ornamental plum

Slightly fragrant, pink semi-double flowers cover the branches of this deciduous shrub or small tree in early and mid-spring. Copper-purple leaves begin to open before flowering finishes. Hardy.
Height and spread: 4m (12ft)
Site: Sun. Moist but well-drained soil
Use: Canopy in border, specimen shrub or tree
Good companions: *Brunnera macrophylla, Tiarella cordifolia, Vinca minor* 'La Grave'

pink and mauve (continued)

1 Prunus cerasifera 'Pissardii'

Cherry plum, Myrobalan, Purple-leaved plum

In early and mid-spring the twiggy stems of this bushy deciduous tree are crowded with pink buds that open to almost white single flowers. The rich red young foliage turns purplish in summer. Edible purple fruits are only rarely produced. Hardy.

Height and spread: 8m (25ft)
Site: Sun. Moist but well-drained soil
Use: Canopy in border, hedge, specimen tree
Good companions: *Anemone* x *hybrida* 'Honorine Jobert', *Fuchsia magellanica* 'Versicolor', *Geranium clarkei* x *collinum* 'Kashmir White'

2 Prunus dulcis

Common almond

This deciduous tree has finely tapered toothed leaves and spreads as it matures. In early spring the naked branches are covered with pink flowers. Velvety green fruits, which contain an edible nut, are freely produced in a warm climate only. Hardy.

Height and spread: 8m (25ft)
Site: Sun. Moist but well-drained soil
Use: Canopy in border, specimen tree
Good companions: *Anemone blanda*, *Colchicum* 'Rosy Dawn', *Colchicum speciosum* 'Album'

3 Prunus mume 'Beni-chidori'

Japanese apricot

Deciduous tree or shrub suitable for training against a wall, preferably warm and sheltered. In late winter and early spring the bare branches carry numerous crimson-pink, sweetly scented, single flowers. Edible fruits are only rarely produced in a cool temperate climate. Hardy.

General care: Delay pruning of wall-trained specimens until midsummer.
Height and spread: 8m (25ft)
Site: Sun. Moist but well-drained soil
Use: Canopy in border, specimen tree or shrub, wall
Good companions: *Abeliophyllum distichum*, *Nerine bowdenii*, *Primula auricula* 'Blue Velvet'

4 Prunus 'Pandora'

Ornamental cherry

This deciduous tree has ascending branches when young, but later becomes more spreading in growth. Specimens are covered with pale pink blossom in early spring, before the leaves appear. The foliage is bronze at first then green, and usually colours bright orange and red in autumn. Hardy.

Height: 9m (30ft) **Spread:** 8m (25ft)
Site: Sun. Moist but well-drained soil
Use: Canopy in border, specimen tree
Good companions: *Anemone blanda*, *Crocus vernus* 'Jeanne d'Arc', *Crocus vernus* 'Purpureus Grandiflorus'

5 Prunus triloba 'Multiplex'

Flowering almond

Deciduous shrub suitable for training against a wall, preferably warm and sheltered. Well-pruned plants will produce masses of clear pink double flowers in early to mid-spring. Hardy.

General care: As soon as flowering is over, cut all flowered shoots hard back.
Height and spread: 3m (10ft)
Site: Sun. Moist but well-drained soil
Use: Border, wall
Good companions: *Anemone coronaria* De Caen Group, *Hyacinthus orientalis* 'Carnegie', *Tulipa* 'Estella Rijnveld'

6 Rhododendron 'Anna Baldsiefen'

The foliage of this small evergreen shrub is light green in summer and bronze-red in winter. The vivid pink funnel-shaped flowers have wavy margins and are densely clustered. Hardy.

Height and spread: 1m (3ft)
Site: Partial shade. Lime-free, humus-rich and moist but well-drained soil
Compost: Soil-based (ericaceous)
Use: Border, container, woodland garden
Good companions: *Acer grosseri* var. *hersii*, *Magnolia* x *loebneri* 'Leonard Messel', *Rhododendron williamsianum*

7 Rhododendron ciliatum

This compact, domed evergreen shrub produces clusters of two to four nodding bell-shaped flowers that are scented and light pink. The dark green leaves are lighter underneath and have hairy margins. Hardy.

Height and spread: 2m (6ft)

Site: Partial shade. Lime-free, humus-rich and moist but well-drained soil

Use: Border, woodland garden

Good companions: *Fothergilla major* Monticola Group, *Halesia carolina, Rhododendron* 'Loder's White'

8 Rhododendron 'Cilpinense'

This evergreen hybrid makes a rounded bush of small dark green leaves with bristly margins. The many trusses of dark pink buds open to paler funnel-shaped flowers. Hardy.

General care: To protect flowers from frost damage, plant where there is overhead cover.

Height and spread: 1.2m (4ft)

Site: Partial shade. Lime-free, humus-rich and moist but well-drained soil

Compost: Soil-based (ericaceous)

Use: Border, container, woodland garden

Good companions: *Cornus kousa* var. *chinensis* 'Satomi', *Davidia involucrata, Magnolia campbellii* subsp. *mollicomata,*

9 Rhododendron 'Razorbill'

The deep pink, upward-facing tubular flowers of this compact evergreen shrub are borne in dense clusters. The small crinkled leaves are dark green. Hardy.

Height and spread: 1.2m (4ft)

Site: Partial shade. Lime-free, humus-rich and moist but well-drained soil

Compost: Soil-based (ericaceous)

Use: Border, container, woodland garden

Good companions: *Acer japonicum* 'Vitifolium', *Kalmia latifolia* 'Ostbo Red', *Rhododendron* 'Vanessa Pastel'

10 Rhododendron Temple Belle Group

Evergreen shrub with rounded pale green leaves that are attractive all year round. The nodding bell-shaped flowers, which are carried profusely in loose clusters, are a soft uniform mid-pink. Hardy.

Height and spread: 2m (6ft)

Site: Partial shade. Lime-free, humus-rich and moist but well-drained soil

Use: Border, woodland garden

Good companions: *Camellia* 'Cornish Snow', *Eucryphia* x *nymansensis* 'Nymansay', *Styrax japonicus*

11 Rhododendron williamsianum

The small heart or kidney-shaped leaves of this evergreen shrub are bright green with a blue-grey underside when mature, but bronze on opening. Red buds, borne singly or in small clusters, open to wide bells that age to pale pink. Hardy.

General care: To protect flowers from frost damage, plant where there is overhead cover.

Height: 1.5m (5ft) **Spread:** 1.2m (4ft)

Site: Sun, partial shade.

Use: Border, woodland garden

Good companions: *Magnolia denudata, Rhododendron* 'Palestrina', *Rhododendron* 'Penheale Blue'

12 Viburnum tinus 'Eve Price'

Laurustinus

Winter and spring-flowering evergreen shrub of dense growth. Ornamental heads of brown-pink buds open to pink-tinged white flowers. This form has relatively small leaves, 8cm (3in) long. Hardy.

General care: Trim or hard prune in spring only if required.

Height and spread: 2.5m (8ft)

Site: Sun, partial shade. Moist but well-drained soil

Compost: Soil-based (John Innes No. 3)

Use: Container, border, informal hedge, topiary

Good companions: *Helleborus argutifolius, Lonicera* x *purpusii* 'Winter Beauty', *Prunus lusitanica*

7

8

9

10

11

12

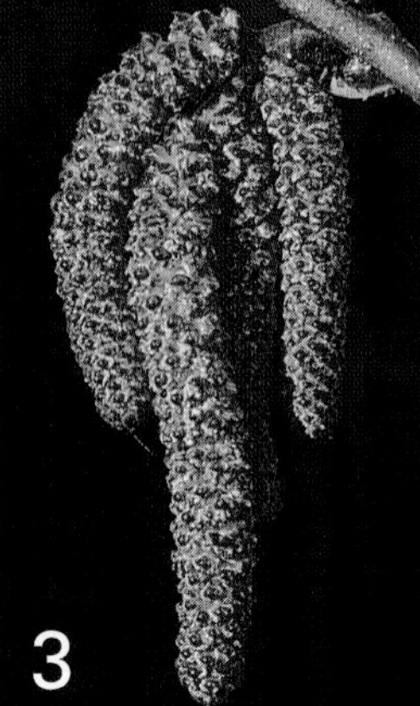

red and russet

1 Aucuba japonica 'Rozannie'
Spotted laurel

This is a plain-leaved cultivar of an evergreen shrub best known for its variegated forms. Small green flowers in early to mid-spring usually go unnoticed, but this self-pollinating cultivar produces a good crop of red berries in autumn that often persist until the following spring. All parts inedible. Hardy.

Height: 1.2m (4ft) **Spread:** 1m (3ft)
Site: Partial shade, sun, shade.
Compost: Soil-based (John Innes No. 3)
Use: Border, container, underplanting for trees
Good companions: *Geranium macrorrhizum* 'Ingwersen's Variety', *Geranium phaeum*, *Helleborus foetidus*

2 Chaenomeles x superba 'Nicoline'
Flowering quince, Japanese quince, Japonica

Spiny deciduous shrub that makes a somewhat tangled spreading bush, but flowers over a long period. The first of the semi-double scarlet cups open in clusters on bare stems. Hardy.

General care: Prune immediately after flowering, on wall-trained specimens cutting back flowered shoots to within three or four buds of a permanent framework of branches.
Height: 1.5m (5ft) **Spread:** 2m (6ft)
Site: Sun, partial shade
Use: Sunny or lightly shaded border, wall
Good companions: *Polemonium* 'Lambrook Mauve', *Tulipa* 'Peach Blossom', *Tulipa* 'Purissima'

3 Corylus maxima 'Purpurea'
Filbert

In late winter or early spring the naked branches of this deciduous large shrub are adorned with dangling purplish catkins that are tinged with pale yellow. From spring to autumn the very rich purple, heart-shaped leaves make a strong impact. The husks surrounding the edible nuts, which ripen in autumn, are also purplish. Hardy.

General care: To produce large leaves, cut stems back to near ground level in early spring and feed and mulch generously.
Height: 6m (20ft) **Spread:** 5m (15ft)
Site: Sun, partial shade. Well-drained soil. Good on chalk
Use: Canopy in border, specimen shrub
Good companions: *Euonymus alatus* 'Compactus', *Narcissus* 'Jack Snipe', *Sorbus sargentiana*

4 Pieris formosa var. forestii 'Wakehurst'

Evergreen shrub with eye-catching young growths that are brilliant scarlet then change to pink and cream before turning green. Although the buds are formed in the preceding autumn, the white flowers, which hang in sprays, do not open until the second half of spring. Not fully hardy.

Height: 4m (12ft) **Spread:** 5m (15ft)
Site: Sun, partial shade. Lime-free, humus-rich and moist but well-drained soil
Use: Border, heather garden, woodland garden
Good companions: *Hamamelis* x *intermedia* 'Diane', *Pieris japonica* 'Blush', *Rhododendron macabeanum*

5 Rhododendron Humming Bird Group

Compact, domed evergreen shrub with glossy round leaves. The nodding bell-shaped flowers have a waxy texture and are bright red with a scarlet glow inside. Hardy.

Height and spread: 1.5m (5ft)
Site: Partial shade. Lime-free, humus-rich and moist but well-drained soil
Compost: Soil-based (ericaceous)
Use: Border, container, woodland garden
Good companions: *Camellia* x *williamsii* 'Francis Hanger', *Rhododendron* 'Bow Bells', *Rhododendron williamsianum*

6 Ribes sanguineum 'Pulborough Scarlet'

Flowering currant

By mid-spring this upright deciduous shrub is usually well covered with numerous drooping sprays of small red flowers. Later the flower sprays are more upright. Despite the somewhat pungent smell, this is a vigorous and easy shrub of great value. Inedible dark berries are occasionally produced. Hardy.

General care: In late spring trim hedges. On free-standing specimens cut back flowered shoots and remove about a quarter of old stems.

Height: 2.5m (8ft) **Spread:** 2m (6ft)

Site: Sun. Well-drained soil

Use: Border, informal hedge

Good companions: *Cercis siliquastrum, Osmanthus* x *burkwoodii, Syringa vulgaris* 'Madame Lemoine'

7

8

9

7 Ribes speciosum

Fuchsia-flowered currant

The stems of this upright deciduous shrub are covered with red bristles. The rich red flowers, which dangle in little clusters, are usually open before mid-spring. Not fully hardy.

General care: In cold areas, worth training against a warm wall. In late spring cut back flowered shoots to within three or four buds of a permanent framework.

Height and spread: 2m (6ft)

Site: Sun. Well-drained soil

Use: Border, wall

Good companions: *Garrya elliptica* 'James Roof', *Iris unguicularis, Nerine bowdenii*

10

11

yellow and orange

8 Aucuba japonica 'Variegata'

Spotted laurel

Rounded evergreen shrub with glossy yellow-speckled leaves that are sparsely toothed. The colour is best in full sun. If there is a male plant nearby, this female cultivar bears good crops of berries that ripen red in autumn and usually last until the following spring. All parts are likely to cause a stomach upset if ingested. Hardy.

Height and spread: 3m (10ft)

Site: Partial shade, sun, shade.

Compost: Soil-based (John Innes No. 3)

Use: Border, container, underplanting for trees

Good companions: *Aucuba japonica* 'Rozannie', *Forsythia* x *intermedia* 'Lynwood', *Syringa vulgaris* 'Katherine Havemeyer'

9 Azara microphylla

Sprays of small dark green leaves make this evergreen small tree or large shrub a good foliage plant. In late winter and early spring fragrant, tiny, yellow petal-less flowers are clustered on the underside of shoots. Hardy.

General care: In late spring cut back flowered shoots of wall-trained specimens to within three or four buds of a permanent framework of branches.

Height: 8m (25ft) **Spread:** 4m (12ft)

Site: Sun, partial shade. Humus-rich and moist but well-drained soil

Use: Border, wall, woodland garden

Good companions: *Cornus alba* 'Elegantissima', *Cornus mas, Fuchsia magellanica* 'Riccartonii'

10 Berberis buxifolia

Evergreen or semi-evergreen shrub with dark green spine-tipped leaves that are grey on the underside. By mid-spring the arching stems carry numerous orange-yellow flowers, which hang singly or in pairs on long stems and are followed by inedible dark purple fruits. The more compact 'Pygmaea' grows to about 1m (3ft). Hardy.

General care: If required, trim after flowering.

Height: 2.5m (8ft) **Spread:** 3m (10ft)

Site: Sun, partial shade. Well-drained soil

Use: Border, informal hedge

Good companions: *Buddleja* 'Lochinch', *Caryopteris* x *clandonensis* 'Heavenly Blue', *Cotoneaster salicifolius* 'Rothschildianus'

11 Corylopsis pauciflora

Before coming into leaf this twiggy deciduous shrub bears short tassels of slightly fragrant pale yellow flowers that hang stiffly from the stems. The leaves open bronze-pink then turn bright green. Hardy.

Height: 1.5m (5ft) **Spread:** 2.5m (8ft)

Site: Partial shade. Lime-free, humus-rich and moist but well-drained soil

Use: Border, woodland garden

Good companions: *Hamamelis* x *intermedia* 'Arnold Promise', *Kirengeshoma palmata, Magnolia* 'Elizabeth'

yellow and orange (continued)

1 Corylopsis sinensis 'Spring Purple'

The sweetly scented, soft yellow flower tassels of this deciduous shrub are up to 10cm (4in) long. The young foliage is deep purple. Hardy.

Height: 3m (10ft) **Spread:** 2.5m (8ft)

Site: Partial shade. Humus-rich and moist but well-drained soil, preferably lime-free

Use: Border, woodland garden

Good companions: *Acer griseum*, *Cercidiphyllum japonicum*, *Leucothoe* Scarletta

2 Corylus avellana 'Aurea'

Hazel

This deciduous shrub is an ornamental rather than a nut-bearing form of the hazel. The drooping male catkins in late winter and early spring are pale yellow; the soft yellow leaves that follow create a more lasting effect. Hardy.

General care: For large leaves cut stems back annually to near base and feed generously.

Height and spread: 4m (12ft)

Site: Sun, partial shade. Well-drained soil. Good on chalk

Use: Border

Good companions: *Corylus maxima* 'Purpurea', *Euonymus alatus* 'Compactus', *Euonymus europaeus* 'Red Cascade'

3 Forsythia 'Beatrix Farrand'

Dense deciduous shrub with upright then arching stems that are covered in spring by numerous bright yellow nodding flowers. These are unusually large for a forsythia. Hardy.

General care: In late spring trim hedges. On free-standing shrubs cut back flowered shoots and cut to the base about a quarter of old stems.

Height and spread: 2m (6ft)

Site: Sun, partial shade. Moist but well-drained soil

Use: Border, hedge

Good companions: *Ceratostigma willmottianum*, *Fuchsia magellanica* 'Riccartonii', *Viburnum opulus* 'Compactum'

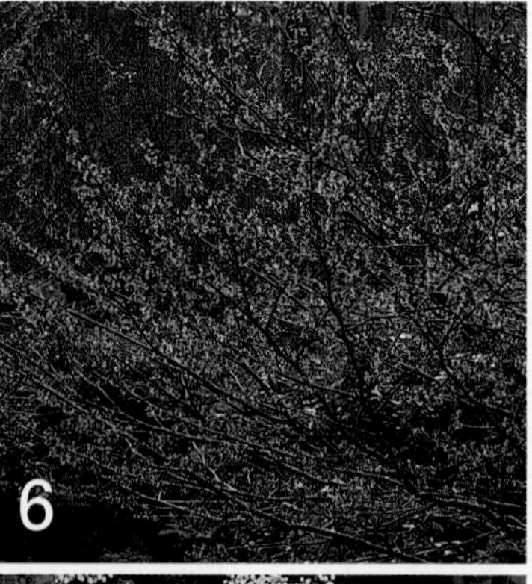

4 Forsythia x intermedia 'Lynwood'

This easy and reliable deciduous shrub is a tangle of branches that carry masses of deep yellow flowers before the leaves appear. Excellent for cutting as flowers will open indoors if stems are gathered while in bud. Hardy.

General care: In late spring trim hedges. On free-standing shrubs cut back flowered shoots and cut to the base about a quarter of old stems.

Height and spread: 3m (10ft)

Site: Sun, partial shade. Moist but well-drained soil

Use: Border, hedge

Good companions: *Hibiscus syriacus* 'Woodbridge', *Rosa* 'Geranium', *Rosa glauca*

5 Forsythia suspensa

Golden bell

Slender-stemmed deciduous shrub that is suitable for training against a wall. Small clusters of yellow starry flowers open on leafless stems in early to mid-spring.

General care: In late spring cut back flowered shoots and cut to the base about a quarter of old stems.

Height and spread: 3m (10ft)

Site: Sun, partial shade. Moist but well-drained soil

Use: Border, wall

Good companions: *Clematis* 'Bill MacKenzie', *Clematis* 'Gipsy Queen', *Rosa* 'Veilchenblau'

6 Hamamelis vernalis 'Sandra'

Ozark witch hazel

In late winter or early spring the bare stems of this deciduous shrub are set with many small, scented, clear yellow flowers. The young leaves that follow open purple then turn green, but retain a purplish colour on the underside. The foliage is brilliantly coloured in autumn. Hardy.

Height: 5m (15ft) **Spread:** 4m (12ft)

Site: Moist but well-drained soil

Use: Canopy in border, woodland garden

Good companions: *Corylopsis pauciflora, Rhododendron luteum, Rhododendron macabeanum*

7 Mahonia aquifolium 'Apollo'

Oregon grape

Compact form of a suckering evergreen shrub with leaves that open copper-tan then turn green and in winter are bronze-purple. Small yellow flowers are borne in dense clusters at the ends of stems in early spring and are followed by blue-black grape-like berries that can be used to make preserves. Hardy.

Height: 60cm (2ft) **Spread:** 1m (3ft)

Site: Partial shade, shade. Humus-rich and moist but well-drained soil

Use: Border, ground cover, woodland garden

Good companions: *Prunus laurocerasus* 'Otto Luyken', *Prunus lusitanica, Viburnum tinus* 'Gwenllian'

8 Ostrya carpinifolia

Hop hornbeam

By mid-spring this round-headed deciduous tree is decorated with dangling yellow male catkins. The fruit clusters that follow are hop-like and white. The toothed leaves are glossy dark green in summer, but turn yellow in autumn. Hardy.

Height and spread: 20m (65ft)

Site: Sun, partial shade. Well-drained soil

Use: Specimen tree, woodland garden

Good companions: *Cyclamen hederifolium, Helleborus hybridus, Polygonatum* x *hybridum*

9 Rhododendron 'Patty Bee'

Compact, rounded evergreen shrub with dark green leaves that become bronzed in winter. Pale yellow funnel-shaped flowers are borne very freely in the first half of spring. Hardy.

Height and spread: 75cm (2ft 6in)

Site: Sun, partial shade.

Compost: Soil-based (ericaceous)

Use: Border, container

Good companions: *Enkianthus campanulatus, Rhododendron* Blue Tit Group, *Rhododendron luteum*

10 Ribes odoratum

Buffalo currant

The yellow flowers of this deciduous shrub are produced in small, slightly drooping sprays. Usually open by mid-spring, they have a delicious and spicy scent. The bright green lobed leaves colour richly in autumn. Hardy.

General care: In late spring cut back flowered shoots and remove about a quarter of old stems.

Height and spread: 2m (6ft)

Site: Sun. Well-drained soil

Use: Border

Good companions: *Geranium* 'Johnson's Blue', *Geranium wallichianum* 'Buxton's Blue', *Rosa xanthina* 'Canary Bird'

11 Salix caprea 'Kilmarnock'

Kilmarnock willow

The branches of this small male tree hang down stiffly like the spokes of an umbrella. In late winter or early spring, silver catkins, yellowed by developing anthers, appear before the leaves open. Plants are grafted, so height varies. Hardy.

Height and spread: 2m (6ft)

Site: Sun. Moist but well-drained soil

Compost: Soil-based (John Innes No. 3)

Use: Border, container, specimen tree

Good companions: *Euphorbia polychroma, Geum rivale* 'Leonard's Variety', *Iris sibirica* 'Ego'

cream and white

12 Chaenomeles speciosa 'Nivalis'

Flowering quince, Japanese quince

The tangled branches of this spiny deciduous shrub are spangled with pure white cupped flowers over a long season, from late winter until late spring. Aromatic yellow-green fruits, often used in preserves, may follow. Hardy.

General care: Prune immediately after flowering, on wall-trained specimens cutting back flowered shoots to within three or four buds of a permanent framework of branches.

Height: 2.5m (8ft) **Spread:** 4m (12ft)

Site: Sun, partial shade. Well-drained soil

Compost: Sunny or lightly shaded border, wall

Use: Border, wall

Good companions: *Paeonia lactiflora* 'White Wings', *Tulipa clusiana, Tulipa* 'Spring Green'

cream and white (continued)

1 Daphne blagayana

Low evergreen or semi-green shrub with trailing stems and leathery oval leaves. The strongly scented milk-white flowers are gathered in clusters of up to 30 at the end of stems. Hardy.

Height: 40cm (16in) **Spread:** 1m (3ft)
Site: Partial shade. Humus-rich and moist but well-drained soil
Use: Border, underplanting for shrubs and trees
Good companions: *Aquilegia vulgaris* 'Nivea', *Erythronium dens-canis, Helleborus niger*

2 Erica x darleyensis 'Silberschmelze'

Darley dale heath

Like other darley dale heaths, this bushy evergreen tolerates lime and flowers over a long season. The scented white flowers are borne from winter and through spring. The foliage is deep green in summer but tinged red in winter, and in spring there is a hint of cream at the tips. Hardy.

Height: 40cm (16in) **Spread:** 75cm (2ft 6in)
Site: Sun. Well-drained soil
Compost: Soil-based, preferably lime-free (ericaceous)
Use: Container, ground cover, heather garden, raised bed, rock garden
Good companions: *Erica* x *darleyensis* 'Kramer's Rote', *Erica vagans* 'Mrs D.F. Maxwell', *Juniperus virginiana* 'Grey Owl'

3 Griselinia littoralis 'Variegata'

Broadleaf

This evergreen large shrub makes an attractive windbreak or foliage plant in seaside gardens. It has glossy leathery leaves that are bright green streaked with grey-green and have creamy white margins. Not fully hardy.

General care: If necessary, trim lightly in late spring.
Height: 3m (10ft) **Spread:** 2m (6ft)
Site: Sun. Well-drained soil
Use: Border, informal hedge
Good companions: *Buddleja davidii* 'Black Knight', *Escallonia* 'Apple Blossom', *Rosa* 'Blanche Double de Coubert'

4 Lonicera fragrantissima

Honeysuckle

Partially evergreen shrub that makes a spreading red-stemmed bush, with dark green leaves that are blue-green underneath. In late winter and early spring, creamy white tubular flowers make little impact visually, but their scent is delicious. Dull red berries follow. Hardy.

General care:
Immediately after flowering cut out up to a quarter of old stems and cut back remaining stems that have flowered to a strong bud.
Height: 2m (6ft) **Spread:** 3m (10ft)
Site: Sun, partial shade. Well-drained soil
Use: Border
Good companions: *Buddleja alternifolia, Ceanothus* x *delileanus* 'Topaze', *Perovskia* 'Blue Spire'

5 Magnolia salicifolia

Willow-leaved magnolia

The fragrant, pure white starry flowers of this deciduous tree are up to 10cm (4in) across and open by mid-spring, before the foliage breaks. The lance-shaped leaves are dull green with a grey underside and are lemon scented when bruised. Usually starts flowering when young. Hardy.

Height: 9m (30ft) **Spread:** 6m (20ft)
Site: Sun, partial shade. Moist but well-drained soil, preferably lime-free
Use: Canopy in border, specimen tree, woodland garden
Good companions: *Clerodendrum trichotomum* var. *fargesii, Hydrangea aspera* Villosa Group, *Hydrangea macrophylla* 'Madame Emile Mouillère'

6 Magnolia stellata

Star magnolia

Slow-growing, compact deciduous shrub that spreads with age. Beautiful grey-green buds open to starry white flowers with up to 15 petals. Many cultivars with blush or pink flowers. Hardy.

Height: 3m (10ft) **Spread:** 4m (12ft)

Site: Sun, partial shade. Moist but well-drained soil

Use: Border, specimen shrub

Good companions: *Narcissus* 'Jack Snipe', *Scilla siberica* 'Spring Beauty', *Tulipa* 'Purissima'

7 Osmanthus x burkwoodii

Rounded, slow-growing evergreen shrub with glossy toothed leaves. By mid-spring there are small sprays of sweetly scented, white tubular flowers. Hardy.

General care: Trim hedges in late spring.

Height and spread: 3m (10ft)

Site: Sun, partial shade. Well-drained soil, preferably moist

Use: Border, hedge, topiary

Good companions: *Cornus alternifolia* 'Argentea', *Sarcococca hookeriana* var. *digyna*, *Viburnum tinus* 'Gwenllian'

8 Pieris floribunda

Fetter bush

In winter upright sprays of greenish white buds, borne at the tips of shoots, stand out against the dark green foliage of this rounded evergreen shrub. They open to small, white urn-shaped flowers. Hardy.

Height: 2m (6ft) **Spread:** 3m (10ft)

Site: Sun, partial shade. Lime-free, humus-rich and moist but well-drained soil

Use: Border, heather garden, woodland garden

Good companions: *Cornus controversa* 'Variegata', *Magnolia stellata*, *Rhododendron* 'Loder's White'

9 Pieris japonica 'Debutante'

Compact low-growing cultivar of a popular evergreen shrub for acid soils. The flower sprays are upright, but the individual white urn-shaped flowers dangle. Hardy.

Height and spread: 1m (3ft)

Site: Sun, partial shade. Lime-free, humus-rich and moist but well-drained soil

Use: Border, heather garden, woodland garden

Good companions: *Gaultheria mucronata* 'Wintertime', *Kalmia latifolia* 'Ostbo Red', *Pieris floribunda*

10 Prunus 'Taihaku'

Great white cherry

Vigorous deciduous tree that is dazzling in mid-spring when it is massed with large white single flowers. The leaves are copper-red when they unfurl, but become dark green as they age. Hardy.

Height: 8m (25ft) **Spread:** 9m (30ft)

Site: Sun, partial shade. Moist but well-drained soil

Use: Canopy in border, specimen tree

Good companions: *Crocus vernus* 'Jeanne d'Arc', *Crocus vernus* 'Pickwick', *Crocus vernus* 'Remembrance'

11 Prunus x yedoensis

Yoshino cherry

The arching branches of this deciduous tree carry masses of pale pink blossom before the leaves appear. The scented single flowers are carried in clusters of five or six. They remain pink in the centre, but age to near white. The foliage in summer is dark green. Hardy.

Height: 12m (40ft) **Spread:** 9m (30ft)

Site: Sun. Moist but well-drained soil

Use: Canopy in border, specimen tree

Good companions: *Colchicum* 'The Giant', *Crocus speciosus*, *Narcissus* 'Dove Wings'

12 Pyrus calleryana 'Chanticleer'

Narrowly upright deciduous tree with thorny branches and glossy leaves that turn red in late autumn. The single white flowers are borne in profusion and usually coincide with the development of the young leaves. They are followed by inedible small brown fruits. Hardy.

Height: 6m (20ft) **Spread:** 5m (15ft)

Site: Sun. Well-drained soil

Use: Avenue, border, specimen tree

Good companions: *Buddleja alternifolia*, *Crataegus persimilis* 'Prunifolia', *Malus* 'John Downie'

7

8

9

10

11

12

cream and white (continued)

1 Rhododendron 'Snow Lady'

Mound-shaped evergreen shrub with somewhat bristly leaves. Scented, pure white funnel-shaped flowers are borne in somewhat loose clusters of two to five. Hardy.

Height and spread: 1m (3ft)

Site: Sun. Lime-free, humus-rich and moist but well-drained soil

Compost: Soil-based (ericaceous)

Use: Border, container, rock garden

Good companions: *Gaultheria mucronata* 'Wintertime', *Rhododendron moupinense*, *Rhododendron* 'Penheale Blue'

2 Skimmia x confusa 'Kew Green'

Compact evergreen shrub that forms a dome of dark green glossy leaves. It is a male form and bears dense heads of scented, creamy white flowers. Old plants may exceed the dimensions given. Hardy.

Height: 2m (6ft) **Spread:** 1.5m (5ft)

Site: Partial shade, sun. Humus-rich, moist but well-drained soil

Use: Shady border, woodland garden

Good companions: *Aucuba japonica* 'Rozannie', *Lonicera* x *purpusii* 'Winter Beauty', *Prunus* 'Taihaku'

3 Spiraea thunbergii

The wiry stems and twigs of this spreading, usually deciduous shrub are covered with a 'snow' of small flowers in early to mid-spring, sometimes with an earlier flurry. The small, bright green narrow leaves turn orange-brown in autumn. Hardy.

General care: In late spring trim hedges. On free-standing specimens cut back flowered shoots and cut to the base up to a quarter of old stems.

Height: 1.5m (5ft) **Spread:** 2m (6ft)

Site: Sun. Moist but well-drained soil

Use: Border, informal hedge

Good companions: *Anemone hupehensis* 'Hadspen Abundance', *Tradescantia* Andersoniana Group 'Osprey', *Viburnum farreri*

4 Viburnum x burkwoodii 'Anne Russell'

Compact semi-evergreen shrub with heads of sweetly scented, waxy tubular flowers that are pink in bud but open white. The blooms last well on the plant, but not when cut. Hardy.

Height: 2m (6ft) **Spread:** 1.5m (5ft)

Site: Sun, partial shade. Moist but well-drained soil

Use: Border

Good companions: *Daphne bholua* 'Jacqueline Postill', *Ilex crenata* 'Convexa', *Prunus* 'Pandora'

5 Viburnum farreri

Deciduous shrub initially of upright growth, but upper parts of mature stems arch out. It is winter flowering, but usually starts in late autumn and continues into early spring. The small, strongly scented tubular flowers are white, sometimes tinged pink, and carried in clusters. Hardy.

Height: 3m (10ft)

Spread: 2.5m (8ft)

Site: Sun, partial shade. Moist but well-drained soil

Use: Border, woodland garden

Good companions: *Aconitum* 'Ivorine', *Cornus kousa* var. *chinensis* 'Satomi', *Fuchsia magellanica* 'Versicolor'

6 Viburnum x juddii

Bushy deciduous shrub that bears sprays of sweetly scented, white tubular flowers that open from pink buds. Usually in flower by mid-spring and may continue into early summer. Hardy.

Height: 1.2m (4ft) **Spread:** 1.5m (5ft)

Site: Sun, partial shade. Moist but well-drained soil

Use: Border

Good companions: *Geranium* x *magnificum*, *Kolkwitzia amabilis* 'Pink Cloud', *Rosa* Mary Rose

silver and grey

7 Juniperus virginiana 'Grey Owl'

Evergreen conifer with almost horizontal branches that spread to make a wide shrub. The foliage is soft grey-green. Hardy.

Height: 2.5m (8ft) **Spread:** 4m (12ft)

Site: Sun. Well-drained soil

Use: Border, heather garden, sunny bank

Good companions: *Artemisia arborescens*, *Buddleja* 'Lochinch', *Cistus ladanifer*

8 Salix hastata 'Wehrhahnii'

Slow-growing deciduous shrub with dark purplish stems thickly set with silver-grey male catkins that turn yellow well before the bright green leaves develop. Hardy.

Height and spread: 1m (3ft)

Site: Sun. Moist but well-drained soil

Use: Border, waterside

Good companions: *Cornus alba* 'Kesselringii', *Salix gracilistyla* 'Melanostachys', *Salix irrorata*

9 Salix helvetica

Swiss willow

Bushy deciduous shrub with rounded silver-grey catkins that open from gold-brown buds at the same time as the leaves emerge. It is a good foliage plant, with grey-green leaves that are white on the underside.

Height: 60cm (2ft) **Spread:** 45cm (18in)

Site: Sun. Moist but well-drained soil

Use: Border, rock garden, waterside

Good companions: *Daphne cneorum* 'Eximia', *Hebe cupressoides*, *Saxifraga* 'Peter Pan'

green

10 Chamaecyparis lawsoniana 'Green Hedger'

Lawson cypress

The lawson cypress, a vigorous evergreen conifer that bears small cones, has numerous cultivars, including large trees and dwarf shrubs. 'Green Hedger' makes a dense conical tree and has bright green foliage. Hardy.

General care: Trim hedges between late spring and early autumn.

Height: 18m (60ft) **Spread:** 5m (15ft)

Site: Sun. Well-drained soil, preferably moist and lime-free

Use: Hedge, specimen tree, windbreak

Good companions: *Acer cappadocicum* 'Aureum', *Nyssa sylvatica*, *Quercus coccinea* 'Splendens'

11 Taxus baccata

Yew

Evergreen slow-growing conifer that makes a large shrub or broad tree. The spreading branches are covered with scaly red-brown bark and the short linear leaves are very dark green, yellow-green on the underside. In autumn female plants carry seeds with a bright red fleshy covering (aril), the only part of the plant that is not poisonous. Yew is an outstanding hedging plant and suitable for large-scale topiary. Do not use as a hedge next to grazing land. Mature free-growing specimens may exceed the dimensions given. Hardy.

General care: Trim hedges and topiary specimens in summer or early autumn.

Height: 9m (30ft) **Spread:** 8m (25ft)

Site: Sun, shade. Fertile well-drained soil

Use: Hedge, specimen shrub or tree, topiary

Good companions: *Anemone* x *hybrida* 'Honorine Jobert', *Aster pringlei* 'Monte Cassino', *Rosa* 'Nevada'

12 Taxus x media 'Hicksii'

Evergreen conifer of which one parent is the common yew (see 11, above). This clone makes a large dark shrub of somewhat open conical shape. Hardy.

General care: Trim hedges in summer and early autumn.

Height: 6m (20ft) **Spread:** 2.5m (8ft)

Site: Sun, partial shade. Fertile, well-drained soil

Use: Hedge, specimen shrub

Good companions: *Crataegus persimilis* 'Prunifolia', *Ginkgo biloba*, *Prunus* x *subhirtella* 'Autumnalis'

camellias

Plant these free-flowering evergreen shrubs in shady borders and woodland gardens in humus-rich and moist but well-drained soil, or in containers filled with soil-based (ericaceous) compost. Although all these are hardy, it is wise to position them under a canopy of trees or against a wall to avoid exposure to early morning sun, as rapid thawing of frost may spoil the delicate blooms.

1 **Camellia japonica 'Lavinia Maggi'**
Spreading dark-foliaged shrub. Double white flowers with random pink and red splashes and no visible stamens.
Height and spread: 5m (15ft)
Good companions: *Acer griseum, Rhododendron moupinense, Rhododendron mucronulatum*

2 **Camellia 'Leonard Messel'**
Hybrid with dark green matt leaves and sumptuous, clear pink semi-double flowers.
Height: 4m (12ft) **Spread:** 3m (10ft)
Good companions: *Camellia* x *williamsii* 'Saint Ewe', *Cercidiphyllum japonicum, Magnolia denudata*

3 **Camellia x williamsii 'Francis Hanger'**
Free-flowering hybrid with wavy leaves and pure white single flowers with golden stamens. Drops its spent blooms.
Height: 5m (15ft) **Spread:** 3m (10ft)
Good companions: *Halesia carolina, Kalmia latifolia* 'Ostbo Red', *Smilacina racemosa*

4 **Camellia japonica 'Jupiter'**
Common camellia
Dark-foliaged upright shrub that bears numerous bright scarlet, single to semi-double flowers filled with a conspicuous bunch of golden stamens.
Height: 5m (15ft) **Spread:** 3m (10ft)
Good companions: *Gaultheria mucronata* 'Bell's Seedling', *Pieris floribunda, Rhododendron* 'Penheale Blue'

5 **Camellia japonica 'Bob's Tinsie'**
Common camellia
Dark-foliaged shrub. Small, red anemone-form flowers with conspicuous pink centre.
Height: 2m (6ft) **Spread:** 1m (3ft)
Good companions: *Camellia* 'Cornish Snow', *Gaultheria mucronata* 'Wintertime', *Leucothoe* Scarletta

6 **Camellia x williamsii 'Donation'**
Outstanding, very free-flowering upright hybrid. Large, bright pink semi-double flowers with darker veining. Drops its spent blooms.
Height: 5m (15ft) **Spread:** 3m (10ft)
Good companions: *Acer japonicum* 'Vitifolium', *Disanthus cercidifolius, Rhododendron* 'Loder's White'

7 **Camellia 'Freedom Bell'**
Compact dense shrub with toothed oval leaves that finish in a neat taper. Red semi-double flowers in late winter and early spring.
Height: 2.5m (8ft) **Spread:** 2m (6ft)
Good companions: *Camellia* x *williamsii* 'Saint Ewe', *Fothergilla major* Monticola Group, *Rhododendron* 'Cilpinense'

8 **Camellia x williamsii 'Saint Ewe'**
Free-flowering hybrid that makes a rounded shrub. Bright pink, cup-shaped single flowers.
Height: 4m (12ft) **Spread:** 3m (10ft)
Good companions: *Erythronium dens-canis, Primula* 'Guinevere', *Styrax japonicus*

alpines

Most small perennials and shrubs that thrive in well-drained conditions do not need a rock garden. They look good in a raised bed and many are suitable for containers or planted among paving. Plant in mild weather, between autumn and early spring.

purple, blue and violet

1 Aubrieta 'Doctor Mules'

Aubrietas produce evergreen mats of small greyish leaves. From early to late spring or even into early summer these are covered with four-petalled flowers in shades of pink, red or purple. 'Doctor Mules' is violet-purple. All are attractive trailing from retaining walls or the ledges of rock gardens. Hardy.

General care: To keep plants compact, trim after flowering in early summer.

Height: 5cm (2in) **Spread:** 60–75cm (2–2ft 6in)

Site: Sun. Well-drained soil. Good on lime

Use: Front of border, ground cover, paving, raised bed, rock garden, sunny bank

Good companions: *Aethionema* 'Warley Rose', *Arabis procurrens* 'Variegata', *Phlox subulata* 'McDaniel's Cushion'

2 Hepatica nobilis

Between late winter and mid-spring this slow-growing semi-evergreen perennial bears numerous upward or outward-facing flowers above a tuft of three-lobed leaves that are often mottled purple. The bowl-shaped flowers are usually purplish blue but can be pink, blue or white. Hardy.

Height: 10cm (4in) **Spread:** 15cm (6in)

Site: Partial shade, sun. Humus-rich and moist but well-drained soil. Good on lime

Use: Rock garden, woodland garden

Good companions: *Cyclamen coum*, *Galanthus* 'S. Arnott', *Saxifraga* 'Peter Pan'

3 Hepatica transsilvanica

The prettily scalloped three-lobed leaves of this semi-evergreen perennial are silvered by a fine down. Mauve-blue flowers are borne between late winter and late spring. Hardy.

Height: 15cm (6in) **Spread:** 20cm (8in)

Site: Partial shade, sun. Humus-rich and moist but well-drained soil. Good on lime

Use: Rock garden, woodland garden

Good companions: *Cyclamen hederifolium*, *Galanthus elwesii*, *Hepatica nobilis*

4 Primula x pubescens 'Mrs J.H. Wilson'

Crosses between *Primula auricula* and *P. hirsuta* produce rosettes of mealy grey-green leaves, above which stems bear several flowers in spring. The colour range extends from white and yellow to pink and purple, but the scented flowers of 'Mrs J.H. Wilson' are purple with a white eye. Hardy.

Height: 10cm (4in) **Spread:** 15cm (6in)

Site: Sun, partial shade. Humus-rich and moist but well-drained soil

Compost: Soil-based (John Innes No. 2) with added leaf-mould and grit

Use: Container, raised bed, rock garden

Good companions: *Adonis vernalis*, *Hepatica transsilvanica*, *Ramonda myconi*

5 Ramonda myconi

Evergreen perennial with dark green, corrugated hairy leaves. From mid to late spring it produces sprays of mauve-purple or violet flowers. Hardy.

General care: Best grown in a vertical crevice.

Height: 10cm (4in) **Spread:** 20cm (8in)

Site: Partial shade. Humus-rich and moist but well-drained soil. Good on lime

Compost: Soil-based (John Innes No. 2) with added leaf-mould and grit

Use: Container, dry wall, rock garden

Good companions: *Hepatica nobilis*, *Polygala chamaebuxus*, *Viola biflora*

6 Soldanella alpina

Alpine snowbell

Evergreen perennial with leathery leaves and mauve-purple bell-shaped flowers. Hardy.

General care: Surround the neck of the plant with a layer of grit and protect from wet in winter.

Height: 10cm (4in) **Spread:** 15–20cm (6–8in)

Site: Sun, partial shade. Humus-rich and moist but sharply drained soil

Compost: Soil-based (ericaceous) with added leaf-mould and grit

Use: Container, raised bed, rock garden

Good companions: *Crocus chrysanthus* 'Ladykiller', *Iris* 'Katharine Hodgkin', *Scilla mischtschenkoana*

purple, blue and violet
(continued)

1 Veronica peduncularis 'Georgia Blue'

Mat-forming evergreen perennial that often flowers through spring into summer. Short spikes of white-eyed blue flowers rise above creeping stems. Hardy.

Height: 10cm (4in) **Spread:** 60cm (2ft)
Site: Sun. Well-drained soil
Compost: Soil-based (John Innes No. 2) with added leaf-mould and grit
Use: Container, front of border, paving, raised bed, rock garden
Good companions: *Hebe cupressoides* 'Boughton Dome', *Leucojum vernum, Picea glauca* var. *albertiana* 'Conica'

pink and mauve

2 Primula clarkei

This miniature deciduous perennial flowers as the pale green, toothed leaves unfold. The flowers have deeply notched pink petals, but are pale yellow at the centre. Hardy.

Height: 5cm (2in) **Spread:** 15cm (6in)
Site: Partial shade. Moist but gritty well-drained soil
Compost: Soil-based (John Innes No. 2) with added leaf-mould and grit
Use: Container, raised bed, rock garden
Good companions: *Campanula carpatica, Polygola chamaebuxus, Primula nana*

3 Primula rosea

Deciduous perennial that flowers before the spoon-shaped toothed or scalloped leaves have fully developed. Up to 12 deep pink flowers with a yellow eye form a cluster at the top of each stem. Hardy.

Height: 15cm (6in) **Spread:** 20cm (8in)
Site: Partial shade. Lime-free, moist soil
Use: Bog garden, rock garden, waterside
Good companions: *Astilbe chinensis* var. *pumila, Hosta lancifolia, Leucojum vernum*

4 Saxifraga 'Cranbourne'
Kabschia saxifrage

The densely packed foliage of many Kabschia saxifrages is heavily encrusted with lime. The tight rosettes of this reliable hybrid are dark green and form a flat mat, over which are scattered almost stemless pink flowers. Hardy.

Height: 2–3cm (1in) **Spread:** 20cm (8in)
Site: Partial shade, sun. Alkaline and moist but gritty, sharply drained soil
Compost: Soil-based (John Innes No. 1) with added limestone chippings
Use: Container, raised bed, rock garden, trough
Good companions: *Saxifraga* 'Gloria', *Saxifraga* 'Gregor Mendel', *Saxifraga* 'Jenkinsiae'

5 Saxifraga 'Jenkinsiae'
Kabschia saxifrage

This fast-growing hybrid is one of the most reliable Kabschia saxifrages for outdoor rock gardens and raised beds. The pale pink flowers have a deep pink centre and are carried on stems above a mound of lime-encrusted rosettes. Hardy.

Height: 8cm (3in) **Spread:** 20cm (8in)
Site: Partial shade, sun. Alkaline and moist but gritty, sharply drained soil
Compost: Soil-based (John Innes No. 1) with added limestone chippings
Use: Container, raised bed, rock garden, trough
Good companions: *Crocus laevigata* 'Fontenayi', *Iris reticulata, Saxifraga* 'Gloria'

6 Saxifraga oppositifolia
Purple saxifrage

In the wild this evergreen perennial is found over an immense area and not surprisingly is variable. Plants in cultivation typically form creeping mats of dark green leaves that in spring are densely covered with stemless purple or pink flowers.

Height: 2–3cm (1in) **Spread:** 20–30cm (8–12in)
Site: Sun, partial shade. Moist but sharply drained soil
Compost: Soil-based (John Innes No. 1) with added leaf-mould and grit
Use: Container, raised bed, rock garden
Good companions: *Crocus laevigatus* 'Fontenayi', *Iris* 'J.S. Dijt', *Tulipa humilis* Violacea Group

red and russet

7 Polygala chamaebuxus var. grandiflora
Ground box

This low evergreen shrub flowers in mid-spring. The cream-and-yellow pea flowers of the species have a keel that ages to purple, but those of *P. chamaebuxus* var. *grandiflora* are more showy, with yellow-lipped purple to brown-crimson flowers. Hardy.

Height: 15cm (6in) **Spread:** 30cm (12in)

5

1

2

3

4

6

7

Site: Partial shade, sun. Humus-rich and moist but sharply drained soil
Compost: Soil-based (John Innes No. 2) with added leaf-mould or soil-less
Use: Container, rock garden
Good companions: *Adonis vernalis, Salix reticulata, Veronica peduncularis* 'Georgia Blue'

8 Rhodohypoxis hybrids

Rhodohypoxis baurii, the most commonly grown species of the genus, and numerous hybrids are tiny deciduous perennials with thickened corm-like rootstocks. Starry flowers are produced freely above narrow hairy leaves in spring and summer. They appear to have no centre because of the way the overlapping segments are arranged. Colours include shades of red, red-purple, pink and white. Not fully hardy.
General care: In winter protect plants outdoors from excessive wet with raised panes of glass.
Height and spread: 10cm (4in)
Site: Sun. Lime-free, moist but well-drained soil
Compost: Lime-free, soil-based (ericaceous) with added leaf-mould and sharp sand
Use: Container, raised bed, rock garden, trough
Good companions: *Lithodora diffusa* 'Heavenly Blue', *Picea mariana* 'Nana', *Salix reticulata*

yellow

9 Adonis vernalis

The very finely cut leaves of this perennial make a bright green tuft topped in early to mid-spring by golden-yellow cup-shaped flowers. Hardy.
Height: 30cm (12in) **Spread:** 40cm (16in)
Site: Partial shade. Humus-rich and moist but well-drained soil
Use: Lightly shaded border, rock garden
Good companions: *Campanula carpatica, Muscari aucheri, Scilla bifolia*

10 Draba rigida var. bryoides
Whitlow grass

The large genus *Draba* includes a number of small cushion or mat-forming species that are equipped to survive mountainous and arctic conditions. The 'cushion' of this example is composed of tiny rigid leaves. In mid-spring short stems carry several small, bright yellow cross-shaped flowers. Hardy.
General care: Surround the neck with a layer of grit and in winter protect outdoor plants from excess moisture with a raised pane of glass.
Height: 5cm (2in) **Spread:** 8cm (3in)
Site: Sun. Sharply drained gritty soil
Compost: Soil-based (John Innes No. 1) with added grit
Use: Container, raised bed, rock garden, trough
Good companions: *Crocus minimus, Iris reticulata, Saxifraga* 'Gregor Mendel'

11 Saxifraga 'Gregor Mendel'
Kabschia saxifrage

Rosettes of pale green leaves make a neat cushion above which short stems carry sprays of light yellow flowers. Good alpine houseplant. Hardy.
Height: 10cm (4in) **Spread:** 30cm (12in)
Site: Partial shade, sun. Moist but gritty, sharply drained, alkaline soil
Compost: Soil-based (John Innes No. 1) with added limestone chippings
Use: Container, raised bed, rock garden, trough
Good companions: *Primula marginata, Saxifraga* 'Gloria', *Saxifraga* 'Johann Kellerer'

cream and white

12 Arabis alpina subsp. caucasica 'Variegata'
Rock cress

This green and creamy yellow-variegated plant is less rampant than its plain-leaved counterpart, but is best used on large rock gardens or sunny banks where it will not overwhelm miniature neighbours. Short-stemmed sprays of fragrant white flowers are borne during spring and into summer. Hardy.
General care: Trim in summer after flowering to keep compact.
Height: 15cm (6in) **Spread:** 45cm (18in)
Site: Sun. Well-drained soil
Use: Front of border, sunny bank, raised bed, rock garden
Good companions: *Aethionema* 'Warley Rose', *Aubrieta* 'Doctor Mules', *Pinus mugo* 'Mops'

cream and white (continued)

1 Arabis procurrens 'Variegata'
Rock cress

Evergreen or semi-evergreen perennial that produces a mat of creamy white-edged green leaves and bears loose sprays of white flowers in spring. Hardy.

General care: Trim in summer after flowering to keep compact.
Height: 8cm (3in) **Spread:** 35cm (14in)
Site: Sun. Well-drained soil
Use: Front of border, sunny bank, raised bed, rock garden
Good companions: *Armeria maritima* 'Düsseldorfer Stolz', *Aubrieta* 'Greencourt Purple', *Phlox douglasii* 'Boothman's Variety'

2 Arenaria balearica
Corsican sandwort

Tiny bright green leaves make a dense mat that closely hugs moist surfaces. In spring and summer white starry flowers spangle this cover. Hardy.

Height: 2–3cm (1in) **Spread:** 45cm (18in)
Site: Partial shade. Moist but well-drained soil
Use: Paving, raised bed, rock garden
Good companions: *Campanula carpatica, Gentiana septemfida, Hebe cupressoides* 'Boughton Dome'

3 Persicaria tenuicaulis
Unlike some of its relatives, this deciduous or semi-evergreen species is slow to spread. It has small leaves and bears short spikes of scented white flowers in spring. Hardy.

Height: 10cm (4in) **Spread:** 30cm (12in)
Site: Sun, partial shade. Moist but well-drained soil
Use: Front of border, raised bed, rock garden
Good companions: *Campanula garganica, Diascia* 'Salmon Supreme', *Gentiana septemfida*

silver and grey

4 Picea pungens 'Montgomery'
Colorado spruce

Several dwarf cultivars of the Colorado spruce, an evergreen conifer from the Rocky Mountains, have blue-tinted foliage. 'Montgomery' slowly forms a broad cone that is dense with pointed grey-blue leaves. Hardy.

Height: 1.5m (5ft) **Spread:** 1.2m (4ft)
Site: Sun. Moist but well-drained soil, preferably lime-free
Use: Border, heather garden, raised bed, rock garden
Good companions: *Campanula cochleariifolia, Diascia barberae* 'Ruby Field', *Picea abies* 'Little Gem'

green

5 Salix reticulata
Willow

The ground-hugging stems of this deciduous dwarf willow are densely covered with dark green leaves that are conspicuously veined on the upper surface and grey with hairs on the underside. The spring catkins are yellow with pink tips and stand erect. Hardy.

Height: 10cm (4in) **Spread:** 30cm (12in)
Site: Sun. Moist but well-drained gritty soil
Use: Front of border, raised bed, rock garden
Good companions: *Astilbe chinensis* var. *pumila, Daphne blagayana, Persicaria tenuicaulis*

6 Thuja occidentalis 'Hetz Midget'
White cedar

There are numerous dwarf cultivars of the white cedar, an evergreen conifer grown for its timber. 'Hetz Midget' develops slowly into an almost spherical bush composed of dense sprays of green foliage. Hardy.

Height and spread: 75cm (2ft 6in)
Site: Sun. Moist but well-drained soil
Use: Border, heather garden, raised bed, rock garden
Good companions: *Campanula poscharskyana* 'Stella', *Thuja occidentalis* 'Rheingold', *Viola biflora*

waterside & water plants

Many of the vigorous waterside plants that require reliably moist soil throughout the year are slow to make growth in early spring, but a few are spectacularly conspicuous because of their flowers. Plant in the dormant season.

purple, blue and violet

1 Primula denticulata

Drumstick primula

Freely self-seeding perennial that produces rounded heads of tightly packed flowers in white as well as in shades of blue, purple, pink and red. The 'globe' appears first at ground level among the developing leaves before being pushed upwards on the stout 'stick'.

General care: Eliminate ruthlessly self-sown plants of poor colour.

Height: 30cm (12in) **Spread:** 25cm (10in)

Site: Partial shade, sun. Humus-rich and moist, even boggy soil

Use: Moist border, waterside

Good companions: *Iris sibirica* 'Ego', *Lobelia* 'Queen Victoria', *Primula pulverulenta* Bartley hybrids

pink and mauve

2 Petasites fragrans

Winter heliotrope

A ground-cover perennial with kidney-shaped leaves and heads of strongly fragrant, pale mauve to purple flowers that emerge with the foliage in late winter and early spring. Although useful for broad landscaping, even doing well on heavy clay, the fleshy roots are too invasive for small or medium-sized gardens. Not fully hardy.

Height: 30cm (12in) **Spread:** Indefinite

Site: Partial shade, shade. Moist soil

Use: Ground cover, waterside

Good companions: *Gunnera manicata*, *Metasequoia glytostroboides*, *Salix alba* subsp. *vitellina* 'Britzensis'

yellow and orange

3 Caltha palustris var. palustris 'Plena'

Giant marsh marigold

The stems of this vigorous perennial spread out widely, even extending over water, and root when they touch moist ground. The heart-shaped leaves are glossy green and the double 'button' flowers are rich yellow. Hardy.

General care: Grows in water up to 15cm (6in) deep.

Height: 60cm (2ft) **Spread:** 1m (3ft)

Site: Sun. Permanently moist soil

Use: Waterside

Good companions: *Euphorbia palustris*, *Iris pseudacorus* 'Variegata', *Myosotis scorpioides* 'Mermaid'

4 Lysichiton americanus

Yellow skunk cabbage

Long-lived perennial with short, thick rhizomes. Green-tinged yellow flowers emerge in early spring, when the waterside is almost bare. The true flowers are tiny and packed on a thick spike, the spadix, which is surrounded by a large bract, or spathe. Glossy 1m (3ft) leaves emerge as the flowers mature and clumps remain impressive throughout summer. Hardy.

Height: 1m (3ft) **Spread:** 1.2m (4ft)

Site: Sun, partial shade. Humus-rich, permanently moist soil

Use: Waterside

Good companions: *Gunnera manicata*, *Lysichiton camtschatcensis*, *Rheum palmatum* 'Atrosanguineum'

cream and white

5 Lysichiton camtschatcensis

Skunk cabbage

Long-lived perennial growing from thick short rhizomes. The flowers, which develop before the leaves are mature, consist of tiny, green true flowers packed on a thick spike, the spadix, surrounded by the swirl of a creamy white bract, or spathe. The large dark green leaves form a handsome clump. Hardy.

Height and spread: 75cm (2ft 6in)

Site: Sun, partial shade. Humus-rich, moist soil

Use: Waterside

Good companions: *Ligularia* 'The Rocket', *Lysichiton americanus*, *Zantedeschia aethiopica* 'Crowborough'

3

4

1

2

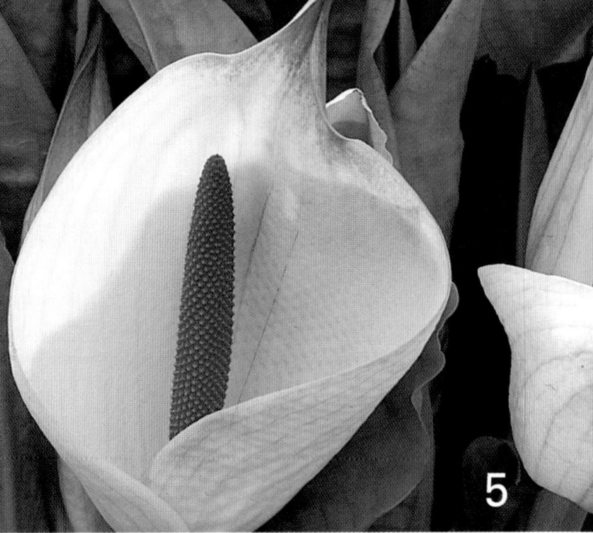
5

herbs & vegetables

Early spring is a busy time in the kitchen garden, for sowing and planting, but there are useful crops to harvest too, including overwintered vegetables such as leeks and sprouting broccoli and fast-growing salad vegetables.

2

herbs

1

1 Alexanders, Black lovage
Smyrnium olusatrum

Almost every part of this biennial or short-lived perennial can be used in salads, soups and stews for its strong angelica-and-celery flavour. Harvest leaves and shoots any time to use fresh, or just before flowering for drying. Hardy.

General care: Sow *in situ* in autumn or early spring, and thin seedlings to groups 45cm (18in) apart. To blanch young shoots for cooking and remove bitterness cover them with soil in March.

Height: 60cm–1.5m (2–5ft) **Spread:** 60cm (2ft)

Site: Sun or light shade. Moist but well-drained soil

Compost: Soil-based (John Innes No. 3)

Use: Border, container, herb garden

2 Anise hyssop
Agastache foeniculum

The fresh aniseed-flavoured leaves of this short-lived perennial can be used in teas, cold drinks, savoury rice and meat dishes. Mauve summer flowers attract bees and butterflies. Pick leaves and flowers for drying just as buds open. Hardy.

General care: Replenish stock by taking soft or semi-ripe cuttings in August or divide in spring.

Height: 1m (3ft) **Spread:** 60cm (2ft)

Site: Sun. Rich moist soil

Compost: Soil-based (John Innes No. 3)

Use: Border, container, herb garden

3 Chinese basil, Japanese shiso, Perilla
Perilla frutescens

The ruffled purple-red or green leaves of this annual have a warm curry-like flavour. It is an essential ingredient of sushi, but young leaves and flower stalks can also be used raw in salads or cooked in soups and pickles. Tender.

General care: Sow under glass in spring, and plant out 30cm (12in) apart after the last frosts. Pick growing tips regularly to encourage bushy growth.

Height: 60cm (2ft) **Spread:** 38cm (15in)

Site: Sun or light shade. Well-drained soil

Compost: Soil-based (John Innes No. 3)

Use: Container, front of border, herb border

3

4 Lemon verbena
Aloysia triphylla (syn. Lippia citriodora)

The penetratingly fragrant pale green leaves of this deciduous shrub are used fresh for flavouring desserts, cakes, summer drinks and tisanes. Pale lilac flowers in summer. Best treated as a pot or summer bedding plant. Tender.

General care: Prune in spring and after flowering for bushy growth. Mulch plants in winter or bring indoors; check indoor plants for whitefly and red spider mites.

Height: 3m (10ft) **Spread:** 2m (6ft)

Site: Sun, sheltered. Light, well-drained soil

Compost: Soil-based (John Innes No. 3)

Use: Conservatory or greenhouse, container, herb border

4

5 Myrtle
Myrtus communis

Aromatic evergreen shrub or small tree. The spicy leaves complement rich meat dishes and the creamy white-and-gold flowers can be dried for potpourri. Harvest fresh leaves any time, leaves and flowers for drying when blooms are fully open. Can be clipped for topiary. Not fully hardy.

General care: Best grown in a container, especially while young. Overwinter under cover. Lightly trim to shape in spring and summer.

Height: 3m (10ft) **Spread:** 2.5m (8ft)

Site: Sun, sheltered. Fertile, well-drained soil

Compost: Soil-based (John Innes No. 3)

Use: Conservatory or greenhouse, container, herb garden, patio

6 Pennyroyal
Mentha pulegium

A compact, prostrate semi-evergreen perennial with tiny pungent leaves and purple flowers in summer. Used sparingly as a substitute for peppermint. Hardy.

General care: Water freely in summer. Plants may die in wet soils below -8°C (18°F), so overwinter some roots under cover.

Height: 15cm (6in) **Spread:** Indefinite

Site: Sun, light shade. Moist but very well drained soil

Compost: Soil-based (John Innes No. 3) with added grit

Use: Container, front of border, paving

Compost: Soil-based (John Innes No. 3)
Use: Border, container, herb garden

7 **Rosemary**
Rosmarinus officinalis
Aromatic evergreen shrub with deep green, needle-like leathery leaves used for flavouring bread, meat, rice and egg dishes. The soft blue flowers are attractive to bees from mid-spring to early summer. There are many forms, including prostrate and variegated kinds. Leaves may be scorched after a cold winter. Plants usually recover if pruned back to healthy wood. Hardy.
General care: Plant 60cm–1m (2–3ft) apart. Trim after flowering and in early spring.
Height and spread: 1.5m (5ft)
Site: Sun, sheltered. Well-drained soil

8 **Sweet cicely**
Myrrhis odorata
Sweet aniseed-flavoured perennial that makes a mound of delicate foliage. Leaves, roots and seeds are all useful for flavouring salads, dressings, ice cream and fruit. Gather seeds for drying in late summer; alternatively, cut down after flowering for more young foliage. Hardy.
General care: Plant 60cm (2ft) apart.
Height: 1m (3ft) **Spread:** 60cm (2ft)
Site: Light shade. Rich, well-drained soil
Compost: Soil-based (John Innes No. 3)
Use: Container, herb garden, wild garden

9 **Sweet woodruff**
Galium odoratum
Attractive ground-covering perennial with the scent of new-mown hay, used for flavouring cold drinks, tisanes and fruit cups. Harvest the foliage as it appears, and flowers and stalks in early summer; dry to heighten their flavour. Hardy.
General care: Plant 15–23cm (6–9in) apart.
Height: 15cm (6in) **Spread:** 30cm (12in)
Site: Light or semi-shade. Rich soil
Compost: Soil-based (John Innes No. 3)
Use: Container, ground cover, underplanting for shrubs

10 **Thyme**
Thymus species and cultivars
There are many upright or creeping evergreen thymes, some variegated, with pink, purple or white summer flowers. All are ornamental aromatic plants, but grey-green garden thyme (*T. vulgaris*) is the most useful for the kitchen. Use fresh at any time for stuffings and bouquet garni. For drying, gather just before flowering. Hardy.
General care: Plant 23cm (9in) apart. Trim after flowering. In very cold areas pot up and overwinter under cover.
Height and spread: 30cm (12in)
Site: Sun. Poor, well-drained soil
Compost: Soil-based (John Innes No. 3)
Use: Container, edging, herb garden

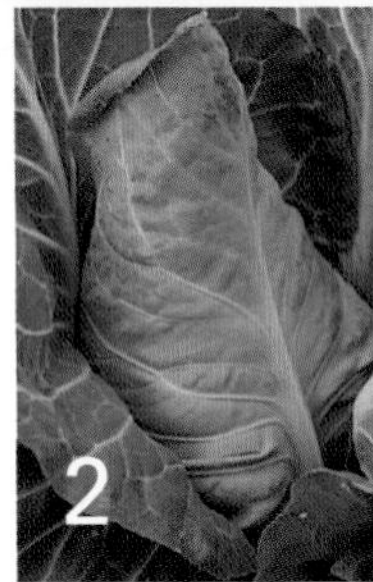

vegetables

1 Broccoli, early sprouting

Brassica oleracea Italica Group

The immature flowering shoots of white or purple sprouting broccoli, available from January to the end of spring, are eaten lightly cooked. For continuity grow early and late varieties (see Late Spring), or sow a prepared mixture. Hardy.

Site: Sun, warm sheltered. Well-drained, non-acid soil

How to grow: Sow in April, thinly in rows in a nursery bed. Thin seedlings to 8cm (3in) apart, and in midsummer transplant 60cm (2ft) apart. Water well in dry weather. Cut shoots when 8–10cm (3–4in) long with sprigs of young foliage. Harvest frequently to encourage new shoots.

2 Cabbage, spring

Brassica oleracea Capitata Group

Varieties such as 'Pixie' and 'Duncan' make small juicy cabbages, while 'Vanguard' and 'Wintergreen' are leafy non-hearting 'greens'. To maximise yields, harvest alternate plants while small, leaving others to grow and heart up. Hardy.

Site: Sun, sheltered. Rich firm soil, with added lime if acid

How to grow: Sow two to three batches from early July to early August, thinly in rows in a nursery bed. Thin to 8cm (3in) apart, and transplant when seedlings are six weeks old, spacing hearted kinds 30cm (12in) apart each way, greens 25cm (10in) apart. Water well in dry weather and net against birds. In late winter feed with high-nitrogen fertiliser. Harvest as soon as large enough, leaving 5cm (2in) stumps to resprout.

3 Cauliflower, winter

Brassica oleracea Botrytis Group

Winter cauliflowers such as 'Armado April', 'Markanta' and richly coloured 'Purple Cape' are hardy varieties for mild areas.

Site: Sun, sheltered. Firm, neutral to alkaline soil

How to grow: Sow in May, in rows in a nursery bed, and thin to 8cm (3in) apart. Transplant when seedlings have four to six true leaves, 75cm (2ft 6in) apart each way. Water in well and keep moist in dry weather. Protect forming heads by breaking some of the outer leaves to lie across the curds. Start cutting heads while still small, as whole batches tend to mature together.

4 Corn salad, Lamb's lettuce, Mâche

Valerianella locusta

This mild salad annual has refreshing, slightly bitter leaves. It can be sown in spring for summer use, but is most valuable as a winter and early spring leaf crop. Hardy.

Site: Sun or light shade. Most soils

How to grow: Sow outdoors in July and August, thinly in broad rows 15cm (6in) wide. Thin seedlings to 10cm (4in) apart, transplanting some thinnings to a coldframe or greenhouse; select only the strongest seedlings. Keep moist at all times. Gather leaves or whole plants as required, first blanching plants under pots for one to two weeks if the flavour is too bitter. Sowings may be left unthinned for harvesting as cut-and-come-again crops – snip strips to 2–3cm (1in) high.

5 Endive

Cichorium endivia

This annual or biennial crop is similar to loose-leaved lettuce, but has a sharper flavour, which is less pronounced if plants are blanched. Curly-leaved varieties are sown in spring for summer use, but hardy varieties, such as 'Golda', can be harvested in winter and early spring, especially if protected to maintain quality.

Site: Sun, warm sheltered. Well-drained soil

How to grow: Sow in August and September, outdoors in a nursery bed or in modules under glass. Thin or transplant to 30cm (12in) apart each way. Water in dry weather. Blanch by covering with an upturned flowerpot or large plate 10–14 days before cutting. In exposed gardens cloche crops or transplant seedlings to a coldframe.

6 Good king henry, Mercury, Poor man's asparagus

Chenopodium bonus-henricus

The early shoots of this undemanding perennial are blanched for cutting in early spring; later the green arrow-shaped leaves can be picked and used like spinach. Self-seeds freely, so deadhead to keep under control. Hardy.

Site: Sun or light shade, sheltered. Well-drained soil

How to grow: Sow in spring in a nursery bed, thin to 10cm (4in) apart, then transplant in autumn

45cm (18in) apart each way. Heap soil 15cm (6in) high over mature plants in autumn and cut shoots in spring as they emerge. Stop cutting and remove soil mound in June, then mulch with compost. Divide plants every three to four years.

7 Leaf beet

Beta vulgaris Cicla Group

There are two main kinds of leaf beet: chard or seakale beet has thick stems and sculpted leaves, while perpetual spinach or spinach beet has large plain leaves that make a long-lasting weather-proof substitute for ordinary spinach, especially on drier soils. Hardy.

Site: Sun or light shade. Fertile, well-drained soil

How to grow: Sow *in situ*, two to three seeds per station 30cm (12in) apart each way, in March or April; sow again in August for transplanting to a coldframe for winter use. Water in dry weather and mulch well. Pick leaves as required or cut whole plants down to 2–3cm (1in). Water and feed with general fertiliser after a heavy picking.

8 Mustard and cress

Sinapsis alba and Lepidium sativum

These cut-and-come-again crops can be sown outdoors as edging or a catch crop between other vegetables. There are various kinds of cress, including Greek and finely cut-leaved varieties. All are sown two to three days before the mustard to ensure seedlings are ready together. Hardy.

Site: Light shade. Moist soils

How to grow: Sow *in situ* every two to three weeks between March and October (November in a greenhouse border). Broadcast the cress seeds in drills 15–30cm (6–12in) wide or in patches and lightly rake in; oversow with mustard seeds two to three days later. Keep moist at all times. Cut with scissors when 5cm (2in) high, leaving short stumps to resprout.

9 Seakale

Crambe maritima

This perennial, which grows wild by the sea, is blanched under pots for cutting in early spring. It may be grown from seed or from root cuttings known as 'thongs'. Produces handsome flower and seed heads up to 60cm (2ft) across, which are popular with flower arrangers. Hardy.

Site: Sun or light shade, sheltered. Light well-drained soil

How to grow: Sow in a nursery bed in spring, and thin seedlings to 15cm (6in) apart. Transplant seedlings or plant thongs 45cm (18in) apart the following spring. Water in dry weather and mulch. Force two-year-old plants in January, covering them with an upturned bucket or forcing pot – the tender, white 15–20cm (6–8in) shoots will be ready for harvest two months later. Feed with general fertiliser after forcing, and replace after five to six years with root cuttings.

10 Shallot

Allium cepa Aggregatum Group

These multiplier onions – each bulb splits to produce a cluster of four to ten new ones – have a distinctive, almost perfumed flavour. Traditional varieties were planted in autumn, but modern kinds bolt if started too early. Not fully hardy.

Site: Sun. Rich, well-drained soil

How to grow: Plant virus-free bulbs 20cm (8in) apart each way in February or March, with their tips just showing. Water in dry weather and keep free of weeds. Gently lift clumps with a fork when leaves die down in midsummer, and leave to dry on the soil's surface. When the skins are papery and dry, separate bulbs and store them in nets or boxes in a cool, airy place for winter and spring use. Save smaller healthy bulbs to replant.

11 Spinach, summer

Spinacea oleracea

The flavour of well-grown spinach amply rewards the extra watering and mulching required. Start sowing this annual early in spring; on hot dry soils grow a bolt-resistant variety. Modern varieties crop all year with winter protection. Hardy.

Site: Sun, but lightly shaded in midsummer. Mulch soil with plenty of added organic matter

How to grow: Sow *in situ* every four to five weeks from April to July, and thin seedlings to 15cm (6in) apart. Water regularly in dry weather and mulch with compost. Harvest when plants have five to six true leaves; cut whole plants to leave stumps for resprouting, or pick some larger leaves. Clear and freeze crops that start to bolt.

12 Turnip

Brassica rapa

For summer use this mild crop is sown from spring onwards and harvested while the round or flat roots are still small and juicy. A winter-hardy variety, such as 'Manchester Market', can be sown late, and forced and blanched for an early spring crop of 'turnip tops'. Add lime to acid soil.

Site: Sun, but lightly shaded in midsummer. Mulch soil with plenty of added organic matter

How to grow: Sow summer crops outdoors every three to four weeks from March to July, thinning seedlings to 10cm (4in) apart in rows 20cm (8in) apart. Water little and often, and mulch when plants are larger. Harvest roots when 5cm (2in) across. For 'tops', sow in September and leave unthinned; give a general feed in February and let tops grow in the open, or feed in January and cover with a ridge of soil 15cm (6in) high to force and blanch the young shoots.

7

8

9

10

11

12

choosing the best plants

The following plant lists draw on all the plants described in the preceding pages of the Plant Selector, but they are grouped together here to help you choose plants for particular conditions, situations and uses.

plants for dry chalky soil

A large number of plants are automatically excluded from this list because they will not tolerate alkaline (limy) soil or they require moist conditions throughout the year. The improvement of shallow chalky soil by the addition of moisture-retaining organic matter allows lime-tolerant but moisture-loving plants, including clematis, hellebores and hepaticas, to be grown successfully. Some lime-loving plants, including many saxifrages, require plentiful moisture as well as gritty free-draining conditions.

- *Arabis alpina* subsp. *caucasica* 'Variegata'
- *Arabis procurrens* 'Variegata'
- *Aubrieta* 'Doctor Mules'
- *Aucuba* japonica (all)
- *Bergenia* (most)
- *Chionodoxa* (all)
- *Corylus avellana* 'Aurea'
- *Corylus maxima* 'Purpurea'
- *Crocus* (all)
- *Erysimum cheiri* 'Blood Red'
- *Euphorbia characias* subsp. *wulfenii*
- *Euphorbia rigida*
- *Hedera colchica* 'Dentata Variegata'
- *Lonicera fragrantissima*
- *Taxus baccata*
- *Taxus* x *meadia* 'Hicksii'
- *Tulipa* (all)

Tulipa turkestanica

plants for clay soil

Although the following plants generally succeed on close-textured clay soils, they do better when the ground has been improved by the addition of grit and organic matter such as well-rotted garden compost.

- *Anemone nemorosa*
- *Aucuba japonica* (all)
- *Berberis buxifolia*
- *Bergenia* (all)
- *Caltha palustris* var. *palustris*
- *Chaenomeles* (all)
- *Corylus* (all)
- *Epimedium* (all)
- *Euphorbia amygdaloides* var. *robbiae*
- *Forsythia* (all)
- *Hamamelis vernalis* 'Sandra'
- *Hedera* (all)
- *Helleborus* (all)
- *Leucojum vernum*
- *Lonicera fragrantissima*
- *Lysichiton* (all)
- *Mahonia aquifolium* 'Apollo'
- *Narcissus* (most)
- *Petasites fragrans*
- *Primula rosea*
- *Prunus* (all)
- *Pulmonaria* (all)
- *Ribes sanguineum* 'Pulborough Scarlet'
- *Salix* (most)
- *Skimmia* x *confusa* 'Kew Green'
- *Symphytum* 'Hidcote Blue'
- *Taxus* (all)
- *Viburnum tinus* 'Eve Price'

Narcissus 'Tête à Tête'

plants for moist shade

The following plants thrive in moist soils and tolerate partial shade and, in a few cases, full shade. Many will also grow in full sun provided the soil is reliably moist.

- *Adonis vernalis*
- *Anemone nemorosa*
- *Arenaria balearica*
- *Aucuba japonica*
- *Camellia* (all)
- *Corydalis flexuosa*
- *Corylopsis pauciflora*
- *Corylopsis sinensis* var. *sinensis* 'Spring Purple'
- *Daphne blagayana*
- *Epimedium* (all)
- *Euphorbia amygdaloides* var. *robbiae*
- *Hamamelis vernalis* 'Sandra'
- *Helleborus* (all)
- *Hepatica* (all)
- *Leucojum vernum*
- *Mahonia aquifolium* 'Apollo'
- *Omphalodes verna*
- *Pachyphragma macrophyllum*
- *Primula* (most)
- *Pulmonaria* (all)
- *Ramonda myconi*
- *Rhododendron* (all)
- *Skimmia* x *confusa* 'Kew Green'
- *Symphytum* 'Hidcote Blue'
- *Viburnum tinus* 'Eve Price'
- *Viola* (all)

Ramonda myconi

plants for acid soil

Plants marked with an asterisk* will only grow satisfactorily on soils that are free of lime. Other plants in the list thrive on acid soils, but may also grow on neutral or slightly alkaline soils.

- *Camellia* (all)*
- *Chamaecyparis lawsoniana* 'Green Hedger'
- *Corydalis flexuosa*
- *Corylopsis pauciflora**
- *Corylopsis sinensis* var. *sinensis* 'Spring Purple'*
- *Erica* (all)
- *Hamamelis vernalis* 'Sandra'
- *Magnolia* (all)
- *Picea pungens* 'Montgomery'
- *Pieris* (all)*
- *Primula rosea**
- *Rhododendron* (all)*
- *Rhodohypoxis* hybrids*

plants for coastal sites

Where windbreaks and hedges give protection from salt-laden winds, a wide range of plants can be grown in coastal gardens. Many benefit from the sea's moderating influence on temperatures.

- *Anemone coronaria*
- *Aubrieta* 'Doctor Mules'
- *Chaenomeles* (all)
- *Chamaecyparis lawsoniana* 'Green Hedger'
- *Chionodoxa* (all)
- *Crocus* (most)
- *Erica* (all)
- *Euphorbia* (all)
- *Forsythia* (all)
- *Griselinia littoralis* 'Variegata'
- *Juniperus virginiana* 'Grey Owl'
- *Narcissus* (most)
- *Osmanthus* x *burkwoodii*
- *Persicaria tenuicaulis*
- *Scilla* (all)
- *Spiraea thunbergii*
- *Veronica peduncularis* 'Georgia Blue'

flowers for cutting

The following list includes several spring-flowering shrubs and trees that if cut judiciously provide excellent material for arrangements. In addition to the following, many other plants, including winter-flowering pansies and early flowering bulbs, provide material for small, sometimes short-lived displays.

- *Anemone coronaria*
- *Camellia* (all)
- *Chaenomeles* (all)
- *Chamelaucium uncinatum*
- *Erysimum cheiri* 'Blood Red'
- *Forsythia* (all)
- *Hyacinthus orientalis* (all)
- *Narcissus* (all)
- *Primula auricula* (all)
- *Primula* Prominent Series
- *Primula* Silver-laced Group
- *Prunus* (most)
- *Salix* (most)
- *Tulipa* (all)
- *Viburnum farreri*

Salix hastata 'Wehrhahnii'

plants for dry shade

The following plants grow most vigorously where there is a regular supply of water, but generally succeed in such difficult conditions as the shady base of walls or where roots of overhead trees and shrubs are near the surface.

- *Aucuba japonica* cultivars
- *Bergenia* (most)
- *Epimedium grandiflorum* 'Rose Queen'
- *Epimedium perralderianum*
- *Euphorbia amygdaloides* var. *robbiae*
- *Hedera colchica* 'Dentata Variegata'
- *Pulmonaria* (all)
- *Symphytum* 'Hidcote Blue'

plants for sandy or gravelly soil

The following plants require free drainage and are mostly drought tolerant, although bulbs generally require a good supply of moisture in the growing season. The range of plants that can be grown in dry sunny gardens will be enlarged if the soil is improved by the addition of well-rotted organic matter.

- *Arabis alpina* subsp. *caucasica* 'Variegata'
- *Arabis procurrens* 'Variegata'
- *Aubrieta* 'Doctor Mules'
- *Berberis buxifolia*
- *Chionodoxa* (all)
- *Crocus* (all)
- *Erysimum cheiri* 'Blood Red'
- *Euphorbia characias* subsp. *wulfenii*
- *Euphorbia rigida*
- *Fritillaria imperialis*
- *Griselinia littoralis* 'Variegata'
- *Juniperus virginiana* 'Grey Owl'
- *Ornithogalum oligophyllum*
- *Puschkinia scilloides* var. *libanotica*
- *Tulipa* (all)

Crocus angustifolius

late spring

practical diary

With late spring comes the busiest planting time. New shrubs and hardy perennials planted during these months will have a whole growing season to become established before winter. Seeds of hardy annuals sown now will provide gorgeous colours in high summer and, once the danger of frost has passed, it is safe to plant out such tender species as pelargonium and heliotrope. As the soil warms up, you can enjoy setting out your kitchen garden, too, and watch with pleasure as the vegetable seedlings emerge. Late spring may be a busy time, but as you plant, prune and sow, you are laying the groundwork for a colourful and rewarding year.

perennials

Herbaceous perennials keep you busy in late spring with a range of tasks that allow plant growth to be as swift and as healthy as possible. On top of routine maintenance, give some thought to the future, as this is the best time to propagate the next generation of plants, either as fillers for gaps in the border or for next year's display.

now is the season to . . .

- **put supports or stakes in place,** well before tall perennials begin to flop over.
- **water thirsty young plants** that are still developing a root system, if more than a few days go by without rain. Soft leafy perennials that have just been planted need plenty of water to maintain their rapid pace of growth – in dry weather this means up to 5 litres (1 gallon) per week per plant.
- **mulch to reduce water loss and suppress weeds:** cover the soil around plants with an organic mulch, such as composted bark, well-rotted manure or garden compost. Before you mulch, make sure the soil is thoroughly moist and clear of perennial weeds. Then lay the mulch at least 7–8cm (3in) deep to prevent light from reaching the soil and stimulating weed seeds to germinate.
- **take steps to control slugs and snails** by a range of means (see opposite).
- **remove weeds regularly,** otherwise they will compete for food, space and moisture.
- **deal with aphids** as they settle on the soft growth of perennials: vigilance is important. Apply a precautionary spray with a systemic insecticide or, if you prefer not to use chemicals, choose an organic oil-based spray that kills the pests as they feed.
- **take basal cuttings from plants** that produce an abundance of new shoots at ground level and insert them in cuttings compost to root (see page 125).
- **acclimatise and plant out young perennials,** to give them time to establish before winter (see right).
- **lift and divide mature perennials** to rejuvenate them as well as to increase stock (see page 124).
- **lift and discard some of the more invasive plants** such as creeping Jenny (*Lysimachia nummularia*) with its low spreading habit; this will check its rapid rate of growth in early summer.
- **encourage sideshoots to grow** from the base of new plants. Whether they have been raised from seed or from cuttings, make them bushier and stronger by removing the growing tip of each shoot, pinching between thumb and forefinger, once they reach a height of 10cm (4in).

supporting perennials

Herbaceous perennials have soft, non-woody stems, so when they reach a certain height they tend to flop. This can result in considerable damage to both stems and flowers, especially after rain when the blooms, heavy with water, cause the stems to keel over and collapse. Once a plant flops or is beaten down by rain it never recovers; however carefully you arrange its stems it will always look awkward.

Put a support of twiggy birch stems in place before tall perennials grow too high.

Give extra support to tall-growing plants long before it is needed, and certainly before they have reached half their mature height. Ideally, the supports should be no more than two-thirds of the plants' ultimate height, so that their shoots and leaves grow through the supports and obscure them. Use any of the following:

- **twiggy stems of birch or hazel,** known as brushwood, with the tips bent over.
- **bamboo canes** (though these are more difficult to obscure).
- **specially designed stakes or supports** that link together to form a frame around the plants as they develop; push these deep into the soil initially and ease them up as plants grow.

acclimatising overwintered plants

It can take perennials raised from seed two full years from germination until they flower. If you sow in late summer or early autumn and grow the plants under the protection of a coldframe, greenhouse or conservatory for the first winter, this period can sometimes be shortened.

Perennials raised in this way, or propagated from root cuttings taken in late autumn or winter, will need to be acclimatised gradually to garden conditions, or 'hardened off'

Dicentra spectabilis 'Alba'

easy **cuttings**
Some plants, such as aster, doronicum, erigeron and phlox, form roots at the base of the new shoots as they develop. Known colloquially as Irishman's cuttings, these roots and shoots can be detached from the parent plant and potted up immediately.

dealing with slugs and snails

The new shoots of herbaceous perennials are soft and succulent and, being at soil level, make easy meals for slugs and snails. Try one of these methods to trap them:

- **hand-pick offenders,** particularly after rain and in the evening.
- **set beer traps,** or a 50:50 beer:water mix; slugs and snails are attracted by the yeasty aroma and then drown.
- **lay a grapefruit half** (flesh scooped out) near vulnerable plants. It will attract large numbers of slugs and snails, so check underneath each morning.
- **grow leafy perennials in pots,** raised off the ground.
- **lay slug pellets** sparingly to act as bait. They are frequently used in far too great a quantity: 10 pellets per m^2 (1 per sq ft) should provide adequate control for one week.

(see page 167), by standing the pots outdoors on warm, sunny days. Bring them under cover at night to protect them from cold and frost. This ensures that the plants will not suffer a serious check in their growth when they are eventually planted out.

Once the plants are fully acclimatised and the risk of heavy frost has diminished, plant them out in the garden (see page 124). With a full growing season ahead of them, they will be strong enough to survive outdoors throughout the following winter season.

PLANTING TIP New perennials raised over winter and divisions from established plants will be smaller in size than those bought at a garden centre, so plant them in groups of three or five of the same species. They will soon appear to merge into a single clump, making much more of a visual impact than if they were planted singly.

Leafy hostas are particularly vulnerable to attack by slugs and snails. Take precautions as soon as their shoots emerge through the soil, otherwise their foliage will be shredded.

perennials/2

planting and propagation

Late spring is a time of rapid growth and lush fresh foliage, so catch the opportunity to lift and divide mature perennials. This is also the time to plant out young plants grown from seed or cuttings, particularly those with hollow stems.

planting perennials

While many perennials can be planted in autumn or early spring, those with hollow stems are vulnerable to weather and must be planted now. They include anchusa, delphiniums, euphorbias, hellebores, helianthus, kniphofias, liatris, phlox, ligularia, poppies (*Papaver orientale*), *Sedum spectabile* and symphytum. If these perennials are planted out in autumn and made to spend their first few months sitting in cold, wet soil, rainwater can collect within their stems and cause them to rot. Disease may then easily be spread to the rest of the plant.

Before planting, dig the site thoroughly, removing all perennial weeds, and incorporate some organic matter, such as well-rotted manure or garden compost. Allow the soil to settle for a week or two, then clear any remaining weeds and roughly rake the soil level before planting begins.

Dig a planting hole large enough to accommodate the whole root system. When you take a bought-in plant from its container, remove the top 1cm (½in) of compost from the surface of the rootball, as it may contain weed seeds and moss that would otherwise be introduced to the garden.

The planting depth of perennials is critical. Most perennials have a shallow root system, with the body or crown of the plant either at or just below soil level.

- **for perennials with fibrous root systems,** such as asters, carex and stachys, the top of the roots should be 1cm (½in) below the soil surface.
- **perennials with fleshier roots,** such as acanthus, bergenias and *Dicentra spectabilis*, need setting slightly deeper, at about 2–3cm (1in) below soil level.
- **it is better to plant slightly too high** and add more soil or mulch later, than too deeply and risk the plant rotting.

PLANTING TIP Buy an established perennial in a large pot rather than several smaller ones. When you get the plant home, remove it from the pot and divide it into smaller pieces, each with several growing shoots and roots, and plant them out as normal.

dividing perennials

Lifting and dividing perennials will rejuvenate mature plants that have formed large congested clumps. This can be done in either autumn or spring. Wait for any that flower early, like bergenias, to finish blooming before you disturb them.

- Lift the clump with a border fork when the soil is moist.
- Divide the clump into pieces by pulling it apart, cutting it

some perennials to divide in spring

• achillea • bergenia (after flowering) • *Geranium sanguineum* • hostas • *Helleborus orientalis* (after flowering) • *Iris sibirica* • *Lysimachia punctata* • *Scabiosa caucasica* • *Sedum spectabile* • thalictrum • *Tradescantia* Andersoniana Group

planting perennials

1 **Water the plant** thoroughly and leave to drain. Remove the plant from its pot by gently supporting the stem and foliage, and tapping the container with the other hand.

2 **Holding the plant** by its rootball, position it in the hole at the correct depth. Pull the soil back around the plant and firm it gently into place with your foot.

3 **Leave a slight depression** round the base of the stem, and water into this straight after planting.

taking a basal cutting

1 **Remove young shoots** from the base of the parent plant at soil level, using a sharp knife. Trim off any leaves from the bottom third of the cutting.

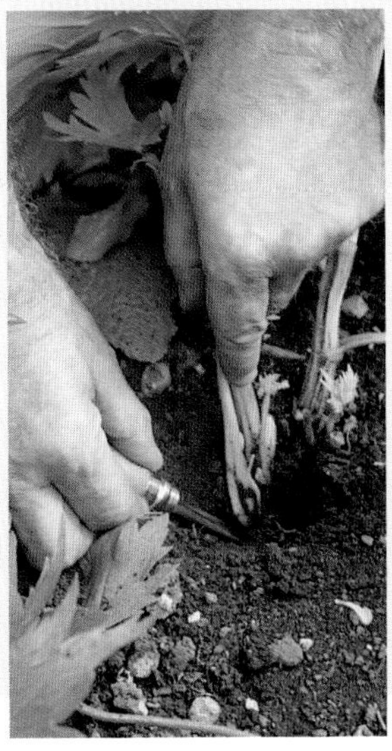

2 **Dip the base** of each cutting into an appropriate rooting hormone preparation. Cover only the cut surface at the base of the cutting as the rooting hormone may injure the stem.

3 **Fill a pot to the rim** with cuttings compost. Strike off the excess so the surface is level with the rim, but do not firm. Holding the cuttings vertically, gently insert them into the compost so their bottom third is covered. Water gently.

looking ahead . . .

☑ LATE SUMMER Sow seeds of perennials and raise under cover.

☑ WINTER Take root cuttings of perennials.

perennials **to raise from basal cuttings**

- achillea • campanula
- chrysanthemum
- delphinium • erigeron
- gaillardia • helenium
- lupin • phlox
- scabious • veronica

with a knife, or using two forks back to back.

- Replant the young outer sections of the clump in the border. They will become established quickly.
- Discard the old central portion and any sections carrying old flower stalks, as they rarely produce any further flowers.

A clear plastic drinks bottle, with the base cut off, makes an ideal cover for a single cutting. Unscrew the cap regularly for ventilation.

taking basal cuttings

Basal cuttings are a variation of softwood cuttings. They are particularly well suited to perennials that produce an abundance of new shoots at ground level in mid to late spring, such as delphiniums or lupins (see above). Select very young, healthy shoots 8–10cm (3–4in) long and insert them into pots of cuttings compost. An 8cm (3in) pot will take a single cutting, a 13cm (5in) pot about six cuttings.

Hostas form large clumps, which can easily be divided. If necessary, cut the clump into pieces using a knife or spade blade.

annuals & biennials

Spring biennials are now drawing to an end and autumn-sown annuals will soon come into bloom: late spring is the time to ensure an abundance of summer-long flowers. It is also the best time to sow next year's spring bedding in a vacant patch outdoors, but if you do not have time or space to raise your own annuals from seed, you can still buy young bedding plants.

now is the season to . . .

- **harden off young plants** sown indoors earlier in spring that are nearly ready for planting out (see page 167). Remove cloches and fleece from protected seedlings outdoors, and open cold frames on mild days to acclimatise young plants.
- **prick out and pot up greenhouse seedlings** to make large specimen plants.
- **clear away exhausted spring bedding plants** and prepare the ground for summer annuals.
- **plant out hardy annuals** sown in spare ground last autumn.
- **buy summer bedding** at the garden centre and plant out (see opposite).
- **sow annuals where they are to grow,** especially those that dislike being transplanted. Do this from mid-April to mid-May in milder areas, two to three weeks later in colder parts of the country or where soils are slow to warm up.
- **sow biennials in drills outdoors** (see opposite) or start under glass for potting up or transplanting later.
- **grow a few annuals for filling seasonal gaps** later or for planting up pockets left in permanent displays; sow in rows in a vacant patch elsewhere in the garden, as for biennials, or sow under glass. Transplant the seedlings when large and robust enough.
- **weed regularly between established annuals,** and protect younger plants from slugs and snails.
- **collect seed** from any outstanding spring annuals and biennials, and sow now or dry and store for later use.

and if you have time . . .

- **sow a few pinches of quick-growing annuals,** like candytuft, where bulbs and early perennials are past their best, and also round spring-flowering shrubs for successional colour.
- **sow fast-growing half-hardy annuals** such as marigolds (*Tagetes*), mexican sunflower (*Tithonia*) and mallow (*Lavatera*) in the greenhouse.
- **take soft-tip cuttings** from vigorous plants of petunias, *Begonia semperflorens* and other tender annuals; choose non-flowering shoots or remove flower buds, and root the cuttings in a propagator or on a windowsill indoors (see page 165).
- **sow leftover seed of taller annuals** in rows at the side of vegetable beds, where they will provide a decorative edging and armfuls of flowers for cutting.
- **sow late flowering annuals** like asters, chrysanthemums and zinnias, either under glass or outdoors with frost protection.

direct sowing hardy annuals

Many hardy annuals will have been sown in autumn or early spring ready for planting out now, but fast-growing annuals like candytuft, as well as those that dislike being transplanted, such as california poppies and love-in-a-mist, can be sown directly into the soil now. Do not add fertiliser as most annuals will flower best in poor soil.

Biennial forget-me-nots (*Myosotis sylvatica*) self-seed freely.

• **prepare the ground thoroughly** as for a seedbed: rake and level the surface to a fine, stone-free texture.

• **scatter the seeds thinly over the area** and rake them in lightly, or cover with a sifting of fine soil, to about twice their depth. Then water the sowings with a fine spray.

buying bedding plants

If you do not have the time or space to raise your own annuals from seed, you can buy young plants in containers during spring. Do not buy them too early unless you can keep them frost free until it is safe to plant them out.

Avoid leggy plants and yellowing foliage, often symptoms that the plants have been growing for too long and have exhausted their compost nutrients. Also steer clear of trays with dry compost or masses of roots growing through the base. Choose compact bushy plants, well spaced out and all the same size, with healthy-looking foliage and plenty of buds, even the first open flower. Water and feed them when you get home, and plant out as soon as possible, or keep them in a warm (but not hot) sheltered place until you are ready.

planting out bedding

Clear the ground of spring bedding and weeds, and rake level. Mark out with sand, or lines scratched in the surface with a cane, the areas where different varieties are to go.

• **most bedding needs** 15–30cm (6–12in) spacings to produce shapely, bushy plants, but ideal planting density varies according to the size and vigour of the variety, so check labels or catalogue descriptions.

Digitalis purpurea

biennials for sowing in late April and May

These plants will flower the following spring and summer:

• brompton stocks (*Matthiola incana*) • canterbury bells (*Campanula medium* and *C. pyramidalis*) • clary (*Salvia sclarea*) • double daisies (*Bellis*) • forget-me-nots (*Myosotis*) • foxgloves (*Digitalis*) • giant thistles (*Onopordum, Silybum*) • honesty (*Lunaria annua*) • iceland poppies (*Papaver nudicaule*) • siberian wallflowers (*Cheiranthus* x *allionii*) • sweet williams (*Dianthus barbatus*) • wallflowers (*Cheiranthus cheiri*) • winter-flowering pansies (*Viola*)

sowing biennials

1 **Prepare a seedbed** outdoors (see page 28) in a spare piece of ground in good light. Mark out straight, parallel drills 15–20cm (6–8in) apart in moistened soil, just deep enough to cover the seeds to double their depth in soil.

2 **Sprinkle the seeds** thinly using finger and thumb (from your palm, not straight from the packet). Carefully cover the seeds and firm gently with the back of the rake.

• **choose a mild, still day** after the threat of frost has passed. Water the plants in their trays and pots, and leave to drain while you dig out planting holes with a trowel. Plant at the same depth as in their containers, firm lightly and water well.

sowing biennials for next spring

Forget-me-nots, wallflowers, sweet williams and foxgloves all need to make plenty of growth this season so that they overwinter outdoors successfully and flower prolifically next year. Sow them outdoors in drills in a nursery bed or vacant piece of ground during May and early June (see above). Cover the bed with netting if you think that birds, squirrels or cats are likely to be a problem.

When the seedlings are large enough to handle, thin to about 5cm (2in) apart. About two weeks later, thin again to leave small varieties 10cm (4in) apart, larger ones 15–20cm (6–8in).

Water as needed and feed once or twice in summer. In autumn, lift plants with a trowel and transfer them to the beds or containers where they are to flower.

looking ahead . . .

☑ SUMMER Deadhead to prolong the life of plants.

☑ AUTUMN Sow hardy annuals. Transfer biennials to their flowering positions.

☑ WINTER Order seed, and protect hardy annuals.

☑ EARLY SPRING Sow annuals under glass.

bulbs & tubers

You can mow bulbs planted in grass six weeks after flowering, or leave them until midsummer if they are intended to seed themselves (see inset picture).

This is the time to tackle spring bulbs that have finished flowering. But remember that bulbs are not exclusively for spring: tender or more exotic species can be planted now, ready to take starring roles in the summer border.

now is the season to . . .

- **plant dahlias and begonias** as dormant or sprouted tubers. Fork the ground deeply and work in plenty of rotted manure or garden compost; just before planting apply a top-dressing of balanced fertiliser at 125g per m^2 (4oz per sq yd).
- **cut large begonia tubers** into sections; ensure each piece has at least one bud, and plant as normal.
- **plant** *Anemone coronaria* in April for flowers in August.
- **plant a batch of gladioli** every two weeks until late May for a succession of blooms.
- **plant lily bulblets** and gladiolus cormlets, saved in autumn, in pots or nursery rows, to flower in a year or two.
- **note dense clumps of spring bulbs** that did not flower well; they are probably overcrowded. Mark their position now for digging up and dividing later in the year.
- **inspect lilies** for bright red lily beetles and their orange-black grubs; remove by hand or spray with permethrin.
- **tie tall flower stems** of lilies, galtonias and gladioli to supporting canes, if your garden is windy.
- **deadhead bulbs** as flowers fade so they conserve energy.

and if you have time . . .

- **feed spring bulbs** with high-potash fertiliser after flowering.
- **sow seeds of summer bulbs** in seed trays in a cold frame.
- **rake soil over holes** left by dead bulb leaves, to deter narcissus flies.

planting dahlias

1 **Dig a hole** about 15cm (6in) deep and wide enough for the tubers. Check the size by placing the rootball in the hole. For tall-growing varieties drive in a 1m (3ft) cane off-centre.

2 **Spread out** the roots carefully before planting, then place in the hole and work soil between them. Cover so the base of the old stem is 5cm (2in) below soil level. Leave a slight depression in the soil surface to act as a watering 'saucer'; water well after planting.

lilies **in pots**

Lilies planted now may bloom two to three weeks later than those planted in autumn, but will readjust to the normal flowering time next year. Choose late flowering cultivars such as 'Sterling Star' or 'Pink Perfection' (left), oriental hybrids like 'Star Gazer', or variants of *Lilium speciosum* and *L. lancifolium*.

looking after your spring bulbs

Bulb foliage continues to build up food reserves for next year's display for several weeks after flowering, so it is important not to remove, trim or knot the yellowing leaves for the sake of tidiness until their work is done.

- In the border hide the dying foliage of permanent bulbs by teaming them with leafy planting partners, such as hardy geraniums, or sow a fast-growing annual such as candytuft (*Iberis umbellata*) to camouflage dying foliage after the bulbs have finished flowering.
- Move bulbs used as spring bedding out of the way if you want to plant out summer flowers. If the leaves are already yellow, fork up the bulbs, clean off most of the soil and spread in a single layer to dry under cover, preferably in a greenhouse or a shed. If the bulbs have just flowered or the leaves are starting to discolour, lift them with as much soil on their roots as possible and replant in groups in a vacant patch (such as the vegetable garden if room), to finish ripening. Give them a liquid feed and let the foliage die down naturally. Then lift, dry and store the bulbs under cover until autumn.

planting bulbs for summer flowers

Whereas spring bulbs make the greatest impact massed in large colonies or naturalised drifts, summer bulbs and tubers look more effective in small, strategic groups. Plant them now to provide local colourful highlights in flower borders as well as to rectify any midsummer gaps in beds and borders left by earlier flowering perennials.

There are many summer-flowering bulbs and tubers to fit the bill. Tigridias and butterfly gladioli are useful 'dot' plants, or high points, or are good for cutting; begonias, cannas and dahlias create hot spots of lively colour; some lilies have a wonderful scent; and galtonias and crinums make stately plants that contrast strikingly with the softer, rounded shapes of many herbaceous perennials.

- **for containers**, use a trowel or bulb planter, and plant most of these bulbs at twice their depth in a pot of rich soil-based compost. Then stand the pots outdoors, feed regularly from six weeks after potting and avoid over-watering.
- **with large bulbs** like lilies, plant three or five (odd numbers tend to look better) halfway down a 25–30cm (10–12in) container. Use them to brighten the summer patio or to plunge into borders where gaps occur.
- **plant begonias, cannas and dahlias** as dormant tubers about six weeks before the last frosts are expected for your locality. Space them 60cm–1.2m (2–4ft) apart, according to expected size.
- **alternatively,** if you took dahlia cuttings in early spring or set the tubers to sprout (see page 495), plant them out once the threat of frost has passed (see opposite).

looking ahead . . .

☑ SUMMER Mulch dahlias and pinch out growing tips.
☑ LATE SUMMER Dig up overcrowded clumps of spring bulbs while dormant.
☑ WINTER Sprout dahlia tubers for taking cuttings or planting out.
☑ EARLY SPRING Take softwood cuttings of dahlias.

Crocosmia x *crocosmiiflora* 'Emily McKenzie'

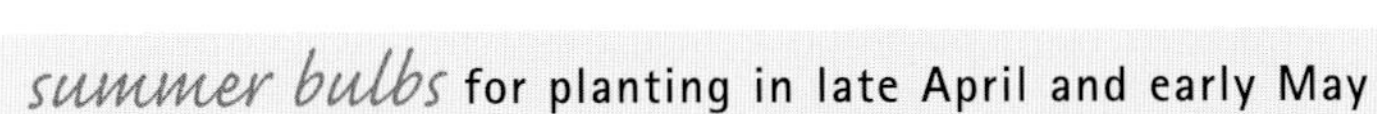

summer bulbs **for planting in late April and early May**

- alstroemeria • *Anemone coronaria* • begonia • bletilla • canna • crinum • crocosmia • eucomis • galtonia • gladiolus • *Nerine bowdenii* • schizostylis • tigridia • *Tropaeolum tuberosum* • zantedeschia • zephyranthes

Explore bulb catalogues for more unusual species.

roses

Roses have begun their transformation, now sprouting fresh foliage and strong new shoots, even a few early buds. By the end of May, the flowers of the earliest-blooming roses could be fully open.

Shrub rose *Rosa xanthina* 'Canary Bird', with its attractive single yellow flowers and fern-like foliage, is one of the first roses to flower.

now is the season to . . .

- **finish pruning,** especially if spring is frosty and late, but try to complete this by mid-April (see page 38).
- **continue planting container-grown roses.** They will benefit from being well established before midsummer.
- **hoe round established plants** regularly to deter weeds and keep bare soil loose and crumbly; hoe only the top 2–5cm (1–2in) of soil to avoid damage to rose roots. Deeper weeds should be hand-pulled or carefully dug out with a trowel, or spot-treated with weedkiller.
- **remedy moss** and green slime on the ground – indicators of soil compaction, especially after a wet winter and spring – by shallow forking and hoeing.
- **feed roses** with a powdered or granular feed once spring pruning is finished, and again in midsummer (see below).
- **give a foliar feed** where soil is poor or plants are ailing, at monthly intervals up to the end of July (see below).
- **mulch roses** as soon as the ground warms up in May and again after feeding (see opposite).
- **plant ground cover** and edging perennials in rose beds.
- **check stakes, supports and ties** on climbing, rambler and standard roses, and loosen or renew them where they are worn or too tight.
- **shorten some of the oldest** and thickest stems of climbing roses by half their length, to stimulate new main branches to appear lower down.
- **start disbudding hybrid tea roses** grown for top-quality blooms by rubbing or pinching out all but the main bud at the end of each shoot.
- **inspect the new growth** on bushes and standards for overcrowded or inward-growing shoots, and pinch them out at their base or at a low bud.
- **check daily for the watering needs** of roses under glass as they come into flower, and give them a liquid feed every 10–14 days. Watch out for health problems, including red spider mites. Ventilate freely and shade the glass to keep temperatures down. When flowering has finished, stand the pots outside.
- **water roses planted in early spring,** especially during prolonged dry weather.

and if you have time . . .

- **sow miniature roses,** in warmth under glass in April. As seeds germinate erratically, sow them thinly in a large seed tray and prick out the individual seedlings when they are large enough.

feeding roses

Roses are greedy plants, and feeding is an important part of their annual care routine. Always use a fertiliser that is specially formulated for promoting flower production. A rose or tomato fertiliser contains all the necessary major nutrients and trace elements. Follow the manufacturer's instructions, and apply the fertiliser to moist soil around all established roses when you have finished spring pruning, ideally before the leaves open fully. Hoe or rake in lightly (see opposite). Repeat this at midsummer to sustain later growth and flowering, but do not feed after mid-July.

Where the soil is poor, plants are ailing or top-quality blooms are wanted, you can supplement this feed with a foliar feed of dilute liquid fertiliser at monthly intervals from now until the end of July.

mulching

Mulch roses after feeding them. Cover the soil around the stem with a 5–8cm (2–3in) layer of garden compost, rotted manure or composted bark, to suppress weeds and keep the soil moist. Leave a small clear space around the plant's stems.

pests and diseases

The first signs of problems can occur as soon as growth revives in spring, and you should decide whether you are going to spray regularly as a precaution, only treat specific ailments as they occur, or leave the plants to cope without your interference. Plants can often tolerate many diseases if they are kept well watered and regularly fed, so control weeds, mulch plants generously, pick off badly affected leaves, and foliar feed infected plants.

MOSAIC VIRUS TIP Look for yellow lines, veins or bands, which show up on new leaves; feed infected plants well and do not use for taking cuttings.

planting roses

Unless there were good reasons for delay (climate or soil conditions, for example), bare-rooted roses will have been planted in early spring and will now be showing signs of life. In more northerly gardens, or where the ground was frozen or waterlogged, plant bare-rooted roses as soon as possible. Container-grown roses can be planted all through the season.

planting container-grown roses

The planting technique for container plants differs only slightly from bare-rooted plants (see page 406).

- Prepare the ground by digging deeply on a site where roses have not grown before, and make sure the drainage is adequate. Remove all weeds and pieces of root, and work in plenty of compost or rotted manure.
- Both the rose and the ground should be moist at planting time. Dig a planting hole 15–20cm (6–8in) wider than the container and a little deeper. Mix garden compost or a tree planting compost with the excavated soil, and line the bottom of the hole with a 5cm (2in) layer of this mixture.
- Stand the container in the hole, with the compost surface at ground level, and cut or slide the container off the rootball. Back-fill around the rootball with the loose, prepared soil mix (see above). Firm it as you go, using your fingers or a trowel handle. Level the surface and rake in a dressing of bone meal or rose fertiliser.
- Prune the main stems of all roses except climbers back to about 15cm (6in) immediately after planting.
- Water well in dry weather, and apply a mulch once the ground warms up in May.

PRUNING TIP Prune the rose while it is still in its container. This saves bending down to ground level later.

tying in new stems of climbers

Space out and secure vigorous new stems on climbing and rambler roses, using soft garden string to attach them to their supports. If possible, arch the stems sideways on walls and trellis, and spiral them around vertical posts to promote flowering. You could, at the same time, remove one or two of the oldest branches and replace them with new stems.

feeding and mulching

1 Hoe the soil lightly round the plant, removing any debris and weeds, before scattering on the fertiliser over the root area.

2 Cover the fertiliser with fresh compost to act as a mulch and soil enricher, as well as to help to suppress weeds.

looking ahead . . .

☑ SUMMER Spray, mulch, feed and deadhead roses.
☑ AUTUMN/WINTER Prune roses and tie in climbers.
☑ EARLY SPRING Plant out bare-rooted roses.

climbers

Many early flowering climbers have finished their display and are ready to prune, while others are just coming into growth. Correct pruning keeps the plants to the desired size and shape, but also encourages strong growth and plenty of flowers for next year.

now is the season to . . .

- **prune early flowering climbers** such as *Clematis alpina, C. armandii* and *C. macropetala.*
- **take cuttings** of late flowering clematis.
- **train the growing stems** of climbers into their supports.
- **plant** new climbers (see page 134).

Flowering wisteria and *Clematis montana* var. *rubens* festoon a house wall in late spring.

routine pruning

With the majority of climbers (honeysuckles, jasmines, early flowering clematis, for example) pruning is only necessary to repair winter damage or restore plants to the desired shape.

- **remove any dead or damaged branches,** and carefully tease out and dispose of old and weak stems.
- **tie in loose stems,** bending them away from the vertical.

WHEN TO PRUNE? The basic rules are simple: if the climber flowers in spring, prune straight after flowering; if it flowers in summer or autumn, prune in late winter or early spring.

herbaceous climbers

Herbaceous climbers like the golden hop (*Humulus lupulus* 'Aureus') and perennial peas, such as *Lathyrus rotundifolius*, die back over winter and leave dead stems. If you have not done so already, get rid of dead stems now, before new shoots grow into them. Ideally, they should be cut back to ground level in late winter, but with young plants, it can be helpful to leave the first year's growth to support this year's stems.

mixed climbers

If you are growing a mixture of climbers some may be expanding at the expense of others. Check all the plants now to ensure that growth is under way.

- **cut out any shoots** that threaten less vigorous neighbours but strike the right balance. Avoid spoiling strong growers just to allow space for a weak plant. If any plant is weak and struggling, consider removing it.

early flowering climbers

These are coming to the end of their display and can be pruned now, to produce a good display next winter and spring. Winter jasmine (*Jasminum nudiflorum*) benefits from having all unwanted long growths removed. Trim them back to the main stems to encourage a mass of short, flowering shoots. This treatment also suits: ornamental quince (*Chaenomeles*), *Coronilla valentina*, flowering currant (*Ribes speciosum*), *Forsythia suspensa* and wintersweet (*Chimonanthus*).

Chaenomeles speciosa

taking leaf-bud cuttings of clematis

1 **Remove a whole stem.** Trim the base and discard the soft, fleshy top, cutting just above a pair of leaf buds. You should now have a stem about 5cm (2in) long.

2 **Take a tray** or shallow pot with plenty of drainage holes and fill with a mixture of equal parts perlite or fine grit and soil-less potting compost. Insert each cutting so that the leaf buds at the top are in contact with the compost.

3 **Place the tray** or pot in a propagator or on a windowsill. Inspect the cuttings regularly and immediately remove any that are turning black or rotting. Pot up once rooted.

pruning clematis

This topic is the cause of much unwarranted anxiety. In fact, clematis are seldom harmed, whether left untouched or pruned almost to ground level. The guidelines are these:

- **summer and autumn-flowering clematis** are pruned in winter or early spring.
- **early flowering species** may need attention now, in late spring, or early summer.

Early flowering clematis include *C. alpina* and any clematis that blooms between the shortest day and late spring. Although they perform well without any pruning, if you need to tidy them or to restrict their size, the best time to act is as soon as the flowers are over. Trimming back encourages the plant to make strong growth on which flower buds will form next year. *Clematis montana*, which is in flower now, is more usually pruned in early summer.

pruning Clematis armandii

Unlike most early flowering clematis, the exceptionally vigorous evergreen *Clematis armandii* benefits from drastic treatment, particularly if it has been neglected or is growing in a restricted space.

- Wait until the last flowers have faded. Then cut off all the growth, right back to the trunk. There may not be a single green leaf or stem left when you have finished.
- If the plant is healthy, it will sprout in a couple of weeks. The young stems will be vigorous but extremely brittle. Tie them in carefully as they emerge, using soft garden string and gently bending them to a horizontal position.
- Continue to train the stems as they extend, arranging them so that they cover as much of the wall or fence as possible. On a mature plant, each stem should have grown to around 3m (10ft) by late summer, and a superb display of fragrant white flowers in early spring will be your reward.

propagating clematis

This is the season to propagate late flowering *Clematis viticella* and its hybrids, by taking cuttings or by layering.

cuttings

To take leaf-bud cuttings (see above), select healthy young stems that are beginning to turn woody. Roots will form at the leaf buds, which will start to grow in five to ten weeks.

layering

This is the easiest method of propagating mature clematis (see also page 139) and now is a good time to begin.

- Take a low-growing stem. On the underside, make a small slanting cut without severing the stem, or simply scrape off the bark.
- Anchor the wounded part in the ground, just below the surface, with a stone or wire staple.
- Within a year, the plant will have grown roots and, as soon as it is dormant, it can be transplanted.

looking ahead . . .

- ☑ SUMMER Continue to train in new growth of *Clematis armandii*.
- ☑ Prune *Clematis montana* and its hybrids.
- ☑ Pot up rooted leaf-bud cuttings of *Clematis viticella* hybrids.

climbers/2

planting and support

Plant herbaceous climbers now to boost vertical displays later in the year. If you provide secure supports and regular attention, your climbers will reward you with a beautiful house wall or boundary.

The soil type is important too, especially if it is limy or chalky, as some plants will not tolerate these alkaline conditions. Sandy soils drain fast and need organic matter added, plus a thick mulch to help to retain moisture, since almost all climbers benefit from a cool, moist root run.

choosing a climber

Assess your site before you buy a climber, as you need to know what kind of conditions prevail on and around your wall or fence.

- **which direction** does the wall or fence face?
- **how much sun** does it receive?
- **are there overhanging eaves** that might prevent rain from reaching the soil below, and reduce the moisture levels?
- **what is** the soil like?

The choice of plants will then depend on the aspect and conditions. A north-facing wall is shaded, whereas one facing south is hot and dry. A west-facing wall catches the afternoon or setting sun, which creates gentler conditions than the rising sun warming an east-facing wall, especially in frosty weather. So plant vulnerable or slightly tender species such as summer jasmine (*Jasminum officinale*) and climbing potato vine (*Solanum*) against a west-facing wall, and tougher species like quince and winter jasmine (*Jasminum nudiflorum*) facing east. Mix climbers to give flower and foliage interest over a long period, but make sure they are of similar vigour and have similar pruning requirements.

planting climbers

Most climbers need supports and these should be put in place first. Before planting, improve the soil generally by digging in compost or other well-rotted organic matter together with a little bone meal or balanced fertiliser. If you are planting into a specially prepared hole in a paved area, fork the sides and base to make sure there is plenty of space for the roots to run, and that it drains freely.

An hour or two before you plant, water the climber thoroughly. Then site your planting hole at least 45cm (18in) from the wall; if there is an overhanging roof or gutter, move it farther out to ensure the roots receive plenty of moisture. Plant climbers very slightly deeper than the level of compost in the container. With clematis, plant more deeply so that 8–10cm (3–4in) of the stems are covered. If the top growth is spindly and thin, cut it back hard to a bud at soil level.

After planting, continue to water the climber at regular intervals until it is established, but do not feed until next year. Once climbers are established, shade their base and therefore their roots with a thick mulch (see page 600), paving slabs or low-growing plants.

planting a climber

1 **Dig a hole** larger and deeper than is needed for the climber's rootball, and tip the bone meal and compost mix into the bottom of the hole. Turn the climber gently out of its pot. If the roots are congested, tease them out.

2 **Place the rootball** in the hole and plant fractionally deeper than the level of compost in the container. Back-fill the hole with soil, firming it down gently with your foot.

3 **Water thoroughly.** If the stems are long enough, tie them to a support. If not, place canes at an angle to encourage young stems to grow towards the fence or wall support.

methods of support

Almost all climbers need to be trained and most need to be tied to a support. Even those that cling by stem rootlets or sucker pads, such as ivy, climbing hydrangea (*H. anomala* subsp. *petiolaris*) or virginia creeper (*Parthenocissus*), will need your help if they are to distribute themselves evenly.

- **horizontal training wires** are the simplest and most effective system. Stretch them taut along the wall or between fence posts, anchoring them at 2m (6ft) intervals with 'vine eyes' (special nails or screws with a hole at one end). Space wires roughly 45cm (18in) apart, with the bottom one this distance above the ground. Use stout galvanised wire, and make sure the anchor points are strong enough to bear the weight of a large climber.
- **trellis is an attractive** alternative to wires. Make sure trellis panels are held clear of the wall or fence so that air can pass freely between plant and structure, and to make tying in easier. Mount panels on wooden battens and secure with long strong screws.

- **tie stems loosely to the wires or** trellis, using soft garden string. Plants that cling by tendrils, such as clematis, or twine, like honeysuckle (*Lonicera*), need little more than to have wayward stems secured. Non-clinging plants such as roses and wall shrubs need their stems tied at several points while they are young and flexible.

training climbers

Train climbers, especially flowering kinds, in a fan formation, gently angling the main stems away from the vertical. Training stems like this promotes flowering and ensures the wall or fence is evenly covered all the way down to the ground, rather than merely at the top.

Keep wall shrubs, roses and other climbers that need regular pruning on the outside of the trellis or wires. If the stems extend between support and wall, they are difficult to unravel and will become jammed, sometimes forcing the trellis or vine eyes away from the wall.

Early in the year, the flowers of *Clematis macropetala* bring colour to walls and fences. This climber does well even in a position of cool, semi-shade.

shrubs & trees

Betula utilis

Many spring-flowering species will be in full bloom, but others, their flowers already finished, will need pruning to restore their shape and good looks. As fresh leaves begin to expand on deciduous shrubs, now is a good time to restore overgrown hedges and plant new evergreens and specimen shrubs.

now is the season to . . .

- **prune shrubs that have flowered already,** and hard-prune shrubs that flower later on new shoots (see right).
- **regularly water shrubs and trees** planted in early spring, especially on light soils. In dry weather occasionally spray new evergreens with clean water during the evening.
- **feed young trees and shrubs,** and any you have pruned hard, with a balanced fertiliser; water in if the soil is at all dry.
- **restore overgrown deciduous hedges** (see page 504) before birds start nesting. Check carefully before starting, and stop work if you find a nest being built.
- **continue protecting foliage and flower buds** at risk from frost (including many silver and grey shrubs, such as cistus, halimium and romneya) with one or two layers of fleece (see page 61); remove as soon as the weather warms up.
- **check for dead and frost-damaged shoots,** once the risk of frost has passed; prune them back to uninjured wood as a precaution against disease.
- **tidy and weed** around established trees and shrubs, but make sure you avoid damaging surface roots with over-zealous hoeing or forking.
- **hand-pull weeds,** or deter them by heavy mulching, around trees and shrubs, such as magnolias, that dislike root disturbance of any kind.
- **watch out for pests and diseases,** especially aphids and caterpillars, on new soft growth, and mildew in a dry season; remove by hand or treat with appropriate insecticide or fungicide.
- **mulch the warmed soil** during May, to conserve moisture around younger plants, those recently planted and any on very light soils.
- **deadhead rhododendrons and azaleas** that have finished flowering (see opposite).
- **plant new evergreens** (see page 138).
- **propagate bushy shrubs** by layering (see page 139).
- **take soft-tip cuttings** of shrubs and hedge plants that produce long new growths (see page 139).

and if you have time . . .

- **prune the stems** of *Buddleja davidii* to varying heights, to produce an attractive tiered display of flowers. Spread the pruning over several weeks to extend the flowering season.
- **plant bareroot deciduous trees and shrubs** in cooler parts of the country, but only if they are still without leaves. Finish the job as early as possible and be prepared to water them regularly throughout the summer; otherwise wait until early autumn.
- **plant bamboos,** both as specimen shrubs and for decorative windbreaks. Where space is limited, choose clump-forming species, rather than spreading varieties with potentially invasive runners.

shrub pruning guide

Keep your secateurs sharp and handy, because there is a lot of pruning to do at this time of year. Some of it is cosmetic, but on many species pruning is an essential stimulus to prolific flowering later in the season or next year.

- **prune shrubs that have already flowered,** such as forsythia and flowering currant, immediately after flowering, by completely cutting out a third of the oldest shoots (thicker and darker than the others). Cut them back to ground level or down to a framework of old branches. Lightly trim the rest by cutting off the flowered tips.

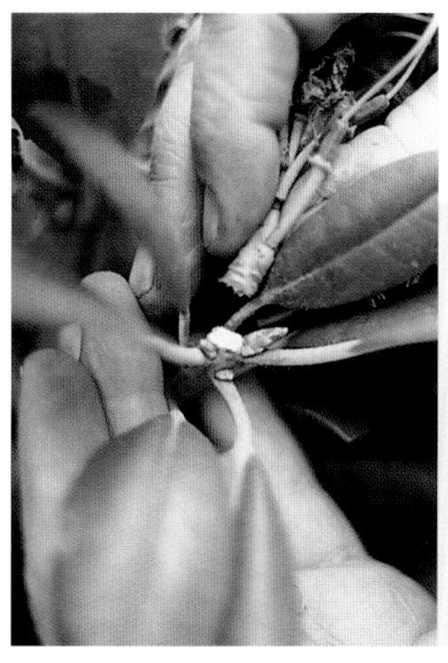

deadheading
Tidy the growth of camellias, magnolias, rhododendrons and azaleas to make room for the new season's shoots. When deadheading, take care not to damage the bud.

- **hard-prune shrubs that flower later** on shoots produced this year, such as hardy fuchsias, *Hydrangea paniculata* and caryopteris: cut all last season's growth either to just above ground level, or to a taller stump if you want a large bush.
- **'stool' ornamental trees** like paulownia, coloured elders and some eucalyptus: that is, cut all stems to just above ground level. These trees produce larger or more decorative leaves when cut back annually to form 'shrubs'.
- **restore grey-leaved shrubs** such as lavender and artemisias to shape. They become leggy and bare at the base if left unpruned. Cut the leafy growth as far back as needed, but stop at least 2–3cm (1in) beyond the older leafless branches. Trim plants again after flowering to encourage bushy growth.
- **prune broad-leaved evergreens** such as laurel and holly to stimulate bright summer foliage and denser growth. Shorten all last year's new shoots by half, using secateurs on large bushes to avoid cutting leaves. Overgrown plants of this kind can be hard-pruned to their original size during April.
- **trim stems of specimen conifers and topiary to shape** with secateurs, but avoid cutting across the sprays of foliage.

Shorten smaller protruding and misplaced shoots to restore shapeliness; larger branches can be tied back in with wire or removed altogether if this does not leave an ugly gap. Where conifers have produced more than one central stem or 'leader', reduce these to the strongest to avoid spoiling the tree's shape. Tip-prune long branches to encourage branching.

hedge care

- **tidy leaves and dead wood** from the base of hedges, and clear weeds. Watch out especially for perennial and twining weeds that can soon infiltrate dense hedges.
- **water newly planted hedges** regularly in dry weather. Concentrate water at the base of each plant rather than giving the hedge an overall sprinkling. Check every two weeks unless rain intervenes.
- **feed young hedges** with a balanced fertiliser at a rate of 125g per m^2 (4oz per sq yd), distributed evenly around the plants. Older hedges need only half this rate, unless they have been hard-pruned to shape. A mulch of rotted manure or garden compost can replace the spring feed on established hedges.
- **mulch young hedges** liberally with grass mowings in dry weather and on light soils. Spread a mulch 5cm (2in) deep over moist soil and keep topped up as the season progresses.

trimming hedges

You can give formal conifer and other fast-growing hedges, such as privet and lonicera, their first clip of the year now, using shears or a hedge trimmer (see below). Stretch a taut line between two canes and use this guide to ensure accurate cutting and to define the new height.

trimming a privet hedge

1 Clip the sides of the hedge first, working from the bottom up. Gently sweep away the trimmings as you go.

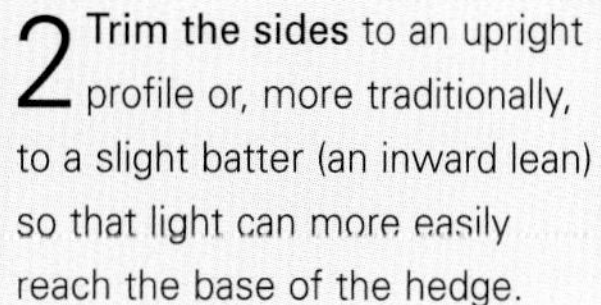

2 Trim the sides to an upright profile or, more traditionally, to a slight batter (an inward lean) so that light can more easily reach the base of the hedge.

3 Clip the top to the string line. Trim a wide hedge in two stages, working to the middle from each side, to ensure a consistent level.

shrubs & trees/2

planting and propagation

Container-grown evergreens are best planted in the spring season as the soil warms up and conditions improve. You can also increase your stock of shrubs and hedge plants using the simple procedures of layering and taking softwood cuttings, which are best done now.

A box hedge is slow growing but makes perfect low edging to a bed if clipped regularly; here, violas form a skirt at its base. Hedge trimmings can be used as a source of soft cuttings to propagate box, privet and lonicera, but they take two to three years to grow into small hedge plants.

planting new evergreens

Evergreen trees and shrubs can be planted safely during mid and late spring, and this is often preferable in cold regions and on heavy wet soils, where autumn planting can result in root injury or disease. Plants that are root-balled (their roots and surrounding soil wrapped in netting) or bare-rooted should be planted by the beginning of April; container-grown specimens are also best established now before a possibly hot and dry summer season (see below).

Remember that trees and shrubs have a potentially long life in one place, so the planting site needs thorough preparation. Dig the soil down two spade depths, and improve the drainage where necessary. Remove all weeds and weed root fragments over an area of $1m^2$ (10 sq ft) to reduce competition from weeds. For a tree, drive in a short upright support stake, slightly off-centre, before planting.

If planting a container-grown evergreen, water the new plant in its pot and allow to drain. Then remove the pot and carefully tease out some of the roots away from the rootball. Put root-balled plants in position, then cut and remove the netting. After planting any kind of shrub or tree, back-fill the hole with excavated soil and firm the plant in place with your foot. Water thoroughly and cover the area with a thick mulch.

Secure a tree to its stake with one or two adjustable tree ties. On exposed sites, it is a good idea to erect a screen of fine mesh or similar windbreak material while the plant is getting established. Place it on the windward side of the plant, to shield it from frost and cold winds.

planting a container-grown conifer

1 **Fork plenty of compost** or similar well-rotted organic material into the soil, then dig a hole two to three times the width of the plant's rootball.

2 **Stand the plant** in the hole, keeping the rootball intact, and adjust the planting depth so that the old soil mark on the stem is at surface level.

3 **After back-filling** the hole with soil, gently shake the tree once or twice to settle the soil around its roots. Then level the soil surface, water and cover the area with a thick organic mulch. Continue to water well in dry weather.

layering bushy shrubs

The lower branches of many shrubs naturally develop roots where they touch the ground. You can exploit this ability to produce new plants with little risk of failure, because the new plant remains attached to its parent until rooted. You may do this at any time of year, although starting now, when growth is at its most vigorous, allows a full season's growth before the new shrub is severed and transplanted in autumn.

- For bushy shrubs such as rosemary, ornamental quince, cistus, virburnums and rhododendrons, select a healthy, flexible low shoot that will bend easily to touch the ground 15–20cm (6–8in) near its tip.
- Where it touches, scoop out some of the soil with a trowel to leave a shallow depression.
- Strip the leaves from the shoot at the point of contact, and wound the underside to expose some of the inner tissues. Do this by slicing off a thin layer of bark with a sharp knife, or by cutting a small slit at an angle to about halfway through, or simply by twisting the stem.
- Peg the stem down and cover the rooting area with soil.
- Should rooting not occur, carefully re-open the wound, dust the surfaces with hormone powder and try again. Wait until spring or the following autumn before detaching the shoot and moving it to its new home.

taking soft-tip cuttings

In mid to late spring, many shrubs produce long new shoots that are firm enough for you to take cuttings. Hebe, lavatera, sage, phlomis and santolina are a few of the many species easily and quickly propagated like this (see page 165).

watering aid

To assist with watering, either lay a porous pipe in the hole, with one end at the soil surface, or bury a pot almost to its rim near the plant as you finish back-filling. This will ensure that water reaches right down to the roots of a newly planted tree or shrub.

- Trim each shoot to about 5–8cm (2–3in) long, cutting just below a leaf joint.
- Remove leaves from the lower half of the cutting and pinch out its soft tip, which can sometimes rot and set up diseases. If the base of the cutting is firm or starting to look woody, dip it in hormone powder or liquid to help stimulate rooting.
- Insert the cuttings to just below the lowest leaves in a pot or tray of cuttings compost or a 50:50 mixture of potting compost and grit or sharp sand. Make sure the cuttings do not touch each other.
- Water in well and leave to drain. Stand the pot in a closed propagator, or cover with a clear plastic bag supported off the leaves with wire hoops. Keep warm and lightly shaded from bright sunshine. New, paler top growth and roots appearing from the base of the pot indicate successful rooting. Cuttings may then be potted up individually.

layering a shrub

1 **Take a young supple stem,** strip off the lower leaves, and tear the bark slightly. Peg the stem down in the soil with a loop of stiff wire.

2 **Cover with fine soil** or fresh potting compost.

3 **Bend the end** of the pegged stem upwards and tie it to a vertical cane to start training the new shrub. Water well, and keep moist in dry weather.

alpine gardens

Late spring is the best season for alpine plants, with more in flower now than at any other time of year. During these months, plan new planting schemes and buy plants while you can see their brilliant colours and exquisite forms.

now is the season to . . .

- **look out for self-sown seedlings,** which are likely to appear now, and take care not to pull them up while weeding. Leave them undisturbed, or transplant any that have popped up in the wrong spot or pot them into small pots to give to friends.
- **tidy up plants that have flowered,** but leave some spent flowerheads if you want seed or self-sown seedlings.
- **trim back invasive plants** to prevent them from swamping neighbours. Where necessary, dig out sections of plants.
- **replenish the grit or gravel mulch** in alpine beds or sinks if it has become buried or scattered.
- **remove cloches or other forms of protection** from alpines that resent winter wetness. Take cloches off as soon as days noticeably lengthen, otherwise the plants will be tricked into premature growth and made more vulnerable to late frosts.
- **watch out for weeds** and remove them as soon as they appear; do not allow any to seed, as weeds can be more troublesome on a rock garden than anywhere else.
- **keep an eye out for pests:** there are few that affect alpines although vine weevils are increasingly common, and most likely to cause problems among primulas, cyclamen and dodecatheon. The tell-tale symptom is sudden wilting. If this occurs, pull up the plant and examine the roots for cream, comma-shaped grubs. If they are present, consider biological treatment (see page 257). Slugs and snails may trouble young plants while they are small and vulnerable.
- **prick out alpines raised from seed** sown in early spring into trays or alpine compost, or individually into 8cm (3in) pots.
- **check cuttings of alpines** taken in early spring and plant them out once they have rooted.

and if you have time . . .

- **divide oversized plants** once they have finished flowering. (If you are busy postpone this job until early autumn.) Lift the plant with a small fork or trowel and carefully tease it apart into small sections; discard the old central part and replant vigorous outer sections.

building an alpine collection

The majority of alpines enjoy cool, moist but very well-drained soil, and need plenty of sun for their bright flowers. Ideally, this means growing them in a south-facing site away from overhanging trees.

Although many are easy to raise from seed, the fastest way to build a collection of alpines is to buy plants and to divide these on a regular basis, although some, like fairy foxglove (*Erinus alpinus*), will obligingly self-seed. Many, such as dwarf campanulas, cover the ground quickly by means of spreading stems or extending rootstocks. Others, including many saxifrages, develop huge cushions that can be gently broken up and the pieces replanted. Alpines are small enough to be handled easily when in bloom, and few will resent planting or moving at this time of year.

In this rock garden, alpine plants including dianthus and saxifrages enjoy the free-draining conditions of a sloping site.

Good places to grow alpine plants include dry-stone walls, cracks and crevices in paving or walls, and gravel or shingle. *Haberlea rhodopensis* (right) grows in a gravel niche.

looking ahead . . .

☑ AUTUMN OR EARLY SPRING Remove any plants that become leggy or untidy and trim or thin the rest.

☑ EARLY SPRING Sow seed of alpines and take cuttings of existing alpines.

sink gardens

The ideal size for an alpine sink garden is approximately 60 x 40cm (24 x 16in) and 20cm (8in) deep. This will allow room for six or seven plants. Choose plants that will flower in different seasons or go for one big bright display that leaves plenty of greenery for the rest of the year. Select a single small shrub or tiny tree (a dwarf conifer or miniature willow, such as *Salix lanata*, for example) to act as a focal point. Water the plants in their containers well, so that they are moist before planting.

Set aside a few small but attractive pieces of rock or large stones. Drill drainage holes in the sink if there is no plug hole, and place a layer of gravel or pieces of terracotta from broken pots in the bottom to make sure that water can escape easily and compost is not washed out.

Fill the sink to the top with a potting compost designed for alpines, then water and allow to settle for a day or two before planting (see below).

COMPOST TIP Make your own free-draining alpine potting compost by blending equal amounts of John Innes No. 2 compost (or a soil-less equivalent) and coarse grit.

rosette-forming alpines to divide now

Divide plants that form cushions of rosettes, such as houseleeks (*Sempervivum*). Gently remove whole rosettes, each with a few roots attached, and replant them in gritty compost.

- *Arabis ferdinandi-coburgi*
- houseleeks • *Saxifraga* x *apiculata* and *S.* 'Tumbling Waters' • *Sedum spathulifolium*

Sempervivum tectorum

flowering plants for an alpine sink

SPRING: *androsaces*, cushion saxifrages, low-growing wallflowers (*Erysimum*), small primulas

SUMMER: alpine pinks, campanulas (especially *C. cochleariifolia*), *Geranium dalmaticum*, *Verbascum* 'Letitia'

AUTUMN: autumn snowflake (*Leucojum autumnale*), *Cyclamen cilicium*, gentians, *Sorbus reducta*

WINTER: snowdrops (*Galanthus nivalis*), winter crocuses

planting an alpine sink

1 With the plants still in their pots, arrange them into a miniaturised landscape, placing the largest plant or plants first as a focal point. Also position one or more of the biggest pieces of rock or stones.

2 Once you are satisfied with your arrangement, bed the rocks into the compost. Remove the plants from their pots and plant using a trowel. Water in well.

3 Place the remaining smaller pieces of rock or stone around the plants. Cover the compost with coarse gravel, 2–3cm (1in) deep. Tuck it carefully round the plants, keeping their leaves free.

water gardens

To maintain the delicate balance of life in your pond, you will need to control rampant water plants and make sure part of the surface is kept clear of water lilies or pond weeds.

Many ponds and pools look their best in late spring, when several water plants are in flower and others are enjoying a surge of new growth.

now is the season to . . .

- **divide bottom-rooted water plants,** marginal (shallow-water) plants and bog plants that are old or overgrown, to provide young replacements (see opposite).
- **top up water features regularly;** hot weather in May can cause rapid evaporation.
- **replenish gravel on baskets** of submerged plants where fish have been foraging.
- **fix a net across the pond** above the surface of the water, if herons are stealing fish.
- **clean the pond** only if absolutely necessary; if it is full of tadpoles it is better to wait till autumn.
- **clear out pond weeds** to keep at least a third of the water surface clear.
- **move or transplant water plants** while they are in active growth; this will give them a long period to establish in their new surroundings, well before the onset of winter weather.
- **grow oxygenating plants** from tip cuttings 15cm (6in) long. Tie six to eight cuttings together at the base with a piece of string and plant each bunch, with the string buried, at the bottom of the pond.
- **plant three small bunches of oxygenating plants** for every square metre of pool (one per sq ft). They absorb minerals and carbon dioxide in the water and are essential to maintain its clarity and quality; choose them according to the scale of your pond as many of these oxygenating plants can be extremely invasive.
- **include small pieces of floating plants** such as duckweed (*Lemna trisulca*), fairy moss (*Azolla filiculoides*) and frogbit (*Hydrocharis morsus-ranae*), which are also oxygenators. Simply toss them onto the surface (they don't need planting) where they will provide useful shade and prevent the build-up of algae and blanket weed.
- **plant up new marginal plants,** either bought in or from your own stock. Plant them along the shallow shelf or at the pond edge, in plastic mesh baskets or directly into the soil.
- **plant deep-water plants** like water lilies in baskets (see page 145).
- **feed fish liberally** as they become more active, to build up their strength and resistance to disease.

good oxygenating plants

• elodea (*Lagarosiphon*) • frogbit (*Hydrocharis morsus-ranae*) • hornworts (*Ceratophyllum*) • water violet (*Hottonia palustris*)

dividing water plants

- Lift the plants out of their baskets, or the pond soil. Depending on their size, chop thick-rooted plants into pieces with a knife or sharp spade, or pull them apart with your hands. If large, use two forks back to back.
- Cut plants with creeping rhizomes into 15cm (6in) lengths, each with one or more fat buds.
- Remove any dead or rotting portions with a knife.
- Replant healthy young pieces either directly into the pond soil, or in baskets as shown on page 145.

clearing weeds

Control pond weeds so that at least a third of the water surface is kept clear. This means removing blanket weed and duckweed if they threaten to block out all the light.

- **duckweed** is mainly found growing on still water. Drag out as much as possible with a net and leave it to dry out and die before adding it to the compost heap.
- **blanket weed** tends to be a greater problem in new ponds or those recently cleaned. Clear thick layers by dragging out as much as possible by hand. For large amounts or big ponds, use a garden rake; in smaller ponds or where there is a liner, twirl the weed around a stout stick. However, blanket weed often contains beneficial insects and water snails, which feed on the weed, so clearing too much can be self-defeating. Leave the piles of blanket weed by the pond overnight to give insects and snails a chance to crawl back into the water.

You might need to clear blanket weed several times from late spring into summer. A long-term solution is to fit an ultra-violet filter to your water-circulating system.

testing the water

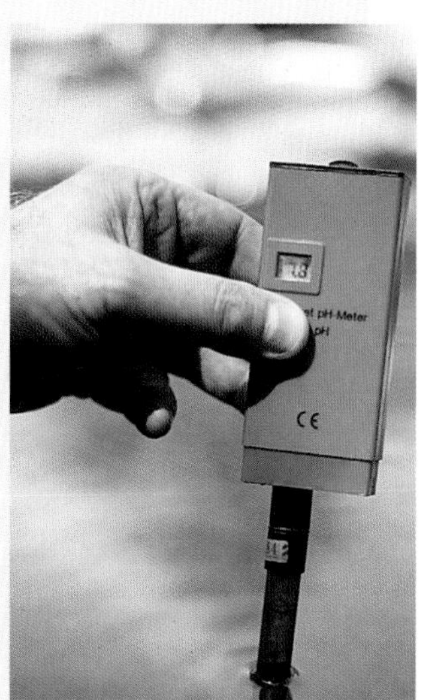

The health of a pond is finely balanced, and one of the factors that will upset its balance is a change in the relative acidity or alkalinity (the pH) of the water. Simple kits are available to test pH accurately. Readings between 6.5 and 8.5 are satisfactory, but above or below these levels plants and fish will suffer. Where the lime content of the water or soil has added too much alkalinity, making the pH reading too high, suspend a fine mesh bag of peat in the pond to lower the pH. Alternatively, add an appropriate pH-boosting agent to the water to redress the balance.

Check the level of the water surface regularly as pond water can evaporate quickly once the weather warms up. Top it up, from a water butt where possible, using a hosepipe.

water gardens/2

Darmera peltata

pond planting

Late spring marks the beginning of the year for pond plants. As water temperatures begin to rise, the cheerful yellow pondside flowers of marsh marigolds and the lovely pink heads of *Darmera peltata* (above) open, while other plants rush into growth. Now is the time to establish new water plants, either bought in or from your own stock.

To make the care and maintenance of the pond and its plant population as easy as possible, always use rigid plastic-mesh planting baskets to contain water plants. The advantages of using baskets are that they give a greater degree of control over the plants' growing environment and they are easier to lift out of the water, compared with growing the plants *in situ*. You should avoid using wooden or metal containers in water because they may produce toxins that are harmful to fish.

Use loamy garden soil, preferably with a high proportion of clay, or a specially formulated aquatic compost. The soil for water plants should not be enriched with organic matter or fertiliser.

planting marginal plants

Marginals are shallow-water plants that prefer no more than 5–10cm (2–4in) of water covering their roots. They fall into two groups according to their root systems: those with a creeping rootstock, or rhizome, like *Iris laevigata*, and those with fibrous roots, such as pickerel weed (*Pontederia cordata*). Grow both types in baskets. Select a planting basket of a suitable size, and line it with hessian or a geotextile, unless you are using a micro-mesh planting basket. Part-fill with soil or aquatic compost (see opposite), before inserting the plant and firming with more soil. Place the basket on the planting ledge, if there is one, or on brick piles to bring the plants up to the required level.

- **to plant marginal plants with rhizomes** remove dead leaves, trim away any old brown roots with a sharp knife and pack the soil fairly firmly around the roots, leaving the horizontal rootstock exposed.
- **to plant marginal plants with fibrous roots** use a sharp knife to trim off any dead and discoloured leaves and old brown roots, then trim back the healthy roots to about 5–10cm (2–4in), and cut back any large shoots. Plant deeply, with the roots going straight down into the soil and the base of the shoots at soil level.

marginal plants with rhizomes

- arrow arum (*Peltandra sagittifolia*)
- bog arum (*Calla*)
- bogbean (*Menyanthes*)
- corkscrew rush (*Juncus effusus* f. *spiralis*)
- great water plantain (*Alisma plantago-aquatica*)
- *Iris laevigata*
- marsh marigold (*Caltha palustris*)
- sweet flag (*Acorus*)

Caltha palustris

marginal plants with fibrous roots

- candelabra primula (*Primula beesiana*)
- cotton grass (*Eriophorum angustifolium*)
- monkey flower (*Mimulus*)
- pickerel weed (*Pontederia cordata*)

Primula beesiana

planting water lilies in a lined basket

1 **Line the basket** with hessian to stop the compost from spilling out through the mesh, and half-fill with soil or aquatic compost.

2 **Place the water lily** in the centre. Add more soil, packing it firmly around the plant. Fill the basket to within 2–3cm (1in) of the rim. Top up with a layer of coarse gravel to prevent the soil from floating away. Trim off any surplus liner. Water the plant with pond water to settle the soil around the roots.

3 **Once the soil** is saturated, lower the basket into the desired position within the pond.

LINER TIP As an alternative to hessian, use geotextile to line the baskets or use micro-mesh planting baskets.

planting water lilies

Water lilies (*Nymphaea*) are deep-water plants, and require a depth of 45–60cm (18–24in) or more. Before planting or replanting them, trim off any large leaves. (If these are left on they will increase the plant's buoyancy, which may result in it floating free of its container and rising to the pond surface.) To encourage new roots to form quickly, trim back the fibrous roots and cut away any dead or rotting sections of the thick fleshy stem, or rhizome. Once the basket is placed in the water, make sure the shoots reach the surface: this may mean standing the basket temporarily on bricks until the leaves grow, then lowering it gradually over a period of weeks until it sits on the bottom of the pool.

flowering plants for deeper water

- golden club (*Orontium aquaticum*)
- *Nuphar lutea*
- water fringe (*Nymphoides peltata*)
- water hawthorn (*Aponogeton distachyos*)
- water lilies (*Nymphaea*)

If bubbles rise from the planting basket as it is lowered into the water, hold it steady until it achieves natural buoyancy, otherwise it will tip onto its side and spill the contents.

patios & containers

Seasonal and permanent plants grown in containers and raised beds rely entirely on you for their care. Feed and water regularly from late spring and they will reward you with a cheerful patio display all summer.

now is the season to . . .

■ **plant out half-hardy bedding** plants as soon as the risk of frost has passed, usually late May. You will still find plenty of summer bedding plants in garden centres and other outlets, even though it is too late to order plants by mail or over the Internet.

■ **prepare the soil** in raised beds and patio borders by clearing any weeds and forking in some organic matter, such as rotted manure or mushroom compost. Apply a general fertiliser before planting.

■ **plant annual climbers** in containers or raised beds to bring an extra colourful dimension to the patio. Nasturtiums and sweet peas look charming growing up a wigwam of bamboo canes or rustic poles.

■ **plant some herbs,** not only for kitchen use, but also for their fragrance. Plant them by hot paving – the heat will help to release their aromatic oils. Lavenders, rosemary, sage, marjoram, coriander and basil all grow in hot, dry conditions.

■ **start to think about summer containers** and hanging baskets for a summer patio display (see page 148). Achieve dramatic results by restricting yourself to simple colour schemes, using foliage as well as flowers to keep schemes lively.

■ **plant up pots or raised beds** with summer bedding to provide a colourful splash from July onwards. Or choose unusual flowering perennial plants, like blue agapanthus, and bulbs such as the glorious South African pineapple lily (*Eucomis*).

■ **direct sow hardy annuals** in pots or raised beds (see page 126).

■ **introduce tender shrubs** in large containers. A lemon or pomegranate plant, for example, will provide a wonderful summer display, but must be taken indoors in late autumn.

care of container shrubs

Most evergreens are at their peak of growth and should not be trimmed or pruned until summer.

- **dwarf rhododendrons and camellias** should have their old flowers and seed heads removed (see page 137).
- **early flowering deciduous shrubs** generally benefit from being pruned as soon as flowering is over; remove branches that have flowered to encourage leafy growth in summer and even more flowers next year (see page 136).
- **few topiary specimens** need clipping in late spring, apart from plants that grow rapidly and need several clips a year. Trim privet (*Ligustrum*) and *Lonicera nitida* now, following the original shape. Use small shears, or even scissors, to get the precise outline.
- **give roses** a light feed in late spring and, if you don't object to using chemical sprays, treat to prevent mildew, black spot and aphid attack (see page 37).

PRUNING TIP Do not prune daphnes – they are prone to virus diseases and can get infected at pruning wounds.

Plant up a group of improvised containers after drilling drainage holes. Violas, azaleas and forget-me-nots make a bright display.

Slow-release fertiliser pellets supply food continuously over several months throughout the growing season.

feeding

Patio plants get hungry, especially during summer. The more permanent shrubs and trees, in the open ground, will need little by way of plant food, since their roots will be searching for nutrients over a wide area. But plants grown in containers, raised beds, or borders where soil is in any way limited will need feeding regularly from late spring onwards.

- **liquid feeds** can be given every 7–14 days, when watering, throughout the growing season. Start six weeks after planting, when the fertiliser in the compost will have run out. Use a high-potash feed, like tomato fertiliser, to promote flowers.
- **slow-release fertilisers** provide all the necessary nutrients container plants require for several months or even the whole growing season – see manufacturer's instructions. They release more nutrients as temperature and available moisture increase – just when plants need them most.

FEEDING TIP Avoid over-feeding plants. It makes them grow too lush and they become disease-prone. The results of over-feeding are more of a problem, especially on patios, than plant starvation. Remember that plants manufacture the bulk of their own food from sunlight, water and carbon dioxide in the air; substances absorbed through the roots are merely supplements – essential, but needed only in tiny quantities.

watering

Watering is the single most important task in container gardening. More plants suffer stress through lack of water than from any other cause.

- **water new plants** thoroughly, not only when planted but regularly later, until their root systems are developed.
- **water plants in containers and hanging baskets** daily as summer approaches.
- **check small patio beds** with shallow soil as they dry out fast. Even after rain it is worth checking just below the surface in case the soil is bone dry. A thorough soaking every two weeks in hot, dry weather makes all the difference to the way your patio plants perform over summer.

WATERING TIP The best means of ensuring adequate water supplies for hanging baskets and containers is to fit an automatic watering system (see page 237). These kits need not be complicated and are operated by a time switch, so that watering will still take place if you are away.

Give container-grown plants a good soaking immediately after planting, preferably through a fine rose attachment. Continue watering until the water runs out of the bottom of the pot.

small trees and shrubs for the patio

• bay (*Laurus nobilis*) • box (*Buxus*) • daphnes • dwarf cherries (such as *Prunus incisa* 'Kojo-no-mai') • japanese maples (hybrids of *Acer palmatum* or *A. japonicum*) • miniature rhododendrons • pieris • christmas box (*Sarcococca*) • strawberry tree (*Arbutus*)

patios & containers/2

creating a summer display

Well-planted pots and hanging baskets will cheer up the patio in summer. Use colourful bedding and plant generously to stage as bright a display as possible.

summer containers

Garden centres have a wide range of bedding and other plants for summer containers. They are often presented in colour groups, so it is easy to choose those that fit a special colour scheme. And why not visit some of the many flower shows and plant fairs that take place at this time of year? You will find a whole range of interesting plants on sale.

- **anchor plants are central to a container,** whether used alone or surrounded by smaller or trailing plants. Fuchsias are a popular choice, but why not try something different, perhaps trained as a standard, such as *Solanum rantonnetii*? Even succulents, like *Aeonium arboreum* and the century plant (*Agave americana*), make fine anchors.
- **trailing or filling plants** to go with the anchors include jolly yellow bidens and cool blue scaevola. New varieties of pelargonium are bred every year, but many older kinds, especially those with aromatic leaves, are just as beautiful and easy to grow.
- **use fragrance, as well as colour.** Heliotrope has a bewitching scent, as do mignonettes (easy annuals), night-scented stocks and sweet peas, especially the older, scented varieties.
- **newly purchased plants** for bedding and containers need to be exposed gradually to cold, windy or excessively wet weather before they go outside. This is known as 'hardening off' (see page 167).

plants for summer containers

anchor plants • *Aeonium arboreum* 'Atropurpureum' • castor oil plant (*Ricinus*) • century plant (*Agave americana*) • daisy bush (*Argyranthemum*), grown as standards • fuchsias • *Solanum rantonnetii* • tree datura (*Brugmansia*)

trailing & filling plants • bacopa • *Bidens ferulifolia* • *Helichrysum petiolare* • laurentia • nasturtiums • pelargoniums • petunias (right) • scaevola

- **water containers daily** from late spring onwards and feed every 7–14 days during the growing season, from six weeks after planting. Use a high-potash feed, such as tomato fertiliser.

hanging baskets

The most attractive baskets are those with plants growing through the sides as well as out of the top. When planting, aim for an almost perfect sphere of foliage and flower.

- **line baskets with natural moss** or with a lining made from coconut-fibre or recycled cardboard. Black plastic is a practical but less attractive alternative.
- **after planting a hanging basket,** wash off any compost that has lodged on the leaves, preferably using rainwater collected in a butt. The plants will take a few days to orientate

planting a summer container

1 **Take a large pot**, at least 40cm (16in) across the top and with a drainage hole. Fill to roughly two-thirds with soil-less potting compost.

2 **Try out the plants** in their eventual positions, placing the anchor plant centrally in the container. Then remove the plants and make a hole large enough for the anchor plant's rootball.

3 **Place the filling** and trailing plants around the 'anchor', encouraging the trailers to grow down over the sides. Add more compost between the plants and gently firm them into position. Water thoroughly.

planting a hanging basket

1 Line a wire mesh basket with a thick layer of moss or an alternative liner. Fill to about a third with soil-less potting compost. Then balance the basket on a bucket or a big pot so that you can work with both hands.

2 Introduce the plants, gently teasing the roots through the sides of the basket and liner. Firm them into the compost. Add more compost and insert more moss and plants, working in layers.

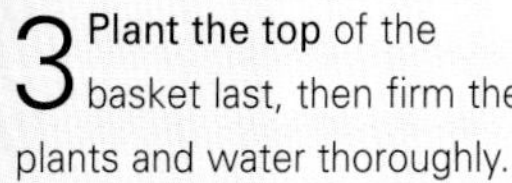

3 Plant the top of the basket last, then firm the plants and water thoroughly.

themselves and will then begin to fill the space around the basket.

- **suspend a hanging basket** from a strong hook well secured to a wall or strong support, and where it is in full light and sheltered from wind. Make sure the basket is easy to reach for watering and that it will not be in your way.
- **for a good display,** hanging baskets require regular feeding and constant watering; in hot weather they may need watering at least twice a day. Mix water-retaining gel into the soil-less compost to reduce the rate at which moisture is lost.

looking ahead . . .

☑ SUMMER Continue to feed and water containers and hanging baskets.
☑ Deadhead plants for a continuous display.

selecting permanent plants

Small shrubs and trees help to give an outdoor seating area a feeling of 'garden', rather than merely an outside room. Those that are evergreen will provide interest all year round and brighten the garden scene in winter. Select the permanent plants in a mixed container first, to create a framework.

trees and shrubs

Choose trees and shrubs that are fairly small or slow growing, because the rooting space is limited. Japanese maples are ideal because they grow at a gentle pace and, provided they have a sheltered, partially shaded spot, are shapely and statuesque. Their autumn colour, winter outline and fresh spring foliage make them great year-rounders, and they grow as well in a roomy container as in open ground.

patio roses

Roses are popular for containers on terraces and patios, but it is important to select those that suit hot, sunny patio conditions.

- **choose disease-resistant varieties** (check with an up-to-date catalogue).
- **check they will flower** all summer. True patio roses, such as the pink, fragrant Queen Mother, yellow Perestroika or Scarlet Patio, keep on flowering, as long as you remove the dead flowerheads throughout summer.
- **make sure** they do not grow too large.
- **try to choose** varieties for fragrance.

patio climbers

Climbing plants can be grown in containers or in the ground. Vigorous grape vines or wisteria trained on frames or pergolas create a shady canopy in summer, but let in more sunshine when their leaves fall in autumn. Climbing roses, too, can be used in this way, or trained over arches around the edge of the patio. Even small climbing roses, such as the bright coppery-hued Warm Welcome, will grow well in a large container.

The shapely, lime-green flowerheads of euphorbia will brighten the patio in late spring. Being semi-evergreen, this perennial provides interest all year.

permanent containers

Trees and shrubs will survive many years in containers as long as they are well tended. Choose plants carefully to stand alone or use them in groups to set off more transient displays of seasonal bedding.

year-round containers

Growing permanently in containers allows you to enjoy plants that require different soil and conditions from those found in your garden. Rhododendrons and pieris, for example, would not thrive in alkaline soil, but you can grow them to perfection in a pot of lime-free ericaceous compost. Spreading plants like many bamboos could overwhelm a small garden, but in a pot they look lovely and are less trouble.

This form of gardening is also very versatile, as you can create different effects with just one permanent plant by surrounding it with temporary plants in smaller pots, changing them from year to year and from season to season (see pages 146–149).

Container-grown trained box, in pairs, bring formality to this spring garden (above).

Shapely perennials such as this agave (right) will give form to a summer patio planting.

selecting plants

Choose trees and shrubs that are naturally slow growing, require little pruning and have appeal throughout the year. Flowering is not essential as evergreens give foliage interest in winter and provide a quiet background to brilliant summer bedding. Some, particularly conifers, have a distinct conical or rounded form; others, like box and small-leaved privets, can be trained as topiary.

grow trees alone

Trees and other permanent plants are best grown alone in a container. Any additional plants, particularly bedding and bulbs, not only compete for the limited amount of moisture and nutrients, but often require different watering and feeding regimes.

Standard plants are another good choice. Fuchsias, ivies, *Hydrangea paniculata* and even wisteria can be grown this way, although they usually need permanent staking.

Do not overlook deciduous trees either. Japanese maples are shapely in and out of leaf and have wonderful foliage that changes with the seasons.

choosing containers

A container must be large enough for the plant to spread its roots and grow well for at least two years. It should be sturdy, broad-based for stability and flaring to the rim, so the rootball can be slid out easily for repotting. Drainage is essential, ideally one hole 2–3cm (1in) across for every 30cm (12in) diameter of rim. Ceramic or terracotta pots must be frost-proof if they are outdoors all winter.

planting a container

The best time to do this is in April. Before you start, water your plant thoroughly and allow to drain. Position the pot where it is to stand (unless you have a wheeled pot trolley) and raise it on bricks or 'pot feet'. Crocking the base creates crevices where adult vine weevils can hide, so instead cover the drainage hole with geotextile membrane to prevent pests from entering and compost from being washed through. Use loam-based rather than soil-less

A mature pittosporum forms the centrepiece of a container grouping, together with a black-stemmed bamboo and an olive tree.

potting compost. As well as being heavier and giving stability, loam-based composts retain nutrients and moisture for longer, and are easier to re-wet.

trees and shrubs for containers

bamboos • bay (*Laurus nobilis*) • box (*Buxus sempervirens*) • camellias • *Cordyline australis* • *Hydrangea paniculata* 'Grandiflora' • japanese maples (*Acer palmatum* var. *dissectum* types) • *Ligustrum lucidum* • pieris • pittosporum • rhododendrons (azalea types)

after planting

- **insert supports** for climbers so that the plants can grow through them from the start. By summer, the supports should be almost invisible amid the flowers.
- **protect the plants** from frost, even if they are hardy. Keep some fleece handy to throw over them, but remove it in the morning as temperatures begin to rise.
- **mulch to conserve moisture,** suppress weeds and improve the pot's appearance. Use an organic material like cocoa shells, or something decorative such as pebbles or fir cones.
- **regular watering** is essential; erratic delivery causes stress to the plant.
- **feed** by lightly forking in a slow-release granular fertiliser that will last all season, or water on liquid feed at regular intervals.

in the following years

Routine pruning of trees and conifers should be unnecessary other than to remove any dead or damage shoots, or crossing branches. Climbers and topiary will need attention (see pages 132 and 146), and flowering shrubs require deadheading (see page 137).

Leave woody plants undisturbed for two to three years before repotting, then move young plants into a larger container; you can leave more mature plants up to five years. 'Refresh' compost annually in March or April by scraping off the top 5cm (2in) of old compost and replacing it with fresh, mixed with a slow-release fertiliser.

In repotting years you may need to do a little root pruning on established shrubs while they are dormant.

planting a tree in a container

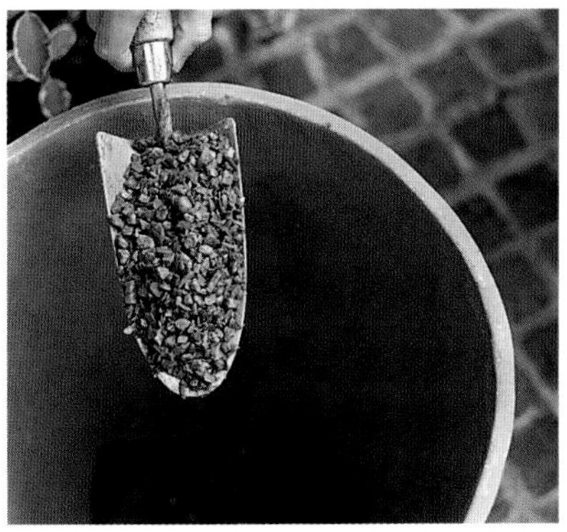

1 **Place a square of geotextile** over the drainage hole and cover with 2–3cm (1in) coarse grit, for good drainage. Add some loam-based compost mixed with a little bone meal, to come about halfway up the sides of the container.

2 **Position the plant centrally.** Pack compost round the sides of the rootball, shaking the plant gently to eliminate air gaps. Push the compost down securely but without over-compacting it.

3 **Fill the container** with more compost and water thoroughly. This will cause the compost to sink to the correct level. Add the mulch of your choice.

lawns

Attention now will influence the appearance of your lawn throughout the summer. Give the lawn a regular spring clean to clear moss, weeds and dead grass, and to encourage strong growth in the future.

now is the season to . . .

- **control isolated weeds** by spot treating with a liquid or gel weedkiller that is sprayed or brushed onto the leaves.
- **treat weed-infested lawns** with a combination method (see right).
- **scarify the lawn** to get rid of thatch.
- **think about laying a new lawn** (see pages 154–157).
- **start mowing the lawn** when the grass begins to grow, which is once the soil temperature has risen to 5–7°C (40–45°F).
- **look out for yellow patches** on your lawn. This may be a sign of 'snow mould' or leatherjacket grubs (see opposite).

weedkiller safety

✓ Read and follow the instructions exactly.
✓ Keep weedkillers locked away from children and pets.
✓ Always wash your hands after using any garden chemicals.
✗ Never mix weedkillers with other garden chemicals.
✗ Never decant weedkillers into unmarked containers.
✗ Never dispose of diluted or undiluted weedkiller down the drain; instead pour it onto a bare patch of soil away from plants. (Once in contact with the soil the chemicals become inactive.)

weed control

In spring the grass grows increasingly fast and so do the weeds. The best time to apply a combined chemical and cultural treatment is in late spring, when the grass is growing vigorously and will not be damaged by the weed-control measures.

Apply a selective hormone weedkiller to the entire lawn. These weedkillers contain chemicals that cause the leaves and stems of weeds to twist, distort and grow upright. The weeds are weakened but are also within reach of the mower blades, making this a combination of chemical and cultural control. If weeds have been allowed to establish in a lawn, it may take several treatments to eradicate them, even to the extent of using different weedkillers on different occasions.

If you prefer not to use chemicals, prise out the weeds individually with an old kitchen knife or a purpose-made tool called a 'grubber'.

A well-maintained lawn forms a fresh green carpet that makes the perfect foil for a colourful border.

dealing with thatch

Over the year small quantities of grass clippings gradually build up in the lawn, even when a collecting box is used. Grass blades die and lie on the soil, as do fragments of moss. If this debris is left it will eventually form a layer of dead material called 'thatch', which often goes unnoticed, hidden by living grasses. The most obvious indicator of thatch is when the lawn feels springy underfoot.

Scarifying, or raking, is the equivalent of giving an established lawn a good scrub and brush up. Use a wire rake to drag out all the thatch, dead grass and dead moss. For large lawns a powered scarifier simplifies this job. Once the debris is removed, air circulates more freely around the grass blades and water can penetrate to the roots.

NEW LAWN TIP Don't scarify a new lawn, even one that has been turfed, because the vigorous action will cause damage.

moss control

To control moss successfully, you must tackle the underlying causes such as shade, compacted soil and poor drainage. Moss can also build up in wet winters on otherwise healthy lawns and if left untreated, it will smother and eventually kill the grass. The use of a lawn sand, that is a combined moss and weedkiller with added fertiliser, saves time and is ideal for the busy gardener. As this product feeds the grass, it will recover quickly and grow over the gaps left by the dead moss.

Choose a day when there is heavy dew so that the chemicals stick to the moss and weed leaves. The moss and other weeds will turn black within five to seven days, but wait until the moss turns brown, which indicates that it is completely dead, before raking. Any patches that return to green should be treated again. Collect and dispose of the dead moss, but not in the compost bin, because the chemical residues will taint its contents.

mowing the lawn

In cold areas, late spring will be the earliest you start cutting your lawn; the heavier the soil, the longer it takes to warm up. In mild areas, where the soil never freezes, you may have mown several times by now. Always begin by giving the shaggy lawn a light trim, with the mower blades on the highest setting. The golden rule is never to reduce the length of the grass by more than a third at a single cut, as this will damage the lawn. Once the grass is under control, progress to a finer, lower cut by adjusting the blades in stages.

pests and diseases

Most lawn problems show up in summer and, even more, in autumn. However, in late spring you may detect yellow circular patches on the lawn.

- **this is the first sign of snow mould,** also known as fusarium patch, which can be troublesome, particularly in wet conditions. Keep it in check by cutting down on applications of high-nitrogen spring fertiliser and spiking the lawn so that moisture does not collect around the base of the grass plants.
- **leatherjacket grubs can also cause yellow patches** on lawns. They feed on grass roots, causing the plants to die. The simplest control is to water the yellow patches and cover them overnight with a sheet of black plastic. In the morning remove the plastic to expose the leatherjackets, which will have come to the surface. Throw bread into the area to attract birds. They will fly in to eat the bread and the grubs.

controlling moss

1 **Scatter lawn sand** evenly over the area, at the rate recommended by the manufacturer.

2 **Use a fan-shaped wire** rake to remove all dead brown moss and debris. Rake from the edges of the area towards the centre to prevent the moss from spreading if any remains alive.

3 **Spiking the lawn** in late spring will help to reduce the incidence of moss by aerating the soil so that grass roots can breathe. Moss is most likely to develop in shady, wet conditions.

new lawns

By late spring the soil is warm and moist, providing the ideal conditions for a new lawn to establish rapidly. Grass grows best from turf or seed in moist but well-drained soil, and good light is usually essential, although lawn mixtures that tolerate some shade are available.

planning your lawn

The size and shape of the lawn depends largely on the size and style of your garden: sweeping curves suit an informal setting while straight lines are more formal. If you are planning narrow strips of grass, make these multiples of the cutting width of your mower. This will make mowing easier and give a more even finish.

Whether grown from turf or seed, make a new lawn slightly larger than its ultimate planned size. This allows you to trim back the edges once the lawn is established to give a crisp outline.

seed or turf?

Before creating a new lawn, the big decision is whether to lay turf or sow seed. Turf provides an instant effect, but it is much more expensive; on the other hand, seed is cheaper, but takes longer to establish. As the soil preparation for turfing a lawn and sowing seed is the same, the deciding factor tends to be how long you are prepared to wait.

preparing the ground

A lawn is a permanent garden feature, so it is worth preparing the ground thoroughly to avoid future problems. You do not want to be continually controlling established weeds or trying to rectify an uneven surface.

Deep and thorough digging is particularly important to ensure that the soil is well cultivated where most root activity occurs, and grass roots penetrate surprisingly deeply. It is essential, first of all, to remove all traces of perennial weeds. Use a spade to dig the area to a depth of at least 25cm (10in). Carefully remove all weed roots and creeping stems. You can do this by hand as you dig, but where the ground contains a high proportion of pernicious perennial weeds, such as horsetail, you may need to use a chemical weedkiller based on glyphosate to eradicate weeds from the soil completely.

SOWING TIP Birds will not eat grass seeds that have been treated with an unpalatable chemical repellent. They may, however, 'dust bathe' in a seedbed before the lawn has started to grow. This is a nuisance, but it is easy to re-seed any resulting small bare patches.

Grass seed will start to germinate in 6–14 days after sowing (above), depending on the seed mixture and the weather.

Turf must be unrolled and laid as soon as possible, ideally within 24 hours of its delivery (left). To avoid unnecessary delay, agree on a delivery date that allows plenty of time to prepare the soil beforehand.

sowing seed

A seeded lawn may be slow to establish but, when sown at the optimum times in spring or autumn, the result is usually of a good quality. You can also select a seed mixture that suits your garden situation. Most reputable seed mixtures are a blend of two or more species of grass that will grow well together and provide an even, dense coverage. The species of grasses usually differ in their mode of growth and at least one will have a creeping habit. The sowing rate will vary depending on the seed mixture and the intended use for the lawn, so check the instructions on the packet.

SOWING TIP Sow at a slightly higher rate than recommended to achieve a thicker-looking lawn in a shorter period of time.

lawn seed mixtures

- **for fine ornamental lawns** These lawns look lush and beautiful, but will not stand up to hard wear. Mow with a cylinder mower for a fine close finish, and one with a roller for stripes. Sowing rate: 35–50g per m^2 (1–2oz per sq yd)
  Mowing height: 1–1.5cm (½–⅝in)
- **for lightly shaded lawns** This is the best mix for lightly or partially shaded areas where the soil is moist, but unsuitable for deep shade, dry soils or under evergreen trees. Sowing rate: 35–50g per m^2 (1–2oz per sq yd)
  Mowing height: 1.5–2cm (⅝–¾in)
- **for hard-wearing lawns** This mix produces a tough, good-looking lawn, tolerant of heavy use and children's games throughout the summer. Sowing rate: 25–35g per m^2 (¾–1oz per sq yd)
  Mowing height: 1.5–2cm (⅝–¾in)

sowing a lawn

1 **After digging thoroughly,** use a garden fork to break up any compacted soil to improve drainage. Level the soil, then allow it to settle for about two weeks. Any emerging weeds can be hoed off or treated with a systemic weedkiller based on the chemical glyphosate.

2 **Rake the soil roughly level.** Incorporate a base dressing of fertiliser applied at the rate of 150–200g per m^2 (4–6oz per sq yd).

3 **Firm the soil thoroughly.** To do this, shuffle over the ground taking short steps and applying pressure with your heels. Rake the soil again and remove any stones.

4 **To sow the seed evenly,** mark out the area into 1-metre squares (1-yard squares) with canes and a string line. Weigh out enough seed for 1 square metre. Pour the seed into a plastic beaker and mark the level on the side. Use this measure to save weighing the seed every time.

5 **For each square,** sow half the seed in one direction and the remainder at right angles. Pour a manageable quantity into your hand at a time and scatter evenly.

6 **When you have sown** all the seed, lightly rake the entire area to incorporate the seed into the soil surface. Water well.

new lawns/2

lawns from turf

Laying turf is the gardener's equivalent of carpet laying and the job must be done just as carefully and as systematically for a good result. So first prepare the soil as described on page 154 and mark out the area slightly larger than required.

Turf may be expensive, but about six weeks from being laid, the lawn should be well established and ready for use. However, this method is not without its drawbacks during the early stages. Newly laid turf needs to be kept well watered, and in warm dry weather this could mean as much as 25 litres per m^2 (5 gallons per sq yd) each week. If turf is allowed to dry out it will shrink and lift, exposing a much greater surface and accelerating the drying process; whereas if there is a spell of dry weather immediately after grass seed has been sown to make a new lawn, the seeds will simply remain dormant until the conditions for germination improve, rather than beginning to grow immediately.

buyimg turf

Turves are usually sold in sections 1m x 30cm (3 x 1ft) and rolled along their length, which makes them easy to stack, transport and store. Many of the more expensive turves are reinforced with a biodegradable plastic mesh, so less soil is needed to hold the root structure together and the turves can be thinner and up to 2m (6ft) in length. For extensive lawns it is possible to buy turf as a large roll, which is laid out by a contractor and cut to the exact dimensions, like a fitted carpet.

turfing a lawn

1 **Starting from one corner**, lay the first row of turf alongside a plank or garden line to get a straight edge. For lawns with curved edges, lay a hosepipe or length of rope to define the boundaries.

2 **Go back to the starting point** to lay the second row of turves at right angles to the first. This ensures that the joints are staggered, like bricks in a wall; it is called 'keying' the turves together. As you work, butt the turves up close to each other.

3 **Work from a wooden plank**; this protects the turves from damage caused by walking on them as subsequent rows are laid. The uniform pressure will also gently firm the turves into position after they are laid, helping the grass to establish.

4 **When all the turves are down**, spread a lawn top-dressing (available from garden centres) over the entire area and brush it into any gaps or cracks with a besom broom or the back of a rake. This will help to stop the turf edges from drying out and shrinking.

care of new lawns

Whether your lawn has been laid from seed or turf, once established it will need regular mowing, watering and feeding to encourage the production of healthy green growth.

mowing new lawns

New lawns sown from seed early the previous autumn or in April will be ready for their first cut at the end of May, but only a very light topping is required for the first two or three cuts. If you use a rotary mower, sharpen the blades well beforehand so that they will cut the grass rather than drag it out by the roots. Rotary mowers rely on the speed of the blades to get a cutting action, but a combination of blunt blades and shallow-rooted grass seedlings can wreak total havoc on a newly establishing lawn.

Whichever type of mower you have, use one with a roller if possible, as the pressure of the roller will bend over the young blades of grass, thus checking their rate of growth. The plants respond by branching from the base to produce many more leaves, which thickens the coverage of the lawn considerably. Some gardeners even roll a new lawn two or three times before the first cut to encourage this branching growth (called 'tillering'). Checking the top growth and stimulating extra root development produces an established lawn more quickly.

The first three or four cuts of a new lawn should be made on a high blade setting, just to 'top' the grass leaves. As the grass starts to thicken, you can gradually lower the height of the cut, but no more than a third of the total height should ever be removed in a single cut (see page 153).

watering new lawns

Young grass plants are very vulnerable in the early stages, before they become established. Freshly laid turf will dry out very quickly if not kept moist, and lawns raised from seed will also dry out rapidly because the grass leaves do not yet cover the soil surface sufficiently to stop it from drying out. One advantage of turf is that immediately after laying the turves and firming them into place, you can brush a 'top-dressing' of loam and sand into the joints to help reduce drying out and therefore shrinkage.

You should water all newly made lawns for at least two to three hours every three or five days if there is no significant rainfall. The gentlest, and most efficient, way to do this is to leave a soaker hose running at a gentle trickle on the lawn, moving it every half hour.

feeding lawns

Regular mowing gradually saps the strength of the grass. If the nutrients taken up by the grass then removed as clippings are not replaced, the lawn will lose its vigour and become vulnerable to attack from disease. Overcome this potential problem by feeding the grass as soon as growth starts in the spring.

All spring lawn feeds contain high levels of nitrogen to promote rapid, green leaf growth. Most consist of a mixture of fertilisers designed to release a constant supply of nutrients during spring and summer. If you are using fertiliser in powder or granular form, water it in if no rain falls within 48 hours of its application.

Apply solutions of lawn feed through a hose dilutor. For small lawns, use a watering can and dilute the solution according to the manufacturer's instructions on the label (see also page 153).

Consider making a hard mowing edge at the same time as laying a new lawn. This will enable the mower to glide smoothly over the lawn edges.

fruit

Now that growth is well under way, flowers must be protected from late frost if fruits are to develop. There are various pruning jobs to be done on trees and vines as well as on trained fruit. The second half of spring can bring a foretaste of fruit to come, with strawberries from the greenhouse and small gooseberries thinned from overladen branches.

Apple blossom
(on 'Cox's Orange Pippin')

now is the season to . . .

- **prune trained fruit trees** such as apples, pears, plums, figs.
- **thin small fruits** such as apricots and gooseberries, as well as wall-trained fruits.
- **uncover forced rhubarb** now that open-air supplies are plentiful; remove pots and boxes, and allow forced plants to recover without further picking.
- **tie in autumn-fruiting raspberry canes** as they develop. Thin them where necessary, keeping only the strongest spaced about 10cm (4in) apart along the wires.
- **weed mature fruit** and, with a fork, lightly cultivate the surface of the surrounding soil, ready for feeding and mulching.
- **apply a general or high-potash fertiliser** to bush and cane fruit and trained trees (see opposite).
- **water new fruit plants** in dry weather at a rate of 25 litres per m^2 (5 gallons per sq yd) a week, and hoe or pull weeds regularly.
- **take steps to prevent pests** and diseases making headway by treating at first sight.
- **keep gooseberries watered** and mulched as a precaution against gooseberry mildew, which tends to be much worse in dry conditions.
- **protect fruit blossom from late frost** with fleece, if hard frost is forecast. This applies to early peach and nectarine fruitlets as well as other small fruit trees and bushes, and wall-trained apples, pears, plums and cherries in flower.
- **net strawberries** to prevent birds from eating the ripening fruits.
- **pull out suckers** growing beside raspberries, gooseberries, apples and pears while they are small.
- **hand-pollinate outdoor peaches,** nectarines and apricots if cold weather is discouraging bees and other pollinating insects; use a soft paintbrush to transfer pollen by gently stroking the centre of each flower. Strawberries under glass may need the same assistance.

fruit cages

- **for an early crop of strawberries outdoors,** cover plants with cloches in cold weather. On warm, sunny days ventilate freely, by removing some or all of the cloches. Water regularly, and feed plants when they start flowering.
- **spread straw or lay mats around strawberries** to keep the fruits clean and dry. Wait to do this until the fruit-bearing stems begin to arch over, as it could prevent the soil from warming up and so delay ripening.
- **mulch raspberries,** using the first few cuts of lawn mowings (provided they haven't been treated with weed or moss killer). Spread a layer of clippings 5–8cm (2–3in) thick on both sides of the rows; alternatively, use garden compost or leaf-mould.

- **check blackcurrants** for any overlooked big buds, conspicuous now as they remain lifeless or produce distorted flowers and leaves. Treat for big bud mite as described on page 523.
- **bees and pollinating insects** can fly through netting cages to pollinate fruit, so there is no need to open the cages specially for this.

pruning

The purpose of pruning now is to improve the health of the fruit plants and ensure maximum cropping later on.

apples and pears

- **remove any surplus new shoots** from trees trained as espaliers, cordons and fans.
- **cut back the ends of branches** on established trained trees and main stems to limit their extent.
- **pinch out flower or fruit clusters** on trees under two years old, to direct energy into growth rather than fruit production.

plums, peaches, nectarines and cherries

Peach blossom is vulnerable to late frost and may need to be protected by horticultural fleece.

- **prune stone fruits** in growth because wounds heal faster than in winter dormancy; this reduces the risk of infection by silver-leaf disease.
- **cut out all dead,** diseased, injured and crossing or overcrowded branches.
- **remove any unwanted** new growth on espalier and fan-trained trees, particularly shoots growing towards the back or front of the tree.

figs

- **hard-prune young trees** to encourage branching; tie in new shoots as they develop.
- **remove any dead or weak** shoots on older trees, and cut off the tips of main branches to stimulate fruiting sideshoots; cut back a few of the old branches to one or two buds, to encourage the formation of some young replacement stems.

grapes

- **cut off the tip from each flowering shoot,** two leaves beyond its first bunch of flowers, and pinch out the tip of any resulting sideshoots after one leaf.
- **tie in the flowering shoots** to training wires.

thinning small fruits

Certain trees and bushes set excessively heavy crops of fruit, which are unlikely to reach good size and quality unless some are removed early.

- **thin trained peaches,** nectarines and apricots, especially those grown under glass, when the fruitlets are the size of hazelnuts. Reduce each cluster to a single fruit, and thin out the rest so that the fruitlets are spaced about 8–10cm (3–4in) apart along the branches.
- **thin gooseberries** now (see below).
- **trained apples and pears** benefit from similar treatment towards the end of May.

feeding bush and trained fruits

Once plants have started growing, usually in April, use a general-purpose or high-potash feed in powdered or granular form, and sprinkle it over the soil area shaded by the stems or branches.

- **for bush or cane fruit,** apply powdered or granular feed at a rate of 70g (2oz) per plant.
- **for trained fruit trees,** apply at a rate of 100g per m^2 (3oz per sq yd).
- **in dry weather,** water in the fertiliser.
- **two or three weeks later** spread a generous mulch of garden compost or well-rotted manure over thoroughly moist, weed-free soil.

thinning gooseberries

1 **Thin gooseberries** when they are roughly the size of grapes.

2 **Leave the fruits** or fruit clusters 5–8cm (2–3in) apart, and use the thinnings for cooking or to make jam.

there is still time to:

- **plant perpetual strawberries** and autumn-fruiting raspberries for crops this year.
- **prune blueberries** and cut down old canes of autumn raspberries, but do this before new growth is well advanced.
- **sow alpine strawberry seeds** under glass or outdoors, if conditions are warm.
- **train and tie in the new fruiting canes** of blackberries, hybrid berries and other brambles, fanning them out in their cropping positions.

vegetables

As the weather starts to warm up, soil preparation begins in earnest. A warm, drying soil is ideal for working a seedbed to a fine tilth and for sowing hardier vegetables outdoors. It is a hectic time for the gardener, but work done now will have a major impact on the success of summer cropping.

now is the season to . . .

- **sow hardier vegetables outdoors** once the soil has warmed to a minimum temperature of 7–7.5°C (44–45°F).
- **sow many of the cabbage family outdoors,** including cauliflowers, kale, kohl rabi and sprouting broccoli, all of which mature much later in the year. Choose different varieties to give a continuity of supply: cauliflowers, for example, can be autumn-maturing (early to late autumn), winter-maturing (late winter through to early spring) and spring-maturing (early spring until early summer the following year).
- **sow root vegetables outdoors** (see page 162). Dig down two spade depths to allow for deeper root penetration, which will give better quality vegetables.
- **begin successional sowings** of quick-maturing crops such as lettuce and radish, and crops that you don't want maturing all at once, such as peas and dwarf beans (see opposite).
- **sow runner beans,** which like a warmed soil, later rather than earlier, in double rows. Position supports as soon as the seedlings emerge, as bean seedlings grow rapidly.
- **plant maincrop potatoes** 10cm (4in) deep (see page 163).
- **plant out autumn and winter-maturing** brussels sprouts.
- **plant out bulb onions** and onion sets (see page 163).
- **make regular patrols** through the vegetable patch with a sharp hoe to keep weeds in check.
- **mulch perennial crops,** such as rhubarb or artichokes, with well-rotted organic matter to help suppress weeds and retain moisture.
- **water regularly:** it is important to give young vegetable plants as much water as they need to keep them growing steadily.
- **look out for signs of potential pests** such as slug damage or early aphid infestation (see pages 53 and 336). Pests are more easily dealt with if spotted early.
- **protect the cabbage family** from flea beetle and cabbage root fly damage by covering with fleece or fitting 'collars' round individual plants.
- **harvest asparagus shoots** ('spears') in established beds, once they are about15cm (6in) high. Slice the stem 2–3cm (1in) below soil level.
- **keep harvesting the flowering shoots** of sprouting broccoli so that more are produced.

and if you have time . . .

- **start a long-term planting** of asparagus (it takes five years to produce spears). Set the crowns in trenches 10cm (4in) deep, 30cm (12in) apart, with 45cm (18in) between the crowns.

Get peas off to a flying start in cold areas by sowing in a length of plastic guttering filled with seed compost. Slide the 'instant' row of peas into a shallow trench outdoors when weather conditions allow.

sowing quick-maturing crops

Many vegetables grow quickly and mature all at once, so sowing little and often – or successional sowing – is the best way to maintain a regular supply.

- **sow peas, spinach, spinach beet and dwarf beans** (also known as french, string or kidney beans); make successional sowings every three weeks. Sow beans in double rows.
- **sow lettuces and radishes** every two to three weeks. You can sow quick-growing salad crops such as lettuce, rocket and radishes between rows of slow growers such as parsnips, for efficient use of space; this is known as intercropping.
- **sow salad onions** at three to four-week intervals, thinly in 7–8cm (3in) wide bands, to avoid the need for thinning. Harvest them about seven weeks after sowing.

recommended cultivars

PEAS (EARLY) • 'Daybreak' • 'Fortune' • 'Kelvedon Wonder'
PEAS (MAINCROP) • 'Bikini' • 'Cavalier' • 'Rondo'
DWARF BEANS • 'Aramis' • 'Masal' • 'Purple Teepee'
RUNNER BEANS • 'Lady Di' • 'Red Rum' • 'White Lady'
SPINACH (SUMMER) • 'America' • 'Trinidad'
SALAD ONIONS • 'Ishikuro' • 'Summer Isle' • 'White Lisbon'
LETTUCE • 'Beatrice' • 'Freckles' • 'Miluna' • 'Revolution'
RADISH • 'Cherry Belle' • 'French Breakfast' • 'Juliette'

Know when the soil is ready: if weed seeds are germinating, then the soil should have warmed enough to prepare a seedbed for hardier vegetable seeds.

sowing sweetcorn

1 **Sow seeds of sweetcorn** individually in biodegradable peat pots in a heated greenhouse.

2 **Peat pots must not be allowed to dry out**, so stand them in a tray of water, which is slowly taken up from the bottom. When in the ground, the roots will grow through the base.

sowing beans

Sow beans directly into the ground, 2–3cm (1in) deep and 15cm (6in) apart.

vegetables/2

Rows of vegetable seedlings (above) are a rewarding sight in late spring. Thinning them leaves space for the remaining young plants to develop.

Thin carrot seedlings under fleece (right), protected from the low-flying pest, carrot root fly. The cultivar 'Fly Away' has lower levels of the chemical that attracts carrot root fly.

growing root crops

Many root crops that mature well into the second half of the year can be sown outdoors now: beetroot, carrot, parsnip, swede and turnip. The timing of sowing is a bit of a balancing act: beetroot, for example, if sown too early, may 'bolt', producing premature seed.

- **beetroot** Space seeds 15cm (6in) apart with 15cm (6in) between rows, to grow medium-sized, nicely rounded beets.
- **maincrop carrots** Sow in shallow seed drills, only 1cm (½in) deep. Sow thinly, 5cm (2in) apart in rows 15cm (6in) apart, to reduce the need for thinning out and reduce risk of carrot root fly. Water the drills immediately after sowing if the soil is dry; do not overwater, as the plants would then produce too much leaf and the roots would split, especially if watered heavily after a dry period.
- **parsnips** Sow in rows or in blocks 10cm (4in) apart with 10cm (4in) between rows, to prevent the roots from becoming too large and misshapen; the longer the growing season, the larger they grow. Do not grow close to carrots as they both attract carrot root fly.

recommended cultivars

BEETROOT • 'Bolthardy' • 'Chioggia Pink' • 'Red Ace'
CARROTS (MAINCROP) • 'Bertan' • 'Fly Away' • 'Parmex'
PARSNIPS • 'Avonresister' • 'Gladiator' • 'White Gem'
POTATOES (MAINCROP) • 'Desirée' • 'Nadine' • 'Romano'
ONION SETS • 'Giant Fen Globe' • 'Sturon' • 'Stuttgart Giant'

growing potatoes and onions

Potatoes and onions like a soil that is fertile but not too rich, otherwise leaf growth is encouraged at the expense of roots. The storage life of the roots will also be reduced.

potatoes

There are two main types of potato: earlies and maincrop. Earlies are planted in early spring and need only 14–15 weeks in the ground to produce tender 'new' potatoes for immediate use. These are the potatoes to grow in a small garden because they take up less space and for a shorter time. Maincrop potatoes have a longer growing season (about 20 weeks) and need more space, but they produce heavier yields, which also store well.

- **earlies** Earth up early potatoes to protect new shoots from late frosts. Once the threat of frost has passed, continue to earth up when the tops (haulms) of early potatoes are about 25cm (10in) high. Draw up the soil to cover the bottom 12–13cm (5in) of the stems so that tubers form on the buried sideshoots.
- **maincrop** Plant maincrop potatoes now. Space them 40cm (16in) apart with 75cm (2ft 6in) between the rows. Grow them apart from other crops, if possible, as they take up a lot of space above ground, with their abundant leafy growth, as well as below ground.

onions

Onions may be planted as seed or sets. It is a race against time to get enough growth on the plant before the bulbs start to swell after midsummer's day. Hand-weed carefully to avoid disturbing their shallow roots.

- **bulb onions** Seeds sown in early spring can be planted out now that the soil is warmer, burying the bulbs just below the soil surface. A spacing of 25–30cm (10–12in) apart and 25–30cm (10–12in) between the rows is ideal, but they must be kept well-watered until they have established.
- **onion sets** Plant out these 'mini-plants' now, 15cm (6in) apart, with 15cm (6in) between rows, and 1cm (½in) deep to give medium-sized, nicely rounded bulbs. If possible, select smaller sets as they are less likely to 'bolt'. 'Golden Ball' is a good cultivar that tolerates later planting.

tender crops

If you wait for the soil to warm up before sowing tender crops, the plants will just produce leafy growth and little or no crop, so they must be started off under protection. Most also hate root disturbance, so sow them in individual small pots. Plants that start growing in a greenhouse or polythene tunnel or on a kitchen windowsill must have two to three weeks of hardening off before being transplanted into the garden soil (for gradual acclimatisation to outdoor growing conditions, see page 167). If you buy your young plants from a garden centre or nursery, they should have already been hardened off, but it is worth checking.

- **aubergines, peppers and** tomatoes can be moved outside to grow successfully when the soil temperature reaches 10°C (50°F).
- **courgettes, marrows and** squashes can all be grown outside, but generally tend to do better in a coldframe or polythene tunnel. They prefer high humidity and may suffer from mildew if grown outside in dry conditions. Transplant them with minimum root disturbance, as even slight damage to the roots can result in the roots rotting and, eventually, in the loss of the plant.
- **young plants of sweetcorn** should be about 15–20cm (6–8in) high before they are planted out. Transplant them in their moist peat pots into square or rectangular blocks (as they are pollinated by wind), with the plants spaced 35cm (14in) apart, with 35cm (14in) between rows.

Pinch out the tops of broad beans once in full flower as a way of controlling blackfly without using chemicals.

harvesting now

- asparagus
- early carrots
- early turnips
- lettuce (overwintered and seedling)
- radishes
- spinach
- spring cabbage (left)
- spring or salad onions
- sprouting broccoli

herbs

The herb garden is full of promise at this time of year, as fresh aromatic leaves unfurl and young plants replace the old. Start to gather the first fragrant tips from established herbs, but also continue sowing, planting and propagating for later harvest.

Herbs such as rosemary, mint, basil, sage and bay revel in the good drainage and extra attention they receive in containers.

now is the season to . . .

- **trim young woody herbs**, such as sage and artemisias, to keep them dense and shapely.
- **clip mature sage, rosemary and santolina** hard, but not into the old wood. Cut out completely any damaged, straggly or misplaced shoots.
- **lightly shear over thyme plants** to remove bare stems.
- **thin early sowings of salad** and other annual herbs to 10cm (4in) apart, then water to settle the disturbed seedlings.
- **pot up strong seedlings** in 10cm (4in) pots for planting in containers or standing on the kitchen windowsill.
- **think of planting a herb hedge** as an edging (see opposite).
- **plant out mint and tarragon** forced from dormant roots under glass in late winter and pot-grown herbs to use out of season.
- **plant up your own seedlings** and home-raised plants in pots and troughs where garden space is limited.
- **top-dress herbs in large containers** by replacing the top 2–5cm (1–2in) of soil with fresh potting compost.
- **harden off cuttings** rooted and potted up in late summer last year under glass, and plant out in permanent positions.
- **take cuttings** of shrubby herbs like bay, rosemary and santolina using sideshoots pulled off with a short 'heel' of woody tissue from the main stem.
- **take soft-tip cuttings** of sage and tarragon (see opposite).
- **harvest herbs** while they are young by pinching off their growing tips. This encourages larger, bushier plants.
- **in exposed positions, support angelica** and other tall herbs before they are damaged by spring winds.
- **harvest sweet woodruff** when the tiny white flowers appear, a sign that you can start cutting and drying flowering stems at their most aromatic for use in tonics and tisanes.
- **crumble leftover dried herbs from last season** as fresh herbs become available; scatter them over newly sown flower and vegetable seeds to confuse soil pests.

and if you have time . . .

- **divide perennial clump-forming herbs**, but keep transplants watered in dry weather.
- **prepare new herb beds** for sowing and planting.
- **sow essential herbs** under glass; many, such as basil and parsley, germinate faster as the weather warms up.

herbs suitable for containers

• basil • bay • chives • curry plant • french tarragon • lemongrass • marjoram • oregano • parsley • rosemary (small plants) • sage (small plants) • salad burnet • thyme

herbs to raise from soft-tip cuttings

• bay • french tarragon • germander • lemon verbena • sage • thyme

planting herb hedges

Small aromatic evergreens like box, lavender, germander and semi-evergreen hyssop have traditionally been used to make low hedges for edging or sheltering herb borders and creating divisions or intricate knots in more formal gardens. Evergreen herbs are best planted in April or in early autumn, when pot-grown plants will establish quickly.

Small-leaved box, which can be tightly clipped, makes an ideal low edging for a herb or vegetable bed.

- Choose small, bushy plants as these settle in faster than larger specimens. Water them well an hour or two before planting.
- Mark the line of the hedge. Use a garden line or string pulled taut for straight edges; for curves, lay a hosepipe on the ground or sprinkle a sand trail.
- Dig or fork over a 30cm (12in) wide trench along the line. Break up the excavated soil, and mix in a little bone meal and garden compost to improve the texture.
- Knock the plants from their pots, and plant them about 23–25cm (9–10in) apart along the row, with the top of the rootballs at ground level. Carefully firm the soil around each plant.
- Water in the plants and lightly trim their shoot tips to encourage early branching.

propagation

Many perennial herbs can be propagated now. This will ensure young, more vigorous replacements for ageing plants.

- **layer thyme, sage and rosemary** (see page 139). Gently pull down a low, strong-growing branch to touch the ground at least 8cm (3in) from its tip, scoop out a small hole and fill with moist potting compost. Peg the stem down just below the surface with a stone or bent wire, mound more compost over the pegged area and leave until autumn.
- **take multiple layers from old rosemary** and other tall woody plants like lavender by bending all the bare, leggy stems to the ground and pegging them down as described above.
- **root the stems by 'dropping'** the whole plant. 'Dropping' means digging up an old woody plant with a sizable rootball and excavating the hole 30cm (12in) deeper. Replant at the lower level and mound soil around the emerging stems to increase the potential rooting area. Leave until autumn.
- **sow short-lived annual** herbs such as chervil, coriander and dill to provide pickings later in the year. Sow under glass in April and plant out in late May after hardening off (see page 167).

Plant invasive herbs such as mint inside a plastic bag filled with soil and lower it into a hole in the ground. This will prevent the roots from spreading.

taking soft-tip cuttings

1 **Propagate sage plants** by taking 'softwood' cuttings from the tips of young shoots. Trim a small piece of healthy stem just below a leaf joint and remove the bottom pair of leaves.

2 **Insert cuttings into pots** of sharp sand and leave them in a mini propagator or on a windowsill out of direct sunlight until they take root.

looking ahead . . .

- ☑ LATE SUMMER Take semi-ripe cuttings of herbs.
- ☑ AUTUMN Check if layered and 'dropped' plants have rooted and are ready to be cut free from the parent plant.
- ☑ WINTER Pot up roots of mint and tarragon under glass.

the greenhouse

Greenhouse plants are completely dependent on you for their welfare. During April and May there is a change of emphasis from keeping plants warm and safe from frost, to protecting them from sudden and extreme heat, as well as a marked increase in watering.

now is the season to . . .

- **increase ventilation** in the greenhouse as temperatures rise by day and, later on, at night.
- **shield plants from hot sunshine**, to protect their leaves from drying and scorching (see below).

Damping down the greenhouse floor and benches reduces the temperature because energy is used up evaporating the water. It also increases humidity, which helps plants by reducing the amount of moisture lost through their leaves.

- **increase humidity** by soaking, or 'damping down', the greenhouse floor and benches with a watering can or hose whenever you water.
- **water and feed plants** regularly; it becomes critical at this time of year.
- **mulch greenhouse beds** with well-rotted organic matter or composted bark, to prevent the soil from drying out quickly. Mulch the compost in large pots with gravel or shingle to help keep plant roots moist.
- **prepare plants for outdoor** conditions: all plants grown under glass, especially half-hardy kinds, must be accustomed to cooler temperatures, or hardened off, before being planted in the garden (see opposite).
- **prick out seedlings** sown earlier in the year as soon as they are large enough to handle; keep shaded with newspaper in sunny weather until they are growing vigorously.
- **pot up especially large seedlings** such as sunflowers and chrysanthemums individually, and move them on to the next pot size when their roots reach the sides.
- **pot up mail-order plants** as they arrive and stand in a well-lit position, but keep separate from other plants for a few days, in case they are carrying pests or diseases. Transfer seedlings and plug plants to trays or small pots as soon as possible.
- **watch out for the first signs of aphids** on the soft growth of fuchsias, carnations and other bedding plants, and also vine weevil damage on many pot plants (see page 336).
- **lightly spray the underside of leaves with water** in hot weather, to deter red spider mites from getting established.
- **inspect woody-stemmed plants** such as grape vines and greenhouse fruits for scale insects.

and if you have time . . .

- **take soft-tip cuttings** (see page 165), using short sideshoots and growing tips of: tender perennials (coleus, fuchsias, pelargoniums, marguerites, heliotropes and dahlias), flowering shrubs (hydrangeas, brooms and azaleas) and woody herbs (lemon verbena or sage).
- **take leaf cuttings** from begonias and streptocarpus (see page 255).

controlling temperature

There are several ways of keeping a greenhouse cool and moist, and you may need to use them all together in really hot weather. Smell the air when you open the greenhouse doors. A good growing atmosphere is moist and earthy, whereas low humidity smells dry and dusty.

- **when using shade paint**, always shade the outside of the glass. Shading the inside keeps out sunlight without reducing the temperature (see picture, opposite).
- **open ventilators** when temperatures rise much above 13°C (55°F) during the day; if possible open them wider on the lee of the greenhouse to prevent draughts from the windy side.
- **by the end of May** vents may need to be left open a little throughout the night.
- **leave the door open** in very warm, still conditions.
- **improve the flow of cool air** by adding louvred panels to the greenhouse sides.
- **think about installing automatic window openers,** adjusted to open once a chosen temperature is reached, to save time and worry about temperature fluctuation.

FROST TIP If an unseasonable cold frosty night should threaten, place a covering of newspaper or fleece over seedlings and tender plants, and remove it in the morning.

shading plants from hot sun

Bright sunshine will quickly scorch young seedlings, dry out compost and reduce humidity to levels at which plants struggle to grow healthily. Provide shade from April onwards with a special shade paint that becomes transparent in wet weather. Wash the greenhouse glass before applying a first, light coat to the outside of the glass with a roller, brush or spray. Follow with a denser second coat in late May.

Alternatively, cover the greenhouse roof with shade netting, sold in various densities, or fit adjustable blinds, which can be operated by hand or controlled automatically.

VENTILATION TIP Most greenhouses are inadequately ventilated, so consider adding more roof vents if it is difficult to keep cool. Ideally the total area of roof vents should equal 15–20 per cent of the ground area of the greenhouse.

getting plants ready for the garden

The best way to acclimatise plants to outdoor conditions (harden off) is to transfer them to a coldframe and keep the lid closed for a week; if frost threatens, cover the frame overnight with a blanket or old mats. Start ventilating the frame on mild days by raising the lid a little; gradually open it farther until it is left off completely after two to three weeks, when plants will be fully acclimatised.

An alternative is to stand plants outdoors on warm days, out of the wind, and bring them back in at night for the first two weeks. Leave them out for a few nights in succession before finally transplanting them into open ground.

watering greenhouse plants

Leafy, tropical and actively growing species require more water than cool or dry-climate plants, such as desert cacti and alpines. All plants are likely to need more in hot or windy weather than when conditions are dull, cool or humid.

- **check established pot plants** at least once daily: they will need more water as the days become warmer.
- **water first thing** in the morning or late in the afternoon. Always avoid wetting the foliage in bright sunlight, otherwise it could scorch.
- **keep water at greenhouse** temperature in a tank if there is room. Alternatively, fill a couple of cans with mains water and leave them in the greenhouse overnight to warm up.
- **stand pots** of young seedlings and very dry plants in a tray of water to soak up as much as they require, then allow them to drain (right).

the greenhouse/2

planting and propagation

There is a lively bustle under glass as a steady flow of plants moves from propagation to planting stage. Crops sown in early spring will need potting on or moving to growing bags and their training started. And there is a range of food plants that can still be sown now to crop this summer.

Greenhouse cucumbers can be trained on vertical strings as single cordons. On traditional varieties it is important to distinguish between male and female flowers as you need to remove the males.

planting greenhouse crops

Start planting tomatoes, cucumbers, peppers, aubergines and melons, sown in early spring, during April, but be prepared to protect them with fleece or newspapers until later in May if frosty nights are forecast. You need to:

- **prepare and water growing bags,** and stand in position in the greenhouse for a few days to warm up before planting.
- **plant tomatoes** only when they have formed their first flowering truss.
- **plant cucumbers and melons** when three or four leaves have grown above the first pair.
- **water plants well beforehand,** then plant them 38–45cm (15–18in) apart in moist growing bags or 25cm (10in) pots, or direct in the greenhouse border.
- **water them into place,** using a diluted liquid feed.

feeding new plants

Most compost mixtures include fertilisers that are sufficient for about six weeks' growth (some contain slow-release fertiliser that lasts for several months), but after that you will need to feed plants regularly.

- **feeding is the most efficient way** to supply extra nutrients. Dilute concentrated organic or inorganic feeds according to instructions and water pots and trays once or twice a week. Use tomato fertiliser because it is cheap and will encourage fruit production. Most liquid greenhouse fertilisers can also be given as foliar feeds, useful for watering or spraying on cuttings, plants with small root systems and those recovering from disease treatment.

training greenhouse plants

Unless you are growing dwarf or bush varieties of tomato, regular training is essential to limit plant growth and maximise cropping.

- **train modern self-pollinating all-female cucumber plants,** which fruit on the main stem, like cordon tomatoes (see opposite). The traditional kinds should have their sideshoots tied laterally to a net suspended vertically from overhead wires. Remove all flowers without a tiny cucumber at their base; these are male flowers, and pollination results in bitter fruit. Pinch off the tip of each sideshoot two leaves beyond a developing fruit.
- **train melons on nets** in the same way as cucumbers, or let them spread over the border as ground cover, under tomato or cucumber plants. Pinch out the growing tip after five leaves have formed, to encourage sideshoots. Be prepared to hand-pollinate female flowers using male blooms.

propagating by seed

The following flowers and vegetables can be raised from seed in late spring.

- **cinerarias and greenhouse primulas** (*Primula obconica, P. sinensis* and *P.* x *kewensis*): grow in pots for early indoor colour from late winter.
- **late flowering annuals** like china asters, chrysanthemums and zinnias.
- **fast-growing half-hardy annuals,** such as marigolds (*Tagetes*), for bedding out in summer.
- **runner beans,** french beans, outdoor cucumbers, sweetcorn, courgettes and squashes: sow seeds individually in small pots or specially formulated root trainers about six weeks before the last expected frosts.
- **cucumbers and melons** for growing in an unheated greenhouse or coldframe.
- **biennials and perennials,** if you have no space for an outdoor nursery bed.

there is still time to . . .

- **sow a late crop of dwarf broad beans** in small pots for planting outdoors in early summer. They will crop before runner and french beans.

Regal pelargoniums are among the plants that can be successfully raised from soft-tip cuttings taken now (see page 165) or in late summer for overwintering in the greenhouse.

training tomatoes

1 **When growing tomatoes** in a greenhouse border as single-stemmed cordons, anchor the string beneath the rootball when planting and attach it to a stong overhead wire or the top of the greenhouse roof.

TIP If growing plants in a growing bag, loop the string under the bag instead.

2 **Tie the stems to the strings** as they grow, or simply twist the string round the stem. (You can also use canes.)

3 **Don't forget** to snap off all sideshoots from the base of the leaves when they are about 2–5cm (1–2in) long.

late spring

plant selector

The sharp yellows and intense greens of early spring are now joined by gentler hues – the pinks, soft mauves and whites of cherry blossom and lilac, the wine or rose-pink of crab apple blooms – and the hotter, more strident tones of tulips, to give a vast palette of colour. With exceptions such as euphorbias, early columbines and honesty, most biennials and perennials have yet to bloom, but spring-flowering clematis are in their full glory on walls and fences, and gem-like alpine auriculas and saxifrages stud rock gardens or alpine sinks. Queens of the late spring floral display, however, are the stunning rhododendrons and azaleas.

Euphorbia x *martinii*

perennials

Although a few are evergreen, most durable non-woody plants are herbaceous, that is they die down in winter and re-emerge in spring. Plant when dormant, in autumn or early spring.

1

2

3

purple, blue and violet

1 Aquilegia 'Hensol Harebell'
Columbine

The ferny leaves are a beautiful feature of this easy perennial, with purplish tints in early spring and more stormy tones as they die down. Spurred blue flowers poised above the leafy clump succeed one another into summer. Self-seeds freely but may not reproduce itself identically. Hardy.
Height: 75cm (2ft 6in) **Spread:** 30cm (12in)
Site: Partial shade, sun. Fertile and well-drained soil, preferably moist
Use: Sunny or lightly shaded border, woodland garden
Good companions: *Chaenomeles speciosa* 'Moerloosei', *Delphinium grandiflorum* 'Blue Butterfly', *Lunaria annua, Viola cornuta* Alba Group

2 Brunnera macrophylla

The blue of the 'forget-me-not' flowers is immediately appealing. The large heart-shaped leaves are less coarse in the white-variegated and spotted kinds, notably 'Langtrees', with aluminium splashes. Hardy.
Height: 45cm (18in) **Spread:** 60cm (2ft)
Site: Partial shade. Humus-rich and moist but well-drained soil
Use: Shady border, woodland garden, ground cover
Good companions: *Erythronium dens-canis, Helleborus orientalis, Hosta sieboldiana* var. *elegans, Primula vulgaris*

3 Geranium phaeum
Dusky cranesbill, Mourning widow

In late spring and early summer the nodding purple-black flowers, with prettily swept-back silky petals, strike a sombre note in shaded parts of the garden. This easy plant often self-seeds. The white-flowered 'Album' form lights up dark corners. Hardy.
Height: 75cm (2ft 6in) **Spread:** 45cm (18in)
Site: Shade, partial shade. Reasonably fertile and well-drained soil
Use: Shady border, woodland garden
Good companions: *Helleborus foetidus, Iris foetidissima, Meconopsis cambrica, Polygonatum* x *hybridum*

4 Geranium sylvaticum 'Mayflower'
Wood cranesbill

Above a base of fingered leaves, masses of purple to violet-blue flowers open over several weeks in spring and early summer. The mixture of a close range of colours is attractive, but the pure white of 'Album' is also lovely. Hardy.
Height: 75cm (2ft 6in) **Spread:** 60cm (2ft)
Site: Partial shade, sun. Moist but well-drained soil
Use: Sunny or lightly shaded border
Good companions: *Campanula lactiflora, Hemerocallis lilioasphodelus, Paeonia mlokosewitschii, Smilacina racemosa*

5 Iris 'Demon'
Dwarf bearded iris

A compact free-flowering iris with fragrant flowers of deep blue-purple, shading to velvety brown-purple around the gold-tipped beard. Hardy.
General care: Do not allow other plants to overshadow the roots (rhizomes). Divide these every three years.
Height: 30cm (12in) **Spread:** 15cm (6in)
Site: Sun. Light and well-drained soil. Does well on lime

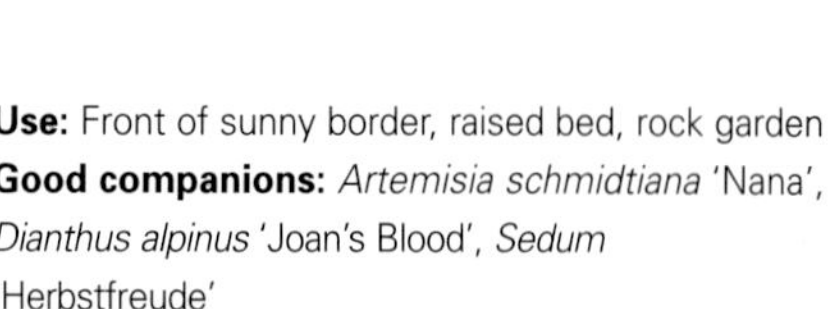
4

Use: Front of sunny border, raised bed, rock garden
Good companions: *Artemisia schmidtiana* 'Nana', *Dianthus alpinus* 'Joan's Blood', *Sedum* 'Herbstfreude'

6 Iris 'Rare Edition'
Intermediate bearded iris

A sturdy stem carries eye-catching flowers clear of the stiff grey-green leaf fans. The erect petals (standards) are violet-purple speckled with white. The slightly drooping outer petals (falls), with pale bluish beards, are white edged with purple. Hardy.
General care: Do not allow other plants to overshadow the roots (rhizomes). Divide these every three years.
Height: 60cm (2ft) **Spread:** 25cm (10in)
Site: Sun. Fertile and well-drained soil. Does well on lime
Use: Raised bed, rock garden, sunny border
Good companions: *Cytisus* x *kewensis, Hebe cupressoides* 'Boughton Dome', *Pulsatilla vulgaris*

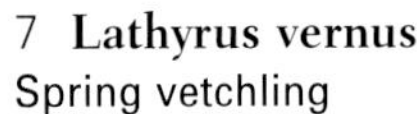

7 **Lathyrus vernus**
Spring vetchling
From mid-spring this bushy plant, dense with divided leaves, is covered with tight sprays of purple pea flowers, nicely varied with tints of crimson and blue. In summer, when flowering has finished, the foliage dies down. Hardy.
Height and spread: 30cm (12in)
Site: Sun. Well-drained, even poor, stony soil
Use: Gravel garden, sunny border
Good companions: *Allium cristophii, Cistus* 'Silver Pink', *Erysimum* 'Bowles' Mauve', *Gladiolus communis* subsp. *byzantinus*

8 **Omphalodes cappadocica**
Navelwort
Sprays of white-eyed blue flowers hover over the dense cover of slightly hairy oval leaves. 'Cherry Ingram' has larger deep blue flowers. Hardy.
Height: 25cm (10in) **Spread:** 45cm (18in)
Site: Partial shade. Humus-rich and moist soil
Use: Ground cover, shady border, woodland garden
Good companions: *Convallaria majalis, Dicentra* 'Luxuriant', *Rubus* 'Benenden', *Viburnum carlesii* 'Aurora'

9 **Pulmonaria 'Mawson's Blue'**
Lungwort
For those who find the spotted leaves of some lungworts unattractive, this has plain dark green foliage and flowers of purplish blue. Hardy.
Height: 40cm (16in) **Spread:** 45cm (18in)
Site: Partial shade. Fertile, humus-rich and moist but well-drained soil
Use: Ground cover, shady border, wild garden, woodland garden
Good companions: *Asplenium scolopendrium, Dicentra formosa alba, Hosta* 'Francee', *Polygonatum* x *hybridum*

10 **Trillium erectum**
Birth root, Stinking benjamin
The nodding flowers, borne above the foliage, have their parts arranged in threes, the reddish purple petals curving back at the tips. The rich green leaves are also arranged in threes. Hardy.
Height: 50cm (20in) **Spread:** 30cm (12in)
Site: Partial shade, shade. Humus-rich and moist but well-drained soil
Use: Lightly shaded border, woodland garden
Good companions: *Arisaema candidissimum, Dryopteris affinis, Mahonia japonica, Uvularia grandiflora*

11 **Viola riviniana Purpurea Group**
Dog violet, Wood violet
In this dark form, purplish green leaves make a sombrely effective base for the violet-purple flowers. Very attractive as an underplanting, but runs too freely to mix with choice plants. Hardy.
Height: 10cm (4in) **Spread:** 40cm (16in)
Site: Partial shade, sun. Fertile and moist but well-drained soil
Use: Ground cover, wild garden, woodland garden
Good companions: *Ajuga reptans, Galanthus nivalis, Milium effusum* 'Aureum'

12 **Viola sororia 'Freckles'**
Sister violet, Woolly blue violet
The appeal of this violet lies in the heavy purple speckling on the white or pale blue flowers. Hardy.
Height: 10cm (4in) **Spread:** 20cm (8in)
Site: Partial shade. Fertile and moist but well-drained soil
Use: Lightly shaded border, underplanting for shrubs, woodland garden
Good companions: *Brunnera macrophylla, Corydalis flexuosa, Dicentra* 'Langtrees', *Dryopteris erythrosora*

purple, blue and violet (continued)

1 Ajuga reptans 'Purple Torch'
Bugle

Bugles are low creeping plants with spoon-shaped evergreen leaves that overlap to make dense ground cover. Most bear spikes of blue flowers in late spring and early summer and some, such as 'Burgundy Glow', have colourful variegated leaves. The misleadingly named 'Purple Torch' form is plain leaved and produces dense spikes of pinkish or mauve flowers. Hardy.

Height: 15cm (6in) **Spread:** 1m (3ft)
Site: Partial shade. Moist but well-drained soil
Use: Ground cover, woodland garden
Good companions: *Convallaria majalis*, *Epimedium* x *youngianum* 'Niveum', *Heuchera cylindrica* 'Greenfinch'

pink and mauve

2 Cardamine pratensis 'Flore Pleno'
Cuckoo flower, Lady's smock

The wild plant, found in damp ground over much of the Northern Hemisphere, has single flowers that are white to purple. An easy and much better plant for the garden is this double form, with spires of mauve-pink flowers rising from dark green, deeply cut leaves. Hardy.

Height: 45cm (18in) **Spread:** 30cm (12in)
Site: Partial shade, shade. Fertile and moist soil
Use: Pond side, shady border, woodland garden
Good companions: *Astilbe* x *arendsii* 'Irrlicht', *Hosta* 'Ginko Craig', *Ranunculus aconitifolius* 'Flore Pleno'

3 Dicentra spectabilis
Bleeding heart

A cottage garden favourite but an elegant plant in any setting, partly because of its attractively cut light green leaves. From an open clump stems arch out, loaded with white-tipped pink lockets. The vigorous white-flowered 'Alba' form is equally beautiful. The foliage dies down in summer. Hardy.

General care: Plant in a sheltered position because the stems are fragile, as are the roots.
Height: 1.2m (4ft) **Spread:** 50cm (20in)
Site: Partial shade, sun. Fertile and moist but well-drained soil
Use: Sunny or lightly shaded border
Good companions: *Clematis alpina* 'Frances Rivis', *Lunaria annua* 'Alba Variegata', *Tulipa* 'Spring Green'

4 Geranium macrorrhizum 'Ingwersen's Variety'
Cranesbill

A semi-evergreen coloniser with pleasantly aromatic leaves that give random touches of autumn colour. All the forms make attractive and effective ground cover. This form has soft mauve-pink flowers. For a stronger effect use 'Bevan's Variety', with crimson-purple flowers. 'Album' is palest pink with deeper pink touches. Hardy.

Height: 50cm (20in) **Spread:** 60cm (2ft)
Site: Partial shade, sun. Reasonably fertile and well-drained soil
Use: Ground cover, mixed border
Good companions: *Dicentra* 'Luxuriant', *Geranium* x *magnificum*, *Viola cornuta*

5 x Heucherella tiarelloides

A low dense cover of evergreen leaves is topped by spires of tiny flowers, which create a salmon-pink haze lasting into summer. Hardy.

Height and spread: 45cm (18in)
Site: Partial shade, sun, shade. Lime-free, moist but well-drained soil
Use: Ground cover, shady or sunny border, woodland garden
Good companions: *Arum italicum* subsp. *italicum* 'Marmoratum', *Exochorda* x *macrantha* 'The Bride', *Hydrangea quercifolia*

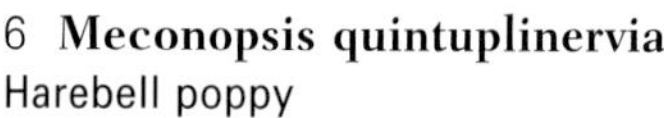

6 Meconopsis quintuplinervia
Harebell poppy

The dark green of the leaves is lightened by rusty or golden bristles. The mauve-blue poppies, darker at the base, dance lightly on hairy stems. Hardy.

Height: 45cm (18in) **Spread:** 30cm (12in)
Site: Partial shade. Lime-free, humus-rich and moist but well-drained soil
Use: Peat bed, woodland garden
Good companions: *Enkianthus campanulatus*, *Fothergilla major* Monticola Group, *Rhododendron* 'Bow Bells'

7 Polemonium 'Lambrook Mauve'
Jacob's ladder

Sprays of bell flowers, which are a silky and delicate mauve, continue into early summer. The

arrangement of paired leaflets has given the polemoniums their common name. Hardy.
Height and spread: 45cm (18in)
Site: Sun, partial shade. Fertile and moist but well-drained soil
Use: Sunny or lightly shaded border
Good companions: *Ajuga reptans* 'Purple Torch', *Aquilegia vulgaris* 'Nivea', *Geranium sylvaticum* 'Mayflower'

8 Primula sieboldii

Heads of pink or purple flowers, with notched petals and a white eye, stand above hairy pale green leaves. An easy plant to grow in moist acid soil. Hardy.
Height: 30cm (12in) **Spread:** 45cm (18in)
Site: Partial shade. Lime-free, moist and humus-rich soil
Use: Pond and stream side, shady border, woodland garden
Good companions: *Matteuccia struthiopteris, Primula japonica* 'Postford White'

9 Tellima grandiflora 'Purpurteppich'
Fringe cups

Swaying slender stems carry little cup-shaped flowers that are green with a pink rim. The attractively scalloped leaves mature to red-purple. Hardy.
Height: 60cm (2ft) **Spread:** 30cm (12in)
Site: Partial shade, sun. Moist but well-drained soil
Use: Ground cover, shady or sunny border, woodland garden
Good companions: *Geranium psilostemon*, x *Heucherella tiarelloides, Philadelphus coronarius* 'Aureus'

bronze and maroon

10 Dryopteris erythrosora
Buckler fern

The young glossy fronds are red-bronze, then mature to dark green. Tattered remnants sometimes survive the winter but this fern is usually deciduous. Plant in a sheltered position. Hardy.
Height: 60cm (2ft) **Spread:** 40cm (16in)
Site: Partial shade. Humus-rich and moist soil
Use: Shady border, woodland garden
Good companions: *Epimedium* x *warleyense* 'Orangekönigin', *Filipendula ulmaria* 'Aurea', *Tiarella cordifolia*

11 Iris 'Holden Clough'
Beardless iris

The yellow flowers are so heavily veined with purple that the overall effect is of rich bronzy maroon. The ribbed leaves often last through the winter. Hardy.
Height: 75cm (2ft 6in) **Spread:** 15cm (6in)
Site: Sun, partial shade. Moist but well-drained soil
Use: Pond and stream side, sunny border
Good companions: *Astrantia major* subsp. *involucrata* 'Shaggy', *Miscanthus sinensis* 'Zebrinus'

12 Podophyllum hexandrum

The white or pale pink cup-shaped flowers have a crystalline beauty as they peep out from the plant's large leaves, which are lobed and handsomely mottled with maroon. The flowering season extends into summer. The ornamental yellowish fruit that follow are highly toxic. Hardy.
Height: 50cm (20in) **Spread:** 1.2m (4ft)
Site: Partial shade, shade. Humus-rich and moist but well-drained soil
Use: Shady border, woodland garden
Good companions: *Dryopteris affinis, Hosta undulata* var. *univittata, Smilacina racemosa*

red and russet

1 Dicentra 'Luxuriant'

Hummocks of ferny fresh green leaves are topped by sprays of red locket-shaped flowers. The season continues into early summer. Hardy.
Height: 30cm (12in) **Spread:** 45cm (18in)
Site: Partial shade. Fertile and moist but well-drained soil
Use: Ground cover, shady border, woodland garden
Good companions: *Erythronium dens-canis, Helleborus orientalis, Pulmonaria saccharata* Argentea Group

2 Epimedium x rubrum

Barrenwort, Bishop's mitre

The new leaflets retain copper-red tints for several weeks before turning light green. The foliage, often with splashes of bright coral in autumn, lasts through the winter. In early spring there are sprays of white-spurred crimson flowers. Hardy.
General care: In winter cut away old leaves so that flowers can be seen when they emerge.
Height and spread: 30cm (12in)
Site: Partial shade. Moist but well-drained soil
Use: Ground cover, shady border, woodland garden
Good companions: *Brunnera macrophylla, Corylopsis pauciflora, Dicentra formosa alba, Lunaria rediviva*

3 Paeonia peregrina

Peony

The scarlet satin petals of the single blooms cup yellow stamens. The flowering season extends into early summer, and the glossy cut leaves remain an attractive deep green throughout the summer. Hardy.
Height and spread: 60cm (2ft)
Site: Sun, partial shade. Fertile and moist but well-drained soil
Use: Sunny or lightly shaded border
Good companions: *Delphinium* Belladonna Group 'Atlantis', *Iris pallida* 'Argentea Variegata', *Veronica gentianoides*

4 Primula 'Wanda'

Primrose

The radiating leaves, often evergreen, are tinged with purple, complementing the wine-red flowers, which are brightened by a yellow eye. The flowers frequently open early and continue for weeks. Hardy.
Height: 15cm (6in) **Spread:** 30cm (12in)
Site: Partial shade, sun. Humus-rich and moist but well-drained soil
Use: Sunny or shady border, woodland garden
Good companions: *Anemone blanda, Galanthus nivalis, Scilla siberica*

yellow and orange

5 Doronicum orientale 'Magnificum'

Leopard's bane

An abundance of yellow daisy flowerheads, up to 5cm (2in) across, make this a cheerful plant to follow on from the yellow-flowered daffodils. Its roots colonise ground but not aggressively. Hardy.
Height: 50cm (20in) **Spread:** 1m (3ft)
Site: Partial shade, sun. Fertile and moist but well-drained soil
Use: Lightly shaded border, sunny border, woodland garden
Good companions: *Alchemilla mollis, Euphorbia polychroma, Lunaria annua*

6 Epimedium x versicolor 'Sulphureum'

Barrenwort, Bishop's mitre

The foliage, tinted red-bronze in spring and autumn, is retained through winter. In spring there are prettily spurred yellow flowers. Hardy.
General care: In winter cut away old leaves so that flowers can be seen when they emerge in spring
Height: 30cm (12in) **Spread:** 1m (3ft)
Site: Partial shade, sun. Moist but well-drained soil
Use: Ground cover, sunny or shady border, woodland garden
Good companions: *Doronicum orientale* 'Magnificum', *Euphorbia griffithii* 'Fireglow', *Geranium* 'Johnson's Blue'

7 Epimedium x warleyense 'Orangekönigin'

Barrenwort, Bishop's mitre

The foliage has lovely coppery tints in spring. The flowers, produced in pretty sprays, are an unusual combination of yellow and orange-brown. Hardy.
General care: In winter cut away old leaves so that flowers can be seen when they emerge in spring.
Height: 50cm (20in) **Spread:** 75cm (2ft 6in)
Site: Partial shade. Moist but well-drained soil
Use: Shady border, woodland garden
Good companions: *Hosta* 'Gold Standard', *Milium effusum* 'Aureum', *Waldsteinia ternata*

8 Euphorbia amygdaloides 'Purpurea'

Milkweed, Wood spurge

The new shoots are eye-catching beetroot-red and gradually turn purplish green. The long-lasting bracts (the petal-like parts around the tiny flowers) are pale yellow, becoming greener with age. Contact with the milky sap may cause a skin reaction. Hardy.
Height and spread: 45cm (18in)
Site: Partial shade. Humus-rich and well-drained but preferably moist soil
Use: Ground cover, shady border, woodland garden
Good companions: *Arum italicum* subsp. *italicum* 'Marmoratum', *Heuchera cylindrica* 'Greenfinch', *Vinca minor* 'La Grave'

9 Euphorbia polychroma

Milkweed, Spurge

The flowers themselves are tiny and inconspicuous, but the bracts surrounding them are a vibrant yellow shading to lime-green. The effect, which lasts well into summer, is of a compact dome studded with arresting flowers. Contact with the milky sap may cause a skin reaction. Hardy.
Height and spread: 45cm (18in)
Site: Sun, partial shade. Well-drained, preferably moist soil
Use: Raised bed, rock garden, sunny or partially shaded border

Good companions: *Allium hollandicum* 'Purple Sensation', *Choisya ternata*, *Iris* 'Jane Phillips', *Tulipa* 'West Point'

10 Filipendula ulmaria 'Aurea'
Meadowsweet, Queen of the meadows

The wrinkled and divided leaves pass through different shades of yellow before turning light green in summer. They scorch in full sun. Hardy.
General care: Remove flowers as they appear to prevent self-seeding.
Height: 75cm (2ft 6in) **Spread:** 60cm (2ft)
Site: Partial shade. Fertile, moist, even boggy soil
Use: Bog garden, pond and stream side, shady border
Good companions: *Astilbe* 'Professor van der Wielen', *Euphorbia griffithii* 'Fireglow', *Rodgersia podophylla*, *Trollius europaeus*

11 Hosta fortunei var. albopicta
Plantain lily

Tightly scrolled leaves unfold to reveal a yellow tongue surrounded by an irregular edge of pale green. By midsummer, when the mauve flowers open, the leaves are two-tone green. Hardy.
Height: 45cm (18in) **Spread:** 1m (3ft)
Site: Partial shade. Fertile, moist, well-drained soil
Use: Ground cover, bog garden, pond and stream side, shady border
Good companions: *Astrantia major* subsp. *involucrata* 'Shaggy', *Kirengeshoma palmata*, *Matteuccia struthiopteris*

12 Meconopsis cambrica
Welsh poppy

Appealing yellow or orange flowers, held trembling above ferny leaves, continue to appear throughout summer. Self-seeds generously. Hardy.
Height: 45cm (18in) **Spread:** 25cm (10in)
Site: Partial shade. Lime-free, moist and humus-rich soil
Use: Shady border, wild garden, woodland garden
Good companions: *Alchemilla mollis*, *Rhododendron luteum*, *Stachyurus praecox*

13 Milium effusum 'Aureum'
Bowles' golden grass, Golden wood millet

Bright yellow ribbon leaves in spring and early summer are joined by shimmering sprays of little golden flowers at the start of summer. Hardy.
Height: 60cm (2ft) **Spread:** 30cm (12in)
Site: Partial shade, sun. Humus-rich and moist but well-drained soil
Use: Lightly shaded or sunny border, woodland garden
Good companions: *Geranium sylvaticum* 'Mayflower', *Hosta fortunei* var. *albopicta*, *Viola riviniana* Purpurea Group

14 Paeonia mlokosewitschii
Caucasian peony, Mollie-the-witch

The lemon-yellow single flowers are soon over but the foliage is of great beauty. The seed pods split in autumn to reveal scarlet and black. Hardy.
Height and spread: 75cm (2ft 6in)
Site: Sun. Fertile and well-drained soil
Use: Sunny border
Good companions: *Allium* 'Globemaster', *Iris* 'Jane Phillips', *Rosa xanthina* 'Canary Bird', *Sisyrinchium striatum* 'Aunt May'

yellow and orange (continued)

1 Uvularia grandiflora
Bellwort, Large merrybells

The drooping leaves and hanging yellow bells, with prettily twisted petals, give an impression of elegant somnolence. Hardy.

Height: 75cm (2ft 6in) **Spread:** 30cm (12in)

Site: Partial shade, shade. Humus-rich and moist but well-drained soil

Use: Shady border, woodland garden

Good companions: *Meconopsis quintuplinervia, Tiarella cordifolia, Trillium erectum*

2 Valeriana phu 'Aurea'
Valerian

This form would not be grown just for the small white flowers in midsummer, but the bright clear yellow of the young leaves makes it a valued foliage plant for several weeks in spring. As the foliage matures it turns lime-green and eventually loses its yellow tint. Hardy.

4

7

8

5

9

1

2

10

3

6

Height: 1m (3ft) **Spread:** 60cm (2ft)
Site: Sun. Well-drained, preferably moist soil
Use: Bedding, sunny border
Good companions: *Fuchsia magellanica* 'Versicolor', *Hyacinthus orientalis* 'Ostara', *Myosotis sylvatica* 'Royal Blue'

3 Waldsteinia ternata

This low-growing evergreen makes a dense and glossy carpet that shows off the sprays of bright yellow flowers into early summer. Hardy.
Height: 10cm (4in) **Spread:** 60cm (2ft)

Site: Partial shade, sun. Reasonably fertile and well-drained, preferably moist soil
Use: Ground cover, wild garden, woodland garden
Good companions: *Euphorbia griffithii* 'Fireglow', *Helleborus argutifolius, Paeonia delavayi* var. *ludlowii, Pleioblastus auricomus*

cream and white

4 Anemone sylvestris
Snowdrop anemone

Rapid coloniser with deeply cut leaves above which dangle white flowers with a yellow boss. The white fluff that follows contains the seeds. Contact with the sap may produce a skin reaction. Hardy.
Height and spread: 45cm (18in)
Site: Partial shade, sun. Humus-rich and well-drained soil
Use: Underplanting for shrubs, wild garden, woodland garden
Good companions: *Colchicum speciosum* 'Album', *Exochorda* x *macrantha* 'The Bride', *Osmanthus delavayi, Viburnum opulus* 'Roseum'

5 Anthericum liliago
St bernard's lily

An easy plant to grow with grey-green grassy leaves and erect spires of starry white flowers. The flowering season continues into early summer. Good for cutting. Often self-seeds but is rarely troublesome. Hardy.
Height: 75cm (2ft 6in) **Spread:** 30cm (12in)
Site: Sun. Well-drained, preferably moist soil
Use: Sunny border, wild flower garden
Good companions: *Agapanthus* 'Lilliput', *Geranium renardii, Veronica spicata* 'Heidekind'

6 Aquilegia vulgaris 'Nivea'
Columbine, Granny's bonnet

The short-spurred flowers of the common columbine are usually in shades of violet, plum or pink. All are worth growing but are outclassed by this white-flowered form in which the beautiful ferny leaves are grey-green. The season spans late spring and early summer. Hardy.
Height: 1m (3ft) **Spread:** 45cm (18in)
Site: Partial shade, sun. Fertile and moist but well-drained soil
Use: Sunny or partially shaded border, woodland garden
Good companions: *Lilium martagon* var. *album, Paeonia lactiflora* 'Bowl of Beauty', *Thalictrum aquilegiifolium* 'Thundercloud'

7 Asphodelus albus
Asphodel

The narrow, keeled leaves make an untidy base for spires of starry flowers. Their whiteness is warmed by the pink veins that run down the centre of each petal. Hardy.
Height: 1m (3ft) **Spread:** 30cm (12in)
Site: Sun. Well-drained, even stony, dry soil
Use: Gravel garden, sunny border, wildflower garden
Good companions: *Allium cristophii, Artemisia ludoviciana* 'Valerie Finnis', *Cistus ladanifer, Ruta graveolens* 'Jackman's Blue'

8 Bergenia 'Beethoven'
Elephant's ears

This is an easy plant, with large and leathery evergreen leaves making impressive clumps; unlike the leaves of some bergenias, these are not noted for taking on strong colours in autumn and winter. Instead of the familiar magenta-pink and purple, the flowers here are white surrounded by a red or pink calyx (the outer ring of parts at the base of each flower). Hardy.
Height and spread: 45cm (18in)
Site: Sun, partial shade. Well-drained, preferably moist soil
Use: Gravel garden, ground cover, sunny or partially shaded border
Good companions: *Buddleja* 'Lochinch', *Eryngium* x *tripartitum, Iris* 'Pearly Dawn', *Lavandula* x *intermedia* Dutch Group

9 Convallaria majalis
Lily-of-the-valley

Where it is happy, this plant makes vigorous and fast-spreading ground cover, but it can fail to thrive where expected. The paired leaves are almost oval, with veins running lengthwise. At the centre nestle little sprays of dangling bells, which are waxy, white and fragrant. Hardy.
Height: 20cm (8in) **Spread:** 30cm (12in)
Site: Partial shade, sun. Fertile, humus-rich and moist but well-drained soil
Use: Ground cover, wild garden, woodland garden
Good companions: *Epimedium* x *youngianum* 'Niveum', *Hydrangea* 'Preziosa', *Syringa vulgaris* 'Madame Lemoine', *Weigela* 'Victoria'

10 Corydalis ochroleuca

Although delicate-looking, this is a great survivor and self-seeder. It can be too vigorous for a rock garden but is completely at home lodged in a wall. Above the ferny, light green leaves, short stems bear showers of curiously curved spurred flowers with yellow throats. Hardy.
Height and spread: 30cm (12in)
Site: Partial shade, sun. Fertile and well-drained soil
Use: Underplanting for shrubs, wild garden, woodland garden
Good companions: *Dryopteris affinis, Euphorbia amygdaloides* 'Purpurea', *Gentiana asclepiadea*

11 Dicentra 'Langtrees'

The hybrid dicentras combine finely cut foliage and pretty dangling flowers, which are produced over weeks in late spring and early summer. The leaves of 'Langtrees' are silvery blue-green and the flowers are white, tinged with pink. Hardy.
Height: 30cm (12in) **Spread:** 45cm (18in)
Site: Partial shade. Humus-rich and moist but well-drained soil
Use: Edging for lightly shaded border, woodland garden, underplanting for shrubs
Good companions: *Ajuga reptans* 'Purple Torch', *Aquilegia* 'Hensol Harebell', *Brunnera macrophylla, Geranium macrorrhizum* 'Ingwersen's Variety'

12 Disporum sessile 'Variegatum'
Fairy bells

The fresh green tapered leaves, irregularly streaked white, are as ornamental as the white tubular flowers, tipped with green, that hang beneath them. The black berries that follow usually go unnoticed. Hardy.
Height and spread: 60cm (2ft)
Site: Partial shade. Humus-rich and moist but well-drained soil
Use: Shady border, peat bed, woodland garden
Good companions: *Helleborus orientalis, Hosta* 'Royal Standard', *Trillium grandiflorum, Uvularia grandiflora*

cream and white (continued)

1 Epimedium x youngianum 'Niveum'
Barrenwort, Bishop's mitre

Above the foliage, which when young is suffused with soft shades of coppery brown, float little sprays of white flowers. Other lovely forms include 'Merlin', which has purplish flowers. Hardy.
Height: 25cm (10in) **Spread:** 30cm (12in)
Site: Partial shade. Moist but well-drained soil
Use: Ground cover, shady border, woodland garden
Good companions: *Dicentra* 'Langtrees', *Omphalodes cappadocica*

2 Hosta undulata var. univittata
The amount of white in the centre of the twisted leaves varies greatly from plant to plant. There are mauve flowers in summer. Hardy.
Height: 45cm (18in) **Spread:** 75cm (2ft 6in)
Site: Partial shade. Humus-rich and moist but well-drained soil
Use: Ground cover, bog garden, pond and stream side, shady border
Good companions: *Aquilegia* McKana Group, *Polemonium* 'Lambrook Mauve', *Tiarella wherryi*

3 Lunaria rediviva
Perennial honesty

The sweetly scented bunched flowers are faintly tinted with mauve and last until early summer. Elliptic papery seedpods follow. Hardy.
Height: 75cm (2ft 6in) **Spread:** 30cm (12in)
Site: Partial shade, sun. Moist but well-drained soil
Use: Sunny or shady border, wild garden, woodland garden
Good companions: *Geranium sylvaticum* 'Mayflower', *Hyacinthoides non-scripta, Prunus avium* 'Plena'

4 Paeonia lactiflora 'White Wings'
Peony

In this single-flowered scented variety, ruffled petals form creamy white cups around golden stamens. In autumn the glossy green leaves take on warm tints. Hardy.
Height: 75cm (2ft 6in) **Spread:** 1m (3ft)
Site: Sun, partial shade. Fertile and well-drained soil
Use: Sunny or lightly shaded border
Good companions: *Iris* 'Florentina', *Lilium regale, Rosa* 'Louise Odier', *Veronica gentianoides*

5 Polygonatum x hybridum
Solomon's seal

This is elegant and easy to grow among shrubs. Veined leaves lie along arching stems, from which dangle green-tipped ivory bells. Inedible blue-black fruits follow. All parts of this plant may be harmful if eaten. Hardy.
Height: 1.2m (4ft) **Spread:** 45cm (18in)
Site: Partial shade, shade. Humus-rich and moist but well-drained soil
Use: Shady border, wild garden, woodland garden
Good companions: *Helleborus foetidus, Hosta* 'Royal Standard', *Pachysandra terminalis*

6 Primula japonica 'Postford White'
Japanese primrose

Whorls of white flowers, each with a yellow or reddish centre, are carried on a sturdy stem above a rosette of pale green leaves. Hardy.
Height and spread: 45cm (18in)
Site: Partial shade, sun. Lime-free, humus-rich and moist soil
Use: Bog garden, pond and stream side, moist border
Good companions: *Cardamine pratensis* 'Flore Pleno', *Hosta sieboldiana* var. *elegans, Rheum palmatum* 'Atrosanguineum', *Rodgersia pinnata* 'Superba'

7 Ranunculus aconitifolius 'Flore Pleno'
Fair maids of France, Fair maids of Kent, White bachelor's buttons

At the base of the plant are fingered leaves with jagged edges. The stems above are almost leafless but carry many white, double button flowers. They are long lasting and their season extends into summer. Contact with the sap may cause skin reactions. Hardy.
Height: 60cm (2ft) **Spread:** 45cm (18in)
Site: Sun, partial shade. Fertile, humus-rich and well-drained soil
Use: Sunny or lightly shaded damp border, woodland garden
Good companions: *Astilbe* x *arendsii* 'Irrlicht', *Iris sibirica* 'Ego', *Zantedeschia aethiopica* 'Crowborough'

8 Smilacina racemosa
False Solomon's seal, False spikenard

Stems, with strongly veined leaves, are topped by tapered tufts of densely packed greenish white or cream flowers that are sweetly scented. Hardy.
Height: 1m (3ft) **Spread:** 60cm (2ft)
Site: Partial shade, shade. Lime-free, humus-rich and moist but well-drained soil
Use: Shady border, woodland garden
Good companions: *Cornus kousa* var. *chinensis, Disanthus cercidifolius, Meconopsis betonicifolia, Trillium grandiflorum*

7

8

9

9 **Tiarella cordifolia**
Foam flower
Spreading by surface runners, this easy colonising plant makes a dense cover of pale green leaves. The creamy froth of small starry flowers is carried on spikes and lasts into summer. Hardy.
Height: 25cm (10in) **Spread:** 30cm (12in)
Site: Partial shade, shade. Humus-rich and moist but well-drained soil
Use: Ground cover, shady border, woodland garden
Good companions: *Hydrangea paniculata* 'Unique', *Omphalodes cappadocica*, *Spiraea* 'Arguta'

silver and grey

10 **Iris 'Florentina'**
Orris root
Pale grey flowers are warmed by purple tints and yellow beards. Combined with fans of grey-green leaves, they give a silvery effect in the garden. Sweetly scented. Hardy.

10

11

12

General care: Do not allow other plants to overshadow the roots (rhizomes). Divide these every three years
Height: 75cm (2ft 6in) **Spread:** 45cm (18in)
Site: Sun. Fertile and well-drained soil. Does well on lime
Use: Sunny border
Good companions: *Allium hollandicum* 'Purple Sensation', *Aubrieta* 'Greencourt Purple', *Clematis alpina* 'Frances Rivis'

green

11 **Dryopteris affinis**
Golden male fern
The green of the unfurling fronds contrasts with the golden-brown midribs. The mature fronds are dark green and often last through winter. Hardy.
Height and spread: 1m (3ft)
Site: Partial shade, shade, sun. Humus-rich and moist soil
Use: Bog garden, pond and stream side, shady border, wild garden, woodland garden
Good companions: *Fargesia murieliae*, *Lobelia* 'Queen Victoria', *Primula florindae*

12 **Euphorbia x martinii**
Milkweed, Spurge
Evergreen and shrubby, the reddish stems and grey-green leaves form a dome-shaped clump topped by lime-green flowerheads. Each small flower-like cup is lit by a red eye. Hardy.
Height and spread: 1m (3ft)
Site: Sun, partial shade. Well-drained soil
Use: Gravel garden, sunny or lightly shaded border, wild garden
Good companions: *Buddleja davidii* 'Black Knight', *Cytisus* x *praecox* 'Allgold', *Onopordum acanthium*, *Stipa gigantea*

13 **Iris 'Green Spot'**
Dwarf bearded iris
A sturdy iris with lightly scented flowers in white and pale green. The outer petals (falls) are nearly horizontal, each printed with a green spot. Hardy.
General care: Do not allow other plants to overshadow the roots (rhizomes). Divide these every three years.
Height: 25cm (10in) **Spread:** 20cm (8in)
Site: Sun. Fertile and well-drained soil. Good on lime
Use: Raised bed, rock garden, sunny border
Good companions: *Campanula carpatica*, *Crocus imperati* subsp. *imperati* 'De Jager', *Cytisus* x *beanii*, *Lavandula angustifolia* 'Nana Alba'

13

annuals & biennials

Most of the short-lived plants that brighten beds and containers in spring are biennials sown the previous summer. Many annuals are sown in spring for summer displays.

purple, blue and violet

1 Myosotis sylvatica 'Royal Blue'
Forget-me-not

Although forget-me-nots have tiny flowers, the numerous sprays create a haze of colour, usually blue, from late spring to early summer. The taller kinds, such as this richly coloured selection, create an airy effect. In the dwarf Ball and Victoria Series the colour range covers blue, pink and white. These easily grown biennials self-seed freely. Hardy.
General care: Sow seed outdoors in early summer and plant out in autumn.
Height: 30cm (12in) **Spread:** 15cm (6in)
Site: Partial shade, sun. Moist but well-drained soil
Compost: Soil-based (John Innes No. 2) or soil-less
Use: Container, sunny or partially shaded border, wild garden, woodland garden
Good companions: *Hyacinthus orientalis* 'Carnegie', *Primula* 'Guinevere', *Tulipa* 'Estella Rijnveld'

2 Viola Sorbet Series
Winter-flowering pansy

Despite being called winter-flowering pansies, the numerous strains of these invaluable plants often reach their peak in spring. The Sorbet Series has small flowers, usually bicoloured and in shades of purple, blue, mauve, yellow and cream. Hardy.
General care: Sow seed outdoors in summer and plant out in autumn. Deadhead regularly.
Height: 15cm (6in) **Spread:** 30cm (12in)
Site: Sun, partial shade. Fertile, humus-rich and moist but well-drained soil
Compost: Soil-based (John Innes No. 2) or soil-less
Use: Bedding, container, raised bed, sunny or lightly shaded border
Good companions: *Crocus vernus* subsp. *albiflorus* 'Purpureus Grandiflorus', *Hyacinthus orientalis* 'Carnegie', *Iris histrioides* 'Major', *Tulipa* 'Queen of Night'

pink and mauve

3 Bellis perennis
Daisy

These double versions of the lawn weed have larger flowerheads in pink, white or red, and they bloom over a long season. The Pomponette Series has neat button flowers. The Habanera Series has shaggier ones. Perennials usually grown as biennials. Hardy.
General care: Sow seed outdoors in early summer and plant out in early autumn.
Height: 10–20cm (4–8in) **Spread:** 15cm (6in)
Site: Sun, partial shade. Moist but well-drained soil
Compost: Soil-based (John Innes No. 2) or soil-less
Use: Bedding, container, edging, sunny or shady border
Good companions: *Chionodoxa luciliae*, *Primula* 'Wanda', *Tulipa* 'Estella Rijnveld', *Tulipa* 'Mount Tacoma'

4 Iberis umbellata Fairy Series
Candytuft

An easy annual producing a low mound of narrow leaves that is almost hidden by clusters of small scented flowers. In this mixture the colours are pink and purple shades with some white. Hardy.
General care: For flowers from late spring to late summer, sow seed *in situ* in autumn and two or three times between early spring and early summer.
Height: 20cm (8in) **Spread:** 25cm (10in)
Site: Sun. Well-drained, even poor soil. Good on lime
Compost: Soil-based (John Innes No. 2) or soil-less
Use: Bedding, container, front of sunny border, raised bed
Good companions: *Clarkia amoena* Satin Series, *Consolida ajacis* Imperial Series, *Nigella damascena* 'Miss Jekyll Sky Blue', *Tulipa* 'Heart's Delight'

5 Primula 'Guinevere'
Polyanthus

Red-tinged stems rising from a base of bronzed, purple-veined leaves carry bunched purplish pink flowers with a yellow eye. Short-lived evergreen perennial often grown as a biennial. Hardy.
General care: Sow seed outdoors in early summer and plant out in early autumn. Divide plants after flowering or in autumn
Height: 20cm (8in) **Spread:** 25cm (10in)
Site: Partial shade, sun. Humus-rich and moist soil, preferably acid
Compost: Soil-based (John Innes No. 2) or soil-less
Use: Bedding, container, raised bed, lightly shaded border
Good companions: *Bellis perennis* Pomponette Series, *Primula vulgaris* 'Alba Plena', *Puschkinia scilloides* var. *libanotica*, *Scilla siberica* 'Spring Beauty'

bronze and maroon

6 Primula Gold-laced Group
Polyanthus

Stems rising from rough leaves support a posy of four to eight jaunty flowers. The mahogany-red

petals are set around a yellow centre and outlined in yellow. Short-lived semi-evergreen perennials often grown as biennials. Hardy.
General care: Sow seed outdoors in early summer and plant out in autumn. Divide plants after flowering or in autumn.
Height: 25cm (10in) **Spread:** 30cm (12in)
Site: Partial shade. Fertile and moist but well-drained soil
Compost: Soil-based (John Innes No. 2) or soil-less
Use: Bedding, container, greenhouse or conservatory, shady border
Good companions: *Muscari armeniacum*, *Narcissus* 'February Gold', *Tulipa* 'Queen of Night'

red and russet

7 Erysimum cheiri 'Fire King'
Wallflower
Upright stems carry velvety, sweetly scented flowers. This selection is vibrant orange-red, but mixtures such as Fair Lady Series include plants with cream, pink, purple or red flowers. Short-lived perennials invariably grown as biennials. Hardy.
General care: Sow seed outdoors in late spring or early summer and plant out in mid-autumn.
Height: 60cm (2ft) **Spread:** 30cm (12in)
Site: Sun. Well-drained soil, preferably limy
Compost: Soil-based (John Innes No. 2) or soil-less
Use: Bedding, container, sunny border
Good companions: *Euphorbia griffithii* 'Fireglow', *Lupinus* 'Chandelier', *Rosa xanthina* 'Canary Bird', *Tulipa* 'West Point'

8 Primula Cowichan Garnet Group
Polyanthus
In the Cowichan strain of polyanthus the leaves are usually tinted bronze and the well-proportioned flowers are in rich and varied colours. The Garnet Group flowers are the colour of old wine. Although often treated as biennials, these short-lived perennials can be maintained by division. Hardy.
General care: Sow seed outdoors in early summer and plant out in autumn. Divide plants after flowering or in autumn.
Height: 25cm (10in) **Spread:** 30cm (12in)
Site: Partial shade, sun. Fertile and moist but well-drained soil
Compost: Soil-based (John Innes No. 2) or soil-less
Use: Bedding, container, greenhouse or conservatory, shady border
Good companions: *Hyacinthus orientalis* 'Carnegie', *Myosotis sylvatica* 'Royal Blue', *Primula vulgaris*, *Veronica peduncularis* 'Georgia Blue'

yellow and orange

9 Erysimum cheiri 'Golden Gem'
Wallflower
Dense trusses of four-petalled flowers provide a bright yellow display over several weeks. Compact evergreen perennial grown as a biennial. Hardy.
General care: Sow seed outdoors in late spring or early summer and plant out in mid-autumn.
Height and spread: 15cm (6in)
Site: Sun. Well-drained soil, preferably limy
Compost: Soil-based (John Innes No. 2) or soil-less
Use: Bedding, container, raised bed, sunny border
Good companions: *Ceanothus thyrsiflorus* var. *repens*, *Jasminum nudiflorum*, *Muscari armeniacum*, *Narcissus* 'Jack Snipe'

10 Erysimum cheiri 'Orange Bedder'
Wallflower
The free-flowering Bedder Series are short-growing wallflowers suited to bedding schemes, often sold as a mixture in shades of yellow, orange and scarlet. The colour of 'Orange Bedder' is intense. Perennial almost invariably grown as a biennial. Hardy.
General care: Sow seed outdoors in late spring or early summer and plant out in mid-autumn.
Height: 25cm (10in) **Spread:** 30cm (12in)
Site: Sun. Well-drained soil. Good on lime
Compost: Soil-based (John Innes No. 2) or soil-less
Use: Bedding, container, raised bed, sunny border
Good companions: *Lupinus* 'Chandelier', *Nepeta* 'Six Hills Giant', *Rosa* 'Golden Wings'

cream and white

11 Erysimum cheiri 'Ivory White'
Wallflower
The fragrant four-petalled flowers are creamy white. Short-lived perennial almost invariably grown as a biennial. Hardy.
General care: Sow seed outdoors in late spring or early summer and plant out in mid-autumn.
Height: 60cm (2ft) **Spread:** 30cm (12in)
Site: Sun. Well-drained soil, preferably limy
Compost: Preferably soil-based
Use: Bedding, container, sunny border
Good companions: *Cytisus* x *praecox* 'Allgold', *Iris* 'Demon', *Tulipa* 'Generaal de Wet', *Tulipa* 'Spring Green'

12 Lunaria annua 'Alba Variegata'
Honesty, Satin flower
The pink-purple spires of honesty are followed by long-lasting mica-like seed discs. In this white-flowered form the leaves have a white variegation. Freely self-seeding biennial. Hardy.
General care: Sow seed outdoors in late spring or early summer and plant out in autumn.
Height: 1m (3ft) **Spread:** 30cm (12in)
Site: Partial shade, sun. Moist but well-drained soil
Use: Lightly shaded border, wild garden, woodland garden
Good companions: *Aquilegia* 'Hensol Harebell', *Hyacinthoides non-scripta*, *Prunus* 'Shirofugen'

bulbs

Much spring colour is provided by bulbs, a group of perennials with underground food storage organs that are described technically as true bulbs, corms, tubers or rhizomes.

purple, blue and violet

1 Fritillaria meleagris
Snake's head fritillary

The leaves are narrow and the stems slender, so when grown in grass the purple or greenish white checquered flowers seem to float. Hardy.

General care: Plant in autumn with the top of the bulb about 8cm (3in) deep.
Height: 30cm (12in) **Spread:** 8cm (3in)
Site: Sun, partial shade. Humus-rich and moisture-retentive soil
Compost: Soil-based (John Innes No. 2) with added leaf-mould
Use: Border, container, damp meadow, rock garden
Good companions: *Camassia leichtlinii* subsp. *suksdorfii* Caerulea Group, *Crocus speciosus*, *Narcissus bulbocodium* var. *conspicuus*

2 Hyacinthoides non-scripta
English bluebell

This spreads freely in its ideal setting of dappled shade under deciduous trees. The leaves are glossy dark green and the tubular bells, usually violet-blue but sometimes white or pink, are carried on a stem that bends at the tip. The larger-flowered Spanish bluebell (*Hyacinthoides hispanica*) tolerates sun and drier conditions. Hardy.

General care: Plant in autumn, with the top of the bulb about 10cm (4in) deep.
Height: 30cm (12in) **Spread:** 10cm (4in)
Site: Partial shade. Humus-rich, moist but well-drained soil
Use: Underplanting for shrubs, wild garden, woodland garden
Good companions: *Davidia involucrata, Magnolia* x *soulangeana, Rhododendron* 'Loderi King George'

3 Hyacinthus orientalis 'Ostara'
Hyacinth

Densely packed flowers make a stocky violet-blue column above the deep green leaves. Hardy.

General care: Plant in autumn with the top of the bulb about 10cm (4in) deep.
Height: 25cm (10in) **Spread:** 10cm (4in)
Site: Sun, partial shade. Fertile, well-drained soil
Compost: Soil-based (John Innes No. 2) or soil-less
Use: Formal bedding, container, raised bed, sunny or lightly shaded border
Good companions: *Erysimum* x *allioni, Fritillaria imperialis* 'Rubra'

4 Muscari armeniacum
Grape hyacinth

Tapered spikes of bright blue bells, white at the constricted rim, stand erect above linear leaves. This robust and easy bulb increases freely by seed and by division, and is best used for massed effect and not for mixing with choice plants. Hardy.

General care: Plant in autumn with the top of the bulb about 10cm (4in) deep.
Height: 20cm (8in) **Spread:** 10cm (4in)
Site: Sun, partial shade. Moist, well-drained soil
Use: Underplanting for shrubs, wild garden, woodland garden
Good companions: *Magnolia* 'Elizabeth', *Magnolia soulangeana, Malus floribunda*

2

1

3

pink and mauve

5 Erythronium dens-canis
European dog's-tooth violet

Nodding flowers, with upturned petals, are poised over maroon-mottled leaves. The flower colour varies from purplish pink to white. 'Pink Perfection' and the darker 'Rose Beauty' are two excellent pink selections. The botanical and common names derive from the tooth-like shape of the corm. Hardy.

General care: Plant in late summer with the top of the corm about 10cm (4in) deep.
Height: 15cm (6in) **Spread:** 20cm (8in)
Site: Partial shade. Fertile, humus-rich and moist but well-drained soil
Use: Rock garden, underplanting for shrubs, woodland garden
Good companions: *Acer palmatum* var. *dissectum* Dissectum Viride Group, *Anemone nemorosa* 'Royal Blue', *Cyclamen hederifolium*

6 Oxalis adenophylla
Shamrock, Sorrel

Neatly pleated leaflets are packed together to make a small grey-green cushion. Furled buds open in late spring and early summer to five-petalled flowers that are near white but have pink veining, centres and tips. Hardy.

General care: Plant in autumn, with the top of the rhizome (the bulb-like root) just below the surface of the soil.
Height and spread: 10cm (4in)
Site: Sun. Gritty and well-drained soil
Use: Paving, raised bed, rock garden
Good companions: *Daphne cneorum* 'Eximia', *Dianthus alpinus* 'Joan's Blood', *Geranium cinereum* 'Ballerina'

4

cream and white

7 Erythronium californicum 'White Beauty'
Dog's-tooth violet

A fine form of one of the easiest of the North American species. The leaves are generally lightly mottled or marbled, and round the centre of each creamy-white flower is a rust-coloured ring. Hardy.

General care: Plant in late summer with the top of the corm about 10cm (4in) deep.

Height: 30cm (12in) **Spread:** 15cm (6in)

Site: Partial shade. Fertile, humus-rich and moist but well-drained soil

Use: Rock garden, underplanting for shrubs, woodland garden

Good companions: *Anemone blanda, Arum italicum* subsp. *italicum marmoratum, Galanthus elwesii, Primula vulgaris*

8 Hyacinthus orientalis 'Carnegie'
Hyacinth

Pure white single flowers, waxy and powerfully scented, are densely packed in a short spike. Hardy.

General care: Plant in autumn with the top of the bulb about 10cm (4in) deep.

Height: 25cm (10in) **Spread:** 10cm (4in)

Site: Sun, partial shade. Fertile and well-drained soil

Compost: Soil-based (John Innes No. 2) or soil-less

Use: Formal bedding, container, raised bed, sunny or lightly shaded border

Good companions: *Bellis perennis* Pomponette Series, *Corydalis flexuosa, Crocus vernus* 'Jeanne d'Arc', *Hedera helix* 'Adam'

9 Leucojum aestivum 'Gravetye Giant'
Summer snowflake

This has rich green linear leaves and the drooping white bells are neatly tipped with green. Hardy.

General care: Plant in autumn with the top of the bulb about 10cm (4in) deep.

Height: 75cm (2ft 6in) **Spread:** 20cm (8in)

Site: Sun, partial shade. Humus-rich and moist soil

Use: Moist border, pondside and streamside

Good companions: *Cardamine pratensis* 'Flore Pleno', *Primula japonica* 'Postford White', *Salix hastata* 'Wehrhahnii'

10 Muscari botryoides 'Album'
Grape hyacinth

Spikes of small white flowers, with constricted rims, rise through the narrow leaves. Some grape hyacinths increase too rapidly to trust them in a rock garden, but this spreads more slowly. Hardy.

General care: Plant in autumn with the top of the bulb about 8cm (3in) deep. Lift and divide congested clumps after leaves have died down.

Height: 15cm (6in) **Spread:** 5cm (2in)

Site: Sun. Moist but well-drained soil

Compost: Soil-based (John Innes No. 2) or soil-less

Use: Container, raised bed, rock garden

Good companions: *Armeria juniperifolia, Crocus chrysanthus* 'Cream Beauty', *Iris* 'Joyce', *Phlox subulata* 'McDaniel's Cushion'

11 Narcissus 'Actaea'
Poeticus daffodil

The tiny, yellow and red-rimmed cup is surrounded by glistening white petals. This and the slightly later-flowering old pheasant's eye (*N. poeticus* var. *recurvus*), with swept back flowers, can extend the spring bulb season into early summer. Hardy.

General care: Plant in autumn with the top of the bulb about 10cm (4in) deep.

Height: 45cm (18in) **Spread:** 15cm (6in)

Site: Sun. Reasonably fertile and moist soil

Use: Sunny border, damp meadow

Good companions: *Camassia leichtlinii* subsp. *suksdorfii* Caerulea Group, *Fritillaria meleagris, Narcissus cyclamineus*

12 Ornithogalum nutans
Star-of-Bethlehem

The colour scheme is cool and restrained. The sprays of white stars have green stripes on the underside of the petals and the leaves are silvered down the centre. Where conditions suit it, this multiplies too freely to include in borders and rock gardens. Hardy.

General care: Plant in autumn with the top of the bulb about 10cm (4in) deep.

Height: 40cm (16in) **Spread:** 10cm (4in)

Site: Partial shade, sun. Well-drained and reasonably moist soil

Use: Underplanting for shrubs, wild garden, woodland garden

Good companions: *Colchicum* 'Rosy Dawn', *Geranium sylvaticum* 'Album', *Lilium martagon* var. *album*

5

6

7

8

9

10

11

12

tulips

Tulips are colourful hardy bulbs for formal spring bedding and containers. Plant them in autumn, 10–15cm (4–6in) deep, in fertile, well-drained soil in sun. In containers use a soil-based (John Innes No. 2) compost.

1 Tulipa 'Spring Green'

A late-flowering Viridiflora tulip, this has flowers that are green or a combination of green and another colour.
Height: 40cm (16in) **Spread:** 10cm (4in)
Good companions: *Buxus sempervirens*, *Primula auricula* 'Osbourne Green'

2 Tulipa 'Mount Tacoma'

Although less elegant than single late-flowering white tulips such as the lily-flowered 'White Triumphator', this double late tulip produces long-lasting flowers of dazzling purity.
Height: 40cm (16in) **Spread:** 10cm (4in)
Good companions: *Syringa vulgaris* 'Katherine Havemeyer', *Tulipa* 'Queen of Night'

3 Tulipa 'West Point'

The single lemon-yellow flowers of this lily-flowered tulip have a waisted goblet shape with elegantly curved tips.
Height: 50cm (20in) **Spread:** 10cm (4in)
Good companions: *Bellis perennis* Pomponette Series, *Primula* 'Guinevere'

4 Tulipa 'Queen of Night'

The sheeny flowers of this single late tulip are an exceptionally dark purple-maroon.
Height: 60cm (2ft) **Spread:** 10cm (4in)
Good companions: *Erysimum* 'Ivory White', *Malus* x *moerlandsii* 'Profusion', *Philadelphus coronarius* 'Aureus'

5 Tulipa 'Estella Rijnveld'

In this parrot tulip, the green-tinged buds have fringed petals and open to an extravagant swirl of white and red.
Height: 60cm (2ft) **Spread:** 10cm (4in)
Good companions: *Bellis perennis* Pomponette Series, *Hyacinthus orientalis* 'Carnegie', *Primula* 'Guinevere'

6 Tulipa 'Red Wing'

The shredded edge of the petals in this Fringed Group tulip gives each vivid red flower a distinctive outline.
Height: 50cm (20in) **Spread:** 10cm (4in)
Good companions: *Bellis perennis* Habanera Series, *Hyacinthus orientalis* 'Ostara', *Primula* Cowichan Garnet Group

7 Tulipa 'Fancy Frills'

A pale fringe encrusts petals that are rich pink with a near-white central blaze.
Height: 45cm (18in) **Spread:** 10cm (4in)
Good companions: *Hyacinthus orientalis* 'Carnegie', *Myosotis sylvatica* 'Royal Blue', *Tulipa* 'Queen of Night'

8 Tulipa 'Shirley'

The ivory-white petals of this Triumph Group tulip (surrounding Late Group tulips) are lightly streaked and edged with purple.
Height: 60cm (2ft) **Spread:** 10cm (4in)
Good companions: *Erysimum cheiri* 'Ivory White', *Tulipa* 'Mount Tacoma'

9 Tulipa saxatilis Bakeri Group 'Lilac Wonder'

In warm sun, the mauve-pink petals of this Species tulip open to reveal a lemon-yellow base. Suitable for a rock garden.
Height: 20cm (8in) **Spread:** 8cm (3in)
Good companions: *Aubrieta* 'Doctor Mules', *Muscari botryoides* 'Album', *Phlox subulata* 'McDaniel's Cushion'

1

2

3

4

5
6
7
8
9

climbers

Trained on architectural structures or other plants, climbers add a vertical dimension to the garden. Many begin flowering in spring and supply welcome early colour. Plant climbers in the dormant season.

purple, blue and violet

1 Clematis alpina 'Frances Rivis'
Alpine clematis

A selection of the slender deciduous species (see 11, opposite) with large, deep blue flowers. Plant with the base in shade. Hardy.
General care: Prune lightly after flowering.
Height: 3m (10ft) **Spread:** 1.5m (5ft)
Site: Sun, partial shade. Fertile, humus-rich and well-drained soil. Good on lime
Compost: Soil-based (John Innes No. 3)
Use: Container, shrub climber, training on tripod, wall
Good companions: *Buddleja crispa, Paeonia mlokosewitschii, Rosa xanthina* 'Canary Bird'

2 Clematis 'Helsingborg'
Alpina Group clematis

This slender deciduous clematis has nodding blue-purple flowers with long, elegant outer petal-like sepals. Plant with the base in shade. Hardy.
General care: Prune lightly after flowering
Height: 3m (10ft) **Spread:** 1.5m (5ft)
Site: Sun, partial shade. Fertile, humus-rich and well-drained soil. Does well on lime
Compost: Soil-based (John Innes No. 3)
Use: Container, shrub climber, training on tripod, wall
Good companions: *Choisya ternata, Hyacinthus orientalis* 'Carnegie', *Tulipa* 'Queen of Night'

3 Clematis macropetala
Clematis

A slender deciduous clematis with violet-blue flowers that have a paler centre filled with petal-like stamens. Ornamental fluffy seed heads follow. Plant with the base in shade. Hardy.
General care: Prune lightly after flowering.
Height: 3m (10ft) **Spread:** 1.5m (5ft)
Site: Sun, partial shade. Fertile, humus-rich and well-drained soil. Good on lime
Compost: Soil-based (John Innes No. 3)
Use: Container, shrub climber, training on tripod, wall
Good companions: *Geranium sylvaticum* 'Mayflower', *Iris* 'Jane Phillips', *Narcissus* 'Peeping Tom', *Tulipa* 'West Point'

pink and mauve

4 Clematis armandii 'Apple Blossom'
Clematis

Thought by many to be the best evergreen clematis, this needs a sheltered position on a warm wall. The glossy leaves provide good year-round cover and are bronze-green when young. The flowers, borne in mid-spring, are white flushed with pink. 'Snowdrift' has white flowers. Plant with the base in shade. Not fully hardy.
General care: Prune immediately after flowering.
Height and spread: 6m (20ft)
Site: Sun. Fertile, humus-rich and moist but well-drained soil. Good on lime
Use: Warm wall
Good companions: *Cynara cardunculus, Passiflora caerulea, Rosa* 'Reine des Violettes', *Vitis vinifera* 'Purpurea'

5 Clematis macropetala 'Markham's Pink'
Clematis

Bright pink and free-flowering cultivar of the deciduous species *Clematis macropetala* (see 3, above). Plant with the base in shade. Hardy.
General care: Prune lightly after flowering.
Height: 3m (10ft) **Spread:** 1.5m (5ft)
Site: Sun, partial shade. Fertile, humus-rich and well-drained soil. Does well on lime
Compost: Soil-based (John Innes No. 3)
Use: Container, shrub climber, training on tripod, wall
Good companions: *Clematis* 'Huldine', *Digitalis purpurea, Nepeta* 'Six Hills Giant'

6 Clematis montana var. rubens 'Elizabeth'
Clematis

The deciduous species is very vigorous, producing masses of white flowers in late spring and early summer. This variety, one of several selections in shades of pink, has purplish foliage and the large scented flowers are pale pink. Plant with the base in shade. Hardy.
General care: Prune immediately after flowering.
Height: 10m (30ft) **Spread:** 5m (15ft)
Site: Sun, partial shade. Fertile, humus-rich and moist but well-drained soil
Use: Pergola, trellis, tree climber, wall
Good companions: *Campanula lactiflora, Lilium regale, Paeonia lactiflora* 'Festiva Maxima', *Rosa* 'Bobbie James'

7 Wisteria sinensis
Chinese wisteria

Very vigorous deciduous climber with attractive large leaves that are divided into many leaflets. Most of the fragrant pea flowers in the trailing sprays open at the same time so that their mauve-blue makes a strong but elegant impression. By pruning it is possible to maintain plants at almost any size. Hardy.
General care: Prune in late summer and again in winter.
Height: 15m (50ft) **Spread:** 6m (20ft)
Site: Sun. Moist but well-drained soil, preferably lime-free
Use: Pergola, trained standard, tree climber, wall
Good companions: *Clematis montana* var. *rubens* 'Elizabeth', *Paeonia lactiflora* 'Bowl of Beauty', *Rosa* 'Madame Alfred Carrière', *Rosa* 'Madame Grégoire Staechelin'

yellow and orange

8 Rosa banksiae 'Lutea'
Yellow banksian rose

Vigorous semi-evergreen rose with slender, almost thornless stems. It takes a few years to settle and needs a sheltered position, but an established plant provides a beautiful display of small, double yellow flowers before the main rose season is under way. Lightly scented. Not fully hardy.
General care: Prune lightly every two or three years, only removing a few of the oldest stems.
Height: 12m (40ft) **Spread:** 6m (20ft)
Site: Sun. Fertile, moist but well-drained soil
Use: Warm wall
Good companions: *Campsis x tagliabuana* 'Madame Galen', *Clematis* 'Perle d'Azur', *Paeonia delavayi* var. *ludlowii*

9 Rosa 'Gloire de Dijon'
Old glory rose

This stiff-stemmed climber starts flowering early and continues over a long season. The fragrant double flowers are buff rather than yellow and have apricot tints. Hardy.
General care: Prune lightly between late autumn and early spring.
Height: 3m (10ft) **Spread:** 1.5m (5ft)
Site: Sun. Fertile, moist but well-drained soil
Use: Sunny wall or screen

2

8

10

11

3

9

12

4

5

Good companions: *Clematis* 'Gipsy Queen', *Clematis* 'Perle d'Azur', *Cleome hassleriana*, *Lilium regale*

10 Rosa 'Maigold'

Climbing hybrid Scots briar rose

Stiff-stemmed and thorny rose with glossy leaves and scented, semi-double, copper-yellow flowers. The display in late spring and early summer is generous but in autumn it is sparse. Can be grown as a free-standing shrub. Hardy.

General care: Prune lightly between late autumn and early spring.

Height: 4m (12ft) **Spread:** 2m (6ft)

Site: Sun. Fertile and moist but well-drained soil

Use: Specimen shrub, well-lit wall or screen

Good companions: *Allium hollandicum* 'Purple Sensation', *Clematis* 'Royal Velours', *Solanum crispum* 'Glasnevin'

cream and white

11 Clematis alpina subsp. sibirica 'White Moth'

Alpine clematis

The species is a slender deciduous climber, which often starts producing its blue flowers in early spring. The moth-like form of this late-flowering white version is due to the double petals. Very suitable for a courtyard or small garden. Plant with the base in shade. Hardy.

General care: Prune lightly after flowering.

Height: 3m (10ft) **Spread:** 1.5m (5ft)

Site: Sun, partial shade. Fertile, humus-rich and well-drained soil. Good on lime

Compost: Soil-based (John Innes No. 3)

Use: Container, shrub climber, training on tripod, wall

Good companions: *Aquilegia vulgaris* 'Nivea', *Clematis alpina* 'Frances Rivis', *Dicentra spectabilis* 'Alba', *Tulipa* 'Estella Rijnveld'

12 Wisteria sinensis 'Alba'

Chinese wisteria

This form of the vigorous *Wisteria sinensis* (see 7, opposite) has powerfully scented white flowers. Hardy.

General care: Prune in late summer and again in winter to control size.

Height: 15m (50ft) **Spread:** 6m (20ft)

Site: Sun. Moist but well-drained soil, preferably free of lime

Use: Pergola, trained standard, tree climber, wall

Good companions: *Clematis montana* var. *rubens* 'Elizabeth', *Clematis* 'Perle d'Azur', *Rosa* 'Gloire de Dijon'

shrubs & trees

Shrubs and small trees have durable frameworks of woody branches. Blossom and tints of new foliage make many conspicuously attractive in spring. Plant in the dormant season – in autumn or early spring.

purple, blue and violet

1 Ceanothus 'Puget Blue'
California lilac

The dense framework of branches and dark leaves of this evergreen shrub is almost hidden in the second half of spring by the rounded heads of small deep blue flowers. Suitable for training against a warm wall. Not fully hardy.

Height and spread: 3m (10ft)
Site: Sun. Well-drained soil
Use: Sunny sheltered border, wall shrub
Good companions: *Actinidia kolomikta*, *Myrtus communis* subsp. *tarentina*, *Solanum laxum* 'Album' (syn. *S. jasminoides* 'Album')

2 Ceanothus thyrsiflorus var. repens
Creeping blueblossom

This low-growing evergreen shrub makes a dark green mound that is covered in late spring and early summer with rounded heads of mid-blue flowers. Hardy.

Height: 1m (3ft) **Spread:** 2.5m (8ft)
Site: Sun. Well-drained soil
Use: Gravel garden, large rock garden, raised bed, sunny border
Good companions: *Artemisia absinthum* 'Valerie Finnis', *Gaura lindheimeri*, *Rosa glauca*, *Verbena bonariensis*

pink and mauve

3 Acer palmatum 'Corallinum'
Japanese maple

One of several Japanese maples, this slow-growing deciduous shrub has brilliant pink foliage in spring. In summer the deeply cut leaves are pale green but usually colour crimson and scarlet in autumn, most vividly on acid soil. Hardy but requires a sheltered position.

Height and spread: 1.2m (4ft)
Site: Partial shade. Humus-rich and moist but well-drained soil, preferably lime-free
Use: Shady border
Good companions: *Enkianthus campanulatus*, *Erythronium dens-canis*, *Rhododendron* 'Cilpinense', *Trillium erectum*

4 Acer pseudoplatanus 'Brilliantissimum'
Sycamore

In spring the young leaves of this slow-growing deciduous tree are an astonishing shade of shrimp pink. As they mature they turn yellow, then later green. Hardy.

Height and spread: 6m (20ft)
Site: Sun. Reasonably fertile and moist but well-drained soil
Use: Canopy in mixed planting, specimen tree
Good companions: *Euonymus alatus*, *Quercus coccinea* 'Splendens', *Taxus baccata* 'Fastigiata'

5 Cercis siliquastrum
Judas tree

This deciduous tree or large shrub bears clusters of bright purple-pink pea flowers on the bare stems or bursting from the trunk. The heart or kidney-shaped leaves are blue-green. Hardy.

Height and spread: 10m (33ft)
Site: Sun. Reasonably fertile and well-drained soil
Use: Canopy in mixed planting, specimen tree
Good companions: *Acanthus mollis* Latifolius Group, *Buddleja alternifolia*, *Cistus ladanifer*, *Helleborus argutifolius*

6 Cornus florida 'Cherokee Chief'
Flowering dogwood

Large petal-like bracts surround the tiny flowers of this deciduous tree or shrub. These are generally white or pink, strongly veined and often twisted, but in this selection they are vivid dark pink. Inedible red fruit follow. The leaves colour well in autumn. Hardy.

4

5

6

2

3

7

1

Height and spread: 6m (20ft)
Site: Sun. Reasonably fertile and well-drained soil, preferably lime-free
Use: Canopy in mixed planting, specimen tree or shrub, woodland garden
Good companions: *Choisya ternata, Cotoneaster frigidus* 'Cornubia', *Euonymus europaeus* 'Red Cascade'

7 Crataegus laevigata 'Paul's Scarlet'
May, Midland thorn

The species, of which this is a selection, and the hawthorn (*Crataegus monogyna*) are thorny deciduous trees of rounded outline that bear masses of pink or white flowers followed by inedible red fruits (haws). They are often used for country hedges, but are also attractive and easily grown trees for the smaller garden. This example carries a profusion of red double flowers. Hardy.
Height and spread: 8m (25ft)
Site: Sun, partial shade. Well-drained soil
Use: Canopy in mixed planting, specimen tree
Good companions: *Malus floribunda, Prunus laurocerasus* 'Otto Luyken', *Sarcococca hookeriana* var. *digyna, Sorbus* 'Joseph Rock'

8 Deutzia x elegantissima 'Rosealind'
The deutzias are mainly easy-going deciduous shrubs. They are covered with pink or white starry flowers in late spring or early summer. The pink flowers of 'Rosealind' are carried on arching stems and bridge the two seasons. Hardy.
General care: Prune immediately after flowering.
Height and spread: 1.5m (5ft)
Site: Sun, partial shade. Reasonably fertile and well-drained soil
Use: Sunny or lightly shaded border, underplanting for shrubs and trees
Good companions: *Exochorda* x *macrantha* 'The Bride', *Osmanthus delavayi, Viburnum opulus* 'Compactum'

9 Enkianthus campanulatus
The leaves of this tree-like shrub turn brilliant red before falling in autumn. The flowers in spring are of a subdued and delicate beauty. Red veining gives a pink tinge to the creamy bell-shaped blooms, which hang in pretty clusters. Hardy.
Height: 3m (10ft) **Spread:** 2.5m (8ft)
Site: Sun, partial shade. Lime-free, humus-rich and moist but well-drained soil
Use: Canopy in mixed planting, woodland garden
Good companions: *Fothergilla major* Monticola Group, *Hamamelis* x *intermedia* 'Pallida', *Rhododendron luteum*

10 Magnolia x soulangeana
Magnolia

A very large deciduous shrub or small tree, this produces a sensational display of chalice-shaped flowers, which open in mid-spring. The magnolia usually seen has cream flowers flushed purplish pink, but all the named white and purple-flowered forms are worth growing. Hardy.
Height and spread: 6m (20ft)
Site: Sun. Humus-rich and moist but well-drained soil, preferably lime-free
Use: Canopy in mixed planting, specimen tree or shrub, woodland garden
Good companions: *Bergenia* 'Beethoven', *Muscari armeniacum, Narcissus* 'Jenny'

11 Malus floribunda
Japanese crab apple

With a dense head of arching branches, this small deciduous tree is suitable for a small to medium garden. Crimson buds open to pale pink or white flowers, which are followed by small red-and-yellow apples. Hardy.
Height and spread: 8m (25ft)
Site: Sun, partial shade. Reasonably fertile, well-drained soil
Use: Canopy in mixed planting, specimen tree
Good companions: *Anemone blanda, Narcissus* 'Jack Snipe', *Spiraea* 'Arguta'

12 Malus x moerlandsii 'Profusion'
Crab apple

Round-headed tree with copper-red young leaves, which mature to bronze-red. In late spring there is a burst of thickly clustered, dark purplish pink flowers. Small red-purple apples follow. Hardy.
Height and spread: 10m (33ft)
Site: Sun. Fertile and moist but well-drained soil
Use: Canopy in mixed planting, specimen tree
Good companions: *Anemone* x *hybrida* 'Honorine Jobert', *Bergenia cordifolia* 'Purpurea', *Narcissus* 'February Gold'

13 Paeonia suffruticosa
Moutan, Tree peony

Despite their common name, tree peonies are deciduous shrubs. The framework of branches is somewhat stiff and awkward, but the leaves are attractively cut and the flowers are breathtaking. There are many magnificent cultivars in shades of pink as well as red, purple and white. Hardy.
General care: Protect young growth from frost.
Height and spread: 2m (6ft)
Site: Sun, partial shade. Fertile, humus-rich and moist but well-drained soil
Use: Sunny or lightly shaded border
Good companions: *Aquilegia* 'Hensol Harebell', *Campanula persicifolia, Rosa* 'Nevada'

pink and mauve (continued)

1 Prunus 'Kanzan'
Ornamental cherry

Although this deciduous tree is less graceful than many ornamental cherries, the upward-sweeping branches make it a useful avenue tree where space is limited. The young leaves are copper-red and the double flowers purplish pink. Hardy.

Height: 10m (33ft) **Spread:** 6m (20ft)
Site: Sun. Well-drained soil, preferably with a trace of lime
Use: Avenue, specimen tree
Good companions: *Crocus speciosus, Crocus tommasinianus, Scilla siberica* 'Spring Beauty'

2 Prunus 'Shirofugen'
Ornamental cherry

This broad-headed and vigorous deciduous tree brings the ornamental cherry season to a magnificent conclusion. Thickly clustered double white flowers open from purple-pink buds to coincide with the copper-red phase of the young leaves. As the long-stalked flowers fade they revert to purple-pink. Leaves usually colour orange-red in autumn. Hardy.

Height: 8m (25ft) **Spread:** 10m (33ft)
Site: Sun, partial shade. Moist, well-drained soil
Use: Canopy in mixed planting, specimen tree, woodland garden
Good companions: *Anemone nemorosa* 'Royal Blue', *Galanthus elwesii, Hyacinthoides non-scripta*

3 Syringa vulgaris 'Katherine Havemeyer'
Lilac

The numerous large-flowered forms of the common lilac are easy deciduous shrubs. They are a glorious feature of spring, when the dense heads of single or double fragrant flowers are borne in profusion. The flowers of 'Katherine Havemeyer' are mauve-pink and double. Hardy.

General care: Deadhead after flowering and remove growth sprouting from the base (suckers).
Height and spread: 6m (20ft)
Site: Sun, partial shade. Reasonably fertile and well-drained soil
Use: Sunny or lightly shaded border
Good companions: *Iris* 'Florentina', *Iris* 'Jane Phillips', *Rosa xanthina* 'Canary Bird'

4 Viburnum carlesii 'Aurora'
Viburnum

One of several forms of a deciduous shrub noted for the delicious fragrance of its waxy flowers, which are pink or red in bud and white or pink on opening. In this case the rounded heads are red and the open flowers pink. The downy leaves, copper tinted when young, may take on purplish or crimson tones in autumn. Hardy.

Height and spread: 2m (6ft)
Site: Sun, partial shade. Moist well-drained soil
Use: Sunny or lightly shaded border
Good companions: *Geranium psilostemon, Hydrangea quercifolia, Viburnum* x *bodnantense* 'Dawn'

5 Viburnum opulus 'Roseum'
Guelder rose, Snowball tree

The guelder rose, of which this is a form, is an attractive shrub with maple-like leaves, heads of white flowers and translucent red berries that glisten among the richly coloured autumn leaves. 'Roseum' produces no berries, the flowers being sterile, but these age to pink. Hardy.

Height and spread: 4m (12ft)
Site: Sun, partial shade. Moist but well-drained soil
Use: Sunny or lightly shaded border, wild garden, woodland garden
Good companions: *Digitalis purpurea, Fuchsia magellanica* 'Versicolor', *Lunaria annua*

red and russet

6 Camellia japonica 'Bob Hope'
Camellia

The common camellia, an evergreen shrub with glossy dark leaves, is the parent of hundreds of cultivars with flowers in a colour range that includes white, red and all shades of pink. Many flower in early spring but the season extends over many weeks. 'Bob Hope' is compact and bears large, semi-double bright red flowers of peony form. Plant in a sheltered position to protect buds and flowers from cold winds and frosts. Hardy.

Height: 3m (10ft) **Spread:** 2.5m (8ft)
Site: Partial shade. Lime-free, humus-rich and moist but well-drained soil
Compost: Soil-based and lime-free (ericaceous)
Use: Container, greenhouse or conservatory, shady border, underplanting for trees
Good companions: *Eucryphia* x *nymansensis* 'Nymansay', *Rhododendron* 'Bow Bells', *Rhododendron* 'Loderi King George'

7 Paeonia suffruticosa 'Hana-daijin'
Moutan, Tree peony

The flowers of tree peonies cover a range of sumptuous colours (see 13, page 191). 'Hana-daijin' bears double flowers with waved petals enclosing a golden centre. Hardy.

General care: Protect young growth from frost.
Height and spread: 2m (6ft)
Site: Sun, partial shade. Fertile, humus-rich and moist but well-drained soil
Use: Sunny or lightly shaded border
Good companions: *Aquilegia* 'Hensol Harebell', *Campanula persicifolia, Geranium psilostemon, Rosa* 'Nevada'

8 Photinia x fraseri 'Red Robin'

The small white flowers of this evergreen shrub count for little, but new growth is brilliant red and makes a striking garden feature in spring and early summer before the leaves turn glossy green. Can be used as an attractive alternative to *Pieris* 'Forest Flame' where there is chalk in the soil. Plant in a sheltered position. Not fully hardy.

Height and spread: 5m (15ft)
Site: Sun, partial shade. Fertile, moist but well-drained soil
Use: Sunny or lightly shaded border, underplanting for trees
Good companions: *Epimedium* x *youngianum* 'Niveum', *Helleborus orientalis, Pulmonaria* 'Mawson's Blue'

9 Pieris 'Forest Flame'

In spring drooping sprays of fragrant white flowers are a lovely feature of this evergreen shrub, but more eye-catching is the brilliant red of its young growth, which turns pink then greenish white and finally green. Plant in a sheltered position. Not fully hardy.

Height: 3m (10ft) **Spread:** 2m (6ft)
Site: Sun, partial shade. Lime-free, humus-rich and moist but well-drained soil
Use: Sunny or lightly shaded border, underplanting for trees
Good companions: *Acer japonicum* 'Vitifolium', *Rhododendron* 'Britannia'

yellow and orange

10 Berberis darwinii
Barberry

Drooping clusters of small bright orange flowers make this evergreen shrub conspicuous in spring. In autumn there are blue-black berries among the glossy spine-tipped leaves. Hardy.

Height and spread: 3m (10ft)
Site: Sun, partial shade. Well-drained soil
Use: Sunny or lightly shaded border
Good companions: *Cytisus* x *praecox* 'Allgold', *Geranium phaeum, Potentilla fruticosa* 'Tangerine'

11 **Berberis x stenophylla**
Barberry
The numerous arching branches of this vigorous evergreen shrub bear fragrant orange-yellow flowers in spring. Generally a light crop of blue-black berries follows. The leaves are prickly. Hardy.
Height: 3m (10ft) **Spread:** 5m (15ft)
Site: Sun, partial shade. Well-drained soil
Use: Informal hedge, sunny or lightly shaded bed
Good companions: *Berberis thunbergii* 'Atropurpurea Nana', *Cotinus* 'Flame', *Syringa vulgaris* 'Katherine Havemeyer'

12 **Cytisus x kewensis**
Broom
This low, spreading deciduous shrub is best sited where the arching stems, laden in spring with creamy-yellow pea flowers, can hang down. Hardy.
Height: 30cm (12in) **Spread:** 2m (6ft)
Site: Sun. Well-drained soil
Use: Bank, large rock garden, raised bed
Good companions: *Euonymus alatus* 'Compactus', *Euphorbia characias* subsp. *wulfenii*, *Pinus sylvestris* 'Beuvronensis'

yellow and orange (continued)

1 Cytisus x praecox 'Allgold'
Broom

The arching stems of this dense and bushy deciduous shrub are closely set with deep yellow pea flowers. Their scent is strong and acrid. Short-lived, but good as a filler. Hardy.

Height and spread: 1.5m (5ft)

Site: Sun. Well-drained soil

Use: Gravel garden, sunny border

Good companions: *Artemisia ludoviciana* 'Valerie Finnis', *Stachys byzantina* 'Silver Carpet', *Verbascum* Cotswold Group 'Gainsborough'

2 Kerria japonica 'Pleniflora'
Jew's mantle

This easy deciduous shrub has slender, glossy green stems that are attractive in winter. Its high season, though, is spring, when the bush carries numerous rich yellow double flowers. Hardy.

General care: Cut out old stems immediately after flowering.

Height and spread: 3m (10ft)

Site: Sun, partial shade. Well-drained soil

Use: Sunny or lightly shaded border, underplanting for deciduous trees

Good companions: *Forsythia* x *intermedia* 'Lynwood', *Fritillaria imperialis*, *Narcissus* 'Peeping Tom'

3 Laburnum x watereri 'Vossii'
Golden rain

This small deciduous tree is often trained on a pergola, a method of growing that shows off the numerous cascades of yellow flowers, which can be up to 60cm (2ft) long. The flowering season extends into early summer. All parts of the plant are highly toxic. Hardy.

Height and spread: 8m (25ft)
Site: Sun. Fertile and well-drained soil
Use: Canopy for mixed planting, pergola, specimen tree
Good companions: *Allium hollandicum* 'Purple Sensation', *Myosotis sylvatica*, *Tulipa* 'Generaal de Wet', *Wisteria sinensis*

4 Magnolia 'Elizabeth'
Magnolia

This conical deciduous tree bears fragrant light yellow flowers, up to 20cm (8in) across, over several weeks in spring. Their cup shape and erect stance are particularly conspicuous on the bare branches before the large leaves unfurl. These open bronze and later change to dark green. Hardy.

Height: 10m (33ft) **Spread:** 6m (20ft)
Site: Sun, partial shade. Humus-rich and moist but well-drained soil, preferably lime-free
Use: Canopy in mixed planting, specimen tree
Good companions: *Acer palmatum* 'Sango-kaku', *Hamamelis* x *intermedia* 'Pallida', *Narcissus* 'February Gold'

5 Paeonia delavayi var. ludlowii
Tree peony

The large, deeply cut, bright green leaves of this deciduous shrub make it worth growing for its foliage alone. The yellow cup-shaped flowers, 13cm (5in) across, open as the leaves are developing, and their season extends into early summer. Hardy.

Height and spread: 2.5m (8ft)
Site: Sun, partial shade. Fertile, humus-rich and moist but well-drained soil
Use: Sunny or lightly shaded border
Good companions: *Brunnera macrophylla*, *Helleborus orientalis*, *Lilium regale*, *Viburnum plicatum* 'Mariesii'

6 Philadelphus coronarius 'Aureus'
Mock orange

There are fragrant single white flowers in late spring and early summer, but this deciduous shrub is grown mainly for the sunny effect of its bright yellow young leaves. By mid-summer these have lost their fresh radiance. Hardy.

Height: 2.5m (8ft) **Spread:** 2m (6ft)
Site: Partial shade. Well-drained soil
Use: Lightly shaded border
Good companions: *Choisya ternata*, *Cotinus* 'Grace', *Euonymus alatus* 'Compactus'

7 Pleioblastus auricomus
Bamboo

This upright evergreen bamboo is grown for its bright foliage. Hollow purplish canes carry blade-like leaves that are yellow streaked with green. The clumps spread but without posing a threat. Hardy.

General care: To promote the growth of fresh leaves, cut the canes down in autumn.
Height: 1.2m (4ft) **Spread:** 1.5m (5ft)
Site: Sun. Humus-rich and moist but well-drained soil
Compost: Soil-based
Use: Container, sunny border, wild garden
Good companions: *Epimedium* x *versicolor* 'Sulphureum', *Milium effusum* 'Aureum', *Paeonia delavayi* var. *ludlowii*

8 Rosa xanthina 'Canary Bird'
Shrub rose

The clear yellow of the small single flowers makes a cheerful start to the long rose season. The blooms have a musky scent and are borne freely along arching stems.The ferny grey-green leaves are attractive throughout summer, and there are odd flowers as a reminder of the generous spring display. Hardy.

Height and spread: 3m (10ft)
Site: Sun. Reasonably fertile and moist but well-drained soil
Use: Specimen shrub, sunny border
Good companions: *Aquilegia* McKana Group, *Iris* 'Jane Phillips', *Rosa* 'Golden Wings'

9 Salix lanata
Woolly willow

This shrubby deciduous willow makes a grey rounded bush. The dark green leaves are covered with silvery wool. Hairy catkins that are yellow with pollen and 5–8cm (2–3in) long sit among the young leaves. Hardy.

Height: 1m (3ft) **Spread:** 1.5m (5ft)
Site: Sun. Moist but well-drained soil
Use: Large rock garden, raised bed, sunny border
Good companions: *Corydalis flexuosa*, *Crocus speciosus*, *Crocus tommasinianus*

cream and white

10 Choisya ternata
Mexican orange blossom

A compact evergreen shrub, this has glossy aromatic leaves and numerous clusters of scented white flowers in late spring. After the main season, the shrub may flower sporadically, often with a little burst in autumn. It is usually seen at its best in a sheltered town garden. Hardy.

Height and spread: 2.5m (8ft)
Site: Sun, partial shade. Well-drained soil
Use: Sunny or shady border, mixed trees and shrubs
Good companions: *Ceanothus thyrsiflorus* var. *repens*, *Cistus ladanifer*, *Melianthus major*, *Wisteria sinensis*

11 Davidia involucrata
Dove tree, Ghost tree, Handkerchief tree

When in flower, this conical deciduous tree seems to be decked with freshly laundered handkerchiefs. The small flowers are clustered in rounded heads, but each cluster is surrounded by a pair, unequal in size, of white leaf-like bracts. Hardy.

Height: 15m (50ft) **Spread:** 10m (33ft)
Site: Sun, partial shade. Fertile and moist but well-drained soil
Use: Canopy in mixed planting, specimen tree, woodland garden
Good companions: *Cornus alba* 'Elegantissima', *Geranium sylvaticum* 'Mayflower', *Hydrangea* 'Preziosa', *Hydrangea quercifolia*

12 Erica arborea var. alpina
Tree heath

This somewhat formless evergreen shrub with needle-like leaves is dramatically transformed in spring when tight conical sprays are covered with small grey-white flowers that have the fragrance of honey. Hardy.

Height: 2m (6ft) **Spread:** 1m (3ft)
Site: Sun. Lime-free and moist but well-drained soil
Use: Heather garden, large rock garden, sunny border
Good companions: *Calluna vulgaris* 'Peter Sparkes', *Erica carnea* 'King George', *Ledum groenlandicum*

cream and white (continued)

1 Exochorda x macrantha 'The Bride'
Pearl bush

This deciduous shrub produces a mound of pliant arching stems, which are garlanded with white flowers. Excellent with late spring bulbs. Hardy.

General care: Cut out about a fifth of the old stems after flowering.

Height: 2m (6ft) **Spread:** 3m (10ft)

Site: Sun, partial shade. Moist but well-drained soil

Use: Sunny or lightly shaded border

Good companions: *Magnolia x soulangeana*, *Tulipa* 'Queen of Night', *Tulipa* 'Spring Green'

2 Fothergilla major Monticola Group
The fragrant bottlebrush flowers, usually white but sometimes tinged pink, are the spring feature of this deciduous shrub. In autumn the leaves turn brilliant shades of yellow, orange and red. Hardy.

Height: 2.5m (8ft) **Spread:** 2m (6ft)

Site: Sun, partial shade. Lime-free, humus-rich and moist but well-drained soil

Use: Sunny or lightly shaded border, woodland garden

Good companions: *Acer japonicum* 'Vitifolium', *Meconopsis betonicifolia*, *Rhododendron* 'Bow Bells'

3 Halesia carolina
Silver bell, Snowdrop tree

This deciduous shrub or spreading small tree starts to flower before the leaves are fully developed. Numerous small clusters of white bells hang from the slender branches in late spring and are followed by inedible four-winged fruits. Plant in a position sheltered from cold winds. Hardy.

Height: 6m (20ft) **Spread:** 8m (25ft)

Site: Sun, partial shade. Lime-free, humus-rich and moist but well-drained soil

Use: Canopy in mixed planting, woodland garden

Good companions: *Acer griseum*, *Hamamelis x intermedia* 'Pallida', *Rhododendron* 'Loderi King George'

4 Ledum groenlandicum
Labrador tree

A rounded bush of dark aromatic leaves, this low evergreen shrub is studded with flat heads of small white flowers. Shoots and the undersides of the leaves are covered with a rusty felt. Hardy.

Height: 1m (3ft) **Spread:** 1.2m (4ft)

Site: Sun, partial shade. Lime-free, humus-rich and moist but well-drained soil

Use: Heather garden

Good companions: *Calluna vulgaris* 'Darkness', *Erica carnea* 'Springwood White', *Gaultheria mucronata* 'Bell's Seedling'

5 Magnolia denudata
Lily tree, Yulan

Provided the fragrant flowers are not spoilt by late frosts, this deciduous shrub or small tree is one of the great delights of spring. The dome of bare branches is liberally covered with upright white blooms. Plant in a sheltered position. Hardy.

Height and spread: 8m (25ft)

Site: Sun. Moist but well-drained soil, preferably lime-free

Use: Canopy in mixed planting, specimen shrub or tree

Good companions: *Narcissus* 'Dove Wings', *Primula* 'Guinevere', *Scilla siberica*

6 Magnolia x kewensis 'Wada's Memory'
Magnolia

The fragrant white flowers of this deciduous small tree or shrub are borne on bare stems. They are large, up to 13cm (5in) across, with fluttering limp petals. The leaves are bronze tinted on opening but later turn dark green, and are aromatic when bruised. Hardy.

Height: 10m (33ft) **Spread:** 6m (20ft)

Site: Sun. Humus-rich and moist but well-drained soil, preferably lime-free

Use: Canopy in mixed planting, specimen tree

Good companions: *Camellia* 'Cornish Snow', *Erythronium californicum* 'White Beauty', *Erythronium dens-canis*, *Eucryphia x nymansensis* 'Nymansay'

7 Osmanthus delavayi

Slow-growing evergreen shrub with small glossy dark green leaves that show off the pure white of the neat tubular flowers. The sweet scent is delicious in the garden and indoors. Hardy.
General care: For a compact shape, prune immediately after flowering.
Height: 4m (12ft) **Spread:** 2.5m (8ft)
Site: Sun, partial shade. Reasonably moist but well-drained soil
Use: Sunny or lightly shaded border, underplanting for deciduous trees
Good companions: *Bergenia* 'Beethoven', *Muscari armeniacum, Sorbus cashmiriana*

8 Prunus avium 'Plena'

Gean, Wild cherry

A somewhat pyramidal deciduous tree, this form of the European species has a fissured trunk banded with peeling red-brown bark. In spring the branches are loaded with drooping clusters of double white flowers. In autumn the leaves turn crimson. Hardy.
Height: 12m (40ft) **Spread:** 10m (33ft)
Site: Sun. Moist but well-drained soil
Use: Canopy in mixed planting, specimen tree, woodland garden
Good companions: *Cyclamen hederifolium, Galanthus nivalis, Helleborus orientalis*

9 Prunus laurocerasus 'Otto Luyken'

Cherry laurel, Laurel

The glossy evergreen foliage of the cherry laurels makes them valuable year-round shrubs and hedging plants. This compact form has narrow lustrous leaves and is one of the most effective in flower. Erect candles, composed of numerous small fragrant flowers, are produced in spring and early summer and occasionally in autumn. Hardy.
Height: 1m (3ft) **Spread:** 1.5m (5ft)
Site: Sun, partial shade. Moist but well-drained soil, preferably lime-free
Compost: Soil-based with added organic matter
Use: Container, informal hedge, sunny or shaded border, underplanting for trees
Good companions: *Cercidiphyllum japonicum, Hydrangea macrophylla* 'Blue Wave', *Mahonia japonica*

10 Prunus 'Shôgetsu'

Ornamental cherry

A good choice for a small to medium garden, this small but rather flat-topped deciduous tree bears numerous clusters of pink buds that open to frilly double white flowers. The foliage usually shows orange and red tints in autumn. Hardy.
Height: 5m (15ft) **Spread:** 8m (25ft)
Site: Sun, partial shade. Moist but well-drained soil
Use: Canopy in mixed planting, specimen tree, woodland garden
Good companions: *Anemone blanda, Colchicum speciosum* 'Album', *Primula vulgaris*

11 Prunus 'Ukon'

Ornamental cherry

The leaves of this spreading deciduous tree are bronze tinted when they open in mid-spring. Their colour goes well with the greenish cream of the semi-double flower clusters. Attractive red-brown foliage in autumn. Hardy.
Height and spread: 8m (25ft)
Site: Sun. Moist but well-drained soil
Use: Canopy in mixed planting, specimen tree, woodland garden
Good companions: *Arum italicum* subsp. *italicum* 'Marmoratum', *Epimedium* x *warleyense* 'Orangekönigin', *Helleborus argutifolius*

12 Rubus 'Benenden'

Related to the blackberry, this thornless deciduous shrub has attractive lobed leaves. Glistening white flowers, each one 5cm (2in) across with a boss of yellow stamens, open along arching stems. Hardy.
General care: Prune after flowering.
Height and spread: 3m (10ft)
Site: Sun, partial shade. Well-drained soil
Use: Sunny or lightly shaded border, wild garden, woodland garden
Good companions: *Forsythia* x *intermedia* 'Lynwood', *Hydrangea aspera* Villosa Group, *Lonicera* x *purpusii* 'Winter Beauty'

cream and white (continued)

1 Sorbus aria 'Lutescens'
Whitebeam

The whitebeam is a columnar, compact deciduous tree. The leaves are an attractive grey-green colour when young, and later turn dark green on the upper surface and grey-white and downy on the underside. White spring flowers are followed by clusters of inedible spherical berries, which ripen to scarlet as the foliage turns gold and russet in autumn. 'Lutescens' is outstanding in spring because of the creamy whiteness of the young leaves. Hardy.

Height: 10m (33ft) **Spread:** 8m (25ft)
Site: Sun. Well-drained soil. Good on chalk
Use: Canopy in mixed planting, specimen tree, woodland garden
Good companions: *Philadelphus* 'Belle Etoile', *Prunus* 'Taihaku', *Syringa vulgaris* 'Katherine Havemeyer'

2 Spiraea 'Arguta'
Bridal wreath, Foam of May

In spring numerous clusters of small white flowers are borne along the whole length of the slender arching branches of this dense deciduous shrub. The toothed narrow leaves are bright green. Hardy.

Height and spread: 2.5m (8ft)
Site: Sun. Fertile and moist but well-drained soil
Use: Sunny border
Good companions: *Abelia schumannii, Osmanthus delavayi, Ribes sanguineum* 'Pulborough Scarlet', *Rosa* 'Céleste'

3 Syringa vulgaris 'Madame Lemoine'
Lilac

Like *Syringa vulgaris* 'Katherine Havemeyer' (see page 192), this is a double form of the popular deciduous shrub, but here the fragrant flowers are creamy yellow in bud and pure white on opening. Hardy.

General care: Deadhead after flowering and remove suckers (growth sprouting from the base).
Height and spread: 6m (20ft)
Site: Sun, partial shade. Reasonably fertile and well-drained soil
Use: Sunny or lightly shaded border
Good companions: *Buddleja* 'Lochinch', *Cynara cardunculus, Rosa glauca*

4 Viburnum plicatum 'Mariesii'
Japanese snowball tree

The spreading branches of this deciduous shrub are arranged in tiers. The bush is already in leaf when the white flowers open in flat-topped heads – small fertile flowers surrounded by large sterile flowers on the outside. The display lasts into early summer. The foliage often colours richly in autumn. Hardy.

Height: 3m (10ft) **Spread:** 4m (12ft)
Site: Sun, partial shade. Moist but well-drained soil
Use: Sunny or lightly shaded border, woodland garden
Good companions: *Campanula lactiflora, Chaenomeles x superba* 'Knap Hill Scarlet', *Geranium sylvaticum* 'Mayflower'

5 Xanthoceras sorbifolium

This large upright deciduous shrub has bright green leaves composed of many sharply toothed leaflets. The starry white flowers, with a yellow to bright red eye, are borne on upright stems. Best in a hot position and suitable for training against a warm wall. Hardy.

Height: 4m (12ft) **Spread:** 3m (10ft)
Site: Sun. Fertile and well-drained soil
Use: Sunny border, wall shrub
Good companions: *Ceanothus* 'Puget Blue', *Clematis alpina* 'Frances Rivis', *Clematis* 'Bill MacKenzie'

green

6 Acer palmatum var. dissectum Dissectum Viride Group
Japanese maple

The Japanese maples are deciduous shrubs and small trees. They are remarkable for the range of leaf shape and size among the various cultivars as well as for the brilliant colours many assume in autumn. Some are slow-growing mound-forming shrubs, with leaves divided into five or more lobes that are cut right to the base. The Dissectum Viride Group have finely divided leaves that are bright green in spring, then plainer in summer before colouring well in autumn, most vividly on acid soil. Plant in a sheltered position. Hardy.

Height: 2m (6ft) **Spread:** 3m (10ft)
Site: Partial shade. Humus-rich and moist but well-drained soil, preferably lime-free
Use: Shady border, underplanting for trees
Good companions: *Cercidiphyllum japonicum, Erythronium californicum* 'White Beauty', *Rhododendron* 'Loderi King George'

1

2 3

4

5

6

rhododendrons

Rhododendrons, which include azaleas, are ornamental shrubs that need neutral to acid soil or an ericaceous compost. Those selected here are all hardy and flower in late spring to early summer.

1 Rhododendron 'Loderi King George'
Large, evergreen and rounded. Huge trusses of scented white flowers open from pink buds.
Height and spread: 4m (12ft)
Good companions: *Camellia japonica* 'Elegans', *Kalmia latifolia* 'Ostbo Red'

2 Rhododendron 'Dopey'
Compact and evergreen, with many trusses of scarlet flowers marked with brown.
Height and spread: 2m (6ft)
Good companions: *Acer palmatum* var. *dissectum* Dissectum Viride Group, *Camellia japonica* 'Bob Hope', *Rhododendron* 'Britannia'

3 Rhododendron 'Strawberry Ice'
Deciduous azalea. Dark-veined pale pink blooms with a yellow-marked throat open from deep pink buds. Suitable for full sun.
Height and spread: 2m (6ft)
Good companions: *Cornus florida* 'Cherokee Chief', *Halesia carolina*, *Rhododendron* 'Vanessa Pastel'

4 Rhododendron 'Lionel's Triumph'
Large-leaved and evergreen with trusses of soft yellow flowers that are pink in bud.
Height and spread: 4m (12ft)
Good companions: *Disanthus cercidifolius*, *Magnolia* 'Elizabeth'

5 Rhododendron macabeanum
Evergreen shrub with huge leaves. Cream or yellow purple-blotched flowers in mid-spring.
Height: 12m (40ft) **Spread:** 6m (20ft)
Good companions: *Eucryphia* x *nymansensis* 'Nymansay', *Hamamelis* x *intermedia* 'Jelena', *Magnolia* 'Elizabeth'

6 Rhododendron 'Vuyk's Scarlet'
Small-leaved and dwarf evergreen azalea. Vivid red flowers. Suitable for full sun.
Height: 75cm (2ft 6in) **Spread:** 1.2m (4ft)
Good companions: *Erica arborea* var. *alpina*, *Ledum groenlandicum*, *Pieris* 'Forest Flame'

7 Rhododendron 'Bow Bells'
Compact and evergreen, with copper-tinted young leaves and pink flowers.
Height and spread: 2m (6ft)
Good companions: *Acer palmatum* 'Corallinum', *Camellia* x *williamsii* 'Donation', *Fothergilla major* Monticola Group

8 Rhododendron 'Golden Torch'
On this compact evergreen shrub pink buds open to peachy-yellow flowers.
Height and spread: 1.5m (5ft)
Good companions: *Acer palmatum* 'Corallinum', *Fothergilla major* Monticola Group, *Hamamelis* x *intermedia* 'Pallida'

9 Rhododendron 'Palestrina'
Small-leaved evergreen azalea. Clusters of two or three white flowers that are pale green in the throat.
Height and spread: 1.2m (4ft)
Good companions: *Camellia* 'Donation', *Kalmia latifolia* 'Ostbo Red'

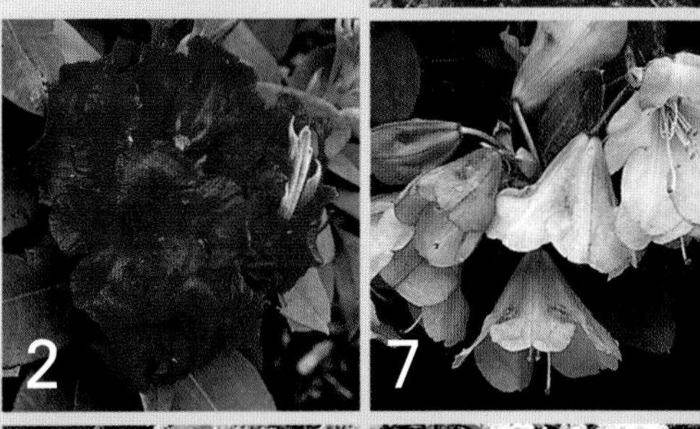

alpines

Most small perennials and shrubs that thrive in well-drained conditions do not need to be grown in a special rock garden. Many flower in spring and early summer. Plant in mild weather between autumn and early spring.

purple, blue and violet

1 Gentiana acaulis
Trumpet gentian

The sensational deep blue of the trumpets, which have green spotting in the throat, make this one of the most celebrated of all alpine plants. Its flowering can be unpredictable. Hardy.

Height: 8cm (3in) **Spread:** 45cm (18in)
Site: Sun. Moist but gritty and well-drained soil
Compost: Soil-based (John Innes No. 1) with added grit and leaf-mould
Use: Alpine house, raised bed, rock garden, scree, trough
Good companions: *Hebe cupressoides* 'Boughton Dome', *Iris histriodes* 'Major', *Narcissus* 'Jack Snipe'

2 Gentiana verna
Spring gentian, Star gentian

The starry flowers are small but their deep azure colour makes a strong impression. This evergreen perennial tends to be short-lived, so it is worth bringing on young plants as replacements. Hardy.

Height: 8cm (3in) **Spread:** 15cm (6in)
Site: Sun. Moist but well-drained and gritty soil
Compost: Soil-based (John Innes No. 1) with added grit and leaf-mould
Use: Alpine house, raised bed, rock garden, scree, trough
Good companions: *Daphne cneorum* 'Eximia', *Muscari botryoides* 'Album'

3 Primula marginata 'Kesselring's Variety'
Primula

The species is an evergreen or semi-evergreen perennial forming rosettes of jagged leaves with silvery margins. The stems are covered with a white mealy powder and carry clusters of lightly scented mauve-blue flowers with a powdery white eye. This selection is richly coloured. Best planted in crevices and protected from excess wet. Hardy.

Height: 15cm (6in) **Spread:** 30cm (12in)
Site: Partial shade. Moist but well-drained and gritty soil
Compost: Soil-based (John Innes No. 1) with added leaf-mould and grit
Use: Alpine house, dry wall, raised bed, rock garden
Good companions: *Alchemilla conjuncta, Geranium cinereum* 'Ballerina'

4 Pulsatilla vulgaris
Pasque flower

This tactile perennial produces a tuft of finely cut leaves that are very hairy when young, and from which rise nodding buds of silky hairiness. The purple or mauve flowers have golden stamens. In summer there are silky seed heads. Hardy.

Height: 25cm (10in) **Spread:** 30cm (12in)
Site: Sun. Fertile and well-drained soil
Use: Front of border, raised bed, rock garden, scree
Good companions: *Armeria maritima* 'Dusseldorfer Stölz', *Crocus imperati* subsp. *imperati* 'De Jager', *Gypsophila repens* 'Rosa Schönheit'

pink and mauve

5 Aethionema 'Warley Rose'
Stone cress

This evergreen or semi-evergreen shrubby perennial is easy to grow. It produces broad spikes of densely clustered rich pink flowers in quantity. Hardy.

Height: 15cm (6in) **Spread:** 30cm (12in)
Site: Sun. Well-drained soil. Good on lime
Use: Dry wall, paving, raised bed, rock garden, scree
Good companions: *Aubrieta* 'Greencourt Purple', *Dianthus deltoides* 'Leuchtfunk', *Silene schafta*

6 Armeria juniperifolia
Sea pink, Thrift

Pink flowers huddle over the small evergreen hummock of narrow rather sharp-tipped leaves. The flowers are richly coloured in the form 'Bevan's Variety'. Hardy.

Height: 8cm (3in) **Spread:** 15cm (6in)
Site: Sun. Well-drained and gritty soil
Compost: Soil-based (John Innes No. 1) with added grit
Use: Paving, raised bed, rock garden, scree, trough
Good companions: *Artemisia schmidtiana* 'Nana', *Lavandula angustifolia* 'Nana Alba', *Raoulia australis* Lutescens Group

7 Aubrieta hybrids
Aubrieta

Mat-forming aubrietas are evergreen perennials. In spring they are covered with four-petalled, sometimes double flowers in mauve, pink, purple or red. 'Rose Queen' has pink flowers; 'Greencourt Purple' is purple. Hardy.

General care: To keep plants compact, trim after flowering in early summer.
Height: 5cm (2in) **Spread:** 60cm (2ft)
Site: Sun. Well-drained soil. Good on lime
Use: Front of border, paving, raised bed, rock garden, sunny bank
Good companions: *Aurinia saxatilis* 'Citrina', *Campanula garganica, Iberis sempervirens* 'Weisser Zwerg'

8 Daphne cneorum 'Eximia'
Garland flower

The daphnes, which are noted for the superlative fragrance of their small flowers, tend to be temperamental. This sprawling evergreen shrub, the most rewarding of the dwarf daphnes, dislikes

root disturbance, so start with a young pot-grown specimen. The starry pink flowers are borne profusely in late spring and early summer. Hardy.
Height: 20cm (8in) **Spread:** 1m (3ft)
Site: Sun, partial shade. Humus-rich and well-drained soil
Use: Dry wall, front of border, raised bed, rock garden, scree
Good companions: *Diascia barberae* 'Ruby Field', *Gypsophila repens* 'Rosa Schönheit', *Tulipa clusiana*

9 Penstemon 'Six Hills'

Several shrubby and sub-shrubby evergreen penstemons are low growing and bear masses of funnel-shaped flowers. This hybrid makes a small bush of grey-green leaves. It produces mauve flowers in late spring and early summer. Hardy.
Height: 15cm (6in) **Spread:** 25cm (10in)
Site: Sun. Well-drained and gritty soil
Use: Paving, raised bed, rock garden, scree
Good companions: *Armeria juniperifolia*, *Artemisia schmidtiana* 'Nana', *Crocus sieberi* 'Hubert Edelsten', *Geranium cinerium* subsp. *subcaulescens*

10 Phlox douglasii 'Boothman's Variety'
Phlox

The species is a shrubby evergreen perennial that makes a bright green mat of narrow leaves. In late spring and early summer saucer-shaped mauve or pink flowers almost hide the foliage. The mauve flowers of this cultivar have a dark eye. Other cultivars have white or crimson flowers. Hardy.
Height: 15cm (6in) **Spread:** 45cm (18in)
Site: Sun. Fertile and well-drained soil
Use: Dry wall, paving, raised bed, rock garden
Good companions: *Convolvulus sabatius*, *Rhodanthemum hosmariense*, *Silene schafta*

11 Phlox subulata 'McDaniel's Cushion'
Moss phlox

The species, like *Phlox douglasii* (see above), is a low-growing evergreen perennial, but the late spring and early summer flowers are more starry and the petals are notched. The colour range in other named forms includes pink, mauve, scarlet and magenta. 'McDaniel's Cushion' has rich pink flowers. Hardy.
Height: 10cm (4in) **Spread:** 45cm (18in)
Site: Sun, partial shade. Fertile, well-drained soil
Use: Dry wall, paving, raised bed, rock garden
Good companions: *Armeria maritima* 'Dusseldorfer Stölz', *Hebe cupressoides* 'Boughton Dome', *Narcissus* 'Jenny'

red and russet

12 Saxifraga 'Peter Pan'
Mossy saxifrage

Tightly packed evergreen leaves form dense hummocks. These are topped in spring by wiry stems carrying saucer-shaped flowers that can be white, yellow, pink or red. The crimson-flowered 'Peter Pan' makes a tidy plant. 'Pixie', another compact hybrid, has deep red flowers. Hardy.
Height: 8cm (3in) **Spread:** 30cm (12in)
Site: Partial shade. Moist but well-drained soil
Compost: Soil-based (John Innes No. 2) with added grit and leaf-mould
Use: Edging, paving, raised bed, rock garden, trough
Good companions: *Alchemilla conjuncta*, *Phlox subulata*, *Viola biflora*

yellow and orange

1 Aurinia saxatilis 'Dudley Nevill Variegated'
Gold dust

This evergreen shrubby perennial has variegated leaves and massed buff-yellow flowers. The species has bright yellow blooms while those of 'Citrina' are lemon-yellow. Hardy.

General care: To keep plants compact, trim when flowering has finished.

Height: 25cm (10in) **Spread:** 45cm (18in)

Site: Sun. Well-drained soil

Use: Dry wall, raised bed, rock garden, sunny bank

Good companions: *Achillea* x *lewisii* 'King Edward', *Aubrieta* 'Greencourt Purple', *Cytisus* x *beanii*

2 Cytisus x beanii
Broom

Like its relative the common broom (*Cytisus scoparius*), this dwarf deciduous shrub makes a sunny impression with sprays of golden pea flowers. It is short-lived, usually achieving its peak in its third year. Hardy.

General care: Prune lightly immediately after flowering.

Height: 60cm (2ft) **Spread:** 1m (3ft)

Site: Sun. Well-drained soil

Use: Front of border, raised bed, rock garden

Good companions: *Aubrieta* 'Doctor Mules', *Crocus tommasinianus, Helianthemum* 'Wisley Primrose', *Iris* 'George'

3 Raoulia australis Lutescens Group

A tight mat of very small blue-grey leaves, this evergreen perennial flows over irregularities. The minute yellow flowers are little more than a powdering in spring. Dislikes winter wet. Hardy.

Height: 1cm (½in) **Spread:** 45cm (18in)

Site: Sun, partial shade. Moist but well-drained and gritty soil

Compost: Soil-based (John Innes No. 1) with added leaf-mould and grit

Use: Paving, raised bed, rock garden, scree, trough

Good companions: *Armeria juniperifolia, Dianthus alpinus* 'Joan's Blood', *Salix boydii*

4 Viola biflora
Twin-flowered violet

The yellow flowers brighten up lightly shaded areas. This perennial has a creeping rootstock, so is likely to spread if it likes the conditions. Hardy.

Height: 8cm (3in) **Spread:** 30cm (12in)

Site: Partial shade. Humus-rich and moist but well-drained soil

Use: Raised bed, rock garden, woodland garden

Good companions: *Alchemilla conjuncta, Galanthus nivalis, Scilla siberica* 'Spring Beauty'

1

2

3

4

cream and white

5 Arabis alpina subsp. caucasica 'Schneehaube'
Rock cress

The species is a robust evergreen perennial that produces numerous spikes of four-petalled white flowers. It tends to bully less vigorous plants. 'Schneehaube' is more compact, as is 'Flore Pleno', which has double flowers. Hardy.

Height: 15cm (6in) **Spread:** 45cm (18in)

Site: Sun. Well-drained soil

Use: Dry wall, paving, raised bed, rock garden

Good companions: *Aubrieta* 'Doctor Mules', *Aurinia saxatilis* 'Citrina', *Cytisus* x *beanii, Juniperus communis* 'Green Carpet'

5

6

6 Iberis sempervirens 'Weisser Zwerg'
Candytuft

The pure white flowers clustered in rounded heads on this evergreen shrubby perennial are dazzling in spring and early summer. The species, does well on a sunny bank, but this compact cultivar is more suitable for growing with other small plants. Hardy.

General care: To keep plants compact, trim when flowering has finished.

Height: 15cm (6in) **Spread:** 25cm (10in)

Site: Sun. Moist but well-drained soil, even poor, and preferably limy

Use: Dry wall, paving, raised bed, rock garden

Good companions: *Gypsophila repens* 'Rosa Schönheit', *Juniperus squamata* 'Blue Star', *Sedum* 'Bertram Anderson'

waterside & water plants

Most of the plants that relish reliably moist conditions are perennials. Some like the ground really wet and others will even grow in shallow water. Plant in the dormant season.

yellow and orange

1 Caltha palustris 'Flore Pleno'
Kingcup, Marsh marigold

Instead of the single, rich yellow flowers shining above deep green kidney-shaped leaves, this double form of the beautiful wild perennial has long-lasting yellow flowers that are tinted green at the centre of tightly packed petals. Hardy.
Height: 40cm (16in) **Spread:** 30cm (12in)
Site: Sun, partial shade. Humus-rich and permanently moist soil or water 10cm (4in) deep
Use: Bog garden, water margin
Good companions: *Acorus calamus* 'Variegatus', *Myosotis scorpioides, Zantedeschia aethiopica* 'Crowborough'

2 Euphorbia palustris
Milkweed, Spurge

This herbaceous perennial makes an impressive clump of bright green leaves topped by clusters of greenish yellow flower-like bracts, which remain attractive well beyond spring. The foliage turns yellow and orange-brown in autumn. Hardy.
Height and spread: 1m (3ft)
Site: Sun. Humus-rich, permanently moist soil
Use: Bog garden, waterside
Good companions: *Iris laevigata* 'Variegata', *Rodgersia pinnata* 'Superba', *Trollius europaeus*

3 Iris pseudacorus 'Variegata'
Yellow flag

The yellow flag is a vigorous plant to fringe a large body of water. Its yellow irises flutter among the tall blades in summer and are followed by attractive seedpods. In this less vigorous variegated form, the fans of young leaves are soft yellow striped with green in spring before turning full green in summer. Hardy.
Height: 1m (3ft) **Spread:** 60cm (2ft)
Site: Sun. Humus-rich and reliably moist soil or water up to 15cm (6in) deep
Use: Bog garden, moist border, waterside
Good companions: *Ligularia* 'The Rocket', *Lysichiton americanus, Matteuccia struthiopteris*

green

4 Matteuccia struthiopteris
Ostrich fern, Shuttlecock fern

In spring the greenish yellow new fronds form a symmetrical 'shuttlecock' on a short trunk, usually less than 30cm (12in) high. Later, a plume of dark, fertile fronds, which carry the spores, rises in the centre to remain as a distinctive feature right through winter, after the outer fronds have died. Spreads freely by underground roots. Hardy.
Height: 1.5m (5ft) **Spread:** 1m (3ft)
Site: Partial shade, sun. Reliably moist, even boggy soil
Use: Bog garden, damp border, waterside
Good companions: *Alnus glutinosa* 'Imperialis', *Osmunda regalis, Rheum palmatum* 'Atrosanguineum'

herbs, vegetables & fruit

Culinary plants are often very ornamental, especially when in blossom or making fresh growth, but the first reason for growing early maturing vegetables and fresh herbs is their produce.

herbs

1 Chive
Allium schoenoprasum

A clump-forming perennial herb with slender, grass-like green leaves that have a mild onion flavour. Spherical bright purple flowers are borne throughout summer. Garlic or Chinese chives (*A. tuberosum*) has broader, garlic-flavoured leaves and white flowers. Snipped chives are a useful garnish for salads, soups and sandwiches. Hardy.
General care: Ensure plants do not dry out, particularly when grown in containers.
Height and spread: 30cm (12in)
Site: Sun, partial shade. Fertile and moist but well-drained soil
Compost: Soil-based (John Innes No. 3) or soil-less
Use: Border edging, container, underplanting roses

2 Fennel
Foeniculum vulgare

A tall-growing perennial, fennel has soft green feathery foliage. In summer it bears flat heads of small yellow flowers, attracting hoverflies that eat aphids. Bronze fennel (*F. vulgare* 'Purpureum') is even more handsome. Fennel leaves are used to season meat and the seeds to flavour sauces and fish dishes. Hardy.
General care: Fennel self-seeds freely so harvest before they have a chance to scatter, or remove the flowers if the seeds are not required.
Height: 1.5m (5ft) **Spread:** 45cm (18in)
Site: Sun. Well-drained soil, preferably fertile
Compost: Soil-based (John Innes No. 3) with added bark and grit
Use: Border, container

3 Lemon balm, variegated
Melissa officinalis 'Aurea'

Grown for its wrinkled green leaves, which give off a lemon scent if crushed, lemon balm looks most attractive in spring when it forms low clumps of neat foliage. This variegated form is one of the most decorative, with green-and-gold leaves. Stems of pale yellow to white flowers, which are attractive to bees, are borne in summer. The leaves are used to make tea. Hardy.
General care: In cold areas plants benefit from winter protection with fleece or straw.
Height: 60cm (2ft) **Spread:** 45cm (18in)
Site: Sun. Fertile and moist soil
Compost: Soil-less with added grit
Use: Border, container

4 Mint, Spearmint
Mentha spicata

This is the most popular of the large and varied mint family. The long, toothed green leaves are borne along upright stems and clusters of mauve flowers appear in summer. Mint is a very invasive perennial, spreading by means of underground runners, so grow it in a large bottomless container sunk in the ground. The leaves are commonly used in mint sauce and drinks. Hardy.
General care: Trim the edges of the clump regularly to limit its spread.
Height: 60cm (2ft) **Spread:** Indefinite
Site: Sun, partial shade. Any soil, except dry
Compost: Soil-based (John Innes No. 3)
Use: Border, container

5 Sorrel
Rumex acetosa

A tall-growing plant, sorrel produces stems clothed with large, lance-shaped, mid-green leaves. In early to midsummer these are topped with inconspicuous greenish flowers that age to reddish brown. The plant has little decorative value, but the strongly flavoured leaves can be used sparingly in soups and omelettes and with meat; the young, more mildly flavoured foliage can be mixed into salads. Hardy.
General care: Remove flowerheads when they appear, as sorrel has a tendency to run to seed early. In warm areas grow in partial shade.
Height: 1.2m (4ft) **Spread:** 30cm (12in)
Site: Sun, partial shade. Acid, humus-rich and moist soil
Use: Border

vegetables

6 Asparagus
Asparagus officinalis

A perennial vegetable with succulent young shoots that grow from asparagus roots or 'crowns'. Although expensive to buy, the plants will crop for many years. 'Fileas' is the earliest variety. Hardy.
Site: Sun. Well-drained soil with plenty of well-rotted manure or compost added
How to grow: In mid-spring plant year-old crowns 45cm (18in) apart in ridges 60cm (24in) apart. Harvest when spears are 15cm (6in) high from mid-spring to early summer; it will be several years before the plants begin to crop well. Feed with a general fertiliser after harvesting is complete, and in autumn cut back top growth and top-dress with manure.

7 Broccoli, late purple-sprouting
Brassica oleracea

Grown for its leafy flowerheads, late purple-sprouting broccoli is a useful vegetable that follows on from winter-cropping varieties. Hardy.
Site: Sun. Fertile, moist and slightly acid soil
How to grow: Sow thinly into a seedbed in mid to late spring. Transplant in early summer to midsummer, allowing 45cm (18in) between each plant and row, and keep well watered until established. Protect from cabbage root fly by fitting 'collars' around the base of individual plants. Harvest from mid to late spring when the flowerheads are well formed but before the flowers begin to open. Pick off flowerheads regularly as production will cease if the flowers are left to develop.

8 Carrot, early
Daucus carota

Carrots can be sown under protection in late winter to provide an early crop. Early varieties include 'Minicor' (syn. 'Amsterdam Forcing', 'Baby Nantes'), 'Early Nantes' and 'Paris Market'. Hardy.
Site: Sun. Well-drained and stone-free soil that has been manured but not in the past year
How to grow: Sow seed thinly under cloches or in frames, in rows 15cm (6in) apart. If necessary, thin seedlings to 5cm (2in) apart. Round-rooted varieties can be sown in a greenhouse, in modular trays with four seeds per cell, and planted out later. Plant out cell-grown clumps 15cm (6in) apart. Keep well watered during dry spells. In spring when the

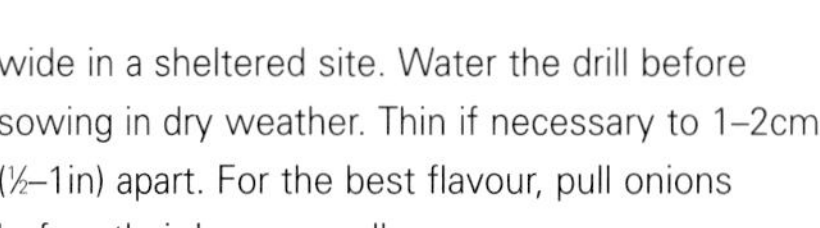

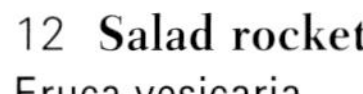

cloche or frame is removed, cover with fleece to protect from carrot root fly. Harvest from late spring onwards.

9 Lettuce, overwintered

Lactuca sativa

Autumn-sown lettuce can be grown under the protection of cloches or frames or in an unheated greenhouse over winter to give a good spring crop. Select a hardy variety that is suitable for winter cultivation.

Site: Sun. Fertile and well-drained soil

How to grow: Sow thinly in rows 23cm (9in) apart from very late summer to mid-autumn. Thin as soon as the seedlings are large enough to handle to 15–23cm (6–9in) apart. Ventilate when weather permits to avoid disease. Harvest as soon as plants are sufficiently large.

10 Radish

Raphanus sativus

A quick-growing salad vegetable that can be grown as a late spring crop by sowing in winter under protection. Hardy.

Site: Sun. Humus-rich and well-drained soil, not freshly manured

How to grow: Sow seed in mid to late winter under cloches or frames in rows 15cm (6in) apart, then thin seedlings to 2–3cm (1in) apart. Or, sow broadcast in a drill 10cm (4in) wide. For the best flavour, pull the radishes when the roots are no larger than 2–3cm (1in) in diameter.

11 Salad onion, Spring onion

Allium cepa

These are young onion plants that are grown close together. If successive sowings are made, spring onions can be harvested for much of the year. Sow seed at fortnightly intervals from late winter to mid-summer. Hardy.

Site: Sun. Well-drained and fertile soil, not freshly manured

How to grow: For a spring crop, sow thinly during midsummer, allowing 10cm (4in) between rows, or sow broadcast in a broad drill up to 10cm (4in) wide in a sheltered site. Water the drill before sowing in dry weather. Thin if necessary to 1–2cm (½–1in) apart. For the best flavour, pull onions before their bases swell.

12 Salad rocket

Eruca vesicaria

An easy and useful leaf vegetable for salads, rocket has a delicious spicy flavour. It can be sown from late winter right through to autumn for harvesting almost all the year round. Hardy.

Site: Sun. Fertile and moist but well-drained soil

How to grow: Sow in late summer for a very early crop the following spring. Allow 30cm (12in) between rows, and thin seedlings to 10cm (4in) apart. Keep plants well watered to avoid them running to seed early. In cold areas, protect plants over winter with cloches. Harvest frequently.

fruit

13 Rhubarb

Rheum x hybridum

Rhubarb is classified as a vegetable but its stalks are eaten as a fruit. Its large green leaves are highly poisonous if eaten. It crops naturally during spring and early summer, but can be forced for a late winter crop. The variety 'Timperley Early' produces the earliest crops outdoors without being forced. Hardy.

Site: Sun. Any soil, preferably heavy and acid

How to grow: Plant a new crown in autumn or spring. Leave the plant untouched for the first year and harvest only a little in the second. From then on, always leave three to four stems on the plant to avoid weakening it. Mulch with well-rotted compost or manure in late winter.

choosing the best plants

The following plant lists draw on all the plants described on the preceding pages of the Plant Selector, but they are grouped together here to help you choose plants for particular conditions, situations and uses to bring interest to your garden in late spring.

plants for clay soil

Although the following plants generally succeed on close-textured clay soils, they do better when the ground has been improved by the addition of grit and organic matter such as well-rotted garden compost.

- *Acer* (all)
- *Berberis* (all)
- *Caltha palustris* 'Flore Pleno'
- *Cardamine pratensis* 'Flore Pleno'
- *Choisya ternata*
- *Cornus florida* 'Cherokee Chief'
- *Crataegus* (all)
- *Doronicum orientale* 'Magnificum'
- *Epimedium* (all)
- *Filipendula ulmaria* 'Aurea'
- *Fritillaria meleagris*
- *Hosta* (all)
- *Philadelphus coronarius* 'Aureus'
- *Pleioblastus auricomus*
- *Polygonatum* x *hybridum*
- *Sorbus aria* 'Lutescens'
- *Viburnum* (all)

Viburnum opulus

plants for dry chalky soil

A large number of plants are automatically excluded from this list because they will not tolerate alkaline (limy) soil. The improvement of shallow chalky soil by the addition of moisture-retaining organic matter allows lime-tolerant but moisture-loving plants, notably clematis, to be grown successfully.

- *Aethionema* 'Warley Rose'
- *Aubrieta* 'Greencourt Purple'
- *Aurinia saxatilis* (all cultivars)
- *Berberis* (all)
- *Bergenia* 'Beethoven'
- *Cercis siliquastrum*
- *Cheiranthus* (all)
- *Choisya ternata*
- *Crataegus* (all)
- *Euphorbia polychroma*
- *Gypsophila cerastioides*
- *Iris* (all bearded)
- *Malus* (all)
- *Muscari* (all)
- *Philadelphus coronarius* 'Aureus'
- *Phlox douglasii* (all cultivars)
- *Phlox subulata* (all cultivars)
- *Prunus* (all ornamental cherries)
- *Pulsatilla vulgaris*
- *Sorbus aria* 'Lutescens'
- *Syringa vulgaris* (all cultivars)
- *Waldsteinia ternata*

Waldsteinia ternata

plants for sandy or gravelly soil

The following plants require free drainage and are mostly drought tolerant, although bulbs generally require a good supply of moisture in the growing season. The range of plants that can be grown in dry sunny gardens will be enlarged if the soil is improved by the addition of well-rotted organic matter.

- *Achillea* x *lewisii* 'King Edward'
- *Aethionema* 'Warley Rose'
- *Arabis alpina* subsp. *caucasica* (all cultivars)
- *Armeria juniperifolia*
- *Asphodelus albus*
- *Aubrieta* 'Greencourt Purple' (and other cultivars)
- *Aurinia saxatilis* (all cultivars)
- *Ceanothus* (all)
- *Cytisus* (all)
- *Erica arborea* var. *alpina*
- *Erysimum* (all)
- *Euphorbia polychroma*
- Fennel (*Foeniculum vulgare*)
- *Gladiolus tristis*
- *Iberis* (all)
- *Iris* (all bearded)
- *Lathyrus vernus*
- *Phlox douglasii* (all cultivars)
- *Raoulia australis* Lutescens Group

Iris 'Holden Clough'

plants for acid soil

Plants marked with an asterisk* will only grow satisfactorily on soils that are free of lime. Other plants in the list thrive on acid soils, but may also grow on neutral or slightly alkaline soils.

- *Acer palmatum* (all cultivars)
- *Bergenia* 'Beethoven'
- *Brunnera macrophylla* (all cultivars)
- *Camellia japonica* (all cultivars)*
- *Cornus florida* 'Cherokee Chief'
- *Disporum sessile* 'Variegatum'
- *Doronicum orientale* 'Magnificum'
- *Enkianthus campanulatus**
- *Erica arborea* var. *alpina**
- *Erythronium* (all)
- *Fothergilla major* Monticola Group*
- *Gentiana* (all)
- *Halesia carolina**
- x *Heucherella tiarelloides**
- *Ledum groenlandicum**
- *Magnolia* (all)
- *Meconopsis cambrica**
- *Meconopsis quintuplinervia**
- *Pieris* 'Forest Flame'*
- *Primula auricula* (all cultivars)
- *Primula japonica* 'Postford White'*
- *Primula sieboldii**
- *Smilacina racemosa**
- *Tellima grandiflora* (all cultivars)

plants for dry shade

The following plants grow most vigorously where there is a regular supply of water, but generally succeed in such difficult conditions as the shady base of walls or where roots of overhead trees and shrubs are near the surface.

- *Ajuga reptans* (all cultivars)
- *Bergenia* 'Beethoven'
- *Brunnera macrophylla*
- *Convallaria majalis*
- *Dicentra* 'Luxuriant'
- *Epimedium* (all)
- *Geranium phaeum*
- *Hyacinthoides non-scripta*
- *Lunaria annua*
- *Polygonatum* x *hybridum*
- *Prunus laurocerasus* (all cultivars)
- *Waldsteinia ternata*

plants for moist shade

The following plants thrive in moist soils and tolerate partial shade and, in a few cases, full shade. Many will also grow in full sun provided the soil is reliably moist.

- *Acer palmatum* (all cultivars)
- *Aquilegia* (all)
- *Brunnera macrophylla* (all cultivars)
- *Camellia japonica* (all cultivars)
- *Dicentra* (all)
- *Disporum sessile* 'Variegatum'
- *Dryopteris affinis*
- *Dryopteris erythrosora*
- *Epimedium* (all)
- *Erythronium* (all)
- *Filipendula ulmaria* 'Aurea'
- *Hosta* (all)
- *Leucojum aestivum* 'Gravetye Giant'
- *Matteuccia struthiopteris*
- *Milium effusum* 'Aureum'
- *Myosotis sylvatica* (all cultivars)
- *Omphalodes cappadocica*
- *Primula* (most)
- *Pulmonaria* 'Mawson's Blue'
- *Rhododendron* (all)
- *Smilacina racemosa*
- *Trillium* (all)
- *Uvularia grandiflora*
- *Viola* (all)

plants for ground cover

The following plants can be used to create an attractive weed-excluding cover if planted in weed-free soil.

- *Ajuga reptans* 'Purple Torch'
- *Bergenia* 'Beethoven'
- *Convallaria majalis*
- *Dicentra* 'Luxuriant'
- *Epimedium* x *rubrum*
- *Epimedium* x *versicolor* 'Sulphureum'
- *Epimedium* x *youngianum* 'Niveum'
- *Euphorbia amygdaloides* 'Purpurea'
- *Geranium macrorrhizum* 'Ingwersen's Variety'
- x *Heucherella tiarelloides*
- *Hosta fortunei* var. *albopicta*
- *Hosta undulata* var. *univittata*
- *Omphalodes cappadocica*
- *Pulmonaria* 'Mawson's Blue'
- *Tellima grandiflora* 'Purpurteppich'

plants for coastal sites

Where windbreaks and hedges give protection from salt-laden winds, a wide range of plants can be grown in coastal gardens. Many benefit from the sea's moderating influence on temperatures.

- *Acer pseudoplatanus* 'Brilliantissimum'
- *Arabis alpina* subsp. *caucasica* (all cultivars)
- *Armeria juniperifolia*
- *Aubrieta* 'Greencourt Purple' (and other cultivars)
- *Aurinia saxatilis* (all cultivars)
- *Berberis* (all)
- *Bergenia* 'Beethoven'
- *Ceanothus* (all)
- *Cheiranthus* (all)
- *Choisya ternata*
- *Crataegus* (all)
- *Cytisus* (all)
- *Erica arborea* var. *alpina*
- *Hyacinthoides non-scripta*
- *Iberis* (all)
- *Laburnum* x *watereri* 'Vossii'
- *Leptospermum scoparium* 'Kiwi'
- *Lunaria annua* (and cultivars)
- *Mysotis sylvatica* (all cultivars)
- *Prostanthera rotundifolia*
- *Pulsatilla vulgaris*
- *Sorbus aria* 'Lutescens'

Choisya ternata

summer

practical diary

In this season of rapid development the speed of plant growth is truly astonishing, and in dry weather plants will need frequent watering. Vigorous climbers spread luxuriantly to cover walls and pergolas, needing to be safely tied in. Your lawn will grow long again soon after mowing. The greenhouse feels like a tropical paradise at this time of year, and while peppers and tomatoes will revel in the sun, cucumbers and easily scorched plants like fuchsias will benefit from a little shade and higher humidity. The sun is warm, the evenings are long, and in summer there is really no better place to be than a garden.

perennials

Perennials are the mainstay of the summer border, and this is the time to increase the display by planting frost-tender varieties for guaranteed colour through to autumn. Keep all perennials at their best by paying attention to staking, thinning out and deadheading.

now is the season to . . .

- **plant tender perennials** as early as possible so they establish quickly and start flowering. Make sure they are first acclimatised to outdoor conditions (hardened off) over a couple of weeks. Do this by standing plants outside during the day for increasing periods of time, eventually leaving them out at night unless frost is forecast.
- **check perennials raised from seed** in spring. Once they are well rooted, pot up into a minimum pot size of 8cm (3in).
- **water newly planted perennials** in dry spells. Soak them every few days, so water penetrates right through the rootball and roots are encouraged to reach down in search of moisture.
- **give regular attention** to perennials in containers. Water them daily, unless the weather is very wet. If they have not been fed so far this year, feed with a controlled-release fertiliser, which will last for the rest of the growing season. If any plant looks sickly, with pale or yellowing leaves, apply a liquid fertiliser first to give quick results.
- **deadhead all faded flowers** to prevent their seed from setting (see opposite).
- **thin overcrowded clumps** of perennials that missed being divided earlier in the year, to increase air circulation and to prevent the stems from flopping over. Cut out a quarter to a third of the stems at ground level.
- **stake tall-growing perennials** early in summer before they begin to flop, because once this happens the stems will never straighten properly (see opposite).
- **hoe and hand-weed** borders regularly. Hoeing off weeds as they germinate saves the more difficult job of tackling large, established weeds later on.
- **protect hostas** from slugs and snails throughout summer. Try growing them in large pots to keep these pests at bay.
- **avoid powdery mildew** on susceptible perennials, such as phlox and pulmonarias, by watering well during dry spells.
- **pick off leaves** affected by fungal disease and throw them away, but not on the compost heap, as disease spores will survive. Plants prone to infection include aquilegias, phlox and pulmonarias. Consider spraying with fungicide to prevent diseases from spreading.
- **propagate some perennials** by cuttings or division (see page 212).

Astrantia major

Once they start to fade, cut the flowered shoots of euphorbias to ground level; wear gloves when doing this as the milky sap can irritate the skin.

staking

Stake tall-growing perennials early in summer using ready-made frames, canes or twiggy sticks. Stake individual stems of very tall plants, like those of delphiniums.

- **tailor-made supports** vary in style and are reusable. Many can be raised as the plants grow or may be interlinked to support clumps of different sizes.
- **place short canes in a circle** round the plant, with string run round and in between them.
- **poke in twiggy branches** of hazel, often referred to as 'pea sticks', round a perennial clump. If bent over at the top, these sticks will make a cage through which the plant will grow.
- **bamboo canes and soft string** or raffia provide reliable support for tall individual stems.

Plant foliage will soon hide tailor-made supports like this.

deadheading

Removing dead or faded flowerheads encourages more blooms over a longer period of time. If this job is neglected, plants will set seed and flower less freely. With regular deadheading, tender perennials will flower well into autumn.

- **self-seeding perennials,** like lady's mantle (*Alchemilla mollis*) and bronze fennel (*Foeniculum vulgare* 'Purpureum'), can produce many seedlings informally throughout a border. To prevent this, cut off faded flowerheads before seeds ripen.
- **spring and early summer-flowering perennials** such as hardy geraniums and oriental poppies (*Papaver orientale*) should be cut back to ground level once they have finished flowering. Feed them with a general fertiliser and water in well, and they will soon reward you with a bushy mound of fresh foliage.
- **deadhead peonies,** but allow foliage to die back naturally.
- **for delphiniums and lupins** cut off dead flower spikes to encourage more flowers on shorter sideshoots.

A low panel of woven willow holds back leafy perennials and prevents them from flopping forwards onto a path or lawn.

perennials/2

Echinops ritro

propagation

Summer is the perfect time to make more plants by taking a variety of cuttings, by dividing and collecting seeds. Although spring is far away, now is also the time to divide polyanthus to ensure a good show of flowers next year.

cuttings and divisions

- **take soft-tip cuttings of tender perennials** like pelargoniums in the cool of the morning (see below). Select strong, non-flowering shoots and cut a length of stem 10cm (4in) long from the top. Put the cut material straight into a plastic bag or bucket of cold water, to prevent it from wilting.
- **plant out basal cuttings** taken in late spring in a nursery bed, or move them into individual 8cm (3in) pots and grow on in a coldframe or sheltered area of the garden.
- **divide polyanthus** and double-flowered primulas after flowering. Dig up the clump with a fork and shake off any loose soil. Use a sharp knife to cut the clump into smaller pieces, each consisting of one or two shoots with plenty of roots attached. Plant out the divisions in rows, in a nursery bed or a spare corner of the garden, spacing them 15–23cm (6–9in) apart. Water them well.
- **split the rhizomes** of bearded irises in established clumps once flowering has finished (see opposite). Replant the divisions in full sun.
- **propagate pinks** (*Dianthus*) from 'pipings' (see opposite) taken from non-flowering shoots. After removing the lower leaves, treat as soft-tip cuttings (see below).

taking soft-tip cuttings

1 **Make the cuttings** with a sharp knife by trimming the base just below a leaf joint.

2 **Carefully take off** the lower leaves and any flowers.

3 **Dip the base** of each cutting into hormone rooting powder before inserting round the edge of a 13cm (5in) pot filled with cuttings compost. Cover the pot with a polythene bag and place it in a shaded coldframe or sheltered spot outside. The exception is geraniums which should not be covered. Rooting usually takes about eight weeks, when the cuttings are potted up individually into 8cm (3in) pots.

dividing bearded irises

1 **Lift the clump**. Cut off the younger, outer pieces of the thick fleshy rootstock, or rhizome, and discard the old central portion.

2 **Trim the leaves** so the plants are not rocked by the wind.

3 **Replant in groups of three** with the fans of foliage to the outside. The top of the rhizome must be just above soil level, as it needs exposure to sun in order to flower well. Feed with a low-nitrogen fertiliser and water thoroughly.

Dianthus are propagated from special cuttings (pipings). Pull out the tips of non-flowering shoots 10cm (4in) long, remove the lower leaves and insert in compost.

collecting seed

Gather seed of spring and early summer-flowering perennials as soon as it is ripe, usually when the seedpods have turned brown. On a dry day cut the seed heads into labelled paper bags (see page 306) and place on a sunny windowsill. Once the seed heads are completely dry, tip them onto a sheet of newspaper, split open the pods and shake out the seed. Store in envelopes or empty film canisters, after writing on the plant name.

The seed of most perennials can be sown immediately, but a few, such as aconitums, meconopsis and primulas, need a cold period in order to germinate, and they should be left until autumn. The best place to store seed for any length of time is in moisture-proof containers in a refrigerator or other cool, dry place.

When you are ready, sow the collected seed thinly into pots of moist seed compost and cover with a thin layer of perlite or horticultural vermiculite. Stand the pots in a coldframe or other sheltered spot outside, and keep the compost moist.

there is still time to . . .

- **take basal cuttings** of clump-forming perennials, such as lupins and delphiniums, before the end of June. Cut strong young shoots about 10cm (4in) long from the base of the plant and treat them as described for soft-tip cuttings (see opposite).

looking ahead . . .

☑ LATE SUMMER Pot up rooted cuttings of tender perennials.
☑ Transplant seedlings of early flowering perennials.
☑ AUTUMN Transplant polyanthus to their flowering positions.
☑ Plant out perennials raised from basal cuttings.

plants that give good results from seed

Aconitum napellus • *Alchemilla mollis* • *Aquilegia* • *Geranium* (some) • *Helleborus* • *Lychnis coronaria* • *Meconopsis* • *Polemonium* • *Primula*

Plants raised from species will resemble their parents, but the offspring of cultivated varieties, or cultivars, will produce plants of differing appearance. *Geranium renardii* is a species, while *Heuchera* 'Palace Purple' is a cultivar.

Geranium 'Ann Folkard'

annuals & biennials

The flower garden becomes a celebration of colour as summer annuals take over from the recently cleared spring bedding. Continue sowing to prolong your display into autumn, and to bring on new plants for next spring.

now is the season to . . .

- **finish hardening off** tender annuals, such as scarlet salvias and busy lizzies (*Impatiens*), and plant them out as soon as the frosts are over. Use them in formal and informal bedding schemes (see opposite).
- **give a weekly liquid feed** to pots and trays of bedding plants, and other seedlings that will flower, if their planting out has been delayed.
- **regularly water** any recently planted bedding and transplanted seedlings in dry weather. Feed annuals in containers with a dilute liquid fertiliser, every seven to ten days.
- **water and feed sweet peas** at regular intervals, and deadhead to prevent seeds from forming. Tie in the stems every two or three days when growing up vertical string supports as a cordon.
- **deadhead annuals,** such as pansies, marigolds, snapdragons and california poppies, to stimulate more flowers.
- **buy seedlings and plug plants** from the garden centre (see opposite).
- **cut flowers for drying** (see opposite).
- **transplant biennials** sown outdoors last month (see page 127) to a spare piece of ground, where they can mature until the autumn (see opposite).
- **pot up individual seedlings,** each in a 5–8cm (2–3in) pot, to make eye-catching feature plants for larger containers.
- **thin seedlings,** such as love-in-a-mist (*Nigella damascena*), sown in late spring where they are to flower, to 5–10cm (2–4in) apart according to vigour. Discard spare seedlings, or carefully transplant them and water immediately (see below).
- **keep weeding,** especially in beds of densely planted annuals, where weeds can flower and self-seed unnoticed.

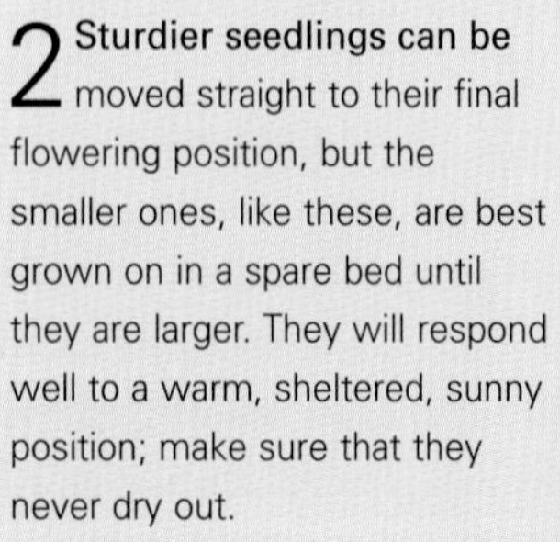

Regularly snip off the dead or fading flowers of annuals, such as these california poppies (*Eschscholzia*), to create a continuous supply of new blooms.

transplanting seedlings

1 **Prick out seedlings** sown in seedbeds or trays in late spring. If they have been growing well they will now need much more space to develop. Handle them carefully by the leaves, and gently tease them apart so that you do not damage their roots. If they really are entangled, place a clump of seedlings with their soil in a large bowl of water; they should be much easier to separate.

2 **Sturdier seedlings can be** moved straight to their final flowering position, but the smaller ones, like these, are best grown on in a spare bed until they are larger. They will respond well to a warm, sheltered, sunny position; make sure that they never dry out.

cutting flowers for drying

'Everlasting' flowers, with a long season, such as statice (*Limonium sinuatum*), helichrysum and helipterum (*Rhodanthe*), sown in March and April, will start to flower in July. Use the earliest young blooms for cutting and drying.

- **cut them off** with a good length of stem as soon as the petals are at their peak, and strip off some lower leaves. Tie in small bundles and hang upside down in a warm, airy place until dry and papery.
- **leave plants** with good seed heads, such as love-in-a-mist (right), until the seed heads form, before cutting.

■ **protect young annuals** from slugs and snails, removing these pests by hand. Also deter red spider mites, which strike in hot, dry weather, by misting plants with water.

planting formal bedding

Most flowers used for formal, organised summer bedding schemes are slightly tender, and cannot be safely planted outdoors until late May, after being acclimatised for a week or two. In an informal bedding scheme the flowers are planted in natural-looking groups and drifts. Work out your colour scheme, and the patterns or shapes you want to create, before preparing the ground.

- Clear the ground of any previous bedding and weeds, lightly fork it over and spread a dressing of granular or powdered general fertiliser. Rake this in, level the bed and remove any stones.
- First plant the tall, showy 'dot' plants, which dominate and catch the eye, where they will be the focus of the display, singly or in small groups, spaced about 1m (3ft) apart. Good examples include fuchsias, heliotropes and pelargoniums grown as standards, as well as cannas, cordylines, castor-oil plants (*Ricinus communis*) and variegated maize.
- Then plant the edging, using dwarf flowers spaced about 10–15cm (4–6in) apart. Try white alyssum, lobelia, marigolds, silver-leaved cinerarias (*Senecio cineraria*) and dwarf phlox.
- Finally, infill the space in between, using flowers of intermediate height, spaced 23–30cm (9–12in) apart, depending on size and vigour. Good plants include pelargoniums, petunias, salvias, bedding dahlias and coleus.
- Water in well after planting, adding a liquid fertiliser to give the plants a flying start.

transplanting biennials

By July, seedlings of biennials such as wallflowers, forget-me-nots and foxgloves (*Digitalis*) sown in late spring will be clamouring for extra space. Now is the time to thin them out.

- **do this where they are sown**, first to 5cm (2in) apart and later to 10–20cm (4–8in).
- **for larger, sturdier plants,** you can transplant them to a spare, lightly shaded bed that has been forked over with added compost and a dressing of general fertiliser. Plant them in rows 23cm (9in) apart. Space hollyhocks (*Alcea*), foxgloves and other large plants 20cm (8in) apart, most other biennials 10–15cm (4–6in) apart. Pinch out the tips of wallflowers to encourage branching. Water in well, and keep moist during dry weather.

buying seedlings

If you are not able to sow your own seeds, you can buy seedlings as plug plants from a garden centre. If the weather is warm enough, plant them straight out where they are to flower, or transplant them into individual pots where they can be kept for two weeks before planting them in the ground. Scattering a layer of horticultural grit on the soil surface of seedlings in coldframes deters pests and keeps the soil surface dry, thus eliminating moss.

Snapdragon seedlings grown as plugs

there is still time to . . .

- **sow fast-growing annuals.** Candytuft (*Iberis*), linaria, night-scented stock and annual chrysanthemums will provide an autumn display if sown where they are to flower or grown in a spare piece of ground for transplanting later.
- **sow spring-flowering biennials,** especially brompton stocks (*Matthiola incana*), forget-me-nots and dwarf varieties of wallflowers. Start them off in a spare bed, then plant out in late September.
- **clear away exhausted spring bedding.** Weed and lightly fork the soil, and rake in a dressing of fertiliser. The bed is then ready for summer.

bulbs & tubers

Summer is a busy bulb season. Some spring bulbs require dividing or storing; summer bulbs need tending; and autumn-flowering bulbs need planting. You can also sow many bulb seeds now, for example if you would like to create your own bluebell wood.

now is the season to . . .

- **lift, dry and store hyacinths,** tulips and, occasionally, daffodils in a cool, dry place (see below).
- **dig up and divide** overcrowded clumps of daffodils (see opposite) once their foliage has completely died down.
- **plant autumn bulbs** such as colchicums (often called autumn crocuses, which is a misnomer, as they are not crocuses), saffron (*Crocus sativus*) and real autumn-flowering crocuses (see opposite).

- **plant autumn-flowering** *Amaryllis belladonna* 5–8cm (2–3in) deep, close to a warm, sunny wall.
- **plant out young begonias** grown from tubers or cuttings taken in late spring, as soon as the frosts are over.
- **plant out dahlias** grown from seed or cuttings, and mulch.
- **plant out arum lilies** that have flowered indoors, for their annual rest. Stand those grown in pots outdoors in a shallow pool for the summer.
- **feed summer-flowering bulbs** planted in pots and keep moist.
- **water summer bulbs,** such as gladioli, during prolonged dry spells, and mulch them to keep the soil moist.
- **stake large-flowered gladioli** in windy gardens, individually or in small groups (see page 211), particularly if you are growing them for cut flowers.
- **watch for early signs** of pests and diseases, especially serious ailments such as narcissus eelworm, which causes stunting, and lily viruses, signalled by failed flowers and mottled foliage.
- **gradually reduce the water** given to amaryllis (*Hippeastrum*) in pots, to allow the bulbs to rest.
- **hand-weed** between groups of lilies and other bulbs that seed freely, to keep them in large clumps rather than letting them spread. Hoe around clumps to create a dust mulch.
- **start planning** next spring's bulb displays. Since bulbs such as daffodils benefit from being planted in August or September, be ready to order them when the bulb catalogues appear in midsummer.
- **sow bluebells** (*Hyacinthoides*) and other bulbs that grow well from seed, in trays or in a nursery bed (see opposite).

and if you have time . . .

- **continue deadheading late spring bulbs** as they fade – unless you want to grow more from seed.

lifting, drying and dividing bulbs

Bedding hyacinths and most hybrid tulips need to be dug up and dried in summer to keep the bulbs in peak condition to replant in autumn. Daffodils benefit from being lifted every few years to prevent overcrowding and reduced flowering.

One of the earliest lilies to bloom, *Lilium martagon* var. *album* makes a fantastic clump of startling white flowers. It grows up to 2m (6ft) high, even in light shade, and is trouble free. Weed the surrounding soil well.

Large clumps of daffodils can be lifted with a fork and either divided into smaller clusters and replanted immediately, or separated into individual bulbs and dried for storing.

- Once the foliage has completely died down and shrivelled, carefully lift the bulbs with a fork; insert it well away to avoid spearing the bulbs.
- Rub off as much soil as possible, then spread out the bulbs on trays or in shallow boxes lined with newspaper. When they are quite dry, with withered roots and papery skins, trim the roots and remove any loose skin.
- Store the sound bulbs in paper bags or boxes in a cool, dry place. Discard any damaged, soft or discoloured bulbs, as well as very small, young bulblets.

BULB TIP Many daffodil varieties have multiple 'noses' – small offset bulbs produced at the side of the parent. These can be left in place or carefully removed for storing until autumn, when you can plant them in rows in spare ground. Leave until they are larger and have reached flowering size.

planting autumn bulbs

The small range of autumn-flowering bulbs provides a welcome late show of colour in beds, borders and containers. Plant them in July, 10cm (4in) deep, in informal groups. The soil should have been well forked over, and fed with plenty of garden compost or a high-potash fertiliser for good flowers.

- **colchicums** have large white or mauve, crocus-like blooms; the large leaves appear in spring. The best is *C. speciosum*.
- **autumn crocuses** flower in shades of lilac, blue, purple and white. The leaves appear in spring. *Crocus speciosus* and its varieties are excellent, but there are many other terrific species, such as the scented, lilac *C. goulimyi*.
- **the brilliant, golden-yellow** crocus-like flowers of *Sternbergia lutea* appear in September and October, accompanied by dwarf, strap-shaped leaves.

SAFFRON TIP You do not have to buy expensive saffron – you can grow your own. It comes from *Crocus sativus*, which has rich purple flowers with bright, orange-red stamens that are harvested to produce saffron. This bulb likes very rich conditions and is traditionally grown along the edges of well-manured vegetable beds or fertile herb borders.

disbudding a dahlia

If you have any dahlias with spectacular flowers, it is well worth looking to see if there are smaller buds to each side of the main bud. Removing them channels the plant's energy into making fewer, larger flowers. Subsequent deadheading of faded blooms stimulates further flowering.

If you have any dahlias still at the seedling stage, try pinching out their growing tips to produce bushy plants.

growing bluebells from seed

Bluebells set masses of black seed, which can be gathered in midsummer from their open seed capsules.

- Sow the seed immediately in rows in a nursery bed, specially created for young plants, or in shallow trays of soil-based compost in a coldframe. Water regularly when dry.
- Prick out the seedlings when they emerge in late winter, or transplant them during spring, about 2–3cm (1in) apart.
- Grow them for another year, then when the leaves die down in their second autumn, plant them out permanently in a moist, shady position.

there is still time to . . .

- **plant winter-flowering** *Anemone coronaria*, outdoors in mild areas, or in pots or coldframes elsewhere. Bury the bulbs individually, or in small groups, 5cm (2in) deep and 10cm (4in) apart.
- **plant autumn-flowering nerines** (cultivars of *Nerine bowdenii*) just below the surface in a warm, sheltered spot.

other bulbs to sow now

• camassia • crocus • foxtail lilies (*Eremurus*) • fritillaries • *Lilium regale* • lily of the valley (*Convallaria majalis*) • sisyrinchium • snowdrop (*Galanthus nivalis*) • tulips

The lovely *Camassia cusickii* flowers in early summer – and sometimes in a warm late spring too.

roses

Summer is the season when roses take centre stage. From late June onwards you can enjoy all the different kinds, including those that flower just once a year. All roses need some attention now – especially those that will carry on blooming.

Rosa 'Francis E. Lester'

now is the season to . . .

- **tie the stems** of young climbing and rambler roses temporarily to supports. This prevents wind damage and keeps the plants tidy. They can be secured permanently in late summer or autumn.
- **deadhead blooms** as soon as they fade (see below), unless hips are required later in the season.
- **water newly planted roses** if the weather is dry for more than two weeks. Give each plant 5 litres (2 gallons) of water. Established roses are deep-rooting and relatively drought-tolerant.
- **regularly water all container-grown roses,** checking the compost daily during hot weather. Add a dilute liquid fertiliser every seven to fourteen days.
- **apply a summer dressing** of rose fertiliser and lightly hoe or rake it in (see opposite). Do this soon after the longest day. Do not feed roses after the end of July.
- **disbud hybrid tea** and floribunda varieties for better flowers (see right).
- **propagate your favourite varieties** from bud cuttings during July (see opposite).
- **keep weeding,** especially around new roses. Hoe and hand-weed, but avoid forking near plants in case you injure the roots and cause suckers to appear.
- **remove suckers** immediately, if they appear (see opposite).
- **spray** a combined insecticide-fungicide at fortnightly intervals if you wish, or need, to take preventative measures against a range of potential problems. In any event, watch out for any signs of mildew, black spot, rust and aphids (see page 258).
- **move roses in pots outdoors** so that they can rest after flowering. Stand them in a sunny, sheltered place, or put each pot in a planting hole so that the compost will not dry out too rapidly.
- **cut blooms for indoors** from late June onwards. Remove only from established, strongly growing plants, and cut off no more than a third of the stem, with a sloping cut, just above an outward-facing bud.

and if you have time . . .

- **harvest fragrant roses** at their best, then dry the petals in layers in a warm, airy room. Use them as the basis of a potpourri.
- **remove all fading and fully open flowers** before going on holiday. This prevents hips from developing while you are away, and wasting the plant's energy.

disbudding roses

Disbudding is the best way to produce top-quality flowers. On hybrid tea varieties cleanly pull off or pinch out the small buds that can form around a central bud. Do this as early as possible to divert all the plant's energy into the single remaining flower and you will get large, fully formed blooms.

Another good idea is to pinch out or snip off the central bud in the flower trusses of floribunda and modern shrub roses. This encourages most of the other buds to open together, creating a better, showier display, and it helps to reduce overcrowding.

deadheading

The removal of faded blooms is a form of light pruning that prolongs flowering on repeat-flowering roses. It also stops roses from making seed, so do not deadhead species roses and once-flowering roses that produce attractive hips.

- **cut off complete floribunda trusses** with a good length of stem to prevent the bushes from producing numerous thin, unproductive shoots.

Use sharp secateurs for deadheading and make an outward-sloping cut.

- **on hybrid tea roses** remove the faded blooms with a portion of the stem. Cut the stem two to three leaves down from the flower and just above a strong leaf bud. Never remove more than half the shoot because this can delay further flowering.

feeding roses

While it is not essential to feed roses to get a good display, they will be healthier and more resistant to disease if you do. So give all roses a summer dressing of high-potash or rose fertiliser, sprinkled evenly around the base of the plant. This is the second of two annual feeds (the first being in early spring), and should be given in the first half of July; later feeding causes soft growth, which will not ripen before autumn frosts.

EXTRA FEEDING TIP You can give young roses, and those growing on 'hungry', light soils, an additional liquid boost one month before the main summer feed. Apply onto the soil, or spray as a foliar feed on a cloudy day when it will not immediately evaporate, nor scorch the leaves.

propagation

Most roses are propagated commercially by budding. This delicate operation joins a bud from a chosen variety onto a wild rose root system (rootstock), which guarantees vigorous growth. This technique requires a lot of skill.

Most gardeners prefer easier methods using cuttings. Many shrub, climbing and rambler roses can be layered or grown from semi-ripe cuttings in summer (see page 227), and most kinds, except hybrid teas, can be grown from hardwood cuttings in September or October (see page 315). But you can also try bud cuttings, taken now from most varieties. It takes two years to make substantial young plants and a further season to flower (see above right).

After planting, stand the pots in a coldframe, water well and close the lid. Shade from bright sun, mist the cuttings weekly with water, and give a liquid feed every four to six weeks until late autumn. Keep in the coldframe over winter, and pot up individually into 8cm (3in) pots when growth revives in spring. Water and feed regularly. In early summer, transplant them 30cm (12in) apart in spare ground, and grow for one or two seasons until they are large enough to plant out.

taking bud cuttings

1 **Cut off a young shoot** about the thickness of a pencil and slice it into sections: cut just above each leaf to produce a number of short pieces, each with a leaf and bud near the top.

2 **Shorten each leaf** to leave just two to three 'leaflets', then dip the base of the cutting in rooting hormone. Insert in a mixture of equal parts grit and perlite with the bud just below the surface. Space four or five cuttings round the edge of a tray or 8cm (3in) pot, without touching.

there is still time to . . .

- **mulch warm, moist soil** around established rose plants, using a 5–8cm (2–3in) layer of rotted manure, garden compost or lawn mowings that are free from weedkillers.

dealing with rose suckers

1 **Clear away soil** at the base of the rose to trace a sucker to its origin on the roots. Suckers are vigorous shoots that grow from below ground on grafted roses, and also from the stems of standards.

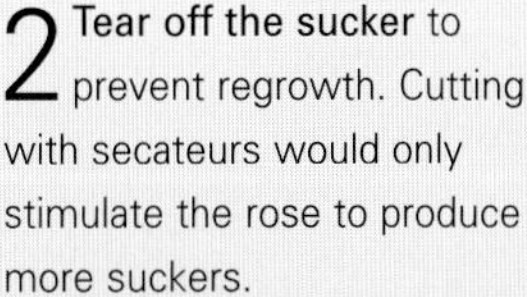

2 **Tear off the sucker** to prevent regrowth. Cutting with secateurs would only stimulate the rose to produce more suckers.

climbers

Climbers and wall shrubs grow fast at this time of year, and the fresh new shoots need tying in regularly. Pruning may be necessary to keep plants tidy and encourage more flowers. This is also a good time to raise more of your favourites by taking cuttings.

now is the season to . . .

- **train and tie in climbers** regularly to produce an attractive display, otherwise many rapidly form a tangled bird's nest of stems that can never be unravelled. Prime candidates for attention are those that climb by means of tendrils or twining leaf stalks, such as clematis, particularly *C. armandii*, and sweet peas (*Lathyrus odoratus*). Use soft string for tying in, not wire.
- **water container-grown climbers** daily unless the weather is very wet. Add a liquid fertiliser to the water once a week over summer, or add slow-release fertiliser to the compost.
- **check climbers against buildings:** even when established they may need watering if the structure keeps off most of the rain.

Clematis 'Jackmanii'

The golden hop (*Humulus lupulus* 'Aureus') is a vigorous perennial climber that will quickly clothe a trellis or fence in summer.

- **prune climbers** that have already flowered if next year's blooms are carried on stems produced this summer.
- **plant permanent climbers** and wall shrubs, but remember to water them regularly during dry spells until the autumn.
- **propagate climbers** and wall shrubs (see opposite).
- **pot up rooted cuttings** taken in spring.
- **watch out for clematis wilt.** This disease causes part or all of the clematis to collapse suddenly. You can help your plant to survive an attack by planting it deep, so that the surface of its compost is about 8cm (3in) deep (buds below ground usually survive to shoot and provide replacement growth). Cut back any affected stems to healthy growth.

pruning

Many climbers and wall shrubs need pruning now to keep them within bounds and to encourage prolific flowering.

- **cut back** *Clematis montana* and its cultivars to keep them within their allotted space. Shorten stems as soon as possible after flowering because next year's blooms are carried on growth produced this summer. To avoid having to prune these rampant climbers, plant the compact cultivar 'Primrose Star', which grows to only 3m (10ft) high.

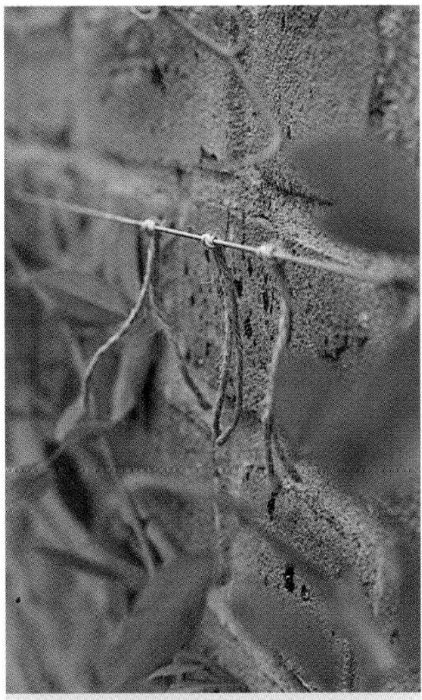

TYING-IN TIP Speed up the training process by attaching string ties to the wires before you start. Move them along as required.

- **prune early flowering** honeysuckles, such as *Lonicera periclymenum* and its cultivars, immediately after flowering. Cut back the flowered stems to strong, young growth to keep the plant neat and bushy.
- **train firethorn** (*Pyracantha*) and flowering quince (*Chaenomeles*) close to their supports. Prune them, and other wall-trained shrubs, immediately after flowering. Cut back all outward-facing shoots to two or three buds and tie in the others.
- **prune wisteria** twice a year, in midsummer (see below left) and again in winter.

summer-pruning wisteria

1 In midsummer, prune young shoots and any long, whippy growths not required to make new branches, to leave five or six buds.

2 This tidies the overall shape of the wisteria, after which the winter prune reduces sideshoots, leaving three buds on all growth that has appeared since the summer pruning. This pruning regime creates a neat shape and plenty of flowers.

propagation

Take advantage of the abundant young growth on climbers and wall shrubs to raise new plants from cuttings.

- **propagate small and large-flowered clematis** (but not the very large kind) by taking 8cm (3in) leaf-bud cuttings (see page 133). Make the cut between leaf joints, instead of immediately below them as with most other plants.
- **take soft cuttings** of climbers and wall shrubs in early June for the best results (see page 139). They should be 10cm (4in) long and have two or three pairs of leaves. Pinch out the top growth, just above a pair of leaves, and remove the lowest leaves. Plant round the edge of a 13cm (5in) pot, filled with cuttings compost, so that the first pair of leaves is just above the surface.
- **pot up any cuttings** taken in late spring once they have rooted. Grow them for six to twelve months in containers, before planting them out.

there is still time to . . .

- **prune spring-flowering clematis** such as *C. alpina* and *C. macropetala*, if necessary.
- **plant bought annual climbers** such as *Cobaea scandens* or morning glory (*Ipomoea*), though you can easily grow them from seed next spring.

looking ahead . . .

☑ LATE SUMMER Pot up cuttings of large-flowered clematis.
☑ WINTER Winter-prune wisteria.

shrubs & trees

Most trees and shrubs are now covered in bright fresh foliage and, in many cases, are in full flower. To keep them in peak condition, maintain a regular routine of watering, weeding, pruning and pest control.

now is the season to . . .

- **trim fast-growing hedges** such as privet and lonicera regularly for an immaculate finish.
- **uncover tender shrubs** after the last expected frost, and move outdoors those given winter shelter under glass.
- **water and feed** during dry weather. Concentrate on freshly planted and container shrubs and trees (see opposite).
- **eradicate weeds** by hoeing and hand-weeding, particularly around new plants and hedges.
- **support and tie in** the new growth of plants being trained against a wall or trellis.
- **prune shrubs** such as broom (*Cytisus*) and flowering quince (*Chaenomeles*) as soon as they finish flowering (see page 224).
- **prune ornamental plums,** cherries and almonds for shape once they are in full leaf. If you do it when they are dormant they are more susceptible to disease.
- **remove the flowers** from grey-leaved shrubs, like senecio or helichrysum, grown for their foliage or as formal hedges.
- **spur prune** wall-trained chaenomeles and pyracantha in July (see page 225). This thins out any congested tangles of spurs – the clusters of mini branches off the main branches – where the flowers grow.
- **thin out the crowns** of congested broad-leaved trees such as crab apples (*Malus*) and acers that heavily shade plants beneath them (see page 225).
- **pot up or transplant seedlings** from earlier sowings, giving them more space to develop.
- **pot up rooted soft-tip cuttings,** and take more if required using the young sideshoots on established plants.
- **start taking semi-ripe cuttings** from conifers using the mid or late summer growth (see page 227).
- **continue layering plants** such as the smoke bush (*Cotinus*) and magnolias (see page 139).
- **watch out for** early signs of pests and diseases, and treat them now before they get serious.

and if there is time . . .

- **feed hardy fuchsias** once or twice with a high-potash fertiliser to encourage prolific flowering.
- **gather lavender flowers** for drying. Hang the stems up in bundles, or spread on trays of absorbent paper in airy shade.
- **protect exposed hydrangeas** from hot, dry winds with a screen of net curtaining or a similar fine material.

Robinia pseudoacacia 'Frisia'

Slate fragments make a decorative and effective mulch for trees grown in large pots, reducing moisture loss.

■ **move camellias in** containers out of bright sunshine into partial shade.

■ **start deadheading lilac** (*Syringa*) and later flowering rhododendrons before new shoots begin developing behind the withered flowers.

watering

Regularly check shrubs, trees and hedges planted earlier in the year, and water if necessary, especially during prolonged dry or windy weather. Limp or lacklustre foliage, and wilting tips, indicate that they desperately need a drink.

- **when watering,** thoroughly soak the ground right round the base of the plant, ideally following with a thick mulch to 'lock' the moisture in the soil. Water early in the morning, or from late afternoon onwards, to avoid the risk of scorching on splashed leaves.
- **add a liquid fertiliser** at the recommended rate when watering new plants, and any that have been hard-pruned or which show signs of poor growth. Apply a foliar feed to the leaves after sunset to give a quick tonic to ailing plants.
- **check plants in containers** daily and move them to a sheltered, lightly shaded position if they dry out rapidly; a mulch of pebbles or gravel helps to prevent moisture loss.

providing support

Tie in the new growth on plants trained up walls, wire or trellis. This is particularly important for young plants still forming their framework of main branches. Space the main stems out evenly, and secure them with soft string. Also ensure that the shoots are pointing in the right direction; pinch off any that are misplaced before they get too long.

weeding

Continue to eradicate weeds by hoeing and hand-weeding. This applies particularly to the immediate area around new shrubs, trees and hedges, as they need a couple of seasons without any competition. Keep at least $1m^2$ (1 sq yd) around the base of the plant weed-free by hoeing, spraying or laying a woven mulching mat.

If you plan to make a new bed or border this autumn, it is best to clear the site now and spray it with glyphosate, or a similar chemical, to kill perennial weeds. This gives surviving roots and weed seeds time to regenerate, and be forked out before planting. The traditional, non-chemical method of getting rid of weed roots is to dig the area thoroughly, removing by hand every trace of weeds, including all root fragments.

acclimatising plants

Now that there is no longer any risk of a late, damaging frost, there are plenty of things to be done.

- **leave the fleece off cold-sensitive shrubs** that were protected from frost at night, now that temperatures are rising.
- **move outdoors any tender shrubs** in containers, such as citrus or oleander (*Nerium*), that were kept under glass during winter. Give them a sunny, sheltered position.
- **check these plants** for any injured or dead stems. Cut them off, together with any unshapely growth.
- **hoe or lightly fork** round the plants, and scatter a balanced fertiliser on the soil surface. Fork it in.

pests and diseases

Watch out for early signs of pests and diseases, and tackle them before they take hold. Look out for aphids on young conifers, beech (*Fagus*), box and camellias, scale insects and mildew on hebes, blackfly on cherries, and red spider mite on a number of shrubs in very dry weather (see page 258).

Silver birches look their best in naturalistic settings, as here in an area of long grass.

shrubs & trees/2

The beauty bush (*Kolkwitzia*) makes a magnificent early summer display. After flowering it will benefit from having about a third of its growth removed by pruning.

pruning early flowering shrubs

Shrubs and informal hedges that flower in May and early June, on stems produced the previous year, need annual pruning. This prevents twiggy growth, and sparse blooms next year. It is best done immediately after flowering to allow plenty of time for new growth to develop and ripen before the end of the season. How hard you prune depends on the age, size and condition of the shrub.

formative pruning

For the first two to three years of a shrub's life, pruning helps form a strong framework of branches and a balanced shape.

- **after planting,** remove any damaged or weak, spindly growth, and lightly trim back the shoot tips to a strong bud, or pair of buds.
- **in the autumn,** cut out any weak shoots and those that unbalance the overall shape.
- **repeat this formative pruning** for the next two years, when you must also prune in midsummer those shoots that carried flowers; cut them back to about 5cm (2in) long.

renewal pruning

This is the simplest way to maintain a compact shape and a vigorous supply of young, floriferous growth on shrubs that are over about three years old. It is often called the one-third prune (see below).

the one-third prune

1 **As soon as the flowers fade,** it is time to prune away a third of a leafy overgrown shrub.

2 **Cut out any weak,** spindly shoots and stems that cross or crowd each other out. Use a sharp pair of secateurs.

early flowering shrubs to prune now

• beauty bush (*Kolkwitzia*) • *Berberis darwinii* • ceanothus (evergreen) • chaenomeles • cytisus • deutzia • escallonia • flowering currant (*Ribes*) • kerria • Mexican orange blossom (*Choisya*) • mock orange (*Philadelphus*) • pyracantha • winter-flowering viburnums • weigela

spur pruning chaenomeles and pyracantha

When trained on a wall, either growing freely or pruned as a fan or espalier, these shrubs will need spur pruning. This maintains their shape and maximises flowering.

- **about two weeks before midsummer,** remove all crossing or inward growing shoots, and shorten those growing away from the wall, to leave four to six leaves. This encourages the formation of flowering shoots and, in the case of pyracantha, exposes the colourful berries.
- **in early autumn,** further shorten the pruned shoots, leaving two to three leaves on each.

pruning broom

If broom (*Cytisus*) is left unpruned it becomes top-heavy and short-lived. It is best to prune young plants in early summer.

- **pinch out the growing tips** of young plants to keep them bushy and cut back the current year's growth by half immediately after flowering to control the shrub's size. Never prune into woody growth as this can kill the plant.

pruning evergreen ceanothus

Evergreen varieties are often injured by frosts unless grown against a sunny, sheltered wall, where they need regular pruning to maintain their shape and vigour. The majority bloom in spring or early summer, and need pruning immediately afterwards.

- **trim back the shoots** growing away from the wall, on which the flowers have just finished, to about 10cm (4in) from their base. Where they meet older main branches, do not cut into these because the main branches do not readily produce new shoots.
- **tie any stems** growing sideways against the wall.
- **check again in early autumn**, and shorten any excessively long new shoots.

3 **Remove a proportion** of the oldest branches just above ground level or to a low, strong sideshoot. You may need to use a pruning saw for this.

4 **Aim to remove a third** of the growth annually, so that no branch on the shrub is more than three years old. This will admit light to the shrub and maintain a good shape.

pruning Viburnum plicatum 'Mariesii'

With its branches arranged in horizontal tiers, *Viburnum plicatum* 'Mariesii' needs careful pruning to maintain its striking architectural shape.

- **as soon as** the flowers fade in early summer, cut off any dead or injured growth.
- **then remove** any misplaced branches growing up or in towards the centre of the shrub, to create clear layers.
- **shorten sideshoots** on the main branches, to leave two to three leaves on each.

crown thinning

A broad-leaved tree with a dense or cluttered canopy of branches may cast so much shade that little will grow beneath it. The technique of crown thinning is used to remove several branches, creating greater penetration of air and light, without altering the tree's size and shape.

Tall trees should be thinned by a qualified tree surgeon, but on a smaller tree you can do this yourself. Do the work in midsummer to assess how much the shade is reduced, and because re-growth will be less vigorous than after winter surgery. The following winter, check to see whether further light pruning is needed to improve the balance and symmetry of the bare branches.

- **start by cutting out dead**, damaged and diseased wood, followed by any branches that cross or rub against each other. Also cut out branches that grow across or into the centre of the tree.
- **reduce pairs of branches** that form narrow angles to a single, strong branch. If necessary, trim back any low branches creating an obstruction at head height, and any that are too long, unbalanced or too close to others.
- **aim to remove** no more than a third of healthy branches.

shrubs & trees/3

propagation

Close to midsummer, the garden will be full of young growth that can be used as cuttings, creating new plants by autumn or the following spring. You can take several kinds of cuttings, while many shrubs can be layered where they grow by pegging branches down in the soil (see page 139).

shrubs to propagate under cloches

• box • buddleja • deutzia • elaeagnus • escallonia • flowering currant (*Ribes*) • forsythia • hebe • hyssop • kerria • potentilla • privet (*Ligustrum*) • st john's wort (*Hypericum*) • tamarisk • viburnum • weigela

soft-tip cuttings

These are the soft tips taken from main stems and sideshoots. They may be rooted in covered pots or trays, in the greenhouse or on a windowsill (see page 139).

semi-ripe cuttings

The sideshoots on shrubs that started growing early in the season are forming woody tissue at their base by midsummer. You can feel this as a slight firmness when you gently bend a shoot with your fingers. Cuttings from these shoots take a little longer to root than soft cuttings, but are less likely to dry out or to rot if conditions are too wet.

Semi-ripe cuttings are normally prepared with the aid of rooting hormone powder or liquid, and are grown in containers or in the ground under a cloche or in a coldframe. Choose a warm, sunny or lightly shaded position. A sheet of bubble polythene makes an excellent cloche cover. Alternatively, coat glass cloches and glazed coldframes with a thin speckling of greenhouse shade paint.

- **fork over the soil** where the cuttings are to go. Remove all weeds and stones, rake level and cover the surface with a 2–3cm (1in) layer of grit and perlite, in equal parts. Mix this into the top 5cm (2in) of soil with a hand fork. Prepare and plant the cuttings (see opposite), then cover them with a cloche or close the coldframe.
- **check after four to six** weeks to see if there is rooting and new growth. If there is, raise the lid or side of the cloche a little to let in some air. Keep the cuttings moist by watering, and mist occasionally with a spray in very hot weather. Rooted cuttings that are growing vigorously may be moved to a 'nursery bed' or spare

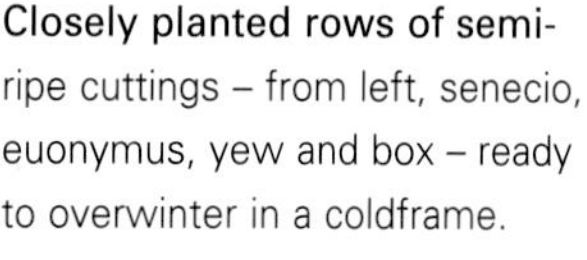

Closely planted rows of semi-ripe cuttings – from left, senecio, euonymus, yew and box – ready to overwinter in a coldframe.

taking semi-ripe cuttings of lavender

1 Prepare the cuttings by gently pulling off 10cm (4in) long sideshoots. This will leave a short 'heel' of tissue at the base, where it is torn from the main stem. Trim the heel with a sharp knife to give a clean edge, and remove all except the top five to ten leaves. Dip the base of the cuttings in hormone powder, and shake off any surplus.

2 Use a dibber to make holes in the soil or cuttings compost. Insert the cuttings, 5cm (2in) deep and 5cm (2in) apart, in rows in the ground, or round the rim of a 13cm (5in) pot; firm in.

3 Water in well, and cover with a cloche or the lid of a coldframe or propagator. Keep closed, but check weekly to see that the soil is not drying out.

piece of ground in autumn, but it is generally safer to wait until next spring before replanting the cuttings 30cm (12in) apart. Plant the young plantlets out permanently the following autumn.

conifer cuttings

Conifers are also easily raised by semi-ripe cuttings. Follow the technique below.

- **Take semi-ripe cuttings**, 5–8cm (2–3in) long, each with a 'heel'. Nip off the sideshoots from the lower half of the cutting, and carefully trim the bark from one side of the lower 2–3cm (1in) with a sharp knife.

Conifer cuttings planted up into cans.

- **Root them** with the aid of hormone powder and plant 1cm (½in) deep in small pots filled with a mixture of equal parts grit and perlite.
- **Keep the cuttings** covered in a propagator, or with a clear plastic bag, and stand them in a warm but shady part of the greenhouse or on a windowsill. New growth should be visible by mid autumn. If they have failed to root, a further batch of cuttings may then be taken in exactly the same way.

azalea cuttings

Some lime-hating plants need slightly different treatment when it comes to propagation. Follow this easy approach for acid-loving plants such as japanese azaleas, enkianthus, gaultheria, kalmia, vaccinium and pieris.

- **Take cuttings** of 5cm (2in) sideshoots and root in a coldframe or gently heated propagator in a greenhouse.
- **Prepare them** as for other semi-ripe cuttings (see left) and insert them 1cm (½in) deep in small pots filled with a mixture of equal parts lime-free grit and perlite.
- **Water well and keep in a closed coldframe** or lidded propagator until late autumn. Then transfer to a cool but frost-free bench in the greenhouse.
- **Feed with a high-potash liquid fertiliser** in early spring. When new shoots appear in early summer, pot them up individually in lime-free compost.

there is still time to . . .

- **prune forsythia,** cutting the flowered shoots almost back to their base. Thin out the older, overcrowded stems on more mature plants.
- **plant container-grown shrubs and trees,** but try to do this before the weather really heats up.

success with rooting hormone

- **never dip cuttings** into the main container: pour a little of the hormone into a dish, and discard any left over after use.
- **keep rooting powder** or liquid in the fridge for prolonged life, and replace annually with a fresh supply.
- **insert only the bottom tip** of the cutting in the hormone, shaking or tapping off any surplus.

alpine gardens

Summer is a relatively quiet time in the alpine garden, enabling you to enjoy its beauty without having to work too hard. Most tasks consist of tidying and deadheading, but summer is also an excellent time to try propagating some of your favourite alpines.

now is the season to . . .

- **tackle any potential weed problems** immediately, before they begin to spread, set seed, and start to detract from the display (see below).
- **keep deadheading** to promote a longer show of flowers. Remove faded blooms and, if plants have become 'leggy', with thin, gangly bare stems, cut them off completely to promote fresh, replacement growth. If you plan to collect seed later, leave some stems untouched to allow their capsules to ripen.

In this small rock garden, dwarf conifers create the framework while flowering plants include meconopsis, aubrieta and gentians.

- **examine plants carefully** to make sure that they are healthy and thriving. Check that rain is not dripping onto them from adjacent rocks. Remove any damaged growth, and lightly prune for shape.
- **water alpines** grown in containers when necessary.
- **increase the shading** if you are growing alpines under glass, as the summer temperatures rise.
- **collect seed** for raising new plants as it becomes ready, enabling you to build up a good show of your favourites (see opposite).
- **take cuttings** to raise more new plants (see opposite).
- **pot up young plants** grown from cuttings in spring.
- **fill any gaps** with colourful pinks (*Dianthus*) and houseleeks (*Sempervivum*).

Houseleeks (*Sempervivum*) are easy to propagate from individual rosettes.

and if you have time . . .

- **occasionally, lightly feed alpines** growing in containers.

eradicating weeds

To a great extent, alpine gardening is small-scale precision gardening, and the rocks, stones and plants need to be thoughtfully placed to produce a good show. But that display can easily be ruined by an invasion of weeds. It is vital that you tackle troublesome weeds promptly, not least because if they scatter their seeds the problem will become even worse. Remove any weeds on the surface compost of containers too.

- **the small, virulent hairy bittercress** can easily lurk behind rocks or under the leaves of plants, so keep an eye out for this. Its tiny, explosive pods scatter seed surprisingly widely, and each seed germinates, grows and flowers within a few weeks. A single plant can cause a widespread infestation in a frighteningly short time.
- **troublesome perennial weeds** pose another problem because their roots run deep, sometimes beneath the rocks, making them difficult to eradicate. Wild species, such as ground

taking soft-tip cuttings of alpines

Remove healthy, non-flowering stem tips, up to 8cm (3in) long. Cut them off just below a leaf joint or node, and trim off their lower leaves. If you have a propagator, rooting will be quick, but at this time of year it is easy to root most potted cuttings in any sheltered spot.

Fill a 9cm (3½in) pot with an equal mix of free-draining compost and horticultural grit or perlite, and insert the cuttings around the sides (see page 227). Water thoroughly and leave them in a warm place; with luck, the cuttings will root in about six weeks.

elder, lesser bindweed and celandine, are problematic, but certain cultivated rock plants can be equally annoying unless carefully controlled. Consequently, plants with creeping stems or rootstocks, such as acaena, some of the campanulas, particularly *C. poscharskyana*, and creeping jenny (*Lysimachia nummularia*), need to be grown with care, keeping their spread under control.

WEED CONTROL TIP Handle free-seeding weeds, such as groundsel, gently, to avoid accidentally spreading the seed, and do not let them hang over the sides of your wheelbarrow or gardening trug when transporting them away.

watering and feeding

It is unnecessary to water a rock garden in all but the driest years, but the compost in pots holding alpines can dehydrate. Give them an occasional, thorough soaking. Intervals between watering will vary according to weather conditions, but once a week should be enough, even in the driest summer.

In the wild, alpines grow in rocky crevices or in poor soil and do not respond well to feeding. But container-grown alpines might benefit from minimal feeding once a year, using slow-release fertiliser or a light dressing of a high-phosphorous fertiliser, such as bone meal.

propagating alpines

The propagation of alpines and rock garden plants can be enormously satisfying and is by far the most economical way to produce more stock.

- **some plants, such as pinks,** primroses (*Primula*), and aquilegias are easy to grow from seed. Check the ripening seed capsules and, when a couple have begun to open, remove the whole stem and place it headfirst in a clean, dry envelope: as the other capsules open, the seed collects in the envelope. Store in a cool, dry place and sow either straight away or in early autumn.

SEED TIP A good way to keep seeds is in the small, semi-transparent envelopes used by stamp collectors. These envelopes can be sealed and inserted into larger ones to keep out light; write on the plant's name and the date.

- **spring and early summer** are excellent seasons for taking soft-tip cuttings from alpines such as penstemon, viola and anthemis (see left).
- **when dividing** certain alpines, such as campanulas, pinks and *Daphne cneorum*, it is best to separate them in autumn, but get them off to a good start now by applying compost to stimulate extra root production at the base of the stems on the parent plant.

Put a handful of gritty compost all round the base of clumps to be divided later.

potting up young plants

1 **Cuttings taken in spring** should be ready for potting up now. Remove them from the propagator and gently separate the rooted cuttings.

2 **Transplant each plant** into its own pot, filled with free-draining compost. Choose a pot that comfortably matches the size of the plant's rootball – with alpines that is unlikely to exceed 8cm (3in). Stand hardy plants outdoors, ready for planting in a few weeks.

water gardens

Ponds and other water features are at their most enjoyable in early summer. This is the best time to divide water lilies and introduce fish, but blanket weed and duckweed need to be controlled.

now is the season to . . .

■ **deadhead flowering plants** in pond and bog gardens once a week, and remove any yellowing leaves. Gather up the debris so it does not rot down and pollute the pond.

■ **weed bog gardens regularly,** by hand rather than by hoe so primulas and other plants can self-seed.

■ **control blanket weed and duckweed,** which grow very fast in warm weather (see opposite).

■ **raise submersible pumps on bricks** to prevent them from sucking up debris from the bottom of the pond.

■ **clean pump filters** every couple of weeks by removing them and rinsing in clean water.

■ **top up ponds** and other water features in hot weather. Use collected rainwater if possible rather than nutrient-rich tap water, which will encourage undesirable green algae.

■ **thin oxygenating plants** by cutting back growth little and often. Pile the trimmings by the pond's edge for a few days so pond creatures can creep back into the water.

■ **add tender floating plants** such as water chestnut (*Trapa natans*) and water lettuce (*Pistia stratiotes*). If these are introduced into the pond before June they may suffer damage from cold and frost.

■ **lift and divide water lilies and irises.**

■ **deal with 'green water'** if this condition, caused by algae, persists. It commonly occurs in late spring, but usually disappears in summer once plants are growing strongly. If it does not, try adding more plants, primarily water lilies, to shade about a third of the pond's surface, and oxygenating plants to take up nutrients that the algae would otherwise feed on. Take care not to over-feed fish, which would add surplus nutrients to the pond.

■ **introduce fish** in summer when the water is warm (see page 233). Float the bag of newly purchased fish in the pond for half an hour so the temperature inside the bag stabilises to match that of the pond. Open it to let some pond water in, and allow the fish to swim out a few minutes later.

■ **give fish somewhere to hide** from predators by putting one or two lengths of drainpipe in the pond.

■ **feed fish daily,** giving only as much food as they will eat in about half an hour.

water lilies

At this time of year, water lilies need extra attention and may suffer from several problems. Catch these early by inspecting leaves regularly. You can divide water lilies now (see opposite).

- **thin overcrowded leaves** using secateurs. If the leaves are being pushed out of the water, the variety is too vigorous for the size of pond. Water lilies vary enormously in vigour, from dwarf varieties suitable for a container pond to fast-growing ones that need a small lake.
- **continue to lower baskets** of water lilies planted in late spring until they sit on the bottom of the pond.

Water-lily leaves shade the pond surface while a variety of flowering and foliage plants, including a variegated iris, bring interest and colour.

keeping the pond clear

Duckweed and blanket weed spread rapidly in warm weather. Blanket weed, resembling green cotton wool, looks unsightly and chokes water plants. Duckweed becomes hazardous if it is allowed to cover the water completely; apart from blocking light and oxygen, it appears to be a firm surface. Try these methods to keep the water clear.

Sink pads of barley straw or lavender stalks in the water; they will slow weed growth as they rot down. Use straw in small ponds and lavender in large ones.

Thin out any overgrown plants on the pond's surface by hand, so sufficient water is left clear. The oxygenating canadian pondweed (*Elodea*) helps control blanket weed but can spread rapidly.

Pull blanket weed out by hand or by carefully twirling it round a rake or bamboo cane.

Use a net, such as a child's fishing net, to remove duckweed from the surface of the pond.

- **look out for** water-lily aphids and water-lily beetle. The beetle comes in two forms: brown adults, 1cm (½in) long, and black grubs. Control these pests by removing the worst affected leaves. Then weigh down the remaining leaves with pieces of wood sufficiently heavy to hold the leaves under the water, so that pond creatures can feast on the pests.
- **water-lily leaf spot** may appear during warm, damp weather. These spots will eventually rot away, leaving holes in the leaves. Control the disease by removing the affected leaves.

looking ahead . . .

☑ LATE SUMMER Top up water during hot weather.
☑ Thin out overcrowded marginals and oxygenators.

propagation

Early summer is the time to split and rejuvenate some of the most popular pond plants.

- **lift and divide water lilies** that are several years old (see page 143). Carefully remove them from their baskets and wash any soil off the fleshy rootstock. Cut the outer branches off the rootstock using a sharp knife and discard the old central portion. Dust cut surfaces with yellow sulphur powder to prevent fungal infection. Plant the divisions individually in mesh baskets lined with hessian, or fine-mesh baskets that do not need lining, and filled with aquatic compost. Top with a layer of fine gravel to prevent the soil from floating away. Water well by soaking in a bowl of pond water until no more air bubbles are produced, before replacing in the pond.
- **divide irises** that have formed large clumps, immediately after flowering.

there is still time to . . .

- **feed established pond plants** with aquatic fertiliser if this was not done in spring.
- **put in new plants** by midsummer.

Trollius chinensis

creating a healthy pond

A pond has a dynamic ecology that needs to develop its own natural balance. This can be achieved fairly easily, but success – as seen in clarity of water, a healthy population of invertebrates and flourishing pond plants – will depend on careful plant choice, and on allowing enough time for the various populations to stabilise. In some situations, this may take more than a year, or even two.

pond plants

Several different kinds of plant are essential for a pond, not only for their decorative value, but also for the positive effect they have on the water. They absorb the nitrogenous waste that is produced by fish, amphibians and other life forms, which in turn helps to prevent too much algae from multiplying and turning the water green. Invasive weeds, however, may need to be kept to a minimum.

oxygenating plants

These are submerged, green plants that give off a constant supply of oxygen, which is dissolved in the water and sustains many small organisms. These in turn provide food for other creatures and process nitrogenous waste. Although underwater plants may not be spectacular to look at, they serve a vital function. If carefully chosen, however, many add subtle beauty, especially if the water is clear enough for them to be seen. Some have feathery, ferny or finely divided foliage. Others, such as the beautiful water crowfoot or water violet, produce flowers above the water's surface.

good oxygenating plants

• canadian pondweed (invasive) • hornwort (*Ceratophyllum demersum*)
• potomogeton, starwort (*Callitriche*) • water crowfoot (*Ranunculus fluitans*)
• water violet (*Hottonia palustris*)

deep-water plants

These plants absorb large amounts of nitrogenous waste and their floating leaves help to shade the water. This reduces light levels and temperature, which inhibits the growth of algae. The best deep-water plants are water lilies (see page 230), but there are others of great value:

- **golden club** (*Orontium aquaticum*) has narrow, blue-green leaves and horn-like yellow flowers (see below).
- **pond crowfoot** (*Ranunculus aquatilis*) has palmate, floating leaves as well as feathery submerged foliage and little white flowers in spring and early summer.
- **spatterdock** (*Nuphar advenum*), for larger ponds, has big, heart-shaped leaves, some of which float while others stand clear of the water, and showy green-tinged yellow flowers.

marginal plants

These also absorb dissolved nutrients and waste and so help to keep down algae and blanket weed (see pages 144 and 23).

Orontium aquaticum is known as golden club for its slender yellow flowers.

floating weeds

Some people dislike such plants as duckweed – a tiny species that grows on the surface of the water and which can be invasive if not controlled. But it is not difficult to control in a small area, and it brings beneficial shade. As fresh, green duckweed is very rich in protein absorbed from the water, removing large amounts is a good way of taking nitrogen from the pond water; furthermore it will benefit your compost heap. Other floating plants include *Azolla caroliniana*, whose ferny leaves will sometimes invade a whole pond, but which may not survive a cold winter. Even less hardy is the water chestnut (*Trapa natans*). This produces 'chestnuts', which can be overwintered in water in a greenhouse, for use the following year.

fauna

Even if you plan not to have any fish in your pond, the water cannot help but attract many different species. Insects like dragonflies or damselflies will arrive, as will birds. At night, hedgehogs and bats will be attracted to the water.

If you are able to encourage the development of this habitat, you will be helping with bio-diversity, but even if wildlife conservation is of no interest to you, your pond will still be more

In a healthy, well-stocked pond the plants and wildlife are in balance and the water is clear.

pleasant if it supports a well-balanced ecosystem. The water will be clearer and sweeter; therefore, the plants that surround it and grow in it will look all the better. Furthermore, with sufficient predators in the water – such as frogs, toads or newts – you will be less likely to be troubled by pests like mosquitoes.

stocking with fish

For fish to thrive, the pond needs to be balanced, with well-established water plants. Fountains or waterfalls are not vital, but they help to oxygenate the water, particularly in the early stages while the plants are settling in. Fish add to the burden of nitrogenous waste, and it is therefore essential that the pond is very well stocked with vegetation, and that you do not overstock with fish.

If you build and plant the pond in spring, allow the plants a month or two to establish before you introduce any fish. Early to midsummer would be an ideal time.

releasing fish

1 **When releasing fish** into your pond, float the whole bag in the water for a while before you open it, so that the temperature change is gentle. Fish are usually purchased in plastic bags, sometimes with a little oxygen added before it is sealed.

2 **Submerge the bag** only when you are ready to release the fish.

3 **Carefully unseal** the bag and allow the fish to swim out into their new home.

patios & containers

This is the season to enjoy your patio. Rearrange the containers to create different colour combinations, give scented plants a prominent position, and make sure there is room for exciting last-minute purchases.

now is the season to . . .

- **hang up baskets** and stand out pots of tender bedding, but make sure they are acclimatised (hardened off) first.
- **water all plants in containers,** and mulch raised beds to conserve moisture (see page 236).
- **keep deadheading** for prolonged flowering (see below).
- **regularly feed plants** in hanging baskets and other containers for optimum performance (see opposite).
- **give all plants a regular check,** even if it means getting on your hands and knees, to make sure they really are healthy. Look under the leaves where aphids might be lurking, and examine the stems closely.
- **check under large planters** from time to time to see that ants are not marching in through the drainage holes, creating nests in the compost.
- **group together pots** and tubs of flowering plants, to create eye-catching combinations.
- **put scented plants** in a sheltered, sunny position by seating areas or near open windows.
- **remove a paving slab** on a patio for planting scented herbs, such as thyme (see right).
- **leave room for impulse buys** to jazz up a raised bed or a container grouping (see right).
- **fill any unintentional gaps.**

For an extravagant globe of colour, water hanging baskets daily and feed weekly. In hot weather they dry out very quickly and may need watering twice a day.

planting thyme

Plant a few permanent thymes in full sun in the patio itself. Their essential oils will be released when they are trodden on.

- **lift a slab** and dig out the soil to a spade's depth. Replace it with a mix of topsoil, compost and horticultural sand for good drainage.
- **plant spreading,** creeping thymes (which can also be planted in the cracks between paving) or taller species that can be pruned to give a rounded shape. Arrange the container-grown plants behind the thymes.

Plant creeping thyme between the slabs in a paved patio; they will release their scent when walked over.

impulse buys

When planting up a patio scheme for containers or a raised bed, do not worry if there are gaps. You will always find a special plant to tempt you at the garden centre or a flower show, possibly something tender or quite flamboyant.

If you buy a tender plant, such as a lemon tree, bear in mind that the conditions on your patio might be cooler and windier than the protected environment in which the plant has been growing and you should acclimatise it gradually.

CITRUS TREE TIP To encourage young potted lemon trees to build up a good framework of branches, remove the flower buds. If they are allowed to flower, the seed heads will develop into lemons and the plant will put all its energy into fruit production, whereas in these early years you want the plant to extend its root, stems and leaf growth. When it has reached a decent size, allow it to produce one lemon, then, as it gets bigger, a few more. When it has reached the height you require, let it flower and fruit all it wants.

deadheading

Promptly snipping off fading or dead flowers does two things. It gets rid of insipid colours that detract from the overall display, and it ensures that plants channel their energy into creating more beautiful flowers instead of developing the seed heads.

- **deadhead patio roses** quite severely after blooming, removing entire flower sprays.
- **radically cut back violas, most geraniums,** campanulas and convolvulus to promote a second flush of bloom.

REVIVAL TIP After cutting the growth back, give the plants a thorough watering and a light application of plant food, such as a dilute liquid feed. This will stimulate new growth and plenty of flowers.

feeding container plants

Regular summer feeding is essential for plants growing in containers or they will develop pale leaves and, ultimately, perform badly.

- **if you have not added a slow-release** fertiliser at planting time, start feeding now, every 7–14 days. Use a high-nitrogen fertiliser for newly planted baskets and containers (see page 604). Swap to a tomato feed after three weeks, to encourage flowering until autumn. Do not exceed the manufacturer's recommended dose, or the concentration of chemicals will do more harm than good.
- **use a liquid feed** or slow-release fertiliser sticks or capsules.

watering and mulching

Plants in pots and raised beds need regular watering.

- **soak pots and baskets** at least once a day in warm weather, until the water runs out of the drainage holes.
- **use a moisture-retaining gel,** available from garden centres, to help prevent the compost in pots and baskets from drying out too quickly. The gel holds water which is then available when the plant needs it.
- **conserve moisture in** raised beds, where the soil can remain dry to a surprising depth, by adding a thick layer of mulch. Use home-made garden compost, especially if it is bulky and fibrous. Grass clippings are an alternative, though they may look rather too unsightly for use on a patio. If you do not have a source of home-produced mulch, most garden centres sell bags of bark chippings, coco husks, or other decorative mulches. Check often to see when watering is required. Organic mulches are porous and let rain through.

Brighten up container displays with floriferous bedding plants such as pelargoniums, penstemon, verbena or phygelius, which will provide pretty colours right through to autumn.

This all-green patio planting displays an astonishing range of shapes and leaf textures. A pair of standard catalpas rise above clipped box, ferns, grasses and the dramatic ornamental rhubarb.

easy patio watering

A patio packed with container-grown plants is a glorious sight in summer, but regular watering is absolutely essential to their survival. Fortunately, there are now many different ways to make watering less labour-intensive and provide precious water even when you are not there.

watering patios

Plants in pots obviously have a limited root area from which to take up moisture, and the situation is compounded by an 'umbrella' of foliage that keeps most rainfall off the compost. Although watering is a relaxing and enjoyable job, it can become a really time-consuming chore in summer when plants can need attention once or even twice a day.

The frequency of watering can be reduced by using water-retaining gels, self-watering containers and large pots. Even better, you can cut the workload dramatically by installing a watering system; the addition of a timer will make the system completely automatic.

compost and water-retaining gel

Soil-based compost dries out more slowly than soil-less types and provides more of a buffer against drought. This is therefore the best type to use for all permanent plants, although its weight makes it an impractical choice for suspended containers such as hanging baskets.

Improve the water-holding capacity of soil-less compost by using water-retaining gel, which is made up of granules that swell to many times their own size when wet (see before and after adding water to the pots, above). Mix just a small quantity of the dry granules into the compost before potting – or you can buy compost that already contains the gel. However, make sure you water whenever necessary, because once the gel has given up its store of moisture, the compost dries out very quickly as air replaces the spaces previously occupied by the swollen gel. Do not use gel for containers that will be outside during autumn, winter or early spring, as the compost would become too wet and cold.

The drip nozzle (below) delivers a fine spray of water to plants in containers.

An effective watering system (left) involves running lengths of microbore tubing, fitted with drip nozzles, to all your pots.

choosing containers

The size and type of container, along with the amount of plant growth it has to support, influences how quickly the compost dries out. Hanging baskets dry out fastest of all, as the whole of the container is exposed to sun and wind. Pots made of porous material like terracotta also dry out quicker than other materials, though you can reduce water loss by lining the inside of the container (not the base) with polythene.

Large containers are best at retaining water as there is more compost to hold the moisture, whereas small pots have only a tiny amount by comparison. If you don't want to bother with a watering system, opt for generous containers and put a selection of plants in each one, rather than having lots of smaller pots.

Self-watering containers are a simple way to reduce the amount of watering required as they incorporate a built-in

Self-watering containers incorporate a reservoir to top up water as needed.

reservoir. The plant can take up water as necessary, but without the roots becoming waterlogged. This design is particularly useful for hanging baskets.

automatic watering

- **make your watering system fully automatic** by fitting an automatic timer or computer-controlled timer, both available from garden centres. Both types are battery-powered: a timer is designed to water once a day and is relatively inexpensive, while a computer gives much greater flexibility of watering times but costs almost twice as much.
- **frequency and length of the watering period** will vary, depending on the site and weather conditions. If you are planning to go on holiday, set up the timer at least a week in advance and monitor the amount of watering required to keep the container compost evenly moist but not waterlogged. The best time to set up a watering system is during hot weather when the pipes will be soft and flexible.
- **in winter,** make sure the system is drained of water, which could otherwise freeze and cause damage. Ideally, it should be dismantled and stored under cover, with open ends of pipes sealed with tape to prevent insects crawling in and creating blockages next year. Timers should be dried and stored with their batteries removed.

patio watering systems

You can plumb your patio containers into a microbore watering system, and tailor it to your own patio. A basic design consists of a rigid hose running to the area to be watered. Flexible microbore tubing travels from the hose to the containers, delivering water to each pot by means of an attached drip nozzle (see below). There are some variations, depending on the kit you buy. The hose itself connects to a tap which you turn on manually as needed, or you can fit a water timer to make the system fully automatic (see above).

A watering system is perfect for containers as the water is delivered slowly and gently, rather than in a rush from a hose. Although fairly costly and time-consuming to set up, such a system can last for years, save time and keep your plants in glowing good health all summer – even during holidays.

constructing a watering system

1 **First stand your containers** exactly where you want them. From the tap, run a length of rigid hose where it will be least obvious, for example, along the base of a wall. Measure the distance from your hosepipe to the first container, then measure the distances between the pots. This will give the number and lengths of microbore tubing needed.

2 **Cut lengths of tubing,** using scissors or the tool provided with the kit. Fit a drip nozzle to the end of the first tube and peg it into a container before joining the next length of tubing up to it. Fix the other end of the first length of tubing to the hosepipe, using the attachment supplied.

3 **Continue to fit** tubes and drip nozzles to all containers. The easiest way to fit the tubes to the drip nozzles is to dip the ends of the tubing into a bowl of hot water. This makes the plastic more flexible to work with.

lawns

As the days become warmer and longer, the lawn demands more of your time to keep it green and lush, with mowing the dominant task. The key to easy mowing is frequency: little and often gives the best results.

now is the season to . . .

■ **increase mowing** to about twice a week, as the grass will be growing rapidly (see opposite).

■ **control lawn weeds** by raking or applying a weedkiller (see opposite).

■ **clear moss** early in the season with an application of lawn sand containing sulphate of iron. In dry weather, water the lawn first so the lawn sand will stick to the moss. As it dies the moss will turn black then brown, at which stage you can rake it out using a fan-shaped rake. Burn or bin the dead moss; do not compost it.

■ **trim lawn edges** after mowing. Use a pair of long-handled shears or an electric edger to save bending and to cut close to the lawn edge, removing the untidy fringe of grass.

■ **feed the lawn regularly** to compensate for frequent mowing, which can starve the grass. In summer give an application of high-nitrogen fertiliser to keep the grass green, healthy and growing rapidly. Two days after mowing, and when the soil is moist, apply a granular feed and water it in (see page 604).

■ **water the lawn** in dry periods (see opposite).

■ **scarify the grass** if it feels soft and spongy to walk on; this is usually a sign that a layer of dead grass and clippings, or 'thatch', has formed. Use a fan-shaped rake in a vigorous combing action to clear off the dead material so that water and fertiliser can penetrate to the grass roots.

However small the lawn, regular mowing, watering and feeding are essential to keep the green sward looking its best.

Move objects standing on the lawn often to prevent pale patches from forming.

mowing

When you mow, aim to remove only the top third of the growth. Fine lawns need frequent mowing, with a cutting height of about 1–2cm (½–¾in). Regular close mowing keeps out the coarser grass and weeds that could otherwise smother fine grasses.

- **change direction** each time you mow to prevent the mower from forming ruts and ridges in the lawn. This will also make it easier for you to mow off taller weeds and any grass flower stalks.
- **in dry conditions** let the grass grow longer, and raise your mower blade to a slightly higher setting, 2–3cm (1in) for fine lawns. The extra length will help to shade grass roots and reduce stress due to water loss.
- **during long periods** of dry weather mow less frequently – about once every seven to ten days should suffice. By leaving a greater leaf area on each plant you are reducing the pressure on it to produce more growth in order to feed itself.

MOSS TIP Moss in the lawn is usually a symptom of poor drainage, heavy shade, an acid soil or of mowing too closely and leaving bare patches, where moss will quickly establish. Killing the moss is only a temporary measure, because if you fail to resolve the original source of the problem, the moss will always return.

weeding

The best way to eradicate spreading weeds, especially over a large area, is to make regular applications of lawn weedkiller in conjunction with frequent mowing. Remember that plants 'drink', rather than 'eat', so any product not already diluted must be accompanied by sufficient liquid to enable it to be taken up through the roots. For this reason water your lawn thoroughly after each application if no heavy rain falls within two to three days. Other useful techniques include:

- **before mowing, rake the grass** to lift weeds like speedwell and yarrow. This enables the cutting blade to slice off their top growth.
- **dig out tap-rooted weeds,** like dandelions, with an old knife or a special tool known as a grubber, to a depth of at least 7–8cm (3in) below soil level. Alternatively, spot-treat such weeds with a herbicide stick.

Sprinklers look effective but can be wasteful and imprecise, whereas a hose (inset) delivers water exactly where it is needed.

watering

Turf can lose about 2–3cm (1in) of water every square metre over a period of one week in hot summer weather. To replace this you need to apply about 25 litres (4 gallons) of water for every square metre of lawn. Using a lawn sprinkler is inexact in delivering water and can be wasteful in view of the volume lost to evaporation. A more effective method is to place a seep or soaker hose on the lawn, connected to a tap, and leave it oozing water for at least half an hour (an hour in dry weather). Then move it to another site 1m (3ft) away and repeat the process. This allows water to penetrate the soil to a good depth, encouraging the grass to root down. If you can, water in the evening to minimise what is lost through evaporation.

looking ahead . . .

☑ AUTUMN Improve poor drainage by aerating and top dressing.

☑ WINTER Lime lawns on acid soil if required.

fruit

This is the season for soft fruit, with luscious strawberries, raspberries and currants ripening on a daily basis. Enjoy the harvest, but do not overlook the routine jobs of weeding, watering, mulching and problem control.

now is the season to . . .

- **water all kinds of fruit** except the largest trees, and mulch to conserve moisture.
- **check ties and supports** on all tree fruit. Stems swell quickly during summer, and ties may need loosening to prevent constriction.
- **keep newly planted fruits** free of weeds by hoeing, hand-weeding or spraying. Those planted in grass establish faster if surrounded by clear soil for the first two years.
- **clear up** and dispose of any fruitlets that fall prematurely, especially if they have holes or signs of damage, as these are probably victims of pest attack.
- **summer-prune** fruits trained as cordons, fans and espaliers, starting with gooseberries and red currants in late June, and finishing with apples at the end of July (see page 242).
- **prune wall-trained figs** by shortening half of all new sideshoots to about six leaves and tie in to training wires those left unpruned. Rub or nip off any shoots growing towards the wall, and shorten the breastwood (shoots growing out from the wall) to three leaves.
- **train grape vines** by tying in new growth to training wires. On fruiting vines, pinch out shoot tips two leaves beyond a truss of flowers or fruit, and the tips of any further sideshoots after one leaf.
- **stop picking rhubarb** by mid July, to give plants time to recover before winter.
- **thin heavy sets of fruit** to prevent overcropping and the risk of breaking laden branches (see page 242).
- **cover ripening fruit with nets** to guard against birds and squirrels, unless already protected by a fruit cage.
- **watch for pests and diseases** and treat them at the first signs, or use appropriate deterrent measures to keep them at bay (see pages 242, 243 and 259).
- **feed alpine strawberries** every two or three weeks with a high-potash fertiliser once they start cropping.

and if you have time . . .

- **propagate blackberries** and hybrid berries in July by layering new canes. Bury the tip of a cane in the soil and peg down with a wire loop. Keep moist, and layers should be ready for transplanting in autumn.

Pick cherries as soon as they ripen, before the birds eat them.

harvesting **now**

• blackcurrants • early peaches and nectarines • early plums • gooseberries • raspberries • red currants (above) • late rhubarb • strawberries • sweet cherries • white currants

harvesting fruit

• **check ripening fruits regularly** and harvest while they are dry and in peak condition, preferably in the morning. This is particularly important for strawberries, but any over-ripe or rotting fruit encourages diseases.

• **strawberries crop** from late May to late July, according to variety. They ripen very quickly in hot weather, so check daily and gather all berries that are fully coloured. Pick them with the stalk, and avoid handling the berries as they bruise easily. Remove all diseased and damaged fruits.

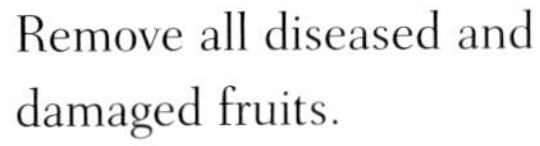

• **gooseberries need thinning** during June, so pick green fruits for cooking until well-spaced berries ripen, from early July onwards. Pick fully ripened berries carefully, as they are soft and burst easily. Crops ripen unevenly, so check over the bushes several times a week.

• **red and white currants ripen** from early July, when they are shiny and with a good colour. Pick whole strings of fruit and remove individual currants back in the kitchen with a table fork. You may need to go over the plants two or three times. In cool, dry weather the ripe berries will often hang quite happily on the bushes for several weeks without deteriorating.

• **blackcurrants** are ready from early or mid-July, when the fruits are a shiny blue-black. Either pick individual currants or wait a week or so, then harvest clusters as for red currants.

• **raspberries** start to ripen during July. They are ready to pick when they are well coloured and part easily from the remains of the flower. Handle with care for these fruits are soft and easily damaged.

• **sweet cherries** are ripe in June. Harvest as soon as they are fully coloured, but test one or two first for flavour. Pick with the stalk, using scissors or secateurs, and use immediately.

• **the first plums** ripen towards the end of July. Test well-coloured fruits to see if they come away easily from the stalk and then check every two or three days, as crops do not ripen all together.

• **early peaches and nectarines** are ripe in July. Check if the flesh around the stalk is soft, then lift the fruit gently in the palm of your hand. If ready, it will come away easily from the stalk. Fruit ripens progressively over several weeks.

there is still time to . . .

• **tuck straw or mats** round strawberry plants before their ripening fruit can touch the soil.

• **mulch gooseberries** as a precaution against mildew.

A heavy crop of raspberries can be supported on a wooden frame.

fruit/2

special fruit care

The best-quality tree fruits are the result of careful thinning and summer pruning, which aids ripening as well as next year's cropping potential. Now is also the time to clear up strawberry beds and prepare new ones.

tree fruit

- **apples** and, to a lesser degree, pears shed some surplus fruits in late June and early July, the so-called 'June drop'. Further thinning is usually necessary to ensure large, good quality fruit. Snip off misshapen and damaged fruits with scissors in mid June. After the June drop, thin the remaining fruits to leave one or, at the most, two fruits in each cluster, to achieve a final spacing of about 10cm (4in) apart for dessert varieties and 15cm (6in) for culinary kinds.

Twist the stems to remove damaged and surplus apples, to leave two in each cluster.

- **thin plums** to 5–8cm (2–3in) apart in early June, and prop up heavily laden branches to prevent breakage.
- **summer-prune apples and pears** trained as bushes, cordons, espaliers and fans, to keep the branch structure open and stimulate next year's fruit buds. Shorten new sideshoots growing from main branches to about five leaves, and those emerging from existing fruit spurs to one leaf; leave the growing tips at the end of branches untouched. Prune pears in mid July and apples slightly later.

Use secateurs to shorten the sideshoots on trained apples and pears in mid to late July.

- **prune plums and sweet cherries** trained on walls between late June and late July. Shorten new sideshoots by a third, but leave shoots at the ends of branches unpruned. After fruiting, these pruned shoots should be further shortened to three leaves.
- **hang pheromone traps** in apple and plum trees to help to control and monitor various moth pests.

bush fruit

As crops of gooseberries and currants develop, avoid overwatering as this can cause fruit to split, but make sure the plants do not suffer from drought. Mulching the plants is a sound precaution against drying out.

- **start summer-pruning gooseberries** and red or white currants in early or mid June. This opens up plants to fresh air, exposes fruit to sunlight and removes soft tips that attract aphids and mildew. Shorten all new sideshoots to about five leaves, but leave the main growing tips unpruned.
- **prune blackcurrants** after the last fruits are picked, or delay until winter. As the best crops are borne on young stems, encourage new growth by cutting out some of the old branches, to just above ground level or to a strong low sideshoot. Aim to remove a third of the branches each year, starting with the oldest and darkest.
- **watch out for reversion** of blackcurrants, indicated by a thick crop of coarse, narrow nettle-like leaves with fewer points on their edges than normal. This is an incurable virus infection, and bushes must be dug up and burned.
- **check gooseberries** for the small 'looper' caterpillars of sawflies. Spray with insecticide or hose off with water.
- **cut off gooseberry shoots** that show signs of mildew.

cane fruit

- **keep cane fruits under control,** otherwise they can get untidy and spread where they are not wanted.

Early plums will need further pruning after they have fruited.

- **tie in new canes of blackberries** and hybrid berries in a temporary bundle (see below).
- **tie in canes of autumn-fruiting raspberries,** spacing them about 10cm (4in) apart on their wires, either individually or by looping a continuous length of string round each cane and over the wire.
- **pull out raspberry suckers** growing out of line while they are small.
- **raspberry beetles** can be troublesome when the maggots hatch out in blackberries and hybrid berries, as well as raspberries. Treat with derris, spraying in the evening when bees are not about. Spray blackberries and hybrid berries when their flowers open, and raspberries when the first berries start to colour and again two weeks later.

looking ahead . . .

☑ LATE SUMMER Plant new strawberries in prepared ground.
☑ AUTUMN Sever and transplant rooted tip layers of blackberries and hybrid berries.
☑ Dig in green manures where fruit has been harvested.

care of blackberries

1 **Tie in the new canes,** which will bear next year's fruit, in a central 'column'. This will keep them tidy and separate from the current year's fruiting canes, and help to prevent damage from wind.

2 **Once the blackberries** have fruited, remove the old fruiting canes at ground level using secateurs.

strawberries

- **clear up strawberry beds** once fruiting has finished.
- **shear off foliage** about 8cm (3in) above ground. Cut off runners unless required for new plants; alternatively, tuck them into rows of two-year-old plants to produce a heavy yield of small fruit for jam-making in the bed's third and final year.
- **dig up three-year-old plants** and burn. Prepare the vacant ground for a late vegetable crop or sow a green manure.
- **remove fruiting mats** and rake off straw for burning.
- **prepare a new strawberry** bed for planting in late summer. Choose a sheltered site that is sunny or lightly shaded, where strawberries have not grown for several years. An area 1.2m (4ft) wide will accommodate two rows spaced 75cm (2ft 6in) apart. Remove all weeds, including perennial roots, before forking in garden compost or rotted manure, one large bucketful a square metre. In heavy clay dig in plenty of grit or coarse compost to improve drainage. Rake the soil roughly level and leave undisturbed for a month before planting the newly rooted strawberry plants.

Root runners for replacement plants by pegging down the small plantlets in the soil or in plunged pots of compost. Perpetual varieties are well worth rooting – these types are best replaced every year because quality deteriorates in subsequent seasons.

vegetables

The vegetable garden is a busy but wonderfully rewarding place at this time of year. Early crops of peas and cabbages are ready to harvest, while later crops need sowing, thinning and planting out. Watering is critical for many vegetables and routine weeding is essential.

harvesting now

• asparagus • asparagus peas • baby sweetcorn • beetroot • broad beans • calabrese • chard and spinach beet • early carrots • early potatoes • french beans • globe artichokes • kohl rabi • lettuces and salad leaves • peas and mangetout • radish • shallots • spinach • spring onions • summer cabbage • summer cauliflower • summer squash • turnips

A collection of beans including french, runner and flageolet beans.

The first french beans appear while the plant is still flowering.

now is the season to . . .

- **sow more seeds** for succession in drills (short single rows) or small blocks, to ensure a continuing supply of fresh vegetables later in the year (see opposite, and pages 246 and 248 for individual crops).
- **thin seedlings** in stages, rather than all at once. If you have space, transplant a few strong thinnings elsewhere. Water the row after thinning to settle the soil so that the remaining plants grow rapidly.
- **watch for slugs** and other pests and diseases. Take action immediately.

watering

Vegetables grow rapidly at this time of year, and plants require plenty of water to sustain them. Ideally, use a method to get water straight to the plant roots, rather than wastefully spraying it over the leaves.

- **lay a seep hose** alongside plants, so water oozes onto the soil exactly where it is needed and loss due to evaporation is minimal. In this way, soil between the rows and pathways remains dry, and weed seeds are not encouraged to germinate.
- **seedlings and crops recently transplanted** or thinned need watering so that they do not dry out and their growth can continue unchecked.
- **leafy vegetables,** such as lettuces and members of the cabbage family, need at least 2 litres (½ gallon) a plant each week to keep growing unhindered in dry weather.

WATERING TIP To increase yields apply water generously at the following times:

- peas and beans at flowering and when the pods begin to swell
- onions as the bulbs start to develop
- carrots, turnips and other roots as they begin to swell
- potatoes when the tubers begin to form
- courgettes, marrows and squashes as fruits start to swell.

controlling weeds

Hoeing with a Dutch hoe (see page 584) is the most effective way to control weeds in vegetable beds, but it must be done with care so as not to disturb crop plants and seedlings.

- **run the hoe blade** just below the surface, no deeper than 1cm (½in). This severs seedling weeds from their roots and minimises moisture loss and soil disturbance, which in turn helps to prevent more weed seeds from germinating.
- **hoe on a hot,** sunny day, so that weeds quickly wilt and die.
- **in wet conditions** rake off the weeds or they will reroot. Leafy annual weeds can be added to the compost heap.

peas and beans

Plant runner beans in early June (see below). Make further sowings of dwarf french beans at three-week intervals. Space seeds 15cm (6in) apart in rows 20cm (8in) apart, as well as using them to fill in the gaps of any plants that failed to grow.

- **harvest peas** sown in spring when the pods are well developed but before they become tightly packed with seeds.
- **sow peas in a broad drill** at three-week intervals. Space the seeds 3–5cm (1–2in) deep in two or three rows 8cm (3in) apart. Sow early varieties for harvesting in late summer and maincrop varieties for harvesting in autumn.

cabbages and calabrese

- **transplant brassicas firmly** to prevent them from drying out and to help their root systems establish. After transplanting, tug one of the larger leaves; if the plant pulls out of the ground, replant and firm in thoroughly with your knuckles.
- **transplant savoy and winter cabbages** to their growing positions at a minimum spacing of 30 x 30cm (12 x 12in), for harvesting from late autumn through to mid spring. Closer spacing will result in more but smaller heads.
- **harvest summer** cabbages when they have developed a good solid heart. Use a sharp knife to cut through the main stem just above the oldest leaves. Leave stalks in the soil and make two cross cuts at right angles; new leaves will sprout from this stump to produce a crop of greens later in the year.
- **early summer cauliflowers** are ready to harvest once the heads have swollen and the outer protective leaves open to show the white curd inside. Cut the head first, then clear the remaining stem and outer leaves.
- **cut broccoli** before the flowers show. Remove the central head with about 15cm (6in) of stem. This encourages smaller sideshoots to develop for harvesting later.
- **sow spring cabbage** in July to transplant later in the year.

there is still time to...

- **sow beetroot,** carrots, courgettes, dwarf french beans, kohl rabi, lettuce, mangetout and peas, outdoor cucumbers, radish, runner beans, swedes and turnips.
- **transplant brussels sprouts** and winter cauliflowers.

Twiggy hazel 'pea sticks' protect peas and dwarf beans from birds and give the plants some support.

planting runner beans

1 Plant beans sown under glass in spring 15cm (6in) apart in double rows 60cm (2ft) apart.

2 Install a sturdy cane support structure and secure it well before the beans start to grow tall.

3 Start guiding the stems up a line or wigwam of bamboo canes from inside the structure.

vegetables/2

harvesting shallots

Shallots planted in winter are ready for harvesting as early as late June if the weather has been warm, dry and sunny. Summer sunshine ripens the bulbs as well as extending their storage life.

- **as the leaves die down,** gently lift each clump of shallots with a border fork. Allow the bulbs to dry in the sun.
- **store bulbs** once the skins are thoroughly dry and the remains of the tops pull off easily. Lay the bulbs in wooden or cardboard trays in a dry, cool, dark, frost-free place until they are required; shallots should keep for up to a year in the right conditions.

Leeks and parsley growing in their final spacings; chives edge the bed.

onions and root vegetables

By now the onion relatives, shallots, sun-ripened and firm, are ready to lift, and it is time to enjoy the first crop of carrots and new potatoes. Meanwhile, earth up maincrop potatoes to prevent them from greening, and pull baby beetroots and turnips to make space for later, larger roots.

transplanting leeks

Leeks sown in spring are ready to transplant when they are about 20cm (8in) tall.

- **lightly trim off** the tops of the leaves and the bottoms of the roots, and drop each young plant into a 15cm (6in) deep hole made with a dibber. Space holes 15cm (6in) apart.
- **water each plant.** There is no need to firm as the soil soon collapses in around the roots, filling the hole.

sowing and harvesting root vegetables

Make several small sowings every few weeks to spread harvesting over a long period. This method of successional sowing goes a long way towards avoiding the peaks and troughs in availability caused by changeable weather during the growing season. Another way to avoid gluts and gaps is to thin in stages, first harvesting baby vegetables to leave more growing space for later, larger roots.

- **sow kohl rabi** at three-week intervals throughout early summer. Sow seed 1cm (½in) deep and thin to a final spacing of 20cm (8in) apart in rows 30cm (12in) apart. Green-skinned types take about eight weeks from sowing to harvest, and mature faster than those with purple skins.

Kohl rabi

- **baby turnips** are ready to eat six weeks after sowing. Try out different cultivars by sowing a different one every three weeks throughout summer. Sow seed 2–3cm (1in) deep and thin to a final spacing of 15cm (6in) apart in rows 25cm (10in) apart.
- **sow round beetroot** at three-week intervals until mid July. Sow seed 2–3cm (1in) deep and thin to a final spacing of 5–8cm (2–3in) apart in rows 30cm (12in) apart; baby beets are ready to pull in eight to ten weeks.
- **carrots sown late in June** are less vulnerable to carrot fly than earlier sowings. Sow seed 1cm (½in) deep, and thin to 10cm (4in) apart in rows 15cm (6in) apart. Extend the

potatoes

The most reliable indication that early potatoes are ready for harvesting is when the flowers have opened.

- **lift early potatoes** as required with a border fork. Drive the fork under the line of the ridge and gently shake the soil to expose the tubers. For the best flavour, harvest only what you need and use them as fresh as possible, leaving the rest of the crop growing *in situ* until required.
- **if potato blight has been a problem** in previous years, cut off and dispose of the leaves and stems, and harvest the entire crop early to prevent the disease re-establishing or spreading.
- **in warm, humid conditions, spray potatoes** with a copper-based or other suitable fungicide. This may prevent potato blight becoming established. Coat both sides of the leaves completely with fungicide for it to be effective.
- **earth up maincrop potatoes** when the plants are about 25cm (10in) high (see right), but first hoe between the rows to loosen the soil surface and remove any weeds. Earthing up keeps the young tubers moist and growing rapidly. More important, it prevents them from turning green and becoming poisonous.

earthing up maincrop potatoes

- **use a rake** to pull the loose soil from the centre of each row into the potato plants, covering the bottom half of each stem.
- **make sure the soil** is in close contact with each stem so that the stems are growing from the top of a soil ridge.
- **firm the sides** of the ridge with a spade blade and leave the top flat so that rain can soak down to the plant roots.

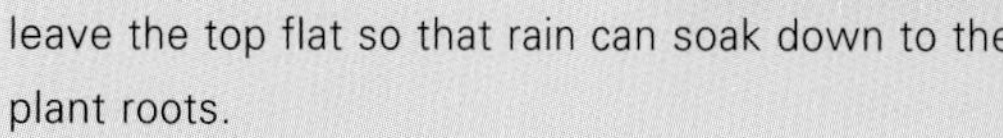

harvest by sowing early varieties, ready in eight weeks, then maincrop varieties, which mature in 10–12 weeks.

- **harvest finger-sized carrots** sown in early to mid spring. Ease the roots with a fork and pull them up by their tops.
- **try not to disturb carrots** more than you need while thinning or harvesting as this releases a scent attractive to carrot root flies. To prevent flies from laying eggs, protect rows of young carrots with insect-proof netting tucked securely in the soil.

The white flowers of garlic open in summer. Unlike onions and shallots, garlic flowers have no adverse effect on the bulbs underground.

Neat blocks of vegetables – radishes, carrots, lollo rosso lettuce and parsley – are planted here in raised brick beds, divided by driftwood. Behind them, seedlings and leeks await their turn to be planted out.

vegetables/3

salads and other crops

Finish planting tender crops like sweetcorn, tomatoes, ridge cucumbers and courgettes once the danger of frost has passed. Globe artichokes are ready to pick, and salads and cut-and-come-again crops, like spinach, need regular harvesting or they may run to seed.

salad crops

- **keep up the supply** of quick-maturing salad leaves by sowing in small batches at two to three-week intervals. Ensure that while one crop is ready for picking, others are at different stages of maturity. Sow seed 1cm (½in) deep.
- **thin lettuces in stages** to 25cm (10in) apart in rows 30cm (12in) apart. Do not transplant thinnings in hot, dry weather as they will run straight to seed.
- **sow radishes and spring onions** in short rows, so as not to produce more than you need. Sow seed 1cm (½in) deep and very thinly indeed.
- **continue to water** at regular intervals if there is no rain, so that leafy salad crops like rocket do not run to seed.

Red and green lettuces grow in timber-edged beds with seedling rows of spring onions and herbs. Pick alternate heads of lettuce for eating while young and leave the rest to hearten up. Spring onions take up little room and are the ideal vegetable for growing between rows of other crops.

Once asparagus has finished cropping and the ferny foliage is growing strongly, apply a granular or liquid feed to the base of the stems two or three times at 10–14 day intervals. This will improve the quality of next spring's crop.

perennial crops

- **pick globe artichokes** from established plants when they are plump and just about to open. Cut them with about 15cm (6in) of stem, to encourage secondary, smaller heads to develop three to six weeks later.
- **feed globe artichoke** plants after harvesting the first crop. Apply a liquid fertiliser round the base of the plants and repeat two or three times at 10-day intervals, to improve the size and quality of a second crop.

tender crops

It is safe to plant tender crops in colder areas now that the danger of frost has passed, but do this early in June to give them as long a growing season as possible.

- **plant tomatoes and peppers** outside in growing bags or fertile soil. Feed and water regularly.
- **support tall-growing cordon tomatoes** and peppers with a stout cane driven in close to each plant. Tie in the stems at intervals of 20–30cm (8–12in) with raffia or soft string to avoid bruising the stems; do not tie too tightly (especially near the base) as this could constrict the stem as it swells.
- **plant out sweetcorn plants** 35cm (14in) apart in blocks (not rows), to aid pollination by the wind (see below).
- **harvest immature 'mini-corns'** from sweetcorn sown under cloches in May or in pots indoors in April. Cut off these young, unpollinated cobs when they are about 10cm (4in) long; the plants are too soft for them to be pulled off like mature cobs.
- **sow courgettes, marrows and ridge cucumbers** in well-drained fertile soil. Dig holes 1.2m (4ft) apart, as deep and as wide as a spade blade. Half-fill with well-rotted organic matter and top with soil to leave a slight mound. Sow three seeds onto the top of each mound; they should germinate in seven to ten days. Allow only the strongest seedling to grow to maturity and remove the other two.
- **plant squashes and pumpkins** in well-drained fertile soil, prepared as described for courgettes and marrows (see above).
- **train squashes** to prevent their vigorous stems becoming a tangled mass. Remove the tip of the main stem once five leaves have developed. This will encourage four or five sideshoots to sprout; as they grow spread them out like the spokes of a wheel.
- **hand-pollinate squash** and pumpkin flowers to ensure good cropping, especially in cool summers (see right). The plants have separate male and female flowers and will produce fruits only if they are cross-pollinated. You can recognise the female by the tiny fruit behind the flower; male flowers have only a thin stalk.

planting sweetcorn

Plant sweetcorn seedlings in a block, 35cm (14in) apart in each direction.

The wind will pollinate the block-grown plants once they flower.

pollinating squashes

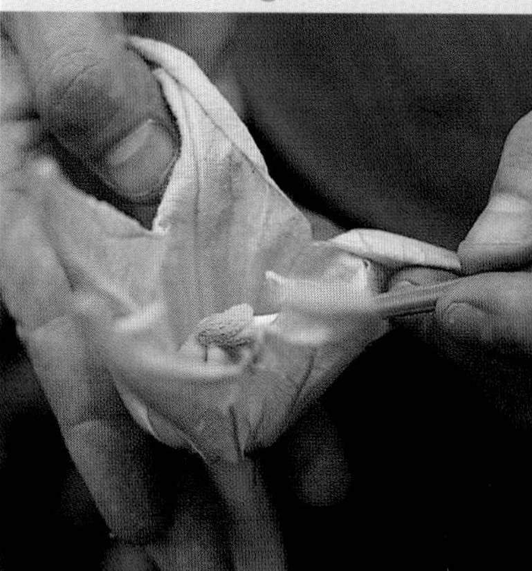

When the flowers are fully open, test a male flower with your fingertip. If pollen grains stick, it is ready to use.

- **pick the flower** and carefully strip off the petals. Gently push the male into the centre of a female flower to transfer the pollen. Use one male flower to pollinate up to four females.
- **repeat** this process three or four days running to ensure pollination has taken place.
- **for large fruits,** allow only one flower to develop on each stem, and remove all flowers once the required number of fruits start to form.

herbs

Herbs are at their most flavoursome now, so pick them regularly for immediate use and to encourage fresh tasty growth. Take special care of tender herbs like basil and don't let vigorous mint plants get out of control.

now is the season to . . .

■ **nip out the growing tips** of bushy herbs, such as basil, savory and marjoram, for kitchen use and to encourage plenty of new sideshoots.

■ **thin or prick out seedlings** sown in late spring before they are too large, and pot up a few for the kitchen windowsill.

■ **plant out tender herbs,** such as basil and lemon verbena, into permanent positions as soon as late frosts are over and young plants are acclimatised to outdoor conditions.

■ **water recently planted herbs** in dry weather, and check those in containers regularly. Chervil, parsley, coriander and sorrel need regular watering, but avoid over-watering basil.

■ **keep on top of weeds,** especially in new beds and borders where herbs are still establishing.

■ **pinch out parsley flowers** forming now on older plants to encourage more leaves, but allow one or two to flower and self-sow to provide seedlings for transplanting in autumn.

■ **gather and dry flowerheads** of chamomile, hyssop and sweet woodruff, as well as lavender and pot marigolds (*Calendula*), to add colour to potpourri.

and if you have time . . .

■ **feed herbs in containers** and perennial herbs planted outside this year, using a high-potash fertiliser.

Shear off the flowers of bushy herbs such as marjoram to promote new leafy growth and prevent seeds from setting.

Against a background of ferns, sage, mint, thyme, parsley and marjoram are grown in pots. They need regular clipping to maintain their rounded shape.

mint

Most mints are vigorous and spreading. To prevent their running roots from invading neighbouring plants, grow them in containers or confine them in open ground by planting in an old bucket or plastic bag. Make sure the container has plenty of drainage holes in the bottom and plunge it in the border soil.

Growing mint in a container is one way to restrain its roots.

- **trim back any wandering** roots once or twice during summer.
- **as mint starts to flower** in July, the quality of the foliage deteriorates. So cut down a proportion of the tall stems to just above soil level, water well and feed with a high-nitrogen fertiliser to stimulate a second crop of young, full-flavoured leaves.
- **watch for mint rust,** distinguished by pale, swollen or distorted stems that later develop dirty orange spots on the leaves. Cut off all affected growth to ground level and burn or dispose of it promptly.

success with basil

To grow well basil needs warmth and shelter, a free-draining rich soil and regular feeding. For these reasons do not plant or sow outdoors until after the last frosts. For a longer cropping period grow basil in a fertile greenhouse border or in 15–20cm (6–8in) pots of soil-based compost with a layer of coarse grit in the bottom for drainage purposes.

- **stand the pots in a warm, sunny corner,** protected from the wind.
- **water before midday** whenever the compost is dry, but avoid overwatering.
- **feed every 10–14 days** with high-nitrogen liquid fertiliser.
- **pinch out the growing** tips regularly, starting while the plants are still small, to encourage bushy growth and prolong the life of the plants by suppressing flowering.

looking ahead . . .

☑ AUTUMN Pot up parsley plants and move under cover.
☑ Scorch beds of mint affected with rust, to kill the spores and sterilise the soil.
☑ Transplant self-sown parsley seedlings.

propagation

A variety of herbs are sown at this time, including a final and generous sowing of parsley for use in autumn from the open garden. With care this sowing should also see you through the winter – some plants can be potted up in September and grown under cover or indoors.

- **sow parsley seeds** sparingly in rows in a warm, sheltered part of the garden in mid July. When the seedlings are large enough to handle, water them well and thin out to leave plants 8cm (3in) apart. Water again to firm.
- **sow basil outside** once the danger of frost has passed.
- **continue to sow annual** herbs, such as chervil, dill and coriander, outdoors, to ensure a continuous harvest all season.
- **sow chives, fennel,** winter savory and other biennials and perennials under glass or in a seedbed outdoors.
- **divide mature clumps of** mint for new plants. After flowering lift ageing clumps and chop them into pieces with a spade. Transplant the younger, outer pieces into a fresh site, where they will grow more vigorously. Discard the exhausted central portion.
- **take semi-ripe cuttings** of woody herbs during July. The sideshoots of bay and rosemary will provide suitable material (see page 227).

Try out a variety of different herbs in their pots before planting up a large container or window box for kitchen use.

there is still time to . . .

- **take soft cuttings** of marjoram, mint, rosemary, sage, thyme and tarragon, and root in a propagator or in a pot on a windowsill (see page 139).
- **layer low branches** of thyme and rosemary by pinning them down in the soil, but keeping the tips above ground (see page 139). They should have rooted by winter.

herbs/2

harvesting herbs

Many herbs reach perfection around midsummer, when their foliage is still fresh and unblemished, and their flavour peaks just before flowering. This is the time to harvest large quantities that you can preserve for winter use.

now is the season to . . .

■ **gather herbs for preserving** on a dry morning, ideally when it is slightly cloudy or before the sun reaches the plants. Harvest only as much as you can deal with straightaway and select only clean, healthy growth. Keep different herbs separate at all times to avoid cross-flavouring.

■ **water and feed herbs** after each mass harvest. Annuals should regrow to supply a second harvest later in the summer and perennials will give another cut or two.

Chop parsley finely, place in ice-cube trays and top up with water – or freeze sprigs.

Preserve borage flowers in ice to float in summer drinks. This works well with other plants.

freezing

This is the best way to preserve the full flavour and colour of most leafy culinary herbs. Freeze them singly or in mixtures, as bouquets garnis, for convenience.

- **pick small sprigs of foliage,** wash in cold water and shake well. Do not pat them dry, as this can bruise the leaves. Place small bunches loosely in plastic bags and freeze.
- **when fully frozen** crush the leaves in their bags, working quickly before they thaw, and pack the bags in a labelled container to save space.
- **alternatively, chop leaves finely** after washing and pack them into the sections of ice-cube trays. Top up with water and freeze. Store the cubes in the trays, or pack them in bags or containers. Use this method to preserve borage flowers and the leaves of variegated mint, lemon balm or scented-leaved pelargoniums for adding to cold drinks.

drying

Dry herbs quickly to retain as much of their colour and their volatile oils as possible. They are ready for storing when crisp, but not so brittle that they crumble to dust. Store dried herbs whole or crushed in airtight, dark jars or tins in a cool place.

- **dry naturally** in a warm, dark and well-ventilated place, such as an airing cupboard, spare room or dry

Tie the stems of thyme, oregano, sage, rosemary and lavender together with soft string before hanging them up to dry.

preserving herbs

HERB	PART	METHOD
BASIL	leaves	freeze; infuse in oil or vinegar
BAY	leaves	dry; infuse in oil or vinegar
BERGAMOT	flowers, leaves	dry
CHAMOMILE	flowers, leaves	dry
CHERVIL	leaves	freeze
CHIVES	flowers leaves	dry freeze; make butter
CORIANDER	seeds	dry
DILL	leaves seeds	freeze; infuse in vinegar dry
FENNEL	leaves seeds	freeze; infuse in oil or vinegar dry
HYSSOP	flowers, leaves	dry; infuse in oil
LEMON BALM	leaves	dry; freeze; infuse in oil or vinegar
LEMON VERBENA	leaves	dry; infuse in oil or vinegar
MARJORAM	flowers leaves	dry dry; freeze; infuse in oil or vinegar
MINT	leaves	dry; freeze; infuse in oil or vinegar; make jelly
PARSLEY	leaves	freeze; mix with butter; infuse in vinegar
POT MARIGOLD	flowers	dry
ROSEMARY	leaves	dry; infuse in oil or vinegar
SAGE	flowers leaves	dry dry; infuse in oil or vinegar
SAVORY	leaves	dry; infuse in oil or vinegar
TARRAGON	leaves	freeze; infuse in oil or vinegar
THYME	leaves	dry; infuse in oil or vinegar

shed. For best results, spread the leaves and stems in a single layer on trays or drying racks and turn several times during the first few days. When the leaves snap easily, they are dry enough to store in airtight jars, tins or wooden boxes in total darkness.

- **alternatively,** tie stems into small bundles and suspend these from hooks or coat hangers to dry gently.

Oven-dry sprigs of rosemary and thyme. Sage and mint can also be oven-dried.

- **oven-drying** speeds up the process. Spread the herbs on trays lined with greaseproof paper and place them in an oven, set at a very low temperature with the door slightly open. Turn and check frequently, making sure the herbs do not get too hot.
- **microwave-drying** is the quickest method, but the trickiest. First remove all stems, which sometimes spark or burn. Spread the leaves on kitchen paper on the turntable with an eggcupful of water in the middle. Dry on full power in 30-second bursts, stirring around and testing after each session. Stop when the leaves are just dry: thyme and other small-leaved herbs take about one minute, large leaves three or four minutes. Leave in the microwave for a few more minutes to complete their drying.
- **allow seeds to dry** for a few days, then store them in airtight jars or tins.

infusions

Infuse the fresh taste of leafy herbs in a medium, such as oil, vinegar, butter or jelly, by first pounding them in a pestle and mortar.

- **add the pulp to an oil** (olive or sunflower), white wine vinegar or cider vinegar and allow to infuse for two to three weeks. Strain out the herbs and bottle the oil or vinegar in a clean bottle or jar with a fresh sprig of the particular herb.
- **blend pounded herbs** with unsalted butter and store in the refrigerator. Basil, oregano and chives are all suitable for this method.
- **make herb jellies** by combining pounded mint leaves, for example, with the cooking apples or crab apples used to make 'jam' or jelly.

the greenhouse

Even though many plants have now been moved outdoors, there is still plenty to get on with. Propagators and coldframes are filling up with seedlings and cuttings, while greenhouse crops need daily attention.

now is the season to . . .

- **take leaf cuttings** of gloxinias and african violets (*Saintpaulia*) (see below) and *Begonia rex* (see right). Take soft-tip cuttings of busy lizzies, houseplant ivies and tuberous begonias (see page 212).
- **take semi-ripe cuttings** of climbers and shrubs (see page 227). Propagate sturdy sideshoots of hydrangeas to root in individual 8cm (3in) pots, making flowering container plants for next year.
- **sow large-flowering cyclamen** to bloom in 18 months, and gently start watering last year's corms after their dormant period (see opposite).
- **sow winter-flowering pansies,** primroses and polyanthus (both *Primula*) in trays in early June. Keep them in a shady part of the greenhouse or in a coldframe, and prick out into small pots when large enough.
- **sow tender perennials** such as gloxinias, tuberous begonias and streptocarpus in early June, and pot up seedlings to make sturdy young plants for keeping over winter.
- **prick out seedlings of cinerarias** (*Pericallis* x *hybrida*), calceolarias and other greenhouse flowers sown in late spring. Transfer them to individual cell-trays or 6cm (2½in) pots. When they fill their containers, move to larger pots and stand in a shady place outdoors.
- **pot up soft cuttings** started in May (see page 139) when new growth indicates successful rooting. Transfer them individually to 8cm (3in) pots, and keep lightly shaded for the first few days.
- **cut back regal pelargoniums** in July after flowering, and reduce watering to allow plants to rest.
- **train tomatoes**, cucumbers and melons as they develop (see page 256), and feed regularly (see page 604). Where necessary, pollinate open flowers by hand. Pick tomatoes as they ripen.
- **thin out fruit on grape vines** to prevent overcrowding (see page 256). Watch out for mildew, and treat it by increasing the ventilation and spraying with fungicide.
- **check plants daily for watering,** more often in hot weather, or use an automatic system (see page 237). Also feed pot plants regularly, starting about six weeks after potting.
- **keep temperatures stable** under glass by a combination of shading, ventilation and damping down (see page 256).
- **inspect plants regularly** for the first signs of pests and diseases, and use biological controls as necessary (see page 257).
- **move greenhouse shrubs,** such as azaleas and camellias,

taking leaf cuttings/1

1 **For african violets** and gloxinias, pull or cut off a leaf stalk and shorten to about 2–4cm (1–1½in) long.

2 **The leaves will root easily** in cuttings compost or a mix of equal parts of grit and perlite, with the base of each leaf just buried. Either cover with a clear plastic lid or stand in a closed and lightly shaded propagator. You can also root african violets by standing the leaves, with their stalks intact, in a jar of water.

taking leaf cuttings/2

1 **A single colourful leaf** of *Begonia rex* can produce several plants when laid on the surface of compost. Cut off a leaf, then make cuts straight across the strongest main veins in a number of places, on the underside, using a sharp knife.

2 **Spread the leaf,** facing up, on the surface of a tray filled with cuttings compost or a grit and perlite mix. Weigh down with pebbles and keep warm and moist in a propagator. Young plants will soon appear where the cuts are in contact with the compost.

outdoors. Stand or plunge their containers in deep sand or leaves, ideally in a coldframe, to keep them cool and moist (see page 257). Christmas cacti (*Schlumbergera*) can spend the summer outdoors in light shade.

■ **clean and store away** all heating equipment now that it is no longer needed.

and if you have time . . .

■ **pot up leftover bedding plants** for indoor colour. Ageratum, coleus, dwarf asters, *Begonia semperflorens* and heliotrope all make attractive windowsill plants in 13cm (5in) pots.

■ **clean out an empty coldframe** and plant with 'self-blanching' celery for late summer and early autumn crops.

■ **scrub out pots** as they are emptied, when the plants are put out. Before re-use, rinse them in a sterilising solution.

leaf cuttings

Some plants, such as *Begonia rex* (left) and streptocarpus, can be grown from a leaf, or portions of it, and they can be propagated during summer. For streptocarpus, choose healthy, full-size leaves that are not too old and insert them vertically in pots or trays of moist cuttings compost (see below). They will root in a few weeks. Pot up new young plantlets individually when large enough to handle.

sowing cyclamen

The best time to sow seed of indoor cyclamen (*C. persicum*) is between June and August, when you should also kick-start last year's corms back into growth.

Streptocarpus can be propagated in much the same way as *Begonia rex* leaf cuttings (see opposite), or you can slice the leaf sideways into several pieces, then bury the lower edge (the one nearest the parent plant) of each strip in the compost. Young plants will then grow from the cut veins.

It is not too late to take soft-tip cuttings of perlargoniums, such as this delicate angel pelargonium grown under glass.

- **Soak the seed in water** for 24 hours. Then space them 2–3cm (1in) apart and just cover with compost, in trays or pots of moist seed compost.
- **Cover the trays or pots** with a sheet of newspaper so that the seeds are completely in the dark, and keep at 13–18°C (55–64°F) for several weeks.
- **Move them into the light** when seedlings emerge, and when large enough to hold, prick them out individually into small pots. Keep in bright light and pot on as necessary, feeding them every 10–14 days. They will usually grow right through the first winter if kept at 10°C (50°F), and flower a year later in 13–15cm (5–6in) pots.
- **To restart cyclamen corms** after their early summer rest, remove them from their pots and clean off all the old compost and as many of the dried roots as possible. Choose a pot that is just a little wider than the corm, fill it with fresh compost, and plant the corm so that its rounded base faces downwards, with its top at surface level and protruding above the compost. Keep it in a warm, shady place, and water whenever dry, either from below or into the compost around the corm. Feed regularly in late summer and autumn.

there is still time to . . .

- **take soft-tip cuttings** of pelargoniums, marguerites and fuchsias (see page 212). Grow them initially in small pots covered with clear plastic bags; prune the tallest cuttings to a single vertical stem if you wish to train them into standards next summer.
- **sow cinerarias** and greenhouse primroses such as *P. obconica*, to flower next spring.

the greenhouse/2

crop care

All greenhouse crops need special care to control their growth and maximise fruiting.

training

Train the following vegetables and fruit in different ways to ensure maximum production.

cucumbers

- **train all-female varieties** in the same way as cordon tomatoes (see page 169). Tie the main stems to canes, or train them up and around vertical string for support; remove any sideshoots that form at the base of leaves.
- **with other varieties,** suspend a wide-meshed net from the roof to provide support, and train the main stem vertically up it, pinching out the tip when it reaches the roof. Tie in the sideshoots to grow horizontally, and pinch out their tips two leaves past a fruit. Remove all the male flowers; they grow on simple stalks, unlike the female flowers which have a tiny cucumber-like swelling behind the petals.
- **for all varieties:** keep the compost moist at all times, damp down daily by spraying to maintain high humidity, and feed like tomatoes (see right).

A fruiting ridge cucumber trained on a string.

A truss of orange tomatoes 'Golden Delight' begins to ripen.

tomatoes

- **spray the open flowers** with water or tap the plants sharply to encourage fruit to set. Water consistently because irregular watering can cause blossom end rot when a sunken patch develops at the base of young fruit.
- **feed every two weeks** with a tomato or high-potash fertiliser.

melons

- **melons enjoy** the same conditions as cucumbers. Train as single-stemmed cordons (see page 169) up vertical nets, keeping the main stem upright, and stop it at the roof.
- **train sideshoots horizontally,** pinching them out or stopping them after five leaves. They then produce flowering sideshoots, which should be stopped two leaves past a female flower (recognised by its swollen stalk, like a tiny fruit).
- **pollinate each female** with an open male flower (which has a simple stalk), by removing its petals and pushing the pollen-bearing tip into the centre of the female flower (see page 249).

summer care of grape vines

- **pinch out the growing tips** of sideshoots two leaves past a flower truss, and any sideshoots that form later to one leaf.
- **help pollinate the open flowers** by sharply tapping the stems daily with a cane.
- **thin the small fruits** while you can still see their stalks. Use long-bladed scissors to nip off the inside berries first, then the smallest of the remainder. Do not touch the grapes with your hands.
- **water each week** in hot, dry weather, and feed with high-potash fertiliser every fortnight. Stop feeding and reduce watering when the grapes show signs of ripening, because the soil and air should then be kept dry.
- **check every week** for split or mouldy grapes, and cut them off. Watch out for mildew, and spray with fungicide when first signs appear.

good growing conditions

Plants under glass often grow at an astonishing rate during summer, and need continuous care for the best results.

- **check their watering needs** morning and evening, more often in hot weather.
- **feed every seven to ten days** with a dilute liquid fertiliser.
- **on hot days, reduce temperatures** and keep the humidity high (see page 166) by damping down (wetting) the staging and floor with a hosepipe or watering can, by fitting blinds or painting the glass with white shading, and by opening ventilators and leaving the doors open for longer.

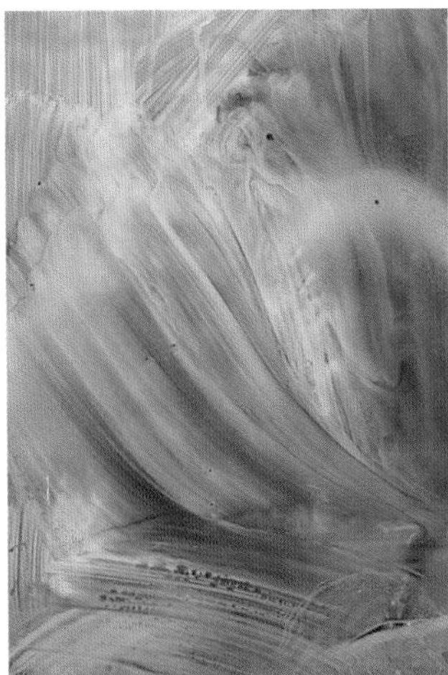

Paint the glass with special greenhouse window paint to reduce temperatures.

Suspend a sticky card from the roof to catch flying insects such as whitefly.

biological control

In the concentrated warmth and humidity of summer, pests and diseases can multiply rapidly under glass, so stay alert for early signs and take prompt action. Simple precautionary measures include keeping the greenhouse atmosphere humid to prevent red spider mites from spreading, hanging up sticky yellow cards as traps (see above), and keeping your plants in peak condition.

Aphids, whitefly, scale insects, red spider mites and vine weevils are the commonest greenhouse pests. They can be kept at acceptable levels by introducing a specific parasite or predator (see top right).

Biological controls are effective all season, but only if the pest is already present and the temperatures are high enough, so wait until you see the first signs in early summer. And remember, you cannot combine biological control with conventional spraying because the biological control will be killed by insecticides.

using coldframes in summer

Once you have finished hardening off tender plants, a coldframe remains a valuable asset all summer.

in June . . .

- **use it as a seedbed** for sowing biennials and perennials, and as a nursery bed for raising transplanted seedlings.
- **revive the soil** with compost or decayed manure, and plant 'self-blanching' celery, or melons or cucumbers 'on the flat', training their stems out from the centre, across the surface, to each corner.

biological control methods

TO CONTROL:	YOU NEED:
• aphids	• *Aphidius* parasite
• red spider mite	• *Phytoseiulus* parasite
• scale insect	• *Metaphycus* parasitic wasp
• vine weevil	• *Heterorhabditis* nematodes
• greenhouse whitefly	• *Encarsia* parasitic wasp

- **partially fill with leaves,** compost or sand to make a 'plunge bed' in which to stand, and keep cool, greenhouse pot plants when they are moved outdoors for the summer.

in July . . .

- **use it to house young cinerarias,** primroses and other winter pot plants. Keep the lid shaded, or filter sunlight with a screen of horticultural fleece.
- **make it into a propagating bed** for soft-tip cuttings (see page 212), semi-ripe cuttings (see page 227) and divisions of perennials (see page 124).
- **sow parsley,** endive and oriental vegetables.
- **dry garlic, shallots and onions** that overwintered in the ground, during a wet season.

Aubergines are in flower now. Pinch off some of the blooms if you do not want the plant to set too many small fruit. When the plant becomes heavy, support it with twiggy sticks.

the greenhouse/3

holiday care

In summer pests and diseases can become established quickly, so keep your eyes open, act fast and consider taking preventative action of the organic kind. You also need to make provision for plants while you are on holiday.

coping with pests and diseases

This is the main growth or migration time for many pests and diseases, with conditions just right for their rapid establishment, so take every precaution to avoid or prevent trouble.

- **inspect plants regularly** for the first sign of problems; hand-pick caterpillars, and collect slugs and snails late in the evening after rain.
- **practise good hygiene** by clearing up fallen fruit, dying leaves and other plant debris that can harbour pests and disease. Burn or dispose of affected material, but not on the compost heap.
- **use mechanical and biological controls** where possible (see page 257).
- **if you need to spray,** use a chemical specifically targeted at a particular pest or disease; always follow the manufacturer's instructions exactly. Afterwards, wash your hands and face, and all equipment, and dispose of any leftover solution safely on a vacant, out-of-the-way patch of soil.
- **never spray in bright sunshine** or windy weather; avoid spraying open flowers or wet leaves, and do not spray when bees are around.

Leaf cutter bees leave a distinctive hole in foliage. They do not harm the plants, and will help with pollination.

Snails congregate in empty containers and cool corners where plant debris has been left to rot.

holiday tips

Before you go on holiday take precautions to prevent problems while you are away.

- **thoroughly water everywhere** the night before you leave if the weather is dry.
- **apply a thick layer of mulch** to drought-sensitive plants after soaking them.
- **water and feed plants,** and move them away from sunny windows to stand in self-watering containers or a bowl or sink of shallow water.
- **deadhead all fading flowers** and remove dying leaves, especially from plants in pots.
- **gather ripe fruit and vegetables,** together with any that are nearly ready.
- **get up to date with pricking out** and potting on so that young plants continue growing unchecked.
- **ensure there is adequate shading**, and invest in an automatic ventilator and watering system.
- **arrange for a neighbour or friend to water** while you are away, and to pick ripening fruit and vegetables.

Mulching the surface of the compost helps to stop it from drying out.

greenhouse plants

Many greenhouse or conservatory plants grow rapidly and need more attention as temperatures rise, which makes early summer a good time to sow seed and root cuttings.

- **regularly water and feed** plants that are in active growth.
- **water cacti and succulents regularly** and stand outdoors if you can, desert species in full sun and forest kinds such as christmas cacti in light shade and with shelter from wind.
- **winter and spring-flowering bulbous plants,** such as lachenalias, hippeastrums and cyclamen, begin to die down and rest in summer, and require little watering.
- **mist leafy plants regularly** to increase humidity; a dry atmosphere encourages red spider mites, which are difficult to control once established.
- **watch out for aphids,** whitefly, mealy bugs and vine weevils, and treat at the first sign. Open windows may admit pests and diseases that readily colonise soft young growth.
- **deadhead plants regularly** and remove all dying leaves to prevent fungal diseases from taking hold.

Group containers together and plunge them into the soil when you go on holiday, to conserve moisture.

- **sow perennials** such as strelitzia, gloriosa, clivia and tender ferns in pots of seed compost and stand on a warm windowsill; they should germinate quickly in the summer heat and make strong seedlings before the winter.
- **take root cuttings** of callistemon, bougainvillea and similar tender woody-stemmed plants. Take soft-tip cuttings from non-flowering shoot tips (see page 212), and semi-ripe cuttings from sideshoots (see page 227).

the organic approach

This puts the emphasis on feeding the soil, raising its fertility with compost, manure and other organic materials, so that plants grow stronger and are better able to cope with problems. Converting to organic gardening methods takes time. You can make the change gradually, by reducing the use of chemical fertilisers, insecticides, fungicides and weedkillers year by year as you introduce these organic practices.

- **recycle vegetable waste** from both kitchen and garden to make compost.
- **seek out local supplies** of rotted animal manure, spent mushroom compost and composted bark.
- **sow green manures** on an empty piece of ground for digging in later to improve the soil.
- **choose plant varieties** that are resistant to pests and diseases and that enjoy the conditions found in your garden; sow or plant them at the right time; and tend them regularly so that they never lack for food, water and growing room.
- **cover the soil** with a 5cm (2in) mulch of rotted compost, composted bark, manure or other organic material to control weeds, conserve moisture and improve the soil structure.
- **feed plants with organic fertilisers** based on dried poultry manure, fishmeal, calcified seaweed or dried blood. Or use a liquid 'tea' made from composted plant materials.
- **avoid pest and disease** problems with good growing methods, a diversity of plants, physical barriers such as fleece, short-lived sprays of plant origin such as derris and pyrethrum, and biological controls like pheromone traps and parasites (see page 257).
- **encourage natural** predators, such as ladybirds, hover flies, toads, ground beetles, hedgehogs and bluetits, into the garden. Create suitable habitats, like a pond; provide cover and overwintering sites, such as a log pile; and leave food in strategic places.

Brightly coloured flowers attract hover flies, whose larvae feed on aphids.

summer

plant selector

Herbaceous plants, including climbers such as clematis and jasmine, are reaching the first of their flowering climaxes, with poppies, foxgloves, geraniums and bellflowers all looking their best. Summer is also the season of roses. With high summer the species roses come into bloom, followed a little later by a vast range of garden hybrids, from small-flowered patio gems to old-fashioned shrub roses and modern hybrid teas. Penstemons, pinks and delphiniums will soon brighten borders while the blooms of early annuals such as cornflowers, larkspurs and bright orange marigolds make the garden sparkle.

Clematis 'Jackmanii'

perennials

Although a few are evergreen, most durable non-woody plants are herbaceous, that is they die down in winter and re-emerge in spring. Plant when dormant, in autumn or early spring.

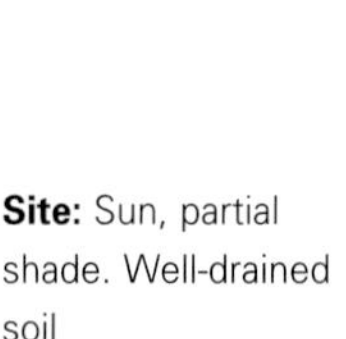

purple, blue and violet

1 Anchusa azurea 'Loddon Royalist'
Alkanet

Usually short-lived plant worth growing for the intense blue of its saucer-shaped flowers, which are carried in upright open sprays. May need to be staked. Hardy.
Height: 1m (3ft) **Spread:** 30cm (12in)
Site: Sun. Moist but well-drained soil
Use: Sunny border
Good companions: *Geum rivale* 'Leonard's Variety', *Hemerocallis lilioasphodelus, Iris sibirica* 'Ego'

2 Campanula lactiflora 'Prichard's Variety'
Milky bellflower

Through summer the leafy stems are topped by crowded sprays of starry bell-shaped flowers. These are usually blue or violet, although the soft pink of 'Loddon Anna' makes a useful exception; 'Prichard's Variety' has rich violet flowers. In exposed gardens it may need to be staked. Hardy.
Height: 1.5m (5ft) **Spread:** 60cm (2ft)
Site: Sun, partial shade. Fertile well-drained soil
Use: Sunny or lightly shaded border
Good companions: *Geranium* x *magnificum, Phlox paniculata* 'Fujiyama', *Rosa* Graham Thomas, *Thalictrum flavum* subsp. *glaucum*

3 Campanula latifolia

Pointed leaves diminish in size up erect stems that are topped by loose spikes of pale blue to deep violet or white narrowly tubular bells. The flowers of 'Brantwood', which grows up to 75cm (2ft 6in), are deep violet. Hardy.
Height: 1.2m (4ft) **Spread:** 60cm (2ft) or more
Site: Sun, partial shade. Well-drained soil.
Use: Sunny or lightly shaded border
Good companions: *Achillea* 'Taygetea', *Crocosmia* 'Lucifer', *Hemerocallis* 'Stella de Oro'

4 Campanula persicifolia
Peach-leaved bellflower

From an overwintering rosette of narrow toothed leaves rise wiry stems that support nicely spaced outward-facing bells. These are in shades of blue or white, and self-seeding populations produce a happy mixture. 'Telham Beauty' has light blue flowers. Those of 'Chettle Charm' are white with a purplish blue edge. There are also doubles in both blue and white. Hardy.
General care: Cut down stems of faded flowers.
Height: 75cm (2ft 6in)
Spread: 20cm (8in)
Site: Sun, partial shade. Well-drained soil
Use: Sunny or lightly shaded border, woodland garden
Good companions: *Achillea* 'Taygetea', *Anthemis tinctoria* 'E.C. Buxton', *Lupinus* 'Chandelier'

5 Delphinium Belladonna Group 'Atlantis'
Belladonna Group delphinium

Belladonna Group delphiniums form clumps of dark fingered leaves from which rise branched wiry stems that support spurred single flowers in shades of blue. The velvet flowers of 'Atlantis' are rich violet-blue. Hardy.
General care: To prolong the flowering season, remove stems of faded flowers promptly.
Height: 1m (3ft) **Spread:** 45cm (18in)
Site: Sun. Fertile and well-drained soil
Use: Sunny border
Good companions: *Geranium psilostemon, Incarvillea delavayi, Paeonia lactiflora* 'Festiva Maxima'

6 Festuca glauca 'Elijah Blue'
Fescue

Evergreen grass that forms a bristling blue-grey tuft of needle-like leaves. In late spring and early summer purplish green flowering spikelets stand above the foliage. Hardy.
Height and spread: 30cm (12in)
Site: Sun. Dry and well-drained soil
Use: Gravel garden, front of sunny border, raised bed, rock garden, ground cover
Good companions: *Campanula carpatica, Euphorbia myrsinites, Geranium cinereum* 'Ballerina'

7 Geranium 'Johnson's Blue'
Cranesbill

This forms a spreading clump of lobed leaves with notched and cut fingers. It creates a dense ground cover from spring to autumn, when the leaves take on warm tints. The production of light blue saucer-shaped flowers reaches its peak in midsummer. Hardy.
Height and spread: 40cm (16in)
Site: Sun, partial shade. Well-drained soil
Use: Ground cover, sunny or lightly shaded border
Good companions: *Ceratostigma willmottianum, Euonymus fortunei* 'Emerald 'n' Gold', *Muscari armeniacum, Sisyrinchium striatum* 'Aunt May'

8 Geranium x magnificum
Cranesbill

This forms a good clump of foliage that is mid-green in summer then develops warm tints in autumn. The rounded leaves are cut into several lobes and are hairy. The violet-blue of the glossy flowers is intensified by the darker colour of the many veins. The blooms are produced abundantly in midsummer. Hardy.
Height and spread: 60cm (2ft)
Site: Sun, partial shade. Well-drained soil
Use: Sunny or lightly shaded border
Good companions: *Clematis* 'Perle d'Azur', *Clematis* 'Royal Velours', *Hemerocallis* 'Stella de Oro', *Rosa* Graham Thomas

9 Geranium pratense 'Mrs Kendall Clark'

Meadow cranesbill

The lobed and cut leaves make attractive and effective ground cover from spring to autumn, when they take on warm tints. For several weeks in early and midsummer the foliage is topped by sprays of grey-blue flowers that may be tinted with palest pink. Hardy.

Height and spread: 60cm (2ft)

Site: Sun, partial shade. Moderately moist but well-drained soil

Use: Sunny or lightly shaded border, woodland garden

Good companions: *Anemone hupehensis* 'Hadspen Abundance', *Aster* x *frikartii* 'Mönch', *Polygonatum* x *hybridum*

10 Hosta 'Halcyon'

Plantain lily

A silvery blue foliage plant with elongated, heart-shaped leaves that are thick and waxy and overlap to form an impressive mound. In summer, smoky mauve flowers stand clear of the foliage. Needs some shade for best leaf colour. Hardy.

Height: 40cm (16in)

Spread: 75cm (2ft 6in)

Site: Partial shade. Fertile and moist but well-drained soil

Compost: Soil-based (John Innes No. 2) with added leaf-mould, or soil-less

Use: Container, ground cover, lightly shaded border, waterside

Good companions: *Cardamine pratensis* 'Flore Pleno', *Geranium macrorrhizum*, *Pulmonaria* 'Mawson's Blue'

11 Iris 'Jane Phillips'

Tall bearded iris

This long-established bearded iris retains its popularity, despite waves of new introductions, on account of its shapely blooms. The clear blue flowers have elegantly ruffled petals with dark veining around the white beards. They are vanilla scented. Hardy.

General care: Do not allow other plants to overshadow the roots (rhizomes). Divide these every three years.

Height: 1m (3ft): **Spread:** 25cm (10in)

Soil: Sun. Light and well-drained soil. Good on lime

Use: Sunny border

Good companions: *Clematis alpina* 'Frances Rivis', *Erysimum cheiri* 'Ivory White', *Paeonia lactiflora* 'Bowl of Beauty', *Tulipa* 'Queen of Night'

12 Iris sibirica 'Ego'

Siberian iris

Nicely shaped rich blue flowers flutter above a clump of grassy leaves. This iris thrives in reliably moist ground, but is also remarkably tolerant of drier conditions. Hardy.

Height: 1m (3ft) **Spread:** 20cm (8in)

Site: Sun. Fertile and moist but well-drained soil

Use: Sunny, moist border, waterside

Good companions: *Aquilegia* 'Hensol Harebell', *Euphorbia palustris*, *Trollius europaeus*

purple, blue and violet (continued)

1 Meconopsis betonicifolia
Himalayan blue poppy, Tibetan blue poppy

At their peak these short-lived plants present a pyramid of open saucer-shaped flowers. These consist of blue petals and yellow stamens around a central cone. The blue is best when the plant is grown in cool conditions. The erect flower stems and the blue-green leaves are covered with rust-coloured hairs. Hardy.

General care: To extend the life of plants prevent flowering in the first year by removing buds.
Height: 1.2m (4ft) **Spread:** 45cm (18in)
Site: Partial shade. Lime-free, humus-rich and moist but well-drained soil
Use: Woodland garden
Good companions: *Kirengeshoma palmata, Rhododendron luteum, Trillium grandiflorum*

2 Nepeta 'Six Hills Giant'
Catmint

Numerous large sprays of mauve-blue flowers emerge from a grey-green clump of small aromatic leaves. This plant blends with a wide range of colour schemes. Hardy.

General care: To encourage renewed flowering in late summer, trim away spent sprays of the first display.
Height: 75cm (2ft 6in) **Spread:** 60cm (2ft)
Site: Sun, partial shade. Well-drained soil
Use: Edging, front of sunny border, gravel garden, ground cover
Good companions: *Achillea* 'Taygetea', *Allium cristophii, Anthemis tinctoria* 'E.C. Buxton', *Verbascum* Cotswold Group 'Gainsborough'

3 Salvia x sylvestris 'Mainacht'
Sage

This softly hairy plant has crinkled leaves and produces numerous dark stems that are crowded with violet-blue hooded flowers from early to midsummer. These emerge from reddish bracts, which remain colourful after the flowers have fallen. Hardy.

Height: 60cm (2ft) **Spread:** 45cm (18in)
Site: Sun. Well-drained soil
Use: Gravel garden, sunny border
Good companions: *Papaver orientale* 'Black and White', *Stipa gigantea, Verbena bonariensis*

4 Veronica austriaca subsp. teucrium 'Kapitän'
Speedwell

Hummock-forming perennial that produces many upright stems set with small flowers of intense blue. 'Crater Lake Blue' also has vivid blue blooms, but is shorter and has a slightly later flowering season. Hardy.

Height and spread: 40cm (16in)
Site: Sun. Well-drained soil
Use: Front of sunny border, raised bed, rock garden
Good companions: *Campanula garganica, Dianthus* 'Gran's Favourite', *Diascia barberae* 'Ruby Field', *Festuca glauca* 'Elijah Blue'

5 Veronica gentianoides
Speedwell

Mat-forming plant with glossy dark green leaves arranged in rosettes. Graceful spires of pale blue flowers may first appear in late spring. Hardy.

Height: 35cm (14in) **Spread:** 45cm (18in)
Site: Sun. Well-drained soil
Use: Front of sunny border, gravel garden, raised bed, rock garden
Good companions: *Achillea* 'Taygetea', *Euphorbia polychroma, Helianthemum* 'Wisley Primrose'

pink and mauve

6 Acanthus spinosus
Bear's breeches

Substantial foliage plant with deeply cut spiny leaves. In late spring and early summer the glossy dark green leafy base is topped by spires of white flowers that are hooded with purplish pink petal-like bracts. Attractive seed heads follow. The Spinossima Group has smaller plants with grey-green leaves that are almost reduced to veins and spines. Hardy.

Height: 1.2m (4ft) **Spread:** 75cm (2ft 6in)
Site: Sun, partial shade. Well-drained soil
Use: Gravel garden, sunny or lightly shaded border
Good companions: *Allium hollandicum* 'Purple Sensation', *Euphorbia characias* subsp. *wulfenii, Stipa gigantea*

7 Dianthus 'Gran's Favourite'
Modern pink

The Modern pinks are evergreen perennials that produce single to double flowers in two or three, flushes between early summer and autumn. Most have prettily fringed petals and some are strongly scented. 'Gran's Favourite' has white double flowers with a purplish mauve centre and

petal margins, and is clove scented. Hardy.
Height: 30cm (12in) **Spread:** 40cm (16in)
Site: Sun. Well-drained soil, preferably limy
Use: Edging, front of a sunny border, raised bed, rock garden
Good companions: *Gypsophila repens* 'Rosa Schönheit', Lavandula angustifolia 'Nana Alba', *Sisyrinchium striatum* 'Aunt May'

8 Erysimum 'Bowles' Mauve'
Wallflower

Shrubby evergreen perennial with grey-green foliage and in spring and summer numerous spikes of four-petalled mauve flowers. Although unscented and often short-lived, it warrants a place for its extended flowering. Hardy.
Height: 75cm (2ft 6in) **Spread:** 60cm (2ft)
Site: Sun. Well-drained soil, preferably limy
Use: Gravel garden, large rock garden, sunny border
Good companions: *Artemisia ludoviciana* 'Valerie Finnis', *Eryngium* x *tripartitum, Lavandula* x *intermedia* Dutch Group

9 Geranium psilostemon
Armenian cranesbill

With above average foliage, this plant makes a large clump of deeply cut leaves that in autumn are randomly tinted red. Arresting, dark-eyed magenta flowers are produced freely throughout summer. Hardy.
Height: 1m (3ft) **Spread:** 60cm (2ft)
Site: Sun, partial shade. Well-drained soil
Use: Sunny or lightly shaded border, woodland garden
Good companions: *Anemone* x *hybrida* 'Honorine Jobert', *Aquilegia vulgaris* 'Nivea', *Polemonium* 'Lambrook Mauve', *Viburnum opulus* 'Compactum'

10 Hemerocallis 'Catherine Woodbery'
Daylily

Evergreen daylily with narrow linear leaves and mauve-pink starry blooms that are wide petalled, slightly ruffled and sweetly scented. Although individually short-lived, these are borne over several weeks from midsummer. Hardy.
Height: 75cm (2ft 6in) **Spread:** 60cm (2ft)
Site: Sun, partial shade. Fertile and moist but well-drained soil
Use: Sunny border
Good companions: *Campanula lactiflora, Geranium* 'Johnson's Blue', *Monarda* 'Prärienacht'

11 Incarvillea delavayi

Rich pink trumpet-shaped flowers, several per sturdy stem, stand above a rosette of divided leaves. The flared mouth of each flower is surrounded by five wavy lobes. Hardy.
General care: Mark the position of the plant as it is late coming into growth.
Height: 60cm (2ft) **Spread:** 30cm (12in)
Site: Sun. Fertile and moist but well-drained soil
Use: Rock garden, sunny border
Good companions: *Galtonia candicans, Liatris spicata, Polemonium* 'Lambrook Mauve'

12 Iris 'Pearly Dawn'
Tall bearded iris

Like most of the tall bearded irises, this has a flowering season that spans late spring and early summer. The gauzy ruffled petals are delicate shades of creamy pink. Hardy.
Height: 75cm (2ft 6in) **Spread:** 20cm (8in)
Site: Sun. Well-drained soil, preferably neutral
Use: Sunny border
Good companions: *Campanula lactiflora, Lupinus* 'Chandelier', *Paeonia mlokosewitschii, Rosa* 'Nevada'

pink and mauve (continued)

1 Paeonia lactiflora 'Bowl of Beauty'
Herbaceous peony

This example of an imperial, or anemone-form, peony has goblet-shaped semi-double flowers with pink petals and creamy petal-like strips (petaloids), which replace true stamens. Hardy.
Height and spread: 1m (3ft)
Site: Sun, partial shade. Fertile and moist but well-drained soil
Use: Sunny or lightly shaded border
Good companions: *Hydrangea paniculata* 'Unique', *Osmanthus delavayi*, *Rosa* Mary Rose

2 Persicaria bistorta 'Superba'
Bistort

Broad basal leaves make a light green weed-excluding clump, above which branching stems hold up short 'bottlebrushes' of tiny soft pink blooms. Starts flowering in late spring. Hardy.
Height and spread: 1m (3ft)
Site: Sun, partial shade. Fertile and moist soil
Use: Ground cover, moist border, waterside, wild garden
Good companions: *Astrantia major* subsp. *involucrata* 'Shaggy', *Hemerocallis* 'Summer Wine', *Rodgersia pinnata* 'Superba'

3 Thalictrum aquilegiifolium
Meadow rue

The light green foliage has a ferny delicacy, above which sprays of tiny purplish buds open to fluffy heads of mauve-pink stamens. In the form 'Thundercloud' the misty flower clusters are dark purple. Hardy.
Height: 1m (3ft) **Spread:** 45cm (18in)
Site: Sun, partial shade, Humus-rich and moist but well-drained soil
Use: Sunny or lightly shaded border
Good companions: *Aconitum* 'Ivorine', *Fuchsia magellanica* 'Versicolor', *Hosta* 'Halcyon'

4 Tiarella wherryi
Foam flower

This forms slow-spreading clumps of hairy maple-like leaves, which usually show bronze tints or flecks on pale green and in winter become coppery. In late spring and early summer there are spikes of tiny starry flowers that are pink-tinted cream. Hardy.
Height: 35cm (14in) **Spread:** 30cm (12in)
Site: Partial shade, shade. Humus-rich and moist but well-drained soil
Good companions: *Erythronium californicum* 'White Beauty', *Trillium grandiflorum, Uvularia grandiflora*

5 Verbascum 'Helen Johnson'
Mullein

The over-wintering grey-green and finely downy leaves of this plant are arranged in a rosette. From this erupts a branched spike that carries flowers in an unusual shade of brown-pink. An attractive and easy plant but often not long-lived. Hardy.
Height: 75cm (2ft 6in) **Spread:** 30cm (12in)
Site: Sun. Well-drained soil. Good on lime
Use: Gravel garden, rock garden, sunny border
Good companions: *Achillea* 'Taygetea', *Eryngium alpinum, Ruta graveolens* 'Jackman's Blue', *Scabiosa caucasica* 'Moerheim Blue'

6 Veronica spicata 'Heidekind'
Speedwell

This useful variation of the blue-flowered mat-forming species produces short spikes of small pink flowers above grey-green leaves over a long flowering season in midsummer. Hardy.
Height: 30cm (12in) **Spread:** 45cm (18in)
Site: Sun. Moist but well-drained soil
Use: Edging, front of sunny border, large rock garden or raised bed
Good companions: *Anchusa azurea* 'Loddon Royalist', *Diascia rigescens, Penstemon* 'Evelyn'

bronze and maroon

7 Geum rivale 'Leonard's Variety'
Water avens

From a clump of divided leaves rise branching mahogany stems that bear drooping bell-shaped flowers. The petals are orange-pink and the calyx (the structure at the base of the flower) is maroon. Hardy.
Height: 40cm (16in) **Spread:** 50cm (20in)
Site: Sun, partial shade. Humus-rich, moist soil
Use: Front of sunny or lightly shaded border, waterside
Good companions: *Astrantia major* subsp. *involucrata* 'Shaggy', *Caltha palustris* 'Flore Pleno', *Phalaris arundinacea* var. *picta* 'Feesey'

red and russet

8 Aquilegia McKana Group
Columbine

Long-spurred flowers in red, yellow or blue, often bicoloured as shown here, are elegantly poised at different angles above divided foliage. Plants are usually short-lived but populations are maintained by self-seeding. Hardy.

Height: 75cm (2ft 6in) **Spread:** 60cm (2ft)
Site: Sun, partial shade. Moist and well-drained soil
Use: Sunny or lightly shaded border, woodland garden
Good companions: *Aconitum* 'Spark's Variety', *Geranium psilostemon, Smilacina racemosa, Viburnum* x *bodnantense* 'Dawn'

9 Astilbe x arendsii 'Fanal'
Astilbe

This is a richly coloured astilbe with dark green, prettily serrated divided leaves. Long-lasting plumes of tiny deep red flowers remain attractive after the colour has faded. Does well in full sun only where the soil is reliably moist. Hardy.

Height: 60cm (2ft) **Spread:** 45cm (18in)
Site: Partial shade, sun. Humus-rich, moist, even boggy soil
Use: Bog garden, moist border, waterside
Good companions: *Astilbe chinensis* var. *taquetii* 'Superba', *Euphorbia palustris, Hosta* 'Royal Standard', *Rheum palmatum* 'Atrosanguineum'

10 Paeonia lactiflora 'Karl Rosenfield'
Herbaceous peony

Double herbaceous peonies may lack the refinement of the singles but they last longer in flower. They all have attractive foliage that is tinted red-brown in spring. This example bears deep wine-red globe-shaped blooms on strong stems and is good for cutting. Hardy.

General care: Insert supports before plants are fully developed.
Height and spread: 75cm (2ft 6in)
Site: Sun, partial shade. Fertile and moist but well-drained soil
Use: Sunny or lightly shaded border
Good companions: *Aconitum* 'Spark's Variety', *Fuchsia magellanica* 'Versicolor', *Rosa* 'Céleste', *Rosa* 'Louise Odier'

yellow and orange

11 Euphorbia griffithii 'Fireglow'
Milkwood, spurge

A colonising euphorbia with running roots, but where there is room for it the orange-red flower-like bracts that stand above the rich green leaves make welcome patches of colour in sun or shade. Hardy.

Height: 75cm (2ft 6in) **Spread:** 1m (3ft)
Site: Partial shade, sun. Moist but well-drained soil
Use: Sunny or lightly shaded border, woodland garden
Good companions: *Epimedium* x *versicolor* 'Sulphureum', *Helleborus argutifolius, Hemerocallis* 'Summer Wine'

12 Kniphofia 'Early Buttercup'
Red hot poker, torch lily

Red hot pokers provide some of the most effective vertical accents in borders. This early flowering deciduous hybrid produces spikes of tubular orange-yellow flowers from a clump of narrow leaves. Hardy.

Height: 1m (3ft)
Spread: 60cm (2ft)
Site: Sun. Humus-rich and moist but well-drained soil
Use: Sunny border
Good companions: *Crocosmia* x *crocosmiiflora* 'Emily McKenzie', *Hemerocallis lilioasphodelus, Miscanthus sinensis* 'Silberfeder'

yellow and orange (continued)

1 Achillea 'Taygetea'
Yarrow

Flat, pale yellow flowerheads, which can be up to 10cm (4in) across, top a clump of silver-grey ferny leaves. Flowering often continues through summer. Good for cutting. Hardy.

Height: 50cm (20in) **Spread:** 45cm (18in)
Site: Sun. Well-drained soil
Use: Gravel garden, sunny border
Good companions: *Coreopsis verticillata* 'Grandiflora', *Iris* 'Rare Edition', *Origanum laevigatum* 'Herrenhausen'

2 Anthemis tinctoria 'E.C. Buxton'
Golden marguerite, Oxeye chamomile

Golden marguerites are stiff-stemmed perennials with ferny leaves. Various cultivars produce large quantities of daisy-like flowers in shades of yellow. Throughout summer 'E.C. Buxton' bears lemon-yellow blooms that complement a range of colour schemes. Often short-lived. Hardy.

General care: Cut back hard immediately after flowering.
Height and spread: 1m (3ft)
Site: Sun. Well-drained soil
Use: Gravel garden, sunny border
Good companions: *Allium cristophii*, *Artemisia* 'Powis Castle', *Gladiolus communis* subsp. *byzantinus*, *Stachys byzantina* 'Silver Carpet'

3 Hakonechloa macra 'Alboaurea'

The arching ribbon-like leaves of this slowly spreading and clump-forming deciduous grass make a soft mound. Their warm yellow variegation is deepened by shades of tan. Hardy.

Height and spread: 45cm (18in)
Site: Partial shade, sun. Humus-rich and moist but well-drained soil
Compost: Soil-based (John Innes No. 2) with added leaf-mould
Use: Container, sunny or lightly shaded border
Good companions: *Heuchera micrantha* var. *diversifolia* 'Palace Purple', *Hosta* 'Royal Standard', *Ophiopogon planiscapus* 'Nigrescens'

4 Hemerocallis lilioasphodelus
Daylily

From a clump of semi-evergreen narrow leaves rise stems carrying star-shaped clear yellow flowers. These are sweetly scented. Hardy.

Height and spread: 1m (3ft)
Site: Sun, partial shade. Fertile and moist but well-drained soil
Use: Sunny or lightly shaded border
Good companions: *Geranium* 'Johnson's Blue', *Geranium* x *magnificum*, *Ranunculus aconitifolius* 'Flore Pleno'

5 Hosta 'Gold Standard'
Plantain lily

This striking foliage plant forms a clump of conspicuously veined, oval to heart-shaped leaves that are

greenish yellow with an irregular, narrow, dark green margin. There are mauve-blue, funnel-shaped flowers in midsummer. Hardy.
Height: 60cm (2ft) **Spread:** 75cm (2ft 6in)
Site: Sun, partial shade. Fertile and moist but well-drained soil
Use: Ground cover, sunny or lightly shaded border
Good companions: *Euphorbia griffithii* 'Fireglow', *Hakonechloa macra* 'Alboaurea', *Miscanthus sinensis* 'Zebrinus', *Tellima grandiflora* 'Purpurteppich'

6 Lupinus 'Chandelier'
Lupin
The leaves of the hybrid lupins have long slender leaflets that are covered with fine hairs. The flowers are ranked in dense vertical spikes and often show a contrast of two colours, as in 'Chandelier', which combines pale and rich yellow. 'The Governor' has deep blue and white flowers. Hardy.
General care: To encourage the production of secondary spikes, remove the first spikes as soon as the flowers have faded.
Height: 1m (3ft) **Spread:** 75cm (2ft 6in)
Site: Sun, partial shade. Lime-free, light and well-drained soil
Use: Sunny or lightly shaded border
Good companions: *Aquilegia* McKana Group, *Aster* x *frikartii* 'Mönch', *Echinacea purpurea*

7 Miscanthus sinensis 'Zebrinus'
Zebra grass
Stiff stems make an upright clump from which gracefully arch narrow leaves. These have yellow crossbanding at broken intervals. This striking grass rarely produces flowers in a northern temperate summer. Hardy.
Height: 1.2m (4ft) **Spread:** 60cm (2ft)
Site: Sun. Moist but well-drained soil
Use: Sunny border, waterside
Good companions: *Cortaderia selloana* 'Sunningdale Silver', *Miscanthus sinensis* 'Silberfeder', *Phormium* 'Sundowner'

8 Thalictrum flavum subsp. glaucum
Yellow meadow rue
The frond-like leaves are blue-grey with hints of purple; excellent for flower arrangements. In midsummer stout stems carrying fluffy heads of pale yellow flowers rise through the foliage. Hardy.
General care: Plants usually need staking.
Height: 1.5m (5ft) **Spread:** 60cm (2ft)
Site: Partial shade, sun. Fertile and moist but well-drained soil
Use: Lightly shaded or sunny border, waterside
Good companions: *Aconitum* 'Spark's Variety', *Ligularia* 'The Rocket', *Miscanthus sinensis* 'Silberfeder'

9 Verbascum Cotswold Group 'Gainsborough'
Mullein
Crinkled grey leaves radiate to form a basal rosette from which rise strong vertical spikes that are set with numerous saucer-shaped flowers of cool lemon-yellow. Not long-lived but an excellent tall upright plant for growing among other sun-lovers. Hardy.
General care: To encourage the development of secondary flower spikes cut down old spikes as soon as flowers fade.
Height: 1.2m (4ft) **Spread:** 40cm (16in)
Site: Sun. Well-drained soil. Good on lime
Use: Gravel garden, sunny border
Good companions: *Artemisia* 'Powis Castle', *Eryngium* x *tripartitum*, *Verbena bonariensis*

cream and white

10 Aconitum 'Ivorine'
Aconite, monkshood
Cut lobed leaves form a rich green clump from which rise spires of creamy-white hooded flowers in late spring and early summer. Excellent in the garden and for cutting. All parts of the plant are toxic and contact with the foliage may cause a skin reaction. Hardy.
Height: 1m (3ft) **Spread:** 45cm (18in)
Site: Partial shade, sun. Fertile, humus-rich and moist but well-drained soil
Use: Border, woodland garden
Good companions: *Astilbe* 'Professor van der Wielen', *Dryopteris wallichiana*, *Hosta lancifolia*, *Polygonatum* x *hybridum*

11 Astilbe x arendsii 'Irrlicht'
Frothy plumes of white flowers rise above an attractive clump formed from dark green divided leaves. Although this plant starts to bloom in late spring, it reaches its peak in early summer. The plumes remain ornamental after the flowers have faded. Hardy.
Height and spread: 50cm (20in)
Site: Partial shade, sun. Humus-rich and moist, even boggy soil
Use: Bog garden, moist border, waterside
Good companions: *Lobelia* 'Queen Victoria', *Persicara bistorta* 'Superba', *Rodgersia pinnata* 'Superba'

12 Geranium clarkei x collinum 'Kashmir White'
Cranesbill
This plant spreads underground to produce a ground-covering carpet of lobed and deeply divided leaves. Throughout summer there are white flowers, which are prettily marked with narrow purple veins. Hardy.
Height: 45cm (18in) **Spread:** 75cm (2ft 6in)
Site: Sun, partial shade. Well-drained soil
Use: Ground cover, sunny or lightly shaded border, woodland garden
Good companions: *Dicentra* 'Langtrees', *Epimedium* x *youngianum* 'Niveum', *Tiarella cordifolia*

cream and white (continued)

1 Hosta 'Francee'
Plantain lily

Rich green puckered and veined leaves, defined by a crisp white margin, make a substantial clump of foliage. In summer arching stems carry mauve funnel-shaped flowers. Hardy.

Height: 60cm (2ft) **Spread:** 1m (3ft)
Site: Partial shade, sun. Fertile and moist but well-drained soil
Compost: Soil-based (John Innes No. 2) with added leaf-mould, or soil-less
Use: Container, lightly shaded or sunny border, waterside, woodland garden
Good companions: *Brunnera macrophylla, Dicentra spectabilis, Dryopteris erythrosora, Tiarella wherryi*

2 Hosta 'Ginko Craig'
Plantain lily

Variegated foliage plant with white-margined dark green leaves and in summer violet-purple trumpet-shaped flowers. In full shade leaves may be completely white. On young specimens leaves are lance shaped, but may be broader on plants left to build up for several years. Hardy.

Height: 25cm (10in) **Spread:** 45cm (18in)
Site: Partial shade, shade. Fertile and moist but well-drained soil
Use: Shaded border, waterside, woodland garden
Good companions: *Aconitum* 'Spark's Variety', *Dicentra spectabilis, Geranium macrorrhizum* 'Ingwersen's Variety'

1

2

3 Iris pallida 'Argentea Variegata'
Bearded iris

Clump of sword-like leaves that are striped vertically grey-green and white. Scented soft blue flowers emerge crinkled from silvered papery bracts for a brief season in early summer. Hardy.

Height: 1m (3ft) **Spread:** 25cm (10in)
Site: Sun. Fertile and well-drained soil, preferably neutral
Use: Gravel garden, sunny border
Good companions: *Artemesia ludoviciana* 'Valerie Finnis', *Lupinus* 'Chandelier', *Verbascum* Cotswold Group 'Gainsborough'

4 Leucanthemum x superbum 'Snowcap'
Shasta daisy

The good show of white blooms has made the shasta daisy hybrids popular summer flowers in spite of their undistinguished dark green foliage. Taller examples, such as the double 'Wirral Supreme', are good for cutting, but in the garden the stems, up to 75cm (2ft 6in) long, often need support. The free-flowering single 'Snowcap' is self-reliant. Hardy.

Height and spread: 45cm (18in)
Site: Sun, partial shade. Moist but well-drained soil
Use: Sunny or lightly shaded border
Good companions: *Ceratostigma willmottianum, Gladiolus* 'The Bride', *Veronica spicata* 'Heidekind'

5 Paeonia lactiflora 'Festiva Maxima'
Herbaceous peony

Stout stems carry scented double flowers, with loosely jumbled petals, above a good clump of leaves. The blooms are white, red tinged at first, and sparingly flecked with crimson. Good for cutting. Hardy.

General care: Insert supports before plants are fully developed.
Height and spread: 75cm (2ft 6in)
Site: Sun, partial shade. Fertile and moist but well-drained soil
Use: Sunny or lightly shaded border
Good companions: *Lilium regale, Paeonia lactiflora* 'Bowl of Beauty', *Rosa* Mary Rose

6 Papaver orientale 'Black and White'
Oriental poppy

Elegantly wavy petals make a white cup that is stained crimson-black at the base and cradles a ring of black stamens. Best sited behind other plants to hide the hairy leaves when flowering is over. Hardy.

Height: 75cm (2ft 6in) **Spread:** 60cm (2ft)
Site: Sun. Well-drained soil
Use: Gravel garden, sunny border
Good companions: *Coreopsis verticillata* 'Grandiflora', *Echinops ritro* 'Veitch's Blue', *Eryngium alpinum*

7 Phalaris arundinacea var. picta 'Feesey'
Gardener's garters

This is a much less invasive plant than the evergreen variegated species. It has ribbon-like leaves that are more white than green and pale green flower spikes with a purplish tinge. Hardy.

General care: Cut down old stems in late spring.
Height and spread: 1m (3ft)
Site: Sun, partial shade. Reasonably moist but well-drained soil
Use: Ground cover, sunny or lightly shaded border, water side
Good companions: *Hemerocallis* 'Summer Wine', *Monarda* 'Prärienacht', *Macleaya cordata* 'Flamingo', *Phormium* 'Sundowner'

3

8 Sisyrinchium striatum 'Aunt May'

Blade-like grey-green leaves, striped lengthwise with creamy yellow, make an iris-like clump out of which zig-zag spikes of cream flowers. Hardy.

Height: 50cm (20in)
Spread: 25cm (10in)
Site: Sun. Well-drained soil
Use: Gravel garden, sunny border
Good companions: *Euphorbia polychroma, Knautia macedonica, Sedum spectabile* 'Brilliant', *Veronica austriaca* subsp. *teucrium* 'Kapitän'

4

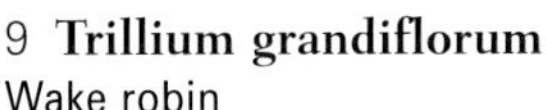

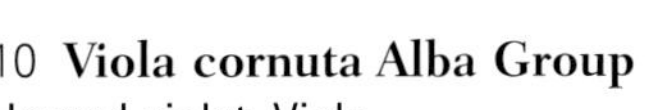

9 Trillium grandiflorum

Wake robin

The leaves and the parts of the flower are arranged in threes. The veined, pristine white flowers are backed by green petal-like sepals and often take on a pink tint as they age. 'Flore Pleno' is a beautifully proportioned double. Hardy.

Height: 40cm (16in) **Spread:** 30cm (12in)

Site: Partial shade, shade. Fertile, humus-rich and moist but well-drained soil, preferably lime-free

Use: Shady border, woodland garden

Good companions: *Buddleja davidii* 'Black Knight', *Verbascum* 'Helen Johnson'

10 Viola cornuta Alba Group

Horned violet, Viola

White flowers are borne in profusion in spring and summer and often again in late summer if the plant is clipped back after the first display. Useful for lighting up the base of shrubs. Blue and purple forms are also worth growing. Hardy.

Height: 20cm (8in) **Spread:** 45cm (18in)

Site: Sun, partial shade. Fertile and moist but well-drained soil

Use: Sunny or lightly shaded border

Good companions: *Geranium* 'Johnson's Blue', *Rosa glauca, Spiraea japonica* 'Anthony Waterer'

silver and grey

11 Artemisia ludoviciana 'Valerie Finnis'

Western mugwort

Foliage plant with silvery-grey cut leaves arranged in flower-like rosettes. Useful for teaming with many summer flowers. Yellow-brown flowerheads appear in the second half of summer. Hardy.

Height and spread: 60cm (2ft)

Site: Sun. Well-drained soil

Use: Gravel garden, sunny border

Good companions: *Allium* 'Globemaster', *Gladiolus communis* subsp. *byzantinus, Lavandula* x *intermedia* Dutch Group, *Stachys byzantina* 'Silver Carpet'

12 Artemisia 'Powis Castle'

Mugwort, Sagebrush, Wormwood

Evergreen shrubby foliage plant. The finely dissected grey foliage makes a dense mound and in a hot dry summer creates the effect of shimmering silver filigree. Not fully hardy.

Height: 75cm (2ft 6in) **Spread:** 1.2m (4ft)

Site: Sun. Well-drained soil

Use: Gravel garden, sunny border

Good companions: *Buddleja davidii* 'Black Knight', *Verbascum* 'Helen Johnson'

silver and grey (continued)

1 Hosta sieboldiana var. elegans
Plantain lily

One of the most distinguished herbaceous foliage plants, this has large, almost heart-shaped blue-green leaves, up to 30cm (12in) long. These are thick and waxy, with a puckered and veined surface that creates a rich pattern of shadows when lit from the side. Pale mauve trumpet-shaped flowers appear in early summer. Hardy.

Height: 1m (3ft) **Spread:** 1.2m (4ft)
Site: Sun, partial shade. Fertile and moist but well-drained soil
Compost: Soil-based (John Innes No. 2) with added leaf-mould, or soil-less
Use: Container, ground cover, sunny or lightly shaded border, waterside
Good companions: *Brunnera macrophylla, Digitalis purpurea, Viola cornuta* Alba Group

2 Stachys byzantina 'Silver Carpet'
Lambs' ears, Lambs' lugs, Lambs' tails, Lambs' tongues

Common names for the species refer to the shape and thickness of the leaves and their woolly texture. This non-flowering form makes a dense carpet of grey-green leaves. Hardy.

Height: 25cm (10in) **Spread:** 60cm (2ft)
Soil: Sun. Well-drained soil
Use: Gravel garden, ground cover, front of sunny border
Good companions: *Gypsophila* 'Rosenschleier', *Nepeta* 'Six Hills Giant', *Origanum laevigatum* 'Herrenhausen'

green

3 Alchemilla mollis
Lady's mantle

Foliage plant with light green rounded leaves that are softly hairy and have a wavy and serrated outline. Airy sprays of tiny greenish yellow flowers froth above and around the clump from early and into late summer. Self-seeds freely. Hardy.

Height: 50cm (20in) **Spread:** 75cm (2ft 6in)
Site: Sun, partial shade. Well-drained soil
Use: Ground cover, sunny or shaded border
Good companions: *Cornus kousa* var. *chinensis*, *Hydrangea paniculata* 'Unique', *Paeonia delavayi* var. *ludlowii*

4 Asplenium scolopendrium
Hart's tongue fern

Bright evergreen fern with glossy, leathery fronds that are strap shaped with a wavy margin. In the Crispum Group the frond margins are more strongly crimped and waved. Hardy.

Height and spread: 60cm (2ft)
Site: Partial shade. Humus-rich and moist but well-drained soil
Use: Shady border, woodland garden
Good companions: *Galanthus nivalis, Helleborus orientalis, Prunus* x *subhirtella* 'Autumnalis'

5 Astrantia major subsp. involucrata 'Shaggy'
Hattie's pincushion, Masterwort

This has deeply cut fingered leaves and each 'pincushion' is surrounded by long bracts that resemble green-tipped petals of pink-flushed flowers. Hardy.

Height: 60cm (2ft) **Spread:** 45cm (18in)
Site: Sun, partial shade. Humus-rich, moist soil
Use: Moist border, waterside, woodland garden
Good companions: *Cardamine pratensis* 'Flore Pleno', *Dicentra spectabilis, Dryopteris affinis*

6 Hosta 'Royal Standard'
Plantain lily

This large hosta is grown mainly for its glossy mid-green leaves. These are of elongated heart shape and deeply veined. In summer the clump is topped by scented white flowers. Hardy.

Height: 1m (3ft) **Spread:** 1.2m (4ft)
Site: Partial shade, sun. Fertile and moist but well-drained soil
Compost: Soil-based (John Innes No. 2) with added leaf-mould, or soil-less
Use: Container, ground cover, sunny or lightly shaded border, waterside
Good companions: *Astilbe* 'Bronce Elegans', *Astilbe* x *arendsii* 'Irrlicht', *Hemerocallis* 'Pardon Me'

pelargoniums

These tender evergreen perennials are grown as bedding and container plants for their colourful flowers and foliage. They need a well-drained soil or soil-based (John Innes No. 2) or soil-less compost, and must be overwintered under glass, at a minimum temperature of 2°C (36°F).

1

1 Pelargonium 'Chocolate Peppermint'

Scented-leaved pelargonium with chocolate-marked dark green leaves. Peppermint scented when bruised. Small mauve flowers in summer.
Height: 45cm (18in) **Spread:** 75cm (2ft 6in)
Good companions: *Helichrysum petiolare*, *Tropaeolum* Alaska Series, *Verbena* 'Peaches and Cream'

2 Pelargonium 'Bird Dancer'

Stellar pelargonium with aromatic leaves and spindly flowers composed of three pale pink bottom petals and two salmon-pink top petals.
Height: 20cm (8in) **Spread:** 15cm (6in)
Good companions: *Helichrysum petiolare*, *Lobelia erinus* 'Cobalt Blue', *Pelargonium* 'Copthorne'

3 Pelargonium 'Caroline Schmidt'

Erect, bushy fancy-leaved zonal pelargonium with bright red double flowers and silvery-white-edged rounded leaves.
Height: 30cm (12in) **Spread:** 20cm (8in)
Good companions: *Antirrhinum* 'Tahiti', *Brachyscome iberidifolia* Splendour Series, *Tropaeolum* 'Alaska'

4 Pelargonium 'Copthorne'

Shrubby scented-leaved pelargonium that releases a cedar-like spicy scent when bruised. The pale mauve flowers are heavily marked on the upper petals.
Height: 50cm (20in) **Spread:** 25cm (10in)
Good companions: *Fuchsia* 'La Campanella', *Lobelia erinus* Cascade Series, *Verbena* 'Imagination'

5 Pelargonium 'Bolero'

Bushy Unique pelargonium with aromatic grey-green leaves and darkly marked salmon-pink trumpet-shaped flowers.
Height: 60cm (2ft)
Spread: 30cm (12in)
Good companions: *Argyranthemum* 'Snow Storm', *Osteospermum jucundum*, *Petunia* Surfinia Purple

6 Pelargonium 'L'Elégante'

Trailing ivy-leaved pelargonium, much used as a foliage plant for containers. The cream variegation of the leaves is often flushed purplish pink if the plant is kept dry. Clusters of single white flowers are lightly tinted mauve.
Height: 20cm (8in) **Spread:** 30cm (12in)
Good companions: *Felicia amelloides* 'Santa Anita', *Scaevola aemula* 'Blue Wonder', *Verbena* 'Silver Anne'

7 Pelargonium 'Paton's Unique'

Vigorous, shrubby pelargonium with strongly aromatic lobed leaves. The magenta-pink funnel-shaped flowers have purple veins and a white throat.
Height: 20cm (8in) **Spread:** 30cm (12in)
Good companions: *Convulvulus sabatius*, *Diascia barberae* 'Ruby Field', *Pelargonium* 'L'Elégante'

8 Pelargonium 'Captain Starlight'

Shrubby Angel pelargonium with small bicoloured single flowers. The upper petals are purple and the lower ones mauve.
Height: 35cm (14in) **Spread:** 20cm (8in)
Good companions: *Fuchsia* 'La Campanella', *Lobelia erinus* Cascade Series, *Pelargonium* 'L'Elégante'

annuals & biennials

Since annuals and biennials quickly reach flowering maturity, they are the ideal plants for filling beds and containers with colourful summer displays.

purple, blue and violet

1 Centaurea cyanus
Blue-bottle, Cornflower

The fringed flowerheads of this annual are usually an intense violet-blue, but white, pink and red cultivars are also available. Tall cultivars are excellent for cutting. Hardy.
General care: Sow seed *in situ* in early autumn or early spring.
Height: 1m (3ft) **Spread:** 20cm (8in)
Soil: Sun. Well-drained soil
Use: Sunny bed or border, wildflower garden
Good companions: *Delphinium grandiflorum* 'Blue Butterfly', *Papaver rhoeas* 'Mother of Pearl'

2 Consolida ajacis Giant Imperial Series
Larkspur

An erect annual with finely dissected leaves and dense spikes of single or double flowers in blue, purple, pink or white. Excellent for cutting. Hardy.
General care: Sow seed *in situ* in early autumn or in mid to late spring.
Height: 1m (3ft) **Spread:** 35cm (14in)
Site: Sun. Well-drained soil
Use: Sunny bed or border
Good companions: *Papaver rhoeas* 'Mother of Pearl', *Salvia viridis* 'Oxford Blue'

3 Delphinium grandiflorum 'Blue Butterfly'
Short-lived perennial usually grown as an annual. The blue funnel-shaped flowers are spurred and carried above a base of fingered leaves. Hardy.
General care: Sow seed under glass at 13°C (55°F) in late winter. Plant out in late spring or early summer.
Height: 50cm (20in) **Spread:** 30cm (12in)
Site: Sun. Well-drained soil
Use: Sunny bed or border
Good companions: *Gladiolus* 'The Bride', *Nigella damascena* 'Miss Jekyll', *Tagetes* 'Lemon Gem'

4 Nigella damascena 'Miss Jekyll'
Devil-in-a-bush, Love-in-a-mist

Bushy annual with feathery foliage and sky-blue semi-double flowers within a ruff of thread-like bracts, over a long summer season. Hardy.
General care: Sow seed *in situ* in early autumn or early spring.
Height: 45cm (18in) **Spread:** 25cm (10in)
Site: Sun. Well-drained soil
Use: Sunny bed or border
Good companions: *Antirrhinum* Sonnet Series, *Eschscholzia californica*, *Papaver nudicaule*

5 Verbena 'Imagination'
Sprawling hybrid verbena raised annually from seed, with heads of small violet flowers above divided leaves throughout summer. Half hardy.
General care: Sow seed under glass at 18-21°C (64-70°F) in late winter to early spring. Plant out in early summer.
Height: 45cm (18in) **Spread:** 50cm (20in)
Site: Sun. Moist but well-drained soil
Compost: Soil-based (John Innes No. 2) or soil-less
Use: Container, sunny bed
Good companions: *Fuchsia* 'La Campanella', *Petunia* 'Surfinia Purple', *Viola* x *wittrockiana* 'Jolly Joker'

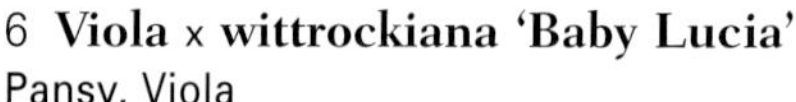

6 Viola x wittrockiana 'Baby Lucia'
Pansy, Viola

Short-lived evergreen perennial grown as an annual for its generous display of small, yellow-eyed blue flowers in spring and summer. Hardy.
General care: Sow seed under glass in late winter or early spring, or outdoors in mid-spring. To prolong flowering deadhead regularly.
Height: 15cm (6in) **Spread:** 20cm (8in)
Site: Sun, partial shade. Humus-rich and moist but well-drained soil
Compost: Soil-based (John Innes No. 2) or soil-less
Use: Container, formal bedding, front of border
Good companions: *Nicotiana* 'Lime Green', *Tropaeolum* 'Alaska', *Tulipa* 'Spring Green'

pink and mauve

7 Ageratum houstonianum
Floss flower

Most cultivars of this annual are compact plants with downy, heart-shaped leaves and clusters of fluffy pompon flowerheads in blue, mauve, pink or white. Flowers until the first frosts. Half hardy.
General care: Sow seed under glass, at 14–16°C (57–61°F), in early to mid-spring. Plant out in early summer.
Height: 15cm (6in) **Spread:** 20cm (8in)
Site: Sun, partial shade. Moist but well-drained soil
Compost: Soil-based (John Innes No. 2) or soil-less

Use: Container, edging, formal bedding, front of bed or border
Good companions: *Verbena* 'Peaches and Cream', *Viola* x *wittrockiana* 'Baby Lucia'

8 Clarkia amoena Satin Series
Godetia, Satin flower

Dwarf annual with numerous clusters of sheeny four-petalled flowers in shades of pink and red, often with contrasting colours. Hardy.

General care: Sow seed *in situ* in early autumn or early spring.
Height: 20cm (8in) **Spread:** 30cm (12in)
Site: Sun. Moist but well-drained soil
Use: Sunny bed or border
Good companions: *Ageratum houstonianum*, *Cleome hassleriana* 'Rose Queen', *Nigella damascena* 'Miss Jekyll Sky Blue'

9 Digitalis purpurea
Foxglove

Biennial or short-lived perennial with spires of pink, purple or white flowers, spotted inside. Self-seeds to excess but suits wild areas. Hardy.
General care: Sow seed *in situ* from late spring to early summer.
Height: 1.5m (5ft) **Spread:** 50cm (20in)
Site: Partial shade, sun. Moist but well-drained soil
Use: Wild garden, woodland garden
Good companions: *Aquilegia* 'Hensol Harebell', *Lilium martagon*, *Myosotis sylvatica* 'Royal Blue'

10 Lathyrus odoratus 'Duke of York'
Sweet pea

Sweetly scented annual tendril climber. Old-fashioned cultivars, such as 'Duke of York' and 'Painted Lady', have small pea flowers in blue, pink or red. Modern cultivars have larger flowers with ruffled petals in many colours. Hardy.
General care: Sow seed under glass in autumn or early spring and plant out in spring. Alternatively, sow *in situ* in mid-spring. Deadhead regularly.
Height: 2m (6ft) **Spread:** 60cm (2ft)
Site: Sun. Humus-rich, fertile and well-drained soil
Use: Screen, tripod climber
Good companions: *Campanula lactiflora*, *Lilium regale*, *Rosa* 'Céleste'

11 Lobelia erinus Cascade Series
Lobelia

This bushy or trailing perennial is grown as an annual. All summer the dark green, sometimes bronzed leaves are obscured by small flowers. Cascade Series is trailing and has pink, purple, blue, red or white flowers. Half hardy.
General care: Sow seed under glass at 16–18°C (61–64°F) in late winter. Plant out in early summer.
Height: 15cm (6in) **Spread:** 20cm (8in)
Site: Sun, partial shade. Fertile and moist but well-drained soil
Compost: Soil-based (John Innes No. 2) or soil-less
Use: Container, raised bed
Good companions: *Fuchsia* 'Leonora', *Petunia* Surfinia Purple, *Verbena* 'Silver Anne'

12 Matthiola incana Ten Week Series
Gillyflower, stock

Ten Week stocks are grown as annuals for their richly scented blooms. Tall and dwarf cultivars bear single or double flowers in pink, mauve, purple or red. Not fully hardy.
General care: Sow seed under glass at 13–15°C (55–59°F) from late winter to early spring. Plant out in late spring.
Height: 45cm (18in) **Spread:** 30cm (12in)
Site: Sun. Moist but well-drained soil, preferably slightly limy
Compost: Soil-based (John Innes No. 2)
Use: Container, sunny bed or border
Good companions: *Amaranthus caudatus*, *Centaurea cyanus*, *Cosmos bipinnatus* Sensation Series

5

8

10

11

6

7

9

12

pink and mauve (continued)

1 Papaver somniferum
Opium poppy
Erect annual with tall stems, deeply lobed grey-green leaves and in summer pink, mauve, red or white bowl-shaped flowers, which are up to 10cm (4in) across and followed by ornamental flat-topped seed pods. Hardy.
General care: Sow seed *in situ* in early to mid-spring. To prevent excessive self-seeding cut seed pods while they are still blue-green.
Height: 1.2m (4ft) **Spread:** 30cm (12in)
Site: Sun. Well-drained soil
Use: Sunny bed or border
Good companions: *Papaver rhoeas* 'Mother of Pearl', *Perovska atriplicifolia* 'Blue Spire', *Verbena bonariensis*

2 Petunia Fantasy Series
Hybrid petunias are bushy or trailing perennials grown as annuals. They produce single or double trumpet-shaped flowers through summer. Some are sweetly scented. Fantasy Series is compact and bears small pink to red flowers. Half hardy.
General care: Sow seed under glass at 15°C (59°F) in early spring.
Height: 15cm (6in) **Spread:** 20cm (8in)
Site: Sun. Well-drained soil
Compost: Soil-based (John Innes No. 1) or soil-less, both with added sharp sand
Use: Container, edging, formal bedding, front of sunny border
Good companions: *Gladiolus* 'The Bride', *Lavatera trimestris* 'Mont Blanc', *Nigella damascena* 'Miss Jekyll Sky Blue'

red and russet

3 Alcea rosea 'Nigra'
Hollyhock
This short-lived perennial is best grown as an annual or biennial to minimise the spread of hollyhock rust. It has rough hairy leaves and a tough stem that shoots up to bear single funnel-shaped flowers. These are dark maroon with a yellow throat. Hardy.
General care: To grow as a biennial, sow seed in a nursery bed in early to midsummer. To grow as an annual, sow seed under glass at 13°C (55°F) in late winter. Plant out in late spring.
Height: 2.5m (8ft) **Spread:** 50cm (20in)
Site: Sun. Fertile and moist but well-drained soil
Use: Sunny bed or border
Good companions: *Clematis* 'Royal Velours', *Lilium regale*, *Rosa* 'Madame Alfred Carrière', *Tulipa* 'Queen of Night'

4 Antirrhinum Sonnet Series
Snapdragon
These short-lived shrubby perennials are grown as annuals in dwarf, intermediate or tall cultivars. The common name derives from the two-lipped flowers, which are carried on spikes. Sonnet Series is intermediate and bears red, pink, yellow or white flowers. It begins its long flowering season early. Half hardy.
General care: Sow seed under glass, at 16–18°C (61–64°F), in late winter or early spring. Plant out in late spring or early summer.
Height: 40cm (16in) **Spread:** 30cm (12in)
Site: Sun. Fertile and well-drained soil
Compost: Soil-based (John Innes No. 2) or soil-less
Use: Container, formal bedding, front of sunny border
Good companions: *Artemisia ludoviciana* 'Valerie Finnis', *Eryngium* x *tripartitum*, *Perovskia* 'Blue Spire'

5 Dianthus barbatus 'Roundabout'
Sweet william
Sweet williams are short-lived perennials grown as biennials for their flat-headed clusters of scented single or double flowers. These are red, maroon or white and often bicoloured and prettily marked. 'Roundabout' is compact and includes many bicolours. The taller kinds are particularly good for cutting. Hardy.
General care: Sow seed under glass at 13°C (55°F) in late winter or early spring. Plant out in late spring or early summer.
Height: 20cm (8in) **Spread:** 25cm (10in)
Site: Sun. Well-drained. Good on lime
Use: Sunny bed or border
Good companions: *Antirrhinum* Sonnet Series, *Delphinium grandiflorum* 'Blue Butterfly', *Tulipa* 'Mount Tacoma'

6 Tropaeolum majus 'Empress of India'
Nasturtium
Compact version of what is often a vigorous scrambling annual. The wavy-edged rounded leaves are blue-green and the scented spurred flowers are velvety scarlet. They are borne

7

8

9

10

11

12

throughout summer if plants are regularly deadheaded. Half hardy.
General care: Sow seed under glass at 13–16°C (55–66°F) in late winter or early spring. Plant out in late spring or early summer. To prolong flowering deadhead regularly.
Height: 30cm (12in) **Spread:** 45cm (18in)
Site: Sun. Moist but well drained soil
Compost: Soil-based (John Innes No. 2) or soil-less, both with added grit
Use: Container, formal bedding, front of sunny border
Good companions: *Amaranthus caudatus, Molucella laevis, Nicotiana* 'Lime Green'

yellow and orange

7 Eschscholzia californica
California poppy
Annual with finely cut blue-green leaves and silky saucer-shaped poppies in yellow, cream, pink or scarlet. The flowering season lasts all summer but individual plants stop blooming when cylindrical seedpods develop. Good for cutting. Hardy.
General care: Sow seed *in situ* in early autumn or mid-spring.
Height: 25cm (10in) **Spread:** 20cm (8in)
Site: Sun. Well-drained, preferably poor soil
Use: Gravel garden, sunny bed or border
Good companions: *Allium cristophii, Artemisia* 'Powis Castle', *Calendula officinalis* 'Fiesta Gitana'

8 Papaver nudicaule
Arctic poppy, Icelandic poppy
Hairy perennial grown as a biennial for its exquisite flowers in yellow, orange, pink or white. 'Summer Breeze' has a long flowering season. Hardy.
General care: Sow seed *in situ* in late spring or early summer.
Height: 40cm (16in) **Spread:** 15cm (6in)
Site: Sun. Well-drained soil
Use: Sunny bed or border
Good companions: *Anthemis tinctoria* 'E.C. Buxton', *Lupinus* 'Chandelier', *Rudbeckia fulgida* var. *sullivantii* 'Goldsturm'

9 Viola x wittrockiana 'Jolly Joker'
Pansy, Viola
Short-lived evergreen perennial grown as an annual. Medium flowers with orange face and rich purple edging, whiskers and upper petals. Hardy.
General care: Sow seed under glass in late winter or early spring or outdoors in mid-spring.
Height: 20cm (8in) **Spread:** 25cm (10in)
Site: Sun or partial shade. Humus-rich and moist but well-drained soil
Compost: Soil-based (John Innes No.2) or soil-less
Use: Container, edging, formal bedding, front of border
Good companions: *Brachyscome iberidifolia* 'Purple Splendour', *Lobelia erinus* ascade Series, *Verbena* 'Imagination'

silver and grey

10 Helichrysum petiolare
This sprawling evergreen shrub with woolly greyish leaves is usually grown as an annual for containers. Variegated cultivars and the yellow-green form 'Limelight' extend the range of foliage effects. Half hardy.
General care: In the growing season pinch back long stems to encourage bushy growth.
Height: 60cm (2ft) **Spread:** 1.5m (5ft)
Site: Sun. Well-drained soil
Compost: Soil-based (John Innes No. 2) or soil-less
Use: Container, sunny bed or border
Good companions: *Argyranthemum* 'Vancouver', *Osteospermum jucundum, Petunia* 'Surfinia Purple', *Scaevola aemula* 'Blue Wonder'

11 Papaver rhoeas 'Mother of Pearl'
Corn poppy, Field poppy, Flanders poppy
The common red annual has been bred for colour variations. 'Mother of Pearl' is in pastel shades of dove-grey, mauve-blue and soft pink. Hardy.
General care: Sow seed *in situ* in early autumn or early to mid-spring.
Height: 1m (3ft) **Spread:** 60cm (2ft)
Site: Sun. Well-drained soil
Use: Sunny bed or border, wildflower garden
Good companions: *Consolida ajacis* Imperial Series, *Convolvulus cneorum, Diascia barberae* 'Ruby Field'

green

12 Nicotiana 'Lime Green'
Tobacco plant
Upright, sticky annual grown for the clusters of yellow-green tubular flowers that are produced all summer. All parts are toxic. Half hardy.
General care: Sow seed under glass at 18°C (64°F) in late winter or early spring. Plant out in early summer.
Height: 60cm (2ft) **Spread:** 25cm (10in)
Site: Sun, partial shade. Moist, well-drained soil
Use: Formal bedding, border
Good companions: *Impatiens walleriana* Tempo Series, *Molucella laevis, Tropaeolum* 'Alaska'

bulbs

Bulbs are perennials with underground food storage organs that are described technically as true bulbs, corms, tubers or rhizomes. The small bulbs of spring are followed by a progression of stately bulbs throughout summer.

purple, blue and violet

1 Allium cristophii
Ornamental onion

Strap-shaped, rather hairy leaves surround a stout stem, which supports a head, up to 20cm (8in) across, of purple-pink starry flowers. These glint with a metallic sheen and remain ornamental when dried. Hardy.

General care: Plant in autumn with the top of the bulb about 10cm (4in) deep.

Height: 45cm (18in) **Spread:** 20cm (8in)

Site: Sun. Well-drained soil

Use: Gravel garden, sunny border

Good companions: *Gladiolus communis* subsp. *byzantinus, Santolina chamaecyparissus, Verbena bonariensis*

2 Allium 'Globemaster'
Ornamental onion

A sturdy stem rises from grey-green strap-like leaves and supports a spherical head, up to 20cm (8in) across, of violet-blue starry flowers. The heads remain attractive when dried. Hardy.

General care: Plant in autumn with the top of the bulb about 10cm (4in) deep.

Height: 75cm (2ft 6in) **Spread:** 20cm (8in)

Site: Sun. Well-drained soil

Use: Gravel garden, sunny border

Good companions: *Buddleja davidii* 'Black Knight', *Eryngium* x *tripartitum, Stipa gigantea*

3 Allium hollandicum 'Purple Sensation'
Ornamental onion

The strap-like leaves begin to wither in late spring when tall stems rise to support spherical heads, about 10cm (4in) across, packed with rich purple-pink starry flowers. Attractive when dried. Hardy.

General care: Plant in autumn with the top of the bulb about 10cm (4in) deep.

Height: 1m (3ft) **Spread:** 15cm (6in)

Site: Sun. Well-drained soil

Use: Gravel garden, sunny border

Good companions: *Artemisia* 'Powis Castle', *Buddleja* 'Lochinch', *Euphorbia characias* subsp. *wulfenii*

4 Camassia leichtlinii 'Electra'

The straight flowering stem rises above linear basal leaves and carries numerous purple-blue starry flowers. Does well in damp meadow-like conditions. Not fully hardy.

General care: Plant in autumn with the top of the bulb about 10cm (4in) deep.

Height: 1.2m (4ft) **Spread:** 20cm (8in)

Site: Sun, partial shade. Humus-rich and moist but well-drained soil

Use: Moist border, wild garden

Good companions: *Cardamine pratensis* 'Flore Pleno', *Fritillaria meleagris, Iris sibirica* 'Ego'

5 Scilla peruviana
Cuban lily, Squill

In late spring and early summer this bulb produces conical heads that are densely packed

8

9

10

11

12

with up to 100 blue starry flowers. It is nearly evergreen, but as the strap-like leaves become untidy in late summer, it is best to plant to hide them. Hardy.
General care: Plant in early autumn with the top of the bulb just covered.
Height: 30cm (12in) **Spread:** 25cm (10in)
Site: Sun. Moist but well-drained soil
Use: Sunny border
Good companions: *Cosmos bipinnatus* Sensation Series, *Lavatera trimestris* 'Mont Blanc', *Lupinus* 'Chandelier'

pink and mauve

6 Arisaema candidissimum

The true flowers are insignificant but arranged around the base of a white to greenish yellow pencil-like structure, the spadix. This is surrounded by a hooded flower-like bract, or spathe, that is white, broadly striped with pink, and suffused with green. The sweet scent is a surprise. Three-lobed leaves expand after the spathe develops. Not fully hardy.
General care: Plant in mid-autumn with the top of the tuber about 15cm (6in) deep.
Height: 30cm (12in) **Spread:** 15cm (6in)
Site: Sun, partial shade. Lime-free, humus-rich and moist but well-drained soil
Use: Peat bed, sunny or lightly shaded border
Good companions: *Erythronium californicum* 'White Beauty', *Trillium erectum, Uvularia grandiflora*

7 Gladiolus communis subsp. byzantinus
Gladiolus

This southern European species produces a fan of narrow leaves and spikes carrying two ranks of about 20 funnel-shaped flowers in piercing magenta. Unlike the South African species and hybrids, it does not need to be lifted annually and often spreads freely. Hardy.
General care: Plant in autumn with the top of the corm about 10cm (4in) deep.
Height: 1m (3ft) **Spread:** 8cm (3in)
Site: Sun. Well-drained soil
Use: Gravel garden, sunny border
Good companions: *Artemisia ludoviciana* 'Valerie Finnis', *Ruta graveolens* 'Jackman's Blue'

red and russet

8 Tulipa sprengeri
Species tulip

The last of the tulips to flower, this extends their season into summer. The narrow glossy leaves develop before the bright scarlet flowers open. These have pointed petals and are about 10cm (4in) across. Self-seeds to form colonies in a wide range of conditions. Hardy.
General care: Plant in late autumn with the top of the bulb about 15cm (6in) deep.
Height: 50cm (20in) **Spread:** 15cm (6in)
Site: Sun, partial shade. Humus-rich and well-drained soil
Use: Sunny or lightly shaded border, wild garden, woodland garden
Good companions: *Anemone blanda, Hyacinthoides non-scripta, Lilium martagon* var. *album*

cream and white

9 Gladiolus 'The Bride'
Miniature gladiolus

Slender hybrid gladiolus with blade-like leaves and spikes of neat white flowers. Half hardy.
General care: Plant in spring on a layer of coarse sand with the top of the corm about 10cm (4in) deep. Lift in autumn.
Height: 60cm (2ft) **Spread:** 8cm (3in)
Site: Sun. Well-drained soil
Use: Sunny bed or border
Good companions: *Paeonia lactiflora* 'Bowl of Beauty', *Nigella damascena* 'Miss Jekyll', *Veronica spicata* 'Heidekind'

10 Lilium candidum
Madonna lily

A stiff flowering stem rises from a rosette of overwintering leaves and carries up to 15 white trumpet-shaped blooms. Richly scented. Hardy.
General care: Plant in mid-autumn with the top of the bulb just covered.
Height: 1.5m (5ft) **Spread:** 25cm (10in)
Site: Sun. Well-drained soil, preferably limy
Use: Sunny border
Good companions: *Campanula persicifolia, Erysimum* 'Bowles' Mauve', *Papaver orientale* 'Black and White'

11 Lilium martagon var. album
Common turkscap lily

Upright stems carry up to 50 white nodding flowers with rolled back segments. Will build up colonies in a wide range of conditions. Hardy.
General care: Plant between mid-autumn and early spring with the top of the bulb about 20cm (8in) deep – the roots develop above the bulb.
Height: 1.5m (5ft) **Spread:** 20cm (8in)
Soil: Sun, partial shade. Well-drained soil. Good on lime
Use: Sunny or lightly shaded border, woodland garden
Good companions: *Geranium phaeum, Helleborus orientalis, Lunaria annua*

12 Lilium regale
Regal lily

Wiry stems carry white funnel-shaped flowers with purple staining on the outside and golden anthers. Scented and good for cutting. Hardy.
General care: Plant between mid-autumn and early spring with the top of the bulb about 20cm (8in) deep – the roots develop above the bulb.
Height: 1.5m (5ft) **Spread:** 30cm (12in)
Site: Sun. Humus-rich, fertile, well-drained soil
Compost: Soil-based (John Innes No. 2) with added leaf-mould and grit
Use: Container, sunny border
Good Companions: *Campanula lactiflora, Geranium* x *magnificum, Rosa* 'Golden Wings', *Rosa* 'Nevada'

climbers

Trained on architectural supports or other plants, climbers assert the vertical dimension of the garden. They twine, cling with aerial roots or clasp with tendrils. Plant in the dormant season.

purple, blue and violet

1 Passiflora caerulea

Blue passion flower

This tendril climber has pliant stems and more or less evergreen fingered leaves. Throughout summer there are showy flowers, with a ring (corona) of blue filaments radiating over white segments. Edible fruits, orange when ripe, follow. Not fully hardy.

General care: In late winter or early spring cut a proportion of stems hard back.

Height: 10m (33ft)

Spread: 5m (15ft)

Site: Sun, partial shade. Well-drained soil

Use: Pergola, screen, wall

Good companions: *Clematis* 'Bill MacKenzie', *Rosa* Golden Showers, *Solanum crispum* 'Glasnevin'

1

2 Wisteria floribunda 'Multijuga'

Japanese wisteria

Vigorous twining climber with elegant deciduous foliage, the leaves composed of numerous leaflets. The fragrant, mauve-blue pea flowers of 'Multijuga' trail in drooping sprays up to 1m (3ft) long. Hardy.

General care: Prune in late summer and winter.

Height: 10m (33ft) **Spread:** 6m (20ft)

Site: Sun, partial shade. Moist but well-drained soil, preferably lime-free

Use: Pergola, trained standard, tree climber, wall

Good companions: *Clematis montana* var. *rubens* 'Elizabeth', *Hedera colchica* 'Dentata Variegata', *Rosa* 'Paul's Himalayan Musk'

3 Wisteria x formosa 'Yae-kokuryû'

Wisteria

Vigorous, twining deciduous climber with attractive large leaves divided into numerous leaflets. In late spring and early summer it bears trailing sprays of violet-purple pea flowers. Hardy.

General care: Prune in late summer and again in winter.

Height: 10m (33ft)

Spread: 6m (20ft)

Site: Sun, partial shade. Moist but well-drained soil, preferably lime-free

Use: Pergola, trained standard, tree climber, wall

Good companions: *Lonicera* x *tellmanniana*, *Rosa banksiae* 'Lutea', *Vitis vinifera* 'Purpurea'

2

3

pink and mauve

4 Actinidia kolomikta

Deciduous twining climber with insignificant flowers but dramatic foliage when grown in full sun. The dark green heart-shaped leaves become tipped with pink and white, some whole leaves starting white and gradually becoming tinged with pink. Hardy.

General care: Little pruning required but when necessary cut back in late winter.

Height and spread: 4m (12ft)

Site: Sun, partial shade. Humus-rich and moist but well-drained soil

Use: Sheltered wall

Good companions: *Jasminum officinale*, *Rosa* 'Aimée Vibert', *Rosa* 'Parade'

red and russet

5 Schisandra rubriflora

Deciduous twining climber with reddish shoots, dark green leaves and deep red flowers – male and female on separate plants. Female plants may produce skeins of small, inedible red fruits if grown near a male plant. Hardy.

General care: Prune back sideshoots to three or four buds in late winter or early spring.

Height: 10m (33ft) **Spread:** 5m (15ft)

Site: Sun, partial shade. Moist but well-drained soil, preferably lime-free

Use: Pergola, wall

Good companions: *Lonicera* x *tellmanniana*, *Rosa* 'Bobbie James', *Vitis coignetiae*

6 Vitis vinifera 'Purpurea'

Grape vine, Vine

Vines are deciduous tendril climbers. This cultivar is grown for its foliage and has white downy young leaves that turn claret-red. The purple grapes taste unpleasant. Hardy.

General care: Prune in midwinter.

Height: 8m (25ft) **Spread:** 5m (15ft)

Site: Sun, partial shade, Fertile and well-drained soil, preferably limy

Use: Arbour, pergola, wall

Good companions: *Clematis montana* var. *rubens* 'Elizabeth', *Lonicera periclymenum* 'Serotina', *Rosa* 'Bobbie James'

4

yellow and orange

7 Lonicera periclymenum 'Belgica'
Early Dutch honeysuckle

Deciduous twining climber with purplish stems and in late spring and early summer purple-and-yellow flowers. Powerfully scented. Hardy.
General care: Prune after flowering, clearing out old stems every two or three years.
Height: 5m (15ft) **Spread:** 2.5m (8ft)
Site: Partial shade, sun. Humus-rich and moist but well-drained soil
Use: Arbour, arch, pergola, tripod, wall
Good companions: *Clematis* 'The Vagabond', *Jasminum nudiflorum*, *Lonicera periclymenum* 'Serotina'

8 Lonicera x tellmanniana
Honeysuckle

Deciduous twining climber. The uppermost pair of leaves on each stem is arranged like a cup below a whorl of bronze-yellow two-lipped flowers, from late spring to midsummer. Unscented. Hardy.
General care: Plant with the base in shade. Prune after flowering, clearing out old stems every two or three years.
Height: 5m (15ft) **Spread:** 2.5m (8ft)
Site: Partial shade, sun. Humus-rich and moist but well-drained soil
Use: Arbour, arch, pergola, tripod, wall
Good companions: *Clematis* 'Royal Velours', *Rosa banksiae* 'Lutea', *Wisteria* x *formosa* 'Yae-kokuryû'

cream and white

9 Hydrangea anomala subsp. petiolaris
Climbing hydrangea

This deciduous climber clings by means of aerial roots. Clusters of tiny, creamy-green fertile flowers surrounded by larger white sterile flowers contrast well with the dark green leaves. Attractive red-brown stems in winter. Hardy.
General care: Prune only if necessary to restrict growth immediately after flowering.
Height: 10m (33ft) **Spread:** 6m (20ft)
Site: Partial shade, sun. Fertile and moist but well-drained soil
Use: Screen, wall
Good companions: *Clematis* 'Royal Velours', *Cotoneaster horizontalis*, *Rosa* 'Madame Alfred Carrière'

10 Jasminum officinale
Jasmine

Deciduous twining climber with dark green divided leaves and sweetly scented, white star-shaped flowers through summer. Not fully hardy.
General care: Thin out overgrown plants after flowering.
Height: 10m (33ft) **Spread:** 5m (15ft)
Site: Sun, partial shade. Moist but well-drained soil
Use: Arbour, pergola, wall
Good companions: *Clematis* 'Comtesse de Bouchaud', *Osmanthus delavayi*, *Rosa* 'Madame Grégoire Staechelin'

green

11 Humulus lupulus 'Aureus'
Hop

Vigorous twining perennial climber with deeply lobed, bristly leaves. 'Aureus' has yellow-green leaves. For best colour grow in full sun. Hardy.
General care: Check tendency to spread too far.
Height: 6m (20ft) **Spread:** 4m (12ft)
Site: Sun, partial shade. Moist but well-drained soil
Use: Arbour, screen, tripod, wall
Good companions: *Aconitum* 'Ivorine', *Clematis* 'Perle d'Azur', *Geranium* 'Johnson's Blue'

12 Parthenocissus henryana
Chinese Virginia creeper

Deciduous tree climber with suckers. The velvety-green, sometimes bronzed leaves have silvery veins and turn red in autumn. Not fully hardy.
General care: Prune after flowering, clearing out old stems every two or three years.
Height: 10m (33ft) **Spread:** 6m (20ft)
Site: Partial shade, sun. Fertile, well-drained soil
Use: Sheltered wall, ground cover
Good companions: *Clematis montana* var. *rubens* 'Elizabeth', *Euonymus fortunei* 'Silver Queen', *Hedera colchica* 'Dentata Variegata'

clematis

Many large-flowered clematis hybrids bloom over a long season and are useful for growing over shrubs, tripods and walls. Plant them in autumn or spring, with the roots in shade, in humus-rich, well-drained soil; clematis do well on lime. For containers use a soil-based compost (John Innes No. 3). Prune in late spring or early autumn, cutting back to a pair of strong buds. All the clematis featured here are hardy and deciduous.

1 Clematis 'Bee's Jubilee'

Dark pink bars along the centre of each petal-like sepal give the mauve-pink single flowers, up to 20cm (8in) across, a starry appearance. Flowers again in early autumn. Ornamental seed heads follow the flowers.

Height: 2.5m (8ft) **Spread:** 1m (3ft)

Good companions: *Anemone* x *hybrida* 'Whirlwind', *Clematis macropetala, Rosa* 'Parade'

2 Clematis 'Gillian Blades'

Single white flowers, up to 20cm (8in) across, with overlapping petal-like sepals that have mauve-tinted crimped margins and soft yellow anthers. Flowers from late spring to early summer and again in early autumn.

Height: 2.5m (8ft) **Spread:** 1m (3ft)

Good companions: *Anemone* x *hybrida* 'Whirlwind', *Clematis* 'Perle d'Azur', *Rosa* 'Parade'

3 Clematis 'Perle d'Azur'

Sky-blue flowers, up to 15cm (6in) across and with pale yellow anthers, are produced over a long summer season. The tips of the petal-like sepals are turned back.

Height: 3m (10ft) **Spread:** 1m (3ft)

Good companions: *Campanula lactiflora* 'Prichard's Variety', *Lathyrus odoratus* 'Noel Sutton', *Rosa* 'Gloire de Dijon', *Rosa* 'Madame Grégoire Staechelin'

4 Clematis 'Niobe'

This versatile hybrid produces deep red single flowers up to 20cm (8in) across. The broad petal-like sepals are ridged lengthwise and the anthers are yellow.

Height: 2.5m (8ft) **Spread:** 1m (3ft)

Good companions: *Clematis* 'Gillian Blades', *Syringa vulgaris* 'Madame Lemoine', *Rosa* 'Parade'

5 Clematis 'Jackmanii'

From early summer to autumn this hybrid bears violet-purple single flowers, about 10cm (4in) across. They open flat and are of velvety texture.

Height: 3m (10ft) **Spread:** 1m (3ft)

Good companions: *Clematis* 'Helsingborg', *Clematis* 'Bill MacKenzie', *Rosa* 'Maigold'

6 Clematis 'The Vagabond'

Short-growing climber suitable for a small garden. Each petal-like sepal of the rich maroon-purple flowers has a central reddish bar. The anthers are creamy yellow. Flowers again in late summer and autumn.

Height: 2m (6ft) **Spread:** 1m (3ft)

Good companions: *Clematis alpina* subsp. *sibirica* 'White Moth', *Rosa* 'Aimée Vibert', *Solanum crispum* 'Glasnevin'

7 Clematis Blue Moon

Flowers are 15cm (6in) or more across. The central bars of the petal-like sepals are at first greenish white and then more silvery, but the ruffled margins are pale mauve-blue. Maroon anthers make a dark, eye-catching centre. Flowers from late spring to early summer and again in early autumn.

Height: 3m (10ft) **Spread:** 1m (3ft)

Good companions: *Aquilegia vulgaris* 'Nivea', *Digitalis purpurea, Lunaria annua, Rosa* 'Madame Alfred Carrière'

8 Clematis 'Lasurstern'

Bears blue flowers, often more than 15cm (6in) across, that consist of 7–8 wavy-margined finely tapered petal-like sepals. There is a crop of smaller flowers in early autumn.

Height: 3m (10ft) **Spread:** 1m (3ft)

Good companions: *Clematis montana* var. *rubens* 'Elizabeth', *Rosa* 'Parade', *Wisteria floribunda* 'Multijuga'

4
5
6
7
8

climbing roses

Ramblers and some climbing roses flower in one spectacular flush in early summer. Others bloom nearly continuously or in several flushes from early summer to autumn. Both are invaluable for arbours, arches, pillars and walls. Plant in autumn or spring in fertile and moist but well-drained soil. All roses featured here are deciduous and hardy.

1 Rosa 'Bobbie James'

Vigorous rambler with glossy, light green foliage and large trusses of strongly fragrant, creamy-white semi-double flowers. At home scrambling up a sturdy tree.

Height: 8m (25ft) **Spread:** 6m (20ft)

Good companions: *Solanum laxum* 'Album', *Vitis coignetiae, Vitis vinifera* 'Purpurea'

2 Rosa Compassion

Climbing Hybrid Tea rose with dark green foliage. Throughout summer apricot-pink blooms, with yellow and copper tints, open from high-centred buds.

Height: 3m (10ft) **Spread:** 2.5m (8ft)

Good companions: *Clematis alpina* 'Frances Rivis', *Clematis* 'Lasurstern', *Solanum laxum* 'Album'

3 Rosa 'Madame Alfred Carrière'

Vigorous old climber with light green leaves and several flushes of fragrant, creamy-pink double flowers that fade to white. Good for siting on a north-facing wall.

Height: 5m (15ft) **Spread:** 3m (10ft)

Good companions: *Clematis* 'Perle d'Azur', *Clematis* 'Royal Velours', *Geranium psilostemon*

4 Rosa 'Madame Grégoire Staechelin'

Vigorous climbing Hybrid Tea rose with a short season of exceptional double flowers that are pink flushed with red and strongly scented. Large red hips follow. Good for a north-facing wall.

Height: 5m (15ft) **Spread:** 3m (10ft)

Good companions: *Clematis* 'The Vagabond', *Lonicera japonica* 'Halliana', *Rosa* 'Madame Alfred Carrière'

5 Rosa 'Veilchenblau'

This vigorous rambler has almost thornless stems and crowded clusters of fragrant semi-double flowers. Mauve buds open to white-centred violet-purple flowers. Their colour intensifies before fading to slate-grey.

Height and spread: 4m (12ft)

Good companions: *Jasminum officinale, Lonicera periclymenum* 'Serotina', *Rosa* 'Aimée Vibert'

6 Rosa 'Paul's Himalayan Musk'

Rampant rambler best trained into a large tree. The small mauve-pink double flowers are borne profusely in a single magnificent burst, often in trailing sprays.

Height: 10m (33ft) **Spread:** 5m (15ft)

Good companions: *Schisandra rubriflora, Vitis coignetiae, Wisteria floribunda* 'Multijuga'

7 Rosa 'Parade'

Modern climber with glossy leaves and deep pink scented flowers, which open almost flat in several flushes from early summer to early autumn.

Height and spread: 3m (10ft)

Good companions: *Ceanothus* x *delileanus* 'Topaze', *Clematis* 'Alba Luxurians', *Rosa* Mary Rose

shrubs & trees

Trees and shrubs have durable frameworks of woody branches. They bring structure to the garden and their foliage creates shade in summer, while the flowers of many provide long-lasting displays. Plant in the dormant season, preferably in autumn or early spring.

purple, blue and violet

1 Buddleja alternifolia

Deciduous shrub or small tree with slender arching branches and alternate lance-shaped leaves. The fragrant mauve-purple flowers encrust the previous year's growths. Hardy.
General care: Immediately after flowering cut back all shoots that have flowered.
Height and spread: 4m (12ft)
Site: Sun. Fertile and well-drained soil
Use: Specimen standard, sunny border
Good companions: *Buddleja davidii* 'Black Knight', *Hibiscus syriacus* 'Oiseau Bleu', *Rosa* 'Golden Wings'

1

2
3

2 Ceanothus 'Italian Skies'

California lilac
Evergreen shrub with a dense framework of branches and dark leaves. In late spring and early summer these are almost hidden by rounded heads of deep blue flowers. Not fully hardy.
Height: 1.5m (5ft) **Spread:** 3m (10ft)
Site: Sun. Well-drained soil
Use: Sunny sheltered border, wall shrub
Good companions: *Actinidia kolomikta, Garrya elliptica, Solanum laxum* 'Album'

3 Hebe 'Youngii'

Compact evergreen shrub with red-edged leaves. Starry flowers, at first violet-blue but later fading to white, are clustered in small spikes. Hardy.
Height: 30cm (12in) **Spread:** 75cm (2ft 6in)
Site: Sun. Moist but well-drained soil
Use: Sunny border, rock garden, ground cover
Good companions: *Diascia rigescens, Monarda* 'Prärienacht', *Sisyrinchium striatum* 'Aunt May'

4 Ruta graveolens 'Jackman's Blue'

Rue
Common rue is a strongly aromatic evergreen shrubby herb, but this form is grown as a foliage plant. The divided leaves make a dense blue-green mound. In summer there are clusters of small yellow flowers. Hardy.
General care: Trim plants in early spring.
Height: 60cm (2ft) **Spread:** 75cm (2ft 6in)
Site: Sun. Well-drained soil
Use: Gravel garden, herb garden, sunny border
Good companions: *Potentilla fruticosa* 'Tangerine', *Rosa* 'Golden Wings', *Verbascum* 'Helen Johnson'

4

5

pink and mauve

5 Abelia schumannii

Bushy deciduous shrub with dark green leaves that are coloured bronze when young. Throughout summer and into autumn lightly scented funnel-shaped flowers are produced prolifically. These are reddish pink on the outside with an orange blotch on the pale inside. Not fully hardy.
Height and spread: 2m (6ft)
Site: Sun. Well-drained soil
Use: Sunny border
Good companions: *Caryopteris* x *clandonensis* 'Heavenly Blue', *Perovskia* 'Blue Spire', *Thalictrum flavum* subsp. *glaucum*

6 Cistus 'Silver Pink'

Rock rose, Sun rose
Compact, mound-forming evergreen shrub that bears clusters of silver-pink saucer-shaped flowers. Individual blooms are short-lived but there is a continuous supply over many weeks. Not fully hardy.
Height: 75cm (2ft 6in) **Spread:** 1m (3ft)
Site: Sun. Well-drained soil
Use: Gravel garden, sunny border
Good companions: *Allium hollandicum* 'Purple Sensation', *Cistus ladanifer*

6

pink and mauve (continued)

1 Cornus kousa var. chinensis 'Satomi'

Flowering dogwood

Cornus kousa itself is a handsome tree or shrub, with tiered branches and conspicuous white petal-like bracts surrounding clusters of tiny flowers. This more upright and richly coloured form has long-lasting bright pink bracts. In autumn the foliage turns red-purple. Hardy.

Height: 6m (20ft) **Spread:** 5m (15ft)

Site: Sun, partial shade. Humus-rich and moist but well-drained soil, preferably lime-free

Use: Specimen shrub, woodland garden

Good companions: *Hydrangea macrophylla* 'Blue Wave', *Hydrangea paniculata* 'Unique', *Magnolia* x *kewensis* 'Wada's Memory'

2 Deutzia x rosea

Most of the deutzias are undemanding deciduous shrubs that bear a profusion of white, pink or purple blooms. During the first half of summer this compact hybrid produces clusters of pink to red-flushed star-shaped flowers. Hardy.

General care: Prune immediately after flowering, cutting back to the base all stems that have flowered.

Height and spread: 1.2m (4ft)

Site: Sun, partial shade. Well-drained soil

Use: Sunny or lightly shaded border, woodland garden

Good companions: *Ceratostigma willmottianum, Choisya ternata, Exochorda* x *macrantha* 'The Bride'

3 Kalmia latifolia 'Ostbo Red'

Calico bush

Dense evergreen shrub with glossy leaves. Most of the calico bushes bear clusters of pink flowers, which are very attractive as curiously pleated buds. Those of 'Ostbo Red' are bright red but open to pale pink bowl-shaped blooms. Hardy.

Height and spread: 3m (10ft)

Site: Partial shade. Lime-free, humus-rich and moist but well-drained soil

Use: Shady border, woodland garden

Good companions: *Camellia* x *williamsii* 'Donation', *Enkianthus campanulatus, Rhododendron* 'Bow Bells', *Rhododendron* 'Loderi King George'

4 Kolkwitzia amabalis 'Pink Cloud'

Beauty bush

During late spring and early summer masses of pink bell-shaped flowers, with yellow-flushed throats, cover the arching stems of this twiggy deciduous shrub. Hardy.

General care: Prune immediately after flowering.

Height: 4m (12ft) **Spread:** 3m (10ft)

Site: Sun. Well-drained soil

Use: Specimen shrub, sunny border

Good companions: *Geranium macrorrhizum* 'Ingwersen's Variety', *Geranium wallichianum* 'Buxton's Variety', *Rosa* 'Nevada'

5 Rhododendron 'Vanessa Pastel'

This compact evergreen hybrid produces trusses of creamy-pink funnel-shaped flowers at the end of the rhododendron season. The crimson eye contrasts with the soft colours of the flowers as does the deeper pink of the buds. Hardy.

Height and spread: 2m (6ft)

Site: Partial shade. Lime-free, humus-rich and moist but well-drained soil

Use: Lightly shaded border, woodland garden

Good companions: *Enkianthus campanulatus, Eucryphia* x *nymansensis* 'Nymansay', *Meconopsis betonicifolia*

6 Weigela 'Victoria'

The hybrid weigelas are showy deciduous shrubs that produce bell-shaped flowers in profusion from late spring to early summer. The colour range includes shades of pink to crimson and sometimes white. 'Victoria' has red-pink flowers

4

5

6

1

2

3

and purplish leaves. Hardy.
General care: Prune after flowering.
Height and spread: 2m (6ft)
Site: Sun, partial shade. Well-drained soil
Use: Sunny or lightly shaded border
Good companions: *Deutzia* x *rosea, Forsythia* x *intermedia* 'Lynwood', *Iris* 'Florentina', *Kolkwitzia amabilis* 'Pink Cloud'

red and russet

7 Fuchsia 'Lady Thumb'
Hybrid fuchsia
The small semi-double flowers of this upright fuchsia have a red-veined white skirt (corolla) below the light crimson tube and spreading sepals. The flowering season lasts from early summer until autumn. Not fully hardy.
General care: Cut back to a low framework in early spring.
Height: 30cm (12in) **Spread:** 45cm (18in)
Site: Sun, partial shade. Fertile and moist but well-drained soil
Compost: Soil-based (John Innes No. 3) or soil-less
Use: Container, sunny or lightly shaded border
Good companions: *Brachyscome iberidifolia* 'Purple Splendour', *Helichrysum petiolare, Lobelia erinus* Cascade Series, *Verbena* 'Silver Anne'

7

8

8 Rhododendron 'Britannia'
Evergreen shrub that makes a somewhat flattened rounded bush with pale green leaves. It bears dense trusses of radiant scarlet bell-shaped flowers. Hardy.
Height: 1.5m (5ft)
Spread: 2.4m (8ft)
Site: Partial shade. Lime-free, humus-rich and moist but well-drained soil
Use: Lightly shaded border, woodland garden
Good companions: *Camellia japonica* 'Bob Hope', *Magnolia denudata, Pieris* 'Forest Flame'

9

10

11

yellow and orange

9 Gleditsia triacanthos 'Sunburst'
Honey locust
Deciduous tree, which, unlike other honey locusts, is thornless and does not produce seedpods. It is grown for its bright yellow young foliage, which becomes light green as summer progresses and turns yellow again in autumn. Hardy.
Height: 12m (40ft) **Spread:** 9m (30ft)
Site: Sun. Well-drained soil
Use: Canopy in mixed planting, specimen tree
Good companions: *Arbutus unedo, Crataegus persimilis* 'Prunifolia', *Genista aetnensis*

10 Potentilla fruticosa 'Tangerine'
Cinquefoil
The numerous cultivars of *Potentilla fruticosa* are mainly compact deciduous shrubs that flower from late spring until autumn in yellow, cream, white, pink or red. 'Tangerine' is a spreading plant with orange-yellow blooms. Hardy.
Height: 1m (3ft) **Spread:** 1.5m (5ft)
Site: Sun. Well-drained soil
Use: Gravel garden, sunny bed, large rock garden
Good companions: *Buddleja* 'Lochinch', *Caryopteris* x *clandonensis* 'Heavenly Blue', *Lavandula* x *intermedia* Dutch Group, *Origanum laevigatum* 'Herrenhausen'

11 Rhododendron luteum
Deciduous azalea
This open deciduous shrub has slightly hairy lance-shaped leaves that turn rich shades of red in autumn. In late spring and early summer clusters of yellow trumpet-shaped flowers exhale a strong, sweet scent. Easy to grow and more tolerant of dry conditions than most azaleas. Hardy.
Height and spread: 4m (12ft)
Site: Sun, partial shade. Lime-free, humus-rich and moist but well-drained soil
Use: Sunny or lightly shaded border, woodland garden
Good companions: *Fothergilla major* Monticola Group, *Halesia carolina, Hamamelis* x *intermedia* 'Diane', *Magnolia* 'Elizabeth'

12

12 Robinia pseudoacacia 'Frisia'
Black locust, False acacia, Locust
Rugged, medium-sized deciduous tree with spiny twigs. The leaves, about 30cm (12in) long and composed of numerous leaflets, are at first rich yellow then become yellow-green during summer and finally orange-yellow in autumn. Hardy.
Height: 15m (50ft) **Spread:** 8m (25ft)
Site: Sun. Well-drained soil
Use: Canopy in mixed planting, specimen tree
Good companions: *Buddleja davidii* 'Black Knight', *Cotinus* 'Grace', *Cryptomeria japonica* Elegans Group

1

cream and white

1 Cistus ladanifer
Common gum cistus, Laudanum

Erect evergreen shrub with sticky, aromatic lance-shaped leaves. The white flowers are yellow at the centre and usually have a crimson-chocolate blotch at the base of each crumpled petal. Although individual flowers are short-lived, the display is long lasting. Not fully hardy.

Height: 2m (6ft) **Spread:** 1.5m (5ft)
Site: Sun. Well-drained soil
Use: Gravel garden, sunny border
Good companions: *Allium cristophii, Lavandula* x *intermedia* Dutch Group, *Lavatera* 'Barnsley'

2 Cornus alba 'Elegantissima'
Red-barked dogwood

Several cultivars of the deciduous species are grown to brighten the winter garden with their colourful stems. 'Elegantissima' has attractive red twigs but is grown chiefly for its foliage of grey-green leaves with an irregular white margin. There are white flowers in late spring and early summer. Hardy.

General care: Cut back to a framework of stems in early spring.
Height: 2.5m (8ft) **Spread:** 3m (10ft)
Site: Sun, partial shade. Moist but well-drained soil
Use: Sunny or lightly shaded border
Good companions: *Clematis* 'Royal Velours', *Thalictrum aquilegiifolium* 'Thundercloud', *Viola cornuta* Alba Group

3 Cornus controversa 'Variegata'
Cornel, dogwood

Small deciduous tree with tiered branches and white-variegated foliage. In early summer there are clusters of creamy-white flowers, which are followed by inedible blue-black fruits. Hardy.

Height: 7.5m (25ft) **Spread:** 6m (20ft)
Site: Sun. Moist but well-drained soil, preferably lime-free
Use: Canopy in mixed planting, specimen tree, woodland garden
Good companions: *Anemone nemorosa* 'Royal Blue', *Erythronium dens-canis, Narcissus* 'Jack Snipe', *Tulipa sprengeri*

4 Magnolia sieboldii
This spreading deciduous shrub has grey-green leaves that are hairy on the underside. In late spring and intermittently throughout summer nodding egg-shaped buds open to fragrant, outward-facing white flowers, 10cm (4in) across, with orange-crimson anthers. Hardy.

General care: Carry out any minimal pruning required in early spring. Avoid heavy pruning.
Height: 6m (20ft) **Spread:** 9m (30ft)
Site: Sun, partial shade. Humus-rich and moist but well-drained soil
Use: Specimen shrub, woodland garden
Good companions: *Cornus kousa* var. *chinensis, Hamamelis* x *intermedia* 'Arnold Promise', *Hydrangea paniculata* 'Unique'

3

5 Philadelphus 'Belle Etoile'
Mock orange

The hybrid mock oranges are deciduous shrubs with white, sometimes tinted, flowers that are usually strongly scented. The largest, such as the white double 'Virginal,' are 3m (10ft) high. The creamy double 'Manteau d'Hermine' is spreading but only 75cm (2ft 6in) high. This example of medium height has single flowers stained purple at the centre. Hardy.

General care: Prune immediately after flowering
Height: 2.5m (8ft)
Spread: 2m (6ft)
Site: Sun, partial shade. Well-drained soil
Use: Sunny or lightly shaded border
Good companions: *Cornus alba* 'Elegantissima', *Fatsia japonica, Geranium psilostemon*

6 Rhododendron 'Loder's White'
This large-leaved evergreen shrub forms a green dome that in summer is studded with cone-shaped trusses of funnel-shaped flowers. These open white from mauve-pink buds and are sparsely flecked with crimson. Hardy.

Height and spread: 3m (10ft)
Site: Sun, partial shade. Lime-free, humus-rich and moist but well-drained soil
Use: Sunny or lightly shaded border, woodland garden
Good companions: *Cornus kousa* var. *chinensis* 'Satomi', *Hydrangea macrophylla* 'Blue Wave', *Kalmia latifolia* 'Ostbo Red'

7 Styrax japonicus
Japanese snowbell

Deciduous large shrub or small tree with drooping growth and glossy foliage that colours subtly in autumn. White snowdrop-like flowers dangle from the underside of the slender stems. Hardy.

Height: 10m (33ft) **Spread:** 7.5m (25ft)
Site: Sun. Lime-free, humus-rich and moist but well-drained soil
Use: Canopy in mixed planting, specimen shrub or tree, woodland garden
Good companions: *Acer japonicum* 'Vitifolium', *Hydrangea aspera* Villosa Group, *Hydrangea paniculata* 'Unique'

silver and grey

8 Artemisia arborescens
This rounded evergreen shrub is grown for the silvery filigree of its aromatic cut leaves. There are small yellow flowerheads in late summer and autumn. Hardy.

General care: Cut back in early to mid-spring.
Height: 1m (3ft) **Spread:** 1.5m (5ft)
Site: Sun. Well-drained soil
Use: Gravel garden, sunny border
Good companions: *Gladiolus communis* subsp. *byzantinus, Lavandula* x *intermedia* Dutch Group, *Verbascum* 'Helen Johnson'

green

9 Melianthus major
Honey bush

Hollow-stemmed evergreen shrub grown mainly for its grey or blue-green foliage. The deeply

divided leaves are up to 50cm (20in) long. Maroon flowers may appear in early summer. Half hardy, but sprouts from the base if hit by frosts.
Height: 2.5m (8ft) **Spread:** 3m (10ft)
Site: Sun. Well-drained soil
Compost: Soil-based (John Innes No. 2)
Use: Container, sunny border
Good companions: *Argyranthemum* 'Vancouver', *Helichrysum petiolare, Pelargonium* 'Chocolate Peppermint'

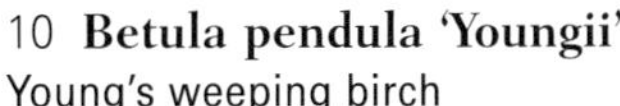

10 Betula pendula 'Youngii'
Young's weeping birch

The common birch is a graceful deciduous tree with white bark and diamond-shaped leaves that move freely on slender stems. 'Youngii' makes a small, dome-shaped weeping tree with mid-green leaves that turn yellow in autumn. Hardy.
Height: 7.5m (25ft) **Spread:** 6m (20ft)
Site: Sun, partial shade. Moist but well-drained soil
Use: Canopy in mixed planting, specimen tree
Good companions: *Helleborus foetidus, Iris foetidissima, Narcissus* 'Peeping Tom', *Pachysandra terminalis*

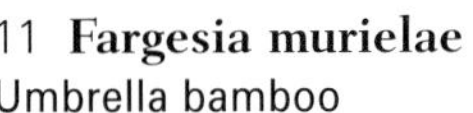

11 Fargesia murielae
Umbrella bamboo

Clump-forming evergreen bamboo with a column of arching yellow-green canes and showers of bright green leaves. Expands slowly. Hardy.
Height: 4m (12ft) **Spread:** 2m (6ft)
Site: Sun, partial shade. Moist, well-drained soil
Compost: Soil-based (John Innes No. 3) with added leaf-mould
Use: Container, hedge, screen, specimen clump, waterside, woodland garden
Good companions: *Acer palmatum* 'Bloodgood', *Asplenium scolopendrium, Dryopteris wallichianum, Fatsia japonica*

12 Trachycarpus fortunei
Chusan palm

Slow-growing evergreen palm with an impressive head of pleated fan-shaped leaves. Mature specimens produce large clusters of creamy-yellow flowers in early summer, sometimes followed by inedible blue-black fruits. Requires a sheltered position. Not fully hardy.
Height: 10m (33ft) **Spread:** 3m (10ft)
Site: Sun, partial shade. Fertile, well-drained soil
Use: Specimen tree, sunny border
Good companions: *Choisya ternata, Fatsia japonica, Phormium* 'Sundowner'

shrub roses

The non-climbing roses are a very mixed group of shrubs, but all flower generously – some in one magnificent flush while others repeat over a long season that may extend into autumn. Plant in autumn or spring in fertile and moist but well-drained soil, in full sun. All roses featured here are deciduous and hardy.

1

1 Rosa 'Céleste'

Alba rose with grey-green foliage and soft pink semi-double blooms. Flowers once only but the fragrant flowers are of exquisite quality.

Height: 2m (6ft) **Spread:** 1.2m (4ft)

Good companions: *Campanula persicifolia, Lilium regale, Viola cornuta* Alba Group

2 Rosa Mary Rose

English shrub rose with dull mat foliage but fragrant, pink, loose-petalled double flowers that are borne almost continuously over a long season.

Height and spread: 1.2m (4ft)

Good companions: *Delphinium* Belladonna Group 'Cliveden Beauty', *Geranium* 'Johnson's Blue', *Penstemon* 'Evelyn'

3 Rosa Bonica

This spreading ground-covering shrub rose has rich green glossy foliage and bears sprays of double pink flowers throughout summer and into autumn.

Height: 1m (3ft) **Spread:** 2m (6ft)

Good companions: *Dianthus* 'Gran's Favourite', *Stachys byzantina* 'Silver Carpet', *Veronica spicata* 'Heidekind'

4 Rosa 'Reine des Violettes'

Hybrid perpetual rose with grey-green leaves and velvety violet-purple double flowers that open flat. Good scent.

Height: 1.5m (5ft) **Spread:** 1m (3ft)

Good companions: *Nepeta* 'Six Hills Giant', *Rosa* 'Céleste', *Rosa* 'Louise Odier'

5 Rosa Alexander

Vigorous hybrid tea rose with glossy dark green foliage and conical buds. The bright vermilion blooms have scalloped petals and repeat well in several flushes during summer and early autumn. Long stemmed and good for cutting.

Height: 2m (6ft) **Spread:** 75cm (2ft 6in)

Good companions: *Diascia barberae* 'Ruby Field', *Geranium × magnificum, Nepeta* 'Six Hills Giant'

6 Rosa 'Complicata'

Gallica rose with single bright pink flowers, paler in the centre and up to 10cm (4in) across, borne along the full length of arching stems. Lightly scented.

Height: 1.5m (5ft)

Spread: 2.5m (8ft)

Good companions: *Campanula persicifolia, Dianthus* 'Gran's Favourite', *Viola cornuta* Alba Group

7 Rosa 'Nevada'

Large arching shrub rose, with almost thornless red stems and lightly scented, creamy white, flat semi-double blooms. These appear from late spring to early summer, when they peak, and again in autumn.

Height and spread: 2.5m (8ft)

Good companions: *Campanula lactiflora, Galtonia candicans, Paeonia mlokosewitschii, Tulipa* 'Spring Green'

8 Rosa 'Golden Wings'

This vigorous thorny shrub rose flowers with few pauses throughout summer and into autumn. The single or semi-double yellow blooms have a sweet fresh scent.

Height : 2m (6ft) **Spread:** 75cm (2ft 6in)

Good companions: *Crocosmia* 'Lucifer', *Geranium × magnificum, Veronica austriaca* subsp. *teucrium* 'Kapitän'

9 Rosa Mountbatten

Vigorous, tall floribunda rose that flowers freely in summer and again in autumn. The conical buds open to bright yellow double flowers that are well scented.

Height: 2m (6ft) **Spread:** 75cm (2ft 6in)

Good companions: *Alchemilla mollis, Buxus sempervirens* 'Suffruticosa', *Lavandula angustifolia* 'Hidcote', *Viola* 'Baby Lucia'

2

3

4

5

7
8
9
6

alpines

Most of these small perennials and shrubs will thrive in any sunny, well-drained conditions, not just in rock gardens. Many are at their flowering peak in early summer. Plant in mild weather between autumn and early spring.

purple, blue and violet

1 Campanula cochleariifolia
Fairies' thimbles

This easily grown dwarf perennial colonises ground with thin running roots, creating mats of shiny green leaves, over which dangle small blue or white bells. Hardy.
Height: 8cm (3in) **Spread:** 45cm (18in) or more
Site: Sun, partial shade. Moist, well-drained soil
Use: Paving, raised bed, rock garden, wall
Good companions: *Armeria maritima* 'Düsseldorfer Stolz', *Geranium cinereum* 'Ballerina', *Hebe cupressoides* 'Boughton Dome'

2 Lithodora diffusa 'Heavenly Blue'

This shrubby evergreen forms wide mats of dark, slightly hairy leaves. In late spring and early summer the trailing stems are sheeted with flowers of intense blue. Hardy.
Height: 15cm (6in) **Spread:** 75cm (2ft 6in) or more
Site: Sun. Lime-free and humus-rich but well-drained soil
Use: Bank, raised bed, rock garden, ground cover
Good companions: *Calluna vulgaris* 'Darkness', *Gaultheria mucronata* 'Bell's Seedling', *Sorbus reducta*

pink and mauve

3 Armeria maritima 'Düsseldorfer Stolz'
Sea thrift

The grass-like leaves of sea thrift, an evergreen perennial, are packed together to form a close hummock, above which small starry flowers are carried in late spring and summer. 'Düsseldorfer Stolz' bears red-pink flowers, but other forms are usually softer pink or occasionally white. Hardy.
Height: 20cm (8in) **Spread:** 30cm (12in)
Site: Sun. Well-drained soil
Compost: Soil-based (John Innes No. 1) with added grit
Use: Paving, raised bed, rock garden, trough, ground cover
Good companions: *Artemisia schmidtiana* 'Nana', *Convolvulus sabatius, Geranium cinereum* 'Ballerina'

4 Dianthus alpinus 'Joan's Blood'
Alpine pink

Although generally short-lived perennials, alpine pinks are worth propagating every two or three years for their fringed single flowers. These are pink to crimson and hide the cushion of dark green leaves. 'Joan's Blood' has bright magenta flowers with a dark red centre. Hardy.
Height: 10cm (4in)
Spread: 15cm (6in)
Site: Sun. Limy, humus-rich, gritty and sharply drained soil
Compost: Soil-based (John Innes No. 1) with added leaf-mould and grit
Use: Raised bed, rock garden, scree, trough
Good companions: *Armeria juniperifolia, Crocus sieberi* 'Violet Queen', *Daphne cneorum*

5 Geranium cinereum 'Ballerina'
Cranesbill

Compact evergreen perennial that forms a mound of lobed grey-green leaves. The dark-eyed veined pink flowers are

7

8

9

10

borne over many weeks. Hardy.
Height: 15cm (6in) **Spread:** 30cm (12in)
Site: Sun, partial shade. Well-drained soil
Use: Paving, raised bed, rock garden
Good companions: *Gypsophila repens* 'Rosa Schönheit', *Lavandula angustifolia* 'Nana Alba', *Muscari botryoides* 'Album'

6 Gypsophila repens 'Rosa Schönheit'

Mound-forming perennial with grey-green leaves, above which hover sprays of small flowers in summer. Hardy.
Height: 20cm (8in) **Spread:** 45cm (18in)
Site: Sun. Well-drained soil, preferably limy
Use: Dry wall, raised bed, rock garden
Good companions: *Aethionema* 'Warley Rose', *Aubrieta* 'Greencourt Purple', *Convolvulus sabatius*

yellow, cream and white

7 Achillea x lewisii 'King Edward'
Yarrow

Mound-forming perennial with soft, ferny grey-green leaves that often last through winter. For many weeks in summer flat heads of biscuit-yellow flowers top the foliage. Hardy.
Height: 15cm (6in) **Spread:** 20cm (8in)
Site: Sun. Well-drained soil
Use: Front of border, raised bed, rock garden
Good companions: *Helianthemum* 'Wisley Primrose', *Linum* 'Gemmell's Hybrid', *Tulipa clusiana* var. *chrysantha*

8 Arenaria montana
Sandwort

The glistening white flowers of this evergreen shrubby perennial spangle trailing stems of dark green foliage. Easily grown in a crevice. Hardy.
Height: 15cm (6in) **Spread:** 45cm (18in)
Site: Sun. Well-drained and gritty soil
Use: Dry wall, paving, raised bed, rock garden, ground cover
Good companions: *Aubrieta* 'Doctor Mules', *Helianthemum* 'Wisley Primrose', *Sempervivum tectorum*

6

9 Helianthemum 'Wisley Primrose'
Rock rose, Sun rose

The dwarf hybrid rock roses are low evergreen shrubs with grey-green or dark green leaves. They bear masses of papery single or double flowers over many weeks. 'Wisley Primrose' has soft yellow single flowers with a more deeply coloured centre, but other rock roses may be yellow, orange, red, yellow, pink or white. Hardy.
General care: To keep compact, trim after flowering.
Height: 30cm (12in) **Spread:** 45cm (18in)
Site: Sun. Well-drained soil. Does well on lime
Use: Front of sunny border, paving, raised bed, rock garden, sunny bank, ground cover
Good companions: *Aubrieta* 'Greencourt Purple', *Campanula carpatica*, *Pulsatilla vulgaris*

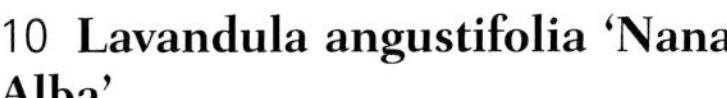

10 Lavandula angustifolia 'Nana Alba'
Lavender, Old English lavender

There are several compact cultivars of *Lavandula angustifolia* but most, including purple-flowered 'Hidcote', grow to at least 45cm (18in) in height. 'Nana Alba' is a particularly neat form with short spikes of white flowers over aromatic grey-green foliage. Hardy.
General care: Trim plants in early spring.
Height and spread: 30cm (12in)
Site: Sun. Well-drained soil
Use: Edging, front of sunny border, raised bed, rock garden
Good companions: *Artemisia stelleriana* 'Boughton Silver', *Hebe cupressoides* 'Boughton Dome', *Helianthemum* 'Wisley Primrose', *Narcissus* 'Jack Snipe'

silver and grey

11 Artemisia schmidtiana 'Nana'
Mugwort, Sagebrush, Wormwood

This evergreen perennial makes a tiny foliage plant. The finely divided leaves have a silky texture and are gathered in a silvery tuft. Hardy.

11

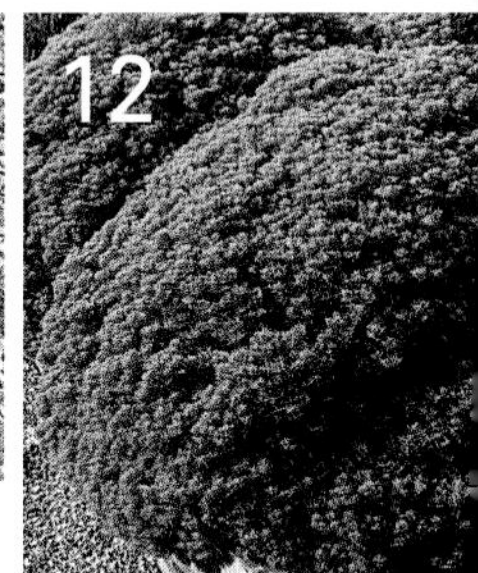
12

General care: To keep compact trim in early spring.
Height: 8cm (3in) **Spread:** 25cm (10in)
Site: Sun. Well-drained soil
Compost: Soil-based (John Innes No. 1) with added grit
Use: Raised bed, rock garden, scree, trough
Good companions: *Dianthus alpinus* 'Joan's Blood', *Crocus* 'Snow Bunting', *Erodium* x *variabile* 'Roseum'

green

12 Hebe cupressoides 'Boughton Dome'

The closely packed stems of this slow-growing, dwarf evergreen shrub are covered with scale-like leaves that form a pale green or olive-green dome. Plants rarely flower. Hardy.
Height: 60cm (2ft) **Spread:** 1m (3ft)
Site: Sun, partial shade. Moist but well-drained soil
Use: Front of border, raised bed, rock garden, ground cover
Good companions: *Alchemilla conjuncta*, *Geranium cinereum* 'Ballerina', *Silene schafta*

waterside & water plants

Most of the plants that relish reliably moist conditions are perennials. Some like the ground really wet and others will even grow in shallow water. Plant in the dormant season.

purple, blue and violet

1 Iris ensata

Japanese iris

Perennial with fleshy creeping stems (rhizomes) from which grow ribbed sword-like leaves. The flowers are violet-purple. Hardy.

Height: 1m (3ft) **Spread:** 20cm (8in)

Site: Sun. Lime-free, humus-rich soil, moist or wet during summer but drier in autumn and winter

Use: Marginal, waterside

Good companions: *Lythrum salicaria* 'Feuerkerze', *Rheum palmatum* 'Sanguineum', *Rodgersia aesculifolia*

2 Iris laevigata 'Variegata'

Beardless water iris

The ivory-and-green variegated sword-like leaves grow from fleshy creeping stems (rhizomes). Soft blue flowers are borne from early to midsummer. Tolerates water to a depth of 15cm (6in). Hardy.

Height: 60cm (2ft) **Spread:** 25cm (10in)

Site: Sun. Humus-rich, wet or reliably moist soil

Compost: Soil-based (aquatic)

Use: Bog garden, marginal, waterside

Good companions: *Iris ensata, Pontederia cordata, Trollius europaeus*

3 Myosotis scorpioides 'Mermaid'

Water forget-me-not

This compact perennial spreads by underground stems (rhizomes) to form small carpets of shiny leaves, topped in early summer by blue flowers. Tolerates water to a depth of 8cm (3in). Hardy.

Height: 25cm (10in) **Spread:** 30cm (12in)

Site: Sun, partial shade. Humus-rich and wet soil

Compost: Soil-based (aquatic)

Use: Bog garden, marginal, waterside

Good companions: *Acorus calamus* 'Variegatus', *Caltha palustris, Pontederia cordata*

pink and mauve

4 Nymphaea 'James Brydon'

Water lily

Perennial water plant with submerged roots and large, rounded floating leaves. These are purplish brown with darker mottling at first but age to brown-green. Crimson-pink floating flowers, with orange-red stamens, are produced throughout summer. Hardy.

Spread: 1m (3ft)

Site: Sun. Still water 45–75cm (18–30in) deep

Compost: Soil-based (aquatic)

Use: Pond

Good companions: *Pontederia cordata, Iris laevigata* 'Variegata', *Zantedeschia aethiopica*

1

5 Primula pulverulenta Bartley hybrids

Candelabra primula

The large, light green crinkled leaves of these perennials form a rosette from which rise several tall stems powdered with white meal (farina). These carry whorls of dark-eyed pink to purple-red flowers. Flowering starts in late spring. Hardy.

Height: 1m (3ft) **Spread:** 60cm (2ft)

Site: Sun, partial shade. Humus-rich and reliably moist soil

Use: Bog garden, moist border, waterside

Good companions: *Filipendula rubra* 'Venusta', *Lobelia* 'Queen Victoria', *Matteuccia struthiopteris*

red and russet

6 Rheum palmatum 'Atrosanguineum'

Chinese rhubarb

The crinkled, jagged lobed leaves of this perennial emerge purplish pink from shiny red buds. By the time the plume of tiny crimson flowers erupts in early summer, the surface of the leaves is dark green. Pink-flushed seed cases follow. Hardy.

Height: 2.5m (8ft) **Spread:** 2m (6ft)

Site: Sun, partial shade. Humus-rich, fertile and reliably moist soil

Use: Bog garden, sunny or lightly shaded border, waterside

Good companions: *Astilbe chinensis* var. *taquetii* 'Superba', *Lobelia* 'Queen Victoria', *Rodgersia pinnata* 'Superba'

2

3

4

yellow and orange

7 Nymphaea 'Pygmaea Helvola'

Water lily

Perennial water plant with submerged roots and olive-green floating leaves that are mottled with purple. Yellow star-shaped flowers with orange stamens are borne freely throughout summer. Slightly fragrant. Hardy.

Spread: 60cm (2ft)
Site: Sun. Still water 15-30cm (6-12in) deep
Compost: Soil-based (aquatic)
Use: Floating aquatic
Good companions: *Iris laevigata* 'Variegata', *Myosotis scorpioides* 'Mermaid', *Nymphaea* 'Frobelii'

8 Primula florindae

Giant cowslip

This perennial forms a dense clump of rounded leaves. In summer several tall flowering stems each dangle up to 40 fragrant yellow bells, which are lightly powdered with white meal (farina). Attractive seed heads follow. Hardy.
Height: 1.2m (4ft) **Spread:** 75cm (2ft 6in)
Site: Sun, partial shade. Humus-rich and reliably moist soil
Use: Bog garden, moist border, waterside
Good companions: *Astilbe* 'Professor van der Wielen', *Hosta sieboldiana* var. *elegans*, *Matteuccia struthiopteris*

9 Trollius chinensis 'Golden Queen'

European globeflower

This perennial forms a mound of deeply lobed glossy leaves. Erect stems carry deep orange-yellow cup-shaped flowers, more than 5cm (2in) across, clear of the foliage. Hardy.
Height: 75cm (2ft 6in) **Spread:** 45cm (18in)
Site: Sun, partial shade. Fertile, reliably moist soil
Use: Bog garden, moist border, waterside, wild garden
Good companions: *Astrantia major* subsp. *involucrata* 'Shaggy', *Primula florindae*, *Rodgersia aesculifolia*

cream and white

10 Acorus calamus 'Argenteostriatus'

Sweet flag

Aromatic perennial with sword-like leaves that grow from underground stems (rhizomes). Striped lengthwise with cream and white, the foliage is shown to good effect when reflected in water. Tolerates water up to 20cm (8in) deep. Hardy.
Height: 1m (3ft) **Spread:** 60cm (2ft)
Site: Sun. Very moist or wet soil
Use: Bog garden, marginal, waterside
Good companions: *Caltha palustris* var. *palustris*, *Ligularia* 'The Rocket', *Myosotis scorpioides* 'Mermaid'

11 Zantedeschia aethiopica 'Crowborough'

Arum lily

Clump-forming perennial with arrow-shaped leaves that survive mild winters. The white spathe swirls around a yellow spadix, on which the tiny true flowers are clustered. Tolerates water to a depth of 30cm (12in). Not fully hardy.
General care: In frost-prone areas protect crown in winter with a mulch.
Height: 1m (3ft) **Spread:** 60cm (2ft)
Site: Sun. Fertile, humus-rich, reliably moist soil
Compost: Soil-based (John Innes No. 2)
Use: Bog garden, container, moist border
Good companions: *Caltha palustris* 'Flore Pleno', *Iris pseudacorus* 'Variagata', *Ligularia* 'The Rocket'

green

12 Gunnera manicata

Deciduous perennial that annually produces massive prickly stems and huge, boldly lobed textured leaves, often more than 2m (6ft) across. A cone-shaped, greenish brown flower spike stands 60cm (2ft) high. Not fully hardy.
General care: Protect the crowns in winter.
Height: 2.5m (8ft) **Spread:** 4m (12ft)
Site: Sun, partial shade. Humus-rich, fertile and reliably moist soil
Use: Bog garden, waterside
Good companions: *Eupatorium purpureum*, *Ligularia* 'Gregynog Gold', *Lysichiton americanus*

herbs, vegetables & fruit

Useful plants are often very ornamental, especially when in blossom or making fresh growth, but the first reason for growing early maturing vegetables and fresh herbs is their produce.

herbs

1 Borage
Borago officinalis
Hairy-leaved annual with blue star-shaped flowers throughout summer and autumn. Young leaves can be added to salads and dressings; the flowers are used as culinary decoration. Hardy.
General care: Sow seed *in situ* from spring to early autumn. Deadhead regularly to avoid over-abundant self-seeding.
Height: 60cm (2ft) **Spread:** 45cm (18in)
Site: Sun. Well-drained soil, low in fertility
Compost: Soil-less
Use: Border, large container

2 Chervil
Anthriscus cerefolium
Feathery foliaged annual with clusters of white flowers from spring to summer. The mild parsley-flavoured leaves are added to salads, soups, sauces and vegetable and egg dishes. Hardy.
General care: Sow seed *in situ* monthly from spring to early autumn.
Height: 45–60cm (18–24in) **Spread:** 30cm (12in)
Site: Partial shade. Light soil with added organic matter to improve moisture retention
Compost: Soil-less
Use: Border, large container

3 Dill
Anethum graveolens
Feathery foliaged annual with flat heads of tiny yellow-green flowers. Leaves and seeds are used to flavour soups, fish and lamb. For a regular supply of young foliage, sow successively. Hardy.
General care: Sow seed *in situ* in spring and early summer. Water during dry weather. Trim container-grown plants regularly. Self-seeds readily, so remove unwanted seed heads.
Height: 1–1.5m (3–5ft) **Spread:** 30cm (12in).
Site: Sun. Well-drained soil, low in fertility
Compost: Soil-less
Use: Border, container

4 Hyssop
Hyssopus officinalis
Semi-evergreen perennial with long, narrow leaves that can be added to salads, soups, stews, stuffing and meat. Throughout summer and into early autumn it is smothered with small blue flowers. Hardy.
General care: To maintain a bushy shape trim the clump in spring and again after flowering.
Height: 60cm (2ft) **Spread:** 1m (3ft)
Site: Sun. Well-drained soil
Compost: Soil-based (John Innes No. 3) with added grit
Use: Border, container, low hedge, edging

5 Mint, apple
Mentha suaveolens
Perennial with apple-and-mint flavoured, oval to rounded mid-green leaves. In summer there are mauve flowers. Very invasive, so grow in a large bottomless container sunk in the ground. Hardy.
General care: Trim edges of clump regularly to limit spread.
Height: 1m (3ft)
Spread: Indefinite
Site: Sun, partial shade. Any soil except very dry
Compost: Soil-based (John Innes No. 3)
Use: Border, container

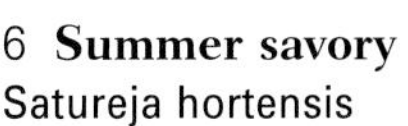

6 Summer savory
Satureja hortensis

Perennial with long, narrow, dark green leaves and in summer sprays of tiny insignificant flowers. Young leaves are used for flavouring vinegar, cooked dishes and salads. The flavour deteriorates in older plants, so replace them every three years. Half hardy.
General care: Protect over winter with deep mulch or a thick layer of straw. Alternatively, grow in a container and move under cover in winter, keeping the compost dry.
Height: 1m (3ft) **Spread:** 45cm (18in)
Site: Sun. Fertile and well-drained soil
Compost: Soil-based (John Innes No. 3) with added grit
Use: Border, container

vegetables

7 Artichoke, globe
Cynara scolymus

Large perennial with edible immature flowerheads. Easy to grow but plants take up a lot of space and need to be replaced after three years. Good varieties include 'Green Globe' and 'Gros Vert de Laon'. Hardy.
Site: Sun. Preferably fertile, well-drained soil
How to grow: Plant rooted offsets in early spring, 60cm (2ft) apart and 75cm (2ft 6in) between rows. Top-dress established plants with fertiliser in early spring and mulch with rotted manure or compost. While the heads are developing, water well during dry weather. Cut the heads when they are fleshy and well formed but while the scales are still closed. After harvest cut down the old stems.

8 Beetroot
Beta vulgaris subsp. vulgaris

Easily grown edible swollen roots with deep red flesh. Choose a bolt-resistant cultivar for early sowings. Hardy.
Site: Sun. Fertile and well-drained soil, not recently manured
How to grow: At the very end of winter or the beginning of spring sow seed, in rows 30cm (12in) apart, under cloches that have been in place for several weeks. Thin seedlings to 10cm (4in) apart. During dry weather water thoroughly once or twice a week. Harvest as required as soon as the roots are sufficiently large.

9 Broad bean
Vicia faba

Broad beans are the earliest outdoor bean to be harvested. For overwintering early plants choose a hardy variety. Sweetly scented flowers. Hardy.
Site: Sun. Fertile and well-drained soil
How to grow: For an early summer crop, sow seed in late autumn, 15–23cm (6–9in) apart with 45–60cm (18–24in) between rows, depending on height. Choose a sheltered site or protect with cloches. In early spring top-dress with fertiliser and lightly hoe into the soil. Support plants with string stretched between canes. When in flower, pinch out the young top growth to boost pod development. Pick before the pods become tough and fibrous. After harvest, cut stems almost to ground level and dig in the roots.

10 Cabbage, summer
Brassica oleracea Capitata Group

Cabbage with a compact rounded head. For an early crop sow under cover. Outdoor sowings, made when the soil is fairly warm at around 7°C (45°F), will mature from late summer onwards. Choose an early maturing variety. Hardy.
Site: Sun. Alkaline, fertile, moisture-retentive soil
How to grow: In late winter or very early spring sow seed in trays under glass in gentle heat – 13°C (55°F). Prick out the seedlings into individual pots and grow on. Harden off then plant out when around 10cm (4in) high, allowing 45cm (18in) all round. Feed established plants with fertiliser. Harvest as soon as the plants are well hearted, using a knife to cut just above soil level.

11 Cauliflower
Brassica oleracea Botrytis Group

Cauliflowers are grown for the white immature flowerheads known as 'curds'. Choose a summer-maturing variety. Can be a difficult crop. Hardy.
Site: Sun. Alkaline, fertile and humus-rich soil, that has been deeply dug
How to grow: Sow seed in mid-autumn in a cold frame or in midwinter under cover in gentle heat – about 13°C (55°F). Grow on young plants in individual pots in a coldframe then harden off and plant out in early spring in a sunny, sheltered site, allowing 45cm (18in) each way. Keep well watered. Harvest individual curds when firm and well developed but before they open.

12 Courgette (zucchini)
Cucurbita pepo

Prolific plant with long green or rounded golden fruits. The large yellow flowers are also edible and can be cooked in batter or used as decoration. Select early maturing varieties. Tender.
Site: Sun. Well-drained and fertile soil with plenty of rotted manure or compost
How to grow: In early spring sow seed under cover in gentle heat – 13°C (55°F). Place two seeds in an 8cm (3in) pot and thin later to one seedling. Grow on and plant out 1m (3ft) apart, in a sheltered site when all danger of frost is past. Keep well watered and feed with liquid fertiliser once the fruits begin to swell. Harvest regularly as soon as the fruits are large enough.

1

2

3

4

5

6

vegetables (continued)

1 French bean, dwarf
Phaseolus vulgaris

Small bushy annual with long edible pods. Select varieties suitable for early sowing. Tender.

Site: Sun. Fertile and well-drained soil

How to grow: In mid-spring sow seed under cover individually in small pots or modular trays. Plant out seedlings under cloches that have been warming the soil for several weeks, 10cm (4in) apart with 45cm (18in) between rows; top-dress the soil with fertiliser before planting. Keep plants well watered, especially once flowers appear. Harvest regularly as soon as pods are sufficiently large but before the seeds are prominent.

2 Garlic
Allium sativum

The underground bulbs of this strongly flavoured member of the onion family keep for many months if they are ripened in the sun. Garlic produced for cultivation is more reliable than bulbs from the greengrocer, as the latter may not be suitable for cooler climates. Hardy.

Site: Sun. Well-drained and fertile soil, not recently manured

How to grow: In early to midwinter plant individual cloves 10cm (4in) apart with the tip just showing, and 23cm (9in) between rows; use a trowel or dibber rather than press the cloves into the ground. If drainage is poor, draw up the soil into low ridges and plant the garlic on top. Lift bulbs in mid to late summer, once the leaves have fallen over and begun to yellow. Spread in the sun to dry thoroughly.

3 Lettuce
Lactuca sativa

Several different types of lettuce can be grown outdoors for cropping from early summer onwards. Choose from crisp cos or Webb's types; loose-leaf or 'cut-and-come-again' lettuces such as 'Lollo Rosso'; or butterhead varieties like 'Tom Thumb'. For a continuous supply, sow every two to three weeks. Cool season plants, some types tolerant of frost.

Site: Sun. Fertile and well-drained soil

How to grow: From mid-spring onwards, sow seed in rows 23–30cm (9–12in) apart. Thin to 15–30cm (6–12in) apart, depending on the size of the variety. In cold areas or for a very early crop, sow under cover, prick out into individual pots then harden off and plant out in late spring. Keep plants well watered during dry spells. Harvest when lettuces are sufficiently large.

4 Mangetout
Pisum sativum

A type of pea grown for its edible pods and seeds. Tall climbing varieties grow 1.5m (5ft) high, while smaller ones reach 75cm (2ft 6in). Varieties include 'Carouby de Maussanne', 'Oregon Sugar Pod' and 'Sugar Snap'. Tender.

Site: Sun. Well-drained and fertile soil with well-rotted compost or manure dug in during winter

How to grow: Sow from early spring onwards and grow as for peas (see 6, below). Harvest when the peas are just visible as tiny swellings; pick regularly to encourage the production of pods.

5 Onion
Allium cepa

Most onions and shallots are grown from 'sets' planted in spring, but seed sown the previous year gives an early summer crop. Not fully hardy.

Site: Sun. Alkaline and well-drained soil

How to grow: In late summer to early autumn, sow in rows or in blocks 30cm (12in) apart in an open, sheltered site. Thin to 5cm (2in) apart in spring and feed with general fertiliser. Harvest for eating as soon as bulbs are large enough. For storing, loosen roots with a fork when leaves flop; leave for a week, then lift and dry in sun.

6 Pea
Pisum sativum

Easy climbing annuals that can provide a crop in early to midsummer. Choose a suitable variety such as 'Douce Provence', 'Early Onward', 'Feltham First' or 'Kelvedon Wonder'. Hardy.

Site: Sun. Well-drained and fertile soil, with well-rotted compost or manure dug in during winter
How to grow: For the earliest crops, sow in late winter under cloches, then outdoors from very early spring onwards. Form a drill with a broad hoe 3cm (1¼in) deep and sow seeds 5cm (2in) apart in a triple row. Net freshly sown seed to protect from birds and put up supports such as netting or twiggy branches when the plants are 10cm (4in) high. Harvest pods when they are well filled but still young; pick regularly.

7 Potato, first early
Solanum tuberosum

These edible tubers are classified according to when they mature, with 'first earlies' maturing in early to midsummer. They can be grown outside with protection or if 'earthed up' with soil. They are ready when the flowers are fully open, around three months after planting. Not fully hardy.
Site: Sun. Acid, fertile and well-drained soil, deeply dug
How to grow: Set seed potatoes to sprout, or 'chit', at the end of winter and plant out in early spring, 15cm (6in) deep with 30cm (12in) between tubers and 60cm (2ft) between rows. Before planting, rake in a general fertiliser. Protect with fleece or polythene, or mound the soil over the rows every two to three weeks. During dry weather, water well once a week. Use a fork to lift carefully as needed.

7

fruit

8 Cherry, sweet
Prunus avium

Compact cherries can be grown in bush, pyramid or fan-trained forms. A number of self-fertile varieties will set a good crop with their own pollen. Best where rainfall is light and in a sheltered position. Hardy.
Site: Sun. Deep, fertile and well-drained soil
How to grow: Plant trees 3–5m (10–15ft) apart depending on the rootstock. To avoid fruit splitting, keep the soil moist but not overwet. Feed in late winter with general fertiliser and mulch with well-rotted manure or compost. Prune if necessary during the growing season. Net fruit to protect it from birds.

9 Gooseberry
Ribes uva-crispa

The green or red berries of this prickly bush are the first soft fruits of the summer season. Usually grown as a bush but can also be trained in half-standard and cordon form. Hardy.
Site: Sun. Well-drained and fertile soil, with plenty of added well-rotted manure or compost
How to grow: Plant 1.2m (4ft) apart with 1.5m (5ft) between rows. In early spring feed each bush with 50g (2oz) sulphate of potash and mulch with plenty of well-rotted manure or compost. Water well while fruit is forming, but stop when it is nearly ripe, otherwise the berries may split. Fruit may need thinning from late spring onwards. Net bushes when the fruit starts to ripen to protect it from birds.

10 Raspberry
Rubus idaeus

Summer-fruiting raspberries crop at different times depending on the variety. They thrive in sun in cool climates but prefer partial shade in hot areas. Hardy.
Site: Sun, partial shade. Fertile and well-drained soil, slightly acid and with plenty of added well-rotted manure or compost
How to grow: Grow on a framework of 1.5m (5ft) high posts and horizontal wires, 30cm (12in) apart. Plant dormant canes in autumn or early winter 40cm (16in) apart, with the topmost roots no more than 5cm (2in) below the surface of the soil, and cut back to 15cm (6in) high. In spring feed with general fertiliser and mulch generously with well-rotted manure or compost. Water well in dry weather but not while the fruit is ripening. After harvest, cut old canes at ground level and tie in new ones 10cm (4in) apart, fanning them out if necessary.

11 Red and white currants
Ribes sativum

Easy and reliable. Grown as bushes, half standards or cordons in warm sheltered sites. Hardy.
Site: Sun. Fertile and well-drained soil, preferably slightly acid and with plenty of added compost or well-rotted manure
How to grow: Plant 1.2m (4ft) apart with 1.5m (5ft) between rows. In early spring feed each bush with 50g (2oz) per bush of sulphate of potash and mulch with well-rotted manure or compost. In summer pull off any suckers produced from below ground.

12 Strawberry
Fragaria x ananassa

Strawberry plants crop well for several years and different varieties can provide a succession of fruit throughout summer. Hardy.
Site: Sun. Fertile and well-drained soil, preferably slightly acid and with plenty of well-rotted manure
Compost: Soil-based (John Innes No. 3)
How to grow: Plant in autumn or early spring in deeply dug well-manured ground, containers or raised beds. Space 30–38cm (12–15in) apart with 1m (3ft) between rows. In late winter feed with sulphate of potash. Feed older plants with a general fertiliser if their vigour declines. After flowering, water thoroughly every two weeks in dry conditions. Net to protect the fruit from birds.

8
9

11

10

12

choosing the best plants

The following plant lists draw on all the plants described in the preceding pages of the Plant Selector, but they are grouped together here to help you choose plants for particular conditions, situations and uses.

plants for clay soil

Although the following plants generally succeed on close-textured clay soils, they do better when the ground has been improved by the addition of grit and organic matter such as well-rotted garden compost.

- *Abelia schumanii*
- *Acanthus spinosus*
- *Alchemilla mollis*
- *Astilbe* (all)
- *Camassia leichtlinii* 'Electra'
- *Cornus alba* 'Elegantissima'
- *Cornus kousa* var. *chinensis*
- *Deutzia* x *rosea*
- *Fargesia murielae*
- *Hemerocallis* (all)
- *Hosta* (all)
- *Humulus lupulus* 'Aureus'
- *Hydrangea anomala* subsp. *petiolaris*
- *Kalmia latifolia* 'Ostbo Red'
- *Kniphofia* 'Early Buttercup'
- *Miscanthus sinensis* 'Zebrinus'
- *Passiflora caerulea*
- *Philadelphus hybrids* (all)
- *Primula florindae*
- *Primula pulverulenta* Bartley hybrids
- *Rheum palmatum* 'Atrosanguineum'
- *Rosa* (all)
- *Thalictrum aquilegiifolium*
- *Weigela* 'Victoria'
- *Wisteria* (all)

Passiflora caerulea

plants for dry chalky soil

A large number of plants are automatically excluded from this list because they do not tolerate alkaline (limy) soil. The improvement of shallow chalky soil by the addition of moisture-retaining organic matter generally improves the performance of the following plants and allows lime-tolerant but moisture-loving plants, notably clematis, to be grown successfully.

- *Acanthus spinosus*
- *Achillea* 'Taygetea'
- *Allium* (most)
- *Antirrhinum* Sonnet Series
- *Anthemis tinctoria* 'E.C. Buxton'
- *Armeria maritima* 'Düsseldorfer Stolz'
- *Campanula cochleariifolia*
- *Campanula latifolia*
- *Centaurea cyanus*
- *Dianthus barbatus*
- *Erysimum* 'Bowles' Mauve'
- *Geranium cinereum* 'Ballerina'
- *Gypsophila repens* 'Rosa Schönheit'
- *Helianthemum* 'Wisley Primrose'
- *Iris* (all bearded)
- *Lavandula angustifolia* 'Nana Alba'
- *Nepeta* 'Six Hills Giant'
- *Papaver orientale* 'Black and White'
- *Philadelphus* 'Belle Etoile'
- *Potentilla fruticosa* 'Tangerine'
- *Salvia* x *sylvestris* 'Mainacht'
- *Salvia viridis* 'Oxford Blue'
- *Verbascum* (all)
- *Weigela* 'Victoria'

Weigela 'Victoria'

plants for sandy or gravelly soil

The following plants require free drainage and are generally drought tolerant. The range of plants that can be grown in dry sunny gardens will be enlarged if the soil is improved by the addition of organic matter.

- *Acanthus spinosus*
- *Achillea* 'Taygetea'
- *Allium* (all)
- *Anthemis tinctoria* 'E.C. Buxton'
- *Artemisia ludoviciana* 'Valerie Finnis'
- *Artemisia* 'Powis Castle'
- *Ceanothus* 'Italian Skies'
- *Cistus* (all)
- *Dianthus* 'Gran's Favourite'
- *Erysimum* 'Bowles' Mauve'
- *Eschscholzia californica*
- *Festuca glauca* 'Elijah Blue'
- *Gleditisia triacanthos* 'Sunburst'
- *Helianthemum* 'Wisley Primrose'
- *Nepeta* 'Six Hills Giant'
- *Papaver orientale* 'Black and White'
- *Philadelphus* 'Belle Etoile'
- *Potentilla fruticosa* 'Tangerine'
- *Robinia pseudoacacia* 'Frisia'
- *Ruta graveolens* 'Jackman's Blue'
- *Salvia* x *sylvestris* 'Mainacht'
- *Tropaeolum majus* 'Empress of India'
- *Verbascum* Cotswold Group 'Gainsborough'

Dianthus 'Gran's Favourite'

plants for acid soils

Plants marked with an asterisk* will grow satisfactorily only on soils that are free of lime. Other plants in the list thrive on acid soils, but may also grow on neutral or slightly alkaline soils.

- *Arisaema candidissimum*
- *Betula pendula* 'Youngii'
- *Cornus controversa* 'Variegata'
- *Cornus kousa* var. *chinensis*
- *Helianthemum* 'Wisley Primrose'*
- *Kalmia latifolia* 'Ostbo Red'*
- *Lithodora diffusa* 'Heavenly Blue'*
- *Lupinus* 'Chandelier'
- *Meconopsis betonicifolia**
- *Primula florindae*
- *Primula pulverulenta* Bartley hybrids
- *Rhododendron* (all)*
- *Schisandra rubrifolia*
- *Styrax japonicus**

plants for ground cover

The following plants can be used to create an attractive weed-excluding cover. Effective cover can only be achieved by planting in soil that is free of perennial weeds.

- *Alchemilla mollis*
- *Arenaria montana*
- *Armeria maritima* 'Düsseldorfer Stolz'
- *Artemisia* 'Powis Castle'
- *Festuca glauca* 'Elijah Blue'
- *Geranium* (most)
- *Hebe cupressoides* 'Boughton Dome'
- *Hebe* 'Youngii'
- *Helianthemum* 'Wisley Primrose'
- *Hosta* (most)
- *Lithodora diffusa* 'Heavenly Blue'
- *Nepeta* 'Six Hills Giant'
- *Parthenocissus henryana*
- *Rhododendron* (small and medium evergreens)
- *Rosa* 'Bonica'

plants for moist shade

The following plants tolerate or, more commonly, thrive in moist shade, although many will also grow in full sun provided the soil is moist. Plants marked with an asterisk* will grow in boggy conditions.

- *Aconitum* 'Ivorine'
- *Alchemilla mollis*
- *Arisaema candidissimum*
- *Astilbe* (all)*
- *Astrantia major* subsp. *involucrata* 'Shaggy'
- *Cornus alba* 'Elegantissima'
- *Cornus kousa* var. *chinensis*
- *Fargesia murielae*
- *Fuchsia* (all)
- *Geum rivale* 'Leonard's Variety'
- *Gunnera manicata**
- *Hosta* (all)
- *Kalmia latifolia* 'Ostbo Red'
- *Myosotis scorpioides* 'Mermaid'*
- *Persicaria bistorta* 'Superba'
- *Phalaris arundinacea* var. *picta* 'Feesey'*
- *Primula florindae**
- *Primula pulverulenta* Bartley hybrids
- *Rheum palmatum* 'Atrosanguineum'*
- *Rhododendron* (all)
- *Tiarella wherryi*
- *Viola cornuta* Alba Group
- *Viola* (all)

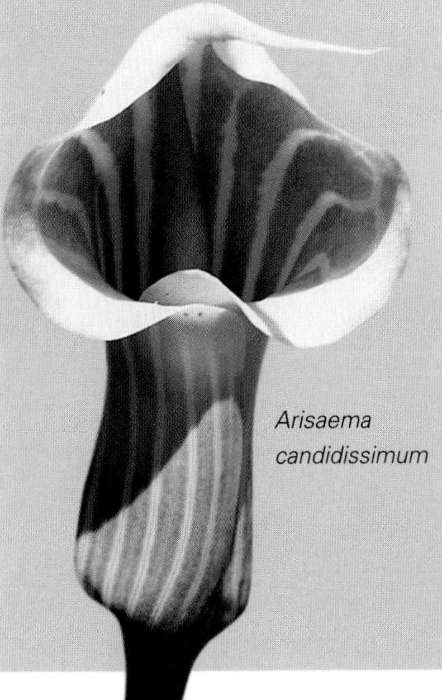

Arisaema candidissimum

plants for coastal sites

Where windbreaks and hedges give protection from salt-laden winds, a wide range of plants can be grown in coastal gardens. Many benefit from the sea's moderating influence on temperatures.

- *Anthemis tinctoria* 'E.C. Buxton'
- *Armeria maritima* 'Düsseldorfer Stolz'
- *Artemisia ludoviciana* 'Valerie Finnis'
- *Artemisia* 'Powis Castle'
- *Campanula cochleariifolia*
- *Centaurea cyanus*
- *Cistus ladanifer*
- *Cistus* 'Silver Pink'
- *Clarkia amoena* Satin Series
- *Dianthus* (all)
- *Erysimum* 'Bowles' Mauve'
- *Eschscholzia californica*
- *Festuca glauca* 'Elijan Blue'
- *Fuchsia* (most)
- *Hebe* (all)
- *Helianthemum* 'Wisley Primrose'
- *Kniphofia* 'Early Buttercup'
- *Nepeta* 'Six Hills Giant'
- *Papaver rhoeas* 'Mother of Pearl'
- *Papaver somniferum*
- *Petunia* (all)
- *Potentilla fruticosa* 'Tangerine'
- *Ruta graveolens* 'Jackman's Blue'
- *Salvia viridis* 'Oxford Blue'
- *Sisyrinchium striatum* 'Aunt May'
- *Veronica austriaca* subsp. *teucrium* 'Kapitan'
- Veronica gentianoides

Cistus 'Silver Pink'

late summer

practical diary

A huge number of flowering plants are at their absolute best in late summer, providing a constant display of colour, but once flowering is over many will need to be cut back or lightly sheared. Roses benefit from deadheading now, if you want plenty of autumn blooms, and removing damaged stems will enhance the appearance of your borders. And there is much tidying to do around ponds and on the patio. But the most enjoyable work at this time of year is without doubt harvesting all the vegetables and fruit that you have been nurturing since the growing season began.

perennials

Give a little care to your flowering perennials and they will continue to perform well into autumn, although there is still time to fill gaps with new plants for late colour. With an eye to the future, take a few cuttings of tender perennials and prepare the ground for autumn planting.

now is the season to . . .

■ **deadhead border perennials regularly,** not only to improve their looks but also to encourage more flowers. Frequent deadheading of tender perennials is particularly worthwhile in order to prolong their display until the first frosts.

■ **stake late flowering tall perennials** such as cimicifugas, michaelmas daisies and phlox, before they start to topple. Surround clumps with a ring of short stakes and run garden string around the stakes. 'Grow-through' plant supports give the best results, but they need to be in place by early summer – something worth remembering for next year.

■ **cut back perennials that have finished flowering** and are flopping over, such as catmint (*Nepeta*), achilleas and hardy geraniums (see opposite).

Daisy-flowered *Echinacea purpurea* is one of the most colourful mainstays of the late summer border.

■ **water and feed** perennials in containers regularly.

■ **keep new plants moist** by watering thoroughly every couple of days if necessary. Established perennials that are not drought tolerant will benefit from a good soaking twice a week during prolonged periods of dry weather.

■ **hoe off weed seedlings** regularly when the weather is warm and dry. Every couple of weeks, look for larger weeds that may be growing unnoticed among mature perennials, and pull them up before they seed. Bindweed and ground elder are a real nuisance once established, so treat them with a weedkiller such as glyphosate. Take care to keep the chemical well away from other plants as it kills everything it touches. The alternative is to dig up every scrap of root.

■ **keep a look out** for pests and diseases.

■ **plant new perennials** for autumn flowers (see opposite).

■ **feed plants** that are coming up to flowering and tender perennials with a high-potash liquid fertiliser.

■ **pot up rooted cuttings** taken earlier and thin seedlings.

■ **propagate new perennials** by layering (see page 306) and taking cuttings (see page 301).

and if you have time . . .

■ **prepare the ground** for autumn planting.

■ **divide established clumps** of the very earliest spring-flowering perennials (see page 306).

■ **collect seed** for sowing or storing; pot up any self-sown seedlings you wish to keep.

pests and diseases

These can take hold very fast in warm weather, so inspect plants regularly and treat if necessary. While perennials are less susceptible than many other groups of plants, there are several problems that commonly occur at this time of year.

- **fungal diseases** include mildew (look out for this on michaelmas daisies) and rust, which can affect dianthus and campanulas. Limit the spread by removing affected foliage and spraying the plant with fungicide. Burn or bin the foliage, or the disease spores will overwinter and attack again next year.
- **vine weevil grubs** commonly feed on the roots of plants growing in containers. If your container plants show signs of ailing, remove them from the pot and look for the white comma-shaped grubs in the compost. Remove and destroy them and repot the plant in fresh potting compost.

Colourful perennials in the late summer border include red hot pokers (*Kniphofia*), seen here alongside the paler blooms of camassias.

Heliopsis

perennials for autumn colour

- heliopsis • kaffir lily (*Schizostylis coccinea*)
- lilyturf (*Liriope muscari*) • michaelmas daisies (*Aster*)
- rudbeckia

planting and transplanting

- **fill gaps in your border** with autumn-flowering perennials (see above right). They can make a handsome display this year provided you buy large plants in 15–20cm (6–8in) pots. Choose bushy, well-grown specimens with plenty of flower buds and avoid any that are tall, leggy or yellow leaved.
- **plant out young perennials** raised from seed or cuttings earlier in the year, so long as the roots are well developed in a minimum pot size of 8cm (3in). Alternatively, pot them on into 13cm (5in) pots and plant out next year.
- **transplant or pot up** young perennials that have self-seeded in the border or on gravel paths. It is worth looking out for such seedlings before hoeing or spraying with weedkiller. Either pot up plants into 8cm (3in) pots or grow them in a row in a nursery bed or a spare piece of ground and plant out next year.
- **plan new borders** and prepare the ground for planting hardy herbaceous perennials. In early September the soil is warm and moist, which encourages plenty of root growth, while the shorter days and falling temperatures ensure the plants do not put their energies into making excess top growth.

cutting back untidy perennials

1 **Once early flowering** perennials like geraniums have finished blooming, they become straggly and untidy. To encourage new growth, cut them back to ground level using shears.

2 **Clear away the trimmings** – they can go on the compost heap – then cut off neatly any remaining straggly stems.

3 **Apply a sprinkling** of general fertiliser and water well. The plant will soon develop a tidy mound of fresh foliage and often more flowers.

perennials/2

propagation

Almost all herbaceous perennials are quick and easy to propagate by at least one method. Give priority to tender perennials, because taking cuttings now is insurance against the parent plant failing to survive the winter.

layering border carnations

Select non-flowering sideshoots for layering, then improve the soil around the plant by forking in some potting compost where the layer is to root.

- **Use a knife to remove** a small sliver, about 1cm (½in) long, from the underside of a sideshoot; the wound will stimulate root production. Peg the wounded area of the stem into the soil using a bent wire.
- **Stake the end of the shoot** to keep it upright. Lightly cover the wounded area with soil.
- **Layers should be well rooted** by autumn, when they can be detached, moved to a nursery bed then planted out next year.

raising from seed

You can raise many hardy perennials from seed, either those you have purchased or those you have collected yourself. Bear in mind when collecting seed that although the offspring of plant species come true, those of cultivated varieties are likely to be variable and often inferior to the parent plant.

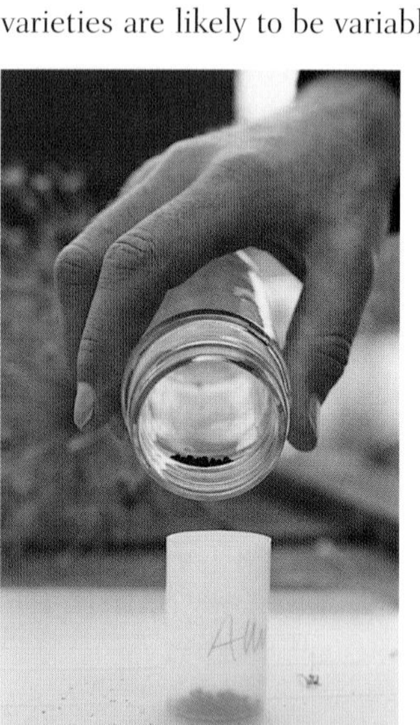

Transfer collected seeds into used film canisters and store in the dark.

- **Collect seed heads** on a dry sunny day as soon as they have turned brown, which indicates the seeds are ripe. Either cover with a paper bag and shake, or cut off the heads and remove the seeds.
- **Store seeds in paper bags,** envelopes or used film canisters. Do not use polythene bags as the seeds could rot. Label each container with the plant name and the date.
- **Sow seeds into pots** or trays of moist compost and cover with a thin layer of perlite or horticultural vermiculite. Stand pots in a coldframe or a sheltered spot outside. Alternatively, sow seeds outside in rows in a well-cultivated nursery bed.

To divide pulmonaria, lift a clump and pull it apart into smaller pieces or individual plantlets. Discard the old central portion and replant the divisions. Water the plants well and keep them moist in dry weather.

helping seed germination

Most perennials are suitable for sowing immediately, but certain varieties need special treatment in order to germinate. The seeds of baptisia and lupin have a hard coating that needs to be chipped carefully with a sharp knife or rubbed with sandpaper to allow water to penetrate before germination can take place. Others, such as certain varieties of campanula and primula, require a cold period, known as stratification. To stratify seeds, mix them with damp potting compost in a plastic bag and keep in the fridge for several weeks. Then sow in autumn.

propagating by division

While most perennials are divided in autumn or spring, those that bloom early in spring, like bleeding heart (*Dicentra spectabilis*), leopard's bane (*Doronicum*) and pulmonaria do better if you divide them in late August or early September. Then they have time to establish before flowering next year. This easy method of propagation also rejuvenates old plants that have formed large congested clumps (see above).

taking cuttings of tender perennials

1 Select young healthy shoots, without flowers if possible. Remove the tip to make a cutting about 10cm (4in) long. Use a sharp knife to trim the base just below a leaf joint and remove the lower leaves. Dipping the base in hormone rooting powder improves the success rate but is not vital.

2 Fill a tray or 13cm (5in) pot with cuttings compost. Though not essential, it aids rooting if you mix compost with a third by volume of horticultural vermiculite or perlite. To reduce the risk of rot, space cuttings so that the leaves do not touch. Water with a fungicide and allow to drain, then cover with a lid or plastic bag.

Brightly coloured coleus come in many different leaf forms.

taking soft-tip cuttings

Take soft-tip cuttings to propagate woody-based tender perennials (see below) and varieties of herbaceous perennials that are difficult or impossible to raise from seed or division, such as penstemon and phygelius. Most tender perennials root easily from cuttings taken during summer (see above), though with non-woody herbaceous perennials it is important to select non-flowering shoots.

A high level of humidity is important for success, so either cover the pots with an inflated clear polythene bag secured with an elastic band or place them in a propagator out of the sun. The exception here is pelargoniums, which are prone to rotting and so best left uncovered.

After about eight weeks, carefully remove the pot to check whether the roots are well developed. If they are, pot up the cuttings individually into 8cm (3in) pots. Overwinter the young plants on a windowsill or in a greenhouse; the parent plant can be left to take its chances outside.

there is still time to . . .

- **divide bearded irises** after flowering (see Summer).
- **take cuttings of pinks** (*Dianthus*), known as 'pipings'.

perennials to raise from soft-tip cuttings

• achillea • anthemis • campanula • coleus • dianthus • diascia • erysimum • euphorbia • nepeta • parahebe • penstemon • phygelius • tanacetum • veronica

Anthemis tinctoria 'Sauce Hollandaise'

looking ahead . . .

☑ AUTUMN Pot up rooted cuttings individually.

☑ Pot up rooted layers of border carnations.

☑ Prick out seedling perennials in pots or thin those in a nursery bed.

annuals & biennials

Give your sweet peas more room to grow upwards and they will reward you with many more blooms, but only if you keep picking. Deadheading other annuals will keep them flowering until autumn approaches, but let some of them set seed for sowing next season.

now is the season to . . .

■ **water plants regularly** in dry weather, especially those growing in containers, and feed with a high-potash fertiliser, such as a tomato feed, every seven to fourteen days.

Cornflowers should be deadheaded as soon as their flowers start to fade, to extend the display.

■ **remove faded flowers** to prolong the display, unless you intend saving the seeds.

■ **control weeds** in beds and borders, if possible without treading on the soil between flowering plants.

■ **watch out for signs of** seasonal problems such as moulds, mildews and virus diseases, earwigs and red spider mites, and vine weevils in containers.

■ **cut and dry flowers,** such as 'everlastings', for long-lasting indoor displays (see page 215).

■ **fill gaps in your display** by planting late-sown annuals, and water them in with a diluted liquid feed.

■ **support tall flowers** such as sunflowers and hollyhocks, and continue tying in sweet peas and other annual climbers.

■ **lower cordon sweet peas** that have reached the tops of their canes (see opposite).

■ **select the best annuals** and allow them to set seed for gathering and drying for storage.

■ **sow some hardy annuals** in early September. These will overwinter and flower early next year (see opposite).

and if you have time . . .

■ **encourage bushy growth** by cutting back by half the long bare stems of sprawling annuals, such as petunias, and by pinching out the tips of long shoots of helichrysums and nasturtiums.

deadheading for long flowering

Some annuals will cease flowering once they have set their first seeds, and for this reason it is important to deadhead pansies, petunias and antirrhinums if you want them to continue into the autumn. Others, such as tagetes, begonias and impatiens, are either 'self-cleaning', dropping their faded flowers naturally, or are unaffected by seed development.

The glaucous seed heads of the annual poppy (*Papaver somniferum*) are eye-catching in the border and scatter seeds freely when ripe.

For these, deadheading is unnecessary, as it is for those special plants you have selected for saving seed.

Deadhead marigolds (*Calendula*) to stop them from seeding too prolifically.

collecting seeds

Many flowers start to set seeds from midsummer, and it is worth collecting the seeds of superior or unusual annuals for sowing next season – but not from F_1 hybrids, which rarely come true. Gather the seed heads before they are fully ripe and start shedding their seed.

Papaver nudicaule 'Summer Breeze'

annuals to sow now

• alyssum • bugloss (*Echium*) • calendula • candytuft • coreopsis • cornflowers • godetia (*Clarkia*) • larkspur • linaria • nigella • poppies (*Papaver*) • scabious • viscaria

Sweet peas, like these *Lathyrus* 'Violet Queen', can be encouraged to produce flowers for longer by lowering them.

- **as soon as the seed heads look dry** or start to change colour, cut them off carefully and invert them into paper bags.
- **tie the bags around the stems** and hang them upside down in a dry, airy place to finish ripening.
- **after a week or two,** shake out the dry seeds, gently blow away the chaff and store them in labelled envelopes in an airtight tin away from extreme cold and heat.

sowing annuals for early display

Although most hardy annuals are sown in spring, many produce larger, stronger plants if sown in late summer and early autumn, and will flower earlier next year, often bridging the gap between spring and summer bedding. Sow them outdoors *in situ* in mild areas, or in rows in a spare piece of ground where they can be covered with cloches or fleece in very cold weather, and thin the seedlings to 8–10cm (3–4in) apart when they are large enough to handle. Alternatively, start them under glass, prick out into trays or individual small pots, and keep these in a coldframe over winter.

lowering sweet peas

Sweet peas growing up individual vertical supports often have several more weeks flowering left after they reach the tops of their tall canes. The plants flower mostly at the top of their stems rather than along their length, so to prolong flowering, remove them from their canes and re-attach them to adjacent ones.

looking ahead . . .

☑ AUTUMN Continue collecting annual seeds.
☑ Thin late sowings of hardy annuals. Plant out biennials.
☑ EARLY SPRING Plant out remaining biennials.

- **Carefully untie each stem** and lay it neatly along the ground from its original cane to the next cane in the row. Re-attach the top 30–45cm (12–18in) of the stem to this new cane.
- **Continue to do this with all the other** sweet pea plants, moving them along the row to the next cane. The first cane will need to be moved to the end of the row.
- **Continue watering and feeding regularly.** Control slugs and cut flowers before they can set seed.

there is still time to . . .

- **transplant biennials** to spare ground (see page 215); even four to six weeks in a nursery bed will improve their quality.
- **use any spare bedding** plants and tender perennials to plant up containers for a late display.
- **pinch out the tips** of young wallflowers to make them bushy, if this was not done at transplanting time (see page 215).

Hollyhocks (*Alcea rosea*) are stately biennials, best suited to cottage-style gardens, but they have to be staked. Choose a rust-resistant variety.

bulbs & tubers

With summer bulbs in full bloom and autumn varieties safely tucked under ground, turn your attention to planting spring bulbs, both in the garden to flower naturally and in pots to force for winter enjoyment indoors.

One of the most colourful stars of the late summer border, *Crocosmia* 'Lucifer' blooms for weeks on end.

now is the season to . . .

- **finish lifting and drying tulips,** daffodils, hyacinths and other spring-flowering bulbs that are dying down in borders or were heeled in to spare ground by early August. Store them in a cool, dry place until planting time (see page 312).
- **lift and divide overcrowded clumps** of bulbs that failed to flower in spring. Discard them if they show signs of disease. You can also lift and divide three or four-year-old clumps of spring-flowering bulbs and reserve some of the largest for potting up to flower indoors.
- **water recently planted bulbs** in a dry season, especially those in containers or close to walls, and species such as galtonias that come from regions of high summer rainfall. A light mulch after watering helps to keep the ground moist.
- **feed summer flowering bulbs** in containers while they are in bloom and for three to four weeks afterwards.
- **cut gladioli spikes** low down the stem when the bottom flower is almost fully open and feed plants every seven to fourteen days with a high-potash fertiliser to encourage more blooms. The cut spikes will continue to bloom indoors.
- **deadhead and stake dahlias** and thin buds for larger flowers (see page 217). Continue feeding regularly, using only high-potash feeds from mid-August onwards.
- **plan spring bulb displays** and send off mail orders as soon as possible. From late August an increasingly diverse selection will be available in large garden centres (see page 312), but these will be more expensive.
- **begin planting spring bulbs** outdoors, starting in late August with daffodils, muscari and erythroniums, followed in September with most other kinds. Tulips are best left until November (see page 425), as earlier planting only encourages diseases such as tulip fire.
- **consider naturalising** patches of spring bulbs in your lawn (see page 313).
- **begin potting up prepared bulbs** in early September to flower over Christmas and the New Year (see page 351).
- **pot up arum lilies** from early September for winter flowering under glass (see page 350).
- **collect lily bulbils** – dark, immature bulbs growing at the base of the leaves – and plant them 2–3cm (1in) apart in trays of compost in a coldframe or under glass.
- **check lilies for lily beetle,** signs of virus and other symptoms of pests and diseases.

Gladioli such as this *Gladiolus callianthus* benefit from a boost with a high-potash liquid fertiliser immediately after flowering.

and if you have time . . .

- **plant autumn flowering bulbs** like colchicums and autumn crocuses. Try to complete planting before the end of August.
- **feed autumn flowering bulbs** naturalised in grass with bone meal, applied once during August at 65g per m^2 (2oz per sq yd), or with a high-potash fertiliser at recommended rates.
- **collect seeds** of spring and summer bulbs and sow immediately in pots or trays, or outdoors in rows in a spare bed. Sow ripe lily seeds now, or keep them cold in the fridge and sow next spring.
- **foliar feed dahlias** using a general fertiliser, to boost late growth and flowering.

feeding summer bulbs in containers

Bulbs growing in containers that are repotted or top-dressed with fresh compost annually benefit from being given a single liquid feed with a high-potash fertiliser immediately after flowering, although this is not essential. However, bulbs left in the same compost for several years require regular feeding throughout their growing period if they are to flower well. This is particularly important for summer bulbs that share containers with bedding plants, as they are all competing for the same nutrients. Here, apply a high-potash liquid feed at recommended strength for alternate waterings, or at half strength every time you water the pot.

growing bulbs near trees and hedges

Although most bulbs prefer to grow in full sun, some kinds are unaffected by, and even appreciate, the shade cast by deciduous trees and hedges (see below). They have usually adapted to woodland conditions by producing flowers or foliage before the tree leaves open and cast shade, or by manufacturing food slowly and wilting if light and heat levels become too intense. Other bulbs grow happily anywhere, but their flowers often last longer out of bright sunshine.

- **before planting** enrich the top few centimetres of soil with moisture-retentive organic material such as garden compost or leaf-mould, and add more every autumn as a mulch.
- **relieve dense shade by thinning** branches unobtrusively to admit extra light and rainfall.
- **always check** the habits and preferences of a particular variety, as not all bulbs will perform well in shady or woodland conditions.

bulbs for beneath trees and hedges

• alliums, especially *Allium triquetrum* and *A. ursinum* • bluebell (*Hyacinthus non-scripta*) • chionodoxa • cuckoo pint (*Arum maculatum*) • cyclamen • dog's tooth violet (*Erythronium*) • Lent lily (*Narcissus pseudonarcissus*) • lilies, especially *L. auratum, L. henryi, L. martagon and L. pyrenaicum* • ornithogalum • snowdrop (*Galanthus*) • winter aconite (*Eranthis*) • wood anemone (*Anemone nemorosa*) • wood lily (*Trillium*)

Autumn-flowering cyclamen

bulbs & tubers/2

buying and planting bulbs

Whether you buy bulbs from a garden centre or by mail-order, plant them as soon as possible after delivery. Erythroniums, trilliums and other bulbs without a skin or 'tunic' should be kept in moist bark or compost.

The best flowers come from the biggest bulbs, so if your bulb catalogue offers a range of sizes, choose the largest you can afford. However, the lower grade or 'second-size' bulbs are more economical for naturalising in large quantities.

Distinguish between a mixture and a collection. A collection is a number of separate and labelled varieties (usually the supplier's choice) sold at a discount. Mixtures can be good value, but be prepared for an unpredictable range of colours. Inexpensive mixtures may comprise undersized bulbs or just a few common varieties.

If you prefer to buy loose and pre-packed bulbs in shops and garden centres, look for bulbs that are clean, firm and plump, with no obvious root or shoot growth. Avoid those that are dirty, soft, damaged, shrivelled, or showing signs of mould or pale, forced shoots and roots. Be wary of bulbs kept in warm conditions, as they are more likely to be soft and actively growing than those in a cool, dry atmosphere.

If you cannot plant your bulbs immediately, unpack them and spread them out in trays in a cool place.

bulbs **to plant now**

• alliums • early spring crocuses • erythroniums • grape hyacinths (*Muscari*) • dwarf bulbous irises (*Iris danfordiae, I. histrioides, I. reticulata*) • narcissus • ornithogalum

planting bulbs

Ideally, you should finish planting your daffodil bulbs by the end of August, as their roots start growing in late summer. However, there is usually no harm in waiting until September, the usual time for planting other spring-flowering bulbs (except for tulips). If you are planning a bedding display with wallflowers and other spring-flowering plants, you can even wait until early October in mild areas.

- **bulbs in borders** look more appealing flowering in informal groups rather than in symmetrical patterns. Before planting it is worth enriching a light soil with plenty of garden compost or well-rotted manure. Or, if your soil is heavy, dig in some coarse sand or grit to improve drainage.
- **many smaller bulbs,** such as fritillaries, snowdrops or crocuses, add charming informality to areas of a lawn or wild garden, especially under deciduous trees.
- **before planting in grass** first mow the area as short as possible. And remember that after flowering you must wait at least six weeks before mowing the grass, to allow the bulb foliage to die down naturally and ensure flowers in future years.

CYCLAMEN TIP You can plant dried tubers now, 15cm (6in) apart and 2–3cm (1in) deep, but the tubers take over a year to establish. A more reliable method is to buy 'green', or growing, plants in pots and plant them in well-drained soil in semi-shade.

spring bulbs
for naturalising in lawns

• *Anemone blanda* • chionodoxa • crocus • dwarf narcissus • ornithogalum • puschkinia • *Scilla siberica* • snakeshead fritillary (*Fritillaria meleagris*) • snowdrop (*Galanthus nivalis*)

Fritillaria meleagris

planting bulbs in the border

1 Dig out a large planting hole. Check that it is wide enough for the bulbs to be at least their own width apart and deep enough so they are covered with soil to two or three times their height.

2 Scatter a little bone meal over the base of the hole and lightly fork in, then water gently before positioning the bulbs.

3 Gently cover the bulbs with soil, making sure you don't knock them over, then tamp the surface firm with the back of a rake and label the area.

rough guide to planting depth

Estimate the height of the bulb from tip to base, then cover it with two to three times that depth of soil, the deeper measurement on light soils.

Muscari botryoides 'Album'

naturalising bulbs in grass

1 Cut the outline of a large 'H' through the turf using a spade. This makes it easier to under-cut the turf from the middle and peel back two panels to expose a rectangle of soil. Loosen the soil underneath with a fork.

2 Fork in bone meal at a rate of 15g per m^2 (½ oz per sq yd). Then scatter the bulbs over the exposed soil and press each one in gently; they should be at least 2–3cm (1in) apart.

3 Make sure the bulbs are upright before carefully replacing the turf.

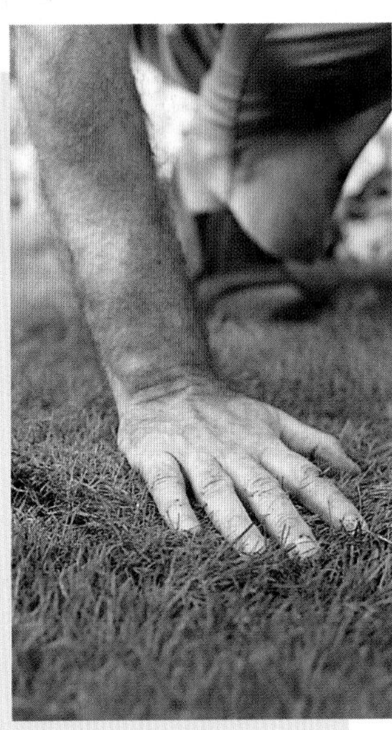

4 Firm the turf gently with your hand and, if necessary, fill the joints with fine soil.

roses

Gather roses for the house and deadhead them regularly to keep plants flowering for longer in the garden. Prune ramblers and remove suckers as soon as you see them then, as autumn looms, take some hardwood cuttings.

now is the season to . . .

- **water recently planted roses** after 10–14 days without rain. Check those growing in containers daily in hot weather.
- **stop feeding roses** at the beginning of August.
- **continue to weed,** as weed seeds germinate quickly at this time. They are easily controlled by hoeing in dry weather.
- **pull off suckers** as soon as you notice them (see right).

Cut roses for the house and at the same time deadhead any spent blooms.

- **deadhead repeat-flowering** roses to encourage more blooms.
- **gather blooms for vases** and combine this with light pruning, cutting the stems just above an outward-facing bud.
- **prune ramblers and** weeping standards from late August onwards (see opposite).
- **start taking hardwood** cuttings from early September.
- **look out for signs of rust** and red spider mite, which are prevalent in late summer, as well as other seasonal pests and diseases. Continue preventative spraying against black spot and mildew, if necessary, with a combined insecticide and fungicide every two weeks.
- **disbud hybrid tea and floribunda roses** to encourage good-quality late blooms (see page 218).
- **plan new plantings,** order roses and start getting beds ready for autumn planting (see opposite).

and if you have time . . .

- **cut off developing seed heads,** unless the hips are decorative, especially if you are about to go away on holiday for any length of time.
- **check supports and ties** are secure on standard, pillar and arch-trained roses, before early autumn winds start to blow.
- **underplant roses** with untreated hyacinth bulbs, which make excellent edging or underplanting.

removing suckers

Suckers growing from the rootstocks of grafted roses are usually conspicuous at this time of year because of their paler colour and smaller, more numerous leaflets. If left uncontrolled they can come to dominate the plant, so remove each one promptly.

- **trace the sucker back** to where it joins the root and pull it off cleanly, wearing strong gardening gloves. Replace the soil and re-firm the rose in the ground (see page 219).
- **suckers on standard roses** sprout from the tall stem; remove any as soon as you spot them, using secateurs.

Rosa 'Lovely Lady'

pruning a rambler on an arch

1 **By the end of summer** rambler roses have finished flowering and their growth will have become tangled. Untie all stems from their supports, and select about six of the strongest, new green stems growing from the ground to retain.

2 **Prune out** all the old, darker stems, cutting them close to ground level. If there is a shortage of new stems from ground level, cut back some of the older ones to a strong new shoot instead of cutting them right down.

3 **Shorten all the fresh green** sideshoots by at least two-thirds and ideally to leave only two to three buds, as shorter sideshoots will produce better regrowth next year. Tie in the retained shoots to their supports, spreading them out evenly.

taking hardwood cuttings

Most roses can be grown from hardwood cuttings. These root easily and the resulting plants grow on their own roots, so there will be no problem with suckers. Take the cuttings between late August and early October, selecting strong, well-ripened stems about the thickness of a pencil.

- **Cut off and discard** the slim, soft growth at the tip. Make the cutting about 30cm (12in) long and trim just below a leaf joint at the base. Remove all lower leaves, but not the buds.
- **Prepare a narrow,** V-shaped trench in the ground, about 23cm (9in) deep; half fill with sharp sand if the soil is heavy.
- **Dip the base of the cuttings** in hormone rooting powder. Plant upright, 15cm (6in) apart, buried to half their length.
- **Replace the soil** and tread it firm round the cuttings. Water them well and label clearly. Check whether they have rooted in April but, preferably, leave until next autumn.

late summer pruning

Prune rambler roses by the first half of September (see above). Weeping standards are also pruned now and in the same way, removing as much older growth as possible and leaving the best of this year's new growth as replacement.

preparing for new roses

Take the opportunity to visit rose gardens to see plants in bloom and read through some rose catalogues. Order plants in good time for autumn delivery. Before then you need to prepare the site thoroughly. Make a start in late summer by digging the soil, two spade blades (spits) deep. Remove weeds and root fragments and work in plenty of well-rotted manure or garden compost. Deep digging helps to improve drainage, but on very heavy ground it might be easier to create raised beds. Lightly fork in a top-dressing of rose fertiliser and leave the soil to settle for at least six weeks.

ROSE SICKNESS TIP Avoid planting new roses where roses grew before as they are unlikely to thrive. If you have nowhere else to plant, you must replace the soil. Dig a hole for each new plant, about 60cm (2ft) wide and 45cm (18in) deep. Remove the excavated soil to elsewhere in the garden and replace it with a mixture of fresh topsoil and garden compost or rotted manure.

there is still time to...

- **take bud cuttings** of most kinds of roses. Root them in a coldframe to make young plants next year (see page 219).
- **layer long flexible branches** of shrub and rambler roses to produce new plants for transplanting next spring.

looking ahead...

☑ EARLY SPRING Transplant rooted layers and pot up bud cuttings.

☑ SPRING OR AUTUMN Check hardwood cuttings.

climbers

Although the pace of growth has slowed, some regular attention in the form of watering, pruning and training continues to pay off. Take advantage of the maturing growth to make semi-ripe cuttings and prepare the ground now for planting new climbers in autumn.

now is the season to . . .

- **prune wisteria** as soon as possible if not already done earlier in summer.
- **train in plant stems** regularly; use soft string where tying is necessary. As growth slows, attend to plants on a fortnightly, rather than a weekly, basis.
- **control self-clinging climbers,** which can damage woodwork and guttering.
- **in dry spells water** climbers in containers and any that are newly planted. Another priority group is established plants growing beside buildings where the soil is sheltered and gets little rain. Give them a soaking every couple of weeks; increase frequency in drought periods.
- **weed regularly** and watch out for bindweed in particular.
- **check leaf-bud cuttings of clematis** taken in late spring once new leaves begin to appear.
- **stay alert for signs of fungal diseases,** which are likely to be a problem if the weather has been extremely wet or dry. An application of fungicide usually limits further spread of the disease but does not cure affected foliage, which should be cut off and removed or destroyed.
- **watch out for pests.** Aphids often infest annual climbers, and nasturtiums are also susceptible to attack by the larvae of the cabbage white butterfly. Regular inspections and hand-squashing caterpillars can keep populations in check.
- **feed annual climbers** every seven to fourteen days with liquid fertiliser to keep them flowering. Do not feed permanent plants, though, as this encourages soft growth that could be damaged later by frost.
- **take semi-ripe cuttings** of many climbers (see opposite).

and if you have time . . .

- **prepare ground for autumn planting** of hardy climbers. Dig the soil to two spade blades deep and incorporate plenty of well-rotted organic matter.

controlling bindweed

Weeds often grow unnoticed through established climbers, and bindweed is a particular nuisance as it twines up their stems. Midsummer is a good time to apply the systemic weedkiller glyphosate to this and other tenacious perennial weeds, before they flower and set seed. Because the chemical kills any growth it touches, train the bindweed away from the host climber by sticking bamboo canes into the ground up which the weed can grow. Then slip the growth off the canes and apply the glyphosate within a polythene bag, to prevent it from coming in contact with other plants.

pruning guide

- **summer prune wisteria** if not already done (see page 221). Tie in new stems left unpruned and train them horizontally if possible, which will boost flowering by slowing the flow of sap along the branches.

The annual morning glory climber (*Ipomoea*) is intertwined with the growth of a grape vine (*Vitis vinifera* 'Olivette').

pruning and training climbers

1 Space out main stems evenly and at an angle from the vertical. Secure them to their support using soft twine tied in a figure of eight.

2 Trim back wayward stems to just above a leaf joint. You may need to do this regularly for vigorous climbers.

- **prune other climbers** if they are extending well beyond their allotted space, but remember that by pruning flowering climbers in late summer you are likely to be removing some of next year's blooms.

The climber *Parthenocissus henryana* clings by sucker pads.

- **cut back self-clinging** climbers like ivy, virginia creepers and *Parthenocissus henryana*. Keep these plants clear of window frames and other woodwork, as their clinging stem roots or sucker pads are likely to cause damage, particularly to paintwork. Trim back growth to at least 30cm (12in) from susceptible areas of the house. Train or prune the stems of all climbers to keep them clear of your roof edges, guttering and downpipes.

propagation

Many climbers can be raised now from semi-ripe cuttings. The chief exception is clematis, which are best propagated by internodal leaf-bud cuttings (see page 133). If you took any of these earlier in the year, check them once new leaves begin to appear by carefully taking off the pot. If roots are developing, pot up cuttings individually into 8cm (3in) pots.

semi-ripe cuttings

- **Select healthy**, non-flowering shoots when the stem is firm but not yet hard and woody. Sever them from the parent plant just above a leaf joint.
- **Make the cuttings** about 10–15cm (4–6in) long by trimming just below a leaf joint, using a sharp knife. Remove the leaves on the lower two-thirds of the shoot.
- **Dip the base of each cutting** in hormone rooting compound, then insert several cuttings around the edge of a 13cm (5in) pot filled with moist cuttings and seed compost. Rooting is improved if the compost is mixed with a third by volume of perlite or horticultural vermiculite.
- **Stand the pot of cuttings** in a propagator or coldframe shaded from the sun. Do not over-water, but do not let them dry out completely. Rooting usually takes between eight and twelve weeks.

Cut back young stems of ivy that have insinuated their way between the wooden panels of sheds and fences. Unless they are cut back, they will eventually force the panels apart.

looking ahead . . .

☑ AUTUMN Choose or order hardy climbers for autumn planting in prepared ground.
☑ Pot up rooted cuttings individually into 8cm (3in) pots.
☑ WINTER Winter-prune wisteria.

climbers to raise from semi-ripe cuttings

- honeysuckle (*Lonicera*)
- passion flower (*Passiflora*)
- solanum
- summer jasmine (*Jasminum officinale*)
- trachelospermum

Jasminum officinale

shrubs & trees

Pruning shrubs and trimming hedges are the main activities this season. In addition, time spent weeding is never wasted and, if you want to make more of your plants, now is the perfect opportunity to propagate lots of different shrubs.

now is the season to . . .

- **trim hedges** to keep them neat (see page 320).
- **check variegated shrubs** and remove any all-green shoots.
- **prune shrubs** that flowered early in summer.
- **keep camellias moist** as they can suffer from bud drop and, consequently, loss of flowers in the coming spring, due to a shortage of water now. Take care not to let the plants dry out, and cover the soil with a 5cm (2in) layer of mulch to help maintain moisture in the soil.
- **water shrubs growing in containers** regularly to keep the compost moist at all times. In dry spells water any recently planted shrubs.
- **weed borders regularly** by hoeing or digging weeds up before they have a chance to establish. Look under spreading branches in case perennial weeds such as dock are growing and shedding seeds unnoticed; the old adage 'one year's seeding means seven years weeding' is a true one.
- **inspect plants for signs of pests or** diseases. These are more likely to be a problem if shrubs have been under stress due to drought or if the weather has been unduly wet. Established shrubs usually shrug off all but severe attacks, but it is worth checking young plants and those growing in containers, and controlling any attacks detected in the early stages.

and if you have time . . .

- **prepare ground** for autumn planting.

Buddleja davidii 'Black Knight' is a beautifully scented shrub. Propagate it now, from non-flowering shoots turning woody.

shrub pruning guide

- **prune early summer-flowering shrubs** such as deutzias, mock orange (*Philadelphus*) and weigelas as soon as possible. Cut back flowered shoots to strong, young lower growth and remove any dead, diseased or damaged stems.
- **trim lavender** and cotton lavender (*Santolina chamaecyparissus*) after their main flowering to keep them neat and bushy.
- **remove green-leaved, or reverted, shoots** that commonly occur on shrubs with coloured or variegated foliage. Prune these out as soon as possible, because they grow fast and, if left, will eventually dominate the coloured plant. Reversion is much less likely to occur on flowering shrubs, but tree mallow (*Lavatera*) may produce shoots with blooms of a different colour and you should prune these out if you wish to stop them dominating the plant.
- **thin out older plants** that are becoming overgrown. Remove a third of the thickest branches close to the ground.
- **assess plants for future pruning now,** while they are in full growth. This is the best time to decide on what action needs to be taken and make a diary note accordingly, rather than viewing leafless plants in winter when they look far less bulky.

shearing lavender

1 Clip over lavender bushes when they are coming towards the end of their flowering.

2 Use shears to clip over the whole plant, taking off the dead flowers complete with stems and the top few centimetres of long new shoots.

shrubs to propagate from semi-ripe cuttings

• aucuba • box • brachyglottis • buddleja • ceanothus • choisya • cistus • cotoneaster • deutzia • escallonia • euonymus • exochorda • hebe • helianthemum • hydrangea • hypericum • kerria • lavender • myrtle • philadelphus • potentilla • pyracantha • santolina • senecio • spiraea • tamarisk • teucrium • weigela

Santolina chamaecyparissus

Check at intervals to see whether cuttings have rooted by pulling one out at random and then replacing if necessary. These yew and box cuttings are now ready to be potted up.

semi-ripe cuttings

These cuttings are taken from this year's growth that is beginning to turn woody. They provide an excellent means of making more shrubs and ensuring the survival of those of borderline hardiness that could be killed in a severe winter. Choose healthy, non-flowering shoots that are starting to turn woody. Sever them from the parent plant by cutting just above a leaf joint to avoid leaving a stump of dead stem.

In some cases you can take cuttings with a 'heel', a strip of older wood at the base of the shoot (see right). These have an even better chance of success because the plant's growth hormones that stimulate rooting are concentrated in the heel.

After inserting the cuttings in a container filled with cuttings compost, water and cover the pot with an inflated clear polythene bag, or stand it in a propagator or coldframe, out of direct sun, and leave. Rooting usually takes from six to ten weeks, but longer in the case of evergreens.

leaf-bud cuttings

- **Leaf-bud cuttings** are an economical method of propagating evergreen shrubs where you want several cuttings from one shoot, or there is not enough suitable material on the parent plant (such as after a poor summer, producing little growth).
- **Select semi-ripe shoots** as described above, but cut each one into sections, 2–3cm (1in) below a leaf joint and immediately above the leaf.
- **Wound the stem** below the leaf joint to stimulate rooting by removing a sliver of bark.
- **Insert the cuttings** into a pot or tray filled with cuttings compost so that the top of the leaf joint is just visible above the surface of the compost. Then treat as described above.

taking heel cuttings

1 **Detach complete sideshoots** from a main stem by pulling gently. You want the shoot to come away complete with a heel where it joins the stem.

2 **Trim off** any bits of bark protruding from the heel.

3 **Dip the base** of each cutting in hormone rooting powder. Arrange in a tray or around the edge of a 13cm (5in) pot filled with seed and cuttings compost, either on its own, or mixed with a third by volume of horticultural vermiculite or perlite to aid rooting.

shrubs & trees/2

trimming hedges

Late summer is the time to give formal hedges their final trim for the year, as pruning in autumn encourages soft new growth that could be damaged by frost. Some informal hedges also benefit from attention now, notably those that have finished flowering.

Established formal hedges require regular trimming along the top and sides to maintain a neat shape, whereas informal hedges, mostly grown for their flowers or berries, should be left to grow more naturally. A neat formal hedge will need to be cut between one and three times during the growing season; the frequency depends on how quickly your chosen hedge plant grows.

Start trimming as soon as a recently planted hedge reaches the required height (except for conifers, see below). If allowed to get out of hand, the hedge may not regrow if pruned hard later on. By beginning regular trimming at an early stage, even leyland cypress (leylandii), that most rampant of hedge plants, can be kept compact. Shape the sides of the hedge so that the top is narrower than the bottom. This makes them less vulnerable to wind and snow.

If pernicious weeds such as bindweed have grown through the hedge, paint a systemic weedkiller onto their leaves. This will cause the plant to wither and die. Avoid getting any weedkiller on the hedge.

hedge-trimming tools

The choice of equipment depends on the size of hedge and the amount of energy you have. Garden shears for hand trimming come in lightweight and heavy-duty models. Choose light ones for a soft-stemmed hedge, but a heavier model for thicker growth. Shears with telescopic handles give extra long reach.

Hedge trimmers come in a range of sizes and are powered by petrol or electricity. For safety, use a circuit breaker, or residual current device (RCD) when operating an electric hedge trimmer from the mains. Wear protective clothing and do not work in wet conditions. Rechargeable battery-powered trimmers are safer.

trimming a formal conifer hedge

1 **Allow conifers to grow** about 60cm (2ft) above the desired height before cutting. Run a string between two canes at the cutting height, which will be around 15cm (6in) below the ultimate level. This will encourage new bushy growth at the top.

2 **Trim the sides,** starting at the bottom and working upwards, and making the hedge narrower at the top than it is at the base. Wear goggles and gloves when using a powered hedge trimmer and, if electric, always use a circuit breaker (RCD) for safety.

3 **Cut the top** of the hedge along your guideline, tapering the edges rather than leaving a flat, wide top. Do not overreach; if necessary, set up a ladder or trestles and make sure they stand on a firm, level base. Get a helper to steady the bottom of a ladder while you are working.

looking ahead . . .

☑ AUTUMN Pot up rooted cuttings to overwinter under cover.

☑ WINTER Renovate overgrown deciduous hedges.

☑ SPRING Renovate overgrown evergreen hedges.

Evergreen hedges and topiary, so characteristic of formal gardens, need regular clipping to maintain their sharp outline. They all need attention in late summer, when they have their final trim of the year.

PRUNING TIP Prune large-leaved hedges, such as laurel (*Prunus laurocerasus*), with secateurs to avoid shearing leaves in half and the unsightly browning remnants of severed leaf blades.

renovating overgrown hedges

Neglected and overgrown hedges can often be rejuvenated by hard pruning. However, there are some plants that do not regrow from old wood, notably the leyland and lawson's cypresses. Such plants are best cut down, dug up and replaced if they have become thin or bare at the base. The best time for hard pruning is mid-spring for evergreens and winter for deciduous plants.

hedge trimming times

FORMAL HEDGES	WHEN TO TRIM
BOX* (*Buxus sempervirens*)	once, late summer
HORNBEAM* (*Carpinus betulus*)	once, mid to late summer
LAWSON'S CYPRESS (*Chamaecyparis lawsoniana*)	twice, spring and autumn
HAWTHORN* (*Crataegus monogyna*)	twice, summer and winter
LEYLAND CYPRESS (x *Cupressocyparis leylandii*)	2–3 times in growing season
BEECH* (*Fagus sylvatica*)	once, late summer
HOLLY* (*Ilex aquifolium*)	once, late summer
PRIVET* (*Ligustrum ovalifolium*)	2–3 times in growing season
LAUREL* (*Prunus laurocerasus*)	once, spring
YEW* (*Taxus baccata*)	twice, summer and autumn
INFORMAL HEDGES	**WHEN TO TRIM**
BERBERIS*	immediately after flowering
ELAEAGNUS	remove straggly shoots only, in spring
ESCALLONIA*	late summer
*Griselinia littoralis**	remove straggly shoots in spring
LAVENDER (*Lavandula angustifolia*)	lightly in spring and again after flowering to remove dead flower stems and tips of new shoots
Pyracantha coccinea	summer
*Rosa rugosa**	remove thin shoots in spring
*Viburnum tinus**	thin out growth in spring

** plants that tolerate hard pruning and renovation*

alpine gardens

As the nights grow cooler and longer, many alpine plants come into flower, but their success depends on time spent weeding, checking invasive neighbours and watering alpine troughs. This is the best season to divide primulas and take cuttings of shrubby alpines.

now is the season to . . .

■ **keep a sharp eye open** for seedling weeds, which come thick and fast after rain, and remove them before they are big enough to cause trouble. Any overlooked weeds that have reached flowering stage must be removed before they have an opportunity to set seed.

■ **freshen up exhausted plants,** such as geraniums, thrift and alpine pinks that have finished flowering. Remove their stems, along with any unsightly dead or dying leaves and snip off any straggly parts. This not only tidies the plants, but also stimulates them into fresh growth.

Dianthus cuttings, as well as seedlings raised earlier in the year, can now be potted up singly in 8cm (3in) pots.

■ **propagate new alpines,** and plant up seedlings or cuttings that were sown or taken earlier in the year.

■ **restrain invasive plants** by taking action with any 'thugs'. Trim them hard back wherever they are threatening to engulf a neighbour and, in extreme cases, consider relocating the more sedate plants under threat – but defer the actual transplanting until autumn or spring.

■ **check creeping plants** that form wide mats, rooting as they go. Remove them from areas where they create a nuisance. Conversely, if you want to speed up their spread, tuck any loose stem ends into the ground and water thoroughly, to encourage extra rooting.

■ **if bare patches have developed** on spreading or ground-covering plants, cover them with a top-dressing of gritty leaf-mould or compost. This will stimulate new root growth, and should encourage the plant to regenerate.

■ **give attention to alpine sinks** and troughs, especially if the weather is hot and dry (see right).

■ **plant dwarf narcissus** at the end of August, when fresh bulbs arrive at garden centres. The tiny bulbs will dehydrate unless planted soon after purchase.

■ **guard against pests** such as vine weevil, particularly in containers. Slugs and snails can ruin delicate young plants, so surround the plants with slug-proof barriers, such as grit, and go out after dark with a torch and hand-pick any slugs and snails found feeding at night.

■ **gather seeds** from plants such as pinks, campanulas and geraniums, and be sure to label whatever you collect (see page 306).

and if you have time . . .

■ **consider building a raised bed** or new rock garden. Summer is a good time for construction and, if you complete the work within a few weeks, it will be ready for planting up in autumn.

Tidy alpine beds and borders by cutting the straggly stems off plants that have flowered. This will stimulate the plants into producing fresh growth.

looking after alpine containers

Although they require little maintenance at other times of the year, alpines in sinks or troughs can suffer in hot and dry summers if you fail to give them the care they need.

- **during the hottest part of the year** give containers an occasional thorough watering to guard plants against stress.
- **as the days shorten,** plants such as gentians and hardy cyclamen begin to grow again. Give your containers a penetrating soak after drought to stimulate this new growth and their flowering performance will be improved.
- **a single dilute liquid feed** will also help, particularly with gentians, but only if the soil has become impoverished. Do not overfeed, however. Late in the season, boost the organic level of the soil in permanent containers by working in a little leaf-mould or friable home-made garden compost.
- **watch out for vine weevil,** whose larvae may be active. The

symptoms are sudden wilting and death of formerly healthy-looking plants. If you search the soil and find the white, comma-shaped grubs among the roots, either re-pot the plant using new compost, or resort to using biological control such as watering with imidocloprid.

propagation

Cuttings of alpines taken in spring should be well rooted by now, and large and hardy enough to survive winter. Where several cuttings are in one pot, carefully turn them out, tease the young plants apart and replant each one in an 8cm (3in) pot filled with free-draining potting compost. Stand the pots in a coldframe or sheltered spot outside. Any plants that are large enough to handle, and have developed a good root system, can be planted directly into the rock garden.

taking semi-ripe cuttings

Woody plants such as dwarf willows, helianthemums, fuchsias and alpine penstemons are propagated in late summer from semi-ripe cuttings (see page 319 for details). Select stems that are just on the turn from soft to woody. Placed in a sheltered spot or a coldframe, the cuttings should develop roots over the coming autumn and winter.

Cut non-flowered helianthemum shoots that are just turning woody and remove the lower leaves. Place the cuttings round the edge of an 8cm (3in) container filled with cuttings compost and gently water them in.

dividing primulas

Most primulas divided now will have time to develop into healthy new plants before autumn advances.

- **primroses and their relatives** form clumps. Lift them, remove soil and dead foliage and gently pull apart the individual leaf 'rosettes'. Replant where you want them to grow.
- **auricula types** produce leaf rosettes at the ends of short, fleshy stems. Break off individual rosettes and use them as 'cuttings'. Insert up to five round the edge of a 8cm (3in) pot filled with gritty, free-draining compost.

A collection of succulents, including the almost black *Aeonium* 'Zwartkop', thrives in pots raised off the ground for free drainage. Again for drainage, the compost is mixed with grit, and more grit has been added as a mulch.

water gardens

Ponds and water features reach their peak of beauty this season, with water lilies in full bloom and marginal plants at their most luxuriant. The essential jobs are to remove dead and dying leaves and to top up water levels regularly.

now is the season to . . .

■ **top up ponds and water features,** especially small ones, whenever levels drop. Where possible, do this with clean rainwater, collected in a water butt, rather than tap water. If tap water is used over prolonged periods, the level of dissolved mineral salts gradually increases, encouraging algae.

■ **oxygenate your pond** in hot weather, especially if you have fish (see right).

■ **keep pond water clear** and sweet by removing blanket weed.

■ **remove dead or dying water lily** leaves and flowers; not only do they look unsightly but they can also foul the water. Take hold of each leaf in turn and pull away as much of its stem as you can.

■ **tidy up marginal plants** by removing dead leaves and fading flowers. Use secateurs, or a pocket knife, to cut away dying leaves or stems from the base of the plants, but take great care not to puncture the pond liner.

■ **thin out oxygenating plants** and surplus water lily leaves.

■ **control weeds in your bog garden.** In lush, moist conditions, weeds can take hold quickly and with devastating results.

■ **ensure that young frogs have an easy exit,** as tadpoles will be entering the last stage of their juvenile lives and, over a few days, will turn into tiny frogs. If your pond has no 'beach' area, rest a plank to bridge the gap from water to dry land to give them access.

Pontederia cordata

maintaining oxygen levels

As the water temperature rises the level of dissolved oxygen drops, which means that the ability of the water to sustain a rich variety of life forms also diminishes. There are several ways in which you can help to minimise the effects of reduced oxygen.

- **run fountains** and other moving water features at night, as well as during the day. As well as helping water to absorb oxygen, this will also bring down the temperature slightly.
- **oxygenate pond water** quickly in hot and sultry weather, especially if you see fish gasping for air at the surface, by playing a hose at least 60cm (2ft) above the water surface. This will carry oxygen down into the pond.
- **make sure oxygenating plants are healthy** and receive enough light to grow. They should be threatening to fill up the pond at this time of year, but if their growth is sparse, try some new species that may be better suited to your pond's conditions.
- **control water snails** if they are too plentiful. In moderate numbers, these are beneficial, helping to clean up algae, but in large numbers they will consume all green leaves under water, including those of oxygenating plants. Pick a few out of the pond every day.

NEW PONDS TIP Deep ponds, or those with relatively large volumes of water, warm up more slowly than do small ones, so if you are building a pond from scratch, or want to expand your existing pond, bear this in mind.

Keep a waterfall running as much as possible during spells of hot weather to lower the temperature and help to oxygenate the water.

controlling surplus growth

Plant growth reaches a climax in late summer, and in a small pond it may be necessary to thin the vegetation to avoid overcrowding. Water lilies can become so congested that the leaves lie on top of each other, or can rear up on their stems, hiding the flowers.

Fairy moss has been allowed to colonise the surface of this container pond. Though it looks pretty, it should be scooped out to control its spread.

- **skim off surplus floating** plants, not only from ponds and smaller water features, but also from water butts. Fairy moss and duckweed should not be permitted to cover every centimetre of the surface. Use a wire rake to pull weeds in one direction, but do this gently and carefully so that plants left behind are not messed up, then remove the weeds by hand to the compost heap. In small ponds a flour sieve does the job more effectively.
- **with water lilies** the aim is to cover no more than 70 per cent of the pond's surface. Remove any excess leaves, starting with older or damaged ones, by giving the stem below the water surface a brisk tug; take off as much of the stem as you can.
- **thin out submerged oxygenating plants** by simply hauling out handfuls at a time. Before taking them along to the compost heap, rescue any stranded fish and leave plants by the waterside for a few hours so that other pond life has a chance to crawl back in.
- **blanket weed,** the green filamentous algae with the texture and consistency of wet wool, can cause an unsightly problem in water features in late summer, especially during spells of hot weather. Remove it by winding up the long filaments round a rake or a strong stick, and take them away for composting.
- **green algae** that clouds the water may not look pretty, but is relatively harmless and a producer of oxygen in daylight. It is often a result of incorrect balance and, although there are chemical algae controls, it is better to allow your pond to develop a good balance naturally (see page 143).

Lush-growing marginal plants by a stream (above) include rodgersias, mimulus, primulas and daylilies. Thin out any that are spreading too far, to prevent overcrowding (left).

patios & containers

Now that the pace of work slows to a gentle crawl, take the opportunity to relax and enjoy your patio. Freshen up plants with regular watering and deadheading, and take some soft-tip cuttings of your favourite flowers for next year's tubs and window boxes.

now is the season to . . .

- **water each container** until you see the surplus running out through the drainage holes, as it is possible for large containers to dry out completely without you knowing.
- **feed flagging plants,** as the growth rate slows down in late summer. An extra boost of plant food should rejuvenate them and help them to flower on until the first frost.
- **deadhead all spent flowers,** and remove faded leaves and straggly stems.
- **trim overgrown topiary** (see right).
- **take soft-tip cuttings** of the tender plants you would like to keep and use again next year.
- **weed** the cracks between paving.

Hand-weed the cracks in between paving stones before plants set seed.

and if you have time . . .

- **plant up a container** or two in September for winter beauty (see page 424).

survival guide for the holidays

This is the traditional season for getting away from the garden, but before you depart make provision for your patio plants so that they survive your absence.

- **arrange for a friend** or neighbour to come in and water your containers, or consider installing an automatic watering system (see page 237).
- **group containers together in one spot,** which is both out of the sun and sheltered from the wind. Not only does this make watering more convenient for your neighbour, it also means pots are less likely to dry out if left unattended for a day or two.
- **plunge small pots** into a bigger container filled with moist sand or potting compost.
- **incorporate water-retaining gel** into the compost of thirsty summer bedding when planting or repotting. The gel mops up excess moisture, preventing waterlogging, but roots are still able to extract the water when they need it.
- **cut off surplus growth,** as plants pruned quite hard will need watering less frequently than those with an excessive amount of leaves and stems. Feed and water plants thoroughly immediately after pruning, to initiate healthy re-growth.
- **pick off flowers and buds,** if these are likely to open while you are away. Removing young flower spikes from such plants as penstemons, phygelius, nemesias and diascias should stimulate a burst of fresh growth to greet your return.

trimming topiary

This is the best time for trimming topiary, as there is still enough growing season left for it to recover from being shorn, but not enough to grow untidy. In this way specimens will retain their neat shape until next summer. The number of trims per year depends on the plant (see Hedge Trimming Times chart on page 321).

keeping topiary in trim

1 **Use shears to trim** small-leaved topiary such as box. Trimming now will define the shape better and neaten the plant.

2 **Follow your eye** to maintain an established shape, like this bird.

tender **perennials suitable for soft-tip cuttings**

- coleus
- fuchsia
- mexican salvia
- mimulus
- nemesia
- pelargonium
- verbena

Fuchsia 'Margaret'

POTTING UP TIP When potting up rooted cuttings, avoid using containers that are too large. The compost could become wet and stagnant, and the young roots rot off. It is better to pot them now into small containers and pot them on later, in February, when the days are lengthening and growth begins in earnest.

looking ahead . . .

☑ WINTER OR EARLY SPRING Pot up rooted cuttings taken in late summer.

Trimming by eye is usually sufficient for simple shapes, although you can use a wooden frame as a guide. More intricate designs are probably best trained on a wire-netting frame, which makes them easier to trim to shape. Shears or mechanical hedge clippers are suitable for topiary work, although shrubs with large evergreen leaves, like laurel, may look unsightly unless trimmed with secateurs. Shears cut across whole leaves, which stain and distort as they heal.

It is easier to trim topiary shrubs in containers than those in borders, which can grow very large. Keep the topiary form in harmony with the container's shape and in proportion to its size.

propagation

This is the season to take cuttings of tender perennials, which are so attractive just now, but so costly at garden centres. Taking soft-tip cuttings now will ensure that you have plentiful stocks of mature plants, ready to set out in beds and containers in late spring next year. Ideally, select non-flowering shoots. If this is not possible, remove the flowers before making and inserting the cuttings in a tray or round the edge of a container (see page 307).

Soft-tip cuttings of scented-leaved pelargoniums should root successfully within a few weeks.

If you plan to grow lots of cuttings, you will need a greenhouse or a well-lit conservatory. But even if you lack these facilities, and space is limited, it should still be possible to overwinter a few of your favourites for next year on a windowsill indoors.

Extend the flowering period of your patio plants by regular feeding, watering and deadheading. This will prolong the colourful display into autumn.

lawns

Regular cutting keeps your lawn looking smart, although if the summer is dry the growth may be very slow without generous watering. If you are planning a new lawn in autumn, prepare the ground well in advance to clear weeds and allow the soil to settle.

now is the season to . . .

- **mow regularly** to maintain a good quality lawn (see opposite).
- **trim edges** every three to four weeks, immediately after mowing. Cut as close to the lawn edge as possible and collect up the trimmings.
- **spike and scarify the grass** if it feels spongy to walk on, a sign that a layer of dead grass clippings, or thatch, has formed. Rake out the thatch with a fan-shaped wire rake, otherwise it can prevent water and fertiliser from reaching the soil around the roots.

Spiking the lawn with a special tool aerates it by removing small plugs of soil, and allows water and nutrients to reach the grass roots.

- **water regularly** in dry periods, particularly if the lawn is in its first season.

Low box hedges frame this fresh green carpet of lawn. The smaller the garden, the more immaculate the lawn needs to look.

The grasses in new lawns will not have developed the large root systems found in established turf and this makes them more vulnerable to drought. The best times to water are in the cool early morning or late evening, so that as much water soaks in as possible rather than being lost through evaporation (see pager 602).

- **at the end of summer, feed the lawn** with an autumn fertiliser containing phosphates and potash to help harden plant growth for autumn and winter. Apply two days after mowing, and be prepared to water the fertiliser in if it does not rain within two days.
- **start preparing the soil** for a new lawn.
- **examine your lawn** for signs of fungal disease, like red thread (see opposite).

FEEDING TIP Applying a soluble fertiliser through an 'in-hose' dilutor saves having to water the lawn after it has been fed by combining the two operations.

preparing for a new lawn

Whether you plan to sow seed or lay turf, you need to prepare the soil well in advance and clear the ground of weeds before laying a new lawn (see page 154).

- **Dig over the ground** to at least the depth of a spade blade, and remove all traces of perennial weeds. Rake over the soil to break down lumps and level the surface.
- **Allow weed seedlings to germinate** and, when they have grown to about 8cm (3in) high, either hoe them off at soil level or kill them by spraying with a weedkiller.
- **Repeat this process several times** to kill off weed seeds that are close to the soil surface. When the time comes to sow, there will be fewer weeds germinating along with the grass seed, which will help the lawn to establish quickly.

A regular mowing regime is best, though the frequency will depend on weather conditions.

mowing frequency

How often you need to mow will vary according to the wetness or dryness of the season and the type of lawn you have. The points to remember, before following the guidelines given here, are never to reduce the height of the grass by more than a third at a single cut, and always to allow it to recover for a couple of days before cutting again.

- **fine ornamental lawns** need cutting as often as two or three times a week, to a height of about 6mm (¼in).
- **cut average-use lawns** once or twice a week to approximately 1cm (½in).
- **hardwearing lawns,** designed for play, need one cut a week to about 2cm (¾in).
- **for new lawns,** leave the grass slightly longer to reduce stress in dry weather. If you have a mower with a roller, alternate between mowing the grass and rolling it lightly. The rolling will bend over the grass shoots, encouraging them to form more leaves and shade for the roots.
- **avoid mowing too closely,** as this can reduce the vigour of the grass plants and make them more susceptible to attack from fungal diseases.
- **infrequent or erratic mowing** encourages moss and weeds to invade the lawn as it struggles to recover.

protecting lawn edges

By late summer, herbaceous plants will be flopping over the edges of borders unless you have put supports in place. This will cause the edges of the lawn to turn brown as well as making them difficult to mow. Insert either purpose-made support frames or twiggy 'pea sticks' (see page 254) to pull plants back, or use canes and string to keep leafy plants off the lawn. The alternative is to lay a hard 'mowing edge' between the edge of the lawn and any border (see page 157).

A home-made support using bamboo canes and hazel twigs stops tall perennials from falling onto the lawn.

red thread disease

This disease can appear as bleached patches of grass, with the leaves taking on a pinkish tinge as summer progresses. The incidence of red thread disease is more common on fine-leaved lawns and those that are underfed, and where soils are sandy as the fertilisers are easily washed through. If you start feeding the grass regularly (with a high-nitrogen fertiliser in spring and early summer and a high-phosphate plus potash feed in late summer and autumn), your lawn will gradually recover, but it can look unsightly for some time. You should also avoid cutting the grass too closely as this will lead to stress, which in turn makes the lawn more vulnerable to fungal diseases.

fruit

The fruit harvest is now in full swing, and in a good season there will be excess for you to store or preserve. In addition to enjoying your fruits, there is also pruning and training to be done, as well as planning new plantings.

now is the season to . . .

- **continue watering** recently planted fruit in dry weather, especially those on light soils and those planted against walls. Mulch after watering to conserve soil moisture.
- **keep on top of weeds** by hoeing or hand-weeding. Pay particular attention to young plants that are still establishing.
- **stay vigilant** for late summer pests and diseases, and take appropriate measures immediately.
- **harvest fruit as it ripens.**
- **plan new fruit plantings,** send off for nursery catalogues and explore locally available varieties. Pay particular attention to the soil, climate and pollination requirements (see right).
- **start preparing** the site where new plants are to grow.

and if you have time . . .

- **clear any fallen fruits,** as these invite pests and diseases.
- **protect ripening fruit** from birds and wasps with fleece or fine-mesh netting. This is particularly important when signs of damage appear, as raiding will continue once started.

harvesting now

- early apples • blackberries
- blackcurrants • cherries
- red currants • white currants
- dessert gooseberries • grapes
- figs • loganberries and other hybrid berries • peaches
- early pears • plums
- raspberries • strawberries

Loganberries

ordering new fruit

It is wise to order new fruit plants early to allow yourself the widest possible choice. Popular varieties are usually available from many outlets throughout the planting season, but unusual, rare or old-fashioned varieties, as well as recent introductions, may sell out early or be available from a limited number of specialist nurseries. Send for catalogues now, and order before the end of September for satisfaction, but before you buy bear in mind the following points:

- **always buy from a reputable source** to avoid introducing diseases or poor quality plants. Where appropriate, choose certified plants: many fruits are inspected regularly to make sure they are healthy and true to type.
- **decide where you want to plant,** then match fruits to the aspect and exposure of your site, and the type of soil. There are some apple varieties, for example, that thrive best in areas of high rainfall; gooseberries enjoy cool districts; raspberries dislike chalky soils; and a single red currant variety can ripen early, mid-season or late according to how warm, sunny, cool or shady is the site.
- **check pollination requirements.** Fruits such as blackcurrants and acid cherries are self-pollinating and will crop well in isolation, whereas sweet cherries, apples, pears and most plums need at least one other compatible tree with which to exchange pollen at flowering time. If you have space for only one tree, make sure it is self-fertile.

Mesh netting will help to protect soft fruit, such as these ripe red currants, from attack by birds.

• **most fruit trees are grafted,** so when you buy avoid plants labelled simply 'bush' or 'standard'. The type of rootstock will decide your tree's vigour, ultimate size and start of cropping, and it is important to choose the appropriate type, identified by a name or number (see page 435). A reputable garden centre or nursery will help you to make the right choice.

preparing for planting

As soon as you have ordered your new fruit, make a start on preparing the site so that the ground has time to settle before planting in autumn. Most kinds of fruit are long-lived and, like other trees and shrubs, grow best where the soil has been thoroughly cultivated.

Begin by clearing all the weeds, particularly perennial kinds. This may mean simply forking out a few weeds here and there, but where the ground is heavily infested, cut down the top growth by hand or with a rotary mower, then spray the entire area with a weedkiller such as glyphosate.

Once the site is cleared you can cultivate, but how you do this depends on your soil type and which fruits you intend to grow. The larger the plant, the deeper the soil needs to be; strawberries will grow in shallow ground 25–30cm (10–12in) deep, whereas tree fruits need 60–75cm (2ft–2ft 6in) of well-drained soil.

• **double dig** sites that are poorly drained or very weedy. This can be strenuous and the work is best tackled in stages.
• **single digging is sufficient** for bush and cane fruits on good soil or ground that has been cultivated previously.
• **fruit trees** need only individually prepared planting sites of about 1m (3ft) square.
• **all soils and sites** benefit from liberal additions of garden compost or rotted manure worked in well as you dig.
• **after cultivation** leave the ground to settle for at least six weeks and then, just before planting in the autumn, hoe or fork out any weeds that have emerged and rake in a dressing of fertiliser appropriate to the type of fruit.

Being trained against a warm wall helps peaches and other fruits to ripen, but they will also need frequent watering.

there is still time to . . .

• **summer prune trained forms** of apples and pears (see page 242), especially in areas of high rainfall, but try to finish before the end of August.
• **prune plums and sweet cherries,** shortening new sideshoots by about a third. Tie in new extension shoots, unpruned.

looking ahead . . .

☑ AUTUMN Finish preparing the ground and planting new fruits.
☑ Propagate cane fruits.

fruit/2

routine care

After your plants have fruited, keep on top of the pruning, training and tidying up; not only will your garden look neater but the plants will be more productive and easier to manage in future.

Remove suckers from the trunks of cherry and other fruit trees if they appear. Use secateurs and cut them cleanly against the trunk.

tree fruit

- **prune acid cherries.** 'Morello' and other culinary cherry varieties produce most of their fruit on shoots made the previous year, so pruning concentrates on encouraging a constant renewal of growth by cutting out old wood and replacing it with new. As soon as the crop is cleared, prune out the sideshoots that have borne cherries, cutting back to a young shoot left as a replacement during spring pruning. Restore weak-growing varieties that produce few new shoots, and neglected trees that only fruit on the outer fringe of the branches, by pruning out about a quarter of the old fruited wood, cutting where possible just above a young sideshoot.
- **prop up heavily laden branches.** Even when thinned to reduce a lavish crop of fruit, branches can be so heavily laden they may break unless supported. Prop them up with forked stakes, using pads of old blanket or sacking to protect the branch from injury, or support them with rope tied to a central stake. This is particularly important for plums, since damage can admit fungal diseases as well as spoiling the shape of the tree.

bush and cane fruits

- **prune blackcurrants** immediately after harvest. Cut out as many of the oldest branches as possible, removing about a third of all growth to make way for the new, more fruitful stems (see page 243).

BLACKCURRANT TIP If you notice blackcurrant stems wilting during August, prune them off halfway down. A dark hole down the centre is symptomatic of the clearwing moth, whose numbers are increasing. The grubs tunnel downwards, so cut back to clean sound wood, and burn the prunings.

- **prune summer raspberry canes** as soon as the remaining fruit has been harvested. Undo the ties attaching the exhausted canes to their training wires, and cut them off at ground level. Remove weak, spindly, damaged or overcrowded new canes (distinguished by their fresh green colour) to leave four to six of the strongest. Tie these to the wires with individual twists or a continuous string looped and knotted over the wires. Space canes evenly about 10cm (4in) apart. Pull up any suckers growing away from the row, and clear any weeds and plant debris.

After harvesting blackcurrants, cut out about a third of the oldest canes to leave room for the newer canes to develop and bear fruit.

- **finally tie in** autumn-fruiting raspberry stems once they reach the top wire. Water well in dry weather as plants come into flower, and mulch with grass cuttings. Birds are seldom attracted to late varieties, so netting is unnecessary.
- **loganberries and other** hybrid berries need to have their old fruited canes cut out; do this

Morello cherries fruit later than sweet cherries and are used for cooking. Pick them when, like these, they are fully coloured.

also for the earliest blackberries immediately after harvest. Trim them at ground level or just above a strong sideshoot if new growth is sparse. Tie the new green canes in place, evenly arranging them on the wires according to the training system used. If your garden is very cold, bundle the canes together for protection and tie them to the lowest wire.

strawberries

When all the fruits have been picked, remove any protective netting and shear off all the foliage and unwanted runners about 5–8cm (2–3in) above ground level; a rotary mower with the blade set high can be used for this on large beds. Remove, clean and store protective mats from around the plants, then rake off and burn the leaves, together with any straw used for mulching. Weed between the plants.

In the third year after planting, fruit quality and size decline, so plants are usually cleared after harvest, although some gardeners leave them for a further year to produce a large crop of small fruits for jam-making. Fork up the plants with all their roots, shake off the soil and burn them (composting can perpetuate diseases), together with all their foliage, unused runners and any straw. Then dig over the bed and manure it, ready for planting a late crop like spring greens.

Plant up new beds on a prepared site (see below) where strawberries have not grown before. The beds need to be dug over thoroughly with plenty of manure or compost worked in, as strawberries prefer organic manures to artificial fertilisers.

perpetual strawberries

These varieties will continue fruiting until the frosts. They benefit from regular watering in dry weather, together with a feed of general fertiliser in early August. As these are best grown for one or, at the most, two years, dig up the plants when cropping finishes, or pick off the oldest leaves and clear away loose debris to leave plants tidy for a second year.

planting a new strawberry bed

1 **Rake in a dressing** of general fertiliser just before planting, then mark out planting positions every 38–45cm (15–18in) in rows 75cm (2ft 6in) apart, using string and canes. Select plants that you have rooted from strong, healthy runners (see page 243) or have bought in as certified virus-free stock. Plant them carefully, at the same level as the compost in the pot.

2 **Firm the plants** in well and water regularly in dry weather during the first few weeks. Try to complete planting by mid-September.

fruit/3

harvesting and storing

With so many fruits ripening at this time of year, it is worth exploring the various methods of preserving and storing. If you harvest fruits gently and avoid bruising them, they will keep for longer.

apples and pears

• **the earliest apples** mature from late July and do not keep, so they should be eaten within a week or so of picking, before the flesh becomes soft and mealy. Some mid-season varieties, which mature in late August and the first half of September, are ripe enough to eat fresh, but others need storing first for a few weeks and will remain in good condition for another month or more.

• **the first pears** are ready to pick during August, but need a few weeks to finish ripening in store, as do all later varieties. Like apples, their harvesting time is indicated by a change of colour and readiness to part easily from the tree, rather than on their readiness for eating.

• **apples and pears ripen** over a long period, so test before you pick by lifting one or two fruits to see if they come away without twisting or tearing; windfalls lying on the ground can be a good indication of ripeness. You might have to spread the harvest over several days, because fruits in the sun or on the outside of the tree often ripen first.

Test apples for ripeness by lifting them gently, rather than by twisting.

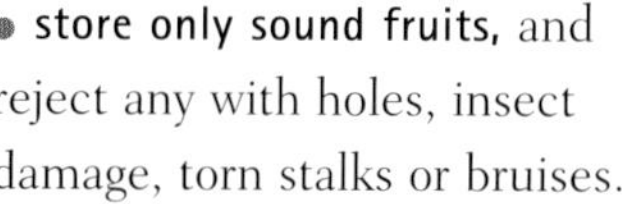

• **store only sound fruits,** and reject any with holes, insect damage, torn stalks or bruises. Handle them carefully and spread them on slatted shelves, or in single layers in boxes, and make sure they do not touch each other. High-quality apples can be individually wrapped in newspaper. Or you can pack about 2kg (4–4½lb) in a clear polythene bag with the bottom corners cut off for ventilation.

• **store all fruit** in a cool but frost-free place with good air circulation. Check fruit every 10 days or so and remove any that are showing signs of rot.

cherries, peaches and plums

• **sweet cherries** are usually cleared in late July, but acid varieties do not ripen until August or early September. Pick when fully coloured; cut the stalks with scissors or secateurs. Bottle or freeze surplus fruits, with or without their stones.

• **plums, damsons and bullaces** continue to be available until late October. Pick them when soft and fully coloured for eating immediately and for freezing (halved and stoned). Or you can gather them slightly under-ripe for bottling and

Pick pears when they part easily from the tree and use only healthy, unblemished fruit for storing. This is 'Louise Bonn de Jersey'.

Tiny cracks in the well-coloured skin of figs indicate that they are ripe and ready to be picked.

jam-making, or for keeping in a cool place for two weeks and eating fresh.

- **late varieties of peaches and nectarines** continue ripening throughout August and into early September. Pick the fruits when they are fully coloured and soft around the stalk, and part easily when gently twisted. Handle them carefully as they bruise easily. They will keep for a few days in a cool place, and surplus fruits can be bottled or frozen.

cane fruits

- **late raspberry varieties** such as 'Leo' continue the summer season into August, often overlapping with the first autumn varieties. Check the ripening crops every two to three days and harvest all that are fully coloured and come away freely, without their stalks and plugs (autumn kinds are a little firmer and part from their plugs less readily). Bottle, freeze or preserve any surplus in syrup or alcohol.
- **hybrid berries** such as loganberries and tayberries ripen in mid to late summer, while the blackberry season extends from midsummer to the first frosts, according to variety. Pick them when fully coloured and soft, complete with their plugs. Check for ripeness every few days, especially in warm, sunny weather. Bottle, freeze or preserve in syrup.

bush fruits

- **black, red and white currants** ripen throughout late summer. Some varieties need harvesting immediately they are ripe, while others remain in good condition for weeks. Pick whole clusters when fully coloured and before they start to shrivel or fall. Cut the stalks with scissors if necessary to avoid damaging the fragile fruit, then use a table fork to strip individual currants from the stalks. Either use straight away, bottle or freeze.
- **any gooseberries** remaining in late summer will be larger, sweeter and of dessert quality, compared with the earlier varieties harvested in June and July. Their skins can be very fragile, so they need careful picking when fully ripe. Freeze or juice surplus fruits.

grapes and figs

- **indoor and outdoor grapes** mature throughout late summer depending on their variety and the amount of heat they receive. It is best to taste them to check for ripeness, as good colour is not a reliable indication and most varieties need several more weeks to develop their full sweetness. Handling grapes removes the bloom from their skins, so harvest by cutting through the stem a short distance away on both sides of the bunch. To store for a few weeks, cut a longer section of branch so that the lower end can be inserted in a jar or bottle of water, securely wedged on a shelf where the grapes can hang freely. Any surplus fruits can be dried or preserved in alcohol.
- **figs are ready to pick** in late summer when they are very soft and hang downwards, with fully coloured skin. Pick them carefully and eat them straight away or store them in a cool place for up to a week or so. You can bottle or freeze surplus fruits.

PRESERVING TIP Many of these fruits can also be preserved by candying or pickling, as well as by being processed into jams, jellies and purées.

vegetables

This is a time of plenty, with many crops approaching maturity. The real skill during late summer is to strike a balance between keeping plants growing rapidly, and encouraging them to crop. In addition, every time you water plants to keep them growing, a new crop of weeds emerges and has to be dealt with.

harvesting now

• aubergines • beetroot • broad beans • broccoli • carrots • chillies • courgettes • florence fennel • french and runner beans • globe artichokes • japanese onions • kohl rabi • lettuces and salad leaves • radish • shallots • spinach • spring onions • summer cabbages • summer cauliflowers • sweetcorn • sweet peppers • tomatoes • turnips

Purple-podded dwarf french beans

now is the season to . . .

- **harvest crops** as they mature and water as necessary.
- **hoe weekly** to kill weed seedlings as they emerge.
- **apply a mulch** of well-rotted compost or other organic matter around the base of plants that occupy the ground for several months, to control weeds and to help keep the soil moist. Leave space to hoe through the centre of each row.
- **control pests,** such as aphids and caterpillars, with sprays containing a non-persistent rapeseed oil at seven to ten day intervals, and cover plants with insect-proof mesh to deter root fly infestation.
- **pick off any discoloured leaves** and other plant parts showing early signs of disease.
- **cut down and burn** potato tops if the leaves show brown markings, the signs of blight.
- **control caterpillars** by hand-picking or spraying affected crops with the biological agent *Bacillus thuringiensis*, which can prove effective without the risk of pesticide residues.
- **sow a green manure** after crops have been cleared, to help improve soil texture and fertility. Alternatively, sow a follow-on crop of quick-maturing peas or french beans, both of which add nitrogen to the soil as well as providing an edible crop.

there is still time to . . .

- **plant winter brassicas:** cauliflower, cabbages and kale.
- **make successional sowings** of lettuce, spinach, spring onions and salad radishes.
- **sow carrots, fennel and turnips**.

watering

Use water efficiently, by applying generous amounts when the plants are going through critical stages of development.

- **water new plants,** both transplants and seedlings, in dry weather. Do this daily for the first four to five days until they have stopped wilting, a sign that new roots have formed and established.
- **leafy plants** and crops with soft, lush growth, such as celery, lettuce and spinach, as well as cabbages and cauliflowers, benefit from 4–5 litres per metre of row (1 gallon per yard) once a week to keep plants actively growing.

- **plants with edible fruits,** such as courgettes, tomatoes, peas and beans, should not go short of water at flowering time and when the fruits or pods are starting to swell.
- **potatoes** benefit from a heavy soaking just as the tubers begin to form, which for a number of cultivars coincides with the start of flowering. Watering at this stage increases the overall yield significantly.
- **water sweetcorn** when the silks (tassels) on the small cobs have just started to shrivel, and again about 10 days before the cobs are due to be picked.

BRUSSELS SPROUTS TIP The very firm planting of brussels sprouts, required to prevent them from falling over as they grow, means that they rarely need water unless the weather is extremely dry.

green manures

Sow green manures on bare ground to improve the soil. They help to retain soil nutrients, the roots open up the soil, and the top growth, when dug in, adds organic matter. Members of the pea family, such as bitter lupins, fenugreek and winter tares, are particularly useful as a rich source of nitrogen.

growing and harvesting

In late summer the work is divided between sowing and transplanting new or successional crops, and harvesting mature vegetables.

peas and beans

- **harvest peas** regularly while the pods are young, bright green and juicy. This encourages further yields and ensures tender peas of good quality. Peas will stop flowering if the pods are left on the plant.
- **harvest french beans** and runner beans every two to three days, and before the seeds start to swell prominently and the pods become stringy and tough.

cabbages, cauliflowers and broccoli

- **finish planting winter and spring cauliflowers** in July and space them 75cm (2ft 6in) apart in rows 75cm (2ft 6in) apart to give them plenty of growing room.
- **transplant winter cabbage** early in the season at a spacing of 50cm (20in) in rows 50cm (20in) apart. Choose the hardier 'January King' types for colder or more exposed areas.
- **transplant kale** into its cropping site in July, spacing plants 45cm (18in) apart in rows 60cm (2ft) apart. The purple forms tend to be less hardy than the green leaf forms.
- **earth up the soil** around the base of sprouting broccoli plants to a depth of about 15cm (6in). This helps to prevent them from falling over during winter if they become top-heavy.
- **sow spring cabbages** in seedbeds outdoors, with a second sowing 10 days later. Grow them as 'hearted' cabbages or cut as spring greens. Transplant spring cabbages sown in early summer, spacing plants 30cm (12in) apart in rows 30cm (12in) apart.
- **sow Chinese cabbage** in July or August. Transplant seedlings sown in modules at a spacing of 30cm (12in) in rows 45cm (18in) apart. Be prepared to protect them from frost in all but the mildest areas.
- **harvest summer cauliflowers,** cutting them with the outer leaves, which protect the curd.
- **continue cutting broccoli;** by now smaller sideshoots will be developing after the main shoots have been harvested.

Winter brassicas and trained runner beans make a colourful sight in the late summer garden.

vegetables/2

• **harvest summer cabbages** while their heads are still firm.

• **be vigilant for caterpillars** and mealy cabbage aphids, which can be a problem at this time, especially on broccoli. Hand-pick caterpillars or control both pests with spray containing a non-persistent rapeseed oil at seven to ten day intervals.

onions

• **lift onions** as soon as the tops have died down. Ease them out of the ground using a fork so as not to damage the roots, and leave them on the soil until the skins turn papery. If the weather is wet, remove them to the greenhouse staging or take indoors until the weather improves.

• **lift shallots** once the tops start turning yellow, if this has not yet been done (see page 246). Allow them to dry in the sun for four or five days, until the skins are papery. Then remove the tops and break the clumps apart.

• **continue to sow spring onions** at three-week intervals for successional crops.

Red-skinned onions (*Allium cepa* 'Noro')

• **sow next year's japanese onions** thinly in August or September about 1cm (½in) deep in rows 30cm (12in) apart. Sow them in the evening in a well-watered seedbed, as they germinate better in a cool soil.

• **lift japanese onions,** which have been growing through the winter. Allow the tops to die back, and leave the bulbs in the ground so that the skins ripen before they are dug up.

root crops

• **sow carrots** in July for a late crop of finger-sized roots.

• **sow turnips** in early August for winter use.

• **sow florence fennel** in July, 1cm (½in) deep, and thin seedlings in stages to 30cm (12in) apart in rows 40cm (16in) apart. You can also sow a little later, but these plants should be protected with cloches in September. Fennel sown at this time should produce good plants, but they rarely develop large bulbs as the days grow shorter.

• **water maincrop potatoes** thoroughly as the tubers are forming. The tubers of healthy plants can be left *in situ* and harvested in autumn or as they are required.

• **harvest immature turnips and carrots** as baby vegetables, as they are required. You can combine this with thinning if you leave thinning until later than normal, so the roots have had a chance to develop. The remaining plants will then have space to develop full-size roots for later harvesting.

• **sow hardy winter radishes** for harvesting over winter. Sow seeds thinly to give the seedlings plenty of room for the large roots to develop. Thin to a final spacing of 15–20cm (6–8in) in rows 25cm (10in) apart, depending on the variety and size of roots required.

tender crops

• **sow lettuce and salad radishes** at weekly intervals for successional crops. Sow radish seeds more thinly than usual. The lettuces will be ready to harvest in autumn.

• **harvest salad crops raised** from earlier sowings as they mature.

• **pick sweetcorn** when the tassels on the ends of the cobs have turned brown and the cobs are at an angle of 45 degrees to the plant's

For maximum sweetness, pick sweetcorn immediately before use, so that the sugar content has no time to convert into starch.

Chard can be grown in a variety of colours – red, yellow and pink – which makes it a decorative crop. Colour does not affect the flavour.

main stem. To be sure that sweetcorn is ready to harvest, press a thumbnail into a kernel – if the sap is creamy it is ready, if clear it is not.

- **pick tomatoes as they ripen.** If the weather is wet, pick the fruits just before they are ripe rather than leave them on the plant for too long, as they may split.
- **harvest peppers and chillies** when the fruits are swollen and the skin smooth. Cut them from the plant with a small stalk attached when green, or leave them until fully ripe and coloured.
- **harvest aubergines** when the fruits are swollen and the skin is clear and glossy, but before the flesh inside becomes soft.
- **gather courgettes** as soon as they reach the required size. If they are left too long the plants will stop producing flowers and cropping will be interrupted.
- **continue to train pumpkins and squashes** by nipping out any new sideshoots. Pinch out the tips of existing sideshoots once a fruit has started to develop.

spinach, celery and chicory

- **continue to sow spinach** at two-week intervals. Choose rough-seeded cultivars at this time of year as they are hardier than those with smooth seeds.
- **sow chicory in beds** for transplanting later. Choose the sugar-loaf types as they can tolerate light frost. They will crop through winter if you protect plants with cloches or a straw mulch in severe weather.
- **sow spinach beet** for early spring harvest. Make two or three sowings at three-week intervals. Sow seed 2cm (¾in) deep and thin plants to 15cm (6in) apart in rows 30cm (12in) apart. Be prepared to protect the plants in winter if the site is cold and exposed.
- **water celery** during dry periods, giving at least 1 litre (2 pints) per plant per week. Keep the plants growing rapidly and the sticks soft and succulent by applying a liquid feed of organic nitrogen every two weeks when you water.

looking ahead . . .

☑ AUTUMN Protect florence fennel from cold weather.

☑ WINTER Protect chicory and spinach beet if your garden is cold and exposed.

holiday care for vegetables

Before you go on holiday, water all plants thoroughly.

- **sink pipes or plant pots** close to the base of larger plants such as artichokes to make watering easier and get the moisture down to the plant roots.
- **lay a seep hose** along the rows or beds of vegetables and link it up to a timing device set to water plants automatically.
- **lay an organic mulch** around wide-spaced plants, such as cabbages, to retain moisture and suppress weeds.
- **remove flowers** from crops that may set seeds or develop fruits while you are absent. This is important if no one is harvesting your crops while you are away.

While you are away, arrange for a friend or neighbour to:

- **harvest vegetables** as they mature, particularly peas, beans, peppers and tomatoes.
- **water plants**, particularly root crops. Carrots often split when subjected to irregular watering, and potatoes will stop swelling if the soil becomes too dry.

perennial crops

- **cut the heads of globe artichokes** when they are plump and green, but before the scales start to open. Water the plants with a liquid feed after harvesting. This will stimulate the production of a second flush of smaller artichokes.
- **harvest late varieties of rhubarb** by cutting through the stalks at ground level.

Globe artichokes are handsome enough to combine with flowering plants and herbs in a border. Pick the heads for eating when plump.

vegetables/3

storing vegetables

One of the main problems at this time of year is what to do with surplus produce. All too often, the sign of a successful season for a particular crop is over-production. Rather than trying to eat your way through everything, consider which crops can be stored. Those harvested young and succulent are ideal for freezing, and gluts of almost any vegetable can be turned into delicious chutneys and pickles. Then you have the double satisfaction of enjoying produce out of season and knowing that you grew and preserved it yourself. After harvesting, inspect your produce and freeze or store only that which is in perfect condition.

If growing beans for drying, wait until the pods are mature and filled out before picking.

peas and beans

- **freeze french** and runner beans whole, after topping and tailing them, or sliced.
- **remove peas** and broad beans from their pods and freeze as soon as possible after picking.
- **for dried peas and beans,** lift whole plants laden with mature pods and hang them up to dry slowly in a cool, dry place, before removing the seeds from the pods. Store the dry seeds in sealed plastic containers or in coloured glass jars; keep them in a cool, dark room.

cabbage family

- **freeze broccoli** (calabrese) and sprouting broccoli as small florets or sideshoots.
- **slice or shred cabbage** and freeze; red cabbage also makes a tasty pickle.
- **winter cabbages** will keep well in the ground, or for two to three weeks after picking, suspended in a net in a cool, dry, dark place such as a shed.
- **although brussels sprouts and kale** can be frozen, there is little point as they are hardy plants and are better left in the ground for picking fresh, as required, from late summer through to winter.

onions

Bulb onions, shallots and garlic are grown with storage in mind. After lifting, leave the crop to dry so that the sun cures the skins. This will seal in the nutrients and improve the storage qualities.

- **once dry, store** the bulbs in a dry, dark, cool but frost-free place such as a shed or garage. Leave them loose in a box or rack, hang them in net bags, or tie them into strings, with the tops tied or plaited together with string.
- **small onions and shallots** can be pickled.

Lift onions and leave them on the soil to dry, a process which also improves their flavour.

root crops

Many roots are safe left in the ground during a mild winter, especially if the soil is light and free-draining. It is a good idea to cover them with straw or bracken against the occasional hard frost. On heavy soils, and for easy access if the ground is frozen, many roots can be dug up and stored in a cool, frost-free place in paper or hessian sacks or cardboard boxes lined with newspaper. Do not wash before storing.

- **maincrop carrots** can be stored in boxes of damp sand (see page 441). Early carrots will keep in a plastic bag in the fridge for two to three weeks, after cutting their tops off.
- **parsnips taste best** after frost has enhanced their aromatic sweetness, so leave in the soil until needed. Mark the end of the rows with a cane as all top growth disappears from sight.
- **turnips and swedes** are best left in the ground until needed.
- **beetroot** may be left in the ground for use as required or dug up in autumn and stored in damp sand, like carrots. Alternatively, it can be pickled in vinegar.
- **kohl rabi** will keep in the fridge for two to three weeks.

potatoes

Maincrop potatoes keep quite well in the ground once they reach maturity. It is only as the weather gets colder and the soil becomes wetter that it is necessary to lift them. This may be well into autumn, unless the ground is required for other crops. But in a very wet September, or if blight has affected your potatoes, it is advisable to lift them early. After the skins have dried, store them in thick paper sacks to exclude light.

preserving vegetables

VEGETABLE	METHOD
ASPARAGUS	blanch and freeze spears
AUBERGINE	slice or dice, blanch and freeze
BEETROOT	store dry; freeze baby beets whole
BROAD BEANS	pod beans, blanch and freeze; dry
BROCCOLI	blanch and freeze florets
CABBAGE	slice or shred, blanch and freeze
CARROTS	slice or dice, blanch and freeze; freeze baby carrots whole; store in damp sand
CAULIFLOWER	blanch and freeze florets
CELERY	slice or dice, blanch and freeze
CHILLIES	hang up to dry, threaded together
COURGETTES	slice or dice, blanch and freeze
FRENCH BEANS	top and tail pods, blanch and freeze; dry
GARLIC	store dry
KOHL RABI	slice or dice, blanch and freeze
MARROWS	store dry
ONIONS	store dry
PARSNIPS	leave in ground; slice, blanch and freeze
PEAS	pod, blanch and freeze; dry
POTATOES	store dry in thick paper sacks
PUMPKIN	store dry
RUNNER BEANS	slice, blanch and freeze; dry
SPINACH	blanch and freeze whole leaves
SPROUTING BROCCOLI	blanch and freeze main shoots and sideshoots
SWEDE	leave in ground; store dry
SWEETCORN	strip off husks and silks; blanch and freeze whole cobs or kernels
SWEET PEPPERS	de-seed, slice or chop and freeze
TOMATOES	chop and freeze
TURNIPS	leave in ground; store dry

salad and fruiting crops

Many salad and fruiting crops can be frozen (see chart above), though some, like tomatoes and peppers, will only be suitable for cooking. Green tomatoes can be made into chutney.

- **store marrows and pumpkins** in a cool, dry, dark room once the skins have been allowed to 'ripen', or harden, in the sun.
- **lettuce and salad leaves** must be eaten fresh. Drench them in icy water and leave to drain, to preserve their freshness.

storing dry and freezing

The best store is a cellar, basement, unheated room or shed where it is cool, dry and inaccessible to mice. It needs to be dark, airy and, ideally, fitted with slatted shelves to keep the produce off the floor. You need wooden boxes or cardboard boxes lined with newspaper for storing root vegetables, net bags for onions, marrows and pumpkins, and hessian or paper sacks for potatoes; it is a good idea to keep the thick paper sacks in which potatoes are sold. Keep insulating materials such as straw, old blankets, rugs or newspapers handy in case temperatures fall. Check your stored produce every few weeks to see that there is no sign of decay.

Blanching involves immersing the prepared vegetables in boiling water for less than a minute, then plunging them into cold water and draining thoroughly. The best way to freeze is to spread the prepared vegetables in a single layer on a tray and open-freeze them, before putting them into plastic bags. In this way they freeze faster and do not stick together.

In a productive walled kitchen garden cabbages are grown in a block, making it easier to protect them from pigeons. Pick alternate plants while young, leaving others to heart up and grow on to maturity.

herbs

It is seed harvesting time in the herb garden, with seed heads ripening in readiness for you to collect for culinary use or for sowing. And it is time, too, to start tidying up and preparing plants for winter use.

now is the season to . . .

- **continue harvesting** herbs while at their best. Pick small sprigs regularly for immediate use, larger quantities for preserving (see page 252).
- **pot on rooted cuttings** taken earlier in summer.
- **prick out seedlings** from sowings made the previous month, and pot up any needed for indoor use over winter.
- **continue sowing parsley,** chervil and winter purslane for winter harvesting, indoors or in a coldframe.
- **gather seed heads** as they near maturity and dry the seeds for storing or sowing (see right).
- **clear leaves and old foliage** from around plants that are being left to self-sow, and lightly loosen the soil as a seedbed.
- **begin tidying the herb garden** in September, deadheading or trimming tall plants and clearing exhausted annual herbs (see opposite).
- **prepare the ground** for new herb beds and borders, early in September, ready for planting in early autumn (see page 346).

and if you have time . . .

- **cut back tarragon** by half to stimulate young growth for late harvest or cuttings.
- **select strong or bushy plants** of chives, parsley and marjoram to pot up later for winter use. Feed them now with a high-potash fertiliser and water in dry weather to maintain quality. You can also lift a few parsley and basil plants and replant in a coldframe or greenhouse border to re-establish before autumn.

harvesting herb seeds

The seeds of many herbs are worth gathering for culinary use or for sowing later. Select from the largest, strongest plants if the seeds are for sowing; for culinary purposes you can gather seeds freely. Label varieties and keep them separate at all times.

- **harvest seeds** before they are fully ripe and shedding. As a guide, look for darkening stalks, seed heads turning yellow or brown, or a papery skin on the seed pods.
- **carefully cut the stems** and either dry the seed heads on trays lined with paper, or loosely bundle them inside paper bags and suspend them in a warm, airy place.
- **most seed heads** take two to three weeks to dry fully. Crush the pods or capsules, or shake out the dry seeds from their

A pot of lemon balm makes a centrepiece for a small geometric herb bed including silver thyme, purple sage, oregano and tarragon.

Gather seed of biennial angelica now to sow in autumn. Winter temperatures encourage the seeds to germinate.

receptacles, and remove as much chaff and plant material as possible.

- **for kitchen use,** store the seeds in airtight tins or jars.

storing seeds to sow

Keep seeds for sowing in a cool, dry place, in small labelled envelopes or used film canisters (see page 306).

- **fresh seeds** usually germinate faster and more evenly than those kept for a year or more. Angelica seeds, for example, should be sown, either *in situ* or in small pots, within three months of gathering to avoid disturbing the taproots later. Alternatively, keep the seeds in a refrigerator through winter, and sow direct in early spring.
- **seeds of many umbellifers,** such as alexanders (*Smyrnium olusatrum*), angelica, aniseed, fennel, lovage and sweet cicely (*Myrrhis odorata*), need a period of cold before they will germinate, so are best sown in autumn or late winter to take advantage of frost and low temperatures.
- **leave one or two plants to self-sow** lavishly, such as angelica, parsley, borage or chervil. When the seedlings germinate, thin them or transplant elsewhere while small. However, results may be less predictable than saving and sowing seeds yourself.

tidying the herb garden

As you harvest seeds, leaves and flowers, start tidying plants and beds ready for autumn. Deadhead or cut back spent flower stems, remove dying leaves and broken stalks, and thoroughly weed around the herbs, especially if any are being left to self-sow. In early September, lightly clip over shrubby herbs such as lavender, hyssop and thyme. Give formal hedges their last light trim of the year.

Even the smallest herb bed is an ornamental as well as a functional asset in the garden. Start making plans for a new herb bed or border now. Once you have decided on its site and layout, prepare the ground while the soil is still warm and there is time to control overlooked weed seeds and root fragments that may appear later.

looking ahead . . .

- ☑ AUTUMN Plan and plant new beds.
- ☑ Tidy beds and top-dress with garden compost.
- ☑ Divide perennials.
- ☑ Sow seeds of umbellifers.

there is still time to . . .

- **take semi-ripe cuttings** of non-flowering shoots of shrubby herbs such as cotton lavender, hyssop, lavender, rosemary, sage, thyme and winter savory (see page 319).

Take semi-ripe cuttings of shrubby herbs such as cotton lavender and thyme now to replenish your stocks for next year.

creating a herb garden

Herbs are adaptable plants that will blend in almost anywhere, from a clump of fennel in a flower bed to a border edging of parsley or a pot of sweet cicely by the back door. But herbs are compelling plants, too, and you may soon find that you amass an expanding collection that deserves a garden setting of its own.

choosing a site

In assessing your garden to find the most suitable place for growing herbs, bear in mind the following points:

- **most herbs prefer heat and sun,** as they come from the Mediterranean. Heat concentrates their aromatic oils. Avoid planting in areas of deep shade.
- **shelter from cold** drying winds is vital, especially for evergreens. A hedge, fence or nearby shrubs will protect them.
- **good drainage** is important, so improve heavy ground with compost or leaf-mould, or make a raised bed to increase the depth of well-drained soil.
- **some herbs** are drought-tolerant but others prefer moist soil.
- **avoid frost pockets,** as damp, cold conditions can be lethal in winter, and overhanging deciduous trees can shed leaves and drip water onto plants.
- **for convenience,** position culinary herbs as near to the kitchen as possible.

themed herb gardens

There are so many herbs to choose from you might want to theme your collection. Here are some suggestions.

FRAGRANT GARDEN: include traditional strewing herbs such as rosemary, thyme and rue, aromatherapy plants like lavender, clary sage (*Salvia sclarea*) and roses, and bergamot or wild strawberries for pot pourri

MEDICINAL BORDER: include sage, valerian, feverfew and calendula

DYE GARDEN: include madder (red), agrimony (yellow), meadowsweet (black), rudbeckia (orange), woad (blue) and lily of the valley (green)

BEE GARDEN: include good flowering herbs such as bergamot, borage and lavender

choosing a style

Think about the herbs you would like to grow and how much space you can allocate to them. You can grow a few basic culinary varieties, such as parsley, sage, thyme, marjoram, savory and bay, in a small rectangular or circular bed up to 1.2m (4ft) wide; arrange the plants according to their heights (see opposite) as well as their soil requirements. A larger collection of herbs will require more planning.

formal herb gardens

These traditional gardens are based on symmetrical geometric shapes, such as squares, triangles or segments of a circle. Herb plants are organised in structured groups within the beds, separated by a pattern of paths in the classic potager, or divided by neatly clipped hedges in a knot garden. This kind of garden needs regular trimming to maintain its disciplined formality.

informal herb gardens

The plants in an informal herb garden are laid out in a relaxed, cottage-garden style, growing and spreading freely as they would in the wild. Although charming in appearance, this style of planting also needs careful planning and maintenance, to avoid a free-for-all of competitive, sometimes invasive plants.

In a scented herb garden based on a circular design, shrubby herbs such as rosemary, thyme and marjoram surround the stems of standard holly centrepieces. In the foreground, meadow plants such as annual poppies and biennial clary (*Salvia sclarea*) bring additional colour.

making a plan

Armed with a clear idea of the proposed layout, draw up a plan on graph paper. Mark in existing features, such as paths, walls or the full spread of a tree – these may need to be incorporated into the design and could affect the final layout. Scale is important, too: it is easy to assume that you have more space than actually exists, so measure the site carefully and use the same scale when adding details like paths to your plan.

To permit easy harvesting and maintenance, make sure that the beds are no more than 1–1.2m (3–4ft) wide, unless you can include stepping stones to give you access without treading on the soil. Try to arrange for frequently used herbs to be no more than 60–75cm (2ft–2ft 6in) from a path or a stepping stone. If you are edging beds with hedges of germander, box or a similar dwarf evergreen, mark in the space that these will occupy to show how much ground is left for planting.

A large pot of nicotiana (right) creates a focus in an informal cottage garden, where herbs including rosemary, rue, golden and purple sage, and thyme spill softly over the paving.

the role of paths

Paths divide beds into manageable units, establish the outline of a formal plan and encourage air circulation around plants, which helps to prevent disease. They need to be a realistic width, ranging from 30cm (12in) for occasional access to 1m (3ft) for main pathways where you might wish to use a wheelbarrow. This is not wasted space because the paths can be edged with rows of chives or sweet violets, or interplanted like an alpine pavement with spreading herbs, such as pennyroyal and creeping thymes.

plants for a herb bed

A herb bed is usually designed so that plants of similar height are gathered together in ranks, with the tallest at the back and the shortest at the front, as in a group photograph. In island beds, the tallest plants go in the centre.

TALL HERBS, 1m (3ft) or more
• angelica • bergamot • fennel • foxgloves • liquorice • lovage • meadowsweet • mullein • rosemary • sea holly • sweet cicely

HERBS FOR THE MIDDLE RANKS, 45cm–1m (18in–3ft) • agrimony • borage • bugloss • caraway • comfrey • curry plant • dill • lavender • lemon balm • rue • sage • santolina • tansy • tarragon • valerian

FRONT RANK AND EDGING HERBS, up to 45cm (18in) • anise • basil • calendula • chamomile • chervil • chives • clary • coriander • cumin • hyssop • marjoram • parsley • savory • sorrel • thyme

In a formally planned herb garden (below), the plants have been allowed to form clumps and to flower, following their natural inclination, to soften the hard edges.

creating a herb garden/2

As soon as you are confident about the shape and style of your new herb garden, you can start constructing it. The best time to do this is in late summer or early autumn, when the weather is still warm enough for you to cultivate in comfort.

preparing the ground

Thorough ground preparation is especially important when constructing a herb garden: you may need to adjust the texture or acidity of the soil, and eliminate any weeds before planting to avoid difficulties later on.

If the ground has already been cultivated, start by marking out the overall shape with pegs and string. Fork over the soil to turn in annual weeds and remove perennials, such as docks, dandelions, bindweed and creeping buttercups. Loosen any deep-rooted weeds first, so that you can lift them out intact, and pick out any small root fragments that might regenerate.

Uncultivated and weed-infested ground will need more extensive preparation. Fork out any perennial weeds, then double-dig the whole bed (see page 595); add well-rotted manure or garden compost below the topsoil as you go. If you do this in late summer or autumn, you can leave the soil to settle over winter and then plant in spring.

path materials

It is best to construct new paths before planting, using any excavated soil to raise the level of the beds. There are several suitable materials you can use.

- **paving stones** are expensive but quick to lay and hard-wearing, although they need a solid, level foundation. They suit formal, squared layouts and allow for prostrate herbs to be grown between them.
- **bricks** are perhaps the most attractive paving material, suitable for both formal and informal gardens.
- **coarse bark** may be laid in an 8cm (3in) layer over landscape fabric.
- **gravel** provides a hard-wearing surface that you can define with edging or allow to merge softly with edging plants. Although a seedbed for weeds, gravel is ideal for planting informally with a range of small herbs.
- **grass** is inexpensive to lay and easy to maintain, but it is not an all-weather surface. It also requires edging, either with a hard material, such as bricks or timber boards, or with regular trimming.

Chamomile (above) forms the centre of a little-used brick path flanked by lavenders.

Part of a potager (left), a geometric bed with a bay tree in the middle, is filled with a mix of herbs, salad crops and flowers. Chives fill one bed, lemon balm is surrounded by marigolds and rue has an edging of lavender.

a herb wheel

A circular island bed of kitchen herbs is attractive and easy to make.

- **Mark out a circle** 2–2.5m (6–8ft) in diameter. Arrange an edging of frost-resistant tiles or bricks laid flat or wedged at an angle.
- **Divide the circle** into four or eight with straight paths of stone slabs or bricks, leaving space in the centre to plant a rosemary or bay tree.
- **Plant up the beds** with basil, parsley, marjoram, sage, thyme, chives, chervil, rosemary and savory for a good selection.

herb lawns and seats

Certain creeping herbs can be used as a good-looking and fragrant alternative to grass for a small lawn or for transforming a raised bed into a perfumed seat. Traditional plants for this are pennyroyal, Corsican mint (*Mentha requienii*), creeping *Thymus serpyllum* varieties, such as 'Goldstream', 'Minimus' or 'Rainbow Falls', and the non-flowering chamomile 'Treneague'. Bear in mind that these herbs cannot withstand heavy traffic and need completely weed-free soil. Space chamomile 10cm (4in) apart, the other herbs 20cm (8in) apart.

planting a box-edged herb bed

YOU WILL NEED
• digging or border fork and spade
• well-rotted garden compost • rake
• trowel • dwarf box plants for edging • specimen centrepiece
• assorted herbs for filling in

1 **Dig over the soil** and fork plenty of well-rotted garden compost into the top layer. Rake level and firm by tamping the soil with the rake head.

2 **Plant dwarf box plants** 8–10cm (3–4in) in from the permanent boards edging the bed. Space them about 15cm (6in) apart, round all four sides.

3 **Find the centre** of the bed by marking where diagonal lines from the corners cross, and plant the centrepiece at the same level that it was growing previously.

4 **Plot the positions** of the remaining herbs by standing them out in their pots at least 10cm (4in) apart. Dig holes and plant each herb firmly. If planting in dry weather, water the whole bed afterwards.

before planting

• **carry out a soil test** with a simple pH kit. If the reading is 6.5 or below, which indicates acid soil, fork a dressing of garden lime into the top 10cm (4in) of the soil. Repeat every two to three years.

• **improve the drainage of clay** soils by incorporating plenty of garden compost, and add lime to the surface in autumn. The compost will aerate and open up the structure, and the lime will help to reduce stickiness. Prepare individual planting areas with plenty of sharp sand or grit. Check the drainage: if the ground stays very wet after rain, consider making a raised bed.

• **sandy soils** can be hungry and will dry out fast in summer, so work in liberal amounts of well-rotted garden compost where you will grow leaf and salad herbs. After planting apply a bark or gravel mulch to conserve moisture.

The square and rectangular beds are laid in a cruciform pattern, separated by 60cm (2ft) wide paths covered with coarse bark. Treated 10cm (4in) timber boards keep the soil in place.

the greenhouse

Inside the greenhouse crops and flowers are at their peak, but in the midst of this bonanza plan ahead. Sow annuals, force bulbs and make time to give the greenhouse a thorough clean ready for the autumn intake of tender plants.

now is the season to . . .

- **keep the greenhouse cool** by a combination of shading, ventilation and damping down.
- **water and feed plants regularly** and remove any dead leaves and flowers.
- **stay alert for diseases and pests;** red spider mite is most likely to appear during August and if it does, introduce biological control in the form of the *Photoseiulus* parasite.
- **prepare for your holiday,** especially if you have to leave plants unattended (see opposite).
- **harvest crops** such as tomatoes, cucumbers, melons, peppers and early grapes, and continue training and supporting them as necessary.
- **prick out and pot on** flowering houseplants such as calceolarias and tender perennials as soon as they need more space. Feed them regularly, and stand in a cool, well-lit place.
- **pot up rooted cuttings** of houseplants and shrubs.
- **gradually cease watering amaryllis** (*Hippeastrum*) as their summer growth period ends, and allow the foliage to die down.
- **thoroughly clean and disinfect** inside the greenhouse in early September (see opposite).
- **bring indoors** all pot plants that have passed the summer outside, before the nights turn cold.
- **take semi-ripe cuttings** of your favourite shrubs, alpines and herbs (see pages 319 and 323).
- **propagate tender perennials** from soft-tip cuttings (see page 307).
- **sow annuals** for flowering under glass during winter and spring, and annual herbs for winter use.
- **plant bulbs in pots** for indoor display (see page 351).
- **pot up arum lilies** after their summer rest (see page 350).
- **collect lily bulbils** and plant in trays.
- **encourage poinsettias** and Christmas cacti to flower at Christmas (see page 351).

and if you have time . . .

- **select strong strawberry runners** and pot them up singly in 13–15cm (5–6in) pots. Stand them in a shaded place. In late November bring them into the greenhouse to force early fruits.
- **cut back violas** growing outdoors, and feed to stimulate plenty of young growth for autumn cuttings.

Anisodontea capensis

■ **plant** *Anemone coronaria* in early September for flowers from late winter on. Space tubers 10–15cm (4–6in) apart and 8cm (3in) deep in a coldframe or greenhouse border.

keeping the greenhouse cool

Temperatures under glass can soar alarmingly in late summer, and it is important to control this for healthy plant growth and to protect foliage from scorching

- **apply a further coat of shade paint** to the outside glass.
- **cover seedlings** with sheets of newspaper on bright days.
- **open all doors and ventilators** to prevent temperatures from rising much above 20°C (68°F); do this at night too in exceptional weather conditions.
- **damp down paths** and staging every day, especially if leaves look dull, a symptom of red spider mite infesting the underside of leaves.
- **water once, preferably twice, daily,** and watch out for early signs of water stress such as flagging or lacklustre leaves and a dry, stale smell as you enter the greenhouse.

preparing for holidays

Before you go away take some of the following precautions.

- **fit automatic ventilators** to open at least one top and one side window above a pre-set temperature.
- **get up to date with your potting** and planting before you go.
- **harvest ripe or nearly ripe fruit;** cut off open flowers and any faded or discoloured leaves.
- **feed all plants** and spray them with a systemic insecticide or suspend sticky traps above their foliage.
- **install an automatic watering system,** using capillary matting or drip tubes, and fill all reservoirs (see page 237). Alternatively, take plants outdoors and group them together in a shady place where rain can reach them, and water them just before leaving.

cleaning inside the greenhouse

The most convenient time to clean out your greenhouse is on a mild day at the end of the season when most crops have finished and before you bring in tender plants for protection. Move any plants in pots outside before you start.

- **remove all used pots**, trays and labels. Clean and store them for later use. Clear out plant remains and brush down the inside structure and the staging to remove cobwebs, loose compost and other debris.
- **repair any broken glass** and make good structural defects.
- **wash inside the glass** using a cloth and warm water mixed with a little washing-up liquid and garden disinfectant; use a scrubbing brush or old toothbrush for the glazing bars. Clean dirt and algae from overlapping panes with a thin seed label. Rinse with a hosepipe or pressure sprayer and clean water.
- **brush down staging** and scrub it with warm water and garden disinfectant.
- **wash surface gravel** on the staging with a pressure sprayer. Sweep and scrub solid floors with water and garden disinfectant, and hose them clean.
- **wash or scrub** the outside of the pots in use before putting the plants back in the clean greenhouse. Shut ventilators in the evening and fumigate the greenhouse with a smoke cone.

cleaning inside the greenhouse

Wash the glass using a sponge and warm water mixed with washing-up liquid.

Brush down the staging with plenty of warm water and garden disinfectant.

Rinse clean using warm clear water and a cloth.

the greenhouse/2

crops and ornamental plants

Most crops under glass will be in full production now. Follow this quick reference guide to keep them in good shape and bearing healthy fruit.

- **peppers** Pick sweet peppers when they are green or have ripened to your preferred colour, and chillies when fully ripe. Water regularly, but decrease watering after the end of August. Maintain good air circulation to prevent grey moulds on leaves and stems.
- **cucumbers** Pick fruits as soon as they are large enough, to encourage further cropping. Continue watering regularly, and cover the surface roots with a top-dressing of fresh potting compost. Maintain high humidity by spraying and damping down regularly to control red spider mite.
- **tomatoes** Pick when fruits are fully coloured. Water regularly but, for maximum flavour, no more than necessary. Feed with a high-nitrogen fertiliser when four trusses have set, and pinch out growing tips after six trusses or, at the latest, by the end of August.
- **aubergines** Allow five or six fruits to set, then remove all others. Feed regularly with tomato fertiliser. Harvest fruits when fully coloured and glossy.
- **melons** Support ripening fruits with 'hammocks' or bags of soft plastic netting or muslin. Let four fruits mature on each plant; remove others and surplus growth. Pick when the stem cracks at the base of the fruit and sweet perfume fills the house.
- **grapes** Feed vines every 10–14 days while fruits are ripening, and ventilate the greenhouse freely to reduce risks of damp-induced fungal diseases. Cut whole bunches with a length of stem, and insert this in water if the fruit needs to be kept for several days (see page 335).

Grape 'Black Hamburg'

sowing for winter and spring

For pots of fragrant flowers in winter and spring, sow stocks (Brompton and Beauty of Nice), mignonette, schizanthus and cornflowers in a shaded coldframe. Prick them out separately into small pots, and pot on in early autumn into 13–15cm (5–6in) pots for flowering.

Sow basil, chervil and parsley in pinches in small pots and move unthinned clumps into 15cm (6in) pots for late autumn picking. Keep these herbs well ventilated at all times.

BULB TIPS

- To compose mixed arrangements in large bowls, start bulbs singly in 8cm (3in) pots, then choose those at the same stage of growth for planting together.
- Grow hyacinth bulbs and some narcissi, especially tazetta varieties, in jars of water or glass bowls filled with pebbles.

potting up arum lilies

The white arum, *Zantedeschia aethiopica*, will keep growing all year, but others, such as the brilliant yellow *Z. elliottiana*, require a dry summer rest. Repot them all in August, when you can also remove young offsets and pot them separately in rich soil-based compost such as John Innes No. 3.

- **Use 15–23cm (6–9in) pots** according to the size of rhizomes; position so the end buds are level with the surface.
- **Stand pots outside** until early October, keeping them moist.
- **Then bring them indoors** to a minimum temperature of 10°C (50°F). Higher temperatures will force earlier flowering.

A young cantaloupe melon ripening under glass.

forcing paper-white narcissi

1 **If the container** has drainage holes, fill it with ordinary moist potting compost; otherwise use prepared bulb fibre. Half fill the bowl with compost and arrange the bulbs in a single layer, close together. Cover with more compost and press it firmly around the bulbs so that their tips just show at the surface.

2 **Stand the container** in a dark shed or cupboard, no warmer than 4°C (40°F), or outdoors in a coldframe or shallow trench in the ground, the pot entirely covered with a 10cm (4in) layer of ash, leaves or sand. Check occasionally that the compost is still moist. When the shoots are about 5cm (2in) high, bring the container into a cool room or greenhouse at about 10°C (50°F). Once the flower buds begin to show colour, move the container to its flowering position.

3 **Twelve weeks after planting** the bulbs, these scented 'paper-white' narcissi are in full bloom and the flowering display should last for weeks.

forcing bulbs

You can force bulbs in pots and bowls to flower indoors in spring, or even earlier if you control temperatures carefully. For Christmas blooms, always choose prepared hyacinths, narcissi and tulips, and plant them by the third week in September. Choose a container at least 10cm (4in) deep. A 15cm (6in) wide bowl will hold three hyacinths, six narcissi or tulips, or 12 smaller bulbs like crocuses. All bulbs need a cold but frost-free period to initiate root growth: allow about 12 weeks for narcissi and hyacinths, 14–15 weeks for other bulbs.

preparing pot plants for Christmas

Poinsettias only start developing their colourful bracts once the flowers are initiated during a period of short days, which is why, left to their own devices, they flower in early spring. But you can trick them into flowering at Christmas by adjusting their growing conditions now.

- **in early September,** keep your poinsettia at 17°C (63°F) or more and expose it to light for a maximum of 10 hours each day, then cover it with a black plastic bag or move it into a dark cupboard for the remaining 14 hours. Do this for three weeks, then grow as normal in full light.
- **Christmas cactus** responds to similar treatment, but needs about 12 hours of darkness per day for six weeks. Keep plants cooler, between 10–15°C (50–60°F).

bulbs suitable for forcing

• crocuses • grape hyacinths • hyacinths • narcissi • reticulata irises • tulips

there is still time to . . .

- **propagate houseplants** from leaf or stem cuttings, including saintpaulias, streptocarpus, begonias (see page 254) and busy lizzies.
- **sow seeds of indoor** cyclamen, and restart old tubers.

looking ahead . . .

☑ AUTUMN Pot up fragrant flowers.
☑ WINTER Bring in strawberries and potted bulbs for forcing, and restart amaryllis.

late summer

plant selector

Perennials come into their own in late summer, with a host of American prairie species such as solidago, asters and eupatoriums. Purple coneflowers bloom ahead of their yellow, tan and orange cousins, the rudbeckias, but there are also huge sunflowers, heleniums that look like flights of bumble bees and pelargoniums which just won't stop blooming. It is a quieter time for shrubs, apart from roses and the buddleias, on whose blossoms hundreds of butterflies will be feasting. The rose season reaches its peak a little after the longest day, but most varieties will produce second and third flushes, and some will go on flowering into winter.

Aster x *frikartii* 'Mönch'

perennials

Durable perennials are the mainstay of attractive summer borders. A few of these non-woody plants are evergreen, but most are herbaceous, that is they die down in winter. Plant when dormant, in autumn or early spring.

3

purple, blue and violet

1 Acanthus mollis Latifolius Group
Bear's breeches

The mound of glossy lobed leaves, each as much as 1m (3ft) long, makes this an impressive foliage plant. It is stately in flower, too, with erect stems stacked with white flowers sheltering under purple bracts from early summer onwards. Hardy.

Height: 1.2m (4ft) **Spread:** 1m (3ft)
Site: Sun, partial shade. Well-drained soil
Use: Sunny or lightly shaded border
Good companions: *Fritillaria imperialis, Helleborus argutifolius, Viburnum opulus* 'Compactum'

1

2 Aconitum 'Bressingham Spire'
Aconite, Monkshood

Above a base of deeply cut, dark green leaves, sturdy stems carry spires of violet-blue hooded flowers. 'Spark's Variety' has branched stems and is taller and wider. Staking is not normally necessary. Highly poisonous if ingested. Hardy.

Height: 1.5m (5ft) **Spread:** 45cm (18in)
Site: Partial shade, full sun. Moist but well-drained soil
Use: Shady or sunny border, woodland garden
Good companions: *Erythronium dens-canis, Hydrangea* 'Preziosa', *Kirengeshoma palmata*

2

3 Agapanthus 'Blue Giant'
African blue lily

The somewhat stiff, strap-shaped leaves of this deciduous fleshy-rooted perennial form a rich green, leafy clump. Tough stems carry rounded heads of bell-shaped blue flowers from mid to late summer. Not fully hardy.

Height: 1.2m (4ft) **Spread:** 60cm (2ft)
Site: Sun. Fertile and moist but well-drained soil
Compost: Soil-based (John Innes No. 3)
Use: Container, sunny border
Good companions: *Dierama pulcherrimum, Galtonia candicans, Salvia uliginosa*

4

4 Agapanthus 'Lilliput'
African blue lily

Fleshy-rooted plant with narrow leaves and heads of trumpet-shaped flowers that are rich blue and darkly veined. Not fully hardy.

Height and spread: 40cm (16in)
Site: Sun. Fertile and moist but well-drained soil
Compost: Soil-based (John Innes No. 3)
Use: Container, sunny border
Good companions: *Agapanthus* 'Blue Giant', *Kniphofia* 'Royal Standard', *Kniphofia triangularis*

5 Aster x frikartii 'Mönch'

The flowering season of this hybrid aster extends into autumn with long-lasting, violet-mauve flowerheads. Disease resistant. Hardy.

Height: 75cm (2ft 6in) **Spread:** 40cm (16in)
Site: Sun. Fertile and well-drained soil
Use: Sunny border
Good companions: *Centaurea hypoleuca* 'John Coutts', *Delphinium* Belladonna Group 'Atlantis'

6 Clematis x durandii

This non-clinging herbaceous clematis has flexible stems. The single saucer-shaped flowers are 10cm (4in) across and indigo blue with a near-white eye. Good for cutting. Not fully hardy.

General care: Subject to mildew if trained against a wall, so tie up to a support in the open garden or drape over a shrub.
Height: 1.5m (5ft) **Spread:** 1m (3ft)
Site: Sun. Fertile, humus-rich and well-drained soil
Use: Sunny border
Good companions: *Delphinium* Belladonna Group 'Cliveden Beauty', *Rosa* 'Céleste', *Weigela* 'Victoria'

7 Delphinium Belladonna Group 'Cliveden Beauty'

This forms a base of deeply cut leaves over which branching wiry stems carry loose spikes of sky blue, spurred flowers from midsummer to autumn. Hardy.

Height: 1m (3ft) **Spread:** 45cm (18in)
Site: Sun. Well-drained soil
Use: Sunny border
Good companions: *Centaurea hypoleuca*

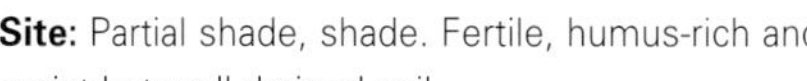

'John Coutts', *Paeonia lactiflora* 'Festiva Maxima', *Phlox paniculata* 'Fujiyama'

8 Echinops ritro 'Veitch's Blue'
Globe thistle

Jagged grey-green leaves, which are white and downy on the underside, are the base for erect stems that carry spherical flowerheads. These are metallic blue in bud and a softer blue when the tiny florets open. Good for cutting. Hardy.
Height: 1m (3ft) **Spread:** 45cm (18in)
Site: Sun. Well-drained, even poor soil
Use: Gravel garden, sunny border, wild garden
Good companions: *Artemisia* 'Powis Castle', *Gladiolus communis* subsp. *byzantinus*, *Helleborus argutifolius*

9 Eryngium alpinum
Eryngo, Sea holly

From basal heart-shaped leaves rise stiff branching stems that carry deeply cut leaves and numerous cone-shaped flowerheads, which are surrounded by ruff-like, exquisitely cut bracts. These look spiny but are soft to the touch. The flowerheads, bracts and the upper parts of stems are metallic blue. Suitable for drying. Hardy.
Height: 75cm (2ft 6in) **Spread:** 45cm (18in)
Site: Sun. Fertile and well-drained soil
Use: Sunny border
Good companions: *Artemisia ludoviciana* 'Valerie Finnis', *Geranium sanguineum*, *Sedum* 'Vera Jameson'

10 Eryngium x tripartitum
Eryngo, Sea holly

Wiry stems branch widely above a basal rosette of coarsely toothed leaves and carry many small cones of violet-blue flowers. Each of these sits on a sparse ruff of grey-blue spines and the broad effect is of hazy metallic blue. Suitable for drying. Hardy.
Height: 75cm (2ft 6in) **Spread:** 50cm (20in)
Site: Sun. Well-drained soil
Use: Gravel garden, sunny border, wild garden
Good companions: *Allium cristophii*, *Festuca glauca* 'Elijah Blue', *Ruta graveolens* 'Jackman's Blue'

11 Gentiana asclepiadea
Willow gentian

A woodland gentian with arching stems, narrow pointed leaves arranged in pairs and rich blue trumpet-shaped flowers that grow from the junction of leaves and stems. Hardy.
Height: 75cm (2ft 6in)
Spread: 45cm (18in)
Site: Partial shade, shade. Fertile, humus-rich and moist but well-drained soil
Use: Shaded border, woodland garden
Good companions: *Dryopteris wallichiana*, *Geranium sylvaticum* 'Mayflower', *Smilacina racemosa*

12 Geranium wallichianum 'Buxton's Variety'
Cranesbill

The trailing stems of this geranium work their way out from the central cluster of marbled leaves and insert the white-centred blue flowers among other plants. Flowers from midsummer to mid-autumn. Hardy.
Height: 30cm (12in) **Spread:** 1.2m (4ft)
Site: Sun, partial shade. Well-drained soil
Use: Sunny or partly shaded border
Good companions: *Diascia rigescens*, *Penstemon* 'Evelyn', *Spiraea japonica* 'Anthony Waterer'

purple, blue and violet
(continued)

1 Platycodon grandiflorus
Balloon flower

Fleshy-rooted perennial that comes into leaf in late spring. Above the blue-green foliage ballooning buds open to blue or violet bell-shaped flowers. Veining intensifies their colour and adds a shadow to white-flowered cultivars. Hardy.

General care: Mark the plant's position so that it is not damaged by digging in spring.

Height: 50cm (20in) **Spread:** 30cm (12in)

Site: Sun. Fertile, reliably moist but well-drained soil

Use: Front of sunny border, raised bed, rock garden

Good companions: *Geranium cinerium* subsp. *subcaulescens*, *Tulipa clusiana*, *Veronica peduncularis* 'Georgia Blue'

2 Salvia uliginosa
Bog sage

This airy and graceful perennial flowers from the end of summer until mid-autumn. The branching, leafy stems wave loose spires of sky-blue flowers above the heads of most border plants. Not fully hardy.

Height: 2m (6ft) **Spread:** 1m (3ft)

Site: Sun. Reliably moist soil

Use: Sunny border

Good companions: *Anchusa azurea* 'Loddon Royalist', *Miscanthus sinensis* 'Variegatus', *Thalictrum aquilegiifolium* 'Thundercloud'

3 Scabiosa caucasica 'Clive Grieves'
Pincushion flower, Scabious

Almost leafless stems rise from a basal clump of long grey-green leaves carrying flowerheads composed of a pale dome of tiny fertile flowers edged with frilly, lavender-blue, petal-like ray-florets. In 'Moerheim Blue' the ray-florets are dark blue. There are also white varieties. All are attractive to bees and butterflies and excellent for cutting. Hardy.

Height: 75cm (2ft 6in) **Spread:** 50cm (20in)

Site: Sun. Well-drained soil. Good on lime

Use: Sunny border, wild garden

Good companions: *Achillea* 'Taygetea', *Artemisia stelleriana* 'Boughton Silver', *Lavandula angustifolia* 'Nana Alba'

4 Thalictrum delavayi 'Hewitt's Double'
Meadow rue

A woodland plant of airy refinement with prettily divided grey-green leaves. Purple-tinted stems carry large open heads composed of tiny 'pompom' flowers, which create a haze of mauve-blue. Hardy.

General care: Avoid staking but position plants so that they are supported by neighbouring perennials or shrubs.

Height: 1.2m (4ft)

Spread: 60cm (2ft)

Site: Partial shade. Humus-rich and moist but well-drained soil

Use: Shaded border, woodland garden

Good companions: *Cornus alba* 'Elegantissima', *Gentiana asclepiadea*, *Viburnum carlesii* 'Aurora'

5 Verbena bonariensis

Stiff branching stems carry clusters of small, scented purple-pink flowers during late summer and autumn. This perennial is often short-lived, but reaches flowering maturity in its first year and self-seeds freely. Not fully hardy.

Height: 2m (6ft) **Spread:** 45cm (18in)

Site: Sun. Well-drained soil

Use: Gravel garden, sunny border

Good companions: *Lavandula* x *intermedia* Dutch Group, *Papaver orientale* 'Black and White', *Stipa gigantea*

pink and mauve

6 Anemone hupehensis 'Hadspen Abundance'
Windflower

This woody-based perennial flowers freely into autumn on erect dark stems rising above the divided leaves. The stems branch to carry more than a dozen single flowers, with light and dark pink around a boss of yellow stamens. Hardy.

Height: 75cm (2ft 6in) **Spread:** 40cm (16in)

Site: Sun, partial shade. Humus-rich and moist but well-drained soil

Use: Sunny or lightly shaded border

6

Good companions: *Anemone* x *hybrida* 'Whirlwind', *Thalictrum aquilegiifolium* 'Thundercloud', *Tiarella cordifolia*

7

8

7 Argyranthemum 'Vancouver'

Woody-based plant with soft stems and deeply cut grey-green leaves. The double flowerheads consist of a bright pink disc of crowded short florets surrounded by well-spaced petal-like ray-florets that fade to pale pink. Half hardy.
General care: In frost-prone areas treat as an annual, or grow in a container and overwinter under glass.
Height: 1m (3ft) **Spread:** 75cm (2ft 6in)
Site: Sun. Well-drained soil
Compost: Soil-based (John Innes No. 2)
Use: Container, sunny border, patio
Good companions: *Convolvulus sabatius, Diascia rigescens, Helichrysum petiolare*

8 Aster novi-belgii 'Heinz Richard'

Michaelmas daisy, New York aster

There are numerous cultivars of michaelmas daisy, a fibrous-rooted perennial that flowers from late summer to mid-autumn. The low leafy clump of 'Heinz Richard' is almost hidden by a mass of bright pink, yellow-eyed semi-double flowers, up to 8cm (3in) across. Hardy.
Height: 30cm (12in) **Spread:** 45cm (18in)
Site: Sun, partial shade. Fertile and moist but well-drained soil
Use: Front of sunny or lightly shaded border
Good companions: *Anemone hupehensis* 'Hadspen Abundance', *Anemone* x *hybrida* 'Honorine Jobert', *Aster divaricatus*

9

9 Astilbe 'Bronce Elegans'

Compact hybrid with finely divided, bronze-tinted leaves. Arching red-green stems carry sprays of tiny salmon-pink-flushed cream flowers. Hardy.
Height: 30cm (12in) **Spread:** 25cm (10in)
Site: Partial shade, sun. Fertile and humus-rich, reliably moist soil
Use: Bog garden, moist border, waterside, woodland garden
Good companions: *Alchemilla conjuncta, Asplenium scolopendrium, Hosta* 'Royal Standard'

10 Astilbe chinensis var. taquetii 'Superba'

Tall erect stems carry fluffy spires of reddish pink flowers over the clump of ferny leaves. Blooms when most astilbes have finished. Hardy.
Height: 1.2m (4ft) **Spread:** 75cm (2ft 6in)
Site: Sun, partial shade. Humus-rich and moist but well-drained soil
Use: Moist border, waterside, woodland garden
Good companions: *Asplenium scolopendrium, Astilbe* x *arendsii* 'Irrlicht', *Astrantia major* subsp. *involucrata* 'Shaggy'

11 Centaurea hypoleuca 'John Coutts'

Knapweed

Clump-forming perennial valued for its long flowering season in summer and autumn. Stiff stems carry deep pink flowerheads, paler at the centre, above light green lobed leaves. Hardy.
Height: 60cm (2ft) **Spread:** 45cm (18in)
Site: Sun. Well-drained soil
Use: Sunny border
Good companions: *Echinacea purpurea* 'Magnus', *Eryngium* x *tripartitum, Geranium* x *riversleaianum* 'Russell Prichard'

12 Chrysanthemum 'Clara Curtis'

Rubellum Group chrysanthemum

The Rubellum Group chrysanthemums are bushy, clump-forming woody-based plants. They flower generously into early autumn. 'Clara Curtis' has pink flowerheads with a central disc that changes from green to yellow. Excellent for cutting. Hardy.
Height: 75cm (2ft 6in) **Spread:** 60cm (2ft)
Site: Sun. Well-drained soil
Use: Sunny border
Good companions: *Anemone* x *hybrida* 'September Charm', *Aster ericoides* 'Pink Cloud', *Penstemon* 'Stapleford Gem'

10

11

12

pink and mauve (continued)

1 Diascia rigescens

Semi-evergreen trailing perennial that sends up stiff erect stems, which are clothed with small heart-shaped leaves and terminate in dense spikes of short-spurred pink flowers. In flower from early summer to mid-autumn. Not fully hardy.
General care: Overwinter cuttings as a precaution against loss.
Height: 30cm (12in) **Spread:** 60cm (2ft)
Site: Sun. Moist but well drained soil
Use: Base of warm wall, front of sunny border, raised bed, rock garden
Good companions: *Geranium* 'Johnson's Blue', *Rosa* Mary Rose, *Spiraea japonica* 'Anthony Waterer'

2 Echinacea purpurea 'Magnus'

Coneflower

Stiff-stemmed plant with rough dark leaves topped by flowerheads that consist of a ring of pink-purple, petal-like ray-florets surrounding a dark orange cone-shaped disc. Hardy.
Height: 1m (3ft) **Spread:** 45cm (18in)
Site: Sun. Humus-rich and well-drained soil
Use: Sunny border
Good companions: *Campanula lactiflora*, *Salvia* x *sylvestris* 'Mainacht', *Sedum* 'Herbstfreude'

3 Geranium 'Ann Folkard'

Cranesbill

From a central clump lax stems make long trails of lobed and toothed leaves. These are an acid yellow-green when young and become greener as they age. From midsummer to mid-autumn the stems also carry numerous dark-eyed magenta flowers. Hardy.
Height: 60cm (2ft) **Spread:** 1m (3ft)
Site: Sun, partial shade. Moist but well-drained soil
Use: Sunny or lightly shaded border
Good companions: *Epimedium* x *versicolor* 'Sulphureum', *Hosta* 'Gold Standard', *Milium effusum* 'Aureum'

4 Geranium x riversleaianum 'Russell Prichard'

Cranesbill

This vigorous perennial sends out trailing stems from a central clump of grey-green lobed leaves. The stems carry light magenta, funnel-shaped flowers throughout summer and into autumn. Hardy.
Height: 30cm (12in) **Spread:** 1m (3ft)
Site: Sun, partial shade. Well-drained soil
Use: Ground cover, sunny or light shaded border
Good companions: *Artemisia ludoviciana* 'Valerie Finnis', *Digitalis purpurea*, *Sedum spectabile* 'Brilliant'

5 Gypsophila 'Rosenschleier'

From mid to late summer the mound of narrow blue-green leaves is enveloped by a cloud of very small double flowers that open white but turn pale pink as they age. Hardy.

8

9

10

12

11

Height: 40cm (16in) **Spread:** 75cm (2ft 6in)
Site: Sun. Well-drained, preferably limy soil
Use: Sunny border
Good companions: *Allium cristophii, Lavandula angustifolia* 'Hidcote', *Lychnis coronaria*

6 Hosta 'Honeybells'

Plaintain lily

Good foliage plant with a clump of fresh green, lustrous leaves. These are nearly heart shaped with slightly wavy margins and are deeply veined. Stems of fragrant white to mauve bells appear in late summer. Hardy.

Height: 75cm (2ft 6in) **Spread:** 1m (3ft)
Site: Partial shade, sun. Fertile and moist but well-drained soil
Use: Ground cover, sunny or shady border, waterside, woodland garden
Good companions: *Astilbe* 'Fanal', *Dicentra spectabilis, Tiarella wherryi*

7 Liatris spicata

Gayfeather

From a base of linear leaves rise sturdy upright stems ringed at intervals with short narrow leaves and packed buds in the top two-thirds. In late summer and early autumn these open from the top down to make mauve-pink plumes. Hardy.
Height: 1.2m (4ft) **Spread:** 45cm (18in)
Site: Sun. Moist but well-drained soil
Use: Sunny border
Good companions: *Astilbe* 'Professor van der Wielen', *Geranium* x *riversleaianum* 'Russell Prichard', *Macleaya cordata* 'Flamingo'

8 Monarda 'Prärienacht'

Bergamot

The bergamot hybrids are aromatic perennials that flower over a long period in late summer and early autumn. The flowering stems of 'Prärienacht' end in heads of purple-mauve flowers arranged in rings. The leaves are prominently veined. Hardy.
Height: 1m (3ft) **Spread:** 45cm (18in)
Site: Sun, partial shade. Humus-rich and moist but well-drained soil
Use: Sunny or lightly shaded border
Good companions: *Anemone* x *hybrida* 'Whirlwind', *Aster* x *frikartii* 'Mönch', *Phlox paniculata* 'Eventide'

9 Origanum laevigatum 'Herrenhausen'

Marjoram, Oregano

Woody-based plant with purplish young leaves that turn dark green with age and are retained in winter. The foliage is not aromatic. Throughout summer and into autumn wiry stems carry dense clusters of small pink flowers, which are surrounded by red-purple bracts. Hardy.
Height: 45cm (18in) **Spread:** 40cm (16in)
Site: Sun. Well-drained soil. Good on lime
Use: Gravel garden, sunny border
Good companions: *Artemisia* 'Powis Castle', *Perovskia* 'Blue Spire', *Verbena bonariensis*

10 Osteospermum 'Jucundum'

Sprawling, woody-based evergreen plant with greyish, aromatic lance-shaped leaves and mauve-pink to magenta daisy-like flowerheads, each on a single stem. The purplish central discs turn gold with age. Blooms throughout summer and into autumn, but buds remain closed in dull weather. Not fully hardy.
General care: In cold areas treat as an annual, or overwinter container-grown plants under glass.
Height: 20cm (8in) **Spread:** 60cm (2ft)
Site: Sun. Well-drained soil
Compost: Soil-based (John Innes No. 2)
Use: Container, front of sunny border
Good companions: *Argyranthemum* 'Vancouver', *Diascia barberae* 'Ruby Field', *Petunia* Surfinia Purple

11 Pelargonium 'Apple Blossom Rosebud'

Rosebud zonal pelargonium

This bushy evergreen perennial has aromatic, green, rounded leaves and produces rounded heads of double flowers with central petals that remain unopened. The outer petals are pink, the central ones white. Plants flower freely in summer and autumn if deadheaded regularly. Tender.
General care: Overwinter in frost-free conditions.
Height: 35cm (14in) **Spread:** 25cm (10in)
Site: Sun. Well-drained soil
Compost: Soil-based (John Innes No. 2) or soil-less with added grit
Use: Conservatory or greenhouse minimum 2°C (36°F), container, formal bedding, sunny patio
Good companions: *Helichrysum petiolare, Pelargonium* 'L'Elégante', *Scaevola aemula* 'Blue Fan'

12 Penstemon 'Evelyn'

From a neat bush of narrow leaves rise spires of deep pink, slender tubular flowers that are paler in the throat. Flowering starts before midsummer and continues into autumn. Hardy.
Height: 50cm (20in) **Spread:** 30cm (12in)
Site: Sun, partial shade. Fertile and well-drained soil
Use: Sunny or lightly shaded border
Good companions: *Aquilegia* 'Hensol Harebell', *Paeonia lactiflora* 'Bowl of Beauty', *Penstemon* 'Stapleford Gem'

pink and mauve (continued)

1 Phlox paniculata 'Eventide'
Perennial phlox

The perennial phloxes are erect plants with linear leaves, often somewhat bare at the base, and rounded heads of scented flowers in a wide range of colours that are good for cutting. The flowers of 'Eventide' are a startling pink. Hardy.

Height: 1m (3ft) **Spread:** 60cm (2ft)

Site: Sun, partial shade. Fertile and moist but well-drained soil

Use: Sunny or lightly shaded border

Good companions: *Geranium psilostemon, Phlox paniculata* 'Fujiyama', *Tradescantia* Andersoniana Group 'Osprey'

2 Sedum spectabile 'Brilliant'
Ice plant

Succulent perennial with fleshy grey-green leaves arranged in rings on erect stems. Flat terminal heads are packed with starry mauve-pink flowers. Attractive to bees. Hardy.

Height and spread: 45cm (18in)

Site: Sun. Well-drained soil

Use: Sunny border

Good companions: *Agapanthus* 'Lilliput', *Caryopteris* x *clandonensis* 'Heavenly Blue', *Perovskia* 'Blue Spire'

bronze and maroon

3 Deschampsia cespitosa 'Goldschleier'
Tufted hair grass, Tussock grass

From a dense evergreen tussock of narrow arching leaves emerge tall stems carrying plumes of silver-purple flowers. In late summer these bleach to straw yellow. Suitable for drying. Hardy.

Height and spread: 1.2m (4ft)

Site: Sun, partial shade. Moist but well-drained soil

Use: Sunny or lightly shaded border

Good companions: *Miscanthus sinensis* 'Variegatus', *Monarda* 'Prärienacht', *Salvia uliginosa*

4 Heuchera micrantha var. diversifolia 'Palace Purple'
Coral flower

This richly textured, evergreen foliage plant is at its best in summer. The jagged, deeply veined leaves have a sheeny bronze-red surface and magenta-pink underside. Showers of tiny white flowers, carried on wiry stems in early summer, are followed by bronze-pink seed pods. Hardy.

Height: 45cm (18in) **Spread:** 60cm (2ft)

Site: Sun, partial shade. Fertile and moist but well-drained soil

Use: Ground cover, sunny or lightly shaded border, woodland garden

Good companions: *Asplenium scolopendrium, Hosta* 'Honeybells', *Tiarella cordifolia*

5 Macleaya cordata 'Flamingo'
Plume poppy

Tall and sometimes invasive perennial but handsome at the back of a border. The large deeply lobed leaves are grey-green, pale grey on the underside. Strong stems carry airy plumes of tiny cream and soft apricot flowers.

Height: 2.5m (8ft) **Spread:** 1m (3ft)

Site: Sun. Moist but well-drained soil
Use: Sunny border
Good companions: *Anemone* x *hybrida* 'September Charm', *Campanula lactiflora*, *Monarda* 'Prärienacht'

6 Phormium 'Sundowner'
New Zealand flax

Large evergreen foliage plant that forms a jagged clump of erect or slightly arching, leathery, broad strap shaped leaves. These are bronze-green with cream and pink lengthwise stripes. In summer yellow-green tubular flowers are arranged in a zigzag along tall woody stems. Not fully hardy.
General care: In cold areas apply a dry winter mulch around the base.
Height and spread: 2m (6ft)
Site: Sun. Moist but well-drained soil
Use: Specimen clump, sunny border
Good companions: *Choisya ternata*, *Cotoneaster conspicuus* 'Decorus', *Hebe* 'Autumn Glory'

7 Stipa gigantea
Giant feather grass, Golden oats

This evergreen or semi-evergreen grass has a mid-green base of arching linear leaves. Tall stems, which stand erect above the clump, carry silver-purple plumes that ripen to spangled gold and remain a feature for many weeks. Plumes can be dried. Hardy.
General care: Cut out dead growths in early spring.
Height: 2m (6ft) **Spread:** 1.2m (4ft)
Site: Sun. Well-drained soil
Use: Gravel garden, sunny border
Good companions: *Anthemis tinctoria* 'E.C. Buxton', *Eryngium alpinum*, *Verbena bonariensis*

red and russet

8 Helenium 'Moerheim Beauty'
Helen's flower, Sneezeweed

The hybrid heleniums are late-flowering upright perennials with narrow leaves and daisy-like flowerheads of petal-like ray-florets around a central disc. They are long-lasting and good for cutting. 'Moerheim Beauty' has a dark brown disc surrounded by copper-red ray-florets. Hardy.
Height: 1m (3ft) **Spread:** 60cm (2ft)
Site: Sun. Fertile and moist but well-drained soil
Use: Sunny border
Good companions: *Helenium* 'Wyndley', *Helianthus* 'Loddon Gold', *Miscanthus sinensis* 'Zebrinus'

9 Hemerocallis 'Pardon Me'
Daylily

In midsummer leafless stems rise from a clump of strap-like leaves carrying red trumpet-shaped flowers that are green-throated with darker veining. Individual flowers are short-lived, but the season lasts for weeks. Hardy.
Height and spread: 60cm (2ft)
Site: Sun. Fertile and moist but well-drained soil
Use: Sunny border
Good companions: *Deschampsia cespitosa* 'Goldschleier', *Helenium* 'Moerheim Beauty', *Thalictrum flavum* subsp. *glaucum*

10 Knautia macedonica

In late summer and early autumn branching stems carry crimson 'pincushion' flowerheads above lobed leaves. Attractive to bees. Hardy.
Height: 75cm (2ft 6in) **Spread:** 45cm (18in)
Site: Sun. Well-drained soil. Good on lime
Use: Sunny border, wild garden
Good companions: *Echinops ritro* 'Veitch's Blue', *Lavandula* x *intermedia* Dutch Group, *Scabiosa caucasica* 'Moerheim Blue'

11 Pelargonium 'Rouletta'
Ivy-leaved pelargonium

This trailing evergreen perennial belongs to a group of hybrid pelargoniums with fleshy ivy-shaped leaves. Throughout summer and autumn it bears rounded clusters of semi-double flowers that are vivid crimson streaked white. Tender.
General care: Overwinter in frost-free conditions.
Height: 20cm (8in) **Spread:** 45cm (18in)
Site: Sun. Well-drained soil
Compost: Soil-based (John Innes No. 2) or soil-less with added grit
Use: Conservatory or greenhouse minimum 2°C (36°F), container, raised bed, sunny patio
Good companions: *Argyranthemum* 'Vancouver', *Convolvulus sabatius*, *Verbena* 'Silver Anne'

12 Penstemon 'Andenken an Friedrich Hahn'

Spires of small, garnet-red bell-shaped flowers rise from this bushy narrow-leaved plant from midsummer until late autumn. Not fully hardy.
General care: In cold areas protect over winter with a dry mulch.
Height: 30cm (12in) **Spread:** 60cm (2ft)
Site: Sun, partial shade. Fertile, well-drained soil
Use: Sunny or lightly shaded border
Good companions: *Anaphalis triplinervis* 'Sommerschnee', *Paeonia lactiflora* 'Karl Rosenfield', *Thalictrum aquilegiifolium* 'Thundercloud'

red and russet (continued)

1 Sedum 'Ruby Glow'
Stonecrop
Succulent perennial with red stems carrying fleshy, purplish green leaves. In late summer and early autumn plants are topped by packed heads of wine-red starry flowers. Hardy.
Height: 25cm (10in) **Spread:** 45cm (18in)
Site: Sun. Well-drained soil
Use: Front of sunny border, raised bed, rock garden
Good companions: *Gypsophila* 'Rosenschleier', *Lavandula angustifolia* 'Hidcote', *Scabiosa graminifolia*

yellow and orange

2 Achillea 'Coronation Gold'
Yarrow
Evergreen perennial with feathery grey-green leaves and flat heads of densely packed, tiny yellow flowers. Flowerheads can be dried for winter decoration. Hardy.
Height: 1m (3ft) **Spread:** 60cm (2ft)
Site: Sun. Well-drained soil
Use: Sunny border
Good companions: *Erysimum* 'Bowles' Mauve', *Potentilla fruticosa* 'Tangerine', x *Solidaster luteus* 'Lemore'

3 Coreopsis verticillata 'Grandiflora'
Tickseed
The finely cut mid-green leaves of this bushy perennial are covered by a profusion of rich yellow daisy-like flowerheads over many weeks. 'Moonbeam' has creamy yellow flowers, which team with a wider range of colours. Hardy.
Height: 60cm (2ft) **Spread:** 40cm (16in)
Site: Sun. Well-drained soil
Use: Sunny border
Good companions: *Aster* x *frikartii* 'Mönch', *Eryngium alpinum, Origanum laevigatum* 'Herrenhausen'

4 Hemerocallis 'Stella de Oro'
Daylily
This low-growing evergreen daylily flowers over many weeks in mid to late summer. The yellow trumpets are a little over 5cm (2in) across and the mouth is almost circular in outline.
Height: 30cm (12in) **Spread:** 45cm (18in)
Site: Sun, partial shade. Fertile and moist but well-drained soil
Compost: Soil-based (John Innes No. 2)
Use: Container, sunny or lightly shaded border
Good companions: *Astilbe* 'Professor van der Wielen', *Carex oshimensis* 'Evergold', *Iris sibirica 'Ego'*

5 Hosta fortunei var. aureomarginata
Plantain lily
The yellow variegation of many hostas fades as summer advances, but in this case the creamy edge of the deeply veined leaves remains distinct until autumn. Mauve flowers in summer. Hardy.
Height and spread: 75cm (2ft 6in)
Site: Sun, partial shade. Fertile and humus-rich but well-drained soil
Use: Ground cover, sunny or partially shaded border, woodland
Good companions: *Milium effusum* 'Aureum', *Tiarella wherryi, Viola riviniana* Purpurea Group

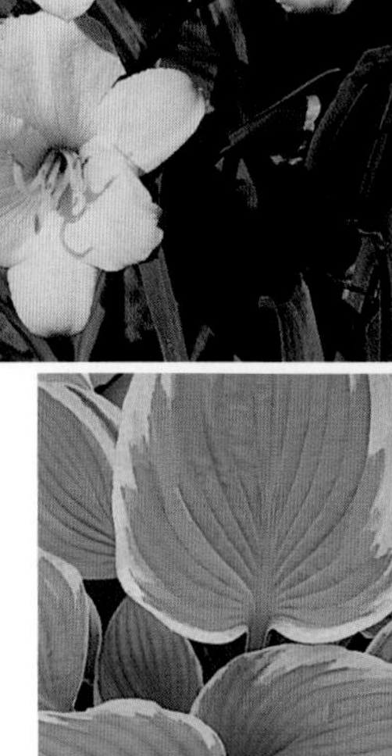

6 Kirengeshoma palmata
This elegant woodland perennial forms a clump of attractively lobed, pale green leaves. In late summer and early autumn black stems carry widely spaced tubular flowers that are composed of fleshy, pale yellow petals. Hardy.
Height: 1.2m (4ft) **Spread:** 75cm (2ft 6in)
Site: Partial shade. Humus-rich and moist soil that is well-drained and lime-free
Use: Peat bed, shady border, woodland garden
Good companions: *Hosta* 'Gold Standard', *Rhododendron luteum, Uvularia grandiflora*

7 Kniphofia 'Royal Standard'
Red hot poker, Torch lily
From a clump of arching narrow leaves rise stiff stems brandishing torches of tubular flowers. These are orange in bud but open yellow from the bottom up. Hardy.
Height: 1m (3ft)
Spread: 60cm (2ft)
Site: Sun, partial shade. Humus-rich and moist but well-drained soil
Use: Sunny or lightly shaded border
Good companions: *Agapanthus* 'Lilliput', *Coreopsis verticillata* 'Grandiflora', *Helenium* 'Wyndley'

8 Rudbeckia fulgida var. sullivantii 'Goldsturm'
Black-eyed susan
This bushy perennial has pointed leaves and slightly hairy branched stems that carry numerous

daisy-like flowerheads up to 8cm (3in) across. The orange-yellow, petal-like ray-florets radiate around an eye-catching, dark brown disc and last well into autumn. Hardy.

Height: 60cm (2ft) **Spread:** 45cm (18in)

Site: Sun, partial shade. Moist but well-drained soil

Use: Sunny or lightly shaded border, wild garden

Good companions: *Deschampsia cespitosa* 'Goldschleier', *Helenium* 'Moerheim Beauty', *Helenium* 'Sonnenwunder'

9 x Solidaster luteus 'Lemore'

These clump-forming perennials are a cross between a golden rod (*Solidago*) and an aster. In late summer and early autumn 'Lemore' bears dense sprays of small daisy-like flowerheads composed of pale yellow ray-florets around a darker central disc. Excellent for cutting. Hardy.

Height and spread: 75cm (2ft 6in)

Site: Sun. Well-drained soil

Use: Sunny border

Good companions: *Achillea* 'Coronation Gold', *Anthemis tinctoria* 'E.C. Buxton', *Helianthus* 'Lemon Queen'

cream and white

10 Anaphalis triplinervis 'Sommerschnee'

Pearl everlasting, Summer snow

Spreading clumps of grey-green spoon-shaped leaves are topped by white, papery everlasting flowerheads. Suitable for drying. Hardy.

Height: 40cm (16in) **Spread:** 50cm (20in)

Site: Sun, partial shade. Moist but well-drained soil

Use: Sunny or lightly shaded border.

Good companions: *Anemone hupehensis* 'Hadspen Abundance', *Aster divaricatus*, *Heuchera* 'Plum Pudding'

11 Anemone x hybrida 'Whirlwind'

Japanese anemone

This woody-based perennial forms an attractive mound of lobed leaves from which rise erect stems carrying white semi-double flowers with yellow centres in late summer and early autumn. Hardy.

Height: 1.2m (4ft) **Spread:** Indefinite

Site: Sun, partial shade. Humus-rich and moist but well-drained soil

Use: Sunny or lightly shaded border, woodland garden

Good companions: *Anaphalis triplinervis* 'Sommerschnee', *Anemone x hybrida* 'September Charm', *Aster novi-belgii* 'Heinz Richard'

12 Argyranthemum 'Snow Storm'

Compact woody-based plant with soft stems and deeply cut grey-green leaves. Through summer and into autumn it bears white daisy-like flowerheads with yellow central discs.
Tender.

General care: In frost-prone areas treat as an annual, or grow in containers and overwinter under glass.

Height and spread: 30cm (12in)

Site: Sun. Well-drained soil

Compost: Soil-based (John Innes No. 2)

Use: Container, sunny border, patio

Good companions: *Argyranthemum* 'Vancouver', *Scaevola aemula* 'Blue Wonder', *Verbena* 'Silver Anne'

cream and white (continued)

1 Astilbe 'Professor van der Wielen'

This large, graceful astilbe hybrid makes mounds of mid-green divided leaves. In midsummer tall stems bear long-lasting arching plumes of tiny creamy flowers. Attractive seed heads in autumn and winter. Hardy.

Height: 1.2m (4ft) **Spread:** 1m (3ft)

Site: Sun, partial shade. Humus-rich and reliably moist soil

Use: Bog garden, moist border, waterside, woodland garden

Good companions: *Miscanthus sinensis* 'Variegatus', *Rheum palmatum* 'Atrosanguineum', *Rodgersia pinnata* 'Superba'

2 Gaura lindheimeri

White flowers hover around the clump of erect or gently arching, slender stems set with narrow leaves. The buds are tinted pink and the flowers age to pale pink. Flowers into autumn. Hardy.

Height: 1.2m (4ft) **Spread:** 1m (3ft)

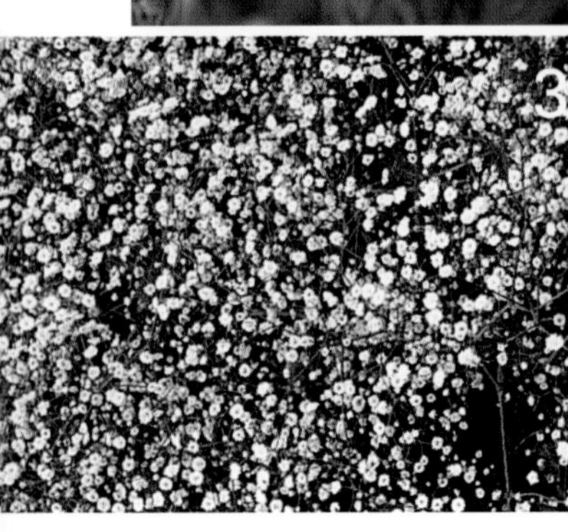

11

12

Site: Sun. Well-drained soil
Use: Gravel garden, sunny border
Good companions: *Artemisia* 'Powis Castle', *Ruta graveolens* 'Jackman's Blue', *Stipa gigantea*

3 Gypsophila paniculata 'Bristol Fairy'
Baby's breath
The base of grey-green grass-like leaves is topped by a tangle of slender branching stems. From mid to late summer these support an airy cloud of small, white double flowers. Good for hiding plants past their best and for cutting. 'Flamingo' has pale pink double flowers. Hardy.
Height and spread: 1m (3ft)
Site: Sun. Well-drained soil. Good on lime
Use: Sunny border
Good companions: *Acanthus spinosus, Papaver orientale* 'Black and White', *Verbascum* Cotswold Group 'Gainsborough'

4 Hosta 'Snowden'
Plantain lily
An impressive clump of foliage with elegant white flowers in mid to late summer. The long pointed leaves are grey-green and deeply veined. Hardy.
Height and spread: 1m (3ft)
Site: Sun, partial shade. Fertile and humus-rich but well-drained soil
Use: Ground cover, sunny or partially shaded border, woodland
Good companions: *Astilbe chinensis* var. *taquetii* 'Superba', *Hosta* 'Ginko Craig', *Pulmonaria* 'Mawson's Blue'

5 Phlox paniculata 'Fujiyama'
Perennial phlox
This erect plant has linear leaves and rounded heads of scented ivory-white flowers. Good in the border and for cutting. Hardy.
Height: 75cm (2ft 6in) **Spread:** 50cm (20in)
Site: Sun, partial shade. Fertile and moist but well-drained soil
Use: Sunny or lightly shaded border
Good companions: *Aster novi-belgii* 'Heinz Richard', *Geranium* 'Johnson's Blue', *Phlox paniculata* 'Eventide'

6 Romneya coulteri
Matilija poppy, Tree poppy
The deeply lobed, grey-green leaves of this deciduous woody-based plant have a blue-grey bloom. Tall stems carry white flowers, which have a boss of yellow stamens and are often more than 10cm (4in) across. Slow to get established, but later may spread vigorously. Not fully hardy.
General care: Grow in a warm, sheltered position and apply a dry mulch in winter. Cut down all of the surviving growth to the ground in late winter.
Height: 2m (6ft) **Spread:** Indefinite
Site: Sun. Humus-rich but well-drained soil
Use: Base of sunny wall, sunny border
Good companions: *Buddleja crispa, Clematis* 'Huldine', *Solanum laxum* 'Album'

7 Tradescantia Andersoniana Group 'Osprey'
Spiderwort, Trinity flower
The tradescantia hybrids grown in borders are leafy plants with pointed strap-shaped leaves that arch away from erect stems. Small sprays of three-petalled flowers emerge at the junction of leaf and stem. 'Osprey' has white flowers with a haze of blue filaments at the centre. Hardy.
Height and spread: 60cm (2ft)
Site: Sun, partial shade. Moist, well-drained soil
Use: Sunny or lightly shaded border
Good companions: *Aconitum* 'Spark's Variety', *Anemone × hybrida* 'Honorine Jobert', *Fuchsia magellanica* 'Versicolor'

silver and grey

8 Cortaderia selloana 'Sunningdale Silver'
Pampas grass
Evergreen grass suitable for a large garden. It forms a substantial mound of narrow arching leaves from which emerge erect stems carrying feathery heads of silky, creamy white flowers. These stand up well to weather and can be used fresh or dried in flower arrangements. Hardy.
General care: Cut down all the old stems in late winter.
Height: 3m (10ft) **Spread:** 2.5m (8ft)
Site: Sun. Well-drained soil
Use: Specimen clump, sunny border
Good companions: *Ceanothus thyrsiflorus* var. *repens, Cortaderia selloana* 'Aureolineata', *Stipa gigantea*

9 Cynara cardunculus
Cardoon
Magnificent foliage plant with large, jagged, grey-green leaves, sometimes grown as a vegetable for the edible leaf-stalks and midribs, which are eaten blanched. In summer and early autumn the violet-purple thistle-like flowerheads are impressive. They are also suitable for dried flower arrangements. Hardy.
Height: 2m (6ft) **Spread:** 1.2m (4ft)
Site: Sun. Fertile and well-drained soil
Use: Sunny border
Good companions: *Artemisia* 'Powis Castle', *Erysimum* 'Bowles' Mauve', *Sedum* 'Herbstfreude'

green

10 Carex comans 'Frosted Curls'
Sedge
This evergreen grass-like sedge makes a dense tuft of arching, pale silvery green, thread-like leaves. There are inconspicuous green cylindrical flower spikes in summer. Not fully hardy.
Height: 60cm (2ft) **Spread:** 45cm (18in)
Site: Sun, partial shade. Moist but well-drained soil
Use: Sunny or lightly shaded border
Good companions: *Miscanthus sinensis* 'Silberfeder', *Molinia caerulea* subsp. *arundinacea* 'Windspiel', *Panicum virgatum* 'Rubrum'

11 Hosta lancifolia
Plantain lily
Grown mainly as a foliage plant, this hosta makes dense dark green clumps of narrow pointed leaves. In late summer numerous stems carry purple, slender funnel-shaped flowers. Hardy.
Height: 45cm (18in) **Spread:** 75cm (2ft 6in)
Site: Shade, partial shade. Humus-rich and moist but well-drained soil
Use: Ground cover, shady border, woodland garden
Good companions: *Dryopteris wallichiana, Viola riviniana* Purpurea Group, *Waldsteinia ternata*

12 Kniphofia 'Percy's Pride'
Red hot poker, Torch lily
From arching leaves that are markedly keeled along the midrib rise upright stems carrying spikes of narrow tubular flowers, which hang down in dense ranks. When open the flowers are pale cream, but there is a strong green tint in the unopened buds. Hardy.
Height: 1.2m (4ft) **Spread:** 60cm (2ft)
Site: Sun, partial shade. Humus-rich and moist but well-drained soil
Use: Sunny or lightly shaded border
Good companions: *Helenium* 'Moerheim Beauty', *Hemerocallis* 'Stella de Oro', *Rudbeckia fulgida* var. *sullivantii* 'Goldsturm'

annuals & biennials

Annuals and biennials often give good value over many weeks. In late summer in particular they brighten beds and containers over a long period if regularly deadheaded.

purple, blue and violet

1 Brachyscome iberidifolia Splendour Series

Swan river daisy

Free-flowering dwarf annual with finely divided leaves and small yellow-centred daisy-like flowers in purple, blue, mauve, pink or white. Half hardy.

General care: Sow seed under glass at 18°C (64°F) in mid-spring. Plant out when there is no longer a risk of frost.

Height and spread: 30cm (12in)

Site: Sun. Well-drained soil

Compost: Soil-based (John Innes No. 2) or soil-less

Use: Container, formal bedding, front of sunny border

Good companions: *Callistephus chinensis* Princess Series, *Lavatera trimestris* 'Mont Blanc', *Nigella damascena* 'Miss Jekyll'

2 Lathyrus odoratus 'Noel Sutton'

Sweet pea

Sweet peas are annual tendril climbers. Modern cultivars have large scented, ruffled pea flowers, which in 'Noel Sutton' are mauve-blue. Hardy.

General care: Sow seed under glass in autumn or early spring and plant out in spring. Or sow *in situ* in mid-spring. Deadhead regularly.

Height: 2m (6ft) **Spread:** 60cm (2ft)

Site: Sun. Humus-rich, fertile and well-drained soil

Use: Screen, tripod climber

Good companions: *Cleome hassleriana* 'Rose Queen', *Lavatera trimestris* 'Mont Blanc', *Penstemon* 'Evelyn'

3 Lobelia erinus 'Crystal Palace'

A bushy narrow-leaved cultivar of a popular bedding and container perennial normally grown as an annual. Covered with dark blue flowers throughout summer and into autumn. Half hardy.

General care: Sow seed under glass at 16–18°C (61–64°F) in late winter. Plant out when there is no longer a risk of frost.

Height and spread: 15cm (6in)

Site: Sun or partial shade. Moist, well-drained soil

Compost: Soil-based (John Innes No. 2) or soil-less

Use: Container, front of sunny or lightly shaded border, formal bedding

Good companions: *Cosmos bipinnatus* Sensation Series, *Impatiens walleriana* Tempo Series, *Nicotiana* Domino Series

4 Salvia viridis 'Oxford Blue'

Annual clary

Erect hairy annual with insignificant flowers, but darkly veined, violet-blue leaf-like bracts. Good for cutting. Hardy.

General care: Sow seed *in situ* in early autumn or mid to late spring. Plant out when there is no longer a risk of frost.

Height: 30cm (12in) **Spread:** 25cm (10in)

Site: Sun. Well-drained soil

Use: Formal bedding, herb garden, sunny border

Good companions: *Allium cristophii*, *Gladiolus* 'Charm', *Verbena bonariensis*

5 Scaevola aemula 'Blue Wonder'

Fairy fan-flower

Shrubby evergreen perennial commonly grown as an annual for containers. The stiff trailing stems carry a profusion of violet-blue fan-shaped flowers from late spring until the first frosts. Tender.

General care: Sow seed at 19–24°C (66–75°F) in spring. Plant out when there is no risk of frost.

Height: 50cm (20in) **Spread:** 75cm (2ft 6in)

Site: Sun. Humus-rich, moist but well-drained soil

Compost: Soil-based (John Innes No. 2) or soil-less

Use: Conservatory or greenhouse minimum 5°C (41°F), container

Good companions: *Anagallis monellii*, *Verbena* 'Peaches and Cream', *Viola* Crystal Bowl Series

6 Viola x wittrockiana Crystal Bowl Series

Pansy

Pansy cultivars are short-lived evergreen perennials grown as annuals or biennials. Their flat flowers are often strongly marked, but some cultivars have single colours. Those of Crystal Bowl are purple, deep blue, rose or white. Hardy.

General care: Sow seed in a coldframe in late winter. Plant out in late spring. To prolong flowering, deadhead regularly.

Height: 20cm (8in) **Spread:** 25cm (10in)

Site: Sun, partial shade. Humus-rich and moist but well-drained soil

Compost: Soil-based (John Innes No. 2) or soil-less

Use: Container, formal bedding, front of border

Good companions: *Lobelia erinus* 'Cobalt Blue', *Nemesia* Carnival Series, *Nicotiana* Domino Series

pink and mauve

7 Cleome hassleriana 'Rose Queen'

Spider flower, Spider plant

Erect annual with a base of 'fingered' leaves topped by rounded heads of fragrant, strong pink spidery flowers. Other colours available. Tender.

General care: Sow seed under glass at 18°C (64°F) from late winter to early spring. Plant out when there is no longer a risk of frost.

Height: 1.2m (4ft) **Spread:** 45cm (18in)

Site: Sun. Free-draining soil

Compost: Soil-based (John Innes No. 2)

Use: Container, sunny border, formal bedding

Good companions: *Antirrhinum* Sonnet Series, *Artemisia* 'Powis Castle', *Verbena bonariensis*

3

4

1 2

5

6

7

8

8 Cosmos bipinnatus Sensation Series

Erect annual with feathery foliage and tall wiry stems supporting large cupped flowerheads that are white or pink and yellow centred. Half hardy.
General care: Sow seed under glass in mid-spring and plant out when there is no longer a risk of frost, or sow *in situ* in late spring.
Height: 1m (3ft) **Spread:** 40cm (16in)
Site: Sun. Moist but well-drained soil
Use: Sunny border, formal bedding
Good companions: *Brachyscome iberidifolia* Splendour Series, *Delphinium* 'Faust', *Lathyrus odoratus* 'Noel Sutton'

9 Dianthus chinensis Baby Doll Series

Chinese pink, Indian pink

Short-lived perennial or biennial grown as an annual. Branching stems carry purplish red to pink and white flowers, usually patterned. Hardy.
General care: Sow seed *in situ* in mid-spring.
Height and spread: 15cm (6in)
Site: Sun. Well-drained soil. Good on lime
Compost: Soil-based (John Innes No. 2)
Use: Container, formal bedding, front of border
Good companions: *Antirrhinum* Sonnet Series, *Convolvulus cneorum*, *Matthiola incana* Ten Week Series

10 Impatiens walleriana Tempo Series

Busy lizzie

The busy lizzies are brittle-stemmed perennials widely grown as annuals. They offer a vast range of intense single colours and mixtures and are free flowering in shade. Tempo Series includes pink, orange, mauve and bicolours. Tender.
General care: Sow seed under glass at 16–18°C (61–64°F) from late winter to early spring. Plant out when there is no longer a risk of frost.
Height: 25cm (10in) **Spread:** 45cm (18in)
Site: Partial shade. Humus-rich and moist but well-drained soil
Compost: Soil-based (John Innes No. 2) or soil-less
Use: Conservatory or greenhouse minimum 10°C (50°F), container, formal bedding
Good companions: *Lobelia erinus* 'Cobalt Blue', *Nicotiana* Domino Series, *Viola* x *wittrockiana* Crystal Bowl Series

9

10

11

12

11 Petunia Surfinia Series

Grandiflora petunia

The Surfinia petunias are perennial hybrids grown as annuals, but available only as young plants raised from cuttings. They are vigorous, branch freely and produce numerous trumpet-shaped flowers on trailing stems throughout summer and early autumn. The colour range includes various shades of pink, red, blue, purple and white. Half hardy.
General care: Plant out when there is no longer a risk of frost.
Height: 35cm (14in) **Spread:** 1m (3ft)
Site: Sun. Well-drained soil
Compost: Soil-based (John Innes No. 1) or soil-less
Use: Container or formal bedding
Good companions: *Helichrysum petiolare*, *Isotoma axillaris*, *Verbena* 'Silver Anne'

12 Verbena 'Silver Anne'

In summer and autumn this stiff-stemmed sprawling plant bears heads of sweetly scented flowers that open bright pink and fade to silvery white. Perennial, but plants raised from cuttings are widely grown as annuals. Not fully hardy.
General care: To propagate take cuttings in late summer, overwinter under glass and plant out in late spring.
Height: 30cm (12in) **Spread:** 60cm (2ft)
Site: Sun. Moist but well-drained soil
Compost: Soil-based (John Innes No. 2) with added sharp sand
Use: Container, formal bedding
Good companions: *Diascia rigescens*, *Helichrysum petiolare*, *Scaevola aemula* 'Blue Wonder'

red and russet

1 Amaranthus caudatus
Love-lies-bleeding, Tassel flower

Bushy annual with large, heavily veined light green leaves. In summer and early autumn tassels of tiny red-purple flowers hang from erect stems. Suitable for cutting and drying. Half hardy.
General care: Sow seed under glass at 20°C (68°F) in mid-spring. Plant out when there is no longer a risk of frost.
Height: 1.2m (4ft) **Spread:** 75cm (2ft 6in)
Site: Sun. Humus-rich, moist but well-drained soil
Compost: Soil-based (John Innes No. 2)
Use: Conservatory or greenhouse minimum 7°C (45°F), formal bedding, sunny border
Good companions: *Cosmos bipinnatus* Sensation Series, *Dahlia* 'Porcelain', *Lathyrus odoratus* 'Noel Sutton'

yellow and orange

2 Calendula officinalis 'Fiesta Gitana'
English marigold, Marigold, Pot marigold

Easy, fast-growing compact annual that bears daisy-like flowers, usually double, above spoon-shaped leaves. Colours are soft yellows and oranges, with some bicolours. Self-seeds. Hardy.
General care: Sow seed *in situ* in early to mid-autumn or in early spring.
Height and spread: 30cm (12in)
Site: Sun. Well-drained, even poor soil
Compost: Soil-based (John Innes No. 2)
Use: Container, front of sunny bed or border
Good companions: *Nigella damascena* 'Miss Jekyll', *Salvia farinacea* 'Victoria', *Salvia viridis* 'Oxford Blue'

3 Nemesia Carnival Series

The cultivars and hybrids of *N. strumosa* are low-growing annuals that produce two-lipped flowers in summer, often with contrasting colours. Carnival Series includes purple-veined orange, yellow, white, pink or red blooms. Half hardy.
General care: Sow seed under glass at 15°C (59°F) in early spring and plant out when there is no longer a risk of frost.
Height: 20cm (8in) **Spread** 15cm (6in)
Site: Sun. Moist but well-drained soil
Compost: Soil-based (John Innes No. 2) or soil-less
Use: Container, edging, front of sunny border, formal bedding
Good companions: *Lobelia erinus* 'Crystal Palace', *Nicotiana* 'Lime Green', *Verbena* 'Peaches and Cream'

4 Tagetes tenuifolia Favourite Series
French marigold

The French marigolds are long-flowering hybrids with divided leaves and upstanding single or double flowerheads in colour mixtures that include yellow, orange and red-brown. Plants in this selection are relatively tall. Half hardy.
General care: Sow seed under glass at 18°C (64°F) in early to mid-spring. Plant out when there is no longer a risk of frost.
Height: 35cm (14in) **Spread:** 30cm (12in)
Site: Sun. Well-drained soil
Compost: Soil-based (John Innes No. 2) or soil-less
Use: Container, formal bedding, front of border
Good companions: *Bidens ferulifolia* 'Golden Goddess', *Felicia amelloides* 'Santa Anita', *Tagetes tenuifolia* 'Lemon Gem'

5 Tagetes tenuifolia 'Lemon Gem'
Signet marigold

The Signet marigolds are low bushy annuals with slender divided leaves. Over a long season they bear sprays of small single flowers in yellow and orange. 'Lemon Gem' is the coolest. Half hardy.
General care: Sow seed under glass at 18°C (64°F) in early to mid-spring. Plant out when there is no longer a risk of frost.
Height: 25cm (10in) **Spread:** 35cm (14in)
Site: Sun. Well-drained soil
Compost: Soil-based (John Innes No. 2) or soil-less
Use: Container, formal bedding, front of border
Good companions: *Bracteantha bracteata* Monstrosum Series, *Convolvulus sabatius*, *Nemesia* Carnival Series

6 Tropaeolum Alaska Series
Nasturtium

Compact variegated version of what is often a vigorous scrambling annual. The scented spurred flowers, in shades of yellow, orange and crimson, stand above wavy-edged leaves that are speckled or blotched with creamy white. Flowers throughout summer and into autumn. Half hardy.
General care: Sow seed under glass at 13°C (55°F) in early spring and plant out in late spring, or sow *in situ* in mid to late spring.
Height: 30cm (12in) **Spread:** 45cm (18in)
Site: Sun, partial shade. Well-drained soil
Compost: Soil-based (John Innes No. 2)
Use: Container, formal bedding, front of border
Good companions: *Bidens ferulifolia* 'Golden Goddess', *Calendula officinalis* 'Fiesta Gitana', *Tagetes tenuifolia* 'Lemon Gem'

1

2

3

4

5

6

7 Verbena 'Peaches and Cream'

Hybrid verbenas raised annually from seed include upright and sprawling plants that produce crowded heads of small flowers throughout summer. 'Peaches and Cream' is a rather stiff sprawling plant with relatively large flowers that combine cream, yellow, orange and salmon-pink. Half hardy.
General care: Sow seed under glass at minimum 18°C (64°F) in late winter or early spring and plant out in early summer.
Height: 45cm (18in) **Spread:** 50cm (20in)
Site: Sun. Moist but well-drained soil
Compost: Soil-based (John Innes No. 2) or soil-less
Use: Container, sunny bed
Good companions: *Brachyscome iberidifolia* 'Purple Splendour', *Helychrysum petiolare, Heuchera micrantha* var. *diversifolia* 'Palace Purple'

cream and white

8 Lavatera trimestris 'Mont Blanc'

Mallow

Erect bushy annual with hairy lobed leaves and white funnel-shaped flowers from midsummer to early autumn. Hardy.
General care: Sow seed *in situ* in early autumn or mid-spring.
Height: 50cm (20in) **Spread:** 35cm (14in)
Site: Sun. Well-drained soil
Use: Formal bedding, sunny bed or border
Good companions: *Echinops ritro* 'Veitch's Blue, *Eryngium* x *tripartitum, Perovskia* 'Blue Spire'

9 Nicotiana Domino Series

Tobacco plant

Upright annual with sticky leaves and stems. Throughout summer and into autumn it bears upward-facing tubular flowers in white, lime-green, pink or purple. Half hardy.
General care: Sow seed under glass at 18°C (64°F) in late winter or early spring. Plant out when there is no longer a risk of frost.
Height: 40cm (16in) **Spread:** 20cm (8in)
Site: Sun or partial shade. Moist but well-drained soil
Compost: Soil-based (John Innes No. 2) or soil-less
Use: Container, sunny or lightly shaded border
Good companions: *Alcea rosea* 'Nigra', *Amaranthus caudatus, Clarkia amoena* 'Satin'

7

8

11

9

10

12

10 Sutera cordata

Bacopa

Trailing perennial grown as an annual and sold as plants, mainly for edging containers. It has small leaves, and throughout summer and into autumn bears numerous tiny white flowers. Tender.
General care: Pinch back stems to encourage branching.
Height: 8cm (3in) **Spread:** 30cm (12in)
Site: Sun, partial shade. Moist but well-drained soil
Compost: Soil-based (John Innes No. 2) or soil-less
Use: Container, sunny or lightly shaded bed
Good companions: *Fuchsia* 'Red Spider', *Petunia* Surfinia Series, *Verbena* 'Silver Anne'

green

11 Molucella laevis

Bells of Ireland, Shell flower

The erect stems of this annual rise above scalloped leaves and are set with numerous shell-like green bracts, each harbouring a small white fragrant flower. Good for cutting and can be dried for winter decoration. Half hardy.
General care: Sow seed under glass in early spring and plant out in late spring, or sow *in situ* in mid-spring.
Height: 60cm (2ft) **Spread:** 20cm (8in)
Site: Sun. Moist but well-drained soil
Use: Sunny border, cutting garden
Good companions: *Alcea rosea* 'Nigra', *Amaranthus caudatus, Tropaeolum majus* 'Empress of India'

12 Zinnia 'Envy'

The annual zinnias usually have double daisy-like flowers that are valuable at the end of summer. Often sold as mixed colours in various heights. 'Envy' is an unusual lime green and readily available as a separate colour. Tender.
General care: Sow seed under glass at 13–18°C (55–64°F) in early spring and plant out when there is no longer a risk of frost, or sow *in situ* in late spring.
Height: 75cm (2ft 6in) **Spread:** 25cm (10in)
Site: Sun. Humus-rich and well-drained soil
Compost: Soil-based (John Innes No. 2) or soil-less
Use: Container, formal bedding, sunny border
Good companions: *Calendula officinalis* 'Fiesta Gitana', *Tagetes* 'French Favourites', *Tagetes tenuifolia* 'Lemon Gem'

bulbs

Perennials with underground food-storage organs – true bulbs, corms, tubers or rhizomes – are a varied group. Many flower in spring, but some of the most distinguished, including lilies, are summer flowering.

pink and mauve

1 Alstroemeria ligtu hybrids

Peruvian lily

These fleshy tubers form extensive colonies. Erect stems carry the narrow leaves and showy flowers, which are pink, purple, red, white or yellow with dark markings. Not fully hardy.

General care: Plant in late summer or early autumn with the top of the tuber about 20cm (8in) deep.

Height: 50cm (20in) **Spread:** 75cm (2ft 6in)

Site: Sun, partial shade. Fertile, moist but well-drained soil

Use: Sunny or lightly shaded border

Good companions: *Alchemilla mollis, Convallaria majalis, Macleaya cordata* 'Flamingo'

2 Cyclamen purpurascens

Sowbread

This tuberous evergreen or deciduous species has lightly silvered leaves and sweetly scented flowers in pink, carmine or white. Hardy.

General care: Plant in autumn with the top of the tuber about 5cm (2in) deep.

Height and spread: 10cm (4in)

Site: Partial shade. Humus-rich, moist but well-drained soil, preferably containing lime

Use: Shady border, woodland garden

Good companions: *Anemone blanda, Helleborus orientalis, Muscari armeniacum*

3 Dahlia 'Kiwi Gloria'

Cactus-flowered dahlia

Tuberous dahlia with small, pink-tinted double flowerheads. The petal-like ray-florets are rolled or 'quilled' for half their length. Half hardy.

General care: Plant in mid to late spring with the top of the tuber 10–15cm (4–6in) deep. Lift tubers in autumn and store in frost-free conditions.

Height: 1.2m (4ft) **Spread:** 60cm (2ft)

Site: Sun. Fertile, humus-rich, well-drained soil

Use: Formal bedding, sunny bed or border

Good companions: *Dahlia* 'Peach Cupid', *Dahlia* 'Porcelain', *Penstemon* 'Stapleford Gem'

bronze and maroon

4 Cosmos atrosanguineus

Chocolate cosmos, Chocolate plant

Tuberous perennial with chocolate-scented divided leaves and in late summer and autumn red-brown cupped flowers. Not fully hardy.

General care: Plant in mid to late spring with the top of the tuber about 10cm (4in) deep. Lift in autumn and store in a frost-free place. In a mild climate leave in ground over winter.

Height: 75 cm (2ft 6in) **Spread:** 45cm (18in)

Site: Sun. Moist but well-drained soil

Use: Sunny border

Good companions: *Echinacea purpurea* 'White Lustre', *Pennisetum alopecuroides* 'Hameln', *Sanguisorba obtusa*

red and russet

5 Begonia 'Memory Scarlet'

Tuberous begonia

Upright tuberous hybrid begonia, suitable for outdoor containers or formal bedding in summer. Branching stems carry white-edged, red double flowers over a long season. Tender.

General care: Start tubers into growth under glass and plant outdoors in early summer. Lift in autumn and store in frost-free conditions.

Height: 75cm (2ft 6in) **Spread:** 45cm (18in)

Site: Partial shade. Humus-rich, well-drained neutral to acid soil

Compost: Soil-based (John Innes No. 2) or soil-less

Use: Conservatory or greenhouse minimum 10°C (50°F), container, formal bedding

Good companions: *Fuchsia* 'Red Spider', *Petunia* Surfinia Series, *Verbena* 'Silver Anne'

6 Crocosmia 'Lucifer'

Montbretia

The sword-like leaves of this vigorous crocosmia develop from a corm. In mid to late summer arching stems bear sprays of upward-facing, vivid orange-red flowers. Not fully hardy.

General care: Plant in spring. Divide congested clumps in spring or autumn. Dry mulch over winter.

Height: 1.2m (4ft) **Spread:** 10cm (4in)

Site: Sun, partial shade. Moist but well-drained soil

Use: Sunny or lightly shaded border

Good companions: *Agapanthus* 'Blue Giant', *Cynara cardunculus, Kniphofia* 'Royal Standard'

7 Dahlia 'Moor Place'

Pompom dahlia

Tuberous hybrid dahlia with small, deep

1

2

3

4

burgundy round flowerheads packed with incurved petal-like florets. They are produced from midsummer until the first frosts occur. Half hardy.
General care: Plant in mid to late spring with the top of the tuber 10–15cm (4–6in) deep. Put in supporting stakes before plants make growth. Lift in autumn and store in frost-free conditions.
Height: 1m (3ft) **Spread:** 60cm (2ft)
Site: Sun. Fertile, humus-rich and well-drained soil
Use: Formal bedding, sunny bed or border
Good companions: *Dahlia* 'Kiwi Gloria', *Dahlia* 'Porcelain', *Penstemon* 'Raven'

yellow and orange

8 Begonia 'Orange Cascade'
Tuberous begonia
Trailing tuberous begonia with double orange flowers, 8cm (3in) across, over a long season. Suitable for growing under glass or for tall pots and hanging baskets outdoors in summer. Tender.
General care: Start tubers into growth under glass and plant outdoors in early summer. Lift in autumn and store in frost-free conditions.
Height and spread: 60cm (2ft)
Site: Partial shade
Compost: Soil-based (John Innes No. 2) or soil-less
Use: Conservatory or greenhouse at minimum 10°C (50°F), container
Good companions: *Bidens ferulifolia* 'Golden Goddess', *Helichrysum petiolare, Tropaeolum majus* 'Empress of India'

9 Crocosmia x crocosmiiflora 'Emily McKenzie'
Montbretia
Small corms produce the sword-like leaves. The sprays of star-shaped orange flowers, splashed mahogany in the throat, appear from late summer and into autumn. Not fully hardy.
General care: Plant in spring. Divide congested clumps in spring or autumn. Dry mulch over winter.
Height: 60cm (2ft) **Spread:** 10cm (4in)
Site: Sun, partial shade. Moist, well-drained soil
Use: Sunny or lightly shaded border
Good companions: *Agapanthus* 'Lilliput', *Deschampsia cespitosa* 'Goldschleier', *Hemerocallis* 'Stella de Oro'

10 Gladiolus 'Green Woodpecker'
Medium-flowered grandiflorus gladiolus
A fan of sword-like leaves grows from a flattened corm. In summer it produces green-yellow, ruffled trumpet-shaped flowers with a deep red mark in the throat. One stiff stem carries up to 25 buds arranged in a closely packed zigzag. The bottom bud opens first and produces the largest flower, about 10cm (4in) across. Ten flowers may be open at a time. Excellent as a cut flower. Half hardy.
General care: Plant in spring with the top of the corm about 15cm (6in) deep. Lift in autumn and store in frost-free conditions.
Height: 1.5m (5ft) **Spread:** 15cm (6in)
Site: Sun. Fertile well-drained soil
Use: Cutting garden, sunny bed or border
Good companions: *Euphorbia marginata, Tropaeolum* 'Alaska', *Zinnia* 'Envy'

cream and white

11 Galtonia candicans
In late summer or early autumn a spike carrying 12 or more green-tinged white flowers rises from a clump of strap-like grey-green leaves. The flowers are pendent and lightly fragrant. Hardy.
General care: Plant in early spring with the top of the bulb 15cm (6in) deep. Cover ground with a mulch in winter.
Height: 1.2m (4ft) **Spread:** 15cm (6in)
Site: Sun. Fertile, moist but well-drained soil
Use: Sunny border
Good companions: *Campanula lactiflora, Geranium x magnificum, Macleaya cordata* 'Flamingo'

12 Gladiolus callianthus 'Murielae'
Narrow blade-like leaves grow from a corm. In late summer or early autumn a stem carries up to ten sweetly scented flowers, about 5cm (2in) across, on thin elegantly arching tubes. The flowers are white with a purplish red mark in the throat. Half hardy.
General care: Pot up corms in early to mid-spring and keep in a greenhouse. Plant out in late spring. Lift in autumn before the first hard frosts and store in frost-free conditions.
Height: 1m (3ft)
Spread: 8cm (3in)
Site: Sun. Well-drained soil
Use: Sunny border
Good companions: *Caryopteris x clandonensis* 'Heavenly Blue', *Gaura lindheimeri, Perovskia* 'Blue Spire'

lilies

Almost all lilies can be grown in pots – in soil-based (John Innes No. 2) or ericaceous (lime-free) compost – as well as in the garden. Plant bulbs between mid-autumn and early spring about 15cm (6in) deep; stem-rooting lilies (which produce roots above the bulb) need to be planted about 20cm (8in) deep.

1 **Lilium 'Olivia'**
Asiatic hybrid lily
Large, outward-facing white flowers with orange-red anthers. The textured petals have warty protuberances. Scented. Hardy.
Height: 1m (3ft) **Spread:** 15cm (6in)
Good companions: *Choisya ternata, Daphne bholua* 'Jacqueline Postill', *Osmanthus delavayi*

2 **Lilium 'Fire King'**
Asiatic hybrid lily
An erect stem supports a head of outward-facing trumpet-shaped flowers that are orange-red with purple spots. Well suited to containers but unscented. Hardy.
Height: 1m (3ft) **Spread:** 15cm (6in)
Good companions: *Aconitum* 'Spark's Variety', *Crocosmia* 'Lucifer', *Philadelphus coronarius* 'Aureus'

3 **Lilium henryi**
Species lily
Easily grown stem-rooting lily with an arching stem that carries about ten deep orange flowers with dark spots. There are warty protuberances on the petals. Does best on a limy soil and usually needs staking. Hardy.
Height: 2.5m (8ft) **Spread:** 20cm (8in)
Good companions: *Paeonia delavayi* var. *ludlowii, Philadelphus coronarius* 'Aureus', *Thalictum flavum* subsp. *glaucum*

4 **Lilium speciosum var. rubrum**
Species lily
In late summer or early autumn this stem-rooting lily bears five to ten or more white or pale pink flowers with pink or crimson warty spots. Strongly fragrant. Requires lime-free soil or ericaceous compost. Hardy.
Height: 1.2m (4ft) **Spread:** 15cm (6in)
Good companions: *Abelia* x *grandiflora, Deutzia* x *hybrida* 'Mont Rose', *Hydrangea* 'Preziosa'

5 **Lilium 'Journey's End'**
Oriental hybrid lily
Vigorous strong-stemmed hybrid with a branched head of scented crimson flowers. The petals are spotted maroon and pale to white at the margins. Hardy.
Height: 1.2m (4ft) **Spread:** 20cm (8in)
Good companions: *Ceratostigma willmottianum, Geranium psilostemon, Rosa glauca*

6 **Lilium 'Star Gazer'**
Oriental hybrid lily
The fragrant upward-facing flowers, five to eight per stem, are deep pink with white margins and dark crimson spots. Hardy.
Height: 1m (3ft) **Spread:** 15cm (6in)
Good companions: *Nicotiana langsdorfii, Thalictrum delavayi* 'Hewitt's Double', *Veronica gentianoides*

7 **Lilium 'Casa Blanca'**
Oriental hybrid lily
This stem-rooting lily has a head of fragrant, dazzling white bowl-shaped flowers with conspicuous orange-red anthers. The petals have warty projections at the base. Hardy.
Height: 1.2m (4ft) **Spread:** 20cm (8in)
Good companions: *Fothergilla major* Monticola Group, *Fuchsia magellanica* 'Versicolor', *Hydrangea* 'Preziosa'

8 **Lilium African Queen Group**
Trumpet hybrid lily
Erect stems each carry a conical head of nodding, outward-facing trumpet-shaped flowers, which are apricot-yellow on the inside and shaded brown-purple on the outside. Fragrant. Not fully hardy.
Height: 1.5m (5ft) **Spread:** 20cm (8in)
Good companions: *Campanula lactiflora, Rosa* 'Golden Wings', *Thalictrum aquilegiifolium* 'Thundercloud'

climbers

Climbers twine, cling with aerial roots or clasp with tendrils. Trained on architectural supports or on other plants, they assert the vertical dimension of the garden. Plant in the dormant season.

purple, blue and violet

1 Clematis 'Warszawska Nike'

Large-flowered clematis

From late summer to early autumn this deciduous twiner bears deep purple velvet-textured flowers, about 15cm (6in) across. The petal-like sepals radiate from a cluster of yellow anthers. Hardy.

General care: Plant with the base in shade. Prune hard in late winter, cutting all growths back to a pair of buds 15–30cm (6–12in) above ground.

Height: 3m (10ft) **Spread:** 2m (6ft)

Site: Sun, partial shade. Fertile, humus-rich and well-drained soil. Does well on lime

Use: Screen, shrub climber, tripod, wall

Good companions: *Buddleja crispa, Clematis* 'Abundance', *Rosa* 'Parade'

pink and mauve

2 Clematis 'Comtesse de Bouchaud'

Large-flowered clematis

In summer and early autumn this deciduous twiner bears a profusion of mauve-pink flowers, about 10cm (4in) across, with cream anthers. The petal-like sepals are strongly ridged. Hardy.

General care: Plant with the base in shade. Prune hard in late winter, cutting all growths back to a pair of buds 15–30cm (6–12in) above ground.

Height: 3m (10ft) **Spread:** 2m (6ft)

Site: Sun, partial shade. Fertile, humus-rich and well-drained soil. Does well on lime

Use: Screen, shrub climber, tripod, wall

Good companions: *Clematis* 'Etoile Rose', *Clematis* 'Perle d'Azur', *Rosa* 'Madame Alfred Carrière'

3 Rosa 'Pink Perpétué'

Climbing rose

Deciduous climber with dark leathery leaves and clusters of lightly scented, bright pink double flowers. Begins flowering in early summer and repeats until the autumn. Hardy.

General care: Prune between late winter and early spring, cutting back sideshoots to three or four buds.

Height: 5m (15ft) **Spread:** 2.5m (8ft)

Site: Sun. Humus-rich, moist but well-drained soil

Use: Arbour, arch, pergola, pillar, wall

Good companions: *Clematis* 'Royal Velours', *Lonicera periclymenum* 'Serotina', *Rosa* 'Parade'

red and russet

4 Clematis 'Kermesina'

Small-flowered viticella clematis

In late summer and early autumn this slender deciduous twiner bears red single flowers with red-brown anthers. Hardy.

General care: Plant with the base in shade. Prune hard in late winter, cutting all growths back to a pair of buds 15–30cm (6–12in) above ground.

Height: 3m (10ft) **Spread:** 2m (6ft)

Site: Sun, partial shade. Fertile, humus-rich and well-drained soil. Does well on lime

Use: Screen, shrub climber, tripod, wall

Good companions: *Choisya ternata, Clematis* 'Gillian Blades', *Solanum laxum* 'Album'

5 Clematis 'Rouge Cardinal'

Large-flowered clematis

This easy and rewarding deciduous twiner flowers in late summer and early autumn. Beige anthers contrast with the deep crimson of the blunt-tipped petal-like sepals. Hardy.

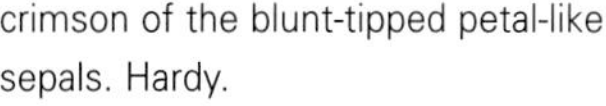

General care: Plant with the base in shade. Prune hard in late winter, cutting all growths back to a pair of buds 15–30cm (6–12in) above ground.

Height: 2.5m (8ft) **Spread:** 1.5m (5ft)

Site: Sun, partial shade. Fertile, humus-rich and well-drained soil. Does well on lime

Use: Screen, shrub climber, tripod, wall

Good companions: *Buddleja crispa, Clematis* 'Abundance', *Rosa* 'Parade'

red and russet (continued)

1 Clematis 'Royal Velours'
Small-flowered viticella clematis

Moderately vigorous deciduous twiner with divided leaves. Bears purple-red velvet-textured flowers in late summer and early autumn. Hardy.
General care: Plant with the base in shade. Prune hard in late winter, cutting all growths back to a pair of buds 15–30cm (6–12in) above ground.
Height: 3m (10ft) **Spread:** 2m (6ft)
Site: Sun, partial shade. Fertile, humus-rich and well-drained soil. Does well on lime
Use: Screen, shrub climber, tripod, wall
Good companions: *Clematis* 'Huldine', *Cornus alba* 'Elegantissima', *Rosa* 'Aimée Vibert'

yellow and orange

2 Campsis x tagliabuana 'Madame Galen'
Trumpet creeper, Trumpet vine

This vigorous deciduous climber clings by aerial roots and has rich green leaves composed of toothed leaflets. In late summer and early autumn orange-red trumpet-shaped flowers are borne on the current season's shoots. Not fully hardy.
General care: Train in growths of young plants until aerial roots take hold. Prune established plants in late winter, cutting back sideshoots to within three or four buds of the main stems.
Height: 10m (33ft) **Spread:** 6m (20ft)
Site: Sun. Humus-rich, moist but well-drained soil
Use: Warm wall
Good companions: *Ceanothus* 'Puget Blue', *Lonicera japonica* 'Halliana', *Wisteria sinensis*

3 Rosa Golden Showers
Climbing rose

Deciduous climber with dark glossy leaves and scented, yellow semi-double flowers in summer and early autumn. The loose-shaped blooms are weather-resistant. Hardy.
General care: Prune between late winter and early spring, cutting back sideshoots to three or four buds.
Height: 3m (10ft) **Spread:** 2m (6ft)
Site: Sun. Humus-rich and moist but well-drained soil
Use: Arbour, arch, pillar, wall
Good companions: *Clematis* 'Bill MacKenzie', *Clematis* 'Perle d'Azur', *Solanum crispum* 'Glasnevin'

cream and white

4 Clematis 'Alba Luxurians'
Small-flowered viticella clematis

In late summer and early autumn this deciduous twiner bears green-tipped, white bell-shaped flowers. Short anthers make a dark eye. Hardy.
General care: Plant with the base in shade. Prune hard in late winter, cutting all growths back to a pair of buds 15–30cm (6–12in) above ground.
Height: 4m (12ft) **Spread:** 2m (6ft)
Site: Sun, partial shade. Fertile, humus-rich and well-drained soil. Does well on lime
Use: Screen, shrub climber, tripod, wall
Good companions: *Ceanothus* x *delileanus* 'Topaze', *Clematis* 'Perle d'Azur', *Solanum crispum* 'Glasnevin'

5 Rosa 'Aimée Vibert'
Rambler rose

Long-stemmed deciduous rose with glossy leaves and, from midsummer to autumn, large clusters of small, white cupped flowers that are tipped deep pink in bud. Slightly fragrant. Hardy.
General care: Prune between late winter and early spring, cutting back sideshoots to three or four buds.
Height: 5m (15ft) **Spread:** 2.5m (8ft)
Site: Sun. Humus-rich, moist but well-drained soil
Use: Arbour, arch, pillar, wall
Good companions: *Clematis* 'Huldine', *Rosa* 'Reine des Violettes', *Rosa* 'Veilchenblau'

6 Solanum laxum 'Album'
Potato vine

Evergreen or semi-evergreen, slender-stemmed climber with twining leaf stalks. From midsummer to autumn it bears sprays of small, white flowers with yellow anthers. Half hardy.
General care: In late winter prune to fit the available space and cut sideshoots to within three or four buds of the main stems.
Height: 6m (20ft) **Spread:** 2.5m (8ft)
Site: Sun. Well-drained soil
Use: Warm wall
Good companions: *Actinidia kolomikta*, *Clematis* 'Perle d'Azur', *Lonicera periclymenum* 'Serotina'

7 Trachelospermum jasminoides
Confederate jasmine, Star jasmine

This evergreen twining climber bears small, scented, white propeller-shaped flowers. The glossy dark green leaves turn bronze-red in winter. Not fully hardy.
General care: Prune in late winter; cut back side-shoots to within three or four buds of main stems.
Height: 6m (20ft) **Spread:** 2.5m (8ft)
Site: Sun. Well-drained soil
Use: Sunny wall
Good companions: *Ceanothus* 'Puget Blue', *Lonicera japonica* 'Aureoreticulata', *Solanum laxum* 'Album'

honeysuckles

These twining, mostly deciduous climbers are excellent for screens, walls and tripods. They need to have their base in shade, in humus-rich and moist but well-drained soil, but tolerate partial shade and sun. Prune from autumn to early spring as required. Honeysuckles that are not fully hardy can be grown in sheltered positions outdoors or under glass.

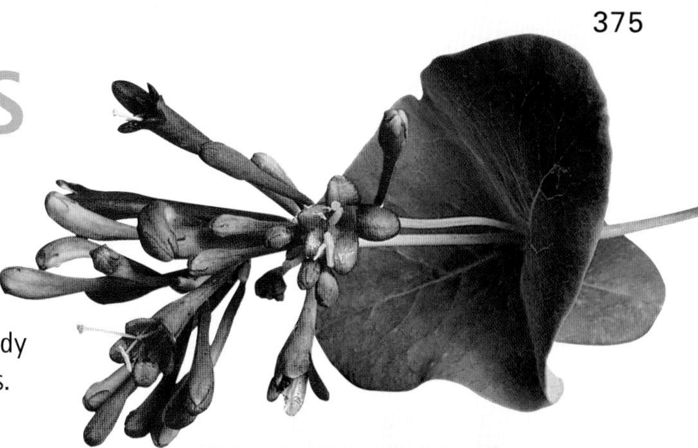

1 Lonicera x brownii 'Dropmore Scarlet'

Deciduous or semi-evergreen honeysuckle with blue-green leaves and, throughout summer, clusters of bright scarlet tubular flowers. This is a colourful climber, but it has no scent. Hardy.
Height: 5m (15ft) **Spread:** 2.5m (8ft)
Good companions: *Campsis* x *tagliabuana* 'Madame Galen', *Chaenomeles* x *superba* 'Knaphill Scarlet', *Clematis* 'Bill MacKenzie'

2 Lonicera sempervirens

Coral honeysuckle, Trumpet honeysuckle

In this deciduous or evergreen species one or two pairs of leaves at the shoot tips are joined to form a cup immediately below each cluster of unscented tubular flowers. These are orange-red on the outside and yellow on the inside and are borne in summer and autumn. Red berries follow. Hardy.
Height: 4m (12ft) **Spread:** 2m (6ft)
Good companions: *Humulus lupulus* 'Aureus', *Rosa* 'Maigold', *Solanum crispum* 'Glasnevin'

3 Lonicera etrusca 'Superba'

Etruscan honeysuckle

Deciduous or semi-evergreen honeysuckle with woody lower stems. From midsummer to mid-autumn it produces clusters of tubular flowers, which are cream at first then turn orange. Red berries follow. Not fully hardy and needs a sheltered sunny position.
Height: 4m (12ft) **Spread:** 2m (6ft)
Good companions: *Ceanothus* 'Puget Blue', *Clematis armandii*, *Myrtus communis* subsp. *tarentina*

4 Lonicera x americana

Deciduous woody climber with dark leaves. The topmost on each stem are joined to form a cup just below a large cluster of sweetly scented flowers. These are yellow flushed with red-purple, produced thoughout summer. Red berries follow. Hardy.
Height: 6m (20ft) **Spread:** 4m (12ft)
Good companions: *Clematis montana* var. *rubens* 'Elizabeth', *Rosa* 'Veilchenblau', *Vitis* 'Brant'

5 Lonicera periclymenum 'Serotina'

Late Dutch honeysuckle

This late-flowering form of the deciduous woodbine, or common honeysuckle, bears clusters of powerfully scented flowers that are creamy white or pale pink on the inside and red-purple on the outside. Red berries follow. Hardy.
Height: 5m (15ft) **Spread:** 2.5m (8ft)
Good companions: *Clematis tibetana* subsp. *vernayi* 'Orange Peel', *Lonicera periclymenum* 'Belgica', *Rosa* 'Gloire de Dijon'

6 Lonicera japonica 'Halliana'

Japanese honeysuckle

Vigorous evergreen or semi-evergreen honeysuckle with bright green leaves. From spring to late summer strongly scented pure white flowers, which age to yellow, are borne in pairs. Hardy.
Height: 10m (33ft) **Spread:** 4m (12ft)
Good companions: *Rosa banksiae* 'Lutea', *Solanum laxum* 'Album', *Vitis coignetiae*

1

2

3

4

5

6

shrubs & trees

Late-flowering trees and shrubs provide end-of-season colour, but equally important is the foliage clothing the framework of branches. Plant in the dormant season, preferably in autumn or early spring.

purple, blue and violet

1 Abies koreana
Korean fir

Slow-growing evergreen conifer of neatly symmetrical cone shape. The needles are dark green above and white on the underside. From an early age it produces erect, violet-blue cylindrical cones. The cultivar 'Silberlocke' has twisted needles, which make the contrast between the dark green and white very conspicuous. Hardy.

Height: 10m (33ft) **Spread:** 6m (20ft)

Site: Sun, partial shade. Moist but well-drained soil, preferably lime-free

Use: Specimen tree

Good companions: *Carpinus betulus, Fagus sylvatica, Taxus baccata,* all as hedges

2 Buddleja davidii 'Black Knight'
Butterfly bush

Wide-spreading deciduous shrub with lance-shaped grey-green leaves on arching stems and, in late summer and autumn, cone-shaped clusters of fragrant dark purple flowers, which are very attractive to butterflies. The colour range in other cultivars includes purple-red, pink, mauve, mauve-blue and white. Hardy.

General care: Cut back annually to a low framework of branches in early spring.

Height and spread: 3m (10ft)

Site: Sun. Well-drained soil

Use: Gravel garden, sunny border

Good companions: *Buddleja* 'Lochinch', *Cistus ladanifer, Philadelphus* 'Belle Etoile'

3 Caryopteris x clandonensis 'Heavenly Blue'

Deciduous shrub with aromatic grey-green leaves and erect stems. In late summer and autumn these bear terminal clusters of small, rich blue flowers. Hardy.

General care: In early spring cut back to a low framework of branches.

Height: 1m (3ft) **Spread:** 1.2m (4ft)

Site: Sun. Well-drained soil

Use: Gravel garden, sunny border

Good companions: *Buddleja* 'Lochinch', *Echinops ritro* 'Veitch's Blue', *Eryngium* x *tripartitum*

4 Ceanothus x delileanus 'Topaze'
California lilac

Dark-leaved, bushy deciduous shrub that bears large sprays of small indigo-blue flowers in summer and autumn. Hardy.

General care: In early spring cut back to a low framework of branches.

Height and spread: 1.5m (5ft)

Site: Sun. Fertile well-drained soil

Use: Sunny border

Good companions: *Lilium henryi, Rosa* Graham Thomas, *Sisyrinchium striatum* 'Aunt May'

5 Ceratostigma willmottianum

Deciduous shrub with a framework of slender stems carrying sharply pointed leaves, some of which take on red tints in autumn. From midsummer to autumn it bears numerous blue saucer-shaped flowers, which open from red-purple tubes and are cut into five distinct lobes. Hardy.

General care: Trim back the previous season's growth in early to mid-spring.

Height: 1m (3ft) **Spread:** 1.5m (5ft)

Site: Sun. Moist but well-drained soil

Use: Sunny border

Good companions: *Anemone hupehensis* 'Hadspen Abundance', *Aster ericoides* 'Pink Cloud', *Spiraea japonica* 'Anthony Waterer'

6 Hibiscus syriacus 'Oiseau Bleu'

Stiffly erect deciduous shrub with dark green, deeply lobed leaves. In late summer and early autumn it bears trumpet-shaped flowers that are 5cm (2in) or more across. In this cultivar, also known as 'Blue Bird', the flowers are blue with maroon veining and cream stamens. Hardy.

Height: 3m (10ft) **Spread:** 2m (6ft)

Site: Sun. Humus-rich, moist but well-drained soil

Use: Sunny border

Good companions: *Aconitum* 'Spark's Variety', *Aster* x *frikartii* 'Mönch', *Geranium* 'Ann Folkard'

7 Lavandula angustifolia 'Hidcote'
Lavender

Aromatic evergreen shrub that forms a neat bush. It has grey linear leaves and produces spikes of dark purple fragrant flowers that are attractive to bees. Hardy.

General care: In spring trim back growth made in the previous year.

Height and spread: 45cm (18in)

Site: Sun. Well-drained soil. Does well on lime

Use: Gravel garden, hedge, rock garden, sunny border

Good companions: *Berberis thunbergii* 'Atropurpurea Nana', *Cistus* 'Silver Pink', *Hypericum olympicum*

8 Lavandula x intermedia Dutch Group
Lavender

Aromatic evergreen shrub that makes a rounded bush of grey-green narrowly linear or spoon-shaped leaves. In summer these are topped by spikes of small, closely packed soft blue flowers that are scented and very attractive to bees. Hardy.

General care: In spring trim back growth made in the previous year.
Height and spread: 75cm (2ft 6in)
Site: Sun. Well-drained soil. Good on lime
Use: Gravel garden, hedge, sunny border
Good companions: *Gypsophila paniculata* 'Bristol Fairy', *Knautia macedonica*, *Verbascum* Cotswold Group 'Gainsborough'

9 Perovskia 'Blue Spire'

Graceful deciduous plant with a woody base and erect, rather soft stems that carry aromatic leaves, which are grey-green on the surface and pale grey on the underside. From late summer to early autumn spires of small flowers create a violet-blue haze. Hardy.
General care: In spring cut stems back to a low woody framework.
Height: 1.2m (4ft) **Spread:** 1m (3ft)
Site: Sun. Well-drained soil
Use: Gravel garden, sunny border
Good companions: *Buddleja davidii* 'Black Knight', *Verbena bonariensis, Yucca gloriosa*

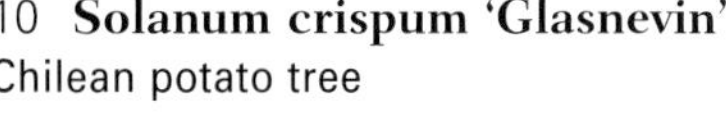

10 Solanum crispum 'Glasnevin'

Chilean potato tree

Bushy semi-evergreen shrub that is best grown with its branches tied in to supports on a sunny wall. Throughout summer it produces numerous clusters of purple-blue star-shaped flowers with a central cone of bright yellow anthers. Inedible yellowish white fruits follow.
General care: Tie in growths regularly and trim in mid to late spring.
Height: 6m (20ft) **Spread:** 5m (15ft)
Site: Sun. Well-drained soil
Use: Sunny wall
Good companions: *Clematis* 'Bill MacKenzie', *Clematis* 'Perle d'Azur', *Rosa* Golden Showers

pink and mauve

11 Buddleja crispa

Deciduous shrub with arching stems and toothed leaves covered in white felt. The small fragrant flowers clustered at the ends of shoots are mauve with an orange throat. Not fully hardy so best trained against a warm wall.
General care: In early spring cut back shoots to within a few buds of a permanent framework.
Height and spread: 3m (10ft)
Site: Sun. Well-drained soil
Use: Sunny wall
Good companions: *Clematis* 'Royal Velours', *Solanum laxum* 'Album', *Trachelospermum jasminoides*

12 Buddleja 'Lochinch'

Butterfly bush

Deciduous shrub with arching stems that are covered in a grey felt when young, as are the leaves. The upper surface of the stems later becomes green and smooth. In late summer and autumn there are numerous cone-shaped heads of small mauve flowers with an orange eye. Strongly fragrant and attractive to butterflies. Hardy.
General care: In early spring cut back to a low framework of branches.
Height: 2.5m (8ft) **Spread:** 3m (10ft)
Site: Sun. Well-drained soil
Use: Sunny border
Good companions: *Buddleja davidii* 'Black Knight', *Ceanothus thyrsiflorus* var. *repens*, *Potentilla fruticosa* 'Tangerine'

pink and mauve (continued)

1 Calluna vulgaris 'Darkness'
Heather, Ling

Heather is a low-growing evergreen shrub that is widely distributed through the Northern Hemisphere, where it turns large areas of acid moorland and heath a vivid purplish pink during late summer and autumn. There are hundreds of cultivars to choose from. This example has short sprays of crimson flowers and bright green foliage. Hardy.

General care: Clip over in early spring.
Height: 25cm (10in) **Spread:** 40cm (16in)
Site: Sun. Humus-rich and well-drained acid soil
Compost: Lime-free (ericaceous) soil-based
Use: Container, ground cover, heather garden
Good companions: *Betula pendula* 'Youngii', *Erica vagans* 'Mrs D.F. Maxwell', *Erica vulgaris* 'Vivelli'

2 Erica vagans 'Mrs D.F. Maxwell'
Cornish heath, Wandering heath

Vigorous evergreen shrub that bears long sprays of rich pink cylindrical to bell-shaped flowers from midsummer to late autumn, when these turn an attractive brown colour. Tolerates slightly alkaline conditions. Hardy.

Height: 75cm (2ft 6in) **Spread:** 1m (3ft)
Site: Sun. Well-drained soil
Use: Ground cover, heather garden
Good companions: *Berberis thunbergii* 'Atropurpurea Nana', *Buddleja davidii* 'Black Knight', *Cistus* 'Silver Pink'

3 Escallonia 'Apple Blossom'

Compact but bushy evergreen shrub with glossy dark leaves. From early summer onwards numerous small pink-and-white flowers are borne. These have five petals formed in a cup shape. Not fully hardy.

General care: Prune immediately after flowering.
Height and spread: 2.5m (8ft)
Site: Sun. Well-drained soil
Use: Hedge, sunny border, windbreak
Good companions: *Cistus ladanifer*, *Laurus nobilis*, *Rosa* 'Fru Dagmar Hastrup'

4 Rosa Gentle Touch
Miniature/Patio rose

Deciduous dwarf shrub with dark green leaves and sprays of pale salmon-pink semi-double flowers over a long period in summer and autumn. Hardy.

General care: Prune in late winter or early spring, cutting back all growth by up to half.
Height: 50cm (20in) **Spread:** 40cm (16in)
Site: Sun. Reasonably fertile and moist but well-drained soil
Compost: Soil-based (John Innes No. 3)
Use: Container, sunny bed or border
Good companions: *Diascia barberae* 'Ruby Field', *Lobelia erinus* 'Crystal Palace', *Viola* x *wittrockiana* 'Baby Lucia'

5 Rosa 'Louise Odier'
Bourbon rose

The Bourbon roses are a group of hybrids developed in the nineteenth century that produce double flowers in several flushes during summer and autumn. In this elegant example, arching stems carry fragrant, mauve-tinted bright pink flowers, which consist of fine-textured, neatly layered petals. Good for cutting. Hardy.

General care: Prune between late winter and early spring, cutting back main stems by up to a third and sideshoots by up to two-thirds.
Height: 2m (6ft) **Spread:** 1.2m (4ft)
Site: Sun. Reasonably fertile and moist but well-drained soil
Use: Sunny bed or border
Good companions: *Dianthus* 'Gran's Favourite', *Geranium* 'Johnson's Blue', *Lilium regale*

6 Rosa Magic Carpet
Shrub/Ground-cover rose

This is an example of a deciduous shrub rose that makes low dense growth and is wider than it is tall. It bears numerous mauve-pink semi-double flowers over a long summer and autumn season. Hardy.

General care: Prune in late winter or early spring, cutting back as required.
Height: 45cm (18in) **Spread:** 2m (6ft)
Site: Sun. Reasonably fertile and moist but well-drained soil
Compost: Soil-based (John Innes No. 3)
Use: Container, ground cover, front of sunny border
Good companions: *Alchemilla mollis*, *Nepeta* 'Six Hills Giant', *Stachys byzantina* 'Silver Carpet'

7 Spiraea japonica 'Anthony Waterer'

Deciduous twiggy shrub with lance-shaped leaves that are sometimes variegated cream and pink. Small crimson-pink flowers are packed in flat-topped heads. Hardy.

General care: Trim plants immediately after flowering.

Height and spread: 1.5m (5ft)

Site: Sun. Moist but well-drained soil

Use: Sunny border

Good companions: *Exochorda* x *macrantha* 'The Bride', *Spiraea* 'Arguta', *Viburnum opulus* 'Roseum'

8

red and russet

8 Rosa Royal William

Hybrid tea rose

A classic hybrid tea rose, this vigorous deciduous shrub is well furnished with dark green leaves. Conical buds open to shapely scented flowers, which are velvety deep red, double and about 12cm (4½in) across. Hardy.

General care: Prune between late winter and early spring, cutting main stems back to a height of about 25cm (10in) and shortening sideshoots to two or three buds.

Height: 1m (3ft)

Spread: 75cm (2ft 6in)

Site: Sun. Reasonably fertile and moist but well-drained soil

Use: Sunny bed or border

Good companions: *Lavandula* x *intermedia* Dutch Group, *Nepeta* 'Six Hills Giant', *Ruta graveolens* 'Jackman's Blue'

yellow and orange

9 Genista aetnensis

Mount Etna broom

Deciduous tree or large shrub with bright green shoots and short-lived linear leaves. Fragrant yellow pea flowers are borne abundantly in mid and late summer. Not fully hardy.

Height and spread: 8m (25ft)

Site: Sun. Light, well-drained soil

Use: Sheltered areas, gravel garden, canopy in mixed planting, specimen tree

Good companions: *Anemone blanda, Crocus speciosus, Helleborus argutifolius*

10 Hypericum 'Hidcote'

St John's wort

Evergreen or semi-evergreen shrub that produces bunches of large, yellow saucer-shaped flowers from midsummer to mid-autumn. Hardy.

General care: Trim lightly after flowering.

Height: 1.2m (4ft) **Spread:** 1.5m (5ft)

Site: Sun, partial shade. Moist but well-drained soil

Use: Sunny or lightly shaded border

Good companions: *Ceanothus* x *delileanus* 'Topaze', *Hydrangea macrophylla* 'Blue Wave', *Mahonia japonica*

11 Koelreuteria paniculata

Golden-rain tree, Pride of India

Spreading deciduous tree with attractive divided foliage that is green in summer but reddish pink when unfurling in spring and yellow in autumn. The small, yellow star-like flowers are carried in large sprays and are sometimes followed by inedible bladder-like fruit that are green at first and then tinged red. Hardy.

General care: Minimal pruning required.

Height and spread: 8m (25ft)

Site: Sun. Well-drained soil

Use: Canopy in mixed planting, specimen tree

Good companions: *Choisya ternata, Philadelphus* 'Belle Etoile', *Weigela* 'Victoria'

12 Rosa Graham Thomas

Shrub rose

This English rose has shiny deciduous foliage and combines in its cupped flowers old-rose qualities with rich yellow, a colour development of the twentieth century. The scented blooms are produced from summer to autumn. Hardy.

General care: Prune in late winter or early spring, cutting back by about a third.

Height and spread: 1.2m (4ft)

Site: Sun. Reasonably fertile and moist but well-drained soil

Use: Sunny bed or border

Good companions: *Campanula persicifolia, Veronica gentianoides, Viola* x *wittrockiana* 'Baby Lucia'

9

10

11

12

cream and white

1 Aralia elata 'Variegata'
Japanese angelica tree

Large, suckering deciduous shrub with spiny stems that is best trained to form a small tree. The large leaves, which mainly grow from the ends of stems, are doubly divided and the leaflets are blotched and margined with creamy white. There are large sprays of small white flowers in early autumn. 'Aureovariegata' has yellow-variegated foliage in spring that fades to creamy white in summer. Hardy.

General care: Remove suckers to control spread and to prevent the plant from reverting to the green-leaved form.

Height and spread: 5m (15ft)

Site: Sun, partial shade. Humus-rich and moist but well-drained soil

Use: Sunny or lightly shaded border, woodland garden

Good companions: *Fuchsia* 'Riccartonii', *Hydrangea paniculata* 'Unique', *Mahonia japonica*

2 Cornus alternifolia 'Argentea'
Green osier,
Pagoda dogwood

This large deciduous shrub can be trained as a small single-stemmed tree. It is grown for the tiered arrangement of the branches and the silvery effect of the white-edged leaves. There are small white flowers in early summer followed by inedible blue-black fruits. Hardy.

General care: Minimal pruning required.

Height: 3m (10ft) **Spread:** 2.5m (8ft)

Site: Sun, partial shade. Humus-rich and moist but well-drained soil

Use: Canopy in mixed border, specimen tree, woodland garden

Good companions: *Acer rubrum* 'October Glory', *Amelanchier lamarckii*, *Hydrangea aspera* Villosa Group

3 Eucryphia x nymansensis 'Nymansay'

Small evergreen columnar tree. In late summer and autumn the dark green, toothed leaves show off white, single cup-shaped flowers that have conspicuous stamens. Not fully hardy.

General care: Minimal pruning required.

Height: 10m (33ft) **Spread:** 3m (10ft)

Site: Partial shade, sun if roots in shade. Humus-rich and moist but well-drained soil, preferably lime-free

Use: Canopy in sheltered border, woodland garden

Good companions: *Cornus kousa* var. *chinensis* 'Satomi', *Enkianthus campanulatus*, *Kalmia latifolia* 'Ostbo Red'

4 Lavatera 'Barnsley'

Fast-growing and relatively short-lived semi-evergreen plant with a woody base and soft erect stems clothed with grey-green leaves. Throughout summer the stems carry numerous funnel-shaped flowers with notched petals. They are white with a red eye and age to pink. Hardy.

General care: In spring cut back to a low framework of branches.

Height and spread: 2m (6ft)

Site: Sun. Well-drained soil

Use: Gravel garden, sunny border

Good companions: *Gaura lindheimeri*, *Lavandula* x *intermedia* Dutch Group, *Origanum laevigatum* 'Herrenhausen'

5 Magnolia grandiflora
Bull bay

Evergreen tree with large dark green leaves that are glossy on the top but downy and often rust-coloured on the underside. Large fragrant flowers, up to 25cm (10in) across, are produced in late summer and autumn. The cultivars 'Exmouth' and 'Goliath' start flowering at an early age. Not fully hardy.

General care: Except where the climate is mild, train as a wall shrub.

Height: 10m (33ft) **Spread:** 6m (20ft)

Site: Sun. Humus-rich, well-drained soil

Use: Warm wall

Good companions: *Solanum laxum* 'Album', *Vitis* 'Brant', *Wisteria sinensis*

6 Myrtus communis subsp. tarentina
Tarentum myrtle

This bushy evergreen shrub is a compact, narrow-leaved cultivar of the common myrtle. In late summer and early autumn it bears masses of pink-tinged white flowers that have

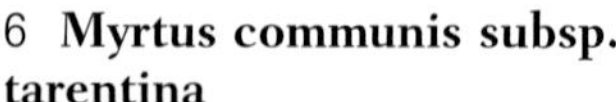

conspicuous tufts of white stamens. The berries that follow are white. Not fully hardy.
General care: Trim lightly in the second half of spring.
Height and spread: 1.5m (5ft)
Site: Sun. Moist but well-drained soil
Compost: Soil-based (John Innes No. 3)
Use: Base of warm wall, container, sunny border
Good companions: *Passiflora caerulea, Rosmarinus officinalis, Solanum crispum* 'Glasnevin'

7 Rosa 'Blanche Double de Coubert'
Rugosa rose
Tough, dense-growing deciduous shrub with prickly stems and bright green leathery leaves. Throughout summer and into autumn it bears scented, pure white semi-double flowers, which are sometimes followed by large orange-red hips. Hardy.
General care: Prune between late winter and early spring, cutting back main stems by up to a third, other growths by as much as two-thirds.
Height: 1.5m (5ft) **Spread:** 1.2m (4ft)
Site: Sun. Well-drained soil
Use: Hedge, sunny border
Good companions: *Rosa* 'Fru Dagmar Hastrup', *Rosa glauca, Stachys byzantina* 'Silver Carpet'

8 Yucca gloriosa
Spanish dagger
Evergreen shrub with a stout, sometimes sparsely branched stem that supports jagged tufts of blade-like stiffly pointed leaves. In late summer and autumn it produces flower spikes with creamy white pendent bells that are often tinged purplish red on the outside. Not fully hardy.
General care: When flowers are spent remove the spike.
Height and spread: 2m (6ft)
Site: Sun. Well-drained soil
Compost: Soil-based (John Innes No. 2)
Use: Container, gravel garden, sunny border
Good companions: *Melianthus major, Stipa gigantea, Trachycarpus fortunei*

silver and grey

9 Pyrus salicifolia 'Pendula'
Weeping pear
This small deciduous tree has weeping branches and narrow silvery leaves that become grey-green as they age. Small, inedible green pears follow the creamy white flowers that are borne in spring. Hardy.
General care: Train and support the main stem until the tree is well established.
Height: 8m (25ft) **Spread:** 6m (20ft)
Site: Sun. Well-drained soil
Use: Specimen tree
Good companions: *Colchicum speciosum* 'Album', *Crocus tommasinianus, Muscari armeniacum*

10 Rosa glauca
Shrub rose
This deciduous shrub of arching growth is grown mainly for the grey-purple tint of its foliage. Single pink flowers are borne in early summer and followed by rounded red-brown hips. Hardy.
General care: Prune lightly in autumn.
Height: 2m (6ft) **Spread:** 1.5m (5ft)
Site: Sun. Humus-rich and moist but well-drained soil
Use: Sunny border
Good companions: *Aquilegia* 'Hensol Harebell', *Campanula lactiflora, Lilium regale*

green

11 Carpinus betulus
Common hornbeam
Deciduous tree with a grey fluted trunk and strongly veined mid-green leaves. In spring it bears fruiting catkins with conspicuous leaf-like bracts. As a specimen tree it is only suitable for large gardens, but is excellent for hedges 1.5m (5ft) or more high. Trimmed hedges retain the tawny dead leaves through winter. Hardy.
General care: Trim hedges in late summer.
Height: 25m (80ft) **Spread:** 18m (60ft)
Site: Sun, partial shade. Well-drained soil
Use: Hedge, specimen tree
Good companions: *Buxus sempervirens, Ilex aquifolium, Taxus baccata* 'Fastigiata'

12 Fargesia nitida
Fountain bamboo
Clump-forming evergreen bamboo with purple-green canes and purplish leaf sheaths. Mature canes arch over with the weight of numerous tapered narrow leaves. Hardy.
Height: 5m (15ft) **Spread:** 2m (6ft)
Site: Sun, partial shade. Moist but well-drained soil
Compost: Soil-based (John Innes No. 3) with added leaf-mould
Use: Container, hedge, screen, specimen clump, waterside, woodland garden
Good companions: *Acer rubrum* 'October Glory', *Cornus controversa* 'Variegata', *Fatsia japonica*

fuchsias

The dangling flowers of fuchsias are borne freely throughout summer and into autumn. Grow them in sunny or lightly shaded borders, in moist but well-drained soil, or in containers filled with soil-based (John Innes No. 3) or soil-less compost. Those described as not fully hardy will usually survive outdoors if planted deeply and given a winter mulch. Overwinter half hardy fuchsias under glass, above 2°C (36°F). In early spring cut back to a framework of stems or, in the case of outdoor plants, to the base. Except in very mild conditions fuchsias are deciduous shrubs.

1 Fuchsia 'Leonora'

Upright shrub producing numerous single pink flowers with green-tipped sepals that are swept back from the skirt of petals. Half hardy.
Height: 75cm (2ft 6in) **Spread:** 50cm (20in)
Good companions: *Fuchsia magellanica* 'Versicolor', *Hebe* 'Autumn Glory', *Hydrangea* 'Preziosa'

2 Fuchsia 'La Campanella'

Ideal for hanging baskets as the pendulous stems of this shrub trail numerous double flowers. The skirt of petals is purple and the tube and spreading sepals are white tinged with pink. Half hardy.
Height: 25cm (10in) **Spread:** 45cm (18in)
Good companions: *Fuchsia* 'Leonora', *Lobelia erinus* 'Cascade', *Pelargonium* 'L'Elégante'

3 Fuchsia 'Red Spider'

Spreading shrub with lax stems from which dangle numerous small single flowers in shades of crimson and red. Half hardy.
Height: 25cm (10in) **Spread:** 45cm (18in)
Good companions: *Fuchsia* 'Margaret', *Heliotropium arborescens* 'Marine', *Viola* x *wittrockiana* 'Baby Lucia'

4 Fuchsia 'Mrs Popple'

This upright vigorous bush freely produces medium-sized single flowers. The tube and sepals are scarlet, the skirt, or corolla, is dark violet. Not fully hardy.
Height and spread: 1m (3ft)
Good companions: *Hosta* 'Snowden', *Hydrangea macrophylla* 'Ayesha', *Spiraea japonica* 'Anthony Waterer'

5 Fuchsia magellanica 'Versicolor'

Shrub of gracefully arching growth with small, pointed variegated leaves that are predominantly grey-green but often tinged with pink. It bears numerous slender, dangling crimson flowers with a purple skirt. Not fully hardy.
Height: 1.5m (5ft)
Spread: 1.2m (4ft)
Good companions: *Hebe* 'Autumn Glory', *Hydrangea macrophylla* 'Madame Emile Mouillère', *Viola cornuta* Alba Group

6 Fuchsia 'Annabel'

Very free-flowering upright bush that produces white double flowers. These are veined and flushed pink while the anthers provide a pink accent. Half hardy.
Height: 60cm (2ft) **Spread:** 45cm (18in)
Good companions: *Geranium wallichianum* 'Buxton's Variety', *Hebe* 'Midsummer Beauty', *Lilium regale*

hydrangeas

Many shrubby hydrangeas flower over a long period in late summer and autumn. The heads are composed of small, fertile central flowers surrounded by larger sterile flowers, or ray-florets, which sometimes fill the whole head, as in hortensias, or mophead hydrangeas. Grow hydrangeas in partial shade or sun in humus-rich, moist but well-drained soil. In pots use soil-based (John Innes No. 3) compost with added leaf-mould, or ericaceous compost. The soil's alkalinity affects the colours of *Hydrangea macrophylla* cultivars.

3

1 **Hydrangea macrophylla 'Altona'**
Hortensia, Mophead hydrangea
Rounded deciduous shrub with large flowerheads composed of overlapping sterile flowers. These are rich pink on neutral to alkaline soils but blue on acid soils, and age to purple. Best in partial shade. Suitable for containers. Hardy.
Height: 1m (3ft) **Spread:** 1.5m (5ft)
Good companions: *Fuchsia* 'Riccartonii', *Hydrangea macrophylla* 'Ayesha', *Lilium* 'Journey's End'

2 **Hydrangea arborescens 'Annabelle'**
Somewhat open deciduous shrub with bright green leaves and 20cm (8in) heads packed with creamy white sterile flowers. These are tinted green at first and age to pale brown. Hardy.
Height and spread: 2.5m (8ft)
Good companions: *Cornus alternifolia* 'Argentea', *Hydrangea* 'Blue Wave', *Magnolia stellata*

3 **Hydrangea serrata 'Bluebird'**
Compact deciduous shrub with somewhat pointed leaves that turn red in autumn. The flowerheads are composed of rich blue fertile flowers surrounded by pale mauve-blue sterile ones. Remains attractive over a long season. Not fully hardy.
Height and spread: 1.2m (4ft)
Good companions: *Acer palmatum* 'Bloodgood', *Amelanchier lamarckii*, *Osmanthus delavayi*

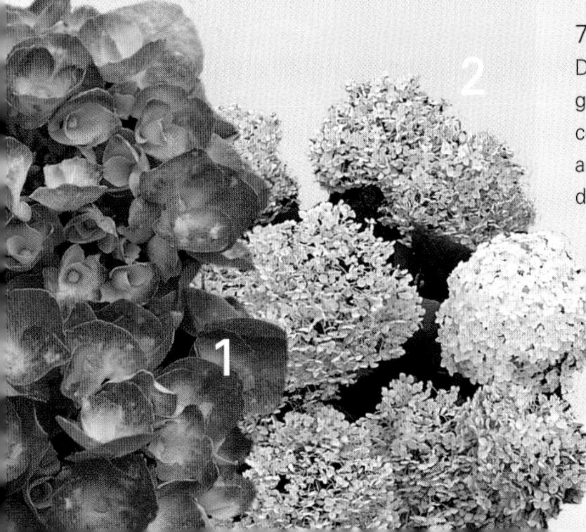
1
2

4 **Hydrangea macrophylla 'Blue Wave'**
Lacecap hydrangea
This rounded deciduous shrub has flattened lacecap flowerheads that consist of closely packed fertile flowers surrounded by a ring of paler-coloured sterile flowers – rich blue on acid soils, mauve to pink on alkaline ones. Hardy.
Height: 2m (6ft) **Spread:** 2.5m (8ft)
Good companions: *Cercidiphyllum japonicum*, *Hamamelis* x *intermedia* 'Pallida', *Hydrangea macrophylla* 'Madame Emile Mouillère'

5 **Hydrangea macrophylla 'Ayesha'**
Hortensia, Mophead hydrangea
Rounded deciduous shrub with glossy, coarsely toothed egg-shaped leaves. The rather open flowerheads are composed of cupped florets that are grey-mauve or pink on alkaline soils but blue on acid ones. Suitable for containers. Hardy.
Height: 2m (6ft) **Spread:** 2.5m (8ft)
Good companions: *Deutzia* x *hybrida* 'Mont Rose', *Hydrangea paniculata* 'Unique', *Spiraea japonica* 'Anthony Waterer'

6 **Hydrangea paniculata 'Unique'**
Upright deciduous shrub with pointed egg-shaped leaves. The large conical flowerheads are packed with small fertile flowers and larger, more conspicuous sterile flowers that at first are creamy white but age to purplish pink. Suitable for growing in containers. Hardy.
Height and spread: 5m (15ft)
Good companions: *Acer griseum*, *Cornus alba* 'Variegata', *Hydrangea* 'Preziosa'

7 **Hydrangea aspera Villosa Group**
Deciduous shrub or small tree with velvety dark green leaves and flowerheads, 15cm (6in) across, composed of small, purplish blue central flowers and larger flowers that are pale mauve with a darker eye. Best in partial shade. Hardy.
Height: 2.5m (8ft) **Spread:** 3m (10ft)
Good companions: *Cornus alternifolia* 'Argentea', *Fargesia murieliae*, *Hydrangea serrata* 'Bluebird'

4

5
6

7

waterside & water plants

All the perennials described here either require reliably moist soil or like to float on the surface of a pool with their roots anchored in the mud below. Plant in the dormant season, in spring or autumn.

purple, blue and violet

1 Pontederia cordata
Pickerel weed

This perennial is for the water's edge. It has glossy, rather arrow-like leaves that are heart-shaped at the base. In late summer and early autumn spikes of bright blue tubular flowers rise above the foliage. Hardy.

Height: 1m (3ft) **Spread:** 75cm (2ft 6in)
Site: Sun. Still water about 10–15cm (4–6in) deep
Compost: Soil-based aquatic compost
Use: Margin of pool
Good companions: *Iris laevigata* 'Variegata', *Myosotis scorpioides* 'Mermaid', *Nymphaea* 'Gonnère'

pink and mauve

2 Filipendula rubra 'Venusta'
Queen of the prairies

Large stately perennial with vine-like leaves. In midsummer red stems carry large heads, up to 30cm (12in) across, crowded with small pink flowers. Spreads to form large clumps. Hardy.

Height: 2.5m (8ft) **Spread:** 1.2m (4ft)
Site: Sun, partial shade. Fertile, reliably moist or wet soil
Use: Bog garden, moist border, waterside
Good companions: *Eupatorium purpureum, Gunnera manicata, Osmunda regalis*

3 Lythrum salicaria 'Feuerkerze'
Purple loosestrife

The stiff stems of this erect perennial are set with narrow pointed leaves. From late summer to early autumn clumps are topped by spikes of small, vivid deep pink starry flowers. Hardy.

Height: 1m (3ft) **Spread:** 45cm (18in)
Site: Sun, partial shade. Reliably moist soil
Use: Bog garden, moist border, waterside
Good companions: *Eupatorium purpureum, Filipendula rubra* 'Venusta', *Rodgersia aesculifolia*

4 Nymphaea 'Frobelii'
Water lily

The rounded floating leaves are bronze at first, then purplish green. Flowers are red-pink with orange-yellow stamens and produced throughout summer. They open from cup shapes into stars. Suitable for a medium-sized pool. Hardy.

Spread: 1.2m (4ft)
Site: Sun. Still water 45–75cm (18–30in) deep
Compost: Soil-based aquatic
Use: Pond or pool
Good companions: *Nymphaea* 'James Brydon', *Pontederia cordata, Zantedeschia aethiopica*

5 Rodgersia pinnata 'Superba'

This clump-forming perennial makes an impressive foliage plant. The large leaves are burnished, heavily veined and usually divided into five or more leaflets. A plume of tiny pink flowers appears in midsummer and is followed by a bold seed head. Hardy.

Height: 1.2m (4ft) **Spread:** 75cm (2ft 6in)
Site: Sun, partial shade. Humus-rich and reliably moist soil
Use: Bog garden, moist border, waterside, woodland garden
Good companions: *Hosta sieboldiana* var. *elegans, Matteuccia struthiopteris, Rheum palmatum* 'Atrosanguineum'

red and russet

6 Lobelia 'Queen Victoria'

Short-lived perennial, but a striking plant for moist soils. The stems and lance-shaped leaves are

6

7

9

10

11

12

beetroot-red and from late summer to mid-autumn they flaunt bright scarlet flowers. Hardy.
General care: Cut down after flowering and cover base with a mulch.
Height: 1m (3ft) **Spread:** 30cm (12in)
Site: Sun, partial shade. Fertile and reliably moist soil
Use: Moist border, waterside
Good companions: *Iris sibirica* 'Ego', *Primula pulverulenta, Rodgersia pinnata* 'Superba'

yellow and orange

7 Ligularia 'Gregynog Gold'
This large perennial forms an impressive mound of heart-shaped leaves and reaches its full stature in late summer with conical spikes of orange-yellow daisy-like flowers. Hardy.
Height: 2m (6ft) **Spread:** 1m (3ft)
Site: Sun. Fertile and reliably moist soil
Use: Moist border, waterside
Good companions: *Ligularia dentata* 'Desdemona', *Miscanthus sacchariflorus, Osmunda regalis*

8 Ligularia 'The Rocket'
This perennial makes a mound of dark green, boldly cut leaves, from which soar nearly black stems brightened by small yellow flowers. Hardy.
Height: 2m (6ft) **Spread:** 1m (3ft)
Site: Sun. Fertile and reliably moist soil
Use: Moist border, waterside
Good companions: *Ligularia* 'Gregynog Gold', *Rodgersia aesculifolia, Trollius europaeus*

cream and white

9 Nymphaea 'Gonnère'
Water lily
The floating leaves of this water lily, bronze at first and then pea green, show off the white fully double flowers with yellow stamens that are produced throughout summer. Fragrant. Suitable for a medium-sized pool. Hardy.
Spread: 1.2m (4ft)
Site: Sun. Still water 60–75cm (24–30in) deep
Compost: Soil-based aquatic
Use: Pool or pond
Good companions: *Acorus calamus* 'Argenteostriatus', *Caltha palustris* 'Flore Pleno', *Iris ensata*

10 Rodgersia aesculifolia
The giant fingered leaves of this clump-forming perennial are deeply veined and crinkled and have a bronzed metallic lustre. The small star-shaped flowers are cream, sometimes tinted pink, and make tall plumes above the foliage. Hardy.
Height: 2m (6ft) **Spread:** 1m (3ft)
Site: Sun, partial shade. Humus-rich, reliably moist soil
Use: Bog garden, moist border, waterside, woodland garden
Good companions: *Hosta* 'Honeybells', *Matteuccia struthiopteris, Rodgersia podophylla*

green

11 Carex pendula
Drooping sedge, Pendulous sedge, Weeping sedge
The grass-like clump of this evergreen perennial consists of shiny green, rather broad leaves with blue-green undersides. Arching stems bear brown flower spikes, which are erect from late spring to early summer but then hang vertically. Hardy.
Height: 1m (3ft) **Spread:** 1.2m (4ft)
Site: Sun, partial shade. Fertile, reliably moist or wet soil
Use: Bog garden, waterside
Good companions: *Iris pseudacorus* 'Variegata', *Matteuccia struthiopteris, Sagittaria sagittifolia*

12 Sagittaria sagittifolia
Common arrowhead
Perennial for pool margins that has distinctive arrow-shaped leaves with extended pointed lobes at the base. Spikes with tiers of small white flowers appear in summer. Hardy.
Height: 1m (3ft) **Spread:** Indefinite
Site: Sun. Still water about 25cm (10in) deep
Compost: Soil-based aquatic compost
Use: Wildlife pond
Good companions: *Carex pendula, Eupatorium purpureum, Iris pseudacorus* 'Variegata'

herbs, vegetables & fruit

In late summer many useful plants make the garden look attractive as they reach maturity, but in most cases, for produce to be of high quality, crops need to be harvested promptly.

herbs

1 Angelica
Angelica archangelica

This tall biennial makes a large leafy clump in its first year and bears flowerheads the following summer. The young scented leaves are used in salads and for flavouring cooked rhubarb. Candied stems are used for cake decoration. Hardy.
General care: Sow fresh seeds *in situ* or allow plants to self-seed and thin to 1m (3ft) apart.
Height: 1.2–1.5m (4–5ft) **Spread:** 1m (3ft)
Site: Shade. Humus-rich and moist soil
Compost: Soil-based (John Innes No. 3) or soil-less
Use: Back of border, large container

2 Basil
Ocimum basilicum

Bushy annual with aromatic green or purple leaves used as an accompaniment to tomatoes, in many Italian dishes and as an ingredient of pesto. Some ornamental varieties are cinnamon, aniseed or lemon flavoured. Often best in pots on a patio or windowsill. Tender.
General care: Shelter from wind and avoid over-watering. Remove flower buds and pick leaves frequently.
Height: 30–45cm (12–18in)
Spread: 23–30cm (9–12in)
Site: Sun. Fertile, well-drained soil
Compost: Soil-based (John Innes No. 3) or soil-less with added grit
Use: Border edging, greenhouse, container

3 Coriander
Coriandrum sativum

This Mediterranean annual has two distinctly different crops: the finely cut pungent leaves and the round, orange-scented seeds, which are an essential ingredient of many Oriental dishes. Grows best in hot dry conditions. Tender.
General care: Do not transplant or over-water. Pick leaves frequently and support seed-bearing plants. Harvest seeds in autumn.
Height: 60cm (2ft) **Spread:** 45cm (18in)
Site: Sun. Light, well-drained soil.
Compost: Soil-less with added grit and extra bottom drainage
Use: Border, container

4 Marjoram
Origanum species

The three main kinds of culinary marjoram, all perennial plants that thrive in containers, are sweet marjoram (*O. majorana*), the warmer pot marjoram (*O. onites*) and pungent oregano (*O. vulgare*). The leaves aid digestion and are an ingredient of bouquet garni. Generally hardy, although sweet marjoram is slightly tender.
General care: Avoid over-watering. Trim after flowering and cut back to 5cm (2in) high in late autumn. Divide or take cuttings every two years.
Height: 15–45cm (6–18in)
Spread: Up to 45cm (18in)
Site: Sun. Dry, well-drained soil
Compost: Soil-based (John Innes No. 3) or soil-less with added grit
Use: Border, edging, container

5 Parsley
Petroselinum crispum

Dark green biennial commonly grown in two forms: the tightly curled version used for garnishing, and the more strongly flavoured French or flat-leaved variety used for both garnishing and cooking. For a year-round supply sow in spring and again in midsummer for growing under cover. Hardy.
General care: Harvest regularly and remove flower stems, leaving one or two plants to self-seed if required.
Height: 40–60cm (16–24in)
Spread: 30–45cm (12–18in)
Site: Light shade in summer, but sun for winter crops. Deep, fertile soil with added compost or rotted manure
Compost: Soil-based (John Innes No. 3) with added bark, or soil-less
Use: Border, container, edging

6 Savory, summer
Satureja hortensis

Annual often referred to as the bean herb as it aids digestion when cooked with beans. Its strong peppery flavour can be added sparingly to rich meat dishes, vegetables and pulses. Tender.
General care: Sow indoors and plant out in a sheltered position when there is no longer a risk of frost. Pick regularly to prevent flowering, and protect in autumn to extend use. Do not feed.
Height: 30cm (12in)
Spread: 20–23cm (8–9in)
Site: Sun. Poor, well-drained soil
Compost: Soil-based (John Innes No. 3) or soil-less with plenty of added grit
Use: Border, container

vegetables

7 Aubergine
Solanum melongena

This has large felty leaves and purple to black or white, generally pear-shaped, fruits. Can be grown under glass or outdoors in a sheltered position. Striking as a container plant for a sunny patio. Tender.
Site: Sun. Rich, well-drained soil
Compost: Soil-based (John Innes No. 3)
How to grow: Sow and grow on as for tomatoes (see 3, Tomato, page 114). Plant out 45cm (18in) apart when there is no longer a risk of frost. Pinch out growing tips when plants are 30cm (12in) high. Allow five or six fruits to set, then pinch out the branch tips. Stake large plants and feed once or twice with high-potash fertiliser when fruits are swelling. Harvest while young.

8 Broccoli, Calabrese
Brassica oleracea Italica Group

This quick-growing plant produces a large central head of tight buds, usually blue-green but sometimes purple or golden yellow. There are many varieties, all highly nutritious and well flavoured: 'Trixie' is particularly fast growing and tolerates club root disease. Not fully hardy.

Site: Sun. Rich firm soil

How to grow: Sow small batches from six to eight weeks before the last frosts until early summer. Make the earliest sowings in small pots under glass and plant out 23–30cm (9–12in) apart each way when there is no longer a risk of frost; make later sowings *in situ* and thin seedlings to the above planting distances. Water regularly and mulch to encourage fast, even growth. Cut the central head before the flower buds open and apply a high-nitrogen feed. Cut the later sideshoots when about 10cm (4in) long.

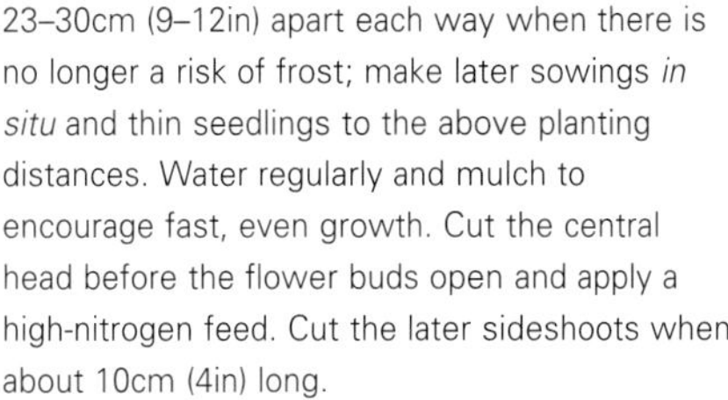

5

6

7

8

9 French bean, climbing

Phaseolus vulgaris

This tender annual is related to the dwarf french bean but is more productive and so useful where space is limited. Early sowings in a greenhouse can be harvested until outdoor beans are available, and, if cut back and fed, will crop again after open-air plants are finished. Varieties with gold, purple or speckled pods, such as 'Borlotto', 'Viola Cornetti' and 'Rob Roy', make decorative features on tall cane wigwams in flower borders.

Site: Sun. Fertile and well-drained soil

How to grow: Sow indoors in small pots in mid-spring or outdoors from late spring until midsummer. Sow greenhouse crops in early spring. Space plants 15cm (6in) apart in rows 20cm (8in) apart or in a 1m (3ft) circle. Provide each plant with a sturdy 2.5m (8ft) cane crossed and tied in rows or as a wigwam. Keep moist, especially once flowering starts. Start picking while beans are young (eight to ten weeks after sowing) and repeat every two to three days.

10 Pepper

Capsicum annuum

Both large-fruited sweet peppers and slimmer hot peppers, or chillies, grow on sun and heat-loving bushy plants. Where summers are cool, peppers are best grown under glass or on a warm patio sheltered from cool winds. Tender.

Site: Sun. Rich well-drained soil

Compost: Soil-based (John Innes No. 3)

How to grow: Sow in late winter as for tomatoes (see 3, Tomato, page 390) or buy young plants in late spring. Pot up seedlings into 8cm (3in) pots, moving them into larger ones as they grow. Harden off outdoor plants and plant out 45cm (18in) apart when there is no longer a risk of frost. Pinch out growing tips when 38cm (15in) high. Water regularly during flowering and fruiting, and feed every 10–14 days. Harvest sweet peppers green or fully coloured; let chillies ripen and then dry on strings for two weeks before storing.

11 Potato, second early

Solanum tuberosum

Ready two to three weeks after 'first earlies', varieties like 'Catriona', 'Marfona' and the salad type 'Belle de Fontenay' give slightly heavier yields of 'new' potatoes or can be left until larger and dug up for storing. Not fully hardy.

Site: Sun. Deeply dug fertile and well-drained soil

How to grow: Sprout tubers in late winter, as for first earlies, and plant in mid-spring 10–15cm (4–6in) deep and 38cm (15in) apart each way. Water and mound soil halfway up the stems every two to three weeks. Start lifting tubers with a fork when flowers are fully open.

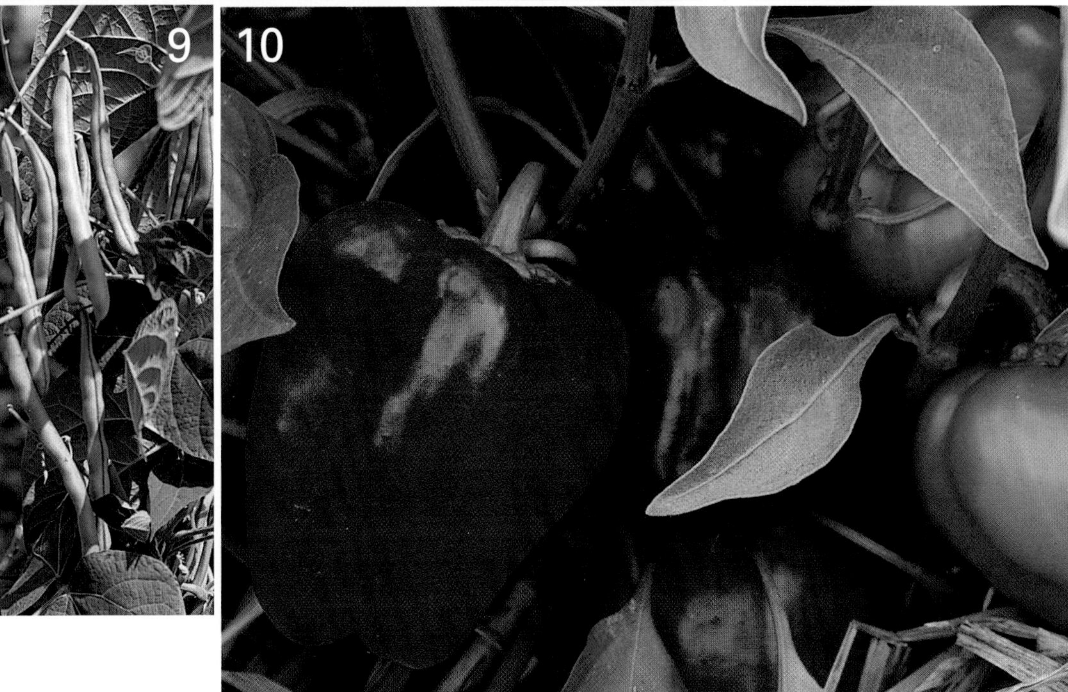

9

10

11

vegetables
(continued)

1 Runner bean
Phaseolus coccineus

A popular tender perennial, usually grown as a half-hardy annual, with lush foliage and decorative scarlet, white, pink or bicoloured flowers. Most varieties are climbers, but a few, such as 'Gulliver' and 'Pickwick', are naturally dwarf, and all can be grown as 45cm (18in) high plants by pinching out growing tips regularly. Train on sunflowers to make a feature. Tender.

Site: Sun, light shade, sheltered from strong winds. Deep, moist and fertile soil

How to grow: Sow as for climbing beans (see 9, French bean, page 389), and plant out after the last frosts, 15cm (6in) apart in rows or circles. Water freely in dry weather, especially during flowering, and mulch. Start harvesting before the seeds are visible through the pods, and pick every few days until the autumn frosts.

2 Sweetcorn
Zea mays

This is a superb crop for home-growing because the flavour and sweetness of the cobs start to deteriorate minutes after picking. The tall plants are decorative and sturdy enough to support climbing beans (see 9, French bean, page 389) planted at their base. In cool gardens, choose early-ripening varieties. Tender.

Site: Sun. Rich, firm well-drained soil

How to grow: Sow seeds individually in small pots in a warm place indoors, about six weeks before the last frosts occur. Harden off outdoors and plant out 35cm (14in) apart each way in blocks. Water well when flowers appear and again when cobs are swelling. Harvest cobs when their tassels turn brown and the kernel contents are milky. Use immediately.

3 Tomato
Lycopersicon esculentum

For the best flavour, tomatoes should be grown outdoors, sheltered from cool winds, but where summers are cool they are an ideal crop for greenhouse borders, containers or growing bags. The most productive kinds are tall varieties, grown on canes or strings as single stems; naturally bushy varieties crop earlier and make decorative pot or hanging basket plants. There is a huge choice available, including red, yellow, green or striped fruits in a range of sizes from small 'cherries' to enormous 'beefsteak' kinds for slicing. Tender.

Site: Sun. Fertile, well-drained soil with plenty of humus

How to grow: Sow indoor crops between midwinter and early spring according to the amount of heat you can provide; sow outdoor varieties 8 weeks before the last frosts. Germinate seed at 15°C (59°F) and prick out seedlings into small pots. Plant out when the first flower truss is visible, after hardening off outdoor plants. Train tall varieties on supports, removing sideshoots; leave bush types unpruned. Water regularly and feed every 10–14 days after flowering starts. Harvest fruits when fully coloured.

fruit

4 Apple
Malus domestica

Apples can be grown in even the smallest garden if the right rootstock is chosen and plants are trained as cordons or espaliers against a fence or wall; if grafted on a very dwarfing rootstock, they will even thrive in large containers. Depending on the variety, apples ripen from late summer until late autumn; later varieties often store until the following year. Early frosts can damage the blossom. Hardy.

Site: Sun. Deep, humus-rich and well-drained soil

How to grow: Plant trees while dormant (spacing will depend on the chosen rootstock). Feed and mulch every spring. Prune trained trees in mid or late summer.

5 Blackcurrant
Ribes nigrum

Blackcurrants are easy to grow and one of the richest sources of vitamin C. They need plenty of space and lavish annual feeding or manuring. 'Ben Sarek' forms a compact bush, but 'Laxton's Giant' has the largest currants. Hardy.

Site: Sun, light shade. Deeply dug, rich soil
How to grow: Plant while dormant, 1.5m (5ft) apart and 10cm (4in) deeper than the previous soil level on the plant; cut down to 8cm (3in) high. Feed and mulch in spring, and water in dry weather. Prune after fruiting, cutting out a third of the old, darker stems. Harvest complete bunches of fruit when fully coloured.

6 Fig
Ficus carica

A handsome Mediterranean tree, this makes an attractive fan when trained on a warm garden or conservatory wall. Figs fruit best when the roots are confined in a large container or a pit lined with buried slabs. Not fully hardy.

Site: Sun. Well-dug soil with a restricted root run
Compost: Soil-based (John Innes No. 3)
How to grow: Plant in spring. Mulch heavily each spring with rotted manure or garden compost. Prune damaged and surplus branches in late spring, and shorten sideshoots in summer. Pick fruits when fully coloured and starting to split. Protect in a hard winter with layers of fleece or by wrapping branches in straw.

7 Loganberry
Rubus x poganbaccus

The long canes of this vigorous raspberry-blackberry hybrid make an excellent screen when trained on a fence of wires. Alternatively, grow it on a wall or training wires. Choose a thornless variety such as 'LY 654' for comfortable harvesting of the richly flavoured berries. Hardy.
Site: Sun. Fertile, well-drained soil
How to grow: Plant while dormant, 3–4m (10–12ft) apart. Mulch with rotted manure or compost each spring, and water in dry weather. Tie in new canes as they develop, and prune out all the old canes after harvesting. Pick fruits when fully ripe and almost purple in colour.

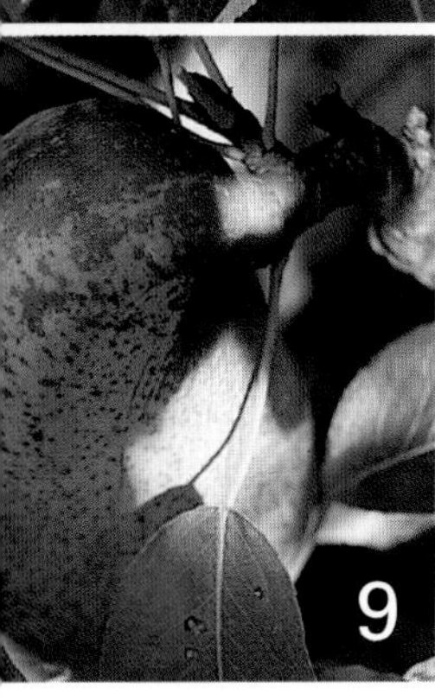

8 Peach
Prunus persica

These attractive trees have a froth of soft pink blossom in late spring followed by richly flavoured fruits. Best grown on a warm sheltered wall where the blossom can be protected from frost. Dwarf plants grow 1.5m (5ft) high and are excellent for large containers. Hardy.
Site: Sun. Fertile, well-drained soil
How to grow: Plant in autumn, spacing full-size trees 4m (12ft) apart. Mulch in spring with well-rotted manure and water in dry weather. Protect against frost and peach leaf curl in late winter and early spring with a sheet of polythene. Prune out surplus growth in spring, leaving a new shoot at the base of each flowering shoot. Pollinate flowers on indoor plants using a soft brush, and thin fruit clusters until fruitlets are about 10cm (4in) apart. Harvest when soft around the stalk.

9 Pear
Pyrus communis

Pears need warm summers for perfection and crop best if fan-trained on warm walls and sheltered from spring frost. Most need a compatible partner for cross-fertilisation. Hardy.
Site: Sun. Fertile, very well-drained soil
How to grow: Plant, grow and prune pears as for apples (see 4, Apple, page 390). Start picking from late summer, while fruits are still hard: test every week and harvest any that come away easily. Store in a cool place until fruits ripen.

10 Plum
Prunus domestica

Plums, gages and damsons are all vigorous trees, even when grafted on a semi-dwarfing rootstock, and are best trained on a wall as fans or left to make large specimen trees, sheltered from cold spring winds. A few varieties like 'Victoria' are self-fertile but most need a pollen partner. Dessert, cooking and dual-purpose varieties are available. Hardy.
Site: Sun. Rich, deep moist soil
How to grow: Plant in late autumn, spacing bushes 2.5m (8ft) apart and other kinds 4.5m (15ft) apart. Mulch generously each spring with rotted manure. Thin fruits in early summer and support heavily laden branches. Only prune trees in leaf, removing misplaced shoots and some that have carried fruit. Harvest ripe fruits, checking every two to three days, and use immediately.

11 Strawberry, alpine
Fragaria vesca

This compact perennial bears flushes of small, intensely fragrant red, yellow or white berries from midsummer until the autumn frosts. The berries are usually overlooked by birds, so rarely need netting. Excellent for edging and containers and as ground cover under fruit trees. Hardy.
Site: Sun, light shade. Well-dug, fertile soil
How to grow: Buy young plants or sow seeds in warmth or outdoors from early spring onwards. Plant out in late spring, about 30cm (12in) apart. Feed each spring and mulch with compost or grass clippings. Water fruiting plants regularly. Harvest fruit when fully coloured and soft. Divide and replant every three to four years.

choosing the best plants

The following plant lists draw on all the plants described in the preceding pages of the Plant Selector, but they are grouped together here to help you choose plants for particular conditions, situations and uses.

plants for clay soil

Although the following plants generally succeed on close-textured clay soils, they do better when the ground has been improved by the addition of grit and organic matter such as well-rotted garden compost.

- *Abies koreana*
- *Acanthus mollis* Latifolius Group
- *Anemone hupehensis* 'Hadspen Abundance'
- *Anemone* x *hybrida* 'Whirlwind'
- *Aralia elata* (all cultivars)
- *Asplenium scolopendrium*
- *Berberis thunbergii* 'Atropurpurea Nana'
- *Campsis* x *tagliabuana* 'Madame Galen'
- *Carex comans* 'Frosted Curls'
- *Carpinus betulus*
- *Cornus alternifolia* 'Argentea'
- *Deschampsia cespitosa* 'Goldschleier'
- *Escallonia* 'Apple Blossom'
- *Fargesia nitida*
- *Hemerocallis* (all)
- *Hibiscus syriacus* 'Oiseau Bleu'
- *Hosta* (all)
- *Hypericum* (all)
- *Kniphofia* (all)
- *Lonicera* (most)
- *Magnolia grandiflora*
- *Rodgersia pinnata* 'Superba'
- *Rosa* (all)

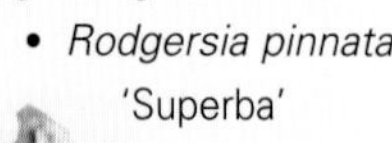

Kniphofia 'Percy's Pride'

plants for dry chalky soil

A large number of plants are automatically excluded from this list because they will not tolerate alkaline (limy) soil. The improvement of shallow chalky soil by the addition of moisture-retaining organic matter allows lime-tolerant but moisture-loving plants, notably clematis, to be grown successfully.

- *Acanthus mollis* Latifolius Group
- *Artemisia stelleriana* 'Boughton Silver'
- *Buddleja* (all)
- *Berberis thunbergii* 'Atropurpurea Nana'
- *Caryopteris* x *clandonensis*
- *Ceanothus* x *delileanus* 'Topaze'
- *Convolvulus sabatius*
- *Coreopsis verticillata* 'Grandiflora'
- *Dianthus chinensis* Baby Doll Series
- *Echinops ritro* 'Veitch's Blue'
- *Eryngium* (all)
- *Gypsophila* (all)
- *Hypericum* (all)
- *Lavandula* (all)
- *Lavatera trimestris* 'Mont Blanc'
- *Origanum* (all)
- *Osteospermum* 'Jucundum'
- *Salvia viridis* 'Oxford Blue'
- *Scabiosa caucasica* 'Moerheim Blue'
- *Sedum* (all)
- *Sempervivum tectorum*
- *Silene schafta*
- *Verbena bonariensis*
- *Yucca gloriosa*

Echinops ritro 'Veitch's Blue'

plants for sandy or gravelly soil

The following plants require free drainage and are generally drought tolerant. The range of plants that can be grown in dry sunny gardens can be enlarged if the soil is improved by the addition of well-rotted organic matter.

- *Agapanthus* (all)
- *Artemisia stelleriana* 'Boughton Silver'
- *Berberis thunbergii* 'Atropurpurea Nana'
- *Brachyscome iberidifolia* Splendour Series
- *Buddleja* (all)
- *Calendula officinalis* 'Fiesta Gitana'
- *Calluna vulgaris* 'Darkness'
- *Caryopteris* x *clandonensis* 'Heavenly Blue'
- *Centaurea hypoleuca* 'John Coutts'
- *Convolvulus sabatius*
- *Coreopsis verticillata* 'Grandiflora'
- *Echinops ritro* 'Veitch's Blue'
- *Erica vagans* 'Mrs D.F. Maxwell'
- *Eryngium* (all)
- *Gaura lindheimeri*
- *Genista aetnensis*
- *Gypsophila* (all)
- *Knautia macedonica*
- *Lavandula* (all)
- *Lavatera* 'Barnsley'
- *Lavatera trimestris* 'Mont Blanc'
- *Oenothera macrocarpa*
- *Origanum* (all)
- *Perovskia* 'Blue Spire'
- *Ruta graveolens* 'Jackman's Blue'
- *Salvia viridis* 'Oxford Blue'
- *Sedum* (all)
- *Sempervivum tectorum*
- *Stipa gigantea*
- *Tagetes* (all)
- *Verbena bonariensis*
- *Yucca gloriosa*

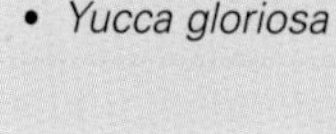

Lavatera 'Barnsley'

plants for moist shade

The following plants tolerate or, more commonly, thrive in moist shade, although many will also grow in full sun provided the soil is reliably moist.

- *Alstroemeria* ligtu hybrids
- *Astilbe* (all)
- *Carex pendula*
- *Fargesia nitida*
- *Filipendula rubra* 'Venusta'
- *Fuchsia* (all)
- *Gentiana asclepiadea*
- *Gentiana septemfida*
- *Hosta* (all)
- *Hydrangea* (all)
- *Kirengeshoma palmata*
- *Impatiens walleriana* Tempo Series
- *Lobelia* 'Queen Victoria'
- *Lonicera* (most)
- *Lythrum salicaria* 'Feuerkerze'
- *Rodgersia* (all)
- *Thalictrum delavayi* 'Hewitt's Double'
- *Viola* x *wittrockiana* Crystal Bowl Series

Astilbe 'Professor Van de Wielen'

plants for coastal sites

Where windbreaks and hedges give protection from salt-laden winds, a wide range of plants can be grown in coastal gardens, including many that benefit from the sea's moderating influence on temperatures.

- *Achillea* 'Coronation Gold'
- *Agapanthus* (all)
- *Alstroemeria* ligtu hybrids
- *Antirrhinum* Tahiti Series
- *Argyranthemum* (all)
- *Artemisia stelleriana* 'Boughton Silver'
- *Aster* x *frikartii* 'Mönch'
- *Aster novi-belgii* 'Heinz Richard'
- *Buddleja* (all)
- *Calendula officinalis* 'Fiesta Gitana'
- *Calluna vulgaris* 'Darkness'
- *Caryopteris* x *clandonensis* 'Heavenly Blue'
- *Convolvulus sabatius*
- *Crocosmia* (all)
- *Dianthus chinensis* Baby Doll Series
- *Echinops ritro* 'Veitch's Blue'
- *Erica vagans* 'Mrs D.F. Maxwell'
- *Eryngium* (all)
- *Escallonia* 'Apple Blossom'
- *Fuchsia* (all)
- *Geranium* (all)
- *Gypsophila paniculata* 'Bristol Fairy'
- *Heuchera micrantha* var. *diversifolia* 'Palace Purple'
- *Hydrangea macrophylla* (all)
- *Hypericum* (all)
- *Kniphofia* (all)
- *Lavandula* (all)
- *Lavatera* 'Barnsley'
- *Lavatera trimestris* 'Mont Blanc'
- *Oenothera macrocarpa*
- *Origanum laevigatum* 'Herrenhausen'
- *Osteospermum* 'Jucundum'
- *Penstemon* (all)
- *Rosa* 'Blanche Double de Coubert'
- *Rosa* Magic Carpet
- *Scabiosa* (all)
- *Scaevola aemula* 'Blue Wonder'
- *Sedum* (all)
- *Sempervivum tectorum*
- x *Solidaster luteus* 'Lemore'
- *Spiraea japonica* 'Anthony Waterer'
- *Yucca gloriosa*

plants for acid soils

Plants in the following list that are marked with an asterisk* will only grow satisfactorily on soils that are free of lime. Other plants in the list thrive on acid soils, although they may also grow satisfactorily on soils that are neutral or to some degree alkaline.

- *Abies koreana*
- *Calluna vulgaris* 'Darkness'*
- *Erica vagans* 'Mrs D.F. Maxwell'
- *Eucryphia* x *nymansensis* 'Nymansay'
- *Kirengeshoma palmata**

plants for ground cover

Close planting of shrubs and perennials will help to create an attractive weed-excluding cover. However, effective cover can only be achieved by planting into soil from which perennial weeds have been eliminated. The following plants are particularly useful because of their dense foliage.

- *Calluna vulgaris* 'Darkness'
- *Geranium* x *riversleaianum* 'Russell Prichard'
- *Heuchera micrantha* var. *diversifolia* 'Palace Purple'
- *Hosta* (all)
- *Erica vagans* 'Mrs D.F. Maxwell'
- *Rosa* Magic Carpet

Rosa Magic Carpet

autumn

practical diary

Mellow autumn weather brings with it the opportunity for garden work put on hold during the hot, dry summer months. Your soil should be moist, though not waterlogged, and still warm, creating ideal conditions for root growth. Don't be in a hurry to clear away the dying stems of herbs and perennials as some are attractive in their own right and, collectively, create delightful outlines when frosted during winter. There is little more satisfying than the glow of working outdoors in the brisk chill of autumn, raking up the leaves and generally setting the garden straight before the onset of winter.

perennials

As the growing season comes to a close there is plenty of weeding and tidying to be done, but leave a few seed heads standing for their winter beauty. This is also a good time to lift and divide large clumps, as new plants will establish well in early autumn.

now is the season to . . .

- **move tender perennials** under cover before the first frosts.
- **cut back to ground level** perennials that have died down, although there are benefits in delaying this job until spring (see below). Remove supports and destroy all diseased growth.
- **mulch plants** on the borderline of hardiness (see opposite).
- **divide clumps of established perennials,** giving priority to those that flower in spring.
- **treat perennial weeds** with systemic weedkiller.
- **inspect container-grown plants** for vine weevils (see below).
- **look for self-sown seedlings** as you weed. Pot these up or transplant to a nursery bed for planting out next year.
- **order new perennials** from mail-order suppliers, who will despatch them in a dormant state.
- **plant out new perennials** in September if possible (see page 398), including polyanthus divided in early summer.
- **pot up rooted cuttings** and layers started in late summer.
- **move under cover** any young plants growing in pots outside.
- **prick out seedlings** sown in late summer into modular trays or small pots once they are large enough to handle, usually when the first pair of true leaves has formed.
- **water plants** in containers occasionally and also new plants in the border if dry spells occur.
- **collect seed** when ripe for sowing now or storing (see page 308).

and if you have time . . .

- **mulch borders** if weather permits (see opposite).
- **move container plants** to a sheltered spot before winter.
- **plant** some winter-flowering perennials.
- **buy and pot up** plug plants and keep under glass until spring (see page 398).

Cut down to the ground the stems of dead and dying perennials that are spoiling the border, but leave those with decorative seed heads.

cutting back perennials

Once the growth of perennials, ferns and ornamental grasses has died back to the ground it can be cut back if you want your garden to look really tidy. However, there are benefits in delaying the traditional autumn tidy-up until late winter or early spring. From an aesthetic point of view, the dead leaves and seed heads of many plants look beautiful when rimed with frost or bejewelled with pearls of moisture on a misty morning. The dead growth also gives the plant extra protection from the cold, and provides shelter for hibernating insects like ladybirds and lacewings, which are natural predators of garden pests such as aphids.

Perennials that must be cut back now, however, are lush-leaved plants like hostas, as their leaves quickly turn to mush, and any plants with diseased foliage. This must be removed and destroyed, not left *in situ* where the disease spores could overwinter, and not put on the compost heap.

Tender perennials rarely tolerate frost and need to be moved under cover in autumn. Lift and pot up any plants

vine weevils

Vine weevil grubs can cause considerable damage to container-grown perennials, as they continue to eat through the roots during autumn and winter. Inspect compost for the creamy white, brown-headed grubs. If any are found treat with the chemical imidocloprid or repot in compost that contains this chemical – or consider using biological control. Primulas and polyanthus are favourite plants, and it is worth growing a few for an early warning of this voracious pest.

Seen here with the golden heads of grasses, *Verbena bonariensis* flowers through to autumn, but will need to be protected with a thick dry mulch over winter.

growing in the border and move them into a well-lit, frost-free place such as a greenhouse, porch or conservatory. Plants in an unheated structure will often survive if the compost is kept on the dry side. However, if you have already rooted some cuttings to overwinter indoors, you could leave the parent plant outside to take its chances.

weeding and mulching

Carry out these jobs at any time from autumn to spring, when the ground is workable. A good guide is that if soil sticks to your boots, it is too wet to work without risk of damaging its structure. The advantage of mulching now is that a blanket of material over the soil helps to keep in warmth, but before you mulch clear the weeds.

- **pull up annual weeds** and dig up the roots of perennial ones.
- **treat perennial weeds** with the systemic weedkiller glyphosate if it is not possible to dig out all the roots. Apply early in autumn so the plant draws the chemical down to its roots as it becomes dormant for the winter.
- **lay a mulch** 5–8cm (2–3in) deep of composted bark, cocoa shells, garden compost or well-rotted manure. The drawback with the latter two materials is that they may contain weed seeds. Cocoa shells have the added advantage that they may also help to repel slugs and snails.
- **plants of borderline hardiness**, such as the african blue lily (*Agapanthus*), penstemons and *Verbena bonariensis*, benefit from a thick, dry covering now in cold and exposed areas. Suitable materials include leaves, bracken or straw, and they should be laid about 8cm (3in) thick. Put a few woody prunings over it or peg some chicken wire over the top to prevent the mulch from being blown away.

MULCHING TIP When applying mulch, first cover the plant with an upturned container or bucket to keep its leaves clean.

perennials/2

planting and propagating

Autumn is the ideal time to plant new hardy perennials as well as to propagate existing ones by division and collect seeds for sowing next spring.

planting

The soil holds plenty of warmth from the summer and is usually moist from autumn rain, creating the perfect environment for plants to develop their roots. This means that new plants can establish a good root system in time for an explosion of growth in spring.

Prepare the ground thoroughly in advance of planting by deep digging and working in lots of organic matter such as garden compost or well-rotted manure. Be sure to remove all weeds, particularly every bit of perennial root. Add planting fertiliser to each planting hole to boost root development and make sure you set the plants at the same depth as they were growing previously.

Red hot pokers are some of the best highlight plants for the autumn border. They form large clumps that can be divided once the plants have died down and are dormant.

propagation

Mail-order suppliers offer a limited range of perennials as 'plug' or starter plants and this is an economical way of quickly building up stocks. When the plugs arrive plant them in 8cm (3in) pots and grow them on in a greenhouse or on a cool, well-lit windowsill.

In addition to buying plug plants, seedlings and cuttings also need attention and it is time to divide established plants.

- **pot up cuttings** taken in late summer into 8cm (3in) pots once they have rooted. Stand them on a warm, well-lit windowsill or in a heated greenhouse.
- **detach rooted layers** of border carnations pegged down in late summer and pot them up or move to a nursery bed for planting out next spring.
- **collect seed** of late flowering perennials and grasses as soon as it is ripe and sow in pots or trays of moist seed compost (see page 308). Stand the containers in a coldframe or in a sheltered spot covered with a cloche to keep off heavy rain.
- **prick out seedlings** of perennials sown in late summer into modular trays or small pots.
- **thin young plants** growing outside in nursery rows to leave them 10cm (4in) apart.

dividing perennials

When your perennials are several years old and have formed established clumps they can be lifted while they are dormant in autumn or winter and divided into several pieces (see opposite). Be sure to replant the divisions at the same depth as they were growing previously. As long as each piece has a reasonable amount of roots and some buds, they will quickly form a new small clump.

perennials to plant now

These excellent gap fillers for the border include those that bloom from late autumn to early spring and some evergreens: • bugle (*Ajuga reptans* varieties) • elephant's ears (*Bergenia*) • *Carex oshimensis* 'Evergold' • euphorbias • stinking hellebore (*Helleborus foetidus*) • Christmas rose (*Helleborus niger*) • Lenten rose (*Helleborus orientalis*) • gladwyn iris (*Iris foetidissima*) • *Liriope muscari* • 'black' lilyturf (*Ophiopogon planiscapus* 'Nigrescens') • *Saxifraga fortunei* • kaffir lily (*Schizostylis coccinea*)

Liriope muscari

• **wash off the soil** if you have trouble seeing the positions of the roots and shoot buds.
• **discard the centre** if the clump has become unproductive and woody, and replant only the young outer portions.
• **hellebores and peonies** dislike being divided and take several years to settle down and start flowering again, so these are best left undisturbed.
• **spring** and summer-flowering perennials are best divided in autumn so they have plenty of time to settle down before flowering.
• **late summer** and autumn-flowering perennials may be divided now or in early spring. In cold areas, delay dividing fleshy-rooted perennials like hostas until spring.

looking ahead . . .

☑ EARLY SPRING Remove dry mulches from plants of borderline hardiness.
☑ LATE SPRING Plant out young perennials raised from seed, cuttings, layers and plug plants.

there is still time to . . .

• **take cuttings** of tender perennials (see page 307), though a heated propagator is usually necessary now for rooting to take place.

dividing sedums

1 Fleshy-rooted plants, like many hostas and *Sedum spectabile*, are best cut into sections using a sharp spade. First, cut back the top growth.

2 Lift the clump using a garden fork. Shake off the excess soil.

3 Use a sharp spade or an old bread knife to cut the root into sections, and replant the divisions.

dividing geraniums

1 Use a garden fork to lift the clump and shake off excess soil.

2 The easiest way of splitting fibrous-rooted plants like geraniums, as well as michaelmas daisies and japanese anemones, is to insert two garden forks back-to-back and lever them apart. Do this several times.

3 Replant the small divisions into soil that has been refreshed with some well-rotted compost or manure and a handful of planting fertiliser. Plant them at the same depth as they were growing previously.

annuals & biennials

Autumn is a gamble. In a mild year continued deadheading can extend the flowering almost into winter, whereas a sudden frost may finish the display prematurely. Many summer bedding plants can be kept over winter, while there is still work to be done to ensure a good show next spring.

Rudbeckia hirta 'Rustic Dwarf' is usually grown as an annual, although it is in fact a short-lived perennial. Its colourful rayed flowers have distinctive cone-shaped centres.

now is the season to . . .

- **continue deadheading plants** regularly to prolong flowering for as long as the weather remains favourable.
- **thin late summer sowings** of annuals so that plants stand 8–10cm (3–4in) apart. If you lift thinnings carefully with a fork they can be transplanted elsewhere or potted up for greenhouse display.
- **remove faded and frosted plants** to the compost heap, weed and rake up fallen leaves so the ground is clear for replanting.
- **lift pelargoniums, argyranthemums** and other tender bedding perennials before the first frosts, and pot up or take cuttings ready for overwintering indoors (see below).
- **buy wallflowers** and plant immediately (see opposite).
- **plant out spring bedding** in display beds and other prepared areas (see opposite).
- **protect seedlings** of hardy annuals with cloches or fleece in the event of severe frost.
- **sow sweet peas** indoors for best results next spring (see page 445).

and if you have time . . .

- **pot up some of the best** summer bedding plants to keep over winter for spring cuttings (see below).
- **cut remaining flowers** if hard frost threatens, and use for indoor decoration.

keeping bedding plants over winter

Some summer bedding plants are perennial and can be kept from one year to the next.

- **Before they are killed** by the frosts, carefully lift some of the best and pot them up in 9–10cm (3½–4in) pots of soil-based compost.
- **Trim the top growth** to about 5–8cm (2–3in) high, and keep just moist in a frost-free greenhouse over winter.
- **Increase heat and watering** in March to induce new growth suitable for soft-tip cuttings. The main plants will often make large specimens for planting out again next summer.

bedding plants to keep over winter

- ageratum • argyranthemum
- *Begonia semperflorens*
- bidens • busy lizzie
- diascia • helichrysum
- pelargonium • petunias (Surfinia and Milliflora types)

buying and planting wallflowers

Wallflowers are popular spring bedding that many gardeners prefer to buy as bare-rooted plants in autumn, rather than devote space to raising them from seed. Choose compact, branching plants with plenty of rich green foliage. Avoid buying thin, drawn specimens, which seldom bush out after planting, or plants with yellow leaves that indicate starvation or stress from being out of the ground too long.

Before planting, apply a little lime to the planting site unless your soil is naturally alkaline, as wallflowers are cabbage relatives and are similarly prone to club-root disease. Plant wallflowers immediately or heel in (bury) the roots in a spare piece of ground until you are ready (see right).

planting spring bedding

Traditional spring bedding displays combine edging plants around a central 'carpet' of wallflowers or forget-me-nots and bulbs such as tulips. Start planting once summer flowers have been cleared and try to finish before November.

perennials as annual bedding

Although often treated as biennials, spring bedding plants such as polyanthus, primroses and double daisies (*Bellis*) are in fact perennials that can be multiplied and re-used year after year. Whether you started by raising your own from seed in May or June, or you bought the plants, in early summer you can dig up plants that have flowered and split them into smaller portions. Planted out in a nursery bed, ideally in moist shade, the segments will develop into full-size plants by autumn. You can now transplant them as part of the usual bedding routine.

Wallflowers are treated differently: tear off sideshoots from the best plants in late spring and use these as cuttings. Dip the bases in rooting hormone and root them under glass.

planting wallflowers

1 **Keep the bare-rooted** plants in a bucket of water before planting them.

2 **Plant several together** to make more of an impact than single spaced plants.

there is still time to . . .

- **sow hardy annuals** under glass to produce early flowers for next year.
- **gather and dry seeds** of favourite plants and unusual varieties to store for sowing next spring (see page 308).
- **take cuttings** from tender perennials, for rooting indoors.

looking ahead . . .

☑ EARLY SPRING Thin autumn-sown annuals to their final spacing.
☑ Prepare sites for hardy annuals, and start sowing *in situ*.
☑ Induce new growth in bedding plants to provide cuttings.
☑ LATE SPRING Sow seed of spring-flowering biennials.

planting spring bedding

1 **Clear all weeds** and prick over the surface with a fork to aerate the soil. Rake the soil level and clear of debris, then leave it for a few days to settle.

2 **Plant the edging first,** spacing plants 15cm (6in) apart. Then plant the other bedding. Space plants closely, 20–23cm (8–9in) apart, because little growth is made before flowering.

3 **Complete the display** by planting bulbs equidistant between the bedding plants.

bulbs & tubers

This is the time to plant spring-flowering bulbs in beds or borders, naturalise them in lawns or line them out in generous rows for cutting. As summer varieties die down, bring them indoors to dry, at about the same time as forced spring bulbs show their first fat buds.

now is the season to . . .

- **continue planting spring-flowering bulbs.** Leave tulips and hyacinths until last (see below); finish planting by November.
- **plant large-flowered anemones** for flowers from January onwards (see below).
- **protect autumn-flowering bulbs,** such as amaryllis and nerines, from frost and heavy rain, particularly those growing in pots, by covering them with cloches, fleece or dry mulch.
- **lift begonias, dahlias and gladioli** before or after frosts (see opposite).
- **prepare new beds for gladioli** (see opposite).
- **check that bulbs potted for forcing** for flowers in late winter or early spring are still sound and moist. Bring indoors any that are forward, with buds above soil level, but keep cool.
- **lift, divide and replant** overcrowded clumps of alliums, summer snowflakes (*Leucojum*) and crocosmias. Collect seeds and bulbils for potting under glass.

and if you have time . . .

- **propagate hyacinths** by scoring or scooping (see opposite).
- **propagate lilies** by scaling for forcing indoors (see opposite).

planting anemones

Plant two or three batches of large-flowered *Anemone coronaria* St Bridgid and De Caen Group between September and early November for a succession of colourful flowers to cut in spring.

- **soak the tubers** in water overnight, and then plant ('claws' uppermost) in rich soil, 5–8cm (2–3in) deep and 10cm (4in) apart in rows or blocks.
- **for early blooms**, cover outdoor rows with cloches or plant some tubers in a coldframe or cool greenhouse.

planting tulips and hyacinths

Once you have planted daffodils and other bulbs that prefer an early start, you can turn your attention to hyacinths and tulips. For outdoor use, smaller 'bedding' hyacinths are preferable to the large bulbs sold for forcing. They can be left permanently in borders, although flower size may decline. For best results in spring bedding use fresh bulbs each year and space them about 20cm (8in) apart each way (see page 401). Use old bulbs for propagation (see opposite).

The ideal time to plant tulips is late October or early November to prevent premature leaf growth and the risk of disease. Give them an open sunny position and plant them deep; 20cm (8in) is sufficient for most soils, but 30cm (12in) is better on light ground. Deep-planted bulbs can be left for three years or more, instead of being lifted annually, which is advisable if shallow planted. Space bulbs 10–20cm (4–8in) apart according to size, or plant more closely in layers in containers (see page 425).

Illuminated by autumn sunshine are the spectacular flowers of *Dahlia* 'Bridge View Aloha', with *Verbena bonariensis* weaving through them. The striped foliage of *Canna* 'Phasion' makes a good backdrop.

scoring hyacinths

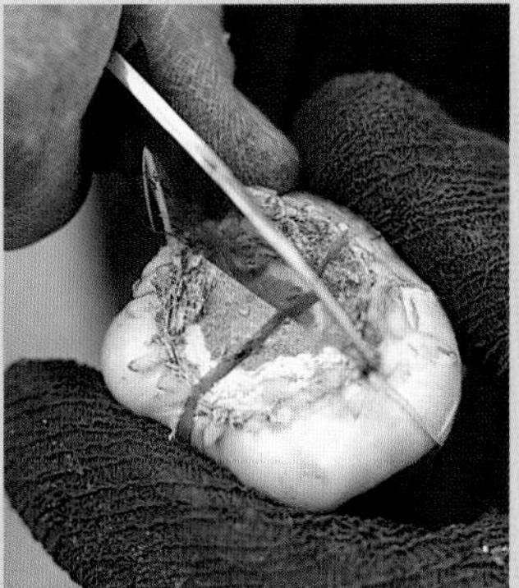

1 Clean off any soil, roots and loose scales. Then make two or three deep cuts across the base, almost a third of the way into the bulb. Pot up the bulb sections with their tips at surface level.

2 Grow in a greenhouse or coldframe over winter until the bulblets have formed.

propagating lily scales

1 Pull the small scales off lily bulbs after cleaning off the soil.

2 Plant them in a seed tray with their base just pushed down into the compost.

propagating from bulbs

Although hyacinths will naturally produce tiny bulblets, they are often extremely slow to multiply. You can speed up propagation by scoring the baseplate on any sound hyacinth (see above). In spring small leaves will appear around the main bulb. Allow growth to die down in summer and remove the bulb from the pot. Up to a dozen bulblets will have formed, and these can be removed for growing on to flowering size.

Scooping is even more productive than scoring. Use a sharp knife to gouge or scoop out a cone of tissue from the baseplate, cutting about a quarter of the way into the bulb. Discard the cone of tissue, then dust the cut surface of the bulb with fungicide, pot up and grow on as for scoring.

lifting summer bulbs

Many summer-flowering bulbs need to be brought indoors just before the frosts or as soon as the first frost has blackened the foliage. This can be early October in some years, or well into November in a mild season.

- **dry bulbs** for two to three weeks, then carefully rub off all soil, roots and papery scales before packing them in dry compost in trays, boxes or bags. Store them in a dry, cool, but frost-free place.

lifting bulbs

BEFORE FROST • begonias

AFTER FIRST FROST • acidantheras • crocosmias • dahlias • gladioli • ixias • sparaxis

Clean begonias, gladioli and dahlias after lifting, and box them up in compost for the winter under glass.

preparing gladioli beds

If you want to grow large-flowered gladioli for cutting, now is the time to prepare a new bed for next season's display. Select a well-drained position in full sun, and thoroughly dig over the site to at least one spade blade deep. If heavy ground lies wet, choose another spot, or create a raised bed with extra topsoil from elsewhere in the garden. Work in plenty of well-rotted manure or garden compost, and leave the ground to settle over winter.

looking ahead . . .

- ☑ WINTER Bring in forced bulbs as buds develop.
- ☑ Check bulbs in store.
- ☑ EARLY SPRING Feed indoor bulbs after flowering.
- ☑ Start planting gladioli.

there is still time to . . .

- **pot up arum lilies** for early flowering under glass (see page 350).
- **plant daffodils**, muscari, early crocuses, erythroniums, ornithogalums and dwarf irises outdoors (see page 312).

roses

In a mild year, roses carry on flowering well into autumn, so continue with deadheading and disease control. The main task this season, though, is to plant new roses so that they have time to establish before winter.

now is the season to . . .

- **plant or heel in new bare-rooted roses** as soon as they arrive (see page 406).
- **water new roses** in a dry season, especially those planted against walls.
- **continue watering roses** in outdoor containers, but reduce the frequency as temperatures fall.
- **tie in new growth** on climbers and ramblers, check their supports for stability, and shorten longer stems to reduce wind damage.
- **prepare sites** ready for planting new roses (see page 406).
- **continue spraying leaves** against black-spot disease.
- **tidy beds for winter** when roses have lost their leaves. Gather and remove or burn fallen leaves, clear away all weeds and lightly fork or hoe in surface mulches.
- **protect newly planted roses** in cold gardens (see right).
- **cut opening buds** for the house if frost threatens, deadhead faded flowers and remove developing hips to conserve the plant's energy, unless keeping for decorative reasons or for future propagation.
- **pot up new roses** for forcing under glass (see opposite).
- **layer climbers**, ramblers and shrub roses (see opposite).
- **gather ripe hips** if you wish to raise new roses from seed (see page 497).

and if you have time . . .

- **continue deadheading** in a mild autumn, but remove only the flower, not a long-stemmed section as in summer.

preparing roses for winter

Tall ramblers and climbers are liable to injury from strong winds unless you take the following simple precautions.

- **finish pruning ramblers** by early October (see page 315) and make sure all new stems are tied in firmly.
- **for climbing roses,** cut back very long stems by up to half their length in November and tie in temporarily. Leave the main pruning until late February (see pages 496–7).
- **check all supports** and repair if necessary (see page 411). Replace any ties that have broken or frayed.
- **make sure labels are securely tied** and legible before winter. This will avoid future frustration, as pruning methods vary according to variety.
- **protect newly planted roses** against frost. Most roses are fully hardy and will survive the winter, but in very cold gardens, where prolonged hard frost is usual, it is worth mounding

Tie in the stems of climbing roses until late winter when they will be pruned.

Heap a layer of straw or dry leaves around a new rose and hold this covering in place until early spring. Remove it before any new growth appears.

In autumn, the single pink flowers of *Rosa glauca* start to be replaced by hips, while the unusual blue-green foliage continues to bring colour and interest to beds and borders.

potting up roses

For perfect blooms under glass from early spring onwards, pot up a hybrid tea or compact floribunda rose in October. Put plenty of drainage material in the bottom of a large pot, 40–45cm (16–18in) deep, and plant very firmly in soil-based compost. Prune stems back to 15cm (6in) and water well. Stand the pots on a hard surface in a sheltered position outside until December, when you should move them into a greenhouse.

straw, bracken or dry leaves over a young plant. Hold this covering in place with fleece or sacking, and leave undisturbed until February or early March, before new growth appears.

layering roses

The usual autumn method of propagating shrub, floribunda, rambler and climbing roses is by hardwood cuttings, but you can also layer any rose with flexible stems (see below). If you do this now, the layers will have rooted by next autumn.

First choose a strong, flexible branch that can be bent easily to meet the ground. Lightly fork over the soil at this position and work in a few handfuls of potting compost. Peg the branch down at least 30cm (12in) back from its tip.

layering roses

1 **Cut into** and along the underside of the chosen branch to produce a 10cm (4in) 'tongue' of stem.

2 **Wedge the cut open** with a thin twig and then place the cut section into loosened soil.

3 **Hold the cut section** of stem down with bent wire, a stone or a forked stick, and cover with a mound of soil.

4 **Tie the tip** of the stem to an upright cane, then water the area. The following autumn, when the layer has rooted, sever it from the parent plant and move to its new home.

roses/2

planting roses

Prepare the soil at least a month before planting by digging thoroughly, adding plenty of organic matter and allowing it to settle (see page 315). It is not too late to do this now, although you might have to tread the soil firm before preparing to plant.

preparing for planting

Just before you expect your bare-rooted roses to arrive, fork over the surface to break up any lumps and remove any weeds. Spread a dressing of rose fertiliser over the whole area, and fork or hoe this in. Finally, rake the site level and mark the position of the roses with short canes.

adapting light soils

Sandy and silty ground can dry out quickly in summer and this will affect the flowering and good health of roses unless you take steps to make the soil more moisture-retentive.

- **dig in ample supplies** of well-rotted manure, garden compost or leaf-mould to increase humus levels and also stimulate beneficial bacteria that aid root growth.
- **mulch established plants** lavishly with an 8cm (3in) layer of well-rotted manure every spring and feed plants in spring and midsummer, because light soils also lose nutrients quickly.

roses for light soils

Most rugosa, gallica, alba and hybrid musk roses tolerate light soils, including:

- 'Alba Maxima' • 'Blanc Double de Couvert'
- 'Fimbriata' • 'Madame Legras de St Germain'
- 'Maiden's Blush' • 'Mrs Anthony Waterer' • 'Nevada'
- 'Queen of Denmark'
- 'Sarah van Fleet'

Rosa x *odorata* 'Pallida'

planting bare-rooted roses

The basic planting method is the same for all roses (see below). On arrival, unpack the plants, check their condition and, if the roots are dry, stand plants in a bucket of water for an hour or two. If you cannot plant them immediately, heel them in to keep their roots moist until you are ready (see page 433). If the weather is very wet or cold, plants can stay heeled in until February without injury.

planting a bare-rooted rose

1 **Before planting**, tidy and trim plants to size. Prune each stem back to three to five buds long (climbers and ramblers to about 1.2m/4ft) and remove any dead wood and weak growth. Trim 5–8cm (2–3in) off the end of each main root.

2 **After placing** the rose in the prepared site, check that the rose is at its original depth, with the bud joint (the bulge immediately above the roots) just below surface level. The hole should be large enough to take the roots comfortably when they are evenly spread out over a small mound of soil.

3 **Carefully replace** the excavated soil over the roots, a little at a time, shaking the plant from time to time to ensure soil fills all air pockets between the roots.

4 **When the hole** is completely filled, firm all round the plant using hands or feet, and level the surface.

Support standard roses with a 5 x 5cm (2 x 2in) treated wooden stake, driven in before refilling the hole to avoid root damage. The top of the stake should reach the lowest rose branch. Use rose ties to hold the stem firmly to its support.

The splendid hips of *Rosa* 'Fru Dagmar Hastrup' can be gathered now and used to raise new roses in winter.

success with roses

Roses will thrive for many years if you prepare the ground well, plant carefully and then foster their positive health.

- **roses prefer slightly acid soils.** Chalky soils and overliming can result in deficiencies of vital nutrients, indicated by yellowing leaves and weak growth. If you garden on chalk choose old shrub roses (damask and hybrid musk), as they are fairly lime-tolerant.
- **cultivate soil thoroughly** and deeply (see page 593). Roses like heavy soils, but these sometimes drain badly. Correct poor drainage before planting as waterlogging is lethal. Improve light soils (see opposite) to improve moisture retention and prevent summer drought.
- **buy strong plants** with plenty of roots and healthy stems.
- **choose disease-resistant varieties** if you prefer not to spray.
- **plant with care:** too deep or shallow planting, inadequate firming, dry or damaged roots, overcrowding and planting under trees all lead to problems.
- **prune for open growth,** so air can circulate, but avoid heavy pruning on shrub and floribunda roses. Clear away all prunings.
- **feed with** a high-potash rose fertiliser. Avoid high-nitrogen feeds, which encourage soft growth that is vulnerable to pests and diseases.

looking ahead . . .

- ☑ WINTER In late winter prune climbing roses.
- ☑ Move pots of roses for forcing into the greenhouse.
- ☑ EARLY SPRING Remove winter protection from young plants.
- ☑ Prune bush roses.
- ☑ Finish planting bare-rooted roses.

there is still time to . . .

- **take hardwood cuttings** up to the end of October, and root in a spare bed outdoors (see page 315).
- **prune rambler roses** and weeping standards, which are ramblers grafted on tall stems (see page 315).
- **dig over** new rose beds.

spacing roses

MINIATURES	30cm (12in)
PATIO	45cm (18in)
HYBRID TEAS	45cm (18in)
FLORIBUNDAS	60–75cm (24–30in)
SHRUB ROSES	1.2–1.5m (4–5ft)
CLIMBERS AND RAMBLERS	2.4m (8ft)
STANDARDS	1.8m (6ft)

Rose varieties vary in vigour so you may need to adjust these guidelines; check catalogue descriptions before planting.

climbers

Virginia creeper (*Parthenocissus quinquefolia*) in its full autumn glory is trained up a bamboo support, with japanese anemones (*Anemone* x *hybrida* 'Whirlwind') at its feet.

The main jobs this season lay the foundations for trouble-free performance next year, and include tying in plants and checking that supports are sound. When the weather is fair, autumn is also a good time to plant new climbers and to continue to take hardwood cuttings.

now is the season to . . .

- **check plant ties** and tie in any new shoots before the autumn gales.
- **inspect layers and cuttings** and pot up those that are well rooted (see below).
- **cut back herbaceous climbers,** such as golden hop and the perennial pea, to ground level once growth has died back. Pull up annual climbers that have been killed by the frost.
- **trim self-clinging climbers** if necessary, to keep growth well away from window frames and downpipes. Trim back all climbers where growth is encroaching into guttering.
- **prune late flowering clematis,** such as *C. tangutica* and *C. viticella*, which are growing through conifers and evergreens, once they have finished flowering. Cut back to 60–90cm (2–3ft) to reveal the full beauty of the host plant in winter.

checking layered climbers

1 **Gently loosen the soil** from under the layer. If plenty of roots have developed, use secateurs to sever the layer from the parent plant. If only a few, poorly developed roots are revealed, replace the soil and re-peg the stem securely.

2 **Plant the severed layer** in potting compost, in a pot that will just accommodate the roots; a 10–13cm (4–5in) pot is usually adequate. After watering well, stand the pot in a coldframe or greenhouse, or under a cloche over winter.

- **plant hardy climbers** and wall shrubs in well-prepared ground (see below).
- **water newly planted climbers** if dry spells occur and give established plants a twice-weekly soaking.

and if you have time . . .

- **take hardwood cuttings.**
- **treat wooden supports** and repair if necessary (see page 411).
- **weed and mulch** around established plants.

propagation

Check semi-ripe cuttings taken in summer. Carefully up-end the pot, with your fingers spread over the compost, and gently slide it off. Pot up any well-rooted cuttings individually into 8cm (3in) pots and grow them on in a greenhouse or indoors on a cool, well-lit windowsill. Leave poorly rooted cuttings to develop further.

Layers started last spring are likely to have rooted by now (see opposite).

planting hardy climbers and wall shrubs

Plant new climbers while the soil is warm and moist. In these favourable conditions the plant can concentrate on building up a good root system rather than trying to make top growth at the same time.

The exceptions to autumn planting are evergreens and climbers that are on the borderline of hardiness in cold areas. Such plants include California lilac (*Ceanothus*), *Clematis armandii, Cytisus battandieri* and *Trachelospermum*, all of which are best planted in spring.

Before planting, clear all weeds and prepare the ground thoroughly by digging in plenty of well-rotted manure or compost. This is particularly important if the site is at the base of a wall where the soil tends to be poorer and drier than elsewhere in the garden. Dig a hole about 45cm (18in) away from the base of the wall, and at least twice the size of the rootball. Mix a bucketful of well-rotted manure or compost into the excavated soil. Plant climbers other than clematis (see below) so that the top of the rootball is at soil level. Where possible, put up any essential supports in advance of planting to avoid damage to the new plant.

After planting mulch the soil with a layer of chipped bark or cocoa shells at least 5cm (2in) deep. This will help to insulate the roots from the worst of frosts, reduce water loss, and suppress weeds.

planting clematis against a wall

1 **Remove the pot** and if the roots are spiralling around the rootball, tease them loose with your fingers.

2 **Place the clematis in the hole**, spreading out any loose roots, and position it so that the top of the rootball is 10cm (4in) below ground level. Then back-fill round the rootball, firm and water.

3 **Spread out the plant's stems** and tie them to several short bamboo canes, stuck into the soil at an angle to the wall. Do this for all climbers whether they are self-clinging or not.

climbers/2

using supports

Most climbers and all wall shrubs need some form of support. The two best options are trellis or wires run through vine eyes. There is also netting made of plastic or wire, but this is rarely used because it is less attractive in appearance.

trellis

Trellis is an extremely adaptable material to use in all sorts of sites around the garden. It instantly transforms any surface as it is decorative in its own right even before the climbing plants become established. Most trellis is made of wood and comes in many different designs, styles and prices.

- **basic 'squared' trellis** is the most economical and comes in 1.8m (6ft) lengths in panel widths from 30cm–1.8m (1–6ft).
- **more decorative styles** include panels with concave or convex tops, diamond lattice and panels open in the centre.
- **criss-crossed willow stems** suit an informal or cottage garden, but expanding willow trellis is not very durable and may last only a couple of years.
- **mount trellis to support climbers** on walls and fences.
- **mount panels** between stout fence posts to act as a free-standing screen around a patio, as a divider within the garden or along the boundary instead of a solid fence.
- **fix trellis on top of low walls** or fences to raise their height, to create privacy or to expand the growing area for plants.

erecting trellis on walls and fences

Whatever the design, the most important point when putting up trellis is to incorporate battens or blocks of wood to create a 3–5cm (1–2in) space between the trellis and the wall or fence to which it is fixed. This gap is essential not only to allow room for plant stems to twine around the trellis, but also to allow air to circulate, which helps to prevent diseases. Birds often take advantage of the gap to build their nests.

wire supports

Strong galvanised wire running through vine eyes provides an inexpensive alternative to trellis on walls and fences, and is especially useful where you plan to cover large areas with climbing plants or wall shrubs.

- **on walls (1)** use flat vine eyes hammered into the mortar.
- **on fences (2)** fix screw-type vine eyes to timber posts.
- **run the wires (3)** horizontally along the mortar lines of a brick wall so they are hardly visible. Space horizontal wires approximately 30cm (12in) apart and vertical wires 1.8m (6ft) apart.
- **strain the wires between the vine eyes (4)** and tighten using pliers, or fit tension bolts to make sure there is no slack.

Ivy and virginia creeper cover a wooden trellis. As both are self-clinging, they do not need to be tied in.

easy access climbers

HERBACEOUS CLIMBERS

• golden hop (*Humulus lupulus* 'Aureus') • perennial pea (*Lathyrus latifolius*) • scotch flame flower (*Tropaeolum speciosum*)

CLIMBERS THAT TOLERATE HARD PRUNING

• blue passion-flower (*Passiflora caerulea*) • *Clematis* 'Bill MacKenzie' • *Clematis tangutica* • *Clematis texensis*: varieties such as 'Etoile Rose' and 'Gravetye Beauty' • *Clematis tibetana* subsp. *vernayi* 'Orange Peel' • *Clematis viticella*: varieties such as 'Abundance', 'Alba Luxurians' and 'Etiole Violette' • japanese honeysuckle (*Lonicera japonica* 'Halliana')

Decorative vines such as this *Parthenocissus* make an unusual, eye-catching subject for an autumn hanging basket.

maintaining supports

Check wooden supporting posts of trellis and other plant supports, paying particular attention to the structure at soil level as this is where rotting is most likely to occur. Rather than buying a replacement, it is sometimes possible to saw off the rotten part and insert the post into a metal post holder, hammered into the hole occupied by the old post. Otherwise, sink a concrete spur into a hole dug next to the existing post, and bolt the two together.

easy-access solutions

Growing climbing plants on certain sites can be a problem if the structure requires occasional maintenance, such as a wooden fence or shed that needs treating with wood preservative every couple of years. The solution is either to put up hinged trellis panels (see below) or to grow climbers that are herbaceous and die down every autumn, or that tolerate hard pruning (see box, above left). It is also worth considering annual climbers such as sweet peas.

mounting trellis

If the trellis is flimsy, mount it on battens all round. Fix top and bottom battens on the wall and secure trellis to them. Sturdy trellis should not need battens (see below).

looking ahead . . .

☑ LATE SPRING Plant out rooted layers that have overwintered under cover.

☑ EARLY SPRING Check semi-ripe cuttings and pot up once they are well rooted.

mounting hinged trellis

1 **Screw a wooden batten** to the wall along the top and bottom of the area to be covered by trellis.

2 **Using hinges,** join the lower edge of the trellis panel to the bottom batten mounted on the wall.

3 **Join the top battens** on trellis and wall with stout hooks and eyes so that, when access is required, you can unhook the panel and lower it to the ground, plants and all.

shrubs & trees

Many shrubs and trees look spectacular in autumn, with late flowering species in bloom and brilliant foliage tints as the season closes. In the midst of this dramatic display, take time to think about planting, renovating and propagating new plants for the years ahead.

now is the season to . . .

- **continue watering regularly** in a dry autumn. Concentrate on shrubs and hedges planted less than a year ago, and trees planted up to two years ago.
- **water container-grown shrubs** and trees in dry weather, but gradually reduce the frequency as autumn advances.
- **keep on top of the weeds,** especially fast-growing annuals like bittercress, which still have time to flower and spread their seeds.
- **pot up rooted cuttings** and overwinter in a coldframe or cool greenhouse.
- **move rooted layers** to their permanent sites (see opposite).
- **transplant rooted** hardwood cuttings, taken last autumn, to their new homes.
- **protect new plants,** especially young evergreens, from cold winds.
- **leave faded flowerheads** on hydrangeas to protect their young shoots from severe weather until early spring.
- **prepare planting sites** for new hedges (see page 414).
- **plant new evergreen shrubs,** trees and hedges between early and mid-autumn for best results, but wait until next spring if your garden is cold or exposed.

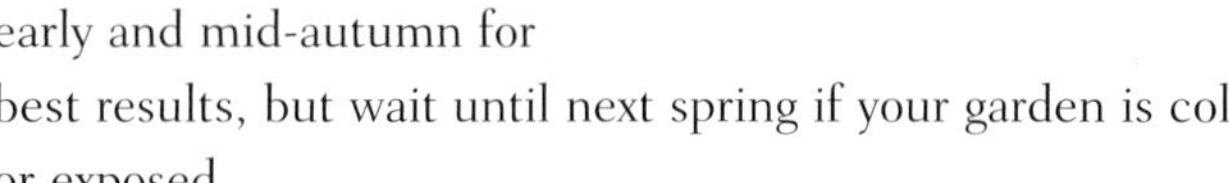

- **start planting new deciduous trees**, shrubs and hedges in prepared sites (see page 414).
- **prune long shoots** of late-summer and early autumn flowering shrubs (see opposite).
- **begin renovating** neglected deciduous hedges in late autumn (see opposite).
- **propagate new shrubs** and hedges from hardwood cuttings (see opposite).

and if you have time . . .

- **collect ripe seeds** from trees and shrubs for sowing now, if exposure to frost is necessary for germination, or to store until spring.
- **net holly branches** laden with berries to protect them from birds until Christmas.

Evergreen hedges, such as privet, should be given a last trim now. Those that are overgrown are best left until spring.

The leaves of *Nyssa sylvatica* turn red and gold before they fall. Use a wire lawn rake or electric blower to clear them from the lawn.

propagation

This is the time to take hardwood cuttings of shrubs and check those taken last year, as they take about a year to root. You can move those that have rooted well to their growing positions, but some shrubs are slow to root and may need to be left a little longer.

taking hardwood cuttings

Hardwood cuttings are 20–30cm (8–12in) portions of ripe, firm stems that have grown this year, either cut just below a bud or pulled from the main stem with a thin strip, or heel, of old bark.

- **first trim any ragged edges** from the heel, then root the cuttings in a sheltered position. (For evergreen cuttings, remove leaves from the lower portion.)
- **dig a V-shaped trench** about 10cm (4in) deep, and fill with equal amounts of soil and grit.
- **push the cuttings** into this mixture, upright and about 15cm (6in) apart, so that only 5–8cm (2–3in) is visible above the surface.
- **firm gently with your foot,** water if the soil is dry and leave until next autumn.

For a hedge, plant hardwood cuttings in threes where they are to grow. Planting through thick plastic insulates the soil and keeps it moist.

shrubs to propagate **by hardwood cuttings**

• buddleja • deciduous ceanothus • cornus • deutzia • forsythia • hydrangea • hypericum • philadelphus • privet • ribes • salix • spiraea • tamarix • weigela • wisteria

moving layers

Layers produced from flexible shoots pegged into the soil in spring or last autumn should have rooted firmly by now. Young shoots are the most visible indication of success, but to be certain gently pull at the layer to test whether there is any resistance.

- **transplant a layer** with plenty of well-developed roots to its permanent prepared site by cutting the branch joining it to the parent plant, then lifting it carefully with a fork.
- **on cold, inhospitable soils** it may be prudent to sever the layer now, but leave it in place and move it next spring.
- **unrooted or poorly rooted** layers can be left for another year without harm.

pruning late shrubs

Late flowering shrubs such as *Buddleja davidii*, caryopteris, leycesteria and brachyglottis were traditionally pruned immediately after flowering, but experience shows that early spring is often a safer time with less risk of frost damage if a warm autumn stimulates new growth. Leaving top growth in place over winter also protects plants and benefits wildlife. So just shorten long shoots that might be damaged by strong winds now, and complete the pruning in early spring.

renovating a beech hedge

1 **Prune the hedge evenly** all over using hedge shears. Trim it to 10–15cm (4–6in) less than the ultimate finished surface to allow room for dense re-growth.

2 **To reduce the size** more severely, cut back one side now and wait for a year before you cut the other side.

renovating neglected hedges

You can cut back overgrown deciduous hedges, such as beech, hornbeam and hawthorn, to restore their shape and fill in bare patches (see left). Use hedge shears and do this any time between late autumn and the end of winter during frost-free weather. Feed the hedge in early spring to support new growth.

shrubs & trees/2

planting trees and shrubs

Dig over sites for new shrubs, trees and hedges well before planting if you can, so that the ground has a month or two in which to settle. If you have no opportunity of preparing the whole area in advance, you can plant immediately after digging individual sites (see below).

To prepare a site for a new hedge, mark out the position by digging a trench 60cm (2ft) wide, with the planting line down its centre. Prepare the ground several weeks in advance or immediately before planting. As you refill the trench after planting, loosen the soil on the sides, especially in heavy soil, to prevent it from becoming a drainage channel for the surrounding ground.

planting a container-grown tree or shrub

Mark out the planting position and dig a hole large enough to allow for 10cm (4in) of planting mixture (see below) beneath and all round the rootball.

- **Thoroughly water the plant** and stand it in the hole to check its position before carefully removing the container.
- **Fill in around the rootball** with planting mix, firming it as you go with your fists or a trowel handle, and level the surface.
- **For trees, position a stake** on the lee side (the side away from the prevailing wind) and drive it in at an angle of 45 degrees to avoid damaging the rootball. Secure the tree with an adjustable tie.

The pink and orange seed capsules of *Euonymus europaeus* 'Red Cascade' make it one of the most conspicuous small trees in autumn.

preparing for planting

1 **Mark out a circle, about** 1–1.2m (3–4ft) across, if you are planting in lawn or a grassed area.

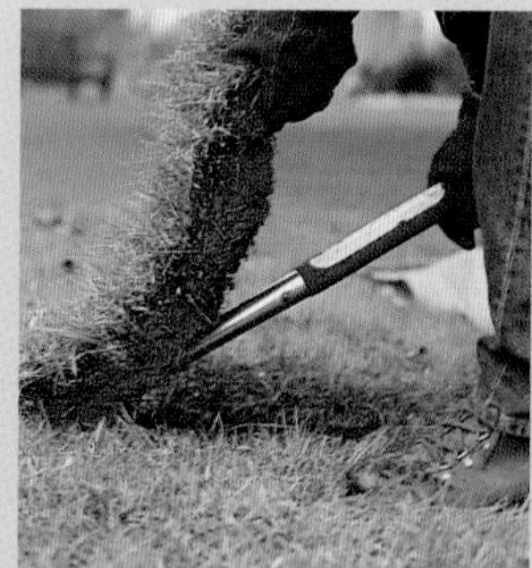

2 **Lift the turf** and fork out any perennial weeds, then dig the area to the depth of a spade blade. Stack this topsoil to one side. Use a fork to loosen the subsoil and work in some garden compost or leaf-mould. Chop up any turf and lay this grass side down in the hole.

3 **Prepare a planting mixture** in the following way. Mix in a bucket 2.5 litres (½ gallon) each of well-rotted manure and garden compost (or leaf-mould), plus 100g (4oz) each of seaweed meal and bone meal, and fork this into the heap of excavated topsoil.

4 **Before planting** the tree or shrub add enough of the planting mix to raise the plant to the right depth.

staking container-grown and bare-rooted trees

A short stake is adequate for sturdy and short-stemmed trees. For bare-root trees, drive the stake in vertically to come a third of the way up the trunk; secure with a tie.

For container-grown trees, drive in a short stake at an angle after planting, so that it misses the rootball and can be attached about 45cm (18in) above the ground.

Alternatively, drive in two short upright stakes 60cm (2ft) apart on opposite sides of the trunk, join with a horizontal batten and attach to the tree with an adjustable tie.

looking ahead . . .

- ☑ WINTER Prune and shape deciduous shrubs and trees.
- ☑ EARLY SPRING Feed hedges that have been renovated.
- ☑ Renovate overgrown shrubs.
- ☑ Prune late flowering shrubs.
- ☑ LATE SPRING Plant evergreen trees and shrubs.
- ☑ Prune hydrangeas.

staking trees

Young trees need staking until their new roots have anchored them securely in the ground (see above). For trees with tall slender trunks or large heads of evergreen foliage, drive in a long stake so the top reaches the lowest branch and secure with one or two tree ties. Use ties with cushioning between tree and stake, or pad the contact point with a wad of sacking.

there is still time to . . .

- **prepare sites** for new trees and shrubs. Plant deciduous species between autumn and spring, but leave evergreens until spring if you cannot plant them by mid-autumn.
- **take semi-ripe cuttings** of evergreens in early autumn and root in a coldframe. Suitable plants include privet, laurel, lavender and lonicera.

planting a bare-rooted tree or shrub

1 **Dig out a hole** large enough to take the roots comfortably when spread out, and check the depth so the soil mark on the stem is at ground level. For trees, drive in a vertical stake 8–10cm (3–4in) off-centre and on the lee side, away from the prevailing wind.

2 **Hold the plant** upright in position, spread a few trowels of planting mix (see 3, opposite) over the roots, and gently shake the plant up and down to settle the mix in place. Repeat and firm the plant lightly with your fist.

3 **Half-fill the hole** and gently tread firm. Check the plant is still at the correct depth and adjust if necessary by adding or removing soil.

4 **Back-fill the hole,** firm again and level the surface. Attach a tree to its support with an adjustable tie fixed near the top of the stake.

planting a hedge

Although it will take several years for a hedge to become an effective screen, your patience will be well rewarded. You will eventually be the proud owner of an attractive living boundary offering great ornamental value in terms of colour, texture and structure.

formal or informal?

First of all you need to decide whether to have a formal or an informal style of hedge. A formal hedge is close-clipped on the top and sides, creating a neat shape that is maintained by trimming two or three times a year. An informal hedge is looser and more open in design, as plants are allowed to grow naturally and are pruned just once a year. Consequently, an informal hedge takes up more space than a formal one. The other main difference between the two types of hedge is that a formal hedge is grown solely for foliage effect, while an informal one is also grown for other ornamental attributes such as flowers and fruit.

Looking its best in autumn, when it produces masses of red berries, *Cotoneaster lacteus* (right) forms a dense evergreen hedge midway between formal and informal in style.

Privet lends itself to tight clipping and makes a superb formal hedge. This immaculate divider (below) incorporates an archway through to another part of the garden.

mixed hedges

Mixed hedges of native plants look very attractive in a rural setting, and are superb for wildlife. They provide flowers for bees, plenty of fruits and berries for birds, as well as shelter for nests. Choose deciduous plants, such as hawthorn, blackthorn, field maple and hazel, for about three-quarters of the hedge, and evergreens, such as holly and yew, for the remainder. It is best to plant this type of hedge in a double staggered row (see page 419).

growth rates

Different plants grow at dramatically different rates, which is usually a prime consideration when deciding what to plant as a hedge. The table below outlines the approximate rates of growth of good hedging plants, but it must be stressed that this is only a general guide. Many other factors influence speed of growth, including the quality of soil preparation prior to planting, attention to watering and feeding after planting, and local climate and weather conditions, such as exposure to wind.

growth rates for hedges

FORMAL HEDGES	GROWTH RATE	SPACING BETWEEN PLANTS
BEECH (*Fagus sylvatica*)	Slow	30cm (12in)
HAWTHORN (*Crataegus monogyna*)	Medium	30cm (12in)
HOLLY (*Ilex aquifolium*)	Slow	45cm (18in)
HORNBEAM (*Carpinus betulus*)	Slow	45cm (18in)
LAUREL (*Prunus laurocerasus*)	Fast	60cm (2ft)
LAWSON'S CYPRESS (*Chamaecyparis lawsoniana*)	Medium	60cm (2ft)
LEYLAND CYPRESS* (x *Cupressocyparis leylandii*)	Fast	75cm (2ft 6in)
LONICERA NITIDA	Medium	45cm (18in)
PRIVET (*Ligustrum ovalifolium*)	Fast	30cm (12in)
WESTERN RED CEDAR (*Thuja plicata* 'Atrovirens')	Medium	60cm (2ft)
YEW (*Taxus baccata*)	Slow	60cm (2ft)

INFORMAL HEDGES	GROWTH RATE	SPACING BETWEEN PLANTS
BERBERIS (many, such as *B. darwinii*, *B.* x *stenophylla*)	Medium	45cm (18in)
ELAEAGNUS x EBBINGEI	Medium	60cm (2ft)
ESCALLONIA	Medium	45cm (18in)
FLOWERING CURRANT (*Ribes sanguineum*)	Fast	45cm (18in)
GRISELINIA LITTORALIS	Medium	45cm (18in)
LAURUSTINUS (*Viburnum tinus*)	Medium	60cm (2ft)
PYRACANTHA COCCINEA	Medium	60cm (2ft)
ROSA RUGOSA	Fast	45cm (18in)
SNOWBERRY (*Symphoricarpos*)	Medium	30cm (12in)

Slow = up to 23cm (9in) of growth per year
Medium = 23–45cm (9–18in) of growth per year
Fast = over 45cm (18in) of growth per year

* not for small gardens; plant only if you are prepared to clip regularly and limit its height.

hedges as windbreaks

In exposed sites, and especially near the coast where the wind is laden with salt, hedges are essential for shelter. They make excellent windbreaks because the wind is filtered through them, unlike solid barriers that create turbulence. If space permits, choose an informal belt of tough, mixed plants rather than a close-clipped hedge. Exceptionally windy sites will benefit from more than one line of protection, such as an informal shelter belt of trees outside a tall hedge.

Coastal windbreaks must be made of salt-tolerant plants. *Elaeagnus* x *ebbingei* and tamarisk (*Tamarix ramosissima*) make lovely informal hedges, as does *Escallonia*, which is widely grown for its colourful flowers. You can also trim *Escallonia* to make a more formal hedge, albeit one that will flower less freely. *Griselinia littoralis* can also be trimmed into a formal shape. In mild areas, *Fuchsia magellanica* and tall hebes such as *Hebe salicifolia* make excellent flowering hedges.

thorns and prickles

Plants packed with vicious thorns or prickly leaves are excellent deterrents to would-be intruders, particularly if you trim them to encourage the growth to form a dense barrier. The following are among the best for hedges.

- *Berberis darwinii*
- *Berberis gagnepainii*
- *Berberis* x *stenophylla*
- holly (*Ilex aquifolium*)
- pyracantha
- *Rosa rubiginosa*
- *Rosa rugosa*

Holly (*Ilex aquifolium*)

planting a hedge/2

A hedge is a long-lasting feature of the garden, so the attention you give to soil preparation, planting and aftercare is particularly important.

the best time to plant

Autumn is the ideal time to plant a hedge because this is the season when plants establish themselves best. You can also make considerable savings during the dormant season: until late winter, you can buy bare-rooted (field-grown) deciduous plants, which are much cheaper than pot-grown ones. You can also buy evergreens, such as holly and laurel, as large, root-wrapped plants for a similar price to smaller container-grown ones. Garden centres and nurseries usually supply a limited range of bare-rooted hedging plants, sold in packs of five or ten. Alternatively, you can buy these by mail order, which is less expensive if you need larger quantities.

preparing the ground

Rather than prepare individual planting sites, tackle the area as one long strip. Its width will range from 60cm (2ft) for a single-row hedge to 1m (3ft) for a double. Most hedges are planted in a single row (see below), but a mixed native hedge or a dense, wide hedge is planted in two rows, with the plants staggered to offset one another. Within each row of a double hedge, position the plants at one-and-a-half times the spacings given on page 417.

Ideally, carry out the preparation of the soil in summer to early autumn. Clear the weeds first, using weedkiller if necessary to get rid of any perennial weeds. Mark out the site carefully using canes and string, to ensure you prepare the strip in a straight line, then double-dig the soil (see page 595) in early autumn, to allow a few weeks for it to settle before planting. Water container-grown plants well, and soak bare-rooted plants thoroughly before planting the hedge.

aftercare

The way you care for a new hedge during its first year can make all the difference. Mulch the soil with a 5cm (2in) layer of chipped bark or cocoa shells straight after planting. This will help to keep the roots moist, even out the soil temperature and prevent weed growth that would compete with the hedge plants. Top-dress with a general fertiliser in early spring and water well during dry spells in the first spring and summer, giving plants a soaking two or three times a week.

planting a single-row holly hedge

1 Set up a string guideline to ensure that you position the plants in a straight line. Cut a bamboo cane to the length of the spacing between plants and use this as a spacer when planting. If the space between plants is uneven, this will be very obvious later, when the plants have grown.

2 Take the plants out of their pots and unwind any roots that are spiralling around the bottom of the rootball. Make individual planting holes and put the plants in the ground at the same depth as they were growing previously.

3 With your toe, firm the soil all around the roots and water well.

A thick layer of bark chippings around new hedge plants acts as a mulch to keep the roots moist and suppress weeds.

low hedges

In open areas where tall planting is inappropriate or not permitted, low hedges can make useful boundaries. Within the garden itself, you can use low hedges in a number of different ways: along paths, fronting borders, and as dividers between different parts of the garden. While box (*Buxus sempervirens*) has long been a favourite for low hedges, the spread of the fungal disease *Cylindrocladium*, to which box is susceptible, may make alternatives more appealing. These include:

- *Berberis thunbergii* 'Atropurpurea Nana'
- hyssop (*Hyssopus officinalis*)
- ivy (*Hedera helix* varieties), growing on a low wire fence
- japanese holly (*Ilex crenata*)
- lavender (most varieties except *Lavandula stoechas*)
- santolina

If your garden is visited by deer or rabbits you will need to protect young hedge plants with plastic tree guards for at least the first six to twelve months after planting.

temporary windbreaks

If the site for planting is at all exposed, put up a temporary windbreak of plastic netting, available from garden centres, to help your plants establish well. Evergreen plants, in particular, need protection because they lose moisture through their leaves all year round. Make sure the netting is at least as high as the plants and secure it to temporary stakes pushed in the ground.

If you want instant privacy as well as a hedge, put up an ornamental screen of reed, bamboo or willow with a view to leaving it in place until the hedge is well established – provided it does not block light to the plants. The hedge will also grow faster in a sheltered environment.

planting a double-row beech hedge

1 **Set up two strings** 45cm (18in) apart as marker lines. Cut a cane to the required plant spacing (one-and-a-half times the spacing given on page 417). Measure out the plant positions, staggering the plants in the second row.

2 **Soak bare-rooted plants** in a bucket for a couple of hours before planting. Then use secateurs to shorten any long roots and to trim off any damaged ones.

3 **Put the plants** in their holes at the same depth as they were growing previously (the part of the stem originally below ground is usually a darker colour). Firm the roots thoroughly. Immediately after planting, cut back all deciduous plants by a third, which includes shortening any long sideshoots. Water well to settle the soil around the roots.

alpine gardens

It is time to start tidying alpine beds and borders, even though some plants are still in flower. The most important tasks are clearing away fallen leaves, topping up the gravel mulch and protecting vulnerable plants from winter wet.

now is the season to . . .

- **clear up fallen leaves** regularly.
- **control weeds** as necessary. Hoe annual weeds to prevent them producing a late batch of seeds. Dig out perennial weeds, or spot treat them with weedkiller to reduce the amount of disturbance to your plants.
- **replenish gravel mulch** on alpine beds and borders, tucking it carefully around stems. A layer at least 2–3cm (1in) deep will allow rain to drain away quickly, keeping the stems dry.
- **protect vulnerable plants** from winter wet (see opposite).
- **trim back straggly plants** or those that have begun to encroach on less vigorous neighbours. Alpines like aubrieta and gold dust (*Aurinia*) often look bare at the base, so cut them back in September to encourage new growth.
- **continue to plant new alpines** in mild weather and sheltered gardens so they will have time to establish before winter.
- **propagate new alpines** from cuttings and divide large clumps (see right).
- **collect seeds** from late-summer-flowering alpines, such as some of the dwarf alliums and gentians, and sow immediately in pots of gritty compost.

propagation

Seeds sown in autumn usually germinate well, especially if you ensure good drainage. Use clay pots filled with gritty compost and sow the seeds thinly. Cover them with a thin layer of compost topped by a 5mm (¼in) layer of grit, but for very fine seeds cover with grit only. Stand the pots in a coldframe where the seeds will benefit from being chilled by winter frosts in a process known as stratification.

dividing alpines

Use this method not only to make more plants but also as a means of controlling them. Divide every three years or so.

- **Lift and divide plants** like campanulas, spring-flowering gentians, violas and sedum, then replant immediately to increase plant numbers.
- **Discard** the old central portion and replant only the young, outer sections.
- **Trim back** long, straggly shoots to about 5cm (2in) to help reduce wilting.

Many rosette-forming plants, such as *Sempervivum* 'Silverine', can be propagated from rooted offsets which can be replanted to fill gaps.

An autumn-flowering gentian (*Gentiana* x *stevenagensis*) brings a splash of colour to an alpine bed. The flowered stems will later die back to semi-evergreen overwintering rosettes.

alpines **to propagate by root cuttings**

- *Ancyclus depressus* • erodium • geranium • morisia
- *Primula denticulata*

taking cuttings

Creeping willows and other woody alpines are easily raised from small hardwood cuttings (see page 413). Insert them in pots of gritty compost and stand in a coldframe.

- **multiply mossy saxifrages** by pulling off individual rosettes. Trim the base and remove any old leaves. Insert the rosettes in clay pots filled with gritty alpine compost and stand them in a coldframe to root over winter.
- **root individual leaves** of *Ramonda myconi* by pushing the base into small pots of gritty alpine compost. Stand them in a coldframe to root over winter.
- **taking root cuttings** in the dormant period is a means of raising some alpine plants, often those with short stems that make conventional cuttings awkward to handle.

taking root cuttings

- **Carefully dig up** the plants and wash the roots.
- **Cut one or two roots** into 2–5cm (1–2in) sections. Fill a half-sized seed tray with a mix of equal parts John Innes No. 1 compost and horticultural grit to within 2–3cm (1in) of the rim.
- **Lay the cuttings** horizontally on the surface of the compost, about 5cm (2in) apart, and cover them with a layer of grit.

protecting vulnerable plants from wet

Alpines can cope with almost any amount of cold, provided their roots and leaves are kept dry, but they will deteriorate rapidly if subjected to cold damp conditions; plants with grey, silver or hairy leaves are particularly vulnerable. Any protection must allow free airflow, because if the plants are too confined they will be harmed by condensation.

- **place an extra layer of grit** around the base of moisture-sensitive plants, such as lewisias (see top right).

Cover low-growing plants with a wire mesh or bamboo cage, or an upturned hanging basket, to prevent falling leaves settling and causing the plants to rot. Clear leaves from the mesh at regular intervals.

adding a layer of grit

1 **Hold back the leaves** with your hand before applying a gravel mulch around individual plants, or cover the plant with an upturned pot. This avoids the laborious task of picking gravel off the leaves.

2 **Spread the mulch** around the stem, tucking it carefully under the leaves, to keep the stem dry and prevent it from rotting at soil level.

keeping alpine beds tidy

1 **Carefully remove** fallen leaves with a hand fork.

2 **Using secateurs,** cut off all dead flowerheads to improve the look of the bed.

3 **Trim back** the straggly growth of trailing alpines to 8–10cm (3–4in) to encourage bushy new growth. Do this in early autumn, so that any new growth will harden before the first frosts.

water gardens

Vital autumn tasks for ponds or water features include cutting back dying plants and netting the pond against falling leaves. These jobs need doing as soon as possible and take very little time, so do not put them off or you are likely to store up problems for the future.

now is the season to . . .

- **give top priority** to netting ponds to keep out fallen leaves. If they blow into the pond, they will rot down and pollute the water. Stretch a fine nylon net over the entire pond and secure it at the edges with bricks or short canes. Make sure the net is kept taut or birds could become entangled.
- **cut back dying foliage** and clear pond debris (see right).
- **protect fish** from herons (see opposite).
- **empty container ponds** and store them for the winter. Move any pond plants or fish to a temporary reservoir in the protection of a greenhouse or conservatory.
- **divide overgrown marginal plants** in the same way as perennials (see page 399). If your garden is in a cold area, delay this job until spring. Divide bog garden plants if they are several years old and have formed large clumps, but take care not to puncture the liner as you work.
- **reduce the amount of food** you give fish as temperatures drop. In winter they will live off their reserves.
- **remove submersible pumps** and store over winter; drain and insulate external pumps (see opposite).
- **transfer tender floating aquatic plants** to a frost-free place for winter (see opposite).

clearing up the pond

- **scoop out** the worst of the debris that builds up through the year in early autumn, before toads settle down to hibernate in the bottom of the pond.
- **pull out blanketweed** by hand or by winding the long filaments round a cane.
- **use a net** or an old kitchen sieve to scoop out any detritus. Pile blanketweed and debris on a plastic sheet spread beside the pond, and leave it for a couple of days so creatures can return to the water, before adding it to the compost heap.
- **cut back the foliage** of marginal plants and water lilies as they die back. You need to do this regularly, as dead leaves rot down quickly and will pollute the water.
- **for marginal plants with hollow stems,** take care not to cut below the water level or the stems will fill with water and the plants may die.

Use a net to remove dead leaves and other debris from the pond surface.

The handsome floating aquatic, water hawthorn (*Aponogeton distachyos*), will flower until the first autumn frost then must be cut back.

• **oxygenating plants** that have formed lots of growth will need thinning. To do this, cut out surplus growth if you can, otherwise use a garden rake to pull some out of the pond, but be careful not to puncture the liner. Leave the prunings by the pond for a couple of days so water creatures can crawl back to the water.

protecting fish against herons

Herons can become much more of a problem from autumn to spring when there is less plant cover to protect fish. First give the fish some secure hiding places, such as short lengths of drainpipe, then put in place some form of heron deterrent.

Placing a length of drainpipe in the pond will give fish a place to hide from predators.

• **the safest,** but not the most attractive means of protection, is to cover the pond with a net, which has the added value of catching fallen leaves (see below).

• **stretch a wire** at a height of 15cm (6in) just back from the pond's edge. This will trip and frighten a heron when it lands near the pond and attempts to walk to the edge.

• **another option** is to buy a movement-detecting bird scaring device.

overwintering floating plants

Floating aquatic plants that are frost-tender, such as water hyacinth (*Eichhornia crassipes*), need to overwinter under cover. Take out a clump and place it in a bowl of water with a layer of soil in the bottom. Keep the bowl in a light place at a minimum temperature of 10°C (50°F): the windowsill of a cool room is ideal. Fruits of the annual water chestnut (*Trapa natans*) can be treated the same way. Hardy floating plants like fairy moss and water soldier survive by sinking to the bottom of the pond for the winter.

pump care

External pumps should be drained and insulated with bubble plastic for the duration of winter. Submersible pumps are best removed from the pond and stored over winter in a shed or garage. This is vital if the pump is in water less than 45cm (18in) deep as there is danger of it becoming frozen and damaged in a severe winter.

• **Disconnect the pump** and cover the connector with a stout plastic bag, tying it securely in place.

• **Remove the filter,** and clean both it and the pump in fresh water. Once it is dry, pack the pump away until spring.

• **If your pump remains in water** through winter, run it for a short time every two weeks.

looking ahead . . .

☑ WINTER If you have fish or wildlife in your pond, keep an area of water ice-free by floating a tennis ball in the water.
☑ EARLY SPRING Reconnect pumps.

netting a pond

1 **Buy a piece of netting** big enough for your pond and anchor one side of it to the pond's edge, using short stakes or tent pegs knocked into the ground.

2 **Unroll the netting** carefully, lifting it over plants in the pond.

3 **Secure the netting** round all sides, using stakes or burying its edge beneath large stones.

patios & containers

Keep the colour going in your containers until the first hard frosts, then plant some seasonal displays to cheer the gloom of winter. Now is also the time to plant spring bulbs, and to tuck up tender plants so they can flourish again next summer.

now is the season to . . .

- **clear out hanging baskets** and other containers of annual plants once flowering has finished. Compost the remains unless they show signs of pests or diseases, in which case remove or burn them. In particular, watch out for the cream grubs of vine weevil in the compost (see page 396).
- **store containers** that are not frost-proof in a shed or garage after cleaning.
- **move frost-tender perennials** and shrubs under cover before the first frost. Keep them in a greenhouse or conservatory that is heated sufficiently to remain frost-free.
- **plant up containers** for autumn colour (see below).
- **plant bulbs** for spring flowers (see opposite).
- **check containers** every couple of days and water the compost sparingly if necessary.

and if you have time . . .

- **plant up containers** for winter colour.

planting containers in autumn

Planting containers at this time of year means paying even more attention than usual to good drainage, for compost that is soggy and poorly drained is liable to freeze solid in winter and kill or damage the plants, particularly bulbs. For this reason, avoid using potting compost containing water-retaining gel. You should also mass plants closely together to ensure a full display as there will be little growth between now and spring. Bear in mind the following:

Lay fine plastic netting over the top of polystyrene pieces or crocks, then fill with compost.

- **Put in a layer of drainage** material about 5cm (2in) deep. Pieces of broken pots, or 'crocks', are ideal, but large stones or chunks of broken polystyrene trays are also suitable.
- **Lay fine plastic netting** over the top of the crocks to prevent the spaces becoming clogged with compost.
- **Part-fill the container** with a free-draining compost. Then pack in the plants closely and so they are at the same depth as they were growing previously.
- **Leave at least a 1cm (½in) gap** between the top of the compost and the rim to allow room for watering.
- **Firm the compost lightly** and water well. Stand the container on pot feet or pieces of tile so that excess water drains away freely.

plants for autumn colour

Seasonal plants for autumn are often overlooked, yet they give a generous display right up until the frosts arrive, and even longer in a sheltered spot or an unheated porch or conservatory. Get the most value from your autumn pots and hanging baskets by planting early. A blend of flowers, fruits

Chrysanthemums in pots will keep the patio colourful and cheerful through autumn. Move them under cover well before the first frosts.

Dismantle container displays once flowering is finished. Put annual plants on the compost heap and move tender perennials to a frost-free place such as the greenhouse.

and foliage ensures a tremendous show of colour and to achieve this don't be afraid to use some plants more usually grown indoors.

- **florists' cyclamen,** the type sold as houseplants, bear masses of flowers in white, pink, red and purple, often with the bonus of scent.
- **winter cherry** (*Solanum capsicastrum*) has small, bright orange fruits.
- **frost-tender heathers** (*Erica gracilis*) bear white, pink or red flowers. These look lovely with ornamental cabbages or kale with frilled leaves patterned in shades of pink, purple, cream and green.
- **winter-flowering pansies** will bloom during mild spells in winter and again in spring.
- **chrysanthemums,** the quintessential flower of autumn, make a glorious show of colourful blooms in a wide range of colours.

bulbs for spring flowers

Bulbs liven up the patio in spring like nothing else, and autumn is the time to get planting. Daffodils, small narcissi and early flowering bulbs like crocuses need to go in as soon as possible, preferably by the end of September so they have enough time to establish a good root system. Tulips, on the other hand, are best planted in late autumn to avoid several diseases that could strike if the bulbs have been sitting in the compost for longer.

To create a really eye-catching display, plant different bulbs in layers in a deep container at least 30cm (12in) deep and 30cm (12in) across. A pot this size will accommodate 8–10 daffodils bulbs, 10–12 tulips or 15–18 crocuses.

Protect pots from the worst of the winter frost and rain in a coldframe or unheated greenhouse. Otherwise, stand them in a sheltered spot against the house wall, and tuck bubble plastic, straw or leaves around the pots to protect them from frost. Give the warmest spot to hyacinths as they are most likely to suffer from the cold.

PROTECTION TIP Make a cover of chicken wire to sit on top of large containers to protect newly planted bulbs against cats and squirrels.

planting bulbs in a large container

1 **Prepare your pot** with a layer of crocks topped with around 5–8cm (2–3in) potting compost, then place the largest bulbs, usually tulips or daffodils, so their tops will be covered by 15cm (6in) of compost. Space them closely but so they do not touch, and cover them with a little compost.

2 **Position medium-sized bulbs** between the tulips, and add more compost. Finish off with small bulbs like crocus, dwarf narcissi or muscari, then cover with a 5cm (2in) layer of compost. Water after planting, then periodically.

Tulips make a spectacular display in late spring. Tall cultivars need a sheltered spot.

lawns

Autumn is the best time to repair damaged turf and prepare your lawn to withstand winter. The grass needs mowing less frequently as temperatures drop, but there are fallen leaves and wormcasts to sweep up.

now is the season to . . .

- **rake up fallen leaves** regularly (see opposite).
- **mow grass less frequently** and raise the height of the cutting blade.
- **scatter wormcasts** by brushing the lawn with a stiff broom or a besom before you mow (see opposite).
- **apply autumn fertilisers,** which are high in phosphates and potash. This slows down the topgrowth of the grass and encourages better root development. Choose a day when the grass is dry and the soil is moist, especially where powder or granular formulations are used, so that they fall off the grass blades and onto the soil.
- **make repairs** to damaged lawns by reseeding bare patches and renewing broken edges (see page 428–9).
- **aerate the lawn** if drainage is poor or moss is a problem; top-dress to relieve compaction (see opposite and page 428).
- **make a last effort** to eradicate moss and weeds before winter sets in (see opposite).
- **sow new lawns or lay turf** on soil well prepared in advance (see page 152–7). The relatively warm moist soil and the likelihood of air temperatures dropping as winter approaches, mean that root development is rapid and leaf growth is slow and steady, so a new lawn laid in autumn will be well established in time for next spring.
- **look out for toadstools** and other fungi. This is the time of year they are visible, even though they may be present in the soil all year round. Most are harmless and just feed on organic matter in the soil, but brush them off if you wish.

This autumn border, featuring *Phormium tenax* 'Variegatum' and *P.* 'Cream Delight', is set off by the crisply edged, immaculately maintained lawn.

mowing

Grass continues to grow while the soil is still relatively warm and moist, but with the first frosts it starts to show signs of slowing down; it is only when the soil temperature drops below 5–7°C (41–45°F) that the grass stops growing for the winter. Before that time, it helps to leave the grass longer to protect the base of the plants from early frosts. Once it shows no signs of growth, cease mowing until the spring.

- **mow less frequently:** once a week should be sufficient.
- **raise the cutting blade** to 2–4cm (1–1½in)
- **remove all grass clippings** as they will encourage the development of moss and worm activity.

MOWING TIP If the grass is too wet to cut and you have a hover mower, remove the blades (or put the mower on its highest setting) and run it over the lawn to 'blow dry' the grass. Then you can mow.

Gather the leaves into a pile with a lawn rake and stack them in a corner of the garden, to rot down into leaf-mould.

clearing leaves from the lawn

If leaves are allowed to accumulate on the lawn or are left in drifts or piles for more than four or five days, the grass will suffer. Moss is encouraged by the dark moist conditions under the leaves, and leaves left lying about will also promote worm activity (see right).

Rake up the leaves and use them to make leaf-mould (see page 597). You can also use your mower to help clear leaves and mow the grass at the same time: a light covering of leaves can be chopped by the mower and collected in the grass box. Add the mixed leaves and grass to the compost heap.

clearing moss and weeds

- **where weeds occur** throughout the lawn, apply a combined weed and autumn feed compound.
- **if few weeds are present,** spot-treat them or paint the centre of each rosette carefully with weedkiller.

Use a weedkiller 'pen' to paint a chemical onto the centre of individual lawn weeds.

Rake out dead moss using a metal-tined lawn rake.

- **to control moss,** first cut the grass short to expose the patches of moss, then apply a mosskiller such as lawn sand. Wait until the moss turns brown, which shows it is dead, before raking it out. If any moss patches appear to recover, treat them again within about three weeks.
- **lawn sand helps** to control spreading weeds such as clover, speedwells, trefoils and silver weeds. All will be severely weakened by frequent applications when the leaves are wet.

wormcasts

Worms are very useful in the garden, recycling dead plant material, aerating the soil and improving its structure, but unfortunately they make disfiguring casts on lawns, especially in autumn when they come up to pull fallen leaves and grass clippings into the soil. If you do not disperse the casts on lawns, the mower or your feet will flatten them, smothering the underlying grass. Wormcasts also contain weed seeds brought up from below ground level, and these will germinate when exposed to daylight.

The worms that form casts tend to prefer alkaline, or limy, soil, so by using an acidic fertiliser such as sulphate of ammonia in spring and summer, the number of worms will gradually reduce as the soil turns more acidic. The worms will move to surrounding borders to carry on their useful work.

Disperse wormcasts with a besom before mowing the lawn.

lawns/2

repairs

Lawns are subjected to much wear and tear through the summer months. This may be due to natural causes, such as drought, but people walking and playing games, and pets, will also take their toll. Rather than allowing damaged areas to deteriorate further, it is best to deal with them in early autumn, when the lawn is little used. This gives the grass plenty of time to recover before next summer.

relieving compaction

The main cause of many lawn problems is soil compaction, usually caused by regular activity or traffic on the lawn pressing air out of the soil. The resulting lack of air causes grass to die from the roots up, leaving sparse or bald patches, unless you take steps to alleviate compaction.

- **Spike the lawn** with a border fork every 15–20cm (6–8in) to a depth of 15cm (6in). Even better is to use a hollow-tine spiker, which allows more air round the grass roots as it takes out small plugs of turf, which can be swept up and composted.
- **Fill the holes** by brushing in a top-dressing (see above right) to encourage new roots to form.

top-dressing mixture

suitable for a clay or poorly drained soil

- 1 part peat or peat alternative
- 2 parts loam or good quality topsoil
- 4 parts horticultural sand

levelling bumps and hollows

Bumps and hollows can develop as the ground settles, with regular foot traffic, and if machinery runs over the same route. Such areas need levelling, with soil added or removed to re-establish the level (see below). Never use a roller to level a lawn, as this will only increase the problem.

dealing with bare patches

Bare patches may be due to weeds smothering the grass or something left lying on it; eventually the grass will die due to lack of light. Spills of concentrated fertiliser or other chemicals may 'burn' the grass, killing it off in patches. These areas can be re-seeded to restore the lawn to its original condition (see page 59).

levelling an uneven lawn

1 **With a half-moon** edging iron, cut two lines through the turf in the form of a cross with its centre in the middle of the affected area.

2 **Use a spade** to cut horizontally under the grass at a depth of about 5cm (2in). Then roll back the sections of turf with your spade to expose the soil, and loosen the surface with a fork.

3 **To level a hump** scrape away enough soil to make the area level with its surroundings. For a hollow, fill the depression with good quality topsoil and gently firm until the level is fractionally higher than the surrounding area.

4 **Replace the rolled-back** turf and firm it gently, using the back of a rake. It should be fractionally higher than the surrounding lawn as it will settle slightly over time.

- **First go over the area** with a spring-tined lawn rake. Rake vigorously to drag out all the old dead grass, including pieces of dead root, and to score the soil surface.
- **Use a garden fork** to break up the surface and ease soil compaction. Jab the tines 2–3cm (1in) into the soil.
- **Rake the soil** to a depth of about 1–2cm (½–¾in) to create a fine seedbed. Sow grass seed evenly over the area, at a rate of about 30g per m^2 (1oz per sq yd), and lightly rake it in.

repairing broken lawn edges

The most vulnerable areas of a lawn are the edges, which can easily become ragged or damaged by walking or mowing. If left alone, damaged edges will gradually crumble away and spoil the overall look of the lawn. Eventually you will need to re-cut the lawn, reducing its area. Far better is to repair damage in the early stages (see below). The repair should be invisible within six weeks.

Choose a fine day in autumn to carry out a grand clear-up of the lawn and to tackle all the repair jobs that need doing before the onset of winter.

repairing a lawn edge

1 **Place a wooden plank** on the lawn to act as a guide and, using a half-moon edging iron, cut out a section of turf behind the damaged edge.

2 **Use a spade** to cut horizontally under the turf at a depth of about 5cm (2in), severing the grass roots.

3 **Lift the section of turf** and rotate it 180 degrees; this will place the damaged area within the lawn and leave a neat edge. Firm the turf until it is just higher than the surrounding lawn, as it will settle over winter.

4 **Fill the gap** around the damaged area with fine garden soil and firm. Sow grass seed and water it in. If the weather is dry, lay a piece of horticultural fleece over the seeded area to prevent it from drying out and to encourage rapid germination, when the fleece is removed.

fruit

As the harvest draws to a close for another year, it is time to start tidying up and planting new fruit while conditions are still pleasant outdoors. Peaches and cane fruits need pruning, and it is worth taking some hardwood cuttings of gooseberries and currants.

harvesting **now**

• apples • apricots • blackberries • blackcurrants • figs • grapes • medlars • nectarines • peaches • pears • plums • quince • raspberries • alpine and perpetual strawberries

now is the season to . . .

- **harvest fruit** as it ripens. Gather everything by the end of October or just before the first frost, and carefully store those varieties that keep well. Check fruit in store regularly (see opposite).
- **prune fan-trained peaches** before the end of September and take measures against peach leaf curl (see page 432).
- **finish preparing the ground** for new fruit by clearing weeds, digging the planting sites, and working in plenty of garden compost or rotted manure (see pages 331 and 436). Dig in green manures sown after strawberries were lifted in early summer.
- **protect fruit trees** by fixing grease bands around their trunks (see opposite).
- **start planting new fruit** if the soil is in a workable condition (see page 436).
- **protect bare roots** of new fruit plants by 'heeling' them in a spare piece of ground if you can't plant immediately (see page 433).
- **pot up strawberries** in 13cm (5in) pots for early fruiting under glass and stand outside until late November, then bring under glass (see page 439).
- **dig up and divide rhubarb** for replanting in fresh ground (see page 432), but leave this until the spring on heavy soils.
- **take hardwood cuttings** of healthy bush fruits and root them in the open (see page 432).
- **start winter pruning** apples and pears in November when crops have been picked and leaves have fallen (see page 522).

Clear fallen leaves and fruits, and burn or thoroughly compost them to defeat overwintering pests and disease spores.

and if you have time . . .

- **remove the roof netting** from fruit cages to allow birds to clear many of the pests remaining on plants or hibernating at ground level, and to reduce the risk of snow damage.

storing apples and pears

1 **Wrap individual fruits** loosely in a sheet of newspaper.

2 **Place wrapped fruits** in a single layer in a shallow wooden or cardboard box.

Alternatively, apples store well in plastic bags, pierced to allow them some air; keep no more than three in each bag. Store in a cool place and check regularly for signs of rotting.

storing apples and pears

Although ideally apples and pears are left on the tree until ripe enough to pick easily, late-maturing varieties are best cleared by the end of October or early November, and stored. This applies particularly to pears such as 'Docteur Jules Guyot' and 'Beurré Hardy', which should be brought indoors to continue ripening before the weather deteriorates.

storage times for late apples and pears

APPLES	
'Annie Elizabeth'	December–May *
'Ashmead's Kernel'	December–March
'Blenheim Orange'	November–January
'Bramley's Seedling'	November–March *
'Crispin' (syn. 'Mutsu')	November–February
'Golden Noble'	October–January *
'Howgate Wonder'	November–February *
'Orleans Reinette'	December–February
'Ribston Pippin'	November–January
'Spartan'	November–January
'Sturmer Pippin'	December–April
'Sunset'	November–December
'Suntan'	December–March
PEARS	
'Catillac'	December–April *
'Joséphine de Malines'	December–January
'Packham's Triumph'	November–December
'Winter Nelis'	November–January

* cooking varieties

- **for long storage,** keep apples and pears in an airy, cool but frost-free place (see page 334).
- **pears benefit from slightly warmer conditions** than apples, and ripen best at about 10°C (50°F). As pears spoil quickly, check them every two or three days to see if they are ready to eat by gently pressing the stalk end for signs of softening.
- **inspect all stored fruit** regularly. Remove any that show signs of damage or disease and use immediately or discard.

preventing fruit tree problems

Trap winter moths by fixing grease bands round the trunks of apple, pear, plum and cherry trees. If left untreated these insects will cause extensive damage to the leaves, blossom and shoots. A barrier of insecticidal grease applied in October will trap the wingless female moths as they emerge late in autumn and winter and climb the tree to lay their eggs.

An espalier-trained pear forms an effective divider in part of a larger garden. Prune once all the fruits have been cropped.

- **spread the grease** directly onto the bark or onto a strip of paper 10cm (4in) wide, fixed to form a continuous band around the trunk; prepared grease bands are also available.
- **tree stakes** provide an alternative route for the moths, so grease these too.
- **check occasionally** that the bands are still sticky, and leave in place until April.

Wrap a prepared grease band around the trunk to prevent damage by winter moths.

bitter pit

Bitter pit is a disorder of apples that renders the fruit inedible. It is the result of calcium deficiency, which causes dark sunken pits on the skin and brown bitter spots within the flesh, especially on the fruit of young trees. Most apple trees outgrow the problem, but useful preventative measures include watering regularly and mulching in dry weather. If a soil test shows the pH is lower than 6.5, lime around the tree (see page 593).

fruit/2

pruning and propagation

Cane fruits and trained peaches will need pruning in autumn, while bush fruit and rhubarb can be propagated.

renewing your rhubarb

Although rhubarb is perennial and seems to thrive even when neglected, it does benefit from regular division and replanting in fresh soil once every four or five years. If your soil is light, divide rhubarb crowns in late autumn, but wait until the following spring if you garden on heavy ground.

Dig up a crown of rhubarb and cut it into segments.

- **Dig up a complete crown** and cut it vertically with a spade into segments, each with two or three fat dormant buds at the top. Alternatively, use a spade to split the crown where it is growing, then lift each division separately.
- **Discard** the old central portion of the crown as well as any rotten pieces.
- **Replant** the healthy outer portions about 1–1.2m (3–4ft) apart, in soil that has been deeply dug and enriched with plenty of rotted manure.
- **Leave surplus segments exposed** on the surface for six to eight weeks. Then you can force them in the greenhouse for an extra early crop (see page 539).

peaches

- **protect late varieties,** such as 'Bellegarde', which may not finish cropping before the first frosts. If low temperatures are forecast, cover unharvested fruit with fine netting or fleece, which will also help to deter birds.
- **prune fan-trained trees** as soon as cropping ends by cutting out the fruited sideshoots back to young low shoots, and tie these in as replacements. Also cut out any dead, broken or old exhausted branches. To avoid disease problems in the future, complete this pruning by the end of September and protect all cuts with wound paint.
- **if peach leaf curl** has been a problem in previous seasons, take steps to prevent its recurrence by spraying trees with copper fungicide just as the leaves are about to fall. Gather up the leaves and burn them. Protecting plants with a polythene screen during winter is a further precaution (see page 499).

cane fruits

- **cut back fruited summer raspberry canes** to ground level, if not done earlier, and tie in the new canes as replacements. Trim very tall canes to 15cm (6in) above the top training wire, or bend the tops down and tie them to the wire.
- **continue harvesting autumn raspberries** until frost finishes the crop. Cover the plants with a layer or two of fleece on cold nights to help to extend the harvest for a week or two.
- **prune blackberries and hybrid berries** by cutting out fruited canes at ground level. In mild areas, fan out the young, replacement canes and tie these to the wires (see page 332).
- **in cold gardens,** bundle the young canes together and tie them on the lowest wire, then fan them out in spring.
- **sever rooted tip layers** of blackberry and hybrid berries taken in summer, and transplant into their growing positions.

Tie young blackberry canes together over winter.

taking cuttings of bush fruit

Take hardwood cuttings from gooseberry and currant bushes as soon as the leaves have fallen (see below). The cuttings root slowly and should be left undisturbed until next autumn, when they can be moved to their final positions.

taking cuttings of blackcurrants

1 **Select strong, straight** stems of this year's growth on healthy plants. Cut the base just below a leaf joint and remove the thin growing tip to leave a cutting about 30cm (12in) long. For gooseberries and red and white currants, rub off all but the top four or five buds. For blackcurrants, leave all buds intact.

2 **Dig a long slit trench** with a spade in a sheltered area of weed-free ground. Push in the cuttings about 10cm (4in) deep and 15cm (6in) apart, and firm with your foot. On heavy soil, cover the bottom of the slit with 5cm (2in) of sharp sand before inserting the cuttings.

Autumn-fruiting raspberries trained decoratively on wires. This makes them easier to harvest and to prune.

strawberries

You can still plant summer-fruiting strawberries (see page 333), but with only a short time to get established they will not crop well in the first summer and it is usual to remove their first flush of flowers next spring to help the plants to build up strength.

- **larger pot-grown strawberry plants** and cold-stored runners (often sold as '60-day' or '80-day' plants) will produce a small crop of fruit next summer but should not be forced during their first year.
- **in a dry autumn,** continue watering summer-planted strawberries regularly until there is substantial rainfall.
- **perpetual strawberries** often continue fruiting until the first frosts, or a little after if you protect plants with cloches or fleece. Do not cut plants down after fruiting, but simply tidy them by removing all mulching material and weeds, and lightly fork over the soil between plants. Transplant runners to a new bed and these will give a full crop next year.

caring for bare-rooted plants

To give new fruit plants the best start you should plant them early in the dormant season, in well-prepared ground that is not frozen or waterlogged. Plant bare-rooted trees and bushes as soon as they are delivered (see page 436); if soil or weather conditions are unsuitable, make sure the roots are kept covered to prevent them from drying out. Well-packed plants will be safe for several days if stored undisturbed in a cool, frost-free place.

Where the delay is likely to be longer, 'heel in' the trees or bushes in a spare piece of ground in a sheltered part of the garden:

- **dig a shallow trench** large enough to take the roots. Unpack the plants soon after delivery and lay them at a shallow angle so that they are safe from wind damage; cover the roots with soil excavated from the trench.
- **alternatively, gather the plants** into a sheltered corner and heap damp straw or autumn leaves over their roots.

looking ahead . . .

☑ EARLY SPRING Fan out young canes of blackberries and hybrid berries.
☑ Remove grease bands.
☑ Remove the first flush of flowers from late planted strawberries.

there is still time to . . .

- **order new fruit soon** for autumn and early winter planting, before choice varieties are sold out (see page 330).

creating a fruit garden

Fruit can be grown in a smaller space than you might imagine possible, but to ensure regular and high-quality crops, you need to select a site that satisfies the requirements of the chosen plant.

assessing the site

Local climate is probably the strongest influence on the type of fruit you can grow. Although you can relieve the effects of high rainfall with efficient drainage, and compensate for too little rain by improving the soil and watering, other factors are critical to productivity.

• **temperature** Fruits such as peaches, apricots and figs do well in long, hot summers, while apples, pears, plums, gooseberries and currants need cooler conditions, especially in winter. Late spring frosts can damage buds, flowers and young shoots.

In very mild districts, the only option is to choose fruits that revel in heat. In cold gardens, note where frost lingers longest and plant elsewhere; never plant at the bottom of a slope, where cold air tends to collect. If you have no choice, plant taller fruit trees and late flowering bush fruit varieties in the cold spots, reserving the warmer sites for smaller and earlier flowering plants.

• **wind** Strong winds discourage pollinating insects, injure flowers and cause fruits to drop prematurely. The best protection is a windbreak of netting or open-board fencing, a hedge of beech, or a row of trees such as willow. Avoid building a wall or solid fence that will block the wind and cause turbulence.

• **sun and shade** Warm-climate crops, like peaches and greengages, and late

A standard red currant bush takes up little room in the centre of a vegetable bed (above), but provides decorative value as well as fruit.

'Stepover' apples make ideal dividers in small spaces, as in this potager (left).

fruit for walls

NORTH WALL (shaded, cool) • acid cherries • blackberries • cooking apples • damsons • gooseberries • red and white currants

EAST WALL (cold, dry, afternoon shade) • blackberries • cherries • early apples and pears • gooseberries • plums • raspberries • red and white currants

SOUTH WALL (sunny, warm, dry) • apples • apricots • cherries • figs • grapes • peaches • pears • plums and gages • red and white currants

WEST WALL (moist, windy, afternoon sun) • all currants and berries • apples • apricots • cherries• grapes • peaches • pears • plums and gages

Pear 'Doyenné du Comice' trained against a south-facing wall.

ripening top, or tree, fruit need the most sunshine, whereas most soft fruits will tolerate some shade for up to half the day. You can train certain fruits on a fence or wall, saving space and allowing the fruits to benefit from the reflected warmth of the sun. Avoid areas of deep shade, especially under overhanging trees.

• **soil** Most soils are suitable for growing fruit, provided they are well drained. You should dig heavy clay deeply to prevent waterlogging and work plenty of compost or well-rotted manure into light soils to improve water retention.

when to start

Ideally, carry out preparation in summer to early autumn, clearing the weeds first and using weedkiller, if necessary, to get rid of any perennial weeds. In early autumn dig the ground, to allow it several weeks to settle before planting.

fruit in small spaces

By using compact varieties and restricted forms, you can assemble a large amount of fruit in a small area. A garden about 6 x 4m (20 x 12ft) could include a row each of gooseberries, red currants and blackcurrants; two rows of raspberries; loganberries, blackberries, cordon apples and pears, and fan-trained peaches around the perimeter on posts and wires or a 2m (6ft) fence.

In a tiny garden, you could plant cordon apples on very dwarfing rootstocks, 75cm (2ft 6in) apart against a fence; train three or four raspberry plants in a cluster round a pillar; and plant a thornless cut-leaved blackberry to make an attractive arch. Strawberries are good edging plants, standard gooseberries and red currants are decorative highlights in flower borders, and many tree fruits will grow well in generous-sized pots.

rootstocks and fruit tree sizes

Most fruit trees are grafted onto a standardised rootstock, which controls the vigour of the tree and reduces its natural size. Some fruits, such as apples and, to a lesser degree, pears, are supplied on a range of rootstocks, from vigorous to very dwarfing, whereas only one or two kinds are available for plums, peaches and cherries. To get the most from a limited space, you need to combine a restrictive form of training with an appropriate rootstock. Good fruit catalogues list the rootstocks available, the trained forms they suit, and their ultimate sizes and recommended spacing.

pruning and training

Top fruits, such as apples, pears and 'stone fruits' like plums, cherries and peaches, grow naturally into large trees, but you can prune and train most of them to create a more attractive and productive shape that occupies much less space (see also Rootstocks, above). Soft fruits that can be pruned and trained into restricted shapes include bushes such as gooseberries and red and white currants.

• **standards, bushes and pyramids** In most open ground, you can train tree fruits like apples, pears, plums and cherries as standards with 1.5–2.2m (5–7ft) trunks, half-standards with 1–1.5m (3–5ft) trunks, bushes with stems up to 1m (3ft) high and cone-shaped dwarf pyramids, 2.2–2.5m (7–8ft) high. Gooseberries and red currants are grown as bushes, with a 15cm (6in) stem, or a standard with a 1–1.2m (3–4ft) stem.

• **cordons, espaliers and fans** You can train all tree and bush fruits (except blackcurrants) flat against walls and fences, or on wires stretched between posts. The commonest forms are cordons, which are upright or angled straight stems with short fruiting sideshoots (see page 436); these are used for apples, pears, gooseberries and red or white currants. The same fruits are also suitable for growing as espaliers, which have a central trunk with pairs of opposite, horizontal branches. Fans, which have branches radiating from a short central trunk, are best for plums, cherries, figs, apricots and peaches; they also suit apples, pears and gooseberries.

Blackberries and hybrid berries can be grown flat on wires, informally or as neat fans, and thornless varieties on pillars and arches, like a climber.

To save space in small gardens, plant four or five strong raspberry canes round a central 8cm (3in) post buried 45–60cm (18–24in) in the ground. Tie the canes in a group with loops of string or, in windy gardens, attach them individually to vertical wires stapled to each face of the post. Grow and prune in the usual way.

creating a fruit garden/2

Unless your soil is already well cultivated, you will need to prepare the site thoroughly at least a month before planting.

preparing the ground

The best way of preparing the ground is to do it in simple stages.

- **mark out the fruit garden area** with canes and string or a garden line, marking approximate planting positions (these depend on fruit type and form).
- **spray weeds** with a systemic weedkiller such as glyphosate, and leave for three weeks for it to take full effect. Alternatively, fork out perennial weeds.
- **dig the whole area** – single digging is sufficient for good soil, but double digging is advisable for soil that is impoverished or overgrown with weeds, or where drainage is poor.
- **feed the soil** and improve drainage by digging in garden compost or well-rotted manure, spreading an 8cm (3in) layer in each trench as you dig.
- **leave to settle** for at least a month before lightly forking and levelling the surface prior to planting.

If making a bed in an old lawn, skim off the top 5–8cm (2–3in) of turf with a spade and bury this upside down while you are digging. This will improve the soil's texture as well as its water-holding qualities.

planting cordon apples

1 **Dig a bed 1m (3ft) wide** and at least one spade blade deep, and add plenty of garden compost or rotted manure (see page 144). Drive in an 8cm (3in) diameter post every 3m (10ft) along the strip, and staple taut horizontal wires to the posts about 60–75cm (2–2ft 6in) apart. Space the cordons 60cm (2ft) apart, marking the position of each with a cane inserted at 45° and tied to the wires.

2 **Plant a cordon beside each cane,** at the same angle, and attach the main stem to the cane with adjustable tree ties. Either prune now, shortening sideshoots by half, or wait until spring. A low sideshoot has been retained on the first tree to train vertically on an upright cane to fill the empty triangular space.

planting the fruit

Store trees and bushes safely if you can't plant them immediately. If they look dry, plunge the roots in a bucket of water for two to three hours before planting. Trim back any damaged roots, and shorten excessively long ones to 30cm (12in).

planting a bare-rooted tree

- **mark the planting position** of the tree with a cane, spacing it an adequate distance from any neighbours. Dig a hole large enough to take the roots comfortably when spread out, and at a depth that leaves the old soil mark on the stem at ground level.
- **drive in a vertical stake** 8–10cm (3–4in) off-centre and on the lee side of the tree (the side away from the prevailing wind). The top of the stake should reach a third of the way up the trunk, or up to the first branches in exposed positions.
- **in a bucket, mix** 5 litres (1 gallon) of planting mix, using equal parts of well-rotted manure and garden compost or leaf-mould, plus 140g (5oz) each of seaweed meal and bone meal. Fork this into the excavated topsoil.
- **hold the tree upright** in its hole, spread a few trowelfuls of the planting mix over the roots, and gently shake the tree up and down so that the mix settles. Repeat and firm the mix lightly with your foot.
- **half-fill the hole** with planting mix, and gently tread firm. Check that the tree is still at the right depth, then fill the hole up, firm again and level the surface. Attach the tree to its support with an adjustable tie fixed near the top of the stake. Water in well.

planting a container-grown tree

- **mark out the planting position** of the tree, and dig out a hole large enough to allow for 10cm (4in) of planting mix below and all round the rootball.
- **water the plant thoroughly** and stand it in the hole on the layer of planting mix. Cut down the side of the container and remove it carefully.

• **fill in around the rootball** with planting mix (see left), firming it as you go with your fists or a trowel handle; level the surface. Water in.
• **position the stake** on the side away from the prevailing wind. Drive it in at a 45° angle to avoid the roots, and secure the tree with an adjustable tie.

soft fruit

Plant bush fruits in the same way as tree fruits, following the appropriate bare-rooted or container-grown method. Bury blackcurrants 5–8cm (2–3in) lower than their original growing depth to encourage branching from below ground. Staking is unnecessary, except for standard red currants and gooseberries, which will need supporting with stakes and adjustable ties near the top of the plant's stem. Blackberries, raspberries and fan or cordon-trained gooseberries and currants need tying in to a system of horizontal wires attached to vertical posts, or to vine eyes screwed into a wall or fence.

RASPBERRY TIP Raspberries dislike wet soils. Where drainage is poor, spread builders' rubble or gravel into the hole as you dig, or add extra topsoil to create planting ridges 8–10cm (3–4in) high.

after planting

Some fruits need pruning at planting time to stimulate plenty of new growth where it is needed. You do not have to prune fruit trees at planting time, unless you are training a restricted form such as a fan or espalier from a one-year-old tree (maiden). Cut down all stems of blackcurrant to 2–3cm (1in) high after planting. Prune the main stems on gooseberry and red or white currant bushes by half, making the cuts just above outward-facing buds. Cut raspberries down to a bud about 23cm (9in) above the ground.

the formative years

For best results, keep an area about 1m (3ft) around the fruits weed-free for at least the first two to three seasons. Do this by hoeing, spraying with weedkiller, or by mulching with manure or compost. Water regularly in dry periods, especially if the soil is light; continue this until the beginning of winter for bush fruits, and for one to two years for tree fruits. Feed plants every spring (see page 159), and prune at the appropriate season for shapely, productive plants (see page 522).

planting raspberries

1 **Dig a strip 1m (3ft) wide** and about one spade blade deep, more if the ground is heavy or poorly drained, then spread a bucketful of garden compost or rotted manure per plant on the surface. Fork this into the top 10–15cm (4–6in) of soil. Space the canes on the surface 38–45cm (15–18in) apart to mark the planting positions.

2 **Make sure the roots** of the raspberries have been soaked for two to three hours beforehand. Dig a hole for each cane so that it sits comfortably at the same depth as it was growing previously, or about 5cm (2in) deeper on light sandy soils. Thin or poorly rooted canes can be doubled up by planting in pairs.

3 **Firm gently** with your foot, continue with the rest of the plants, then level the surface.

4 **Prune each cane** to about 23cm (9in) high to stimulate strong buried buds to start growing in the coming season – they will produce fruit the following year. Once this new growth appears next spring, tie it to the wires and cut the pruned stumps to ground level.

vegetables

With many crops approaching maturity it is time to harvest and store your produce before frost strikes. Plan for next year as you clear the ground; thorough preparations made now will improve plant growth and yields in future.

now is the season to . . .

- **harvest crops regularly** and store excess produce (see below and page 440).
- **clear crops** after harvest. Put any green waste or crop residue onto the compost heap unless affected by pests and disease, in which case they should be burned or disposed of in the dustbin.
- **dig over and manure the soil** as it is cleared of crops. This is particularly important on heavy soils, which will benefit from being broken down by winter frosts. By leaving the soil in ridges it will also keep drier through the winter.
- **plan, sow, plant and prepare** for next year, once the ground is clear and cultivated. Then you can start off next year's crops, or leave the soil vacant so the frost can help to improve its structure.
- **earth up winter brassicas** to prevent wind rock.
- **remove supports** used for climbing crops and detach remnants of the spent plants. Then sort, bundle and store the supports somewhere dry until next year.
- **continue to hoe regularly** to kill weed seedlings as they emerge.
- **remove and burn** the stems of maincrop potatoes if they are affected by potato blight.

sowing early peas and beans

1 **Sow peas in a block** after taking out a spade-width of soil. Sow in three rows, staggering the spacing. Cover with cloches.

2 **Sow broad beans** 15cm (6in) apart in rows 60cm (2ft) apart, to overwinter and crop in summer.

3 **On exposed** sites, protect young broad bean plants with fleece, or grow them under cloches.

peas and beans

Continue to harvest peas, french beans and runner beans as they become ready, or leave some for drying. Sow broad beans and early peas for cropping next spring to summer.

- **sow early cultivars of peas** under cloches to be ready for picking in early summer. The cloches will be essential for winter protection after the seedlings have emerged.
- **sow broad beans** to crop from late spring to early summer. Longpod cultivars are the hardiest.
- **harvest maincrop peas** for using fresh when the seeds have swollen and the pods are still green (see pages 337 and 340).
- **for dried peas and beans cut the plants** off at ground level when the seeds are visibly swollen. Allow the vines to hang on the support and dry out before harvesting the pods.

SOIL IMPROVEMENT TIP Leave the roots of peas and beans in the ground after the crop has finished: they contain high levels of nitrogen, which will benefit a follow-on crop of brassicas (see page 531).

cabbages, cauliflowers and other brassicas

Some jobs need doing at the start of autumn, while others are better left until the end of the season.

in early autumn:

- **use up summer** and autumn cabbages. Harvest these less hardy crops that will not store for long periods before cutting the hardier winter cabbages.
- **transplant spring cabbages** into their cropping site (see opposite). In order to achieve a succession, sow more seed under cloches ready to transplant in early spring. Where headed cabbages and loose-leaved spring greens are both required, plant the cabbages closer together in the rows. Then remove alternate plants to eat as spring greens and leave the others to form a head.

harvesting now

• beetroot • carrots • celeriac • celery • chinese cabbage • florence fennel • french and runner beans • jerusalem artichokes • kale • leeks • lettuces and salad leaves • maincrop potatoes • marrow • onions • parsnips • peas • pumpkins and squash • salad radish • salsify • scorzonera • spinach and spinach beet • spring onions • summer and autumn cauliflowers • summer, autumn and winter cabbages • swedes • turnips

The blue-green foliage of leeks shows up well in front of the flowering evening primrose and lavatera. Young box plants will grow to form a low edging, while at the end of the row is a standard euonymus.

• **sow summer cauliflowers** under the protection of a cloche or in modular trays in a coldframe.

Net young brassica plants, especially in cold weather, against attack by wood pigeons.

• **earth up the soil** around the stems of cabbages, cauliflowers and brussels sprouts, to help to prevent them from rocking in the wind and loosening their roots in wet soil conditions.

• **sow turnips** for a leafy crop of greens, or turnip tops, but choose a hardy variety such as 'Green Stone Top'.

• **transplant chinese cabbage** and chinese broccoli sown in trays in late summer. Plant them out under the protection of cloches or low polythene tunnels.

• **sow texsel greens** early under similar protection as a cut-and-come-again crop for late autumn and early winter. Keep sowings well watered to ensure swift germination and rapid early growth. Cut leaves in five to six weeks when they are about 25cm (10in) high.

in late autumn:

• **cut and store winter cabbages** of the Dutch winter-white type. They will keep in a cool, frost-free place with good air circulation for up to three weeks.

• **harvest Savoy and 'January King'** cabbages as required. These are hardy enough to stand over winter in the garden.

• **protect spring cabbages** with cloches or fleece when long periods of frost are forecast.

• **cover chinese cabbages** with low polythene tunnels, cloches or fleece during cold weather as they can only withstand very light frost.

• **protect cauliflowers** by drawing up the outer leaves and tying them to cover the curd when frosty weather is forecast. It is the rapid thaw on mild sunny days that damages the curd rather than the cold weather itself.

looking ahead . . .

☑ WINTER Protect new seedlings of peas and broad beans with cloches or fleece.

☑ Protect crops from attack by birds, as food becomes scarce.

☑ EARLY SPRING Transplant autumn-sown spring cabbages.

transplanting spring cabbages

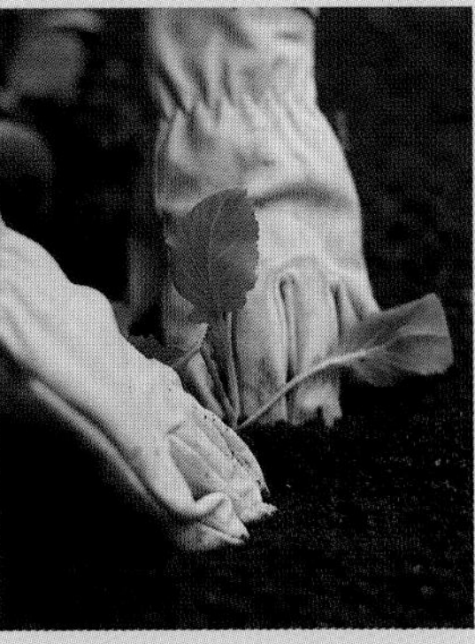

1 **Space young cabbages** 30cm (12in) apart in rows 30cm (12in) apart and plant very firmly.

2 **To test for firmness,** tug an indivdual leaf; the plant should remain bedded in the soil. If it becomes dislodged, plant again more firmly.

vegetables/2

onions, roots and salad crops

Autumn is the ideal time to clean up the vegetable garden and make a fresh start for next year. As the various crops come to the end of their production cycles, dispose of their debris as you harvest, rather than leaving remnants *in situ* where they could harbour pests and diseases. This also leaves the soil clear for digging.

onions

- **finish lifting bulb onions** as soon as possible. Leave them on the ground or in trays to allow the skins to cure in the sun, but bring them inside if persistent rain threatens and before the first frost.
- **store the onions** after the tops have died and dried off. Clean off any soil and all withered roots, twist off the old dead leaves and hang in strings or nets, or simply place on open trays in a cool, airy and frost-free place.

HARVESTING ONIONS TIP In a wet season, if the onion tops are slow to die down, bend the leaves over just above the swollen part, or neck. This speeds the dying down process.

If your soil is heavy, plant garlic cloves on top of a ridge for improved drainage.

Harvest leeks when you need them by digging them up with a garden fork.

- **plant garlic cloves now,** as they need at least two months of cold weather in order to grow well, and a longer growing season produces larger bulbs the following year.
- **plant sets** (small bulbs) of the hardier types of onion, but only if your soil is light and free draining.
- **harvest leeks** with a garden fork as you need them; they are hardy enough to stand through the coldest winter months.

root crops

There are various ways in which you can extend the harvest of your root crops. Many can be stored in or out of the ground to last through the coming months and still taste good. The method you choose will depend on the amount of excess produce you have and how long you wish to store it (see also page 340).

- **cover carrots and parsnips** in the row with loose straw, after the foliage has died down. In this way you can store them in the ground over winter, but keep a watch for mice hiding in the straw and eating the roots.
- **harvest maincrop carrots** and store in sand (see opposite).
- **earth up florence fennel** once the stem bases begin to swell and protect with cloches to extend the harvesting season.
- **dig up beetroot** as soon as the foliage starts to die down and store in clamps or boxes of moist sand (see opposite).
- **lift maincrop potatoes** as the foliage dies down. If possible, leave the tubers on the soil surface for a few hours to allow the skins to harden.

Ripen pumpkins after harvesting by leaving them on the ground, where the sun can 'cure', or harden, their skins.

- **store large quantities of potatoes** in a 'clamp' outdoors (see below). The straw and soil casing will insulate the tubers and protect them from frost.
- **lift salsify** and store in boxes of damp sand in a cool shed.
- **lift and store turnips** in clamps, or cover them in the row with loose straw where they will keep until Christmas.
- **cover scorzonera roots** in the row with loose straw and lift as required.

building a clamp

A clamp is a protective casing in which to store potatoes and other root crops outdoors during inclement weather. It is important to choose a well-drained site for a clamp, or the potatoes, or other roots, may become waterlogged and rot. Choose a north-facing position, so that the clamp has a cool, even temperature, which encourages the tubers to stay in good condition.

Spread straw over the soil, about 20cm (8in) thick, and pile the potatoes on this base. Cover the tubers thickly with more straw and top this with a 10cm (4in) layer of soil, taken from around the clamp to leave a drainage 'moat'. Pull some wisps of straw through the top to make a ventilation chimney, then pat firm the earthen sides with the back of a spade. Other roots like beetroots, carrots, celeriac and turnips can also be stored in a clamp after you have removed any leafy tops.

salads and tender crops

- **cut down tomato plants** and hang them in a cool dry shed or greenhouse to allow the remaining fruits to ripen.
- **sow seeds of winter lettuce** and winter spinach under fleece or cloches at 14-day intervals to ensure a continuity of crop.
- **cover spinach plants** with cloches or a polythene tunnel to extend the harvesting season into early winter.
- **cut and harvest marrows** before the first frosts. They will store for several months laid on open trays in a cool, frost-free place with a good flow of air.
- **harvest pumpkins** and squash and leave them outdoors to ripen their skins.
- **leave dead sweetcorn** stems in place on exposed sites to provide some wind protection for those crops that remain.

Grow young winter lettuce plants in a soil bed under the protection of a coldframe.

perennial crops

- **cut asparagus stalks** down to ground level, and burn.
- **prune jerusalem artichoke** stems to the ground and compost, or cut and lay them over the row of tubers as winter protection and to make lifting easier in frosty weather.

storing carrots in sand

1 **After harvesting the carrots,** wash off the dirt and cut off the feathery tops.

2 **Store in single layers** in boxes, alternating with layers of damp sand.

3 **Cover with a final layer** of sand and store in a cool, frost-free shed.

herbs

Although many herbs are still providing useful pickings for the kitchen, the emphasis in the herb garden now is on clearing, tidying and planting. Make sure that herbs in pots for winter use are healthy and growing strongly.

now is the season to . . .

- **continue harvesting** the leaves of basil, mint and rosemary, and the stems or roots of horseradish, liquorice and orris for immediate use or storage (see opposite).
- **pot up selected herbs,** including self-sown parsley, early in the season for winter use. Later on, bring a batch indoors for growing on a windowsill (see below).
- **extend the picking season** of outdoor herbs, such as parsley, as temperatures fall, by covering them with cloches or fleece.
- **insulate potted herbs** outdoors or bring them under cover if frost threatens. Before the first frost, move under glass tender herbs such as lemon verbena, pineapple sage and french lavender.

Bronze fennel can be cut down in autumn. Or you might leave the stems to be frost enhanced.

- **continue clearing** old growth and spent flowerheads, but leave some of the more decorative for foraging birds. Top-dress bare soil with garden compost.
- **scorch beds of mint** affected by rust with a flame gun or a small fire of straw and kindling, to kill the spores and sterilise the soil.
- **dig the site** for a new herb garden and leave rough over winter for spring planting.
- **start planting hardy perennials** such as mint and comfrey (see opposite).
- **make final sowings of chervil and lamb's lettuce** in a coldframe, spent growing bag or cool greenhouse border.
- **lift and divide large clumps of perennial herbs** such as fennel, tarragon, lemon balm and lovage (see opposite).
- **plant evergreen herbs,** such as box, curry plant or lavender, to edge beds and borders on light soils and in mild gardens; elsewhere, especially on heavy or cold ground, planting is best done in April or late summer.
- **check layers of thyme and rosemary** pegged down in early summer as well as leggy plants 'dropped' in spring or winter (see page 537), and separate the young plants if they have rooted. If not, re-peg and look again in early spring.

and if you have time . . .

- **take hardwood cuttings** of elderberries to root outdoors. Once rooted, plant them as traditional guardians of herbs and herb gardens.
- **cut back chives** as the leaves brown and start to die down.
- **sow seed of umbellifers** such as angelica, caraway and lovage in a coldframe or greenhouse.

potting up winter supplies

If you have not already potted up plants of basil, chives, parsley, small tarragons, marjoram and mint from the garden for winter use, do so as soon as you can. Keep them in the greenhouse or a lightly shaded place outdoors, sheltered from

Divide clumps of chives and pot up ready to bring them indoors for winter use.

Mint is one of the herbs that can be potted up in autumn for use during winter.

Hyssop is a semi-evergreen shrub with aromatic leaves. Its dark blue flowers are attractive

cold winds, and water them if necessary. Before moving plants indoors, check carefully for signs of aphids or other pests; a precautionary spray of insecticidal soap will help to control pest numbers.

Augment herb supplies by exploring garden centres for end-of-season bargains. Young plants of thyme, sage, rosemary and salad burnet are a good size for indoor windowsills, before planting out next spring.

dividing herbs

Every three to four years, lift and divide vigorous clump-forming herbs to control and rejuvenate their growth (see below). Do this early in autumn in mild, protected areas, otherwise wait until March or April.

herbs to divide

- comfrey • fennel
- liquorice • lovage
- saponaria • sorrel
- tansy • tarragon
- variegated lemon balm

planting hardy herbs

Plant new perennial herbs in September, while the soil is still relatively warm. Water the plants and allow them to drain before planting them in prepared sites (see page 346); large plants can be cut into two or more portions using a sharp knife.

- **dig a hole large enough** to accommodate the roots comfortably. Fork over the soil in the bottom and mix in a little potting compost.
- **loosen any tightly wound roots** before planting. Make sure that the top of the rootball is at surface level and replace the excavated soil.
- **firm gently and water** if conditions are dry.

harvesting and drying roots

Dig up roots when growth has ceased and plants are dormant. Lift them carefully with a spade or fork to avoid damage, wash off the soil, remove any top growth and cut off thin, fibrous roots.

Small roots of arnica, angelica, liquorice and marshmallow dry well whole, but larger ones, such as dandelions, horseradish, lovage, orris and sweet cicely, are better split lengthways and sliced. Dry the roots in a microwave on full power in 30-second bursts, or in a conventional oven set at 50°C (120°F), until they are light and fragile. Allow the roots to cool, then store them in airtight tins.

dividing lemon balm

1 **Cut back** old top growth close to the ground, then ease out the clump by inserting a digging fork all round the outside and levering upwards.

2 **Use a spade to chop** the clump into smaller segments. You may find it easier to split very large clumps *in situ* and then fork up the segments.

3 **Replant** only the young outer sections in fresh soil, then firm. Water in dry weather.

there is still time to . . .

- **gather seed heads** to dry for kitchen use or to sow in spring.
- **prepare new herb borders** for planting during late autumn.

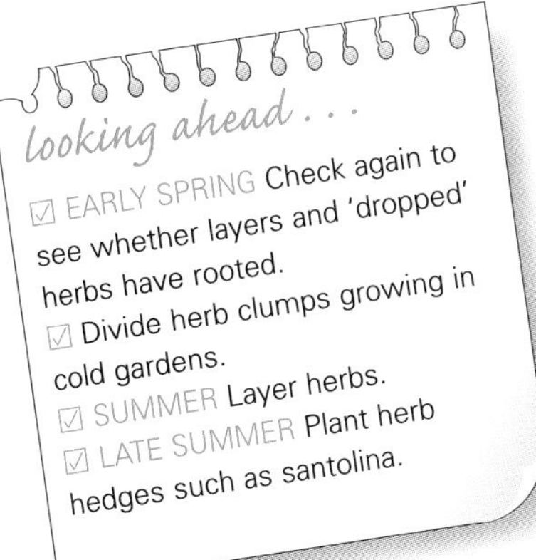

looking ahead . . .

☑ EARLY SPRING Check again to see whether layers and 'dropped' herbs have rooted.

☑ Divide herb clumps growing in cold gardens.

☑ SUMMER Layer herbs.

☑ LATE SUMMER Plant herb hedges such as santolina.

the greenhouse

With shortening days and falling temperatures, the greenhouse offers a safe haven from conditions outdoors. Make preparations now for an influx of tender plants that need to share frost-free space with rooting cuttings and fresh sowings.

now is the season to . . .

- **reduce watering** and feeding as growth slows. Stop damping down, only water in the mornings and avoid wetting foliage to prevent fungal diseases, which thrive in a damp atmosphere.
- **open ventilators on mild days,** but keep them closed during frost or fog.
- **harvest remaining crops** as they mature, and clear out exhausted plants.
- **allow permanent plants** a little more space, to improve the movement of air between them.
- **remove shade netting and paint** and wash down the outside of the glass. Shield young seedlings from very bright sunshine with sheets of newspaper or a layer of fleece.
- **pot up seedlings** of annuals and other plants sown in late summer.
- **pot up well-rooted cuttings** of tender perennials and other plants propagated in late summer.
- **sow hardy annuals,** prick out into trays and overwinter in a coldframe for early flowers next year.
- **sow sweet peas** in deep pots or paper tubes (see opposite).
- **sow winter lettuces** for spring cutting and leaf lettuce as a seedling crop for winter use (see below).
- **pot up lilies** in deep pots for flowering in their containers or for transplanting outdoors in spring.

Plump, healthy-looking lily bulbs are ready for potting up. They can be moved outdoors in spring, left in their pots or transplanted to beds.

- **make space** for tender perennials lifted from outdoors.
- **dry bulbs and tubers** ready for their winter rest (see page 403).
- **stop watering cacti** to keep them dry and safe from frost.
- **pot up some hardy perennials** such as astilbes, aquilegias, dicentras and hellebores, to flower early indoors.
- **prune climbers** under glass (see opposite).
- **check for pests,** especially whitefly and red spider mite, and spray with insecticide. It is too late to introduce biological controls, which are only effective in warm conditions.
- **pick off fading leaves,** dead flowers and any sign of decay or mould, to reduce the risks from fungal diseases.

Scrub out containers before storing or re-using them.

- **clean and sort pots.** Clean out gutters and water butts or tanks when leaves have finished falling (see page 446).
- **from November,** bring in batches of potted strawberries for forcing in a well-lit position.
- **bring potted spring bulbs** into light and warmth once they have shoots about 5cm (2in) high.
- **move potted herbs inside** for winter supplies (see page 442).
- **in late autumn insulate** the greenhouse (see page 447), and test heaters before they are needed. If you plan to install heating, decide on the kind of plants you wish to grow and the temperature regime they prefer.
- **make repairs** to greenhouse and coldframes before winter.

sowing winter lettuce

Choose a suitable variety, such as 'Arctic King', green or red 'Parella' or the greenhouse iceberg-type 'Kelly's'. Sow seeds in pots and prick out seedlings into trays. About six weeks later plant the lettuces in a greenhouse border or coldframe, or keep them in trays in a coldframe for planting outdoors under cloches in late winter.

For earlier harvest under cover, sow mixed lettuces or misticanza (a lettuce, chicory and endive mixture) in rows in a greenhouse border or deep box, and cut the leaves with

sowing sweet peas in paper tubes

1 Fold a sheet of newspaper or pages from an old telephone directory to make a long strip about 10cm (4in) wide. Roll this round a rolling pin or thick piece of dowel and fasten with sticky tape. Then slide off the paper tube.

2 Pack the tubes in a seed tray so they stand upright. Use a plastic funnel to fill them with compost and sow two seeds in each tube, about 1cm (½in) deep. Stand the tray in a little water until the top of the compost is moist.

3 When seedlings have four pairs of leaves, remove the weaker plant and pinch out the tip of the other to encourage strong sideshoots to develop.

scissors when 8–10cm (3–4in) high. Several harvests are possible during the winter.

sweet peas from seed

For top-quality blooms sow sweet peas in deep pots of moist soil-based seed compost during mid-October. Stand the pots in a coldframe or unheated greenhouse, and ventilate well in mild weather. Keep the seedlings in a coldframe until March, when they can be planted out.

You can also raise sweet peas in home-made paper tubes (see above). This method avoids any root disturbance because you keep the tubes in the tray over winter and plant them intact; the paper will disintegrate in the soil.

pruning climbers under glass

Tender climbers such as passionflowers, stephanotis and Plumbago auriculata can make a lot of new growth during summer, and you can cut this back in October or November to admit more light to the greenhouse and improve air circulation around the plant's stems. You should check the specific pruning requirements for each species, but in general you can cut out some of the older stems, thin new growth and shorten it to fit the space available, then remove any weak shoots. This should leave a well-spaced arrangement of branches, which you tie securely to their supports.

The fast-growing evergreen climber *Allamanda cathartica* is frost tender and best grown in a greenhouse. Its golden trumpet-shaped flowers appear from late summer to early autumn.

the greenhouse/2

preparing for winter

The autumn clean-up in preparation for overwintering tender plants is a good opportunity to wash pots and cloches. Used plant containers can be a source of disease if they are left in a dirty condition under the greenhouse staging. Water butts and gutters also benefit from a scrub so they do not become a source of damping-off disease and other problems. Don't forget to wash the outside of the glass – this is particularly important as light levels fall and you fix up winter insulation.

cleaning greenhouse equipment

- **examine your containers.** You can sometimes mend cracks and breaks in large clay pots with strong waterproof glue, with a tight wire hoop round the outside for reinforcement. Discard broken, cracked and brittle plastic containers. Repair wooden trays and boxes with slats, perhaps from an old fence panel or pallet.
- **scrub pots and trays** in warm soapy water with added horticultural disinfectant. Use a stiff washing-up brush to get well into the corners and under rims, where pests often hide. There is no need to scrape chalky deposits from clay pots, but do remove all traces of green algae.
- **dry containers** thoroughly before packing away according to size. Keep clay and plastic pots separate. Paint wooden trays with diluted horticultural disinfectant or a wood preservative.
- **plastic labels** are re-useable. If you soak them in a container filled with a diluted bleach solution they will be easy to scrub clean with a scourer or wire-wool pad. Rinse and spread out to dry.
- **drain water tanks** and rain butts and scrub the insides with warm soapy water and disinfectant. Rinse very well before re-filling.
- **clear leaves** from roof gutters and clean with disinfectant as a precaution against disease.

CLEANING TIP Clean and wash coldframes and cloches now, before their main season of use.

The cup-and-saucer vine (*Cobaea scandens*) grows rapidly in greenhouse conditions and needs support (left). Its greenish cream flowers gradually turn purple.

Remove leaves from gutters that supply water butts.

By late autumn you should insulate the greenhouse, even though late crops such as this cucumber 'Pepinex' are still to be harvested.

saving heat

- **insulate the greenhouse** after cleaning the glass.
- **seal gaps** to reduce draughts. Repair cracked and broken glass, and fill holes with clear silicon sealant. Make sure the door fits well, but do not make the greenhouse totally draught-proof, because some air movement is essential for reducing condensation.
- **save up to 10 per cent** of heat by insulating the floor. You can do this by laying plastic sheeting underneath paving, spreading gravel over a woven geotextile membrane, or simply covering the floor with a temporary carpet of bark.
- **group plants** that need extra warmth at one end of the greenhouse, lined with thick insulation and separated off by a curtain of fleece or polythene. Cover seedlings and small tender plants with propagator lids. Move larger tender plants onto windowsills indoors.
- **keep newspapers handy** for covering plants on cold nights.
- **draw down external roller blinds** at night to trap heat in.

insulating the greenhouse

About 80 per cent of the heat in a greenhouse is lost through the glass, but you can reduce this dramatically by insulating the inside during the coldest months, from late September or October until April.

Double glazing is the most efficient way to conserve heat, but it is expensive and only a serious option for a conservatory that is also used as a living area. A far cheaper method is to line the greenhouse inside with a skin of clear polythene sheeting, pinned to the glazing bars or attached with special plastic clips to leave a 2–3cm (1in) air gap. This can save 30 per cent of the heat lost. By using bubble plastic for lining, the saving increases to 40 per cent. Thicker materials save even more heat, but reduce light levels proportionally. An effective compromise is to use thick triple-layer bubble plastic with large bubbles for the lower half of the walls, and thinner material above bench level.

Instead of insulating the roof, install a thermal screen above head height to pull across on horizontal wires at night and on cold days. Use fleece, clear woven plastic or a similar porous material to reduce condensation, which is sometimes a problem with polythene-sheet insulation.

VENTILATING TIP Remember to trim and fix insulation materials around ventilators so that these can be opened during mild weather.

looking ahead . . .

- ☑ WINTER Bring in strawberries and more potted bulbs for forcing.
- ☑ Plant out winter lettuces under cloches.
- ☑ EARLY SPRING Plant out sweet peas and hardy annuals.
- ☑ LATE SPRING Remove insulation.

there is still time to . . .

- **pot up spring bulbs** for early flowers indoors.
- **clean the greenhouse** before it fills up with tender plants.
- **bring in tender plants** that have stood outdoors during summer before the frost comes, but first scrub the pots and spray the plants with insecticide.

autumn

plant selector

Fresh blooms of dahlias, nerines, fuchsia and autumn crocus mingle with glowing rose hips, cotoneaster berries and structural seed heads, just as leaves turn yellow, red, orange and purple. This crescendo of colour and texture at the end of the growing season provides the grand finale of the gardening year. The ingredients are easy to assemble. Choose shrubs and trees like the japanese maples and liquidambars for their autumn leaf tints. Plant clumps of swaying grasses in a tapestry of late flowering perennials. Plan surprises, like the dazzling orange lanterns of physalis, or the turquoise berries and fiery red calyces of clerodendrum. Then stand back and enjoy the show.

Physalis alkekengi var. *franchetii*

perennials

Many perennials continue to flower well into autumn. A few of these non-woody but durable plants are evergreen, but most are herbaceous, that is they die down in winter. Plant in the dormant season, preferably in autumn or early spring.

purple, blue and violet

1 Aconitum carmichaelii 'Arendsii'
Aconite, Monkshood

The glossy, dark green fingered leaves contribute to borders throughout spring and summer. In early autumn branching spires of rich blue helmeted flowers are carried on sturdy stems. All parts are highly toxic if ingested. Hardy.

Height: 1.2m (4ft) **Spread:** 35cm (14in)
Site: Partial shade, sun. Moist but well-drained soil
Use: Lightly shaded or sunny border, woodland garden
Good companions: *Aconitum* 'Spark's Variety', *Anemone* x *hybrida* 'Whirlwind', *Viburnum* x *bodnantense* 'Dawn'

2 Liriope muscari
Lilyturf

The dense clumps of evergreen grassy leaves may look a little untidy, but the spikes of knobbly violet-blue flowers, which never fully open, are eye-catching in autumn. Hardy.

Height: 30cm (12in) **Spread:** 45cm (18in)
Site: Sun, partial shade. Well-drained soil
Use: Ground cover, sunny or lightly shaded border
Good companions: *Aster* x *frikartii* 'Mönch', *Echinacea purpurea* 'White Lustre', x *Solidaster luteus* 'Lemore'

3 Penstemon 'Raven'

In late summer and autumn, this tall slender-stemmed hybrid bears numerous red-purple, broad tubular flowers with a white throat. A taller and tougher hybrid is 'Blackbird', which has black-purple, narrow tubular flowers. Good for cutting. Not fully hardy.

Height: 75cm (2ft 6in) **Spread:** 45cm (18in)
Site: Sun, partial shade. Fertile well-drained soil
Use: Sunny or lightly shaded border
Good companions: *Aster amellus* 'Veilchenkönigin', *Penstemon* 'Evelyn', *Sedum* 'Herbstfreude'

4 Tricyrtis formosana
Toad lily

Wiry stems set with glossy, near-oval leaves carry intriguing upturned waxy flowers. These are pale

mauve-purple heavily speckled with red-purple. Hardy.
Height: 75cm (2ft 6in) **Spread:** 45cm (18in)
Site: Partial shade. Humus-rich and moist but well-drained soil
Use: Shaded border, woodland garden
Good companions: *Asplenium scolopendrium*, *Helleborus foetidus* Wesker Flisk Group, *Hosta sieboldiana* var. *elegans*

pink and mauve

5 Anemone x hybrida 'September Charm'
Japanese anemone
Branched wiry stems rise from a handsome base of dark divided leaves to carry upward-facing flowers. These are purple on the outside with pink inner petals around yellow stamens. Distinguished and long flowering. Hardy.
Height: 75cm (2ft 6in) **Spread:** 45cm (18in)
Site: Sun, partial shade. Humus-rich and moist but well-drained soil
Use: Sunny or lightly shaded border
Good companions: *Fuchsia magellanica* 'Versicolor', *Hydrangea* 'Preziosa', *Viburnum* x *bodnantense* 'Dawn'

6 Chrysanthemum 'Emperor of China'
Rubellum Group chrysanthemum
In autumn the foliage of this hybrid is suffused with crimson as the flowering season reaches its climax. The quilled petal-like ray-florets are silvery pink but with a glow of deep crimson in the centre of the flowerhead. Hardy.
Height: 1.2m (4ft) **Spread:** 60cm (2ft)
Site: Sun. Well-drained soil
Use: Sunny border
Good companions: *Anaphalis triplinervis* 'Sommerschnee', *Fuchsia magellanica* 'Versicolor', *Geranium wallichianum* 'Buxton's Variety'

7 Gaura lindheimeri 'Siskiyou Pink'
At first this gives the impression of being a lightweight perennial, but over weeks in late summer and autumn graceful stems carry clouds of small pink flowers. Hardy.
Height and spread: 60cm (2ft)
Site: Sun. Well-drained soil
Use: Gravel garden, sunny border
Good companions: *Allium hollandicum* 'Purple Sensation', *Eryngium* x *tripartitum*, *Erysimum* 'Bowles' Mauve'

8 Geranium sanguineum
Bloody cranesbill
The species and its cultivars make tidy clumps of finely cut leaves that are brightened throughout summer and autumn by an almost unflagging succession of cupped flowers. The usual colour is magenta-pink; 'Album' is pure white; and var. *striatum* is pale pink with dark veining. Hardy.
Height: 25cm (10in) **Spread:** 30cm (12in)
Site: Sun, partial shade. Well-drained soil
Use: Front of sunny or lightly shaded border, raised bed, rock garden
Good companions: *Gladiolus* 'The Bride', *Lavandula angustifolia* 'Hidcote', *Origanum laevigatum* 'Herrenhausen'

9 Penstemon 'Stapleford Gem'
From midsummer to early autumn, sometimes later, the erect stems of this large-leaved hybrid carry outward-facing, lipped tubular flowers. Their colour is a subtle blend of mauve-blue and pink, with purple lines in the pale throat. Hardy.
Height: 60cm (2ft) **Spread:** 45cm (18in)
Site: Sun, partial shade. Well-drained soil
Use: Sunny or lightly shaded border
Good companions: *Aster* x *frikartii* 'Mönch', *Caryopteris* x *clandonensis* 'Heavenly Blue', *Penstemon* 'Evelyn'

10 Physostegia virginiana 'Vivid'
False dragonhead, Obedient plant
The pink or white tubular flowers cluster in short spikes on square stems. They are 'obedient' in that, if moved, they stay in their new position. The plant has running roots and makes dense clumps. The flowers of this cultivar are bright purple-pink. Good as a cut flower. Hardy.
Height: 45cm (18in) **Spread:** 30cm (12in)
Site: Sun, partial shade. Moist, well-drained soil
Use: Sunny or lightly shaded border
Good companions: *Anemone* x *hybrida* 'Honorine Jobert', *Galtonia candicans*, *Phlox paniculata*

11 Sanguisorba obtusa
Burnet, Japanese burnet
In late summer and early autumn the grey-green leaves, which are composed of numerous leaflets, are topped by fluffy 'bottlebrush' spikes of rich mauve-pink flowers. Hardy.
Height and spread: 60cm (2ft)
Site: Sun, partial shade. Moist, well-drained soil
Use: Sunny or lightly shaded border
Good companions: *Astilbe* x *arendsii* 'Irrlicht', *Veronica gentianoides*, *Viola cornuta* Alba Group

12 Schizostylis coccinea 'Sunrise'
Kaffir lily
The grassy clumps of this rhizomatous perennial are almost evergreen. In autumn and early winter slender spires thrust up through the blade-like leaves bearing salmon-pink cup-shaped flowers. 'Major' has bright red flowers. Good as a cut flower. Not fully hardy.
Height: 60cm (2ft) **Spread:** 30cm (12in)
Site: Sun. Moist but well-drained soil
Use: Sunny border
Good companions: *Anemone* x *hybrida* 'Honorine Jobert', *Aster novi-belgii* 'Heinz Richard', *Diascia rigescens*

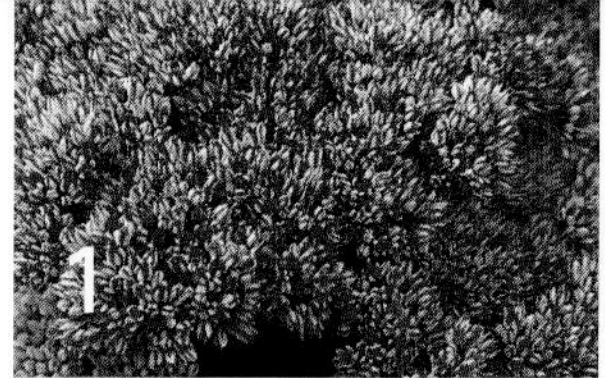

pink and mauve (continued)

1 Sedum 'Herbstfreude'
Ice plant

The clump of fleshy grey-green leaves is attractive long before the small starry flowers, which are clustered in flat heads, open in early autumn. These are pink at first then darken to orange-red. Red-brown seed heads follow and add interesting texture to the winter garden. Hardy.

Height and spread: 60cm (2ft)
Site: Sun. Well-drained soil
Use: Gravel garden, sunny border
Good companions: *Caryopteris* x *clandonensis* 'Heavenly Blue', *Festuca glauca* 'Elijah Blue', *Stipa gigantea*

2 Sedum 'Vera Jameson'
Stonecrop

In late summer and early autumn arching purple stems, clothed with fleshy purple-pink leaves, carry heads of pink starry flowers. Hardy.

Height: 25cm (10in) **Spread:** 45cm (18in)
Site: Sun. Well-drained soil
Use: Front of sunny border, raised bed
Good companions: *Eryngium alpinum*, *Gaura lindheimeri* 'Siskiyou Pink', *Knautia macedonica*

bronze and maroon

3 Galax urceolata
Wandflower

In autumn and winter the toothed, nearly heart-shaped evergreen leaves are burnished bronze. Slender spires of tiny white flowers are borne in late spring or early summer. Hardy.

Height: 30cm (12in) **Spread:** 1m (3ft)
Site: Partial shade. Lime-free, humus-rich, moist but well-drained soil
Use: Ground cover, lightly shaded border, woodland garden
Good companions: *Disanthus cercidifolius*, *Hamamelis* x *intermedia* 'Pallida', *Rhododendron luteum*

4 Ophiopogon planiscapus 'Nigrescens'
Black lilyturf

This produces creeping clumps of near-black grassy leaves, which are usually relieved by a hint of green at the base. Shiny black berries, which follow on from tiny mauve flowers, mature in autumn and last into winter. Hardy.

Height: 20cm (8in) **Spread:** 30cm (12in)
Site: Sun, partial shade. Humus-rich, moist but well-drained soil
Use: Front of border
Good companions: *Galanthus elwesii*, *Saxifraga fortunei*, *Tiarella wherryi*

5 Panicum virgatum 'Rubrum'
Switch grass

The ribbon-like leaves of this deciduous perennial grass turn from green to light yellow then bronze in autumn, coinciding with airy sprays of tiny similarly coloured seed heads. Good for cutting. Hardy.

Height: 1.2m (4ft) **Spread:** 75cm (2ft 6in)
Site: Sun. Well-drained soil
Use: Sunny border
Good companions: *Berberis thungergii* f. *atropurpurea*, *Eryngium alpinum*, *Sedum* 'Herbstfreude'

red and russet

6 Canna 'Assaut'
Indian shot plant

The hybrid cannas are impressive foliage plants with large paddle-like leaves, which in late summer and autumn are topped by spikes of brightly coloured broad-petalled flowers. In the case of 'Assaut' the leaves are brown-purple and the flowers intense orange-scarlet. Half hardy.

General care: Plant out in early summer. In frost-prone areas, lift the rhizomatous perennials before the first frost, remove leaves and stems and store in frost-free conditions in boxes of barely moist compost. Plant while dormant in spring.
Height: 2m (6ft) **Spread:** 60cm (2ft)
Site: Sun. Fertile, moist soil
Use: Formal bedding, moist border
Good companions: *Lobelia* 'Queen Victoria', *Musa basjoo*, *Ricinus communis* 'Impala'

7 Imperata cylindrica 'Rubra'

In a hot summer this grass produces spikes of silvery flowers, but its main ornamental value is the red stain that extends down from the tips of the erect leaf blades in summer and early autumn. Not fully hardy.

Height: 50cm (20in) **Spread:** 30cm (12in)
Site: Sun, partial shade. Moist, well-drained soil
Use: Sunny or lightly shaded border
Good companions: *Ceratostigma willmottianum*, *Geranium sanguineum*, *Phlox paniculata* 'Fujiyama'

8 Iris foetidissima
Gladwyn iris, Stinking iris

It is only when the evergreen strap-shaped leaves are crushed that this plant gives off an unpleasant smell. The beardless flowers, mauve with

touches of yellow, do not count for much in early summer, but the seedpods split in autumn to show their bright orange contents. Var. *citrina* flowers freely and has large pods. All parts can be harmful if ingested. Good for cutting. Hardy.
Height: 60cm (2ft) **Spread:** 45cm (18in)
Site: Sun, shade. Well-drained, even poor, soil
Use: Shady border, underplanting for trees and shrubs, wild garden, woodland
Good companions: *Euphorbia characias* subsp. *wulfenii, Pachysandra terminalis, Vinca minor*

9 Kniphofia triangularis
Red hot poker, Torch lily

From a clump of narrow grassy leaves rise slender wiry stems that terminate in a cluster of narrow tubular flowers of intense scarlet paling to yellow at the mouth.
Height: 75cm (2ft 6in) **Spread:** 45cm (18in)
Site: Sun, partial shade. Moist, well-drained soil
Use: Sunny or lightly shaded border
Good companions: *Agapanthus* 'Lilliput', *Galtonia candicans, Schizostylis coccinea* 'Sunrise'

yellow and orange

10 Canna 'King Midas'
Indian shot plant

This hybrid has erect, dark green paddle-like leaves and in late summer and early autumn orange-marked, rich yellow flowers. Half hardy.
General care: Plant out in early summer. In frost-prone areas, lift the rhizomatous perennials before the first frost, remove leaves and stems and store in frost-free conditions in boxes of barely moist compost. Plant while dormant in spring (see Late Spring).
Height: 2m (6ft) **Spread:** 60cm (2ft)
Site: Sun. Fertile, moist soil
Use: Formal bedding, moist border
Good companions: *Canna* 'Assaut', *Dahlia* 'Bishop of Llandaff', *Dahlia* 'Zorro'

11 Chrysanthemum 'Mary Stoker'
Rubellum Group chrysanthemum

From late summer this bushy, woody-based clump-forming perennial bears sprays of long-lasting flowerheads. The orange-yellow, petal-like ray-florets radiate from a boss that is green at first then yellow. Good for cutting. Hardy.
Height: 75cm (2ft 6in) **Spread:** 60cm (2ft)
Site: Sun. Well-drained soil
Use: Sunny border
Good companions: *Anemone* x *hybrida* 'September Charm', *Aster ericoides* 'Pink Cloud', *Penstemon* 'Stapleford Gem'

12 Helenium 'Sonnenwunder'
Helen's flower

Branching stems carry clear yellow flowerheads with yellow-brown centres. The sprays are long lasting and good for cutting. Hardy.
Height: 1.5m (5ft) **Spread:** 60cm (2ft)
Site: Sun. Fertile and moist but well-drained soil
Use: Sunny border
Good companions: *Helenium* 'Moerheim Beauty', *Miscanthus sinensis* 'Silberfeder', *Rudbeckia fulgida* var. *deamii*

yellow and orange (continued)

1 Helianthus 'Lemon Queen'
Sunflower

This perennial has running roots and needs staking, but for several weeks from late summer the branched stems bear numerous lemon-yellow daisy-like flowerheads. Good for cutting. Hardy.
Height: 2m (6ft) **Spread:** 1.2m (4ft)
Site: Sun. Moist but well-drained soil
Use: Back of sunny border
Good companions: *Aster amellus* 'Veilchenkönigin', *Echinacea purpurea* 'White Lustre', *Helenium* 'Sonnenwunder'

2 Kniphofia 'Prince Igor'
Red hot poker, Torch lily

Majestic, incandescent red hot poker with erect stems set with red-orange tubular flowers, making giant 'torches' that last from early to mid-autumn. Hardy.
Height: 2m (6ft) **Spread:** 1m (3ft)
Site: Sun. Moist but well-drained soil
Use: Sunny border
Good companions: *Agapanthus* 'Blue Giant', *Cortaderia selloana* 'Sunningdale Silver', *Miscanthus sinensis* 'Silberfeder'

3 Molinia caerulea subsp. arundinacea 'Windspiel'
Purple moor grass

This deciduous grass forms a clump of flat leaves through which rise erect stems bearing purple flowerheads. By autumn these are full of tiny seeds and the whole plant is honey tinted.
Height: 1.8m (6ft) **Spread:** 50cm (20in)
Site: Sun, partial shade. Moist but well-drained soil, preferably acid
Use: Sunny or lightly shaded border, waterside, woodland garden
Good companions: *Alchemilla mollis*, *Epimedium* x *versicolor* 'Sulphureum', *Miscanthus sinensis* 'Zebrinus'

4 Physalis alkekengi var. franchetii
Chinese lantern, Japanese lantern

A rather untidy plant with running roots and insignificant flowers, but the orange papery 'lanterns' that enclose inedible scarlet berries are brightly decorative and suitable for drying. All parts can cause stomach upset if ingested and contact can cause skin reactions. Hardy.
Height: 60cm (2ft) **Spread:** 1m (3ft)
Site: Sun, partial shade. Well-drained soil
Use: Sunny or lightly shaded border
Good companions: *Cotoneaster conspicuus* 'Decorus', *Helleborus argutifolius*, *Rosa glauca*

5 Rudbeckia fulgida var. deamii
Black-eyed susan

Bushy perennial with pointed leaves and hairy stems that branch to carry numerous daisy-like flowerheads. The orange-yellow, petal-like ray-florets radiate from the brown-black eye. Hardy.
Height: 75cm (2ft 6in) **Spread:** 45cm (18in)
Site: Sun, partial shade. Moist but well-drained soil
Use: Sunny or lightly shaded border, wild garden
Good companions: *Chrysanthemum* 'Mary Stoker', *Helenium* 'Moerheim Beauty', *Miscanthus sinensis* 'Silberfeder'

6 Rudbeckia 'Herbstsonne'
Coneflower

In late summer and early autumn, tall leafy branching stems carry masses of bright yellow daisy-like flowers. The petal-like ray-florets droop to form a wide skirt around the central green cone. Excellent for cutting. Hardy.
Height: 2m (6ft) **Spread:** 1m (3ft)
Site: Sun, partial shade. Moist, well-drained soil
Use: Back of border
Good companions: *Kniphofia* 'Prince Igor', *Molinia caerulea* subsp. *arundinacea* 'Windspiel', *Rudbeckia fulgida* var. *deamii*

6

5

1

3

2

4

cream and white

7 Anaphalis margaritacea
Pearl everlasting

In late summer and early autumn, spreading clumps of dull green leaves, woolly and white underneath, are topped by clusters of long-lasting, white daisy-like flowers. The leaves of the shorter var. *yedoensis* are outlined in white. Hardy.
Height and spread: 60cm (2ft)
Site: Sun, partial shade. Moist, well-drained soil

Use: Ground cover, sunny or lightly shaded border
Good companions: *Anemone hupehensis* 'Hadspen Abundance', *Anemone* x *hybrida* 'Honorine Jobert', *Hydrangea macrophylla* 'Blue Wave'

8 Anemone x hybrida 'Honorine Jobert'

Japanese anemone

A star of the autumn garden, but can be invasive. Wiry branching stems rise above lobed dark leaves and bear a long succession of white flowers with yellow stamens. Hardy.
Height: 1.2m (4ft) **Spread:** Indefinite
Site: Sun, partial shade. Humus-rich and moist but well-drained soil
Use: Sunny or lightly shaded border
Good companions: *Anemone hupensis* 'Hadspen Abundance', *Anemone* x *hybrida* 'September Charm', *Aster novi-belgii* 'Heinz Richard'

9 Cimicifuga simplex Atropurpurea Group [syn. Actaea]

Bugbane, Cohosh

In early to mid-autumn sinuous slender stems carry 'bottlebrushes' of small, sweetly scented cream flowers. The stems and deeply cut leaves develop their rich purple best in full sun. Hardy.
Height: 1.5m (5ft) **Spread:** 60cm (2ft)
Site: Sun, partial shade. Humus-rich, moist soil
Use: Moist border
Good companions: *Anemone* x *hybrida* 'Honorine Jobert', *Astilbe* 'Professor van der Wielen', *Astrantia major* 'Claret'

10 Cortaderia selloana

Pampas grass

This evergreen grass makes a substantial clump of arching leaves. In late summer stout stems carry long-lasting, silky cream plumes, which are good for drying. 'Aureolineata' has yellow-margined leaves, which become more pronounced as they age. Hardy.
Height: 2.2m (7ft) **Spread:** 1.5m (5ft)
Site: Sun. Well-drained soil
Use: Specimen clump, sunny border
Good companions: *Buddleja davidii* 'Black Knight', *Lavandula* x *intermedia* Dutch Group, *Verbena bonariensis*

11 Echinacea purpurea 'White Lustre'

Coneflower

Stiff upright plant with branching stems that carry flowerheads nearly 15cm (6in) across. Each flower consists of a glistening orange-brown central cone and drooping, greenish white, petal-like ray-florets. Other cultivars have purple or crimson ray-florets. Hardy.
Height: 1m (3ft) **Spread:** 45cm (18in)
Site: Sun. Humus-rich, well-drained soil
Use: Sunny border
Good companions: *Centaurea hypoleuca* 'John Coutts', *Deschampsia cespitosa* 'Goldschleier', *Liatris spicata*

12 Saxifraga fortunei

Saxifrage

Deciduous or semi-evergreen species with lobed and toothed round leaves that are deep green on the surface, red on the underside. In late autumn branching stems suspend showers of white starry flowers above the foliage. Each flower has one petal longer than the others. Hardy.
Height and spread: 35cm (14in)
Site: Partial, full shade. Humus-rich and moist but well-drained soil
Use: Shady border
Good companions: *Alchemilla mollis*, *Helleborus foetidus* Wester Flisk Group, *Sarcococca hookeriana* var. *digyna*

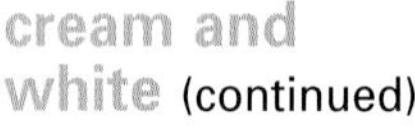

cream and white (continued)

1 Scabiosa caucasica 'Miss Willmott'

Pincushion flower, Scabious

Like its blue counterparts, this scabious flowers over many weeks in late summer and early autumn. The pincushion effect referred to in its common name is produced by protruding styles at the centre of the greenish white to cream flowerheads. Excellent for cutting. Hardy.

Height: 1m (3ft) **Spread:** 50cm (20in)
Site: Sun. Well-drained soil. Good on lime
Use: Sunny border, wild garden
Good companions: *Eryngium alpinum, Lavandula angustifolia* 'Hidcote', *Verbascum* 'Helen Johnson'

green

2 Euphorbia schillingii

Milkweed, Spurge

This spurge has attractive foliage, with a central white vein highlighting the dark green of the leaves. Lime-yellow bracts, which remain ornamental from mid-summer through to mid-autumn, cup the relatively insignificant but specialised flowers. All parts of this plant can be harmful if ingested and contact with the sap can cause allergic skin reactions. Hardy.

Height: 1m (3ft) **Spread:** 30cm (12in)
Site: Partial shade, sun. Moist but well-drained soil
Use: Lightly shaded or sunny border, woodland garden
Good companions: *Aconitum* 'Ivorine', *Epimedium* x *versicolor* 'Sulphureum', *Helleborus argutifolius*

3 Euphorbia seguieriana subsp. niciciana

Milkweed, Spurge

For many weeks in late summer and early autumn this spurge adds a fresh note with heads of lime-green flowers over blue-grey leaves. All parts can be harmful if ingested and contact with the sap can cause skin reactions. Hardy.

Height: 50cm (20in) **Spread:** 45cm (18in)
Site: Sun. Well-drained soil
Use: Gravel garden, sunny border
Good companions: *Bergenia* 'Ballawley', *Stipa gigantea, Verbascum* Cotswold Group 'Gainsborough'

4 Kniphofia 'Green Jade'

In late summer and early autumn, stout stems rise up through the arching leaves of this evergreen perennial to carry a 'torch' of green buds. When fully open, the tubular flowers are white. Hardy.

Height: 1.2m (4ft)
Spread: 60cm (2ft)
Site: Sun, partial shade. Humus-rich and moist but well-drained soil
Use: Sunny or lightly shaded border
Good companions: *Helenium* 'Sonnenwunder', *Pennisetum alopecuroides* 'Hameln', *Rudbeckia* 'Herbstonne'

5 Pachysandra terminalis

This evergreen perennial makes a dense cover of glossy leaves arranged in neat rosettes. In autumn, small inedible white fruits follow insignificant but scented white flowers, borne in spring. Tolerant of dry shade. Hardy.

Height: 20cm (8in) **Spread:** Indefinite
Site: Shade, sun. Moist but well-drained soil
Use: Ground cover, woodland garden
Good companions: *Geranium macrorrhizum, Helleborus foetidus, Lunaria annua*

6 Pennisetum alopecuroides 'Hameln'

Fountain grass

This evergreen grass makes a dense clump of linear arching leaves. It is transformed in autumn when fuzzy caterpillar-like flowerheads weigh down their thin stems. The flowerheads are green at first then pale brown. Not fully hardy.

Height: 1m (3ft) **Spread:** 1.2m (4ft)
Site: Sun. Moist but well-drained soil
Use: Sunny border
Good companions: *Cosmos atrosanguineus, Kniphofia* 'Percy's Pride', *Sanguisorba obtusa*

asters

The asters include some of the most useful perennials for autumn borders as they flower profusely in a wide range of colours, often yellow centred. The daisy-like blooms are long lasting on the plant or cut. All of the following are hardy but vary in their requirements.

1 **Aster amellus 'King George'**
This makes a rather dull clump of narrow hairy leaves in spring and summer, but in autumn it bears large violet-purple flowerheads.
Height: 45cm (18in) **Spread:** 40cm (16in)
Site: Sun. Well-drained soil. Good on lime
Good companions: *Eryngium alpinum*, *Lavandula angustifolia* 'Hidcote', *Verbascum* 'Helen Johnson'

2 **Aster novae-angliae 'Andenken an Alma Pötschke'**
New England aster
In late summer and the first half of autumn sprays of bright reddish pink flowerheads top a stiff clump of foliage. Other New England asters are mainly mauve, pink or white.
Height: 1m (3ft) **Spread:** 75cm (2ft 6in)
Site: Sun, partial shade. Moist but well-drained soil
Good companions: *Gaura lindheimeri* 'Siskiyou Pink', *Penstemon* 'Blackbird', *Sedum spectabile* 'Brilliant'

3 **Aster lateriflorus 'Horizontalis'**
In mid-autumn this stiff-stemmed bushy plant bears masses of white starry flowerheads with fluffy pink centres.
Height: 60cm (2ft) **Spread:** 30cm (12in)
Site: Partial shade. Moist but well-drained soil
Good companions: *Aconitum carmichaelii* 'Arendsii', *Anemone* x *hybrida* 'Whirlwind', *Geranium* x *magnificum*

4 **Aster ericoides 'Pink Cloud'**
Over several weeks in autumn this bushy perennial with needle-like leaves produces a mass of small, pale pink flowers.
Height: 1m (3ft) **Spread:** 30cm (12in)
Site: Sun. Well-drained soil
Good companions: *Bergenia* 'Ballawley', *Geranium* 'Johnson's Blue', *Verbena bonariensis*

5 **Aster pringlei 'Monte Cassino'**
Erect branching stems, which are set with tiny narrow leaves, are liberally sprinkled with white starry flowerheads throughout autumn.
Height: 1m (3ft) **Spread:** 30cm (12in)
Site: Partial shade, sun. Moist but well-drained soil
Good companions: *Anaphalis triplinervis* 'Sommerschnee', *Phlox paniculata* 'Fujiyama', *Tradescantia* Andersoniana Group 'Osprey'

6 **Aster novi-belgii 'Kristina'**
Michaelmas daisy, New York aster
In late summer and early autumn the dense 'cushion' of dark green leaves is almost hidden by white semi-double flowerheads.
Height: 30cm (12in) **Spread:** 45cm (18in)
Site: Sun, partial shade. Fertile and moist but well-drained soil
Good companions: *Anemone* x *hybrida* 'September Charm', *Aster novi-belgii* 'Heinz Richard', *Phlox paniculata* 'Eventide'

7 **Aster amellus 'Veilchenkönigen'**
This makes a neater plant than 'King George', with smaller flowerheads of intense violet carried on stiff stems.
Height: 40cm (16in) **Spread:** 30cm (12in)
Site: Sun. Well-drained soil. Good on lime
Good companions: *Aster ericoides* 'Pink Cloud', *Delphinium* Belladonna Group 'Cliveden Beauty', *Echinacea purpurea* 'White Lustre'

annuals & biennials

These short-lived plants often give good value over many weeks. If deadheaded regularly in summer, many continue to flower and brighten beds and borders in autumn until stopped by frosts.

purple, blue and violet

1 Anagallis monellii
Blue pimpernel

Evergreen perennial commonly grown as an annual raised from cuttings. In summer and early autumn, low branching stems clothed with narrow pointed leaves carry small saucer-shaped flowers of intense blue. Not fully hardy.
General care: Buy young plants in early summer or take cuttings between late spring and early summer and overwinter under glass.
Height: 15cm (6in) **Spread:** 40cm (16in)
Site: Sun. Moist but well-drained soil
Compost: Soil-based (John Innes No. 2) or soil-less
Use: Container, front of sunny bed or border
Good companions: *Cosmos bipinnatus* 'Sea Shells', *Heliotropium arborescens* 'Marine', *Nicotiana* Domino Series

2 Convolvulus tricolor 'Royal Ensign'
Bushy then sprawling short-lived perennial grown as an annual. The funnel-shaped flowers, borne from midsummer to early autumn, are vivid deep blue with a yellow-and-white centre. Hardy.
General care: Sow seed *in situ* or in pots in mid-spring.
Height: 30cm (12in) **Spread:** 35cm (14in)
Site: Sun. Well-drained soil
Compost: Soil-based (John Innes No. 1)
Use: Container, front of sunny bed or border
Good companions: *Cleome hassleriana* 'Rose Queen', *Delphinium grandiflorum* 'Blue Butterfly', *Salvia viridis* 'Oxford Blue'

3 Heliotropium arborescens 'Marine'
Cherry pie, Heliotrope

Short-lived shrub usually grown as an annual. This compact cultivar has dark, deeply veined leaves and large heads of small, violet-blue flowers during summer and early autumn. Half hardy.
General care: Sow seed under glass at 16–18°C (61–64°F) in mid-spring.
Height: 45cm (18in) **Spread:** 35cm (14in)
Site: Sun. Moist but well-drained soil
Compost: Soil-based (John Innes No. 3) or soil-less
Use: Container, formal bedding, sunny border
Good companions: *Lobelia erinus* 'Crystal Palace', *Verbena* 'Imagination', *Viola* x *wittrockiana* 'Jolly Joker'

4 Isotoma axillaris
Perennial usually grown as an annual. It forms a mound of dark green, slender narrow-lobed leaves and bears a profusion of scented, blue starry flowers in summer and autumn. Tender.
General care: Sow seed under glass at 16–18°C (61–64°F) in mid-spring.
Height and spread: 30cm (12in)
Site: Sun, partial shade. Well-drained soil
Compost: Soil-based (John Innes No. 2)
Use: Container, sunny bed or border
Good companions: *Pelargonium* 'Bird Dancer', *Petunia* Fantasy Series, *Scaevola aemula* 'Blue Wonder'

5 Pennisetum villosum
Feathertop

Deciduous perennial grass usually grown as an annual. In late summer and early autumn soft 'bottlebrush' plumes weigh down arching stems above the loose tuft of narrow leaf blades. The plumes are greenish white at first but age to purple. Not fully hardy.
General care: Sow seed under glass at 13–18°C (55–64°C) in early spring.
Height and spread: 60cm (2ft)
Site: Sun. Well-drained soil
Use: Sunny bed or border
Good companions: *Eryngium* x *tripartitum*, *Gaura lindheimeri*, *Sedum* 'Herbstfreude'

6 Salvia farinacea 'Victoria'
Mealy sage

Short-lived perennial grown as an annual. In summer and autumn mealy stems carry spikes of small flowers clear of glossy green foliage. Stems and flowers are intense purple-blue. Half hardy.
General care: Sow seed under glass at 16–18°C (61–64°F) in mid-spring.
Height: 60cm (2ft) **Spread:** 30cm (12in)
Site: Sun. Moist but well-drained soil
Compost: Soil-based (John Innes No. 2) or soil-less
Use: Container, sunny bed or border
Good companions: *Cosmos bipinnatus* 'Sea Shells', *Lobelia erinus* 'Crystal Palace', *Verbena* 'Imagination'

7 Verbena rigida
Perennial with toothed lance-shaped leaves grown as an annual as it is too tender to survive winters except in favoured coastal gardens. Tight clusters of fragrant purple-violet flowers are borne in summer and early autumn. Not fully hardy.
General care: Sow seed at 18–20°C (64–68°F) under glass in early spring.
Height: 50cm (20in) **Spread:** 40cm (16in)
Site: Sun. Moist but well-drained soil
Use: Sunny border
Good companions: *Cosmos bipinnatus* Sensation Series, *Dahlia* 'Porcelain', *Nicotiana* Domino Series

2

3

4

1

5

6

pink and mauve

8 Begonia semperflorens Organdy Series
Wax begonia

Fibrous-rooted perennial usually grown as a bedding annual. It has glossy, dark green or bronze foliage and sprays of pink, red or white flowers from early summer to mid-autumn. Tender.

General care: Sow seed under glass at 16°C (61°F) in late winter or early spring or take cuttings from overwintered plants in spring.

Height and spread: 15cm (6in)

Site: Sun. Well-drained soil

Compost: Soil-based (John Innes No. 2) or soil-less

Use: Container, formal bedding

Good companions: *Bassia scoparia* f. *tricophylla*, *Brachyscome iberidifolia* Splendour Series, *Dianthus chinensis* Baby Doll Series

9 Callistephus chinensis Princess Series
China aster

Numerous dwarf and taller cultivars of china aster flower in late summer and autumn. The semi-double flowerheads of the tall Princess Series, in a range of colours that includes shades of pink, red, purple and white, have quilled and incurved petal-like ray-florets. Half hardy.

General care: Sow seed under glass at 16°C (61°F) in early spring or *in situ* in mid-spring.

Height: 60cm (2ft) **Spread:** 30cm (12in)

Site: Sun. Moist, well-drained soil. Good on lime

Use: Sunny border, formal bedding

Good companions: *Dahlia* 'Porcelain', *Fuchsia* 'Leonora', *Heliotropium arborescens* 'Marine'

10 Cosmos bipinnatus 'Sea Shells'
Erect annual with feathery foliage. Tall wiry stems support large starry flowerheads, the florets of which are rolled into tubes. The colour range includes pink, red and white. Half hardy.

General care: Sow seed under glass in mid-spring or *in situ* in late spring.

Height: 1m (3ft) **Spread:** 45cm (18in)

Site: Sun. Moist but well-drained soil

Use: Sunny border, formal bedding

Good companions: *Alcea rosea* 'Nigra', *Clarkia amoena* Satin Series, *Nicotiana* Domino Series

11 Lavatera trimestris 'Silver Cup'
Mallow

Erect and bushy annual with somewhat coarse lobed leaves. Pink funnel-shaped flowers, which are heavily veined in a darker shade, are borne in profusion during summer and early autumn. Suitable for cutting. Hardy.

General care: Sow seed *in situ* in early autumn or mid-spring.

Height: 75cm (2ft 6in) **Spread:** 40cm (16in)

Site: Sun. Well-drained soil

Use: Formal bedding, sunny bed or border

Good companions: *Centaurea cyanus*, *Consolida ajacis* Giant Imperial Series, *Xeranthemum annuum*

12 Petunia 'Purple Wave'
Multiflora petunia

The multiflora petunias are bushy hybrid perennials grown as annuals. They produce trumpet-shaped flowers, up to 5cm (2in) across, in great profusion in summer and early autumn. Those of 'Purple Wave' are an intense magenta. Half hardy.

General care: Sow seed under glass at 13–18°C (55–64°F) in early spring.

Height: 45cm (18in) **Spread:** 75cm (2ft 6in)

Site: Sun. Well-drained soil

Compost: Soil-based (John Innes No. 1)

Use: Container, formal bedding, front of sunny border

Good companions: *Brachyscome iberidifolia* Splendour Series, *Pelargonium* 'L'Elégante', *Verbena* 'Silver Anne'

7

8

9

10

11

12

pink and mauve (continued)

1 Xeranthemum annuum

Annual with silver-green leaves and wiry upright branching stems that carry papery, single or double daisy-like flowerheads through summer and early autumn in shades of pink, red, purple or white. Suitable for cutting and drying. Half hardy.

General care: Sow seed under glass at 16°C (61°F) in early spring.

Height: 60cm (2ft) **Spread:** 35cm (14in)

Site: Sun. Well-drained soil

Use: Sunny bed or border

Good companions: *Brachyscome iberidifolia* Splendour Series, *Dianthus chinensis* Baby Doll Series, *Nigella damascena* 'Miss Jekyll'

red and russet

2 Arctotis x hybrida 'Flame'

African daisy

The hybrid African daisies are perennials usually grown as annuals, many easily raised from seed. They have felted silver-green leaves and produce flowerheads in a wide range of colours from mid-summer to early autumn. 'Flame' is raised annually from cuttings and bears a profusion of vivid orange-red flowers. Tender.

General care: Buy plants in early summer or take cuttings in summer and overwinter young plants under glass.

Height: 45cm (18in) **Spread:** 30cm (12in)

Site: Sun. Moist but light, well-drained soil

Compost: Soil-based (John Innes No. 2) with added grit

Use: Container, formal bedding, front of border

Good companions: *Ageratum houstonianum*, *Layia platiglossa*, *Viola* x *wittrockiana* 'Jolly Joker'

3 Bassia scoparia f. tricophylla

Burning bush, Summer cypress

Fast-growing annual that forms a cone-shaped bush packed with narrow leaves. In summer these are light green but in late summer or autumn they turn deep purplish red. The green flowers are insignificant. Half hardy.

General care: Sow seed under glass at 16°C (61°F) in early to mid-spring or *in situ* in late spring.

Height: 75cm (2ft 6in) **Spread:** 45cm (18in)

Site: Sun. Well-drained soil

Compost: Soil-based (John Innes No. 2)

Use: Container, formal bedding, sunny border

Good companions: *Antirrhinum* Sonnet Series, *Cleome hassleriana* 'Rose Queen', *Nigella damascena* 'Miss Jekyll'

4 Dahlia 'Figaro Red'

Dwarf bedding dahlia

Low-growing dahlia raised annually from seed with a long flowering season if regularly deadheaded. The Figaro Series includes plants with double or semi-double flowerheads in a range of colours. Half hardy.

General care: Sow seed under glass at 16°C (61°F) in early spring. Deadhead regularly.

Height and spread: 40cm (16in)

Site: Sun. Fertile, humus-rich, well-drained soil

Compost: Soil-based (John Innes No. 2) or soil-less

Use: Container, formal bedding

Good companions: *Amaranthus caudatus* 'Viridis', *Canna* 'Assaut', *Fuchsia* 'Lady Thumb'

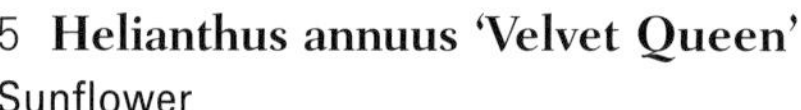

5 Helianthus annuus 'Velvet Queen'

Sunflower

Sunflowers are fast-growing annuals with stout stems bearing large daisy-like flowerheads. 'Velvet Queen' is moderately tall with red-brown velvet florets surrounding the darker brown centre. Suitable for cutting. Hardy.

General care: Sow seed under glass at 16°C (61°F) in late winter or *in situ* in mid-spring.

Height: 1.5m (5ft) **Spread:** 45cm (18in)

Site: Sun. Moist, well-drained soil. Good on lime.

Use: Sunny bed or border

Good companions: *Layia platiglossa*, *Nicotiana* 'Lime Green', *Rudbeckia hirta* 'Rustic Dwarf'

6 Impatiens New Guinea Group

Balsam, Busy lizzie

These sub-shrubby hybrid perennials are usually grown as annuals raised from seed or from cuttings for their brightly coloured flowers and colourful foliage, which may be red, bronze or variegated yellow. 'Spectra' includes soft and intense colours, sometimes bicoloured. Tender.

General care: Buy plants in early summer or take cuttings from overwintered plants in spring.

Height: 35cm (14in) **Spread:** 30cm (12in)

Site: Partial shade. Humus-rich and moist but well-drained soil

Compost: Soil-based (John Innes No. 2) or soil-less

Use: Conservatory or greenhouse minimum 10°C (50°F), container, formal bedding

Good companions: *Begonia* 'Orange Cascade', *Fuchsia* 'Gartenmeister Bonstedt', *Solenostemon* 'Crimson Ruffles'

yellow and orange

7 Bidens ferulifolia

Short-lived perennial usually grown as an annual. The sprawling stems, which are lightly clothed with finely divided leaves, carry numerous small, yellow daisy-like flowerheads throughout summer and early autumn. Not fully hardy.

General care: Sow seed under glass at 13–18°C (55–64°F) in mid-spring, or take cuttings from overwintered plants in spring.

Height: 30cm (12in) **Spread:** 1m (3ft)

Site: Sun. Well-drained soil
Compost: Soil-based (John Innes No. 2) or soil-less
Use: Container, sunny bed or border
Good companions: *Helichrysum petiolare, Petunia* Surfinia Series, *Scaevola aemula*

8 Cosmos sulphureus 'Sunset'

Upright annual with narrow-lobed leaves and long-stemmed flowerheads produced freely from mid-summer until the first frosts. The usual colour is yellow but 'Sunset' is rich orange. Tender.
General care: Sow seed under glass at 16°C (61°F) in mid-spring.
Height: 50cm (20in) **Spread:** 35cm (14in)
Site: Sun. Moist but well-drained soil
Use: Sunny bed or border
Good companions: *Nicotiana langsdorffii, Nicotiana* 'Lime Green', *Viola* x *wittrockiana* 'Baby Lucia'

9 Layia platyglossa
Tidy tips

Bushy annual with narrow grey-green leaves. In summer and the first half of autumn it produces numerous daisy-like flowers that have white-tipped, yellow petal-like ray-florets and rich yellow centres. Cut flowers are long lasting. Hardy.
General care: Sow *in situ* in autumn or spring.
Height: 45cm (18in)
Spread: 25cm (10in)
Site: Sun. Moist but well-drained soil
Use: Sunny bed or border
Good companions: *Molucella laevis, Nemesia* 'Carnival', *Zinnia* 'Envy'

10 Limonium sinuatum Forever Series
Statice

Perennial usually grown as an annual with stiffly branching winged stems that are rough to the touch. In late summer and early autumn these carry sprays of tiny flowers that are surrounded by colourful papery bracts in yellow, white, blue or pink. Suitable for cutting and drying. Not fully hardy.
General care: Sow seed under glass at 13–18°C (55–64°F) in spring.
Height: 60cm (2ft) **Spread:** 40cm (16in)
Site: Sun. Well-drained soil
Use: Sunny bed or border
Good companions: *Antirrhinum* Sonnet Series, *Bidens ferulifolia, Brachyscome iberidifolia* Splendour Series

11 Rudbeckia hirta 'Rustic Dwarf'
Black-eyed susan

Short-lived branching perennial or biennial usually grown as an annual. The stems and leaves are bristly. The large flowerheads are composed of dark centres surrounded by petal-like ray-florets in shades of yellow, bronze or chestnut; sometimes they are bicoloured. Suitable for cutting. Hardy.
General care: Sow seed under glass in early to mid-spring.
Height: 60cm (2ft) **Spread:** 35cm (14in)
Site: Sun, partial shade. Moist but well-drained soil
Compost: Soil-based (John Innes No. 2)
Use: Container, formal bedding, sunny or lightly shaded border
Good companions: *Cosmos sulphureus* 'Sunset', *Nicotiana langsdorffii, Verbena* 'Peaches and Cream'

12 Scabiosa stellata 'Paper Moon'

In summer this hairy annual bears pale mauve-blue flowerheads on wiry stems. The intriguing yellowish seed heads that follow are up to 8cm (3in) across and composed of tightly clustered, cup-shaped papery bracts with maroon centres. The seed heads are suitable for drying. Hardy.
General care: Sow *in situ* in mid-spring.
Height: 45cm (18in) **Spread:** 25cm (10in)
Site: Sun. Well-drained soil
Use: Sunny bed or border
Good companions: *Lagurus ovatus, Papaver rhoeas* 'Mother of Pearl', *Salvia viridis* 'Oxford Blue'

yellow and orange (continued)

1 Tagetes Zenith Series
Afro-French marigold

Bushy annual hybrid with deeply cut leaves and yellow, orange or bicoloured double flowerheads throughout summer and early autumn. Half hardy.
General care: Sow seed under glass at 21°C (70°F) in early spring.
Height: 30cm (12in) **Spread:** 25cm (10in)
Site: Sun. Well-drained soil
Compost: Soil-based (John Innes No. 2) or soil-less
Use: Container, formal bedding, front of sunny border
Good companions: *Euphorbia marginata, Lagurus ovatus, Tagetes tenuifolia* 'Lemon Gem'

2 Tithonia rotundifolia 'Goldfinger'
Mexican sunflower

Compact bushy annual that in late summer and autumn produces orange flowerheads. Half hardy.
General care: Sow under glass in mid-spring at 15°C (59°F) or *in situ* in late spring.
Height: 75cm (2ft 6in) **Spread:** 25cm (10in)
Site: Sun. Well-drained soil
Use: Sunny bed or border
Good companions: *Bidens ferulifolia, Tagetes* Zenith Series, *Tropaeolum* Alaska Series

cream and white

3 Lagurus ovatus
Hare's tail

This annual grass forms a tuft of pale grey-green leaves. Fluffy oval flowerheads age from greenish white, often tinged purple, to buff-cream. Hardy.
General care: Sow seed *in situ* in mid-spring.
Height: 40cm (16in) **Spread:** 30cm (12in)
Site: Sun. Well-drained soil
Use: Border, gravel garden
Good companions: *Eschscholzia californica, Euphorbia marginata, Nigella damascena* 'Miss Jekyll'

4 Nicotiana sylvestris
Tobacco plant

Short-lived perennial usually grown as an annual. Stout stems rise from large basal leaves and carry scented, white long-tubed flowers. Half hardy.
General care: Sow seed under glass at 18°C (64°F) in mid-spring.
Height: 1.2m (4ft) **Spread:** 50cm (20in)
Site: Sun, partial shade. Fertile and moist but well-drained soil
Use: Sunny or lightly shaded border
Good companions: *Amaranthus caudatus* 'Viridis', *Molucella laevis, Nicotiana* 'Lime Green'

green

5 Amaranthus caudatus 'Viridis'
Love-lies-bleeding, Tassel flower

Bushy annual with large, heavily veined, light green leaves. In summer and autumn dangling tassels are packed with tiny green flowers that fade to cream. Half hardy.
General care: Sow seed under glass at 20°C (68°F) in mid-spring.
Height: 1.2m (4ft) **Spread:** 75cm (2ft 6in)
Site: Sun. Humus-rich, moist but well-drained soil
Compost: Soil-based (John Innes No. 2)
Use: Conservatory or greenhouse minimum 7°C (45°F), container, formal bedding, sunny border
Good companions: *Amaranthus caudatus, Dahlia* 'Claire de Lune', *Dahlia* 'Moor Place'

6 Nicotiana langsdorffii
Tobacco plant

Short-lived perennial grown as an annual. From a rosette of large sticky basal leaves rise branching stems that carry sprays of pale green flowers in late summer and early autumn. Half hardy.
General care: Sow seed under glass at 18°C (64°F) in mid-spring.
Height: 1.2m (4ft) **Spread:** 45cm (18in)
Site: Sun, partial shade. Fertile and moist but well-drained soil
Use: Sunny or lightly shaded border
Good companions: *Impatiens* New Guinea Group hybrids, *Nicotiana sylvestris, Viola* x *wittrockiana* Clear Crystal Series

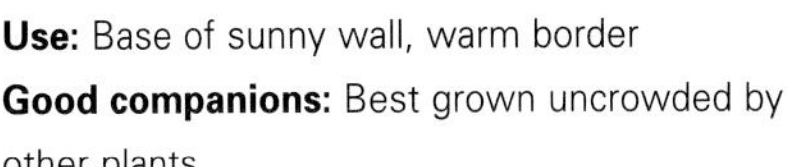

bulbs

Perennials with underground organs are a very varied group, encompassing true bulbs, corms, tubers and rhizomes. Many bloom in spring or summer, but others flower in autumn after a period of summer dormancy.

purple, blue and violet

1 Crocus banaticus

This crocus produces blue-purple flowers in early autumn. Hardy.
General care: Plant in late summer with the top of the corm about 10cm (4in) deep.
Height: 10cm (4in) **Spread:** 5cm (2in)
Site: Sun. Well-drained soil
Use: Raised bed, rock garden, sunny border
Good companions: *Campanula poscharskyana* 'Stella', *Crocus tommasinianus*, *Juniperus squamata* 'Blue Star'

2 Crocus speciosus

Darkly veined, pale to deep mauve-blue goblets, supported by long pale tubes, appear before the leaves. Increases steadily. The form 'Albus' is white. Hardy.
General care: Plant in late summer with the top of the corm about 10cm (4in) deep.
Height: 10cm (4in) **Spread:** 5cm (2in)
Site: Sun. Well-drained soil
Use: Raised bed, rock garden, underplanting for shrubs, wild garden
Good companions: *Anemone blanda*, *Colchicum* 'The Giant', *Crocus tommasinianus*

pink and mauve

3 Amaryllis belladonna

Red-purple flowering stems support funnel-shaped flowers that are usually bright pink. The fan of strap-shaped leaves emerges later and persists through winter. Not fully hardy.
General care: Plant in late summer with the top of the bulb just covered by soil.
Height: 75cm (2ft 6in) **Spread:** 15cm (6in)
Site: Sun. Well-drained soil
Use: Base of sunny wall, warm border
Good companions: Best grown uncrowded by other plants

4 Colchicum 'Rosy Dawn'

Autumn crocus, Naked ladies

In autumn, this hybrid produces up to six white-centred, lightly chequered mauve-pink flowers. The large leaves emerge in spring. Hardy.
General care: Plant in summer or early autumn with the top of the corm about 10cm (4in) deep.
Height: 15cm (6in) **Spread:** 20cm (8in)
Site: Sun, partial shade. Well-drained soil
Use: Front of border, planting in grass, underplanting for shrubs and trees
Good companions: *Galanthus elwesii*, *Helleborus hybridus*, *Tiarella wherryi*

5 Colchicum 'The Giant'

Autumn crocus, Naked ladies

White-throated, rich mauve-pink goblet-shaped flowers, faintly chequered inside, emerge before the large leaves, which develop in spring. Hardy.
General care: Plant in summer or early autumn with the top of the corm about 10cm (4in) deep.
Height: 20cm (8in) **Spread:** 10cm (4in)
Site: Sun, partial shade. Well-drained soil
Use: Front of border, planting in grass, underplanting for shrubs and trees
Good companions: *Colchicum speciosum* 'Album', *Crocus speciosus*, *Crocus tommasinianus*

6 Crinum x powellii

The stems support heads of up to ten fragrant, pink, flared trumpet-shaped flowers, which emerge from a base of bright green, strap-shaped leaves. 'Album' is white. Not fully hardy.
General care: Plant in spring with the tip of the bulb's neck above ground. Leave established clumps undisturbed. Dry mulch in winter.
Height: 75cm (2ft 6in) **Spread:** 30cm (12in)
Site: Sun. Well-drained soil but with a plentiful supply of moisture in summer
Use: Warm border
Good companions: *Agapanthus* 'Lilliput', *Passiflora caerulea*, *Solanum crispum* 'Glasnevin'

pink and mauve (continued)

1 Crocus kotschyanus

In late summer or early autumn, mauve flowers are borne on slender white tubes before the leaves develop. Inside the flowers there are orange dots at the base. Hardy.

General care: Plant in summer with the top of the corm about 8cm (3in) deep.

Height: 8cm (3in) **Spread:** 5cm (2in)

Site: Sun. Well-drained soil

Use: Front of border, raised bed, rock garden

Good companions: *Crocus chrysanthus* 'Zwanenburg Bronze', *Euphorbia myrsinites*, *Muscari botryoides* 'Album'

2 Cyclamen hederifolium

Sowbread

Although the first flowers often appear in late summer, the main season is early autumn, when well-established tubers, which can be more than 15cm (6in) across, may produce as many as 50 blooms. These have swept-back twisted petals, usually a shade of pink but sometimes white. The leaves are normally marbled and remain attractive from autumn to early summer. Hardy.

General care: Plant in the first half of summer, just after the leaves have died down. Set the corm indented side (from which the roots grow) uppermost just below the surface of the soil and cover with leaf-mould. Mulch with leaf-mould in summer.

Height: 10cm (4in) **Spread:** 15cm (6in)

Site: Partial shade, sun. Well-drained soil

Compost: Soil-based (John Innes No. 1) with added leaf-mould and grit

Use: Container, raised bed, rock garden, underplanting for shrubs, woodland garden

Good companions: *Crocus tommasinianus*, *Galanthus nivalis*, *Primula vulgaris*

3 Nerine bowdenii

Stiff stems bear three to nine glistening pink flowers, which have narrow wavy-edged petals. The flowers open before the strap-shaped leaves develop and are good for cutting. Best at the foot of a sunny wall. 'Mark Fenwick' is a vigorous selection. Hardy.

General care: Plant in early spring with the neck of the bulb just below the surface of the soil. Leave established clumps undisturbed for best flowering display.

Height: 50cm (20in) **Spread:** 10cm (4in)

Site: Sun. Well-drained soil

Use: Sunny border

Good companions: *Myrtus communis* subsp. *tarentina*, *Origanum laevigatum* 'Herrenhausen', *Passiflora caerulea*

yellow

4 Sternbergia lutea

The rich yellow flowers, which are goblet-shaped and lustrous, show up well against the glossy dark green of the grass-like leaves. These do not reach their full length, up to 30cm (12in), until spring. Best planted at the foot of a sunny wall. Not fully hardy.

General care: Plant in late summer with the top of the bulb about 10cm (4in) deep.

Height: 15cm (6in) **Spread:** 8cm (3in)

Site: Sun. Well-drained soil

Use: Sunny border, rock garden

Good companions: *Euphorbia myrsinites*, *Sedum spathulifolium* 'Cape Blanco', *Sempervivum tectorum*

cream and white

5 Colchicum speciosum 'Album'

Autumn crocus, Naked ladies

The usual flower colour of the species is pink-mauve and 'Atrorubens' is a fine red-purple form. These are excellent autumn plants, but this white cultivar, with its elegant weather-resistant goblets supported on green-tinted tubes, is outstandingly beautiful. The large lance-shaped leaves appear in spring. Hardy.

General care: Plant in summer and early autumn with the top of the corm about 10cm (4in) deep.

Height: 15cm (6in) **Spread:** 20cm (8in)

Site: Sun, partial shade. Well-drained soil

Use: Front of border, planting in grass, underplanting for shrubs and trees

Good companions: *Geranium macrorrhizum*, *Helleborus argutifolius*, *Vinca minor* 'La Grave'

6 Leucojum autumnale

Autumn snowflake

The tuft of grassy leaves starts to develop in late summer or early autumn, at the same time as the flower stems. The stems carry one, occasionally several, white bell-shaped flowers that are tinged pink. Hardy.

General care: Plant in late summer with the top of the bulb about 8cm (3in) deep.

Height: 20cm (8in) **Spread:** 5cm (2in)

Site: Sun. Moist but well-drained soil

Use: Sunny border, raised bed, rock garden

Good companions: *Alchemilla conjuncta*, *Hebe cupressoides* 'Boughton Dome', *Saxifraga* 'Peter Pan', *Viola* 'Molly Sanderson'

dahlias

Dahlias make a colourful show in moist beds and borders from late summer until first frost. The flowerheads vary in shape and size, from neat pompoms and daisies to huge shaggy domes, in pastels, vibrant tones and deep velvety hues. Lift these half-hardy tuberous perennials after frost has blackened the foliage and overwinter in cool, dry frost-free conditions.

1

2

1 Dahlia 'Claire de Lune'

Collerette dahlia

This belongs to a group with flowers that have an outer row of petal-like ray-florets around a 'collar' of shorter florets and a central disc. Here the ray-florets and collar are pale yellow and the disc is orange-yellow.

Height: 1m (3ft) **Spread:** 60cm (2ft)

Good companions: *Dahlia* 'Bishop of Llandaff', *Dahlia* 'David Howard', *Tagetes tenuifolia* 'Lemon Gem'

2 Dahlia 'Peach Cupid'

Miniature ball dahlia

This belongs to a group with small ball-shaped flowerheads packed with incurved petal-like florets arranged in a spiral. Here the blooms are warm pink and open from midsummer.

Height: 1.2m (4ft) **Spread:** 75cm (2ft 6in)

Good companions: *Dahlia* 'Porcelain', *Penstemon* 'Blackbird', *Penstemon* 'Stapleford Gem'

3 Dahlia 'Yellow Hammer'

Dwarf bedding dahlia

This bronze-foliaged dahlia bears orange-centred, yellow single flowerheads and is suitable for containers or as a bedding plant.

Height: 50cm (20in) **Spread:** 40cm (16in)

Good companions: *Canna* 'King Midas', *Dahlia* 'Bishop of Llandaff', *Dahlia* 'David Howard'

4 Dahlia 'Bishop of Llandaff'

Peony-flowered dahlia

The bright red flowerheads consist of two or more rings of flat petal-like ray-florets and a central disc of conspicuous yellow anthers. The purple-black foliage is highly ornamental.

Height: 1m (3ft) **Spread:** 60cm (2ft)

Good companions: *Canna* 'Assaut', *Cosmos antrosanguineus*, *Dahlia* 'Zorro'

5 Dahlia 'Zorro'

Giant decorative dahlia

This is a deep red example of a group with double flowerheads that have no central disc but are composed of layers of blunt-tipped, slightly twisted petal-like ray-florets.

Height: 1.2m (4ft) **Spread:** 60cm (2ft)

Good companions: *Amaranthus caudatus*, *Cosmos atrosanguineus*, *Gladiolus callianthus* 'Murieliae'

6 Dahlia 'David Howard'

Miniature decorative dahlia

The orange double flowerheads are composed of layers of blunt-tipped, slightly twisted petal-like ray-florets. The blooms are about 8cm (3in) across and there is no central disc.

Height: 1m (3ft) **Spread:** 60cm (2ft)

Good companions: *Dahlia* 'Bishop of Llandaff', *Dahlia* 'Claire de Lune', *Dahlia* 'Yellow Hammer'

7 Dahlia 'Porcelain'

Water lily dahlia

This is a small-flowered example of a group that bears shallowly cup-shaped double flowerheads composed of relatively few rounded, broad, petal-like ray-florets. The white flowerheads are tinted purple-mauve.

Height: 1.2m (4ft) **Spread:** 60cm (2ft)

Good companions: *Dahlia* 'Peach Cupid', *Dahlia* 'White Moonlight', *Penstemon* 'Evelyn'

8 Dahlia 'White Moonlight'

Miniature semi-cactus dahlia

This belongs to a group with double flowerheads, in which the pointed petal-like ray-florets are rolled under for up to half their length, giving them a quilled appearance. The pure white flowers are up to 20cm (8in) across.

Height: 1.2m (4ft)

Spread: 60cm (2ft)

Good companions: *Dahlia* 'Kiwi Gloria', *Dahlia* 'Peach Cupid', *Dahlia* 'Porcelain'

6

7

3

4

5

8

climbers

Climbers twine, cling with aerial roots or clasp with tendrils. Trained on architectural supports or other plants, they assert the vertical dimension of the garden. Plant in the dormant season.

red and russet

1 Parthenocissus quinquefolia

Virginia creeper

Vigorous, woody-stemmed self-clinging climber grown for its foliage, which turns from green to brilliant crimson in autumn. Inconspicuous greenish flowers in late spring or early summer are followed by inedible blue-black berries. Hardy.

General care: To prevent shoots invading gutters and covering windows, cut back in winter or early spring to about 1.2m (4ft) from vulnerable areas.

Height and spread: 18m (60ft)

Site: Sun, partial shade. Well-drained soil

Use: Large mature tree climber, wall

Good companions: *Hedera colchica* 'Dentata', *Vitis coignetiae, Vitis vinifera* 'Purpurea'

2 Parthenocissus tricuspidata 'Veitchii'

Boston ivy

Vigorous, woody-stemmed self-clinging climber. The three-lobed leaves, smaller than those of the typical Boston ivy, open purple-red and become more richly coloured in autumn. Hardy.

General care: Cut back shoots in winter or early spring to about 1.2m (4ft) from vulnerable areas.

Height and spread: 18m (60ft)

Site: Sun, shade. Well-drained soil

Use: Large mature tree climber, wall

Good companions: *Ilex* x *altaclarensis* 'Camelliifolia', *Prunus lusitanica, Taxus baccata*

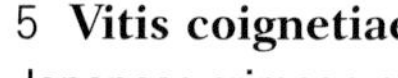

3 Rosa 'Crimson Shower'

Rambler rose

The pliant stems of this deciduous rambler are well furnished with glossy, bright green leaves. Clusters of crimson semi-double flowers are borne from midsummer to early autumn. Hardy.

General care: Prune between late winter and early spring, cutting up to a third of the oldest stems to near ground level and reducing sideshoots to three or four buds.

Height: 5m (15ft) **Spread:** 2.5m (8ft)

Site: Sun. Humus-rich, moist but well-drained soil

Use: Arbour, arch, wall

Good companions: *Clematis* 'Alba Luxurians', *Rosa* 'Aimée Vibert', *Trachelospermum jasminoides*

4 Vitis 'Brant'

Vine

The boldly lobed leaves of this vigorous woody vine colour splendidly in autumn, turning bronze-red. The edible red-purple grapes are sweet if there has been enough sun to ripen them. Hardy.

General care: Prune in late winter, cutting back main stems within the available space and reducing sideshoots to three or four buds.

Height: 6m (20ft) **Spread:** 4m (12ft)

Site: Sun, partial shade. Well-drained soil. Good on lime

Use: Pergola, wall

Good companions: *Clematis rehderiana, Lonicera* x *brownii* 'Dropmore Scarlet', *Rosa* Golden Showers

5 Vitis coignetiae

Japanese crimson glory vine, Vine

Vigorous deciduous vine with stout woody stems. The dark green, often huge, heart-shaped leaves, with a reddish felted underside, turn vivid red in autumn. Inconspicuous green flowers in spring are followed by inedible black grapes. Hardy.

General care: Prune in late winter, cutting back main stems within the available space and reducing sideshoots to three or four buds.

Height: 6m (20ft) **Spread:** 4m (12ft)

Site: Sun, partial shade. Well-drained soil. Good on lime

Use: Pergola, wall

Good companions: *Clematis montana* var. *rubens* 'Elizabeth', *Lonicera* x *americana, Vitis vinifera* 'Purpurea'

yellow and orange

6 Celastrus orbiculatus

Oriental bittersweet, Staff vine

Vigorous deciduous twiner with yellow autumn leaves and showy yellow berries. Hardy.

General care: To control growth on a pergola or wall, prune in late winter or early spring.

Height: 12m (40ft) **Spread:** 8m (25ft)

Site: Sun, partial shade. Well-drained soil

Use: Pergola, tree climber, wall

Good companions: *Clematis montana, Vitis coignetiae, Wisteria sinensis*

late flowering clematis

These deciduous clematis are hardy twining climbers that flower from late summer into early autumn. All do well on lime but need rich, well-drained soil. Grow in sun or partial shade, but with the base shaded. Most can be pruned in late winter or early spring, cutting all growths back to a pair of strong buds 30–60cm (1–2ft) above the ground.

1

1 Clematis 'Gipsy Queen'

Large-flowered clematis

The velvety single flowers, 15cm (6in) across, are violet-purple with deep red anthers.

Height: 3m (10ft) **Spread:** 1.5m (5ft)

Good companions: *Clematis* 'Ernest Markham', *Rosa* 'Crimson Shower', *Rosa* 'Madame Alfred Carrière'

2 Clematis 'Etoile Rose'

Texensis Group clematis

Small-flowered clematis ideal for growing through shrubs. The nodding urn-shaped flowers are deep pink with silver margins. Dies back to ground level in winter.

Height: 3m (10ft) **Spread:** 2m (6ft)

Good companions: *Choisya ternata*, *Clematis* 'Lasurstern', *Rosa* 'Pink Perpétué'

3 Clematis 'Ernest Markham'

Large-flowered clematis

The vivid red flowers with cream-brown anthers are produced most freely in full sun. For a flowering season from early summer to mid-autumn, prune in late winter, trimming half the stems lightly and cutting back the remaining stems to a pair of buds 30–60cm (1–2ft) above ground level.

Height: 5m (15ft) **Spread:** 2.5m (8ft)

Good companions: *Clematis* 'Jackmanii', *Jasminum officinale*, *Solanum laxum* 'Album'

4 Clematis 'Abundance'

Viticella Group clematis

Small-flowered clematis that bears darkly veined, wine-red flowers with greenish yellow anthers from midsummer to late autumn.

Height: 3m (10ft) **Spread:** 2m (6ft)

Good companions: *Ceanothus* x *delileanus* 'Topaze', *Clematis* 'Gillian Blades', *Rosa* 'Madame Grégoire Staechelin'

5 Clematis rehderiana

Vigorous twiner with elegantly divided foliage. It bears sprays of nodding, straw-yellow, bell-shaped flowers that have a sweet but light scent. Flowers most freely in full sun.

Height: 6m (20ft) **Spread:** 3m (10ft)

Good companions: *Rosa* 'Bobbie James', *Vitis* 'Brant', *Wisteria floribunda* 'Multijuga'

6 Clematis 'Bill MacKenzie'

The nodding yellow single flowers have red anthers. They are borne in profusion over a long season and are followed by fluffy seed heads.

Height: 6m (20ft) **Spread:** 2.5m (8ft)

Good companions: *Rosa banksiae* 'Lutea', *Vitis* 'Brant', *Wisteria floribunda* 'Multijuga'

7 Clematis 'Huldine'

Viticella Group clematis

Vigorous twiner with slightly cupped flowers, about 10cm (4in) across. Their upper surface is clean white, the underside tinted mauve.

Height: 4m (12ft) **Spread:** 2m (6ft)

Good companions: *Buddleja crispa*, *Clematis* 'Warszawska Nike', *Rosa* 'Parade'

shrubs & trees

In autumn, late flowering trees and shrubs have to compete with others that have brilliantly coloured foliage, which shows up well against sombre evergreens. Plant in the dormant season, preferably in autumn or early spring.

purple, blue and violet

1 Callicarpa bodinieri var. giraldii 'Profusion'

Beauty berry

Deciduous shrub with narrow toothed leaves that are bronze-purple when young. Small mauve-pink flowers in midsummer are followed by tight clusters of inedible violet-purple berries. Hardy.

General care: In late winter or early spring cut back the previous season's growth.

Height and spread: 2.5m (8ft)

Site: Sun, partial shade. Well-drained soil

Use: Sunny or lightly shaded border

Good companions: *Fuchsia magellanica* 'Versicolor', *Lonicera* x *purpusii* 'Winter Beauty', *Rosa glauca*

2 Caryopteris x clandonensis 'Kew Blue'

Grey-green-leaved aromatic deciduous shrub with clusters of deep blue flowers borne on erect stems from late summer to early autumn. Hardy.

General care: In early to mid-spring cut stems back to a low framework.

Height: 1m (3ft) **Spread:** 1.5m (5ft)

Site: Sun. Well-drained soil. Good on lime

Use: Sunny border

Good companions: *Eryngium* x *tripartitum*, *Erysimum* 'Bowles' Mauve', *Lilium candidum*

3 Ceanothus 'Autumnal Blue'

California lilac

The bright glossy foliage of this evergreen hybrid shows off large sprays of sky-blue flowers in late summer, autumn and occasionally spring. Hardy.

General care: Trim in early to mid-spring.

Height and spread: 3m (10ft)

Site: Sun. Well-drained soil

Use: Sunny border, warm wall

Good companions: *Myrtus communis* subsp. *tarentina*, *Rosa* 'Parade', *Vitis* 'Brant'

4 Clerodendrum trichotomum var. fargesii

Deciduous bushy shrub or small tree that bears sprays of fragrant white flowers in late summer and autumn. These emerge from the red-tinged base of the calyces, which are retained even when the berries ripen to a startling blue.

Height and spread: 5m (15ft)

Site: Sun. Humus-rich, moist but well-drained soil

Use: Sunny border

Good companions: *Fargesia nitida*, *Hydrangea macrophylla* 'Blue Wave', *Hydrangea paniculata* 'Unique'

5 Hebe 'Autumn Glory'

Spreading evergreen shrub with purplish stems and dark green leaves outlined with purplish red. Bears spikes of mauve-blue tubular flowers in late summer and autumn. Not fully hardy.

Height: 60cm (2ft) **Spread:** 1m (3ft)

Site: Sun, partial shade. Moist but well-drained soil

Compost: Soil-based (John Innes No. 2)

Use: Container, sunny or lightly shaded border, raised bed, rock garden

Good companions: *Euonymus fortunei* 'Emerald Gaiety', *Fuchsia* 'Riccartonii', *Hydrangea macrophylla* 'Blue Wave'

pink and mauve

6 Calluna vulgaris 'Peter Sparkes'

Ling, Scots heather

The single species of heather, a low evergreen shrub with scale-like leaves, has given rise to a very large number of cultivars. The spikes of small single or double flowers remain colourful over several months in late summer and autumn. 'Peter Sparkes' has double pink flowers. Hardy.

General care: Clip over in early to mid-spring.

Height: 40cm (16in) **Spread:** 50cm (20in)

Site: Sun. Lime-free, humus-rich soil

Compost: Ericaceous

Use: Container, front of sunny border, ground cover, heather garden, wild garden

Good companions: *Erica carnea* 'King George', *Erica* x *darleyensis* 'Furzey', *Pinus mugo* 'Mops'

7 Euonymus europaeus 'Red Cascade'

Spindle tree

Deciduous shrub or small tree often bare at the

1

2

3

base but with a bushy head. Inconspicuous until autumn, when leaves turn red and branches arch over with the weight of scarlet-pink capsules, which split to reveal orange seeds. Hardy.
Height: 3m (10ft) **Spread:** 2.5m (8ft)
Site: Sun, partial shade. Well-drained soil. Good on lime
Use: Border, wild garden
Good companions: *Acanthus mollis* Latifolius Group, *Berberis darwinii, Cotoneaster lactaeus*

8 Fuchsia 'Alice Hoffman'

Upright deciduous shrub with dense purple-green foliage. Throughout summer and autumn pink semi-double flowers, with a pink-veined white 'skirt', dangle from stem tips. Not fully hardy.
General care: Cut stems down to the base in early spring.
Height and spread: 50cm (20in)
Site: Sun, partial shade. Moist, well-drained soil
Compost: Soil-based (John Innes No. 3)
Use: Container, sunny or lightly shaded border
Good companions: *Fuchsia* 'Riccartonii', *Hydrangea* 'Preziosa', *Viburnum* x *bodnantense* 'Dawn'

9 Fuchsia 'Mrs Popple'

This upright deciduous hybrid fuchsia blooms profusely throughout summer and early autumn. The tube and long sepals are glossy red, the petals violet-purple and the long stamens and style are crimson. Not fully hardy.
General care: Cut stems down to the base in early spring.
Height and spread: 1m (3ft)
Site: Sun, partial shade. Moist, well-drained soil
Compost: Soil-based (John Innes No. 3)
Use: Container, sunny or lightly shaded border
Good companions: *Ceratostigma willmottianum, Fuchsia* 'Alice Hoffman', *Hydrangea macrophylla* 'Madame Emile Mouillère'

10 Hibiscus syriacus 'Woodbridge'

Upright deciduous grey-stemmed shrub that bears lobed dark green leaves, and from late summer to mid-autumn pink flowers with dark centres. Suitable for training as a standard. Hardy.
Height: 3m (10ft) **Spread:** 2m (6ft)
Site: Sun. Humus-rich and moist, well-drained soil
Use: Sunny border
Good companions: *Anemone hupehensis* 'Hadspen Abundance', *Penstemon* 'Evelyn', *Veronica gentianoides*

11 Rosa 'English Miss'
Floribunda rose

Throughout summer and early autumn this compact deciduous bush carries large sprays of scented, pale pink fully double flowers. Hardy.
General care: Prune between late winter and early spring, cutting main stems back to a height of about 30cm (12in) and shortening sideshoots to two or three buds.
Height: 75cm (2ft 6in) **Spread:** 60cm (2ft)
Site: Sun. Fertile and moist but well-drained soil
Use: Formal bedding, sunny border
Good companions: *Geranium macrorrhizum, Stachys byzantina* 'Silver Carpet', *Veronica peduncularis* 'Georgia Blue'

12 Rosa 'Felicia'
Hybrid musk rose

The arching stems of this vigorous deciduous bush bear sprays of scented, apricot-tinted light pink flowers in early summer then intermittently, often with a strong flush in autumn. Hardy.
General care: Prune in late winter to early spring, removing about a third of stems; select the oldest and cut back main stems by up to a third and sideshoots by half.
Height and spread: 1.5m (5ft)
Site: Sun. Reasonably fertile and moist but well-drained soil
Use: Hedge, sunny bed or border
Good companions: *Nepeta* 'Six Hills Giant', *Rosa* 'Buff Beauty', *Viola riviniana* Purpurea Group

4

5

6

7

8

9

11
12

10

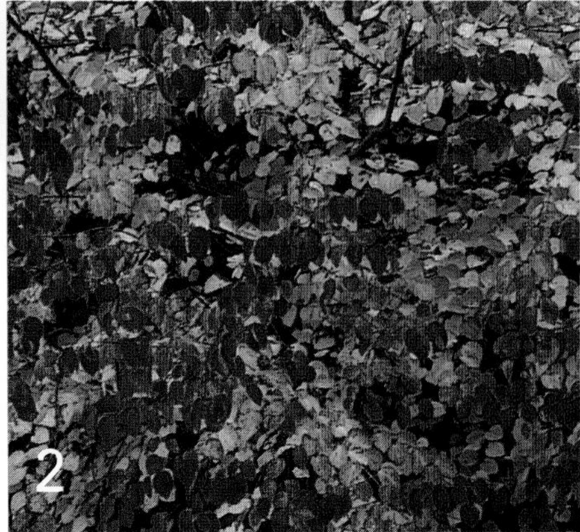

red and russet

1 Amelanchier canadensis
Shadbush

In autumn the foliage of this deciduous shrub or small tree turns brilliant orange and red. In spring it produces white starry flowers, which are followed by edible blue-black fruits. Hardy.

Height: 7m (23ft) **Spread:** 2m (6ft)

Site: Sun, partial shade. Moist but well-drained soil, preferably lime-free

Use: Specimen tree

Good companions: *Acer griseum*, *Cornus florida* 'Cherokee Chief', *Sorbus hupehensis*

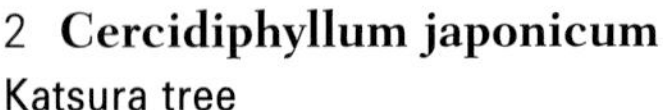

2 Cercidiphyllum japonicum
Katsura tree

Deciduous tree with heart-shaped leaves that are bronze when young, green in summer then shades of red, pink and yellow in autumn. There are tiny red flowers in spring. Hardy.

Height: 20m (65ft) **Spread:** 12m (40ft)

Site: Sun, partial shade. Humus-rich and moist but well-drained soil, preferably lime-free

Use: Specimen tree, woodland garden

Good companions: *Acer pensylvanicum* 'Erythrocladum', *Hamamelis* x *intermedia* 'Diane', *Picea breweriana*

3 Cotinus 'Flame'
Smoke bush

Deciduous large shrub or small tree with light green, rounded leaves that turn brilliant orange-red in autumn. Tiny pink flowers in summer are followed by inedible purple-pink fruits that form smoke-like plumes. Hardy.

General care: To promote the growth of large leaves, cut stems down to near ground level in early spring.

Height: 6m (20ft) **Spread:** 5m (15ft)

Site: Sun, partial shade. Moist, well-drained soil

Use: Canopy in border, specimen

Good companions: *Cotoneaster frigidus* 'Cornubia', *Ilex aquifolium* 'Handsworth New Silver', *Philadelphus* 'Belle Etoile'

4 Cotoneaster conspicuus 'Decorus'

This small-leaved evergreen shrub forms a mound of arching stems. In early summer these are covered with white flowers, which are followed in autumn by bright red berries that usually last well into winter. Hardy.

Height: 1.5m (5ft) **Spread:** 2.5m (8ft)

Site: Sun, partial shade. Well-drained soil

Use: Bank, ground cover, raised bed, large rock garden

Good companions: *Euonymus alatus* 'Compactus', *Prunus lusitanica*, *Pyracantha* 'Orange Glow'

5 Crataegus persimilis 'Prunifolia'
Hawthorn

Broad-headed deciduous tree armed with strong thorns. The glossy green leaves turn orange and red in autumn. In late spring there are clusters of small white flowers, which are followed by bright red haws that last into winter. Hardy.

Height: 8m (25ft) **Spread:** 10m (33ft)

Site: Sun, partial shade. Well-drained soil

Use: Canopy in border, specimen tree, woodland garden

Good companions: *Crocus speciosus*, *Galanthus nivalis*, *Primula vulgaris*

6 Disanthus cercidifolius

Rather spidery, slightly fragrant flowers are borne in autumn, but the value of this deciduous shrub lies in the blue-green foliage, which in autumn turns shades of yellow, red and purple. Hardy.

Height and spread: 3m (10ft)

Site: Sun, partial shade. Lime-free, moist but well-drained soil

Use: Canopy in border, woodland garden

Good companions: *Erythronium californicum* 'White Beauty', *Fothergilla major* Monticola Group, *Kirengeshoma palmata*

7 Euonymus alatus 'Compactus'
Winged spindle

This is a compact form of a dense-growing deciduous shrub, the twigs of which often develop corky wings. It makes little impact until autumn when the leaves turn brilliant shades of deep pink and red, and purplish capsules split open to reveal scarlet seeds. Hardy.

Height: 1m (3ft) **Spread:** 1.5m (5ft)

Site: Sun, partial shade. Well-drained soil

Use: Hedge, sunny or lightly shaded border

Good companions: *Cotoneaster salicifolius* 'Rothschildianus', *Helleborus argutifolius*, *Prunus lusitanica*

7

8

9

8 Fuchsia 'Riccartonii'

Vigorous deciduous shrub with neat pointed leaves that are dark green with a bronze tint. Throughout summer and autumn there are showers of small red flowers with purple petals. In mild climates specimens can exceed the dimensions given here. Not fully hardy.
General care: Cut stems back to a low framework in early spring.
Height: 2.5m (8ft) **Spread:** 1.5m (5ft)
Site: Sun, partial shade. Moist but well-drained soil
Use: Hedge, sunny or lightly shaded border
Good companions: *Daphne bholua* 'Jacqueline Postill', *Hydrangea aspera* Villosa Group, *Spiraea japonica* 'Anthony Waterer'

9 Fuchsia 'Snowcap'

Upright deciduous hybrid fuchsia that blooms freely from midsummer to mid-autumn. The semi-double flowers are red with a 'skirt' of pink-veined white petals. Not fully hardy.
General care: Cut stems down to the base in early spring.
Height: 1m (3ft) **Spread:** 75cm (2ft 6in)
Site: Sun, partial shade. Moist but well-drained soil
Compost: Soil-based (John Innes No. 3)
Use: Container, sunny or lightly shaded border
Good companions: *Exochorda macrantha* 'The Bride', *Fuchsia* 'Leonora', *Hydrangea macrophylla* 'Ayesha'

10

11

10 Gaultheria mucronata 'Mulberry Wine'

Evergreen shrub making a dense thicket covered with small lustrous leaves. When this female clone is grown close to a male plant the small, white urn-shaped flowers, which are borne in late spring and early summer, are pollinated. The long-lasting berries that form ripen from magenta to deep purple-red in autumn. Hardy.
General care: Remove suckers to limit spread.
Height and spread: 1.2m (4ft)
Site: Partial shade. Lime-free, moist soil
Use: Heather garden, peat bed, rock garden, woodland garden
Good companions: *Acer palmatum* 'Corallinum', *Leucothoe* 'Scarletta', *Rhododendron* 'Praecox'

11 Hydrangea 'Preziosa'

Mophead hydrangea

Deciduous shrub with purple-tinted stems and young leaves, which also take on attractive tints in autumn. The heads of sterile flowers, which in summer are red-pink or, on acid soils, mauve-blue, deepen to purple-red in autumn. Hardy.
General care: Deadhead and in early to mid-spring cut out up to a quarter of old stems.
Height and spread: 1.5m (5ft)
Site: Sun, partial shade. Moist but well-drained soil
Compost: Soil-based (John Innes No. 3)
Use: Container, sunny or lightly shaded border, woodland garden
Good companions: *Fuchsia* 'Riccartonii', *Hydrangea paniculata* 'Unique', *Viburnum opulus* 'Roseum'

12 Liquidambar styraciflua 'Worplesdon'

Sweet gum

Deciduous tree of broadly conical shape grown principally for its foliage. The fingered leaves, which have five to seven lobes and are dark green in summer, turn purple-red and orange-yellow in autumn. In winter the corky bark of some twigs can be a feature. Hardy.
Height: 25m (80ft) **Spread:** 12m (40ft)
Site: Sun. Moist but well-drained soil, preferably lime-free
Use: Specimen tree, woodland garden
Good companions: *Acer cappadocicum* 'Aureum', *Acer grosseri* var. *hersii*, *Hamamelis* x *intermedia* 'Pallida'

12

red and russet (continued)

1 **Malus 'John Downie'**
Crab apple
Young specimens of this deciduous tree are narrow and upright but older plants tend to spread. In late spring white flowers open from pink buds. The crimson-flushed yellow crab apples that follow are highly ornamental. Hardy.
Height: 10m (33ft) **Spread:** 6m (20ft)
Site: Sun. Moist but well-drained soil
Use: Canopy in border, specimen tree
Good companions: *Colchicum* 'Rosy Dawn', *Galanthus nivalis, Narcissus* 'Actaea'

2 **Metasequoia glyptostroboides**
Dawn redwood
Fast-growing, deciduous conical conifer with bright green, feathery foliage that turns russet and gold before falling. Mature trees may exceed the dimensions given. Hardy.
Height: 25m (80ft) **Spread:** 5m (15ft)
Site: Sun. Humus-rich, moist but well-drained soil
Use: Specimen tree, waterside
Good companions: *Fargesia murieliae, Gunnera manicata, Salix alba* subsp. *vitellina* 'Britzensis'

3 **Prunus sargentii**
Sargent's cherry
Round-headed deciduous tree that is very attractive in mid-spring when young foliage, unfurling bronze-red, coincides with single pink flowers, and again early in autumn when the leaves turn brilliant orange and red. Inedible, glossy crimson fruits follow the flowers. Hardy.
Height: 20m (65ft) **Spread:** 15m (50ft)
Site: Sun. Moist but well-drained soil
Use: Specimen tree
Good companions: *Gentiana asclepiadea, Hydrangea* 'Preziosa', *Sarcococca hookeriana* var. *digyna*

4 **Quercus coccinea 'Splendens'**
Scarlet oak
When mature, this fast-growing deciduous tree develops a broad head. The lobed leaves are glossy green throughout summer then turn rich scarlet in autumn. Hardy.
Height: 20m (65ft) **Spread:** 15m (50ft)
Site: Sun, partial shade. Lime-free, well-drained soil
Use: Specimen tree, woodland garden
Good companions: *Amelanchier canadensis, Disanthus cercidifolius, Pseudolarix amabilis*

8

10

11

12

9

5 Rosa 'Fru Dagmar Hastrup'

Rugosa rose

Compact prickly rose with matt leaves. Scented, pink single flowers are borne throughout summer and followed by impressive red hips. Hardy.

General care: In late winter or early spring cut back main stems by about a third and sideshoots by up to two-thirds.

Height: 1m (3ft) **Spread:** 1.2m (4ft)

Site: Sun. Well-drained soil

Use: Hedge, sunny border

Good companions: *Geranium sanguineum* var. *striatum*, *Rosa* 'Blanche Double de Coubert', *Stachys byzantina* 'Silver Carpet'

6 Rosa 'Geranium'

Shrub rose

Blood-red single flowers spangle this deciduous open, thorny bush in summer, but the late summer and autumn display of large, scarlet, curiously shaped hips is longer lasting. Hardy.

General care: Cut out about a quarter of the oldest stems and trim other stems lightly in late winter or early spring.

Height: 2.5m (8ft) **Spread:** 1.5m (5ft)

Site: Sun. Moist but well-drained soil

Use: Sunny or lightly shaded border

Good companions: *Rosa xanthina* 'Canary Bird', *Viburnum opulus* 'Compactum', *Viburnum tinus* 'Gwenllian'

7 Rosa The Times Rose

Floribunda rose

In summer and autumn this deciduous bush rose bears clusters of lightly scented, dark crimson double flowers over purplish green foliage. Hardy.

General care: Prune between late winter and early spring, cutting back main stems to a height of about 25cm (10in) and shortening sideshoots to two or three buds.

Height: 60cm (2ft) **Spread:** 75cm (2ft 6in)

Site: Sun. Fertile and moist but well-drained soil

Use: Formal bedding, sunny border

Good companions: *Nepeta* 'Six Hills Giant', *Paeonia lactiflora* 'White Wings', *Rosa* Elina *Sorbus commixta* 'Embley'

8 Sorbus sargentiana

Slow-growing deciduous tree with large leaves, composed of many leaflets, opening from sticky crimson buds. White flowers in early summer are followed by red fruits that ripen to coincide with the orange and red of the autumn foliage. Hardy.

Height and spread: 10m (33ft)

Site: Sun, partial shade. Well-drained soil, preferably lime-free

Use: Specimen tree, woodland garden

Good companions: *Ilex aquifolium* 'Bacciflava', *Malus* 'Red Sentinel', *Viburnum tinus* 'Gwenllian'

9 Viburnum opulus 'Compactum'

Guelder rose

In late spring and early summer this deciduous shrub bears flat heads of heavily scented white flowers surrounded by showy sterile florets. Inedible translucent red berries ripen before the lobed leaves turn red. Hardy.

Height and spread: 2m (6ft)

Site: Sun, partial shade. Moist, well-drained soil

Use: Sunny or lightly shaded border, woodland garden

Good companions: *Eranthis hyemalis*, *Erythronium dens-canis*, *Galanthus elwesii*

yellow and orange

10 Cotoneaster salicifolius 'Rothschildianus'

Large evergreen shrub with arching stems and narrow tapered leaves. Small white flowers in early summer are followed by long-lasting clusters of inedible, creamy yellow fruits. Hardy.

Height and spread: 5m (15ft)

Site: Sun, partial shade. Well-drained soil

Use: Canopy in border

Good companions: *Colchicum speciosum* 'Album', *Corylus avellana* 'Contorta', *Osmanthus delavayi*

11 Ginkgo biloba

Maidenhair tree

This upright deciduous tree is a survivor of a primitive plant group most closely allied to the conifers. The leaves, which form a notched fan up to 8cm (3in) across, are bright green in summer then turn clear yellow in autumn. Female trees may produce fruits, which have an edible kernel but a rank-smelling outer coating. Hardy.

Height: 25m (80ft) **Spread:** 8m (25ft)

Site: Sun. Fertile, well-drained soil

Use: Specimen tree

Good companions: *Euonymus alatus* 'Compactus', *Prunus laurocerasus* 'Otto Luyken', *Sorbus sargentiana*

12 Malus tschonoskii

Crab apple

Deciduous tree of upright, loosely conical shape with glossy green leaves that colour yellow, orange, red and purple in autumn. The pink-tinged, white single flowers of spring are followed by red-flushed yellow-green crab apples. Hardy.

Height: 12m (40ft) **Spread:** 8m (25ft)

Site: Sun. Moist but well-drained soil

Use: Canopy in border, specimen tree

Good companions: *Geranium macrorrhizum* 'Ingwersen's Variety', *Hosta* 'Halcyon', *Tiarella cordifolia*

yellow and orange
(continued)

1 Nyssa sylvatica
Black gum, Sour gum, Tupelo

A dense head and drooping lower branches give this deciduous tree a broadly columnar shape. The dark green leaves turn brilliant yellow, orange and scarlet in autumn. There are insignificant yellow-green flowers in early summer. Hardy.
Height: 20m (65ft)
Spread: 10m (33ft)
Site: Sun, partial shade. Lime-free, moist but well-drained soil
Use: Specimen tree, woodland garden
Good companions: *Acer japonicum* 'Vitifolium', *Hamamelis* x *intermedia* 'Arnold Promise', *Rhododendron luteum*

2 Rhus typhina
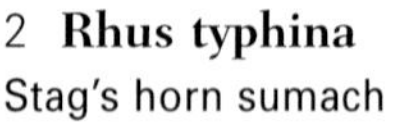

Stag's horn sumach

Deciduous suckering shrub or small tree with few but wide-spreading branches, with red hairs on young shoots. The leaves, which are composed of numerous dissected leaflets, turn brilliant yellow, orange and red in autumn. Female cultivars, such as 'Dissecta', carry inedible, furry, crimson fruits in autumn. Hardy.
General care: To encourage large leaves, cut stems to near base in late winter or early spring.
Height: 3m (10ft) **Spread:** 5m (15ft)
Site: Sun. Moist but well-drained soil
Use: Border, specimen shrub, woodland garden
Good companions: *Cornus alba* 'Sibirica', *Cornus stolonifera* 'Flavirimea', *Cotinus* 'Flame'

3 Sorbus 'Joseph Rock'
Deciduous small tree with a compact head of branches. The green leaves are composed of numerous leaflets and turn rich shades of red, orange and purple in autumn. Heads of creamy white flowers in late spring are followed by clusters of inedible, pale yellow fruits, which ripen to amber and persist after leaf fall. Hardy.
Height: 9m (30ft) **Spread:** 6m (20ft)
Site: Sun, partial shade. Moist but well-drained soil, preferably lime-free

Use: Specimen tree, woodland garden
Good companions: *Cornus kousa* var. *chinensis* 'Satomi', *Malus* 'John Downie', *Prunus sargentii*

cream and white

4 Arbutus unedo
Strawberry tree

Evergreen small tree, often with multiple stems, with deep brown and shredding bark. The glossy, nearly oval leaves are toothed. Pendent clusters of small white flowers are borne in late autumn and coincide with unpalatable orange-red fruits from the previous season's flowers. Hardy.
Height and spread: 8m (25ft)
Site: Sun. Well-drained soil
Use: Canopy in border, specimen tree
Good companions: *Bergenia* 'Ballawley', *Helleborus foetidus, Pachysandra terminalis*

5 Hydrangea macrophylla 'Madame Emile Mouillère'
Mophead hydrangea

Deciduous rounded shrub with coarsely toothed leaves, topped in late summer and early autumn by globular heads of sterile white florets. On alkaline soils the eye of each floret is red, on acid soils it is blue. The florets themselves usually

develop a pink tinge as they age. Hardy.
General care: Deadhead and, in early to mid-spring, cut out up to a quarter of old stems.
Height: 2.5m (8ft) **Spread:** 2m (6ft)
Site: Sun, partial shade. Moist but well-drained soil
Compost: Soil-based (John Innes No. 3)
Use: Container, sunny or lightly shaded border, woodland garden
Good companions: *Fuchsia magellanica* 'Versicolor', *Halesia carolina, Viburnum plicatum* 'Mariesii'

6 Rosa Elina
Hybrid tea rose
Deciduous bush rose with dark green foliage. During summer and early autumn it bears scented, white double flowers with a pale yellow centre. The buds are cone shaped. Hardy.
General care: Prune between late winter and early spring, cutting back main stems to a height of about 25cm (10in) and shortening sideshoots to two or three buds.
Height: 1m (3ft) **Spread:** 75cm (2ft 6in)
Site: Sun. Fertile and moist but well-drained soil
Use: Formal bedding, sunny border
Good companions: *Alchemilla mollis, Campanula persicifolia, Viola cornuta* Alba Group

7 Rosa Iceberg
Floribunda rose
Deciduous bush rose well covered with light green leaves. Throughout summer and autumn it bears numerous clusters of creamy white double flowers. Hardy.
General care: Prune between late winter and early spring, cutting back main stems to a height of about 35cm (14in) and shortening sideshoots to two or three buds.
Height: 1m (3ft) **Spread:** 75cm (2ft 6in)
Site: Sun. Fertile and moist but well-drained soil
Use: Formal bedding, sunny border
Good companions: *Geranium* x *magnificum, Paeonia lactiflora* 'Bowl of Beauty', *Viola cornuta*

8 Sorbus hupehensis
Hubei rowan
Deciduous tree with a compact head of purplish brown branches clothed with foliage that is conspicuously blue-green throughout summer but colours red in autumn. Heads of white flowers in late spring are followed by clusters of round white berries, sometimes tinged with pink, which last into winter. Hardy.
Height: 8m (25ft) **Spread:** 6m (20ft)
Site: Sun, partial shade. Moist but well drained soil, preferably lime-free
Use: Specimen tree, woodland garden
Good companions: *Acer griseum, Hamamelis mollis, Malus tschonoskii*

green

9 Eucalyptus gunnii
Cider gum
Evergreen tree with striking greenish white bark that is shed in late summer to reveal new grey-green bark, usually warmed by an orange-pink flush. Juvenile leaves are rounded and silver-blue while mature leaves are sickle shaped and grey-green. In favourable conditions trees bear clusters of small cream flowers during late summer and early autumn. Not fully hardy.
General care: To maintain as a shrub with colourful juvenile foliage cut back all stems to near base in early spring.
Height: 20m (65ft) **Spread:** 9m (30ft)
Site: Sun. Moist but well-drained soil, preferably lime-free
Use: Border (as shrub), formal bedding (as shrub), specimen tree
Good companions: *Cortaderia selloana* 'Sunningdale Silver', *Eucalyptus pauciflora* subsp. *niphophila, Genista aetnensis*

10 Fatsia japonica
Evergreen shrub with handsome, glossy green fingered leaves up to 40cm (16in) long. In mid-autumn stiff sprays made up of rounded clusters of tiny creamy flowers stand out against the foliage. Small, inedible black berries follow. Hardy.
General care: Trim lightly in mid-spring to keep shape balanced.
Height and spread: 3m (10ft)
Site: Sun, partial shade. Moist, well-drained soil
Compost: Soil-based (John Innes No. 3)
Use: Container, sunny or lightly shaded border
Good companions: *Fargesia nitida, Hedera colchica* 'Dentata Variegata', *Pleioblastus auricomus*

11 Ilex x altaclarensis 'Camelliifolia'
Highclere holly
Large conical shrub or tree with almost spineless glossy leaves, which are red-purple when young and carried on purplish stems. This female clone produces red berries if near a pollinating male plant. Hardy.
General care: Trim hedges in mid-spring, clip shaped specimens in late summer.
Height: 15m (50ft) **Spread:** 12m (40ft)
Site: Sun, partial shade. Moist, well-drained soil
Use: Hedge, topiary, specimen tree, woodland garden
Good companions: *Corylus avellana* 'Contorta', *Hamamelis mollis, Magnolia stellata*

12 Juniperus scopulorum 'Skyrocket'
Rocky mountain juniper
The shoots of this slow-growing evergreen conifer are covered with scale-like leaves that hug the stem to form a grey-green column. Hardy.
Height: 6m (20ft) **Spread:** 35cm (14in)
Site: Sun, partial shade. Well-drained soil
Use: Avenue, gravel garden, heather garden, specimen tree
Good companions: *Calluna vulgaris* 'Peter Sparkes', *Erica carnea* 'Vivellii', *Erica* x *darleyensis* 'Arthur Johnson'

acers

Among the deciduous maples, several shrubs and trees are outstanding for their rich autumn colouring and are suitable for specimen planting or for woodland gardens. Although most tolerate some lime in the soil, the best results are on moist but well-drained acid soil in sun or partial shade. All of the following are hardy.

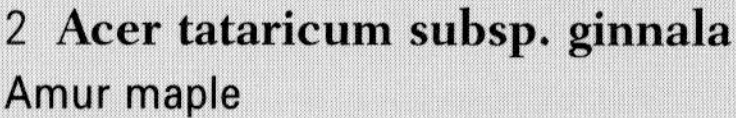

1 Acer capillipes
Snake-bark maple

The young shoots of this small tree are coral-red, but the mature bark is bright green with white vertical stripes. The small greenish flowers develop into more conspicuous tassels of winged fruits, and the three-lobed leaves turn vivid shades of orange and red in autumn.
Height and spread: 10m (33ft)
Good companions: *Acer griseum, Enkianthus campanulatus, Magnolia* x *kewensis* 'Wada's Memory'

2 Acer tataricum subsp. ginnala
Amur maple

In summer the three-lobed leaves of this large shrub or small tree are bright green, but in autumn they turn vivid crimson. Reasonably tolerant of dry conditions.
Height: 8m (25ft) **Spread:** 6m (20ft)
Good companions: *Cotoneaster lacteus, Gaultheria mucronata* 'Bell's Seedling', *Ilex aquifolium* 'Pyramidalis'

3 Acer japonicum 'Vitifolium'
Full-moon maple, Japanese maple

Slow-growing tree or large shrub with multi-lobed fan-shaped leaves that colour magnificently in autumn. In spring, produces drooping clusters of red flowers.
Height and spread: 8m (25ft)
Good companions: *Acer grosseri* var. *hersii, Amelanchier canadensis, Picea breweriana*

4 Acer rubrum 'October Glory'
Red maple, scarlet maple, swamp maple

Tree with a rounded crown grown mainly for the brilliant red of the glossy five-lobed leaves in autumn.
Height: 20m (65ft) **Spread:** 9m (30ft)
Good companions: *Eucryphia* x *nymansensis* 'Nymansay', *Magnolia denudata, Rhododendron* 'Palestrina'

5 Acer palmatum 'Sango-kaku'
Japanese maple

Shrub or round-headed small tree with deeply cut five-lobed leaves. These are warm yellow in spring, green in summer and soft yellow in autumn, when they stand out against the red twigs, which remain a feature over winter.
Height: 6m (20ft) **Spread:** 5m (15ft)
Good companions: *Acer cappadocicum* 'Aureum', *Halesia carolina, Magnolia* 'Elizabeth'

6 Acer circinatum
Vine maple

The red-purple-and-white flowers of this large shrub or small tree are a mid-spring feature, but it is the orange to red autumn foliage that makes the plant worth growing. The deeply lobed leaves are almost circular. More tolerant of dry conditions than most maples.
Height: 5m (15ft) **Spread:** 6m (20ft)
Good companions: *Betula pendula, Cercis canadensis* 'Forest Pansy', *Lonicera* x *purpusii* 'Winter Beauty'

7 Acer cappadocicum 'Aureum'
Cappadocian maple, Caucasian maple

Rounded tree with fingered leaves up to 10cm (4in) long that are yellow in spring, green in summer and yellow again in autumn.
Height: 15m (50ft) **Spread:** 10m (33ft)
Good companions: *Acer palmatum, Davidia involucrata, Magnolia denudata*

alpines

These small perennials and shrubs generally thrive in well-drained conditions and do not need a rock garden. Most look well in a raised bed and many are suitable for containers or paving. Plant in mild weather between autumn and early spring.

purple, blue and violet

1 Campanula poscharskyana 'Stella'

Dalmatian bellflower

In the second half of summer and early autumn mats of neat toothed leaves are almost covered by violet-blue starry flowers. This perennial is too vigorous for small rock gardens. Hardy.

Height: 15cm (6in) **Spread:** 60cm (2ft)

Site: Sun, partial shade. Moist, well-drained soil

Use: Dry wall, paving, raised bed, rock garden

Good companions: *Hebe cupressoides* 'Boughton Dome', *Saxifraga* 'Peter Pan', *Viola biflora*

2 Gentiana sino-ornata

Gentian

Semi-evergreen perennial that forms dense mats of prostrate stems clothed with narrow green leaves. The trumpet-shaped flowers are usually brilliant blue with greenish white and blue-purple stripes on the outside and in the throat. Hardy.

Height: 15cm (6in) **Spread:** 35cm (14in)

Site: Sun, partial shade. Lime-free, humus-rich and moist but well-drained soil

Compost: Ericaceous with added sand and leaf-mould

Use: Container, front of border, raised bed, rock garden

Good companions: *Erythronium dens-canis, Fritillaria meleagris, Lithodora diffusa* 'Heavenly Blue'

3 Gentiana 'Strathmore'

Gentian

Hybrid perennial producing sprawling stems with paired linear leaves. In autumn it bears sky-blue, trumpet-shaped flowers that are silver streaked on the outside and just under 8cm (3in) in length. Hardy.

Height: 15cm (6in) **Spread:** 30cm (12in)

Site: Sun, partial shade. Lime-free, humus-rich and moist but well-drained soil

Compost: Ericaceous with added sand and leaf-mould

Use: Container, front of border, raised bed, rock garden

Good companions: *Erythronium californicum* 'White Beauty', *Narcissus* 'Cedric Morris', *Viola cornuta*

4 Viola 'Belmont Blue'

Cornuta hybrid viola

The horned violet (*Viola cornuta*) and the violas derived from it are evergreen perennials that usually produce an autumn flush of flowers if plants are trimmed over after the main spring and summer season. The pale flowers of 'Belmont Blue' have clearly separated petals. Hardy.

Height: 15cm (6in)

Spread: 35cm (14in)

Site: Sun, partial shade. Humus-rich and moist but well-drained soil

Compost: Soil-based (John Innes No. 2) or soil-less

Use: Container, front of border, raised bed, rock garden

Good companions: *Primula marginata* 'Kesselring's Variety', *Saxifraga* 'Peter Pan', *Thuja occidentalis* 'Danica'

pink and mauve

5 Astilbe chinensis var. pumila

In late summer and autumn slender spikes of dark mauve-pink flowers top the reddish green, broadly cut leaves of this perennial. Ideal for the edge of a rock garden pool. Hardy.

Height: 30cm (12in) **Spread:** 45cm (18in)

Site: Partial shade. Humus-rich and moist soil

Use: Ground cover, front of border, rock garden, waterside

Good companions: *Campanula poscharskyana* 'Stella', *Tiarella wherryi, Viola* 'Belmont Blue'

6 Diascia 'Salmon Supreme'

Throughout summer and autumn this perennial produces slender spires of salmon-pink spurred flowers over mats of heart-shaped leaves. Not fully hardy.

Height: 15cm (6in)

Spread: 45cm (18in)

Site: Sun. Moist but well-drained soil

Compost: Soil-based (John Innes No. 2) or soil-less

Use: Container, front of sunny border, raised bed, rock garden

Good companions: *Campanula carpatica, Festuca glauca* 'Seeigel', *Geranium cinereum* 'Ballerina'

pink and mauve (continued)

1 Erodium 'County Park'

Heron's bill, Stork's bill

The common names refer to the pointed beaks of the fruits, but the appeal of this modest perennial lies in the long succession of mauve-pink flowers borne in clusters over the finely cut grey-green leaves throughout summer and autumn. Hardy.

Height and spread: 25cm (10in)

Site: Sun. Gritty well-drained soil

Compost: Soil-based (John Innes No. 1) with added grit

Use: Container, paving, raised bed, rock garden

Good companions: *Crocus chrysanthus* 'Zwanenburg Bronze', *Euphorbia myrsinites, Lavandula angustifolia* 'Nana Alba'

2 Origanum amanum

Marjoram, Oregano

In summer and autumn this compact evergreen bush bears numerous long-tubed curved flowers that emerge from among pale green bracts, which take on pink tints as they age. Hardy.

General care: Protect from excessive winter wet.

Height: 15cm (6in) **Spread:** 30cm (12in)

Site: Sun. Well-drained, preferably alkaline soil

Compost: Soil-based (John Innes No. 1) with added grit

Use: Container, raised bed, rock garden

Good companions: *Erodium* 'County Park', *Geranium cinereum* 'Ballerina', *Lavandula angustifolia* 'Hidcote'

3 Persicaria vacciniifolia

This semi-evergreen perennial produces upright spikes packed with small, deep pink flowers in late summer and autumn. The tiny glossy leaves on red-tinted stems turn red in autumn. Hardy.

Height: 20cm (8in) **Spread:** 50cm (20in)

Site: Sun, partial shade. Moist, well-drained soil

Use: Ground cover, front of border, raised bed, rock garden

Good companions: *Astilbe chinensis* var. *pumila, Hebe cupressoides* 'Boughton Dome', *Viola* 'Belmont Blue'

4 Scabiosa graminifolia

Pincushion flower, Scabious

Easily grown evergreen perennial that makes a tuft of narrow grey-green leaves. Slender stems carrying soft mauve flowerheads with 'pincushion' centres emerge in summer and early autumn. Good for cutting. Hardy.

Height: 25cm (10in) **Spread:** 35cm (14in)

Site: Sun. Well-drained soil. Good on lime

Use: Front of sunny border, raised bed, rock garden

Good companions: *Aubrieta* 'Greencourt Purple', *Gypsophila repens* 'Rosa Schönheit', *Iberis sempervirens* 'Weisser Zwerg'

red and russet

5 Sedum 'Bertram Anderson'

Stonecrop

From late summer to mid-autumn the arching to prostrate purple stems of this perennial, which are clothed with small purple-blue leaves, bear loose clusters of wine-red starry flowers. Hardy.

Height: 15cm (6in) **Spread:** 30cm (12in)

Site: Sun. Well-drained soil

Use: Front of border, raised bed, rock garden

Good companions: *Artemisia schmidtiana* 'Nana', *Campanula cochleariifolia, Festuca glauca* 'Seeigel'

6 Zauschneria californica 'Dublin'

Californian fuchsia

In late summer and early autumn this narrow-leaved woody-based perennial produces sprays of bright orange-red tubular flowers that flare at the mouth. Not fully hardy.

General care: Grow in a sheltered position.

Height: 25cm (10in) **Spread:** 35cm (14in)

Site: Sun. Well-drained soil

Use: Dry wall, front of sunny border, raised bed, rock garden

Good companions: *Aubrieta* 'Doctor Mules', *Aurinia saxatilis* 'Citrina', *Cytisus* x *beanii*

1

4

2

3

5

6

7

8

9

10

11

12

cream and white

7 Rhodanthemum hosmariense

In autumn this shrubby perennial continues to produce yellow-centred, white daisy-like flowers over deeply cut silver leaves. Not fully hardy.
Height: 25cm (10in) **Spread:** 35cm (14in)
Site: Sun. Well-drained soil
Compost: Soil-based (John Innes No. 2) with added grit
Use: Container, front of sunny border, raised bed, rock garden
Good companions: *Lavandula angustifolia* 'Hidcote', *Muscari botryoides* 'Album', *Tulipa saxatilis* Bakeri Group 'Lilac Wonder'

silver and grey

8 Festuca glauca 'Seeigel'

Fescue

Evergreen perennial grass grown for the hair-like, silvery blue-green leaves, which make a spiky clump, rather than its blue-green flowers. Hardy.
Height and spread: 15cm (6in)
Site: Sun. Well-drained soil
Use: Front of sunny border, gravel garden, raised bed, rock garden
Good companions: *Armeria maritima* 'Düsseldorfer Stolz', *Crocus chrysanthus* 'Ladykiller', *Oxalis adenophylla*

green

9 Chamaecyparis lawsoniana 'Gimbornii'

Lawson cypress

Slow-growing, dwarf evergreen conifer valued as a foliage plant. This dense globular bush has blue-green leaves with tips that are tinged purple in cold winters. After many years it may double the dimensions given. Hardy.
Height and spread: 60cm (2ft)
Site: Sun. Moist but well-drained soil
Compost: Soil-based (John Innes No. 3)
Use: Container, heather garden, sunny border, raised bed, rock garden
Good companions: *Campanula poscharskyana* 'Stella', *Persicaria vacciniifolia, Viola* 'Belmont Blue'

10 Chamaecyparis lawsoniana 'Green Globe'

Lawson cypress

Dwarf conifer with congested sprays of bright green foliage that make a neat bun when young, but are less regular with age. Hardy.
Height and spread: 25cm (10in)
Site: Sun. Moist but well-drained soil
Compost: Soil-based (John Innes No. 3) with added leaf-mould
Use: Container, raised bed, rock garden
Good companions: *Campanula carpatica, Hebe cupressoides* 'Boughton Dome', *Viola biflora*

11 Thuja occidentalis 'Danica'

White cedar

The white cedar is itself a large evergreen conifer, but there are numerous attractive dwarf forms grown as foliage plants. This slow-growing example, which may eventually exceed the dimensions given, makes a rounded bush composed of erect stems carrying sprays of bright green leaves. Hardy.
Height and spread: 45cm (18in)
Site: Sun. Moist but well-drained soil
Compost: Soil-based (John Innes No. 3)
Use: Container, heather garden, sunny border, raised bed, rock garden
Good companions: *Daphne cneorum* 'Eximia', *Gentiana verna, Hebe cupressoides* 'Boughton Dome'

black

12 Viola 'Molly Sanderson'

Viola

Although it may be short-lived, this compact evergreen perennial flowers freely throughout summer and into autumn. A yellow eye brightens the medium-sized velvet-black flowers. Hardy.
General care: Deadhead to prolong flowering.
Height: 10cm (4in) **Spread:** 25cm (10in)
Site: Sun, partial shade. Humus-rich, moist but well-drained soil
Compost: Soil-less or soil-based (John Innes No. 2)
Use: Container, front of border, raised bed, rock garden
Good companions: *Astilbe chinensis* var. *pumila, Erythronium dens-canis, Viola biflora*

waterside & water plants

As the days shorten, a few perennials that thrive in reliably moist soil put on a late show. Plant in the dormant season.

purple, blue and violet

1 Lobelia syphilitica

Blue cardinal flower

Short-lived perennial with leafy upright stems and light green foliage. In late summer and early autumn it produces spikes of clear blue flowers that are tubular but open at the lips. Hardy.

General care: Divide plants every few years and move to fresh soil.

Height: 1m (3ft) **Spread:** 30cm (12in)

Site: Sun, partial shade. Fertile and moist soil

Use: Moist border, waterside

Good companions: *Lobelia* 'Queen Victoria', *Lythrum salicaria* 'Feuerkerze', *Primula pulverulenta* Bartley hybrids

pink and mauve

2 Eupatorium purpureum

Joe-pye weed

Large impressive perennial with stiff upright stems that are conspicuously purple among the toothed mid-green leaves, which sometimes also have a purple tinge. In late summer and autumn, domed heads of pink flowers top the foliage. Hardy.

Height: 2.5m (8ft) **Spread:** 1.2m (4ft)

Site: Sun, partial shade. Moist soil

Use: Moist border, waterside, wild garden

Good companions: *Cortaderia selloana* 'Sunningdale Silver', *Lythrum salicaria* 'Feuerkerze', *Miscanthus sinensis* 'Silberfeder'

bronze and maroon

3 Azolla filiculoides

Fairy moss, Mosquito plant

This aquatic fern forms patches of scale-like fronds that float freely on the water's surface and trail fine roots. The foliage is light green in summer but turns red-bronze in autumn. Half hardy.

General care: In frost-prone areas overwinter several fronds on damp soil under cover. When there is no longer risk of frost scatter them on the water's surface.

Spread: Indefinite

Site: Sun, partial shade

Use: Pond

Good companions: *Aponogeton distachyos*, *Caltha palustris* 'Flore Pleno', *Myosotis scorpioides* 'Mermaid'

4 Rodgersia podophylla

This rhizomatous perennial produces a modest display of rounded sprays of tiny, greenish cream flowers in late summer but bears magnificent foliage. The leaves are up to 40cm (16in) long and consist of five jaggedly lobed leaflets. Newly unfolded, these are crinkled and dark brown. They then turn green and in autumn become bronze-red. Hardy.

Height and spread: 1.5m (5ft)

Site: Sun, partial shade. Humus-rich and moist soil

Use: Moist border, waterside

Good companions: *Miscanthus sinensis* 'Silberfeder', *Rheum palmatum* 'Atrosanguineum', *Rodgersia aesculifolia*

red and russet

5 Osmunda regalis

Flowering fern, Royal fern

Large deciduous fern that forms a substantial mound of broadly triangular fronds, which are copper tinted when they unroll in spring. In summer upright, rust-coloured partially fertile fronds contrast with bright green infertile fronds, which in autumn turn yellow, tan and buff. Hardy.

Height and spread: 1.5m (5ft)

Site: Sun, partial shade. Humus-rich and reliably

moist soil, preferably lime-free

Use: Damp border, waterside

Good companions: *Cornus alba* 'Sibirica', *Matteuccia struthiopteris, Salix irrorata*

yellow and orange

6 Ligularia dentata 'Desdemona'

Golden groundsel

This perennial makes an impressive clump of large, bronze-purple heart-shaped leaves with magenta-purple undersides. In late summer and early autumn sturdy stems carry clusters of orange-yellow daisy-like flowers. Hardy.

Height: 1.2m (4ft) **Spread:** 1m (3ft)

Site: Sun, partial shade. Reliably moist soil

Use: Moist border, waterside

Good companions: *Ligularia* 'The Rocket', *Miscanthus sinensis* 'Zebrinus', *Rodgersia aesculifolia*

7 Luzula sylvatica 'Aurea'

Greater woodrush

In summer the tussock of glossy leaves, topped early in the season by warm brown flowers, is yellow-green. In late autumn and winter the leaves turn bright yellow. Hardy.

Height: 75cm (2ft 6in) **Spread:** 45cm (18in)

Site: Partial shade, sun. Humus-rich and reliably moist but well-drained soil

Use: Ground cover, moist border, waterside, woodland garden

Good companions: *Carex pendula, Filipendula ulmaria* 'Aurea', *Trollius europaeus*

cream and white

8 Aponogeton distachyos

Cape pondweed, Water hawthorn

This perennial aquatic may be evergreen in mild winters. The floating light green leaves are frequently mottled maroon. The heavily scented, forked flower clusters are white at first then fade to green, their season extending from early summer until mid-autumn. Not fully hardy.

Spread: 1.2m (4ft)

Site: Sun. Still water 30cm–1m (1–3ft) deep

Compost: Soil-based (aquatic)

Use: Pond

Good companions: *Myosotis scorpioides* 'Mermaid', *Nymphaea* 'James Brydon', *Zantedeschia aethiopica* 'Crowborough'

silver and grey

9 Miscanthus sacchariflorus

Silver banner grass

Non-invasive perennial grass that makes a magnificent summer and autumn feature for large gardens. Leaves, up to 1m (3ft) long and blue-green in summer, flutter from bamboo-like canes. Their rustling movement remains appealing when they turn beige-brown in autumn. Silky, silvery brown flowers are produced only after a hot summer. Hardy.

General care: Leave foliage for winter effect but cut to the ground by early spring.

Height: 2.5m (8ft) **Spread:** 1.2m (4ft)

Site: Sun. Moist but well-drained soil

Use: Moist border, waterside, wild garden

Good companions: *Eupatorium purpureum, Ligularia* 'Gregynog Gold', *Rodgersia pinnata* 'Superba'

10 Miscanthus sinensis 'Silberfeder'

The value of most cultivars of this clump-forming grass lies in their foliage. The blue-green ribbon-like leaves of 'Silberfeder' arch elegantly from tall stems that in autumn are topped by feathery, pink-tinted silver-beige plumes. These remain attractive throughout winter. Hardy.

Height: 2.5m (8ft) **Spread:** 1.2m (4ft)

Site: Sun. Moist but well-drained soil

Use: Sunny border, waterside

Good companions: *Aconitum carmichaelii* 'Arendsii', *Cimicifuga simplex* Atropurpurea Group, *Molinia caerulea* subsp. *arundinacea* 'Windspiel'

11 Molinia caerulea subsp. caerulea 'Heidebraut'

Purple moor grass

This perennial grass makes a tussock of narrow tapered blades. In autumn, even after these have died down, stiff columns of straw-coloured stems topped with glittering seedheads remain eye-catching. Hardy.

Height: 1.5m (5ft)

Spread: 40cm (16in)

Site: Sun, partial shade. Moist soil, preferably lime-free

Use: Moist border, waterside

Good companions: *Astilbe* 'Professor van der Wielen', *Carex pendula, Hosta* 'Royal Standard'

7

8

9

10

11

herbs, vegetables & fruit

Autumn is the traditional season for harvesting fruit and vegetables, but it is also when gardeners need to plan for early crops the following year.

herbs

1 Aniseed
Pimpinella anisum

With a froth of feathery leaves this annual makes a dainty edging and container plant. The strongly flavoured fresh foliage and dried seeds are used in Indian and Middle Eastern cooking. Tender.
General care: Sow seed in late spring in pots or *in situ,* then thin to 20cm (8in) apart. Harvest seeds in early autumn when seedpods turn grey and hang up to dry in a cool dark place.
Height: 45cm (18in) **Spread:** 30cm (12in)
Site: Sun, sheltered. Light, well-drained soil
Compost: Soil-based (John Innes No. 3)
Use: Container, edging, front of border

2 Bay
Laurus nobilis

Large shrub or small tree with evergreen foliage that can be trimmed into simple topiary shapes and kept to required size. In very hot summers, creamy white flowers are produced. The leaves are used to flavour soups, stews and stocks. Use fresh or harvest to dry in early summer. Fairly hardy when established, but frost-sensitive while young and in exposed gardens.
General care: Plant in spring or autumn and protect from frosts for two years. Insulate containers against frost. Water regularly in dry summers. Trim to shape in late spring.
Height: 12m (40ft) **Spread:** 3m (10ft)
Site: Sun, sheltered. Well-drained soil
Compost: Soil-based (John Innes No. 3) with good drainage
Use: Large container, specimen tree in border, topiary

3 Caraway
Carum carvi

Easily grown biennial herb. Although young leaves are used in salads, the seeds, used for flavouring bread and biscuits, are the main crop. Harvest these in autumn just before they ripen, as the capsules change colour. Hardy.
General care: Sow seed outdoors in rows in autumn or indoors in a plug tray in early spring. Thin or plant out 20cm (8in) apart each way. Mark the position of the plants as they die down completely over winter. Check for carrot root fly.
Height: 1m (3ft) **Spread:** 30cm (12in)
Site: Sun. Well-drained soil
Use: Herb or vegetable garden

4 Winter savory
Satureja montana

This semi-evergreen perennial is an attractive plant for indoor and patio containers. It is more strongly flavoured than summer savory. Hardy.
General care: Sow seed indoors in small pots in early spring and plant out 15cm (6in) apart, or divide established clumps. Pick or trim regularly to maintain good shape and condition.
Height and spread: 45cm (18in)
Site: Sun. Fairly poor, well-drained soil
Compost: Soil-based (John Innes No. 3) with added grit
Use: Container, edging, front of border

vegetables

5 Brussels sprout

Brassica oleracea Gemmifera Group

Sprouts are normally picked after the first frost, which improves their flavour. Firm ground or staking is essential for taller varieties. The leafy tops make tasty 'greens', especially if cut off when the lowest sprouts are nearly ready. 'Oliver' and 'Peer Gynt' are the first to crop. Hardy.

Site: Sun, light shade. Deep, rich very firm soil, limed to pH7 or higher

How to grow: Sow seed outdoors in mid-spring. Thin seedlings to 8cm (3in) apart and transplant 60cm (2ft) apart each way when five or six weeks old. Water freely in dry weather. Feed with high-nitrogen fertiliser in midsummer. Remove yellowing leaves and net against birds. Snap off sprouts cleanly, starting at the bottom.

6 Cabbage, autumn

Brassica oleracea Capitata Group

Hardier and slower growing than summer cabbage, this produces large heads that remain in good condition for weeks. Varieties include pointed 'Winnigstadt', round 'Stonehead', white 'Polinius', savoy 'Celtic' and red 'Hardoro'. Hardy.

Site: Sun. Rich firm soil, with added lime if acid

How to grow: Sow outdoors in mid-spring. Thin seedlings to 8cm (3in) apart and transplant 50cm (20in) apart, less for compact varieties, when six to eight weeks old; plant firmly. Water in dry weather and protect from birds. Cut heads off when large enough. If hard frost threatens, dig up mature heads and hang in a cool frost-free place.

7 Carrot, maincrop

Daucus carota

Large autumn and winter carrots are maincrop varieties, sown later than summer kinds and allowed to grow for at least 12 weeks. Whole crops can be dug up for storing when mature, but in mild gardens with light soils, roots remain sound over winter if mulched. Varieties include 'Autumn King' and 'Major'. Hardy.

Site: Sun. Light, well-drained soil with plenty of added compost

How to grow: Sow seed outdoors in late spring, in rows 15cm (6in) apart. Thin seedlings to 5–8cm (2–3in) apart and mulch. Water every two to three weeks in dry weather. Start forking up roots when large enough. Clear crops in mid-autumn; twist off tops and store in boxes in just damp sand, or mulch rows with straw or leaves 15cm (6in) deep, held down with netting or soil.

8 Celery, self-blanching

Apium graveolens var. dulce

Self-blanching and green (American) celery is Fast-growing and harvested from late summer until the first frosts, or later if grown under cover. The tasty green leaves can be picked at any time for use as flavouring. Good varieties include 'Celebrity', 'Lathom Self Blanching', 'Green Utah' and 'Greensleeves'. Tender.

Site: Sun, sheltered or in a coldframe. Moist soil with plenty of added compost

How to grow: Sow seed indoors in early spring and prick out into trays or small pots. Harden off and plant out in late spring, at least 23cm (9in) apart each way in blocks. Water weekly during dry weather and feed with high-nitrogen fertiliser in midsummer. Start harvesting when large enough and clear before the first frosts.

9 Jerusalem artichoke

Helianthus tuberosus

This produces nutritious tubers and tall leafy stems, which make an effective 3m (10ft) high windbreak if grown in rows. Stems can be shortened in midsummer to 2m (6ft). 'Fuseau' has the smoothest tubers; 'Dwarf Sunray' is short. Hardy.

Site: Sun, light shade. Fertile soil with plenty of added compost

How to grow: Plant small tubers in early spring, 10–15cm (4–6in) deep and 30cm (12in) apart. Water freely in dry weather. Earth and mulch stems for extra support. For larger tubers remove flowers. Lift as required from very early autumn.

10 Kohl rabi

Brassica oleracea Gongylodes Group

This cabbage relative has smooth swollen stems that are crisp and mildly flavoured. Ready just seven to eight weeks after sowing, even on soils that are too dry for other brassicas. The 'bulbs' are best when the size of tennis balls, although modern varieties grown on moist soils remain crisp when much larger. Not fully hardy.

Site: Light shade. Fertile sandy soil

How to grow: Sow small batches of seed *in situ* about every three to four weeks, in rows 30cm (12in) apart, from mid-spring until midsummer. Thin seedlings to 15–20cm (6–8in) apart. Water regularly in dry weather and mulch. Pull plants when large enough. Late crops can be cleared and stored in boxes of sand, or left outdoors in mild weather.

11 Leek, early

Allium porrum

Mild-flavoured member of the onion family with non-bulbing white stems. Early varieties, such as 'Albinstar' and 'King Richard', are juicy but cannot withstand frost. Mini-leeks, grown by thinning leek seedlings to 2.5cm (1in) apart, are ready when the size of spring onions. Tender.

Site: Sun, light shade. Deep rich soil with plenty of added compost

How to grow: Sow seed under glass in late winter then prick out into trays, or outdoors in mid-spring, thinning seedlings to 4cm (1½in) apart. Plant out from late spring onwards, when 20cm (8in) high, dropping a single seedling into a 15cm (6in) deep hole, spaced 15cm (6in) in rows 30cm (12in) apart. Water occasionally in dry weather. Start lifting with a fork when large enough.

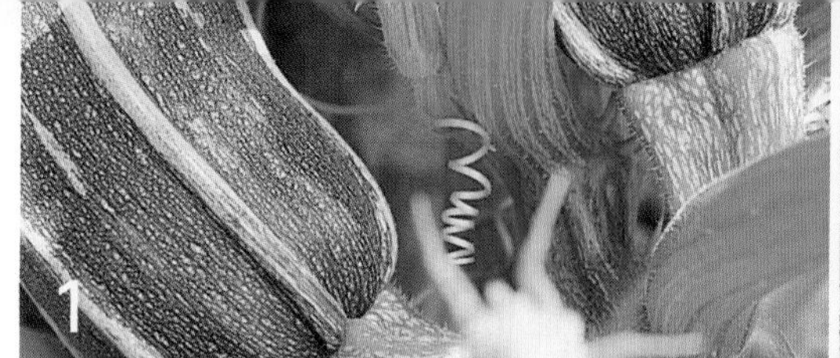

vegetables (continued)

1 Marrow
Cucurbita pepo

Marrows can be cut eight weeks after planting and will continue cropping until the first frosts. The last can be 'cured' (see below), then stored in a dry airy place at about 10°C (50°F) for several weeks. Trailing varieties can be planted on a compost heap. Varieties include 'Long Green Trailing' and 'All Green Bush'. Tender.

Site: Sun, sheltered. Rich, deeply dug soil with plenty of added compost

How to grow: Sow seed indoors in small pots two to three weeks before the last frosts and plant out when all risk of frost is past. Space bush varieties 1–1.2m (3–4ft) apart and trailing kinds 2m (6ft) apart. Water and mulch liberally. Pinch out trailing kinds when five leaves have opened and spread out resulting sideshoots across the ground or tie to trellis. Harvest regularly. To cure fruits for storing, dry them in the sun (in a greenhouse or on a windowsill) for two weeks.

2 Onion, maincrop
Allium cepa

Can be raised from seed or, more easily, from sets (immature bulbs). A combination of spring and autumn sowing or planting (see 5, Onion, page 298) can ensure a year-round supply. Check varieties for flavour, which can range from mildly sweet to ferociously hot. Not fully hardy.

Site: Sun. Fertile, well-drained soil with plenty of added compost

How to grow: Sow seed *in situ* in early spring in rows 30cm (12in) apart and thin seedlings to 5cm (2in) apart for small bulbs and 10–15cm (4–6in) for large ones. Plant sets at the same distances, with their tips just covered. Water frequently until midsummer. In late summer to early autumn fork up bulbs carefully and spread out on trays or under glass to dry. When skins are papery, store in nets or boxes; they will keep until spring.

3 Potato, maincrop
Solanum tuberosum

Maincrop potatoes yield heavily on most soils. Although they occupy space for most of the growing season, they can be stored until spring. Good varieties are 'Marfona', 'Cara', 'Romano', 'Sante' and 'Picasso'. Not fully hardy.

Site: Sun. Fertile, deeply dug and well-drained soil

How to grow: Set seed potatoes to sprout, or 'chit', in late winter and plant out in mid-spring 10–15cm (4–6in) deep, spaced 40cm (16in) apart with 75cm (2ft 6in) between rows. Mound soil half-way up the stems every two to three weeks until the leaves of adjacent plants meet. Water well once or twice after flowering starts. Cut down the foliage when it turns brown in autumn, then lift the tubers with a fork two weeks later. Allow to dry on the surface for a few hours, then store in an insulated clamp or in thick paper sacks in a cool dry place.

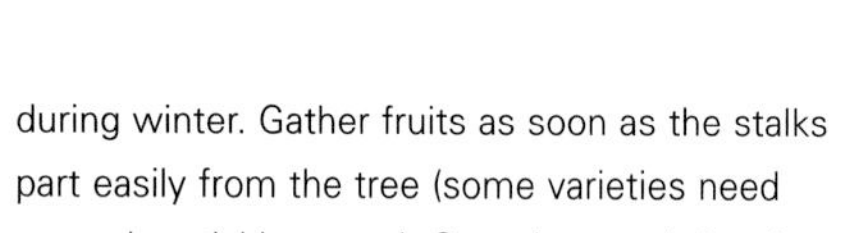

4 Squash, winter
Cucurbita maxima and C. moschata

With thick skins protecting their well-flavoured flesh, pumpkins and other winter squashes can be stored for months over winter. These vigorous trailing plants need plenty of space, but tolerate light shade so make good ground cover under sweetcorn, runner beans and fruit trees. Tender.

Site: Sun, light shade. Rich, deeply dug soil with plenty of added compost or rotted manure

How to grow: Sow and plant as for marrows (see 1, Marrow), or sow *in situ* after the last frosts. Water well in dry weather and feed every two to three weeks while fruits are swelling. To grow large squashes, thin fruitlets to three to four on each plant. Move or remove leaves to expose ripening fruits to the sun. Cut when large enough or, for storing, leave until fully coloured in early autumn. Cure and store as for marrows.

fruit

5 Apple
Malus domestica

Apart from the earliest varieties, most apples ripen at various times during the autumn and need regular inspection to judge the best moment to start harvesting. Some kinds, such as 'Sunset', can be eaten straight after picking, while others, especially late keepers such as 'Ribston Pippin' and 'Orleans Reinette', need storing for a few weeks after harvest before they are ready to eat. These will keep well into winter or early spring. Hardy.

Site: Sun, sheltered. Deep, fertile, well-drained soil

How to grow: Plant during the dormant season. Support if necessary, especially dwarf trees in exposed gardens. Water regularly during the first season, and feed and mulch in spring. Prune trained trees in mid or late summer, other kinds during winter. Gather fruits as soon as the stalks part easily from the tree (some varieties need several partial harvests). Store in a cool airy place.

6 Blackberry
Rubus fruticosus

Cultivated blackberries have larger fruit than wild plants, but are still vigorous and need firm training on wires or a fence. A range of varieties offers fruit from late summer until the frosts. 'Ashton Cross' and 'Fantasia' have good flavour; parsley-leaved 'Oregon Thornless' is thornless. Hardy.

Site: Sun, sheltered. Fertile, well-drained soil

How to grow: Plant while dormant, spacing the plants 4m (12ft) apart. Water in dry weather, and feed and mulch in spring. Train in new canes and prune out fruited ones after harvest. Pick fruit when fully coloured and soft.

7 Damson
Prunus insititia

Grow as specimen trees for spring blossom and heavy crops of blue-black, richly flavoured fruits. 'Farleigh Damson' and 'Prune Damson' are among the best varieties. Hardier but less vigorous than other plums.

Site: Sun, sheltered. Rich, deep soil with plenty of added compost

How to grow: Plant in late autumn, 5m (15ft) apart. Mulch in spring with rotted manure. Prune while in leaf. Harvest fruit when fully coloured and starting to fall.

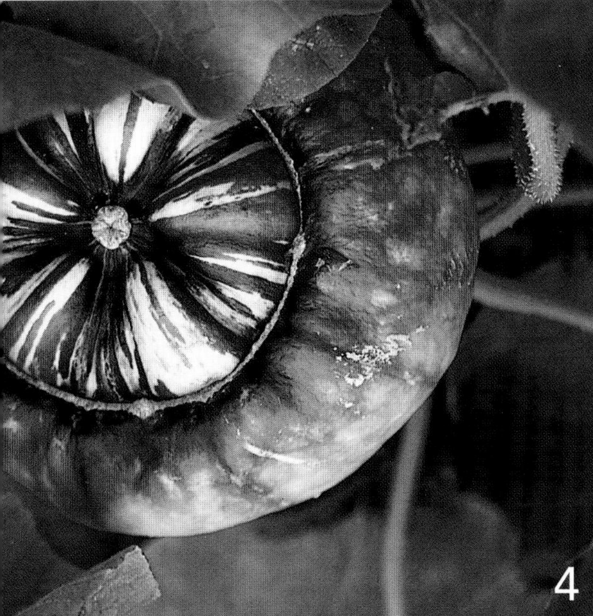

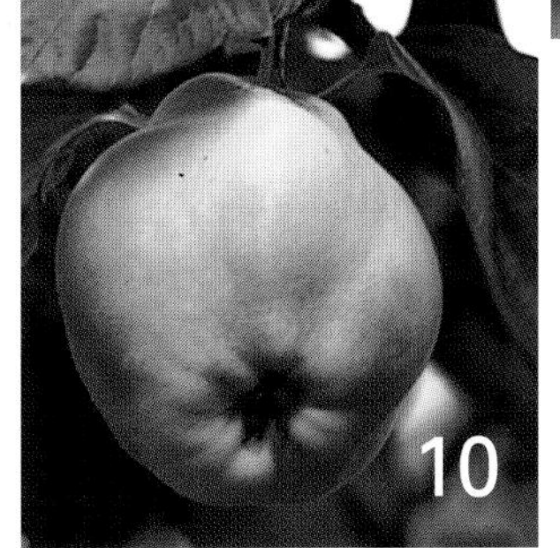
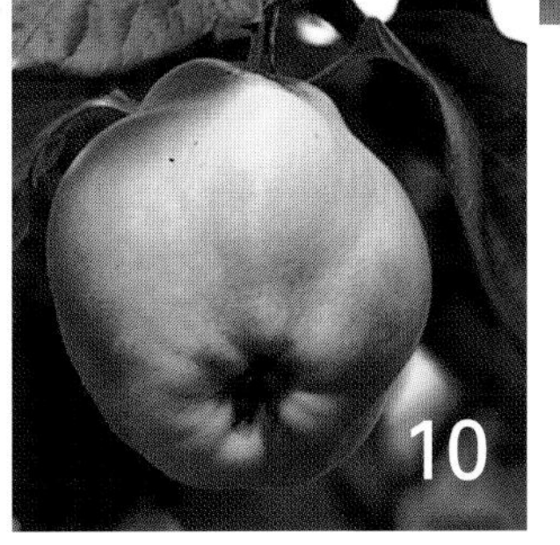

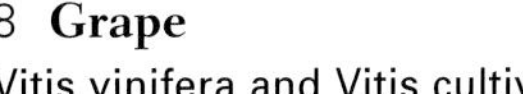

8 Grape

Vitis vinifera and Vitis cultivars

With firm training these elegant vines may be grown as an intensive fruit crop, or they can be used as decorative climbers for screens and pergolas. Outdoor dessert grapes are best trained on a warm wall; wine grapes are hardier and can crop heavily after a hot summer. Good varieties include 'Siegerrebe' (white) and 'Brant' (black, good autumn colour). Hardy.

Site: Sun, sheltered. Fertile, well-drained soil

How to grow: Plant while dormant, 1.2–1.5m (4–5ft) apart. Mulch in spring with rotted manure and water regularly during dry weather. Train climbers on wires, with a maximum of three to four stems. Prune after fruiting, cutting all sideshoots back to the main branches.

9 Melon

Cucumis melo

For the best crops, grow in a greenhouse or coldframe, but cantaloupe varieties can be grown in the open, especially if trained over a hard surface such as paving, which absorbs heat. Tender.

Site: Sun, sheltered. Fertile, well-drained soil.

How to grow: Sow seed indoors in mid-spring in small pots. Plant out 1m (3ft) apart, after danger of frosts is past. Pinch out the growing tip after five leaves and spread out resulting sideshoots on the ground or on vertical wires. Select the best fruit on each shoot, remove any others and pinch out the growing tips. Flowers on indoor plants may need hand pollinating. Harvest when melons are strongly fragrant, with cracking around the stalk base.

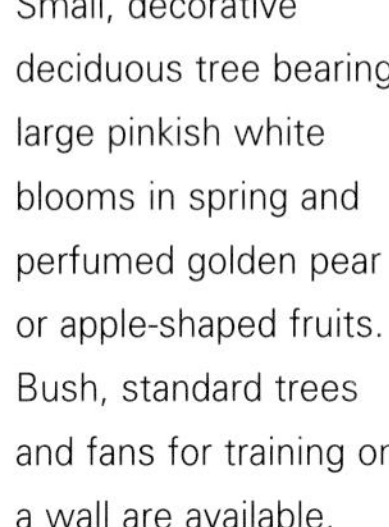

10 Quince

Cydonia oblonga

Small, decorative deciduous tree bearing large pinkish white blooms in spring and perfumed golden pear or apple-shaped fruits. Bush, standard trees and fans for training on a wall are available. Look for 'Vranja' and 'Meech's Prolific'. Hardy.

Site: Sun, sheltered. Deep, light, fertile soil

How to grow: Plant while dormant, 4.5–6m (15–20ft) apart. Feed or mulch with rotted manure annually in early spring. Prune in winter, removing misplaced, crossing and congested shoots. Leave fruits until fully coloured but harvest before frosts. Store in boxes in a cool airy place for a month to allow the powerful flavour to develop; keep away from other fruit to avoid cross-flavouring.

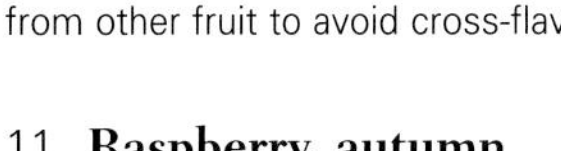

11 Raspberry, autumn

Rubus idaeus

Autumn-fruiting raspberries yield heavy crops of firm red, sometimes golden fruits until the frosts. They need plenty of space and produce a dense screen of tall canes, which can be useful for shading leafy vegetables in a hot summer. Try 'Autumn Bliss', 'Heritage' or yellow 'Fallgold'. Hardy.

Site: Sun. Deep, light soil with added compost

How to grow: Plant while dormant, 45–60cm (18–24in) apart in rows 1.2m (4ft) apart, and cut down to 23cm (9in) high. In early spring feed and mulch with compost. Train in the canes as they grow, fanning them evenly about 10cm (4in) apart on parallel wires. Harvest fruit when fully coloured. Leave canes over winter, cutting to ground level in late winter to allow for the new season's canes.

choosing the best plants

The following plant lists draw on all the plants described in the preceding pages of the Plant Selector, but they are grouped together here to help you choose plants for particular conditions, situations and uses.

plants for coastal sites

Where windbreaks and hedges give protection from salt-laden winds, a wide range of plants can be grown in coastal gardens, including many that benefit from the sea's moderating influence on temperatures.

- *Amaryllis belladonna*
- *Arbutus unedo*
- *Arctotis* x *hybrida* 'Flame'
- *Aster* (short-growing kinds)
- *Calluna vulgaris* (all)
- *Campanula poscharskyana* 'Stella'
- *Caryopteris* x *clandonensis* 'Kew Blue'
- *Ceanothus* 'Autumnal Blue'
- *Cotoneaster conspicuus* 'Decorus'
- *Cyclamen hederifolium*
- *Erodium* 'County Park'
- *Euphorbia seguieriana* subsp. *niciciana*
- *Festuca glauca* 'Seeigel'
- *Fuchsia* (most)
- *Geranium sanguineum*
- *Hebe* 'Autumn Glory'
- *Hydrangea* (all)
- *Ilex* x *altaclarensis* 'Camelliifolia'
- *Isotoma axillaris*
- *Juniperus communis* 'Green Carpet'
- *Kniphofia* (all)
- *Lagurus ovatus*
- *Lavatera trimestris* 'Silver Cup'
- *Limonium sinuatum* Forever Series
- *Nerine bowdenii*
- *Penstemon* (all)
- *Rhodanthemum hosmariense*
- *Rosa* 'Fru Dagmar Hastrup'
- *Scabiosa* (all)
- *Schizostylis coccinea* 'Sunrise'
- *Sedum* (all)
- *Sternbergia lutea*

Penstemon 'Raven'

plants for moist shade

The following plants tolerate or more commonly thrive in moist shade, although many will also grow in full sun provided the soil is reliably moist. Plants marked with an asterisk* will grow in boggy conditions.

- *Acer* (all)
- *Amelanchier canadensis*
- *Anemone* x *hybrida* (all)
- *Aster divaricatus*
- *Aster lateriflorus* 'Horizontalis'
- *Astilbe chinensis* var. *pumila*
- *Cercidiphylum japonicum*
- *Cimicifuga simplex* Atropurpurea Group
- *Disanthus cercidifolius*
- *Euphorbia schillingii*
- *Fatsia japonica*
- *Fuchsia* (all)
- *Galax urceolata*
- *Gaultheria mucronata* 'Mulberry Wine'
- *Hydrangea macrophylla* 'Madame Emile Mouillère'
- *Hydrangea* 'Preziosa'
- *Impatiens* New Guinea Group
- *Iris foetidissima*
- *Lobelia syphilitica**
- *Molinia* (all)
- *Nicotiana langsdorffii*
- *Nicotiana sylvestris*
- *Ophiopogon planiscapus* 'Nigrescens'
- *Osmunda regalis**
- *Rodgersia podophylla**
- *Saxifraga fortunei*
- *Tricyrtis formosana*
- *Viburnum opulus* 'Compactum'
- *Viola* 'Belmont Blue'
- *Viola* 'Molly Sanderson'

Acer palmatum

plants for acid soil

Plants in the following list that are marked with an asterisk* will only grow satisfactorily on soils that are free of lime. Other plants in the list thrive on acid soils, although they may also grow satisfactorily on soils that are neutral or to some degree alkaline.

- *Acer* (all)
- *Amelanchier canadensis*
- *Calluna vulgaris* (all)*
- *Camellia sasanqua* 'Narumigata'*
- *Disanthus cercidifolius**
- *Eucalyptus gunnii*
- *Galax urceolata**
- *Gaultheria mucronata* 'Mulberry Wine'
- *Gentiana sino-ornata**
- *Gentiana* 'Strathmore'*
- *Lapageria rosea**
- *Liquidambar styraciflua* 'Worplesdon'
- *Molinia* (all)
- *Osmunda regalis*
- *Quercus coccinea* 'Splendens'*
- *Sorbus* (most)

plants for dry chalky soil

A large number of plants are automatically excluded from this list because they will not tolerate alkaline (limy) soil. The improvement of shallow chalky soil by the addition of moisture-retaining organic matter allows lime-tolerant but moisture-loving plants, notably clematis, to be grown successfully.

- *Arbutus unedo*
- *Aster amellus*
- *Caryopteris* x *clandonensis* 'Kew Blue'
- *Cotoneaster conspicuus* 'Decorus'
- *Crocus kotschyanus*
- *Crocus speciosus*
- *Cyclamen hederifolium*
- *Euonymus europaeus* 'Red Cascade'
- *Euphorbia seguieriana* subsp. *niciana*
- *Iris foetidissima*
- *Lavatera trimestris* 'Silver Cup'
- *Liriope muscari*
- *Origanum amanum*
- *Scabiosa* (all)
- *Sedum* (all)
- *Sternbergia lutea*

plants for clay soil

Although the following plants generally succeed on close-textured clay soils, they do better when the ground has been improved by the addition of grit and organic matter such as well-rotted garden compost.

- *Acer* (most)
- *Amelanchier canadensis*
- *Anemone* x *hybrida* (all)
- *Chamaecyparis lawsoniana* 'Gimbornii'
- *Clematis* (some)
- *Cotinus* 'Flame'
- *Cotoneaster* (all)
- *Crataegus persimilis* 'Prunifolia'
- *Eucalyptus gunnii*
- *Hibiscus syriacus* 'Woodbridge'
- *Ilex* x *altaclarensis* 'Camelliifolia'
- *Juniperus communis* 'Green Carpet'
- *Kniphofia* (all)
- *Malus* 'John Downie'
- *Miscanthus* (all)
- *Molinia* (all)
- *Panicum virgatum* 'Rubrum'
- *Parthenocissus quinquefolia*
- *Parthenocissus tricuspidata* 'Veitchii'
- *Prunus sargentii*
- *Rodgersia podophylla*
- *Rosa* (all)
- *Sorbus* 'Joseph Rock'
- *Sorbus sargentiana*
- *Thuja occidentalis* 'Danica'
- *Viburnum opulus* 'Compactum'
- *Vitis coignetiae*

Acer circinatum

plants for sandy or gravelly soil

The following plants require free drainage and are generally drought tolerant. The range of plants that can be grown in dry sunny gardens can be enlarged if the soil is improved by the addition of organic matter.

- *Bassia scoparia* f. *tricophylla*
- *Bidens ferulifolia*
- *Calluna vulgaris* (all)
- *Caryopteris* x *clandonensis* 'Kew Blue'
- *Convolvulus tricolor* 'Royal Ensign'
- *Cotoneaster conspicuus* 'Decorus'
- *Cotoneaster salicifolia* 'Rothschildianus'
- *Crocus kotschyanus*
- *Crocus speciosus*
- *Erodium* 'County Park'
- *Euphorbia seguieriana* subsp. *niciciana*
- *Festuca glauca* 'Seeigel'
- *Gaura lindheimeri* 'Siskiyou Pink'
- *Isotoma axillaris*
- *Juniperus communis* 'Green Carpet'
- *Juniperus scopulorum* 'Skyrocket'
- *Lagurus ovatus*
- *Lavatera trimestris* 'Silver Cup'
- *Limonium sinuatum* Forever Series
- *Nerine bowdenii*
- *Origanum amanum*
- *Pennisetum villosum*
- *Rhodanthemum hosmariense*
- *Sedum* (all)
- *Sternbergia lutea*
- *Tagetes* (all)
- *Tithonia rotundifolia* 'Goldfinger'
- *Vitis* 'Brant'
- *Xeranthemum annuum*
- *Zauschneria californica*

Erodium 'County Park'

flowering plants for containers

As well as the plants listed here as suitable for general container gardening, a number of alpine, or rock garden, plants are suitable for troughs.

- *Amaranthus caudatus* 'Viridis'
- *Anagallis monellii*
- *Arctotis* x *hybrida* 'Flame'
- *Begonia semperflorens* Organdy Series
- *Calluna vulgaris* (all)
- *Convolvulus tricolor* 'Royal Ensign'
- *Dahlia* 'Figaro Red'
- *Diascia* 'Salmon Supreme'
- *Fuchsia* (most)
- *Heliotropium arborescens* 'Marine'
- *Hydrangea macrophylla* 'Madame Emile Mouillère'
- *Hydrangea* 'Preziosa'
- *Impatiens* New Guinea Group
- *Isotoma axillaris*
- *Petunia* 'Purple Wave'
- *Rudbeckia hirta* 'Rustic Dwarf'
- *Salvia farinacea* 'Victoria'
- *Tagetes* (all)
- *Viola* 'Belmont Blue'
- *Viola* 'Molly Sanderson'

plants for ground cover

Close planting of shrubs and perennials will help to create an attractive weed-excluding cover. However, effective cover can only be achieved by planting into soil from which perennial weeds have been eliminated. The following plants are particularly useful because of their dense foliage.

- *Astilbe chinensis* var. *pumila*
- *Calluna vulgaris* (all)
- *Cotoneaster conspicuus* 'Decorus'
- *Galax urceolata*
- *Liriope muscari*
- *Persicaria vaccinifolia*

winter

practical diary

Winter gives the gardener time to draw breath after the busy growing season. There are still important jobs to be done, but these need not be tackled with the urgency of spring and summer work, and they often deserve more thought. The siting of new trees and shrubs, and the pruning and training of existing ones, requires some artistry and consideration. Other tasks, like winter digging and clearing the vegetable plot, ensure that, bit by bit, the garden is brought back under control. This is a good time for cleaning tools and pots, for tidying sheds and repairing fences. And as the days lengthen in late winter, the new year's early sowings can be made under glass.

perennials

Most perennials become dormant in winter, which makes the few that flower or hold their leaves an especially welcome sight. Lift your spirits in winter by bringing on new plants for the year ahead, from plug plants or root cuttings.

now is the season to . . .

- **plant bare-rooted perennials** such as lily of the valley, which are sold dormant, usually by mail order, at this time of year. (You can also plant container-grown plants, though with less urgency as they are available year-round.)
- **in late winter buy and pot up young plants,** or 'plugs', available by mail order. Grow them on in a coldframe or an unheated greenhouse.
- **in cold or exposed gardens,** protect perennials on the borderline of hardiness if not done in autumn.
- **group pot-grown plants** together in a sheltered spot to reduce the risk of their rootballs freezing.
- **check new plants** put in during autumn and refirm any lifted by frost.
- **look for vine weevil larvae** in the compost of container-grown perennials if you suspect damage (see page 396).
- **pick off old and tattered foliage** of early flowering evergreen perennials, such as bergenias, Lenten rose (*Helleborus orientalis*) and epimediums in late winter.
- **protect flowers for cutting** of Christmas rose and *Iris unguicularis* from severe weather and bird damage, using cloches, or sheets of glass or rigid plastic balanced on bricks.
- **in fair weather, prepare new borders** for spring planting. Dig them over to two spades' depth (see page 595, double digging), incorporating plenty of well-rotted organic matter, but be sure to bury annual weeds and remove the roots of perennial weeds.
- **remove and clean plant supports,** and store ready for spring. Paint metal supports if necessary.
- **in late winter, divide** any summer-flowering perennials and herbaceous climbers that have formed large clumps, so long as the ground is not frozen or waterlogged (see page 398).

perennials and grasses for winter interest

Evergreen and winter-flowering perennials may be few in number, but they create welcome colour in the garden through the darkest months of the year. The pure white blooms of the Christmas rose (*Helleborus niger*) and the wonderful blue, honey-scented flowers of *Iris unguicularis* are also both good for cutting. Other plants offer double value: bergenias bloom white, purple or pink in late winter while their rounded leathery leaves develop red and bronze tints; the daintier Lenten rose (*Helleborus orientalis*) bears its beautiful flowers above jagged dark green leaves.

Ornamental grasses and phormiums enhanced by a dusting of frost.

Most ornamental grasses die back in winter, but their parchment-coloured foliage gives an ethereal beauty to the garden, particularly when each fragile leaf is silvered with frost. A few evergreen grasses bring more substantial foliage interest, notably the golden-leaved *Carex oshimensis* 'Evergold', and the dramatic black lilyturf (*Ophiopogon planiscapus* 'Nigrescens').

taking root cuttings

1 **Dig up** a strong, healthy plant and wash the soil off the roots.

2 **Select young,** vigorous roots of pencil thickness and cut them from the parent plant near the crown.

divide container-grown perennials that have outgrown their pots, but delay dividing pot-grown grasses until early spring.
take root cuttings of selected perennials (see below).
occasionally water tender perennials that are overwintering under glass, to keep the compost just moist. Check plants once a week, and remove dead leaves and flowers that could become infected with grey mould (botrytis).
water evergreen perennials in containers or very sheltered spots if no rain has fallen for several days.

and if you have time . . .

top-dress perennials and grasses in containers.
weed, tidy and mulch borders when soil conditions permit in late winter, cutting dead stems to ground level.

root cuttings

This type of cutting is a useful way to propagate perennials with thick fleshy roots (see below). No special equipment is needed and the cuttings can be left outdoors during winter, although standing them in a coldframe is preferable. In spring or early summer, when leaves appear, pot up the cuttings individually and grow them on for planting outside in autumn or the following spring.

After taking the cuttings, replant the parent plant immediately into soil that you have improved by forking in some well-rotted organic matter and a little slow-release fertiliser.

The Lenten rose (*Helleborus orientalis*) is one of the earliest hellebores to come into bloom.

looking ahead . . .
☑ EARLY SPRING Divide grasses and late flowering perennials.
☑ LATE SPRING Pot up root cuttings when leaves appear.

***perennials* to raise from root cuttings**
• acanthus • *Anchusa azurea* • japanese anemone (*Anemone* x *hybrida*) • echinops • gypsophila • oriental poppy (*Papaver orientale*) • romneya • verbascum

3 **Cut each root** into 7–10cm (3–4in) lengths, cutting straight across the top and slanting at the bottom (so you know which way up to plant them).

4 **Fill a deep** 13cm (5in) pot with moist cuttings compost. Insert six to eight cuttings round the rim, 2–5cm (1–2in) apart, their tops level with the surface.

5 **Cover the compost** with a fine layer of grit and place the pots in a coldframe, a sheltered place outdoors, or on the windowsill of a cool room.

annuals & biennials

Enjoy taking time out to scan catalogues for new varieties, and make your preparations for spring sowings. Check biennials are still in good condition after hard weather and start sowing half-hardy annuals under glass.

now is the season to . . .

- **clear beds where late annual displays** have finished. Weed, then cover the ground with a layer of garden compost ready to be forked in early in spring.
- **check biennials after bad weather** and firm in plants loosened by winds and frost. Remove any that are severely frosted, but do not replace them until early spring.
- **thin autumn-sown seedlings** to leave young plants at least 5cm (2in) apart as a precaution against damping-off disease, which is often encouraged by overcrowding.
- **in very cold weather, cover seedlings** and young plants with

Universal pansies are one of the few annuals to bloom in the depths of winter. If planted in a hanging basket or container, they will need to be watered sparingly in dry weather.

choosing annuals

Besides the many popular annuals, such as marigolds, tagetes, ageratums and salvias, that are happy in a sunny position in most garden soils, the following plants will suit particular requirements:

FOR CUTTING • antirrhinum • calendula • china aster • chrysanthemum • gypsophila • larkspur • molucella • nigella • scabious • sunflower • sweet peas • verbena

FOR FRAGRANCE • alyssum (*Lobularia*) • evening primrose • heliotrope • mignonette • mirabilis • nicotiana • petunia • stocks • sweet peas

FOR FOLIAGE • amaranthus • atriplex • *Begonia semperflorens* (bronze-leaved varieties) • castor oil plant (*Ricinus*) • coleus • kochia • nasturtiums (*Tropaeolum* Alaska Series) • variegated pelargoniums • perilla

FOR SHADE • alyssum (*Lobularia*) • begonias • cleome • coleus • impatiens • lobelia • mimulus • nicotiana • pansies • schizanthus

FOR MEADOWS • borage • candytuft • clarkia • corncockle • cornflower • cosmos • eschscholzia • larkspur • nasturtiums • pansies • poppies • sunflowers

FOR CLIMBING • *Cobaea scandens* • *Eccremocarpus scaber* • morning glory • sweet peas • *Thunbergia alata* • trailing nasturtiums

QUICK FILLERS • candytuft • chrysanthemums • linaria • nigella • night-scented stocks

Eschscholzia californica

cloches, fleece, polythene tunnels or newspaper.

■ **plan next year's display** by exploring catalogues. Order seeds early to ensure a wide selection of varieties.

■ **start cultivating sites** for annuals towards the end of winter when the weather is fair (see page 28). Prepare a small area of ground as a nursery bed in which to sow hardy annuals for transplanting. Delay this until early spring in a wet season or if your soil is heavy clay.

■ **sow half-hardy annuals** under glass from January onwards, and prick them out when they are large enough to handle (see below).

■ **in February, place your orders** for seedlings and plug plants for spring delivery; this is often an easier and less expensive alternative to raising your own in a heated greenhouse.

and if you have time . . .

■ **pot up some of the seedlings** sown in autumn under glass, and grow them on in a greenhouse or coldframe for early flowers indoors.

looking ahead . . .

☑ EARLY SPRING Finish preparing beds and start sowing outdoors.
☑ Plant out sweet peas and spring biennials raised under cover.
☑ Direct sow sweet peas in warmed soil.
☑ Continue sowing half-hardy annuals under glass.

sowing half-hardy annuals

Pelargoniums benefit from early sowing, in January or even late December, but most other half-hardy annuals that need a long growing season can wait until the first week of February. These early sowings will germinate reliably in a propagator kept at a steady temperature of 13–15°C (55–60°F).

Use clean seed trays and fresh seed compost, pre-warmed by keeping it in the greenhouse for a week. Many seeds will germinate in a few days, but some, such as *Begonia semperflorens*, can take several weeks. Protect seedlings against damping-off disease (see page 76), and as soon as they are large enough to handle, prick them out into trays or small pots. Bushy and trailing lobelia are small and slender when young, and are usually pricked out in clusters of six to eight seedlings, rather than singly. This is made easier by sowing in rows (see below), rather than evenly across the seed tray.

there is still time to . . .

● **sow sweet peas during January** in pots under glass. Alternatively, cover an outdoor bed with polythene to warm the soil, and sow direct early in March.

timetable **for sowing half-hardy annuals**

JANUARY • antirrhinums • *Begonia semperflorens* • pelargoniums

FEBRUARY • anagallis • brachyscome • impatiens • kochia • lobelia • nemesia • nicotiana • petunia • *Phlox drummondii* • scarlet salvia • verbena

MARCH • ageratum • cosmos • bedding dahlias • tagetes (including french and african marigolds) • zinnia

raising lobelia

1 **Fill a seed tray** with moist seed compost and lightly firm and level. Use a pencil or thin cane to press parallel grooves about 1cm (½in) deep in the compost. Sow seeds sparingly along these channels, but do not cover with compost, as light is essential for germination. Cover the tray with polythene or a clear lid and stand in a warm place.

2 **When the seedlings** are about 1cm (½in) high, fill another tray with moist potting compost, and make holes about 5cm (2in) apart. Lift small clumps of seedlings with a dibber and transfer to the holes in the new tray.

3 **Lightly firm** with your fingers, water through a fine rose, then put the tray in a propagator or cover it with a clear lid.

bulbs & tubers

In pots and outdoors, the first flowers will be opening before the turn of the season. While you are enjoying these harbingers of the new year, get ahead with sprouting summer bulbs and preparing their ground, for the longest possible display.

now is the season to . . .

■ **clear leaves and other debris** from around the shoots of snowdrops, scillas, muscari and other early bulbs, but do not fork or hoe the surface as this can cause damage.

■ **protect buried bulbs,** especially tulips, from mice and squirrels. Lay panels of chicken wire on the ground and secure at the corners with large stones or bent wires.

■ **move or divide snowdrops** while they are in flower or have green leaves (see opposite).

■ **cover spring bulbs with cloches** or a low polythene tunnel to advance flowering if you planted them in rows for cutting. Remember to ventilate plants on mild days to keep them free from rot.

■ **start moving forced bulbs** into light and gentle warmth in December, no more than 10°C (50°F); hyacinths should have plump shoots with buds visible, and narcissi should be about 10cm (4in) high, with visible flower buds. Tulips and crocuses are often not ready until late January or February, when they show flower colour.

■ **remove dead blooms** after flowering, then feed with a high-potash fertiliser. Move plants to a coldframe or sheltered position outside to continue growing and storing food to fuel next year's display.

■ **buy lilies** for growing in pots or outdoors. Refresh any that look dry and shrivelled by burying them in a tray of leaf-mould or moist compost for a week or two before planting.

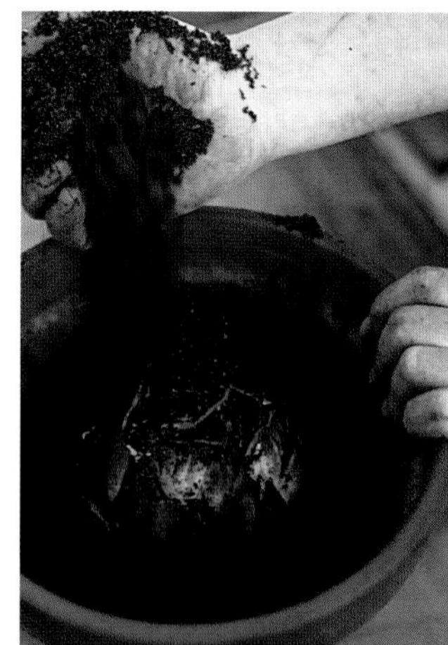

If your lily bulbs look dry and shrivelled, place them in a pot or tray and cover with moist compost to plump them up.

■ **pot up amaryllis,** a few at a time for a succession of blooms (see opposite).

■ **carefully empty pans of** lilies propagated two years ago from seed or bulbils. These are usually large enough to separate and pot up individually in small pots. Leave one-year-old bulbs for another year.

■ **prepare sites during February** for summer-flowering bulbs such as gladioli, alliums, lilies and tigridias. Fork the ground thoroughly, removing perennial weeds and mixing in plenty of leaf-mould or garden compost. Delay this work until spring on frosted, wet or heavy soils.

Low-growing winter aconites (*Eranthis hyemalis*) push up through the leaf litter, their golden yellow flowers a cheering sight in late winter.

planting amaryllis

1 **Choose a pot a little larger** than the bulb, and part fill with moist potting compost so the bulb sits with its tip above the rim. Fill round the bulb with compost to within 2–3cm (1in) of the rim, then water.

2 **Do not water** again until the flower bud shows, then keep just moist.

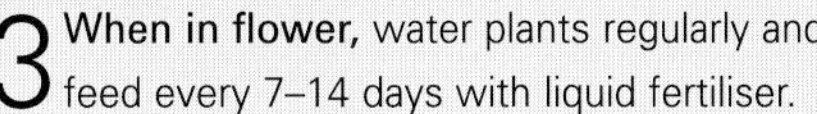

3 **When in flower,** water plants regularly and feed every 7–14 days with liquid fertiliser.

■ **sprout begonias and dahlias** in boxes under glass, either for taking cuttings in early spring or for planting out in late spring (see right).

moving snowdrops

1 **Lift large clumps of** snowdrops carefully with a fork while they are still in flower ('in the green').

2 **Tease into smaller** clumps and replant immediately in ground you have already forked over and enriched with leaf-mould or compost.

growing amaryllis

These popular bulbs, correctly called *Hippeastrum*, are easy to grow indoors and often flower six to eight weeks after potting. Although they are evergreen, the bulbs flower best if rested annually, so start to reduce watering in August and allow the leaves to die down. Keep the bulbs dry for two to three months, then force into growth in early winter at a temperature of 13–15°C (55–60°F). Amaryllis will also grow well in cooler surroundings and start to flower in February or March. Repot the bulbs every two to three years (see above).

sprouting dahlias and begonias

If you want to multiply your stocks from cuttings or division, start tubers into growth in January or February in a warm greenhouse (see page 68) or on a windowsill. By April, the shoots should be about 10–15cm (4–6in), long enough to remove and root as soft-tip cuttings (see page 139).

there is still time to . . .

- **plant tulips, hyacinths** and early flowering *Gladiolus nanus*.
- **clean dried gladiolus corms** after autumn lifting by removing the old withered corm from the base, together with any loose skins. Check corms in store, and remove and destroy any that are spongy or shrivelled. Dust others with an insecticide if you notice any grubs present.

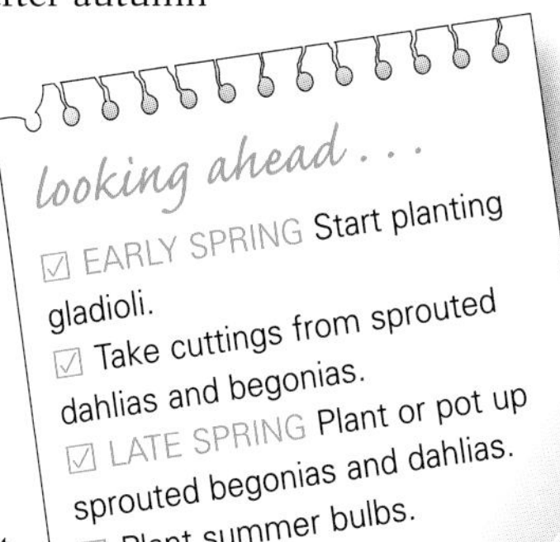

roses

Although apparently lifeless, roses are merely resting during their winter dormancy. You can plant or move them now and, as winter draws to an end, prune them to concentrate their energy for the coming season.

The large hips of the sweet briar (*Rosa rubiginosa*), shine out in the winter garden, their shapes enhanced by a riming of frost.

now is the season to . . .

- **continue tidying rose beds.** Cut back any ground-covering herbaceous perennials and edging plants around the roses, clear weeds and pick up all fallen rose leaves.
- **give plants a final spray of fungicide** if black spot, rust or mildew have been serious that year. Choose a mild December day, drenching all stems to the point of run-off.
- **check recently planted roses** after frost and tread firm any that have lifted from the ground. If it gets very cold, cover young plants with straw (see page 404–5).
- **continue preparing** the ground for new roses. In January break down with a fork heavy soil roughly dug in autumn, ready for planting in late winter.
- **plant new roses** as they arrive, or heel them into some vacant ground until you are ready. Plant only when the soil breaks up easily and is not frozen or waterlogged.
- **protect roses** of borderline hardiness with two or three layers of fleece. Varieties sensitive to frost include the banksian roses (*R. banksiae* cultivars), *R.* x *odorata* 'Mutabilis' and, in exposed positions, the yellow climber 'Mermaid'.
- **inspect supports and ties,** especially after high winds, and readjust where necessary (see page 501).
- **start pruning climbing roses** during February, but delay the work until March in a cold or frosty season (see opposite).
- **move potted roses** into the greenhouse during January for forcing early blooms (see below).

and if you have time . . .

- **in February increase the resistance** of roses that have been badly affected by black spot by spreading 35g per m^2 (1oz per sq yd) sulphate of potash over soil shaded by the branches.
- **in mild areas, begin pruning** shrub roses (see page 38).

replacing rose-sick soil

1 **Dig out an area** roughly 60cm (2ft) square around where the old rose grew, removing the top 38–45cm (15–18in) of soil. This soil is fine for growing other plants, so exchange it for the same amount dug from an area where roses have not been grown before.

2 **Work plenty of compost** or rotted manure into the replacement soil.

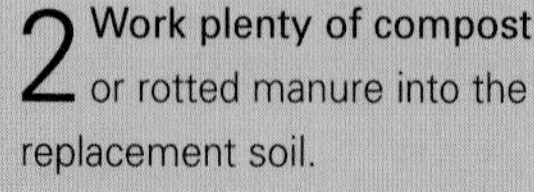

3 **Leave the soil to settle** for a few weeks before planting a new rose or moving one from elsewhere.

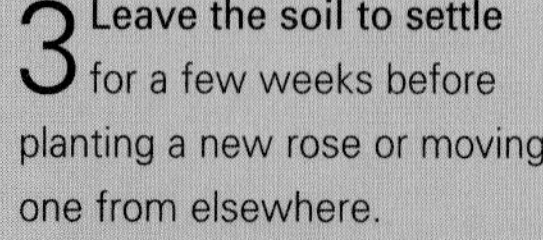

dealing with rose-sick soil

Where a rose has been grown for eight years or more, a replacement planted in the same spot is likely to grow sickly, with stems dying back. This is due to specific replant disease, or 'rose sickness', a combination of soil exhaustion and a build up of diseases. It is better to plant a new rose somewhere fresh, but you can replant successfully in the same spot if you either replace the soil (see left) or use a soil-sterilising concentrate, following the manufacturer's instructions.

forcing roses

Roses that were pruned back to 15cm (6in) and potted up in autumn for early forcing can be brought inside from late December onwards.

- **wash the outsides** of the pots, and weed and loosen the surface of the compost, then stand the plants in a well-lit greenhouse or conservatory, maintained at a minimum temperature of 5°C (40°F).

- **ventilate well** in mild weather, and water so the compost is evenly moist but not saturated.

pruning climbing roses

Healthy climbers will have produced several new shoots during the summer. Retain the best and strongest of these when pruning to replace some of the older framework stems being cut out, or to fill in gaps (see right).

pruning climbing roses

1 **Prune out all dead stems** and ends of stems, cutting back to healthy wood, then cut out two or three of the oldest branches, either to ground level or to where a strong replacement stem originates.

2 **Stimulate flowering** by shortening all sideshoots to leave two to four buds.

3 **Tie new stems** to their supports to make an even spread of branches; some may need re-tying to avoid overcrowding or crossing growth.

raising roses from seed

Rose seeds need exposure to frost before they will germinate. This process is called stratification. After a hard winter, you may notice rose seedlings growing under parent plants and you can move these to a nursery bed to grow on. If you want to raise your own plants from a special variety or one you have deliberately cross-pollinated, you can do this using seed from hips (see below).

there is still time to . . .

- **gather hips** for sowing your own seeds (see below).
- **pot up new roses** for forcing early flowers under glass.
- **cut back tall stems** on climbing and shrub roses to safeguard the plants against wind damage.

looking ahead . . .

☑ EARLY SPRING Continue pruning bush, shrub and climbing roses.
☑ Finish planting bare-rooted roses.
☑ LATE SPRING Plant out and feed roses forced in pots.

raising roses from seed

1 **Gather hips** when they are almost fully coloured but before they start to shrivel. Bury them whole in a potful of moist sharp sand or grit and keep in a warm place for three to four weeks. Then stand the pot outdoors, protected from mice and birds but not from frost.

2 **In late winter** bring the pot indoors and squeeze the seeds out of the hips into a bowl of water; discard any that float. Sow the remaining seeds in pots on the surface of seed compost and cover them with a layer of grit. Keep under glass, unheated or heated.

3 **The seedlings** will come through erratically. Carefully prick them out individually into final pots when the first true leaves appear, and leave the rest to germinate.

climbers

Winter is the time to get to grips with deciduous climbers, for while they are dormant you can see what lies beneath their cloaks of growth. This is the best season to prune certain climbers and service their supports. During very cold spells, evergreen and slightly frost-tender climbers will benefit from protection.

now is the season to . . .

- **protect climbers** on the borderline of hardiness during cold, frosty periods (see opposite). If any leaves or shoots become damaged by frost, leave them in place until early spring because, although unsightly, they give protection to undamaged shoots below.
- **continue to plant hardy** climbers when the soil is workable, and not frozen or sodden (see page 409).
- **lift and divide herbaceous** climbers that have formed well-established clumps (see page 500).
- **propagate selected climbers** by layering or taking hardwood cuttings (see page 500).
- **prune ornamental vines,** winter jasmine, wisteria and any overgrown deciduous climbers (see opposite).
- **check trellis** and other supports before growth begins, and repair or treat if necessary (see page 501).
- **tie in climber stems firmly** to avoid wind damage, and loosen existing ties if they threaten to cut into stems.
- **trim self-clinging climbers** away from woodwork and guttering.
- **occasionally water climbers** that are growing in sites sheltered from rain, such as beneath the overhanging eaves of a roof, if necessary.

and if you have time . . .

- **weed and mulch** around established plants.

pruning deciduous climbers

Early winter is the time to prune ornamental vines (*Vitis*), when the pruning cuts are least likely to 'bleed' sap. Shorten shoots as necessary. Prune back weak or thin stems hard, to encourage more vigorous growth, but prune strong growing stems lightly.

Prune winter jasmine (*Jasminum nudiflorum*) as soon as flowering has finished because next winter's flowers open on new shoots produced during the coming year (see opposite).

Hard pruning ornamental vines while they are still dormant will stimulate vigorous new growth in spring.

The star-shaped flowers of winter jasmine brighten a wooden fence. Once flowering is finished, prune to promote the growth of new shoots that will carry flowers the following winter.

You can also prune overgrown deciduous climbers that will bloom on new wood produced in the coming year, such as trumpet vine (*Campsis*), summer jasmine (*Jasminum officinale*) and honeysuckle (*Lonicera periclymenum*). Late flowering clematis are better left until early spring unless February is particularly mild.

winter-pruning wisteria

Wisteria is pruned twice a year: initially around midsummer, then again in winter to stimulate the formation of short sideshoots that will bear summer flowers. Plants left unpruned tend to put their energy into producing leafy growth, not flowers.

The winter pruning of wisteria is intended to encourage the formation of short flower-bearing sideshoots.

- **cut back to** two or three buds those sideshoots that were shortened to five or six buds from the main stem in summer.
- **at the same time,** cut back any long shoots that have developed since summer, pruning them to 15cm (6in).
- **if your plant is shy** to flower, feed it with sulphate of potash towards the end of winter.

protecting plants of borderline hardiness

You can increase the chances of these plants surviving by growing them against a sunny south-facing wall in a site sheltered from winds, as the wall will hold some warmth and create a 'storage-heater' effect. However, plants such as ceanothus, evergreen clematis (*C. armandii* and *C. cirrhosa*), and trachelospermum, need additional protection during very cold weather or in cold and exposed gardens.

A protective screen is simple to make and quick to install when frost threatens:

- **you will need two long wooden battens** and a large piece of fine windbreak netting or thick horticultural fleece of a size that is sufficient to cover the whole plant.
- **secure the battens** along the top and bottom of the netting or fleece using a staple gun or other means.
- **fix two or more** large hooks along the top of the wall or fence. Hang one batten from the hooks and let the other rest on the ground, close to the base of the plant.
- **insulate tender plants** or those in very exposed sites by packing straw or dry bracken behind the netting or fleece and around the plant.
- **for the blue passionflower** (*Passiflora caerulea*) it is usually sufficient to pack straw around the base of the stems and over the root area, as it tends to regrow from the base even if the top growth is killed by frost.

pruning winter jasmine

1 **Cut back all sideshoots** that have borne flowers to around three buds from the main stem.

2 **Shorten the main framework** shoots if necessary to restrict growth.

3 **On well-established plants,** take out several of the older, more woody stems close to ground level.

climbers/2

planting and propagation

Winter is the time not only to propagate more climbers and check their supports, but also to plant them. One of the most beautiful combinations of all is a climber growing through the branches of an established tree to give an extra season of colourful flowers or foliage.

climbers for trees

The golden rule is to match the vigour of the climber to the size of the tree, as a rampant climbing plant would overwhelm a small specimen. For the climber to grow successfully you need to pay particular attention to soil preparation, planting and aftercare, because it will have to compete with the roots of the tree for water and nourishment (see opposite). The planting position should not be close to the trunk but towards the edge of the branch canopy, where the soil should have fewer roots and more moisture.

climbers for trees

FOR SMALL TREES • annual climbers such as morning glory and canary creeper (*Tropaeolum peregrinum*) • *Clematis alpina* • *C. macropetala* • *C. tangutica* • *C. viticella* • large-flowered clematis hybrids • golden hop (*Humulus lupulus* 'Aureus') • rambler roses 'Emily Gray' and 'Phyllis Bide'
FOR LARGE TREES • *Clematis flammula* • *Clematis montana* • parthenocissus • vigorous rambler roses such as 'Bobbie James', 'Paul's Himalayan Musk', 'Rambling Rector' and 'Seagull' • ornamental vines (*Vitis*) • wisteria

propagation

There are various methods of propagating climbers at this time of year. Mature herbaceous climbers, such as golden hop, perennial pea (*Lathyrus latifolius*) and flame flower (*Tropaeolum speciosum*), are divided in the same way as herbaceous perennials when soil conditions are suitable.

Many deciduous climbers and wall shrubs, including *Actinidia kolomikta*, honeysuckles, parthenocissus and vines (*Vitis*), are simple to propagate by hardwood cuttings once their leaves have dropped. Take cuttings 15cm (6in) long and root them outdoors in well-drained soil (see page 413). They should be ready for planting by next autumn or the following early spring.

layering

The chocolate vine (*Akebia*), trumpet vine (*Campsis*) and ornamental vines (*Vitis*) are liable to 'bleed' sap if cut when in leaf, so they are best layered in late winter when dormant.

- **select a long, pliable,** healthy shoot that can be bent down to touch the ground. About 30cm (12in) from the end of the stem, use a sharp knife to remove a sliver of bark from the underside, close to a leaf joint, to stimulate rooting.
- **peg the wounded stem** to the ground with loops of wire, cover with a layer of soil and tie the tip of the shoot to a short stake to keep it upright. Leave for at least six months before severing, after checking that it has rooted.

The cream-centred leaves of *Hedera helix* 'Goldheart' brighten even the dullest of vertical structures in winter.

Use a stiff brush to clean dirt and algal growth off wooden trellis and supports, then check for signs of decay.

Renew ties where necessary on wall shrubs such as this early flowering *Chaenomeles* x *superba* growing against trellis.

looking after supports

Keep trellis and other wooden plant supports in good condition by treating them with a preservative every few years. An annual inspection of the wood during winter will show when the coating begins to deteriorate and you can take advantage of a spell of dry weather to make it good.

- **first clean the wood** using a wire brush to remove algal growth and stubborn patches of dirt. Then scrub it well with a stiff brush and clean water, and allow to dry. Treat any small areas of rotting wood with wood hardener.
- **choose a preservative paint or stain,** making sure it is non-toxic if plants are growing close by. Follow the instructions for application, and wear protective gloves and safety glasses if necessary.
- **check support posts,** particularly where they go into the ground as this part is the most prone to rot. If rotting has occurred, you can often repair the post by bolting the sound part to a metal spike or a concrete spur, rather than putting in a new one.
- **remove rust** and flaking paint from metal supports with a wire brush. Then wash the structure and allow to dry before painting.

looking ahead . . .

☑ EARLY SPRING Plant evergreen climbers and wall shrubs, and any plants of borderline hardiness.
☑ Prune late flowering clematis.
☑ SUMMER Summer-prune wisteria.
☑ AUTUMN Plant or pot up rooted cuttings and layers.

training a climber into a tree

1 At the edge of the tree's canopy of branches dig a planting hole about 60cm (2ft) wide and 45cm (18in) deep. Incorporate plenty of well-rotted organic matter and some slow-release fertiliser or, if the soil is very poor, replace it with good-quality topsoil mixed with organic matter and fertiliser.

2 Plant the climber at the same depth as it was growing previously, with the exception of clematis, which benefit from deep planting with 10cm (4in) of soil covering the top of the rootball.

3 Set up one or several training canes or lines of string to lead the climber into the branches and attach the climber to these using soft string.

4 Water and mulch the new climber and make sure that it does not dry out during its first year.

shrubs & trees

Apart from routine matters such as planting and protection, winter is pruning time for many shrubs and trees and an opportunity for you to use your artistic skills to shape and train them to suit your garden.

now is the season to . . .

- **check recently planted shrubs** and trees after any high winds or hard frost. Make sure their supports and ties are secure, and refirm any plants that have lifted.
- **brush snow off** hedges and shrubs, as the weight can damage the dense growth of evergreens in particular.
- **continue planting** deciduous shrubs and trees in prepared sites if the ground is not frozen or waterlogged (see page 414).
- **move misplaced shrubs and trees** to more suitable sites if the soil is workable (see page 504).
- **repair damaged hedging** and fill gaps (see page 505).
- **prune established shrubs and trees,** and shape young specimens (see page 508).
- **protect flowering cherry buds** from birds in late winter with fleece, or use harmless deterrent sprays and bird scarers.

Wintersweet (*Chimonanthus praecox*) often opens its sweetly fragrant blooms during December. It should be pruned once it has finished flowering.

Cover early rhododendrons with fleece to protect flower buds against frost damage.

- **protect early rhododendron** flower buds against frost with fleece, and pull up any suckers that you see.
- **clear hedge bases** (see opposite).
- **trim back invasive roots** where hedges grow next to borders, by plunging a spade full depth along a line about 45cm (18in) away from the hedge.
- **tidy shrubs** such as *Buddleja globosa* and tree peonies, which do not need regular pruning. Remove dead or diseased wood, and any live branches that spoil the shape of the plant.
- **prune** wintersweet and witch hazel (see opposite).
- **prepare planting sites** for rhododendrons (see below).
- **take hardwood cuttings** of deciduous plants while they are leafless.
- **transplant suckers** to propagate new plants (see opposite).

and if you have time . . .

- **pot up small specimens** of early flowering shrubs like deutzia, hydrangea and viburnum. Stand them in a cool greenhouse for early blooms.
- **cut spindly flowering stems** from ribes, cornus, prunus, willows and viburnums, and bring indoors to flower.
- **paint or spray deciduous trees** that have a history of pest and disease attack while leafless, using winter wash to kill moss and overwintering insect eggs, but first spread plastic sheeting to protect surrounding plants (see page 523).

preparing for new rhododendrons

Rhododendrons and azaleas are acid-loving plants so it is important to test the soil on the proposed site before you do any work or buy plants. If the pH is higher than 5.5 these shrubs will not survive, so plant them in containers or raised beds filled with lime-free (ericaceous) compost instead. In addition to an acid soil, rhododendrons also need a very well-drained spot in light shade, shielded from early morning sun.

About six weeks before planting, dig over an area $1m^2$ (10sq ft) and 45cm (18in) deep, working in at least one large bucketful of leaf-mould or garden compost per plant. Level the soil, rake in a granular fertiliser formulated for acid-loving plants, and leave to settle until planting time in mid-spring.

transplanting suckers

Some trees and shrubs produce suckers from their own roots – these are separate shoots, growing from shallow roots or close to the base of the parent plant. You can lift these and grow them on, ready for planting out in a year's time.

The spidery blooms of witch hazel (*Hamamelis mollis*).

pruning winter-flowering shrubs

Wintersweet (*Chimonanthus praecox*) can take many years to reach flowering size, and is best left unpruned until then. After flowering, cut out one stem in three to encourage vigorous new growth from the base of the plant.

Winter-flowering witch hazels (*Hamamelis*) are similarly slow growing and should not be pruned until mature. Then, as soon as the flowers fade, shorten or remove surplus branches, and tidy or lightly trim the rest of the shrub to maintain shape and size.

Gather up and dispose of the debris at the foot of a hedge as it can harbour disease.

clearing the base of hedges

Fallen leaves and other wind-blown debris collects in large quantities at the bottom of hedges. Although this may provide winter shelter for wildlife, it also harbours pests and diseases.

- **rake out loose material** to expose overwintering pest eggs and grubs for birds. Add leaves and rotting vegetation to the compost heap, but burn woody material as a precaution against diseases.
- **clear weeds** and use a fork to prick over the soil.

transplanting a lilac sucker

1 **Identify the sucker** and dig down to its base to make sure the sucker has plenty of roots of its own.

2 **Cut the sucker off** where it joins a main root and pot it up in a 15–20cm (6–8in) pot of soil-based potting compost (lime-free for acid-loving gaultherias). Alternatively, space several suckers 45cm (18in) apart in a nursery bed. Leave tree suckers unpruned, but cut back shrub suckers by half.

plants to raise from suckers

- dogwoods (*Cornus*) • gaultheria • kerria • lilacs • quince
- snowberry (*Symphoricarpos*)
- sumachs (*Rhus*)

there is still time to . . .

- **screen recently planted shrubs** and trees against cold winds with plastic mesh or sacking. Mulch well to prevent frost heave.
- **cut back overgrown** deciduous hedges (see page 413).

looking ahead . . .

☑ EARLY TO LATE SPRING
☑ Prune late flowering shrubs.
☑ Renovate overgrown shrubs and evergreen hedges.
☑ Plant evergreens.
☑ Start pruning conifers, topiary and most hedges.
☑ Move evergreens.
☑ SUMMER Prune spring shrubs after flowering.

shrubs & trees/2

moving misplaced plants

Despite careful planning, it sometimes happens that a tree or shrub is obviously in the wrong place. If it is well established, consider first whether it might be easier to move neighbouring plants or even sacrifice them for the sake of a prized specimen that might not survive transplanting. Do not attempt to move magnolias or other plants with fleshy roots.

In general, the younger the plant the greater the chances of it surviving the move, but all plants, even small ones, need special care before, during and for two or three years after transplanting. Bear in mind also the weight of a heavy rootball and get some help if the plant is fairly large.

Prepare the new site in advance in the same way as you would for planting a tree (see page 414). Move deciduous plants while they are dormant, between late November and late February, but leave evergreens until spring or autumn on heavy soils. Larger plants will need some root preparation a year or two in advance, and after transplanting they will need staking or guying with thin rope attached to short stakes to keep them upright. Younger plants should not need root preparation.

root preparation for larger shrubs and trees

To reduce the shock of transplanting trees and shrubs larger than 1m (3ft) across, prepare the rootball in late autumn or early winter a year in advance, as follows:

- **Mark a circle round the plant** just within the area shaded by its branches.
- **Dig a trench as described below**, but continue downward until you meet the thicker roots. Cut through these.
- **Refill the trench with the excavated soil** mixed with plenty of garden compost or a proprietary tree-planting mixture; firm and water well. Make sure the area of refilled soil does not dry out during summer.
- **When you come to move the plant** the following winter, you will find the rootball already defined and showing signs of healthy new fibrous roots.
- **You could extend the preparation** over two years: cut and refill one half of the trench in the first year, complete the circle the second year and move the tree in the third.

repairing a damaged hedge

Bare or damaged areas are often more noticeable when the hedge is dormant during winter, which is the best time to assess hedges for repair.

large gaps caused by plants dying

Open these up by pruning the healthy growth on either side so you can remove the remains of the dead plant and its roots. Then fork over the soil, adding compost and fertiliser, and replant with young specimens. Keep the adjacent growth tied back through the year so the new plants get as much light as possible.

moving young trees and shrubs

1 **Excavate a hole** about 1m (3ft) across and 45cm (18in) deep in the new site. Then use a spade to mark a circle 60–75cm (2–2ft 6in) in diameter around the plant to be moved. Tie up arching branches with string.

2 **Dig a trench** one spade blade deep outside the circle. With a fork loosen some of the soil from the fibrous roots to reduce the weight of the rootball.

3 **Undercut the rootball** by digging down at an angle, slicing through woody roots. Work round until the rootball is free. Check that the new hole is big enough, and adjust if necessary.

4 **Tilt the plant to one side** and ease a piece of strong sacking or plastic sheet underneath. Lean the plant the opposite way and pull the sheet through.

5 **Tie up the sheet securely** to keep the rootball intact, and lift or drag the plant on the sheet to its new home. Plant at the same depth as before, firm in, water well and mulch.

To avoid specific replant disease, which can affect young plants growing where closely related species grew previously, dig out the soil to a depth of 30–38cm (12–15in) and replace with soil from elsewhere in the garden (see 'dealing with rose-sick soil', page 496).

small gaps

You can 'patch' smaller holes in a healthy hedge by training neighbouring branches across the gap (see right). Alternatively, insert a cane vertically in the middle of the gap and tie branches from each side to this. Another solution is to layer plants with pliable growth by bending some of the lower branches across the gap and pegging them down in the soil in one or more places. Tie back any growth that heavily shades the layers until they have rooted, then either sever them from the parent plants or leave attached.

tall conifer hedges

If the weight of snow or high winds force branches out of place, clip back slender sideshoots to the face of the hedge, then push larger branches that may have moved back into the foliage. To keep the large branches in place, tie them with plastic string or soft wire to strong upright stems deep within the hedge.

patching gaps in a hedge

1 **First cut out** all the dead or damaged growth using sharp secateurs.

2 **Tie healthy shoots** together across the gap with soft string. Snip off their tips to encourage bushy side growth.

The dormant winter season is the best time to transplant misplaced trees and shrubs to a more suitable place in the garden, but avoid doing this in frosty conditions (right).

shrubs & trees/3

pruning essentials

Many people find pruning intimidating, or feel that cutting off healthy growth must be counter-productive. On the contrary, however, judicious pruning at the right time can do much to improve the shape, flowering and fruitfulness of plants compared to those left to grow naturally.

why prune?

Pruning entails the selective removal of parts of a plant for a particular reason. The main purposes of pruning are:

- **maintaining health** Controlling disease is an important part of keeping plants vigorous and attractive. Cutting out dead and diseased portions of branches, as well as removing rubbing branches, prevents further spread and disfigurement and, in the case of trees, ensures that they are safe.
- **early training** Young trees and shrubs flower or fruit sooner, and develop into more attractive specimens, if they are pruned in ways that emphasise a well-spaced framework of branches. Early formative pruning aims to correct misshapen or excessive growth.
- **keeping a balance** Strongly growing plants can make a lot of leaf and stem growth at the expense of flowers, while mature specimens may stop producing new growth and only flower erratically or at the branch tips. Routine annual pruning encourages a regular supply of young productive shoots while controlling more mature growth.
- **improving quality** Sometimes less is more; pruning can divert energy from heavy yields of small flowers and fruits into fewer, but higher quality, blooms. Similarly, some shrubs and trees with handsome foliage or bark are pruned to ensure plenty of young growth with enhanced colour or shape.
- **limiting size** All healthy plants continue growing until they reach maximum size, which in many cases is too big for their allotted space. Hedges must be clipped to keep them in shape and the growth of shrubs and trees restricted to keep them in balance with a garden.

how pruning works

Several different hormones regulate plant activity. Those responsible for producing new growth tend to be concentrated in the top few buds of shoot tips, where they encourage stems to lengthen while suppressing the growth of buds lower down.

If you cut off these active areas of growth, the plant redirects its energies elsewhere, usually into the buds just below the pruning cut. In this way, pruning is not just the removal of excess, misplaced or unwanted growth, but also the creative and predictable redirection of new growth.

pruning equipment

- **garden knife** Use a garden knife to trim young, thin growth, to tidy round large cuts, and to take cuttings.
- **secateurs** A pair of secateurs is the essential pruning tool to cut stems up to 1cm (½in) thick. Check out the various types to find the one you prefer (see page 586).
- **long-handled pruners, or loppers** Secateurs with long handles give greater reach and more leverage when cutting stems up to 2cm (¾in) thick.

A valuable winter-flowering evergreen shrub, *Mahonia* x *media* 'Winter Sun' needs little pruning, other than to cut out dead branches and maintain its overall shape.

the correct pruning cut

Pruning cuts through the bark, which is what protects a plant from disease. The cleaner the cut, the faster the wound will dry and heal, so it is important to keep tools sharp, and avoid ragged cuts and torn bark. Plants have natural defences against injury concentrated in certain places, such as in the joint where a bud or leaf grows. Cutting close to this point helps the wound to heal quickly.

Always prune just above a bud, sloping the cut to direct water away from the bud.

Where buds are in pairs on opposite sides of the stem, cut straight across, no more than 5mm (¼in) above the buds.

A correctly pruned cut (below) will heal quickly, whereas using blunt secateurs produces a ragged cut and torn bark, which will take longer to heal.

- **tree pruners** Ideal for removing high branches up to 2–3cm (1in) thick, tree pruners are basically a pole, sometimes telescopic, topped with a secateur-like cutting blade.
- **pruning saw** A narrow-bladed saw deals with branches up to 8cm (3in) thick. Straight, curved and folding models are available, with large teeth for cutting sappy wood or smaller teeth for dry material.
- **bow saw** This has a bent metal frame and a slim detachable blade; use a bow saw to cut through large tree branches.

pruning buddleia

1 **At winter's end,** prune buddleias by cutting shoots back to a strong pair of buds or shoots at the preferred height.

2 **To rejuvenate older plants** and improve flower size, use loppers or a saw to shorten some stems just above the trunk or main framework branches.

when to prune

EARLY FLOWERING DECIDUOUS SHRUBS

Plants that flower during the first half of the growing season – for example forsythia, philadelphus and weigela – generally do so on stems that grew the previous year. Prune immediately after flowering to allow plenty of time for new growth in the second half of the growing season.

LATE FLOWERING DECIDUOUS SHRUBS

Plants that flower late in the year do so on shoots developed earlier in the same year; for example, *Buddleja davidii* (see left), caryopteris and perovskia. Prune during winter, or wait until March or April as this helps to avoid frost damage to new growth.

BROAD-LEAVED EVERGREENS

Most evergreens need little pruning except to remove dead material and maintain shape. Regardless of whether they are flowering species, such as skimmia, or foliage plants, such as spotted laurel, prune if necessary in April or May, since their new growth can easily be damaged by frost.

CONIFERS

Apart from removing dead material, you can trim ornamental specimens occasionally to encourage bushy growth and cut back the main shoot if it is growing too tall. Prune if necessary during autumn or early winter, to avoid the excessive gumming that occurs when the sap is rising.
Do not prune in frosty weather. Trim coniferous hedges in late summer.

shrubs & trees/4

routine pruning

Before you prune make sure your tools are sharp and clean, and that you have plenty of time. Choose a pleasant day when you will enjoy doing the job well and the plants will not be under stress due to severe weather.

the basic routine

Never prune without a good reason and always cut off less rather than too much, because you can always remove more later. It is better not to prune at all rather than do the wrong kind of pruning in the wrong season or in unsuitable conditions, such as frost or drought.

The deciduous *Viburnum farreri* bears clusters of pinkish white scented flowers throughout winter and into early spring; it needs minimal pruning.

pruning young shrubs

Early training and formative pruning determine the future shape of a young plant and, if done correctly, will avoid pruning problems later on.

- **immediately after planting** select the strongest three or four shoots as main branches and shorten them by half their length, cutting just above an outward-facing bud. Remove completely any weak and badly placed shoots.
- **after one year,** cut out weak and misplaced shoots, and any that cross the centre. Shorten the longest main branches to establish a shapely outline.
- **in the following years,** start a regular routine of pruning the established shrub according to its type and flowering season (see page 507).

pruning young trees

A one or two-year-old tree is supplied either as a single stem with few or no sideshoots (a whip, or maiden), or as a stem with several strong sideshoots (a feathered whip, or feathered maiden). After planting, keep the main stem supported by a sturdy

pruning an overgrown deciduous shrub

1 **Take a close look** at your overgrown shrub in winter: even with evergreens it is easier to see its structure then, especially at the end of winter when frost injuries should be apparent.

2 **First cut out** all dead, damaged and diseased wood, then remove any weak, spindly stems.

3 **Using loppers** or a puning saw, cut out any stems that interfere with the growth of a more important branch, or that cross the centre of the shrub. Then thin out any overcrowded stems.

4 **Only then prune** the main flowering or structural branches, according to variety.

5 **You may need** to cut back almost to the base of shoots that have recently flowered to restrict size, but prune less severely if you want a large shrub.

6 **The pruned shrub** admits light and air to the centre of the plant, promoting healthy growth.

Newly planted trees benefit from protection by plastic spiral tree guards for the first few years. A mulch of plastic sheeting will suppress weeds.

stake and protected by a guard around the base if rabbits are a problem. (For what to do if the main stem is damaged, see page 511; for special effects, see page 512).

- **three or four years** after planting, remove the stake and cut off any low shoots growing from near the base of the tree.

for standard trees

The presence of sideshoots supports a tree's early growth and also helps to thicken the main stem. But if a standard tree with a clear stem about 1.5–2m (5–6ft) high is required, remove the sideshoots while they are small to avoid large pruning scars later.

shrubs and trees that need little or no pruning

• amelanchier • *Buddleja globosa* • caragana • chimonanthus • corylopsis • daphne (deciduous) • enkianthus • eucryphia (deciduous) • fothergilla • hoheria (deciduous) • japanese maples (*Acer palmatum*) • magnolia • poncirus • rhamnus (deciduous) • viburnum (deciduous)

PRUNING PRUNUS TIP Do not prune ornamental cherries, plums, peaches and apricots in winter. Wait until late spring or early summer to avoid infection from disease.

raising the crown of an established tree

The branches of a maturing tree often bend under the weight of foliage, casting excessive shade and even becoming a hazard to anyone passing underneath. Raising the crown improves the situation by removing the lowest branches (see below); this can involve taking off one or more sizable boughs (see page 511). Where several large branches are involved, it is a good idea to spread the work over two to three years, re-assessing the shape of the tree each summer.

thinning the crown

Trees such as malus or sorbus develop a cluttered head of twiggy growth that may eventually cast unwanted shade and offer high resistance to wind, sometimes resulting in wind damage and disease. Removing some smaller branches and sideshoots during winter can improve the air circulation. Carry out any further thinning the following midsummer, when you can assess how much reduction in shade you have already achieved.

PRUNING MATURE TREES TIP Any pruning should retain the characteristic shape of the tree, and it is advisable to have the job done by a qualified tree surgeon, especially if much of the work needs to be done off the ground.

pruning a young tree

1 **The autumn** after planting, cut out the sideshoots (or feathers) on the lowest third of the stem to clean the trunk. This is sometimes known as 'feathering'.

2 **Shorten sideshoots** on the next third of the trunk by half, and leave the top third unpruned. Repeat this each year until the clean trunk is the required height, above which natural branching can be allowed to develop.

raising the crown

1 **When the tree is dormant,** work your way up the trunk, removing enough of the lowest branches to raise the tree's crown, or head, of branches.

2 **While the tree retains** its distinct profile, the crown is then carried on a taller trunk.

shrubs & trees/5

pruning out problems

Frost, wind and shade as well as age, pests and diseases all modify growth in various ways. Remedial pruning can often restore good health and shapeliness.

pruning for health

Although easily overlooked in a busy garden, pruning for health is an important part of the annual routine, and if done in time will often prevent a condition from spreading.

Make a point of inspecting all shrubs and trees during the dormant season, and prune back any dead or damaged shoots to live, healthy wood, cutting just above an outward-facing bud to encourage bushy regrowth away from the plant's centre. Check again in spring, after the worst frosts, to cut out frost-damaged shoots, especially on evergreens and conifers.

Pruning can be the quickest and most effective treatment for disease, and it is worth inspecting all woody plants every month in the growing season for initial signs. Shoots affected by mildew, canker and die-back, for example, should be cut back to healthy wood before starting other remedial treatments and this may even be sufficient to control the problem. Before and after cutting diseased wood, dip your pruning tools in horticultural disinfectant; this is essential for serious diseases such as fireblight, which disfigures and even kills cotoneasters and pyracanthas.

The variegated *Euonymus japonicus* is a valuable shrub in winter. It should only need pruning if it outgrows its allotted space.

Some variegated shrubs, such as euonymus and hollies, produce plain yellow or white shoots, and these should be removed.

preventing reversion

Many variegated shrubs and trees show an occasional tendency to revert to their original all-green form, by producing more vigorous green shoots. Left untreated these can eventually crowd out the variegated foliage. Cut out reverted shoots at their point of origin, removing a whole stem or branch if necessary. Do this in winter for evergreens, and deciduous shrubs as you see them.

removing suckers

Suckers are shoots produced from the base or the roots of a tree or shrub, especially if the variety has been grafted on a different rootstock. They often look distinctive and grow vigorously, spoiling the shape of the plant, and if derived from a rootstock can come to dominate the rest of the shrub – so they must be cut out while young (see below).

Thin stems, known as water shoots, often grow on a trunk, especially around the edge of a wound left after the removal of a branch. Although these are not, strictly speaking, suckers, they too spoil the look of a plant and should also be removed.

removing suckers

1 **Suckers grow** vigorously and must be removed.

2 **Cut off larger suckers** as close to the stem or roots as possible. For the best results, scrape back the soil and pull them off at source. You can use suckers from ungrafted plants as a method of propagation (see page 503).

If a tree has competing main shoots (leaders), select the strongest shoot and cleanly cut out its rivals at their base. Check in a year or two that no shoots are growing from the pruning wounds.

Remove an over-vigorous leading shoot with loppers before it is too large, cutting at or just below the main outline. Trim the tips of other main shoots to check their growth and encourage them to branch.

keeping a tree symmetrical

Sometimes the growing tip of a tree splits to produce two or more competing main shoots (leaders). As well as spoiling the overall symmetry of the tree, these usually branch at a narrow angle, creating a weak point that can later be damaged by strong winds. Some trees and shrubs, such as holly, produce vigorous new leading shoots that spoil the shape of the bush or tree if they are left to grow and these need to be cut out so a more balanced profile can develop (see above).

weeping trees

Encourage a young weeping tree to gain height by tying the topmost shoot vertically to a strong cane. Once this shoot develops sideshoots, you can trim off some of the lower branches to raise the crown (see page 509).

- **if the main shoot** gets broken or damaged, train the nearest branch vertically to a cane, or to the broken shoot, provided it is healthy. The replacement will later take over, then you can remove the damaged shoot at its base.
- **some weeping trees**, especially standards, are grafted, or joined, onto a straight, clear stem of a different variety, which may suddenly produce upright shoots. These should be cut right out before they spoil the shape of the tree's head.

The weeping pear looks just as beautiful when pruned to a mophead as when it trails down.

pruning large branches

Before cutting off a large tree branch, make sure you feel able to do the work safely. If in doubt, or if the branch is more than 20cm (8in) in diameter, consider hiring a qualified tree surgeon, especially if the branch is well above ground level. Make the final cut flush not with the trunk but with the branch collar, the swollen area where branch and trunk join.

removing a large branch

1 **To prevent** the branch splitting and tearing the bark, use a sharp pruning saw to make a preliminary upward cut, about a quarter of the way through the branch and 30–45cm (12–18in) away from the trunk.

2 **Saw through the branch** from above, cutting 2–3cm (1in) outside the first cut, which will close and absorb the weight of the branch, making it easier for you to saw.

3 **Saw off the stub** by making a small cut on the underside, close to the trunk but not quite flush with it, and finish by sawing from above to meet this cut.

shrubs & trees/6

pruning for special effects

You can enhance the ornamental value of some trees and shrubs using special pruning techniques that emphasise the colour or shape of leaves and bark.

coppicing and pollarding

Woody plants react to pruning by producing fresh growth. The harder they are pruned, the more vigorous is their response, and this predictable behaviour is often exploited in hard pruning shrubs and trees whose young stems and foliage are more colourful or shapely than those of mature plants. Two traditional methods of hard pruning are coppicing (or stooling), and pollarding. Both styles are useful but they produce dramatically different effects.

- **coppicing shrubs** produces a large crop of new shoots of medium height and allows a number of plants to be grown in a relatively small space. All growth is cut back regularly, usually annually, close to ground level.
- **pollarding** is like coppicing, but leaves permanent main stems of manageable size. It allows plants to retain single or multiple main stems of a certain height, above which all growth is hard pruned.

HEAVY PRUNING TIP Frequent heavy pruning can weaken plants unless they are fed and well mulched afterwards.

for colourful stems

Hard prune coloured willows, red, green and yellow-stemmed dogwoods and the white-stemmed bramble, *Rubus cockburnianus*, in spring to stimulate plenty of young regrowth with the brightest winter colouring (see opposite).

- Immediately after planting, cut all stems down almost to ground level. This helps shrubs like dogwoods to form a low woody base, while the bramble responds by producing numerous young canes.
- Thereafter, cut stems back hard in late winter to mid-spring.
- To enjoy the flowers of dogwoods in combination with the bright young stems, coppice half the stems and leave others untouched. This also helps the shrub to build up strength, and is a useful compromise if new growth has been poor.

for improved foliage

Some trees produce their most handsome leaves on young stems, and coppicing is a useful technique for displaying these to advantage. Tree of heaven (*Ailanthus*), paulownia and many ornamental elders such as the golden cut-leaved *Sambucus racemosa* 'Plumosa Aurea', all produce luxuriant foliage, often brightly coloured or of enormous size, when coppiced in spring. The smoke bush, *Cotinus coggygria*, has fine foliage if coppiced, or attractive wispy flowers when left unpruned. Young *Eucalyptus gunnii* has rounded, blue-green juvenile leaves that are more attractive than the grey-green adult foliage. This and other eucalyptus can be coppiced or pollarded to 1–1.2m (3–4ft) high in March or April, with all growth trimmed annually to 5–8cm (2–3in) from its base.

Young green-stemmed dogwoods (*Cornus stolonifera* 'Flaviramea') need to be coppiced in spring in order to produce brightly coloured stems.

coppicing hazel

1 **Purple hazel** produces more vividly coloured foliage and also useful crops of peasticks if coppiced when two to three years old.

2 **Cut off all growth** to ground level, leaving cuts that slope away from the centre of the plant; feed afterwards for maximum regrowth.

Chaenomeles trained against a wall on horizontal wires will display its flowers to best effect.

training standard trees

Standard trees with a single stem 1.5–2m (5–6ft) high are rewarding tree forms in gardens because the clear trunk allows easy access all round, and other plants can be grown beneath without competition for light. There are two kinds.

- **central-leader standard** retains a central main stem for the tree's full height and is the shape favoured for forest and woodland trees, such as oak and beech. Cut out any competing main shoots (see page 511) and prune sideshoots off the trunk as the tree develops (see page 509).
- **branched-head standard** is the preferred shape for most small ornamental trees like crab apples, cherries and rowans. Trained like this, they achieve a symmetrical arrangement of similar-sized main branches radiating from the top of the trunk. To create a branched-head standard tree:
- For the first three to four years prune as described on page 509.
- When four or five strong branches have developed above the required height of the main stem, prune back the central upright or 'leading' branch to a strong bud.
- Afterwards, thin out resulting sideshoots to help develop an open, symmetrical crown; remove strong vertical branches.

training shrubs against a wall

Hardy shrubs such as cotoneaster, chaenomeles, ceanothus and ornamental prunus varieties occupy less space, yet cover a large area to good effect, if trained against a wall as fans and espaliers. Start training early for the most complete coverage and provide support in the form of trellis or wires (see page 410).

- After planting, tie the main shoot and branches in a well-spaced arrangement. Prune out weak and surplus shoots, shorten outward-growing sideshoots to two or three buds or leaves, and remove any growing towards the wall.
- Keep tying in developing growth to create a framework of branches; prune out redundant shoots to define the shape.
- Once a framework is established, prune yearly according to the shrub's flowering season (see page 507). In midsummer remove inward-growing shoots and cut back those growing out from the wall to keep the shrub neat and densely leaved.

tiered shrubs

Shrubs with a naturally tiered structure, such as *Viburnum plicatum* 'Mariesii' and some japanese maples, need careful pruning to retain this habit. The removal of dead and diseased wood is often all that is needed, but you may need to cut out a crossing branch or uncharacteristic upright shoot. On mature plants, be prepared to cut out one or two older branches for replacement by younger shoots, and to shorten some sideshoots.

hard pruning dogwoods

1 **Shrubs such as dogwoods** (*Cornus*) can be coppiced (see opposite) or pollarded annually to leave taller main stems. Either method will stimulate plenty of regrowth with the brightest bark.

2 **Once the coloured stems** begin to bud, in late winter, cut the stems back hard, in stages, until the shrub is reduced to its framework of permanent branches.

3 **After pruning,** feed the shrub with a balanced fertiliser and mulch.

alpine gardens

Now that there is little likelihood of damaging plant growth, you can spruce up alpine plantings in rockeries, raised beds and containers. So pick off dead foliage, clear weeds, add more top-dressing, if necessary, and protect susceptible plants from the worst of the winter wet.

now is the season to . . .

■ **ensure good drainage** for alpines growing in containers as they dislike wet soil. Raise the containers just off the ground so water drains away freely.

■ **remove dead leaves** and flowers to prevent the spread of fungal diseases.

■ **pull up weeds,** taking care to remove all the roots of perennial weeds. If any weeds are growing through plants, dig up the clump and tease out the roots. Otherwise make a note to treat the weeds with systemic weedkiller in spring. Lift up the foliage of carpeting plants where weeds may grow undetected.

■ **protect alpines with fleshy or woolly leaves** from excess wet with cloches or panes of glass, unless already done in the autumn. Susceptible plants growing in containers should be moved to an unheated greenhouse or coldframe.

A pane of glass supported on upturned pots can protect fleshy-leaved alpines from wet winter weather.

The fleshy-leaved *Saxifraga spathularis* will survive a dusting of frost, but it is important that this succulent is not allowed to get too wet.

■ **top up mulches** of stone chippings or fine gravel to keep a thickness of at least 2–3cm (1in). These materials prevent rotting by creating a 'collar' of good drainage around plants, where moisture could otherwise collect.

■ **propagate more alpines** from seed, by scooping out rosettes, or by taking root cuttings (see below and opposite).

propagation

Winter is the time to sow seeds of alpines as many require a period of cold, known as stratification, in order to germinate. There are exceptions, and these include anemone, corydalis, primula and pulsatilla, all of which need sowing when the seed is freshly collected.

A few alpines, such as *Anacyclus depressus*, erodiums and *Primula denticulata*, are propagated from root cuttings in autumn and winter. Follow the method described on page 491 for perennials, but take smaller cuttings about 5cm (2in) long.

Plants that form rosettes, such as many saxifrages and *Primula denticulata*, can be propagated by scooping out rosettes to encourage new, young plants to develop. Select healthy, strong-growing rosettes and cut them off using a sharp knife to expose the top of the root, then discard. Brush the exposed area with fungicide powder to prevent disease. Soon, a cluster of shoots should develop all round the edge of the cut area and, when 2–5cm (1–2in) tall, these can be separated from the parent. Pot up individually, using the compost mix described opposite for sowing, to give the sharp drainage required.

alpines to sow now

- campanula
- chiastophyllum
- dianthus
- dodecatheon
- draba
- saxifraga
- scutellaria
- sedum

Sedum spurium

sowing seeds

To give alpines the sharp drainage they need, mix a special potting compost of equal parts by volume of seed and cuttings compost and perlite or sharp sand. Water the compost before sowing to avoid washing the seeds down deeply where they would not germinate.

After sowing stand the pots in a coldframe. The seedlings may take several months to show. Prick them out carefully once two true leaves have formed, then put the pot back in the coldframe. It can take up to a year for some seeds to germinate.

SOWING TIP Large seeds with hard coats will germinate more readily if chipped with a sharp knife or soaked overnight in tepid water before sowing.

sowing seeds

1 **Fill pots with compost,** firm gently and water using a can fitted with a fine rose. Spread the seeds thinly and evenly over the surface.

2 **Cover the seeds** to their own depth with sieved compost, unless the seeds are very fine, and top with a 1cm (½in) layer of grit to protect the seeds and prevent moss from growing. For fine seeds cover only with grit.

3 **Once the seedlings start** to show through, prick out those that have two true leaves, then return the pot to the coldframe to encourage others to germinate.

looking ahead . . .

☑ EARLY SPRING Transplant root cuttings.
☑ Prick out seedlings.
☑ LATE SUMMER Check sowings and prick out any germinated seedlings.

water gardens

Once you have cleared the pond of leaves and plant remains, and taken care of the pump, there is little to do until the frosts arrive. Then it is essential to keep an area of water ice-free, so that fish and other pond creatures can survive the sub-zero conditions.

now is the season to . . .

- **remove dead plant growth** if not done earlier (see page 422), or it will rot down and pollute the water. Cut back the stems of marginal aquatic plants to just above the water level.
- **always keep** a small area of water ice-free in freezing weather (see below).
- **plan new planting** for the spring (see opposite).
- **sweep off snow** lying on the ice after a couple of days, so that light can penetrate to the depths.
- **scoop out leaves** that have blown into the pond and are starting to sink using a child's fishing net or an old kitchen sieve. Take care not to dredge the bottom where frogs and toads are likely to be hibernating.
- **do not feed fish** in winter as they live off their reserves during cold weather.
- **run pumps** that remain in water, insulate external pumps and service those that have been removed (see right).

keeping the pond ice-free

A solid layer of ice on the pond is potentially lethal to fish, and to frogs and toads that may be hibernating at the bottom, as it prevents vital oxygen from entering the water and toxic gases from escaping. It is essential, therefore, to keep a small area of open water. One solution is to install a pond heater, which can replace a pump removed for the winter. Otherwise, you can buy an ice-guard device and float it on the surface of the water; this will also provide a hibernation place for frogs and toads. If a thick layer of ice does form, never break it with a sharp blow as the shock waves can kill fish and other pond-dwellers. Instead, set a pan of boiling water on the surface of the ice to gently melt a hole in it.

If your pond is ice-bound, stand a saucepan of boiling water on it to melt a hole. Never break it with a sharp blow.

winter pump care

If you have not already done so, remove submersible pumps from the water. Clean them thoroughly in fresh water, drain and allow to dry before storing over winter. If necessary, send the pump for servicing while it is not needed. Any pumps that remain in water over winter should be at least 45cm (18in) deep to prevent them from freezing. Run the pump for a short time once a fortnight to prevent the build-up of scale or silt. Drain external pumps and insulate them with bubble plastic.

Once the edges of a pond start to freeze, take steps to keep at least part of the water ice-free for the sake of the wildlife within it.

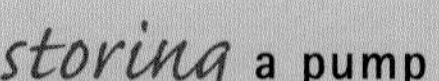

a pump

Lift the submersible pump out of the water, with the brick on which it is mounted.

Carefully remove the filter in order to clean the pump before putting it away for winter.

plants for ponds

SMALL PONDS *(minimum size 1 x 1.5m/3 x 5ft)*

1 water lily (*Nymphaea*) such as: 'Aurora', 'Froebelii', 'Hermine', 'James Brydon', 'Laydekeri' varieties and 'Sioux'. Plant in water 30–45cm (12–18in) deep.

4–5 marginal plants such as: • marsh marigold (*Caltha palustris*) • *Iris laevigata* 'Variegata' • corkscrew rush (*Juncus effusus* f. *spiralis*) • american water mint (*Mentha cervina*) • water forget-me-not (*Myosotis scorpioides* 'Mermaid') • arum lily (*Zantedeschia*)

MEDIUM-SIZED PONDS *(minimum size 1.8 x 2.4m/6 x 8ft)*

1 water lily (*Nymphaea*) such as: 'Conqueror', 'Marliacea Albida', 'Marliacea Chromatella', 'Paul Hariot', 'Rosennymphe'. Plant in water 45–75cm (18–30in) deep.

6–8 marginal plants such as: • *Acorus calamus* 'Variegatus' • flowering rush (*Butomus umbellatus*) • manna grass (*Glyceria maxima* var. *variegatus*) • *Houttuynia cordata* 'Chameleon' • *Iris pseudacorus* 'Variegata' • water mint (*Mentha aquatica*) • water forget-me-not (*Myosotis scorpioides*) • pickerel weed (*Pontederia cordata*)
All plants listed for small ponds are also suitable.

choosing plants for your pond

While pond planting should be done in spring or early summer, now is a good time to plan new planting and to order aquatic and marginal plants for delivery as soon as the weather warms up. The most important aspect is to choose plants of a suitable size to match that of your pond, because marginal plants and water lilies vary considerably n spread and vigour. This is crucial for small to medium ponds as plants that are too large will produce profuse quantities of foliage that needs regular trimming, but comparatively few flowers.

Ensure that your pond looks good from spring to autumn by choosing a mixture of foliage plants that provide long-lasting interest and flowering plants for each season. Always have oxygenating plants to help keep the water clear, planting three small bunches to each square metre of pond surface area (one bunch per square foot).

looking ahead . . .

- ☑ SPRING Remove pond heater.
- ☑ Start feeding fish, sparingly at first.
- ☑ Install submersible pumps.

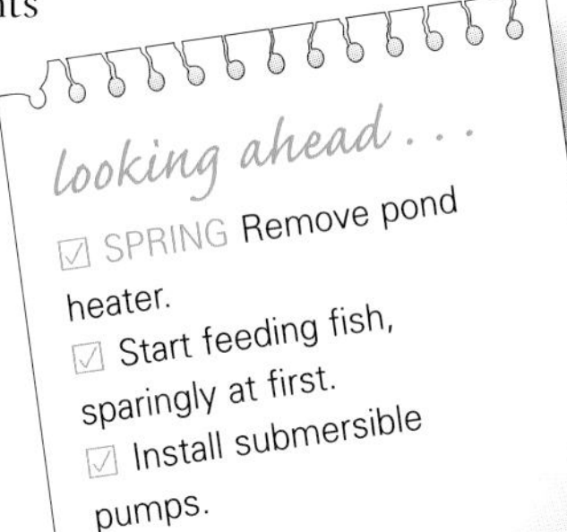

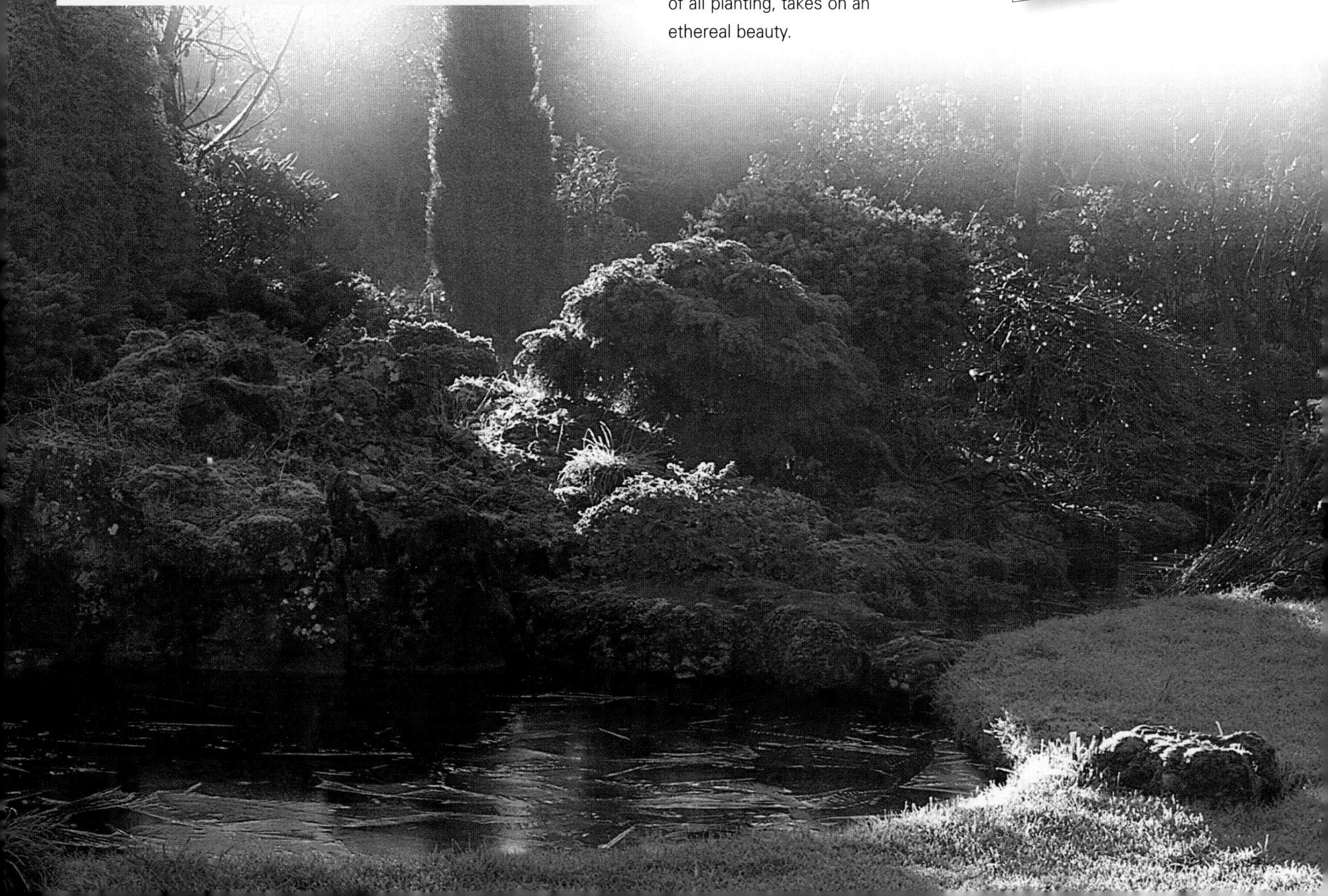

A pond in winter, devoid of all planting, takes on an ethereal beauty.

patios & containers

Hardy shrubs and seasonal flowers in tubs and window boxes keep the patio cheerful throughout the winter, but in all but the mildest areas containers will need protection from frost. Towards the end of winter, take time to tidy up and clean patios and any other hard surfaces to prevent them from becoming slippery.

now is the season to . . .

- **move containers** that are not frost-proof under cover, to a greenhouse, conservatory or coldframe.
- **clean paved paths,** patios and decking (see page 57).
- **empty out containers** of frost-tender plants that are dead. Scrub the containers using hot water and a mild detergent, rinse and leave to dry, then store under cover.
- **protect container-grown plants** against frost (see right). The extent of the protection required depends on the hardiness of the plant.
- **top-dress pot-grown lilies** while the bulbs are dormant by replacing the top 10cm (4in) of old soil with fresh loam-based potting compost.
- **water occasionally** if the compost begins to dry out. Regularly check containers that are standing close to a wall and so may not receive any rainfall.

frost protection

All container-grown plants need some degree of protection from frost, because both rootball and topgrowth are above the ground. Evergreens are particularly vulnerable, as they continue to lose water through their leaves and are unable to replenish their stocks if their roots are in frozen compost. The ideal solution is to move any susceptible plants into an unheated greenhouse, porch or conservatory, but if there is no such structure available plants have to be protected outside.

ensuring good drainage

It is vital to provide good drainage as soggy compost that freezes can result in severe damage to plants. When planting up pots, first put in a 5cm (2in) layer of drainage material, such as pieces of broken pot or chunks of polystyrene. Make

Stalwarts of winter containers, evergreen *Skimmia japonica* 'Rubella', *Heuchera micrantha* var. *diversifolia* 'Palace Purple' and ivy (left), are brightened by the cheerful 'faces' of universal pansies (*Viola* 'Ultima Scarlet').

protecting plants

Tall plants, such as standard evergreens and tree ferns, benefit from individual protection. Remove coverings during the day unless very low temperatures persist.

Tie up the leaves of cordylines, then wrap the whole plant in fleece or bubble plastic.

sure that surplus water can drain away by raising all containers just off the ground, either on 'pot feet' or pieces of tile, or by standing them on gravel.

looking ahead . . .

☑ LATE SPRING Remove protection and dead foliage from plants and containers.

☑ SUMMER Move tender plants outdoors.

grouping containers

If severe weather threatens, move all containers against a wall, standing them shoulder to shoulder; this will raise the temperature around the pots by a valuable few degrees.

- **wrap insulating material,** such as bubble plastic, sacking or thick wads of straw around the pots.
- **cover the plants** with thick horticultural fleece during very cold spells, but remove this during the day or as soon as the weather improves, otherwise fungal disease may become a problem.
- **remember that** well-protected plants may need watering.

A window box planting for winter relies on colourful foliage. This one includes silver-leaved cineraria, grey-leaved senecio, variegated ivy and the winter cherry (*Solanum capsicastrum*).

Insulate container-grown plants that are not fully hardy with an 'overcoat' of sacking and straw in severe weather (above).

Wrap the stems of standard evergreens in pipe insulation (top left), then cover the pot and the head of the plant with fleece (left).

Fold the dead fronds of tree ferns over the top of the crown (below), before encasing the whole plant in a 'jacket' of bubble plastic (bottom).

lawns

Although we think of winter as a time when the lawn takes a rest, this really only applies when conditions are very cold. During mild spells the grass will often grow and you can mow, repair turf or even make a new lawn.

now is the season to . . .

- **rake up any leaves,** which if left will block out light, hold moisture and encourage moss to establish.
- **scatter worm casts** with a stiff broom or besom to prevent the mounds of soil being smeared by feet or by the mower and killing the grass.
- **make a final winter cut** with the mower blades on a high setting (see opposite). Rake off any clippings to prevent them from killing the grass beneath. In mild winters you may need to cut the grass more than once if it continues to grow.
- **avoid walking over a frosted lawn** as the pressure damages the grass, causing it to turn brown and, possibly, to die.
- **'top' newly established lawns** with the mower blades on their highest setting to encourage more shoots from the base of the plants. If the new grass is quite low, roll it lightly to encourage branching and a denser lawn (not in frosty conditions).
- **apply lime** to lawns on acid soil if moss has been a particular problem.
- **improve drainage** by spiking or slitting (see right).
- **in mild conditions carry out minor repairs,** such as mending damaged lawn edges, and even out bumps and hollows that have formed as parts of the lawn settle (see page 428).
- **prepare the soil for new grass** in mild weather. You can lay turf or sow seed in winter, but growth will be slow if the soil temperature drops below 5°C (40°F). In early winter, seed is the better option, as turf may dry out along its edges if there are any hard frosts within the first weeks after laying.

improving drainage

The problem that causes most damage in winter is wet, rather than cold, as long periods of mild wet weather starve the roots of air as they are trying to grow. During the summer lawns often develop a compacted, impervious layer just below the surface from regular foot traffic, and this impedes drainage unless it is opened up by spiking or slitting.

- **spike** with a garden fork, or preferably, a hollow-tine lawn spiker, to help air get to the grass roots. Drive in the tines 15cm (6in) deep every 15–20cm (6–8in).

This specimen cherry tree in the middle of a contoured lawn is a striking centrepiece even in winter, with its tracery of bare branches outlined against the frosted grass.

Stepping stones set into a lawn prevent people having to walk on the grass in frosty weather, which can damage the grass blades and make them turn brown.

- **slitting** with a powered scarifying machine is an easier and quicker way to deal with a large lawn and also gathers surface debris, such as dead grass and moss. Blades cut into the top 2–3cm (1in) of soil. As well as improving drainage, scarifiers prune the grass roots, encouraging them to branch.
- **after spiking or slitting,** top-dress lawns on heavier soils with a mixture of equal parts of sand and loam, brushing it into the holes. This will help to improve drainage.
- **for areas that get very wet,** you can lay land drains; do this early in winter before the ground is too wet.

CLEANING TIP Use a plastic scraper to clean off any caked grass stuck to the mower. This not only makes it easier to examine, but also protects your mower, as grass sap stains plastic and corrodes metal. Where grass is lodged in places that are difficult to clean, blow it out with a few blasts from a bicycle pump.

equipment overhaul

In late autumn and winter, when the grass hardly grows, take the opportunity to check over your mower and other lawn equipment. Clean electrically powered machinery such as mowers and scarifiers. Check and oil all moving parts, and sharpen blades with a file to regain a sharp edge, or replace them if necessary.

- **petrol-driven mowers** can be washed clean with a power hose and left to dry, but this is not recommended for machinery powered by battery or electricity.
- **cylinder mowers** need to be serviced by a specialist, who will sharpen the blades on a grinding lathe.

raising the blades of a rotary mower

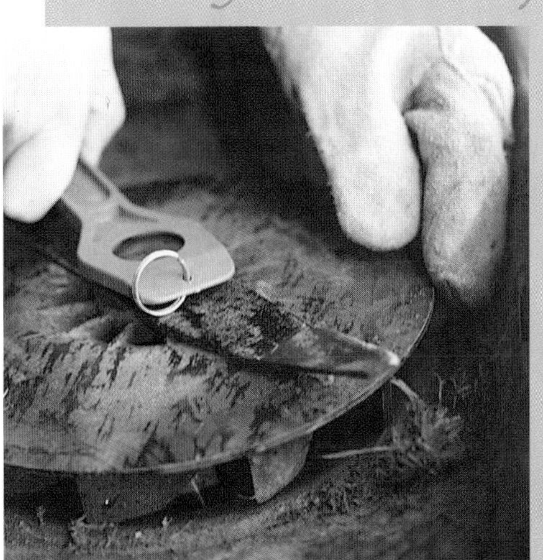

1 **Using the spanner** provided, slacken the spindle nut that holds the cutting blade onto the underside of the mower. Always wear a thick leather glove to grip the blade as it may be sharp.

2 **Carefully remove** the spindle nut, the cutting blade and the spacer washer from the mower.

3 **Now re-attach** the blade and spindle nut (but not the spacer washer – keep this safe); tighten the spindle nut. Without the spacer washer, the blade is raised and the mower will cut at a higher setting.

fruit

With all fruit crops harvested and safely stored, winter is mainly a time for maintenance, pruning and taking precautions against pests and diseases, but even now some fruits are nearly ready for forcing into early life.

now is the season to . . .

- **inspect stored fruit** every two to three weeks. Use any that is showing signs of deterioration, and discard rotting fruits before decay can spread.
- **continue planting** new fruit whenever conditions are suitable.
- **check ties and supports:** secure, adjust or repair if needed.
- **clear weeds** for a distance of 60cm (2ft) around fruit plants and hoe the surface, to expose pest eggs and larvae to foraging birds.
- **prune gooseberries and autumn-fruiting raspberries** by cutting all canes down to 5–8cm (2–3in).
- **finish taking hardwood cuttings** of bush fruits while plants are dormant.
- **carry out essential winter pruning** before the end of January (see right).
- **look over blackcurrant bushes** for big bud (see opposite).
- **check grease bands** on fruit trees; reapply grease if needed.
- **deal with canker** on apple and pear trees (see opposite).
- **apply a winter wash** to dormant fruit trees (see opposite).
- **protect fruit buds** from birds.
- **guard peaches** and nectarines from peach leaf curl with screens of polythene as described for climbers on page 499, and spray with copper-based fungicide.
- **grass down** established fruit trees if yields are low (see opposite).
- **start fruits under glass** into growth (see page 539–40).

and if you have time . . .

- **place cloches** over strawberry plants to force early crops.
- **cover rhubarb** with boxes or forcing pots for an early harvest (see page 539).

winter pruning guide

A simple winter pruning routine applies to all tree and bush fruits except plums, cherries, peaches and other stone fruits (see page 61). These are pruned in spring after the buds have opened, to reduce the chance of disease.

Prune apple trees in winter, when they are completely dormant.

- **cut back any dead,** damaged and diseased stems to healthy live wood.
- **remove branches that cross** others or grow towards the centre of the plant; bushes, in particular, should be kept open-centred in a goblet shape.
- **further shorten sideshoots** on cordons, espaliers and fans, which were summer-pruned to four or five leaves, to just one or two buds. For gooseberries and red and white currants, prune back the tips of main branches at the same time.
- **thin out congested spurs** on mature trained forms of apple and pear; shorten long spurs by half, and remove completely some that are growing closely together.
- **encourage sideshoots** and spurs to develop on young espalier and fan-trained fruit by shortening main branches by half. Cut to a downward-facing bud.
- **on overgrown** or neglected trees, cut out completely one or two main branches to admit more light and air and encourage new growth.

Snow settles on a row of neatly trained raspberry canes, forming a ghostly structure in the garden.

treating pests and diseases

There are measures you can take now to protect plants from pests and counteract several serious diseases.

blackcurrant big bud

Blackcurrant gall mites overwinter inside buds, causing them to swell and fail to develop. The mites also spread reversion virus, a serious and incurable disease. Check bushes in winter and early spring for the characteristic fat, rounded buds. Pick off any you find, and burn or otherwise destroy them.

apple and pear canker

This fungal disease can be serious if allowed to spread unchecked. Cracks and lesions develop on branches and at the base of spurs and sideshoots, often causing them to die back altogether if infection rings the stem. The disease is most prevalent on wet soils and is often controlled by improving drainage. Some apple varieties, such as 'Cox's Orange Pippin', are particularly vulnerable, whereas 'Bramley's Seedling', 'Lane's Prince Albert' and 'Newton Wonder' are more resistant.

Canker is a potentially serious fungal disease of apple and pear trees, most often caused by wet conditions.

- **remove diseased** and mummified fruits.
- **prune back affected shoots** and cut out lesions on main stems; paint the cuts with fungicidal wound paint.
- **grass down** older trees to prevent rain splashes, which spread the spores (see below).
- **remove and destroy** badly infected trees.

winter washing fruit

Painting or spraying fruit trees with a tar-oil winter wash is a traditional way of killing overwintering pest larvae and eggs, disease spores, moss and lichen. This wash is a very toxic substance so the whole area under the trees should be covered with plastic sheeting or thick layers of newspaper before treatment to keep splashes off neighbouring plants. It is also indiscriminate in its treatment, killing eggs and the larvae of beneficial insects as well as fruit pests.

grassing down to improve yields

If fruiting on mature trees is in decline, sow grass seed or turf right up to their trunks to help restore the balance of nutrients in the soil. Don't feed the trees for two or three years, or use a high-potash, low-nitrogen fertiliser.

looking ahead . . .

☑ LATE SUMMER Summer-prune trained fruit.
☑ AUTUMN Spray against peach leaf curl just before the leaves fall.

there is still time to . . .

- **prune blackberries** and summer-fruiting raspberries (see page 432).

pruning gooseberries

1 **Shorten to two buds** all sideshoots that were summer-pruned to five leaves, and completely remove any thin or spindly shoots.

2 **Cut out one or two of the old,** dark branches where young shoots are growing and tie these in, as replacements.

3 **Remove any surplus shoots** growing from the base, clear weeds and mulch with straw, bracken or well-rotted manure.

vegetables

Take advantage of mild spells to get ahead in the vegetable garden by digging and preparing seedbeds. There are still some fresh crops to pick to supplement those stored away in late summer and autumn. On dark, chilly days draw up plans for next year, so you can get your orders for seeds, young plants and potatoes in early.

now is the season to . . .

- **plan next year's crop rotation** (see pages 530–1) and order seeds and potatoes for the coming season.
- **create a seedbed** early in winter. Cover the area with plastic sheeting to warm the soil for early crops (see opposite).
- **hoe off weed seedlings.**
- **watch for pest and diseases** in mild periods. Look for aphids hiding in the outer leaves of cabbages, cauliflowers and other overwintering vegetables.
- **be prepared to control slugs** with baits or chemicals. Young slugs start feeding on plants almost immediately the eggs hatch in warm spells.
- **watch for bird damage:** crops will be attacked as food supplies become scarce, and hungry wood pigeons can devastate a crop of cauliflowers. Protect vegetables with netting or use bird scarers. A length of twine or old video tape stretched just above the crop deters many birds but not wood pigeons, which tend to walk in to feed, rather than fly direct.
- **use stored vegetables** and check those that remain; discard any with signs of mould or rot. Watch for vermin damage, as mice may nest and feed in your store during cold periods.

harvesting now

• brussels sprouts • celeriac • jerusalem artichokes • kale • leeks • parsnips • swedes • winter cabbage • winter cauliflower • winter radish • winter spinach

Celeriac ready for lifting

- **check storage temperatures:** if stored vegetables start to sprout, this indicates the store is too warm, and produce will deteriorate rapidly.
- **put in place cloches** or low polythene tunnels to warm the soil and help it to dry out after wet weather.
- **make early sowings** of beetroot, broad beans, carrots, lettuce, peas, radishes, spinach or turnips when the soil has warmed sufficiently and spring is approaching.

In a colourful winter vegetable bed, leeks 'Longbow' grow with two varieties of brussels sprout ('Rubine Red' and 'Icarus'). Pick the sprout tops for eating as greens, and to reduce the plants' exposure to wind.

winter cultivation

Complete winter digging when conditions allow. The heavier the soil, the earlier it should be dug to let frost break it down; lighter, free-draining soils can be left until later. The depth of cultivation depends on your soil and the plants you grow.

single digging

Single digging is ideal for shallow-rooted salad crops and small round-rooted vegetables. It entails digging trenches to a depth of about 30cm (12in), or one spade blade deep and wide. Work systematically across the plot; bury any plant debris and old mulch from the surface in the base of the previously opened trench, and cover it with soil as you dig the next.

double digging

Double digging improves poor drainage and is good preparation for deep-rooted crops, such as carrots and parsnips, and long-term crops like asparagus and rhubarb. It is similar to single digging but more strenuous, as you cultivate to approximately 60cm (2ft) or the depth of two spade blades. Well-rotted manure or garden compost is forked into the base of each trench. It is vital not to mix the darker topsoil with the paler, infertile subsoil as you work (see page 595).

Double digging incorporates manure or garden compost, giving root crops a good start.

preparing a seedbed

Dig over the soil in autumn or early winter, especially if it is heavy. Roughly level the surface and leave for a month or two so the frost can break up the clods and make final preparation easier. This time lag also allows weeds to germinate, for easy removal later on.

Two or three weeks before sowing, when the weather is fair and the soil is not so wet it clings to your tools, lightly fork over the surface to break up any remaining clods and rake the surface level (see below). After the seedbed is prepared, warm the soil by covering it with cloches, low polythene tunnels, or black or clear plastic sheeting. Black plastic excludes light and heats up the soil more quickly, whereas the advantage of clear plastic is that it provides ideal conditions for weed seeds to germinate, for easier removal before sowing.

EARLY SOWING TIP Don't be tempted to sow seeds in periods of mild weather without first checking the soil temperature, as many seeds need the soil to be between 5–7°C (40–45°F) before they will germinate. Insert a thermometer into the top 8–10cm (3–4in) of soil regularly.

making a seedbed

1 **Break up any lumps of soil** on the prepared bed with the back of a fork, then rake the surface until it is fine and level.

2 **To warm the soil** for early sowings, cover the seedbed with plastic sheeting. Spread the plastic over upturned plant pots so that condensation drains to the edges rather than dripping on the prepared surface.

3 **Hoe off any seedling weeds** after two or three weeks, disturbing the soil as little as possible, or treat with weedkiller for a clean start.

vegetables/2

winter crops

Early winter is the time to browse through catalogues and order seeds and young plants. By late winter you can begin to sow for the year ahead in pots or cellular trays under cover and outside, if conditions are suitable. The success of your vegetable garden hinges on careful planning, both in terms of what you grow (see page 534) and how you operate your crop rotations (see page 530).

Winter cabbages can stay in the ground until you need them. This variety, with its distinctive crinkled leaves, is 'Winter Savoy'.

peas and beans

- **inspect autumn-sown broad beans** in spells of very cold weather and protect the plants with cloches or a covering of horticultural fleece.

Young broad beans may need to be protected with fleece.

- **sow broad beans** into 8–10cm (3–4in) pots, one or two per pot, in a cool greenhouse, ready to transplant in early spring.
- **check autumn-sown peas** under cloches and insulate with thick fleece or a layer of loose straw if very cold days and nights are anticipated.
- **sow early varieties of peas** in 8–10cm (3–4in) pots, two or three seeds per pot, in a cool greenhouse. These will be large enough for transplanting in mid-March and should crop in May.
- **sow early peas outdoors** under cloches to follow on the batches you have raised under glass.

cabbage family

- **harvest brussels sprouts:** pick the largest first from the base and work up the stem. Support the plants with short canes and string ties to prevent them from blowing over in exposed areas. Pick the leafy tops for eating and to reduce their vulnerability to wind rock.
- **when harvesting kale,** remove and compost larger outer leaves each time the young shoots are picked over.
- **cut winter cabbages** as required. Cut off the head, leaving 8–10cm (3–4in) of stalk protruding from the ground. Cross-cut these stalks to encourage a secondary crop of leafy greens in mid-spring.
- **in cold spells,** protect spring cabbages from pigeons by covering the crop with nets or by using bird scarers.

Pests may strip the leaves of brussels sprouts, but this will have no detrimental effect on the sprouts themselves.

Jumbo garlic cloves can be planted in cellular trays under glass, to plant outdoors once they have sprouted.

onion family

- **use stored onions,** shallots and garlic. Check bulbs and remove immediately any that show signs of rot or mould, before the infection can spread.
- **the last chance** to plant garlic is in February. Plant cloves 2–3cm (1in) deep and spaced 15–20cm (6–8in) apart, on a ridge if your soil is heavy.
- **plant shallots early,** from December to March. Plant the small bulbs, or sets, setting them 1cm (½in) deep and 10–15cm (4–6in) apart.
- **lift mature leeks** as required during mild spells; lifting them when the ground is frozen will cause bruising and stem rot.
- **during late winter, sow leeks** and onions in cellular trays or small pots and place in a cool greenhouse; sow four or five onion seeds per pot for transplanting in mid-spring.

salad crops

- **protect** overwintering lettuce with cloches or low polythene tunnels, allowing some ventilation to reduce the risk of fungal rots.
- **sow short rows of lettuce,** radish and spinach in late winter under cloches on previously warmed soil.

other crops

- **lift jerusalem artichoke** tubers as required. If cold weather is forecast, lift and temporarily store some for immediate use.
- **order asparagus crowns** for planting in early spring. Prepare planting trenches for the new beds by double digging (see page 595).

Rows of lettuce seedlings are protected in a coldframe. Pick alternate plants and allow the others to develop a heart.

looking ahead . . .

☑ EARLY SPRING Plant early potatoes and asparagus crowns.

☑ Begin to plant out hardy crops started off under glass.

potatoes and root crops

- **use carrots and beetroot** in store, discarding any that are showing signs of rot.
- **lift celeriac, parsnip and winter** radish as required when the weather is mild and the soil is not frozen or waterlogged. If a cold spell is forecast, lift and store some roots in a shed so they are ready for use.
- **sow early varieties** of beetroot, carrot and turnip in open ground if the soil conditions are suitable. Pre-warming the soil and cloche protection will be necessary for the earliest sowings in all but the mildest gardens.
- **sow celeriac** in late winter in cellular trays in a cool greenhouse for transplanting in late spring.
- **order seed potatoes early** and sprout, or chit, early varieties indoors from February.

Early potatoes are sprouted, or 'chitted', in late winter or early spring. Lay them in seed trays or egg trays, rose end up (this is the end with most buds, or 'eyes'), in a cool, light frost-free place. About six weeks later, in early spring, each potato will have formed four to five shoots 2–3cm (1in) long. When conditions are suitable the tubers can then be planted.

making a vegetable plot

It is possible to include a few favourite vegetables almost anywhere in the garden, but the time may come when you want to grow a more ambitious selection of crops in a dedicated kitchen garden or vegetable plot. At this stage, some thought and planning will pay dividends.

the right site

Choosing the best place to grow vegetables is important, as it can make the difference between success and failure. Factors to consider include:

- **shelter** Cold winds seriously affect cropping, with even light winds reducing yields by 20 per cent or more, especially in winter. Fences and hedges filter winds and limit their impact, and both can be used to protect vegetables and fruit crops, adding to the total productivity of your garden. Walls can be a mixed blessing. They are valuable for supporting trained fruit, but solid barriers can produce strong wind turbulence within the garden and trap frost. Make sure that boundary or internal walls are not affecting the proposed site adversely.
- **sun and shade** Most crops need plenty of sunlight, particularly winter crops, if they are to yield well. Light shade can be welcome in summer to protect leafy vegetables like lettuce and kohl rabi from drying out, but heavy shade from buildings or trees is best avoided.
- **good drainage** Heavy waterlogged soil causes all kinds of problems for vegetables. If puddles lie on the surface for any length of time after prolonged rain, you might have to dig the site deeply to improve drainage, or consider raising the soil level in beds or ridges to increase the depth of well-drained earth.
- **soil** No soil is perfect, but most can be improved over time. Incorporating large amounts of organic material, such as garden compost and rotted manure, adds body to light soils and opens up heavy clays. With regular cultivating and mulching, your soil and crops will steadily improve in quality.
- **size** Even a small area can be productive, but plot size will influence the choice of plants you will be able grow. If you have a small plot, choose vegetables that can grow close together. Include tall varieties that use vertical space, like beans, and crop the ground intensively by close-spacing the plants.

Winter in this kitchen garden (below) reveals the skeletons of fan-trained and tree fruit. The low box hedges edging the half-empty vegetable beds have chicken wire at their base to deter rabbits.

a practical design

In drawing up a plan for your vegetable plot, do your best to incorporate the permanent features detailed below. Some of these will make your day-to-day gardening easier, while others, like paths, form a key part of the layout.

permanent features

- **one or two compost bins** allow you to dispose of annual weeds and vegetable waste, and to recycle their fertility back into the garden.
- **space to stack** manure, leaf-mould and other bulky materials for digging into and improving the soil.
- **water** – you don't want to carry this far, so consider installing a tap and standpipe, or a tank to collect rainwater.
- **a coldframe**
- **borders** or other space for herbs and perennial vegetables, such as asparagus and globe artichokes.
- **fruits are permanent** and should be considered early in the planning stage.
- **paths** provide essential access, both for cultivation and for harvesting, particularly on a wet day. Depending on the size of your plot, you will need at least one all-weather path, ideally wide enough to manoeuvre a wheelbarrow. Narrower paths between beds can be of beaten earth or made from more durable materials.
- **edges to beds** such as treated timber boards, bricks or a low hedge of perennial herbs, keep the paths clean.

making a traditional vegetable plot

YOU WILL NEED • spade • rake • string and pegs • measuring tape • 16 treated timber boards 8–10cm (3–4in) wide by 2.5cm (1in) thick • 16 battens 30cm (12in) long • sledgehammer • screwdriver and screws • cocoa shells and grit, or bark

1 **Dig the whole site,** removing as many weeds as possible, especially the roots of perennial species. Rake the area level.

2 **Using the string and pegs,** mark out the plot as a square. Divide this into quarters by marking out two central paths 50cm (20in) wide, crossing at right angles in the centre.

3 **Edge the beds** with the treated boards. Drive the battens firmly into the ground at the corners of the beds and screw the boards to these.

4 **Surface the paths** with a layer of cocoa shells and grit or shredded bark. For a permanent surface, such as brick or slabs, dig out some of the soil and spread this on the beds before laying the paving material.

5 **Allocate the beds** as 1, 2, 3 or 4 for crop rotation (see page 142) and prepare as follows: **bed 1**, fork in rotted manure for peas and beans; **bed 2**, fork in garden compost and fertiliser for potatoes or green manure; **bed 3**, rake in fertiliser for root crops; **bed 4**, fork in compost and fertiliser for brassicas.

6 **Rake the beds level,** and plant any edging crops of perennial herbs, flowers or low hedges. You are now ready to plan plantings for each bed.

making a vegetable plot/2

crop rotation

Growing vegetables in a new position each year is an important precaution against building up soil pests and diseases, and depleting soil nutrients. The traditional method is to divide the ground into three or four plots or beds, then move groups of vegetables with similar needs and disorders from one bed to the next in annual sequence. The three main groups are legumes (peas and beans), brassicas (the cabbage family), and root crops, including onions, with potatoes and squashes in a fourth bed. Fit in salad leaves and sweetcorn wherever there is space. Additions of rotted manure or garden compost are made to each bed when digging and preparing it for planting, depending on the type of crop grown in it (see below). Fertiliser, where required, is applied just before planting the crop. In small gardens, where only a few vegetables are grown, simply avoid growing a particular group or individual crop in the same place for two consecutive years.

rotation groups

	YEAR 1	YEAR 2	YEAR 3	YEAR 4
BED ONE	legumes (add well-rotted manure)	brassicas (add compost and fertiliser)	roots and onions (add fertiliser)	potatoes (add manure or compost and fertiliser)
BED TWO	potatoes (add manure or compost and fertiliser)	legumes (add well-rotted manure)	brassicas (add compost and fertiliser)	roots and onions (add fertiliser)
BED THREE	roots and onions (add fertiliser)	potatoes (add manure or compost and fertiliser)	legumes (add well-rotted manure)	brassicas (add compost and fertiliser)
BED FOUR	brassicas (add compost and fertiliser)	roots and onions (add fertiliser)	potatoes (add manure or compost and fertiliser)	legumes (add well-rotted manure)

Crop rotation is clearly at work in this vegetable garden, with box-edged square beds dedicated to different groups of crops that have varying requirements in terms of soil and fertilisers. The all-weather brick paths are wide enough for a wheelbarrow. Cloches are used to protect young plants until they become established.

style and layout

There are alternative layouts to the traditional one shown on page 529, which make efficient use of the space. And a vegetable garden need not always be strictly functional, as many crops are ornamental as well as edible.

- **traditional kitchen gardens** were quartered by crossing paths, a system that allowed for efficient crop rotation and a large number of bed edges to plant with herbs, fruit or flowers for cutting.
- **raised or narrow beds,** up to 1.2m (4ft) wide, are very productive; they make the most of small spaces and organic matter and are useful in planning crop rotations too. Several can be arranged to form a kitchen garden, or you can include them as an integral part of a flower border.
- **potagers** are plots that exploit the decorative potential of vegetables by arranging them like bedding plants, balancing their shapes and colours in a pattern of formally shaped beds.
- **a cottage garden patchwork** can be made by organising small square beds in a flexible layout for any size or shape of site, perhaps combined with flowers.

no-dig beds

The deep bed, or no-dig, system of cultivation is based on the concept that routine cultivation damages the soil structure and can lead to a reduction in the population of worms and other beneficial organisms within the soil. Instead of digging the soil to work in organic matter, the organic matter is spread over the surface and left for worms and other organisms to gradually draw it down into the upper layers, improving fertility in the area penetrated by most plant roots. Worm activity not only breaks down organic matter but improves the soil's aeration, drainage and water-holding capacity.

Narrow beds, edged by boards, are one way to grow vegetables in a small space. The soil level drops slightly as the organic matter rots down.

The no-dig system is ideal for dealing with heavy clay soils, which are difficult to work and are easily compacted. By protecting the surface with organic matter structural damage is avoided, while below worms open up the soil's close structure and improve its drainage.

preparation

A once-only, very thorough cultivation is essential to the success of the no-dig system. Double digging, incorporating large quantities of organic matter, enriches the soil and improves texture (see page 525). But from this point on, any cultivation and walking on beds must be avoided to prevent disturbance or compaction, and to allow a natural soil structure to develop. For this reason you need to be able to reach to the middle of the bed comfortably from either side, which limits the width to about 1.2m (4ft).

maintenance of no-dig beds

After the initial preparation is done you should mulch annually (see left). After harvesting leafy vegetables, leave the roots in the soil to decay naturally, trim vegetables near to where they were growing, and lay any leaf litter or waste on vacant areas of the bed to rot down.

maintaining a no-dig bed

1 **Mulch the surface every year** with well-rotted organic matter to a depth of about 10cm (4in) to keep soil fertile. This deep mulching will reduce moisture loss, suppress the germination of weed seeds and keep the soil warmer, extending the growing season. Always work from a path.

2 **When you want to plant,** scrape back the mulch to expose the soil surface and replace it afterwards, keeping it clear of young stems. The timber edging helps to retain the mulch layer within the bed until it rots down.

making a vegetable plot/3

choosing your crops

To some extent, deciding what to grow is a matter of trial and error, but it is a good idea to start with vegetables that are favourites with your family and also those that are expensive, or hard to find, in the shops.

- **list your favourite vegetables** and decide what not to grow. Good quality maincrop potatoes and cabbages may be available locally, whereas salad leaves, sweetcorn or early baby carrots taste better picked fresh.
- **match your list** to the available space, and the time and energy you can devote to their cultivation. Recognise the difference between vegetables that sprint to maturity, allowing you to grow something else afterwards, and slow crops such as brussels sprouts that need a long growing season (see pages 534–5).
- **use your space** to best effect. Do you want to harvest a wide variety of produce for as long as possible, or simply raise large amounts of a few varieties for storing or self-indulgence?
- **find out** what does well locally. As your soil and skills improve, your range of produce will increase, but some crops may not suit your ground or local climate.
- **keep a garden diary.** Note your most successful crops and varieties, with their sowing or planting dates, to help you plan for the next year.

raising from seed

The cheapest and possibly the most rewarding way to grow vegetables is to raise them from seed, but this depends on having a greenhouse or at least a coldframe (see page 606), to start plants off in the warmth. Growing from seed also gives you a wider choice of vegetables and allows you to select more unusual varieties.

Small plug plants of lettuce, beetroot and brassicas are ready to pot on or plant out.

buying plug plants

Where space is at a premium, it is a good idea to visit a garden centre and buy plug plants or small trays of seedlings. This allows you to buy just as many plants as you have space to grow, without the trouble of raising them from seed. You can buy a wide range of crops in this form, both direct and through mail-order and internet outlets.

Plug plants and seedlings are also an invaluable way of raising vegetables if you do not have a greenhouse or even a coldframe, and prefer not to fill your windowsills with propagating cases and pots of seedlings for the first few months of every year. Instead, let the professionals germinate the seeds and grow on the young plants in controlled conditions. You can then take over in spring, when growing conditions are more favourable.

Mesclun (right) is a mixture of spicy salad leaves best freshly picked. Since it is not readily available in shops, it is an ideal crop to grow yourself.

Turnips are a brassica; they take up relatively little space and the tops can be eaten as greens (below).

cropping continuity

The challenge of vegetable growing is having a range of crops available all year round. There are various ways in which you can make the most of your vegetable plot and keep it healthy.

• **successional sowing** Usually it is the quick-maturing crops like spinach, beetroot, radishes and lettuce that are most likely to produce gluts and gaps, but this can be avoided if you sow small amounts of seed at regular intervals. Timing can be difficult to gauge, but a good guide is to sow a new batch of seed when the first true leaves (those forming after the seed leaves) start to emerge on the previous sowing. In this way you avoid 'bolting' lettuces, woody roots or bitter spinach leaves.

• **intercropping** This means using the space between slow-growing crops as a seedbed for vegetables that will later need transplanting or are quick maturing. Radishes, rocket, lettuce, turnips and beetroot (pulled young) are all suitable for growing between crops such as winter cabbages, brussels sprouts or parsnips, spaced a little further apart than usual.

• **catch crops** Take advantage of vacant soil by growing a 'catch', or quick-maturing, crop. For example, rapidly maturing lettuce, spinach or peas could precede a tender crop of runner beans, tomatoes, sweetcorn or courgettes, none of which can be planted in the ground until the risk of frost is over. The catch crop is harvested before the tender crop is planted, or at least before it gets established.

maximising your space

Make full use of available ground by spacing plants equally in each direction rather than in rows. This planting 'on the square' (or in staggered rows) works well in a bed system, where equally spaced plants grow evenly and weeds are quickly crowded out. You can also space plants closer than recommended to produce 'baby' vegetables, a method particularly suited to root crops.

vegetables in small gardens

If you have a really tiny garden that cannot encompass dedicated vegetable beds, it is still possible to grow a few vegetables. Here are some ideas, but try to experiment too.

• **flower borders** A number of vegetables have handsome foliage, which will look attractive among the flowers. There are varieties of chard with rainbow-coloured stems in yellow, orange, pink and ruby red, while beetroots have dark red-veined leaves and stems. Carrot foliage is soft and ferny, and in winter there are few plants that can match the majestic curly kale. Spinach beet and frilly loose-leaved lettuces are always worth growing as cut-and-come-again crops. Sweetcorn is another possibility, planted in a group in a sunny spot. Runner or climbing french beans trained up vertical canes at the back of a border, or along a boundary, give both privacy and produce during summer months. Don't expect the yields to be quite as high as they would be in a dedicated vegetable plot, however.

• **containers** Many vegetables are easy to grow in large containers, tomatoes and salad crops especially, but also peas, beans, courgettes and squashes. Early potatoes are particularly successful when grown in a deep, barrel-like container. Fill it about a third full of soil-based compost, space out the sprouted seed tubers and cover with more compost. As the foliage appears, earth it up with more compost until the container is full. To harvest, just scrape away the compost and lift a helping at a time, then cover up the remaining potatoes to grow on.

• **window boxes** Choose shallow-rooted crops for a window box, although carrot varieties with ball-like roots and radishes should also succeed. Peppers and cherry tomatoes crop well in a sunny aspect, so long as they are well fed and watered. Bush tomato varieties like 'Tumbler' need no training and will even grow successfully in a hanging basket. Lettuces and salad leaves do best on a windowsill shaded from the midday summer sun.

Quick-maturing spring onions and lettuces are grown here as an intercrop between rows of slower-growing maincrop carrots.

vegetables in containers

Vegetables grown in containers must be watered regularly (daily in hot weather) and fed every 7–14 days with an appropriate fertiliser if they are to do well.

• **feed fruiting crops** like tomatoes, beans, courgettes, peppers, aubergines and cucumbers with a tomato fertiliser, which is high in phosphate and potash, to develop flowers and seeds.

• **leafy vegetables,** such as spinach, ruby chard, cut-and-come-again salad crops and lettuces, need a high-nitrogen feed to promote leafy growth.

making a vegetable plot/4

implementing crop rotations

To rotate crops efficiently you need to know which vegetables fall into which group, and this is not always obvious. For example, turnips and swedes grow alongside cabbages because they are also brassicas, whereas potatoes, though they grow underground, need more in the way of organic matter than root vegetables like carrots or onions, and so are more easily treated on their own.

The vegetables here are listed under their crop rotation group, where relevant. Perennial vegetables need a permanent home, so should be grown in a separate bed, while tender fruiting crops, though annuals, need plenty of space and are therefore also grown in a bed of their own. To make the best use of space, fit in quick-maturing salads and spinach as a catch crop or an intercrop (see page 533), to provide a continuous succession of fresh pickings.

SEED PACKET TIP Read the seed packet:

- before buying – it will tell you if the variety is appropriate for the season
- before sowing – it gives precise growing instructions for the best results.

spacing

The spacings given are final, maximum spacings based on vegetables growing in rows. The between-plants distance is given first, followed by the distance between rows. If you prefer to grow plants equidistant from one another, follow the between-plant spacings.

feeding

Most plants grow well without additional feeding as long as the soil has been well-prepared and is mulched regularly with organic matter. With vegetables, however, an application of fertiliser in advance of planting makes a real difference to the quantity and quality of your harvest. Extra feeding during growth is not essential for crops growing in open ground, but vital for those in containers.

ROOTS & ONIONS

Root vegetables, such as carrots, onions and parsnips, do not need a great deal of space, but they prefer a deep soil to allow good root development and do not do well on shallow soils. Rake in a balanced fertiliser before planting or sowing.

bulb onions Raise onions from seed or from plant sets, which is easier.
sow February–March **plant sets** February–March or September–October
spacing 10–15 x 30cm (4–6 x 12in)

garlic Plant individual cloves in autumn. for the biggest bulbs. Grows well in pots.
plant February or October
spacing 20 x 20cm (8 x 8in)

leeks There are varieties for autumn and winter use, so check the packet.
sow February–March **plant** June–August
spacing 15 x 30cm (6 x 12in)

shallots Traditionally planted on Christmas Day.
plant December–March
maximum spacing 15 x 25cm (6 x 10in)

spring or salad onions Successional sowing, or as an intercrop.
sow March–June
spacing 2–3 x 25cm (1 x 10in)

beetroot Easy to grow. For successional sowing, or as an intercrop for baby beets.
sow March–July
spacing 5–8 x 30cm (2–3 x 12in)

carrots Sow early varieties as successional sowings or as an intercrop to be pulled young. Sow Nantes types early and late in the season. 'Sytan' is resistant to carrot fly. Stony ground may create forked roots.
sow March–July
spacing 5–10 x 15cm (2–4 x 6in)

celeriac Tolerates light shade.
sow April **plant** June
spacing 30 x 40cm (12 x 16in)

parsnips Stony ground may split roots.
sow March–May
maximum spacing 8–15 x 30cm (3–6 x 12in)

LEGUMES

These follow root crops or potatoes in rotation. Add well-rotted manure when preparing the soil in Autumn. Before sowing or planting, rake in a balanced fertiliser. After harvesting, leave the roots in the ground or dig them in for the benefit of a following brassica or other leafy crop.

broad beans Tall varieties need support.
sow November or April–May
maximum spacing 25 x 30cm (10 x 12in)

dwarf beans These need no support but crop less heavily than climbing varieties.
sow April–July
spacing 20 x 60cm (8 x 24in)

french & runner beans Canes, arranged in single or double rows or as wigwams, are essential for support. Raise these tender plants in pots under cover for an early start, or direct sow in late May.
sow April–May
maximum spacing 15 x 60cm (6 x 24in)

peas & mangetout Make successional sowings about 5–10cm (2–4in) apart in a broad row and as an early catch crop. Put in place netting or twiggy branches to support the growing plants.
sow earlies March–April; maincrop April–July
maximum spacing 8 x 90cm (4 x 36in)

POTATOES

Potatoes need a deep soil. They can follow brassicas in a rotation and are best grown on their own. Dig in garden compost when preparing the soil and rake in a general-purpose fertiliser a couple of weeks before planting. They can also be grown under black plastic sheeting tucked in round the edge of the bed. Plant tubers 10–15cm (4–6in) deep through a cross cut in the plastic. To harvest, lift the plastic, remove as many tubers as you want and replace the plastic.
plant earlies March–May; maincrop April–May
spacing earlies 30 x 50cm (12 x 20in); maincrop 38 x 75cm (15 x 30in)

BRASSICAS

Brassicas follow legumes to benefit from the residual nitrogen. Dig in compost when preparing the soil and rake in a balanced fertiliser before planting. Dress acid and neutral soils with lime to reduce the risk of club root disease. Leafy brassicas benefit from a high-nitrogen feed in summer.

LIMING TIP Apply lime well in advance of planting, and at least a month after any organic matter has been added, to avoid a chemical reaction taking place that would result in loss of nitrogen from the soil.

broccoli Pick regularly for long harvest.
sow March–April **plant** June–July
maximum spacing 60 x 60cm (2 x 2ft)

brussels sprouts Easy to grow, but tall varieties need support, especially in windy gardens in winter.
sow March–April **plant** May–June
maximum spacing 60 x 60cm (2 x 2ft)

cabbages Easy to grow, especially winter varieties. Choose a variety appropriate for the season. Winter cabbages need the widest spacing.
sow March–September **plant** September–July
spacing 30–50 x 30–50cm (12–20 x 12–20in)

cauliflowers A challenging crop. Raise or buy young plants in pots so that there is no check to growth when transplanting, and never let them dry out. Choose a variety appropriate for the season.
sow/plant April–May
spacing 50–75 x 60–75cm (20–30 x 24–30in)

kale Decorative and easy to grow. Pick shoots regularly for long harvesting.
sow April–August
spacing 45 x 60cm (18 x 24in)

kohl rabi Tolerates light shade. Successional sowing.
sow April–August
spacing 20 x 30cm (8 x 12in)

radishes For successional sowing or an early catch crop or intercrop.
sow March–September
spacing 2–3 x 15cm (1 x 6in)

swedes Easy to grow.
sow April–June
spacing 25 x 40cm (10 x 16in)

turnips Easy to grow. For successional sowing, or pull as baby turnips for an early or late catch crop and intercrop.
sow April–August
maximum spacing 15 x 25cm (6 x 10in)

PERENNIAL VEGETABLES

Because these vegetables grow in the same place for many years, they must be planted in well prepared soil enriched with plenty of rotted manure or garden compost and given a general-purpose feed every year.

asparagus Have patience and wait two years after planting before cutting any spears. In the third year, begin to cut for 4–6 weeks and in subsequent years up to 8 weeks. Earthing up emerging shoots gives a longer blanched stem. After harvesting, apply fertiliser and in autumn mulch with rotted manure after ferns are cut down.
plant March–April
spacing 30 x 45cm (12 x 18in)

globe artichokes These need time to establish before you crop them heavily. The second year after planting limit yourself to one head per plant, the next year cut two or three. In subsequent years you can pick the smaller side heads after picking the main buds. Apply a balanced fertiliser in early spring and in autumn mulch with rotted manure and compost.
plant February–April
spacing 1 x 1m (3 x 3ft)

jerusalem artichokes Tubers can be lifted in the first year. Apply fertiliser in spring and mulch with organic matter in autumn. Will tolerate light shade.
plant February–May
spacing 30 x 60cm (12 x 24in)

LETTUCE & SPINACH

Fit these in wherever there is space, with brassicas or in a bed devoted to salad crops.

lettuce It is most important to sow the appropriate variety for the time of year. Mix with spinach and other salad leaves for a cut-and-come-again seedling crop. Good for successional sowing and intercropping.
sow all year round according to variety
maximum spacing 25 x 30cm (8 x 12in)

spinach & chard Choose a variety appropriate to the season or grow spinach beet, which will crop throughout the year.
sow true spinach in small batches for succession, or as an early catch crop; summer spinach March–May; winter spinach August–October; chard April–August
spacing 15–20 x 30cm (6–8 x 12in)

TENDER FRUITING CROPS

These need plenty of space and are best grown in a bed of their own. Like legumes they need well-manured ground so they can follow roots in a crop rotation.

outdoor cucumbers Train plants up wigwams or other supports. You may need to pollinate the flowers to ensure a crop. Also grow well in growing bags.
sow April–May **plant** May–June
maximum spacing 60 x 60cm (2 x 2ft)

outdoor tomatoes Support tall-growing, or cordon, varieties with canes or other means and remove sideshoots regularly. Pinch out the growing tips two leaves above the third or fourth fruit truss; the fifth or sixth truss in the case of cherry tomatoes. Allow bush varieties to sprawl and do not remove fruit-bearing sideshoots. Outdoor tomatoes also do well in growing bags.
sow April–May **plant** May–June
spacing 75 x 75cm (30 x 30cm)

squash, courgettes, marrows & pumpkin Plant out on mounds of soil, to ensure good drainage, or even on top of your compost heap. You may need to pollinate the flowers to ensure fruits form.
sow April–May **plant** May–June
spacing Give each plant about 1m^2 (1sq yd); pumpkins and large-fruiting winter squash need 1.5m^2 (1½sq yd). Alternatively, plant them two to a growing bag.

sweetcorn Plants are wind pollinated so plant in a block, rather than in rows.
sow April–May **plant** May–June
spacing 35 x 35cm (14 x 14in)

herbs

Fresh pickings come mostly from herbs in pots now that all but a few evergreens have died down in the garden. Most herb care is confined under glass, but outside you can rejuvenate leggy sage and thyme, and prepare to make early sowings.

Salad burnet is one of the few herbs to keep growing through winter, and makes a tasty salad crop.

now is the season to . . .

- **ventilate herbs under glass** in mild weather as a precaution against fungal disease.
- **water sparingly** lemon verbena and other overwintering tender herbs.
- **lay hard paths** in a new herb garden and start constructing new beds (see page 346).
- **protect containerised herbs** outdoors. In severe weather, bring the most vulnerable indoors or gather pots together and cover with fleece or bubble plastic (see page 518).
- **in early winter, pot up roots** of mint and tarragon for fresh early supplies.

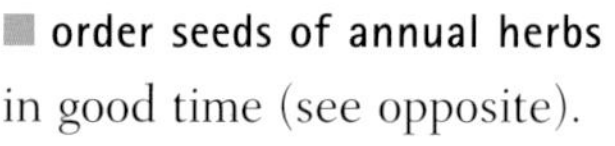

Pot up root cuttings of mint in a box of compost to force under glass.

- **order seeds of annual herbs** in good time (see opposite).
- **clear annual crops** and tidy beds. Mulch with garden compost or well-rotted manure, which can be forked in just before sowing in early spring.
- **cultivate new beds** for annual herbs (see opposite).
- **prepare a mint bed** where the roots will not invade other plants. Buy mint plants in late winter or lift and divide existing healthy roots for replanting 30cm (12in) apart.
- **propagate old leggy plants** of sage, thyme and other woody herbs by mound layering or dropping (see opposite).
- **protect bay trees** from cold and remedy any frost damage in late winter (see below).
- **cover a few parsley** and chive plants with cloches to revive growth for early pickings.

protecting bay trees in winter

The shallow roots of bay trees less than three or four years old are vulnerable to frost, and severe cold weather can scorch the foliage of even mature trees. To guard against injury, plant bay in a sunny sheltered position, and screen from cold winds. In winter bring potted bay plants indoors, or protect both plant and container with fleece or bubble plastic and clad bare stems in foam pipe insulation (see page 519). A thick mulch of leaf-mould or straw over the roots helps to prevent freezing in pots or open ground.

Bay trees are susceptible to frost, which can scorch their leaves in winter.

- **if a few leaves turn brown,** remove them, but leave shoots intact in case fresh growth appears later in the year.
- **extensive leaf browning** usually indicates the death of the top growth, but provided the roots have been kept frost-free, new shoots may sprout from the base. So cut down the tree at the end of winter, leaving stumps about 10cm (4in) long, and apply a balanced fertiliser.

growing annual herbs

Annual or biennial herbs such as parsley, chervil and dill are usually sown in rows or in a special bed within the kitchen garden. Every two or three years it is advisable to prepare a new bed in a different position.

- **dig clay soil in autumn,** leave it rough and break it up finely with a fork in late winter. Add plenty of leaf-mould or garden compost to improve the texture and drainage.
- **dig light soils in late** winter, adding plenty of garden compost or well-rotted manure to improve water retention. Many annual herbs are leafy and grow fast, so need moister conditions than many aromatic perennials.
- **just before sowing** or planting, fork a balanced fertiliser into the top 8cm (3in) of soil. Then rake to leave a fine, level seedbed.

Sow parsley *in situ* in late winter; once germinated, and with cloche cover, it will rapidly put on leafy growth.

dropping a rosemary

1 Dig up the leggy plant in late winter or early spring and excavate the hole 30cm (12in) deeper than it was.

2 Replant in the same hole, spreading out the branches. Return the soil to cover the centre of the plant and the bare portions of the branches.

3 Keep moist in dry weather and transplant any rooted layers in autumn, or leave them to form a wider clump.

annual & biennial herbs

to raise from seed

- basil (tender) • borage
- caraway • chervil
- coriander • dill • parsley
- summer savory

Dill (*Anethum graveolens*)

propagating leggy herbs

Some woody herbs get very bare at the base if they are not clipped back regularly to keep them compact. If your herbs have become leggy you can take cuttings or layer some of the lower branches, and then discard the old plants. The alternative methods of 'dropping' (see left) or mound layering in late winter will give you numerous new plants while improving the appearance of the parent shrub until it is superseded. Dropping is best suited to sage, rosemary and lavender.

mound layering

This works well for thymes as well as other small woody herbs.

- **Mix together** equal parts of soil-based compost and grit and heap it over the bare centre of the plant, working it well in between the branches.
- **Keep the plant moist** in dry weather during the summer months.
- **In early autumn,** carefully explore around the branches, most of which will have formed roots. These layers can now be detached for transplanting.

Heap a mixture of compost and grit over the middle of a leggy thyme and keep it moist in dry weather to encourage layers to develop roots.

there is still time to...

- **plant new perennial herbs** and hedges when the ground is in a workable condition.

looking ahead...

☑ EARLY SPRING Sow annual and biennial herbs.
☑ Continue dividing perennials.
☑ AUTUMN Detach and pot up layers from mounded or dropped plants.

the greenhouse

A greenhouse is a comfortable sanctuary for gardeners as well as for tender plants. Visit it regularly to sow, prune and check that all is well; air it on fine days and water growing plants occasionally. Forced bulbs and early strawberries will be coming into flower if you have provided a little warmth.

now is the season to . . .

- **water plants sparingly** in cold weather, and avoid wetting foliage (see opposite).
- **open ventilators** for a short period on frost-free and fog-free days to prevent the air from stagnating.
- **make sure heaters are working** properly, and monitor temperature levels with a maximum-minimum thermometer.
- **keep insulation materials** securely in place, and have newspapers, blankets or fleece handy for covering plants in extreme weather, especially in unheated greenhouses.
- **remove dead flowers** and leaves, diseased plants and mildewed cuttings to keep healthy plants free from infection.
- **check for vine weevils** if any of your plants suddenly collapse (see page 541).
- **inspect stored bulbs** and tubers to make sure that they are still sound.
- **continue to bring potted bulbs** in from outdoors as they show signs of growth and flower buds (see page 494).
- **pot up amaryllis** and restart older bulbs (see page 495).
- **continue potting up lilies** for early flowers.
- **prune indoor grape vines,** and lower their stems (see page 540).
- **prune greenhouse climbers** and tie in any new stems (see page 540).
- **start under glass fruit trees** such as apricots for early fruit; hand-pollinate once flowers appear (see page 540).
- **bring in potted strawberries** and rhubarb crowns for forcing (see opposite).
- **from midwinter, sow greenhouse flowers** such as begonias and gloxinias, and the first half-hardy annuals.
- **start begonia and gloxinia tubers** in trays for a supply of cuttings (see page 540).
- **sow half-hardy annuals and early vegetables** in pots or trays.
- **sow lettuce and radish** in the greenhouse border if you have one. Sow tomato seeds in pots in mid-February for planting under glass in early April.
- **cut down greenhouse chrysanthemums** and encourage new growth for cuttings (see page 540).

Strawberries that were potted up last autumn and left outside should be brought into the greenhouse to force early fruits.

forcing early fruits

Strawberries and rhubarb (see below) are two fruits you can enjoy early with a frost-free greenhouse.

strawberries

Bring in batches of strawberry plants potted up in late summer or autumn and left outside to stimulate the production of flower buds. Clean the pots and remove any dead leaves, then stand the plants on a high shelf in the light.

- **Water lightly at first,** but increase as growth revives. Feed with a balanced liquid fertiliser every 14 days once in flower.
- **Pollinate the flowers** by gently brushing their centres with a soft paintbrush.
- **Support developing fruit trusses** with twigs. After harvest, harden the plants off and transplant into the garden.

On fine days open top ventilators slightly for an hour or two in the morning.

Use a maximum-minimum thermometer to check temperatures as these are critical in winter.

winter greenhouse management

Special care is essential in winter to keep plants healthy. Temperature and light levels are low, and knowing how much water and air to give plants can be tricky.

watering

Only plants in active growth will need much water. To keep these evenly moist, stand pots and trays in water until the surface starts to look damp; watering from above may just moisten the surface and leave the roots dry. Take care to avoid overwatering sensitive plants such as calceolarias and cinerarias, which can collapse suddenly if too wet. Most other plants need just enough to prevent the compost from drying out. Try to water in the mornings, so that surplus dries before nightfall, and avoid wetting the foliage.

ventilation

A dry atmosphere with a gentle circulation of air without cold draughts is the ideal, so open one or two top ventilators for an hour or so during the day, unless it is foggy or frosty. If possible, open vents on the side away from the wind, and close them by midday so that warmth has time to build up before sunset.

heat

Most plants benefit from temperatures above 5–7°C (40–45°F); use a thermometer to check. You can economise by gathering tender plants in a well-insulated spot and heating only this area. Germinate seeds on a windowsill or in a warm cupboard in the house, or invest in a heated propagator.

forcing rhubarb

1 **Bring in the strong crowns** you dug up and left exposed to frost in autumn, from December onwards. Place them under the greenhouse staging, blacking out the light with plastic or blankets. Pack straw, dry leaves or used potting compost between the plants, water well and drape another blanket from the front of the staging to ensure total darkness.

2 **Check weekly for watering** and to monitor growth. Pull sticks when they are a useable length. Discard the crowns once picking is over.

the greenhouse/2

plant care

Fruit trees growing under glass, such as peaches, nectarines and apricots, can be started into growth during January for fruits from June, if you provide a minimum temperature of 7°C (45°F). Keep ventilators closed until buds break, and mist the branches and sideshoots with warm water every other morning to stimulate growth. When flowers open, fertilise them by brushing the centres with a soft brush, or open the ventilators on a warm day to admit bees and other pollinating insects.

pruning climbers

In midwinter, clear all dead flowers and leaves from climbers, and then prune them according to size and variety. Strong-growing plants such as passionflower and bougainvillea can take over a small greenhouse unless pruned hard annually.

- **Thin the congested growth,** aiming for a balanced arrangement of main branches. Remove any weak or spindly stems, then shorten sideshoots almost to their base.
- **You may need to cut out** one or two older branches to allow replacement with young, more vigorous shoots. Sort the prunings for potential cuttings before discarding them.
- **Finally,** check the plant is symmetrical and well shaped, with plenty of light reaching all the stems.
- **Clean the glass or wall** behind the climber, prick over and weed the soil, and mulch plants growing in the ground.

pruning vines in winter

Prune greenhouse grape vines as soon as they have lost all their leaves. They are usually grown with a system of parallel main branches, or rods, from which fruiting sideshoots grow each year.

- **Cut back** sideshoots to one or two buds.
- **Rub or pull** any loose bark from the rods to expose and eliminate hiding places for pests.
- **After pruning,** untie the rods and lower them until they are horizontal or a little lower. This encourages all buds to start growing together, after which the rods can be retied in place. Do this in December, January or February: it depends on whether the variety is early, mid-season or late.

starting begonias, dahlias and gloxinias

Encourage tuberous-rooted begonias, dahlias and gloxinias into growth now to make large flowering plants and also to supply early shoots for cuttings (see below).

chrysanthemums from cuttings

When greenhouse and slightly tender border chrysanthemums finish flowering, cut down their topgrowth to 5–8cm (2–3in) high. Overwinter them in a cool frost-free place: indoor varieties in their pots, border kinds dug up and packed in soil in a coldframe or under the greenhouse staging. Keep watering to a minimum, just enough to prevent the plants from drying out. New shoots appear from late December onwards,

starting begonias into growth

1 **Fill a tray** with moist potting compost and press tubers into this, 5cm (2in) apart, so their tops are just above surface level. Make sure they are the right way up, with the rounded base downwards and the hollowed area uppermost, then water.

2 **Cut very large tubers in half** with a sharp knife to increase the number of plants, but dust the cut edges with yellow sulphur powder as a precaution against rotting. Use a propagator or cover the tray with a clear lid and keep moist at 13–15°C (55–60°F). In a cooler greenhouse, delay planting until early spring.

3 **When growth appears,** pot up the tubers individually.

Even in the coldest winter weather, plants inside the sheltered environment of the greenhouse will be safe and warm.

depending on the variety. Use these for cuttings when they are about 8cm (3in) long.

- **Cut off** all the lower leaves and trim each cutting just below a leaf joint.
- **Insert them** 2–3cm (1in) deep in pots of cuttings compost mixed with added sharp sand; five will fit comfortably in a 15cm (6in) pot.
- **Water,** cover with a clear plastic bag and keep in a light, warm position until rooted.

Yellow-flowered *Lachenalia* enjoys the protection of a greenhouse, along with *Pelargonium graveolens* cuttings and a tray of developing seedlings.

vine weevils

The damaging effects of this troublesome weevil whose grubs feed on roots can be obvious in winter. If plants start to look sick and then suddenly collapse, tip them out carefully and explore the compost for the curved larvae, creamy white with brown heads.

- **inspect plants** in the evening for irregular holes round the edges of leaves, typical evidence of adults feeding, and crush any you find.
- **during summer,** when the temperature is at least 12°C (54°F), use a biological control: water plants with a parasitic nematode (*Heterorhabditis*) to kill the grubs.
- **throughout the year,** tip out plants occasionally to check for grubs and inspect new plants before introducing them to the greenhouse.
- **surround the rims** of precious plants with double-sided sticky tape to trap adults before they can lay eggs.
- **try using** an insecticidal compost containing imidocloprid.

looking ahead . . .

☑ LATE SPRING Plant forced strawberries in the garden.
☑ Start hardening off young plants.
☑ SUMMER Introduce biological pest controls.

there is still time to . . .

- **clean out the greenhouse,** and wash the glass and all equipment (see page 446).

winter

plant selector

There is a surprising variety of star turns and solid garden performers to lift the spirits during the darker months. Evergreens are the stalwarts of the season, and their myriad forms and leaf shapes will weave a tapestry of greens. Tightly clipped box, walls of deep green yew and jazzy variegated hollies lend themselves to hedges and topiary, and provide the backbone that knits a garden together. There can be flowers in winter, too – scented viburnums and daphnes, spidery witch hazels and yellow mahonias. Berries can last well into winter on malus, cotoneasters and holly, while hellebores, marbled-leaved arums and the earliest of bulbs beautify beds and borders.

Hamamelis x *intermedia* 'Pallida'

perennials

Although most perennials are herbaceous, a few are evergreen and some flower in winter. Most are best planted in late autumn or early spring.

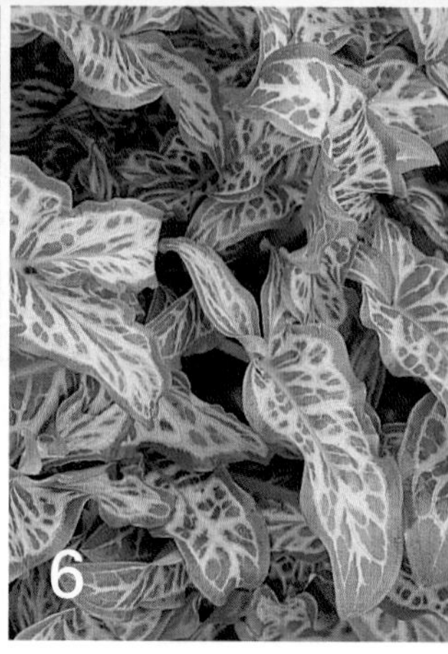

blue, violet and purple

1 Pulmonaria angustifolia 'Munstead Blue'

Blue cowslip, Lungwort

Unlike most lungworts, this is not evergreen nor is the foliage spotted. The bristly lance-shaped leaves appear with the first flowers in late winter. The clear blue, funnel-shaped blooms are carried on erect stems well into spring. Hardy.

Height: 20cm (8in) **Spread:** 45cm (18in)

Site: Partial shade, shade. Moist but well-drained soil

Use: Border, underplanting for shrubs

Good companions: *Aquilegia* 'Hensol Harebell', *Dicentra* 'Langtrees', *Geranium sylvaticum* 'Mayflower'

2 Viola odorata

English violet, Garden violet, Sweet violet

Semi-evergreen perennial that spreads by underground runners to form dark green mats of almost heart-shaped leaves. Scented violet to white flowers emerge through the foliage from late winter to mid-spring. Hardy.

Height: 15cm (6in) **Spread:** 30cm (12in)

Site: Sun, partial shade. Moist but well-drained soil

Use: Wild garden, woodland garden

Good companions: *Ajuga reptans* 'Purple Torch', *Galanthus nivalis, Primula vulgaris*

pink and mauve

3 Bergenia x schmidtii

Evergreen hybrid with rounded leaves on long stalks. Against the rich green sprays of pink flowers stand out in late winter and early spring. Hardy.

Height: 30cm (12in) **Spread:** 60cm (2ft)

Site: Sun, partial shade. Well-drained soil

Use: Border, ground cover, woodland garden

Good companions: *Epimedium* x *youngianum* 'Niveum', *Prunus* x *subhirtella* 'Autumnalis', *Sarcococca hookeriana* var. *digyna*

bronze and red

4 Bergenia 'Ballawley'

This evergreen hybrid makes a substantial green clump in summer, but takes on rich purple and bronze tones when touched by frost. In spring it produces sprays of bright red-pink flowers. Hardy.

Height: 60cm (2ft) **Spread:** 50cm (20in)

Site: Sun, partial shade. Well-drained soil

Use: Border, gravel garden, ground cover

Good companions: *Allium hollandicum* 'Purple Sensation', *Euphorbia* x *martinii, Gladiolus communis* subsp. *byzantinus*

5 Pulmonaria rubra 'Redstart'

Lungwort

Evergreen lungwort that bears small clusters of coral-red flowers from midwinter, but often peaks in late winter or early spring. Hardy.

Height: 30cm (12in) **Spread:** 75cm (2ft 6in)

Site: Partial shade, shade. Moist but well-drained soil

Use: Border, underplanting for shrubs, woodland garden

Good companions: *Asplenium scolopendrium, Dicentra* 'Luxuriant', *Viola riviniana* Purpurea Group

cream and white

6 Arum italicum subsp. italicum 'Marmoratum'

Clusters of red berries on erect stems are eye-catching in autumn, but in winter it is the glossy foliage that counts. The spear-shaped leaves are rich green with ivory veining; they emerge in winter and attain their full size in early to mid-spring. Toxic if ingested and contact can cause allergic reactions. Hardy.

Height: 40cm (16in) **Spread:** 45cm (18in)

Site: Sun, partial shade. Humus-rich and well-drained soil

Use: Border, underplanting for shrubs

Good companions: *Galanthus* 'Atkinsii', *Helleborus argutifolius, Rubus* 'Benenden'

7 Helleborus niger

Christmas rose, Hellebore

Evergreen hellebore valued for the glistening white flowers that stand on purplish stems above dark evergreen fingered leaves. It often starts to bloom in early winter and continues until early spring, the petals usually taking on a pink flush as they age. Harmful if ingested and the sap can cause allergic skin reactions. Hardy.

Height: 30cm (12in) **Spread:** 45cm (18in)

Site: Partial shade. Humus-rich and moist but well-drained soil. Good on lime

Use: Lightly shaded border, woodland garden

Good companions: *Cyclamen purpurascens, Dryopteris erythrosora, Tiarella wherryi*

7

8

9

8 Helleborus x nigercors

Hellebore

The leathery evergreen leaves of this hybrid have three to five toothed lobes and the flowers, borne in clusters on short stems from midwinter to early spring, resemble white or pale pink saucers. Harmful if ingested and the sap can cause allergic skin reactions. Hardy.

Height: 30cm (12in) **Spread:** 75cm (2ft 6in)

Site: Partial shade. Humus-rich and moist but well-drained soil. Good on lime

Use: Lightly shaded border, woodland garden

Good companions: *Helleborus hybridus, Hosta lancifolia, Polygonatum* x *hybridum*

green

9 Helleborus argutifolius

Corsican hellebore

Stiff-stemmed bushy evergreen plant with deep green leathery leaves that are lighter underneath and divided into three conspicuously toothed and veined leaflets. Clusters of yellow-green flowers first open in late winter, but last for many weeks. Harmful if ingested and the sap can cause allergic skin reactions. Hardy.

Height: 1m (3ft) **Spread:** 1.2m (4ft)

Site: Sun, partial shade. Moist but well-drained soil

Use: Border, underplanting for shrubs

Good companions: *Epimedium* x *rubrum, Euphorbia amygdaloides* 'Purpurea', *Tricyrtis formosana*

10 Helleborus foetidus Wester Flisk Group

Bear's foot, Dungwort, Stinking hellebore, Stinkwort

Evergreen hellebore with deep to grey-green, divided fan-shaped leaves that smell unpleasant if bruised. The drooping thimble-like flowers, which are green with a maroon rim, are borne in large clusters from midwinter to mid-spring. The stems, stalks and leaf bases are all tinted red. Harmful if ingested and the sap can cause allergic skin reactions. Hardy.

Height: 60cm (2ft)

Spread: 45cm (18in)

Site: Partial shade, shade, sun. Moist but well-drained soil

Use: Border, underplanting for shrubs and trees, woodland garden

Good companions: *Anemone sylvestris, Galanthus nivalis, Iris foetidissima*

10

11 Helleborus x sternii Blackthorn Group

Hellebore

The grey-green leaves of this evergreen hybrid are composed of three conspicuously veined leaflets and carried on purple stems. The nodding green flowers, borne from late winter to mid-spring, are overlaid with purple or pink. Harmful if ingested and the sap can cause skin reactions. Not fully hardy.

Height and spread: 40cm (16in)

Site: Sun, partial shade. Moist but well-drained soil. Good on lime

Use: Border, underplanting for shrubs

Good companions: *Cyclamen hederifolium, Disporum sessile* 'Variegatum', *Lilium martagon* var. *album*

12 Polystichum munitum

Sword fern

Clump-forming evergreen fern with glossy, dark green arching fronds. Each one is composed of numerous paired narrow segments that are spiny toothed. Hardy.

Height and spread: 1m (3ft)

Site: Shade, partial shade. Humus-rich and moist but well-drained soil

Compost: Soil-based (John Innes No. 2) with added leaf-mould

Use: Container, shady border, woodland garden

Good companions: *Anemone nemorosa, Galanthus elwesii, Helleborus foetidus* Wester Flisk Group

11

12

annuals & biennials

A few perennials that are usually grown as annuals or biennials are particularly valued in the winter garden because they produce colourful flowers with gay abandon. They are suitable for bedding and containers.

lilac, pink and mauve

1 Viola x wittrockiana Mello Series

Winter-flowering pansy

Mello Series is sufficiently hardy for winter and spring displays and the upward-facing flowers come in a wide range of simple colours. Hardy.

General care: Sow seed in early to midsummer and plant out in autumn. Deadhead regularly.

Height: 15cm (6in) **Spread:** 20cm (8in)

Site: Sun, partial shade. Humus-rich and moist but well-drained soil

Compost: Soil-based (John Innes No. 2) or soil-less

Use: Container, formal bedding, front of border

Good companions: *Hyacinthus orientalis* 'Ostara', *Primula* Cowichan Garnet Group, *Tulipa* 'Couleur Cardinal'

2 Viola x wittrockiana Ultima Series

Winter-flowering pansy

The rich green, almost heart-shaped leaves form a spreading tuft. The flowers are available in a wide range of single and mixed colours. Hardy.

General care: Sow seed in early to midsummer and plant out in autumn. Deadhead regularly.

Height: 15cm (6in) **Spread:** 20cm (8in)

Site: Sun, partial shade. Humus-rich and moist but well-drained soil

Compost: Soil-based (John Innes No. 2) or soil-less

Use: Container, formal bedding, front of border

Good companions: *Narcissus* 'Dove Wings', *Scilla siberica* 'Spring Beauty', *Tulipa* 'Madame Lefeber'

red and russet

3 Primula Pacific Giant Series

From late winter to mid-spring these polyanthus bear scented, usually yellow-eyed flowers in a range of vivid colours above an evergreen or semi-evergreen rosette of crinkled leaves. Hardy.

General care: Sow seed in summer and plant out in autumn.

Height and spread: 20cm (8in)

Site: Sun, partial shade. Moist but well-drained soil

Compost: Soil-based (John Innes No. 2) or soil-less

Use: Container, formal bedding, front of border

Good companions: *Hyacinthus orientalis* 'Carnegie', *Narcissus* 'Dove Wings', *Viola* x *wittrockiana* Universal Series

4 Viola x wittrockiana Universal Series

Winter-flowering pansy

Flowers reliably in mild weather from late autumn to late spring. Some single colours are available, but the seed is usually sold as mixtures. Hardy.

General care: Sow seed in early to midsummer and plant out in autumn. Deadhead regularly.

Height: 15cm (6in) **Spread:** 20cm (8in)

Site: Sun, partial shade. Humus-rich and moist but well-drained soil

Compost: Soil-based (John Innes No. 2) or soil-less

Use: Container, formal bedding, front of border

Good companions: *Bellis perennis*, *Puschkinia scilloides* var. *libanotica*, *Tulipa* 'Heart's Delight'

yellow and orange

5 Primula Crescendo Series

These evergreen perennial polyanthus are grown as biennials for their scented yellow-centred flowers in late winter and early spring. Seed is available as mixtures or as separate colours. Hardy.

General care: Sow seed in summer and plant out in autumn.

Height and spread: 20cm (8in)

Site: Sun, partial shade. Moist, well-drained soil

Compost: Soil-based (John Innes No. 2) or soil-less

Use: Container, formal bedding, front of border

Good companions: *Anemone coronaria* De Caen Group, *Crocus vernus* 'Remembrance', *Narcissus* 'Jack Snipe'

bulbs

Perennials with underground food-storage organs – bulbs, corms, tubers and rhizomes – are a very varied group. Early flowering species give a strong foretaste of the riches that will follow in spring.

3

5

1

2

4

6

purple, blue and violet

1 Anemone blanda

Wood anemone

In late winter or early spring flowers are borne freely over prettily divided foliage. Colours include shades of blue, white and pink. Hardy.

General care: Plant in autumn with the top of the tuber about 8cm (3in) deep.

Height and spread: 15cm (6in)

Site: Sun or partial shade. Well-drained soil

Compost: Soil-based (John Innes No. 2) with added leaf-mould

Use: Container, planting in grass, raised bed, rock garden, underplanting for shrubs and trees

Good companions: *Colchicum* 'Rosy Dawn', *Eranthis hyemalis, Narcissus* 'February Gold'

2 Crocus chrysanthus 'Ladykiller'

In late winter or early spring each corm produces honey-scented, white globular flowers with rich purple outer markings and scarlet styles. Hardy.

General care: Plant in autumn with the top of the corm about 8cm (3in) deep.

Height: 8cm (3in) **Spread:** 5cm (2in)

Site: Sun. Gritty, well-drained soil

Compost: Soil-based (John Innes No. 1) with added grit

Use: Container, raised bed, rock garden, sunny bed

Good companions: *Campanula carpatica, Iris* 'Natascha', *Rhodanthemum hosmariense*

3 Crocus tommasinianus 'Whitewell Purple'

In late winter or early spring red-purple flowers, which teeter on white tubes, open in sun to reveal a silvery mauve inside. The leaves appear with the flowers and have a white midrib. Hardy.

General care: Plant in autumn with the top of the corm about 8cm (3in) deep.

Height: 8cm (3in) **Spread:** 5cm (2in)

Site: Sun. Gritty, well-drained soil

Compost: Soil-based (John Innes No. 1) with added grit

Use: Container, front of sunny border, raised bed, rock garden, planting in grass

Good companions: *Aubrieta* 'Doctor Mules', *Colchicum speciosum, Crocus speciosus*

4 Scilla mischtschenkoana

In late winter produces up to four very pale blue starry flowers marked with darker stripes. Hardy.

General care: Plant in late summer or autumn with the top of the bulb about 8cm (3in) deep.

Height: 10cm (4in) **Spread:** 8cm (3in)

Site: Sun or partial shade. Moist, well-drained soil

Compost: Soil-based (John Innes No. 2) with added leaf-mould

Use: Container, front of border, rock garden, planting in grass, underplanting for shrubs and trees

Good companions: *Eranthis hyemalis, Galanthus* 'S. Arnott', *Scilla siberica* 'Spring Beauty'

pink and mauve

5 Crocus imperati subsp. imperati 'De Jager'

The flowers produced with the dark green leaves in late winter or early spring are mauve inside and buff outside with purple lines. Hardy.

General care: Plant in autumn with the top of the corm about 8cm (3in) deep.

Height: 10cm (4in) **Spread:** 5cm (2in)

Site: Sun. Gritty, well-drained soil

Compost: Soil-based (John Innes No. 1) with added grit

Use: Container, raised bed, rock garden

Good companions: *Chionodoxa sardensis, Hypericum olympicum, Tulipa humilis* Violacea Group

6 Crocus laevigatus 'Fontenayi'

The white to mauve-blue flowers are feathered on the outside with mauve-purple and the feathery stigma is orange. Hardy.

General care: Plant in autumn with the top of the corm about 8cm (3in) deep.

Height: 5cm (2in) **Spread:** 2–3cm (1in)

Site: Sun. Gritty, well-drained soil

Compost: Soil-based (John Innes No. 1) with added grit

Use: Container, raised bed, rock garden

Good companions: *Crocus chrysanthus* 'Ladykiller', *Muscari botryoides* 'Album', *Tulipa turkestanica*

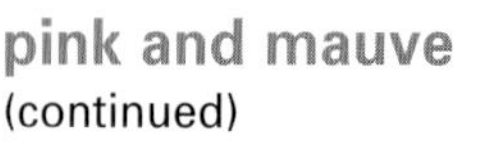

pink and mauve
(continued)

1 Cyclamen coum

From early or midwinter this tuber produces glossy foliage and 'shuttlecock' flowers. These are white, pink or carmine-red with dark stains above the white mouth. The rounded leaves are plain deep green or patterned in silver. Hardy.

General care: Plant in early summer, just after the leaves have died down, with the top of the corm just below the surface of the soil and cover with leaf-mould. Mulch with leaf-mould annually in summer.

Height: 8cm (3in) **Spread:** 10cm (4in)

Site: Partial shade. Well-drained soil

Compost: Soil-based (John Innes No. 1) with added leaf-mould

Use: Container, raised bed, rock garden, underplanting for shrubs, woodland garden

Good companions: *Cyclamen hederifolium, Galanthus nivalis, Helleborus hybridus*

2 Tulipa humilis Violacea Group

In late winter or early spring the egg-like bud opens to form a pink to violet-purple star with yellow or blue-black markings. The leaves develop fully after the flowers and often lie flat. Hardy.

General care: Plant in late autumn with the top of the bulb about 15cm (6in) deep. Plants usually persist for several years without lifting.

Height and spread: 15cm (6in)

Site: Sun. Well-drained soil

Compost: Soil-based (John Innes No. 1)

Use: Container, front of sunny border, raised bed, rock garden

Good companions: *Erodium* 'County Park', *Geranium cinereum* 'County Park', *Oxalis adenophylla*

yellow and orange

3 Crocus chrysanthus 'Zwanenburg Bronze'

The honey-scented globular flowers appear in late winter or early spring with the grass-like leaves. They are bronzed tan outside and open wide in sun to reveal a deep gold interior and orange style. Hardy.

General care: Plant in autumn with the top of the corm about 8cm (3in) deep.

Height: 8cm (3in) **Spread:** 5cm (2in)

Site: Sun. Gritty, well-drained soil

Compost: Soil-based (John Innes No. 1) with added grit

Use: Container, raised bed, rock garden, sunny bed

Good companions: *Crocus chrysanthus* 'Cream Beauty', *Euphorbia myrsinites, Iris reticulata*

4 Crocus korokolwii

The deep yellow flowers have brown or bronze markings on the outside. They appear in the second half of winter with the leaves. Hardy.

General care: Plant in autumn with the top of the corm about 8cm (3in) deep.

Height: 10cm (4in) **Spread:** 5cm (2in)

Site: Sun. Gritty, well-drained soil

Compost: Soil-based (John Innes No. 1) with added grit

Use: Container, raised bed, rock garden

Good companions: *Crocus imperati* subsp. *imperati* 'De Jager', *Festuca glauca* 'Seeigel', *Iris* 'George'

5 Eranthis hyemalis
Winter aconite

Each pale yellow flower is set off by a ruff of bright green leaves in winter and early spring. Best naturalised in large drifts. Hardy.

General care: Plant in early spring before growth dies down or in autumn with the top of the tuber about 5cm (2in) deep.

Height: 8cm (3in) **Spread:** 5cm (2in)

Site: Sun or partial shade. Humus-rich, well-drained soil

Use: Planting in grass, underplanting for shrubs

Good companions: *Anemone blanda, Galanthus nivalis, Muscari aucheri*

6 Narcissus 'Cedric Morris'
Trumpet daffodil

Short-growing bulb with prettily frilled 'trumpets' that often flowers throughout winter. Hardy.

General care: Plant in early autumn with the top of the bulb about 8cm (3in) deep.

Height: 20cm (8in) **Spread:** 8cm (3in)

Site: Sun or partial shade. Moist, well-drained soil

Compost: Soil-based (John Innes No. 2)

Use: Border, container, planting in grass, rock garden, underplanting for shrubs and trees

Good companions: *Chionodoxa luciliae* Gigantea Group, *Primula* 'Miss Indigo', *Scilla siberica* 'Spring Beauty'

7 Narcissus 'Rijnveld's Early Sensation'

Trumpet daffodil

Produces long-lasting yellow trumpet-shaped flowers in late winter with the leaves. Hardy.
General care: Plant in early autumn with the top of the bulb about 8cm (3in) deep.
Height: 30cm (12in) **Spread:** 10cm (4in)
Site: Sun or partial shade. Moist, well-drained soil
Compost: Soil-based (John Innes No. 2)
Use: Border, container, planting in grass, underplanting for shrubs and trees
Good companions: *Narcissus* 'Jack Snipe', *Puschkinia scilloides* var. *libanotica, Tulipa sprengeri*

cream and white

8 Crocus chrysanthus 'Cream Beauty'

In late winter or early spring each corm produces scented, rich cream globular flowers with a pale bronze-green base. They have a golden throat and a vivid scarlet style. Hardy.
General care: Plant in autumn with the top of the corm about 8cm (3in) deep.
Height: 8cm (3in) **Spread:** 5cm (2in)
Site: Sun. Gritty, well-drained soil
Compost: Soil-based (John Innes No. 1) with added grit
Use: Container, raised bed, rock garden, sunny bed
Good companions: *Crocus chrysanthus* 'Zwanenburg Bronze', *Iris danfordiae, Iris histrioides* 'Major'

9 Galanthus 'Atkinsii'

Snowdrop

Strong-growing early flowering snowdrop hybrid that does not set seed, but quickly forms colonies from offsets. Often one segment of the white drooping flowers is malformed. Each of the smaller inner segments carries a green heart-shaped mark. Hardy.
General care: Plant in early spring immediately after flowering and before leaves die down with the top of the bulbs about 8cm (3in) deep.
Height: 20cm (8in)
Spread: 8cm (3in)
Site: Partial shade. Humus-rich and moist but well-drained soil
Compost: Soil-based (John Innes No. 2) with added leaf-mould
Use: Container, planting in grass, rock garden, underplanting for shrubs and trees
Good companions: *Bergenia* 'Ballawley', *Narcissus* 'Dove Wings', *Pulmonaria saccharata* 'Frühlingshimmel'

10 Galanthus elwesii

Snowdrop

Late-flowering honey-scented snowdrop with grey-green broad leaves. Each inner segment has two green marks that are often merged. Hardy.
General care: As for 9, above.
Height: 20cm (8in) **Spread:** 8cm (3in)
Site: Partial shade. Humus-rich and moist but well-drained soil
Compost: Soil-based (John Innes No. 2) with added leaf-mould
Use: As for 9, above
Good companions: *Colchicum speciosus* 'Album', *Crocus speciosus, Crocus tommasinianus* 'Whitewell Purple'

11 Galanthus nivalis

Common snowdrop

The scented pendulous flowers are globular and the inner segments bear a green inverted V-shaped mark. Colonies expand from offsets and seeding, especially in light woodland. Hardy.
General care: As for 9, above.
Height: 10cm (4in) **Spread:** 8cm (3in)
Site: Partial shade. Humus-rich and moist but well-drained soil
Compost: Soil-based (John Innes No. 2) with added leaf-mould
Use: As for 9, above
Good companions: *Asplenium scolopendrium, Hamamelis* x *intermedia* 'Pallida', *Scilla bifolia*

12 Galanthus 'S. Arnott'

Snowdrop

This vigorous, sweetly scented snowdrop flowers in late winter or early spring. The relatively large blooms just reveal a green inverted V on the inner segments. The leaves are grey-green. Hardy.
General care: As for 9, above.
Height: 20cm (8in) **Spread:** 8cm (3in)
Site: Partial shade. Humus-rich and moist but well-drained soil
Compost: Soil-based (John Innes No. 2) with added leaf-mould
Use: As for 9, above
Good companions: *Colchicum* 'The Giant', *Leucojum vernum, Scilla mischtschenkoana*

8

9

10

11

12

dwarf irises

Hardy reticulata irises form the largest group of dwarf irises. Their fragile-looking flowers, composed of inner petals (standards) and outer petals (falls), usually appear in late winter, but stand up to inclement weather. Plant in autumn in well-drained sunny borders, raised beds or rock gardens, with the top of the bulb 8cm (3in) deep. In containers use soil-based compost (John Innes No. 2) with added grit.

1 Iris 'Natascha'

There is a hint of blue in the white of this slender flower and blue lines surround the orange crests on the falls.

Height: 5cm (2in) **Spread:** 8cm (3in)

Good companions: *Origanum amanum*, *Tulipa humilis* Violacea Group, *Tulipa saxatilis* Bakeri Group 'Lilac Wonder'

2 Iris danfordiae

Sturdy greenish yellow flowers appear in mid to late winter before the leaves. Very small standards give the flowers a squat appearance. Happiest in small groups.

Height: 10cm (4in) **Spread:** 5cm (2in)

Good companions: *Crocus imperati* subsp. *imperati* 'De Jager', *Lavandula angustifolia* 'Hidcote', *Tulipa clusiana*

3 Iris reticulata

This species, a parent of numerous dwarf hybrids, has slender, deep violet-blue flowers with a yellow ridge on each fall. They are scented and appear while the leaves are still short.

Height: 15cm (6in) **Spread:** 5cm (2in)

Good companions: *Armeria juniperifolia*, *Iris* 'Joyce', *Pulsatilla vulgaris*

4 Iris histrioides 'Major'

In mid to late winter this sturdy iris produces one or two large flowers before the leaves appear. They are royal blue with deeper markings and have a yellow ridge on the falls.

Height: 13cm (5in) **Spread:** 8cm (3in)

Good companions: *Crocus laevigatus* 'Fontenayi', *Gypsophila repens* 'Rosa Schönheit', *Tulipa* 'Heart's Delight'

5 Iris 'Joyce'

Deep sky-blue flowers, with bright yellow crests over white markings on the falls, appear when the leaves are just emerging.

Height: 13cm (5in) **Spread:** 8cm (3in)

Good companions: *Artemisia schmidtiana* 'Nana', *Ipheion uniflorum* 'Wisley Blue', *Tulipa* 'Shakespeare'

6 Iris 'J.S. Dijt'

Slender but vigorous iris that produces scented red-purple flowers with an orange-yellow ridge on the falls. Leaves are short at flowering time.

Height: 13cm (5in) **Spread:** 8cm (3in)

Good companions: *Crocus chrysanthus* 'Zwanenburg Bronze', *Geranium cinerium* subsp. *subcaulescens*, *Helianthemum* 'Wisley Primrose'

7 Iris 'Katharine Hodgkin'

This vigorous hybrid has flowers of unusual colouring. The pale creamy blue petals are overlaid by yellow and sea-green and the standards are marked with blue. It usually flowers in midwinter.

Height: 13cm (5in) **Spread:** 8cm (3in)

Good companions: *Dianthus alpinus* 'Joan's Blood', *Iris* 'Natascha', *Tulipa* 'Red Riding Hood'

8 Iris 'George'

Vigorous plant with relatively large flowers. The standards are red-purple and the darker falls are marked with yellow on white.

Height: 13cm (5in)

Spread: 8cm (3in)

Good companions: *Armeria maritima* 'Düsseldorfer Stolz', *Crocus chrysanthus* 'Ladykiller', *Iris* 'J.S. Dijt'

7

climbers

Climbers twine, cling with aerial roots or clasp with tendrils. Trained on architectural supports or other plants, they assert the vertical dimension of the garden. Plant in the dormant season.

blue, violet and purple

1 Ampelopsis glandulosa var. brevipedunculata

This deciduous tendril climber is worth growing for its handsome lobed foliage alone, but where summers are warm enough, bead-like fruits form and persist after the leaves have fallen They ripen from green to purple-pink then blue. Hardy.

General care: If necessary to restrict growth prune in early spring.

Height: 5m (15ft) **Spread:** 4m (12ft)

Site: Sun, partial shade. Moist, well-drained soil

Use: Pergola, tree climber, wall

Good companions: *Clematis armandii* 'Snowdrift', *Rosa* 'Parade', *Solanum laxum* 'Album'

red and russet

2 Clematis cirrhosa 'Freckles'

Evergreen twining climber with leaves composed of three to six leaflets. Nodding, creamy pink flowers heavily speckled with red are borne in late winter or early spring. Silky seedheads follow. Not fully hardy.

General care: Plant with the base in shade. Prune immediately after flowering.

Height: 3m (10ft) **Spread:** 1.5m (5ft)

Site: Sun, partial shade. Fertile, humus-rich and well-drained soil. Good on lime

Use: Screen, shrub climber, tripod, wall

Good companions: *Clematis* 'Etoile Rose', *Forsythia suspensa, Narcissus* 'Jack Snipe'

3 Euonymus fortunei 'Coloratus'

Like most other cultivars of the evergreen shrub *E. fortunei*, 'Coloratus' is capable of performing as a climber. The usually green leaves turn red-purple in winter, especially on poor soils. Hardy.

General care: If necessary to restrict growth prune in early spring.

Height: 5m (15ft) **Spread:** 4m (12ft)

Site: Sun, partial shade. Well-drained soil

Use: Ground cover, tree climber, wall

Good companions: *Cotoneaster conspicuus* 'Decorus', *Ilex* x *altaclerensis* 'Golden King', *Prunus lusitanica*

silver

4 Clematis vitalba

Traveller's joy

Rampant, twining deciduous climber. Small, lightly scented greenish white flowers in late summer or early autumn are followed by fluffy seedheads that last through winter. Hardy.

General care: If necessary cut back stems to near ground level in early spring.

Height: 9m (30ft) **Spread:** 5m (15ft)

Site: Sun, partial shade. Well-drained soil. Good on lime

Use: Wild garden

Good companions: *Cotoneaster salicifolia* 'Rothschildianus', *Euonymus europaeus* 'Red Cascade', *Philadelphus* 'Belle Etoile'

green

5 Hedera colchica 'Dentata'

Bullock's heart ivy, Persian ivy

In its long-lasting juvenile stage, evergreen Persian ivy is self clinging. This cultivar has large dark green leaves and purplish stems. When it reaches the non-clinging mature stage, it bears clusters of yellow-green autumn flowers, which are followed by poisonous black fruits. Hardy.

General care: Prune at any time to restrict growth.

Height: 9m (30ft) **Spread:** 6m (20ft)

Site: Partial shade, sun, shade. Well-drained soil

Use: Ground cover, wall

Good companions: *Camellia* 'Freedom Bell', *Camellia* x *williamsii* 'Francis Hanger', *Rhododendron* 'Cilpinense'

6 Hedera colchica 'Sulphur Heart'

Bullock's heart ivy, Persian ivy

This cultivar of Persian ivy (see 5, above) has large plain leaves that are light green with patches of lighter green and yellow. Poisonous black fruits follow yellow-green autumn flowers. Hardy.

General care: Prune at any time to restrict growth.

Height: 9m (30ft) **Spread:** 6m (20ft)

Site: Sun, partial shade. Well-drained soil

Use: Ground cover, wall

Good companions: *Aucuba japonica* 'Rozannie', *Choisya ternata, Fatsia japonica*

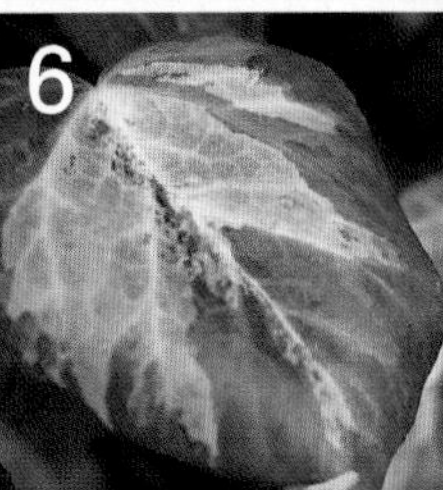

common or english ivy

The common ivy is an evergreen climber and its many cultivars offer a wide variety of leaf size, shape and colour. Leaves in the juvenile stage are usually lobed and stems cling by aerial roots. Plants may develop the adult bushy form, without aerial roots; they produce unlobed leaves and in autumn heads of yellow-green flowers, followed by poisonous black fruits. Ivy generally prefers partial shade and well-drained soil, but will tolerate sun and shade; variegated forms need a well-lit position. In containers, use soil-based (John Innes No. 2) or soil-less compost.

1 Hedera helix 'Adam'

Small shallow-lobed leaves with grey-green mottling and creamy white margins. Hardy.
Height: 5m (15ft) **Spread:** 2.5m (8ft)
Use: Container, houseplant, wall
Good companions: *Fuchsia* 'Leonora', *Hydrangea macrophylla* 'Madame Emile Mouillère', *Skimmia japonica* 'Rubella'

2 Hedera helix 'Manda's Crested'

The large five-lobed leaves have downward-pointing tips and waved edges. In summer they are mid-green, but take on bronze tints in winter. Not fully hardy.
Height: 2m (6ft) **Spread:** 1.2m (4ft)
Use: Ground cover, wall
Good companions: *Epimedium* x *versicolor* 'Sulphureum', *Euphorbia amygdaloides* 'Purpurea', *Pachysandra terminalis*

3 Hedera helix 'Parsley Crested'

The medium-sized, glossy deep green leaves are almost rounded and if there are lobes these are obscured by the strongly waved and crimped margins. Not fully hardy.
Height: 2m (6ft) **Spread:** 1m (3ft)
Use: Wall
Good companions: *Celastrus orbiculatus*, *Chaenomeles speciosa* 'Nivalis', *Osmanthus delavayi*

4 Hedera helix 'Goldheart' (syn. 'Oro di Bogliasco')

The neat, finely tapered, three-lobed leaves of medium size are rich green with an irregular bright yellow central splash. Young shoots are tinted pink. Hardy.
Height: 8m (25ft) **Spread:** 5m (15ft)
Use: Wall
Good companions: *Chimonanthus praecox*, *Clematis* 'Bill MacKenzie', *Clematis* 'Perle d'Azur'

5 Hedera helix 'Ivalace'

Versatile ivy with medium-sized, glossy dark green leaves that have five shallow lobes and are stiffly waved. Hardy.
Height: 1.2m (4ft) **Spread:** 75cm (2ft 6in)
Use: Container, ground cover, houseplant, wall
Good companions: *Fargesia nitida*, *Fatsia japonica*, *Viburnum davidii*

6 Hedera helix 'Buttercup'

Slow-growing ivy with large five-lobed leaves. In full sun, young leaves are bright yellow, older leaves yellow-green; in shade, leaves are pale or deeper green. Hardy.
Height: 2m (6ft) **Spread:** 1m (3ft)
Use: Wall
Good companions: *Clematis alpina* 'Frances Rivis', *Coronilla valentina* subsp. *glauca*, *Ipheion uniflorum* 'Wisley Blue'

7 Hedera helix 'Goldchild'

The small three to five-lobed leaves have an irregular centre with various overlays of green surrounded by a creamy yellow margin. Not fully hardy.
Height: 1.2m (4ft) **Spread:** 75cm (2ft 6in)
Use: Container, houseplant, wall
Good companions: *Clematis alpina* 'Frances Rivis', *Clematis* 'Gipsy Queen', *Clematis* 'Helsingborg'

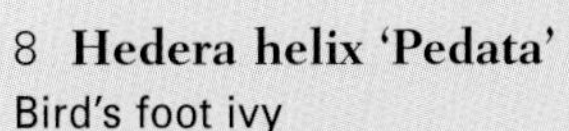

8 **Hedera helix 'Pedata'**
Bird's foot ivy
The medium-sized glossy leaves are divided into five narrow lobes. Hardy.
Height: 4m (12ft) **Spread:** 2m (6ft)
Use: Wall
Good companions: *Jasminum nudiflorum*, *Lonicera periclymenum* 'Belgica', *Lonicera periclymenum* 'Serotina'

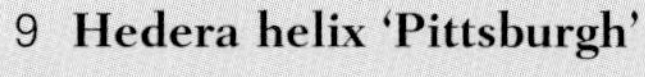

9 **Hedera helix 'Pittsburgh'**
The glossy dark green leaves are of medium size and elegantly cut into five lobes. Not fully hardy.
Height: 1.2m (4ft) **Spread:** 75cm (2ft 6in)
Use: Container, ground cover, houseplant, wall
Good companions: *Epimedium* x *rubrum*, *Euphorbia griffithii* 'Fireglow', *Fargesia murielae*

10 **Hedera helix 'Atropurpurea'**
Purple-leaved ivy
The pattern of green veins stands out against the purple-green of the large five-lobed leaves. Hardy.
Height: 6m (20ft) **Spread:** 4m (12ft)
Use: Wall
Good companions: *Forsythia suspensa*, *Jasminum nudiflorum*, *Rosa* 'Madame Alfred Carrière'

11 **Hedera helix 'Glacier'**
The small three to five-lobed leaves are grey-green with silvery grey markings and cream variegation. Hardy.
Height: 2.5m (8ft) **Spread:** 2m (6ft)
Use: Container, ground cover, houseplant, wall
Good companions: *Chaenomeles* x *superba* 'Pink Lady', *Clematis* 'Jackmanii', *Clematis macropetala* 'Maidwell Hall'

12 **Hedera helix 'Glymii'**
The medium-sized three-lobed or unlobed leaves, are often curled, especially in cold weather. They are glossy dark green, but in winter become red-purple with conspicuous green veins. Hardy.
Height: 2m (6ft) **Spread:** 1.5m (5ft)
Use: Wall
Good companions: *Clematis* 'Alba Luxurians', *Garrya elliptica* 'James Roof', *Lunaria annua*

shrubs & trees

Shrubs and trees are the mainstay of the winter garden. Whether with leaves or without, they bring substance and shape, and evergreen foliage also gives colour. Late fruits and colourful stems add their rich tones, and early blossom heralds new life. Plant in the dormant season, preferably in autumn or early spring.

purple and blue-grey

1 Chamaecyparis lawsoniana 'Ellwoodii'
Lawson cypress

The species is a large columnar evergreen conifer, but this form makes a compact cone densely packed with sprays of grey-green foliage, which in winter turns blue-grey. Hardy.

Height: 9m (30ft) **Spread:** 8m (25ft)

Site: Sun, partial shade. Humus-rich and moist but well-drained soil, preferably lime-free

Use: Avenue, heather garden, large rock garden

Good companions: *Camellia japonica* 'Lavinia Maggi', *Pieris japonica* 'Debutante', *Rhododendron* 'Praecox'

2 Cornus alba 'Kesselringii'

The young stems of this deciduous shrub are striking purplish black in winter. In autumn the green leaves turn red-purple. Hardy.

General care: To maintain a supply of young wood, cut all or a proportion of stems to near ground level in early spring.

Height and spread: 3m (10ft)

Site: Sun. Well-drained, preferably moist soil

Use: Sunny border, waterside

Good companions: *Astilbe* x *arendsii* 'Irrlicht', *Miscanthus sacchariflorus, Salix gracilistyla*

3 Picea pungens 'Hoopsii'
Colorado spruce

Several forms of the colorado spruce, a broadly conical evergreen conifer, have silvery blue foliage. The stiff needles of dense-growing 'Hoopsii' are silvery white when young but become more blue as they age. The cones, 10cm (4in) long, are green at first, later pale brown. Hardy.

Height: 15m (50ft) **Spread:** 5m (15ft)

Site: Sun. Moist but well-drained soil, preferably lime-free

Use: Canopy in mixed planting, specimen tree

Good companions: *Bergenia* 'Ballawley', *Chamaecyparis lawsoniana* 'Tamariscifolia', *Cotoneaster conspicuus* 'Decorus'

4 Salix daphnoides
Violet willow

In winter the stems of this fast-growing, deciduous small tree are a conspicuous violet-purple overlaid with a white bloom. Grey catkins are borne in late winter or early spring before the leaves emerge. Hardy.

Height: 9m (30ft) **Spread:** 8m (25ft)

Site: Sun, partial shade. Humus-rich and moist but well-drained soil, preferably lime-free

Use: Canopy in mixed planting, specimen tree

Good companions: *Eupatorium purpureum, Salix gracilistyla* 'Melanostachys', *Salix irrorata*

5 Viburnum davidii

Spreading evergreen shrub that makes a mound of dark green foliage. The leaves have three prominent veins that run to a pointed tip. Metallic blue egg-shaped berries follow the dull white flowers of early summer. For a good show of these long-lasting inedible fruits grow several plants together. Hardy.

Height: 1.2m (4ft) **Spread:** 1.5m (5ft)

Site: Sun, partial shade. Humus-rich and moist but well-drained soil

Use: Front of border, ground cover, underplanting for shrubs and trees

Good companions: *Bergenia* 'Sunningdale', *Betula utilis* var. *jacquemontii* 'Silver Shadow', *Helleborus argutifolius*

pink and mauve

6 Acer pensylvanicum 'Erythrocladum'
Moosewood, Striped maple

This small deciduous tree is outstanding for the brilliant pink of its young shoots, which become striped white with age. The white-striped green bark of *A. pensylvanicum* itself is also arresting. The leaves of both trees have forward-pointing lobes and turn bright yellow in autumn. Hardy.

Height: 9m (30ft) **Spread:** 8m (25ft)

Site: Sun, partial shade. Humus-rich and moist but well-drained soil, preferably lime-free

Use: Canopy in mixed planting, specimen tree

Good companions: *Acer griseum, Enkianthus campanulatus, Fothergilla major* Monticola Group

7 Camellia x williamsii 'J.C. Williams'

Between late winter and mid-spring this camellia bears soft pink single flowers with a conspicuous cluster of stamens. Flowers fall when they are over. Glossy green evergreen foliage. Hardy.

Height: 4m (12ft) **Spread:** 3m (10ft)

Site: Partial shade. Lime-free, humus-rich and moist but well-drained soil

Compost: Soil-based (ericaceous)

Use: Container, shady border, underplanting for trees

Good companions: *Camellia* x *williamsii* 'Donation', *Eucryphia* x *nymansensis* 'Nymansay', *Rhododendron* 'Cilpinense'

8 Chaenomeles speciosa 'Moerloosei'

This deciduous shrub makes a spreading bush of tangled spiny branches, but is also suitable for training against a wall. The first of its pink-and-white flowers open in late winter, before the leaves appear, but the display continues, with thick clusters, into spring. Hardy.

General care: Prune immediately after flowering, on wall-trained specimens cutting back flowered shoots to within three or four buds of a permanent framework of branches.

Height: 2.5m (8ft) **Spread:** 4m (12ft)
Site: Sun, partial shade. Well-drained soil
Use: Sunny or lightly shaded border, wall
Good companions: *Garrya elliptica* 'James Roof', *Muscari armeniacum*, *Narcissus* 'Dove Wings'

9 Daphne bholua 'Jacqueline Postill'

Upright evergreen or semi-evergreen shrub with narrow leathery leaves. Dense clusters of sweetly scented, small pink flowers open in mid and late winter from purplish red buds. Not fully hardy.

Height: 2.5m (8ft) **Spread:** 1.5m (5ft)
Site: Sun, partial shade. Humus-rich and moist but well-drained soil
Use: Border, woodland garden
Good companions: *Magnolia stellata*, *Prunus subhirtella* 'Autumnalis', *Sorbus cashmiriana*

10 Daphne odora 'Aureomarginata'

This variegated evergreen shrub, with a fine cream line edging its leaves, is said to be hardier than the plain-leaved species. Fragrant, small, pink-purple flowers are in tight clusters. Half hardy.

Height and spread: 1.5m (5ft)
Site: Sun, partial shade. Humus-rich and moist but well-drained soil
Use: Border
Good companions: *Anemone blanda*, *Galanthus nivalis*, *Primula* 'Miss Indigo'

11 Prunus incisa 'February Pink'

Fuji cherry

This form of the deciduous shrubby Fuji cherry often starts flowering in midwinter and continues into early spring. The pale pink blossom is rarely followed by fruit. The leaves are bronzed when young and orange-red in autumn. Hardy.

Height: 8m (25ft) **Spread:** 6m (20ft)
Site: Sun. Moist but well-drained soil
Use: Canopy in border, specimen tree
Good companions: *Galanthus* 'Atkinsii', *Narcissus* 'Dove Wings', *Scilla siberica* 'Spring Beauty'

12 Prunus x subhirtella 'Autumnalis'

Higan cherry, Rosebud cherry

From late autumn to early spring this deciduous small tree provides a trickle and in late winter a flush of pink-tinged white blossom. When the leaves first appear they are lightly bronzed; after their summer green they turn yellow. Hardy.

Height and spread: 8m (25ft)
Site: Sun. Moist but well-drained soil
Use: Canopy in border, specimen tree
Good companions: *Crocus speciosus*, *Crocus tommasinianus* 'Whitewell Purple', *Cyclamen hederifolium*

pink and mauve (continued)

1 Rhododendron mucronulatum

The bare branches of this deciduous dwarf shrub carry clusters of pink-purple funnel-shaped flowers throughout winter. Hardy.

Height and spread: 1m (3ft)

Site: Sun or partial shade. Lime-free and moist but well-drained soil

Use: Sunny or lightly shaded border, woodland garden

Good companions: *Camellia* 'Cornish Snow', *Halesia carolina, Magnolia* x *loebneri* 'Leonard Messel'

2 Rhododendron 'Praecox'

Small-leaved evergreen shrub bearing clusters of red-purple funnel-shaped flowers at the end of stems in late winter or early spring. Hardy.

Height and spread: 1.2m (4ft)

Site: Sun or partial shade. Lime-free, moist but well-drained soil

Use: Sunny or lightly shaded garden, rock garden, woodland garden

Good companions: *Acer palmatum* var. *dissectum* Dissectum Viride Group, *Kalmia latifolia* 'Ostbo Red', *Rhododendron* 'Bow Bells'

3 Viburnum x bodnantense 'Dawn'

The naked stems of this upright deciduous shrub carry tight clusters of powerfully scented pink flowers from late autumn to early spring. Hardy.

Height: 3m (10ft) **Spread:** 2m (6ft)

Site: Sun, partial shade. Moist but well-drained soil

Use: Border, woodland garden

Good companions: *Ceratostigma willmottianum, Geranium* 'Johnson's Blue', *Viburnum davidii*

4 Viburnum tinus 'Gwenllian'

Compact form of an evergreen bushy shrub. From late autumn to early spring small pale pink flowers open from tight heads of carmine buds. Inedible blue-black fruits follow. Hardy.

General care: Trim or hard prune in spring only if required.

Height and spread: 3m (10ft)

Site: Sun, partial shade. Moist, well-drained soil

Compost: Soil-based (John Innes No. 3)

Use: Container, border, informal hedge, topiary

Good companions: *Hydrangea macrophylla* 'Blue Wave', *Prunus serrula, Rhamnus alaternus* 'Argenteovariegata'

bronze and maroon

5 Cryptomeria japonica 'Elegans Compacta'

Japanese cedar

This form of the Japanese cedar, a fast-growing, columnar evergreen conifer, is compact and retains its soft juvenile foliage when it matures. In winter the foliage changes from blue-green to purplish or reddish bronze. Hardy.

Height: 8m (25ft) **Spread:** 5.5m (18ft)

Site: Sun, partial shade. Moist but well-drained soil

Use: Heather garden, specimen tree or shrub, woodland garden

Good companions: *Acer palmatum* 'Corallinum', *Corylus avellana* 'Contorta', *Nandina domestica* 'Fire Power'

6 Leucothoe Scarletta

Graceful evergreen shrub grown for its glossy foliage. In summer the lance-shaped leaves are dark green, but are red-purple when young and in winter turn dark bronze. Hardy.

Height: 1.2m (4ft) **Spread:** 1.5m (5ft)

Site: Partial shade, shade. Lime-free, moist but well-drained soil

Use: Woodland garden

Good companions: *Eucryphia* x *nymansensis* 'Nymansay', *Gaultheria mucronata* 'Wintertime', *Uvularia grandiflora*

red and russet

7 Acer griseum

Paper-bark maple

The three-lobed leaves of this slow-growing deciduous tree turn brilliant shades of red in autumn, but of lasting beauty is the peeling bark.

Brown-coloured old bark curls back to reveal orangey new bark beneath. Hardy.
Height and spread: 9m (30ft)
Site: Sun, partial shade. Moist but well-drained soil
Use: Specimen tree, woodland garden
Good companions: *Erythronium californicum* 'White Beauty', *Galanthus* 'S. Arnott', *Primula vulgaris*

8 Arbutus x andrachnoides
Strawberry tree
This evergreen tree has a tapering canopy of dark green, finely toothed leaves above trunks and branches with peeling red-brown bark. Hardy.
Height: 8m (25ft)
Spread: 6m (20ft)
Site: Sun. Well-drained soil
Use: Canopy in border, specimen tree, woodland garden
Good companions: *Bergenia* 'Sunningdale', *Colchicum* 'The Giant', *Ribes laurifolium*

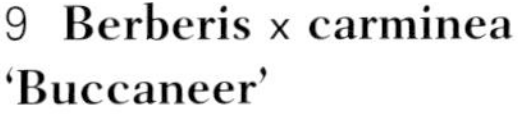

9 Berberis x carminea 'Buccaneer'
Spiny deciduous or semi-evergreen shrub with small yellow flowers in late spring or early summer followed by dense clusters of glowing scarlet berries. Hardy.
Height: 1.5m (5ft)
Spread: 2.5m (8ft)
Site: Sun, partial shade. Well-drained soil
Use: Border, informal hedge
Good companions: *Berberis* x *stenophylla*, *Cytisus* x *praecox* 'Allgold', *Genista aetnensis*

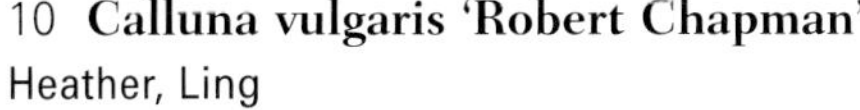

10 Calluna vulgaris 'Robert Chapman'
Heather, Ling
The heathers are low evergreens valued for their long-lasting flowers in late summer and autumn and in some cases for their richly coloured foliage. That of 'Robert Chapman' turns from gold in summer to red in winter; the flowers, from midsummer to autumn, are soft purple. Hardy.
General care: Clip over in early spring.
Height: 25cm (10in) **Spread:** 60cm (2ft)
Site: Sun. Lime-free, humus-rich, well-drained soil
Compost: Soil-based (ericaceous)
Use: Container, ground cover, heather garden, raised bed, rock garden
Good companions: *Calluna vulgaris* 'Darkness', *Erica carnea* 'Vivellii', *Gaultheria mucronata* 'Bell's Seedling'

11 Chaenomeles x superba 'Knap Hill Scarlet'
Flowering quince, Japanese quince, Japonica
Spreading deciduous shrub that often starts flowering in late winter. Hardy.
General care: Prune immediately after flowering; on wall-trained specimens cut back flowered shoots to within three or four buds of the permanent framework of branches.
Height: 1.5m (5ft) **Spread:** 2m (6ft)
Site: Sun or partial shade. Well-drained soil
Use: Sunny or lightly shaded border, wall
Good companions: *Clematis* 'Helsingborg', *Rosa* 'Parade', *Solanum laxum* 'Album'

12 Cornus alba 'Sibirica'
Red-barked dogwood
Thickets of glossy red stems are the main feature of this deciduous suckering shrub in winter. The leaves turn red and orange in autumn. Hardy.
General care: To maintain a supply of young wood, cut all or a proportion of stems to near ground level in early spring.
Height and spread: 3m (10ft)
Site: Sun. Well-drained, preferably moist soil
Use: Sunny border, waterside
Good companions: *Cornus stolonifera* 'Flaviramea', *Salix alba* subsp. *vitellina* 'Britzensis', *Salix irrorata*

red and russet (continued)

1 Cotoneaster frigidus 'Cornubia'

Vigorous semi-evergreen shrub or small tree with arching branches and dark green leaves that turn purplish bronze in winter. Clusters of small white flowers in summer are followed by prodigious crops of inedible bright red fruits in autumn, which weigh down the branches. The brilliant display continues well into winter. Hardy.

Height and spread: 6m (20ft)
Site: Sun, partial shade. Well-drained soil
Use: Canopy in border, specimen tree or shrub
Good companions: *Berberis* x *carminea* 'Buccaneer', *Bergenia* 'Ballawley', *Cotoneaster conspicuus* 'Decorus'

2 Cotoneaster 'Hybridus Pendulus'

Low-growing, spreading evergreen or semi-evergreen shrub with glossy leaves. Inedible, long-lasting brilliant red fruits follow the clusters of small white flowers of early summer. It is sometimes grown as a standard on a stem to make a small weeping tree about 2.5m (8ft) high. Hardy.

Height: 1.2m (4ft) **Spread:** 2m (6ft)
Site: Sun, partial shade. Well-drained soil
Use: Canopy in border, ground cover, large rock garden, raised bed, specimen tree
Good companions: *Bergenia B*allawley', *Galanthus elwesii, Helleborus foetidus*

3 Cotoneaster lactaeus

Large evergreen shrub with leathery oval leaves that are dark green with grey undersides. Clusters of small creamy flowers in summer are followed by berries that ripen red in late autumn and remain colourfully conspicuous until midwinter. Hardy.

Height and spread: 4m (12ft)
Site: Sun, partial shade. Well-drained soil
Use: Canopy in border, specimen shrub
Good companions: *Berberis darwinii, Choisya ternata, Syringa vulgaris* 'Katherine Havemeyer'

4 Fagus sylvatica

Common beech

This large deciduous tree is magnificent in broad landscapes, as are purple-leaved forms such as 'Riversii'. In gardens, however, it is excellent for hedges 2–5m (6–15ft) high. When trimmed in the summer it retains its dead leaves until the following spring, when their warm copper gives way to the acid-green of young foliage. Hardy.

General care: Trim hedges in late summer.
Height: 25m (80ft) **Spread:** 15m (50ft)
Site: Sun, partial shade. Well-drained soil. Good on chalk and lime but also on acid soils
Use: Hedge, specimen tree
Good companions: *Ilex aquifolium* 'Pyramidalis', *Pachysandra terminalis, Taxus baccata*

5 Gaultheria mucronata 'Bell's Seedling'

Compact evergreen shrub that makes thickets of wiry stems covered with glossy deep green leaves and flowers in late spring and early summer. The edible berries are produced by female plants if a male plant is growing nearby, but 'Bell's Seedling' is hermaphrodite and produces long-lasting dark red berries if grown on its own. Hardy.

Height and spread: 1.2m (4ft)
Site: Partial shade, sun. Lime-free, moist but well-drained soil

7

8

Use: Ground cover, raised bed, woodland garden
Good companions: *Camellia* 'Freedom Bell', *Camellia* x *williamsii* 'Francis Hanger', *Rhododendron* 'Palestrina'

6 Hamamelis x intermedia 'Diane'
Witch hazel

Deciduous large shrub or tree that bears small, fragrant spidery flowers of rich copper-red in winter or early spring. In autumn the leaves usually colour well. Hardy.
Height and spread: 4m (12ft)
Site: Sun, partial shade. Moist but well-drained soil, preferably lime-free
Use: Canopy in border, specimen tree, woodland garden
Good companions: *Cornus mas, Disanthus cercidifolius, Magnolia* 'Elizabeth'

7 Malus x robusta 'Red Sentinel'
Crab apple

Deciduous small tree with arching branches that make a spreading canopy. White blossom in late spring is followed by edible, shiny scarlet crab apples, which persist through winter. Hardy.
Height and spread: 6m (20ft)
Site: Sun. Moist but well-drained soil
Use: Canopy in border, specimen tree
Good companions: *Digitalis purpurea, Hyacinthoides non-scripta, Lunaria annua*

8 Nandina domestica 'Fire Power'
Heavenly bamboo

This compact form of an evergreen bamboo-like shrub is grown mainly for its attractive foliage. The large leaves, composed of elegantly pointed leaflets, turn red in autumn and remain colourful throughout winter. Not fully hardy.

9

Height: 45cm (18in) **Spread:** 60cm (2ft)
Site: Sun, partial shade. Moist, well-drained soil
Use: Border, ground cover
Good companions: *Epimedium* x *rubrum, Osmanthus delavayi, Viburnum* x *bodnantense*

9 Parrotia persica
Persian ironwood

Spreading deciduous tree that usually branches close to the ground. On old wood the bark flakes off in patches, creating a grey-and-beige pattern. In late winter or early spring tiny petal-less flowers with red stamens are borne on the naked branches. In autumn leaves turn yellow and orange, shaded with purple and crimson. Hardy.
Height: 9m (30ft) **Spread:** 10m (33ft)
Site: Sun, partial shade. Moist but well-drained soil, preferably lime-free
Use: Specimen tree, woodland garden
Good companions: *Acer japonicum* 'Vitifolium', *Amelanchier canadensis, Prunus sargentii*

10

10 Prunus serrula
Ornamental cherry

The bark of this deciduous tree is its main ornamental feature. A pattern of rough bands breaks up the polished red-brown surface of new bark. White flowers appear in mid to late spring at the same time as the tapered leaves. Hardy.
Height and spread: 9m (30ft)
Site: Sun. Moist but well-drained soil
Use: Specimen tree
Good companions: *Cryptomeria japonica* 'Elegans Compacta', *Hydrangea macrophylla* 'Blue Wave', *Ilex* x *altaclerensis* 'Camelliifolia'

11

11 Pyracantha 'Mohave'

Bushy and spiny evergreen shrub. Heavy crops of red berries follow the dense clusters of small white flowers of early summer. Although eventually eaten by birds, the display usually persists well into winter. Hardy.
General care: Trim hedges and prune wall-trained specimens in the first half of summer.
Height: 4m (12ft) **Spread:** 5m (15ft)
Site: Sun, partial shade. Well-drained soil
Use: Border, hedge, wall
Good companions: *Hedera colchica* 'Sulphur Heart', *Kerria japonica* 'Pleniflora', *Pyracantha* 'Soleil d'Or'

red and russet (continued)

1 Salix alba subsp. vitellina 'Britzensis'

White willow

White willows are fast-growing deciduous trees. They bear slender catkins in spring and their leaves are silky-hairy when young, giving them a general silvery appearance. The main ornamental feature of this male clone is the brilliant orange-red of its young shoots, a supply of which can be maintained by severe pruning; this will also keep it below the dimensions given. Hardy.

General care: For a supply of strongly coloured young growths cut back stems to a permanent framework every two or three years.

Height: 18m (60ft) **Spread:** 12m (40ft)

Site: Sun. Moist but well-drained soil

Use: Specimen tree, waterside

Good companions: *Cornus alba* 'Kesselringii', *Osmunda regalis, Rodgersia pinnata* 'Superba'

2 Skimmia japonica 'Rubella'

Female and hermaphrodite clones of *Skimmia japonica*, usually domed evergreen shrubs, are grown for their fragrant white flowers in spring, which are followed by inedible, long-lasting red fruits. This male form has dark green leaves edged in red and red-tinted stems. From autumn through winter it carries eye-catching heads of red flower buds. Hardy.

Height: 1m (3ft) **Spread:** 1.2m (4ft)

Site: Partial shade, shade. Humus-rich and moist but well-drained soil

Compost: Soil-based (John Innes No. 3)

Use: Container, shady border, woodland garden

Good companions: *Hydrangea* 'Preziosa', *Sarcococca hookeriana* var. *digyna, Sorbus hupehensis*

3 Sorbus aucuparia 'Beissneri'

Mountain ash, Rowan

The amber or russet bark and red shoots of this form of the mountain ash make it an arresting deciduous tree in winter, but it is attractive at other seasons, too. In spring and summer the rather upright branches are clothed in ferny yellow-green leaves, which colour well in autumn. Heavy crops of inedible bright red fruits ripen in late summer. Hardy.

Height: 9m (30ft) **Spread:** 5m (15ft)

Site: Sun, partial shade. Moist but well-drained soil, preferably lime-free

Use: Canopy in border, specimen tree

Good companions: *Cornus mas, Mahonia japonica, Malus* 'Winter Gold'

yellow and orange

4 Aucuba japonica 'Crotonifolia'

Spotted laurel

Although very tolerant of a wide range of conditions, this variegated evergreen shrub does best in a well-lit position, where it will make a dense rounded bush well covered with large leaves heavily spotted and blotched with rich yellow. If there is a male plant nearby this female clone produces inedible berries that ripen red in spring. Hardy.

Height and spread: 2.5m (8ft)

Site: Sun, partial shade. Well-drained soil

Compost: Soil-based (John Innes No. 2)

Use: Border, container, specimen shrub, underplanting for trees

Good companions: *Lonicera fragrantissima, Mahonia aquifolium* 'Apollo', *Taxus × media* 'Hicksii'

5 Calluna vulgaris 'Beoley Gold'

Heather, Ling

The ever-gold foliage earns this vigorous low-growing shrub a place in the winter garden. There are white flowers in autumn. Hardy.

General care: Trim in early to mid-spring.

Height: 40cm (16in) **Spread:** 60cm (2ft)

Site: Sun. Lime-free, humus-rich soil

Compost: Soil-based (ericaceous)

Use: Container, front of sunny border, ground cover, heather garden, wild garden

Good companions: *Calluna vulgaris* 'Firefly', *Pinus mugo* 'Mops', *Thuja occidentalis* 'Rheingold'

6 Calluna vulgaris 'Firefly'

Heather, Ling

In autumn there are short sprays of deep mauve flowers, but the foliage makes this low evergreen attractive throughout the year. In summer it is red-brown, but in winter it turns a more intense rust-orange. Hardy.

General care: Trim in early to mid-spring.

Height: 45cm (18in) **Spread:** 60cm (2ft)

Site: Sun. Lime-free, humus-rich soil

Compost: Soil-based (ericaceous)

Use: Container, front of sunny border, ground cover, heather garden, wild garden

Good companions: *Calluna vulgaris* 'Robert Chapman', *Juniperus communis* 'Hibernica', *Juniperus × pfitzeriana* 'Wilhelm Pfitzer'

7 Chimonanthus praecox

Wintersweet

Deciduous large but twiggy shrub grown for the spicy scent of its winter flowers. These are waxy and pale yellow with purplish centres, somewhat larger and more deeply coloured in 'Grandiflorus'. Hardy.

General care: Shorten growths of wall-trained plants immediately after flowering.

Height: 4m (12ft) **Spread:** 3m (10ft)

Site: Sun. Well-drained soil

Use: Border, specimen shrub, wall

Good companions: *Alchemilla mollis, Clematis* 'Abundance', *Galanthus nivalis*

8 Cornus mas

Cornelian cherry

Deciduous twiggy shrub or small tree that bears numerous small yellow flowers on naked stems in late winter and early spring. Edible red fruits sometimes follow the blooms and the foliage

frequently colours well in autumn. Hardy.
Height: 5m (15ft) **Spread:** 4m (12ft)
Site: Sun, partial shade. Well-drained soil
Use: Canopy in border, specimen shrub or tree, woodland garden
Good companions: *Cornus alba* 'Elegantissima', *Hyacinthoides non-scripta, Mahonia aquifolium* 'Apollo'

9 Coronilla valentina subsp. glauca

Lightweight evergreen shrub with blue-green foliage. It bears scented yellow pea-flowers in late winter and early spring, and again in summer. Benefits from the favourable conditions at the base of a warm wall. Hardy.
General care: No regular pruning required but to rejuvenate leggy plants cut hard back in mid-spring.
Height and spread: 1.5m (5ft)
Site: Sun. Well-drained soil
Use: Border
Good companions: *Clematis* 'Bill MacKenzie', *Narcissus obvallaris, Solanum crispum* 'Glasnevin'

10 Corylus avellana 'Contorta'

Corkscrew hazel

In late winter and early spring yellow catkins dangle from the twisted stems of this deciduous tree-like shrub. Cut stems provide interesting material for arrangements. Hardy.
Height: 3m (10ft) **Spread:** 2.5m (8ft)
Site: Sun, partial shade. Well-drained soil. Good on lime
Use: Border, specimen shrub
Good companions: *Buddleja* 'Lochinch', *Caryopteris* x *clandonensis* 'Heavenly Blue', *Cercis siliquastrum*

11 Elaeagnus pungens 'Maculata'

Evergreen shrub with lustrous leaves with a bold yellow mark in the centre. In autumn small silvery flowers, hidden among the leaves, are betrayed by their intense scent. Hardy.
General care: Remove promptly any green-leaved shoots. Trim hedges in early summer and again in early autumn.
Height: 3m (10ft) **Spread:** 4m (12ft)
Site: Sun, partial shade. Well-drained soil
Use: Border, hedge
Good companions: *Genista aetnensis, Potentilla fruticosa* 'Tangerine', *Prunus lusitanica*

yellow and orange (continued)

1 Euonymus fortunei 'Emerald 'n' Gold'

The various cultivars of evergreen *E. fortunei* make bushy shrubs or, when given support, vigorous climbers. They are mainly valued for their foliage. This cultivar is usually seen as a low bush with deep green leaves that are edged yellow, often with a pink flush in cold winters. Hardy.

Height and spread: 1m (3ft)

Site: Sun. Well-drained soil

Compost: Soil-based (John Innes No. 3)

Use: Border, container, ground cover

Good companions: *Allium* 'Globemaster', *Cytisus* x *praecox* 'Allgold', *Helianthemum* 'Wisley Primrose'

2 Forsythia giraldiana

This is a more lanky deciduous shrub than the later-flowering forsythias, but its early display of pale yellow flowers hanging from arching naked stems in late winter or early spring gives it special value. Grey to mid-green oval leaves follow the flowers. Hardy.

General care: Immediately after flowering cut back to base up to a quarter of old stems and cut back all remaining shoots that have borne flowers.

Height and spread: 4m (12ft)

Site: Sun, partial shade. Moist, well-drained soil

Use: Border, wall

Good companions: *Lonicera* x *purpusii* 'Winter Beauty', *Rosa* 'Golden Wings', *Rosa xanthina* 'Canary Bird'

3 Hamamelis x intermedia 'Arnold Promise'

Witch hazel

Like other hybrid witch hazels, this deciduous shrub or small tree is principally grown for its scented flowers. In mid and late winter the naked stems are encrusted with small ribbon-like petals that are bright yellow. The rounded leaves usually turn yellow in autumn. Hardy.

Height and spread: 4m (12ft)

Site: Sun, partial shade. Moist but well-drained soil, preferably lime-free

Use: Canopy in border, specimen tree, woodland garden

Good companions: *Fothergilla major* Monticola Group, *Sarcococca hookeriana* var. *digyna*, *Sorbus cashmiriana*

4 Hamamelis x intermedia 'Pallida'

Witch hazel

The spreading canopy of naked branches thickly covered with lemon-yellow spidery flowers is a luminous sight in a dark winter garden. The scent of the flowers is delicate but sweet. Hardy.

Height and spread: 4m (12ft)

Site: Sun, partial shade. Moist but well-drained soil, preferably lime-free

Use: Canopy, specimen tree, woodland garden

Good companions: *Hosta sieboldiana* var. *elegans*, *Narcissus* 'Jack Snipe', *Pulmonaria angustifolia* 'Munstead Blue'

5 Hamamelis mollis

Chinese witch hazel

Deciduous large shrub or small tree with a somewhat irregular canopy of ascending and spreading branches. In mid to late winter the bare stems are covered with small, bright yellow many-petalled flowers. Their sweet scent carries well. The rounded soft leaves turn yellow in autumn. Hardy.

Height and spread: 4m (12ft)

Site: Sun, partial shade. Moist but well-drained soil, preferably lime-free

Use: Canopy in border, specimen tree, woodland garden

Good companions: *Cryptomeria japonica* 'Elegans Compacta', *Hamamelis* x *intermedia* 'Diane', *Prunus serrula*

6 Hippophae rhamnoides

Sea buckthorn

Bushy, spiny deciduous shrub, sometimes tree-like, with narrow silvery leaves. If a male plant is present, female plants bear thickly clustered crops of inedible bright orange berries that remain on the branches through winter. Hardy.

Height and spread: 6m (20ft)

Site: Sun. Moist but well-drained soil

Use: Border, hedge, windbreak

Good companions: *Escallonia* 'Apple Blossom', *Fuchsia* 'Riccartonii', *Griselinia littoralis* 'Variegata'

7 Jasminum nudiflorum

Winter jasmine

Deciduous shrub with lax green stems and bright yellow scentless flowers, red tinted in bud, between late autumn and early spring. Hardy.

General care: Immediately after flowering remove up to a quarter of old stems and trim back all shoots that have flowered to strong buds.

Height and spread: 3m (10ft)

Site: Sun, partial shade. Well-drained soil

Use: Bank, wall

Good companions: *Cotoneaster conspicuus* 'Decorus', *Hedera helix* 'Goldheart', *Pyracantha* 'Soleil d'Or'

8 Lonicera nitida 'Baggesen's Gold'

Bushy evergreen shrub that in sunny positions is an alternative to shade-tolerant plain green forms. The small leaves are yellow in summer and yellow-green in autumn and winter. Hardy.

General care: Trim hedges at least twice between early summer and early autumn.

Height and spread: 1.5m (5ft)

Site: Sun, partial shade. Well-drained soil

Use: Hedge, ground cover

Good companions: *Epimedium* x *versicolor* 'Sulphureum', *Forsythia* x *intermedia* 'Lynwood', *Lonicera* x *purpusii* 'Winter Beauty'

9 Mahonia japonica

Evergreen shrub with rosettes of bold leaves composed of dark green, leathery spiny leaflets. It flowers between late autumn and early spring, the lax sprays of small yellow blooms falling over the leaves. The sweet scent carries well on the air. Strings of inedible dark blue fruits follow. Hardy.

Height: 3m (10ft) **Spread:** 4m (12ft)

Site: Partial shade, shade, sun. Moist but well-drained soil

Use: Border, specimen shrub, woodland garden

Good companions: *Aconitum* 'Ivorine', *Aucuba japonica* 'Crotonifolia', *Hydrangea quercifolia*

10 Mahonia x media 'Winter Sun'

This hybrid bears many similarities to one of its parents (see 9, above), but its flowers are not so strongly fragrant and are borne in sprays that are more upright. Hardy.

Height: 5m (15ft) **Spread:** 4m (12ft)

Site: Partial shade, shade, sun. Moist but well-drained soil

Use: Border, specimen shrub, woodland garden

Good companions: *Elaeagnus pungens* 'Maculata', *Forsythia giraldiana*, *Geranium* x *magnificum*

11 Malus 'Winter Gold'

Crab apple

Small deciduous tree with a rounded canopy. The white blossom opens from pink buds in the second half of spring. The edible lemon-yellow crab apples that follow remain on the tree well into winter. Hardy.

Height and spread: 6m (20ft)

Site: Sun. Moist but well-drained soil

Use: Canopy in border, specimen tree

Good companions: *Narcissus* 'Actaea', *Narcissus* 'Cedric Morris', *Tulipa sprengeri*

7

9

8

10

11

yellow and orange (continued)

1 Prunus maackii

Manchurian cherry

The lasting feature of this deciduous tree or large shrub is the bark; the old layer peels away to reveal yellow-brown new bark beneath. Inedible, glossy black spherical fruits follow scented white spring flowers. Hardy.

Height: 9m (30ft) **Spread:** 8m (25ft)
Site: Sun. Moist but well-drained soil
Use: Canopy in border, specimen tree
Good companions: *Anemone blanda, Crocus vernus* 'Pickwick', *Narcissus* 'Dove Wings'

2 Pyracantha 'Orange Glow'

Evergreen spiny shrub of upright but irregular shape. Numerous clusters of inedible orange fruits follow dense heads of small, white late spring flowers and last well into winter. Hardy.

General care: Trim hedges and prune wall-trained specimens in the first half of summer.
Height and spread: 3m (10ft)
Site: Sun, partial shade. Well-drained soil
Use: Border, hedge, wall
Good companions: *Forsythia suspensa, Hedera colchica* 'Dentata Variegata', *Pyracantha* 'Mohave'

3 Pyracantha 'Soleil d'Or'

Moderately vigorous evergreen shrub with red-tinted spiny stems and glossy green leaves. Large clusters of inedible amber-yellow fruits follow heads of small white early summer flowers and persist for many weeks. Hardy.
General care: Trim hedges and prune wall-trained specimens in the first half of summer.
Height: 3m (10ft) **Spread:** 2.5m (8ft)
Site: Sun, partial shade. Well-drained soil
Use: Border, hedge, wall
Good companions: *Jasminum nudiflorum, Narcissus* 'Tête-à-Tête', *Tulipa* 'Orange Emperor'

4 Stachyurus praecox

Deciduous shrub with red-brown stems, from which hang stiff sprays studded with pale yellow buds from late autumn until they open as bell-shaped flowers in late winter or early spring. Tapered leaves emerge after the flowers. Hardy.
Height and spread: 3m (10ft)
Site: Sun, partial shade. Moist but well-drained soil, preferably lime-free
Use: Border, woodland garden
Good companions: *Hamamelis* x *intermedia* 'Diane', *Smilacina racemosa, Sorbus sargentiana*

cream and white

5 Abeliophyllum distichum

Deciduous shrub best grown against a sunny wall to encourage flowering. The sprays of fragrant, white four-petalled flowers open from pink-tinted buds in late winter or early spring. The rounded leaves usually turn purple before falling. Hardy.
General care: After flowering cut back all shoots to a low framework or, if wall trained, to within three or four buds of a permanent framework.
Height and spread: 1.5m (5ft)
Site: Sun. Well-drained soil
Use: Border, wall
Good companions: *Clematis armandii* 'Snowdrift', *Clematis* 'Etoile Rose', *Ribes speciosum*

6 Acer grosseri var. hersii

Snakebark maple

Small deciduous tree with variable lobed leaves that turn orange and yellow in autumn. Dangling clusters of fruits are often conspicuous in late summer and autumn, but the main feature is the bold white striation of the bark, which is particularly eye-catching in winter. Hardy.
Height: 9m (30ft) **Spread:** 8m (25ft)
Site: Sun, partial shade. Humus-rich and moist but well-drained soil, preferably lime-free
Use: Canopy in mixed planting, specimen tree, woodland garden
Good companions: *Acer palmatum* 'Corallinum', *Chionodoxa luciliae* Gigantea Group, *Colchicum* 'Rosy Dawn'

7 Camellia 'Cornish Snow'

Evergreen shrub with tapered leaves that emerge bronze before turning dark green. Small white single flowers, tinted very pale pink, are borne profusely in late winter and early spring. Hardy.
Height: 3m (10ft) **Spread:** 1.5m (5ft)
Site: Partial shade. Lime-free, humus-rich and moist but well-drained soil
Compost: Soil-based (ericaceous)
Use: Container, shady border, underplanting for trees
Good companions: *Camellia japonica* 'Bob's Tinsie', *Gaultheria mucronata* 'Wintertime', *Rhododendron* 'Razorbill'

8 Daphne mezereum f. alba

Mezereon

In late winter and early spring the naked shoots of this upright deciduous shrub are densely clad with small white stemless flowers. It is a well scented alternative to the usual mezereon, which has purplish pink flowers. Poisonous fleshy yellow fruits follow the flowers. Hardy.
Height: 1.2m (4ft) **Spread:** 1m (3ft)
Site: Sun, partial shade. Humus-rich, well-drained soil
Use: Border, woodland garden
Good companions: *Anemone blanda, Exochorda* x *macrantha* 'The Bride', *Geranium sanguineum*

9 Eucalyptus pauciflora subsp. niphophila

Alpine snow gum, Snow gum

In late summer and autumn the grey-and-brown bark of this evergreen tree flakes to reveal colourful patches of new bark. Rounded grey-green juvenile leaves give way to scimitar-shaped pendent leaves with a blue-green bloom. Hardy.
Height: 9m (30ft) **Spread:** 6m (20ft)
Site: Sun. Well-drained soil, preferably lime-free
Use: Specimen tree
Good companions: *Artemesia arborescens, Ceanothus thyrsiflorus* var. *repens, Cistus ladanifer*

10 Euonymus fortunei 'Emerald Gaiety'

Evergreen bushy foliage shrub. The leaves have bright green and grey-green centres and irregular white margins, often tinged pink in winter. Hardy.
Height and spread: 1.5m (5ft)
Site: Sun. Well-drained soil
Compost: Soil-based (John Innes No. 3)
Use: Border, container, ground cover
Good companions: *Choisya ternata, Fatsia japonica, Hypericum* 'Hidcote'

11 Gaultheria mucronata 'Wintertime'

This evergreen shrub makes dense thickets of wiry stems covered with small, glossy deep green leaves and bears white flowers in late spring. This female clone bears heavy crops of long-lasting, white fruits if grown near a male plant. Hardy.
Height and spread: 1.2m (4ft)
Site: Partial shade, sun. Lime-free, moist but well-drained soil
Use: Ground cover, raised bed, woodland garden
Good companions: *Gaultheria mucronata* 'Bell's Seedling', *Ledum groenlandicum, Rhododendron* 'Praecox'

12 Lonicera x purpusii 'Winter Beauty'

Shrubby honeysuckle

Deciduous or semi-evergreen rounded shrub. From midwinter sweetly scented cream flowers are borne over several weeks on naked stems. Hardy.
General care: Immediately after flowering cut out up to a quarter of old stems and cut back remaining stems that have flowered to a strong bud.
Height: 2m (6ft) **Spread:** 2.5m (8ft)
Site: Sun, partial shade. Well-drained soil
Use: Border
Good companions: *Campanula lactiflora* 'Prichard's Variety', *Geranium pratense* 'Mrs Kendall Clark', *Rosa* 'Golden Wings'

9

10

11

12

cream and white (continued)

1 Prunus davidiana

Small deciduous tree of upright growth worth planting in a sheltered position for its early blossom. The white or pink saucer-shaped flowers appear on leafless stems from midwinter. The glossy dark green leaves are finely tapered. Hardy.

Height and spread: 8m (25ft)
Site: Sun. Moist but well-drained soil
Use: Canopy in border, specimen tree
Good companions: *Anemone blanda*, *Crocus vernus* 'Jeanne d'Arc' and 'Remembrance'

2 Rhamnus alaternus 'Argenteovariegata'

Italian buckthorn

Evergreen shrub grown mainly for its foliage. The green and grey-green leaves have an irregular bright white margin. It requires hot sunny summers to produce fruits, which are red then black. All parts are harmful if ingested. Hardy.

Height: 5m (15ft) **Spread:** 4m (12ft)
Site: Sun, partial shade. Well-drained soil
Use: Border
Good companions: *Ceanothus* 'Italian Skies', *Euonymus alatus* 'Compactus', *Ruta graveolens* 'Jackman's Blue'

3 Rhododendron 'Christmas Cheer'

Compact evergreen hybrid that bears trusses of pink buds, which open to white trumpet-shaped flowers in late winter and early spring. If grown under glass it can be brought into flower by early winter, hence its name. Hardy.

Height and spread: 2m (6ft)
Site: Sun or partial shade. Lime-free, moist but well-drained soil
Compost: Soil-based (ericaceous)
Use: Container, sunny or lightly shaded border, rock garden, woodland garden
Good companions: *Acer palmatum* 'Sango-kaku', *Omphalodes cappadocica*, *Viburnum carlesii* 'Aurora'

4 Rhododendron moupinense

A parent of many compact hybrids, this evergreen dwarf species has shiny, mid-green rounded leaves that are light coloured and scaly on the underside. The white or pink funnel-shaped flowers, sometimes speckled red, are borne in twos or threes in late winter or early spring. Hardy.

Height and spread: 1.2m (4ft)
Site: Sun, partial shade. Lime-free, moist but well-drained soil
Compost: Soil-based (ericaceous)
Use: Container, sunny or lightly shaded border, rock garden, woodland garden
Good companions: *Kalmia latifolia* 'Ostbo Red', *Rhododendron* 'Palestrina', *Rhododendron* 'Vanessa Pastel'

5 Sarcococca hookeriana var. digyna

Christmas box, Sweet box

This evergreen shrub makes a dense thicket of upright green stems that are well covered with narrow tapered leaves. Small, pink-tinged white flowers add a delicious fragrance to the winter garden. Inedible black fruits follow. Hardy.

Height: 1.5m (5ft) **Spread:** 2m (6ft)
Site: Shade, partial shade. Humus-rich and moist but well-drained soil
Use: Informal hedge, underplanting for shrubs and trees, woodland garden
Good companions: *Cercidiphyllum japonicum*, *Saxifraga fortunei*, *Viburnum davidii*

6 Sorbus cashmiriana

Deciduous small tree with an open canopy and leaves up to 20cm (8in) long composed of numerous narrow leaflets. White or pale pink flowerheads in late spring are followed by drooping clusters of inedible, white, or pink-tinged, berries that last well into winter. Hardy.

Height: 8m (25ft) **Spread:** 6m (20ft)
Site: Sun, partial shade. Moist but well-drained soil, preferably lime-free
Use: Canopy in border, specimen tree
Good companions: *Hydrangea macrophylla* 'Madame Emile Mouillère', *Magnolia soulangeana*, *Viburnum opulus* 'Roseum'

7 Symphoricarpos x doorenbosii 'White Hedge'

Snowberry

Hybrid deciduous shrub that makes a steadily increasing thicket. Inconspicuous summer flowers are followed by long-lasting, eye-catching white fruits. These are suitable for indoor arrangements, but harmful if ingested. Hardy.

Height: 1.5m (5ft) **Spread:** Indefinite
Site: Sun, partial shade. Well-drained soil
Use: Border, informal hedge
Good companions: *Cotinus* 'Flame', *Euonymus europaeus* 'Red Cascade', *Euonymus fortunei* 'Emerald Gaiety'

8 Viburnum farreri

Deciduous shrub with very upright main stems, although mature plants develop a rounded outline. The oval leaves are bronze-tinted when they open. Sweetly scented, white tubular flowers, sometimes tinted pink, are borne in small clusters over a remarkably long period from late autumn until early or even mid-spring. Hardy.

Height: 3m (10ft) **Spread:** 2.5m (8ft)
Site: Sun, partial shade. Moist but well-drained soil
Use: Border
Good companions: *Epimedium* x *youngianum* 'Niveum', *Galanthus nivalis*, *Geranium* 'Johnson's Blue'

silver and grey

9 Betula utilis var. jacquemontii 'Silver Shadow'

Himalayan birch

The trunk and ascending branches of this deciduous tree are silvery white but terminate in a haze of dark twigs. The large drooping leaves are dark green. Hardy.

Height: 18m (60ft) **Spread:** 9m (30ft)
Site: Sun. Moist but well-drained soil
Use: Specimen tree, woodland garden
Good companions: *Clerodendrum trichotomum* var. *fargesii*, *Taxus baccata*, *Tsuga heterophylla*

10 Juniperus communis 'Hibernica'

Common juniper

Evergreen conifer that forms a dense slender column of grey-green foliage in which there is a hint of blue. The vertical accent remains shapely without any training or clipping. Hardy.

Height: 4m (12ft) **Spread:** 30cm (12in)

Site: Sun. Well-drained soil

Use: Avenue, heather garden, rock garden, specimen shrub

Good companions: *Erica carnea* 'Vivellii', *Erica arborea* var. *alpina*, *Euonymus alatus* 'Compactus'

11 Rubus cockburnianus

White-stemmed bramble

Deciduous shrub that forms thickets of arching purple stems. These are conspicuous in winter because of the overlay of white bloom. The ferny leaves are dark green, grey-white on the underside. Purple flowers in summer are followed by unpalatable black fruits. The larger, more spreading white-washed bramble (*R. biflorus*) produces edible yellow fruits. Hardy.

General care: For the best stem colour cut all growths back to near ground level in early spring.

Height and spread: 2.5m (8ft)

Site: Sun, partial shade. Moist, well-drained soil

Use: Border, woodland garden

Good companions: *Anemone nemorosa*, *Omphalodes verna*, *Taxus baccata*

12 Salix irrorata

Willow

Deciduous shrub of upright growth. Purple stems covered with a white bloom, which are particularly conspicuous in winter, are its main ornamental feature. Grey catkins appear in spring before the leaves; the male catkins have red anthers that turn yellow. Hardy.

General care: For a supply of young growths, cut back stems to a permanent framework every two or three years.

Height: 3m (10ft) **Spread:** 4m (12ft)

Site: Sun. Moist but well-drained soil

Use: Border, waterside

Good companions: *Alnus glutinosa* 'Imperialis', *Cornus alba* 'Sibirica', *Salix daphnoides*

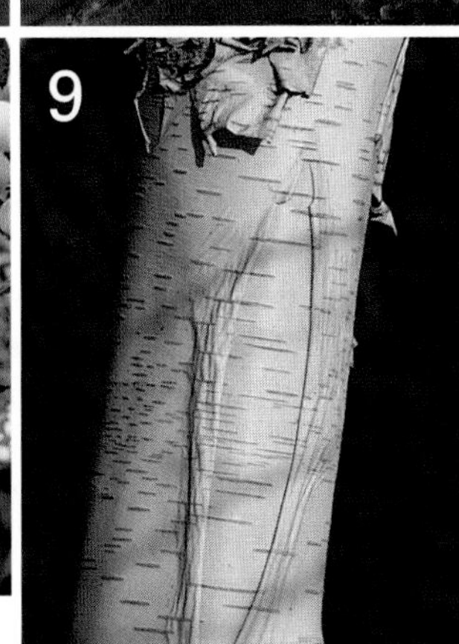

green

1 Buxus sempervirens

Common box

Slow-growing evergreen shrub or small tree with dense, glossy dark green foliage, traditionally used for hedging and topiary. The numerous cultivars include 'Suffruticosa', which because of its compact slow growth is used as a clipped edging as little as 15cm (6in) high. The dimensions may, after many years, exceed those given below. Hardy.

Height: 3m (10ft) **Spread:** 2m (6ft)
Site: Partial shade, sun. Well-drained soil
Compost: Soil-based (John Innes No. 3)
Use: Border, container, hedging, topiary
Good companions: *Rosa* 'Céleste', *Rosa* 'Louise Odier', *Viola cornuta* Alba Group

2 Cedrus deodara

Deodar cedar

Magnificent evergreen conifer for large gardens and landscapes. It is broadly conical, with spreading branches and drooping sprays of needle-like leaves that vary in colour from grey-green to dark green. Hardy.

Height: 25m (80ft) **Spread:** 8m (25ft)
Site: Sun. Well-drained soil
Use: Specimen tree
Good companions: *Crataegus persimilis* 'Prunifolia', *Liquidambar styraciflua* 'Worplesdon', *Prunus sargentii*

3 Chamaecyparis lawsoniana 'Tamariscifolia'

Lawson cypress

The species is a columnar evergreen conifer of considerable vigour, but this slow-growing form is of irregular spreading growth with no main stem and branches that splay out from a high centre. The foliage is deep green with a hint of blue. Hardy.

Height: 3m (10ft) **Spread:** 4m (12ft)
Site: Sun. Moist but well-drained soil, preferably lime-free
Use: Sunny bank, border, ground cover, large rock garden
Good companions: *Berberis* x *stenophylla*, *Cotinus* 'Flame', *Cotoneaster salicifolius* 'Rothschildianus'

4 Cornus stolonifera 'Flaviramea'

Red osier dogwood

Deciduous shrub that makes a thicket from a base of spreading underground stems. After the elegantly tapered leaves have coloured red and fallen, the bare greenish yellow stems remain conspicuous throughout winter. Hardy.

General care: To maintain a supply of young wood, cut all or a proportion of stems to near ground level in early spring.
Height: 3m (10ft) **Spread:** 4m (12ft)
Site: Sun. Moist but well-drained soil
Use: Border, waterside
Good companions: *Cornus alba* 'Sibirica', *Metasequoia glyptostroboides*, *Salix* x *sepulcralis* var. *chrysocoma*

5 Garrya elliptica 'James Roof'

Silk-tassel bush

Evergreen shrub or small tree with leathery leaves. In late winter and early spring, male specimens bear pale green to grey-green dangling catkins up to 20cm (8in) long. The silver-grey female catkins are smaller and less showy, but are followed by inedible purplish fruits. Hardy.

Height: 4m (12ft) **Spread:** 3m (10ft)
Site: Sun, partial shade. Well-drained soil
Use: Border, wall
Good companions: *Clematis* 'Gipsy Queen', *Myrtus communis* subsp. *tarentina*, *Vitis* 'Brant'

6 Juniperus x pfitzeriana 'Wilhelm Pfitzer'

This evergreen conifer has tiers of branches that rise at an angle of 45 degrees to make a somewhat flat-topped shrub. The scale-like leaves are green or grey-green. The fruits are purplish. Hardy.

Height: 1.2m (4ft) **Spread:** 2.5m (8ft)
Site: Sun, partial shade. Well-drained soil
Use: Border, ground cover, heather garden, large rock garden, specimen shrub
Good companions: *Artemisia* 'Powis Castle', *Buddleja davidii* 'Black Knight', *Cistus ladanifer*

7 Picea breweriana

Brewer spruce

Evergreen conifer of broad conical shape with horizontal main branches and hanging shoots that make a curtain of deep green or blue-green foliage. The backs of the flattened leaves are marked by two white lines. Mature specimens bear female cones that are green at first and later purple-brown. Hardy.

Height: 12m (40ft) **Spread:** 6m (20ft)
Site: Sun. Moist but well-drained soil
Use: Specimen tree
Good companions: *Betula utilis* var. *jacquemontii* 'Silver Shadow', *Parrotia persica*, *Quercus coccinea* 'Splendens'

8 Prunus lusitanica
Portugal laurel

Evergreen large shrub or small tree grown mainly for its dense foliage. The glossy dark green leaves have red stalks. Upright sprays of small white flowers with a cloying scent are borne in early summer, followed by inedible red fruits that turn black. Specimens can be clipped to make simple topiary shapes. Hardy.
General care: Clip topiary in early to mid-spring.
Height: 9m (30ft) **Spread:** 6m (20ft)
Site: Sun, partial shade. Moist but well-drained soil
Use: Canopy in border, specimen tree, topiary
Good companions: *Bergenia* 'Sunningdale', *Helleborus argutifolius, Pachysandra terminalis*

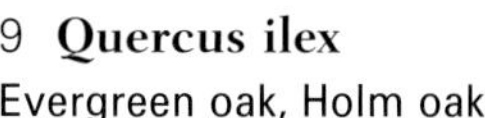

9 Quercus ilex
Evergreen oak, Holm oak

Majestic evergreen broad-leaved tree with a trunk or sometimes several stems supporting a large canopy of dark green leaves that are lighter on the underside. The bark is dark grey. Bears acorns, singly or in twos or threes. Suitable for trimming into simple geometric shapes. Hardy.
General care: Trim shaped specimens in late summer.
Height: 25m (80ft) **Spread:** 20m (65ft)
Site: Sun. Fertile, well-drained soil
Use: Hedge, shelter belt, specimen tree, topiary
Good companions: *Arbutus unedo, Cytisus* x *praecox* 'Allgold', *Genista aetnensis*

10 Ribes laurifolium
Flowering currant

Evergreen shrub with smooth, dark green leathery leaves. It flowers in late winter or early spring, the yellow-green male or female blooms being borne on separate bushes. The larger male flowers are carried in drooping sprays. The smaller female flowers are more upright and may be followed by inedible red fruits that ripen to black. Hardy.
Height: 1m (3ft) **Spread:** 1.5m (5ft)
Site: Partial shade, sun. Well-drained soil
Use: Border, underplanting for shubs and trees
Good companions: *Cyclamen hederifolium, Iris foetidissima, Osmanthus delavayi*

11 Taxus baccata 'Fastigiata'
Florence court yew, Irish yew

The yews are impressive and long-lived evergreen conifers that make large shrubs or trees, many being excellent for hedging and topiary. This female form is best grown to show it off as a dark green column composed of densely packed branches. As a young plant it is narrow but steadily acquires girth. In autumn it carries seeds with a bright red fleshy covering (aril), which is the only part of the plant that is not poisonous. Hardy.
Height: 9m (30ft) **Spread:** 6m (20ft)
Site: Sun, partial shade. Fertile, well-drained soil
Use: Avenue, specimen tree
Good companions: *Prunus* 'Taihaku', *Pyrus calleryana* 'Chanticleer', *Sorbus cashmiriana*

12 Tsuga heterophylla
Western hemlock

Tall-growing evergreen conifer of narrowly conical growth, with purplish brown bark and dense dark green foliage that hangs from slightly upturned branches. Small, pale brown female cones develop on mature trees. Excellent for hedging, but too large as a specimen tree for most gardens and will eventually exceed the dimensions given. Hardy.
General care: Trim hedges in summer.
Height: 25m (80ft) **Spread:** 8m (25ft)
Site: Sun, partial shade. Humus-rich and moist but well-drained soil
Use: Hedge, specimen tree
Good companions: *Aconitum* 'Ivorine', *Fuchsia magellanica* 'Versicolor', *Hydrangea macrophylla* 'Madame Emile Mouillère'

holly

The best-known hollies are hardy evergreen shrubs and trees grown for their glossy, often spined leaves and colourful inedible berries. For a crop of berries, most female plants require a male plant nearby. Grow in sun or partial shade on moist, well-drained soil. Clip hedges and topiary specimens in spring or late summer.

1 **Ilex aquifolium 'Handsworth New Silver'**
Common holly, English holly
Female large shrub or small tree with purplish stems. The long spiny leaves are green and grey-green with cream margins. Heavy crops of red berries.
Height: 8m (25ft) **Spread:** 5m (15ft)
Good companions: *Anemone hupehensis* 'Hadspen Abundance', *Aster* x *frikartii* 'Mönch', *Kolkwitzia amabilis* 'Pink Cloud'

2 **Ilex crenata 'Convexa'**
Box-leaved holly, Japanese holly
Slow-growing female shrub with small, dark green convex leaves and shiny black berries. Suitable as a low hedge or for a border or rock garden.
Height: 2m (6ft) **Spread:** 1.5m (5ft)
Good companions: *Dicentra* 'Langtrees', *Nandina domestica* 'Fire Power', *Tiarella wherryi*

3 **Ilex aquifolium 'Ferox Argentea'**
Hedgehog holly
This relatively slow-growing male cultivar has small puckered leaves that bristle with numerous spines. These, like the leaf margins, are white.
Height: 8m (25ft) **Spread:** 5m (15ft)
Good companions: *Anemone* x *hybrida* 'Whirlwind', *Aster pringlei* 'Monte Cassino', *Deutzia* x *rosea*

4 **Ilex x meserveae 'Blue Princess'**
Blue holly
Female shrub with blue-tinted spiny leaves and glossy red berries if there is a male plant, such as 'Blue Prince', nearby. Useful as specimen, canopy in border or for a woodland garden.
Height: 3m (10ft) **Spread:** 2.5m (8ft)
Good companions: *Betula utilis* var. *jacquemontii* 'Silver Shadow', *Lonicera* x *purpusii* 'Winter Beauty', *Nandina domestica* 'Fire Power'

5 **Ilex aquifolium 'Bacciflava'**
Common holly, English holly
Female tree or large shrub with dark green spiny leaves. Heavy crops of long-lasting bright yellow berries.
Height: 6m (20ft) **Spread:** 5m (15ft)
Good companions: *Epimedium* x *versicolor* 'Sulphureum', *Epimedium* x *warleyensis* 'Orangekönigin', *Hosta fortunei* var. *albopicta*

6 **Ilex aquifolium 'J.C. van Tol'**
Dark green leaves, which have few spines, and large crops of bright red berries. Self-fertile. Best used as a specimen shrub or tree.
Height: 8m (25ft) **Spread:** 4m (12ft)
Good companions: *Amelanchier canadensis, Crataegus persimilis* 'Prunifolia', *Prunus sargentii*

7 **Ilex aquifolium 'Pyramidalis'**
Common holly, English holly
This self-fertile shrub or small tree is narrowly conical when young, more open when mature. It has green stems, spiny or spineless leaves and heavy crops of long-lasting bright red berries. Useful as a specimen or for topiary. For a formal shape, clip in summer.
Height: 6m (20ft) **Spread:** 5m (15ft)
Good companions: *Bergenia* 'Sunningdale', *Hedera helix* 'Ivalace', *Skimmia japonica* 'Rubella'

8 **Ilex x altaclerensis 'Golden King'**
Female tree or large shrub with almost spineless leaves that are rich green with an irregular bright yellow margin or sometimes entirely yellow. Heavy crops of red berries.
Height: 6m (20ft) **Spread:** 5m (15ft)
Good companions: *Doronicum orientale* 'Magnificum', *Eranthis hyemalis, Narcissus obvallaris*

heaths

These low-growing evergreen shrubs resemble heathers (*Calluna vulgaris*), but most flower from winter to spring. Although many are natives of acid moorland or heathland, those described here are tolerant of lime. Most are hardy and require a sunny well-drained site; in a container use soil-based, preferably lime-free (ericaceous) compost. Trim in spring after flowering.

1 Erica carnea 'Springwood White'
Alpine heath, Winter heath

From midwinter white flowers almost hide the small bright green leaves.

Height: 25cm (10in) **Spread:** 50cm (20in)

Good companions: *Calluna vulgaris* 'Peter Sparkes', *Erica* x *darleyensis* 'White Perfection', *Gaultheria mucronata* 'Mulberry Wine'

2 Erica x darleyensis 'Arthur Johnson'
Darley dale heath

Long-flowering heath with long slender sprays of pink flowers that are good for cutting.

Height: 30cm (12in) **Spread:** 60cm (2ft)

Good companions: *Cotoneaster conspicuus* 'Decorus', *Erica carnea* 'Vivellii', *Juniperus communis* 'Green Carpet'

3 Erica x darleyensis 'White Perfection'
Darley dale heath

Bright green foliage and spikes of pure white, urn-shaped flowers that open between early and late winter and last for many weeks.

Height: 40cm (16in) **Spread:** 75cm (2ft 6in)

Good companions: *Chamaecyparis lawsoniana* 'Ellwoodii', *Erica arborea* var. *alpina*, *Picea glauca* var. *albertina* 'Conica'

4 Erica x darleyensis 'Furzey'
Darley dale heath

Deep green leaves and deep pink flowers. Can flower over a long period, sometimes starting in late autumn and continuing until mid-spring.

Height: 30cm (12in) **Spread:** 60cm (2ft)

Good companions: *Calluna vulgaris* 'Robert Chapman', *Erica* x *darleyensis* 'White Perfection', *Juniperus communis* 'Compressa'

5 Erica carnea 'King George'
Alpine heath, Winter heath

This is one of the first heaths to flower, with dark pink blooms in early winter. Hardy.

Height and spread: 25cm (10in)

Good companions: *Calluna vulgaris* 'Peter Sparkes', *Erica carnea* 'Springwood White', *Picea pungens* 'Montgomery'

6 Erica erigena 'Brightness'
Irish heath, Mediterranean heath

The dense foliage of this heath takes on a purple tint in winter. Honey-scented, deep pink flower spikes from late winter until mid or late spring. Not fully hardy.

Height: 1.2m (4ft) **Spread:** 1m (3ft)

Good companions: *Erica carnea* 'Springwood White', *Juniperus communis* 'Compressa', *Picea glauca* var. *albertiana* 'Conica'

7 Erica carnea 'Vivellii'
Alpine heath, Winter heath

Compact plant with bronze-red foliage and deep carmine flowers in winter.

Height: 15cm (6in) **Spread:** 35cm (14in)

Good companions: *Erica arborea* var. *alpina*, *Erica carnea* 'King George', *Erica* x *darleyensis* 'Furzey'

1

2

3

7

6

5 4

alpines

Small perennials and shrubs that thrive in well-drained conditions look good in a raised bed or rock garden and many are suitable for containers or paving. Most can be planted during any mild spell in the dormant season, but dwarf conifers are best planted in late autumn or mid-spring.

pink and mauve

1 Primula nana (syn. P. edgeworthii)

In winter the leaves of this perennial form a congested rosette covered with a mealy powder. They extend in summer and become mid-green. Clusters of yellow-eyed, usually mauve flowers are borne in late winter or early spring. Hardy.

General care: Protect from excessive wet in winter.

Height: 10cm (4in) **Spread:** 15cm (6in)

Site: Partial shade or shade. Lime-free, moist but gritty and sharply drained soil

Compost: Soil-based (John Innes No. 2) with added leaf-mould and grit

Use: Container, raised bed, rock garden

Good companions: *Acer palmatum* var. *dissectum* Dissectum Viride Group, *Leucojum vernum*, *Salix* 'Boydii'

2 Saxifraga 'Johann Kellerer'

Kabschia saxifrage

Evergreen perennial with grey-green wedge-shaped leaves packed in small silvery rosettes. In late winter and early spring there are sprays of tubular pink flowers. Valued as an early flowering saxifrage for the alpine house, but can be grown successfully outdoors. Hardy.

General care: Plant in early autumn or early spring.

Height and spread: 15cm (6in)

Site: Partial shade. Moist but gritty and sharply drained soil. Good on lime

Compost: Soil-based (John Innes No. 1) with added limestone chippings

Use: Container, raised bed, rock garden

Good companions: *Primula marginata*, *Saxifraga* 'Gloria', *Scilla mischtschenkoana*

yellow and orange

3 Adonis amurensis

The yellow bowl-shaped flowers of this perennial are borne in late winter and early spring. They can have as many as 30 petals, sometimes bronzed on the backs. The fern-like leaves develop fully after the flowers are over. Hardy.

General care: Plant in autumn with the crown about 2–3cm (1in) deep.

Height: 35cm (14in) **Spread:** 30cm (12in)

Site: Partial shade. Humus-rich and moist but well-drained soil

Use: Raised bed, rock garden, shaded border

Good companions: *Alchemilla conjuncta*, *Cyclamen hederifolium*, *Erythronium californicum* 'White Beauty'

4 Chamaecyparis lawsoniana 'Minima Aurea'

Lawson cypress

One of many dwarf cultivars of the Lawson cypress, a large, evergreen conical conifer much used as a specimen tree and for hedging and shelter belts. It is globular to conical with erect sprays of soft golden foliage. Hardy.

Height and spread: 1m (3ft)

Site: Sun. Moist but well-drained soil

Compost: Soil-based (John Innes No. 3)

Use: Container, heather garden, raised bed, rock garden, sunny border

Good companions: *Campanula cochleariifolia*, *Hebe cupressoides* 'Boughton Dome', *Narcissus* 'Tête-à-tête'

5 Thuja occidentalis 'Rheingold'

White cedar

This slow-growing dwarf form of the white cedar, a medium-sized evergreen conifer, is of roughly conical shape. Young leaves are tinged pink, but the deep old-gold colouring of mature foliage

makes it a good contrast to deep greens, particularly in winter. Hardy.
Height: 1.5m (5ft) **Spread:** 1m (3ft)
Site: Sun. Moist but well-drained soil
Compost: Soil-based (John Innes No. 3)
Use: Container, heather garden, raised bed, rock garden, sunny border
Good companions: *Salix reticulata, Thuja occidentalis* 'Hetz Midget', *Viola biflora*

10

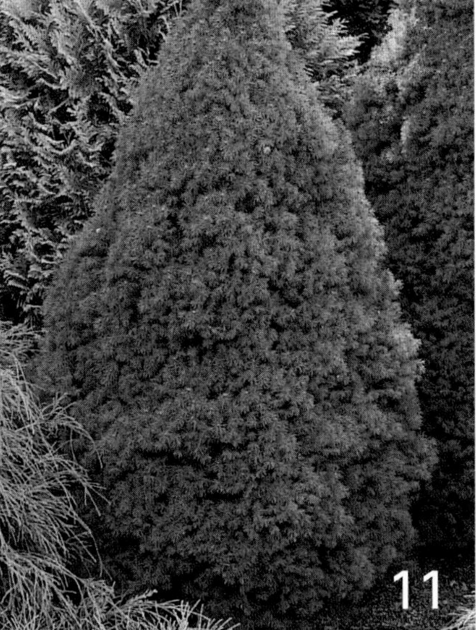
11

12

8

9

cream and white

6 Saxifraga 'Gloria'
Kabschia saxifrage
Perennial with tight rosettes of grey-green spiky leaves that make firm lime-encrusted cushions. In late winter or early spring yellow-centred white flowers stand on reddish stems. Hardy.
General care: Plant in early autumn or in early spring.
Height: 5cm (2in) **Spread:** 15cm (6in)
Site: Partial shade. Moist but gritty and sharply drained soil. Good on lime
Compost: Soil-based (John Innes No. 1) with added limestone chippings
Use: Container, raised bed, rock garden
Good companions: *Campanula carpatica, Gentiana verna, Saxifraga* 'Johann Kellerer'

silver, grey and blue

7 Juniperus squamata 'Blue Star'
Flaky juniper
Dwarf evergreen conifer that makes a hummock of silver-blue narrow leaves. It is most silvery when growing in relatively dry conditions. Hardy.
Height: 40cm (16in) **Spread:** 1m (3ft)
Site: Sun, partial shade. Well-drained soil
Compost: Soil-based (John Innes No. 3)
Use: Container, ground cover, heather garden, raised bed, rock garden
Good companions: *Geranium cinereum* 'Ballerina', *Tulipa saxatilis* Bakeri Group 'Lilac Wonder', *Tulipa turkestanica*

8 Picea mariana 'Nana'
Black spruce
This dwarf form of the black spruce, a slow-growing evergreen conifer, makes a dense mound composed of radiating stems closely covered with small blue-grey leaves. If bruised leaves smell of menthol. Hardy.
Height: 45cm (18in) **Spread:** 60cm (2ft)
Site: Sun, partial shade. Moist but well-drained soil
Compost: Soil-based (John Innes No. 3)
Use: Container, heather garden, raised bed, rock garden
Good companions: *Erica carnea* 'King George', *Erica carnea* 'Vivellii', *Picea glauca* var. *albertiana* 'Conica'

green

9 Juniperus communis 'Compressa'
Common juniper
The common juniper is a very variable evergeen shrubby conifer that has several compact upright forms. The miniature column of the slow-growing 'Compressa' is composed of erect, closely held sprays of dull green to blue-green leaves. Hardy.
Height: 75cm (2ft 6in) **Spread:** 35cm (14in)
Site: Sun, partial shade. Well-drained soil
Compost: Soil-based (John Innes No. 3)
Use: Container, front of border, heather garden, raised bed, rock garden
Good companions: *Aubrieta* 'Greencourt Purple', *Helianthemum* 'Wisley Primrose', *Tulipa* 'Cape Cod'

10 Picea abies 'Little Gem'
Christmas tree, Norway spruce
One of several dwarf forms of the Norway spruce, a tall-growing evergreen conifer, this makes an almost globular bush of tiny, tightly packed dark green leaves. Hardy.
Height and spread: 40cm (16in)
Site: Sun. Moist but well-drained soil
Compost: Soil-based (John Innes No. 3)
Use: Container, heather garden, raised bed, rock garden
Good companions: *Chamaecyparis lawsoniana* 'Gimbornii', *Picea glauca* var. *albertiana* 'Conica', *Thuja occidentalis* 'Danica'

11 Picea glauca var. albertiana 'Conica'
White spruce
This slow-growing form of the white spruce, a large blue-green evergreen conifer, usually makes a remarkably symmetrical cone of dense bright green foliage. It may take more than 30 years to achieve the dimensions given. Hardy.
Height: 2m (6ft) **Spread:** 1.2m (4ft)
Site: Sun. Moist but well-drained soil
Compost: Soil-based (John Innes No. 3)
Use: Container, front of border, heather garden, raised bed, rock garden
Good companions: *Calluna vulgaris* 'Firefly', *Calluna vulgaris* 'Robert Chapman', *Erica* x *darleyensis* 'Furzey'

12 Pinus mugo 'Mops'
Dwarf mountain pine
This is a slow-growing globular form of the dwarf mountain pine, an evergreen conifer that usually develops as a gnarled shrub. Hardy.
Height: 35cm (14in) **Spread:** 50cm (20in)
Site: Sun. Well-drained soil
Compost: Soil-based (John Innes No. 3)
Use: Container, heather garden, raised bed, rock garden
Good companions: *Crocus chrysanthus* 'Ladykiller', *Cytisus* x *beanii, Pulsatilla vulgaris*

herbs, vegetables & fruit

In winter the kitchen garden provides a store of hearty vegetables and flavourings that are the basis of sustaining recipes. It is also the season to make sowings, as weather permits, of early succulent crops.

herbs

1 Horseradish
Armoracia rusticana

The hot, pungent flavour of this robust perennial's roots is used to flavour sauces and dips. Mild in spring but fiery in autumn. Hardy.

General care: Sow or plant in spring. Control spread of older plants by chopping out wayward roots before they establish. To grow as an annual, plant root cuttings in spring for lifting in late autumn or winter.

Height: 1m (3ft) **Spread:** Indefinite

Site: Sun or dappled shade. Light moist soil

Use: Herb or vegetable garden

2 Sage
Salvia officinalis

Aromatic shrubby evergreen with grey-green leaves used as a flavouring, especially for stuffing and meat dishes. Milder-flavoured variegated and coloured kinds are good for shrub borders. Hardy.

General care: Prune hard to shape in spring and trim after flowering. Replace after four to five years. Sow under glass in March and plant out after the last severe frosts 45cm (18in) apart or take softwood cuttings in early summer. Protect in the first winter.

Height and spread: 1m (3ft)

Site: Sun. Well-drained soil, not acid

Compost: Soil-based (John Innes No. 3) or soil-less, both with added grit

Use: Border, container, herb garden

3 Salad burnet
Sanguisorba minor

Drought-tolerant evergreen perennial best treated as an annual for culinary use. The soft divided leaves have a fresh nutty flavour and are useful in salads. Naturalises well in grass. Hardy.

General care: Sow indoors in spring or autumn and plant out 30cm (12in) apart. Cut young leaves from early summer onwards; frequent cutting encourages plenty of young growth.

Height: 60cm (2ft) **Spread:** 30cm (12in)

Site: Sun or light shade. Well-drained soil

Compost: Soil-based (John Innes No. 3)

Use: Container, edging, herb garden, wild garden

4 Scented-leaved pelargonium
Pelargonium species and cultivars

A huge range of very different pelargoniums has soft, sometimes variegated leaves packed with aromatic oils that smell variously of mint, lemon, eucalyptus, eau-de-cologne or spicy nutmeg; these can be used as culinary flavouring. Pink or white flowers in summer. Grow in pots and harvest young leaves as required. Half hardy.

General care: Take cuttings in summer, pot up individually when rooted and overwinter in a cool room or greenhouse. Feed and trim to shape regularly. Keep fairly dry over winter, but well watered at other times.

Height and spread: 30cm–1m (1–3ft)

Site: Sunny, sheltered and frost-free

Compost: Soil-based (John Innes No. 3) or soil-less, both with added grit

Use: Container, houseplant, sunny patio

vegetables

5 Brussels sprout, late
Brassica oleracea Gemmifera Group

As mid-season varieties finish cropping in early winter, late varieties, such as 'Wellington' and 'Fortress', extend supplies until spring. Hardy.

Site: Sun or light shade, sheltered. Deep, rich very firm soil, limed to pH7 or higher

How to grow: Sow in late April in a nursery bed outdoors and thin seedlings to 8cm (3in) apart. Transplant 60cm (2ft) apart each way when five to six weeks old. Water freely in dry weather; use a high-potash feed in midsummer only. Stake in windy sites. Remove yellow leaves and net against birds. Pull up whole stems for stripping indoors. Harvest leafy tops to eat as greens.

6 Cabbage, winter
Brassica oleracea Capitata Group

These often large plants have solid heads and a distinctive flavour. Many varieties have dark crinkled leaves, often tinted blue or red. Hardy.

Site: Sun. Rich firm soil, limed to pH7

How to grow: Sow in late April in a nursery bed outdoors and thin seedlings to 8cm (3in) apart. Transplant 50cm (20in) apart each way when six to eight weeks old. Water in dry weather and protect from birds. In exposed gardens earth up the stems for stability in early winter. Cut heads as required or pull up with the roots and suspend in a frost-free shed if bad weather is forecast. Use by early spring.

7 Celeriac
Apium graveolens var. rapaceum

Rugged vegetable with celery-flavoured bulbous stem. The firm flesh is delicious in winter stews or grated raw in salads. Hardy.

Site: Sun or light shade. Rich moist soil

How to grow: Sow indoors in mid-spring and prick out seedlings individually into cell trays or small pots. Plant out 30cm (12in) apart when about 8cm (3in) tall. Water freely in dry weather and mulch. Gently pull off lower leaves and any secondary growing tips every few weeks. Harvest from autumn onwards, when large enough, and leave in the ground over winter.

8 Chicory, heading
Cichorium intybus

Crunchy salad crop with a slightly bitter flavour. The large green 'sugar loaf' type and various red chicories, often called radicchio, are both outdoor crops for autumn and early winter, or throughout winter if grown under cover. Not fully hardy.

Site: Sun. Fertile and well-drained soil

How to grow: Sow in succession from April to July for harvesting from August to December. Plants can be sown *in situ* and thinned to 25–30cm (10–12in) apart each way; transplant midsummer thinnings to a coldframe or cool greenhouse for winter use. Water well in dry weather. Harvest complete heads as required.

9 Chicory, witloof
Cichorium intybus

This produces loose heads of leaves and thick roots that can be dug up and forced in an airing cupboard or cellar to produce fat buds called chicons. Surplus plants can be left to produce exquisite blue flowers the following year and may be transplanted to a wild garden. Hardy.

Site: Sun. Fertile and well-drained soil

How to grow: Sow outdoors in mid to late spring and thin seedlings to 23–25cm (9–10in) apart each way. Water well in dry weather. In early winter, dig up a few roots at a time, trim the thickest to 15cm (6in) long and cut off the leaves about 2–3cm (1in) from their base. Pack the roots upright in a box or pot of moist soil and put in a dark place; chicons will appear after three to six weeks in a warm place, twice that in a cool place. Cut when 10–15cm (4–6in) long; discard exhausted roots.

10 Claytonia
Montia perfoliata

An undemanding salad plant with succulent, mildly flavoured leaves, stems and flowers. This annual can self-sow and naturalise in the garden. Needs some shelter in cold gardens. Hardy.

Site: Sun or shade. Most soils

How to grow: For winter use, sow in August, indoors in cell trays or outdoors in rows 15cm (6in) apart. Plant out or thin to clusters 10–15cm (4–6in) apart, and transplant some seedlings to a coldframe or unheated greenhouse. Cut the whole plant when large enough, leaving a 2–3cm (1in) basal tuft of stems to regrow and provide several more pickings throughout winter. Can be sown in May for summer use.

vegetables (continued)

1 Kale

Brassica oleracea Acephala Group

This annual or biennial leaf crop often supplies juicy 'greens' when other vegetables have succumbed in a hard winter. Different varieties have plain, sometimes red-tinted leaves or curly green or rich red foliage that is tightly crimped like parsley. Hardy.

Site: Sun. Most, even light soils with added compost or rotted manure

How to grow: Sow outdoors in May in a nursery bed and thin seedlings to 8cm (3in) apart. Transplant when about eight weeks old, 60cm (2ft) apart and keep well watered. Surplus kale can be transplanted to flower borders for winter bedding. Pick young leaves and whole shoots regularly from November until April.

2 Land cress, upland cress

Barbarea verna

Biennial usually grown as an annual that resembles watercress but is a brighter green. Ready about eight weeks after sowing, it remains green all winter and can be used like spinach. Young shoots can be added to salads. Hardy.

Site: Most soils, with plenty of added compost

How to grow: Sow in July or August, indoors in cell trays or outdoors in rows 15cm (6in) apart, and thin or transplant 10–15cm (4–6in) apart. Transplant some seedlings to a coldframe or greenhouse or cover outdoor sowings with cloches where winters are very cold. Cut or pick young leaves. May also be sown in early spring for early summer crops.

3 Leek, late

Allium porrum

Versatile and richly flavoured undemanding crop that can withstand the harshest weather. Winter leek varieties are bulkier than early ones, with thicker squat stems and dark, sometimes steely blue or purple-tinted foliage; 'Cortina', 'Apollo', 'Giant Winter' and 'Bleu de Solaise' are all good. Hardy.

Site: Sun or light shade. Deep, rich soil with plenty of added compost

How to grow: Sow in late April and May in a nursery bed outdoors and thin seedlings to 4cm (1½in) apart. Plant out 20–23cm (8–9in) apart when 15–20cm (6–8in) tall, dropping each seedling into a 15cm (6in) deep hole made using a dibber. Water after planting and regularly throughout summer. Dig up leeks as needed from early winter onwards; when hard frost is likely, lift several plants, trim leaves and roots, and store in a cool, frost-free place, wrapped in newspaper.

4 Lettuce, winter
Lactuca sativa

Fresh lettuce can be available even in the depths of winter by using greenhouse varieties that are tolerant of short days and low light levels, such as 'Kellys', 'Novita' and 'Valdor'. In mild gardens these may be grown outdoors, preferably under cloches. Hardy.

Site: Sun. Moist and well-drained soil

How to grow: Sow in September in modular trays indoors and transplant 20–25cm (8–10in) apart each way when 5–8cm (2–3in) high. Keep moist, but avoid overwatering. Ventilate freely if under glass except in frosty weather. Cut either complete heads or a few leaves from each young plant as loose-leaf lettuce.

5 Parsnip
Pastinaca sativa

Sweetly flavoured and popular as a roast vegetable, parsnips are a reliable winter root that improves as the season progresses. Long varieties such as 'Tender and True' suit deep, light soils, but for shallow soils a shorter kind like 'Avonresister' is preferable. Always use fresh seeds, as they do not keep well. Hardy.

Site: Sun. Deeply dug soil that is not acid or recently manured

How to grow: Sow outdoors in March to May in rows 30cm (12in) apart and thin seedlings to 8–15cm (3–6in) apart, depending on the size of root required. Water regularly in dry weather to prevent splitting, and pull weeds by hand – hoeing can damage the tops of roots and admit canker disease. Start digging up roots in mid-autumn. To make lifting easier in a severe winter, cover rows with straw or leaves.

6 Radish, winter
Raphanus sativus

Although small summer radishes may still be available in a cold frame or greenhouse, the most reliable kinds for winter use are the large Spanish or Chinese varieties, such as 'China Rose' or red-fleshed 'Manhangtong', and the long white Japanese mooli or daikon. Flavour and use are as for summer radishes. Not fully hardy.

Site: Sun. Light soil

How to grow: Sow outdoors in August, in rows 25cm (10in) apart, and thin seedlings to about 15cm (6in) apart according to variety. Keep moist, but avoid over-watering. Crops are mature after about three months' growth and can be lifted as required.

7 Salsify
Tragopogon porrifolius

A biennial crop with delicious white-skinned roots for winter use and edible flower buds in summer followed by pretty purple daisy-like flowers. The roots are best skinned after cooking. High in insulin, a sugar acceptable to diabetics. Hardy.

Site: Sun. Deeply dug light soil, not recently manured

How to grow: Sow outdoors in April, in rows 15cm (6in) apart, and thin seedlings to 10cm (4in) apart. Keep well watered during dry weather, and feed with high-potash fertiliser in midsummer to encourage large roots. Start lifting as required from late autumn onwards; remaining roots can be left in the ground.

8 Scorzonera
Scorzonera hispanica

Winter crop with slim black-skinned roots that have a delicate, slightly nutty flavour and are high in insulin, a sugar acceptable to diabetics. Bright yellow summer flowers. Hardy.

Site: Sun. Deeply dug light soil, not recently manured

How to grow: As for salsify (see 7, Salsify). Plants can be left for a further year for larger roots, but older plants become woody.

9 Spinach, winter
Spinacia oleracea

Fast-growing annual leaf vegetable. Varieties such as 'Bergola' and 'Sigmaleaf' are available from December, but with cloche protection can be cropped throughout winter. In very cold gardens, perpetual spinach or spinach beet (see 7, Leaf beet, page 117) may be a more productive alternative. Hardy.

Site: Sun. Fertile, well-drained soil

How to grow: Sow outdoors in August and September, in rows 30cm (12in) apart, and thin seedlings to clusters 15cm (6in) apart. Keep well watered at all times. Cover with cloches from late October. Harvest a few leaves from each plant.

10 Swede
Brassica napus var. napobrassica

This sweet yellow-fleshed root needs a long growing season. Swedes can be overwintered in the ground, but keep their quality better if stored in boxes of sand. Ridging up surplus roots with soil in midwinter will produce young, semi-blanched 'spring greens'. Hardy.

Site: Sun or light shade. Rich, moist soil, limed to pH7

How to grow: Sow outdoors in June for winter use and in April for autumn use. Space rows 40cm (16in) apart and thin seedlings to 25cm (10in) apart. Water regularly in dry weather. Dig roots as required; lift for storing in early winter.

fruit

11 Rhubarb, forced
Rheum x hybridum

Established crowns are covered with cloches where they grow for early spring use, but can be forced in warmth and darkness for an even earlier harvest. Plants are useless after forcing, but divisions can be taken for replanting before forcing takes place. Hardy.

Site: Dark frost-free place

How to grow: Dig up two to three year old crowns in November. Leave on the soil surface exposed to frost for two to three weeks then pack side by side in soil, old potting compost, straw or leaves and put in a dark place. Water well and do not allow to dry out. Ready to harvest after five to six weeks at 10°C (50°F), or a little longer at lower temperatures.

choosing the best plants

The following plant lists draw on all the plants described in the preceding pages of the Plant Selector, but they are grouped together here to help you choose plants for particular conditions, situations and uses.

plants for acid soils

Plants in the following list that are marked with an asterisk* will only grow satisfactorily on soils that are free of lime. Other plants in the list thrive on acid soils, although they may also grow satisfactorily on soils that are neutral or to some degree alkaline.

- *Acer* (most)
- *Calluna vulgaris**
- *Camellia* (all)*
- *Chamaecyparis lawsoniana* (all)
- *Erica carnea* (all)
- *Erica* x *darleyensis* (all)
- *Erica erigena* 'Brightness'
- *Eucalyptus pauciflora* subsp. *niphophila*
- *Gaultheria mucronata* (all)*
- *Hamamelis* (all)
- *Leucothoe* Scarletta*
- *Parrotia persica*
- *Picea pungens* 'Hoopsii'
- *Rhododendron* (all)*
- *Salix daphnoides*
- *Sorbus* (most)
- *Stachyurus praecox**

plants for sandy or gravelly soil

The following plants require free drainage and are generally drought tolerant, although bulbs generally require a good supply of moisture in the growing season. The range of plants that can be grown in dry sunny gardens can be enlarged if the soil is improved by the addition of organic matter.

- *Anemone blanda*
- *Calluna vulgaris* (all)
- *Cotoneaster* (all)
- *Crocus* (most)
- *Iris* (most)
- *Juniperus* (all)
- *Pinus mugo* 'Mops'
- *Tulipa humilis* Violacea Group

plants for dry chalky soil

A large number of plants are automatically excluded from this list because they will not tolerate alkaline (limy) soil. The improvement of shallow chalky soil by the addition of moisture-retaining organic matter allows lime-tolerant but moisture-loving plants, notably hellebores and clematis, to be grown successfully. Some lime-loving plants, including many saxifrages, require plentiful moisture as well as gritty free-draining conditions.

- *Anemone blanda*
- *Aucuba japonica* 'Crotonifolia'
- *Bergenia*
- *Cornus mas*
- *Cotoneaster*
- *Crocus* (many)
- *Cyclamen coum*
- *Euonymus fortunei*
- *Iris* (all)
- *Juniperus communis*
- *Juniperus* x *pfitzeriana* 'WilhelmPfitzer'
- *Lonicera nitida* 'Baggesen's Gold'
- *Lonicera* x *purpusii* 'Winter Beauty'
- *Pinus mugo* 'Mops'
- *Pyracantha* (all)
- *Symphoricarpos* x *doorenbosii* 'White Hedge'
- *Taxus baccata*

Crocus imperati subsp. *imperati* 'De Jager'

plants for clay soil

Although the following plants generally succeed on close-textured clay soils, they do better when the ground has been improved by the addition of grit and organic matter such as garden compost.

- *Acer* (all)
- *Aucuba japonica* 'Crotonifolia'
- *Berberis* x *carminea* 'Buccaneer'
- *Bergenia* (all)
- *Chaenomeles* (all)
- *Chamaecyparis lawsoniana* (all)
- *Cornus* (all)
- *Cotoneaster* (all)
- *Euonymus* (all)
- *Forsythia giraldiana*
- *Galanthus* (most)
- *Garrya elliptica* 'James Roof'
- *Hamamelis* (all)
- *Hedera* (all)
- *Helleborus* (all)
- *Ilex* (all)
- *Juniperus* (all)
- *Lonicera* (all)
- *Mahonia* (all)
- *Malus* (all)
- *Prunus* (all)
- *Pyracantha* (all)
- *Salix* (all)
- *Sorbus* (all)
- *Taxus baccata* 'Fastigiata'
- *Viburnum* (all)

Viburnum x *bodnantense* 'Dawn'

plants for moist shade

The following plants thrive in moist soils and tolerate partial shade and, in a few cases, full shade. Many will also grow in full sun provided the soil is reliably moist.

- *Acer* (all)
- *Adonis amurensis*
- *Arum italicum* subsp. *italicum* 'Marmoratum'
- *Camellia* (all)
- *Cryptomeria japonica* 'Elegans Compacta'
- *Gaultheria mucronata* (all)
- *Hamamelis* (all)
- *Helleborus* (all)
- *Leucothoe* Scarletta
- *Mahonia japonica*
- *Mahonia* x *media* 'Winter Sun'
- *Nandina domestica* 'Fire Power'
- *Polystichum munitum*
- *Primula* Polyanthus Group
- *Pulmonaria angustifolia* 'Munstead Blue'
- *Pulmonaria rubra* 'Redstart'
- *Rhododendron* (all)
- *Rubus cockburnianus*
- *Sarcococca hookeriana* var. *digyna*
- *Skimmia japonica* 'Rubella'
- *Stachyurus praecox*
- *Viburnum davidii*
- *Viola* (all)

plants for ground cover

Close planting of shrubs and perennials can create a weed-excluding cover. However, effective cover can be achieved only by planting into soil from which every trace of perennial weed has been eliminated.

- *Bergenia* 'Ballawley'
- *Bergenia* x *schmidtii*
- *Calluna vulgaris* (all)
- *Chamaecyparis lawsoniana* 'Tamariscifolia'
- *Cotoneaster* 'Hybridus Pendulus'
- *Erica* (all)
- *Gaultheria mucronata* (all)
- *Hedera* (most)
- *Juniperus* x *pfitzeriana* 'Wilhelm Pfitzer'
- *Juniperus squamata* 'Blue Star'
- *Lonicera nitida* 'Baggesen's Gold'
- *Nandina domestica* 'Fire Power'

plants for coastal sites

Where windbreaks and hedges give protection from salt-laden winds, a wide range of plants can be grown in coastal gardens, including many that benefit from the sea's moderating influence on temperatures.

- *Anemone blanda*
- *Calluna vulgaris* (all)
- *Chaenomeles* (all)
- *Chamaecyparis lawsoniana* (all)
- *Cornus stolonifera* 'Flaviramea'
- *Crocus* (most)
- *Elaeagnus pungens* 'Maculata'
- *Erica* (all)
- *Euonymus fortunei* (all)
- *Garrya elliptica* 'James Roof'
- *Hippophae rhamnoides*
- *Ilex* x *altaclerensis* (all)
- *Ilex aquifolium* (all)
- *Iris* (most)
- *Juniperus* (all)
- *Lonicera nitida* 'Baggesen's Gold'
- *Pinus mugo* 'Mops'
- *Pyracantha* (all)
- *Quercus ilex*
- *Rhamnus alaternus* 'Argenteovariegata'
- *Salix alba* subsp. *vitellina* 'Britzensis'
- *Sorbus aucuparia* 'Beissneri'
- *Viburnum tinus*

flowers for cutting

Several spring-flowering shrubs and trees provide excellent material if cut judiciously in winter, while winter-flowering pansies and early bulbs suit small displays.

- *Abeliophyllum distichum*
- *Chaenomeles* (all)
- *Chimonanthus praecox*
- *Forsythia giraldiana*
- *Galanthus* (all)
- *Hamamelis* (all)
- *Helleborus niger*
- *Jasminum nudiflorum*
- *Mahonia japonica*
- *Narcissus* 'Cedric Morris'
- *Narcissus* 'Rijnveld's Early Sensation'
- *Primula* Polyanthus Group
- *Prunus incisa* 'February Pink'
- *Prunus* x *subhirtella* 'Autumnalis'
- *Viburnum* x *bodnantense* 'Dawn'
- *Viburnum davidii*

plants with aromatic foliage

In the case of many aromatic plants the scent of the leaves is only detectable when they are bruised.

- *Chamaecyparis lawsoniana*
- *Eucalyptus pauciflora* subsp. *niphophila*
- *Hedera colchica*
- *Pelargonium* (scented-leaved forms)
- *Picea mariana* 'Nana'
- *Picea pungens* 'Hoopsii'
- *Rhododendron* 'Praecox'
- Sage *(Salvia officinalis)*
- *Skimmia japonica* 'Rubella'
- *Thuja occidentalis* 'Rheingold'

trees for small gardens

None of the following plants is really suitable for very small gardens, but some can be grown as large shrubs rather than as trees.

- *Acer griseum*
- *Acer grosseri* var. *hersii*
- *Acer pensylvanicum* 'Erythrocladum'
- *Arbutus* x *andrachnoides*
- *Chamaecyparis lawsoniana* 'Ellwoodii'
- *Cornus mas*
- *Cotoneaster* 'Hybridus Pendulus'
- *Cryptomeria japonica* 'Elegans Compacta'
- *Eucalyptus pauciflora* subsp. *niphophila*
- *Garrya elliptica* 'James Roof'
- *Hamamelis* x *intermedia* (all)
- *Hamamelis mollis*
- *Ilex* (most)
- *Malus* 'Winter Gold'
- *Prunus* (most)
- *Salix daphnoides*

Prunus incisa 'February Pink'

gardening basics

Gardening will always be easier and more pleasurable if you get the basics right. Ensuring that you have the right tools for each job, and looking after them carefully, will make even the heaviest tasks more enjoyable. Understanding the type of soil you have is crucial to successful planting, and learning how to improve it by careful composting and mulching, watering and feeding, will make sure you are handsomely rewarded for your efforts. You can protect the plants you have nurtured, and even extend their growing season, by using cloches and coldframes in your garden. And after the hard work, take some time to sit back and enjoy the fruits of your labour – a garden you can enjoy all year round.

tools & equipment

Looking after a garden is easier and more pleasurable when you have the right tools for the job you are doing. A bewildering range is available, but all you need to get started is a simple kit of a few good-quality tools.

essential tools

A few basic tools will enable you to accomplish most garden tasks, but some extra items designed for particular jobs will add versatility to your tool kit. You may also want to try out a few more specialised items of equipment, some of which you may eventually find indispensable. A fertiliser spreader, for instance, could prove a worthwhile investment (see page 589) if you have a large lawn to feed but little spare time. And if you want to grow plants from seed or take cuttings, you will need propagation tools and equipment (see pages 590–1).

Cultivation tools are described on pages 584–5, pruning tools on pages 586–7 and lawn tools on pages 588–9.

the basic kit

The equipment shown here is described in detail on the following pages:

- spade (see page 584)
- fork (see page 584)
- trowel (see page 585)
- secateurs (see page 586)
- lawnmower (see page 588)
- watering can (see page 587)
- pocket knife (see page 587)
- gardening gloves (see opposite)

useful extras

The following additional tools and equipment will almost certainly be useful:

- rake (see page 584)
- hoe (see page 584)
- shears (see page 587)
- hand fork (see page 585)
- hand cultivator (see page 585)
- bucket (see page 587)
- hosepipe (see page 589)

buying tools

Durable, well-made tools are a pleasure to handle and can make light work of gardening tasks, so always buy the best you can afford. Anything less will prove a false economy, especially for the tools you rely on most, such as your spade.

Make sure the tool is right for the job and ask for advice if you are in doubt. Before buying, test it for comfort, balance, size and weight; a tool that is too heavy will be tiring to use over a long period of time, while a handle that is too short or long for you can cause wrist or back injury.

Compare the relative merits of the different materials the tool may be made of. For example, wooden handles are more shock-absorbent than metal ones. Stainless steel or teflon-coated blades, although more expensive, are easier to use and to clean, especially if you garden on clay.

gardening gloves

Often overlooked, these are invaluable for messy work and essential when handling prickly plants or applying garden chemicals. Two pairs are ideal: one of suede or supple leather for general use, and a thicker pair for rough work.

caring for tools

Tools that are regularly cleaned and neatly stored are always ready for use.

- **allocate storage space** for each tool where it is easily accessible and cannot be damaged. Suspend large items with cutting edges, such as spades and hoes, from hooks or clips on a wall or door and keep smaller tools together in a drawer or a box.
- **clean all tools after use.** Scrape or brush off soil and plant debris, especially from the handles, where hardened soil can cause discomfort during use. Wipe metal blades with an oily rag to prevent rust.
- **keep cutting tools sharp.** Pruning equipment needs regular honing to keep it sharp so that it cuts without damaging the plant, and without undue effort. Spade and hoe blades are easier to use if you hammer out any dents that may form and occasionally file the edge sharp.

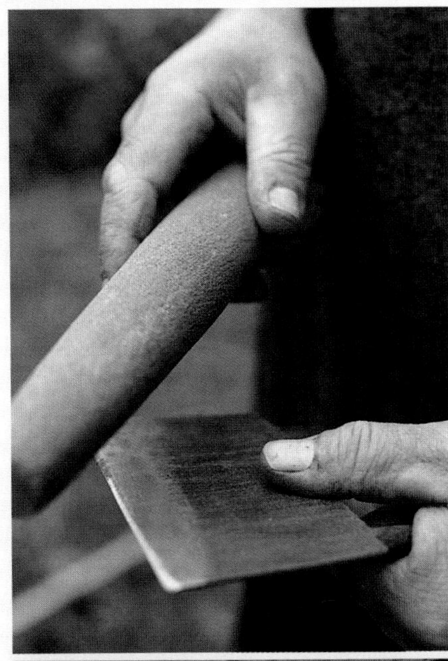

Regular use of a sharpening stone will keep blades sharp, making spades and hoes easier to use (top).

Fix purpose-made hooks or brackets to make the most of hanging space around the walls and doors of a shed (above).

- **clean, sharpen and oil or grease** all metal parts.
- **at the end of the growing season,** inspect tools before storing them over winter. Clean them all thoroughly. Check and repair or replace damaged handles, and wipe those made of wood with linseed oil.

hiring tools

Gardening equipment, especially larger or occasionally used items such as rotavators, hedgetrimmers and powered lawn rakes can be hired, saving you the cost and trouble of purchase and maintenance, as well as storage space. Book equipment in advance, particularly at busy times of year, and check if the hire firm can arrange delivery and collection if necessary. Inspect the tool's condition before accepting delivery or signing a hiring contract. Make sure you are shown how to use it safely if it is unfamiliar, and check whether any protective clothing is advisable.

Keep frequently used small tools and items of equipment, such as secateurs, trowel and sharpening stones, readily to hand (above).

tools & equipment/2

cultivation tools

Several versatile tools are designed for soil preparation, planting and weeding tasks. Stainless steel models, especially of spades and forks, are more expensive but easier to use and to clean.

spades, forks and rakes

• **spade** Used primarily for digging, making planting holes and moving or mixing soil, a spade is also useful for skimming off weeds, tidying border edges and mixing compost. The blade – of stainless, forged or coated steel – is attached to a wooden or metal shaft fitted with a plastic or wooden D or T-shaped handle. In a good-quality spade, the blade and tubular neck are forged from a single piece of metal for strength, and the blade has a tread for comfort.

Standard spades have a 28 x 20cm (11 x 8in) blade and a 70cm–1m (2ft 4in–3ft) shaft, but a border spade has a smaller blade for working in small spaces or where a lighter model is better.

• **fork** A garden fork is used for general cultivation work, such as breaking down soil after digging, pricking over and loosening the surface. It can also be used for moving or lifting crops, plants and bulky manure. Most forks have four metal prongs, or tines, forged from a single piece of metal, and are fitted with the same kinds of shafts and handles as spades. On a standard fork, the head or tines are 30 x 20cm (12 x 8in) long, but a border fork has smaller tines.

TOOL TIP Gardeners who find digging and cultivating difficult may find a spade and fork with special cranked handles or a spade with a sprung blade useful.

• **rake** A soil rake is used for levelling and surface preparation, especially when making a seedbed. The long wooden or plastic-covered metal handle is attached to a steel head fitted with forged steel tines. As you move the head backwards and forwards over soil, the tines loosen the surface and break up lumps as you level the ground. Held in a more upright position, a rake can be used to comb stones and weeds across the surface. Once you have prepared a seedbed, you can turn the rake over and use a corner to draw out a drill for sowing. Cover seeds by drawing soil over them with the back of the rake, then tamp the head along the row, holding the rake upright.

Border fork (top) and rake (above).

using a fork or spade

- keep your back straight
- insert the full head vertically into the soil to its maximum depth
- when lifting soil or plants, steady the handle with one hand and move the other close to the head
- clean the head regularly during use by plunging it into a bucket of sand or scraping it with a flat piece of wood or a paint scraper

hoes

There are many kinds of hoe, but the most important are the dutch, or push, hoe and the draw, or swan-necked, hoe. These can be used for making sowing drills and covering seeds with soil, as well as for weeding. Choose one you can use without bending your back.

• **dutch hoe** The flat rectangular blade is attached to a long handle at a slight angle. To loosen soil and destroy weeds while still small, push the hoe to and fro, with the blade just below the surface, as you walk backwards.

Dutch hoe (left) and draw hoe (right).

• **draw hoe** The rectangular or semi-circular head, joined to the handle at a right angle, is used to chop out weeds and break up the surface while moving forwards. It is also good for scraping off stones and earthing up potatoes.

other types of hoe

• **tined hoe** The curved prongs of this hoe are effective for deeper cultivation as well as for weeding.

• **onion hoe** This is a short-handled draw hoe to weed between close-spaced plants.

hand tools

• **trowel** This small tool is used for surface cultivation – planting, removing weeds, loosening the soil surface and marking out seed drills – as well as for measuring small amounts of soil, compost or fertiliser. The rounded, tapering blade, sometimes with cranked neck, is fitted with a 10–15cm (4–6in) wooden or plastic handle. Make sure that the head is forged from a single piece of steel and fitted to the handle with a separate ring or ferrule.

• **hand fork** Of similar construction and size to a trowel, this has three or four flattened tines and is used for weeding in confined spaces, lifting young plants and lightly cultivating small areas such as pots, window boxes and growing bags.

• **hand cultivator** This tined tool is used to loosen and aerate soil between plants and in spaces where a hoe cannot reach.

• **bulb planter** Used to bore holes in soil or a lawn when planting bulbs, this can save time when transplanting small pot-grown plants, which often neatly fit the 8cm (3in) wide holes, or even planting potatoes. It is a tapering steel cylinder attached to a short or long handle at one end, with cutting teeth at the other.

garden line

A garden line is simply two canes or spikes joined by a length of plastic twine, sometimes sold knotted at intervals to help identify distances.

cultivating a large area

Petrol-powered rotavators or cultivators are excellent for tilling a larger garden, turning in weeds and mixing in manure or compost. Attachments are available for earthing up, making seedbeds and tilling between crops. Most machines can be set to work at different depths and some have adjustable handles, allowing you to walk to one side on uncultivated soil. Buy a sturdy, easily managed model, suited to the size of the garden, and maintain it regularly, or hire an appropriate type and cultivate as much ground as possible in one go.

When working the soil, you will need a rake and hoe as well as a garden spade and fork. A garden line, used to mark out seed drills and areas of soil for digging, can be made from two spikes and some brightly coloured nylon string.

Hand trowel and fork (left), hand cultivator (above) and bulb planter (right).

tools & equipment/3

Clockwise from left: tree pruners on fixed pole; pruning saw; bow saw; garden shears; one-handed shears; anvil loppers; bypass loppers; folding pruning saw; bypass secateurs.

Select the best secateurs you can afford (inset); if you have a lot of woody shrubs, anvil types (right) may be a better choice than bypass (left).

pruning and maintenance

Having the right tools for routine jobs like pruning, watering and tidying will make them seem less of a chore.

secateurs and loppers

The two main types of secateurs are for use on stems up to 1cm (½in) thick. Ratchet types can make cutting easier, as does a rubber stop fitted between the handles. Before buying, check that hand grips are comfortable and fit the span of your hand when open. Avoid cheap models, which are suitable only for light work. Left-handed models are available.

- **bypass secateurs** Operating with a scissors action, these are used for most kinds of pruning, deadheading and trimming plants to size and shape.
- **anvil secateurs** A single sharp blade cuts against a flat surface, making these ideal for cutting hard, woody stems.
- **loppers** These are long-handled pruners for cutting stems up to about 2.5cm (1in) in diameter. They are fitted with anvil or bypass secateur heads, often with a ratchet to reduce the effort needed to cut hard, thick stems. Test for balance and weight before buying.
- **tree loppers or long-arm pruners** The cutting heads are on the end of fixed or extending poles up to 5m (15ft) long.

saws

- **pruning saw** A fixed or folding pruning saw will cut branches thicker than 2.5cm (1in) in diameter. The straight or curved handle and blade are designed for easy access in confined places between branches. Unlike wood-working saws, the large toughened teeth often cut only on the pulling stroke.
- **bow saw** This consists of a disposable blade tensioned between the ends of a bent tubular handle. It is used for the largest tree branches.

powered hedgetrimmers

An electric or petrol-powered hedge-trimmer can save time and effort if you have a large hedge to clip. They are available to buy or hire. Fitted with either single or double-sided reciprocating blades, these powerful machines require great care during use. Always keep power cables safely out of the way, and use a circuit breaker. Wear thick gloves, goggles or a face guard, and ear defenders.

Good-quality carrying equipment will make gardening less tiring. Shown here is a pneumatic-tyred wheelbarrow with galvanised watering can and bucket, plastic carrying sheet and bags, and an all-purpose black carrier made of recycled materials.

shears

- **garden shears** Lightweight and heavy-duty models are available for trimming hedges, shrubs and small areas of grass. Straight-edged kinds are easy to sharpen and maintain, while those with wavy cutting edges are effective for cutting thicker stems, but need care with sharpening. Some shears have long or extending handles for greater reach. Test a pair for weight and balance before buying.
- **one-handed shears** Sprung to open automatically, these are useful for light trimming, deadheading and for cutting small areas of grass. They may be fitted with swivelling blades to adjust the angle of cut.

garden knives

- **pruning knife** This has a curved, folding blade and is used for trimming off thin sideshoots, cleaning up the edges of pruning wounds and taking cuttings.
- **pocket knife** A sharp pocket knife has a multitude of uses, from cutting string and opening bags of fertiliser to trimming and pruning plants (see page 591). Most models have a blade that folds away.

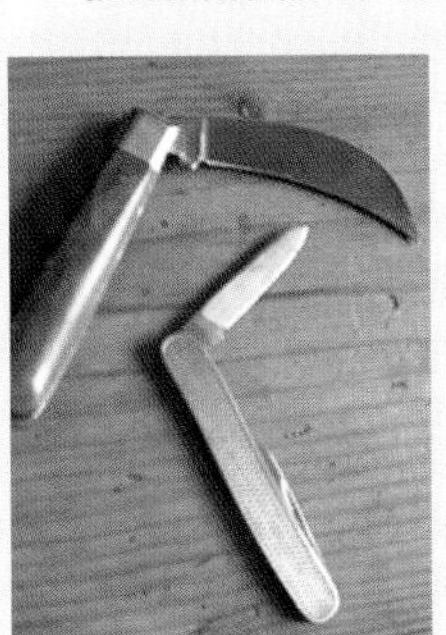

Pruning knife and pocket knife.

carrying equipment

- **bucket** This indispensable and versatile item can be used for carrying materials, storing water and soaking plants, and can even double up as improvised seating. Plastic buckets are cheaper than metal ones, but have a shorter life.
- **carrying sheets and bags** Made of tear-proof woven plastic, carrying sheets and bags are useful for tidying the garden and for carrying prunings, trimmings and soft weeds. They are light and easily stored.
- **watering can** Made of plastic or metal, watering cans come in several sizes, often with volume levels marked on the side. For general use, choose one that holds 9 litres (2 gallons), but for the greenhouse choose a lighter 4.5 litre (1 gallon) model with a long spout. You will need two roses (sprinkler heads): fine for watering seeds and seedlings, and coarse for general watering. Buy the largest you can carry comfortably when full. Make sure it has a large enough opening for easy filling.
- **wheelbarrow** Useful for transporting heavy materials such as soil, compost and larger tools, wheelbarrows are made of plastic or metal. They are usually fitted with a single wheel; for frequent use over long distances, a pneumatic tyre is more comfortable than a solid one. Two-wheeled barrows are more stable on uneven ground. Some models can be fitted with side extensions for carrying leaves, and collapsible models are also available for use where storage space is limited.
- **trug** An elegant, lightweight container, a trug is useful for carrying garden tools as well as for transporting cut flowers and freshly harvested produce. Treat wooden trugs annually with preservative or linseed oil to keep them in good condition.

Watering can roses and a wooden garden trug.

tools & equipment/4

caring for lawns

A range of specialised lawn-care tools is available to help keep a lawn looking good throughout the growing season. A lawnmower and other cutting tools are essential for keeping grass under control, while additional tools are designed to keep it healthy.

lawnmowers

The type and size of lawnmower you need will depend on the size of your lawn, your budget and how much effort you want to put into mowing. Mowers are generally defined by their cutting action and how they are powered.

cutting action

- **cylinder mowers** These have a number of blades arranged in a spiral to form a rotating cylinder. Cutting occurs as the blades pass close to a fixed blade set just below the cylinder, rather like the action of scissor blades. The quality of the cut depends on the rotation speed of the cylinder, how closely the rotating blades are passing the fixed blade and the number of blades on the cylinder – the more blades, the finer the cut.

Mains electricity-powered cylinder mower.

- **rotary mowers** A single blade or several blades, made from toughened metal or a hardened plastic, rotate horizontally at high speed, slicing through the grass. The effectiveness of the cut depends on the speed of rotation and the blades' sharpness.

Both types of mower produce a good finish if used correctly, but only rotary mowers are able to cope with cutting down long grass. Both will also produce a striped effect if equipped with a roller behind the cutting blades – stripes result not from the cutting action but from the roller pressing down the grass.

means of power

The models discussed here are all walk-behind mowers; ride-on mowers are too large for the average garden.

- **non-powered cylinder mowers** are driven entirely by human energy. They have a restricted cutting width of 25–45cm (10–18in) and can be tiring to use, especially on a large lawn, but are useful for a small grassed area.
- **petrol or diesel-powered mowers** are fitted with a two or four-stroke engine. Models may be cylinder, rotary or rotary hover (which float just above the ground rather than rely on wheels).
- **mains electricity-powered mowers** have a heavy-duty electric motor, and cylinder, rotary and rotary hover types are all available. They can be light to use, but there must be a handy power socket and the working area is restricted by the length of cable. It is important to follow a cutting pattern to avoid accidental damage to the cable, which can get in the way; always use a residual circuit breaker (RCB) in case of accidents.
- **battery-operated cylinder mowers** incorporate a motor and a heavy-duty battery, with a charger. The weight of the battery tends to make this type of mower heavier than others.

Edging shears (top) and strimmer (above).

other cutting tools

An assortment of cutting implements has been designed for specific trimming jobs around lawn edges and for awkward places where lawnmowers cannot be used.

- **strimmers** These light, hand-held machines are useful for trimming long grass around trees or in difficult corners. Powered by a two-stroke petrol engine or mains electricity, they cut through grass using a length of nylon cord rotating horizontally at high speed.
- **shears** With straight handles set as an extension of the cutting blades, garden shears (see page 587) cut like scissors. They are useful for grass where the mower cannot reach. Edging shears have long handles set at right angles to the cutting blades and are used from a standing position to trim grass growing over the lawn edge.
- **half-moon edger** With a curved metal blade mounted onto a spade shaft and handle, the half-moon edging tool is used to trim lawn edges and cut turf.

Seep hose

lawn watering equipment

Watering a lawn in dry weather is essential to keep it looking green throughout the summer.

hosepipes

• **hosepipe** For larger gardens, a hosepipe will prove invaluable. The best kind is reinforced with nylon, which prevents kinking and increases its life; make sure it will reach to the end of the garden. You need an appropriate connector to attach it to a tap and possibly a spray nozzle for the other end. A wall-mounted reel is convenient for storing and a freestanding reel on wheels for storing and moving the hose around.

• **leaky pipe and seep hose** These perforated hosepipes can be laid on a lawn and moved around every so often to deliver a fine spray or a gentle trickle of water. They are less wasteful of water than sprinklers.

sprinklers

Attached to the end of a hosepipe, a sprinkler is convenient for watering a large area of grass.

• **static sprinklers** spray a circular area of the lawn.

• **oscillating sprinklers** revolve or swing from side to side and cover a large area; their reach can be adjusted.

• **travelling sprinklers** creep slowly across the lawn, powered by the water flow.

• **'pop up' sprinklers** are permanently installed below lawns and rock gardens; they remain out of sight until water pressure pushes them above ground.

Clockwise from top left: hollow-tined aerator; lawn scarifier; fertiliser spreader; lawn rake; leaf blower.

lawn health

To stay green and healthy, grass needs more attention than simply mowing. Debris in the form of moss or dead grass builds up over time and needs to be removed, as do fallen leaves in the autumn. Lawns also benefit from being aerated.

• **aerator** This introduces air into the soil and aerates grass roots. It consists of a set of tines or blades held in a frame; these are simply pushed into the ground all over the lawn. Some have hollow tines, which remove tiny cores of soil that can be replaced with a top-dressing or sand, if required.

• **scarifier** A scarifier will remove surface debris and dead grass. It is pushed over the lawn, rotating a series of tines or blades that rake through the grass.

• **fertiliser spreader** To feed a large area of lawn, this drum on wheels is a great asset. When it is pushed along, rotating blades below the drum spray out the granular fertiliser for up to 1m (3ft) on either side.

• **lawn rake** With spring tines arranged in a fan shape, this tool is ideal for raking out moss, collecting leaves and removing surface debris.

• **leaf blower or vacuum** This hand-held machine incorporates a strong fan powered by a two-stroke petrol engine or mains electricity. It blows leaves and debris into one area or sucks them into a chamber or bag within the machine. A push-along leaf sweeper is available too, whose rotating stiff bristles are driven by the land wheels. It collects leaves, debris and dead grass but is not very effective if leaves and grass are wet.

tools & equipment/5

propagation equipment

When sowing seed and taking cuttings, the right compost (see page 599) and equipment, with a few specialised tools, will increase your chances of success.

containers

• **pots** Stock up with a selection of pots, ranging in size from 6–8cm (2½–3in) for individual seedlings and cuttings to 20–25cm (8–10in) for large plants and greenhouse shrubs. Square pots hold more compost than round ones and pack closer together on the greenhouse staging. Extra-deep pots (growing tubes or long toms) are for long-rooted seedlings such as sweet peas.

A selection of plastic seed trays, including modular trays and cellular inserts, are shown here, together with plastic pots, long paper tubes and degradable coir pots standing in a home-made wooden seed tray.

home-made seed trays

You can make your own sturdy seed trays from wooden slats. They need to be 4cm (1½in) deep for sowing, but for pricked out seedlings 7cm (2½in) deep trays will allow stronger root systems to develop.

Pots can be made from plastic or clay, but degradable pots made of peat, coir or paper are ideal for propagating plants that resent root disturbance, as they are planted out with their contents to gradually decompose in the soil.

• **trays** Full or half-size trays are usually shallow and made of thin plastic that lasts for only a few seasons. Most can be fitted with a clear lid for germinating seeds and rooting cuttings. Some are divided into 6, 12 or more cells for growing plants separately, or can be fitted with cellular inserts (modules) for sowing large seeds or pricking out individual seedlings.

Terracotta pans for raising alpines.

• **pans** Like pots but only a third or half as deep, pans are useful for sowing seeds and raising shallow-rooted, slow-growing plants like alpines and dwarf bulbs.

A metal compost tidy separates off an area of staging for potting up. Also useful are rooting hormone, diluted copper fungicide, long-spouted small watering can, mister, sieve and scoop.

other items

• **rooting hormone** The lower tips of cuttings are dipped in this liquid or powdered hormone suspension to aid rooting. Do not contaminate, store in a refrigerator and discard after a year.

• **copper fungicide** This powdered or liquid concentrate is diluted, then watered onto seedlings and freshly sown seeds as protection against damping-off and other fungal diseases.

• **scoop** A compost scoop is handy for decanting compost from large bags.

• **sieve** A meshed sieve, or riddle, is used to separate coarse compost or soil from finer particles, especially when covering seeds and preparing a seedbed. Buy sieves with different meshes or buy one with a selection of graded inserts. Wire mesh is more durable than plastic.

• **knife** A folding pocket knife, or craft knife with disposable blades, is essential for cuttings. Keep it dry and very sharp, and sterilise the blade after use.

• **dibber** This slim, tapered tool is used when transplanting seedlings to make holes in compost. Some kinds have a two-pronged fork at the other end for separating and lifting seedlings. Larger dibbers, sheathed with a metal nose, are for planting and transplanting outdoors. Improvise with a pencil under glass and sharpened broken spade handle outdoors.

• **widger** Shaped like a narrow, fluted spatula, this is useful for lifting out seedlings and rooted cuttings without disturbing their neighbours.

• **labels** You will need a supply of plastic labels and a soft lead pencil to identify seeds and seedlings. Brightly coloured ones are useful if you wish to distinguish between batches of plants. Labels used outdoors must be weather-resistant and conspicuous; use a waterproof marker.

• **thermometers** Temperature levels are important under glass, especially in a propagator, where the right amount of heat can be critical for germination. Use a maximum-minimum thermometer to record the daily range of temperatures, and a soil thermometer to test composts, cuttings beds in propagating cases and outdoor seedbeds.

• **propagator** For a controlled environment in which to root cuttings and germinate seedlings, a propagator is almost essential. The simplest type is a clear plastic-covered box that takes a few seed trays. Electrically heated propagating trays are available for use on windowsills. The most sophisticated type is a large frame for staging, fitted with a hinged lid, soil heating cable and thermostat, and automatic misting unit.

• **glass** Small panes of clear glass are useful for covering pots and trays of seeds to prevent them from drying out.

• **plastic bags** Keep a stock of new or used clear bags to enclose pots and trays of cuttings to keep humidity levels high.

Capillary matting is laid over plastic sheeting on the staging (right). It absorbs water from a reservoir at the side so that the pots and trays standing on it can take up moisture as required.

Thermometers, plant labels and pocket knife are invaluable for sowing and propagating under glass.

watering equipment

• **water trays** These are useful for pots and trays that need watering from below. You can buy purpose-made shallow plastic trays or use an old roasting tin.

• **long-spouted watering can** A small watering can with a long spout fitted with a very fine rose is ideal for gently watering seed trays and seedlings and for reaching over the staging.

• **mister** Several 500ml (1 pint) hand sprays will be useful for misting cuttings and young plants. Keep one filled with water and others, labelled, for copper fungicide solution or diluted liquid feed.

• **capillary matting** This reduces the need to water and is useful if you are away for any length of time.

understanding your soil

We cannot all achieve the perfect loam treasured by gardeners, but we can go a long way towards improving our soil, provided we understand it and know how to treat it.

soil type and texture

Soil is the raw material of a garden, made up of four basic components: sand, silt, clay and organic material. The varying proportions of these will determine soil texture and how well plants grow.

You need to know what type of soil you are dealing with and its pH value (acidity/alkalinity), as this will influence how you cultivate the soil and the time of year you do it. Heavy clay soils are best cultivated in autumn before they become too wet, and sandy soils in late winter and spring. The pH will to an extent dictate the plants you can grow – you should avoid trying to grow acid-loving plants on chalk soil, for example. You can test the pH using a kit; it is a good idea to take samples from different areas of the garden.

- **sandy soils** are at least 70 per cent sand and gravel and no more than 15 per cent clay. The colour varies, depending on their organic matter content. They are very free-draining and often lack fertility, but do have the advantage of warming up quickly in spring. They feel gritty when rubbed between finger and thumb.
- **clay soils** contain at least 45 per cent clay, and less than 40 per cent sand. Their high water-holding capacity means they drain slowly; some are prone to waterlogging. Most are quite fertile and good at holding plant nutrients, but they can be difficult to cultivate and are slow to warm up in spring. They have a smooth, soapy texture when moistened and rubbed between finger and thumb.
- **chalky soils** have a high concentration of chalk or limestone (it may be visible as pieces of rock) and are often shallow, with soil depth less than 30cm (12in) over the rock below. They can be very fertile and are usually biologically active, with high populations of worms and beneficial bacteria. They tend to be free-draining, but high pH limits the range of plants they can support.
- **peaty soils** are correctly termed 'organic' as a relatively high level of organic matter (minimum 15 per cent) influences their characteristics. They are good at retaining water and can be very fertile (unless they are pure peat). Although this type of soil is usually associated with plants that love acid conditions, there are many alkaline organic soils. They are crumbly and fibrous when handled.
- **silty soils,** often referred to as loams, contain at least 70 per cent silt with a clay content below 12 per cent. Many gardeners view these as ideal soils. They are usually good at holding water and are also free-draining, fertile, productive and easier to work than other types. They are smooth but slightly gritty when moistened and rubbed between finger and thumb.

soil testing

1 **Following the instructions with** the kit, use an old spoon or a trowel to dig up a sample of moist soil from the top 15cm (6in) and place it on a sheet of absorbent paper. With the back of the trowel or spoon, crush the sample lightly to break down lumps, and remove and discard any stones or roots. Put a measured amount of soil into the test tube with a measured amount of test chemical, and add distilled water to the level indicated on the tube. Seal the top and shake the contents vigorously for about a minute, then allow the solution in the tube to settle and clear.

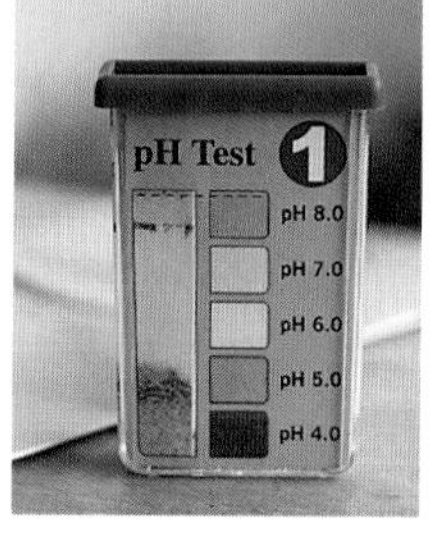

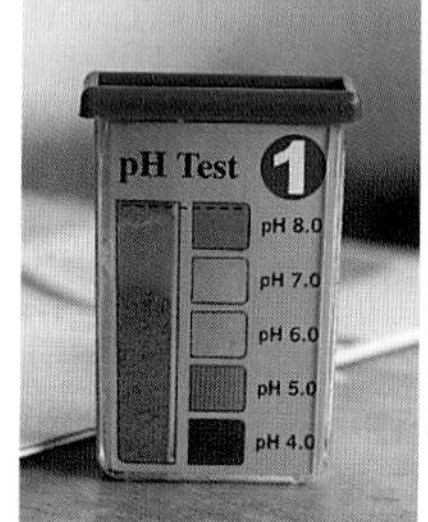

2 **The liquid will gradually** change colour as it settles. Check its final colour against the pH indicator card to get a reasonably accurate reading of the lime content in the soil. The three samples tested above show a range of soils from the acid end of neutral to the alkaline.

pH scale

0	1	2	3	4	5	6	7	8	9	10	11	12	13	14
acid						neutral								alkaline

understanding pH values

Whether soil is acid, alkaline or neutral will determine the range of plants that can be grown in it. Acidity and alkalinity are measured using the pH scale, which ranges from 0–14; pH 7 is neutral, neither acid nor alkaline (see opposite).

Most natural soils range from pH 4 to pH 9; few plants grow in soil with pH above 9 or below 4. Gardeners usually aim at a soil of pH 6.5–7 to ensure they can grow the maximum range of plants.

TESTING TIP Avoid handling soil samples with your bare hands as the pH of your skin may affect the final reading.

adding lime

Lime raises the pH and neutralises soil acidity. This often benefits plant growth because many plant nutrients are more readily available when there is lime present in the soil, and many soil organisms can only function well in a soil where there is lime. Ideally, lime should be added to the soil after digging but before it is cultivated down to a finer tilth – this ensures that the lime is evenly distributed. Apply lime in small quantities rather than run the risk of overliming.

single digging

The most commonly practised form of digging cultivates the soil to the depth of a spade blade (called a spit), usually about 25–30cm (10–12in) deep. Cultivation is concentrated in the area where most plant roots naturally grow, in the top 10–20cm (4–8in) of soil.

If the plot is large, mark out the extent to be dug using canes and a garden line, then dig a trench at one end (see right). A new trench is created each time a section of the plot is dug. Repeat this process until the entire plot has been dug. Keep your back as straight as possible when lifting spadefuls of soil.

single digging

YOU WILL NEED

• garden line and canes to mark out plot (optional) • spade • fork to loosen soil • wheelbarrow

1 **Dig the first trench** to one spade width and one spade depth.

2 **Place the soil** from this trench in a wheelbarrow and take it to the far end of the plot – or place it in a corner of the plot. It will be used to fill in the final trench.

3 **Dig a second trench,** adjacent to the first, and throw the soil from the second trench into the first. (You can put manure or garden compost in the bottom of the trench first, if you wish to improve the soil's texture). Turn each block of soil upside down as it is moved, so that the surface soil goes into the bottom of the trench to cover weeds and prevent new weed seeds from germinating.

4 **Continue to dig** trenches across the whole plot. Use the soil from the wheelbarrow to fill the last trench.

understanding your soil/2

improving soil structure

Structure is the term given to the way the individual particles of soil bond together in clusters. If soil particles are fine, they are packed together so that water drains through slowly and the soil stays wet. By adding organic materials the structure can be improved by 'opening' the soil, allowing air and water to penetrate. Conversely, if a soil is too open (drains too quickly), adding organic matter will help the soil particles to stick together more closely, allowing the soil to hold more water.

why add organic matter?

Animal manures and fresh green plant waste provide small amounts of nutrients quite quickly, mainly nitrogen (N), phosphate (P) and potash (K). However, fibrous and woody materials are much better for improving soil structure and 'opening' heavy soils, while on lighter, free-draining soils, they improve moisture retention. The ideal garden compost is a mixture of the two (see page 596).

All bulky organic materials have low levels of nutrients when compared with inorganic concentrated fertilisers, but as the organic matter rots, it produces organic acids that dissolve nutrients already in the soil, making them available to plants.

- **for green manure,** grow borage, comfrey, mustard, red clover or ryegrass and dig into the top soil when the plants are six to eight weeks old. This will improve organic matter and nutrient levels, particularly nitrogen content, and smother germinating weeds.

ORGANIC MATTER TIP For maximum nutrient benefit from bulky organic materials such as manures, incorporate them into the soil when they have only partly rotted. The longer they are stored, the lower their nutritional value, because nutrients can leech away.

improving soil fertility

A healthy, fertile soil must have a biologically active community of different organisms, capable of releasing and recycling nutrients so that plants can feed. For this activity to take place, there must be a balance between the amount of air in the soil (so that the beneficial organisms can live) and water (so that chemical changes can take place).

Time the application of manures, organic mulches or fertilisers so plants gain maximum benefit, applying them either just as growth starts as a base dressing, or part-way through the growing cycle as a top dressing. Apply dry fertilisers to moist soil, as plants absorb nutrients in soluble form.

Bear in mind that over-feeding with high concentrations of fertilisers and manures can severely damage or kill plants by chemically burning their roots.

adding mulches

ORGANIC MULCHES ARE USED TO:

- **suppress weeds;** the mulch needs to be at least 8cm (3in) deep to block out the light.
- **reduce moisture loss;** the mulch needs to be at least 5cm (2in) deep.
- **improve soil fertility** by encouraging high levels of biological activity while the organic material is broken down and incorporated into the soil's upper layers.

FOR BEST RESULTS:

- **in order to work well,** mulches should be spread evenly over the soil, and left to work their way into it. This is particularly important on heavy soil. If they are dug in, decomposition stops due to lack of oxygen. The soil structure may also be damaged when digging takes place.

the benefits of digging

Digging over vacant ground within flower borders and vegetable plots at least once each year is a good way of incorporating organic matter into the soil, improving drainage and root penetration. It is the most effective way of preparing the soil for the next growing season and also keeps the garden tidy by burying unwanted plant waste and weeds. However, especially when soil is being brought back into cultivation from a neglected state, disturbing the soil in this way will lead to the emergence of weeds, as most of their dormant seeds will start to germinate once exposed to daylight.

For shallow-rooted plants, it may not be necessary to dig to a greater depth than about 30cm (12in) unless the soil is compacted or badly drained. For single digging, see page 593.

double digging

This technique is often used where a hard sub-surface layer of soil has formed, or on land that is being cultivated for the first time. It involves digging to the equivalent depth of two spade blades (see opposite). The aim is to improve the crumbliness of the subsoil without bringing it up to the surface, while keeping the most biologically active layer of soil (the topsoil) close to the young roots of the plants. This makes it a useful technique for an area where long-term, deeper-rooted plants, such as roses, shrubs, trees or fruit bushes, are to be grown. The benefits of double digging a plot can last for up to 15 years.

DOUBLE DIGGING TIP Avoid mixing the subsoil with the topsoil. If the two are mixed together, the fertility of the topsoil is diluted, rather than the fertility of the subsoil improved.

double digging

1 Mark out the plot with canes and line, and remove the turf. Dig a trench 60cm (2ft) wide and one spade deep, then place the soil from this trench in the wheelbarrow and take it to the far end of the plot, to be used to fill the final trench.

2 Fork over the subsoil in the base of the trench to the full depth of the fork's tines. You may need to use a pickaxe to break through very compacted soil.

YOU WILL NEED

• garden line and about 10 bamboo canes to mark out plot • spade • wheelbarrow • fork to loosen soil • pickaxe (optional) • organic matter

3 Mix organic matter into the lower layer of soil to improve its structure and its drainage.

4 Using a spade, dig the topsoil from an adjacent second trench and throw it into the first, making sure that it gets turned over. (On new ground, or if the soil is not very fertile, you can incorporate a further dressing of compost or manure into the top layer of soil.) Fork over the bottom of the second trench in the same way as the first.

5 Repeat the process until the entire plot has been dug to a depth of about 50cm (20in). Use the soil from the wheelbarrow to fill the last trench and finish the plot.

CLEANING TIP Clean the spade blade regularly, using a scraping tool such as a trowel. A clean spade slices through the soil more easily.

compost & leaf-mould

Gather up your garden and kitchen waste and recycle it to provide a free supply of nutrients for the garden. Composting is not difficult or smelly – it is a means of speeding up the natural process of decomposition.

how composting works

Left to itself, a heap of garden waste will warm up in the centre as the softer, greener ingredients start to ferment and rot. This warmth encourages worms and other organisms to feed on the waste and, in time, turn it into a crumbly, sweet-smelling substance rich in plant foods that holds water like a sponge.

making compost

The secret of making good compost is to mix quick-rotting green waste and tougher fibrous materials in roughly equal amounts, and keep them warm and moist in a container, preferably insulated, as the beneficial aerobic bacteria need warmth, moisture and air in order to break down waste. A lid ensures that the compost does not become too wet or dry out, and helps to retain much of the heat, which accelerates decay.

- **add a mixture of materials** (see page 598) in 15cm (6in) layers, or fork them into the heap. If you have a lot of one type of material stack it to one side and cover with black plastic sheeting until there is sufficient variation to mix together. Large quantities of grass cuttings will not go slimy if mixed with torn crumpled paper or egg boxes, while fibrous waste will rot faster mixed with grass cuttings, nettle tops or comfrey leaves.
- **continue to add waste** until the container is full, although the level will sink as the contents rot.
- **check that the heap is moist;** water it occasionally in hot weather.
- **cover the top** with an old blanket, piece of carpet or a layer of straw if there is no lid, and leave to rot for at least six months in summer – rotting will tend to slow down over winter.
- **turn the heap** once or twice to speed up the rotting process, mixing the outer materials into the centre. The easiest way to do this is to fork the materials into a second bin.

A box on wheels is used to gather up fallen leaves from the garden to turn into leaf-mould.

recycling perennial weeds

The roots of perennial weeds can survive and even multiply in a compost heap, while seeds and spores on mature or diseased weeds will only be killed if the temperature is sufficiently high. You can compost these weeds separately in a black plastic bag, mixed with a bucketful of mowings to help build up heat. Tie the bag tightly and leave for at least six months in summer, longer over winter, after which the contents can safely be added to the compost heap.

In six to twelve months, raw kitchen and garden waste (top) will have rotted down into a dark, crumbly mass at the bottom of the heap (above) – a valuable source of organic matter.

making leaf-mould

1 Rake up autumn leaves, preferably after rain. Stack them outdoors in a simple low enclosure. (You can make one easily by driving four stakes into the ground and wrapping them round with chicken netting.) Tread down the leaves to make room for more. Leave the heap open, or cover with old carpet or sacking.

2 The level of leaf-mould will fall dramatically as the leaves decay, and you can sometimes combine two heaps into one after a year. By this time, the partially decomposed leaf-mould makes an excellent soil conditioner and mulching material.

3 If you allow leaf-mould to rot for two years, you can sieve out the finer material and add it to potting composts and top-dressings for lawns.

shredding woody waste

Thick stems and tough prunings take years to decompose unless you chop them into fragments in a shredder. Petrol or electric models are available, usually capable of dealing with bundles of plant stems and branches up to 2–3cm (1in) in diameter. Make sure that the blades are kept sharp and don't overload the machine. Add the fibrous shreddings to the compost heap to aerate the mixture and break it down much more quickly.

resolving problems

- **unpleasant smells** Turn or fork the heap, working in fibrous materials such as torn newspapers and straw.
- **a dry heap that does not rot** Water it well or, if the contents are mostly fibrous, mix in plenty of soft green waste such as grass cuttings.
- **a cold wet heap** Turn or remix the contents, adding plenty of fibrous material. In cold weather, cover with old blankets, a piece of carpet, sacking or bubble plastic.
- **flies** They are harmless and part of the decomposition process, but if you find flies unpleasant cover the bin with a close-fitting lid.

composting autumn leaves

You can mix small amounts of leaves into the compost heap, but large quantities are better stacked separately (see above). Leaf-mould is slower to make than compost but should need no attention after you have packed the leaves into netting cages or plastic bags.

making leaf-mould in bags

Rake up fallen leaves after rain and pack them into black plastic bags; tie the tops and punch a few holes in the sides with a garden fork. Stack the bags in a hidden corner of the garden for a year while the leaves decay.

COMPOST TIP For faster leaf-mould, spread the leaves on the lawn and use a rotary mower to chop them into fragments before bagging them up. The grass cuttings help the leaves to decay faster.

An electric shredder makes quick work of chopping up thick plant stems. For safety, wear gloves as well as face and ear protectors when using a shredder.

compost & leaf-mould/2

compost containers

Although garden waste can be left in a heap, it is tidier and more efficient to contain it in a bin. Various models are available, or you can easily make your own wooden compost containers.

Timber is one of the best materials for a compost bin as it is an efficient insulator and you can recycle old pallets or wooden boards in its construction. The minimum sized container to make sure you get sufficient heat at the centre measures 1 x 1 x 1m (3 x 3 x 3ft) and the loose front panels allow you easy access. Attach a second bin alongside the first if you have enough space, so that the contents of the first mature while you fill up the other.

Timber is one of the best materials for a compost bin and blends well into the garden.

alternative compost containers

- **wire-mesh cage** with four corner posts and lined with cardboard or straw.
- **large plastic barrel** with 2–3cm (1in) holes drilled 30cm (12in) apart around the base and halfway up the sides.
- **proprietary square or conical** plastic bin with a close-fitting lid.
- **compost tumbler,** a barrel that is turned daily for fast results, mounted on a frame.
- **old beehives** with removable wooden slats.
- **whole builders' pallets** make excellent 'instant' compost bins set on end and lashed together. For extra insulation, fill the gaps with straw or newspaper.

worm compost

Small amounts of kitchen waste can be recycled in a worm bin or 'wormery' to produce a very rich compost that you can use as a fertiliser for potting mixtures, lawn top-dressings, fruit or large container plants. Kits are available supplying everything you need, including the worms. The container usually has a facility for draining off a concentrated solution that you can dilute and use as a liquid feed.

A wormery can run for a year or more before it is full, depending on how much it is 'fed', and you can remove the finished compost from the bottom of most proprietary bins.

compost ingredients

QUICK-ROTTING MATERIALS These are the active ingredients of a compost heap.

- soft, sappy, green waste such as weeds, young plants, soft prunings, fruit and vegetable peelings.
- lawn cuttings and nettles – these heat up very fast, and are used as accelerators to stimulate a dry compost heap into life.
- horse and poultry manure, tea and coffee grounds, and litter from small pets (rabbits, guinea pigs and pigeons).

SLOW-ROTTING MATERIALS These add bulk and prevent the softer materials from turning into a wet and evil-smelling mass.

- fibrous materials such as shredded paper and card products, straw, vegetable stems, leaves, eggshells and soft hedge prunings.
- thick stems and woody material: these need to be chopped or crushed with a spade, or shredded (see page 597).

DO NOT USE: meat and fish scraps; cat and dog faeces; plastic and synthetic fibres; coal ashes; wood, metal or glass; diseased plant material; perennial and seeding weeds.

types of potting compost

Choosing the right container for container-grown plants is all-important, as their rooting area is more limited than in the ground. Potting compost is designed to retain water while remaining well aerated, ensuring that plant roots are never short of oxygen. Buy compost little and often to ensure it is fresh, store it in a shed or greenhouse where it will stay at indoor temperatures, and keep open bags covered to prevent them from drying out.

soil-less compost

Usually sold as 'multi-purpose', soil-less compost is light and clean to use. It is excellent for short-lived seasonal displays and where weight is an issue, such as in hanging baskets. However, its structure breaks down rapidly, rendering it unsuitable for long-lived container plants. Regular watering is vital as this type of compost dries out quickly and is hard to moisten again. Waterlogging can also be a problem during very wet weather, or if plants are over-watered. Fertiliser levels are short-lived, so plants will need feeding about six weeks after potting.

Traditionally, soil-less composts were peat based, which today has serious ecological implications, but many alternatives are available (see right).

soil-based compost

Compost that contains soil, also referred to as loam, has much more 'body' than soil-less types and is excellent for permanent plants that will remain in containers for more than a few months. The loam provides a good buffer against drought and is also less liable than soil-less types to suffer from waterlogging. This category includes composts made to the John Innes formulae, which are numbered according to the amount of fertiliser contained. John Innes No. 1 is suitable for propagation, while Nos. 2 and 3 are for established plants. When planting bulbs that need sharp drainage, such as lilies, add a third by volume of coarse grit to the compost.

Always use potting compost in containers. Different types have been devised for a range of purposes, so success will often depend on making the correct choice for the plant's needs.

alternatives to peat

Many potting composts are based on peat harvested from bogs, which are valuable wildlife habitats. Home gardeners use about two-thirds of all the peat sold in Britain, so buying alternative composts based on recycled waste materials will make a real contribution towards protecting wildlife. The chief ones are coir (ground coconut husk fibres); wood waste from forestry and sawmills; and recycled 'green' household waste. If you do not want to change from peat, at least look for compost that is based on 'reclaimed' peat that has been filtered out of streams that feed into reservoirs.

ericaceous compost

Plants that dislike lime, such as azaleas, rhododendrons and pieris, need to be grown in ericaceous (lime-free) compost.

seed and cuttings composts

While multi-purpose compost can be used for seeds and cuttings, better results are achieved using compost designed for propagation. Fertiliser levels in both types are low, as high nutrient levels can damage delicate new roots. It is important to pot on or prick out young plants once cuttings are rooted or seedlings are large enough to handle, as they will be in need of more nutrients as well as more space.

- **seed compost** is fine textured to ensure good contact with the seed, especially small seeds, and developing roots; it retains moisture well.
- **cuttings compost** is free draining to avoid waterlogging, as cuttings are kept in a humid environment.

perlite and vermiculite

These lightweight, granular materials can be mixed into different composts to improve aeration and control drainage, especially for cuttings where a half-and-half mixture gives very good rooting.

Fine perlite retains moisture while still letting light through, so it is useful for covering seeds that need light in order to germinate.

mulches

Mulching brings many benefits over and above its primary role in improving the soil. It gives your garden a neat, well-tended finish and reduces the amount of time and effort you need to spend on routine care.

Extreme weather is unkind to bare soil. Hot sunshine and winds dry and harden the surface, which causes heavy ground like clay to crack. Pounding rain turns the surface to a caked crust, and it washes away plant foods and even the topsoil itself. To protect your soil from these effects, cover the surface with a mulch. Depending on the material you use, mulching can also:

- **improve** soil texture
- **increase** the soil's ability to retain water and nutrients
- **suppress** weeds
- **provide** plant nutrients
- **deter** some pests
- **protect** plant roots from temperature extremes, including moderate frost
- **give** a decorative finish to beds or containers, especially for alpines.

using mulches

All bare cultivated soil benefits from mulching. Mulches tend initially to preserve the conditions they cover; for example, moist soil is prevented from drying out, while cold soil takes longer

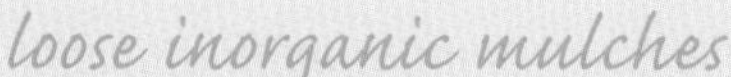

loose inorganic mulches

gravel (1), **shingle** and other loose aggregates, such as crushed shells **(2)**, help to keep soil cool and moist, and improve the drainage around plants that need dry conditions, such as alpines and herbs. They also give a decorative finish to beds and containers (see page 599). Grit mulches help to protect plants from slugs.

small pebbles (3) and cobbles (4) form a decorative mulch around plants.

loose organic mulches

shredded bark (5) must decompose for a year or be bought ready composted, as fresh bark removes nitrogen from the soil when it decays. It is a decorative mulch for shrubs, borders and herb gardens, often laid over geotextile membrane.

mushroom compost is a mixture of manure and straw or wood shavings left over from commercial mushroom cultivation. Use it around all plants except acid-lovers, because it contains lime, and make sure it is sterilised.

to warm up. So the best times to mulch are late spring, when soil temperatures are rising, and early autumn, before they begin to fall. Before covering the soil with a mulch, remove weeds, apply any fertilisers and ensure that the ground is thoroughly moist.

types of mulch

There are permanent inorganic mulches, such as gravel and shingle, and seasonal mulches, which include the various organic materials applied while plants are growing as well as being forked in later to improve the soil. There are also synthetic sheet mulches that are effective at suppressing weeds but which tend to look unattractive.

For maximum benefit spread loose organic mulches 5–10cm (2–4in) deep, depending on the plants. Young perennials, for example, need only a shallow mulch, which can be topped up as the plants develop, whereas shrubs, trees, fruit and potatoes can have a thicker layer. Leave a 5–8cm (2–3in) gap round the stems of trees and shrubs when spreading an organic mulch, to prevent rotting.

It is easier to mulch after sowing and planting but, where a mulch is in place, just scrape it aside to reveal the soil and replace it once you finish planting. Mulches are more effective insulators if they are kept loose, so check organic materials after heavy rain and gently loosen any compacted surfaces with a garden fork.

sheet mulches

black plastic is widely used for mulching strawberries, potatoes and other crops. Lay the plastic over prepared soil and secure the edges by burying them in slits made with a spade, then plant through smaller slits, cut with a sharp knife. Black plastic absorbs heat and excludes light, effectively suppressing weeds, but it is impermeable. It can successfully be used to clear a large area of weedy ground, such as a new vegetable plot, if it is left in position for a year or two.

clear plastic is sometimes spread over the soil to warm it up in early spring or to protect a prepared seedbed until needed.

black mulching paper is permeable and, like black plastic, used for short-term vegetable crops.

geotextile membranes are long-lasting materials that suppress weeds while allowing water to penetrate. They are widely used under shredded bark and gravel.

floating mulches include fleece and thin perforated plastic sheeting. They are spread over plants to help retain heat and moisture. They also protect crops from many flying insect pests as long as the edges are well secured (see black plastic). Since the materials are permeable and very light, they can be laid in position immediately after sowing and will rise with the plants as they grow. Use them in early autumn to protect crops against one or two degrees of frost.

manure allowed to rot down for at least a year makes a nutritious mulch for spreading generously around fruit, vegetables and roses. Dried and composted manure in bags is expensive and too concentrated for mulching, so is best used as a soil improver.

garden compost is nourishing and free of charge, but it must be well made or it can introduce persistent weeds to previously clean soil.

leaf-mould is an excellent soil conditioner. Sieve out the finer material for making potting compost, and use the coarse residue for mulching around any type of plant.

cocoa shells are a waste material that is light, pleasant to handle and both decorative and natural looking. This mulch may form an impervious surface after heavy rain.

grass cuttings are a useful mulch around well-established acid-loving plants such as rhododendrons and raspberries. Do not use for several mowings after weedkiller has been applied to the lawn.

straw (6) is spread around strawberries, cucumbers and squashes to ensure clean fruit. It is also useful for keeping greenhouse beds moist and for protecting frost-sensitive perennials in winter.

summer watering

All plants need adequate water to survive, which means that artificial watering is usually necessary during dry spells. With supplies often running low in summer, it makes sense to use water as wisely as possible in the garden, both for environmental reasons and to save money on metered supplies.

An oscillating sprinkler, though it tends to be somewhat wasteful of water, is useful to cover a large area of vegetable garden.

conserving water

Well-established plants in the ground should be able to survive all but long periods of drought without extra water, so concentrate watering on those plants that must not be allowed to dry out (see right). However, the key to successful plant survival starts way back at the soil preparation and planting stage, with the addition of organic matter to the soil; this improves its water-holding capacity as it acts like a sponge.

You should also 'lock in' valuable moisture by mulching the ground every spring to reduce evaporation from the soil. Apply a 5–8cm (2–3in) layer of organic material such as chipped bark, garden compost or well-rotted manure (see page 601). Work in co-operation with nature: if you garden on free-draining, fast-drying soil, opt for drought-tolerant plants that thrive in such sites. Conserving water also brings labour-saving benefits for the gardener, as artificial watering takes up valuable time.

watering techniques

Timing is all-important to make maximum use of water and keep plants looking their best. In hot weather, water in the evening or early morning, which is when less moisture is lost by evaporation, and when plants can take up water more efficiently. This also avoids the danger of water-splashed leaves becoming scorched in bright sunshine. In cooler seasons, water early in the day so that the foliage then has a

priority plants

In dry weather, concentrate on watering those plants that need it most.

- **new plants** Do not allow these to dry out during their first year, as they are unlikely to have established enough of a root system to take up sufficient moisture.
- **new lawns** Whether they have been made from seed or turf, new lawns need to be kept moist for several months until established. Fine, bowling green-type lawns also need watering regularly throughout their lives. Existing general-purpose lawns can be left to their own devices – despite turning brown, they will green up surprisingly quickly once rain arrives.
- **annuals and newly sown seed** These must not dry out for the first few weeks after planting; after that you can get away with an occasional soaking during dry spells, with the exception of thirsty varieties like sweet peas that prefer regular watering.
- **plants in containers** You will need to water these frequently, even daily, in summer (see page 234).
- **vegetables** To produce good crops, all vegetables benefit from regular watering, particularly leafy vegetables such as salad crops and spinach, and those with large or succulent fruits such as tomatoes or courgettes.
- **soft fruit** Strawberries and raspberries, especially, need watering while the fruit is developing.

chance to dry out, as moist leaves provide an attractive environment for disease. This is particularly important for plants growing under cover.

How to water is also important. Remember to water the soil – not the plant. During the growing season, always give plants a thorough soaking as a sprinkling of water can be more harmful than none at all, encouraging roots to quest towards the surface.

A rotating sprinkler is a convenient way to water a small flower garden at regular intervals.

watering equipment

There is an extensive range of watering equipment, varying from simple watering cans to more technical and costly equipment such as sprinklers and automatic watering systems.

• **watering can** At least one can is essential: choose a size that you can lift comfortably when full. Although galvanised cans look handsome, plastic ones are lighter and easier to use. For watering seedlings and young plants, fit a rose attachment. Never use the same can for applying weedkiller, but buy another one just for this purpose.

• **plastic bottle** While a small can is useful for watering raised containers such as hanging baskets, a large plastic bottle does the job more easily and costs nothing at all. Such bottles can be fitted with special 'bottle top waterers' for more effective watering.

• **garden hose** A hose is essential unless your garden is very small. Check how long it needs to be as hoses come in a variety of lengths from 15–60m (50–200ft). Cheaper hoses have a tendency to 'kink' readily, while good quality types have reinforced or double walls and are much less trouble.
To keep your hose tidy and out of the way, store it on a wall-mounted reel or trolley – it is usually best to buy this complete with hose. Hose end attachments allow the water to be delivered in a variety of ways, and a lance or a rigid extension is useful for watering hard-to-reach plants like those in hanging baskets.

• **garden sprinklers** These are fixed to hose ends and automatically deliver a fine spray of water over a large area. A static sprinkler is the simplest design and waters a circular area, though it usually needs to be moved around for an even coverage. Oscillating and rotating sprinklers give better coverage.

• **soaker or seep hose** Large areas of new plants, rows of vegetables or lawns can be watered easily and efficiently with a soaker hose. Made of plastic or rubber, these hoses have small perforations all along their length, which let the water seep out gently. For temporary watering, lay the hose on the soil covered with a 2–5cm (1–2in) layer of mulch. Alternatively, bury the hose about 10cm (4in) deep if it is to be a permanent fixture, but mark its position to avoid accidental damage.

Mircobore tubes deliver water to individual plants in a window box.

• **microbore watering systems**
These are perfect for watering container-grown plants in the garden or greenhouse, and automatic water timers can be used with any watering system (see page 237).

• **capillary matting** This thick matting holds water, which is taken up by the plants in pots standing on it. It is useful in the greenhouse to ensure thorough watering; remove it in winter to avoid making the atmosphere too humid.

recycling and saving water

Collecting rainwater in a water butt is one way to reduce your use of mains water – and many plants prefer it. Models range from inexpensive standard plastic butts to dearer wooden ones or slim wall-mounted models. If looks do not matter, any large watertight container will do, like plastic barrels thrown out from factories or an old water tank. Make sure it has not previously contained anything toxic that could harm your plants.

Position a water butt where the downpipe from a gutter can direct rainwater into it.

You can use recycled or 'grey' water from baths and sinks on the garden provided it is reasonably clean and free from strong detergents. Water from washing machines and dishwashers, however, should not be used as it will damage plants.

summer feeding

All plants need feeding in order to perform at their best and remain healthy. In a garden plants grow closely in a limited space, which takes more out of the soil than goes back in naturally. The situation is compounded by the removal of untidy plant debris and cut grass, which would otherwise rot down and return nutrients to the soil.

nutrients

Knowing what plants need makes it easier to choose and apply fertiliser correctly. The nutrients required by plants divide into three groups: major nutrients that need to be added to all soils, and secondary and trace nutrients that only need to be applied on soils that are very poor or have extreme pH levels (too acid or too alkaline). All these nutrients are chemical elements and have a chemical symbol, which is given in brackets.

The three main nutrients required for healthy growth are nitrogen (N), phosphorus (P) and potassium (K). Most general-purpose, or compound, fertilisers contain all three. The actual balance of each nutrient does vary, so check the packet before buying. Fertilisers are also available 'straight' – that is, supplying only one nutrient. These are used to correct deficiencies rather than for general feeding. Do not confuse fertilisers with soil improvers like manure and garden compost, which contain only limited nutrients.

- **nitrogen** encourages strong growth and should be applied early in the growing season. Do not use high-nitrogen fertiliser on permanent plants after midsummer as the resulting soft, young growth could be frost-damaged.
- **phosphorus** boosts strong root growth and is particularly important when planting all permanent plants.
- **potassium** improves both fruiting and flowering. Apply a high-potassium fertiliser (such as a tomato feed) in spring and early summer.
- **secondary nutrients** such as calcium (Ca), magnesium (Mg) and sulphur (S) are needed in relatively large amounts, but are present in sufficient quantities in most soils. In some cases, deficiency is actually caused by insufficient water in the soil, making it hard for plants to extract all they need.
- **trace nutrients** include iron (Fe), boron (Bo) and molybdenum (Mb). While important, they are required only in small amounts and rarely require artificial application. One common exception is lime-hating plants growing on soil that is insufficiently acid, where they often become deficient in iron.

easy fertiliser application

For easy and accurate distribution of nutrients, make your own applicator using two small plastic pots of the same size, placed one inside the other with the drainage holes just offset to leave small gaps. Fill with granular fertiliser and simply shake the pot to distribute the fertiliser evenly.

Mix a combination of granular fertiliser and water-retaining granules into the compost when planting up containers.

applying fertilisers

Whatever the fertiliser, always follow the manufacturer's instructions. Never be tempted to apply more on the basis that double the feed will do twice as much good – over-feeding can do more harm than giving nothing at all.

granular fertiliser

Fertiliser granules or powder are scattered on the soil surface around plants and hoed or raked into the soil. Apply at the recommended rate by weighing out the amount per metre, then marking a pot or small container at this level for future reference.

Plants can only take up fertiliser when it becomes dissolved in water, so in dry weather water well after feeding.

- **ideally, apply** when the ground is moist but plants are dry, or fertiliser could stick to and scorch damp leaves.
- **always wear gloves** and take care not to breathe in any dust.

Magnolia x soulangeana

specialist fertilisers

Certain fertilisers are formulated for specific plants in order to achieve their best performance.

- **lawn fertiliser** is usually labelled according to the time of year it should be applied, spring or autumn, as this affects the balance of nutrients.
- **lime-hating or ericaceous** plants like magnolias benefit from an ericaceous fertiliser that contains iron, in which they often become deficient.
- **some specific fertilisers** can be used for a wide range of plants – rose or tomato fertiliser can also be used on all flowering plants.

controlled-release fertiliser

These polymer-coated granules or tablets are designed to release nutrients gradually over a period of months, as and when conditions are sufficiently warm and moist for the plant to utilise the food. While more expensive than other types, controlled-release fertilisers are also more effective. They are particularly useful for feeding plants in containers as they do away with the time-consuming weekly job of liquid feeding.

liquid fertiliser

Soluble or liquid fertiliser is dissolved before application, then watered onto the soil around the roots. The plants take up the nutrients rapidly as they are already in solution. But regular feeding is needed as the nutrients quickly leach away through the soil, particularly on light, free-draining ground.

- **water liquid fertilisers** onto the soil using a watering can. Over a large area, a hose end diluter (see above right) cuts down a lot of work – just attach the filled applicator and turn on the hose.
- **apply morning or evening** to avoid the risk of sun scorch on splashed foliage.

You can buy liquid fertiliser in an applicator that clips onto the end of a hose. This is invaluable for feeding plants over a large area.

- **do not apply on dry soil** as scorching could occur, and avoid applying before rain which would wash off the fertiliser.

foliar fertiliser

This liquid fertiliser is designed to be absorbed through a plant's leaves. Spray onto the leaves using a pump-action hand sprayer. The plant absorbs the nutrients very quickly, which is particularly useful if it is showing signs of nutrient deficiency such as pale, yellowing or discoloured leaves. Follow the guidelines for applying liquid fertiliser (left), and never spray when the sun is on the leaves or it could cause severe scorching.

feeding guidelines

TYPE OF PLANT	TYPE OF FERTILISER	WHEN TO FEED
NEW PLANTS IN BORDERS	Slow-release, high in phosphorus to aid root growth	On planting
ESTABLISHED PLANTS IN BORDERS	Slow-release (general) or controlled-release	Late winter and late spring
PERMANENT PLANTS IN CONTAINERS	Controlled-release, along with a top-dressing of fresh potting compost	Early spring
ANNUALS IN CONTAINERS	Controlled-release followed by high-nitrogen liquid fertiliser. Add controlled-release fertiliser to compost when planting	Liquid feed from midsummer
VEGETABLES	Balanced compound fertiliser	Scatter on the soil, several days before sowing
FRUIT	Compound fertiliser high in potassium	Spring and early summer
LAWNS	Lawn fertiliser suitable for the time of year	Spring and autumn

cloches & coldframes

In cooler climates, or where the weather is unpredictable, cloches and coldframes allow you to extend the season and protect vulnerable plants. Whether you regard them as accessories or substitutes for a greenhouse, they have their own unique merits.

the value of plant protection

Cloches and coldframes are invaluable in the attempt to protect plants from extreme weather conditions. They also enable you to extend the growing season by several weeks so that you can grow more crops for longer with less risk from the elements.

They will shield plants from frost, fog, cold winds, persistent rain and, if shaded, from scorching sunshine. By trapping the sun's energy, they gather and retain warmth in spring and autumn, the seasons when they are most useful, and allow tender plants and seedlings to continue growing or cropping throughout the winter. They can also be used to keep plants dry at critical times of the year: alpines, bulbs and winter lettuce, for example, can all be sensitive to lingering dampness.

The use of cloches and coldframes relieves pressure on limited greenhouse space. Overall, they provide a considerable measure of control over the unpredictability that can make unprotected gardening a gamble in some climates and seasons.

some advantages of cloches and coldframes

Compared to a greenhouse,

- **they are cheap and versatile** and damage is easily repaired.
- **they occupy less space** than a greenhouse, warm up more quickly and are easier to insulate.
- **cloches are portable,** to some extent frames too, and can be moved round the garden as needed.
- **they act as a half-way house,** hardening off plants in their journey from greenhouse to the open air.
- **cloches and movable frames** can be used to warm the soil before planting and to protect transplants while they get established.
- **they can be opened** or removed completely to admit rain or fresh air in hot weather.
- **pests and diseases** are unlikely to invade and multiply, and are more easily dealt with if they do.

glazing materials

Maximum light and adequate warmth are essential for healthy plant growth and, as with greenhouses, the choice of glazing material can affect conditions in the protected environment.

- **glass** admits more light and retains heat better than other materials, but it is heavy (possibly an advantage for cloches in windy gardens), and potentially dangerous if broken, especially where children and pets are concerned. It is possible to fit toughened glass for safety; otherwise 3mm (⅛in) horticultural glass is adequate.
- **flat or corrugated glass-reinforced polyester** is the best substitute for glass among the rigid plastics.
- **polycarbonate** is cheaper, with lower light transmission but good heat retention if twin or triple-walled.
- **acrylic** is a clearer glazing material, but very brittle and easily cracked.
- **flexible plastic sheets,** widely used for tunnel cloches and lightweight frames, has good light transmission but a limited life, even when treated with an ultra-violet inhibitor to delay yellowing. There is also an increased risk of condensation, which can be a problem with disease-susceptible plants in winter, and heat is rapidly lost at night.

using with a greenhouse

- **coldframes** are the equivalent of an unheated greenhouse, and can be used for growing and storing plants that do not need cosseted conditions, or for

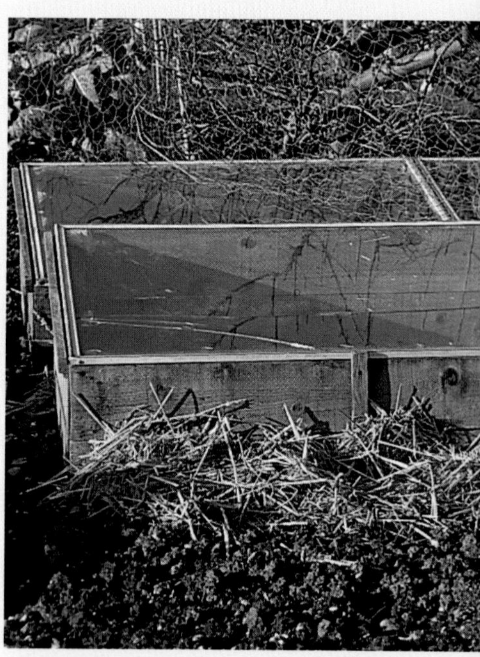

In severe weather, a line of glass barn cloches, constructed with special wire clips, have been joined together and closed at the ends to form a continuous insulated row over young broad bean plants (top right).

A coldframe on open ground is insulated with straw to give extra protection for young vegetable plants in winter (above).

Tent cloches, made using two sheets of glass joined with wire and a wooden spacer, are the simplest form of movable protection. Here, they shelter young lettuce seedlings (right).

those being prepared for the open air after being started in heat. Coldframes with a soil base can be used for sowing and growing out-of-season plants like salads and flowers that would take up excessive space in a greenhouse border. Since it is also possible to heat a coldframe either by electricity or with a small paraffin heater, using the frame as an extension to the greenhouse can relieve congestion within it.

- **cloches** are mainly for open ground use, although they can provide extra protection for crops growing in the border of an unheated greenhouse. Their role is to help plants on the final stage of their journey from the greenhouse or coldframe to the open air, and their greatest value lies in protecting young plants during the first few days after being transplanted or moved outdoors.

Cloches also have an important role, independent of the greenhouse, as temporary, movable protection. Use them to warm the soil before sowing, to cover early outdoor sowings, to provide warmth for tender summer crops and to extend the growing time for crops in autumn.

a year in a coldframe

JANUARY • force rhubarb, kale and witloof chicory
• sow sweet peas in pots
• sow early lettuce

FEBRUARY • sow carrots and radishes
• sow onions, leeks, brassicas for transplanting
• transplant lettuces into the soil

MARCH • plant early potatoes in the soil or in boxes or buckets
• sow dwarf french beans
• root chrysanthemum cuttings

APRIL • sow runner beans and sweetcorn for transplanting
• sow half-hardy annuals
• harden off hardy annuals

MAY • harden off tender flowers and vegetables
• plant ridge cucumbers, melons and self-blanching celery

JUNE • sow biennials and perennials
• train melons and cucumbers
• fork over the soil and add compost after clearing crops grown in it

JULY • sow parsley for winter
• root soft and semi-ripe cuttings

AUGUST • root semi-ripe cuttings and strawberry runners
• house cuttings from pelargoniums and other tender perennials
• dry garlic and shallots

SEPTEMBER • plunge early forced bulbs
• sow hardy annuals
• ripen onions

OCTOBER • plant lettuce
• transplant annual herbs for winter use
• store chrysanthemum roots

NOVEMBER • harvest salads and herbs
• overwinter brassica seedlings

DECEMBER • sow carrots, turnips and radishes in heated frames
• start forcing rhubarb

types of cloche

Cloches are the simplest of glazed structures for protecting plants, and come in all shapes and sizes. From the original bell jar and ornate lantern cloche to functional plastic tunnelling, they all do a useful job in protecting growing plants from the weather.

simple cloches

The earliest kinds of cloche, still available today, were made from two panes of glass joined in the form of a tent to cover sowings and low plants. For taller plants, the barn cloche uses two more panes to raise the basic tent on low walls (see page 606). The glass panes are joined with wires, or metal or plastic clips, or you can improvise with clothes pegs or short canes. Although heavy and breakable, well-made glass cloches are stable in windy positions.

Plastic cloches have now largely superseded glass models. Some use rigid or semi-rigid plastic in the form of tents, squares or short tunnels to cover small areas. Others use plastic sheeting supported on wire hoops to make a low tunnel, 60cm–2m (2–6ft) wide, to cover rows of plants and seedlings.

Plastic sheeting stretched over wire hoops forms a continuous open-ended cloche. The plastic can be tied at the end for greater insulation in winter (top).

Decorative as well as functional, this Victorian lantern cloche forms a cosy environment for overwintering plants (above).

Bell jars and a lantern cloche protect individual plants while they are establishing (left). The cloche lid is angled to allow some ventilation.

Young lettuces are protected under a row of flat-topped cloches (right). Clay pots on top help to prevent them from lifting in windy weather.

other kinds of cloche

- **bell jar** This is the original cloche (*cloche* is French for a bell), formerly glass but increasingly made from plastic. It is used to cover individual plants.
- **flat-topped cloche** Similar to the glass barn cloche, this is a wide, heavy type with a central horizontal panel, adjustable for watering and ventilation. A modified plastic version with slots or small perforations is known as the self-watering cloche.
- **dome cloche** A moulded plastic enclosure, this has a handle and open ends, so several can be arranged in a row.
- **lantern cloche** A square, free-standing cloche, this has a lid like a pitched roof. Victorian models were made of leaded glass panels, but modern replicas are available in plastic.
- **floating cloche** The hoops deployed for continuous plastic tunnels can be used to support fleece over plants to give them temporary protection from light frost as well as from various winged insect pests.
- **improvised cloches** Many kinds of individual cloche made from waxed paper or bottomless clear plastic bottles are used for protecting single plants.

using cloches in strip cropping

This is the most efficient method of using cloches. Plan the crops you wish to grow, so that their starting times are staggered. Set the cloches over the first row until they are no longer needed, then move them to cover new sowings or plantings in the adjacent row. Continue in this way across the plot, or move the cloches back to the first row to cover the next crop. Here is an example of how cloches might be used throughout the year in a kitchen garden.

OCTOBER–APRIL

- cover autumn-sown lettuces, intercropped with peas, in row 1.

APRIL–JUNE

- as lettuces and peas mature, move cloches to cover transplanted bush tomatoes in row 2.

JUNE–SEPTEMBER

- transfer cloches back to row 1, now replanted with melons, and keep plants covered until harvest.

SEPTEMBER–OCTOBER

- move cloches to row 2, to ripen late tomato fruits.

managing cloches

Covering and warming seeds and plants promotes more rapid growth and intensive production, so cultivate the ground well, increase fertility, and rake the surface level and free from stones so that the base of the cloche makes good contact with the ground. This also helps to reduce the risk of breaking glass cloches.

- **most cloches are open-ended** so that they can be joined together to cover a row of plants. If then left open, however, they will become wind tunnels, defeating the object of using them and often injuring plants. Close rigid cloches with end panels of glass or plastic held in place with bricks or other means. Tie the loose ends of polythene tunnels to stakes or bury them securely in the ground.
- **warm the soil** by setting cloches in place two weeks before sowing or planting (see right).
- **check underneath regularly** during the growing season to see what is happening. The soil dries out faster, the weeds grow rapidly, and pests and diseases may not be visible from outside, especially through plastic cloches.
- **when watering is necessary,** it can often be done lightly and steadily over the top of narrow cloches, allowing the water to run down and soak the edges, where it will be accessible to the plant roots. Wider cloches will need to be moved or opened before watering the plants, or you could run a seep hose down the centre.
- **keep the cloches clean,** and shade them in a hot bright spring or autumn by covering them with fleece, fine netting or old sheets.
- **ventilate in warm weather** by lifting the side of polythene tunnels, especially if plants such as strawberries need pollinating. With rigid cloches, remove one and move the others slightly to make gaps in between, or lift up one side onto small stones.

CLOCHES TIP When hoeing, thinning or weeding under a row of cloches, remove the first two and take them to the far end of the row. You can then move a pair at a time along the row as you cultivate in stages.

warming the soil

Setting out cloches a week or two before sowing or planting warms the soil and ensures rapid germination and establishment. The same principle can be used in a cold or wet spring, to dry and warm the ground before preparing a seedbed, and also to keep it in good condition afterwards until sowing is possible. In early winter, cover root crops like parsnips and swedes before a hard frost so you can lift supplies when the rest of the ground is frozen.

index

Page numbers in *italic* refer to the illustrations and captions

A

Abelia schumannii 285, *285* , 300
Abeliophyllum distichum *564*, 565, 579
Abies koreana 376, *376*, 392, 393
Abutilon 'Souvenir de Bonn' *33*
acacia, false 287, *287*
Acacia dealbata *72*
Acaena 229
A. saccaticupula 'Blue Haze' 384, *384*
Acanthus 124
A. mollis Latifolius Group 354, *354*, 392
A. spinosus *19*, 264, *265*, 300
acclimatising
shrubs and trees 223
see also hardening off
Acer 206, 486, 487, 578, 579
A. capillipes 476, *476*
A. cappadocicum 'Aureum' 476, *476*
A. circinatum 476, *476*, *487*
A. griseum 556–7, *557*, 579
A. grosseri var. *hersii* *564*, 565, 579
A. japonicum 'Vitifolium' 476, *476*
A. palmatum 207, *486*
'Corallinum' 190, *190*
var. *dissectum* Dissectum Viride Group 198, *198*
'Sango-kaku' 476, *476*
A. pensylvanicum 'Erythrocladum' 554, *555*, 579
A. pseudoplatanus 'Brilliantissimum' 190, *190*, 207
A. rubrum 'October Glory' 476, *476*
A. tataricum subsp. *ginnala* 476, *476*
Achillea 'Coronation Gold' 362, *362*, 393
A. x *lewisii* 'King Edward' 206, 293, *293*
A. 'Taygetea' 268, *268*, 300
acid soils
pH value 592, *592*, 593
plant selectors 119, 207, 301, 393, 486, 578
aconite 269, *269*, 354, *354*, 450, *450*
winter 35, *35*, *494*, 548, *548*
Aconitum 213
A. 'Bressingham Spire' 354, *354*
A. carmichaelii 'Arendsii' 450, *450*
A. 'Ivorine' 269, *269*, 301
Acorus calamus 'Argenteostriatus' 295, *295*
Actinidia kolomikta 280, *280*, 500
Adonis amurensis 572, *572*, 579
A. vernalis 111, *111*, 118
Aeonium arboreum 75, *75*, 148
A. 'Zwartkop' *323*
aerating lawns *58*, *153*, *328*, 428, 520
aerators 589, *589*
Aethionema 'Warley Rose' 200, *201*, 206
african blue lily 354, *354*, 397
african daisy 460, *460*
african violet, leaf cuttings *254*
Agapanthus 392, 393, 397
A. 'Blue Giant' 354, *354*
A. 'Lilliput' 354, *354*
Agastache foeniculum 114, *114*
Agave *75*
A. americana 148
Ageratum houstanianum 274, *275*
Ailanthus 512
air layering 46, 47, *47*
Ajuga reptans 207
'Purple Torch' 174, *174*, 207
Akebia 500
A. quinata 95, *95*
Alcea 215
A. rosea *309*
'Nigra' 276, *276*
Alchemilla mollis 211, 272, *272*, 300, 301
alexanders 114, *114*, 343
algae
on patios 57
in ponds 55, 232, 325
alkaline soils 592, *592*, 593
alkanet 262, *262*
Allamanda cathartica *445*
Allium 300
A. cristophii 278, *278*
A. 'Globemaster' 278, *278*
A. hollandicum 'Purple Sensation' 278, *278*
A. schoenoprasum 204, *204*
almond 98, *98*
aloe *75*
Aloysia triphylla 114, *114*
alpine strawberries 62, 63, *63*
alpines
in autumn 420–1
beds 53
in containers 322–3
cuttings 229, 323, 421
division 141, 229, 420
in early spring 52–3
fertilisers 229, 322
in late spring 140–1
in late summer 322–3
mulching 421, *421*
plant selectors 109–12, 200–2, 292–3, 384–5, 477–9, 572–3
planting *141*
potting up *229*
propagation 53, 229, *229*, 420–1, 514–15
sink gardens 141
sowing 420, 514–15, *515*
in summer 228–9
tidying beds *421*
watering 229
weeding beds 228–9
in winter 421, 514–15
Alstroemeria ligtu hybrids 370, *370*, 393
alyssum 215
Amaranthus *18*
A. caudatus 368, *368*
'Viridis' 462, *462*, 487
Amaryllis 495, *495*
A. belladonna 216, 463, *463*, 486
Amelanchier canadensis 470, *470*, 486, 487
Ampelopsis glandulosa var. *brevipedunculata* 551, *551*
Anacyclus depressus 514
Anagallis monellii 458, *458*, 487
Anaphalis margaritacea 454–5, *455*
A. triplinervis 'Sommerschnee' 363, *363*
Anchusa 124
A. azurea 'Loddon Royalist' 262, *262*
anemone 402, 514
japanese 363, *363*, *408*, *450*, 451, 455, *455*
snowdrop *178*, 179
Anemone blanda *15*, 547, *547*, 578, 579
A. coronaria 119, 217
De Caen Group 88, *88*, 402
Saint Bridgid Group 86, *86*, 402
A. hupehensis 'Hadspen Abundance' 356–7, *357*, 392
A. x *hybrida* 486, 487
'Honorine Jobert' 455, *455*
'September Charm' *450*, 451
'Whirlwind' 363, *363*, 392, *408*
A. nemorosa 91, *91*, 118
A. sylvestris *178*, 179
Anethum graveolens 296, *296*, *537*
angelica 343, *343*, 388, *388*, 443
Angelica archangelica 388, *388*
angelica tree, japanese 380, *380*
animal manure *see* manure
aniseed 343, 482, *482*
Anisodontea capensis *348*
annuals
in autumn 400–1
bedding plants 32–3, *33*, 127, 215
choosing 492
climbers 41, 492
cut flowers 29
deadheading 308
in early spring 28–33
fertilisers 605
herbs 537
in late spring 126–7
in late summer 308–9
plant selectors 85, 182–3, 274–7, 366–9, 458–62, 546
sowing 28–30, *32*, 126–7, 215, 309, 493
in summer 214–15
transplanting seedlings *214*
watering 602
in winter 492–3
Anthemis 229, *229*
A. tinctoria 'E.C. Buxton' 268, *268*, 300, 301
'Sauce Hollandaise' *307*
Anthericum liliago *178*, 179
Anthriscus cerefolium 296, *296*
Antirrhinum 30, 308
A. Sonnet Series 276, *276*, 300
A. Tahiti Series 393
anvil secateurs 586, *586*
aphids
biological control 257

aphids (continued)
in greenhouses 258
mealy cabbage aphids 338
on roses *37*
on trees and shrubs 223
on vegetables 65
water-lily aphids 231
Aponogeton distachyos 422, 481, *481*
apples 390, *390*, 484, *485*
'Annie Elizabeth' 431
'Ashmead's Kernel' 431
bitter pit 431
'Blenheim Orange' 431
'Bramley's Seedling' 431, 523
buying trees 330
canker 523, *523*
cordons 435, *436–7*
'Cox's Orange Pippin' *158*, 523
'Crispin' 431
'Golden Noble' 431
harvesting 334, *334*
'Howgate Wonder' 431
'June drop' 242
'Lane's Prince Albert' 523
'Newton Wonder' 523
'Orleans Reinette' 431
planning a fruit garden 434
pollination 330
pruning 159, 242, *242*, 435, *522*
'Ribston Pippin' 431
'Spartan' 431
'Stepover' *434*
storing 334, 430–1, *430*
'Sturmer Pippin' 431
'Sunset' 431
'Suntan' 431
thinning 61, 159, 242, *242*
apricots
in greenhouses 540
japanese 98, *98*
planning a fruit garden 434
pollinating 62
thinning 62, 159
aquatic plants *see* water plants
Aquilegia 50, 207, 229
A. 'Hensol Harebell' 172, *172*
A. McKana Group 267, *267*
A. vulgaris 'Nivea' *178*, 179
Arabis alpina subsp. *caucasica* 206, 207
'Schneehaube' 202, *202*
'Variegata' *51*, 111, *111*, 118, 119
Arabis alpina (continued)
A. procurrens 'Variegata' 112, *112*, 118, 119
Aralia elata 392
'Variegata' 380, *380*
Arbutus x *andrachnoides* 557, *557*, 579
A. unedo 51, 474, *474*, 486
Arctotis x *hybrida* 'Flame' 460, *460*, 486, 487
Arenaria balearica 112, *112*, 118
A. montana 293, *293*, 301
Argyranthemum 73, 393
A. 'Snow Storm' 363, *363*
A. 'Vancouver' 357, *357*
Arisaema candidissimum 278, 279, 301, *301*
Armeria juniperifolia 200, *201*, 206, 207
A. maritima 'Düsseldorfer Stolz' 292, *292*, 300, 301
Armoracia rusticana 574, *574*
arnica 443
arrowhead 387, *387*
Artemisia 137
A. arborescens 288, *289*
A. ludoviciana 'Valerie Finnis' 271, *271*, 300, 301
A. 'Powis Castle' 271, *271*, 300, 301
A. schmidtiana 'Nana' 293, *293*
A. stelleriana 'Boughton Silver' 385, *385*, 392, 393
artichokes *see* globe artichokes; jerusalem artichokes
Arum italicum subsp. *italicum* 'Marmoratum' 544, *544*, 579
arum lily 295, *295*, 350
asparagus 204, *205*, *249*, 535
cutting down 441
planting 69, *69*, 527
storing 341
asphodel *178*, 179
Asphodelus albus 178, 179, 206
Asplenium scolopendrium 272, *272*, 392
aster *123*, 124
china 30, 169, 459, *459*
new york 357, *357*, 457, *457*
Aster 486
A. amellus 486
'King George' 457, *457*
'Veilchenkönigen' 457, *457*
Aster (continued)
A. divaricatus 486
A. ericoides 'Pink Cloud' 457, *457*
A. x *frikartii* 'Mönch' *352–3*, 354, *355*, 393
A. lateriflorus 'Horizontalis' 457, *457*, 486
A. novae-angliae 'Andenken an Alma Pötsche' 457, *457*
A. novi-belgii 'Heinz Richard' 357, *357*, 393
'Kristina' 457, *457*
A. pringlei 'Monte Cassino' 457, *457*
Astilbe 300, 301, 393
A. x *arendsii* 'Fanal' 267, *267*
'Irrlicht' 269, *269*
A. 'Bronce Elegans' 357, *357*
A. chinensis var. *pumila* 477, *477*, 486, 487
var. *taquetii* 'Superba' 357, *357*
A. 'Professor van der Wielen' 364, *364*, *393*
Astrantia major 210
subsp. *involucrata* 'Shaggy' 272, *272*, 301
aubergines 163, *257*, 388, *389*
in greenhouses 168, 350
harvesting 339, 350
storing 341
Aubrieta 200, *201*, *228*
A. 'Doctor Mules' 109, *109*, 118, 119
A. 'Greencourt Purple' 206, 207
Aucuba japonica 118, 119
'Crotonifolia' 560, *560*, 578
'Rozannie' 100, *100*
'Variegata' 101, *101*
auricula, border 80–1, *80*, *82*, 83, 323
Aurinia saxatilis 206, 207
'Dudley Nevill Variegated' 202, *202*
automatic watering systems 237, *237*, 603, *603*
autumn crocus 463, *463*, 464, *464*
avens, water 266, *267*
azaleas 287, *287*
in containers *146*
cuttings 227
deadheading 137
soil 502–3
Azara microphylla 101, *101*
Azolla caroliniana 232
A. filiculoides 142, 480, *480*

B

baby's breath *364*, 365
bachelor's buttons, white 180, *181*
bacopa 369, *369*
balloon flower 356, *356*
balsam 460, *460*
bamboo 150, *151*, *194*, 195
fountain 381, *381*
heavenly 559, *559*
umbrella 289, *289*
bamboo canes, supporting plants 122, 211
banana plants *19*
baptisia 306
barberry 192, 193, *193*, 384, *385*
bare-rooted plants
fruit 433
'heeling' in 433
planting 138, 406, *406*, *415*, 436
bark
mulches 397, *419*, 600, *600*
paths 346
barrenwort 81, *81*, 82, *82*, 176, *176*, 180, *180*
basal cuttings 125, *125*, 212, 213
basil 388, *388*
chinese 114, *114*
in containers 251
division *70*
potting up 442–3
preserving 253
sowing 251, 350
baskets, planting water plants in 144, *145*
Bassia scoparia f. *tricophylla* 460, *460*, 487
bats 232
bay *346*, 482, *482*
cuttings 251
preserving 253
topiary 48, *48*
winter protection 536, *536*
beans
in containers 533
crop rotation 530
drying 438
extending harvest 67
sowing 161, *161*
storing 340

beans (continued)
watering 244, 337
see also individual types of bean
bear's breeches 264, *265*, 354, *354*
bear's foot 545, *545*
beauty berry 468, *468*
beauty bush *224*, 286, *286*
bedding plants
buying 127
over-wintering 400
planning bedding schemes 32–3, *33*, 51
planting 127, 215, 401, *401*
sowing *32*, 33
beds and borders
alpines 53
designing 50–1
growing vegetables in flower beds 533
herb gardens 345, 346
maintenance 26–7, *27*
no-dig beds 531, *531*
patio beds 147
planting bulbs 312, *313*
beech 558, *558*
hedges 321, 413, *413*, 417, *419*
pests 223
training standards 513
beer traps, slugs 123
bees *258*, 344
beet, leaf 117, *117*
beetroot 297, *297*, 533
crop rotation 534
intercropping 533
plug plants *532*
sowing 69, 162, 246, 527
storing 340, 341, 440, 527
successional sowing 533
begonia
deadheading 308
planting 129
sowing 33, *74*
starting into growth 495, 540, *540*
tuberous 370, 371, *371*
wax 459, *459*
Begonia 'Memory Scarlet' 370, *371*
B. 'Orange Cascade' 371, *371*
B. rex 254, 255
B. semperflorens 30, 126, 493
Organdy Series 459, *459*, 487
bell jars *608*, 609
bellflower 384, *384*
dalmatian 477, *477*
milky 262, *262*
peach-leaved 262, *263*
Bellis 401
B. perennis 29, 182, *182*
'Kito' 85, *85*
bells of ireland 369, *369*
bellwort 178, *178*
Berberis 206, 207, 321, 417
B. buxifolia 101, *101*, 118, 119
B. x *carminea* 'Buccaneer' 557, *557*, 578
B. darwinii 192, *193*, 417
B. x *media* 'Red Jewel' *20*
B. x *stenophylla 51*, 193, *193*, 417
B. thunbergii 'Atropurpurea Nana' 384, *385*, 392
bergamot 71, 253, 359, *359*
Bergenia 118, 119, 124, 490, 578
B. 'Ballawley' *51*, 544, *544*, 579
B. 'Beethoven' *178*, 179, 206, 207
B. ciliata 83, *83*
B. x *schmidtii* 544, *544*, 579
B. 'Schneekönigen' 81, *81*
B. stracheyi 81, *81*
B. 'Sunningdale' *22*, 81, *81*
Betula pendula 'Youngii' 289, *289*, 301
B. utilis 136
var. *jacquemontii 22*
'Silver Shadow' 566, *567*
Bidens 148
B. ferulifolia 460–1, *461*, 487
bidi-bidi 384, *384*
biennials
in autumn 400–1
in early spring 28–33
in late spring 126–7
in late summer 308–9
plant selectors 85, 182–3, 274–7, 366–9, 458–62, 546
sowing 127, *127*
in summer 214–15
transplanting seedlings *214*, 215
in winter 492–3
big bud mites 63, 158, 523
bindweed 229, 316, *320*, 384, *384*
biological pest control, greenhouses 257
birch
himalayan *22*, 566, *567*
birch (continued)
silver *223*
young's weeping 289, *289*
birds
protecting brassicas *439*
protecting fish 423, *423*
protecting fruit *330*
birth root 173, *173*
bishop's mitre 81, *81*, 82, *82*, 176, *176*, 180, *180*
bistort 266, *266*
bitter pit 431
bittercress, hairy 228
black-eyed susan 362–3, *363*, 454, *454*, 461, *461*
black flowers, alpines 479
black gum 474, *474*
black locust 287, *287*
black spot *37*
blackberries 484, *485*
pests 243
pruning 61, *243*, 432
training 435
tying-in 60, 243, *243*, *432*, 437
blackcurrants 390–1, *390*
big bud mites 63, 158, 523
cuttings 432, *432*
harvesting 241, 335
pests 332
planning a fruit garden 434
planting 436, 437
pollination 330
pruning 61, 242, 332
reversion 242
tying-in 437
blackfly 223
on broad beans 65, *163*
blackthorn hedges 416
blanching vegetables 341
blanket weed 143, *143*, *231*, 325, 422
bleeding heart 174, *174*, 306
blight, potato 247
blue-bottle 274, *274*
blue-eyed mary 80, *80*
blue flowers and foliage
alpines 109–10, 200, 292, 384, 477, 573
annuals and biennials 85, 182, 274, 366–7, 458
bulbs 86–7, 184, 278–9, 463, 547
climbers 95, 188, 280, 373, 551
blue flowers and foliage (continued)
perennials 80–1, 172–3, 262–4, 354–6, 450–1, 544
shrubs and trees 96, 190, 285, 376–7, 468, 554
water plants 113, 294, 386, 480
bluebell, english 184, *184*, 217
blueblossom, creeping 190, *190*
borage 296, *296*, 343
Borago officinalis 296, *296*
borders *see* beds and borders
boron 604
boston ivy 466, *466*
bougainvillea 259, 540
bow saws 507, 586, *586*
bowles' golden grass 177, *177*
box 568, *568*
in containers *235*
cuttings *226*, *319*
hedges 43, *43*, *138*, 165, *165*, 321, *328*
pests 223
planting *347*
topiary 48, 150, *150*, *326*
brachyglottis 413
Brachyscome iberidifolia Splendour Series 366, *366*, 392
bramble, white-stemmed 512, 567, *567*
brassicas
crop rotation 530, 534, 535
pests 338
plug plants *532*
protecting from birds *439*
transplanting 245
see also individual types of brassica
brick paths 346
bridal wreath 198, *198*
broad beans 297, *297*
blackfly 65, *163*
crop rotation 534
pinching out tops *163*
sowing 68, 169, 438, *438*, 526
storing 341
winter protection 526, *526*
broadleaf 104, *104*
broccoli *65*, 116, *116*, 204, *205*, 388–9, *389*
crop rotation 535
earthing up stems 337
harvesting 245, 337
sowing 68
storing 340, 341

brodiaea 35
bronze flowers and foliage
annuals and biennials 182–3
bulbs 370
perennials 175, 266, 360–1, 452, 544
shrubs and trees 556
water plants 480
broom 193, *193*, 194, *194*, 202, *202*
mount etna 379, *379*
pruning 43, 222, 225
Brunnera macrophylla 172, *172*, 207
brushwood, supporting perennials 122
brussels sprouts *482*, 483, *526*, 574, *575*
crop rotation 535
earthing up 439
harvesting 68, 526
'Icarus' *524*
intercropping 533
'Rubine Red' *524*
sowing 68
storing 340
watering 337
bubble plastic
insulating greenhouses 447
protecting containers 519, *519*
buckets 587, *587*
buckler fern 175, *175*
buckthorn, italian 566, *566*
bud cuttings
clematis 221
roses 129, *129*
budding roses 129
Buddleja 392, 393, *507*
B. alternifolia 285, *285*
B. crispa 377, *377*
B. davidii 43, 45, 136, 413
'Black Knight' *318*, 376, *376*
B. 'Lochinch' 377, *377*
buds
disbudding dahlias *217*
disbudding roses 218
bugbane 455, *455*
bugle 174, *174*
bulb planters 585, *585*
bulbs
in autumn 402–3
bedding schemes 32
buying 312
in containers 129, 311, 425, *425*
bulbs (continued)
drying 403
in early spring 34–5
fertilisers 311
foliage *35*, 129
forcing 351, *351*
growing in water 350
in late spring *14–15*, 128–9
in late summer 310–13
lifting 129, 216–17, *217*, 403
naturalising in lawns 35, *128*, 312, *313*
near trees and hedges 311
planning borders 50, 51
plant selectors 86–94, 184–7, 278–9, 370–1, 463–4, 547–9
planting 35, 129, 217, 312, *313*, 350, *425*
planting depth 313
propagation 403, *403*
storing 217
in summer 216–17
in winter 494–5
bull bay 380, *380*
bullaces 334–5
bullock's heart ivy 551, *551*
burnet 451, *451*
japanese 451, *451*
burning bush 460, *460*
burr, new zealand 384, *384*
busy lizzie 367, *367*, 460, *460*
butterfly bush 376, *376*, 377, *377*
Buxus sempervirens 321, 568, *568*
buying
bedding plants 127
bulbs 312
fruit plants 330–1
plug plants 215
roses 315
tools 583
bypass secateurs 586, *586*

C

cabbages 297, *297*, *337*, *341*, *482*, 483, 532, 574, *575*
crop rotation 530, 534, 535
earthing up 439
harvesting 68, 245, 338, 438, 526
intercropping 533
'January King' 337, 439
planting 337
savoy 245, 439
cabbages (continued)
sowing 68, 245, 337
spring cabbages 116, *116*
storing 340, 341, 439
transplanting 68, 245, 337, 438, *439*
watering 244, 336
winter protection 439
'Winter Savoy' *526*
cacti, watering 258
calabrese 340, 388–9, *389*
Calamagrostis brachytricha 20
calcium 604
calcium deficiency, apples 431
Calendula 30, *308*
C. officinalis 'Fiesta Gitana' 368, *368*, 392, 393
calico bush 286, *286*
california lilac 190, *190*, 285, *285*, 376, *376*, 409, 468, *468*
californian fuchsia 478, *478*
Callicarpa bodinieri var. *giraldii* 'Profusion' 468, *468*
callistemon 259
Callistephus chinensis Princess Series 459, *459*
Calluna vulgaris 44, 486, 487, 578, 579
'Beoley Gold' 560, *561*
'Darkness' 378, *378*, 392, 393
'Firefly' 560, *561*
'Peter Sparkes' 468, *469*
'Robert Chapman' 557, *557*
'Spring Torch' *21*
Caltha palustris 54, *144*
'Flore Pleno' 203, *203*, 206
var. *palustris* 118
'Plena' 113, *113*
Camassia cusickii 217
C. leichtlinii 'Electra' 278, *278*, 300
camellia 118, 119, 578, 579
in containers 146
deadheading 137
pests 223
Camellia 'Cornish Snow' *564*, 565
C. 'Freedom Bell' 108, *108*
C. japonica 207
'Akashigata' *42*
'Bob Hope' 192, *193*
'Bob's Tinsie' 108, *108*
'Jupiter' 108, *108*
'Lavinia Maggi' 108, *108*
C. 'Leonard Messel' 108, *108*
Camellia (continued)
C. sasanqua 'Narumigata' 486
C. x *williamsii* 'Donation' 108, *108*
'Francis Hanger' 108, *108*
'J.C. Williams' 554–5, *555*
'Saint Ewe' 108, *108*
campanula
deadheading 235
division 229, 420
dwarf 140
germination 306
rust 304
Campanula carpatica 384, *384*
C. cochleariifolia 292, *292*, 300, 301
C. lactiflora 'Prichard's Variety' 262, *262*
C. latifolia 262, *263*, 300
C. persicifolia 262, *263*
C. poscharskyana 229
'Stella' 477, *477*, 486
campion 384, *385*
Campsis 41, 499, 500
C. x *tagliabuana* 'Madame Galen' 374, *374*, 392
candytuft 129, 202, *202*
sowing 126, 215
canker 510, 523, *523*
Canna 129, 215
C. 'Assaut' *33*, 452, *452*
C. 'King Midas' 453, *453*
C. 'Phasion' *402*
C. 'Rosemond Coles' *18*
capillary matting 591, *591*, 603
caraway 482, *482*
Cardamine pratensis 54
'Flore Pleno' 174, *174*, 206
cardinal flower, blue 480, *480*
cardoon *364*, 365
Carex 124
C. comans 'Frosted Curls' *364*, 365, 392
C. oshimensis 'Evergold' 490
C. pendula 387, *387*, 393
carnations, layering 306, 398
Carpinus betulus 321, 381, *381*, 392, 417
carrots 204–5, *205*, *247*, 483, *483*, 532, 533
carrot fly 69, 162, *162*, 246, 247
in containers 533
crop rotation 534
harvesting 247, 338, 440

carrots (continued)
sowing 66, 69, 162, 246–7, 338, 527
storing 340, 341, 440, *441*, 527
watering 244
carrying equipment 587, *587*
carrying sheets 587, *587*
Carum carvi 482, *482*
Caryopteris 45, 137, 413
C. x *clandonensis* 392
'Heavenly Blue' 376, *376*, 392, 393
'Kew Blue' 468, *468*, 486, 487
castor-oil plant 215
catalpa *235*
catch crops 533
catchfly 384, *385*
caterpillars, on brassicas 338
catmint 264, *264*
cauliflowers 116, *116*, 297, *297*
crop rotation 535
earthing up 439
harvesting 245, 337
planting 337
'Purple Cape' *66*
sowing 68, 439
storing 341
watering 336
winter protection 439
ceanothus *16*, 206, 207, 409
pruning 225
training 513
winter protection 499
Ceanothus 'Autumnal Blue' 468, *468*, 486
C. x *delileanus* 'Topaze' 376, *376*, 392
C. 'Italian Skies' 285, *285*, 300
C. 'Puget Blue' 190, *190*
C. thyrsiflorus var. *repens* 190, *190*
cedar
deodar 568, *568*
japanese 556, *556*
western red 417
white 112, *112*, 479, *479*, 572–3, *572*
Cedrus deodara 568, *568*
celandine 229
Celastrus orbiculatus 466, *466*
celeriac *524*, 575, *575*
crop rotation 534
harvesting 527
sowing 69, 527
celery 483, *483*
in coldframes 257
storing 341
watering 336, 339
Centaurea cyanus 274, *274*, 300, 301
C. hypoleuca 'John Coutts' 357, *357*, 392
century plant 148
Ceratostigma willmottianum 376, *377*
Cercidiphyllum japonicum 470, *470*, 486
Cercis siliquastrum 190, *190*, 206
chaenomeles 118, 119, 132, 221, 222, 578, 579
spur pruning 225
training 513, *513*
Chaenomeles speciosa 132
'Moerloosei' 555, *555*
'Nivalis' 103, *103*
C. x *superba 501*
Chaenomeles speciosa (continued)
'Knap Hill Scarlet' 557, *557*
'Nicoline' *44*, 100, *100*
'Pink Lady' 96, *97*
chalky soils 592
plant selectors 118, 206, 300, 392, 486, 578
Chamaecyparis lawsoniana 321, 417, 578, 579
'Ellwoodii' 554, *554*, 579
'Gimbornii' 479, *479*, 487
'Green Globe' 479, *479*
'Green Hedger' 107, *107*, 119
'Minima Aurea' 572, *572*
'Tamariscifolia' 568, *568*, 579
Chamelaucium uncinatum 119
chamomile
cuttings 7741
lawns 346, *346*
oxeye 268, *268*
preserving 253
'Treneague' 346
chard *339*, 533, 535
Cheiranthus 206, 207
cherries *240*, 299, *299*
buying trees 330
harvesting 241, 334
'Morello' 332, *332–3*
pollination 330
pruning 159, 242, 331, 332, 435, 522
suckers *332*
cherry, flowering 98, *98*, 192, *192*, 197, *197*, *520*, 555, *555*, 559, *559*
great white 105, *105*
manchurian 564, *564*
pests 223
sargent's 472, *472*
training standards 513
wild 197, *197*
yoshino 105, *105*
cherry pie 458, *458*
chervil 296, *296*
preserving 253
self-seeding 343
sowing 165, 251, 350, 537
chicory 339, 575, *575*
chillies 339, 341
Chimonanthus 132
C. praecox 502, 503, 560, *561*, 579
chinese broccoli 439
chinese cabbage 337, 439
chinese lantern 454, *454*
Chionodoxa 118, 119
C. forbesii 'Pink Giant' 87, *87*
C. luciliae Gigantea Group 86, *86*
C. sardensis 86, *86*
chitting potatoes 69, 527, *527*
chives 204, *204*, *246*, 345, *346*
division 71, *442*
potting up 442–3
preserving 253
sowing 251
chocolate plant 370, *370*
chocolate vine 95, *95*, 500
Choisya ternata 51, *194*, 195, 206, 207, *207*
christmas box 566, *567*
christmas cacti 258, 351
christmas rose 490, 545, *545*
christmas tree 573, *573*
chrysanthemum
in containers *424*, 425
cuttings 540–1
sowing 31, 169, 215
winter protection 540–1
Chrysanthemum 'Clara Curtis' 357, *357*
C. 'Emperor of China' *450*, 451
C. 'Mary Stoker' 453, *453*
C. Rubellum Group 357, *357*, *450*, 451
chusan palm 289, *289*
cider gum 475, *475*
Cimicifuga simplex Atropurpurea Group 455, *455*, 486
cineraria 169, 215, 257, *519*
cinquefoil 287, *287*
cistus 139, 300
common gum 288, *288*
Cistus ladanifer 288, *288*, 301
C. 'Silver Pink' 285, *285*, 301, *301*
citrus trees 223, 234
clamps, storing vegetables 441
Clarkia amoena Satin Series 274–5, *275*, 301
clary 30, *344*
annual 366, *366*
clay soils 592
drainage 347
no-dig beds 531
soil, plant selectors 118, 206, 300, 392, 487, 578
claytonia 575, *575*
clearwing moth 332
clematis 487
alpine 188, *188*, 189, *189*
clematis wilt 220
cuttings 221
layering 133
leaf-bud cuttings 133, *133*, 317
planting 134, *409*
pruning 41, 132, 133, 220, 499
supports 135
winter protection 499
Clematis 'Abundance' 467, *467*
C. 'Alba Luxurians' 374, *374*
C. alpina 132, 133, 221
'Frances Rivis' 188, *188*
'Ruby' 95, *95*
subsp. *sibirica* 'White Moth' 189, *189*
C. armandii 95, *95*, 132, 133, 220, 409, 499
'Apple Blossom' 188, *189*
C. 'Bee's Jubilee' 282, *282*
C. 'Bill MacKenzie' 467, *467*
C. Blue Moon 282, *283*
C. cirrhosa 499
'Freckles' 551, *551*
C. 'Comtesse de Bouchaud' *16*, *17*, 373, *373*
C. x *durandii* 354, *355*
C. 'Early Sensation' *41*
C. 'Ernest Markham' 41, 467, *467*
C. 'Etoile Rose' 467, *467*

Clematis (continued)
C. 'Gillian Blades' 282, *282*
C. 'Gipsy Queen' 41, 467, *467*
C. 'Helsingborg' 188, *189*
C. 'Huldine' 467, *467*
C. 'Jackmanii' 41, *220*, *260–1*, 282, *283*
C. 'Kermesina' 373, *373*
C. 'Lasurstern' 41, 282, *283*
C. macropetala 132, *135*, 188, *189*, 221
'Maidwell Hall' 95, *95*
'Markham's Pink' 188, *189*
C. 'Maroon Velours' *17*
C. montana 133, 220
'Primrose Star' 220
var. *rubens 132*
'Elizabeth' 188, *188*
C. 'Nelly Moser' 41
C. 'Niobe' 282, *283*
C. 'Perle d'Azur' 282, *283*
C. 'The President' 41
C. rehderiana 467, *467*
C. 'Rouge Cardinal' 373, *373*
C. 'Royal Velours' 374, *374*
C. tangutica 41
C. 'The Vagabond' 282, *283*
C. vitalba 551, *551*
C. viticella 41
C. 'Warszawska Nike' 373, *373*
Cleome hassleriana 'Rose Queen' 366, *367*
Clerodendrum trichotomum var. *fargesii* 468, *469*
climate
planning borders 50
planning a fruit garden 434
planning a herb garden 344
climbers
annual climbers 41, 492
in autumn 408–11
choosing 134
in containers 40, 149
cuttings 221, 317, 409, 500
division 500
in early spring 40–1
in greenhouses 445
in late spring 132–5
in late summer 316–17
layering *408*, 409, 500
mulching 409
plant selectors 95, 188–9, 280–4, 373–4, 466–7, 551–3
climbers (continued)
planting 134, *134*, 409, *409*
propagation 500
pruning 41, 132–3, 220–1, 316–17, *317*, 445, 498–9, 540
in summer *16–17*, 220–1
supports 135, 410–11, 501
training 135, *317*
in trees 500, *501*
tying-in *135*, 220, *221*
weeding around 316
in winter 498–501
climbing roses
pruning 38, 404, 497, *497*
spacing plants 407
tying-in *131*
clivia 259
cloches 67, 606–9, *606–8*
coastal gardens
planning borders 50
plant selectors 119, 207, 301, 393, 486, 579
windbreaks 417
Cobaea scandens 221, *446*
cobble mulches 600, *600*
cocoa shell mulches 397, 409, 601
cohosh 455, *455*
Colchicum 217
C. 'The Giant' 463, *463*
C. 'Rosy Dawn' 463, *463*
C. speciosum 217
'Album' 464, *464*
coldframes 606–7, *607*
cuttings in *226*
hardening off plants 167
sowing vegetables in *67*
in summer 257
coleus 33, 73, 215
colour
bedding schemes 33
late summer *18–19*
see also individual colours
columbine 172, *172*, *178*, 179, 267, *267*
comfrey *80*, 81
liquid fertilisers 77, *77*
compost
ingredients 598
making 596–7, *596*
as mulch 601
trench composting 64, *64*
worm compost 598
compost bins 529, 598, *598*
compost heaps 259, 596–7
composts, potting 599
for alpines 141, 515
cuttings compost 599
ericaceous composts 599
in permanent containers 150–1
seed compost 599
sterilising soil 76
water-retaining gel 236, 424
concrete, cleaning 57
coneflower 358, *358*, 454, *454*, 455, *455*
confederate jasmine 374, *374*
conifers
in containers 150
cuttings 227, *227*
hedges 137, *320*
pests 223
planning gardens 51
pruning 137, 507
repairing hedges 505
in rock gardens *228*
Consolida ajacis Giant Imperial Series 274, *274*
container-grown plants, planting 138, *138*, 414
containers
alpines in 322–3
in autumn 424–5
bulbs in 129, 311, 425, *425*
cleaning *444*, 446
climbers in 40, 149
composts 599, *599*
drainage 424, *424*, 518–19
in early spring 56–7
fertilisers 147, 235, 605
flowering plants for 487
frost protection 518–19, *519*
herbs in 70, *71*, 164, *250*, 251
holiday care *259*, 326
in late spring 146–51
in late summer 326–7
mulching 151, *258*
perennials in 57
permanent containers 150–1
planting *148*, 150–1, *151*, 424
potting on 73, *73*
for propagation 590, *590*
shrubs in 146, 147, 149, 150–1
sink gardens *53*, 141
sowing seeds in 74, *74*
in summer 148, 234–7
trees in 147, 149, 150–1, *151*
vegetables in 533
containers (continued)
watering 147, 235, 236–7, *236–7*, 602
in winter 425, 518–19
Convallaria majalis 178, 179, 207
Convolvulus 235
C. sabatius 384, *384*, 392, 393
C. tricolor 'Royal Ensign' 458, *458*, 487
copper fungicide 591
coppicing 512, *512*
cordons
fruit trees 435, *436–7*
pruning 242, 522
cordyline 215, *518*
Coreopsis verticillata 'Grandiflora' 362, *362*, 392
coriander 388, *388*
preserving 253
sowing 165, 251
Coriandrum sativum 388, *388*
corn salad 116, *116*
cornel 288, *288*
cornelian cherry 560–1, *561*
cornflower 274, *274*, *308*, 350
Cornus 43, *513*, 578
C. alba 'Elegantissima' 288, *288*, 300, 301
'Kesselringii' 554, *554*
'Sibirica' 557, *557*
C. alternifolia 'Argentea' 380, *380*, 392
C. controversa 'Variegata' 288, *288*, 301
C. florida 'Cherokee Chief' 190–1, *190*, 206, 207
C. kousa var. *chinensis* 300, 301
'Satomi' 286, *286*
C. mas 560–1, *561*, 578, 579
C. sanguinea 'Winter Beauty' *23*
C. stolonifera 'Flaviramea' *512*, 568, *568*, 579
Coronilla valentina 132
subsp. *glauca* 561, *561*
Cortaderia selloana 455, *455*
'Sunningdale Silver' *364*, 365
Corydalis 514
C. flexuosa 80, *80*, 118, 119
C. lutea 56
C. ochroleuca 178, 179
C. solida 'George Baker' 87, *87*
Corylopsis pauciflora 101, *101*, 118, 119

Corylopsis (continued)
C. sinensis var. *sinensis* 'Spring Purple' 102, *102*, 118, 119
Corylus 118
C. avellana 43
'Aurea' 102, *102*, 118
'Contorta' 561, *561*
C. maxima 'Purpurea' 100, *100*, 118
cosmos, chocolate 370, *370*
Cosmos atrosanguineus 370, *370*
C. bipinnatus 'Sea Shells' 459, *459*
Sensation Series 367, *367*
C. sulphureus 'Sunset' *33*, 461, *461*
Cotinus 45, *45*
C. coggygria 512
C. 'Flame' 470, *470*, 487
Cotoneaster 487, 510, 513, 578
C. conspicuus 'Decorus' 470, *470*, 486, 487
C. frigidus 'Cornubia' *23*, 558, *558*
C. horizontalis 22
C. 'Hybridus Pendulus' 558, *558*, 579
C. lacteus 416, 558, *558*
C. salicifolius 'Rothschildianus' 473, *473*, 487
cottage gardens, vegetable plots 531
cotton lavender 318, *343*
courgettes 163, 297, *297*
catch crops 533
in containers 533
crop rotation 535
harvesting 339
planting 248
sowing 169, 249
storing 341
watering 244, 337
cowslip
blue 544, *544*
giant 295, *295*
crab apple 191, *191*, 472, *472*, 473, *473*, 559, *559*, 563, *563*
japanese 191, *191*
training standards 513
cranesbill 174, *174*, 262, *263*, 269, *269*, 292–3, *292*, 355, *355*, 358, *358*, 384, *385*
armenian 265, *265*
bloody 451, *451*
cranesbill (continued)
dusky 172, *172*
meadow 263, *263*
wood 172, *172*
Crataegus 48, 206, 207
C. laevigata 'Paul's Scarlet' *190*, 191
C. monogyna 321, 417
C. persimilis 'Prunifolia' 470, *470*, 487
cream flowers
alpines 111–12, 202, 293, 479, 573
annuals and biennials 183, 369, 462
bulbs 91, 185, 279, 371, 464, 549
climbers 95, 189, 281, 372
perennials 179–81, 269–71, 363–5, 454–6, 544–5
shrubs and trees 103–6, 195–8, 288, 380–3, 474–5, 565–6
water plants 113, 295, 387, 481
creeping jenny 122, 229
crimson glory vine, japanese 466, *466*
Crinum 129
C. x *powellii* 463, *463*
Crocosmia 19, 393
C. x *crocosmiiflora* 'Emily McKenzie' *129*, 371, *371*
C. 'Lucifer' *310*, 370, *371*
crocus 118, 119, 578, 579
cloth of gold 94, *94*
in containers 425
dutch 94, *94*
forcing 351
naturalising 35, 312
planting 217
Crocus angustifolius 94, *94*
C. banaticus 463, *463*
C. chrysanthus 'Cream Beauty' 549, *549*
'Ladykiller' 547, *547*
'Zwanenburg Bronze' 548, *548*
C. flavus 94, *94*
C. goulimyi 217
C. imperati subsp. *imperati* 'De Jager' 547, *547*, *578*
C. korokolwii 548, *548*
C. kotschyanus 464, *464*, 486, 487
C. laevigatus 'Fontenayi' 547, *547*
Crocus (continued)
C. x *luteus* 'Golden Yellow' 94, *94*
C. minimus 94, *94*
C. sativus 216, 217
C. speciosus 217, 463, *463*, 486, 487
C. tommasinianus 13
'Whitewell Purple' 547, *547*
C. vernus 'Jeanne d'Arc' 94, *94*
'Pickwick' 94, *94*
'Purpureus Grandiflorus' 94, *94*
'Remembrance' 94, *94*
crop rotation, vegetables 530, 534–5
crowfoot, water 232
crown imperial *14*, 90, *90*
crown thinning, trees 225
Cryptomeria japonica 'Elegans Compacta' 556, *556*, 579
cuckoo flower 54, 174, *174*
cucumbers
in coldframes 257
crop rotation 535
flowers *168*
in greenhouses 168, 350
harvesting 350
'Pepinex' *447*
planting 168, 248
sowing 169, 249
training 168, 256, *256*
cultivation tools 584–5, *584–5*
cultivators, power-driven 585
cup-and-saucer vine *446*
x *Cupressocyparis leylandii* 321, 417
currant
buffalo *102*, 103
flowering *100*, 101, 132, 136, 417, 569, *569*
fuchsia-flowered 101, *101*
cut flowers
annuals 29, 492
drying 215
plant selectors 119, 579
cuttings
alpines 53, 229, 323, 421
basal cuttings 125, *125*, 212, 213
bud cuttings 129, *129*, 221
climbers 221, 317, 409, 500
conifers 227, *227*
fruit 432, *432*
greenhouse plants *254–5*, 255, 259
cuttings (continued)
hardwood cuttings 129, 315, 413, 421, 432, *432*, 500
heel cuttings 319, *319*
herbs 71, 164, *165*, 251
irishman's cuttings *123*
leaf-bud cuttings 133, *133*, 221, 319
leaf cuttings *254–5*, 255
perennials 27, 212, *212*, 213, 307, 398, *490–1*, 491
potting up 327
root cuttings 46, 71, 259, 421, *490–1*, 491
rooting hormone 139, *212*, 227, 591
roses 129, *129*, 315
semi-ripe cuttings 226, *226–7*, 251, 317, 319, 323, 409
shrubs 46, *47*, 139, 226–7, *226–7*, 319, *319*, 413
soft-tip cuttings 139, 164, *165*, 212, *212*, 221, 226, 229, 251, 307, 327, *327*
stem cuttings *47*
succulents 75, *75*
tender perennials *307*, 327, *327*
trees 46
see also individual plants
cuttings compost 599
cyclamen
in containers 322, 425
planting 312
restarting corms 255
resting 258
sowing 255
Cyclamen 311
C. coum 12, 548, *548*, 578
C. hederifolium 464, *464*, 486
C. persicum 255
C. purpurascens 370, *370*
C. repandum 14
cylinder mowers 588, *588*
Cynara cardunculus 364, 365
cypress
summer 460, *460*
see also lawson cypress; leyland cypress
Cytisus 43, 206, 207, 222, 225
C. battandieri 409
C. x *beanii* 202, *202*
C. x *kewensis* 193, *193*
C. x *praecox* 'Allgold' 194, *194*

D

Daboecia cantabrica 44
daffodils *13*
  bedding schemes 32
  in containers 425
  cyclamineus 92, *92*
  deadheading 34, *34*
  double 93, *93*
  dwarf trumpet 92–3, *93*
  large-cupped 93, *93*
  lifting 216–17, *217*
  offsets 217
  plant selector 92–3
  planting 312
  poeticus 185, *185*
  small-cupped 93, *93*
  tenby 93, *93*
  triandrus 93, *93*
  trumpet 92, *92*, *548*, 549
  see also Narcissus
dahlia *18*, *19*
  bedding schemes 215
  cactus-flowered 370, *370*
  cuttings 35
  disbudding *217*
  planting *128*, 129
  pompom 370–1, *371*
  sowing 30
  starting into growth 495, 540
Dahlia 'Bishop of Llandaff' 465, *465*
  D. 'Bridge View Aloha' *402*
  D. 'Claire de Lune' 465, *465*
  D. 'David Howard' 465, *465*
  D. 'Figaro Red' 460, *460*, 487
  D. 'Kiwi Gloria' 370, *370*
  D. 'Moor Place' 370–1, *371*
  D. 'Peach Cupid' 465, *465*
  D. 'Porcelain' 465, *465*
  D. 'White Moonlight' 465, *465*
  D. 'Yellow Hammer' 465, *465*
  D. 'Zorro' 465, *465*
daisy
  african 460, *460*
  double *29*, 85, *85*, 182, *182*, 401
  mexican 56
  shasta 270, *270*
  swan river 366, *366*
damask roses 407
damping down, greenhouses 256
damping-off disease 31, 76
damsons 334–5, 484, *484*
dandelions 58, 239
  drying roots 443
Daphne 146
  D. bholua var. *glacialis* 'Gurkha' 96, *97*
    'Jacqueline Postill' 555, *555*
  D. blagayana 104, *104*, 118
  D. cneorum 229
    'Eximia' 200–1, *201*
  D. mezereum f. *alba* *564*, 565
  D. odora 'Aureomarginata' 555, *555*
Darmera peltata 144, *144*
Davidia involucrata *194*, 195
daylily 265, *265*, 268, *268*, *325*, 361, *361*, 362, *362*
deadheading
  annuals 308
  bulbs 34, *34*
  herbs *250*
  patio plants 234–5
  perennials 211
  roses 218–19, *314*
  shrubs *137*
  see also individual plants
decking, cleaning 57
deep bed system, vegetables 531, *531*
deep-water plants 232
deer, protecting new hedges from 419
delphinium
  cuttings 125, 213
  deadheading 211
  planting 124
  supporting 211
Delphinium Belladonna Group
    'Atlantis' 262, *263*
    'Cliveden Beauty' 354–5, *355*
  D. grandiflorum 'Blue Butterfly' 274, *274*
derris 243
Deschampsia cespitosa
    'Goldschleier' 360, *360*, 392
    'Tautrager' *21*
Deutzia 318
  D. x *elegantissima* 'Rosealind' 191, *191*
  D. x *rosea* 286, *286*, 300
devil-in-a-bush 274, *274*
Dianthus *140*, 212, *213*, 301, *322*
  D. alpinus 'Joan's Blood' 292, *292*
  D. barbatus 300
    'Roundabout' 276, *276*
Dianthus (continued)
  D. chinensis Baby Doll Series 367, *367*, 392, 393
  D. 'Gran's Favourite' 264–5, *265*, 300, *300*
dianthus rust 304
Diascia 326
  D. barberae 'Ruby Field' 384, *385*
  D. rigescens 358, *358*
  D. 'Salmon Supreme' 477, *477*, 487
dibbers 591
Dicentra 207
  D. 'Langtrees' 179, *179*
  D. 'Luxuriant' 176, *176*, 207
  D. spectabilis 124, 174, *174*, 306
    'Alba' *123*
die-back 510
digging 331, 594
  double digging 525, *525*, 594, *595*
  new lawns 154
  single digging 593, *593*
  winter cultivation 525, *525*
Digitalis 215
  D. purpurea *127*, 275, *275*
dill 296, *296*, *537*
  preserving 253
  sowing 165, 251, 537
dimorphotheca 30
Disanthus cercidifolius 470, *470*, 486
  D. gunnii 486
disbudding
  dahlias *217*
  roses 218
diseases 258
  fruit 523
  lawns 153, 329
  organic gardening 259
  perennials 304
  roses 37, *37*, 131
  trees and shrubs 223
  see also individual plants and diseases
Disporum sessile 'Variegatum' 179, *179*, 207
division
  alpines 141, 229, 420
  climbers 500
  grasses *27*
  herbs 70, *70*, 71, *442–3*, 443
division (continued)
  perennials 124–5, 212, *213*, 306, 398–9, *399*
  water plants 143, *143*
  see also individual plants
docks 58
dog's-tooth violet 185, *185*
  american *14*
  european 184, *185*
dogwood 288, *288*, 557, *557*
  coppicing 512, *512*
  flowering 190–1, *190*, 286, *286*
  pagoda 380, *380*
  pruning *513*
  red-barked 288, *288*
  red osier 568, *568*
dome cloches 609
Doronicum *123*, 306
  D. orientale 'Magnificum' 176, *177*, 206, 207
double digging 525, *525*, 594, *595*
dove tree *194*, 195
Draba rigida *52*
  var. *bryoides* 111, *111*
dragonflies 232
dragonhead, false 451, *451*
drainage
  alpines 53
  containers 424, *424*, 518–19
  lawns 520–1
  soil 347
  vegetable plots 528
draw hoes 585, *585*
'dropping' 165, 537, *537*
dry soil, plant selectors 118, 119, 206, 207, 300, 392, 486, 578
drying
  bulbs 403
  cut flowers 215
  herb seeds 342–3
  herbs 252–3, 443
  peas and beans 340
  vegetables 438
Dryopteris affinis 181, *181*, 207
  D. erythrosora 175, *175*, 207
duckweed 142, 143, *231*, 232, 325
dungwort 545, *545*
dutch hoes 244–5, 584, *585*
dwarf beans 298, *298*, 534
dyes, herbal 344

E

earthing up
  brassicas 439, 440
  potatoes 246, 247, *247*
earthworms, wormcasts 427, *427*
echeveria 75
Echinacea purpurea 304
  'Magnus' 358, *358*
  'White Lustre' 455, *455*
Echinops ritro 212
  'Veitch's Blue' 355, *355*, 392, *392*, 393
edgers, half-moon 588
Eichhornia crassipes 423
Elaeagnus 321
  E. x *ebbingei* 417
  E. pungens 'Maculata' 561, *561*, 579
elder 137
  golden 512
elephant's ears 81, *81*, 83, *83*, *178*, 179
endive 116, *116*, 257
Enkianthus 227
  E. campanulatus 191, *191*, 207
Epimedium 118, 206, 207
  E. grandiflorum 'Rose Queen' 81, *81*, 119
  E. perralderianum 82, *82*, 119
  E. x *rubrum* 176, *176*, 207
  E. x *versicolor* 'Sulphureum' 176, *177*, 207
  E. x *warleyense* 'Orangekönigin' 176, *177*
  E. x *youngianum* 'Niveum' 180, *180*, 207
equipment 582–91
  basic kit 582
  buying 583
  caring for 583
  carrying equipment 587, *587*
  cultivation tools 584–5, *584–5*
  hedge-trimming 320
  hiring 583
  lawn care 521, 588–9, *588–9*
  propagation 590–1, *590–1*
  pruning tools 506–7, 583, 586–7, *586–7*
  watering 589, *589*, 591, *591*, 603
Eranthis hyemalis 494, 548, *548*
Erica 119, 579
  E. arborea var. *alpina* 195, *195*, 206, 207
  E. carnea 578
    'King George' 571, *571*
    'Springwood White' 571, *571*
    'Vivellii' 571, *571*
  E. ciliaris 44
  E. cinerea 44
  E. x *darleyensis* 44, 578
    'Arthur Johnson' 571, *571*
    'Furzey' 571, *571*
    'Kramer's Rote' 96, *96*
    'Silberschmelze' 104, *104*
    'White Perfection' 571, *571*
  E. erigena 'Brightness' 571, *571*, 578
    'Irish Dusk' 96, *97*
  E. gracilis 425
  E. tetralix 44
  E. vagans 'Mrs D.F. Maxwell' 378, *378*, 392, 393
ericaceous plants 599, 605
Erigeron 123
  E. karvinskianus 56
Erinus alpinus 140
Erodium 514
  E. 'County Park' 478, *478*, 486, 487, *487*
Eryngium 392, 393
  E. alpinum 355, *355*
  E. x *tripartitum* 355, *355*
Erysimum 206
  E. 'Bowles' Mauve' 265, *265*, 300, 301
  E. cheiri 'Blood Red' 85, *85*, 118, 119
    'Fire King' 183, *183*
    'Golden Gem' 183, *183*
    'Ivory White' 183, *183*
    'Orange Bedder' 183, *183*
Erythronium 307, 312
  E. californicum 'White Beauty' 185, *185*
  E. dens-canis 184, *185*
  E. oregonum 14
Escallonia 321, 417
  E. 'Apple Blossom' 378, *378*, 392, 393
Eschscholzia 214
  E. californica 277, *277*, 300, 301, *492*
espaliers
  fruit trees *431*, 435
espaliers (continued)
  pruning 242, 522
  training 513
Eucalyptus 137, 512
  E. gunnii 475, *475*, 487, 512
  E. pauciflora subsp. *niphophila* 565, *565*, 578, 579
eucomis 35
Eucryphia x *nymansensis* 'Nymansay' 380, *380*, 393
Euonymus 226, 578
  E. alatus 'Compactus' 470, *471*
  E. europaeus 'Red Cascade' *414*, 468–9, *469*, 486
  E. fortunei 578, 579
    'Coloratus' 551, *551*
    'Emerald Gaiety' 565, *565*
    'Emerald 'n' Gold' 562, *562*
  E. japonicus 510
Eupatorium purpureum 480, *480*
euphorbia 119
  in containers *149*
  cutting back *211*
  planting 124
Euphorbia amygdaloides
    'Purpurea' 176, *177*, 207
    var. *robbiae* 82, *82*, 118, 119
  E. characias subsp. *wulfenii 82*, 83, 118, 119
  E. griffithii 'Fireglow' 267, *267*
  E. x *martinii* 181, *181*
  E. palustris 203, *203*
  E. polychroma 176–7, *177*, 206
  E. rigida 82, 83, 118, 119
  E. schillingii 456, *456*, 486
  E. seguieriana subsp. *niciciana* 456, *456*, 486, 487
evening primrose 385, *385*, *439*
evergreens
  in containers 146, 150
  frost protection 518, *518*, *519*
  hedges *321*, 416
  planning gardens 51
  planting 138, *138*, 409
  pruning 43, 137, 507
  topiary 48, *48–9*
  transplanting 504
'everlasting' flowers 215
Exochorda x *macrantha* 'The Bride' 196, *196*
exposed gardens
  windbreaks 417
  see also coastal gardens

F

Fagus 223
  F. sylvatica 321, 417, 558, *558*
fair maids of france 180, *181*
fair maids of kent 180, *181*
fairies' thimbles 292, *292*
fairy bells 179, *179*
fairy fan-flower 366, *367*
fairy foxglove 140
fairy moss 142, 325, *325*, 423, 480, *480*
fans
  fruit trees 432, 435
  pruning and training 242, 513, 522
Fargesia murielae 289, *289*, 300, 301
  F. nitida 381, *381*, 392, 393
Fatsia japonica 475, *475*, 486
feather grass, giant *360*, 361
feathertop 458, *459*
feeding plants *see* fertilisers
fences, trellis on 410
fennel 204, *204*, 206
  bronze 211, *442*
  preserving 253
  seeds 343
  sowing 251
fennel, florence
  earthing up 440
  sowing 338
fenugreek, green manures 337
ferns *50*, *235*, 259
  flowering 480–1, *480*
  royal 480–1, *480*
fertilisers 594, 604–5
  alpines 229, 322
  annuals 605
  applying 604–5, *604–5*
  bulbs 311
  container plants 147, 235, 605
  controlled-release 605
  ericaceous plants 605
  fruit 60, 159, 605
  greenhouse plants 168, 256
  hedges 137
  lawns 59, 157, 605
  liquid fertilisers 77, *77*, 147, 605, *605*
  organic gardening 259
  over-feeding plants 147
  roses 129, 130, *131*, 407
  slow-release fertilisers 147, *147*

fertilisers (continued)
spreaders 589, *589*
vegetables 534, 605
fescue 262, *263*, 479, *479*
Festuca glauca 'Elijah Blue' 262, *263*, 300, 301
'Seeigel' 479, *479*, 486, 487
fetter bush 105, *105*
figs *335*, *390*, 391
harvesting 335
planning a fruit garden 434
pruning 159
filbert 100, *100*
Filipendula rubra 'Venusta' 386, *386*, 393
F. ulmaria 'Aurea' 177, *177*, 206, 207
fir, korean 376, *376*
fireblight 510
firethorn 221
fish
cleaning out ponds *55*
frozen ponds 516
protecting against herons 423, *423*
stocking ponds 233, *233*
flageolet beans *244*
flame flower 500
fleece 601
flies, on compost heaps 597
floating cloches 609
floating mulches 601
floribunda roses
deadheading 218
disbudding 218
pruning 38
spacing plants 407
floss flower 274, *275*
foam flower 181, *181*, 266, *266*
foam of may 198, *198*
Foeniculum vulgare 204, *204*, 206
'Purpureum' 211
foliage
annuals 492
bedding schemes 33
bulbs *35*, 129
and coppicing 512
reversion 318, 510, *510*
scented 579
see also individual colours
foliar fertilisers 605
forcing
bulbs 351, *351*
kale *68*
forcing (continued)
rhubarb 62, 63, *539*
roses 496–7
strawberries 62, 63, *538*, 539
forget-me-not *126*, 182, *182*
as bedding plants 32, 401
in containers *146*
creeping 80, *80*
sowing 127, 215
transplanting seedlings 215
water 294, *294*
forks 584, *584*, 585, *585*
formal hedges 320, 321, 416, 417
formal herb gardens 344, *345*
formative pruning, shrubs 224, *224–5*
forsythia 118, 119
pruning 136, 227
Forsythia 'Beatrix Farrand' 102, *102*
F. giraldiana 562, *562*, 578, 579
F. x *intermedia* 'Lynwood' *102*, 103
F. suspensa *102*, 103, 132
Fothergilla major Monticola Group 196, *196*, 207
fountain grass 456, *456*
fountains, oxygenating ponds 233, 324
foxglove 275, *275*
sowing 127
transplanting seedlings 215
fragrance *see* scented plants
frames, topiary *49*
freezing
herbs 252
vegetables 340, 341
french beans *244*, *336*, 533
climbing 389, *389*
crop rotation 534
dwarf 298, *298*
harvesting 337
sowing 161, 169, 245
storing 340, 341
fringe cups 175, *175*
Fritillaria imperialis *14*, 90, *90*, 119
F. meleagris *14*, 184, *184*, 206, *312*
fritillary
naturalising 35, 312
snake's head *14*, 184, *184*
frogbit 142
frogs 233, 516
frost damage, shrubs 42, *42*
frost protection
cloches and coldframes 606–7, *606–7*
containers 518–19, *519*
fruit 61, *61*
greenhouse plants 166
planning a fruit garden 434
topiary 48
fruit 484–5, *484–5*
in autumn 430–7
bare-rooted plants 433
buying plants 330–1
creating a fruit garden 434–7
cuttings 432, *432*
diseases 523
in early spring 60–3
fertilisers 60, 159, 605
frost protection 61, *61*
fruit cages 158, *158*
in greenhouses 62, 540
harvesting 241, 330, 334–5, 430
in late spring 158–9
in late summer 330–5
mulching 60
pests 431, 523
plant selectors 205, 299, 390–1, 484–5, 577
planting 436–7
pollination 62, 158, 330
preparing soil 331
protection from birds *330*
pruning 61, 159, 242, 331, 332–3, 432, 435, 437, 522, *522*, *523*
rootstocks 331, 435
in small gardens 435, *435*
soil 435, 436
storing 334–5, 430–1, *430*
in summer 240–3
supporting branches 332
thinning 159, *159*
training 435, *436–7*
tying-in 243, *243*
watering 602
in winter 522–3
winter washing 523
see also individual types of fruit
fuchsia
bedding schemes 32, 215
in containers 148, 150
cuttings 323
frost protection 42
pruning 45, 137
reviving 73
Fuchsia 301, 393, 486, 487
F. 'Alice Hoffman' 469, *469*
F. 'Annabel' 382, *382*
F. 'La Campanella' 382, *382*
F. 'Lady Thumb' *33*, 287, *287*
F. 'Leonora' 382, *382*
F. magellanica 417
'Versicolor' 382, *382*
F. 'Margaret' *327*
F. 'Mrs Popple' 382, *382*, 469, *469*
F. 'Red Spider' 382, *382*
F. 'Riccartonii' 471, *471*
F. 'Snowcap' 471, *471*
fuji cherry 555, *555*
fumitory, yellow 56
fungal diseases
fungicides 247, 591
perennials 304
fusarium patch 153

G

Galanthus 578, 579
G. 'Atkinsii' 549, *549*
G. elwesii 549, *549*
G. nivalis 549, *549*
G. 'S. Arnott' 549, *549*
Galax urceolata 452, *452*, 486, 487
Galium odoratum 115, *115*
Galtonia 35, 129
G. candicans 371, *371*
garden lines *585*
gardener's garters 270, *271*
garland flower 200–1, *201*
garlic 298, *298*
crop rotation 534
drying 257
planting 440, *440*, 527, *527*
storing 68, 341, 527
Garrya elliptica *51*
'James Roof' 568, *568*, 578, 579
Gaultheria 227
G. mucronata 578, 579
'Bell's Seedling' 558–9, *558*
'Mulberry Wine' 471, *471*, 486
'Wintertime' 565, *565*
Gaura lindheimeri 364–5, *364*, 392
'Siskiyou Pink' *450*, 451, 487
gayfeather *358*, 359
gean 197, *197*
Genista aetnensis 379, *379*, 392
gentian *228*, 322, 420
spring 200, *200*
star 200, *200*

gentian (continued)
trumpet 200, *200*
willow 355, *355*
Gentiana 207
G. acaulis 200, *200*
G. asclepiadea 355, *355*, 393
G. septemfida 384, *384*, 393
G. sino-ornata 477, *477*, 486
G. x *stevenagensis 420*
G. 'Strathmore' 477, *477*, 486
G. verna 200, *200*
geotextile membrane 150, *151*, 601
geranium
deadheading 211, 235
division *399*
see also pelargonium
Geranium 301, 393
G. 'Ann Folkard' *213*, 358, *358*
G. cinereum 'Ballerina' 292–3, *292*, 300
subsp. *subcaulescens* 384, *385*
G. clarkei x *collinum* 'Kashmir White' 269, *269*
G. 'Johnson's Blue' 262, *263*
G. macrorrhizum 'Ingwersen's Variety' 174, *174*, 207
G. x *magnificum 51*, 262, *263*
G. phaeum 172, *172*, 207
G. pratense 'Mrs Kendall Clark' 263, *263*
G. psilostemon 265, *265*
G. x *riversleaianum* 'Russell Prichard' 358, *358*, 393
G. sanguineum 451, *451*, 486
G. sylvaticum 'Mayflower' 172, *172*
G. wallichianum 'Buxton's Variety' 355, *355*
germander 165
germination
annuals 30
failure of 77
perennials 306
testing old seeds 77, *77*
Geum rivale 'Leonard's Variety' 266, *267*, 301
ghost tree *194*, 195
gillyflower 275, *275*
Ginkgo biloba 473, *473*
Gladiolus 129, 403
G. 'The Bride' 279, *279*
G. callianthus 311
'Murielae' 371, *371*
Gladiolus (continued)
G. communis subsp. *byzantinus* *278*, 279
G. 'Green Woodpecker' 371, *371*
G. tristis 206
gladwyn iris 452–3, *453*
glass
cloches and coldframes 606, *606–7*
protecting seed trays 591
Gleditsia triacanthos 'Sunburst' 287, *287*, 300
globe artichokes 297, *297*, *339*, 535
fertilisers 249
harvesting 248, 249, 339
planting 69
globe thistle 355, *355*
globeflower, european 295, *295*
gloriosa 259
glory of the snow 86, *86*, 87, *87*
gloves 583
gloxinia
leaf cuttings *254*
starting into growth 540
glyphosate 223, 316, 397, 436
godetia 274–5, *275*
gold dust 202, *202*
golden bell *102*, 103
golden club 232, *232*
golden rain *194*, 195
golden-rain tree 379, *379*
good king henry 116, *116*
gooseberries *241*, 299, *299*, 330
cuttings 432
harvesting 241, 335
planning a fruit garden 434
planting 436
pruning 61, 242, 522, *523*
sawflies 242
thinning 159, *159*, 241
training 435
tying-in 437
granny's bonnet *178*, 179
granular fertiliser 604, *604*
grape hyacinth *86*, 87, 184, *184*, 185, *185*
grape vines 280, *281*, *316*, 485, *485*
in greenhouses 62, 350
harvesting 335, 350
mildew 256
on patios 149
pollination 256
grape vines (continued)
pruning 159, 540
thinning grapes 62, 256
watering 256
grapefruit, trapping slugs 123
grass
mulching with grass cuttings 601
paths 346
under fruit trees 523
see also lawns
grasses, ornamental *20–1*
collecting seed 398
in containers *235*
division *27*
sowing 31
in winter 490, *490*
gravel
mulches 600, *600*
paths 346
gravelly soil, plant selectors 119, 206, 300, 392, 487, 578
grease bands, on fruit trees 431
Great Dixter, Sussex *19*
green flowers and foliage
alpines 112, 293, 479, 573
annuals and biennials 277, 369, 462
climbers 95, 281, 551
perennials 181, 272, 365, 456, 545
shrubs and trees 107, 198, 289, 381, 475, 568–9
water plants 203, 295, 387
green manures 259, 337, 594
greenfly *see* aphids
greengages 434–5
greenhouses
in autumn 444–7
cleaning 349, *349*, 446
damping down 349
in early spring 72–7
fertilisers 168
fruit 62, 540
heating 539
holiday care 349
insulation 447
in late summer 348–51
planting crops in 168
propagation in 74–7
shading 166–7, 349
sowing seeds in 30, 74, *74*, 169
in summer 254–9
temperature control 166
training plants 168
greenhouses (continued)
vegetables in 256–7, 350
ventilation 166, 167, 349, 539, *539*
watering 167, 539
in winter 446–7, 538–41
grey foliage
alpines 112, 293, 479, 573
annuals and biennials 277
perennials 181, 271–2, 365
shrubs and trees 288–9, 381, 566–7
water plants 481
Griselinia littoralis 321, 417
'Variegata' 104, *104*, 119
grit, mulching alpines 421, *421*
ground beetles 259
ground box 110–11, *110*
ground elder 228–9
ground-cover plants
plant selectors 207, 301, 393, 487, 579
roses 38, 378, *378*
groundsel 229
golden *480*, 481
guelder rose 192, *193*, 473, *473*
Gunnera manicata 54, 295, *295*, 301
Gypsophila 392
G. cerastioides 206
G. paniculata 'Bristol Fairy' *364*, 365, 393
G. repens 'Rosa Schönheit' 293, *293*, 300
G. 'Rosenschleier' 358–9, *358*

H

Haberlea rhodopensis 141
hair grass, tufted 360, *360*
Hakonechloa macra 'Alboaurea' 268, *268*
Halesia carolina 196, *196*, 207
half-hardy annuals *see* annuals
half-moon edgers 588
Hamamelis 23, 503, *503*, 578, 579
H. x *intermedia* 579
'Arnold Promise' 562, *562*
'Diane' *558*, 559
'Pallida' *542–3*, 562–3, *562*
H. mollis 562, 563, 579
H. vernalis 'Sandra' *102*, 103, 118, 119
hand cultivators 585, *585*
hand forks *585*, 585

handkerchief tree *194*, 195
hanging baskets
  planting 148–9, *149*
  watering 147, 149, 236
  in winter *492*
  see also containers
hardening off
  in coldframes 167
  container plants 148
  perennials 122–3
hardwood cuttings
  alpines 421
  climbers 500
  fruit 432, *432*
  roses 129, 315
  shrubs 413
hardy annuals *see* annuals
hare's tail 462, *462*
hart's tongue fern 272, *272*
harvesting
  extending harvest 67
  fruit 241, 330, 334–5, 430
  herbs 252, 342–3, 443
  root vegetables 246–7
  seeds 306, 308–9
  vegetables 336, 337–9, 350, 439, 524
  see also individual types of fruit and vegetable
hattie's pincushion 272, *272*
hawthorn 470, *470*
  hedges 321, 413, 416, 417
  topiary 48
hazel *43*, 102, *102*
  coppicing *512*
  corkscrew 561, *561*
  hedges 416
heaters, ponds 516
heath 571, *571*
  alpine 571, *571*
  cornish 378, *378*
  darley dale 96, *96*, 104, *104*, 571, *571*
  irish 96, *97*, 571, *571*
  mediterranean 96–7, *97*, 571, *571*
  tree 195, *195*
  wandering 378, *378*
  winter 571, *571*
heather *22*, 378, *378*, 557, *557*, 560, *561*
  in containers 425
  scots 468, *469*
  trimming 44, *44*
heating
  greenhouses 539
  propagators 75
Hebe 139, 223, 301
  H. 'Autumn Glory' 468, *469*, 486
  H. cupressoides 'Boughton Dome' *51*, 293, *293*, 301
  H. salicifolia 417
  H. 'Youngii' 285, *285*, 301
Hedera 118, 578, 579
  H. colchica 579
    'Dentata' 551, *551*
    'Dentata Variegata' 95, *95*, 118, 119
    'Sulphur Heart' 551, *551*
  H. helix 'Adam' 552, *552*
    'Atropurpurea' 553, *553*
    'Buttercup' 552, *553*
    'Glacier' 553, *553*
    'Glymii' 553, *553*
    'Goldchild' 552, *553*
    'Goldheart' *500*, 552, *552*
    'Ivalace' 552, *552*
    'Manda's Crested' 552, *552*
    'Parsley Crested' 552, *552*
    'Pedata' 553, *553*
    'Pittsburgh' 553, *553*
hedgehogs 232, 259
hedges
  boundary hedges 416–17
  clearing base of 503, *503*
  dwarf hedges *328*
  fertilisers 137
  growing bulbs under 311
  growth rates 417
  hedge trimmers 320, 587
  herb hedges 165, *165*
  low hedges 419
  maintenance 137
  mulching 137, 418, *419*
  overgrown 43, *43*, 321, *413*
  planting 413, *413*, 414, 418–19, *418–19*
  repairing 504–5, *505*
  thorns 417
  trimming 137, *137*, 320–1, *320*
  watering 137, 223
  weeding under 223, *320*
  windbreaks 417
heel cuttings, shrubs 319, *319*
'heeling' in, bare-rooted plants 433
Helenium 'Moerheim Beauty' 361, *361*
  H. 'Sonnenwunder' 453, *453*
helen's flower 361, *361*, 453, *453*
Helianthemum 323, *323*
  H. 'Wisley Primrose' 293, *293*, 300, 301
Helianthus 124
  H. annuus 'Velvet Queen' 460, *460*
  H. 'Lemon Queen' 454, *454*
Helichrysum 33, 215
  H. petiolare 277, *277*
Heliopsis 305
heliotrope 458, *458*
  bedding schemes 215
  in containers 148
  reviving 73
  winter 113, *113*
Heliotropium arborescens 'Marine' *33*, 458, *458*, 487
helipterum 215
hellebore 124, 399
  corsican 545, *545*
  stinking 545, *545*
Helleborus 118, 578, 579
  H. argutifolius 545, *545*
  H. foetidus 57
    Wester Flisk Group 545, *545*
  H. hybridus 12, 84, *84*
    'Pluto' *78–9*
  H. niger 490, 545, *545*, 579
  H. x *nigercors* 545, *545*
  H. orientalis 490, *491*
    subsp. *guttatus* 84, *84*
  H. x *sternii* Blackthorn Group 545, *545*
    'Boughton Beauty' 84, *84*
  H. torquatus Party Dress Group 84, *84*
Hemerocallis 300, 392
  H. 'Catherine Woodbery' *51*, 265, *265*
  H. lilioasphodelus 268, *268*
  H. 'Pardon Me' 361, *361*
  H. 'Stella de Oro' 362, *362*
hemlock, western 569, *569*
Hepatica 118
  H. nobilis 109, *109*
  H. transsilvanica 109, *109*
herbaceous perennials *see* perennials
herbs 482, *482*
  annuals 537
  in autumn 442–3
  in containers 70, *71*, 164, *250*, 251
herbs (continued)
  creating a herb garden 344–7
  cuttings 71, 164, *165*, 251
  deadheading *250*
  division 70, *70*, 71, *442–3*, 443
  'dropping' 165
  drying 443
  in early spring 70–1
  harvesting 252, 342–3, 443
  hedges 165, *165*
  herb towers *71*
  herb wheels 346
  infusions 253
  in late spring 164–5
  in late summer 342–7
  lawns 346
  layering 165, 251
  plant selectors 114–15, 204, 296–7, 388, 482, 574
  planting *347*, 443
  potting up 442–3, *442*
  propagation 251, 537, *537*
  repotting 70
  seats 346
  sowing 165, 537
  storing 252–3, *252–3*
  in summer 250–3
  tidying herb gardens 343
  in winter 536–7
  see also individual herbs
herons, protecting fish from 423, *423*
heron's bill 478, *478*
Heuchera micrantha var. *diversifolia* 'Palace Purple' 360, *360*, 393, *518*
x *Heucherella tiarelloides* 174, *174*, 207
Hibiscus syriacus 'Oiseau Bleu' 376, *377*, 392
  'Woodbridge' 469, *469*, 487
higan cherry 555, *555*
Hippeastrum 216, 258, 495, *495*
Hippophae rhamnoides 562, 563, 579
hips, roses *407*, *496*, *497*
hiring equipment 583
hoes 583, 584–5, *585*
  weeding vegetable beds 244–5
Holboellia coriacea 95, *95*
holiday care 258
  containers *259*, 326
  greenhouses 349
  vegetables 339

holly 570, *570*
blue 570, *570*
box-leaved 570, *570*
english 570, *570*
hedgehog 570, *570*
hedges 43, 321, 416, 417, *417*, 418, *418*
highclere 475, *475*
japanese 570, *570*
pruning 43, 137, 511
topiary 48
hollyhock 215, 276, *276*, *309*
honesty 183, *183*
perennial 180, *180*
honey bush 288–9, *289*
honey locust 287, *287*
honeysuckle 104, *104*, 375, *375*
coral 375, *375*
cuttings 500
early dutch 281, *281*
etruscan 375, *375*
japanese 375, *375*
late dutch 375, *375*
pruning 41, 132, 221, 499
shrubby 565, *565*
supports 135
trumpet 375, *375*
hop 281, *281*
golden 132, *220–1*, 500
hormone rooting powder 139, *212*, 227, 591
hornbeam 381, *381*
hedges 321, 413, 417
hop *102*, 103
horseradish 443, 574, *574*
hortensia 383, *383*
hosepipes 589, 603
hosta *123*, 206, 207, 300, 301, 392, 393
cutting back 396
division *125*
Hosta fortunei var. *albopicta* 177, *177*, 207
var. *aureomarginata* 362, *362*
H. 'Francee' 270, *270*
H. 'Ginko Craig' 270, *270*
H. 'Gold Standard' 268–9, *268*
H. 'Halcyon' 263, *263*
H. 'Honeybells' *358*, 359
H. lancifolia 365, *365*
H. 'Royal Standard' 272, *272*
H. sieboldiana var. *elegans* 272, *272*
H. 'Snowden' *364*, 365
Hosta (continued)
H. undulata var. *univittata* 180, *180*, 207
houseleek *228*, 385, *385*
hover flies 259, *259*
Humulus lupulus 'Aureus' 132, *220–1*, 281, *281*, 300
Hyacinthoides non-scripta 184, *184*, 207
hyacinths 88, *88*, 184, *184*, 185, *185*
bedding schemes 32
deadheading 34, *34*
forcing 351
growing in water 350
lifting 216–17
planting 402
scooping 403
scoring 403, *403*
Hyacinthus orientalis 119
'Amethyst' *13*
'Anna Marie' 88, *88*
'Carnegie' *15*, 185, *185*
'Jan Bos' 88–9, *88*
'Ostara' 184, *184*
hybrid berries
harvesting 335
pests 243
pruning 61, 332–3, 432
training 435
tying-in 60, 243
hybrid musk roses 407
hybrid tea roses
deadheading 219
disbudding 218
pruning 38
spacing plants 407
hydrangea
frost protection 42
lacecap 383, *383*
mophead 383, *383*
pruning 43, 45
supports 135
Hydrangea *19*, 393, 486
H. anomala subsp. *petiolaris* 135, 281, *281*, 300
H. arborescens 45
'Annabelle' 383, *383*
H. aspera Villosa Group 383, *383*
H. macrophylla 45, 393
'Altona' 383, *383*
'Ayesha' 383, *383*
'Blue Wave' 383, *383*
Hydrangea (continued)
'Madame Emile Mouillère' 474–5, *474*, 486, 487
H. paniculata 45, 137, 150
'Unique' 383, *383*
H. 'Preziosa' 471, *471*, 486, 487
H. serrata 'Bluebird' 383, *383*
Hydrocharis morsus-ranae 142
hygiene, cleaning greenhouses 349, *349*, 446
Hypericum 392, 393
H. 'Hidcote' 379, *379*
H. olympicum 385, *385*
hyssop 296, *296*, *442–3*
anise 114, *114*
cuttings 71
hedges 165
preserving 253
shearing 343
Hyssopus officinalis 296, *296*

I

Iberis 206, 207
I. sempervirens 'Weisser Zwerg' 202, *202*
I. umbellata 129
Fairy Series 182, *182*
ice, on ponds 516, *516*
ice plant 360, *360*, 452, *452*
Ilex 578, 579
I. x *altaclerensis* 579
'Camelliifolia' 475, *475*, 486, 487
'Golden King' 570, *570*
I. aquifolium 321, 417, *417*, 579
'Bacciflava' 570, *570*
'Ferox Argentea' 570, *570*
'Handsworth New Silver' 570, *570*
'J.C. van Tol' 570, *570*
'Pyramidalis' 570, *570*
I. crenata 'Convexa' 570, *570*
I. x *meserveae* 'Blue Princess' 570, *570*
Impatiens 33, 308
I. New Guinea Group 460, *460*, 486, 487
I. walleriana Tempo Series 367, *367*, 393
Imperata cylindrica 'Rubra' *20*, 452, *453*
Incarvillea delavayi 265, *265*
indian shot plant 452, 453, *453*
informal hedges 321, 416, 417
informal herb gardens 344
infusions, herbal 253
insects
beneficial 259, 396
and ponds 232
insulation
containers 519, *519*
greenhouses 447
intercropping 161, 533, *533*
Ipheion uniflorum *86*, 87
Ipomoea 221, *316*
iris
bearded 263, *263*, 265, *265*, 270, *270*
beardless 175, *175*
beardless water 294, *294*
division 212, *213*, 231
dwarf bearded 172, *173*, 181, *181*
japanese 294, *294*
siberian 263, *263*
Iris 206, 300, 578, 579
I. 'Demon' 172, *173*
I. ensata 294, *294*
I. 'Florentina' 181, *181*
I. foetidissima *22*, 452–3, *453*, 486
I. 'George' 550, *550*
I. 'Green Spot' 181, *181*
I. histrioides 'Major' 550, *550*
I. 'Holden Clough' 175, *175*, *206*
I. 'J.S. Dijt' 550, *550*
I. 'Jane Phillips' *51*, 263, *263*
I. 'Joyce' 550, *550*
I. 'Katharine Hodgkin' 550, *550*
I. laevigata 144
'Variegata' 294, *294*
I. 'Natascha' 550, *550*
I. pallida 'Argentea Variegata' 270, *270*
I. 'Pearly Dawn' 265, *265*
I. pseudacorus 'Variegata' 203, *203*
I. 'Rare Edition' 172, *173*
I. reticulata 550, *550*
I. sibirica 'Ego' 263, *263*
I. unguicularis 490
irishman's cuttings *123*
iron 604
ironwood, persian 559, *559*
Isotoma axillaris 458, *458*, 486, 487
ivy 551, *551*, 552–3, *552–3*
bullock's heart 95, *95*
in containers *57*, 150, *518*, *519*

ivy (continued)
persian 95, *95*, 551, *551*
pruning 317, *317*
supports 135, *410*
topiary *49*

J

jacob's ladder 174–5, *174*
japanese lantern 454, *454*
japanese onions 338
japonica 100, *100*, 557, *557*
jasmine
pruning 41, 132, 498, 499, *499*
summer 134
winter 132, 134, 498, *498–9*, 563, *563*
Jasminum nudiflorum 132, 134, 498, *498–9*, 563, *563*, 579
J. officinale 41, 134, 281, *281*, *317*, 499
jellies, herb 253
jerusalem artichokes 483, *483*, 535
cutting down 441
planting 69
storing 527
jerusalem cowslip 83, *83*
jerusalem sage *80*, 81
jew's mantle 194, *194*
joe-pye weed 480, *480*
John Innes composts 599
jonquil 93, *93*
judas tree 190, *190*
'June drop', apples 242
juniper
flaky *572*, 573
rocky mountain 475, *475*
Juniperus 578, 579
J. communis 578
'Compressa' 573, *573*
'Green Carpet' 486, 487
'Hibernica' *51*, 567, *567*
J. x *pfitzeriana* 'Wilhelm Pfitzer' 568, *569*, 578, 579
J. scopulorum 'Skyrocket' 475, *475*, 487
J. squamata 'Blue Star' *572*, 573, 579
J. virginiana *23*, *51*
'Grey Owl' 106, *107*, 119

K

kaffir lily 451, *451*
kalanchoe 75
kale 533, 576, *576*
crop rotation 535
forcing *68*
harvesting 68, 526
storing 340
transplanting 337
Kalmia 227
K. latifolia 'Ostbo Red' 286, *286*, 300, 301
katsura tree 470, *470*
Kerria japonica 'Pleniflora' 194, *194*
kingcup 54, 203, *203*
Kirengeshoma palmata 362, *363*, 393
knapweed 357, *357*
Knautia macedonica 361, *361*, 392
Kniphofia 124, *305*, 392, 393, 486, 487
K. 'Early Buttercup' 267, *267*, 300, 301
K. 'Green Jade' 456, *456*
K. 'Percy's Pride' 365, *365*, *392*
K. 'Prince Igor' 454, *454*
K. 'Royal Standard' 362, *363*
K. triangularis 453, *453*
knives 506, 587, *587*, 591, *591*
Koelreuteria paniculata 379, *379*
kohl rabi *246*, 483, *483*
crop rotation 535
sowing 69, 246
storing 340, 341
Kolkwitzia 224
K. amabilis 'Pink Cloud' 286, *286*

L

labels 591, *591*
re-using 446
labrador tree 196, *196*
Laburnum x *watereri* 'Vossii' *194*, 195, 207
lacewings 396
Lachenalia 258, *541*
ladybirds 259, 396
lady's mantle 211, 272, *272*
lady's smock 174, *174*
Lagurus ovatus 462, *462*, 486, 487
lambs' ears 272, *272*
lamb's lettuce 116, *116*
lambs' lugs 272, *272*
lambs' tails 272, *272*
lambs' tongues 272, *272*
land cress 576, *576*
land drains 521
lantern cloches *608*, 609
Lapageria rosea 486
larkspur 30, 274, *274*
Lathyrus latifolius *17*, 500
L. odoratus 220
'Duke of York' 275, *275*
'Noel Sutton' 366, *366*
L. rotundifolius 132
L. vernus 173, *173*, 206
L. 'Violet Queen' *309*
laudanum 288, *288*
laurel
cherry 197, *197*
hedges 321, 417, 418
portugal 48, 569, *569*
pruning 43, *43*, 137, 321
spotted 100, *100*, 101, *101*, 560, *560*
Laurus nobilis 48, 482, *482*
laurustinus 99, *99*, 417
Lavandula 392, 393
L. angustifolia 321
'Hidcote' 376, *377*
'Nana Alba' 293, *293*, 300
L. x *intermedia* Dutch Group 376–7, *377*
L. stoechas 70
lavatera
cuttings 139
pruning 45
sowing 30
Lavatera *32*, 126, 318, *439*
L. 'Barnsley' 380, *380*, 392, *392*, 393
L. trimestris 'Mont Blanc' *29*, 369, *369*, 392, 393
'Silver Cup' 459, *459*, 486, 487
lavender *252*, 293, *293*, *346*, 376–7, *377*
cuttings *227*
'dropping' 537
french 70
frost protection 42
hedges 165, 321
layering 165
old english 293, *293*
pruning 137
repotting 70
shearing 318, *318*, 343
lawnmowers *see* mowers
lawns
aerating *58*, *153*, *328*, 428, 520
in autumn 426–9
bare patches 59
clearing leaves 427, *427*
diseases 153, 329
drainage 520–1
in early spring 58–9
edges 429, *429*
equipment 588–9, *588–9*
fertilisers 59, 157, 605
herb lawns 346
in late spring 152–7
in late summer 328–9
moss in 58, 153, *153*, 239, 427, *427*
naturalising bulbs in 35, *128*, 312, *313*
new lawns 154–7, 328–9
pests 153
protecting edges 329, *329*
repairing 428–9, *428–9*
scarifying 521
soil compaction 428
sowing 154–5, *154–5*
stepping stones *521*
in summer 238–9
thatch 153
top-dressing 428, 521
trimming edges 59, *59*
turf 154, *154*, 156, *156*
watering 157, 239, 602
weeds in 58, 152, 154, 239, 427, *427*
in winter 520–1
wormcasts 58, 427, *427*
see also mowing
lawson's cypress 107, *107*, 479, *479*, 554, *554*, 568, *568*, 572, *572*
hedges 321, 417
layering
air layering 46, 47, *47*
carnations 306, 398
clematis 133
climbers *408*, 409, 500
herbs 165, 251
mound layering 537, *537*
roses 405, *405*
shrubs 139, *139*, 413
Layia platyglossa 461, *461*
leaf blowers 589, *589*
leaf cuttings, greenhouse plants *254–5*, 255

leaf-bud cuttings
clematis 133, *133*, 221
roses 129, *129*
shrubs 319
leaf-mould 597, *597*
as mulch 601
leatherjackets 153
leaves
clearing from lawns 427, *427*
see also foliage
Ledum groenlandicum 196, *196*, 207
leeks *246*, *439*, 483, *483*, 576, *576*
crop rotation 534
harvesting 68, 440, *440*, 527
'Longbow' *524*
sowing 68, 527
spacing *67*
transplanting 246
legumes
crop rotation 530, 534
see also beans; peas
Lemna trisulca 142
lemon balm 204, *204*, *342*, *346*
division 71, *443*
preserving 253
lemon trees 234
lemon verbena 70, 114, *114*, 253
lenten rose *12*, 84, *84*, 490, *491*
leopard's bane 176, *177*, 306
Leptospermum scoparium 'Kiwi' 207
lettuces *65*, 205, *205*, *247*, *248*, 298, *298*, *576*, 577
'Arctic King' 444
catch crops 533
in containers 533
crop rotation 535
cut-and-come again crops 533
harvesting 341
intercropping 533, *533*
'Kelly's' 444
'Parella' 444
plug plants *532*
sowing 69, 161, 338, 441, 444–5, 527
successional sowing 533
thinning 248
watering 244, 336
winter protection *441*, 527, *527*
Leucanthemum x *superbum* 'Snowcap' 270, *270*
Leucojum aestivum 15
'Gravetye Giant' 185, *185*, 207
Leucojum (continued)
L. autumnale 464, *464*
L. vernum 91, *91*, 118
Leucothoe Scarletta 556, *556*, 578, 579
leycesteria 45, 413
leyland cypress
hedges 320, 321, 417
Liatris 124
L. spicata 358, 359
Ligularia 124
L. dentata 'Desdemona' *480*, 481
L. 'Gregynog Gold' 387, *387*
L. 'The Rocket' 387, *387*
Ligustrum 48, 146
L. ovalifolium 321, 417
lilac 192, *193*, 198, *198*
deadheading 223
suckers *503*
Lilium African Queen Group 372, *372*
L. candidum 279, *279*
L. 'Casa Blanca' 372, *372*
L. 'Fire King' 372, *372*
L. henryi 372, *372*
L. 'Journey's End' 372, *372*
L. lancifolium 129
L. martagon var. *album 216*, 279, *279*
L. 'Olivia' 372, *372*
L. 'Pink Perfection' *129*
L. regale 51, 279, *279*
L. speciosum 129
var. *rubrum* 372, *372*
L. 'Star Gazer' 129, 372, *372*
L. 'Sterling Star' 129
lily
african blue *see* african blue lily
arum *see* arum lily
asiatic hybrid 372, *372*
bulbs *444*, *494*
in containers *129*
kaffir *see* kaffir lily
madonna 279, *279*
oriental hybrid 372, *372*
peruvian *see* peruvian lily
planting 129
regal 279, *279*
scaling *403*
st bernard's *178*, 179
torch *see* torch lily
trumpet hybrid 372, *372*
turkscap 279, *279*
lily tree 196, *196*
lily-of-the-valley 73, *178*, 179
lilyturf 450, *450*, 490
black 452, *452*
liming soil 535, 593
Limonium sinuatum 215
Forever Series 461, *461*, 486, 487
linaria 215
ling 378, *378*, 468, *469*, 557, *557*, 560, *561*
liquid fertilisers 77, *77*, 147, 605, *605*
Liquidambar styraciflua 'Worplesdon' 471, *471*, 486
liquorice 443
Liriope muscari 398, 450, *450*, 486, 487
Lithodora diffusa 'Heavenly Blue' 292, *292*, 301
loam 592
lobelia
bedding schemes 215
pricking out 493
sowing *493*
Lobelia erinus Cascade Series 275, *275*
'Crystal Palace' 366, *366*
L. x *gerardii 19*
L. 'Queen Victoria' 386–7, *387*, 393
L. syphilitica 480, *480*, 486
locust 287, *287*
loganberries *330*, 391, *391*
harvesting 335
pruning 332–3
lollo rosso lettuces *247*
lonicera
hedges 137
supports 135
Lonicera 392, 393, 578
L. x *americana 51*, 375, *375*
L. x *brownii* 'Dropmore Scarlet' 375, *375*
L. etrusca 'Superba' 375, *375*
L. fragrantissima 104, *104*, 118
L. japonica 'Halliana' 375, *375*
L. nitida 146, 417
'Baggesen's Gold' 563, *563*, 578, 579
L. periclymenum 41, 221, 499
'Belgica' 281, *281*
'Serotina' 375, *375*
Lonicera (continued)
L. x *purpusii* 'Winter Beauty' 565, *565*, 578
L. sempervirens 375, *375*
L. x *tellmanniana* 281, *281*
loosestrife, purple 54, 386, *386*
loppers 506, 586, *586*
lovage 443
black 114, *114*
division 71
seeds 343
love-in-a-mist 126, *215*, 274, *274*
love-lies-bleeding 368, *368*, 462, *462*
Lunaria annua 207
'Alba Variegata' 183, *183*
L. rediviva 180, *180*
lungwort *80*, 81, 82, *82*, 83, *83*, 173, *173*, 544, *544*
lupin *268*, 269
cuttings 125, 213
deadheading 211
germination 306
green manures 337
Lupinus 'Chandelier' *268*, 269, 301
Luzula sylvatica 'Aurea' 481, *481*
Lysichiton 118
L. americanus 113, *113*
L. camtschatcensis 113, *113*
Lysimachia nummularia 122, 229
Lythrum salicaria 54
'Feuerkerze' 386, *386*, 393

M

Macleaya cordata 'Flamingo' 360, *360*
magnesium 604
magnolia
star *104*, 105
transplanting 504
willow-leaved 104, *104*
Magnolia 119, 207
M. campbellii subsp. *mollicomata* 97, *97*
M. denudata 196, *196*
M. 'Elizabeth' *194*, 195
M. grandiflora 380, *380*, 392
M. x *kewensis* 'Wada's Memory' 196, *197*
M. x *loebneri* 'Leonard Messel' 97, *97*
M. salicifolia 104, *104*
M. sieboldii 288, *289*

Magnolia (continued)
M. x *soulangeana* 191, *191*
M. stellata 104, 105
mahonia
mahonia rust 44
propagation *47*
pruning 44, *44*
Mahonia 578
M. aquifolium 44
'Apollo' *102*, 103, 118
M. japonica 44, 563, *563*, 579
M. x *media* 'Winter Sun' *506*, 563, *563*, 579
M. x *wagneri* 'Moseri' *23*
maidenhair tree 473, *473*
maize, variegated 215
male fern, golden 181, *181*
mallow 126, 369, *369*, 459, *459*
tree 318
Malus 206, 509, 578
M. floribunda 191, *191*
M. 'John Downie' 472, *472*, 487
M. x *moerlandsii* 'Profusion' 191, *191*
M. x *robusta* 'Red Sentinel' 559, *559*
M. tschonoskii 473, *473*
M. 'Winter Gold' 563, *563*, 579
mangetout 298, *298*, 534
manure
improving soil structure 594
as mulch 397, 601
organic gardening 259
manures, green 337, 594
maple
amur 476, *476*
cappadocian 476, *476*
caucasian 476, *476*
full-moon 476, *476*
hedges 416
japanese 149, 150, 190, *190*, 198, *198*, 476, *476*, 513
paper-bark 556–7, *557*
red 476, *476*
scarlet 476, *476*
snake-bark 476, *476*, *564*, 565
striped 554, *555*
swamp 476, *476*
vine 476, *476*
marginal plants 232, 517
cutting back 422
planting 144
thinning *325*
marguerite 73
golden 268, *268*
marigold *346*
afro-french 462, *462*
bedding schemes 215
deadheading *308*
english 368, *368*
french 368, *368*
giant marsh 113, *113*
marsh 144, 203, *203*
pot 253, 368, *368*
signet 368, *368*
sowing 126, 169
marjoram *250*, *344*, 359, *359*, 388, *388*, 478, *478*
division 71
potting up 442–3
preserving 253
maroon flowers and foliage
annuals and biennials 85, 182–3
bulbs 370
perennials 175, 266, 360–1, 452
shrubs and trees 556
water plants 480
marrows 163, 484, *484*
crop rotation 535
sowing 249
storing 341, 441
trench composting 64, *64*
watering 244
marshmallow 443
masterwort 272, *272*
Matteuccia incana 215
M.i. Ten Week Series 275, *275*
M. struthiopteris 13, 203, *203*, 207
matting, capillary 591, *591*, 603
mauve flowers and foliage
alpines 110, 292–3, 384, 477–8, 572
annuals and biennials 182, 274–6, 459–60, 546
bulbs 87–8, 184, 279, 370, 463–4, 547–8
climbers 95, 188, 280, 373
perennials 81, 174–5, 264–6, 356–60, 451–2, 544
shrubs and trees 96–9, 190–2, 285–7, 377–9, 468–9, 554–6
water plants 113, 294, 386, 480
may *190*, 191
meadow rue 266, *266*, 356, *356*
yellow 269, *269*
meadows 492
meadowsweet 177, *177*
mealy bugs 258
mealy cabbage aphids 338
Meconopsis 213, *228*
M. betonicifolia 264, *264*, 301
M. cambrica 177, *177*, 207
M. quintuplinervia 174, *174*, 207
medicinal herbs 344
Melianthus major 288–9, *289*
Melissa officinalis 'Aurea' 204, *204*
melons *350*, 485, *485*
in coldframes 257
in greenhouses 168, 256
harvesting 350
planting 168
pollination 256
sowing 169
supporting 350
training 168
Mentha pulegium 114, *115*
M. requienii 346
M. spicata 204, *205*
M. suaveolens 296, *296*
mercury 116, *116*
merrybells, large 178, *178*
mesclun *532*
Metasequoia glyptostroboides 472, *472*
mexican orange blossom *194*, 195
mezereon *564*, 565
michaelmas daisy 357, *357*, 457, *457*
mildew 304
microbore watering systems *236–7*, 237, 603, *603*
microwave-drying herbs 253
midland thorn *190*, 191
mignonette 148, 350
mildew
on grapes 256
on michaelmas daisies 304
on roses *37*
on trees and shrubs 223, 510
Milium effusum 'Aureum' 177, *177*, 207
milkweed *82*, 83, 176–7, *177*, 181, *181*, 203, *203*, 267, *267*, 456, *456*
mimosa *72*
mimulus *325*
miniature roses
pruning 38–9
spacing plants 407
mint 204, *205*, *250*
apple 296, *296*
in containers 251, *251*
corsican 346
cuttings 71
division 71, 251
mint rust 251
planting *165*
potting up 442–3, *442*
preserving 253
Miscanthus 21, 487
M. sacchariflorus 481, *481*
M. sinensis 'Silberfeder' *51*, 481, *481*
'Zebrinus' *268*, 269, 300
misters 258, 591, *591*
misticanza 444–5
mock orange *194*, 195, 288, *289*
pruning 318
modular trays, sowing vegetables in 67
moist shade, plant selectors 118, 207, 301, 393, 486, 579
moisture-retaining gel 235, 236, 424
Molinia 486, 487
M. caerulea subsp. *arundinacea* 'Windspiel' 454, *454*
subsp. *caerulea* 'Heidebraut' *20*, 481, *481*
mollie-the-witch 177, *177*
Molucella laevis 369, *369*
molybdenum 604
Monarda 'Prärienacht' 359, *359*
monkshood 269, *269*, 354, *354*, 450, *450*
montbretia 370, 371, *371*
moor grass, purple *20*, 454, *454*, 481, *481*
moosewood 554, *555*
morning glory *41*, 221, *316*
mosaic virus 131
mosquito plant 480, *480*
mosquitoes 233
moss, on lawns 58, 153, *153*, 239, 427, *427*
moths
clearwing moth 332
pheromone traps 242
winter moth 431
mound layering 537, *537*
mountain ash 560, *560*
mourning widow 172, *172*

moutan 191, *191*, 192, *193*
mowers 588, *588*
cleaning *521*
raising blades *521*
servicing 521
mowing
in autumn 427
in early spring 59
equipment 521
in late spring 153
in late summer 329, *329*
new lawns 157
in summer 239
mrs robb's bonnet 82, *82*
mugwort 271, *271*, 293, *293*, 385, *385*
western 271, *271*
mulching 594, 600–1, *600*
alpines 421, *421*
climbers 409
containers 151, *258*
fruit 60
hedges 137, 418, *419*
no-dig beds 531, *531*
perennials 397, *397*
raised beds 235
roses 131, *131*, 406
slate mulches *223*
water conservation 602
mullein 266, *266*, 269, *269*
Muscari 206
M. armeniacum 184, *184*
M. aucheri *86*, 87
M. botryoides 'Album' 185, *185*, *313*
mushroom compost 259, 600
mustard and cress 117, *117*
Myosotis scorpioides 'Mermaid' 294, *294*, 301
M. sylvatica *126*, 207
'Royal Blue' 182, *182*
myrobalan 98, *98*
Myrrhis odorata 115, *115*, 343
myrtle 114, *115*
tarentum 380–1, *380*
Myrtus communis 114, *115*
subsp. *tarentina* 380–1, *380*

N

naked ladies 463, *463*, 464, *464*
Nandina domestica 'Fire Power' 559, *559*, 579
narcissi
in containers *57*, 425
narcissi (continued)
forcing 351, *351*
growing in water 350
naturalising 35
'paper-white' 351, *351*
Narcissus 118, 119
N. 'Actaea' 185, *185*
N. 'Barrett Browning' 93, *93*
N. 'Cedric Morris' 548, *548*, 579
N. 'Dove Wings' 92, *92*
N. 'Dutch Master' 92, *92*
N. 'February Gold' 92, *92*
N. 'Jack Snipe' 92, *92*
N. 'Liberty Bells' 93, *93*
N. 'Little Gem' 92–3, *93*
N. obvallaris 93, *93*
N. pseudonarcissus *15*
N. 'Rijnveld's Early Sensation' *548*, 549, 579
N. 'Rip van Winkle' 93, *93*
N. 'Saint Keverne' 93, *93*
N. 'Sun Disc' 93, *93*
N. 'Tête-à-tête' 92, *92*, *118*
nasturtium *74*, 368, *368*
sowing 30, *74*
navelwort 173, *173*
nectarines
in greenhouses 540
harvesting 241, 335
peach leaf curl 63
pruning 159
thinning 159
neglected shrubs and hedges 43, *43*, 321, *413*
nematodes, pest control with 53, 541
Nemesia 30, 326
N. Carnival Series 368, *368*
Nepeta 'Six Hills Giant' 264, *264*, 300, 301
Nerine bowdenii 217, 464, *464*, 486, 487
Nerium 223
netting
protecting brassicas *439*
protecting fish 423, *423*
protecting fruit *330*
protecting new hedges 419
nettles, liquid fertilisers 77, *77*
new zealand flax *360*, 361
newts 233
Nicotiana *345*
N. Domino Series 369, *369*
N. langsdorfii 462, *462*, 486
Nicotiana (continued)
N. 'Lime Green' 277, *277*
N. sylvestris 462, *462*, 486
Nigella damascena 'Miss Jekyll' 274, *274*
nitrogen 604
improving soil 438, 594
no-dig beds 531, *531*
Nuphar advenum 232
Nymphaea 145
N. 'Frobelii' 386, *386*
N. 'Gonnère' 387, *387*
N. 'James Brydon' 294, *294*
N. 'Pygmaea Helvola' 294–5, *295*
Nyssa sylvatica *412*, 474, *474*

O

oak 513
holm 569, *569*
scarlet 472, *472*
oats, golden *360*, 361
obedient plant 451, *451*
Ocimum basilicum 388, *388*
Oenothera macrocarpa 385, *385*, 392, 393
oils, herbal infusions 253
oleander 223
olive trees *151*
Omphalodes cappadocica 173, *173*, 207
O. verna 80, *80*, 118
onion hoes 585
onions 298, *298*, 484, *484*
crop rotation 530, 534
drying 257
lifting 338, 340, *340*, 440
ornamental 278, *278*
planting 68, *68*, 163, 440
red-skinned *338*
sowing 161, 163, 527
storing 68, 340, 341, 440, 527
watering 244
Ophiopogon planiscapus 'Nigrescens' 452, *452*, 486, 490
orange flowers
alpines 202, 385, 572–3
annuals and biennials 183, 277, 368–9, 460–2, 546
bulbs 90–1, 371, 548–9
climbers 188–9, 281, 374, 466
orange flowers (continued)
perennials 176–9, 267, 362–3, 453–4
shrubs and trees 101–3, 192–5, 287, 379, 473–4, 560–5
water plants 113, 203, 294–5, 387, 481
oregano *252*, *342*, 359, *359*, 478, *478*
oregon grape *102*, 103
organic gardening 259
organic matter
improving soil structure 594
no-dig beds 531, *531*
organic mulches 600–1, *600*
oriental vegetables, sowing 257
Origanum 388, *388*, 392
O. amanum 478, *478*, 486, 487
O. laevigatum 'Herrenhausen' 359, *359*, 393
Ornithogallum nutans 185, *185*
O. oligophyllum 91, *91*, 119
Orontium aquaticum 232, *232*
orris root 181, *181*, 443
osier, green 380, *380*
Osmanthus x *burkwoodii* 105, *105*, 119
O. delavayi *51*, 197, *197*
Osmunda regalis 480–1, *480*, 486
Osteospermum 'Jucundum' 359, *359*, 392, 393
ostrich fern 203, *203*
Ostrya carpinifolia *102*, 103
Oxalis adenophylla 184, *185*
oxygenating plants 142, 232, 324, 517
thinning 325, 423
oxygenating ponds 233, 324, *325*
ozark sundrops 385, *385*

P

Pachyphragma macrophyllum 83, *83*, 118
Pachysandra terminalis 456, *456*
Paeonia delavayi var. *ludlowii* *194*, 195
P. lactiflora 'Bowl of Beauty' 266, *266*
'Festiva Maxima' 270, *271*
'Karl Rosenfield' 267, *267*
'White Wings' 180, *180*
P. mlokosewitschii 177, *177*
P. peregrina 176, *176*

Paeonia (continued)
P. suffruticosa 191, *191*
'Hana-daijin' 192, *193*
pampas grass *364*, 365, 455, *455*
Panicum virgatum 'Rubrum' 452, *452*, 487
pans, for propagation 590, *590*
pansy 85, *85*, 274, *275*, 277, *277*, 366, *367*
bedding schemes 32
in containers 425, *492*, *518*
deadheading *56*, 308
winter-flowering 182, *182*, 546, *546*
Papaver nudicaule 277, *277*
'Summer Breeze' *309*
P. orientale 124, 211
'Black and White' 270, *271*, 300
P. rhoeas 'Mother of Pearl' 277, *277*, 301
P. somniferum 276, *276*, 301, *308*
paper tubes, sowing sweet peas in 445, *445*
Parrotia persica 559, *559*, 578
parsley *246*, *247*, *250*, 388, *389*
potting up 442–3
preserving 253
self-seeding 343
sowing 251, 257, 350, 537, *537*
parsnips *576*, 577
crop rotation 534
harvesting 527
intercropping 533
sowing 69, 162
storing 340, 341, 440
Parthenocissus 135, *411*, 500
P. henryana 281, *281*, 301, 317, *317*
P. quinquefolia *408*, 466, *466*, 487
P. tricuspidata 'Veitchii' 466, *466*, 487
pasque flower 200, *200*
Passiflora caerulea 280, *280*, 300, *300*, 499
passion flower
blue 280, *280*
in greenhouses 445
pruning 540
winter protection 499
paths
in herb gardens 345, 346
paths (continued)
herb paths *346*
vegetable plots 529, *529*
patio roses 149, 378, *378*
deadheading 235
spacing plants 407
patios
in autumn 424–5
cleaning 57, *57*
deadheading plants 234–5
in early spring 56–7
in late spring 146–51
in late summer 326–7
planting thyme between slabs 234, *234*
in summer 234–7
watering plants 236–7, *236–7*
weeding *326*
in winter 518–19
paulownia 137, 512
paving stones, paths 346
pea, perennial *17*, 132, 500
pea sticks 211, *245*, 329
peaches *159*, *331*, 391, *391*
'Bellegarde' 432
in greenhouses 540
harvesting 241, 335
peach leaf curl 63, 432
planning a fruit garden 434–5
pollinating 62
pruning 159, 432, 435, 522
thinning 62, 159
winter protection 432
pearl bush 196, *196*
pearl everlasting 363, *363*, 454–5, *455*
pears 391, *391*
'Beurré Hardy' 430
buying trees 330
canker 523, *523*
'Catillac' 431
'Docteur Jules Guyot' 430
'Doyenné du Comice' *434*
espalier *431*
harvesting 334
'Joséphine de Malines' 431
'June drop' 242
'Louise Bonn de Jersey' *334*
'Packham's Triumph' 431
planning a fruit garden 434
pollination 330
pruning 159, 242, *242*, 435, 522
storing 334, 430–1, *430*
pears (continued)
thinning 61, 159, 242
weeping trees 381, *381*, *511*
'Winter Nelis' 431
peas 298–9, *298*
catch crops 533
in containers 533
crop rotation 530, 534
drying 438
extending harvest 67
harvesting 245, 337, 438
sowing 68, *160*, 161, 245, 438, *438*, 526
storing 340, 341
trench composting 64, *64*
watering 244, 337
winter protection 526
peat, alternatives to 599
peaty soils 592
pebble mulches 600, *600*
pelargonium
bedding schemes 32, 215
in containers 148, *235*
cuttings 212, *212*, 307, *327*
ivy-leaved 361, *361*
regal *169*
reviving 73
pelargonium (continued)
rosebud zonal 359, *359*
scented-leaved 574, *574*
sowing 30, 493
Pelargonium *255*, 579
P. 'Apple Blossom Rosebud' 359, *359*
P. 'Bird Dancer' 273, *273*
P. 'Bolero' 273, *273*
P. 'Captain Starlight' 273, *273*
P. 'Caroline Schmidt' 273, *273*
P. 'Chocolate Peppermint' 273, *273*
P. 'Copthorne' 273, *273*
P. 'L'Elégante' 273, *273*
P. graveolens *541*
P. 'Paton's Unique' 273, *273*
P. 'Rouletta' 361, *361*
Pennisetum alopecuroides 'Hameln' 456, *456*
P. villosum 458, *459*, 487
pennyroyal 71, 114, *115*, 345, 346
penstemon
in containers *235*
cuttings 229, 323
winter protection 397
Penstemon *18*, 326, 393, 486
P. 'Andenken an Friedrich Hahn' 361, *361*
P. 'Evelyn' 359, *359*
P. 'Raven' 450, *450*, *486*
P. 'Six Hills' 201, *201*
P. 'Stapleford Gem' 451, *451*
peony *26*, 176, *176*, 180, *180*, 266, *266*, 267, *267*, 270, *271*
caucasian 177, *177*
deadheading 211
division 399
tree 191, *191*, 192, *193*, *194*, 195
peppers 163, 389, *389*
in containers 533
in greenhouses 168, 350
harvesting 339, 350
planting 249
storing 341
supports 249
perennial vegetables 535
see also asparagus; globe artichokes; jerusalem artichokes
perennial weeds
in alpine gardens 228–9
in borders 397
in compost heaps 596
perennials
in autumn 396–9
as bedding plants 401
collecting seed 213, 398
in containers 57
cutting back *305*, 396–7, *396*
cuttings 125, *125*, 212, *212*, 213, 307, *307*, 398, *490–1*, 491
deadheading 211
diseases 304
division 124–5, 212, *213*, 306, 398–9, *399*
in early spring 26–7
in greenhouses 74–7
hardening off 122–3
in late spring 122–5
in late summer 304–7
mulching 397, *397*
pests 304
planning borders 50, 51
plant selectors 79–84, 172–81, 262–73, 384–5, 450–7, 544–5
planting 124, *124*, 305, 398
propagation 27, 306–7, 398–9
seedlings 398
sowing 306

perennials (continued)
in summer 210–13
supports 122, *122*, 211, *211*, 329, *329*
in winter 490–1
see also tender perennials
pergolas 149
Perilla frutescens 114, *114*
periwinkle, lesser 96, *97*
perlite 599, *599*
Perovskia 45
P. 'Blue Spire' 377, *377*, 392
Persicaria bistorta 'Superba' 266, *266*, 301
P. tenuicaulis 112, *112*, 119
P. vacciniifolia 478, *478*, 487
peruvian lily 370, *370*
pests 258
biological control 257
brassicas 338
fruit 431, 523
in greenhouses 73, 258
lawns 153
organic gardening 259
perennials 304
pheromone traps 242
roses 37, *37*, 131
trees and shrubs 223
vegetables 64–5
see also individual plants and pests
Petasites fragrans 113, *113*, 118
Petroselinum crispum 388, *389*
petunia
bedding schemes 215
deadheading 308
grandiflora 367, *367*
sowing *74*
Petunia 18, 301
P. Fantasy Series 276, *276*
P. 'Purple Wave' 459, *459*, 487
P. Surfinia Series 367, *367*
pH values
soil 592, *592*, 593
testing pond water *143*
Phalaris arundinacea var. *picta* 'Feesey' 270, *271*, 301
pheromone traps 242
Philadelphus 300, 318
P. 'Belle Etoile' 288, *289*, 300
P. coronarius 'Aureus' *194*, 195, 206
phlomis 139
phlox
bedding schemes 215
cuttings *123*
moss 201, *201*
planting 124
Phlox 50
P. douglasii 206
'Boothman's Variety' 201, *201*
P. paniculata 'Eventide' 360, *360*
'Fujiyama' *364*, 365
P. subulata 206
'McDaniel's Cushion' 201, *201*
Phormium 490
P. 'Cream Delight' *426*
P. 'Sundowner' *51*, *360*, 361
P. tenax 'Variegatum' *426*
phosphorus (phosphate) 594, 604
Photinia x *fraseri* 'Red Robin' 192, *193*
phygelius *235*, 326
Physalis alkekengi var. *franchetii 448–9*, 454, *454*
Physostegia virginiana 'Vivid' 451, *451*
Picea abies 'Little Gem' 573, *573*
P. breweriana 568, *569*
P. glauca var. *albertiana* 'Conica' 573, *573*
P. mariana 'Nana' 573, *573*, 579
P. pungens 'Hoopsii' 554, *554*, 578, 579
'Montgomery' 112, *112*, 119
pickerel weed 144, 386, *386*
Pieris 57, 119, 150, 227
P. floribunda 105, *105*
P. 'Forest Flame' 192, *193*, 207
P. formosa var. *forestii* 'Wakehurst' 100, *100*
P. japonica 'Blush' 97, *97*
'Debutante' 105, *105*
pimpernel, blue 458, *458*
Pimpinella anisum 482, *482*
pincushion flower 356, *356*, 456, *456*, 478, *478*
pine, dwarf mountain 573, *573*
pink flowers
alpines 110, 200–1, 292–3, 384, 477–8, 572
annuals and biennials 182, 274–6, 459–60, 546
bulbs 87–8, 184, 279, 370, 463–4, 547–8
climbers 95, 188, 280, 373
pink flowers (continued)
perennials 81, 174–5, 264–6, 356–60, 451–2, 544
shrubs and trees 96–9, 190–2, 285–7, 377–9, 468–9, 554–6
water plants 113, 294, 386, 480
pinks 264–5, *265*
alpine 292, *292*
chinese 367, *367*
cuttings *322*
division 229
indian 367, *367*
'pipings' 212, *213*
sowing 229
Pinus mugo 'Mops' 573, *573*, 578, 579
'pipings', pinks 212, *213*
Pistia stratiotes 230
Pittosporum 151
P. tobira 51
planning
borders 50
herb gardens 345
lawns 154
vegetable plots 529
plantain lily *see Hosta*
planting
alpines *141*
bedding plants 127, 215
bulbs 35, 129, 217
climbers 134, *134*
containers *148*, 150–1, *151*
evergreens 138, *138*
hanging baskets 148–9, *149*
perennials 124, *124*, 398
shrubs 138, *138*
trees 138, *138*
water plants 144–5, *145*
see also individual plants
plastics
bags 591
cloches and coldframes 606
mulches 601
Platycodon grandiflorus 356, *356*
Pleioblastus auricomus 194, 195, 206
plug plants *56*
annuals and biennials 215, *215*
potting on *30*
vegetables 532, *532*
plum
cherry 98, *98*
ornamental 97, *97*
purple-leaved 98, *98*
Plumbago auriculata 445
plume poppy 360–1, *360*
plums *242–3*, *390*, 391
buying trees 330
harvesting 241, 334–5
planning a fruit garden 434
pollination 330
pruning 159, 242, 331, 435, 522
supporting branches 332
thinning 242
pocket knives 587, *587*
Podophyllum hexandrum 175, *175*
poinsettia 351
Polemonium 'Lambrook Mauve' 174–5, *174*
pollarding trees 512
pollination
fruit 62, 158, 330
greenhouse fruit 540
melons 256
squashes and pumpkins 249, *249*
polyanthus 85, *85*, 182–3, *182–3*
as bedding plants 401
division 212
Polygala chamaebuxus var. *grandiflora* 110–11, *110*
Polygonatum x *hybridum* 180, *180*, 206, 207
Polystichum munitum 545, *545*, 579
ponds
algae 232, 325
in autumn 422–3
cleaning out 55, *55*
clearing up 422–3
controlling surplus growth 325
in early spring 54–5
healthy ponds 232–3
ice on 516, *516*
in late spring 142–5
in late summer 324–5
oxygenating 233, 324, *325*
oxygenating plants 142, 232, 324, 325, 423, 517
plants for 232, 517
stocking with fish 233, *233*
in summer 230–3
testing water *143*
weeds 143, *143*, *231*, 232
wildlife 232–3
in winter 516–17
pondweed, cape 481, *481*

Pontederia cordata 144, *324*, 386, *386*
poor man's asparagus 116–17, *116*
poppy *308*, *344*
arctic 277, *277*
california 126, *214*, 277, *277*
corn 277, *277*
deadheading 211
field 277, *277*
flanders 277, *277*
harebell 174, *174*
himalayan blue 264, *264*
icelandic 277, *277*
matilika *364*, 365
opium 276, *276*
oriental 270, *271*
planting 124
tibetan blue 264, *264*
tree *364*, 365
welsh 177, *177*
potagers *346*, *434*, 531
potassium (potash) 594, 604
potato tree, chilean 377, *377*
potato vine *17*, 134, 374, *374*
potatoes 484, *484*, 532
chitting 69, 527, *527*
in containers 533
crop rotation 530, 534
early potatoes 163, 247, 299, *299*, 389, *389*
earthing up 163, 246, 247, *247*
harvesting 247, 440
maincrop potatoes 163
planting 69, *69*, 163
potato blight 247
storing 340, 341, 441
watering 244, 337, 338
Potentilla 45
P. fruticosa 'Tangerine' 287, *287*, 300, 301
potting composts *see* composts, potting
potting up
alpines *229*
cuttings 327
herbs 442–3, *442*
roses 405
predators 259, 396
pressure washers 57, *57*
pricking out seedlings 31, *31*, 398
pride of india 379, *379*
primrose *80*, 81, *82*, 83, *83*, 176, *176*, 257
as bedding plants 401
primrose (continued)
division 323
japanese 180, *180*
sowing 229
primula *325*
candelabra 294, *295*
division 212, 323
drumstick 113, *113*
primula (continued)
germination 306
sowing 213, 229, 514
Primula 118, 207
P. auricula 119, 207
'Blue Velvet' 80–1, *80*
'Old Yellow Dusty Miller' *82*, 83
P. beesiana 144
P. clarkei 110, *110*
P. Cowichan Garnet Group 183, *183*
P. Crescendo Series 546, *546*
P. denticulata 113, *113*, 514
P. florindae 295, *295*, 300, 301
P. Gold-laced Group 182–3, *183*
P. 'Guinevere' 81, *81*, 182, *182*
P. japonica 'Postford White' 180, *180*, 207
P. x *kewensis* 169
P. marginata 'Kesselring's Variety' 200, *200*
P. 'Miss Indigo' *80*, 81
P. nana 572, *572*
P. obconica 169
P. Pacific Giant Series 546, *546*
P. Polyanthus Group 579
P. Prominent Series 85, *85*
P. x *pubescens* 'Mrs J.H. Wilson' 109, *109*
P. pulverulenta Bartley hybrids 294, *295*, 300, 301
P. rosea 110, *110*, 118, 119
P. sieboldii 175, *175*, 207
P. Silver-laced Group 85, *85*, 119
P. sinensis 169
P. vulgaris 82, 83
'Alba Plena' 83, *83*
P. 'Wanda' 176, *176*
privet
golden 48
hedges 137, *137*, 321, *412*, *416*, 417
topiary 48, 146, 150
propagation
alpines 53, 229, *229*, 420–1, 514–15
bulbs 403, *403*
climbers 500
equipment 590–1, *590–1*
herbs 165, 251, 537, *537*
perennials 27, 306–7, 398–9
shrubs and trees 46–7, *47*
see also cuttings; division; layering; sowing *and individual plants*
propagators 75, *75*, 591
Prostanthera rotundifolia 207
pruners 506–7, 586, *586*
pruning
climbers 41, 132–3, 220–1, 316–17, *317*, 445, 498–9, 540
conifers 507
crown thinning trees 225
cuts *507*
early-flowering shrubs 224
equipment 506–7, 583, 586–7, *586–7*
evergreens 43
fruit 61, 159, 242, 331, 332–3, 432, 435, 437, 522, *522*, *523*
knives 587, *587*
neglected hedges 43, *43*, 321, *413*
one-third prune 224, *224–5*
roses 38–9, *38–9*, 315, *315*, 404, 497, *497*
shrubs 43–5, 136–7, 224, *224–5*, 318, 413, 503, 506–8, *507*, *508*, 510
spur pruning 225
topiary 326–7, *326*
trees 506–13, *507–13*
see also individual plants
Prunus 118, 119, 206, 513, 578, 579
P. avium 'Plena' 197, *197*
P. x *blireana* 97, *97*
P. cerasifera 'Pissardii' 98, *98*
P. davidiana 566, *566*
P. dulcis 98, *98*
P. incisa 'February Pink' 555, *555*, 579, *579*
P. 'Kanzan' 192, *192*
P. laurocerasus 207, 321, 417
'Otto Luyken' 197, *197*
P. lusitanica 48, 569, *569*
Prunus (continued)
P. maackii 564, *564*
P. mume 'Beni-chidori' 98, *98*
P. 'Pandora' 98, *98*
P. sargentii 472, *472*, 487
P. serrula 50, 559, *559*
P. 'Shirofugen' 192, *192*
P. 'Shôgetsu' 197, *197*
P. x *subhirtella* 'Autumnalis' 555, *555*, 579
P. 'Taihaku' 105, *105*
P. triloba 'Multiplex' 98, *98*
P. 'Ukon' 197, *197*
P. x *yedoensis* 105, *105*
Pulmonaria 118, 119, 306, *306*
P. angustifolia 'Munstead Blue' 544, *544*, 579
P. 'Mawson's Blue' 173, *173*, 207
P. officinalis 26
P. rubra 'David Ward' 82, *82*
'Redstart' 544, *544*, 579
P. saccharata 'Frühlingshimmel' *80*, 81
P. 'Sissinghurst White' 83, *83*
Pulsatilla 514
P. vulgaris 200, *200*, 206, 207
pumpkins
crop rotation 535
harvesting *440*, 441
planting 249
pollination 249
storing 341
training 339
trench composting 64, *64*
pumps, winter care 423, 516, *516*
purple flowers and foliage
alpines 109–10, 200, 292, 384, 477
annuals and biennials 85, 182, 274, 366–7, 458
bulbs 86–7, 184, 278–9, 463, 547
climbers 95, 188, 280, 373, 551
perennials 80–1, 172–3, 262–4, 354–6, 450–1, 544
shrubs and trees 96, 190, 285, 376–7, 468, 554
water plants 113, 294, 386, 480
Puschkinia scilloides 86, 87
var. *libanotica* 119
pyracantha
fireblight 510
spur pruning 225

Pyracantha 221, 222, 578, 579
P. coccinea 321, 417
P. 'Mohave' 559, *559*
P. 'Orange Glow' 564, *564*
P. 'Soleil d'Or' *564*, 565
pyramids, fruit trees 435
Pyrus calleryana 'Chanticleer' 105, *105*
P. salicifolia 'Pendula' 381, *381*

Q

queen of the meadows 177, *177*
queen of the prairies 386, *386*
Quercus coccinea 'Splendens' 472, *472*, 486
Q. ilex 569, *569*, 579
quince, flowering *44*, 96, *97*, 100, *100*, 103, *103*, 134, 557, *557*
japanese 96, *97*, 100, *100*, 103, *103*
layering 139
pruning 132, 221, 222
quinces 485, *485*

R

rabbits, protecting new hedges from 419
radishes 205, *205*, *247*
crop rotation 535
harvesting 527
intercropping 533
sowing 69, 161, 248, 338, 527
successional sowing 533
winter *576*, 577
rain butts 446, 603, *603*
rainwater, conserving 603
raised beds
mulching 235
vegetables *247*, 531
rakes 584, *584*, *585*
lawn rakes 589, *589*
scarifying lawns 153
rambling roses
pruning 38, 315, *315*, 404
spacing plants 407
Ramonda myconi 109, *109*, 118, *118*, 421
Ranunculus aconitifolius 'Flore Pleno' 180, *181*
R. aquatilis 232
Raoulia australis Lutescens Group 202, *202*, 206
raspberries *241*, 299, *299*, 485, *485*
harvesting 241, 335, 432
raspberries (continued)
mulching 158
pests 243
planting 437, *437*
pruning 61, 332, 432
in small gardens *435*
soil 330
suckers 243
training *433*
tying-in 243, 332, 437
raspberry beetle 243
recycling water 603
red cabbage 340
red currants *241*, 299, *299*, 330, *330*, *434*
cuttings 432
harvesting 241, 335
planning a fruit garden 434
planting 436, 437
pruning 61, 242, 522
training 435
tying-in 437
red flowers and foliage
alpines 110–11, 201, 384–5, 478
annuals and biennials 85, 183, 276–7, 368, 460, 546
bulbs 88–90, 279, 370–1
climbers 280, 373–4, 466, 551
perennials 82, 176, 267, 361–2, 452–3, 544
shrubs and trees 100–1, 192, 287, 379, 470–3, 556–60
water plants 294, 386–7, 480–1
red hot poker 267, *267*, 305, 362, *363*, 365, *365*, *398*, 453, *453*, 454, *454*
red spider mite
biological control 257
in greenhouses 258
prevention 349
on shrubs 223
red thread disease 329
redwood, dawn 472, *472*
renewal pruning, shrubs 224, *224*
reversion
blackcurrants 242
variegated foliage 318, 510, *510*
Rhamnus alaternus 'Argenteovariegata' 566, *566*, 579
Rheum palmatum 'Atrosanguineum' 294, *295*, 300, 301
rhizomes, planting marginal plants 144
Rhodanthe 215
Rhodanthemum hosmariense 479, *479*, 486, 487
rhododendron
air layering *47*
in containers 146, 150
deadheading *137*, 223
layering 139
pruning 43
soil 502–3
winter protection *502*
Rhododendron 118, 119, 207, 301, 578, 579
R. 'Anna Baldsiefen' 98, *98*
R. Blue Tit Group 96, *96*
R. 'Bow Bells' *51*, 199, *199*
R. 'Britannia' 287, *287*
R. 'Christmas Cheer' 566, *566*
R. ciliatum 99, *99*
R. 'Cilpinense' 99, *99*
R. 'Dopey' 199, *199*
R. 'Golden Torch' 199, *199*
R. Humming Bird Group 100, *100*
R. 'Lionel's Triumph' 199, *199*
R. 'Loderi King George' 199, *199*
R. 'Loder's White' 288, *289*
R. luteum 287, *287*
R. macabeanum 199, *199*
R. moupinense 566, *567*
R. mucronulatum 556, *556*
R. 'Palestrina' 199, *199*
R. 'Patty Bee' *102*, 103
R. 'Penheale Blue' 96, *97*
R. 'Praecox' 556, *556*, 579
R. 'Razorbill' 99, *99*
R. 'Snow Lady' 106, *106*
R. 'Strawberry Ice' 199, *199*
R. Temple Belle Group *46*, 99, *99*
R. 'Vanessa Pastel' 286, *286*
R. 'Vuyk's Scarlet' 199, *199*
R. williamsianum 99, *99*
Rhodohypoxis 111, *111*, 119
rhubarb 205, *205*, 577, *577*
chinese 294, *295*
forcing 62, 63, *539*
harvesting 339
ornamental *235*
renewing plants 432, *432*
Rhus typhina *46*, 474, *474*
Ribes laurifolium 569, *569*
R. odoratum *102*, 103
R. sanguineum 417
Ribes (continued)
'Pulborough Scarlet' *100*, 101, 118
R. speciosum 101, *101*, 132
Ricinus communis 215
Robinia pseudoacacia 'Frisia' *222*, 287, *287*, 300
rock cress 111, *111*, 112, *112*, 202, *202*
rock gardens *228*
see also alpines
rock rose 285, *285*, 293, *293*
rocket 205, *205*
intercropping 533
sowing 161
Rodgersia *325*, 393
R. aesculifolia 387, *387*
R. pinnata 'Superba' 386, *386*, 392
R. podophylla 480, *480*, 486, 487
Romneya coulteri *364*, 365
root cuttings 46
alpines 421
greenhouse plants 259
perennials *490–1*, 491
root vegetables
in autumn 440–1
crop rotation 530, 534
harvesting 246–7
sowing 69, 162, 246–7, 338
storing 340
watering 244
see also individual vegetables
root-balled plants, planting 138
rooting hormone 139, *212*, 227, 591
roots
drying herb roots 443
transplanting trees and shrubs 504, *504–5*
see also planting
rootstocks, fruit trees 331, 435
Rosa 300, 392, 487
R. 'Aimée Vibert' 374, *374*
R. Alexander 290, *290*
R. banksiae 'Lutea' 188, *189*
R. 'Bantry Bay' *17*
R. 'Blanche Double de Coubert' 381, *381*, 393
R. 'Bobbie James' 284, *284*
R. Bonica 290, *290*, 301
R. 'Céleste' 290, *290*
R. Compassion 284, *284*
R. 'Complicata' 290, *291*
R. 'Crimson Shower' 466, *466*

Rosa (continued)
R. 'Elina' *474*, 475
R. 'English Miss' 469, *469*
R. 'Felicia' 469, *469*
R. 'Félicité Perpétue' *16*
R. 'Francis E. Lester' *218*
R. 'Fru Dagmar Hastrup' *407*, *472*, 473, 486
R. 'The Garland' *38*
R. Gentle Touch 378, *378*
R. 'Geranium' *472*, 473
R. glauca 381, *381*, *404–5*
R. 'Gloire de Dijon' 188–9, *189*
R. Golden Showers 374, *374*
R. 'Golden Wings' 290, *291*
R. Graham Thomas 379, *379*
R. 'Iceberg' *474*, 475
R. 'Louise Odier' 378, *378*
R. Lovely Lady *314*
R. 'Madame Alfred Carrière' 284, *284*
R. 'Madame Grégoire Staechlin' 284, *284*
R. Magic Carpet 378, *378*, 393
R. 'Maigold' 189, *189*
R. Mary Rose 290, *290*
R. 'Minnehaha' *17*
R. Mountbatten 290, *291*
R. 'Nevada' 290, *291*
R. x *odorata* 'Pallida' *406*
R. 'Parade' 284, *284*
R. 'Paul's Himalayan Musk' 284, *284*
R. 'Perestroika' 149
R. 'Pink Perpétué' 373, *373*
R. 'Queen Mother' 149
R. 'Reine des Violettes' 290, *290*
R. Royal William 379, *379*
R. rubiginosa *496*
R. rugosa 321, 417
R. 'Scarlet Patio' 149
R. The Times Rose *472*, 473
R. 'Veilchenblau' 284, *284*
R. xanthina 'Canary Bird' *130*, *194*, 195
rosebud cherry 555, *555*
rosemary 115, *115*, *252*, *344*, *345*
in containers 443
cuttings 251
'dropping' 537, *537*
frost protection 42
layering 139, 165
preserving 253, *253*
roses
in autumn 404–7
bourbon 378, *378*
budding 129
buying 315
in containers 146, 149
cuttings 129, 315
deadheading 218–19, *314*
disbudding 218
diseases 37, *37*, 131
in early spring 36–9
fertilisers 129, 130, *131*, 407
forcing 496–7
ground-cover 38, 378, *378*
hips *407*, *496*, *497*
hybrid tea 379, *379*
in late spring 130–1
in late summer 314–15
layering 405, *405*
miniature 378, *378*
mulching 131, *131*, 406
old glory 188–9, *189*
patio 149, 235, 378, *378*, 407
pests 37, *37* , 131
planting 131, 406
potting up 405
pruning 38–9, *38–9*, 315, *315*, 404, 497, *497*
rose-sick soil 315, 496, *496*
rugosa 381, *381*
scots briar 189, *189*
shearing 39
shrub 379, *379*, 381, *381*
soil 406, 407
sowing 37, 497, *497*
spacing plants 407
standards 407, *407*
suckers *219*, 314
in summer 218–19
supports 135, *407*
underplanting 36, 37
in winter 404–5, *404*, 496–7
yellow banksian 188, *189*
Rosmarinus officinalis 115, *115*
'Prostratus' 70
rotary mowers *521*, 588, *588*
rotation of crops 530, 534–5
rotavators 585
rowan 560, *560*
hubei *474*, 475
training standards 513
royal fern 480–1, *480*
Rubus 'Benenden' 197, *197*
R. cockburnianus 512, 567, *567*, 579
R. thibetanus *22*
Rudbeckia fulgida var. *deamii* 454, *454*
var. *sullivantii* 'Goldsturm' 362–3, *363*
R. 'Herbstsonne' 454, *454*
R. hirta 'Rustic Dwarf' *400*, 461, *461*, 487
rue 71, 285, *285*, *345*, *346*
Rumex acetosa 204, *205*
runner beans *244*, *337*, 390, *390*, 533
catch crops 533
crop rotation 534
harvesting 337
planting 245, *245*
sowing 169
storing 340, 341
trench composting 64, *64*
runners, strawberries *243*
russet flowers and foliage
alpines 110–11, 201, 384–5, 478
annuals and biennials 85, 183, 276–7, 368, 460, 546
bulbs 88–90, 279, 370–1
climbers 280, 373–4, 466, 551
perennials 82, 176, 267, 361–2, 452–3
shrubs and trees 100–1, 192, 287, 379, 470–3, 556–60
water plants 294, 386–7, 480–1
rust
mahonia 44
on perennials 304
Ruta graveolens 'Jackman's Blue' 285, *285*, 300, 301, 392

S

saffron 216, 217
sage *250*, *252*, 264, *264*, 574, *574*, 579
bog 356, *356*
in containers 443
cuttings 139, *165*
'dropping' 537
golden *345*
layering 165
mealy 458, *459*
preserving 253
purple *342*, *345*
sagebrush 271, *271*, 293, *293*, 385, *385*
Sagittaria sagittifolia 387, *387*
salad burnet 574, *574*
in containers 443
division 71
salad crops 532
in autumn 441
in containers 533
in greenhouses 444–5
harvesting 248, 338
sowing 161, 338
storing 341
in summer 248
under cloches 69
watering 248
in winter 527
salad onions 205, *205*
sowing 68, 161
Salix 118, 119, 578
S. alba subsp. *vitellina* 'Britzensis' 560, *560*, 579
S. caprea 'Kilmarnock' 103, *103*
S. daphnoides 554, *554*, 578, 579
S. gracilistyla 'Melanostachys' 96, *97*
S. hastata 'Wehrhahnii' *12*, 106, *107*
S. helvetica 106, *107*
S. irrorata 567, *567*
S. lanata 141, *194*, 195
S. reticulata 112, *112*
salsify 441, *576*, 577
salt-tolerant plants *see* coastal gardens
Salvia 215
S. farinacea 'Victoria' 458, *459*, 487
S. officinalis 574, *574*, 579
S. sclarea *344*
S. x *sylvestris* 'Mainacht' 264, *264*, 300
S. uliginosa 356, *356*
S. viridis *32*
'Oxford Blue' 300, 301, 366, *366*, 392
Sambucus racemosa 'Plumosa Aurea' 512
sandwort 293, *293*
corsican 112, *112*
sandy soils 592
improving 347

sandy soils (continued)
plant selectors 119, 206, 300, 392, 487, 578
Sanguisorba minor 574, *574*
S. obtusa 451, *451*
Santolina 45, 139
S. chamaecyparissus 318, *319*
Sarcococca hookeriana var. *digyna* 566, *567*, 579
satin flower 183, *183*, 274–5, *275*
Satureja hortensis 297, *297*, 388, *389*
S. montana 482, *482*
savory
preserving 253
summer 297, *297*, 388, *389*
winter 71, 251, 482, *482*
savoy cabbages 245, 439
sawflies 242
saws, pruning 507, 586, *586*
Saxifraga 'Cranbourne' 110, *110*
S. fortunei 455, *455*, 486
S. 'Gloria' *572*, 573
S. 'Gregor Mendel' 111, *111*
S. 'Jenkinsiae' 110, *110*
S. 'Johann Kellerer' 572, *572*
S. oppositifolia 110, *110*
S. 'Peter Pan' 201, *201*
S. spathularis 514–15
saxifrage *140*, 455, *455*
division 140
kabschia 110, *110*, 111, *111*, 572, *572*, 573
mossy 201, *201*, 421
propagation 514
purple 110, *110*
Scabiosa 393, 486
S. caucasica 'Clive Grieves' 356, *356*
'Miss Willmott' 456, *456*
'Moerheim Blue' 392
S. graminifolia 478, *478*
S. stellata 'Paper Moon' 461, *461*
scabious 356, *356*, 456, *456*, 478, *478*
Scaevola 148
S. aemula 'Blue Wonder' 366, *367*, 393
scale insects 63, *63*, 223, 257
scarifiers 589, *589*
scarifying lawns 153, 521
scented plants
annuals 492
scented plants (continued)
in containers 148
foliage 579
herbs 344
Schisandra rubrifolia 280, *281*, 301
schizanthus 350
Schizostylis coccinea 'Sunrise' 451, *451*, 486
Scilla 119
S. bifolia 86, 87
S. mischtschenkoana 87, *87*, 547, *547*
S. peruviana 278–9, *278*
S. siberica 'Spring Beauty' 87, *87*
scooping, hyacinths 403
scoops, compost 591, *591*
scoring, hyacinths 403, *403*
scorzonera 441, *576*, 577
screens, protecting climbers 499
sea buckthorn *562*, 563
sea holly 355, *355*
sea pink 200, *201*
sea thrift 292, *292*
seakale 117, *117*
seats, herb 346
secateurs *242*, 506, 586, *586*
security, thorny hedges 417
sedge *364*, 365
drooping 387, *387*
sedum
division *399*, 420
propagation 53
Sedum 392, 393, 486, 487
S. 'Bertram Anderson' 478, *478*
S. 'Herbstfreude' 452, *452*
S. 'Ruby Glow' 362, *362*
S. spathulifolium 'Purpureum' 385, *385*
S. spectabile 124
'Brilliant' 360, *360*
S. spurium 515
S. 'Vera Jameson' 452, *452*
seed compost 599
seed tape *66*
seed trays 590, *590*
seedbeds, preparation 28–9, *28*, 525, *525*
seedlings
alpines 515
biennials 127
damping-off disease 31, 76
pricking out 31, *31*, 398
slug protection *65*
thinning 29, *29*, 31, 67
seedlings (continued)
transplanting biennials *214*, 215
vegetables *162*
watering 244
seeds
collecting 213, 398
germination 306
harvesting 306, 308–9, 342–3
storing 213, 229, 306, *306*, 343
stratification 306, 497, 514
see also sowing
seep hose 235, 244, 339, 589, *589*, 603
semi-ripe cuttings
alpines 323
climbers 317, 409
herbs 251
shrubs 226, *226–7*, 319
Sempervivum 228
S. 'Silverine' *420*
S. tectorum 141, 385, *385*, 392, 393
Senecio 33, *226*, *519*
S. cineraria 215
'Silver Dust' *33*
shadbush 470, *470*
shade
annuals 492
growing bulbs in 311
planning a fruit garden 434–5
plant selectors 118, 119, 207, 301, 393, 486, 579
shading greenhouses 166–7, 349
vegetable plots 528
shallots 117, *117*
crop rotation 534
drying 257
lifting 246, 338
planting 68, 527
storing 340, 527
shamrock 184, *185*
sharpening tools 583, *583*
shears
edging shears 588, *588*
garden shears *586*, 587
one-handed *586*, 587
trimming hedges 320
sheet mulches 601
shell flower 369, *369*
shelter belts 417
shingle mulches 600, *600*
shiso, japanese 114, *114*
shredders 597, *597*
shrub roses 290, *290–1*
pruning 38, *39*
spacing plants 407
shrubs
acclimatising 223
air layering 47, *47*
in autumn 412–15
in containers 146, 147, 149, 150–1
coppicing 512
cuttings 46, *47*, 139, 226–7, *226–7*, 319, *319*, 413
deadheading *137*
in early spring 42–9
frost damage *42*
in late spring 136–9
in late summer 318–19
layering 139, *139*, 413
overgrown 43
pests and diseases 223
planning gardens 51
plant selectors 96–108, 190–9, 285–91, 376–81, 468–76, 554–71
planting 138, *138*, 414, *414–15*
potting on *73*
pruning 43–5, 136–7, 224, *224–5*, 318, 413, 503, 506–8, *507*, *508*, 510
reversion 318
suckers 503, *503*, 510, *510*
in summer 222–7
tiered shrubs 513
topiary 48, *48–9*, 326–7, *326*
transplanting 504, *504–5*
watering *139*, 223
weeding around 223
in winter 502–13
see also wall shrubs
shuttlecock fern *13*, 203, *203*
sieves 591, *591*
Silene schafta 384, *385*, 392
silk-tassel bush 568, *568*
silty soils 592
silver banner fern 481, *481*
silver bell 196, *196*
silver foliage
alpines 112, 293, 479, 573
annuals and biennials 277
perennials 181, 271–2, 365
shrubs and trees 288–9, 381, 566–7
water plants 481
silver-leaf disease 159

single digging 593, *593*
sink gardens *53*, 141
Sisyrinchium striatum 'Aunt May' 270, *271*, 301
Skimmia x *confusa* 'Kew Green' 106, *106*, 118
S. japonica 'Rubella' *51*, *518*, 560, *560*, 579
skunk cabbage 113, *113*
yellow 113, *113*
slate mulches *223*
slugs 64
and alpines 53
protecting seedlings *65*
slug pellets 123
traps 123
small gardens
fruit *435*, 435
trees 579
vegetables 533
Smilacina racemosa 180, *181*, 207
smoke bush 470, *470*
coppicing 512
pruning 45, *45*
Smyrnium olusatrum 114, *114*, 343
snails 123, *258*
water 324
snapdragon *215*, 276, *276*
sneezeweed 361, *361*
snow damage, hedges 505
snow gum 565, *565*
snow mould 153
snowball tree 192, *193*
japanese 198, *198*
snowbell
alpine 109, *109*
japanese 288, *289*
snowberry 417, 566, *567*
snowdrop 549, *549*
planting 312
transplanting *495*
snowdrop tree 196, *196*
snowflake
autumn-flowering 464, *464*
spring-flowering 91, *91*
summer-flowering *15*, 185, *185*
soaker hose 235, 603
soft-tip cuttings 35, 139, 164, *165*, 212, *212*, 307
alpines 229
climbers 221
herbs 251
perennials 307
soft-tip cuttings (continued)
shrubs 226
tender perennials 327, *327*
soil 592–5
alpines 53
drainage 347
fruit gardens 435, 436
green manures 337
herb gardens 346
improving fertility 594
improving nitrogen content 438
improving structure 594
liming 535, 593
mulching 594, 600–1, *600*
no-dig beds 531, *531*
pH value 592, *592*, 593
planting water plants 144
preparing for fruit 331
preparing for new lawns 328–9
rose sickness 315, 496, *496*
for roses 406, 407
seedbeds 525, *525*
sterilising soil for composts 76
temperature *64*
testing 347
texture 592
trench composting 64, *64*
types of 592
vegetable plots 528
warming 525, *525*, 609
winter cultivation 525, *525*
see also digging; planting
soil-based composts 236, 599
soil-less composts 236, 599
Solanum 134
S. capsicastrum 425, *519*
S. crispum 'Glasnevin' *17*, 377, *377*
S. laxum 'Album' 374, *374*
S. rantonnetii 148
Soldanella alpina 109, *109*
x *Solidaster luteus* 'Lemore' 363, *363*, 393
solomon's seal 180, *180*
false 180, *181*
Sorbus 486, 509, 578
S. aria 'Lutescens' 198, *198*, 206, 207
S. aucuparia 'Beissneri' 560, *560*, 579
S. cashmiriana 566, *567*
S. hupehensis *474*, 475
S. 'Joseph Rock' 474, *474*, 487
S. sargentiana 473, *473*, 487
sorrel 184, *185*
sorrel (herb) 71, 204, *205*
sour gum 474, *474*
sowbread 370, *370*, 464, *464*
sowing
alpines 53, 229, 420, 514–15, *515*
annuals 28–30, *32*, 126–7, 215, 309, 493
biennials 127, *127*
catch crops 533
in drills *66*
germination failure 77
in greenhouses 74, *74*, 169
herbs 165, 251, 537
intercropping 161, 533, *533*
lawns 59, 154–5, *154–5*
perennials 27, 306
root vegetables 246–7, 338
seed tape *66*
successional sowing 67, 533
testing old seeds 77, *77*
vegetables 66–9, *66–7*, 161–2, *161*, 532–3
see also individual plants
spades 584, *584*, *585*
cleaning *595*
sharpening 583
spanish dagger 381, *381*
sparaxis 35
spatterdock 232
spearmint 204, *205*
specific replant disease 496, 505
speedwell 239, 264, *264–5*, 266, *266*
spider flower 366, *367*
spider plant 366, *367*
spiderwort *364*, 365
spikenard, false 180, *181*
spinach 117, *117*
catch crops 533
crop rotation 535
harvesting 248
sowing 69, 161, 339, 441, 527
storing 341
successional sowing 533
watering 336
winter protection 441
winter spinach 577, *577*
spinach beet 161, 533
spindle tree 468–9, *469*
winged 470, *471*
Spiraea 'Arguta' 198, *198*
S. japonica 'Anthony Waterer' *378*, 379, 393
S. thunbergii 106, *106*, 119
spotted dog 83, *83*
sprays 258
spring greens 68
spring onions 205, *205*
crop rotation 534
intercropping *533*
sowing 248, 338
spring vetchling 173, *173*
sprinklers 235, *235*, 589, *602*, 603, *603*
spruce
black 573, *573*
brewer 568, *569*
colorado 112, *112*, 554, *554*
norway 573, *573*
spur pruning 225
spurge *82*, 83, 176–7, *177*, 181, *181*, 203, *203*, 267, *267*, 456, *456*
wood 176, *177*
squashes 163
in containers 533
crop rotation 530, 535
harvesting 441
planting 249
pollination 249, *249*
sowing 169
training 249, 339
trench composting 64, *64*
watering 244
winter 484, *485*
squill *86*, 87
siberian 87, *87*
st john's wort 379, *379*, 385, *385*
Stachys 124
S. byzantina *21*
'Silver Carpet' 272, *272*
Stachyurus praecox *564*, 565, 578, 579
staking
fruit trees 436
supporting perennials 122
trees 415, *415*
see also supports
standards
in containers 150
fruit trees 435
roses 39, 407, *407*
trees 509, 513
weeping trees 511

star jasmine 374, *374*
star-of-bethlehem 91, *91*, 185, *185*
statice 215, 461, *461*
stem cuttings *47*
stems
 colourful 512
 coppicing 512, *512*
 pollarding 512
stephanotis 445
stepping stones, in lawns *521*
sterilising soil 76
Sternbergia lutea 217, 464, *464*, 486, 487
stinking benjamin 173, *173*
stinking hellebore 545, *545*
stinking iris 452–3, *453*
stinkwort 545, *545*
Stipa aurundinacea 22
 S. gigantea 360, 361, 392
 S. tenuissima 21
stock 275, *275*
 'Beauty of Nice' 350
 brompton 215, 350
 night-scented 148, 215
stone cress 200, *201*
stonecrop 362, *362*, 385, *385*, 452, *452*, 478, *478*
'stooling' trees 137
storing
 bulbs 217
 fruit 334–5, 430–1, *430*
 herbs 252–3, *252–3*
 seeds 213, 229, 306, *306*, 343
 tools 583, *583*
 vegetables 340–1, 440–1, *441*
stork's bill 478, *478*
stratification, seeds 306, 497, 514
straw, as mulch 601, *601*
strawberries 299, *299*
 alpine 62, 63, *390*, 391
 clearing beds 243
 early crops 158
 forcing 62, 63, *538*, 539
 frost protection 61
 harvesting 241
 new beds 243
 perpetual varieties 333, 433
 planting 333, *333*, 433
 pollinating 62
 runners *243*
 thinning fruit 62
 tidying beds 333
 watering 433
strawberry tree 474, *474*, 557, *557*
strelitzia 259
streptocarpus 255, *255*
strimmers 588, *588*
strip cropping, cloches 609
Styrax japonicus 288, *289*, 301
successional sowing 67, 533
succulents *323*
 in containers 148
 cuttings 53, 75, *75*
 watering 258
suckers 510, *510*
 cherry trees *332*
 raspberries 243
 roses *219*, 314
 transplanting 503, *503*
sulphur 604
sumach, stag's horn 474, *474*
summer snow 363, *363*
sun rose 285, *285*, 293, *293*
sunflower 454, *454*, 460, *460*
 mexican 126, 462, *462*
sunny sites
 planning a fruit garden 434–5
 vegetable plots 528
supports
 climbers 135, 410–11, 501
 fruit 436–7
 pea sticks 211, *245*, 329
 perennials 122, *122*, 211, *211*, 329, *329*
 roses *407*
 tomatoes 249
 wall shrubs 223
 see also staking
Sutera cordata 369, *369*
swedes 577, *577*
 crop rotation 534, 535
 sowing 162
 storing 340, 341
sweet box 566, *567*
sweet briar *496*
sweet cicely 115, *115*
 cuttings 71
 drying roots 443
 seeds 343
sweet flag 295, *295*
sweet gum 471, *471*
sweet peas 220, 275, *275*, *309*, 366, *366*
 in greenhouses 445
 lowering 309
 planting out 28, *28*
 scent 148
 sowing 41, *74*
sweet peas (continued)
 sowing in paper tubes 445, *445*
sweet william 127, 276, *276*
sweet woodruff 71
sweetcorn 390, *390*, 532, 533
 catch crops 533
 crop rotation 535
 harvesting 249, 338–9, *338*
 planting 163, 248, 249, *249*
 sowing *161*, 169
 storing 341
 watering 337
 as windbreak 441
sword fern 545, *545*
sycamore 190, *190*
Symphoricarpos 417
 S. x *doorenbosii* 'White Hedge' 566, *567*, 578
Symphytum 124
 S. 'Hidcote Blue' *80*, 81, 118, 119
Syringa 223
 S. vulgaris 206
  'Katherine Havemeyer' 192, *193*
  'Madame Lemoine' 198, *198*

T

tagetes
 deadheading 308
 sowing 30, 31
Tagetes 126, 169, 392, 487
 T. tenuifolia Favourite Series 368, *368*
  'Lemon Gem' 368, *368*
 T. Zenith Series 462, *462*
tamarisk 417
Tamarix ramosissima 417
tar-oil winter wash 523
tarragon *342*
 cuttings 71
 division 71
 potting up 442–3
 preserving 253
tassel flower 368, *368*, 462, *462*
Taxus 118
 T. baccata 107, *107*, 118, 321, 417, 578
  'Fastigiata' 569, *569*, 578
 T. x *media* 'Hicksii' 107, *107*, 118
tayberries 335
teasel *21*
Tellima grandiflora 207
 'Purpurteppich' 175, *175*, 207
tender perennials
 cuttings *307*, 327, *327*
 reviving 73, *73*
 winter protection 396–7
terracotta pots, watering 236
texsel greens 439
Thalictrum aquilegiifolium 266, *266*, 300
 T. delavayi 'Hewitt's Double' 356, *356*, 393
 T. flavum subsp. *glaucum* 269, *269*
thatch, lawns 153
thermometers 591, *591*
thinning
 fruit 159, *159*
 seedlings 29, *29*, 31, 67
thorns, hedges 417
thrift 200, *201*
Thuja occidentalis 'Danica' 479, *479*, 487
  'Hetz Midget' 112, *112*
  'Rheingold' 572–3, *572*, 579
 T. plicata 'Atrovirens' 417
thyme 115, *115*, *250*, *252*, *343*, *344*, 345, *345*
 in containers 443
 division 71
 in herb towers *71*
 layering 165
 mound layering 537, *537*
 planting 234, *234*
 preserving 253
 shearing 343
 silver *342*
Thymus 115, *115*
 T. serpyllum 'Goldstream' 346
  'Minimus' 346
  'Rainbow Falls' 346
Tiarella 50
 T. cordifolia 181, *181*
 T. wherryi 266, *266*, 301
tickseed 362, *362*
tidy tips 461, *461*
tiered shrubs 513
tigridia 35, 129
tined hoes 585
Tithonia 126
 T. rotundifolia 'Goldfinger' 462, *462*, 487
toad lily 450–1, *450*
toads 233, 259, 422, 516

tobacco plant *18*, 277, *277*, 369, *369*, 462, *462*
tomatoes 163, 390, *390*
catch crops 533
in containers 533
crop rotation 535
'Golden Delight' *256*
in greenhouses 168, 256, 350
harvesting 339, 350, 441
pinching out sideshoots *169*
planting 168, 248, 249
storing 341
supports 249
training *169*
watering 337
tools *see* equipment
top-dressing, lawns 428, 521
topiary 48, 150, *150*, *321*
in containers 146
frames 48, *49*
trimming *48*, 137, 326–7, *326*
torch lily 267, *267*, 362, *363*, 365, *365*, 453, *453*, 454, *454*
trace elements 604
Trachelospermum 409, 499
T. jasminoides *51*, 374, *374*
Trachycarpus fortunei 289, *289*
Tradescantia Andersoniana Group 'Osprey' *364*, 365
trailing plants, in containers 148
training
climbers 135, *317*
fruit 435, *436–7*
greenhouse plants 168, 256, *256*
standard trees 513
topiary 48
wall shrubs 513, *513*
transplanting
biennial seedlings *214*, 215
brassicas 245
suckers 503, *503*
trees and shrubs 504, *504–5*
Trapa natans 230, 232, 423
traveller's joy 551, *551*
trays, for propagation 590, *590*
tree fern, winter protection *518*, *519*
tree of heaven 512
trees
acclimatising 223
in autumn 412–15
climbers in 500, *501*
trees (continued)
in containers 147, 149, 150–1, *151*
coppicing 512, *512*
crown thinning 225
in early spring 42–9
growing bulbs under 311
in late spring 136–9
pests and diseases 223
planning gardens 51
plant selectors 96–108, 190–9, 285–9, 376–81, 468–76, 554–71
planting 138, *138*, 414, *414–15*
pollarding 512
propagation 46–7
pruning 506–11, *509–11*
raising crown 509
shelter belts 417
for small gardens 579
staking 415, *415*
standards 513
'stooling' 137
suckers 503, 510, *510*
in summer 222–5
symmetry 511, *511*
thinning crown 509
training stems 49, *49*
transplanting 504, *504–5*
tree guards *509*
watering *139*, 223
weeding around 223
weeping trees 511
windbreaks 138
in winter 502–13
see also individual fruit trees
trellis
hinged trellis 411, *411*
preservatives 501
supporting climbers 135, 410–11, *410–11*
trench composting 64, *64*
Tricyrtis formosana 450–1, *450*, 486
Trillium *50*, 207, 312
T. erectum 173, *173*
T. grandiflorum 271, *271*
trinity flower *364*, 365
tritonia 35
Trollius chinensis *231*
'Golden Queen' 295, *295*
Tropaeolum Alaska Series *74*, 368, *368*
T. majus 'Empress of India' 276–7, *276*, 300
T. speciosum 500
trowels 585, *585*
trugs 587, *587*
trumpet creeper 374, *374*
trumpet vine 374, *374*, 499, 500
Tsuga heterophylla 569, *569*
tubers
in autumn 402–3
in early spring 34–5
in late spring 128–9
starting into growth 540, *540*
in summer 216–17
in winter 494–5
see also bulbs
tulip
bedding schemes 32
in containers 425, *425*
diseases 425
forcing 351
fosteriana 89, *89*, 90, *90*, 91, *91*
greigii 89, *89*, 90, *90*
kaufmanniana 89, *89*, 90, *90*
lady 89, *89*
lifting 216–17
planting 402
Triumph Group 88, *88*, 90, *90*
Tulipa 118, 119
T. 'Apeldoorn' *15*
T. 'Apeldoorn's Elite' *15*
T. 'Apricot Beauty' 88, *88*
T. 'Cape Cod' 90, *90*
T. clusiana var. *chrysantha* 89, *89*
T. 'Couleur Cardinal' 88, *88*
T. 'Estella Rijnveld' 186, *187*
T. 'Fancy Frills' 186, *187*
T. hageri 'Splendens' 89, *89*
T. 'Heart's Delight' 89, *89*
T. humilis Violacea Group 548, *548*, 578
T. 'Madame Lefeber' 89, *89*
T. 'Mount Tacoma' 186, *186*
T. 'Orange Emperor' 90, *90*
T. orphanidea Whittallii Group 90, *90*
T. 'Peach Blossom' 88, *88*
T. praestans 'Fusilier' 89, *89*
T. 'Prinses Irene' 90, *90*
T. 'Purissima' 91, *91*
T. 'Queen of Night' 186, *186*
T. 'Red Riding Hood' 89, *89*
Tulipa (continued)
T. 'Red Wing' 186, *187*
T. saxatilis Bakeri Group 'Lilac Wonder' 186, *187*
T. 'Shakespeare' 90, *90*
T. 'Shirley' 186, *187*
T. sprengeri 279, *279*
T. 'Spring Green' 186, *186*
T. turkestanica *36*, 91, *91*, *118*
T. urumiensis *90*, 91
T. 'West Point' *14*, 186, *186*
tupelo 474, *474*
turf, lawns 154, *154*, 156, *156*
turnips 117, *117*, *532*
crop rotation 534, 535
harvesting 246, 338
intercropping 533
sowing 69, 162, 338, 439, 527
storing 340, 341, 441
watering 244
tussock grass 360, *360*
tying-in
climbers 220, *221*
fruit 243, *243*, 332

U, V

Uvularia grandiflora 178, *178*, 207
vaccinium 227
valerian 178–9, *178*
Valeriana phu 'Aurea' 178, *178*
variegated foliage, reversion 318, 510, *510*
vegetables *482–4*, 483–4
in autumn 438–41
'baby' vegetables 533
blanching 341
buying plug plants 532, *532*
choosing crops 532
in coldframes 607
in containers 533
crop rotation 530, 534–5
drying 438
in early spring 64–9
fertilisers 534, 605
in greenhouses 168, 256–7, 350
harvesting 336, 337–9, 350, 439, 524
holiday care 339
intercropping 533, *533*
in late spring 160–3
in late summer 336–41
making a vegetable plot 528–35
maximising space 533

vegetables (continued)
pea sticks *245*
pests 64–5
plant selectors 116–17, 204–5, 297–8, 388–90, 483–4, 574–7
seedlings *162*
in small gardens 533
sowing 66–9, *66–7*, 161–2, *161*, 532–3
spacing 67, *67*, 534
storing 340–1, 440–1, *441*
strip cropping 609
in summer 244–9
trench composting 64, *64*
watering 244, 336–7, 602
weeding 244–5
see also individual vegetables
in winter 439, 524–35, *528*
ventilation
cloches 609
greenhouses 166, 167, 349, 539, *539*
Verbascum 300
V. chaixii 'Gainsborough' 269, *269*, 300
V. 'Helen Johnson' 266, *266*
Verbena 235
V. bonariensis *19*, 356, *356*, 392, 397, *397*, *402*
V. 'Imagination' 274, *275*
V. 'Peaches and Cream' 369, *369*
V. rigida 458, *459*
V. 'Silver Anne' 367, *367*
vermiculite 599
Veronica austriaca subsp. *teucrium* 'Kapitän' 264, *264*, 301
V. gentianoides 264, *265*, 301
V. peduncularis 'Georgia Blue' 110, *110*, 119
V. spicata 'Heidekind' 266, *266*
Viburnum 119, 139, 206, 578
V. x *bodnantense* 44
'Dawn' 556, *556*, *578*, 579
V. x *burkwoodii* 44
'Anne Russell' 106, *106*
V. carlesii 'Aurora' 192, *193*
V. davidii 554, *554*, 579
V. farreri 106, *107*, *508*, 566, *567*
V. x *juddii* 106, *107*
V. opulus *206*
'Compactum' 473, *473*, 486, 487
Viburnum (continued)
'Roseum' 192, *193*
V. plicatum 'Mariesii' 198, *198*, *225*, 513
V. tinus *51*, 321, 417, 579
'Eve Price' 99, *99*, 118
'Gwenllian' 556, *556*
Vinca minor 'La Grave' 96, *97*
vine eyes, supporting climbers 135, 410, *410*
vine weevils 396
and alpines 322–3
biological control 257
in containers 150, 304
in greenhouses 258, 541
vines, ornamental 466, *466*
cuttings 500
layering 500
pruning 498, *498*
see also grape vines
viola
cornuta hybrids 477, *477*
cuttings 229
deadheading 235
division 420
Viola 118, *146*, 207, 301, 579
V. 'Belmont Blue' 477, *477*, 486, 487
V. biflora 202, *202*
V. cornuta Alba Group 271, *271*, 301
V. 'Molly Sanderson' 479, *479*, 486, 487
V. odorata 544, *544*
V. riviniana Purpurea Group 173, *173*
V. Sorbet Series 182, *182*
V. sororia 'Freckles' 173, *173*
V. 'Ultima Scarlet' *518*
V. x *wittrockiana* 'Baby Lucia' 274, *275*
Crystal Bowl Series 366, *367*, 393
'Jolly Joker' 277, *277*
Mello Series 546, *546*
Princess Series 85, *85*
Ultima Series 546, *546*
Universal Series 546, *546*
violet 544, *544*
dog 173, *173*
english 544, *544*
horned 271, *271*
sister 173, *173*
sweet 345, 544, *544*
violet (continued)
twin-flowered 202, *202*
water 232
wood 173, *173*
woolly blue 173, *173*
violet flowers
alpines 109–10, 200, 292, 384, 477
annuals and biennials 85, 182, 274, 366–7, 458
bulbs 86–7, 184, 278–9, 463, 547
climbers 95, 188, 280, 373, 551
perennials 80–1, 172–3, 262–4, 354–6, 450–1, 544
shrubs and trees 96, 190, 285, 376–7, 468
water plants 113, 294, 386, 480
virginia creeper *408*, 466, *466*
chinese 281, *281*
pruning 317
supports 135, *410*
Vitis 498, 500
V. 'Brant' 466, *466*, 487
V. coignetiae *51*, 466, *466*, 487
V. vinifera 'Olivette' *316*
'Purpurea' 280, *281*

W

wake robin 271, *271*
Waldsteinia ternata *178*, 179, 206, *206*, 207
wall shrubs
cuttings 500
planting 409
supports 135, 223
training 513, *513*
see also climbers
wallflowers 85, *85*, 183, *183*, 265, *265*
bedding schemes 32
buying 401
planting 401, *401*
sowing 127, 215
transplanting seedlings 215
walls
growing fruit on 434
planting climbers against 499
trellis on 410, *411*
wandflower 452, *452*
water
conservation 602, 603
testing pond water *143*
see also drainage; watering
water chestnut 230, 232, 423
water gardens
in autumn 422–3
in early spring 54–5
in late spring 142–5
in late summer 324–5
in summer 230–3
in winter 516–17
water hawthorn *422*, 481, *481*
water hyacinth 423
water lettuce 230
water lily 230–1, *230*, 294–5, *294*, *295*, 386, *386*, 387, *387*, 517
division 231
pests and diseases 231
planting 145, *145*
thinning 230, 325
water-lily aphids 231
water-lily beetle 231
water-lily leaf spot 231
water plants 480–1
division 143, *143*
plant selectors 113, 203, 294–5, 386–7, 480–1
planting 144–5, *145*
winter protection 423
water-retaining gel 235, 236, 424
water shoots 510
water soldier 423
water supply
vegetable plots 529
water butts 446, 603, *603*
water tanks 446
waterfalls, oxygenating ponds 233, 324, *325*
watering 602–3, *602–3*
alpines 229
annuals 602
container plants 147, 235, 236–7, *236–7*, 602
equipment 589, *589*, 591, *591*, 603
fruit 602
greenhouse plants 167, 256, 258, 539
hanging baskets 147, 149, 236
hedges 137, 223
holiday care 339
lawns 157, 239, 602
patio plants 236–7, *236–7*
salad crops 248
shrubs *139*, 223
trees *139*, 223
vegetables 244, 336–7, 602

watering (continued)
water trays 591
watering cans 587, *587*, 591, *591*, 603
watering systems 147, 236, *236–7*, 237, 603, *603*
weedkillers
lawns 152
in new beds and borders 223
safety 152
systemic *320*
weeds
in alpine gardens 228–9
amongst climbers 316
around shrubs and trees 223
in compost heaps 596
in hedges *320*
in lawns 58, 152, 154, 239, 427, *427*
on patios *326*
in perennial borders 397
perennial weeds 228–9, 397, 596
in ponds 143, *143*, *231*, 232
vegetable gardens 244–5
weeping trees, training 511, *511*
Weigela 318
W. 'Victoria' 286–7, *286*, 300, *300*
wheelbarrows 587, *587*
white currants 299, *299*
cuttings 432
harvesting 241, 335
planning a fruit garden 434
planting 437
pruning 61, 242, 522
training 435
tying-in 437
white flowers
alpines 111–12, 202, 293, 479, 573
annuals and biennials 183, 369, 462
bulbs 91, 185, 279, 371, 464, 549
climbers 95, 189, 281, 372
white flowers (continued)
perennials 179–81, 269–71, 363–5, 454–6, 544–5
shrubs and trees 103–6, 195–8, 288, 380–3, 474–5, 565–6
water plants 113, 295, 387, 481
whitebeam 198, *198*
whitefly 257, 258
whitlow grass 111, *111*
widgers 591
wildlife, ponds 232–3, 516
willow 112, *112*, 567, *567*
coppicing 512
cuttings 323
kilmarnock 103, *103*
swiss 106, *107*
violet 554, *554*
white 560, *560*
woolly *194*, 195
windbreaks
hedges 417, 505
planning a fruit garden 434
planting trees 138
protecting new hedges 419
vegetable plots 528
windflower 86, *86*, 88, *88*
window boxes
vegetables in 533
winter displays *519*
see also containers
winter cherry 425, *519*
winter moth 431
winter protection
alpines 421, *514*
aquatic plants 423
bedding plants 400
cloches and coldframes 606–7, *606–7*
containers 425
greenhouses 446–7
roses 404–5, *404*
tender perennials 396–7
vegetables 439
winter sweet 560, *561*
winter tares, green manures 337
winter washing, fruit 523
wintersweet 132, *502*, 503
wires, supporting climbers 135, 410, *410*
wisteria
chinese 188, *188*, 189, *189*
in containers 150
japanese 280, *280*
on patios 149
pruning 221, *221*, 316, 499, *499*
Wisteria 16, 132, *132*, 300
W. floribunda 'Multijuga' 280, *280*
W. x *formosa* 'Yae-kokuryû' 280, *280*
W. sinensis 188, *188*
'Alba' 189, *189*
witch hazel *23*, 503, *503*, *558*, 559, 562–3, *562*
chinese *562*, 563
ozark *102*, 103
witloof chicory 575, *575*
wood anemone 91, *91*, 547, *547*
wood millet, golden 177, *177*
woodruff, sweet 115, *115*
woodrush, greater 481, *481*
worms
no-dig beds 531
worm compost 598
wormcasts 58, 427, *427*
wormwood 271, *271*, 293, *293*, 385, *385*

X

Xanthoceras sorbifolium 198, *198*
Xeranthemum annuum 460, *460*, 487

Y

yarrow 239, 268, *268*, 293, *293*, 362, *362*
yellow flag 203, *203*
yellow flowers and foliage
alpines 111, 202, 293, 385, 572–3
yellow and foliage flowers (continued)
annuals and biennials 183, 277, 368–9, 460–2, 546
bulbs 90–1, 371, 464, 548–9
climbers 188–9, 281, 374, 466
perennials 82–3, 176–9, 268–9, 362–3, 453–4
shrubs and trees 101–3, 192–5, 287, 379, 473–4, 560–5
yellow and foliage flowers (continued)
water plants 113, 203, 294–5, 387, 481
yew 107, *107*
cuttings *226*, *319*
florence court 569, *569*
hedges 43, 321, 416, 417
irish 569, *569*
topiary 48, *48*
Yucca gloriosa 381, *381*, 392, 393
yulan 196, *196*

Z

Zantedeschia aethiopica 350
'Crowborough' 295, *295*
Z. elliottiana 350
Zauschneria californica 487
'Dublin' 478, *478*
zebra grass *268*, 269
Zinnia 30, 31, 169
Z. 'Envy' 369, *369*
zucchini *see* courgettes

acknowledgments

Photographs were supplied by the following people and organisations. Where relevant, the number of a picture as it appears on a page is given. Abbreviations are used as follows:

t top, c centre, b bottom, l left, r right.
DA David Askham, MB Mark Bolton, PB Philippe Bonduel, MBr Martin Brigdale, LB Lynne Brotchie, NB Nicola Browne, JB Jonathan Buckley, CB Chris Burrows,BC Brian Carter, EC Eric Crichton, SC Sarah Cuttle, RD Reader's Digest, JD Jacqui Dracup, RE Ron Evans, CF C Fairweather, VF Vaughan Fleming, OBG Oxford Botanical Garden, JG John Glover, GH Gil Hanly, FH Fran Harpur, JH Jerry Harpur, MH Marcus Harpur, SH Sunniva Harte, NH Neil Holmes, PH Photos Horticultural, GWL GardenWorld Images, ML Michelle Lamontagne, AL Andrew Lawson, GPL Garden Picture Library, MM Marianne Majerus, S&OM S & O Mathews, DM David Murphy, MN Mike Newton, CN Clive Nichols, JP Jerry Pavia, SSP Sea Spring Photos, LP Laslo Puskas, HR Howard Rice, GR Gary Rogers, MLS Mayer le Scanff, JS J Sira, GGS Georgia Glynn-Smith, RS Ron Sutherland, BT Brigitte Thomas, MT Maddie Thornhill, JWh Jo Whitworth, DW Didier Willery, JW Justyn Willsmore, MW Mark Winwood, SW Steven Wooster

Front cover, clockwise from top left: soft-tip cuttings, MW/RD; *Clematis* 'Jackmanii', MN/RD; *Amaryllis* in winter, SC/RD; *Rosa* 'Iceberg', SC/RD; *Verbascum* 'Helen Johnson', SC/RD; *Physalis alkekengi* var. *franchetii*, RD.
Back cover, clockwise from top left: Trailing lobelia Cascade Series, MT/RD; MBr/RD; *Astrantia major* SC/RD; apples MT/RD. **1** MW **2-3** GPL/Lamontagne **4** GPL/HR **6** SC **7** MW

year-round garden

10-11 MH (Lakemount, Co. Cork, Ireland) **12 r** GPL/HR **13 t** JH, **bl** MB, **bc** GPL/MB, **bl** CN **14 tl** JB, **tr & br** MB, **bl** GPL/C Burrows **15 tl** GPL/MB, **tr** RD, **bl** MM (Design: Peter Chan) **br** MM **16 t** MN, **c** JH (Sun House, Suffolk), **b** S&OM **17 tl** S&OM (Closewood House, Hants), **tr** GPL/HR, **bl & br** JH **18 t** GPL/SW (Priory, Kemerton), **bl** MM (Old Vicarage, East Ruston, Norfolk), **br** MN **19 tl** MM (Design: W Giles), **tr** MH (Lakemount, Co. Cork, Ireland), **b** JB (Great Dixter, E. Sussex) **20 tl** JWh, **bl** R Whitworth, **r** CN (RHS Wisley) **21 tl** JWh, **tr** MB (Lady Farm, Somerset), **c** GPL/François de Heel, **b** GPL/M Heuff **22 tl** GPL/HR, **tr** GPL/NH, **br** GPL/HR, **bl** NB **23 tl** GPL/HR, **tr** GPL/M Heuff, **br** GPL/NH, **bl** GPL/R Evans

early spring

24-25 GPL/HR **26 l** SC, **r** MW **27 tl, tc & tr** MW, **b** SC **28** MW **29 tl & b** MW, **tr** GPL/D Cavagnaro **30** SC **31** MW **32 bl, bcl & bcr** MW, **br** AL **33** Illustration by Ian Sidaway.**34 l** SC, **c & r** MW **35 t** MW, **cl, cr, bl & br** SC **36 t & c** MW, **b** SC, **37 tl & c** SC, **tr & b** MW **38 l** MW, **r** SC **39** SC **40 tl** SC, **tr** MW, **b** JWh **41** MW **42 l** SC, **r** RD **43 tl** MW, **tr** GWI, **bl & br** MW **44 tl, tr & c** MW, **b** JWh **45 t** MW, **b** SC **46 l** JWh, **r** S&OM **47 t** MW, **cl, cr, c inset & br** SC, **bl** RD **48 t** SC, **bl, bcl, bcl inset & bcr** MW, **br** MB **49 tl, tc, bl & bc** SC, **tr & br** MW **50 l** CN, **r** AL **52 t** MW, **c** SC, **b** GWI **53** SC **54** MW **55 tl & tr** SC, **bl, bc & br** MW **56 l & r** SC, **bc** SC **57 l** SC, **r** MB (Design: Bob Purnell) **58-9** MW **60** MT **61-64** MW **65 tl, tc, bl, bc & br** MW, **tr** SSP **66 l** SC, **tr** MT, **bl** MW, **br** SC **67 tl** MW, **tc** MW, **tr** SC, **c** MW, **b** SC **68 l** MT, **c & r** MW **69-70** MW **71 tl, tr, bl & bc** MW, **br** SC **72-3** MW **74-5 all** SC **except bl & br** MW **76 tl & b** SC, **tr** MW **77 tl, tr & cl** SC, **c, cr & br** MW **78-9** GWI **80-1 (1)** GPL/MLS, **(2, 10, 11)** RD, **(3)** AL, **(4 & 5)** JWh, **(6)** GPL/MLS, **(7)** S&OM, **(8)** GPL/NH, **(9)** GPL/R Butcher **82-3 (1)** GPL/JG, **(2)** GPL/HR, **(3)** GPL/MLS, **(4, 7, 11)** JWh, **(5)** GPL/NH, **(6)** HSC, **(8)** RD, **(9)** GPL/SH, **(10)** PH **84 (1)** JWh, **(2, 4, 5, 8)** S&OM, **(3)** RD, **(6)** GWI, **(7)** SC **85 (1)** Colegrave Seeds Ltd, **(2)** GWI, **(3)** A-Z Botanical, **(4)** GPL/HR, **(5)** GPL/JG **86-7 (1, 5)** GWI, **(2)** GPL/JS, **(3, 7, 9)** RD, **(4)** MB, **(6)** MB, **(8)** S&OM, **(10)** GPL/JS, **(11)** GPL/SH **88-9 (1, 2, 3, 8, 11, 12)** RD, **(4)** MB, **(5)** GPL/A I Lord, **(6)** GPL/B Carter, **(7)** S&OM, **(9)** GPL/JG, **(10)** GWI **90-1 (1,10)** GPL/CB, **(2, 4, 6, 9)** RD, **(3)** GPL/NH, **(5)** GWI, **(7)** GPL/JG, **(8)** GPL/SH, **(11)** SC **92-3 (1)** RD, **(2, 3, 4, 9,12)** MB, **(5)** GPL/P Bonduell, **(7)** GPL/NH, **(6, 8, 10)** GWI, **(11)** GPL/CB **94 (1)** GPL/J Beedle, **(2, 6)** PH, **(3)** GPL/JG, **(4)** RD, **(5)** GPL/CB, **(7)** GPL/B Challinor, **(8)** GPL/E Rooney **95 (1)** PH, **(2)** GWI, **(3)** GPL/E Crichton, **(4)** GPL/JG, **(5)** AL, **(6)** MW **96-7 (1)** GPL/JG, **(2)** GPL/S Wooster, **(3)** GWI, **(4)** GPL/R White, **(5, 9)** GPL/CF, **(6)** GPL/JG, **(7, 8, 10, 11)** JWh, **(12)** GWI **98-9 (1)** GPL/Lamontagne, **(2, 5, 7)** GWI, **(3)** GPL/HR, **(4, 6, 9, 10)** JWh, **(8)** GPL/NH, **(11)** RD, **(12)** JD **100-101 (1)** GWI, **(2, 7)** JWh, **(3)** GPL/D Willery, **(4, 5, 8, 9)** RD, **(6)** S&OM, **(10, 11)** GPL/JS **102-103 (1, 9, 10)** JWh, **(2, 11)** GWI, **(3, 4, 5)** RD, **(6)** S&OM, **(7)** GPL/HR, **(8)** PH, **(12)** JD **104-105 (1, 3, 6)** RD, **(2, 4, 5, 7, 10)** JD, **(8, 11)** GWI, **(9, 12)** GPL/JG **106-107 (1)** GPL/D England, **(2, 3, 4, 12)** JD, **(5)** GPL/J Hurst, **(6)** GPL/R Butcher, **(7, 8)** RD, **(9)** A-Z Botanical, **(10)** GWI, **(11)** GPL/BT **108 (1, 2, 3, 7, 8)** JD, **(4)** S&OM, **(5)** JD, **(6)** GWI **109 (1, 2)** RD, **(3, 5)** GPL/JG, **(4)** GPL/R Hyam, **(6)** GWI **110-111 (1)** MB, **(2)** GWI, **(3, 6)** GPL/JG, **(4)** RD, **(5, 10)** GWI, **(7, 11, 12)** JD, **(8)** GPL/NH, **(9)** GPL/HR **112 (1)** JD, **(2, 5)** GWI, **(3)** GPL/HR, **(4)** GPL/J Pavia, **(6)** RD **113 (1)** GPL/JG, **(2)** GPL/P Bonduel, **(3)** A-Z Botanical, **(4, 5)** S&OM **114-115 (1, 2, 4, 6, 7, 8, 9, 10)** MT, **(3)** GPL/J Pavia, **(5)** MW **116-117 (1, 11)** SSP, **(2, 3, 6, 7, 8, 9, 10)** MT, **(4, 5, 12)** MN **118 l** SC, **c** MB, **r** GPL/JG **119 l** RD, **r** GPL/JG

late spring

120-1 GPL/HR (Design: B Chatto) **122** MW **123 l** MW, **t** MB, **b** MN **124** SC **125** MW except **br** SC **126** SC **127 t** SC, **b** RD **128** SC except **c insert** MW **129 t** SC, **b** RD **130** CN **131 t** MW, **b** SC **132** MB **133** MW **134** SC **135 l** SC, **r** GPL/HR **136** MN **137 t** SC, **b** MW **138 t** JB, **b** MW **139 t** SC, **b** MB **140** GPL/J Pavia **141 t & cr** MN, **bl & br** SC, **bc** MW **142** GR **143** MW **144 t** MB, **bl** NB, **br** SC **145** MW **146** GPL/L Brotchie **147** SC **148** SC **149 tl & tc** SC, **tr** MN, **b** GPL/J Wade **150 t** AL, **b** JB (RHS Chelsea 2001, Design: A Sturgeon) **151** SC except **t** MN **152 l** GPL/JG, **r** MW **153** MW **154 l** GPL/J Legate, **r** MW **155** MW **156** MW **157** GPL/JG **158 t** GPL/HR, **b** GPL/M Howes **159 l** MT, **r** SC **160 t** SSP, **b** MW **161 t** MBr, **b** MW **162 t** MT, **b** MN **163 t** MT, **b** SSP **164** GPL/A Lord **165** MW except **t** GPL/SH **166** MW **167 t** MW, **b** GPL/P Windsor **168** MW **169 t** GPL/M Howes, **bc & bl** SC, **br** MW **170-171** RD **172-73 (1, 5, 6)** GWI, **(2, 4, 10)** RD, **(3)** MB, **(7)** GPL/NH, **(8)** GPL/JG, **(9)** GPL/JS, **(11)** GPL/M Heuff, **(12)** SC **174-75 (1)** MT, **(2)** GPL/SH, **(3, 4, 6, 10)** RD, **(5)** GWI, **(7)** SC, **(8)** GPL/JS, **(9, 12)** MB, **(11)** S&OM **176-77 (1)** JWh, **(2)** GPL/JG, **(3)** GPL/JS, **(4, 6, 10, 11)** RD, **(5)** GPL/NH, **(7)** GPL/HR, **(8)** MB, **(9)** SC, **(12)** GPL/J Wade, **(13)** GPL/C Fairweather, **(14)** GPL/MLS **178-79 (1, 5, 6, 7, 12)** RD, **(2)** GPL/HR, **(3, 4)** AL, **(8, 9)** GPL/JG, **(10)** GPL/J Pavia, **(11)** GPL/ D Willery **180-81 (1, 3, 10, 12)** RD, **(2)** GPL/R Evans, **(4)** GPL/NH, **(5, 7)** GPL/ J Hurst, **(6, 13)** GWI, **(8)** GPL/MLS, **(9)** GPL/J Pavia, **(11)** MB **182-83 (1, 4)** GPL/JG, **(2, 6, 8)** GPL/SH, **(3, 5)** RD, **(7, 9, 10, 11)** GWI, **(12)** MB **184-85 (1, 2, 7)** MB, **(3, 11)** GPL/HR, **(4, 5, 8, 9, 10, 12)** RD, **(6)** GPL/JG **186-87 (1, 9)** SC, **(2, 3, 4, 5)** RD, **(6, 7)** GPL/C Burrows, **(8)** RD **188-89 (1)** GPL/JS, **(2)** MB, **(3, 5, 7, 9)** GPL/HR, **(4)** GPL/JG, **(6, 8)** RD, **(10)** GPL/B Carter, **(11)** GWI, **(12)** GPL/JS **190-91 (1, 4, 9)** MB, **(2, 5, 7, 8, 10)** RD, **(3, 6, 11)** GPL/JG, **(12, 13)** GPL/B Carter **192-93 (1, 2, 3, 9, 10)** RD, **(4)** GWI, **(5)** SC, **(6)** GPl/HR, **(7)** GPL/NH, **(8, 11)** MB, **(12)** S&OM **194-95 (1, 4)** GPL/JG, **(2, 10)** MB, **(3, 6, 7, 11, 12)** RD, **(5)** Ray Cox/Glendoick Gardens Ltd, **(8)** GPL/D Clyne, **(9)** GWI **196-97 (1, 8, 9)** MB, **(2, 3)** GPL/HR, **(4)** JWh, **(5, 6, 7, 10, 11)** RD, **(12)** GPL/E Crichton **198 (1)** GPL/R Sutherland, **(2)** GPL/JG, **(3, 4)** RD, **(5)** GPL/B Carter, **(6)** MB **199 (1)** GPL/D Askham, **(2, 7)** RD, **(3)** GPL/B Carter, **(4)** Ray Cox/Glendoick Gardens Ltd, **(5, 9)** GPL/J Glover, **(6)** GPL/B Challinor, **(8)** GPL/D England **200-201 (1)** GPL/J Hurst, **(2, 3, 4, 6, 7, 11)** RD, **(5)** GPL/S Harte, **(8)** GPL/JS, **(9, 12)** GWI, **(10)** SC **202 (1, 4)** GPL/HR, **(2, 6)** RD, **(3, 5)** GWI **203 (1, 3, 4)** RD, **(2)** MB **204-205 (1)** GWI, **(2)** GPl/NH, **(3)** GPL/J Wade, **(4)** GPL/C Boursnell, **(5)** GPL/B Thomas, **(6, 8, 13)** GPL/M Howes, **(7)** GPL/HR, **(9)** C Carter, **(10)** GPL/M Watson, **(11)** SSP, **(12)** GPL/SH **206 l** SC, **c** AL, **r** S&OM **207** MB

summer

208-9 MBr 210 SC 211 MW except br MB (Design: M Payne) 212 MW except t SC 213 MW except b SC 214 l MT, tr & br SC 215 t MW, b MT 216 GPL/RE 217 tl & tr MW, b GPL/JG 218 FH 219 MW except tl SC 220 l MN 220-1 S&OM, 221 r MW, bl & br SC 222 JWh, 223 t & b MT 224 t JW, c & b SC 225 t GPL/JS, c & b SC 226-27 MW, 228 l MB (RHS Chelsea, Lifetime Care Garden, Design: P Stone), r MN 229 SC 230 MB (Design: M Payne) 231 t MW, b GPL/JG 232 AL, 233 t JH (Design: B Hicks, Australia), b MW 234 t GPL/JG, b MT 235 t & b MN 236 t MW, c GPL/GGS, b GPL/J Sorrell 237 t GPL/F Strauss, b MN 238 GPL/GH 239 MW 240 SC 241 t & br MT, bl SC 242 MW 242-43 MT 243-44 MW 245 t MB, b MW 246 l CN (Design: S Irvine), r MT 247 t MW, c JB (Design: M Crosby-Jones), b GPL/JP 248 MT 249 MW 250 t MW, b MN 251 t MN, b SC 252 tl SC, tr MW, b MBr 253 SC 254 MW 255 t MN, b MW 256-57 MW 258 SC 259 l JB (Design: V Kennedy) 260-261 MN 262-263 (1, 9) MB, (2, 5, 6, 8, 10) JWh, (3) GPL/JG, (4, 7, 11) RD, (12) GWI 264-265 (1, 5, 7, 8, 9, 11) RD, (2) MB, (3) GWI, (4) GPL/HR, (6, 10) JWh, (11) RD, (12) CN 266-267 (1, 11) MB, (2, 3) GPL/JS, (4, 6, 7, 12) RD, (5) SC, (8) GPL/JG, (9) JD, (10) AL 268-269 (1, 4) AL, (2, 3, 9, 11, 12) RD, (5, 6, 7, 8) JWh, (10) GWI 270-271 (1, 2) GPL/JG, (3, 12) AL, (4, 11) RD, (5) GPL/Lamontagne, (6) CN, (7) MB, (8, 10) GWI, (9) GPL/MLS, 272 (1, 4, 6) JWh, (2, 3) MB, (5) GPL/MB 273 (1, 2, 4, 5) JWh, (3) GPL/EC, (6) AL, (7) GPL/D Askham, (8) GPL/CB 274-275 (1, 4, 5, 7, 8, 9, 10, 11) MT, (2) GPL/JS, (3, 12) GWI, (6) GPL/JG 276-277 (1, 11) GPL/HR, (2, 3, 4, 5, 6, 7, 12) MT, (8) GPL/J Hurst, (9) RD, (10) GPL/CB, 278-279 (1, 2, 3, 5, 6, 8) RD, (4) GPL/RS, (7) GPL/J Wade, (9) GPL/JS, (10) GPL/JG, (11) GPL/HR, (12) GPL/RE 280-281 (1) RD, (2) S&OM, (3) GPL/C Fairweather, (4) SC, (5) GPL/JS, (6) JW, (7, 8, 10) MT, (9) MB, (11) GPL/R Wickham, (12) AL 282-283 (1) RD, (2, 8) GPL/HR, (3) GWI, (4) MT, (5) MN, (6) CN, (7) JH, 284 (1, 2, 4, 5, 6) MT, (3) AL, (7) RD 285 (1) S&OM, (2, 4, 6) RD, (3) GPL/D England, (5) GPL/NH 286 (3) GPL/Lamontagne, (8) GPL/MB, (10) GPL/JG 286-287 (1, 4, 5) GWI, (2, 6, 7, 9, 11, 12) RD 288-289 (1, 5, 6, 7, 8, 9) RD, (2, 11) AL, (3) MB, (4) GPL/B Thomas, (10) GWI, (12) S&OM 290-291 (1) GPL/JG, (2, 4) MB, (3) JH, (5, 9) GPL/LP, (6) GPL/EC, (7) GPL/D Clyne, (8) RD 292-293 (1, 3, 4, 5, 7, 9, 11) RD, (2) GPL/NH, (6) GWI, (8, 12) GPL/HR, (10) GPL/B Carter 294-295 (1) GPL/K Blaxland (2, 7) GPL/HR, (3, 4, 8, 9) RD, (5) S&OM, (6) GPL/RE, (10) MH, (11) AL, (12) MB 296-297 (1) MB, (2, 4) GPL/J Hurst, (3) GPL/C Boursnell, (5, 7, 10) MT, (6, 11) GWI, (8, 12) SSP, (9) GPL/M Howes 298-299 (1) GWI, (2, 4, 5, 7) SSP, (3, 9) GPL/JG, (6) GPL/M Howes, (8) SC, (10, 11) MT, (12) GPL/M Watson 300-301 GPL/ J Legate

late summer

302-303 GPL/SW (Priory, Kemerton) 304 MB 305 tl MT (Cokes Barn, W. Burton, W. Sussex), tr SC, b MW 306 MW 307 tl & tr MW, tc MN, b SC 308 l MT, tr & br SC 309 MT 310 MW 311 t GPL/D England, b SC 312 l SC, r MB 313 all MW 314 l MW, r SC 315 MW 316 GPL/MLS 317 t all MW, br MT, bl JW 318 l JWh, r MW 319 all MW except tr GPL/MB 320 all MW 321 JH (King Henry's Hunting Lodge) 322 SC 323 all SC except r FH 324 SC 325 tl N Browne, br S&OM (Lower Mill, Hants), bc & bl MW 326 SC 327 tl JWh (Little Brook Fuchsias, Ash Green, Hants), br CN (Design: L Pleasance, Ldn), bl SC 328 t MW, b MH (Design: J Baillie) 329 MW 330 l GPL/MLS, r GPL/Lamontagne 331 GPL/J Hurst 332 l SC, b MT 332-333 GPL/E Craddock 333 b MW 334 l MT, r MW 335 GPL/HR 336 MW 337 JH (Barnsley House, Glos.) 338 l MT, r GPL/R Butcher 339 t MN, b CN (Design: Hedens Lustgard, Sweden) 340 MW 341 CN (Little Court, Hants) 342 CN (RHS Chelsea 1993, National Asthma Campaign. Design: Lucy Huntington) 343 l GPL/RS, r JB (Hollington Herbs, Berks) 344 AL 345 t JH (Design: M Runge), b AL 346 l AL (RHS Chelsea 1992. Design: D Pearson), r JB (Clinton Lodge, Sussex) 347 SC 348 GPL/NH 349 MW 350 l GPL/R Asser, r MW 351 SC 352-353 RD 354-355 (1, 5, 8, 10, 11) RD, (2) AL, (3, 4, 6) MT, (7) SC, (9) GPL/RE, (12) GWI 356-357 (1, 2, 5, 7, 8, 9,12) RD, (3) GPL/M Watson, (4) GPL/JG, (6) GPL/MB, (10)GPL/DW, (11) GPL/SH 358-359 (1, 2, 5, 7, 10) RD, (3) GPL/PB, (4) GPL/SH, (6) GPL/J Greene, (8) GPL/J Sorrell, (9, 11) MT, (12) GPL/CB 360-361 (1, 4, 9, 10, 11) RD, (2, 3, 5, 7, 8, 12) MT, (6) GPL/HR 362-363 (1) GPL/DW, (2) MT, (3, 4, 5, 8, 9, 11) RD, (6, 12) GWI, (7) GPL/BC, (10) GPL/DA 364-365 (1, 3, 4, 7, 8) RD, (2, 5, 9, 10) MT, (6) GPL/MB, (11) AL, (12) GPL/JG 366-367 (1, 2, 3, 9, 10) GWI, (4) MT, (5) GPL/N Kemp, (6, 7) GPL/JP, (8) MW, (11) GPL/EC,(12) GPL/HR 368-369 (1) RD, (2, 5, 6 ,11) MW, (3) GPL/BC, (4) MT, (7) GPL/HR, (8) GPL/D Cavagnaro, (9) GPL/NH, (10, 12) GWI 370-371 (1, 2, 9, 10) RD, (3) GPL/M Howes, (4) GPL/NH, (5) GPL/BC, (6) MW, (7) JW, (8) GWI, (11) GPL/PB, (12) GPL/JG 372 (1) GPL/JS, (2) GPL/B Forsberg, (3, 4, 7) RD, (5) GPL/CB, (6, 8) GPL/JG 373 (1, 3) RD, (2, 5) MT, (4) GPL/BC 374 (1) S&OM, (2) MT, (3) GPL/Z McCalmont, (4) RD, (5) GWI 375 (1, 2, 6) RD, (3) GPL/HR, (4) GPL/J Ferro Sims, (5) MT 376-377 (1, 2, 3, 4, 5, 8, 9, 10, 11) RD, (6, 12) JWh, (7) GPL/HR 378-379 (1, 7) GPL/NH, (2, 10) JWh (3) GPL/CF, (4) GWI, (5, 6) JWh (Seale Nursery, Surrey), (8, 12) JWh (Apuldram Roses, Chichester, W. Sussex), (9) GPL/JS, (11) A-Z Botanical 380-381 (1, 2, 5, 10) JWh, (3,7, 8, 9) RD, (4, 12) GPL/JG, (6) GWI, (11) GPL/MB 382 (1, 2) JWh (LittleBrook Fuchsias, Hants), (3) JWh (Seale Nursery, Surrey), (4) GPL/JS, (5) JWh, (6) GPL/JG 383 (1) GPL/MB, (2) GPL/NH, (3) GPL/MLS, (4) GPL/JG, (5) JWh, (6, 7) RD 384-385 (1, 2, 3, 4, 8, 9, 12, 13) RD, (5) A-Z Botanical,(6) GWI, (7, 11) GPL/BC, (10) MN 386-387 (1, 2, 3, 4, 5, 6, 7, 9, 11) RD, (8) GPL/MB, (10) GPL/BT, (12) GWI 388-389 (1, 3) GPL/JP, (2) GPL/D Cavagnaro, (4, 7) GPL/MLS, (5, 6) GPL/JG, (8, 11) SSP, (9) GPL/DA, (10) GPL/C Carter 390-391 (1) MW, (2, 5) GPL/M Howes, (3) GPL/SH, (4, 10) RD, (6) GPL/HR, (7) GPL/Lamontagne, (8) GPL/JS, (9) MT, (11) SSP 392 l GPL/JG, c RD, r GPL/JG 393 l GPL/JG, c JWh, r AL

autumn

394-95 MW 396 MW 397 t MB (Design: Sheila White), b MW 398 l OBG, 398-399 MW except bl SC 400 GPL/MB 401 t SC,b MW 402 S&OM 403 tl & tcl SC, tcr, tr & b MW 404-405 t S&OM, bl MW 406 t GWI, b MW, 407 l SC, r S&OM 408 l MB (Design: Sheila White), c & r MW 409 MW 410 t MW bl JH, bc & br MW 411 MW 412 l GPL/MB r SC 413 t MW, bl & br SC 414 MW 415 t SC, b MW 416 t GPL/HR, b CN 417 RD 418 MW 419 MW 420 t SC, b S&OM 421 MW 422 t MW, b RD 423-424 MW 425 t, bl & bc SC, br MN 426 CN (Lakemount, Cork, Eire) 427-429 MW 430 t S&OM, c & b MW, 431 t GPL/MLS (Domaine de St Jean de Beauregard, France), b MW 432 tl, bl, br MW, tr SC 433 GPL/GGS 434 t JH (Eck & Winterrowd, Vermont, USA), c JH (Old Rectory, Sudborough, Hants), b S&OM 435 SC 436 SC except b MW 437 SC 438 MW 439 t GPL/C Perry, c MN, bl & br MW 440 tl & tr MW, b GPL/C Carter, 441 t MN, b MW, 442 b SC 442-443 t RD 67 b MW 444 MW 445 t MW, b RD 446 l GWI, r MW 447 GPL/M Howes 448-449 RD 450-451 (1, 9) GPL/JG, (2) GPL/SH, (3) GPL/CB, (4, 8, 11, 12) RD, (5) GPL/JS, (6) GPL/D Askham, (7, 10) AL 452-453 (1, 4, 5, 7) RD, (2) GPL/SH, (3) PH, (6) GPL/EC, (8) MH, (9) GPL/MB, (10) GPL/E Peios, (11, 12) GPL/HR 454-455 (1, 4, 5) RD, (2, 6, 8, 11, 12) GWI, (3) S&OM, (7) J Willsmore, (9) GPL/JG, (10) SC 456 (1, 2) GWI, (3, 6) RD, (4) GPL/JS, (5) GPL/HR 457 (1, 2, 4) RD, (3) GPL/SH, (5, 6) GWI, (7) GPL/HR 458-459 (1, 4, 8, 9) GWI, (2, 11) GPL/B Carter, (3) GPL/EC, (5) GPL/M Heuff, (6) GPL/JS, (7, 12) RD, (10) AL 460-461 (1, 3, 6, 8, 9, 11, 12) GWI, (2, 4, 5, 10) RD, (7) GPL/JS 462 (1, 2, 4, 6) RD, (3) GPL/HR, (5) GPL/JS 463 (1) GPL/CB, (2, 4) MB, (3) GPL/P Bonduell, (5, 6) RD 464 (1) RD, (2, 3, 4, 5) MB, (6) JH 465 (1, 3, 4, 5, 6, 7) RD, (2) GPL/CB, (8) GPL/NH 466 (1, 4) MB, (2) JD, (3) GPL/J Sorrell, (5) GPL/JS, (6) S&OM 467 (1) RD, (2, 7) GWI, (3, 5) MB, (4) RD 468-469 (1, 9) JWh, (2, 5, 8, 12) RD, (3) GWI, (4) MM, (6, 10) GPL/NH, (7) MT, (11) JD 470-471 (1, 2, 3, 5, 6, 7, 9, 10) RD, (4, 12) JWh (8) HSC, (11) S&OM 472-473 (1, 10, 11) RD, (2, 8, 12) GPL/HR, (3) JWh, (4) GPL/Ron Evans, (5, 7) GWI, (6) JH, (9) MW 474-475 (1, 9, 11) RD, (2) S&OM, (3, 4, 5, 10) JWh, (6, 8, 12) GWI, (7) SC 476 (1, 7) GPL/HR, (2, 3, 5) RD, (4) GWI, (6) GPL/JS 477 (1) SC, (2) GPL/Lamontagne, (3)

GPL/JS, **(4, 5)** RD, **(6)** GPL/JG **478-479 (1)** SC, **(2)** AL, **(3)** GPL/B Carter, **(4, 6, 9, 11)** RD, **(5)** GPL/C Fairweather, **(7)** GPL/HR, **(8)** GPL/J Pavia, **(10)** GPL/NH, **(12)** GPL/SH **480-481 (1, 5, 10)** RD, **(2)** GPL/JS, **(3, 4, 6)** GWI, **(7)** GPL/HR, **(8, 11)** SC, **(9)** JH **482-483 (1, 4)** PH, **(2, 3, 5, 6, 7, 11)** MT, **(8)** GPL/MLS, **(9)** GPL/JG, **(10)** GPL/C Carter **484-485 (1, 3 ,4, 5, 6, 7, 8, 10, 11)** MT, **(2)** SSP, **(9)** S&OM **486 l** S&OM, **r** MH **487 l** GPL/JS, **r** SC

winter

488-489 SC **490 l** S&OM, **c & r** MW **491** MW **492 l** MW, **r** MT **493** MW **494-495** SC **496 l** SC, **r** GPL/HR **497 t** MW, **b** SC **498 l** GPL/JG, **r** MW **499** MW **500** MW **501** MW except **tl** SC **502** MW **503** MW except **tl** GWI **504** MW **505** MW except **br** GPL/M O'Hara **506** RD **507 t** SC, **b** MW **508** SC except **tr** GPL/BT **509** MW **510** MW **511** MW except **ct & tr** SC **512 t** CN, **b** SC **513** MW except **t** MB **514** MW **514-515** S&OM **515** SC except **br** MW **516** MW except **bl** GPL/JG **517** JH (Design: K Akers, Essex) **518 l** CN (Design: L Hampden), **r** MW **519** SC except **t** GPL/LB **520** GPL/HR **521** MW except **tl** GPL/HR **522 l** S&OM, **r** MW **523** MW **524 t** MT, **b** S&OM **525** MW **526 l** GPL/J Wade, **c** MW, **br** SC **527 tl** MW, **tr** MT, **b** MN **528** GPL/CN (Chenies Manor Garden, Bucks) **529** SC **530** S&OM **531 t** GPL/M Howes, **b** SC **532 t** SC, **br** MT, **bl** MN **533** GPL/MB **534 r** GPL/M Howes **534 l** MT **535** GPL/C Carter **536 l** MW, **tr** MT, **b** SC **537** MW except **tr** GPL/C Boursnell **538** SC **539** MW **540** MW **541 t** GPL/MLS, **b** SC **542-543** JWh **544-555 (1, 2, 7, 8, 9)** RD, **(3)** GPL/NH, **(4, 6, 11)** JWh, **(5)** GPL/JP, **(10)** GPL/MB, **(12)** S&OM **546 (1)** Courtesy of Thompson & Morgan, **(2, 3, 4, 5)** GWI **547 (1, 4)** GPL/NH, **(2)** RD, **(3)** S&OM, **(5)** GPL/JG, **(6)** GPL/CB **548-549 (1)** GPL/JS, **(2, 4)** GWI, **(3)** GPL/SH, **(5, 8, 9, 11, 12)** RD, **(6)** PH, **(7)** GPL/JG, **(10)** SC **550 (1)** GPL/CB, **(2, 6)** MB, **(3, 4, 5, 8)** RD, **(7)** GPL/JG **551 (1, 2)** GPL/JS, **(3)** GWI, **(4)** GPL/BT, **(5)** GPL/P Bonduell, **(6)** RD **552-553 (1, 4, 7, 11)** RD, **(2, 3, 12)** GWI, **(5)** GPL/JG, **(6)** GPL/D Willery, **(8, 9)** MW, **(10)** JWh **554-555 (1)** MB, **(2)** GWI, **(3)** GPL/VF, **(4, 12)** S&OM, **(5)** GPL/NH, **(6, 7, 9, 11)** JWh, **(8)** GPL/C Fairweather **556-557 (1)** RD, **(2, 3, 4, 8)** JWh, **(5, 6)** GWI, **(7, 9)** GPL/HR, **(10)** J Willsmore, **(11)** GPL/BC, **(12)** SC **558-559 (1)** GWI, **(2)** GPL/JG, **(3, 7, 11)** RD, **(4)** GPL/ML, **(5)** GPL/VF, **(6)** JWh, **(8)** S&OM, **(9)** CN, **(10)** GPL/CN **560-561 (1, 9, 10, 11)** RD, **(2, 4, 5)** JWh, **(6)** JD, **(7)** CN, **(8)** S&OM **562-563 (1, 2, 6, 7, 9)** RD, **(3, 10)** JWh, **(4)** SC, **(5)** S&OM, **(8)** GPL/JG, **(11)** GWI **564-565 (1)** S&OM, **(2, 3, 4, 5, 6, 7, 8, 9)** RD, **(10)** MB, **(11, 12)** GPL/JS **566-567 (1, 8)** GPL/HR, **(2)** GPL/CN, **(3, 7, 12)** GWI, **(4, 6, 9, 10, 11)** RD, **(5)** GPL/JS **568-569 (1)** GPL/Joanne Pavia, **(2, 4, 8, 9, 11)** RD, **(3, 6, 12)** GWI, **(5)** MB, **(7)** S&OM, **(10)** GPL/JS **570 (1)** J Willsmore, **(2)** GPL/SH, **(3)** RD, **(4)** JWh, **(5, 7, 8)** RD, **(6)** GPL/NH **571 (1)** GPL/NH, **(2)** S&OM **(3)** RD, **(4, 6, 7)** JWh, **(5)** GPL/JG **572-573 (1, 2, 6, 11)** GWI, **(3)** GPL/SH, **(4, 7, 8, 10, 12)** RD, **(5)** GPL/ML, **(9)** GPL/JG **574-575** MT except **(8, 10)** MN **576-577 (1)** GPL/SH, **(2, 8)** MN, **(3, 4, 6, 9, 11)** MT, **(5, 10)** SSP, **(7)** GPL/P Bonduell **578 l** GPL/JG, **r** JWh **579** JWh **116 l** RD, **r** GPL/JS **579 l** RD, **c** GPL/CB, **r** SC

gardening basics

580-581 SC **582** SC **583 t & br** MW, **bl** SC **584 all** MW **585 tl, tr, bl & bcl** MW, **bcr & br** SC **586** SC **587 t, bc & br** SC, **bl** MN **588 t** MW, **c & b** SC **589** MW **590** SC **591 tl & tr** SC, **br** MW **592-593** MW **594-595** MW **596 t & br** MW, **bl** SC **597 t** SC, **b** MN **598** MW **599 t** MB (Lady Farm, Somerset), **b** JH (Charney Well Design: Christopher Holiday) **600-601 tl** GPL/G Glynn-Smith, **c** MN, **br** SC, **bl** JB (Design: D Buckley) **cl** GPL/JS **602** S&OM **603 t** GPL/GGS, **c** GPL/M Watson, **b** GPL/A Jones **604** MW **605 tl** RD, **tr & b** MW **606** GPL/M Howes **607 t** GPL/B Carter, **b** GPL/MB **608 t** GPL/M Howes, **br & c** GPL/HR, **bl** GPL/G Dann

Amazon Publishing would like to thank Adrian Hall Garden Centres, Lotus Water Garden Products Ltd (www.lotuswatergardens.com), and, for supplying tools shown on pages 582–587, Bulldog Tools and Burgon & Ball Ltd. Thanks also to the following, who allowed us to use their gardens for photography: Martin Brigdale and Helen Trent, Andi and Meg Clevely, Katia Demetriardi, Bridget Heal, Gaye Prescott, Jenny Raworth, Alison Shackleton, Ian Sidaway and Capel Manor Limited.

The Complete Guide to Gardening – Season by Season

is based on material first published in a series entitled *Reader's Digest All-Season Guide to Gardening*. It was created for Reader's Digest by Amazon Publishing Ltd.

Series Editor Carole McGlynn
Art Director Ruth Prentice
Editors Barbara Haynes, Jackie Matthews, Alison Freegard; also Norma MacMillan
Design Jo Grey, Mary Staples; also Alison Shackleton
Special photography Sarah Cuttle, Mark Winwood, Martin Brigdale
Writers Steve Bradley, Andi Clevely, Nigel Colburn, Sue Fisher, David Joyce, Anne Swithinbank
Picture research Clare Limpus, Mel Watson, Sarah Wilson
DTP Felix Gannon, Gerard Gannon, Claire Graham
Editorial Assistants Elizabeth Woodland, Lucy Doncaster

Consultant Jonathan Edwards
Indexer Hilary Bird

For Reader's Digest
Project Editor Christine Noble
Project Art Editor Kate Harris
Pre-press Accounts Manager Penny Grose

Reader's Digest General Books
Editorial Director Cortina Butler
Art Director Nick Clark

www.readersdigest.co.uk

Reprinted 2005

We are committed to both the quality of our products and the service we provide to our customers. We value your comments, so please feel free to contact us on **08705 113366**, or via our website at **www.readersdigest.co.uk**
If you have any comments about the content of our books, you can email us at **gbeditorial@readersdigest.co.uk**

Origination Colour Systems Limited, London
Printed and bound in Europe by Arvato Iberia

ISBN 0 276 42925 7
BOOK CODE 400-215-02
CONCEPT CODE UK1942/IC
ORACLE CODE 250008683H.00.24